SMYTHE LIBRARY

Stamp this label with the date for return.
Contact the librarian if you wish to renew this book.

BY ROBERT LOWELL

Land of Unlikeness (1944)

Lord Weary's Castle (1946)

The Mills of the Kavanaughs (1951)

Life Studies (1959)

Phaedra (translation) (1961)

Imitations (1961)

For the Union Dead (1964)

The Old Glory (plays) (1965)

Near the Ocean (1967)

The Voyage & other versions of poems by Baudelaire (1969)

Prometheus Bound (translation) (1969)

Notebook 1967–68 (revised and expanded edition, *Notebook*, 1970)

History (1973)

For Lizzie and Harriet (1973)

The Dolphin (1973)

Selected Poems (1976) (revised edition, 1977)

Day by Day (1977)

The Oresteia of Aeschylus (translation) (1978)

Collected Prose (1987)

Collected Poems (2003)

The Letters of

ROBERT LOWELL

The Letters of

ROBERT

LOWELL

Edited by Saskia Hamilton

ff

First published in Great Britain in 2005
by Faber and Faber Limited
3 Queen Square London WC1N 3AU
and in the United States by Farrar, Straus and Giroux LLC, New York
Printed in the United States

Copyright © 2005 by Harriet Lowell and Sheridan Lowell
Compilation, editorial work and introduction copyright © 2005 by Saskia Hamilton

Portions of this work previously appeared in *The Kenyon Review* and *Harvard Review*

Designed by Jonathan D. Lippincott

A CIP record for this book
is available from the British Library

ISBN 0—571—20204—7

2 4 6 8 10 9 7 5 3 1

Contents

Introduction:

"I Was Naked Without My Line-Ends"

When Robert Lowell lived in New York City in 1941, he took typing classes at the W.P.A. His experiments with typewriters as a young writer were intermittent, however. Jean Stafford typed his manuscripts. Letters, which he mostly penciled in longhand, tended to be brief. In his first typewritten one, to his mother, he declares that "learning to type has almost annihilated any potentialities I ever had for correspondence." After a few desultory sentences, he ends: "Typewriters give one a stamped-collar-button style." He did not return to the instrument for some years. But his attraction to prose and his ease with it grew with his ability to type. He inherited his father's typewriter in 1950 and took it to Europe. For some reason, lonely for his friends and faced with the machine, he discovered he could dress his prose style differently. Obsessed with writing, he began to think of a letter not as a duty but as a formal challenge: how to make his company travel such a long distance.

He sometimes had to make himself companionable after long silences. He did so with a mix of candor and what he half-apologetically called "shop talk." He also did so by testing the lengths of his sentences and paragraphs. He wrote to John Berryman after reading Berryman's "Skunk Hour" essay:

> What a Longfellow-note after your searching essay! Forgive me, I am trying to break the ice and start talking where we left off ten years ago. In our insides we never stopped. Still one has to grunt and sweat a bit to get the talk going.

To get back inside an old intimacy he declares, disarmingly, that it never stopped. But to get it running again—to overcome what he called the "lassitude, the inertia of original sin or whatever" that makes him "put off from day to day answering *anyone*"—requires an effort equivalent to hard physical labor. Lowell often overcame his inertia and engaged his will by attending to

the musical problems in sentence making. He typed as fast as he could think but his ear reached for work. In the Berryman letter, having answered the essay ("there's both a wish and a fear of annihilation" in the skunk vision, he says), he fingers a phrase from *Hamlet* and uses it to make the sentence do just what it describes:

Stíll one hás to grúnt and swéat a bít to gét the tálk góing.*

A sudden intimacy—in my mind we've never been separated—is deepened by an allusion that has a "nervous underside," whether witty or despairing one isn't sure.† From "still" to "going." The rhythm and sound patterns push the sentence into motion, as if the ear is impatient to make new meanings out of these connections. Or, to change the metaphor, it's as if, writing prose, he is a racehorse in a stall tensed for release onto the track of a poem.

The just-starting quality of the thought, the mixture of tones—warm, playful, testing—are typical of Lowell's correspondence, the excitement of his intelligence and the liveliness of his prose. "Let me get this scrappy, whistling little letter into the afternoon mail," he writes to Elizabeth Bishop. "I want to write you something with a little thought soon, but this is just to relieve your mind." Although Lowell was an intrepid and compulsive reviser of his poetry, his correspondence was rarely drafted. Written on the fly, glancingly corrected, the letters are grammatically and visually messy. The paper often looks like a worksheet. They are composed in his distinctive prose— odd, intricate, sinewy sentences that seem to run several syntaxes together.

During the mid-1950s, when he was struggling to find a new form for his poems, Lowell experimented with autobiographical prose. He had written intelligent, tonally varied essays but had never before tried to work at prose in this consistent way. "I found the problems and possibilities of a sentence, a paragraph as charming as anything I'd done," he recalled in a letter to Richard Tillinghast. Sustaining his energy in prose did not please him as much as working within the tighter space of a poem, however, and he abandoned the project. "I had other difficulties—a dread of more of the same, impossibility of honestly showing the living, at loss for a plot to pass beyond childhood." If the formal shape of a poem (whether metrical or free-verse) created an interesting tension with his in-line revisions, prose was much more

*"Who would fardels bear, / To grunt and sweat under a weary life, / But that the dread of something after death, / The undiscovered country from whose bourn / No traveller returns, puzzles the will" (*Hamlet*, 3.1.76–80).
†Robert Hass, "Lowell's Graveyard," 11.

ungainly, "a hell of a job, it starts naked[,] ends as fake velvet." Not one to shy away from work, he nevertheless found that "revision and retyping so much was detestable—so impossible not to find holes, so tedious to ~~retype~~ plug them." As distinct from prose, "verse, whatever else it may or may not be, is itself a system of punctuation," T. S. Eliot suggests. "The usual marks of punctuation themselves are differently employed."* Revising, without the line breaks and white space on the right side of the text—important elements of a poem's punctuation—Lowell lost the fun in the labor. Prose was at first too undressed, then, when he worked at it, too clotted; finally, the arbitrariness of its possibilities exhausted him.

The labor of retyping was such that he did not feel the need to redraft his letters; their prose never became "fake velvet." For this reason and others, his correspondence invites us into an intimacy with his inner life in a different way from his other writing. Letters stand in awkward relation to other literary production. As if the writer is on a short visit to a friend, letters require of him a certain willing sociability. They are meant neither for the privacy of a journal nor the public space of print. They carry the particular voice of the social person in relation to a specific other. They are, as Tom Paulin describes in an essay about Elizabeth Bishop's letters,

> throwaway, disposable, unique holographs which aim to flower once and once only in the recipient's reading and then disappear immediately . . . What the posthumous reader desires is a privileged entrance to each text's primal, absolutely best performance, a cross-wired connection which is yet somehow random—what Charles Lamb in his essay "Distant Correspondents" calls "this grand solecism of *two presents*" where "*my Now*" collides with "*your Now*."[†]

The letters give us Lowell's life as he lived it, inside out. We find him not just in history but in his house, on a particular morning, taking a break from his other work to write for a friend's ear. "It's an iron-black warm New York morning that reminds me of Europe," he writes to Bishop. "With the heat turned off in my study, I hear the great huffle of nature outside and almost feel I were voyaging off into the Atlantic, till I look up and see the stationary skyline of little sky-scrapers and wooden water towers." Wishing his New York morning were a European one, he feels his ship of an apartment drift from its

TLS, 27 September 1928, quoted in Ricks, *The Force of Poetry*, 89.
[†]Paulin, 216.

mooring, but finds himself, at the end of the paragraph, arriving back in his own city. (Bishop loved to travel by freighter.)

How Lowell managed both the loneliness of writing to an absent person and the labor of writing recurs in the letters. He writes to the Dutch critic W. F. van Leeuwen:

> I feel like a dog not having written sooner—there's something abstract and distant about letters even at their best. As you overlook the black keyboard of your typewriter, it's as though you were facing yourself in the mirror and trying to hold the attention of what you see there by what you see there.

The attempt to write a sentence that will capture and hold his own attention has no reward, makes possible no sudden warmth or intimacy. But Lowell's need to crash through self-consciousness to get going undoes the narcissism:

> This opening is meant as a counterthrust to your classified list of depressions, which I find very sympathetic—as long as it's not myself, I feel like cheering when one of my friends grows darkly thoughtful and philosophic, what the expression *self-possessed* should mean literally, but doesn't. I mean to . . . I'm trying to get around to some good optimistic New England American moralizing, such as saying it's only our long aimless periods that prove we are alive; I guess they do do something, but I mustn't put it that way. You know there's a wintry, wordy American character, half manic-depressive and half booster, who puts the tragic European to shame.

Thinking of his friend's mood elicits a cheer of recognition. The New England moralist in him wants to assert some value in depression: to become possessed or imprisoned by the self, to dwell in a "long aimless period" and get through the experience does "do something," does "prove we are alive." Like thought moving from the mirror to the "counterthrust," Lowell is able to escape his self-absorption by commenting on his own process. This energy—noticing what is going on behind what is going on—is in all of Lowell's writing. The tension between feeling self-possessed and wanting to be released from the mirror, back in good company, works itself out as he carries his sentences into effect. And his American ambition is stimulated by the thought that a "wintry, wordy" character can put "the tragic European to shame."

When thinking about the New England character, Lowell has as a model Henry Adams, who writes:

> The habit of doubt; of distrusting his own judgment and of totally rejecting the judgment of the world; the tendency to regard every question as open; the hesitation to act except as a choice of evils; the shirking of responsibility; the love of line, form, quality; the horror of ennui; the passion for companionship and the antipathy to society—all these are well-known qualities of New England character in no way peculiar to individuals but in this instance they seemed to be stimulated by the fever, and Henry Adams could never make up his mind whether, on the whole, the change of character was morbid or healthy, good or bad for his purpose.*

Deeply troubled by his own fevers, Lowell was equally ambivalent about whether they served his education. His New England character, which had been "stimulated by the fever," is now "wintry, wordy"—cold, exposed, reaching for words to clothe it, self-possessed or "what the expression . . . should mean literally." But self-possession is associated with composure or command, enviable traits of the "booster" personality. He wants a word (less pejorative than, say, *self-absorbed*) to describe what it's like to be haunted or colonized by problems of the self. If the expression were understood literally, the self would stand in relation not to a noun of condition or a noun of state but to a noun of action. Lowell never took for granted the idea that he could possess the self. Self-possession, he recognized, is an action one has to perform; in his experience of madness, he discovered that it is not an action one always can perform.

Some of the letters were written during manic episodes; many more were written during periods of depression. Lowell's first experience of profound depression came in 1949, after his first manic episode. He described it in a letter to Gertrude Buckman:

> I've written you and started to write you and thought about you and writing to you daily. Nothing I can say will really do to tell you every-

*Adams, *Education*, 6.

thing that happened, or why. By the time I reached the hospital I was completely out of my head—strange physical sensations—I was a prophet and everything was a symbol; then in the hospital: shouting, singing, tearing things up—religion and antics. Then depression (extreme) aching, self-enclosed, fearful of everyone and everything anyone could do, feeling I was nothing and could do nothing.

After being possessed by sensations, "religion and antics," Lowell found himself in the enclosure not of a monastery but of a hospital, and later even more remotely removed inside himself, the walls or boundaries marked by an "(extreme) aching." "I am now in the Payne-Whitney Clinic. . . . I seem to be in the other half, the down half of what you saw in Bloomington–self-inclosed, unable to function, depressed," he wrote in a letter he never sent to Peter Taylor. Images of enclosure also appear in the poetry:

> Given a year
> I walked on the roof of the West Street Jail, a short
> enclosure like my school soccer court,
> and saw the Hudson River once a day
> through sooty clothesline entanglements
> and bleaching khaki tenaments.*

One can see how writing hovers behind the narrative. Lowell was "given," figurative for "sentenced to," a year. The sentences fill the "short enclosure" of the stanza. The entanglements of the clotheslines call up the enjambed lines of Lowell's early poems, which he revised for *Land of Unlikeness* while serving out his actual jail term.

In letters Lowell wrote during depressions, his sentences of despair are accompanied by ones that try to alter or clothe the mood. He was unable to finish the letter to Taylor. The letters he mailed to Elizabeth Hardwick from that period have such self-correcting shifts as "O Lord, how empty I am. However, this letter is just to tell you ~~that the depression~~ that I am well. Please don't worry." This habit persisted. He wrote to Elizabeth Bishop in 1963, for example:

> I am at the end of something. Up till now I've felt I was all blue spots
> and blotches inside, more than I could bear really, if I looked at myself,

*"Memories of West Street and Lepke," *Life Studies* (1959).

and of course I wanted to do nothing else. So day after day, I wrote, sometimes too absorbed to even stop for lunch and often sitting with my family in a stupor, mulling over a phrase or a set of lines for almost hours, hypnotized, under a spell, often a bad spell. Now out of this, I have seven poems and seven translations, just about a book when added to what I had before. Now I say to myself, "Out of jail!" I look back on the last months with disgust and gratitude. Disgust because they seem so monstrous, gratitude, because I have lived through the unintelligible, have written against collapse and come out more or less healed. Oh dear, have you ever felt like a man in an unreal book?

The self-analytic mind wants to describe what he has reached the end of and the New England moralizing mind wants to speak from the present moment—"Now out of this," "Now I say." He has written "against collapse." His will declares that the jail doors are open, as if to startle him out of his stupor—to count the number of poems written, survey the past, and declare the depression is over. But where is he, "more or less healed"? He leaps from analysis to metaphor. The final sentence begins in exhaustion with the exhaled "Oh" and rises like a balloon to the peculiar qualification of an "unreal book," as if, at the last moment, before letting go the string, he must bat the sentence in a new direction. He feels real enough, but the place he inhabited—or inhabits?—is not. The declaration of freedom and the metaphor sit tentatively beside each other.

"Unreal" seems to have been code in his marriage for his illness. In manic states, he was lost to his family and society in allegories of interconnecting symbols, texts, and characters. Whether that world was real or unreal was an open question to him and to others. People who witnessed his manic episodes were often puzzled by his erratic behavior, trying to determine what was due to his illness and what was not. In "mixed mania," which seems to have been a feature of Lowell's form of the illness, mania and depression arise together, making a patient feel simultaneously elated and lethargic. Xandra Bingley described what Lowell's descent into illness could be like:

At the beginning the horror was when he started to say awful things about people he was really very fond of. And when Cal said awful things about people they were always spot on, so people sort of quailed, and got very angry. He'd say it absolutely direct to them . . .

Eventually he'd go to bed and he'd wake earlier and earlier in the morning just collapsed by remorse. Because Cal had an extremely kind character in most ways. So he'd wake up horrified by what he'd said. Drunken abuse is usually quite stupid, and so is drunken remorse, sort of maudlin. But Cal's remorse was quite exact. He knew exactly what he'd said and exactly how it might hurt somebody. And he wasn't caught up in [thinking], "what can I say to make it all right" . . . It was the remorse in a way that pushed him into a worse and worse depression, because he minded so much about the cruelty. The logistics of it were that he woke earlier and earlier, he felt worse and worse about it, he drank earlier and earlier in the day to forget it, so that by the end of October he was drinking vodka and milk by half past ten in the morning. And then he'd be high again, so that the remorse would turn into a high again, with the next day's vitriol. And then he couldn't sleep. So it turned into a sort of 24-hour binge.*

Lowell's friends struggled to understand what happened to this "extremely kind character" who was so changed and yet seemed aware of his own behavior. If part of the disarming charm of his company was the impression he gave that "to be candid does not annihilate the self,"† when he was sick he became the pejoratively candid friend (telling Flannery O'Connor, for instance, that "Bowden Broadwater says, 'I still can't read Flannel Mouth'").

Because of the cyclical nature of Lowell's illness, people's social experience of him was not consistent. He was neither always mad nor always sane; he was also *either* mad *or* sane. This confounded and strained the people he knew. Perhaps for this reason, one finds, in the interviews Ian Hamilton conducted for his biography shortly after Lowell's death, that many people who knew him judged his manic behavior as a moral failing, as if the manic Lowell were the "real" Lowell, as if a mask had dropped, revealing his true character. Others, including his family and closest friends, thought that his "real" self was the person they knew when he was well. Having to integrate his different experiences of self was a pressing and unsolvable problem for Lowell throughout his life, both as he interpreted it and was encouraged to interpret it through the psychiatric and psychotherapeutic treatments he received. His ambivalent relationship to the insights of his manic episodes—contorted

*Xandra Bingley interview, Ian Hamilton Notebooks, British Library.
†Frank Bidart in conversation with SH, July 31, 2003.

and privately patterned as they were—is illuminated by the way he used the word *unreal* in his correspondence and his work.*

The letters Lowell wrote in the spring of 1954 after the death of his mother in Italy document most fully what happened to his mind during a manic episode. By the time he arrived in Rapallo, his psychosis was well under way (the mania likely exacerbated by exhaustion and jet lag); however, his delusional state was not necessarily obvious or evident to correspondents. Letters to Giovanna Madonia, a woman he knew slightly and with whom he took up while arranging to ship his mother's body back to America, show many signs of mania. But despite his increasing volubility, his aggressive asides, letters to others seem lucid and controlled. (Only those alert to the symptoms—Elizabeth Hardwick, Blair Clark—recognized that he was ill.) While instigating a separation from Hardwick, he wrote Madonia ardent, electric letters full of bold associative leaps, ambitious travel plans, fantasies about their future life, and worry, keening—one ends, "YOU HAVE SAVED MY LIFE," printed in small capitals like a sinking joy. At the same time, he began a warm and polite letter to Katherine Biddle, "Thank you for your very kind, slow-paced and human letter"—typing his appreciation as if to modulate his own pace. He sustained it for a paragraph but then jauntily added: "Elizabeth and I are getting a divorce—we are quite chatty and cozy about it, and there is no bitterness. I am getting married again, to an Italian girl whom I have known for some two years. She too is getting a divorce from a husband who is *not* d'accordo, which makes a hell of a mare's-nest in Italian law—a reform of the Italian legal code should, by the way, have been part of the peace treaty. What's the per centage in an unconditional surrender, if you can't at least do that. I protest as an American citizen!" The fantasy that his separation from Hardwick is "chatty and cozy," painless for them both, the impression he tries to make that he has "known" (not known of) Madonia "for some two years," as if to say his decision is not impulsive, the joke about the Italian legal code (Biddle's husband was attorney general when Italy surrendered) are features of one kind of "unreality"—masking suffering, blind to suffering, while consumed by the manic excitement—which, after recovery, he admits "was sincere enough, but a stupid pathological mirage, a magical orange grove in a nightmare. I feel like a son of a bitch."

Psychiatrists at the private East Coast hospitals where Lowell was institu-

*See, for example, *Notebook* (1970), 262. Barbara Estrin analyzes Lowell's uses of *unreal* in *The American Love Lyric after Auschwitz and Hiroshima* (2001).

tionalized before lithium treated his severe mania with a combination of organic therapies—shock treatment and sedatives like Thorazine, which temporarily controlled his symptoms—and psychotherapy. Although he did not consider a course of strict psychoanalytic treatment until 1958, the therapy he received in and out of the hospital before then was influenced by psychoanalytic theory.* Psychodynamic models of the causes of his disorder were highly influential not only in American psychiatry—particularly for patients who could afford private treatment—but also in American culture, affecting the way he and his society understood his manic behavior.† When he discusses his illness and his therapy in letters, what seems implicit is the hope that insight will one day prevent him from relapsing. He also writes to apologize:

> For many fairly obvious reasons I have not wanted to write about coming here—but ashamed and puzzled by it. . . . I've been trying to understand my first six or seven years, and have many questions to ask you.
> (1949)

> It's like recovering from some physical injury, such as a broken leg or jaundice, yet there's no disclaiming these outbursts—they are part of my character—me at moments; hence the protracted stay here, hence the continued therapy . . . I feel like a son of a bitch.
> (1954)

> I feel rather creepy and paltry writing now to announce that I am all healed and stable again. So it is. Five attacks in ten years make you feel rather a basket-case . . . Maybe when ten years have passed I'll be a sort of monument of the norm—Eberhart and Wilbur combined.
> (1959)

> You shouldn't feel dead—of all people you seem to have most escaped the kind of hollowness and airy disorder that so vexes me. I wake up

*"Cal is now in the hands of a first-rate Freudian analyst, a man who was on the staff of a hospital (a city hospital, it was!) and who will now have been in the position of having seen Cal both well and ill. . . . There is no doubt in my mind that Cal needs depth analysis—and it is in any case a last resort, like an amputation, since everything else has been tried" (Elizabeth Hardwick to Elizabeth Bishop, January 20, 1958, Vassar College Libraries).

†See Nathan G. Hale, Jr., "The Rise of a Psychoanalytic Psychiatry, 1945–1965," *The Rise and Crisis of Psychoanalysis in the United States* (1995), 245–256. "The doctor thinks that his kind of illness with long 'therapy' can be brought a good deal under the control of the will—and that this time showed the ability to control certain symptoms and there would be more improvement, or at least that it was possible if Cal worked at it" (Elizabeth Hardwick to Elizabeth Bishop, June 24, 1959, Vassar College Libraries).

thinking I have perhaps twenty more years, that they are whizzing by . . . I think about my ragged conduct, unreality, squabbling uncontrollable desires, etc. (1960)

Maybe I'll get well, this doctor is the first I've had who is really much like an artist, though it took several days for us to speak a language intelligible to the other. (1966)

Lowell could not control his illness with the power of his will or understanding. When he was prescribed lithium in his fiftieth year, he was given a new medical explanation: "All the psychiatry and therapy I've had, almost 19 years, was as irrelevant as it would have been for a broken leg. Well, some of it was interesting, tho most was jargon." Lithium treatment relieved him from suffering the idea that he was morally and emotionally responsible for the fact that he relapsed. However, it did not entirely prevent relapses. And whether his symptoms were meaningless, whether it was true that "'Where you are going, Professor, / you won't need your Dante,'" was a harder question to answer.* He did not stop trying to find language for the experience of being terribly drawn from himself. And he was troubled and anxious about the impact of his relapses on his family and friends until the end of his life.

Although he was deeply marked by his illness and went in dread of it—he called it "shades of the future prison"—he was not obsessed with it. He got back to work. He and his family clearly considered his fame for instability tiresome. ("Anecdotes about John could be made up for miles by his cronies and students, monotonous, wearying, like Dylan Thomas's, because the escapades even when they happened, lived on the imagination," he wrote after Berryman's death.) Most of his letters were written when he was well; they document the force of his will to recover from each breakdown and rebuild his relationships and his work. By the 1960s, during the time when he was well, he was, as Frank Bidart recalls, "more 'well' than most people I know," free of small neuroses, pettiness, and malice. Hardwick writes:

His fate was like a strange, almost mythical two-engined machine, one running to doom and the other to salvation. Out of the hospital he returned to his days, which were regular, getting up early in the morn-

*"Visitors," Day by Day (1977).

ing, going to his room or separate place to work. All day long he lay on the bed, propped up on an elbow. And this was his life, reading, studying and writing. The papers piled up on the floor, the books on the bed, the bottles of milk on the window sill, and the ashtray filled . . . Since he was in no sense an autodidact, and not the sort of poet, if there are any, for whom beautiful things come drifting down in a snowfall of gift, the labor was merciless. The discipline, the dedication, the endless revision, the constant adding to his store, by reading and studying—all of this had, in my view, much that was heroic about it. Fortunately, Cal was 'well' much more of his life than he was not; otherwise his large and difficult, for him, production would not exist.*

But he was deeply disturbed by the harm he caused when he was sick; he "thought hard, and felt deeply, about violence" and power, Christopher Ricks observes. "Violence was Lowell's essential subject, terrible in its variety (of time, of place, of motive, of nature) and terrible in not changing."† If in his mania Lowell was attracted to the Caesars, Napoleon, Hitler, Stalin, in his politics he was antiauthoritarian and against violence. He identified with no single political philosophy; he voted Democratic and was attracted to Henry Adams's definition of the "anarchical conservative." ("My socialist-anarchist earned income half-person will be at Harvard by the first of February," he joked to Hardwick.) The letters document the maturation of his political views and the ways he chose to resist power. As a young man, he began to be troubled by the conservatism that he had absorbed from his class, his local culture (Boston, Nashville, Kenyon College), and his literary culture (the Fugitives, the modernists). In a letter to Robert Bridges that Lowell refers to in 1942, Gerard Manley Hopkins exhorts his friend to be bold enough to give alms "to the point of sensible inconvenience" and to examine "the difference between paying heavily for a virtue and not paying at all. It changes the whole man, if anything can; not his mind only but the will and everything."‡ After the firebombing of Hamburg, to protest the violence the Allies were inflicting on civilian populations to win an unconditional surrender, he refused to fight and was sent to jail. He wrote to Peter Taylor, "The best comment on the war I heard is what the Italians wrote on the walls of some of their towns when we entered: 'Fanno shifo tutti'"(They're all disgusting). Lowell was profoundly

*Elizabeth Hardwick to Ian Hamilton, n.d., Ransom Humanities Center, University of Texas.
†Ricks, "Robert Lowell: 'The War of Words,'" 261, 256.
‡*The Letters of Gerard Manley Hopkins to Robert Bridges*, ed. Claude Colleer Abbott, 60–61.

changed—in his understanding of himself and in his work—by taking this stand. "To be thoroughly *in act* is human perfection," he wrote about Hopkins. "In other words, it is to be *thoroughly made*."* He drifted from his conservative Catholic anti-Communism after the war. While the "jaunty . . . old crusade for international democracy" was turning into American imperialism, he read Hannah Arendt's *The Origins of Totalitarianism* in Amsterdam in the early 1950s:

> I felt landless and alone, and read Hannah as though I were going home, or reading *Moby-Dick*, perhaps for the second time, no longer seeking adventure, but the voyage of wisdom, the tragedy of America. Writing when Stalin was still enthroned and the shade of Hitler still unburied, Hannah believed with somber shrewdness, like Edmund Burke, that totalitarian power totally corrupts. . . . *Origins*, like many of her books, is apparently a defense of America, one that overstates and troubles us by assuming that we must be what we declared ourselves to be in our Revolutionary and post-Revolutionary beginnings. Her dream, it is both German and Jewish, now perhaps seems sadly beyond our chances and intentions. Yet the idea is still true, still taunting us to act. What is memorable, and almost uniquely rare and courageous in a thinker, is that Hannah's theory is always applied to action, and often to immediate principles of state. Her imperatives for political freedom still enchant and reproach us.†

Lowell's horror of violence included the violence of doctrines. His awareness of the "problems and paradoxes" of political action gave his radical political pronouncements an air of apology—he could be described as possessing a "triumphant diffidence."‡ "I had the idea that a simplistic, idealistic, coherent view of life turned out to be too brittle for the facts and so leads people to violence," he remarked in an interview.§ Freud was "not like Freudians, but marvelous, like Proust, the most revealing mind of our age." The principles of the Founding Fathers "are necessary for us, but they are curiously fragile in action." Applied political theory, applied psychoanalytic theory, worried him. He makes the link to his experience of illness explicit in a letter about "Waking Early Sunday Morning":

*"Gerard Manley Hopkins," *Collected Prose* (1987), 168.
†"On Hannah Arendt," *New York Review of Books*, May 13, 1976.
‡Ricks, 257; Meyers, 114.
§Meyers, 127.

The poem is about energy (Too much and too little, both dangerous, a sort of non-clinical manic-depressive state, resembling the world and the American national character[,] mine too)—then about the pathos and impotence of the old religion, belief in the state etc. Then, of course about American imperialism, Viet Nam, etc.

The old belief in the state continued to "enchant and reproach" him, but he was as distrustful of it as he was of the desire for power. He aligned himself with Eugene McCarthy over Robert Kennedy in the 1968 presidential campaign in part "for McCarthy's negative qualities: lack of excessive charisma, driving ambition, machinelike drive, and the too great wish to be president."

Some years earlier, after a Kennedy White House dinner, he wrote to Edmund Wilson, "Except for you, everyone there seemed addled with adulation at having been invited. It was all good fun but next morning you read that the President has sent the 7th fleet to Laos . . . I feel we intellectuals play a very pompous and frivolous role—we should be windows, not window-dressing. Then, now in our times, of all times, the sword hangs over us and our children, and not a voice is lifted." However hesitant he may have been to get in a fight, he never avoided one if he felt it was right. He took part in countless protests, famous and obscure, against the Vietnam War. After the 1968 Columbia student uprising, Diana Trilling took him to task for supporting student protesters whose behavior she found unseemly. "She seems more preoccupied with the little violence of the unarmed student uprisings than with the great violence of the nation at war," he wrote in rebuke. "She implies that we who are horrified by napalm on human flesh are somehow indifferent to the piss on President Kirk's carpet. She wants to be sure where I stand on this." He ended with an antideclaration of his position: "I want to explain . . . that I have never been New Left, Old Left, or liberal. I wish to turn the clock back with every breath I draw, but I hope I have the courage to occasionally cry out against those who rule us, and wrongly lecture us."

"It's like life, only I'm allowed to talk enormously more," Lowell wrote to Hardwick about a film documenting a Castine dinner party. Reading his correspondence is not dissimilar—one overhears him develop his friendships over a collection of "now"s that took a lifetime to write. That it was a lifetime of intense concentration, discipline, and study is clear enough. But there is something else about him that his letters reveal, "the original moment that his presence always was," as Hardwick remarks. "That is the very person so

many people loved and whom scarcely any friend, and certainly no woman . . . ever repudiated." In the "fray, shamble, and conversational idiom" of letters written when he was well, one hears in his tone his fearless tenderness. Writing to older men like Ezra Pound, George Santayana, William Carlos Williams, contemporaries like Bishop, Arendt, Randall Jarrell, Mary McCarthy, Peter Taylor, younger writers like Bidart and Seamus Heaney, Lowell sought to learn from them—about writing, philosophy, politics—with all the wit and regret he could bring to bear. The character that emerges is affectionate, courtly, attentive, and gregarious, hungry for company, hungry for fathers.

His "love of line, form, quality" and his willful revision of his other writing might suggest that he did not value letter writing as a formal activity (as, say, Bishop did); yet his correspondence is very writerly. "I think letters ought to be written the way you think poetry ought be," he wrote to Allen Ginsberg. "So let this be breezy, brief, incomplete, but spontaneous and not dishonestly holding back." His letters are not reshaped, dismantled, and made again in the daylight of his attention the way his poetry was, but they exhibit the same intelligence and character as his more formally controlled writing. And as loose and spontaneous as his letters might seem in relation to his other work, there is an unmistakable degree of composure in the correspondence of a poet whose fame—his life in rumor, as it were—is based in part on the impression that his work is ruthlessly open about the "acts and facts" of his personal life ("the reader [of *Life Studies*] was to believe he was getting the *real* Robert Lowell").* In writing a letter, Lowell chose not to express but to compose his moods and desires—he had to "grunt and sweat a bit to get the talk going." "The notion of composure," Adam Phillips writes, "is a clue about the fantasies—all the unspoken words—we have about excitement. . . . 'To compose,' as Ruskin wrote, 'is to arrange unequal things.'"† Lowell's letters are attempts to arrange his companionable, social self with his "ragged conduct, unreality, squabbling uncontrollable desires etc." The shape of that arrangement—what he describes, what he leaves out—is very different from his other writing. The letters have the immediacy of the first rhythm and the first thought that occurred to him—the very thing he revised away in his poems. Their interest lies in the different way they dress themselves. Near the end of his life, he wrote to Bishop:

*Frederick Seidel, "The Art of Poetry: Robert Lowell," *Paris Review*, Winter–Spring 1961, reprinted in *Collected Prose*, 247.
†Phillips, *On Kissing, Tickling, and Being Bored*, 42.

I liked your interview but must disappoint you by saying I'm still in free verse, written in the blue period after sickness, when I felt I could nothing else well. On the balance side and on the side of formality, I am told all my lines are lines. I do scores of revisions to make them so. I use iambics often loosened into anapests. I suppose definitions of words in the dictionary can be made to do this—anything can be scanned but not be made into decisive lines. I meant to say that I agreed with everything you said, but not in practice. How different prose is; sometimes the two mediums ~~just~~ refuse to say the same things. I found this lately doing an obituary on Hannah Arendt. Without verse, without philosophy, I found it hard, I was naked without my line-ends.

A Note on the Text and Selection

A printed edition of letters makes their original physicality—the creases in the paper, the imprint of the characters, the handwritten corrections—invisible. This edition does not attempt to present facsimiles of Lowell's letters, but I have preserved some sense of Lowell's interaction with the page. I hope readers will have a vivid sense of the letters as documents, as well as writing intended for specific recipients. The text follows as closely as possible the handwritten or typed originals. Editorial changes—either to amend something or to suggest something omitted—are indicated by brackets. I have put the many marginal corrections where he clearly intended them to go; several instances call for bracketed parentheses or dashes. If a letter is undated, I provide the postmarked date in brackets. If there is a conflict between the actual day a letter was written and the postmarked date, I give the actual date.

Lowell was not a fastidious letter writer. Where errors in grammar and punctuation interfere with the sense of the sentence, I have inserted clarifications in brackets. This judgment being somewhat subjective, I have done so rarely. To preserve the rhythm of his sentences, I have not otherwise set mistakes right or called attention to them. However, I have silently corrected insignificant misspellings, typos, and canceled words, except where they seemed to indicate something of the way Lowell's mind worked and corrected itself (for example, in one instance he types "I was mostly waste," probably intending "It was mostly waste").

To save space, I have omitted Lowell's address in sequences written from the same place, except for the first letter in the series. Lowell lived a peripatetic life, as the list of his addresses indicates (see Lowell's Addresses).

Two important correspondences are either missing or broken: his letters to Jean Stafford and Caroline Blackwood. Lowell presumably wrote to Stafford often during their courtship and marriage; Stafford destroyed those letters in a moment of rage. A few arrived later and are printed here. When Ian Hamil-

ton was writing his biography, Caroline Blackwood showed him Lowell's letters to her. He transcribed the portions of these letters that he found useful. Some years later, according to her daughter, a trunk containing silver, letters, and other items was stolen from Blackwood's London house. What remains is Ian Hamilton's transcriptions. The silences and broken pieces of the conversation, which I have replicated here, are striking elements of our encounter with it. Perhaps, over time, these letters will surface again; for the moment, fragments from them are what we have, suggestive and elusive as they are.

To produce a single-volume, readable selection, I had to cut many lively and interesting letters to friends, acquaintances, and colleagues. (Even letters of incidental interest—fixing the date for a reading, thanking a friend for a gift—contain at least a few startling turns of phrase.) Lowell sometimes wrote several letters in a single afternoon and repeated stories and jokes. Omissions of these passages and occasional bits of information (a phone number, the address of a mutual friend) are indicated by bracketed ellipses; unbracketed ellipses are Lowell's own. Small omissions to maintain the pace of the narrative in a selection this size were also unavoidable; but I have tried as often as possible to preserve whole letters. I hope and trust the many wonderful letters I have not been able to include, as well as the brief omitted passages, will eventually be printed in a multivolume collection. In the meantime, I refer scholars who wish to work with them to the library collections that house them (see Location of Letters and Manuscripts).

The privacy of two people is disturbed by the publication of their correspondence. Some recipients, among them Lowell's children, have preferred to keep their letters separate from the public. In a handful of instances (fewer than ten), I have omitted sentences that do not illuminate Lowell's work, life, or character but intrude on a living person's privacy or the privacy of someone's family. Lowell made his own life the subject of his work, however— three biographies about him and many biographies about writers in his circle have rendered incidents in his life part of the public record. In the interest of accurate literary history, I have not tried to protect his privacy. If a letter contained information about him that was disturbing, my impulse was to include it. In his work, he could be merciless with his own "persona" and, though he was ardent, earnest, and sometimes defensive, he never tried to make himself look good or to mask his faults.

Chronology

1917 Born March 1 to Charlotte Winslow Lowell and Robert Traill Spence Lowell III, a naval officer, in his grandfather Arthur Winslow's house at 18 Chestnut Street, Boston, Massachusetts. He is the couple's only child.

1919 Family moves to Philadelphia, where his father works in Philadelphia Naval Yard. Swallows a tiny ivory elephant, one of his earliest memories.

1921 Family moves back to Boston. Father works in Charlestown Naval Yard. Spends summers at his grandfather's house near Mattapoisett, where he learns to fish.

1922 Attends Brimmer School.

1923–24 Uncle Devereux Winslow dies. Family moves to Washington, D.C., where he attends the Potomac School.

1924–25 Father named second in command of Charlestown Naval Shipyard in Massachusetts and family moves to 91 Revere Street, Boston. Returns to Brimmer School.

1927 Father resigns from the navy and family moves to 170 Marlborough Street. Attends Rivers Country Day School, an open-air school. Collects books on Napoleon.

1930–34 Boards at St. Mark's School in Southborough, Massachusetts. Acquires "Cal" as a nickname. Befriends Blair Clark and Frank Parker. Is a poor student until his final two years, when he develops an interest in art and poetry.

1934–35 In the summer of 1934, works as a counselor at Brantwood Camp with Frank Parker. Starts to write poetry. In the summer of 1935, goes to Nantucket Island with Parker, staying in a house near a Coast Guard station in Madaket.

1935 Enrolls at Harvard College. Meets Robert Frost.

1936 Spends second summer at Madaket with Parker and Clark. Becomes engaged to Anne Dick. Fights with father.

1937 Leaves Harvard before the end of spring term, travels to Nashville, Tennessee. Attends John Crowe Ransom's lectures at Vanderbilt University. Lives in tent on Allen Tate and Caroline Gordon's lawn in Clarksville, Tennessee. Attends writers' conferences in Michigan and Colorado and works as a secretary for Ford Madox Ford. Meets Jean Stafford. Attends Kenyon College in the fall, boarding with John Crowe Ransom and rooming with Randall Jarrell. Befriends Peter Taylor. Breaks off engagement to Anne Dick.

1938 Grandfather dies in the spring. In the fall, moves into Douglass House on the Kenyon campus with Taylor, Jarrell, Robie Macauley, John Thompson, David McDowell, John Nerber, and other students of Ransom's. During Christmas vacation, while driving Jean Stafford home, crashes car, injuring Stafford's face.

1939 Stafford sues the Lowell family's insurance company for medical expenses. Trial in the summer, which Stafford wins. Lowell and Stafford become engaged. Ransom publishes two of Lowell's poems in the newly founded *Kenyon Review*. Meets William Empson.

1940 Marries Jean Stafford on April 2 in New York City. Graduates summa cum laude from Kenyon with highest honors in classics. Moves to Baton Rouge and begins graduate studies at Louisiana State University, planning to write on Jonathan Edwards. Befriends Robert Penn Warren and Cleanth Brooks.

1941 Received into the Catholic Church. Spends fall in New York City working for Sheed & Ward, publishers.

1942–43 Volunteers several times for the navy and the army but is not inducted due to poor eyesight. During the winter, shares house with Tate and Gordon in Monteagle, Tennessee. Abandons a book on Jonathan Edwards to write poems. Stafford writes *Boston Adventure*.

1943 Allies fire-bomb Hamburg and other German cities and declare policy of unconditional surrender. Moves to New York. Called up for military service. Refuses military induction; sentenced to a year and a day. Serves five-month term, first at the West Street Jail in New York City, then at federal prison in Danbury, Connecticut. Some signs of mild mania before and during imprisonment.

1944 Cousin Warren Winslow killed in New York Harbor when USS *Turner* sinks in explosion. Released on parole. Moves to Black Rock, Connecticut. Mops corridors at army cadet nurses' dormitory in

Bridgeport, Connecticut, for the duration of his sentence. Publishes *Land of Unlikeness*. Stafford publishes *Boston Adventure*. During the summer, reads nineteenth-century French poetry and writes many poems for *Lord Weary's Castle*, including "Colloquy in Black Rock" and "The Quaker Graveyard in Nantucket." Moves to Westport, Connecticut, at the end of parole.

1945 "The Quaker Graveyard in Nantucket" published in the *Partisan Review*. Stafford buys house in Damariscotta Mills, Maine. Ezra Pound arrested for treason.

1946 Lowell and Stafford spend part of the winter with Delmore Schwartz in Cambridge, Massachusetts, then returns to Damariscotta Mills. Befriends John Berryman. Separates from Stafford. Moves to New York City. Begins affair with Gertrude Buckman. Publishes *Lord Weary's Castle*. Elizabeth Bishop publishes *North & South*. Ezra Pound incarcerated at St. Elizabeth Hospital.

1947 Randall Jarrell introduces him to Elizabeth Bishop. Awarded the Pulitzer Prize for *Lord Weary's Castle* and a Guggenheim Fellowship. Meets T. S. Eliot. William Carlos Williams publishes *Paterson*. Summer at Yaddo writers' colony in Saratoga Springs, New York; meets Theodore Roethke and J. F. Powers, visits Frost. Moves to Washington, D.C., in the fall to begin job as poetry consultant to the Library of Congress. Meets Pound and Williams.

1948 Begins correspondence with George Santayana. Ends affair with Buckman. Begins affair with Carley Dawson (some signs of mild mania evident). Divorces Jean Stafford. Ends affair with Dawson; visits Bishop in Maine. Moves back to Yaddo. Pound publishes the *Pisan Cantos*; Eliot wins Nobel Prize. Serves on the Bollingen Prize committee with Eliot, Léonie Adams, Conrad Aiken, W. H. Auden, Louise Bogan, Katherine Anne Porter, Karl Shapiro, Allen Tate, and Robert Penn Warren, among others.

1949 Pound awarded the 1948 Bollingen Prize. First acute manic episode. Controversies at Yaddo and the Cultural and Scientific Conference for World Peace in New York. Hospitalized at Baldpate Hospital in Massachusetts. Marries Elizabeth Hardwick on July 28 in Boston. Moves to Red Hook, New York. First major depression; hospitalized at the Payne Whitney Clinic in New York City.

1950 Teaches at the Iowa Writers Workshop and at Kenyon Summer School. Father dies. Leaves for Europe, settling in Florence. Meets George Santayana.

1951 Publication of *The Mills of the Kavanaughs*. Lives in Florence; travels in Italy, Turkey, Greece, France, and England. Moves to Amsterdam. Hannah Arendt publishes *The Origins of Totalitarianism*. Writes very little.

1952 Leaves Amsterdam for Munich and Salzburg; teaches at the Salzburg seminars. Second acute manic episode; hospitalized in Munich and Switzerland. Moves to Rome. Writes "Beyond the Alps" and other poems in the first section of *Life Studies*.

1953 Returns to America. Teaches at Iowa Writers Workshop.

1954 Teaches at the University of Cincinnati. Mother has a stroke in Rapallo, Italy. Flies to Italy but arrives just after mother's death; takes a freighter home with her coffin. Third acute manic episode; hospitalized in Cincinnati and at Payne Whitney in New York City. Moves to 33 Commonwealth Avenue, Boston. Begins to write autobiographical prose.

1955 In the summer, visits cousin Harriet Winslow in Castine, Maine, for the first time. In the fall, moves to 239 Marlborough Street, Boston. Begins to teach at Boston University. Hardwick publishes *The Simple Truth*.

1956 Publication of "91 Revere Street" in *Partisan Review*.

1957 Harriet Winslow Lowell born on January 4. Tours West Coast in March–April, sees Roethke in Seattle, and meets Allen Ginsberg and other Beat writers in San Francisco. Although behavior mildly manic on his return, manages to avert an episode. Writes the first stanza of "Man and Wife." For the summer settles in Castine, where Bishop visits. Again manages to avert a manic episode. Writes "Skunk Hour" and other poems for the "Life Studies" sequence of *Life Studies* in the late summer and fall.

1958 Fourth acute manic episode; hospitalized at McLean Hospital. Returns home, writes more *Life Studies* poems and begins translations for *Imitations*. Divides summer between Castine and Boston. Anne Sexton attends his class at Boston University. Befriends Adrienne Rich. Pound released from St. Elizabeths.

1959 Sylvia Plath attends his class at Boston University. Publication of *Life Studies*. Manic episode; hospitalized at McLean. Summer in Castine and fall in Boston.

1960 Wins National Book Award for *Life Studies*. Receives Ford Foundation grant to study opera and spends fall in New York City.

1961 Publication of *Imitations* and *Phaedra*. Manic episode in spring; hospitalized at Columbia Presbyterian Hospital in New York. Hardwick and Lowell buy apartment at 15 West 67th Street in New York City. Begins to write *The Old Glory*.

1962 *Imitations* receives Bollingen Prize for translation. Teaches at the New School for Social Research. Visits Bishop in Brazil during the summer. Manic episode in Brazil and Argentina; hospitalized in Argentina and then at Institute for Living in Hartford, Connecticut. Hardwick publishes *A View of My Own*.

1963 Begins to teach at Harvard. Founding of *The New York Review of Books*. Visits England and France. Deaths of Robert Frost and Theodore Roethke. Manic episode late in the year; hospitalized at Institute for Living.

1964 Publication of *For the Union Dead* and *The Old Glory*. *My Kinsman, Major Molineux*, and *Benito Cereno*, directed by Jonathan Miller, premiere at the American Place Theater. Death of Harriet Winslow. Manic episode in the fall; hospitalized at the Institute for Living.

1965 To protest the Vietnam War, refuses Lyndon Johnson's invitation to the White House. Visits Egypt. *Phaedra* premieres at Wesleyan University. Death of Randall Jarrell. Manic episode late in the year; hospitalized at McLean.

1966 Travels to Italy. Begins to write *Prometheus Bound*. Befriends Frank Bidart and Grey Gowrie. Manic episode in winter; hospitalized at McLean.

1967 Publishes *Near the Ocean*. Prescribed lithium. *Prometheus Bound* premieres at Yale. Begins writing sonnets. Participates in March on the Pentagon and other antiwar demonstrations. Spends ten days at Center for Intercultural Documentation in Cuernavaca, Mexico.

1968 Continued involvement in antiwar movement. Supports Eugene McCarthy's campaign for the presidency. *Endecott and the Red Cross* premieres at the American Place Theater. Attends Democratic National Convention in Chicago.

1969 Publishes *Notebook 1967–68*. Visits Israel and Spain.

1970 Visits Italy and the Netherlands. Fellow at All Souls College, Oxford. Affair with Caroline Blackwood. Manic episode; hospitalized at Greenways Nursing Home, London. Hardwick visits, then returns to New York. Settles alone in London at 33 Pont Street. Begins

to write *Dolphin* sonnets. Teaches at Essex University. Publication of *Notebook*. Visits New York at Christmas.

1971 Returns to London; moves in with Blackwood at 80 Redcliffe Square. Behavior mildly manic in late spring, but manages to avert an episode. Moves with Blackwood and her daughters to Milgate Park, Maidstone, Bearsted, Kent. Robert Sheridan Lowell born on September 27. Teaches at Essex.

1972 Teaches at Essex. Works closely with Frank Bidart on *History, For Lizzie and Harriet*, and *The Dolphin*. Travels to New York and Santo Domingo in the fall to divorce Hardwick and marry Blackwood.

1973 Teaches at Essex in spring. Publishes *History, For Lizzie and Harriet*, and *The Dolphin*. Moves with Blackwood to Brookline, Massachusetts, in the fall to teach at Harvard. Blackwood publishes *For All That I Found There*. Returns to Milgate at the end of term.

1974 Wins Pultizer Prize for *The Dolphin*. Goes on a reading tour of the American South in the spring. Returns to Milgate. Begins to write poems in *Day by Day*.

1975 Manic behavior in January, spends some days in Greenways Hospital. Spring term at Harvard. In April, takes too much lithium, fearing an impending manic episode; checks into Mount Sinai Hospital in New York for observation and to reduce toxicity. Hardwick publishes *Seduction and Betrayal*. Summer and fall at Milgate. Prepares *Selected Poems* for publication and begins to work on a collection of his prose. Manic episode in November, hospitalized at the Priory in Roehampton, discharges himself, hospitalized at Greenways in December.

1976 Committed to St. Andrews in Northampton for two weeks in January. Returns to Milgate, writes more poems for *Day by Day*. Publishes *Selected Poems*. Blackwood publishes *The Stepdaughter*. Travels to New York City for American Bicentennial production of *The Old Glory*. Summer at Milgate. Manic episode in September; hospitalized at Greenways. Blackwood leaves for Cambridge, Massachusetts. Lowell follows at the end of October, staying at Blackwood's rented house and Frank Bidart's apartment. Blackwood departs; Lowell returns to England. Christmas in Scotland.

1977 Moves back to Cambridge in January. Hospitalized at McLean for congestive heart failure. Teaches at Harvard. Publishes *Day by Day* and *Selected Poems* (revised edition). Blackwood publishes *Great Granny Webster*. Blackwood moves to Castletown House, Ireland,

where he visits her. At the end of Harvard term, moves back to 15 West 67th Street in New York. Receives Gold Medal for Literature from the American Academy of Arts and Letters. Blackwood visits Lowell in New York and attends ceremony. Spends summer with Hardwick in Castine. Travels to Russia. Travels to Ireland to visit Blackwood and Sheridan. Dies in taxi from Kennedy Airport on his return to New York.

1936–1940

Education at Harvard and Kenyon Colleges • Marriage to Jean Stafford

Harvard • Tennessee • Kenyon

Lowell in Nantucket, Massachusetts, 1935 (courtesy Judith and Francis S. Parker)

1. To Ezra Pound

<div align="right">

A-12 Wigglesworth Hall
Harvard College
Cambridge, Mass.
May 2, [1936]

</div>

Dear Mr. Pound:

I have been wanting to write you for several months, but haven't quite had the courage to until now. You will probably think that I am very impudent and presumptuous, but I want to come to Italy and work under you and forge my way into reality. I have no right [to] ask this of you, yet let me try to describe myself and explain my desire.

I am 19, a freshman at Harvard, and some relation, I don't know what, to Amy Lowell. All my life I have been eccentric according to normal standards. I had violent passions for various pursuits usually taking the form of collecting: tools; names of birds; marbles; catching butterflies, snakes, turtles etc; buying books on Napoleon. None of this led anywhere, I was more interested in collecting large numbers than in developing them. I caught over thirty turtles and put them in a well where they died of insufficient feeding. I won more agates and marbles than anyone in school, and gradually amassed hundreds of soldiers; finally leaving them to clutter up unreachable shelves. I could identify scores of birds, at first on charts, later it led me into nature. Sometime overcome by the collecting mania I would steal things I wanted. At 14 I went to St. Mark's and never mixed well or really lived in the usual realities. At one point I became very strong but never got very far in athletics because I didn't think in terms of the necessary technique. I was proud, somewhat sullen and violent.

The summer before last I was a counsellor at a charity camp, hit the swing of it, and felt for the first time that I was driving ahead and breathing thru all my pores. I determined to keep it rolling tried very hard at football, didn't make the team but did well and gained a tremendous amount from the experi-

<div align="right">

| *3*

</div>

ence, then drifted along till winter. At that time I began reading Homer thru the dish-water of Bryant's 19th century translation. I mulled over the ideas for some time, and somehow they gradually became very real. The tremendous growth of Achilles and above all Zeus the universal symbol which has ~~begun~~ become almost a religion with me. I had always chafed against what I thought was Christianity, the immortality of the soul, the idealistic unreal morality and the insipid blackness of the Episcopalian church. Homer's world contained a God higher than anything I had ever known, and yet his world blinked at no realities. The whoring of Zeus and the savagery of the heroes. I know that the beauty and richness of Homer are what impress you most. I found this later in Chaucer, but a poor translation is an ugly photograph.

Last spring I began reading English poetry and writing myself. All my life I had thought of poets as the most contemptible moth so you can see how violently I was molded and bent. I was encouraged by Richard Eberhart, whom you have perhaps heard of. I spent the summer alone with a friend reading and writing. Since then I have been sucking in atmosphere, reading; and ~~writing~~ dreaming. Writing and trying to help one or two friends have been the only real things in life for me. At college I have yearned after iron and have been choked with cobwebs. I have had a good chance to read, I have gained a lot of inevitable experience; but no one here is really fighting. The courses are catalogues rather than windows.

I am enclosing a few poems as samples, you will probably think they are not enough to prove me. I pray you to take me! I can bring sufficient money to support myself, in a few year[s] I'll have to make my own living and am glad of it. I am ignorant of languages, but want to do nothing more than to learn. Your *Cantos* have re-created what I have imagined to be the blood of Homer. Again I ask you to have me. You shan't be sorry, I will bring the steel and fire, I am not theatric, and my life is sober not sensational.

Very sincerely yours,
R. T. S. Lowell

2. *To Ezra Pound*

[n.d. May? 1936]

Dear Mr. Pound:

I have to apologize in advance for this letter, because I am still in the dusk as to the exact meaning of "Why not try mediating on a few MORE of the im-

plications of yrl letter." Probably you expected me to mediate for several months and not 3 days. My interpretation is: "Work out specifically the various problems involved with leaving college and working under me and then I'll consider letting you come." You may have meant: "You're not wholly damned before you start but I don't see much hope." I assume that you made your wording intentionally vague so that I would throw myself into the future and push troops into all possible conjectures. That's fine but your tone is hard to catch. Rightly or wrongly I look on your note as sober and kindly rather than contemptuous or insulted.

Of course I don't actually know you, but I have felt increasingly enthusiastic about you for some time. Thru the indirect medium of your writing I can tell pretty well what I am up against. The main outline is hardly doubtful. If the 20th century is to realize a great art comparable to that of Chaucer or Shakespeare, the foundation will have to be your poems. You have re-created quantity, music, directness, and realism; your craftsmanship, your blood, and your ideals must be continued, but [I] don't think in exactly the same form. Can the main current of English literature float such a vast quantity of spondées and compound nouns? After all—

> Ear, ear for the sea-surge
>> rattle of old men's voices

(Justified by success) is just as peculiar as—With hollow shriek the steep of Delphos leaving. Your *Cantos* practically ignore hard narrative and motion. They are like lily pads on a lake: a flat surface swaying with vigorous and beautiful images. "Near Perigord" and the narrative in the *Cantos* are more impressionistic than the paintings of Monet and Renoir. Cantos XIV, XV, are completely static when set against the conclusion of the *Pardoner's Tale*. I would like to push both action and image to the limits.—

> nor can
> Her heart inform her tongue: the swan's down feather
> That stands up on the swell at full of tide
> And neither way inclines.
>> *(Antony and Cleopatra)*

For the exact word and the *fewest* possible *words* you ought to substitute *Real-*

ity [(]boredom, religion, anything[)] expressed with the utmost vitality. Eliot's "Ariel" poems are closely and skillfully expressed but lack vitality. I would like to bring back momentum and movement in poetry on a grand scale, to master your tremendous machinery and to carry your standard further into the century; and I think I have life enough to withstand the years of pounding and grinding before accomplishment. More specifically to work in Italy under your personal direction: plenty of work and plenty of leeway for initiative.

Please don't feel insulted, I have no delusions as to your bulk and my smallness, I am only trying to show you more clearly why I wish to become your disciple. Let me join you in September. You will have no cause to be ashamed of me. As soon as I get acclimated I will make myself felt as an exponent of your ideals. I shan't bring any strings of principles, but will throw myself into the fight and stay there.

Sincerely yours,

R. T. S. Lowell

P.S. Relatives have nothing to do with the question.

Address will be:

Nantucket, Mass.

3. To Frank Parker

[Madaket, Mass., n.d. Summer 1936]

Plump
As camel's hump
Or elephant's rump
Plump
As mountain's bump
Or walrus' dump.

Plump and plump and twice so plump
As plump as any may be
The rump is plump for thee alone
And for no other lady

Dear Frank:

I suppose I am the goat and write first. Of course I don't dare to affirm positively that you have not written. Perhaps you wrote a letter and forgot to mail, perhaps you mailed and forgot to stamp, perhaps you stamped and forgot to envelope, perhaps you dreamt your epistle etc. etc. etc. ad infinitum. With this off my chest I can begin.

I was sorry not to see you before leaving and especially to have missed your "Christ before Pilate." Is work proceeding pretty solidly? My [work] is doing well. Blair is a kindly dull creature who ruminates about the house and life much like a clumsy, slow, methodical moose calf. One night he even had a tantrum, magnified all his peculiarities and wouldn't speak. Even taking this into consideration, however, I can truthfully say that he is literally always sweet natured. Cooks every morning, smiles under any amount of jeering, and will always consent to anything I want. I think he is making steady headway, of course his progress is rather unexciting, yet I find that I grow fonder of him as the days go by and what I thought might be a very tedious summer is turning out very pleasantly.

I have written two fairly long poems and a mess of scrap work. Extracts are hardly worth while, you will see what I have done when you arrive here. When do you think you can join us? I am looking forward to seeing you tremendously.

Anne wrote me about the 25th and her day with you, and your bewitching. I swear Sunswick has the weirdest power: sorcery and death. I think "Cousin Annie" deserves a sound spanking. I don't know how much Anne has told you, but we are engaged. Reality and time crawl on us fast before we know it. 2 months ago marriage, working for a living etc. seemed far away at least 3 or 4 years in the future and now the curtain appears to have fallen almost overnight. I love her and know her as deeply and as much as anyone could in a few weeks, but must admit that she has not yet the same reality to me as you have and that the trial and tempering of the blade all lies in the future. The realities and problems are extremely powerful perhaps glorious, but at the same time infinitely sober. Can she or should she burn thru her neuroses? My indirect work with her this summer will partially answer the question perhaps. Will we be able to float our feather against the winds. All I should like to consider definite about the future is that you and I and Anne ([and] Bobo) will live and fight thru life together always working toward realizing our ideals. We have got to think about living conditions, making money; we must not compromise

and sink into school teaching, we must break away from our relations and throw aside all convention that we cannot believe in. I want you to think on those things, to be a friend of Anne's just as you are mine, to help her and tell me what is happening and to realize that you are and always will be a definite and imperative factor. I am afraid this letter has the tone of a campaign speech, but after all that's what we are beginning.

Could [you] buy a cheap volume [of] Shakespeare for Bobo. The Oxford at Grolier (Cambridge) also Marlowe *complete* you can get one of those green volumes in Cambridge for a dollar or two. Let me hear from you in a day or two.

Cal

P.S. Try and persuade Anne to come down to Nantucket with you.

4. *To Anne Dick*

[n.d. summer 1936]

[. . .]No one is a "he's a good fellow except for—." No weakness is in itself worse than another. Regard people as glass spheres, filled with stained water, the bottom dark blue, the top almost clear, gradual suffusion forming the space between.

All law, morals, and rewards are based by necessity on the black and white of action. No notice can be taken of the individual's utter depravity or suffering. For some warfare is a lark, they are incapable of being terrified. They are dull amiable cows, munching buttercups. There is also the man whose heart's blood flows consciously to his fingers and the bottoms of his feet, whose every nerve is a glowing filament, and whose soul flounders in his mouth. Both receive the same reward. In the staggering zig-zag to a machine gun nest[,] one endure[s] little more annoyance than the keeper of the beehives caught without his gloves, the other goes through the darkest horrors of hell.

5. To Charlotte Winslow Lowell and Robert T. S. Lowell

POSTCARD

[August 7, 1936]

We wish you joy
We wish you health
But would destroy
You for your pelf
The water's fine and so are we
One + one + one makes 3

Affectionately,
 Cal
 Frank
 Blair

Might be more
If we were 4

6. To Charlotte Winslow Lowell and Robert T. S. Lowell

August 9, 1936

Dear Mother and Daddy:

Thinking it over soberly for several weeks, I feel no motive for particular gratitude or acceptance of your stand. Outwardly you assume an attitude of gossipy indifference, and inwardly compliment yourselves with the belief that unaided you can run everything according to your own whimsies. Another year of college will do no harm. Aside from that I might as well list out my position on all fundamental points:

(1) I consider a *college education* and degree as not only valueless but detrimental. One does not meet interesting or useful people. I have no interest in college life or athletics of any sort. The courses (English in particular, also the others) are largely conservative hack work conducted by mediocrities. Any profit that I have so far gotten, except for a valuable insight into the stupidity of academic methods, has been from my own reading etc. almost in spite of the authorities.

(b) The last thing I'd want to do would be to teach or profess, or get a fellowship.

(2) I regard your attitude toward a *self-supporting job* as sentimental. Perhaps if Daddy had been slower to self support himself he'd do better off now. Apart from necessity (which incidentally is not very pressing) the honor of earning one's own living, is a very small thing when set against the honor of writing lasting literature. Writing that is worth while seldom pays especially at first. I doubt if there is any poet of real ability alive, who supports himself by his writing. The sort of jobs I could get: English instructor at Harvard, comma-pruner for *Atlantic Monthly* or head pencil sharpener at Elmer Bright's, would necessitate long hours of drudge work on things for which I have only 2nd rate ability and the practical abandonment of really first rate talent for writing.

(3) I have no intention of leading a sort of platonic-non-money-making existence. I have already made a few valuable connections, not because I was a Lowell at Harvard but by my writing and general attitude. I expect in a year or so to show my power in perfectly definite ways.

(4) For reasons hardly worth mentioning I intend to marry Anne as soon as possible. Direct dependence on you or anyone else cannot be considered. I have no hopes that you will grant it but the only possible way you can help is the *gift* (not allowance) of a moderate sum of money.

Apparently there has been some sort of crazy correspondence between you and Frank. (I paraphrase Blair's account for substantiation.) While Blair and Frank were alone in Nantucket, Frank received a letter from Daddy upon the reading of which Frank tore it into minute pieces stamped on it, all the time shouting this is the most absurd, hypocritical, insolent nonsense I have ever read. The most colossal fabrication of false Back Bay morality and true sophistry. Did you really button-hole John Parker for 2¾ hours! I think Frank is writing a violent reply but am not sure whether he has mailed it. I must say if you go gunning mosquitoes with cannon expect to ooze out your life in yellow fever, or rather if you make an ass of yourself expect to get the scab. For heaven's sake don't antagonize any more people until you have conferred with me.

I conclude with wishing you may find wealth, health, and happiness in

Germany, and hope that you may bathe in the spring of everlasting goodness and beauty (if it hasn't been transformed into sulphurious bath tubs).

Affectionately,

Cal.

7. To Richard Eberhart

Aug. 23, 1936

Dear Dick:

Owe an apology for the mix-up at the end of the term unconnected telephone calls etc. also for not having written sooner (or does one apologize for not writing?) I have had a full summer besides quarrelling with my parents, reading 15 Elizabethan plays, practically tutoring Clark, writing a quantity of verse and prose; I have become thoroughly and firmly engaged, almost married. As letters are a rather unsatisfactory medium I'll only state facts. Anne Dick, 1st cousin of the St. Mark's Elkins and Kinnicutt[,] a distant relative of Frank's. 24 years old and very much the real thing.

As a result I have [been] sandwiching my time between Ipswich and Nantucket and am leaving here for good in a couple of days. I read your two poems in some magazine or other at Grolier, both familiar. Your "Alphabet" is effective enough as a tour-de-force, but only an etymological fanatic armed with a Webster's dictionary could read through it. Admired your second with the portraits, but wonder if the art in it isn't a bit too obvious. Anyhow it wasn't as impressive as some of your simpler pieces. What are the facts about your book, what are the reviews saying? When does the American edition come out? How is this? in the same line as your "Alphabet"[:] "a cryptical cricket consciously cutting elliptical capers across a circular cobweb." I have been wrestling most of the summer with technique, realizing that vigorous expression wasn't enough, tried my hand at both satire and prose. Beginning to feel my judgment hardening, recognize calibre more easily. I'll send you a few little pieces so you can decide for yourself.

I was awfully sorry not to have seen you this spring, and have a last talk about our summers. Looking forward to reading *Reading the Spirit* and your novel. How far have you gotten? Started to read Huxley's *Eyeless in Gaza* found it so insipid and dull that I could endure but sixty pages. Apparently all the critics want is tons of biology, anthropology, sociology etc. dumped into seas of unnatural, over-elaborate psychology, colored here and there by a few loose metaphors. Read also Wyndham Lewis' *Snooty Baronet*. Although it

lacks structure and is at times hardly articulate, the conversations, the firm satire, and the rough hewn craftsmanship of the prose ought to make it lasting in these days. Wonder if the old Anglo-Saxon alliterative poetry isn't coming back, loosened up a bit and strengthened by assonances and off rhymes? Pardon the hap-hazardness of this letter. I find it difficult to express but what you are doing means much to me.

 Affectionately
 Cal Lowell

If you want to reply my address will be
c/o Mrs. Bayard Tuckerman
Appleton Farms
Ipswich, Mass.

Will try to get in touch after school opens in September sometime.

Do [you] know anything about a fellow at Harvard called McCreary? I showed him some of my stuff (written after I saw you last). He said none of them were really poems but that he had never seen anything like the images from some one of 19.

8. To Charlotte Winslow Lowell

[170 Marlborough Street]
Boston
August 24, [1936]

Dear Mother:

 I am just up in Boston for the day, buying necessary books. Have you ever read Dryden's operas[,] they are as intriguing as Agatha Christie. Found it necessary to open the house in order to dig up some old Napoleana; what did you do with Sir William Napier's *Peninsula War* I couldn't find it anywhere[,] 6 green volumes. 170 was awfully musty and cobwebby but I have been opening windows, pulling up shades and so forth and now things are really quite livable. Mr. Herne was very agreeable about keys, telling us where to go.

 For the past 3 days I have been to Rock and expect to return tonight. Things are very pleasant and quiet there, although hardly carried on with their usual éclat. Gaga and Aunt Sarah are very well, leading their usual existence, shut up days, out to water the garden, pounce in the evening. Gaga is reading the mem-

oirs of St.-Simon in French, which she finds very dull and keeps wondering why she took it out of the Athenaeum. Granpa is in fine style we have had 4 very close matches at pool, of which I won one by the skin of my teeth. The fishing has been rather poor, but tell Daddy I caught a small-mouth bass weighing 2 lbs. ¼ over near the island. Yesterday I went out with Mr. Thomas and only caught a few perch and a small pickerel. Granpa wonders why I am not doing more lazing. The tennis court has been abandoned. I have never seen Cinder looking better, although she boards at Macdonald's, she is constantly about the house, accompanied by the world's little dogs with whom she is really very intimate. All my energies have gone in to avoiding dances (barn dances) for Aunt Sarah's god-children you know how I hate them, i.e. the dances.

Anne is at Bar Harbor staying with some relatives, and hopes to be here in a week or two, perhaps I will visit her then. Blair has returned to Newark and is attending his father's wedding. He is marrying a certain Mrs. Russell Black. Everyone thinks it was the best thing he could have done considering the circumstances. Frank is at 55 Pickney Street, working hard, thru the influence of his Aunt Molly he expects to get some cartoons in the *New Yorker*, satires on Boston stock broking. I am so glad he is getting a definite start. I had lunch with Mr. Eberhart, who has just completed a novel and is highly exuberant about it. Harper's has practically accepted.

Gaga and Aunt Sarah join me in sending their love to both of you and Granpa. I hope all three of you are enjoying Carlsbad.

Very affectionately,
 Cal

P.S. I wish you could be with me to enjoy the blackberries. I have never seen them so large and tasty. No one else will eat them. I hope you will write about all you are doing. Are you really in Nazi Germany? It must be exciting! [. . .]

9. *To Robert T. S. Lowell*

[Cambridge, Mass., March 4, 1937]

Dear Daddy:

 I have been churning about and turning things over for the last two months or so, and have at last come to realize I have been very foolish, very weak, aside from the fact that what I did might have had far more disastrous results; one can not get away with striking his father or for that matter using violence to anyone. I am sorry and wish to be forgiven.

Things in the past have been very wrong, and of course the blame must be divided. Relations were not cordial, but cold, distrustful, and deceptive, and if I am allowed to re-enter the family I hope we can establish a condition of mutual confidence. I believe that many of the provisions you have made for me have proven sound, but I do not believe they were made with sympathy and understanding. My objections have not been to *what* you have done but to *how* you have done it. Our aims and desires, I think will turn out to be much less opposed than they have appeared, if discussed openly without prejudice. I think that given a fair chance I can work with and not against you, and hope if you will permit it to have a much more intimate relationship than was ever possible in the past. I will be glad to apologize whenever you find it convenient.

Affectionately,

Cal

10. To Sarah Winslow

[March 24, 1937]

Dear Aunt Sarah:

I have been in a state of inertia for the past two weeks: wondering, writing and watching the time go by. This is no excuse for not thanking you for your "timely" handkerchiefs. As you know I usually have a cold (sniffles) all winter. Pajamas and handkerchiefs seemed to have given out simultaneously.

You probably know that I am back in the family. Daddy could not have been more reasonable, and I think everyone realizes that a great deal of friction was needless and merely the result of misunderstanding. Nevertheless I sometimes feel rather uncertain about the future, the atmosphere is strained, my father is leaning over backwards too much, more than he can enjoy. Intercourse creaks: I have been home once, I haven't spoken to my mother, set times are made for meeting. All this is inevitable after a wide rupture. I hope above all that a mutual sympathy can be reached. Individual demands are relatively trivial.

I want to formally thank you for being so kind to both Anne and myself during this awkward "interregnum." It has meant a great deal to both of us. Are you back at your home again. Can we arrange for a tea sometime this week? I am busy Thursday and Friday, how about Saturday.

Very affectionately,

Cal (I don't know how to sign myself.[)]

I hope this is legible, I had to submit myself to the interesting but unenjoyable experiment of sharpening my pencil with a sealing knife in order to write.

11. To Anne Dick

<div align="right">
Hotel William Penn

Pittsburgh, Pennsylvania

[n.d. April 1937]
</div>

Dearest Anne:

I am beginning a long day; from 8 to 8 I am free and vacant. The trip to Pittsburgh was neither particularly dull nor particularly exciting. Merrill has 4 children, for the most part too young to be articulate. Their names are Adam (after my grandfather), Leslie (after Mrs. Moore), Hesperus and Eve (after our primal parent). Hesperus mirrors Merrill down to the eyebrows.

I am daying in Pittsburgh, nothing to do from 8 to 8. M. speaks of taking you on as an independent patient which I suppose means pay cut and Miss Rogers. Your point is not how can you be occupied but, how can you work with me toward marriage, how you can profitably develop [in] the interim. See that your talk is on that basis. The less of Miss Rogers the better. He has several "voluntary" jobs up his sleeve and is going to pass on all his literary invitations to you, i.e. going to parties not giving them. Keep on the point of marriage! Perhaps you'll get an invitation to dinner with Robert Frost in a few days.

Reading over the "Fugitive" poets on the train I decided Allen Tate is very topnotch, a painstaking technician and an ardent advocate of Ezra Pound. Three things I want to do. I doubt if Moore is in sympathy with any: Read Ezra, keep up my organization, *and have you prepare for our marriage.*

Merrill is a fine fellow but somehow I feel he has four children because it is psychologically ~~bad~~ unwise to have less. Sounds in the sleeping car after lights. Merrill="Do you want to go pee" (pea?). Hesperus="nooo" (no). Just the exact amount of enlightening on sex-consciousness realism. I think he will forward what we want if kept an eye on.

Have Frank tell Norman to get in touch with Merrill as soon as possible. Tuesdays at the Hygiene Building. What is Frank's address? Be[tter] think it over so you can tell me when I send mine. I have spoken about McCreary and will more.

I miss you terribly but refuse to say anything. Granny gave me a little pic-

ture of you bonneted[,] send the dark eyed one. Blair took my picture as we were leaving and has agreed to go to tea at 170. I can nam(M)oore.

 love
 Cal

P.S. Why it is a letter I could show my grandmother!

12. To Norman Johnson

[Clarksville, Tenn., n.d. 1937]

Dear Norman:

[...]I have been spending the past 3 weeks in a translucent green umbrella tent, obliquely under a fragile green lotus tree on the front lawn of the agrarian poet Allen Tate. His wife writes serious and extremely fine novels and together they scrape up a shabby living writing. You would probably find things in common with them, that is they churn their buttermilk, make buttermilk cake etc. but then they are strong on tradition family etc.

My writing has been developing more or less on the lines you suggested, no more free verse, use of rimes, rational use of material instead of impressionistic fanworks of sympathetic particles. I feel strongly now that one should establish his thread and then logically elaborate. For a single sentence (a) I ran down the hill (b) I hurried down the hill with a bundle of straw, stumbling. Of course to be a poem several sentences realizing a definite effect would be necessary. The ~~sowing~~ plowing would [be] more valuable than the buried pot of gold i.e. the energies called for to realize the effect would stand on themselves once lured out in definite form. Apparently today the ~~greatest~~ problem is to discover a substance or symbolism dense enough and concentrated enough to bear and coordinate the huge energies necessary to produce poetry of vital impact. In the past various love and pastoral conventions were used and almost every emotion had some established device to give it a more clear cut and ritual truth. On a larger scale the Fall of Man and the Christ legend served the same purpose. I find it nearly impossible to shape a poetic form out of my feelings. [...]

Mr. Ransom is moving from Vanderbilt College in Tenn. to Kenyon College in Ohio. I am planning to follow him there and board with him, taking certain courses at the college. There is mention of some sort of going abroad [to] Oxford but I don't think it would be for at least two years. I hope to settle down and really learn Greek and Latin. Ransom is going to be at Boulder, so that when I am thru there I will have a definite knowledge of the potentialities

of the future and hope we can work out some course together, we might both go to Oxford or something of the sort.

I miss your advice and friendship. But real connections are never broken. I don't believe I will ever meet anyone with as sound an outlook. Everyone is down here now, and there is great confusion. Such as being driven 97 miles an hour by Harry Brown and burning a bearing to the distress of Blair. I don't know that the change of scenery has brought much serenity but I feel littler and solider, and know better what I need to do to advance, and less inflated with my doings and writings.

Write and tell me about Merrill Moore, your plans for a scholarship and begin to think about how we can spend some more time together. Any news is thirsted for.

Affectionately,
Cal

13. To Richard Eberhart

[n.d. Summer 1937]

For the past 3 weeks I have been camping on the Tates lawn in a translucent green umbrella tent obliquely under a lotus tree. Barnyard stock meander all around me, occasionally scratching the tent sides or pawing the mosquito netting. The Tates live in a shabby plantation house which is not ancestral, high on the top of a slope overlooking the brown Cumberland River[. . .]

Everyone seems to have his own theme or foible instead of puzzling about the materialistic and ideal worlds as you do[. . .]All here is land vs. industry. Tate is sold on sectionism ("The South of course should have seceded it would even have been better for the North, Communism is just a ruse to maintain the New York supremacy." etc.)

[Ford Mrs. Ford ½ Jewish, Francophile, ex. comm.—her sister in law, Ford's secretary Jewish. comm. m. to comm. painter]

The Fords are spending two months with the Tates and there is a certain amount [of] buried conflict. Water is supplied by a cistern, toilets must hardly ever be flushed, French as opposed to Tennessee cooking.

I am not on speaking terms with Mr. Ford, the explanation given, being that he is afraid I will write memoirs 30 or 60 years from now, in which I will describe him as an ever stout, gouty old gentleman deluded by the poetry of Christina Rossetti and potentialities of the ideograph, as opposed to the alphabet which [belongs?] with the printing press.

[Jarrell going to Kenyon with Ransom]

I have written several poems since coming here, moving toward greater simplicity and more direct expression of emotion. [Poems rejected by "Gregory Review"] I'm in no hurry for recognition. I have no doubt in my ability to produce in the end.

14. To Charlotte Winslow Lowell

[August 23, 1937]

Dear Mother:

Sorry to have written so seldomly this last month but a month of Writers' Conferences leaves one exhausted and particularly undesirous of writing in his spare time. I am at Olivet College and will be until about the 12th, serving as a sort of conscripted secretary to Mr. Ford, taking dictation in the mornings and typing it out afternoons. As he is a very great master of English prose the training is very valuable, and I would not miss the opportunity.

Bill arrived here several days ago saying that he had been to see you, and your letter arrived this morning so that I feel more in touch with my family than I might otherwise. I do not know whether I like the far West or not, all seasons and familiar touches of scenery disappear there. Many of the writers want to go East, and many are harassed by foolish problems such as whether mountains and extending skies are legitimate subjects for poetry. The Middle-West is non-descript. Where the country isn't flat it might be anywhere, part of New Hampshire perhaps only the fields are greener, the roads are better and the people are fewer.

Kenyon begins on the 14th and I will board with Mr. Ransom who was out at Boulder and whom I saw a lot of and liked extremely. Probably it would be a good idea if Daddy got in communication with [him] about prices for boarding, tuition etc. as he is making the negotiations for my enrollment at Kenyon.

The summer has been very hard work and very much worth all the sweat that has gone into it. Much credit is due to Dr. Moore for his initial decisions which made it all possible. Many of the people I have met are above average but the Tates and Ford and Ransom are in a class by themselves. Give my love to Daddy. I would like to have my allowance sent here.

love

 Bobby

Give my best to Granpa, Gaga and Aunt Sarah.

15. To Anne Dick

[Kenyon College
Gambier, Ohio,
n.d. 1937]

[. . .]But without putting my head into [a] well I want to say I am sorry and that although it would be doing a favor to neither of us I'd like to see you again.

Even now I hear the steps of "horrentia Martis" my football acquaintance. ["]Mr. Ransom and I are going to drink some beer and we want you to drink with us."—Ransom not in the least an even casual drinking sort of man.

But let me any way see you again and as Frank of old times would say: We're hardly less than friends. My letter is sort of pigeon-feathered but I mean more seriously. That is[,] I hardly as ever yet want to let go[,] and want you to let me do something for—but preferably with you.

love
Cal

16. To Frank Parker

[November 9, 1937]

Dear Frank:

Condolements and greetings—and behold a voice sprang from the shadows. I was glad to get your letter and sorry to hear, what I might have expected, that you are sick. I was thinking of visiting the Tates on Thanksgiving but if you could come here, I would either put it off or we could drive to Nashville together. Did I tell you that I am taking Greek under a classmate of Mr. Manzur's—ambi-vociferous in phonetics and choir-practice—; he has one expression: "hie you to the blackboard." I am not sure how one should obey such a request but surely the student's not greatly delayed approach to the blackboard is implied. So: "hie you to Kenyon Ohio."

My sheets of paper seem to wither in the wind! I have written Cousin Lawrence, Blair and Norman. Perhaps the mere "Harvard College" doesn't land a letter; so could you give me Blair's precise address? You gather, I have written and gotten no answers. Only Cousin Ghormley is faithful, and on blue-type he says: "This sounds awful but I haven't got time to write a letter instead I enclose a poem, you may send it back or not as you please. What do you think of it?["]

And now Arcadia is in full bloom, the happy shepherd, having forsaken his rustic tennis rackets, pursues the nymphs. Mr. Randall Jarrell, at best an epicene in a state of pre-puberty, has found a girl who comes for him in a gray car. She teaches French and perhaps as Katherine the daughter of the mad King of France she teaches her King Harry to say: "la plus belle de la monde."

I am glad to hear you have taken up Virgil, who is a much better writer than Shakespeare: if simplicity and urbanity are of importance. Compare Shakes. with either Milton or Chaucer and see how gilded his vocabulary is. How many Shakespearean profundities are merely inexactitudes of phrasing? However, I speak out of half of my head. Why don't you get Dr. Pharr's edition of Virgil bks 1-6 put out by Heath? The vocabulary is at the bottom of the page.

I seem by circumstance to be drawn more and more into a realm oblivious to music, but envy your grasp. I now realize why Blair wrote Dave "*seems* to be pretty busy." Letters which appear unfulfilled always seem to tell almost everything so you should not complain of yours.

Sorry the league is Art and not art. Why don't you visit Chirico, or do you think he's varnish now. Ransom has a friend who is just like Dave only he is Jewish. On the subject of actresses on poetry, have you seen Anne Hegira? Are there any girls of body and brain in New York I mean excellent in body and brain.

Write back

Cal

P.S. Let me know if my "calligraphy" is impossible.

This crazy printed envelope is my mother's gift to encourage correspondence.

17. To Richard Eberhart

[November 27, 1937]

[. . .]If you mention my relapsing into the soft arms of a Harvard background—I'll ask you what about becoming a celibate in a fancy boarding school. You need not fret about winning or losing and no one knowing the difference. You have already established yourself as a poet—any intelligent person knows the difference—and Poverty has only partially come. I have had little praise that would allow me to spoil and am not expecting to peter out at 25. The underlined words in your letter are undecipherable. Please reproduce them using the established alphabet. Even your more composed letter had difficult places. In my defense I might add that mis-spelling seldom obscures meaning.

18. To Merrill Moore

[December 3, 1937]

Dear Merrill:

Ever since I received and later lost your letter from Mr. Jeffers and your enclosed return envelope I have been meaning to write, wondering vaguely if I had really forgotten your address.

The testy letter from my grandfather resulted from my writing him because it got on my conscience that I was neglectful. Doubtless my letter fell flat and never should have been mailed. An answer probably could be composed that would be neither sparing, insolent or insincere but I hardly feel up to it now. So I will say nothing to him until Christmas. Comforting him on his illness would be insulting.

I have always been a great admirer of H.D.'s work although it is hardly up my alley. As you foresaw I feel like settling here at Kenyon studying the classics in a leisurely and thorough manner and perhaps competing for a Rhodes scholarship. Ransom is on the committee for this section. Looking forward to seeing you this vacation.

Sincerely,
Cal

19. To Arthur Winslow

Mercy Hospital
[Mount Vernon], Ohio
March 21, [1938]

Dear Granpa:

A limit to tardiness is perhaps even better than adequacy—so I shall take advantage of an enforced vacation in this holy institution (a day or two for an insignificant sore throat) to write thanking you for your appropriate but over handsome birthday present, and as soon as I get back to school mail you without comment pictures of Kenyon.

My life here has altered somewhat with the opening of spring football. A few days ago we had a game which I played in for the whole period. This was not an athletic achievement since both teams were made up of Kenyon students. Nevertheless, the exercise is stiff.

I cannot remember your letter entirely but it appears to have been the most

favorable I have ever received from you; therefore I am on my mettle to extract another from you. I hope you will not be displeased with my having fallen back on the sisters of Nazareth.

I was glad to hear that you are better than when I last wrote, but very sorry to hear that you are still pretty unwell. Probably you wouldn't be encouraged to know that the meals at Phillips House are incomparably better than those of the Sisters of Mercy. I am surrounded by sacred effigies, statuettes and colored photographs of the Virgin, all the officials are hooded.

From time to time I answer a list of questions. One is: "What is your religion?" Despondently I mumble, "Episcopalian." Then all the Sisters lower their eyes awed by their charity. However, they lose nothing by their contract with the college.

I won't ask you to get better for my vacation but want you to anyway.
Love
 Bobby

20. *To Robert T. S. Lowell*

[Kenyon College
Gambier, Ohio]
October 30, 1938

Dear Daddy:

Your letters have been so kind and pleasant that I hardly feel that we haven't been in the closest communication. I'm really very sorry and hope you won't attribute my not writing to any lack of affection or bohemian belief that nothing matters.

You will be so glad to hear that Bill is doing splendidly, working harder than ever in his life and yet enjoying it. His family are gradually coming around and I suppose I'll get my money back.

My work is more satisfactory than last year—particularly my Latin. I think I shall probably major in classics. To do this I shall have to spend some time this summer studying. Santee, my professor, has offered to teach me Latin composition for a month. I would stay at his house and he insists that all instruction should be free. Next year when I graduate I should know Latin fluently even to the extent of writing verses. I should also be in an extremely strong position for a Rhodes scholarship—as confident as one should be.

I have submitted poems to the *Review* and hope to write you of the out-

come, but I shan't know for several weeks. Chances are favorable. You should subscribe not to the college newspaper but the literary magazine which sails under the unattractive name *HIKA*. I'll have McDowell send copies. I have a sort of essay in this issue.

Robert Frost lectured here and in spite of my moustache and glasses remembered me. Apparently he is now living right below Cousin Alfred near Louisburg Square.

I have stopped football partly so that I can do more studying. Tell Mother I shall write her in a few days and that [I] appreciate the things and socks she sent me. Two letters written the same night must overlap. I hope you'll forget my being so neglectful.

Affectionately,
Cal

21. *To Merrill Moore*

[Harvard Faculty Club, Cambridge, Mass., n.d. June 1939]

Dear Merrill:

Engagements seemed to be unfortunately spaced for both of us during the past two weeks. I wanted very much to talk with you. However, I shall probably be back again by the middle of August and possibly even July for the trial. At either time or both we can get together.

My family are still a trifle difficult, but I think that with your aid and my diplomacy and good will everything will go on amicably. In asking for your potential assistance, I believe I am acting with justification; for the past year has been the most enlightening and fundamental I have ever spent. So I am confident that given anything like an even break, I shall in the future achieve things of considerable value. By an even break I mean chiefly to be able to act without autocratic guidance from friends and parents.

My career, I hope, will be exceptional rather than queer. That is I have become more and more aware of the need for an at least surface conformity, dressing inconspicuously and neatly, living by a stable economy, flaunting convention by penetration rather than by eccentricity. Poetry depends on beauty, passion and comprehension, but even here the above remarks on conduct have a preliminary appropriateness.

Could you send me Milton Starr's address. I want to thank him for his summer invitation. Also I feel that in this era of accumulating inhumanity

every artist and thinker should do all he can to preserve and maintain the rights of the Jews.

Hoping you have a pleasant summer,

Cal

22. To Charlotte Winslow Lowell

[July 19, 1939]

Dear Mother:

I started to write you before and wrote a considerable amount but the content seemed unsatisfactory. This summer, between physics and the trial[,] is terribly busy.

I was glad to hear you were enjoying your trip and that Daddy's health is improving. I have been healthy but only partly enjoyed myself.

The money arrangement is this I believe: $500 have been transferred from my savings account to a checking account and each month Daddy pays Merrill $100. There are certain advantages to this which we discussed but both Merrill and I are distressed with the secrecy with which it was done, as I explained before $100 is insufficient for July with the trial.

I apologize for my irritable behavior on the night of your departure which was inexcusable. I am always infuriated by uncritical praise.

About Boston, I gather many people think you have behaved shabbily about Jean's accident. Such opinion is not my concern yet I cannot feel the action of my family has in all cases been ethically ideal. I say this not in anger but as a suggestion for a better understanding, an understanding which seemed to be making such strides this winter. Gaga sends her love and I send mine to Daddy

love

Bobby

23. To A. Lawrence Lowell

[Kenyon College, Gambier, Ohio, February 1940]

Dear Cousin Lawrence:

I appear to be embarked on the turbid waters of poetry and scholarship. And a career in poetry and knowledge is as hard to guide as Plato's horses. On the one hand I must range about discovering the fundamentals of knowledge,

dipping into science, politics and other arcana, forever seeking an education that is both profound and practical; on the other, I must keep spiritually alive and brilliantly alive, for poetry is, as the moral Milton conceded in practice and precept, a sensuous, passionate, brutal thing. I put in the last adjective because I am modern and angry and puritanical.

So much for my rhetoric, but something such as the above must be stated. My qualifications are a wide reading in English and an ability to read poetry extremely closely; a knowledge of the classics which should enable me, in say three or four years, to read fluently not only Greek and Latin but all the Romance Languages. I have need of a thorough acquaintance with history, particularly with American history (I use the term *history* widely and vaguely but mean cultural history: and again I use *cultural* widely and mean the varieties of life man has been through). I have need of a knowledge of sciences and mathematics, and here I am totally ignorant.

The relevance of such schedule to poetry is obvious. I cannot think it a pedantry that a man desiring to speak (or sing) something important should also desire to speak with certainty. Also if he lack scope, such as an acquaintance with science and an acquaintance with other languages, he will be romantic and an anachronism.

This letter is written principally for general advice. I also wanted to ask you about "Harvard Fellowships." I remember, when I was a freshman or a sophomore at Harvard, that you mentioned such. I think their advantages are that they pay well, demand no thesis, suggest a variety of fields along with men with various proficiencies. Then, as you said last vacation Caesar was probably wrong about being "second in Rome"; success in a big place counts for more than in a small. There is some question as to whether I am qualified for a Harvard Fellowship.

This letter might pleasantly be re-written in English and with something less disgusting than a soft lead pencil; that would be much better but I am not sure of the gain.

I was distressed that you were unwell when I left, and I would say much more that I really feel; but there is something gross and mercenary about concluding a letter of rant with amenities.

Affectionately,

Robert

24. *To Charlotte Winslow Lowell*

Dear Mother:

Kenyon has an unfortunate location. Everything said in Boston blows in my ears. I might as well be sitting in Dr. Moore's office or dining at the Chilton Club. You may enjoy talking about my sacrificed fellowship and forced marriage. The first is uncertain and the second untrue. Naturally I find such gossip very undignified and annoying. I beseech you to observe [the] negative virtue of keeping quiet.

I am not flattered by the remark that you do not know where I am heading or that my ways are not your ways. I am heading exactly where I have been heading for six years. One can hardly be ostracized for taking the intellect and aristocracy and family tradition seriously.

Affectionately,
Cal

1940–1946

Writing of *Land of Unlikeness* and *Lord Weary's Castle* • Imprisonment for
refusing military induction

Baton Rouge • New York City • Tennessee •
New York City • Jail • Black Rock • Damariscotta Mills

Lowell, Jean Stafford, and Robert Giroux in Damariscotta, Maine, 1945 (courtesy Robert Giroux)

25. To Mr. and Mrs. R.T.S. Lowell

[1106 Chimes Street, Apartment 3, Baton Rouge, L.A., n.d. June 1940]
Dear Mother and Daddy:

I had the leisure but little news to answer your letters and telegrams. Now Kenyon is past and our course is mapped out for the next twelve or twenty months.

Monday I graduated summa cum laude, phi beta kappa, highest honors in classics, first man in my class and valedictorian. For next year I will have a junior fellowship at Louisiana State University and probably will take a master's degree next spring. Jean is secretary of the *Southern Review.*

As we are just moving into our apartment, Cousin Belle's furnishings, my tea set, and any odds and ends of plate, glass or linen you can spare would be very welcome, if sent post-haste. None of these things are bare necessities, but you will understand, how, when one has a thread-bare purse[,] they make life pleasanter.

The climate, here, is humid, the people are affable, the architecture parvenu and the work is tough but useful. Our address is 1106 Chimes St. Apartment 3 Baton Rouge Louisiana. I hope you both have a cool and easy summer.

love,
 Cal

26. To Mary Devereux Winslow

[n.d. Summer 1940]

Dear Gaga:

Of course we have been daily enjoying your furniture and my slowness in answering is not a sign of ingratitude. Other articles from other people have also come until our apartment has grown to opulence; nothing more is needed.

I wonder where you have been this summer, I think Mother mentioned Mattapoisett. Baton Rouge is the utter opposite, inland, windless, waterless, suburban. In place of Mrs. Curtiss, the Casino, the wharf, the ocean etc. are immense twentieth-century-Mexican dormitories, iron pipes blazing with crude oil, palm-beachy trees and Huey Long's two million dollar sky-scraper capitol. This world is new to me; so is a coeducational summerschool and a Negro woman, named Loyola who arrives at six-thirty every other day to give us a grand house-cleaning. We have entertained with an elaborate dinner and now have a guest.

The war and our coming draft are "leveling." Nobody, conventional or unconventional, has good, unclouded prospects. I am neither a member of our military reserve, nor driving an ambulance in England; I am not looking for avocation or marking time. If war comes and they want me, I'll gladly go; if not, I'll continue in this peaceful and sedentary occupation of university work. I suppose writing is something of a career, something that steadily grows more secure and substantial.

We are immured in three ages of furniture: Cousin Belle, Rock, and Montgomery-Ward.

love,

Bobby.

27. To Robie Macauley

[n.d. Summer 1940]

Dear Robie:

You and Santee have hit, both with a tone of persecution, on one aspect of Gambier, pregnant women. His words were "*all* except, of course, Kitty Rice." Well, somebody (Nerber?) in Gambier has lifted fifty or sixty of my books, all the new expensive twentieth century books I can never again afford and which L.S.U. under the directorship of its bawdy, Victorian head-librarian neither has nor ever will have.

About L.S.U. I have taken as my motto, "in Rome consort with the Romans and never do as they do." Here reign the "critical approach," "the aesthetic approach," "metaphysical poetry" "drama in the lyric" etc.; the students are weak and wormy; Brooks and Warren/Brooksandwarren are excellent especially Warren; result: I am reading English theology.

This, as perhaps Randall Jarrell would say, is not as crazy as it sounds, but it's pretty crazy and must not be amplified. My poetic terminology using:

heresy, diabolic, frivolous gnosticism etc. should worry the solemn and liberal English majors. You might study theology and rewrite your monograph on Dave and anathematize him so he looks like a naked goose crucified.

I can list the summer's news: for myself, twenty-three chairs (we have three rooms) and twenty-two imitation Navajo carpets arrived from Boston, an arrangement called "the toastmaster" from Merrill Moore—his favorite wedding present, two courses finished, my hell and damnation poem against England lent to Brooks and since sporadically mentioned but never seen, an amusing rather disconcerting visit from Peter—Virginia Jett has just married; Peter, about to marry someone else, is planning to come here. I started my list with myself and there is little else.

Baton Rouge is a mushroom fake Mexican set-up, very relieving after the gothic-heavy North. We are really unexpectedly normal and happy.

Cal

P.S. The *Review* is taking Peter's story: $160. In their files repose Nerber's aesthetics and aspirations.

28. To Charlotte Winslow Lowell and Robert T.S. Lowell

[October 13, 1940]

Dear Mother and Daddy:

My circumstances in writing this are embarrassing: I am shut out on the porch, indefinitely into the night, until an excellent letter to you be finished. I have been told that I do not know why/what for I am writing; and I have replied "to thank my mother and father for three letters, two postal-cards, a box of S. S. Pierce food and a check for fifty dollars." This is the bond and curse of marriage.

How much news have I given you? Some of this may be repetition. People have been collecting: one and [a] half months ago, Peter Taylor to enroll; last week, Blair and Frank on a tour westward; finally for the last two months, members of the faculty, senior fellows etc. Result: a good deal of conviviality, entertainments, suppers and gossip. Then, of course, college has begun. There is nothing remarkable about it. Classes are now less frequent, assignments are longer; the students are more phlegmatic and study ~~harder~~ forever.

We were very touched by your pilgrimage to Saint Mark's Church. Perhaps you met the Reverend Brocklebank, who is a Kenyon graduate and something worse than secular in his manner.

As I go out to mail this, I go to register for the draft. Of course, no students will be taken for a while yet.

love,

Bobby

29. *To Peter Taylor*

Dear Peter:

Whenever I feel inclined to agree with you on anything, I should try to write. Two attitudes toward the war are morally plausible: a tempered isolationism or a tempered defeat [of] fascism. The first has the insurmountable defect of requiring a practical, reforming or rejuvenating program; the second can float along on its weary, negative catchwords "we still can do such and such" or "the world is made up of two sorts, people who want to work out things for themselves and people who take orders." Six months ago Middleton Murry said: "England can't win a Christian victory because she is not Christian." As the tide of movies, radios and speeches sweeps ahead, one wonders whether any other victory can be worth the frightful carnage and hooey.

Well, there it rests. I am now taking Communion daily. Yesterday was the feast of the martyrs Philip and Bartholomew. We may suppose that Saint Philip, when he was crucified in a world not worse than this, ~~remembered~~ understood the famous rebuke. Our Lord had said: I am the Way, the Truth and the Life. And Philip had answered: Yes, but show us the way, that will be sufficient. Then the rebuke: Philippe, qui videt me, videt et Patrem meum.

No, I am not being maudlin, but we should become hard-headed and remember the Germans are human and that no more comes out of a war than goes in.

My only news from Jean is a maddening telegram. "Cannot stay here. Can I have fifty dollars more, will go to Colorado Springs. Explanation follows." Her consumption is not serious and Witter thinks it quite likely flu. But she must rest.

I think Houghton is taking her novel. "The writing is very extraordinary—almost Proustian in its delicacy and imaginative insight."

Good luck,

Cal

30. To Peter Taylor

Southern Review
Louisiana State University
Baton Rouge, Louisiana
[July 1941]

Dear Peter:

The problem of Proust's memory fascinates me. Jean is writing a Proustian novel and you have turned to remembrance. I'll dash off a few definitions and aversions, not to Proust who is one of the world's few tremendous writers but to his method and its implications.

Memory is not an end but an invaluable means for selecting and accumulating, for holding an experience as in a pair of tongs so that the intellect may intuit from many angles, distort, refine, invent and develop etc. Memory is only a power for summoning images and consequently sub-intellectual and a fortiori sub-mystical. As an idol, as "something terribly important" (precious?), it leads to illusions. 1) The nostalgia of recapturing mentally what can never be recaptured in life, i.e. the past as passed, there mysterious, pathetic. 2) A perilous severance from substantial objects, a subjective state to be distinguished from Plato's realism viz. the Ideals are external, more in opposition to Aristotle by terminology than intention. 3) A solipsism: What I think, what I reconstruct, what I feel is reality. This results in hideous violence to nature and tendencies to pamper one's faculties of introspection and self-criticism. Proust has five or six marvelous stratagems for escaping such pit-falls.

If you must use religious vocabulary, don't use it with such luxuriant abandon. Many people we know will undoubtedly go to Hell. But what insolence and arrogance to say so-and-so is a lost-soul. Actions and operations not people are "lost." Who are the damned? Unless you have some criteria other than talent and sensibility your language is mere, ornery, perverse, insipid name-calling.

There! I have made my retreat and would give my left arm to have had you with me. At least you are not military. I am exempted on account of my eyes.

Love,
Cal

31. To Charlotte Winslow Lowell

[63 West 11th Street, New York, N.Y., November 2, 1941]
Dear Mother:

Learning to type has almost annihilated any potentialities I ever had for correspondence. I move slowly and pencil-writing is a lingering reproach.

We are able and delighted to be in Boston for the wedding. We will arrive on Friday at 8:45. Shipping from Louisiana has been very dear, so let me accept your offer of expenses.

My work is particularly enjoyable and going well I think. Give our love to Daddy.

Love,

P.S. Typewriters give one a stamped-collar-button style.

32. To Peter Taylor

[New York, N.Y., n.d. 1942?]
Dear Peter:

An "advice" letter or question is always a lot of psychological vexation and disturbance. Probably you should have gone to a priest at random, that way you would have gotten hold of the books at least. But then he might have been curious or given you Father Scott's pamphlets.

I'll list six or seven different categories and one book per category. Other titles by the same authors will do well enough. 1) History Christopher Dawson *Progress and Religion*. 2) Psychology Rudolf Allers *The Psychology of Character*. 3) History of Philosophy Etienne Gilson *The Spirit of Medieval Philosophy*. 4) Polemic Jacques Maritain *Three Reformers*. 5) Basic Philosophy Garrigou-Lagrange *God, [His] Existence and Nature*. 6) Autobiography St. Teresa of Avila, *Life*. If you want sheer information say on St. Anne, the Mass, or Purgatory go to the *Catholic Encyclopedia* which is dry, compact and exhaustive.

We who have accreted illusions all our lives must read just to be able to see. Actually, a good deal of it is pretty obvious the rest can be known with a little trouble, it is desperately hard, nearly impossible to do. Christians have to be perfectionists and so on and on. On the other hand, the Catholic Church always makes great pragmatical claims so that one might almost say common sense is impossible without faith in Christ. However, neither books nor letters nor talks will convert you, but only prayers principally your own with God's

grace. Read Hopkins's letters, he says this to Bridges who wrote that before joining any religion he would have to be intellectually convinced—a stubborn and typically late Victorian bit of irrationality. The correspondence nearly ended on the unfeeling suggestion that Bridges give alms for self-discipline.

Well so it goes. We all do what we can and what we will. But surely now that our world and our lives are washing out or turning to an awkward savagery and everyone is either utterly self-cynical or patting himself on the back for those very things he is spinelessly dishing . . . this is getting absurdly grandiose but it is not foolish to advise the people we love (O and the people we should love) to plunge into Christianity.

I've been having tonsil trouble too (ulcerous tonsillitis which is cured with pills). Your unpaid rent was no go with the income-tax man. While Jean was making a short trip, I took a Turkish Bath and was approached by horrible young men.

Cal

P.S. Will we ever see you again?

33. To Violet Otis Parker

[Monteagle, Tenn., December 1942]

Dear Mrs. Parker:

I have had you in mind several months and can hardly say why I haven't written before. The news of Frank's disappearance depressed me almost more than anything I have ever experienced. The day before John's letter arrived, a friend of ours told us that the losses on the Dieppe raid had been much greater than anyone had imagined and almost all Canadians. I remember waking Jean up that night and saying that I supposed it was foolish to hope any longer. A German prison-camp seems relatively close to home and secure. Frank is probably morose and all his friends are enormously relieved.

I know that [it] is quite unnecessary to defend Frank to you and that in any case I am not the appropriate person to do it. Still I want to go on record as saying that I think the people who sneeringly spoke of Frank as eccentric or a "problem" were talking through their hats. Of course, anyone's life is a problem, but while almost everyone else was resting, Frank was literally sweating blood to learn his craft. I never worked a tenth as hard myself, and imagine the same could be said of almost anyone I have met. When the war broke out he was already an accomplished painter and in the future I am sure he will have a

reputation and all the other pleasant things that come with age and practice. I could go on like this indefinitely but this is hardly the moment for an elegy.

I hope you are not too distressed by his failure to write letters. That is only a personal quirk and not at all indicative of his feelings. What Blair and I both most envied in him was his very natural and dogged love for his family. He never showed any signs of losing it.

I have just undergone my sixth physical examination for the army and am rather disgruntled. Jean is about to finish her book. The future is unsettled but things are going as well as one could wish. Thank John for writing us. I am afraid this note is a bit tedious and impertinent, which is not at all what I mean.

Affectionately,
Cal

34. To Charlotte Winslow Lowell

[12 Gansevoort Street, New York, N.Y., July 23, 1943]
Dear Mother:

This is just a note to tell you that I am well and happy. There are plenty of jobs but the problem is to get the right one. Right now I am looking about and doing odd jobs whenever my money gets low.

Jean is safely at Yaddo but still running a low fever. On the whole the conditions there are favorable to work and relaxation.

The other day I got notice from my draft board and expect to be examined (the 7th time) sometime in the next ten days. The chances are that I will be rejected on account of vision. However, there is no telling. My love to Daddy
Bobby

35. To Charlotte Winslow Lowell and Robert T.S. Lowell

[n.d. August 1943]
Dear Mother & Daddy:

Thank you for your letters and the check. I am glad you like my poem on Granpa, it is the first of a series of four in the same meter. They are the clearest and most positive writing in the book. All the other poems have been revised—I think you will like them better in their final form. What I am saying will be much more obvious and constructive. All of them are cries for us to re-

cover our ancient freedom and dignity, to be Christians and build a Christian society. I think of Blake's hymn:

I shall not cease from mental fight
Nor shall my sword sleep in my hand
Till we will have built Jerusalem
In England's green and pleasant land.

You see the meaning of my title: *Land of Unlikeness*.

Two days ago I met Caroline Tate in New York and she said she had written you to send Jean the money to be thoroughly diagnosed. I confess I was quite taken aback. On second thought I think you must do it. I shall be inducted on September 8th and can't manage it myself. Jean has been having these fevers off and on for three years. No one has been able to cure her or tell her what the matter is. I worry about this night and day and can't resign myself to the army with her illness still unsettled. Dr. Wolf has had an almost miraculous record; I believe he never fails. I don't [know] how I can overemphasize the importance to us of Jean's recovery. Our whole lives depend on it.

I'll try to get up to Manchester for a few days at the end of the month. My status debars me from any permanent job but there are any number of things I'd like to accomplish here. Give my love to Gaga.

love,
Bobby

36. To Franklin Delano Roosevelt

20 Harbor Street
West Manchester
Massachusetts
September [5 or] 7, 1943

Dear Mr. President:

I very much regret that I must refuse the opportunity you offer me in your communication of August 6, 1943, for service in the Armed Forces.

I am enclosing with this letter a copy of the declaration which, in accordance with military regulations, I am presenting on September 7 to Federal District Attorney in New York, Mr. Matthias F. Corres. Of this declaration I am sending copies also to my parents, to a select number of friends and

relatives, the heads of the Washington press bureaus, and to a few responsible citizens who, no more than yourself, can be suspected of subversive activities.

You will understand how painful such a decision is for an American whose family traditions, like your own, have always found their fulfillment in maintaining, through responsible participation in both the civil and the military services, our country's freedom and honor.

I have the honor, Sir, to inscribe myself, with sincerest loyalty and respect, your fellow-citizen,

Robert Traill Spence Lowell, Jr.

A DECLARATION OF PERSONAL RESPONSIBILITY

ORDERS FOR MY INDUCTION INTO THE ARMED FORCES ON SEPTEMBER EIGHTH 1943 have just arrived. Because we glory in the conviction that our wars are not won by irrational valor but through the exercise of moral responsibility, it is fitting for me to make the following declaration, which is also a decision.

Like the majority of our people I watched the approach of this war with foreboding. Modern wars had proved subversive to the Democracies and history had shown them to be the iron gates to totalitarian slavery. On the other hand, members of my family had served in all our wars since the Declaration of Independence: I thought—our tradition of service is sensible and noble; if its occasional exploitation by Money, Politics and Imperialism is allowed to seriously discredit it, we are doomed.

When Pearl Harbor was attacked, I imagined that my country was in intense peril and come what might, unprecedented sacrifices were necessary for our national survival. In March and August of 1942 I volunteered, first for the Navy and then for the Army. And when I heard reports of what would formerly have been termed atrocities, I was not disturbed: for I judged that savagery was unavoidable in our nation's struggle for its life against diabolic adversaries.

Today these adversaries are being rolled back on all fronts and the crisis of the war is past. But there are no indications of peace. In June we heard rumors of the staggering civilian casualties that had resulted

from the mining of the Ruhr Dams. Three weeks ago we read of the razing of Hamburg, where 200,000 non-combatants are reported dead, after an almost apocalyptic series of all-out air raids.

This, in a world still nominally Christian, is *news*. And now the Quebec Conference confirms our growing suspicions that the bombings of the Dams and of Hamburg were not mere isolated acts of military expediency, but marked the inauguration of a new long-term strategy, endorsed and coordinated by our Chief Executive.

The war has entered on an unforeseen phase; one that can by no possible extension of the meaning of the words be called defensive. By demanding unconditional surrender we reveal our complete confidence in the outcome, and declare that we are prepared to wage a war without quarter or principles, to the permanent destruction of Germany and Japan.

Americans cannot plead ignorance of the lasting consequences of a war carried through to unconditional surrender—our Southern States three quarters of a century after their terrible battering down and occupation, are still far from having recovered even their material prosperity.

It is a fundamental principle of our American Democracy, one that distinguishes it from the demagoguery and herd hypnosis of the totalitarian tyrannies, that with us each individual citizen is called upon to make voluntary and responsible decisions on issues which concern the national welfare. I therefore realize that I am under the heavy obligation of assenting to the prudence and justice of our present objectives before I have the right to accept service in our armed forces. No matter how expedient I might find it to entrust my moral responsibility to the State, I realize that this is not permissible under a form of government which derives its sanctions from the rational assent of the governed.

Our rulers have promised us unlimited bombings of Germany and Japan. Let us be honest: we intend the permanent destruction of Germany and Japan. If this program is carried out, it will demonstrate

to the world our Machiavellian contempt for the laws of justice and charity between nations; it will destroy any possibility of European or Asiatic national autonomy; it will leave China and Europe, the two natural power centers of the future, to the mercy of the USSR, a totalitarian tyranny committed to world revolution and total global domination through propaganda and violence.

In 1941 we undertook a patriotic war to preserve *our lives, our fortunes, and our sacred honor* against the lawless aggressions of a totalitarian league; in 1943 we are collaborating with the most unscrupulous and powerful of totalitarian dictators to destroy law, freedom, democracy, and above all, our continued national sovereignty.

With the greatest reluctance, with every wish that I may be proved to be in error, and after long deliberation on my responsibilities to myself, my country, and my ancestors who played responsible parts in its making, I have come to the conclusion that I cannot honorably participate in a war whose prosecution, as far as I can judge, constitutes a betrayal of my country.

SIGNED <u>ROBERT TRAILL SPENCE LOWELL JR</u>

37. To Charlotte Winslow Lowell

12 Gansevoort St.
New York
[September 5?, 1943]
Sunday,

Dear Mother:

After your touching letter about my picture and poems, I fear you will think this a rather shocking return. Please believe that I have taken the only course that was honorable for me.

I cannot ask you to support or even in any way concern yourself with my ideas. I do ask for your love, above all for Jean whose part in this is much the hardest. Don't be too alarmed about any consequences to me, they will be within just limits.

love,
Bobby

38. To Mary Devereux Winslow

[September 6?, 1943]

Dear Gaga:

I hardly know what to say in writing you and have hesitated to send you the enclosed statement. Finally I decided that writing you was my duty. You know more about American history than I do and can certainly judge whether our recent actions in this war are justifiable. I think only a Southerner can realize the horrors of a merciless conquest.

I love you immensely and want you to pray for us.

love,

 Bobby

39. To Frank Sheed

[September 9?, 1943]

Dear Mr. Sheed:

I owe you the deepest apologies for the disturbance on Wednesday. What happened was this. My mother in West Manchester woke up to find herself besieged by reporters, so she sent them on to Sheed & Ward, my mailing address. What she said to me on the telephone was: "I knew you wouldn't be there."

If you wish me to, I shall be glad to make a general statement clearing you or your firm of in any way countenancing or sympathizing with my position.

After two reporters—one was drunk and stayed for three hours—we have had no trouble. Perhaps if you are not sick of us, we could all get together for a non-political luncheon some time next week.

I am enclosing a copy of my statement.

Very sincerely,

 R.T.S. Lowell

40. To Peter and Eleanor Taylor

[n.d. September 10?, 1943]

Dear Peter and Eleanor:

I have been intending to write you all summer and thank you for the most delightful visit I have ever had. I am remorseful about having been so frantic and peevish,—pills and suitcases are a horrible mixture.

I send you this statement as friends not supporters. It's an unhappy business but one I cannot escape. Jean feels as strongly as I do.

Jean has had a hard but I think triumphant time at Yaddo. Yaddo is another Stephens College. She speaks on the inmates with copious eloquence. The novel is done.

love,
　　Cal

Good luck to your writing.

41. To Peter Taylor

<div align="right">

315 East 17th Street
New York, New York
[October 11, 1943]

</div>

Dear Sub:

Many thanks for your telephone call and your letters and your anxiety. You can hardly guess what a comfort you have been.

Here's how matters stand. For the past month I have been treated with almost alarming courtesy. No one has questioned my sincerity. Bail has been waived. Etc. This morning I was arraigned. On Wednesday I will be sentenced. I will certainly go to jail, but possibly for a very short time[,] a matter of weeks. Or maybe it will be longer: I really don't know what's up.

Jean is in very good health. The novel (still unnamed) is done and accepted except for some minor revisions. We have an apartment that delights her so, she has spent 20 hours a day for nearly a month playing with it. She hardly ever has time to speak to me. She will be as well off as I could hope under the circumstances which are bad.[. . .]

Jean will write you on Wednesday, and I'll write when I can. We have seen or heard from everyone under the sun and almost all have been warm-hearted beyond belief.

　　My love to Eleanor,
　　　　Cal

42. To Mary Devereux Winslow

[October 12, 1943]

Dear Gaga:

I don't know what to say to you except that I love you and am sorry to have caused you so much worry. That troubles me more than anything else.

I have talked at great length to my priest in New York and written the priest who baptized me in Louisiana. They are both very shrewd and experienced men. They are also very good men. They have told me to *follow my conscience and trust in God.* I have prayed for light and tried to persuade myself that I was mistaken; I cannot.

I shall be sentenced this Wednesday. I shall have to go to jail, but there is good reason to hope that in a short time I shall be transferred to the medical corps or to an objectors' camp.

Please forgive me for your disappointment and anxiety, and pray for us.

love,

 Bobby

43. To Richard Eberhart

St. Vincent's Hospital
Bridgeport Conn.
[March 24, 1944]

Dear Dick:

I am settling down to mop-work in the underground of this hospital, a little like your involuntary working your way around the world. The day after I was released from Danbury notice was sent to me to report for pre-induction physical examination. What comes next I don't know.

About the play: it is personal with a vengeance, in about a thousand details. It will be recognized by everyone and, of course, I am not crazy about that kind of free advertising. But that doesn't matter! It will be cruel to my parents and Anne Dick. So as far as I am concerned don't print it.

Some of the poet's speeches are excellent (I imagine he is you with a mask rather than me). The rest is little more than gossip, sometimes good sometimes commonplace, in a fancy style. Why don't you work it up into something that stands on its own feet rather than on our 2 necks? Good luck to your gunnery. By the way I am not a pacifist but a Catholic.

love,

 Cal

68 Ocean Avenue
Black Rock, Conn.
[July 10, 1944]

Dear John:

We are living in a really splendid apartment with great windows, but it rests on a dump and looks out on a mud-flat. My parole consists of getting up at 5:15 and mopping the corridors of a dormitory for student-nurses. This work has a harsh somehow moral monotony rather like my health swimming and running at Kenyon. Jean is in wonderful health and lies in bed all day reading novels.

I am mailing you my long satirical poem on England. I doubt if you can use it in the *Review* but I have been writing it for five years and am almost hysterical with relief at getting it off.

I have read your four articles on Hopkins. They are fine but not enough. I hoped Hopkins would get the same expert treatment as Yeats and Hardy. Here are my first, probably very superficial impressions.

McLuhan: good particularly the point about *buckle* which I missed, but perhaps more an example of how critical analysis is improving than a brilliant essay.

Miles: true enough but very limited and academic.

Warren: excellent description, but surely Hopkins' best poems are more than wonderful experiments. No attempt at real criticism.

Whitehall: this is terrific if it is true. But how could Hopkins have used this elaborate dipodic system without knowing it? His normal line seems to be an iambic line varied with sprung-rhythm. I read him that way without much difficulty. However, I want to try out Whitehall's scheme. I hope you will get him to write a long essay on *Piers Plowman*.

I feel disorganized and rush[ed] for time, very tired and wanting to loaf after mopping. I will try to write an essay or at least some notes.

Please give me an estimate of my long poem *soon*.

Affectionately,
 Cal [...]

45. *To Allen Tate*

[July 31, 1944]

Dear Allen:

Thanks for the two books to review. Hopkins and Baudelaire are an inter-

esting juxtaposition but I wonder if the two books *on* them will combine. The Ruggles is a very usual uncritical biography. Bennett's will be something else. I know very little about Baudelaire.

Last week I was given three days off. My blood-pressure is a *little* low and I am a *little* anemic. I spent the whole time, day and night, writing. (Oddly enough I feel much better.)

I think the seven poems I am sending you are a new style, more lyrical and lucid. There may be echoes from Eliot. Two you have seen in earlier versions. Two others are pillaged from my long poem on England, which John Ransom described as "big and oppressive" and I have decided to scrap. I have also heavily revised my sonnets and written two more.

I think the story of Peter's that Jean sent you is his best, more serious and toned down than any of his others. He is safe in England and won't do any fighting.

There was a nasty article in the *Commonweal* on the Fugitives. I thought I would answer and then decided not to. Their politics are mad, almost as bad as the *New Republic*'s.

The best thing about this job is that every night is like a Christmas holiday. We are really thriving on it. Give my love to Caroline,

> Cal [. . .]

46. To Peter Taylor

> The Barn
> Sturges Highway
> Westport, Conn.
> Saturday, 6/9, [1945]

Dear Peter:

Jean has probably written you that our house has been sold over our heads. The owner is a horrible Mrs. Newman who, literally, keeps her husband's skeleton in a panelled compartment over the piano. Our cat, Frederick Kuh, has disappeared. Jean said "Do you know how many kittens are missing?" I, "How many?" Jean: "ONE!"

The best comment on the war I heard is what the Italians wrote on the walls of some of their towns when we entered: "Fanno schifo tutti." I'll leave you the labor of looking up what this means.

Frank is out of prison, and married. If you have time look him up at the Cavendish Hotel 81 Jermyn St. London.

Did you hear Harry Brown's V. Day ode recited by Alfred Lunt and Lynn Fontaine? All I remember is a relay of orotund, capital-D Deaths peering and wailing about a lot of [illegible] cities. When it finally came round to "But the job only half done" alliterated with Japs I turned the radio off.

Very grateful for *Orthodoxy* which I want and don't have. After packing 14 cartons of books, I can't think of anything for you to send.

Too bad in a way about your not hearing Eliot. I imagine he would enjoy meeting you.

Have another book of poems about done. Can't think of anything else to tell you except Allen's disgraceful trip to New York.

Last night I met a Catholic poet who is tormented by voices. "On 23rd St. I heard as many as 250 speaking as clearly as you are in the space of three minutes . . . There are some idiot fiends who seem to have nothing else to do but talk to me. I imagine they waste their whole lives at it." Apparently he really has them.

Glancing over this letter I realize I haven't heeded the instructions I heard yesterday over the radio: "Every G.I. thinks that in America the streams flow with malted milk and every girl is a pin-up No. 1. When you write tell them the truth but emphasize what's good." Well I haven't bellyached about "rationing."

God bless you,

Cal

We must get together this year hope you don't go to the Pacific. Frank's brother was just killed on Okinawa.

47. To Selden Rodman

[Damariscotta Mills, M.E., n.d. 1945]

1917, b. Boston, Mass.
1940, g. Kenyon College
1944, *Land of Unlikeness*, Cummington Press
At present working on a second volume of poems
Contributor to *Sewanee Review, Kenyon Review, Partisan*

Dear Rodman:

I am afraid autobiography is not a s[ubject] on which I can feel loquacious, I think the on[ly word to] apply to War and war-poetry is .

The partly unrhymed sonnet should g[o] with the other six. I would like to have them printed without a space between the octave and sestet. Could you send me a copy of the first number of *Portfolio* c.o.d.

Sincerely yours,

Robert Lowell

48. To Peter Taylor

Sept. 27, [1945]

Dear Peter:

I can't remember whether I wrote you about your *Partisan Review* story. I gather from your letter I didn't. I think it is one of the great stories of the age. The detail is incredibly acute and solid. The Aunt and Scoutmaster are wonderful characters and unusual ones. The Aunt is the best I can think of, of her type. The way you have the boy narrate it is masterly. I had to rub my eyes to realize it was yours; not that I don't extremely admire some of your other stories, but with this one I think you can be said to have arrived. Delmore Schwartz who was staying with us admired it very much too. Have I written this before?

We have just bought a house and lived a month in it. Not even you could imagine the state of sustained ecstasy Jean is in. Every day I say: "Let's make a list of things that don't absolutely *have* to be done." I've worked pretty hard though I don't think we have ever been so happy. In the 17th century this region was Catholic and has the oldest Catholic Church in New England. The congregation is scattered and the priest, a round Irishman from Portland who has been stationed here for eight years, is about to go out of his mind. He loathes the country and wants to go to prize-fights. When I went to call on him, I saw two enormous black book-cases empty. He said: "You [see] I was so sure I wouldn't be here long, that I didn't even unpack my books." He is up to his neck in land-litigation with the widow of the deceased Bishop of Vermont.

> A clergyman in want
> Of a second-hand movable font
> Would barter the same
> For a portrait in frame
> Of the Bishop-elect of Vermont.
> Ronald Knox

I have just finished the manuscript of my second book *Lord Weary's Castle* and hope to have it published by spring. I hope it's a lot better than my first, on which I made $4.82 and a few anthologies.

While you are on autobiographies read Tolstoy's (I haven't but Delmore says it's as good as Adams) Gibbon's, Trollope's, Stendhal's, Hopkins', Arnold's, Flaubert's letters and perhaps Santayana's *Persons and Places*. Probably you know these already.

I think we are at an age when one is concerned with time in every form. It's in all my poems now, even the personified Time. By the way I think Ransom misled us on Plato. P's *ideas* are not Aristotelian abstraction but intelligible essences, more like God and the angels, at least midway there. Augustine's attitude about his mother's burial is no doubt a half-truth. Like Christ's forsaking all, which isn't altogether irreconcilable with what seems to be its opposite.

When you get home you must spend two weeks with us and drink as much as you want to. You are in much the state I was in jail only there no outlet except reading, work and argument.

 love,
 Cal

P.S. Hope you really do get out much sooner than 5 months.

I caught my first bass in ten years here. We expect to go to Sewanee in November.

49. To Caroline Gordon

[n.d. Fall 1945]

Dear Caroline:

We leave here on Friday, and will spend the weekend with my Mother and Father and be in New York on Monday. We are taking a furnished room and will stay about two weeks.

Your divorce is a night-mare and even now I find myself rubbing my eyes and expecting it to vanish. I am sure you will be delighted with Damariscotta once you get here. This part of Maine is old, wildish and unmodern. The "autochthons" are affable and much like Mr. Francis. With a few stoves we will be quite snug and even being snowed-in will be merry. You will get on well with our next-door neighbor the widow of the Episcopalian Bishop of Vermont. She bakes her own bread and chops her wood. We can see both salt and fresh

water from our house. The village is about a quarter of a mile away but we are quite out of it.

Two days after your first letter Allen wrote: "Caroline has left me—permanently." After that he asked us to come and keep house with him but that we might possibly feel our loyalty to you prevented this, and that his side was not the one to be taken. I wrote that it was physically impossible for us to come, that I assumed there were no *sides*, and that I thought we could be loyal to both of you. We've asked him to spend a week or so with us before December 15.

Of course our sympathies are entirely with you. If matters come to the point of formal hostilities, we will break with Allen or do whatever you wish. From your letters I gather and hope it won't come to that.

I think I once said to you that I thought of you as almost my mother. I hope you accept everything that is flattering and good in that comparison. Jean and I are very excited about what we will all do during the winter. You must stay with us indefinitely and make this house your home.

love,

Cal[. . .]

50. *To Selden Rodman*

Dec. 1 [1945]

Dear Rodman:

I've just come across the following sentence in the Dec. 3 issue of *Time*: "Random House hastily dropped Pound from a forthcoming poetry anthology." This would seem to refer to your anthology, although I'm sure there must be some mistake. However, publishers sometimes interfere this way with their writers and editors. If such should be the case I want to withhold permission for the inclusion of my own poems. I can't for a minute imagine you guilty of an action so time-serving and foolish.

I forget whether you include Blackmur, Agee, Berryman, Jean Garrigue, Louise Bogan and Léonie Adams. I think they all have a few wonderful poems.

We enjoyed meeting you and your wife and very much regret that my appendix prevented our spending a long evening together. Thanks for showing me Alan Lowes.

We are getting to work at last after New York.

Sincerely,

Robert Lowell

51. To Selden Rodman

[n.d. December 1945]

Dear Selden:

I didn't think for a minute that you had anything to do with Pound's exclusion. I hope Random House gets some unpleasant publicity for putting pressure on Aiken. I suppose it's the doing of that great patriot Cerf. I hope you run into no trouble with them. [. . .]

Much to our surprise our house is warm and sunny—much warmer than most New York apartments during the coal-shortage.

I hope you use "Where the Rainbow Ends" rather than one of the other poems.

Let me know if you have any trouble with Random House,

Yrs,

Cal

52. To James Laughlin

1/19 [1946]

Dear Mr. Laughlin:

I was surprised to hear this morning that your symposium on Hopkins in which I have an essay is on sale. I assume you are going to do something about sending me copies of the book and whatever is due to me in the way of royalties. It strikes me as rather odd that I should have to propose this to you.

Sincerely,

Robert Lowell

53. To Blair Clark

Jan. 20 [1946]

Dear Blair:

I hope you all arrived in New York safely and are by now rested. The interview with Frank was so complex that I haven't really analyzed it. Jean says we should have emphasized the positive side of marriage more.

I finally decided that it would do less harm to tell Jean about Lesley's matchbox analysis than to keep it to myself any longer. I had no idea that Frank

agreed and grow more appalled the more I think of it. That Lesley should have such an illusion is perhaps excusable, though very odd and eccentric; but Frank should have known better. Jean doesn't want to see Frank or Lesley again. Though you must be tired of nursing people through phantoms, I wish you would do everything in your power to enlighten Frank. Frank's numbness has kept pace with his tremendous growth in intelligence and maturity.

All that can be said to excuse our lashing of Frank, is that it was better than silence and that in time [he] will agree with us when the ice dissolves. Please let me know the latest developments. I feel we see eye to eye as we used to years ago. We will see you in February.

My love to Holly,

Cal

P.S. I'm afraid I did very badly but it was like chopping through a knot of wood.

54. To Peter Taylor

c/o Schwartz
20 Ellery St
Cambridge, Mass.
[February 16, 1946]

Dear Peter:

Your statement is a sad surprise, but I respect your honesty. I myself find the Episcopalian dogma on the Eucharist confusing and perhaps that is some of your difficulty. You might when you are in Monteagle look up St. Thomas on the sacraments and then some modern apologetic work. Claudel has a good essay.

Belief here, as Matthew Arnold would say, is "at bottom" belief in Christ i.e. that when he said "This is my Body" and the other passages He really meant it. Only prayer can bring this faith. But it will help you to know just what your church means. Even if you think you know, you probably have mis-construed or passed by some principle of importance. I assume you have no silly philosophico-scientific notions that transubstantiation has or can be proven impossible. I wish you could talk to Wood Carper, but Father Flye or some-one else ought to be able to give you realistic advice.

We are staying with Delmore Schwartz and are recovering from a grotesque cocktail party. We started praising you and then O'Donnell made a loud, im-

pressive oration on you and two Harvard professors wrote your name down in little note-books.[...]

Wish I heard your lecture, a mere reading makes me tremble like a leaf. We think it's marvelous about Eleanor's story.

love,

Cal

55. To Peter and Eleanor Taylor

Damariscotta Mills, Maine

[May 23, 1946]

Dear Peter & Eleanor:

[...]You must come to Maine soon. Peter, we now have new interests in common: Napoleon and birds, to say nothing of theology. *Lord Weary's Castle* is full of Napoleon[ic] picture and I go birding with field glasses every day and read a set of books called *Birds of New England* by a Mr. Forbush who is the most eccentric writer of our times. His running attacks on the "pernicious activities" of cats sets Jean's teeth on edge. Did you know that the catbird interrupts its melodious mating warble with the harsh squawks of the great crested fly-catcher? And I have heard him!

Please come here before your surroundings purple your skins and souls.

Love,

Cal

56. To John Berryman

[August 16, 1946]

Dear John:

The Brandy Bingos and the Ruma Ricas have been quite a treat, and we admire the pepper-grinder. Gertrude arrived Tuesday by sea-plane in the late [afternoon] and is here now. You both missed a fabulous fishing trip with the Rahvs and the sheriff's daughter and a man named Asa.

Jean is probably going to Boston on the 26th to see a nose doctor and will be away for a week; but I'll be here and would be delighted to have you both come, if Eileen could bear to be put in charge of the household (a euphemism for doing the cooking).

I am inclosing your stanza which I read and envy, for it's a subject I have wanted to try for years. As for your heart, we intend to hold on to it through the formless future.

Affectionately,
Cal

P.S. I really hope you will come back, and will promise not to be too slip-shod a host.

57. To Peter Taylor

[August 19, 1946]

Dear Peter:

Your letter arrived just as mine left. I would be interested in a job that left me time to write, but not in a lot of freshman composition courses.

I don't care for confessions, but I suppose I must tell you that everything is chaos with us. Jean is driving like a cyclone, and we both have had about all we can stand and more. Right now I think I'll go to New York sometime in September, and stay with the Jarrells a little, and then get a room and pick up some sort [of] temporary work. Jean has a lot of plans, none of them too good, including going to Hollywood. Anyhow we have got to *leave each other alone*, and the future to time. Please just be an ear for this letter, and don't say anything to me or anyone else.

love,
Cal

58. To Gertrude Buckman

[early September 1946]

Dear Gertrude:

I wish you had come in September and stayed a month; the weather has turned, and we have turned with it, and are no longer frantic and restless. The Rahvs have left, Mr. Brigham's linoleum shears have turned up, and we are both writing things that must, alas, be finished.

Bigless and Arms are on their way to New York to soften up the Jarrells,

and find us a coldwater flat with two air-tight, sound-proof studies. We expect to join them in October. Maurice Mulligan is convinced that you are a Mulligan.

Yours,
 Cal

1946–1949

Separation from Stafford • Writing of *The Mills of the Kavanaughs*

New York City • *Yaddo* • *Washington, D.C.* • *Yaddo*

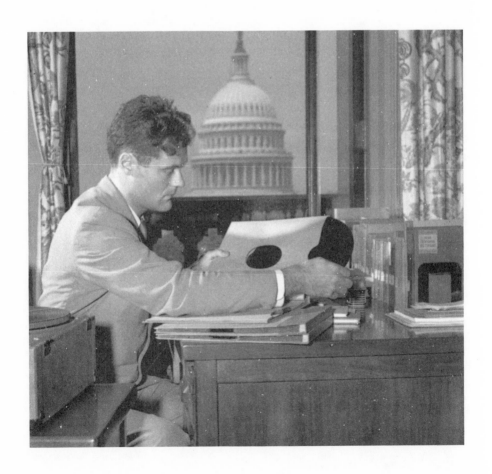

Lowell in Washington, D.C., 1948 (courtesy Associated Press)

59. To Peter Taylor

<div style="text-align: right;">

131 3rd Ave
New York, NY
[November 18, 1946]

</div>

Dear Peter:

This is really a letter to you and Eleanor, but I find it more confusing to write two people at once than you do.

I gather from Jean that she has written you, although I have little idea of the tone of what she said. We are getting a divorce and I shall be going to Florida or Nevada sometime in the next two or three weeks.

I hope neither of you will feel compelled to take sides or advise, but that you will remain our friends as before. I'm afraid only stubbornness prevented our separation two years ago, for it would have been better if our last two years had never been.

Love to you both,
Cal

P.S. If I go to Florida and you are willing to see me I might stop by for a day or two on the way back.

60. and 61. To Charlotte Winslow Lowell and R. T. S. Lowell

<div style="text-align: right;">

[November 20, 1946]

</div>

Dear Mother:

The enclosed is self-explanatory. If you feel that it would be too much of a shock for Daddy, please don't show it to him. I hope things will be settled without publicity of strife.

I'll probably come to visit you for a day or two sometime in the next two or three weeks.

Love,
 Bobby

Dear Daddy:

I hope what I am going to write will pain and trouble you as little as possible; for it grieves me that you should be hurt by anything I do or suffer.

Jean and I are getting a divorce; she will probably be the plaintiff but the decision is mutual. There is the unpleasant question of alimony which involves my trust and possibly yours. My lawyer is Julien Cornell and Jean's is Melville Cane of Ernst, Cane & Berner.

My legal position is that I want the divorce to go through without needless delay; as for a settlement, I want to be reasonable but not much more than that. If you are willing and will not be very upset, I'd be grateful for your advice on technicalities.

I can't go into the personal part in a letter beyond saying that this is not unpremeditated and that for both of us it is undoubtedly a change for the better.

I know that I have caused you much unhappiness, so please don't feel that you need be involved in my problem. I can take care of myself.

Love,
 Bobby

P.S. Cornell is writing Cousin Alfred in two days about your trust; but I will make no settlement without asking your advice.

62. *To Peter Taylor*

[December 7, 1946]

Dear Peter:

Thanks for your letter—you are so much better than I was with the Tates—not that I want to urge any similarity.

You'll have to take my word that there is nothing I can do about your advice. But I *do* want [to] talk to you—slowly and without any pressures of time or place—for there is no one else I can talk to in the same way. But this can wait.

I have no immediate plans. Jean's lawyer is working up his demands for a

settlement. And Jean is mysterious and contradictory. We had an excruciatingly unpleasant meeting in which she said that she loved me and her one desire was to drive me wild. Something like that—largely subconscious—has been wrong with us for a long time. But there is no point in my cutting out little snippets from the whole picture.

The Jarrells are very keen on North Carolina for the summer, and I am counting on coming too if I get a Guggenheim and this business is over.

My love to you and Eleanor,

 Cal

63. To Peter Taylor

<div align="right">Dec. 27, [1946]</div>

Dear Peter:

If you can make the ending friendly, I will do almost anything you say. But that would be the only purpose in "holding up[,]" the time for considering and reconsidering is long past. I'll only be counting the days.

Your letter was an honorable and warm-hearted one for you to have written. But what you imagine is not the same as my remembrance. You mustn't idealize what someone else has to live. You mustn't.

I wish you could replace the lawyers, for the way things are being done is abominable; and I think no one else in the world could help much.

I should tell you that I hope to re-marry after all this is over; but whether I do or not will make no difference.

So do what you can. I had hoped that our divorce would be accomplished without involving anyone. But since you offer, I am glad. I'll do nothing till I hear from you. I'm not optimistic, I fear.

My love to you both,

 Cal

P.S. Yes, it would be worlds better, if you could do anything.

64. To Peter Taylor

<div align="right">[January 20, 1947]</div>

Dear Peter:

I wrote you a letter a week or so ago that was sort of an apology, but never

mailed it. Jean told me that of course I'd lose many friends before I was through and I felt a little hysterical. You and Eleanor mustn't judge me unheard.

A week and a half ago I saw Jean at her hospital where she is taking a psycho-alcoholic cure. Physically she is in fine shape, but not otherwise. It costs $125 a week, the doors lock and she is supposed to be there about 3 months. Otherwise the place is fairly luxurious and pleasant.

Our interview was miserable. The psychiatrist, a well-trained unimaginative young woman, insisted that I stop stalling and get the divorce over with as soon as possible so that Jean's cure might begin. I've signed a quit claim to the Maine house and we are up to our necks in difficulties about alimony. The demands are roughly ⅓ of my income until my father dies, then ⅓ of my trust fund $33,000. There are a few other complications, and the whole business is a mess.

I would be delighted to have your mediation, but I'm afraid it would be to no purpose. A long delay would be agonizing in itself, and we would be just where we started at the end.

Your transplanted southerners makes very good sense. It has all kinds of structural possibilities and is backed by personal experience. But I'm frightened by your 3 points of view confessions. I take it you are the Henry Adams reflection and Nerber the Rousseau.

I don't like New York and I am not getting much done, but that's not the city's fault, I suppose. I'd like to drive down with the Thompsons to your conference and perhaps stay over a little while after everyone is gone. But I really can['t] plan anything at the moment.

I've got a new dramatic 2-points of view theory for poems and have written a couple about David and Bathsheba. A horrible couple live in the next room to mine and I know all about life.

Love to you both,
Cal

P.S. Thanks for what you have done for Jean.

To go with your squirrels: I know what working like a beaver means to a beaver; it's the Life of Reilly.

65. To Louis Untermeyer

202 E 15th
New York
[February 20, 1947]

Dear Mr. Untermeyer:

I first read modern poetry in one of your anthologies, which was required reading for our third form English. I remember declaiming James Whitcomb Riley, and being baffled by Stephen Crane's grass. Why was each blade "a singular knife," or something of the sort. I am flattered that you want to include me. I have my own preferences if you would like suggestions.

I was born in Boston in 1917. My education was nearly ended by an open-air school where we worked in sleeping-bags—it was healthy and nothing much learned. After that I went to St. Mark's, Harvard, Kenyon and L.S.U. During the war I was a conscientious objector and spent five months in jail. Except for editing at Sheed & Ward for a year, I have had no occupation but writing. It's a poor business, and I am keeping my fingers crossed about your "something more substantial."

I'm sure your revised anthology will include Shapiro; but I hope it will also have selections from Randall Jarrell and Elizabeth Bishop and some of the later work of R. P. Warren.

Sincerely yours,
Robert Lowell

66. To Gertrude Buckman

1204 West Market
Greensboro, NC
[March 25?, 1947]

Darling K:

This is the first pause since last Tuesday, and everyone has returned. I've had a marvelous time, but so much has happened that I can only make notes.

Bed-bugs on the way down. Morning scene: Bob Giroux staggers into the Taylors' kitchen in pajamas, wipes percolator with his bath-towel, lights already lit burner, makes coffee but forgets to put coffee in. Dilly with a beer can in one hand and a huge ham-bone in the other. And so it went—all wonderful except the official conference.

Untermeyer's surprise was the Academy reward $1000, to be received May 22. *Life* tracked me down here, and I had my picture taken, after refusing to be photographed under a statue of General Greene, a colonnade, a student's New England landscape in the exhibition.

Haven't really talked to Peter, but he seems to agree pretty much about Jean. For a while she was writing almost daily and he began to dread looking in the mail-box.

Had a sort of offer to direct the Cummington Summer Conference $200 six weeks, pretty sure I'll refuse. I'm writing like the villain in Pickwick.

At last got Cornell on the telephone and he is negotiating. I will offer $5,000, to be paid in ten years.

There's lots that will make good talk that would take forever to write. Red was wonderful and I impressed everyone that I shouldn't of.

Your letter was swell; I've missed you and loved you all the time. Perhaps everything will be settled by May.

Love,

Cal

67. To Gertrude Buckman

[n.d. April 9?, 1947]

Dear Honey,

I think my mail has been hung up at 202 15th, for I've heard nothing from anyone since your second letter. I've sent them a check for rent and asked them to forward. I'm hoping for a flood of letters.

Peter has had several letters from Jean and thinks that she has gone back to making obstacles. He wants the divorce to go through right away (but that we should wait awhile afterwards) and has written Jean a long letter. In a few days I should have some definite news.

The Taylors are wonderful and seem to be trying to adopt me, but I feel lonely and dreary underneath. And put off thinking of the confusion of the immediate future by reading incessantly.

Please love me as much as I do you, and don't have too rough a time of it.

Love

Cal

P.S. Will be back in a week or so.

68. To Peter Taylor

202 E. 15
New York, N.Y.
[May 19, 1947]

Dear Sub:

I hate to think of Yaddo without you and Eleanor; the only people I know of that are going are a former student of Paul Engle's and a former secretary of Ferris Greenslet and a former friend of John Sweeney's and a former wife of Louis Untermeyer and former reviewer of political books for Randall.

Apparently the Friedlaender House hangs on Kitten—please don't repeat the malicious (with cause!) story of Kitten and my black suit.

Awards and pictures are pouring in and out, but no good offers. Allen told me that your Iowa offer was mine for the asking. So I asked. And he offered me $1000 for one class, $1500 for two or a full time instructorship. However, Robie's offer went from $600 a class to $3000 so I still have hopes. Engle is obviously a lunatic.

I had an Eliot encounter almost as good as your raven. I was going to a party in a building constructed to house Luce (Luce studied Latin under Uncle Ransom and didn't think he was a good teacher) employees. Coming to the self-help elevator, I saw that it was wavering about the 5th floor, so I pushed the down button six times (you can't push too often to get a self-help elevator) great struggles—the elevator starts to go up, starts down, finally floats slowly down. The door opens and there is Mr. Eliot. But instead of getting out he cowers against the back of the elevator and says "I can't work this thing. I was just getting out when the door shut."

Not much real news. Jean made a trip to Maine which upset her a good deal. The settlement negotiations are about to be settled, I hope. Terrifying prospect of a visit from my mother and father on the 29th.

Hope you can work something at Chapel Hill. Engle after Mrs. Ames would be enough to put anyone in a strait-jacket,

My love to you both,
Cal

69. To Elizabeth Bishop

[May 23, 1947]

Dear Miss Bishop:

Sorry to have missed dining with you yesterday, and the time before, and reading with you. I'm afraid that you have had a miserable winter.

You are a marvelous writer, and your note was about the only one that meant anything to me.

Last night at three we had a fire. The man who started it fell asleep drunk and smoking. He ran back and forth from his room to the bathroom carrying a waste-basket with a thimble-full of water shouting at the top of his lungs: "Shush, shush no fire. Stop shouting you'll wake everyone up." Then the engines came out on the street. He kept saying: "An accident. Nobody injured," until a policeman shouted: "Nobody injured? Look at all the people you've gotten up." After it was over he went on talking: "I'm an American. I fought the fire. If it hadn't been for me you'd all be dead." Today my room smells like burnt tar-paper.

I'm going to Boston on the 2nd and then to Yaddo on the 9th. I hope that I will see more of you some day. The Jarrells and I had hoped to get you to go on a picnic with us tomorrow. Good luck on your illness.

Robert Lowell

70. To Paul Engle

[June 4, 1947]

Dear Mr. Engle:

I'm afraid that I have decided to take the Library of Congress job. The pay is $5700 and the work is nominal. I feel sorry to do this after our pleasant correspondence and all the trouble that you have taken. I hope that I can come to Iowa sometime in the future.

If you are interested in filling my position, you might be able to get John Berryman. He has been teaching writing at Princeton under R. P. Blackmur. He is a wonderful person, a good poet and probably fifty times as good a teacher as I would have been. His address is 20 Prospect Ave. Princeton New Jersey.

Sincerely yours,
Robert Lowell

71. To Gertrude Buckman

Yaddo
 Saratoga Springs
 [N.Y., June 10, 1947]

Dear Pumble:

I had dinner between Mrs. Ames and Marguerite Young—in my room are a 12 foot fire-place, leaded windows, a bust of Augustus, buttons marked butler and maid, a stone stair-case leading to the ground, and two horrible framed dog poems by some one named W.C.D. And yet it seems a marvelous place to rest and work.

The people seem friendly and harmless. There are Lexei, M. Hauser, A. Warren, Ruth Domino, a colored composer named Ulysses Cane, Mr. & Mrs. Krim[,] a novelist named Doremus, a novelist named Jean Pedrick, a storywriter named Michael Seide, a Kafka critic named Neider (who spent last evening reading the Song of Songs aloud[)]. My nearest neighbor is a Mr. Bontemps a colored librarian from Nashville who writes juveniles. All pleasant enough.

Eliot talked to me a good bit about Pound, said he wanted to do my selected poems after I had another volume. Said it was wonderful to be introduced as Cousin Annie's nephew for a short time. MacLeish was a better librarian than poet. Dylan Thomas was getting much better. Empson was good the way Marianne Moore was. Ford had seemed like a café wit and a little senile. Was very happy when Ted Spencer got his professorship. He had introduced a monk with apples into *Murder in the Cathedral* and didn't know how to make him leave the room. Richards' delivery was too excited. Eliot was quite worn out, very kind and at great pains to speak fully on whatever subject came up.

Levin was savage on I. A. Richards and [a] number of people, but pleasant enough to me. His wife pointed out your house and said that all their acquaintances of six years ago were divorced.

Could you send me the address of the Guggenheim Foundation and Cornell?

Tell me all about your week-end and the Berrymans'. Wish you could be here with me in this country that you enjoyed so much.

Love,
Cal

72. To Gertrude Buckman

[July 8, 1947]

Dear Sweet-Heart:

A fine autumn feeling last night & today with many memories. Played Beethoven's 15th quartet, as marvelous as the 16th in its way, with the screeching and sweetness more diffused, and a terrific wild last movement.

Yaddo has improved. Roethke is a ponderous, coarse fattish, fortyish man; well-read and likes the same things I do, and quite a competent poet. He reminds me of Sam Newberry. I think we'll visit Frost some week-end. Also a Catholic C.O. short story writer named J. F. Powers, whom Randall admires. I haven't read him but he is a fine person. Spent several evenings with Alexei and heard him play his music and like him better & better. Marguerite Young really crucifyingly odd and garrulous, poor thing!

Roskolenko is a petulant, phony mediocrity in his reviews, as you know. I hope he isn't coming here.

John turned down the Iowa, a mistake one would think.

Wouldn't you go to Garden City to hear Faulkner? Or Christina Stead?

I wish we could spend a week in the country before Washington, but perhaps it would be perilous. I'm enclosing Mother's violent letter on Jean and am writing Cornell to see if Cousin Alfred's plan is feasible.

Did you read Tolstoy's great story about some Mohammedan leader who goes over to the Russians and is killed trying to escape? Gorky on Tolstoy is fascinating and worth thousands of pages of Simmons.

Ah, the lovers in Central Park!

Love,
Cal

73. To Robert Frost

[n.d. Summer 1947]

Dear Mr. Frost:

Theodore Roethke and I would like to take a bus trip to Bread-Loaf and visit you some week-end in July, if you have the time & disposition to see us.

Compliments are a dirty business, but I want to tell you that I have been reading over your poems many times in the past year or so; and nothing being written in English strikes me as better. I'm thinking particularly of some of the blank verse pieces: "The Fear," "Servant to Servants," "The Witches," "Home

Burial," "Old Man's Winter Night" etc. To have characters whose lives are definite and who come from a definite place; who have a language that *speaks*, and that never uses verbal excitement except when there is substance and observation behind it—I think no other poet does these things as well as you. Your people and plotting remind me much of Faulkner.

This is badly put, but it's better than saying nothing. I don't flatter.

I hope you will be able to see us. I remember when I first called on you in Cambridge in 1936. You were the first real writer I had ever met.

Very sincerely,
 Robert Lowell

74. To Robert Frost

[n.d. late July 1947]

Dear Mr. Frost:

We plan to leave here on the 31st (Roethke has to leave here then) and spend two or three days with you and then go on to Boston. Is there a place at Breadloaf for us to stay? We have no car.

Yes, Merrill is wonderful to watch, if you can watch most of his ideas pour by you. Last fall he wanted me to sail around the world on a square-rigger or/and to go to Hollywood.

Thanks for what you said in your letter. We are really old friends now. Anyway eleven years seems a long time to me at thirty, and worlds have "changed and decayed" since 1936.

I've done a lot of bass fishing and some poems, and it's sad to see the summer sliding away.

Yours
 Robert Lowell

P.S. Your farm sounds like Ezra Pound's child; but Homer's a good New England name.

75. To J. F. Powers and Bucklin Moon

POSTCARD

[Vermont, July 31, 1947]

Mishaps—Ripton

Rutland—forgot laundry bag—lock Skidmore book in room—leave rain-
coat in car—bus station moved—miss bus—$100 taxi—champagne for lunch
Beast's slugged brandy—meet woman whose aunt has Thornton Wilder sig-
nature—Ripton area dry for miles around—no one knows about Frost farm.

76. To Gertrude Buckman

Yaddo
Saratoga Springs, N.Y.
[August 16, 1947]

Dear Gertrude:

My two weeks away from here are too much to tell. The Frost visit was
good; a marvelous devil of a man, very inquisitive about Jean and in the
process of having his mad daughter committed. "I always said, let her run
loose till she kills someone." Seeing Roethke's face drop. "I suppose I shouldn't
talk that way, but . . ."

[. . .]Found a stack of letters a foot high waiting for me. Nothing but
proofs from Ransom, your letter and a pleasant note from W. C. Williams on
my review; and 10 postals from my mother & father.

You'll see how Jean is from the enclosed letter. She's not much worse, but
one can say little with certainty beyond that. Perhaps the Brustleins got their
information from me. They sail on Sept. 23. They *are* nice. Did Jean go
south? Peter never mentioned it. The Taylors & Jarrells have bought a duplex
house!

I'll be in New York between the 1st & the 7th.

Love,
Cal

77. To Elizabeth Bishop

[August 21, 1947]

Dear Elizabeth:

(You must be called that; I'm called Cal, but I won't explain why. None of the prototypes are flattering: Calvin, Caligula, Caliban, Calvin Coolidge, Calligraphy—with merciless irony.)

I'm glad you wrote me, because it gives me an excuse to tell you how much I liked your New Yorker Fish poem. Perhaps, it's your best. Anyway I felt very envious in reading it—I'm a fisherman myself, but all my fish become symbols, alas! The description has great splendor, and the human part, tone etc. is just right. I question a little the word *breast* in the last four or five lines—a little too much in its context perhaps; but I'm probably wrong.

Practically everything in the *Sun* was lousy; but it's exciting for us to be grouped with Nims, Ciardi and Brinnin and Howard Moss and Nerber as promising "youngsters" as W. T. Scott puts it.

I was in Nova Scotia a long time ago with my Grandfather trout-fishing. All I remember of the coast is Yarmouth Harbor at low-tide from a steamer called the Yarmouth, and some dismal low-tide gulls and a horrible after sea-sick feeling—something like death which as a boy I assumed I was immune to.

Glad the review was alright. I suppose what you said that night at the Jarrells started me off on a theme for your poems. I think Randall deserves the credit for reviewing you properly—mine was only later and longer.

Puffins are in my book of New England birds, but I've never seen one.

I expect to be in New York sometime between Sept. 1 & 14 on my way to Washington, and if you're there then we'll try to have the dinner we missed last spring.

The Jarrells are at the Woman's College in North Carolina.

Sincerely yours,

Robert Lowell

P.S. Thanks for all the pleasant undeserved things you said in your letter.

[Library of Congress
Washington, D.C.
n.d. September 1947]

Darling Gertrude:

Bad news. Jean now wants $7000 in cash, next five years; $800 a year for life; and ⅓ interest in the trusts for life. Cornell calls this "by far the largest settlement yet discussed" and "it seems to me hopeless to continue negotiations." We're going [to] take up the matter of a contested Maine suit. But I'm not hopeful. Cane's letter was harsh & unpleasant, called this demand "final" & "minimum" and hinted "instituting a proceeding for support." Damn it!

This job reminds me of Kafka's castle. But I think it will work well. I spoke to the librarian about Brinnin, Spencer, Engle & Mrs. Biddle being included in our first album of 20 poets; and [a] few other things and he said, "Why this is a breath of fresh air. None of the other fellows said anything to me about this." He was O.K. This is for you alone.

My office is good & I'll have plenty of time to write. You'd better write me at the Cosmos Club; they object to personal mail here.

I haven't gotten over the shock of the last Jean business. Oh lonely and disheartened and I feel guilty writing you about it—and God knows . . . I'm sure there'll be clear weather for the patient.

Love, my darling,
Cal

This big envelope is not a disguise but all I've got in the office.

79. To Ezra Pound

[n.d. September 1947]

Dear Mr. Pound:

They tell me that one has to have special permission from Dr. Overholser to see you. So I return. Hope to see you when arrangements can be made. Good luck.

Robert Lowell

80. To Ezra Pound?

[n.d. September 1947]

During the war, I spent a few months in jail as an objector, so I suppose we have a little of that in common as well as verse, which is what matters.

Yours,

Robert Lowell

81. To Elizabeth Bishop

September 25, [1947]

Dear Elizabeth:

It looks as though I'll be gone from Oct. 6–12, just wrong. I could easily make arrangements for you to be recorded while I'm away. But then you'd miss the otters, and me, and my New Brunswick nun poem, and all kinds of talk. Couldn't you push your reservations ahead four days and come here on the 13th.

I'm pretty sure I can find you a cheapish hotel $3.00, or you could stay with my friends the Starrs, who would love to have you and wouldn't impose on your time.

When poets come here, I can take off as much time as I want, and nothing said. So try and come. I'll be grieved, you know, if you don't.

Yours,

Cal

P.S. Your post-card baffled me for a minute or two. It seemed an anonymous threat. Then memory stirred, and I read the instructions for opening it. Last year, when I was at one of my disreputable rooming houses, I was told that a tall stoutish dark man with a brief case had called and refused to leave his name. I thought it was the Law. It was Allen Tate with his violin.

82. To William Carlos Williams

[n.d. late September 1947]

Dear Dr. Williams:

Saturday the 18th will be fine. Let me know as soon as you are certain.

What would you infer from the fact that I have Van Buren's autobiography on my desk? You ought to know about American names. Thanks.

Sincerely yours,

83. To Gertrude Buckman

<div align="right">
Cosmos Club

Madison & H

[Washington, D.C.]

10/1 [1947]
</div>

Dear Gertrude:

Cornell is off for a week, so there's nothing new. Did I tell you that I talked it all over with Milton Starr and his lawyer? We concluded that the best thing to do was to fight it out this fall, unless the Maine lawyer vetoes it. I'm not sure (not at all) that I know what Jean's up to. The demands are so fantastically high. I try not to contemplate the trial, but at times I'm nervous and fearful. Life's like that.

Tomorrow morning I start for Iowa with Powers, who came thru here in his poor ancient car. We'll spend a day or so at Kenyon.

Haven't seen much of anyone except the Starrs, Pound (twice). He's just like his later prose, and absolutely the most naive and simple man I've ever met. Still sure that the world will be alright, if people only read the right books. Pathetic and touching. Told about snatching up Confucius odes when the Communists with Tommy guns came for him. And this was all that saved his mind in the ensuing months. Then he was in a specially constructed cage—America's number one war-criminal. Then a comparatively idyllic period with the army. Given a tent and called Uncle Ezra, and did all the writing he's done since he was taken. Then here in something called the snake-pit with "a lot of imbecilic mad niggers" which was tough. Then as he is. Every day from one to four his wife comes and sits with him and he talks politics, jumps up for chairs, gobbles saltines and more or less mad people go wandering and raging past. Very sad and silly; and yet there [is] something wonderfully honest and innocent about him and he knows & loves books & he's absorbed in Chinese and he won't write "while I'm in this cess-pool."

Karl is terribly nice and unassuming. He'll be at Johns Hopkins this winter. Evelyn is alright, I suppose, but heavy and masterful.

Sunday, I went up to the Washington Monument (one of the stones is from

the Stark house) found the house I used to live in, the school etc. Went to the zoo.

That was my busiest day. The job's O.K. But I feel a little like a dressed up idiot with nothing to do but pretend dignity. I haven't tried to write anything. But I've read at Pound's book list for American history: Woodward, Brooks Adams, Van Buren's auto-biography.

It's a waste of spirit to get righteous about Jean. She's driven and a desert somewhere at the center. We can't do anything about her. Just try not to be hurt.

This isn't much of a letter; and I don't know why exactly—except that it's the turmoil and being blown about. Whatever I'll come to will be what comes out of this period—hard times in a way, but they discovered what you are.

But it will all shine sometime. Darling, try not to suffer & question yourself.

How is the Colliers working?

Love,
 Cal

P.S. I'll be back here Monday 13th. Keep hold of our calm for us.

84. To Theodore Roethke

Library of Congress
Washington, D.C.
Oct. 20 [1947]

Dear Ted:

Walking in Lafayette Square my eye fell on these words in bronze: "Ordnung! Ordnung!" Above an old Greek soldier giving a young Greek soldier lessons in swordsmanship. Higher above, I saw your stern cherubic face above a bronze fancy dress, then, Baron van Steuben born in Prussia 1730.

Sorry to hear that Seattle is so in the sticks, but in Iowa City where I've just been you can't even buy martinis in restaurants. I had a room without a bath. O.K., but there was no public bath in the hotel. When I read I stank.

I haven't been able to get hold of your recordings yet. The first series (half of it is lousy) is all made up for publication. You'll go in the second, which I hope will be out before I leave.

Seen Williams twice, once here for recording and he was as you said, very easy to talk to.

Sorry to miss the champagne and chickies (not if they were like Shirley) anyway the champagne. I called you at your various hotels.

Drove with Jim to Chicago. Hope the town loosens up.

Affectionately,

Cal

85. To William Carlos Williams

Dear Bill:

You might get some usable quotations from Lyle—the paragraph with *Forever Amber* & Faulkner listed together; or the one about the contradictions of capitalism being necessities which the German staff learned, which the Russians etc.

I guess he's really read *Paterson*, but there's so much confusion, simplification, dogma and jargon in his piece that it seems more crack-pot than to the point. It's up Burke's alley, though. Did you see B's piece of what the new epic would have to be? (*Chimera*—I think summer 47) Perhaps Burke's machinery is too much—yes, it really is, and something of a game—but it's fascinating to read—bits at a time.

Reread Book One, and almost all the things that puzzled me are now clear. I see for the first time that your overall form is the interior monologue that old Ford exploited and always claimed to have invented.

Jarrell writes me: "The people that think *Paterson* either mediocre or bad would bewilder me if I weren't used to such fools. Did you see that unspeakably dumb *Sewanee Review* article?" I did. And thought of writing a nasty reply—but what's the use? As more parts come out such people will fade—most of them.

I hadn't meant to write such a shop-talk letter, but Lyle started me off.

I'm still brimming with my visit and Williams' hospitality. When I come again, come May, for the pilgrimage to Paterson and the fishing I'll try to have a Spanish phrase for your mother—pronounced with a Church-Latin accent.

Affectionately,

Cal

86. To Gertrude Buckman

<div align="right">

Cosmos Club
Washington 5, D.C.
[November 30, 1947]

</div>

Darling Gertrude:

I've just finished reading all the published *Cantos*—the most self-indulgent long poem in English, and what wasted grace! Someone ought to do a fifty page book of selections.

Had a grand week-end at the Williams's. I told him your story about his reading "Sweeney Agonistes" and he laughed, and said, "Oh, I can't be that bad." He says anything that comes into his head—rather like Cousin Ghormley—with far other content. "No, she was never anything to me, not that I didn't try to make her." "What's the use of writing? They admit that all the cheap paper will rot. That's the only kind of immortality I can think of." Then with his old 92 year mother with wonderful black eyes, slapping her hands and laughing and making her laugh—like what's his name in *Great Expectations*—and saying, "Would you rather see us or twenty beautiful blonds?" And his wife: "Bill gets so angry when I criticize his poems, that if I don't like them I don't say anything. But he knows." So it was when *Paterson* Book I was read, then he slashed it to pieces. Book Two is marvelous.

Thanks for the pretty posy. Where did it come from? Not from the Colliers' offices?

Thanksgiving comes and with it the Jarrells. Nothing much comes to me except reading. Met a) an old friend of Grandpa's b) Mrs. Lowell Conger whose poems are dictated by her dead son; c) Mayor Dyer who takes E.P. icecream, taught Miss Truman fencing and writes awful little poems; d) Dr. Swiggett—horrible terza-rima translations of Dante; Polish cultural attaché, poet, seems to be a red, with bullet pierced volume; e) Spanish cultural attaché, poet and nice, and is going to trace Carlos for me f) and . . . But that's about it. O, a friend of a friend of Jim Powers, who set one of my poems to music; mixed feelings! December, Allen comes.

Two letters from Jean and maybe she'll ask something like what I can pay. She's really better.

I've been thinking about Christmas and somehow New York doesn't seem right. I think things will have to clear and that fugitive meetings won't help us, while nothing is settled. It's just an instinct and I don't know how to state it— there isn't much rationality.

Just got a Thanksgiving box from home with things like jars of jelly in it, which we could use in New York, but I can't here.

I've read: Henry Adams *History of Jeff. & Mad.*; *Life of John Randolph*; Van Buren *Autobiography*; Woodward's *History of the U.S.*; Brooks Adams *New Empire*; *Canterbury Tales*; Dickens' *Hard Times* (better than *Expectations* even) James' *Awkward Age*; Ransom's *Poems*; M. Moore's *What Are Years*; a big hunk of Léger; Corbière selections; hunks of Saintsbury's *History of Eng. Prosody*; and am starting Froissart's *Chronicles*. Ah me! And a new poem in 25 line stanzas.

Love,
Cal

87. To J. F. Powers

Lib. of Congress
Washington, D.C.
Dec. 1 [1947]

Dear Jim:

The Jarrells have been here and gone. I have been talking and listening steadily for five days, and seen the largest living rodent at Rock Creek Park— a rather transcendently hideous creature—a guinea pig pretending to be a wild boar—in [a] larger cage than any two lions.[. . .]

Mrs. P. took me to dinner and confessed that Ezra's economics bore her to death, but she has faith. I said how much I liked one of his translations (which turned out to be her favorite) and compared it to *By the Waters of Babylon*. She: "Yes, but we hope it's better than *that*."

What does Delmore Schwartz say about the child at the end of his story? You must revere it for its namesake; and why not make K.A.P. a godmother and send it off to stay with her in her 15 room house? That's what St. Anne did, you know.

Miss Armstrong is sick and if I had anything to do my job would be incomprehensible. As it is, paper and chaos pile up and I'm out of stamps and every day a retired major calls me and asks me to identify obscure quotations which may help him win a radio contest, whose answer last year was Clara Bow, and I say that Miss Armstrong who knows about such things will soon be well; but she too is trying to win the contest and get a million dollars and get a new Packard and go to California and leave me to my incompetence.

Oh, across the hall a senate committee has been moved into the division for the adult blind. No one sees the joke.

I liked what you did in *Great Expectations*; but, old friend, I've read the book, one of D's two or three best.

Goodbye Jim Betty and Katherine Anne,

Cal

88. To Elizabeth Bishop

[December 8, 1947]

Dear Elizabeth:

Some of your questions accord remarkably with the revisions I'd made in my *Kenyon Review* galleys. 1) *Mass* is now service & *church*. 2) The *Johnny comes marching* is out for something else. 3) *Shadows* is *stands by*.

Apologia: 1) The first 3 lines *are* prose. 2) *Filings*: one of my few puns— files of soldiers, steel filings—something uniform, filing cabinets, metal, shining, unbearably monotonous. 3) *It asks*: the corpse. *Arrow eye*: the eye used for sighting arrows. 4) The *sword* is the one Aeneas left behind him at Carthage and Dido killed herself with it. 5) It is the feet of the *men* wheeling past the bier. 5) Teeth lather works for me; it's a grotesque surrealistic image not meant to be like anything else in the poem. 6) The aunt laughs because she's a proud mad old lady, one side of her despises the Negroes and thinks the war and the parading a lot of stuff.

Of course, your objections may hold good and I'll ponder them. It's flattering to get such a thorough going reading.

I'll mail you my new 25 line stanza poem in a few days—I just got it in decent shape. I like your two spigots and hope you'll have luck with them and send them to me before long. You know, when the next atom bombs fall there won't be any more inhabitable Atlantic coast in our life-time—so you'd better hurry. Randall has written a wonderful poem on the death of a colored child, which I think you'll like.

Sat in back of the Trumans at the symphony. They never stirred. Next to them Admiral Nimitz and his daughters smiling, craning around, saying *this is it* (when the Tchaikovsky came on) then—having ignored each other thru the music and a long intermission—the Trumans and Nimitzes suddenly recognized and shook hands with unnecessary heartiness.

Randall's something with people he doesn't like: A pompous man of some political importance here, and a professor of political economy at Harvard, who claimed to have started Ransom (whom he called Johnnie) writing po-

etry (this is all one man). We were reading the galleys of *Paterson* and some manuscript of Randall's.

Pompous Man: "Can I see some of that?"

Randall, leaping up with unbelievable speed: "Oh yes!" Hands Pompous Man the galleys he's already read of *Paterson*.

Pompous Man: "No, I want to see yours."

Endless pause

Randall: "Uh . . . uh . . . uh oh yes, I guess, but I think some one's reading them." Pompous Man finally buries himself in Randall-manuscript. Lavish praise, "You're not obscure like the Fugitives etc. etc." Pompous Man questions the meaning of a phrase. Randall, pause, looks at Pompous Man with quiet contemptuous compassion: "You wouldn't understand it, but I think most people would. Why even my students etc . . . etc." This went on for about five hours on Thanksgiving till Mackie & I were almost dead. I've promised to write Randall a poem like Donne's "Will" (the coals to Newcastle legacies) in which I leave him my candor.

Your records are on the way to Key West—see what you think?

Allen's here now—I'm going to leave him my tact in the presence of humbugs.

Affectionately,
Cal

89. To Katherine Anne Porter

Dec. 15 [1947]

Dear Miss Porter:

Just a note to tell you how much I enjoyed your Stein piece—the best critical essay I've read for ages, and so much better than the academic analytical stuff, that everyone is learning to do. I was delighted with the shot at Laughlin; it's hard to accomplish such things without losing one's balance.

In a few days you'll hear from Dr. Evans about the Fellows meeting—something about the end of January, but the date hasn't been settled yet. I hope you can come and tell me about the evils of the Mathers and the Essex Junto and all such things that should be innate knowledge with me.

Sincerely yours,
Robert Lowell

90. To J. F. Powers

Dec. 18 [1947]

Dear Jim:

No snap-shots arrived, except the one of my old friend the car. Did he rise from his bed of snow and slip it in the envelope when you weren't looking?

I took a poet from the Spanish Embassy out to see Ezra, and you can guess what happened—a torrent of oracular advice on how to run Spain. "Do you get any papers that really tell you what's going on." " . . . " "They're several—supposed to sell about 2000 copies but they can't sell more than 350 . . . The *New Bedford Sentinel* occasionally really says something. They've gotten around to defending Quisling." " . . . " "Gesell is the only man worth reading in 1947. Major Douglas can spot any sort of financial shit, but he never discovered Europe."

Finished another long poem which I'll send you, when it has cooled a bit, like the car.[. . .]

This is a dull letter but I'm on the brink of a two hour staff meeting: to choose a new staff-leader and discuss "what are the cataloguing needs of the Library as seen by units . . . " I wish I had your bottle of whiskey and bottle of rum—in me!

Merry Christmas to you and Betty and flowering Judas.

Cal

P.S. Read Miss Porter's piece on Miss Stein in *Harper's* or the *Atlantic*.

91. To George Santayana

Jan. 12 [1948]

Dear Mr. Santayana:

Here is some of my story: I am 30, the son of a retired naval officer; J. R. Lowell was my great grand-uncle, Amy was about a fourth cousin; long long ago Jonathan Edwards was one of my ancestors. I went to St. Mark's School, Harvard (a year & a half, and didn't like it) then Kenyon College, where John Ransom is teaching. In 1940 I was married to Jean Stafford, the novelist, and became a Catholic. In 1943, it seemed to me that the continuance of the war was unjust (the all-out bombings, unconditional surrender and the letting of Russia into Europe) and refused to ~~answer~~ be inducted. For this, a sentence of a year and a day (the day makes me a felon and I am not yet a citizen again)[,]

5 months in jail and 7 mopping floors in a hospital. I am separated from my wife and am trying to get a divorce. I'm not in the Church any longer—I think that what Catholics believe is true, in a way—has a world of experience behind it—but not *the truth*. I don't know exactly what I believe, and am just as glad.

Perhaps, the oddest thing about my poems is the locale. I spent a couple summers on *Nantucket*—just after I got out of school and did most of my first writing there. "Dunbarton" is where our family burial ground is—the Winslows' my Mother's people; it is near Concord New Hampshire. The Maine stuff is Damariscotta Mills, a village where I lived two years ago—about 30 miles north of Bath. It has a Catholic Church, said to be the oldest north of St. Augustine.

This sounds rather pompous, but it covers some of the ground. In my life, I suppose I'm ~~nothing~~ something of a mild, secular quietist—usually in trouble though—and an anarchical conservative. But I blush to toss these rude terms to a philosopher!

I can only say inadequately what your letters meant to me. My relatives, and people who don't read modern poetry, tell me that my poems are unintelligible. I've never thought them so, and never wrote them just for a few enthusiasts who like to be up on things.

I've read your writings, since I was about 20. I suppose my favorites are *Opinion in America*, *The Autobiography*, the *Browning* and *Whitman Essays* and the book *On Christ*. I haven't really the right sort of mind for straight philosophy—about the only philosopher I'm wild about is Plato, but I read the *Dialogues* as I would read *Antony & Cleopatra* or the Gospels.

I see poor old Pound here at his hospital and he repeats things you told him. It amuses me to imagine your meetings.

Sincerely yours,

Robert Lowell

P.S. I'm enclosing two new poems. My next book will be these, another about the same length, but more dramatic, and a long poem (600 or 700 lines) laid in Maine, a little like my "Death of the Sheriff," on a large scale with all the characters really worked out. I have 300 lines written and 200 more in rough shape. My job here is Consultant in Poetry for the Library of Congress—a one year sinecure.

Rereading your letter, I see that you ask about books that I've read. "The Quaker Graveyard" is built on *Moby-Dick*. Five lines from section one are lifted from Thoreau's *Cape Cod* Journal. "After the Surprising Conversions" is a re-working of a few paragraphs from Jonathan Edwards' book with the

same title. "Mr. Edwards" takes lines from his sermons, and the first stanza comes from the little essay he wrote on the spider when he was 13 (?). In college I majored in classics, mostly Latin, alas.

Health to you for the New Year!

92. *To Carley Dawson*

[January 27, 1948]

Dear Carley:

Finally found Dr. Gosse's notes on your engravings folded up in an obscure corner of my bill-fold, where if they'd been serpents . . . I wouldn't be here. I enclose with them Miss Armstrong's second and more coherent version. There's no money in them, I fear.

Dreary day going over minutes and reading *Age of Anxiety*—the ruins of one of the first talents of the century; but he'll recover, I hope.

You gave me a hell of a jolt—unpleasant, but I should have done it to myself months ago. As I was waiting for a turkey sandwich at the bakery, I heard my voice whispering to myself with a sad restlessness: "Fool, fool, fool."

Well, we shall hear Rubinstein,

Cal

93. *To George Santayana*

Feb. 2 [1948]

My Dear Friend—

(For so it is after your letter) In the last few hours I have been contemplating what you have written me, and it moves tears of joy.

So well have you understood all that I hoped my two poems would become! Down to the versification, even! Yes, the Trojans and Italians are meant to have the barbarous dignity of Red-Skins—of the Germans, for the devil must have justice.

I think Browning had all the right ideas about what the poetry of his time should take in—people and time. But (this is presumptuous) how he muffed it all! The ingenious, terrific metrics, shaking the heart out of what he was saying; the invented language; the short-cuts; the hurry; and (one must say it) the horrible self-indulgence—the attitudes, the cheapness! I write strongly, for he

should, with patience, have been one of the great poets of the world. Anyway, he was on the side of the angels a lot of the time.

You're very right about me too; I marvel that you could have intuited so much from my crude summary.

I suppose it's the will of adolescence to be self-centered, Calvinist and blind. We believe that unless things come hard, they are somehow phony. It's only in the last two or three years that I have begun to know and treasure *patience* and *pity* and "the sacredness of ~~nature~~ things." I was talking to a lady last night, and we agreed that only age brought these things. Those poor blind years—and perhaps it's always that way, but less so.

I was a Catholic, when I went to jail, and my confessors said what you said they would, only they allowed that in the end a man must do what he believes, even if it's heresy and madness. So they did well enough by me.

I love my country, because it's mine, and all I know. And [I] think our culture can stand comparison with others of the last 150 years—it's better than most, probably. And, of course, we have Roman virtues—energy, and even clarity of a kind. But there are times . . . Oh yes, when one trembles, and wonders if a people have ever been so dehumanized, when "the man in the street" lacked so much—had so little chance for grace and ability. But one must accept this too; and life is good after all.

I don't regret my Latin—some of the writers are marvelous: Propertius, Vergil, Horace, Catullus, Tacitus, Petronius, and some of Juvenal. And it connects with us historically through the church. And how can one understand what English words mean without it? And yet to read Homer fluently, what a happiness that would be!

This is such a pretentious letter I'm writing. I'm mailing it though because I imagine it will tell you more about me than if I'd written in a more fitting style. I can't very well express my awe at being so understood by you. I "take it right kind" that you have written.

Yours sincerely,

Robert Lowell

P.S. Looking forward to your new dialogues. I'll mail you my new poem later this month—not the long one, now about 550 lines, that will be another year yet.

94. To J. F. Powers

Dear Jim:

I got the Bennington woman's letter yesterday and will write them this morning. I don't think you need have any fears for your Guggenheim. I believe they're announced about the second week in March.

I hope you didn't mean that Ted business too seriously. My final judgment on his poetry is pretty complicated—a fairly small thing done, at its best, with remarkable clarity and freshness. But this wouldn't please him or sell his book like hot cakes. If somehow he could forget about renown and arriving and all that . . . but it's easy to say this about someone else—hard to practice.

I'll tell you about yesterday with Pound. I come into the story too much but it gives a good picture of him.

Ezra: "I've just re-read Bill Williams' attack on Eliot's Milton essay. It's good stuff."

Cal: "You know, I think you and Williams are talking thru your hats about Milton."

Ezra: "Well, a young man who'd been reading Eliot brought me the *Areopagitica*. You're not going to tell me a young writer can read that garbage."

Cal: "I'm talking about the poems and so was Williams."

Conversation drifts Yeats, Lady Gregory.

Ezra: "I don't think Synge will be read much longer but his plays will always be acted."

Cal: "Yeah, a thing doesn't have to be much good, if it gives the actors a little air. You know, *The Waste Land* is a much better poem as Eliot reads it than it is on paper."

Ezra: "Why, it's a damn good poem anyway."

Cal: "Yes, but it's a better one read."

Ezra: "You ought to be able to do that for yourself. What you're saying is that Eliot is a better piano player than you are."

Slight pause, Ezra draws himself up in a mock pontifical attitude and roars: "Your mind is so corrupted by your rhetorical reading that to appreciate really good poetry you have to hear it read aloud." (Only there was more)

Then we all (Mrs. Pound too) burst out laughing.

Ezra: "One of my pleasantest experiences is to watch the startled expression on a young man's face when he realized that Granpa is right on some small particular."

Cal: "How about the reverse?"

Long pause, then Ezra smiles: "I can't ever remember having had that humiliating experience."

He's really a wonderful old creature, but he has a scheme on now for 12 writers living here and in England to keep each other informed about reading—"Action within 24 hours." I now have his Gesell, which he wants me to re-write, and I won't. Judas!!!

I've finished another longish poem, and am mid-way in a really long one 550 lines so far. I hope to have it done in a year.

Glad to hear you are working. Did I tell you that you have a new admirer, Caroline Gordon? She has become a Catholic, by the way. I was invited to join the Catholic Gallery of Living Authors, and I had to break the bad news to them, and now masses are being said for me—God rest my soul; you seem to be the only one that doesn't go in for that sort of thing.

Love to you both,
Cal

95. To Gertrude Buckman

[Cosmos Club
Washington, D.C.]
Feb. 19, [1948]

Dear Gertrude:

I suppose I understand what is to be read in and behind the lines of your letter. Not to write in a canting, confusing and self-excusing style is almost impossible—I'm not at all clear on either the present or the future, so I can't really explain or defend myself, and I shan't.

I'd better cast back a little. You know better than anyone how all things changed for me—as though I were re-born, as though I were suffering a second adolescence, with all the first to guide or mislead or what you will. And all this due to you, though I'd been having stirrings (half-listened to at best) or else nothing would have happened. This is pompous, but how else can I say it?

Anyway, all I know is that the past year and a half is transitional—a new world, and worlds better; but where on earth is it taking me? As I was saying to Williams last fall, I know my directions, where I'm going in the end, but the waters to be crossed are mysterious; completely! When I'm sure I foresee, I find I'm wrong; and yet it hangs together, so far.

So much for that; this is not a defense (though my unwieldy abstract style must make it seem so) but a description.

I want to drift a while before I marry. As my friend you can understand this, but in another way you can't, and it will all seem heartless and irresponsible. I suppose, it is so. And yet there is nothing ~~I can, or~~ I even believe ~~in doing~~ I can do about it.

This is a lousy return to you who have saved my life and always been perfect and kind to me. I think we've never quarreled or been unhappy together. I must be frightened to death of marriage and being tied down. I don't know enough—not about myself even, or above all.

About meeting, I think when I said will be the right time. I have nothing to add to what I've written right now. They're plenty of particulars, of course, but they wouldn't do any good, and this isn't the time for them. What's true now won't be true at the end of April. What will be though? You see how little I know.

I'm going to Greensboro on the ninth of March for about a week. Then back here to record Frost. And the water, all the while, must and will go flowing under the bridge.

Love,
Cal

P.S. Reading this over, I feel that this letter has been cursory and off-hand, perhaps, very kind to myself; but it's honest enough, and as near the truth as I can get in a preliminary.

96. To Gertrude Buckman

Feb. 24, [1948]

Dear Gertrude:

I must grasp it now. Your letter is all true—both for what it doesn't say and what it doesn't omit saying. You've given me all a person could—"only love." What can I say? Just that I *do* understand it, feel it, live with it.

What will happen, will. But I think last year was quite as wonderful as we thought it was. I have no right to say it, and I'm not sure I know what I mean; but, perhaps, it's the *anchor* we can always hold to—come what will.

I get garrulous friendly letters from Jean about her science courses and people she's met; and I still have the uneasy feeling that it's someone talking from behind a mask. But she now wants to get the divorce herself. So it will be $6000 + $500 if I can raise it on my trust fund—all fair enough.

Flint is the fellow who used to, who still does, write Randall and Haggin

innumerable argumentative letters. The praise is pleasant and embarrassing—John's too.

Well, your suffering recoils on me, and I take it to heart—you've always soothed so much of mine!

Till April,

Love,

Cal

97. To Elizabeth Bishop

Library of Congress
Washington, D.C.
February 25, [1948]

Dear Elizabeth:

Here's my poem, in time I hope to cheer you on your voyage to Haiti. Reading the "Poète contumace" after my nun poem, I felt with a shock all the things he could say that I couldn't. So this came—not much like Corbière, but starting there. I suppose it and the nun complement each other.

Sorry to hear you were ailing and glad you found a good doctor. I've been thinking of Paris too, as one does come spring; but, alas, I'm a felon and can't leave the United States, except to go to "greater America." Patriot though I am, I find the newness of Washington rasping at times.

Did I write you about my Santayana letters? Some one gave him my book, and he wrote me, asking me a lot of questions, and saying that my poetry was the first since Trumbull Stickney's that seemed to inhabit the same mental and moral world that he did. So I answered his questions and sent him my nun and Aeneas. He managed to get about everything I'd intended. The comments paralleled yours, even down to the Browning. It all was rather indescribably moving to me.

I have been reading masses of Pope and Faulkner—a wonderful pair to have together.

Randall's colored child will be in the next *Partisan*. I hope you'll like it as much as I do.

Isn't Ted Spencer an odious nerveless thing! What's on the inside of this page is something Ezra wants sent to 12 writers: me, Randall, Allen, Williams, Cummings, Wyndham Lewis, Auden, Spender—I forget the rest—"action within twenty-four hours" whatever that means. When Spencer saw him, he offered to be our academical advisor, and Pound said: "No, you're to be one

of the advised." See if you can guess to whom he's sending his Confucius translation *The Unwobbling Pivot*. It's the most unlikely person in the world.

Affectionately,

Cal

P.S. Excited about your poems.

98. *To John Berryman*

[mid-March 1948]

Dear John:

Three sorries—very sorries! 1) For helping to make you a link—it's no fun, but I am grateful. 2) For being dispersed, but what can I do about it? I do intend to read your new poems with friendly care and be one of [the] exceptions who does read his friend's work. Randall & Ransom agree with me that they're a great stylistic development. 3) The seven dollars—please let me pay it—and take a rain check on the future, when I'll be down & out and you—rolling in yachts and books.

I've just gotten back from Greensboro where Randall's lost all his early enthusiasm for the faculty—and how! Are you tempted by his Salzburg idea? I would be, if I weren't a felon and locked up in this nation.

Had a note from Delmore saying that he'd be delighted to read here—so perhaps we'll make up, if one ever does in this world.

Beginning tomorrow with Frost's arrival to read the next two months look like almost steady activity—fun but frightening & overwhelming!

Goodbye & love to you both,

Cal

99. *To Carley Dawson*

Cosmos Club
Washington 5, D.C.
[March 20–21, 1948]

Dearest Carley:

It's nice and hot here—outside the things of the city are moving, sounding and shining.

I'm writing so that you can hear from me right away, and so that my head can stop milling with the problem fruitlessly—for tonight, maybe.

The answer to your three-fold analysis is! I love you with all I have and want you to marry me.

But a lot of water is going to flow under the bridge before that happens. Come April, come Jean's divorce, come September. I want to let them come.

You're afraid of getting in deeper, and that's just as well. But I'm already in over my head. I'm carried away with love.

Love,

Robert

P.S. I'll try to answer whatever your imperious orderly mind asks me.
Sunday,

It's still hot—sweltering and budding outside, alas.

Last night's page sounds too brusque and full of *I*'s and self-assertion as I re-read it.

But good-bye for today—two colored maids have just come to my door saying "Can we come in? We're getting ready to go home." And I, to your friend's church.

100. *To Carley Dawson*

[March 24 or 25, 1948]

Dearest Carley:

You're a hell of a correspondent—I mean, what a wonderful one I've been—as far as stamps, ink and paper go.

I've just been to *Tenebrae* at the Cathedral—a choir of Franciscans in their order's brown, starched white ropes looped downwards, awkward gangling young men, looking like minor employees at the Library. And the psalms and lamentations were good, and I thought: "Why should anyone, who wants to believe, have much trouble?" And I was in the middle of the sermon, the grim pomposity of the Irish-American voice (all you say of the Jews is of course true of the Irish—they're about 20 million too many; what a benign, cultured old world country this would be if they were all illiterate mutes)

" . . . and right then and there it was
A bitter thing for Judas Iscariot
 And right then and there . . .

And right then and there . . .

And right then and there etc . . .

"That heart was a reeking cess-pool. My dearest brethren, you might think Judas Iscariot was in a class by himself, apart from all betrayers and murderers."

At this point, fresh from *Murder for Profit*, I almost commented out loud: "What about bath-tub Smith and the homosexual Haarmann." I was prepared. No I wasn't!

"No, my dearest brethren, Judas Iscariot is not unique."

Guess who?

"All who willingly sleep through Sunday Mass (looking at the green leaves and listening to the cardinals and reading the funnies with a word or a look for their friends at one o'clock breakfast)

"All who willingly eat meat on Fridays." This is the gospel truth.

You won't have a personal word from me till you write

your faithful correspondent,

Robert

101. *To Carley Dawson*

[March 24, 1948]

Dearest Carley:

I trust I've left you far behind in letters—the third before I've had an answer—this must be my record.

Anyway I've taken the liberty of inviting Elizabeth to stay with you. She plans to come on either the 10th or the 15th of April (I wrote that the latter would be better; and "why don't you stay with my friend Mrs. Dawson, who'd be delighted to have you and whom I'd like you to meet.[)]" So, if you're not horrified and planning to flee away from me to California, why don't you invite her: Miss Elizabeth Bishop 630 Dey St. Key West Florida. She plans to stay a week, but you'll like knowing her and she won't be any trouble. She's an independent shy soul, and probably will stay somewhere else anyway. (My paragraph begins and ends with the same word)[. . .]

Been reading more Bolitho (Library copies) an ingenious, restless, delightful mind—but not a wise one, in love with, and absorbed in its objects. One thinks of his heroes and villains as loaded with fire-works that go off as they move into universalizations and epigrams. He rather naively complains that

Casanova might have told us what woman really is "if he'd been interested in generalizations or utilities." But I must hold off on *utilities* till I've read more.

Two days of rain—last night a thunder-storm, which I slept through! Washington colder and not much greener.

Went to hear Vals' lecture on modern Spanish poets—very green, enthusiastic and unintellectual—lots of talk about schools, so and so's Classical period, poems read in Spanish and dull translations. Perhaps, Spanish poets are about like English sculptors or Canadian poets. No, probably not. What do you know about Carmen Conde, Jiménez's discovery?

Carmen Vals said: "When are you coming to dinner, you lead such a social life." I: "Why, I never go in for that sort of thing." She: "I mean by *social* everything that might be included in that word. Is my meaning clear." I: "I guess you're clear enough." She: "I can't express what I mean in English." She said to people who asked her how she liked the lecture "It's an old record," with a shy girlish Catalan smile.

"How slowly do the hours their numbers spend; how slowly does sad time his feathers move! Ah when will this long weary day have end, and lend me leave to come unto my love?"

If you ask your mother who wrote this you'll be embarrassed; but I wrote it myself.

Auden says: "When a man starts writing love poems, one thing is certain: He is not writing about his love but about himself; she should be suspicious." But what does Auden know about it?

I miss and miss you dear love,

 Robert.[...]

102. To Peter Taylor

[April 3, 1948]

Dear Old Sub:

You owe me a letter; but I know your time is valuable.

Well, the old man is on his way home to you with not so many adventures in Washington. An evening with Dwight Macdonald during which he was more than usual genial—we'd said goodbye to Macdonald and separated about ten feet when Randall began doing gigantic ballet leaps in the air giggling.

The reading of the war-poems went quite well, but Mr. Steele had rather expected autobiographical comments about buddies etc. "How did the read-

ing go?" "Oh, pretty well. Of course, I didn't tell Mr. Jarrell that they'd have gone better with someone else reading. Still, I'd buy them even with Jarrell. Who knows, in twenty years he may be a polished poet like Eliot."

There are two new bears—Ezrable and Randible, the ideo-types of Filth & Fabbidge. There they sat, big as life and queer as hell, Pound rather the more conventional. I: "How have you been?" Pound: "Rather languid." Squinting at Randall, scrolled up in the exposed chair, "Let me study the animal before I map out a program for him . . . "

Long economico-political monologue. Pound: "I must give a vignette. Lowell likes anecdotes some of the time."

Randall: "What do you mean *some* of the time?"

Rambling story about Wyndham Lewis looking at cave paintings and saying "they're fakes. Just Picasso."

Pound: "You see the valuable thing is to knock different kinds of minds against each other."

Randall—scrolled-up sphinx tone: "And what was the *value* of Lewis's observation?"

I think they thought of each other as enduring eccentrics.

I've been *alone* the last ten days. And how I wish I'd had the comfort of your years and experience to chew the rag with. Don't you think a little trip in May would do you good? It's only eight hours. When you open your eyes you're here with me and Arms waiting for you with open arms.

The idea of a visit to *Scuppernong* in late July—just a day or two—has taken hold of me greatly. But if you and Eleanor have enough on your hands, I'll try to understand. I've never had a baby, you know.

Got Uncle Ransom $500 to read at the Library. "The honorarium astounds me. I'm writing editor Grove Paterson of the *Toledo Blade* that his is not the only cutting edge."

My father had another thrombosis. Very slight and painless, but he's in bed for a month and the California trip is off. They may go to Florida this fall.

My love to you both—my mail-box has been emptied for a letter.

Cal

P.S. Wish we'd talked sooner & longer.

I had a long telephone conversation with Jean, which went fairly well. We're not meeting. I suppose you've heard how the lawyers gummed up everything just as it seemed settled.

Your reviews are really rolling.

Lib. of Congress
Washington, D.C.
4/6 [1948]

Dear Mr. Stevens:

I know that the enclosed form is an old story to you, and that you have always refused to record your poems.

I don't suppose I can say much of anything to change your mind. But with the exception of Ezra Pound (and he would if his strength were up to it and the government would let him out of St. Elizabeth's) you are the only important American poet who has not been recorded, we have Eliot, Frost, Williams, Moore, Ransom, Tate and Auden.

If you should be willing, we would like to do an album of five records—or if that seemed too many we might do an album of you and Williams or Ransom.

I hope you will reconsider.

Yours sincerely,

Robert Lowell

104. To Theodore Roethke

4/9 [1948]

Dear Ted:

It's good to see all the familiar poems in a book at last. The best are the flowers and the long ones—the clear eye and the spring and rush like a child's. How evil and world-worn I feel for a moment—not, not really. Spring has come here and I'm thinking of fishing and I have one of those new spinning reels.

Also the poets come. Wytter Bynner, Spender, Frost, Jarrell, Blackmur, Ransom, Fletcher, Eliz. Bishop, Herbert Read[,] Tate (many times)[,] Berryman, Auden—most of it fun, but I'll be glad to descend from this tower to the ground again in September.

The consultant for next year is Léonie Adams. They say she's separated from Troy, but it's all vague. After that Williams. Recently, he had a heart attack (angina pectoris[)] (not vagina pectoris as he said in his letter) very painful, but apparently not serious in the long run.

My father's had another thrombosis. It was painless and won't do him any damage the doctors think. Still he's laid up in bed and can't go to California as he'd planned—growing old's a sorrowful thing. It's in the cards.

I'm going to Boston in a couple of weeks and hope to see and drink a lot of the Parkers.

Affectionately,

Cal

P.S. What are your plans? Has Washington mellowed?

105. To Elizabeth Bishop

Cosmos Club
Washington 5, D.C.
4/10 [1948]

Dear Elizabeth:

There are no bears, or cats or dogs among the roses at Mrs. Dawson's, only a negress named Florence. If you arrive on the 16th, we can go to the Budapest recital at the Library—a good Hayden, Mozart, Beethoven program.

Will you read again for us on Monday, the 19th, I think? I have some Jack Daniels and can start you off properly slugged this time.

The German pictures are grand, but with crowds like the World Fair.

2,000 Illustrations is very brilliant, but I want to read it many more times before saying anything.

Affectionately,

Cal

106. To George Santayana

Lib. of Congress
Washington, D.C.
4/20 [1948]

Dear Mr. Santayana:

This is just a note to warn you that I'm mailing you a box of food. Perhaps, this is an impertinence, but I think we are good enough friends now for me to presume. Please write me if there is anything you really want that I can send.

Well, my poem was meant to have a chronological order with gaps—rather like the ghost of Cynthia in Propertius. I have been letting it lie for several weeks meaning to come back to it fortified by your criticism and my own. But work and distractions . . .

I went ahead and read the first two [new] dialogues in spite of your instructions, and am waiting for an all out battle between Socrates and the new man, with Alcibiades insulting them both.

Spring has come here, and with it many poets and old friends—all good fun, but too strenuous for more than the few months remaining me at this job.

I look forward to your interview. I'm naturally embarrassed, and naturally delighted that you mentioned your interest in me.

Tomorrow, I go to Boston to read poems at Harvard. I can say: "When I was here 13 years ago["]; but what else?

Yours sincerely,
Robert Lowell

107. To Jean Stafford

[April 23, 1948]

GOODBYE GOOD LUCK AND GOD BLESS YOU—
CAL.

108. To Carley Dawson

170 Marlboro St.
Boston, Mass.
[April 25, 1948]
Sunday morning 7.15 in bed,

Dearest Carley:

The visit was painful. We had a sandwich and milk lunch at Gertrude's apartment and talked mostly about New York people. She was very nervous and tore up bits of paper or played with rubber bands. Several times we were in tears though neither is given that way. Then she played some Bach as she had done many times. "What happened to us was good, and it was good that it ended, as it had to. But, you're funny, Cal; how could it have passed from you so quietly. It took longer for me to twist it out." I felt as though I were abandoning my child. I called her up from Boston when I got in, and she said, "I've been talking to you all afternoon. But you haven't heard me."
5 p.m.

This gives a wrong impression—all was warm. But poor child, alone and insecure with few friends and they with their problems. Life deals badly some-

times, and I don't think I helped. I hope you'll meet and become close friends; but, perhaps, this is a mad notion.

I had a long conversation with Mother this afternoon. From marriage in general to you in particular. I guess she'd have been keen on you except for a conversation with Harriet. If there is a marriage she wants to be there to bless it. At the end she produced a bottle of Mary Chess White Lilac: "Do you think I might be sent some of this for Christmas?" "I'll try to bribe you." I didn't produce my Mary Chess bottle.

Comments: —

Her visit was too perfect; I'm afraid she's clever.

Won't you quarrel over the son?

You know how you'll resent anyone trying to make you dress properly, brush your hair, & entertain.

Harriet must know a good deal about Washington.

You want to lead a quiet life.

This is the worst. Remembering the past (Anne & Jean) Mother was very affable. Daddy, who probably doesn't know about the Harriet conversation, was enthusiastic. Our parents seem to take about the same attitude and won't be a problem.

Monday 2 p.m.

An evening with Frost; tonight the Parkers. More talk. Daddy: "I suppose you're thinking of getting married again. That's the natural way to live." I: "Yes, I guess I am." "Have you anyone in ~~might~~ mind?" I: "Sort of." Mother came in & out; we digressed on his future. He feels he must justify his no longer having a regular job. He hasn't the art of doing nothing. Poor things! And Mother frankly dreading the prospect of having him as an invalid, giving up her therapy, nothing to do together, or talk about, much.

Women! Mother thinks I should see your people etc. I think your call on the whole at least neutralized Harriet's one hour long distance talk. Mother seemed to think Harriet had picked out Marcella (not du Pont) for me.

So many events, I've not paused to say I love you, miss you, and don't think I phrased my last inquiries and reflections to you with much tact, gentleness or imagination.

God help me, I love you,

Love,

Cal

P.S. God help you!

109. *To R. W. Flint*

Lib. of Congress
Washington, D.C.
5/5 [1948]

Dear Mr. Flint:

A few bones to pick. It seems to me that maturity of experience makes Williams so wonderful—by comparison a gorgeous poet like Thomas seems wordy, green, living in an imaginative darkness. Only a man past fifty who knew his town and its people long and inside out could have written *Paterson*.

The description of the water coming down in Part One is a dazzling handling of motion. "Gallant," an expected and yet startling word, with a quiet fi- nality jerk to it (in its context) that shows Williams as a master of language. Eliot (in the *Quartets*, but always) and Williams seem to me almost infallible in their use of words—the spoken, the conventional, the technical, the flat the intense etc.

E. Bishop is genuine—as Eliot said of Moore—you never doubt her solidity, her tone, her sense intuition for material that is hers—a touch-stone, except for Jarrell, her contemporaries seem pretentious, faked, empty etc.

Randall has a better mind than I have, more contemporary interests, is more articulate and talented. I too find him emotionally immature, puritanical, monstrous, odd; but his peculiarity is part of his excellence.

Thanks for the praise and more for the enthusiasm. I wonder what you'll make of my new poems? There's one in the winter *Kenyon* and another in the issue to come.

Yes, someday I'll probably lap up Tillich; but now I'm filled to the gills with theology and churches.

Yours,

Robert Lowell

110. *To Robie Macauley*

5/17 [1948]

Dear Robie:

I don't think I've even written you to congratulate you. The last New York marriage I attended was my own at St. Mary's of the Bowery—April second (?) 1940 with only the Tates, two of their cousins whom we'd never met and

Blair Clark. It was election day and no one could get us anything to drink. When we came out we were surrounded by strange and excited children.

I want to come and I [will] write Peter and ask him if he's getting too old to travel.

Spender came here and I liked him better than I was prepared to, I saw the sensitive, reasonable, not overly high-powered side of him. Also since October I've seen every friend and every writer I've ever known, and started a long poem which I'll pick up again in September.

I have many inchoate plans—but one I'm certain of—to get away and take my Guggenheim and write.

I'll be seeing you both at the wedding.

Affectionately,
Cal

111. To Elizabeth Bishop

May 20, [1948]

Dear Elizabeth:

Why don't we and Miss Moore (and maybe the Tates, she and they are friendly) have dinner before hand. There's nothing official arranged.

The Modern Library Chaucer is a convenient size with a glossary in the back. He's the author who has all the slow, open, common-sense, loving, secure, wise in people etc. virtues that we were talking about and that the modern world has little of. I've been reading *Middlemarch*,—she too, very mature, powerful wise, if one forgets her stretches of blank Victorian prose. Not easy-going like Chaucer and Dryden—more like Milton and Wordsworth a kind of sustained tense Protestant adultness.—Herbert is in between the two groups, though these categories are too vague to be worth much.

I read Carley "The Grave," "The Sweet Dead Whale" "Silence," and a few others and with the momentum of your stories, more or less converted her. My admirer Flint who writes me so many letters, wrote me about how Blackmur was all wrong about her—her poems being as personal as they could be. I can't write essays as letters but this fits my theory on re-reading. All the animals and places [are] analogues (roughly) of Miss Moore and her art—so I take the Canadian mountain which you got me to really read for the first time. What a massive overwhelming poem it is. Now you must sell Carley on James. We had quite an agitated argument: "You must feel uncertain or you

wouldn't be so aroused." I: "But damn it, you haven't *read* him." Then I named her a list of 50 world authors, important as James, James's peers. She: "I can't think of one except Carlyle that I wouldn't rather read than James." But I'd never dreamed of naming Carlyle in any list.

How much I enjoyed your visit—and yet it will be September before I get my poem rolling again—it worries me not writing and yet it seems right and sensible to wait. But will the inspiration come when I call it? No peace in this world for the poet! Poor poets!

I just met someone who knew Randall since the fourth grade when he had the most beautiful Indian suit in the world, it's a fascinating subject to pursue—and the day he discovered tennis.

Be seeing you, affectionately,

Cal

112. *To George Santayana*

May 20 [–June 20?] [1948]

Dear Mr. Santayana:

Your "He tried. That's Bostonian." hits home nicely. We're a little more earnest and a little more hypocritical than is natural—a failing and a peculiarity, sometimes a distinction. Hawthorne, Melville, Adams and James are full of it. They all had something else and so must I. Chaucer and Homer are models of all that I would desire.

Tell me more about Robert Bridges. He's a poet I've admired for many years. "I Heard a Linnet[,]" "The Summer House on the Mound," "Nightingales," "Eros," the end of "The Isle of Achilles," "Milton Senex," "Low Barometer" and many others. But I've always bogged down in the *Testament*. Once I thought of him as a model. But his style is not one I can use—good to remember as an idea of craftsmanship and modulation. Stickney, I've never been able to admire much except in intention—such an impossible language. If he'd only lived earlier or later or longer or been a Frenchman!

I'm going to send you [a] few books for your amusement, if I can get hold of them. Stevens is a man in his late sixties, with many affinities in thought and temperament to you—though from a very different tradition. You may find his organization disquieting and he tosses off far too much. But he has a wonderful ear, a richness and a moderation. I've sometimes wondered if some of his ideas didn't derive from yours.

Bishop and Jarrell are about my age, and the best new poets in my judg-

ment. The anthology is made up by a fool who used to be in advertising, but it's an easy way to send you a lot of poems. I've marked ones I like for your amusement. Some of the best poets are appalling[ly] represented: Hardy, Frost, Auden, Pound, Williams, Ransom—that I've been almost unable to mark them.

Perhaps, you'll have fun with these books, though I can't imagine you burdened with superfluous time.

I suppose [nothing] in my "Thanksgiving" is as obscure as the break toward the end of the stanza on page 2. [In] the quotes the *he* is recollecting [her speech]. Beginning with the quotes his wife is talking in the dream. She looks out of her window in the asylum at the hills and children etc. feeling at one with them. Then "what if they're stone, indifferent to me?" She imagines her husband fishing outside. He comes into the ~~guest~~ visiting-room with its stuffed seal, stuffed owls etc. but the owls are talking. Her husband's visit gives her a shock, she's put in a cage, or thinks so. She stops talking and he sees her, fantastic; then more recollection and she vanishes. Then morning at church, —the smile a sort of reconciliation but mysterious and uncertain.

Yes, the Propertius is decadent Christian John Webster, Baudelaire— grim, sordid, tortured, damned, pathetic—like *Hamlet* rather than *Antony and Cleopatra*.

Is there religion in Shakespeare? Perhaps, negatively. Macbeth is damned and disintegrating[,] a better picture of damnation in some ways than Milton's Lucifer, and similar, though human.

I've been reading many of your essays and begin to have a picture of the consistent philosophy behind them. It would be an illusion for me to ever expect to rid myself of all my American oddities and heresies of thought and temperament (this most of all) and hardly desirable. But it's medicinal to get a dose of the other—and most of all now when I have [been] changing and re-assembling myself somewhat in your direction. Not too consciously—the urge preceded the conscious desire. Once I wished for intensity more than wisdom. I was never as bad as your philosophical visitor with the brow of Josiah Royce.

Two women—one angular and embarrassed, the other never pausing for breath. "Do you know that Ohio sets apart a day to honor her poets. It was my dream . . . " Well, she edited a poetry column,—somebody's magnificent elegy on Vachel Lindsay etc. and contests for all four Ohio high-school grades competing for four prizes. "Do you know W. H. Bumer (?) and some of the boys made a survey of all the poetry columns and mine they said, you know, was superior to all of them." She made a scrap-book of her column, and

Joseph Auslander (a hack poet who had a sinecure at Library for many years and many years ago) "coaxed" it from her. "I've always had a feeling that it was somewhere in the Library of Congress."

You can't say that the United States neglects its arts.

Yours sincerely,

 Robert Lowell

A MONTH LATER

Meant to get this off, but I had trouble getting the books. A few changes— the Williams seems to have most of the virtues of Whitman—the great "American" poet of our time, or will be if he can bring off the next two books. He is about 65, a doctor and a good one, just outside of New York, in Rutherford N.J.

You might like some of these in the anthology.

Hopkins
Ransom
Tate—"Mediterranean," first two "Sonnets at Christmas"
Stevens—"Sunday Morning," "Le Monocle"
Frost—"Gift Outright," "Acquainted"
Yeats

There are a lot more, but that's enough. I've been having vicissitudes: in, and alas, out of love, and divorced at last. I'll be glad to be just writing again, come September.

113. *To Gertrude Buckman*

Cosmos Club
Washington, DC
May 22, [1948]

Darling Gertrude:

It was a joy to see you, especially the second time. But I have been eating bitter bread. It's been as though I were pounding my soul with two stones to wash it. Perhaps that's where *no soap* comes from.

Why? Because there's some one else, and because the past keeps coming back, and because . . . But I and what I'm going through are useless to you at the moment—to anyone except myself.

You were good to see me; but I know that seeing you now is being selfish, irresponsible and self-indulgent. It's hard not to be with one's friend when one is troubled.

I wrote you a long twisted letter; here's a short one—not much of one.
Love,
Cal

P.S. I enclose a ticket for the reading, if you feel inclined to go. Say anything you feel like to me.

114. To William Carlos Williams

[n.d. June 1948?]

Dear Bill:

No; you're in the last *Cantos*; very lovingly on the whole.

Glad you liked my review, but the only good writing is in my quotations.

I'm off to a friend's wedding, so this is brief.

Best to all of you,
Cal

115. To Gertrude Buckman

[n.d. Summer 1948]

Dear Gertrude:

I've been on the edge of writing for several weeks to say that I'm still in this world and would like to see you if I could, if you could.

More has been happening than I ~~can~~ want to say in a letter, but I've almost pulled the lining out of myself.

No plans except to go to Yaddo in September and work on my poem. I know I've been mad and abominable to you.

Love,
Cal

116. To Elizabeth Bishop

Library of Congress
Washington, D.C.
July 2, [1948]

Dear Elizabeth:

All the prose parts of *Paterson* are lifted, not made up. I don't know whether your point is right or not—the first two books cry out for the next two, and perhaps the proportions will come out right in the end. As it is the letters are literally left hanging. I think of their ~~function~~ effectiveness in two ways 1) so terrifyingly and typically real, and yet I don't think I'd want to read many of them straight—too monotonous, pathological. Yet in the poem they are placed and not pathological, the agony is absorbed. 2) Aren't they really hardest on Williams himself (Paterson)[,] a damning of his insensitivity. She's mad, but he, like Aeneas can't handle her and shows up badly. I think that's their purpose in the poem. *Paterson* has been like water to me, and judgment may be subjective. But doesn't true criticism come that way—the only way to penetrate an author—then after a while the intuitions become objective.

Read a good essay on Burns in an anthology of essays gotten together by F. R. Leavis. I guess he's really quite first-rate, and I've followed fashion in ignoring him. It's funny, because his rhymes and stanzas are technical fireworks just on the surface. Then so much experience or observation. I don't know which, for I've never soaked in him and have trouble with Scots—more words I have to look up than a French poet.

My feeling about babies is mostly a joke—an imitation of Frank Parker. Still a howling one for long periods—not so hot! Then Randall thinks nothing adult is human, and how can a poor single man talk the way parents do—one's affable indifference against the afflicted mother's affectionate fury. This is meant to be non-sense.

I dropped a hint to Giroux (Harcourt Brace) about trying to get the Fontaine. You should like him, in French, at least—so solid, shrewd, tender, unromantic, worldly wise, full of people—hard and soft where he should be—a perfect craftsman. He might be much larger than the other extreme Rimbaud.

Enough talk about verse! Would you like me to write Mrs. Ames about inviting you to Yaddo? Get Miss Moore to write too. You can't invite yourself, though, of course, almost all the invitations are planned. It would be marvelous to have you there. I know the solitude that gets too much. It doesn't *drug* me, but I get fantastic and uncivilized.

At last my divorce is over. Looking back, it seems strange that we could

survive it, and now the conclusion is allaying and satisfying. While I was in New York, I saw Jean—all very affectionate and natural, thank God.

It's funny at my age to have one's life so much in and on one's hands. All the rawness of learning, what I used to think should be done with by twenty-five. Sometimes nothing is so solid to me as writing—I suppose that's what vocation means—at times a torment, a bad conscience, but all in all, purpose and direction, so I'm thankful, and call it good as Eliot would say.

Rodman was here, but I couldn't rise to the occasion: praise his anthology, care much about my ignorance of Haitian painting, pretend I hadn't read *Annus Mirabilis* and wanted to. He suggested that he be included in the record albums, and that one of his friends had found me indifferent and abstracted. What do you do with such people!

Now that Carley is away, I feel that I have been trying to force something that wouldn't work. I suppose this has happened to people again and again, sad, foolish, confusing—but that's enough for a letter, enough to give substance to what must have struck you as odd generalities in my letters.

I may drive to Maine on the 1st with some cousins in that case how would the 6th or 7th do instead of the 14th?

Affectionately,
Cal

117. *To J. F. Powers*

Lib. of Congress
Washington D.C.
[July 17, 1948]

Dear Jim:
Note from Peter saying he wanted to send Eliz. Hardwick your review. She "patronized" him in *P.R.*

Pound wrote the *Four Pages* man about me. Pound: "He won't touch you at any price!" Took Mrs. Longworth to see him; she chattered for half an hour about everything under the sun ending with a synopsis of two 1880 novels she'd read as a girl. Pound (restless, silent, but not motionless misery) "You like reading more than I do."

My term here is drawing to an end, and you know I see a resemblance to my year of jail and floor-mopping—all intake[,] nothing much done, passing activity.

I guess it pays off.[. . .]

Long arguments with Robert Fitzgerald about faith and the classics. Experience makes even the better Catholic apologist look like some one memorizing—precise about this world but threadbare—while the best of the other side is full worldly substance, truths that don't fit in etc. But foolish in its imprecision; the harnessed again the unharnessed, neither very happy.

All I can say for my nun's Rabelais is "but that's what she *was* reading!" She was full of eccentricities and that was one of them. For me it "fits" but after a point she became real to me and I find it hard to unmake her. Is it odder than the book your monks were reading? Let me hear from you—

Cal

118. To Carley Dawson

<div align="right">
Cosmo Club

Washington 5, D.C.

[July 29, 1948]
</div>

Dear Carley:

No, not silent or sick—a letter sent c/o Mrs. Ryan has been trailling you for more than a month, unless it's dead. Just as well, perhaps. I tried to call spades and say what was wrong. Worrying through it all again—from the beginning in wonder to the end in impasse—seems useless. It all seems [to] have been in the cards or stars; alas.

I've been reading and writing up my 60 Modern English Poets. After the best 20 it's a graveyard—they were alive and are dead.

I've been accepting invitations and find it distracting—no one I'll ever ~~no~~ know well I guess. I wrote *no* for know—no go, just a spectacle, for them and for me.

I have been toying with the idea of going to Italy and seeing Santayana, and discovered that I have nationality and not citizenship. Passports are complicated, conditions disturbed and expenses too expensive. It looks like Yaddo.

What a summer! If there's a breath of air we all rejoice as though we were in the mountains. The office is not too bad; the club is bad. But fanned.

No, there's no use in saying the thousand things that might be said now. I'm so glad you liked Cummington. Cairns said he'd heard from you, that you were happy and going to go to California. Are you? I was impassive and didn't question him.

Elizabeth seems to be flitting from place to place, so I'll mail this to O St.

Robert

After Elizabeth's phone. Hope I'll see you at Stonington. Mrs. Gross will be astonished, first I came by myself, then with Jean and now with you and Elizabeth—then a fisherman, now a librarian.

119. To Ezra Pound

POSTCARD of a fisherman's memorial: "They that go down to the sea in ships 1623–1923"

[Manchester, Massachusetts, August 6, 1948]

Dear Mr. Pound:

The first stop Northward to Maine. The statue is a memorial for Eliot.

Cal

120. To Elizabeth Bishop

Cosmos Club
Washington 5, D.C.
[August 23, 1948]

Dear Elizabeth:

A sticky Boston day, a lunging walk with Frank Parker half way across Boston ending with a call on Hyman Bloom—against my better judgment. We talked about painting, compared the arts, oriental mysticism, suffering, why you were always on some littoral move, why he never moved; and had five or six beers. I have misgivings but I think it went off—he's going to Ipswich if Frank will fetch and return him—probably Stonington if you could get the Summers to do the same. Seemed very real and witty in a somber way.

A sticky New York day, went to the end of the 3rd Avenue El alone, lunch with my publisher, said your manuscript had been refused over his head, lot of shop talk, long milk and lemonade session with Jean at the Grand Central Station and we listed about 100 useless and sordid preventatives for restlessness and solitude—but you'll laugh us to scorn.

A gummy Sunday in Washington, slept, went to the office and read my mail, the papers, went to *Henry VIII*, which I'd wanted to see for years because someone said I should or shouldn't, and a ghastly Douglas Fairbanks Jr. movie called *Catherine the Great*, did the *Times* crossword, read *Apes of God*, sleep.

Now I'm back in my loose harness. I'm unhappy about the Carley business when I think of it, but it's too near and I forget as much as I can. Have you

ever read Constant's *Adolphe*—it's all there, a bit worked up and romanticized, but not much.

Legend: Through Betty Sortwell, through Emily Dick, through Anne Dick—sordid Bohemian parties in Stonington with odd Bohemians drinking absinthe. I restored our vodka.

A shocking surprise—a library official with incredible diligence has written critical biographies of all the recorded poets. My pencil drops from paralyzed fingers when I try to set about cutting.

I have acquired a phony, spruce disillusioned tone—but it's only Washington.

Affectionately,
Cal

121. *To Charlotte Winslow Lowell*

Library of Congress
Washington, D.C.
August 24 [1948]

Dear Mother:

I'm back on the job—pretty much renewed and looking forward to Yaddo. I feel that you and Daddy and Emma and even Apple Sauce did their best for me.

I meant to ask you about something and forgot. I'm making a will which gives you everything I have during your life-time and then splits my trust between Randall Jarrell and Peter Taylor, the most needy of my friends. This would include Daddy's trust so as to cover every contingency. To do this I'll have to have a copy of the deed. I wonder if Daddy could mail me my copy?

Tell me about the Christening. Washington is moist and hot, but quite tolerable.

My love to everyone,
Bobby

122. *To Richard Eberhart*

[August 27, 1948]

Dear Dick:

I have no objection to the poem being published—there was gossip in the

play and it would have hurt my parents; but this is another matter—pretty general. Like lines, but the whole seems a bit first draftish and jerky. I feel somewhat the same way about the females—more so.

Washington is fearfully hot and wet after Maine. We had a wonderful time with the kites, out-board[,] Dikkon, the Manhattans, the drive and the Parkers.

My parents' address is Apple Sauce Cottage, Apple St. Essex Mass.

Meant to write my bread and butter letter sooner—you are wonderful hosts. Hope Betty finds a house and I'll see you in it before long.

Yours,
Cal

I do think you should write some of your poems over and over—so often you stifle what is alive in them in great fluffs of Eberhart rhetoric. The burst of inspiration is just as deceptive as the other extreme of polishing nothing into polish. But enough criticism!

123. To Elizabeth Bishop

August 27, [1948]

Dear Elizabeth:

I started to write you a letter—after a page the heat reduced me to inertia—about my morning of being photographed for the Associated Press's rotogravure section—from all angles, sometimes as consultant, sometimes as an expert on recording, holding a metal "mother" disc, sometimes as a typical poet reading, and all I had to read was Randall, "It was not dying. Everybody died," and "When my mother died it made me nervous," over and over again.

I too had a letter from "Poetry" Hayden Carruth, "We admired your poem in the *Kenyon* etc." Unlike with you their comments stopped with admiration; I'm esteemed but not loved by them. Do you think their letters are the result of run-down sensibilities?

I spent a blissful two days reading *Les Liasons Dangereuses*, one of the great books; I wish there were more. I don't know what it's like, *Troilus and Cryseyde* combined with Clarissa Harlowe, with the villains made as horrible as they could without becoming lurid.

I guess I've emphasized all the charms of Yaddo: large house, trees, autumn, space and economy and irresponsibility, and you can't be disturbed before 5 or 6. Perhaps, you should combine your alternatives—try Yaddo, and if

it becomes oppressive, fly away on a freighter. If I can stand it, and they'll let me, I'm going to stay through the winter.

Today I record myself—the hangman with no one left to hang but himself.

From the enclosed you'll see that the poem on me has already been written. You probably would rather read his "Viable Women," it begins, "Maia was one, all gold, fire and sapphire . . . she was of Roman vocables the disburser." Parody proof; I'll mail it when I finish reading it. Thinking it over, your 1 line, "My feet were cut by barnacles," doesn't sound as though you were risking much.

Ever since I've left Jean, my tongue gets blacker and blacker. I *did* enjoy Stonington.

Affectionately,
 Cal

P.S. I put in Flint's letter out of vanity—the analysis seems right to me—all I know about Canada is Maine and Francis Parkman. Flint is the man who wrote Randall so many letters, and started out objecting to my Catholicism. The shoe is on the other foot.

Wish my "Kavanaughs" were done—then I'd be free and you'd have your review to write—so far off it seems!

Dick's letter isn't quite accurate; this must be the poem he sent Randall as a review—still the kites, cold Manhattans and drive were fun.

124. To Richard Eberhart

Cosmos Club
Washington 5, D.C.
[August 28, 1948]

Dear Dick:

After my carping letter I read—re-read, I guess, but it never seemed to stick in my mind before—your Wisconsin Lawrence poem and was much moved. I'm not sure why it seems so much better to me than some of your poems which I've seen lately, but I think you have a real subject and your rhythm wavers and moves as the mind and voice would. Even what usually strike me as your vices—diffuseness, confusion, odd million-dollar words, echoes from Hopkins—somehow work and make the reverie felt and yours.

This is said heavily, but it had to be said after my fault-finding.
 Cal

125. To John Berryman

Dear John:

Many apologies for not thanking you for *The Possessed*—we've got to be-ware of Richard and choose new titles—what are fellaheen? Not good Euro-peans; anyhow he's caught in the same net.

The new difficult poems seem to me the most wonderful advance that anyone has made. I rather agree with Randall that they exist in bits and pas-sages—so many breaks, anacolutha etc. that the whole poem usually escapes me. You seem to have the equipment to do almost anything now. I think it needs to be docked in some overwhelming and unifying object. Maybe this is stupid criticism.

I go to Yaddo like a turtle with my house on my back i.e. I have no place to store anything and so must carry it all. This makes any stop almost impossi-ble. After I'm settled, we must arrange a visit or a meeting in New York.

I didn't realize Eileen had had so much trouble, and I gather she's better but not well. I'm so sorry.

Had lunch with Omar Pound and he's bubbling with you and Cummings. I don't see how anyone could be Ezra's wife, son, mistress or friend without yearl[y] making a long retreat, a trip to some other country and five or six other things. (Maybe getting drunk and gossiping wildly about Ezra to some-one who'd forget it.)

Fitzgerald is good on the classics, and good (very strident Catholic, though) on religion. Terribly patient and earnest and somehow surprisingly subtle at times—and completely unselfish. I liked his Tate and Pound reviews—great saturation effort and fairness—a bit florid and pious. I think you'd have hit it off, if he'd talked.

Go to Maine, if you can and stay as long as you can—I feel re-born. You might look up Elizabeth Bishop in Stonington.

Love to you both,

Cal

126. To John and Heather Keeler Thompson

[September 3, 1948]

Dear Jack & Dilly:

Wonderful pictures, but libellous: either I can bear children or . . . God knows what. I'm having all the copies burned.

I look like Mussolini shot, hanged and terrified in the wedding picture.

I've so much baggage, I think I'll go direct to Yaddo.

Love to all but the child.

Cal

127. To George Santayana

Sept. 7–13 [1948]

Dear Mr. Santayana:

Many things seem to converge to put off my trip to Rome; but the most important is that I shan't be happy till my book is done; and that's no way to see you and Europe. I want to try it though next summer or fall if things go well and I can scrape the money together. I've been urging the idea on Elizabeth Bishop, my one close unmarried friend.

I'm completing a hack-work bibliography on 60 modern British poets for the Library and am pretty sour on most of them, so your comments are welcome. But I don't agree. Hopkins, Hardy, Yeats, some of Housman, and Bridges, Stevens[,] Frost, Williams, Marianne Moore, Tate, Crane, Auden, Ransom, Pound's translations and Eliot seem very brilliant—more good writers of short poems than at any time since the 17th century. But I guess we can agree to differ.

Well, one more week and I'm done here. It's been an interesting shaking-up year; and I'm glad it's over.

This is no time for an unhurried, un-American letter—this is my last week, I have to record myself, pack, induct the new consultant, be de-processed from the library, say good-bye to quantities of friends and relatives (usually at dinners) listen to all the records made this year, squirm out of last minute correspondence without leaving too much for the next consultant and so on and so on—two friends have picked this week to visit Washington—one with a girl whom he loves and who doesn't love him. Ah me!

Had an exhausting and touching farewell day with Pound—in the morning I brought him my editor[. . .]Pound was full of gay obscenities, funny

nutty jokes on notables "If you're the Possum's or Parson's (T. S. Eliot) publisher why aren't you mine." Sang songs, read his translations, scribbled out lists of books that must be published. "Robert, what did you bring this guy for anyway?" It must be wonderful to be young and indestructible.

I've just received *Dialogues in Limbo*. I thought it was something called "Poets at Work," which had been promised me, and nearly didn't open it. Thank you, I'll read it in the quiet of Yaddo.

It must be maddening to have more than one copy of O. Williams sent you. He's a worm of a man, poet then advertiser then poet, but always Williams, the new Untermeyer.

At the moment I feel as though I were on a 6 day roller-coaster, but I'll write properly soon.

My address will be
Yaddo
(the sons of the former owners saw their reflections in the lake, and said "Yaddo" and waded after them and were drowned.)
Saratoga Springs
N.Y.
Yours sincerely,
 Robert Lowell

128. To Elizabeth Bishop

Yaddo
Saratoga Springs, [N.Y.]
[October 1, 1948]

Dear Elizabeth:

The place swarms with Elizabeths—Elizabeth Ames, though one wants to call her and thinks of her as Mrs. Ames, she won't allow it,—and Elizabeth Hardwick, just left, who brought back to me those days—when it was glorious and horrible to be alive—of the Tate divorce. There was even an Elizabeth Fenwick, but she was gone.

Now there are an introverted and an extroverted colored man; a boy of 23 who experiments with dope; a student of a former Kenyon class-mate of mine, who at the age of six was in a Pathe News Reel for having a chicken that walked backwards; and Malcolm Cowley, nice but a little slow.

I'm all set up with a small dark room to sleep in, and large sunny room to work in—with five windows, four tables, three chairs and one work-bed. The

"Kavanaughs" seems to be moving—I figure if I can do about two stanzas a week, come spring I'll have it. For December through February (possibly March) I'll pay $50 a month, "to help with the frightful fuel bill."

Léonie Adams is a queer one, so shy she mumbles inaudibly half the time, and very funny telling New York stories or about her induction tour of the library—all for the intense lyrical Blakean kind of poetry, and though she hasn't published for almost 20 years carries around a little child's green copybook with scribblings for poems, and occasionally loses it. She said you'd told her Auden was much better than Yeats. And she'd said you'd outgrow it; and you'd said, "How old are *you*?" She's a great admirer of your poetry.

An emotional last meeting with Pound—"Cal, God be with you, if you like the company."

No use describing Yaddo—run down rose gardens, rotting cantaloupes, fountains, a bust of Dante with a hole in the head, sets called *Gems of Ancient Literature*, *Masterpieces of the World*, cracking dried up sets of Shakespeare, Ruskin, Balzac, *Reminiscences of a Happy Life* (the title of two different books), pseudo Poussins, pseudo Titians, pseudo Reynolds, pseudo and real English wood, portraits of the patroness, her husband, her lover, her children, lit with tubular lights, like a church, like a museum . . .

I'm delighted.

Why don't you come?

Affectionately,

 Cal

129. *To Peter Taylor*

Oct. 22 [1948]

Dear Peter:

A month gone, and my spirits go up and down with my poem—35 stanzas are now 52 (a couple pretty ragged) so I'm fairly delighted. But what a haul: it now looks like [it will be] 100[,] about the length of an Elizabethan play—I work all day[,] a bit most nights. I hope by April it will be substantially done— then many months of revision. It's a dog's life; and none of the verses will write themselves.

I've been wondering walking if one should think of one's writing—I find unless I have some lines in my head I get as far away as possible.

Yaddo would be ideal, if one's friends turned up occasionally. Can't you be looked over at Bard and spend a week here?

There's a man here who is an elixir of unpleasant characteristics. He is writing a pious history of Harvard, is a cautious fellow-traveller and likes . . . well here are some quotations[. . .]"I think Wallace has a good *platform.*" Slyly, after I said some mean things about Longfellow: "Do you think Rembrandt would be thought a good painter if he were painting today." After I've been telling some Pound stories: "I wouldn't give the life of one American soldier he betrayed for Pound's." I. "But no one lost his life because of Pound." This argument got really heated, especially after I found a review in the *Nation* which ended "and if anyone has to be drowned or put before a firing-squad, I'd rather [it] were Bennett Cerf or even Clifton Fadiman." Then I was telling [the] Uncle Ransom and Chattanooga-only-God-can-make-a-tree controversy: "*Trees* will be knocking around a lot longer than Mr. Ransom." I fear he doesn't fancy me much.

Sub-kai-pie, Sub-kai-pie
Sired a baby; I asked him why
"Mine" he said
"Chubby-red,
And better than money can buy.["]

Love to the 3 of you,
 Cal & BIG

130. *To Elizabeth Bishop*

[November 11, 1948]

Dear Elizabeth:
 The train connections were O.K. and next morning I felt wonderful at breakfast; but I noticed that I held on to my coffee cup with both hands, and when I got back to my room with the typed first draft of a stanza ugly and awful as life before me, after half an hour I discovered I was just staring at it, so I read the third book of the *Dunciad*, where the dunces contend in unmentionable contests and end by trying to see who can stay awake the longest over each other's books. Then I went to bed, then I went for a long walk, then I had a really profound sleep. Now I'm back in the groove briefly before next week.
 Except for the glugg (I quickly substituted it for mulled claret in my poem) the readings and the sacerdotal canon on divorce it was a marvelous week-end.
 I wrote Allen and Caroline suggesting they get in touch with you and the

Frankenbergs for dinner Tuesday night. If you're free let's have lunch together Wednesday—out of all the turmoil.

The Taylors are coming to New York for Christmas if they can get an apartment. If you're still around I want you to meet. I can promise you'll like each other.

One's sins catch up with one—when I started writing, it was about like Rexroth—no, not quite, but bad enough not to make any difference.

It was a lot of fun talking to you, and the long walk and meeting the Frankenbergs and Summers.

Hope you make your dentist and have survived the *glugg*.

Affectionately,

Cal

131. To Ezra Pound

[n.d. Fall 1948]

Dear Ezra:

I've been meaning to write you for weeks, but I've been working like hell on my poem, and somehow that doesn't go well with letters.

Yaddo is a sort of St. Elizabeths without bars—regular hours, communal meals, grounds, big old buildings etc. Details: a bust of Dante with a hole in the top and cigarette ashes inside, framed poems by Henry van Dyke, a man writing a history of Harvard.

Liked the Uberti; but it's awesome that you are now *un profeta* as though I were going to visit Isaiah; but you wouldn't like the comparison. Afraid I don't have Vals' address. You might write him through the Spanish Embassy.

I've been reading the *Unwobbling Pivot* slowly and trying to look into my heart. Also *Faust* with a trot.

Bill's bristling at the thought of meeting Eliot. "*I'm indifferent to him and what he does.*"

I was much touched by your note to me in Washington, and miss seeing you both. I'll see you Friday or Saturday.

Affectionately,

Cal

P.S. Omar is coming up here after Thanksgiving.

Nov. 14, [1948]

Dear Mr. Santayana:

Yaddo is an enormous mansion, called the "Mansion," built as a reproduction of another enormous house owned by a Romanian queen (?) who flourished about 1900, and wrote verses. The Yaddo poet of that time was Henry van Dyke and framed copies of his verses hang about—incredible brick-a-brack: stained glass, bad paintings, thrones, real English wood that looks fake, books with such titles as *Gems of Ancient Literature*[,] *Reminiscences of a Happy Life*[,] *Free Not Bound* (a ~~cautious~~ timid, ill-written thing on female emancipation, written by the old owner) a bust of Dante with a hole in the top and cigarette ashes inside, many busts, a famous race track, Negro bars, a great rose garden in disrepair, local literary people who seem as though they'd come out of one of Balzac's provincial novels and so on, and so on. I live at the farmhouse in two rooms. There are painters outside, and I just heard one say: "I guess, they wouldn't be here, if they had anything else to do."

I've done a lot—about 500 lines in the last two months. The whole poem is to be in six books, I think, between 2500 & 3000 lines. Probably it will take me two more years. It's in the revisions that one really goes to town. Maybe, it'll be pretty hot—my own experience keeps flooding up—anyhow, for the first time, I feel I'm doing all I'm capable of.

There are four others here—pleasant people who'll probably never set a river on fire, but easy to get on with. We eat breakfast & dinner together and play ping-pong. The lady who runs Yaddo is deaf and repeats herself—the details in her stories change without somehow giving them novelty. She is like a well-meaning early Hanoverian king—but she's a liberal and doesn't approve of kings. One of her subjects is how many people King George's income would feed.

A week or so ago I went to a conference of poets (Elizabeth Bishop & Williams and other friends) drank a lot of vodka and talked a lot and had a grand time. This week I'm going to another in Washington with Eliot and Auden and many others. Otherwise, I stay here and write all day and sometimes at night.

I read the piece on you in *Time* (do you feel your *system* is lost in "flourishes of naturalistic fencing"), also Edmund Wilson's interview. I wish I could get to Rome, I'd gladly *listen*.

I haven't yet read your first *Dialogues in Limbo*; but am looking forward to a passive contemplative period sometime this winter—then I'll pause and reflect. For the first time in my life I have no desire to read—just old things,

very carefully and in small quantities—*Lear* & *Antony and Cleopatra*[,] *The Dunciad*, bits of Milton, a little of *Phèdre*. After your essay and Mann's I'm trying Faust, but my German's lousy even with a trot. I can almost take Goethe as gospel, though there's no one I'm less like. Our age has little knack for being adult and yet alive. Pound's son finds that the *Conversations with Eckermann* remind him of his father!!

Ezra has translated all the Confucian odes with pages and pages of footnotes in the insane asylum—he's like a child, full of un-understanding, ignorant, often dazzling, exuberance. Fun, but maddening.

Well, the three of us have somewhat similar quarters.

Affectionately,

Robert

P.S. Your three books described in *Time* sound very exciting.

133. To Caroline Gordon

[n.d. November 1948]

Dear Caroline:

I don't know how my soul is—pretty uncombed, I guess; but my spirits are fine. I have a small black room to sleep in (fine, but last night the mattress suddenly dropped through the frame) and a largish light room to work in— five windows, four tables, three chairs, two lamps and one work-bed.

I liked Washington, but what a delight to be done with it; and back to work. With what I've saved from the library and Yaddo and my Guggenheim; I can easily last two years before I have to think of teaching.

Would you ask Allen to reserve a room for me at the Cosmos Club for the fellows meeting. I was only an associate member, and have expired.

There's a girl here named Flannery O'Connor, an admirer of yours, a Catholic and probably quite a good writer, who is looking for a teaching job. Is there anything at Columbia?

Did the Sacred Heart deceive you?

Love to you both,

Cal

134. To William Carlos Williams

[n.d. November 1948]

Dear Bill:

It was good seeing you and Flossie in Washington. Do you remember meeting my Cousin Harriet? She picked you and Eliot out as her favorite poets—"You can tell somehow by their faces." Eliot was very disappointed to have seen so little of you and wants to make a pilgrimage to Rutherford if he can get away from Princeton before he flies. I know you'd hit it off, if you really knew each other!!!

How about inviting me and Auden out sometime late in December or early in January—set a definite date and we'll come bearing bottles of bourbon and all set to wallow in prosody, until . . . but anyway we'd have good time.

How grand the world is after Yaddo and Yaddo after the world.

Affectionately,

Cal

A's address is 7 Cornelia Place (or Street) N.Y.C.

135. To T. S. Eliot

[November 25, 1948]

Thanksgiving,

Dear Uncle Tom:

(A letter's no place to begin this sort of thing; but someone in the Tate's kitchen said: "Shall we slug Uncle Tom's drink?" And I said "He'll know and not finish it." Which turned out to be true. Well, after the Barnes kiss and Cousin Mary's Léger kiss, you're part of the family—no, I don't mean that, I mean we're related. Her way of referring to Léger is something: "That greasy little Frenchman who dyes his hair, whom Bobby says is a good poet." But I didn't dare say this before Allen.)

I'll have a little more than I thought for the Faber volume—there are two more poems which I have since re-written for the *Kavanaughs*, in all about 500 lines. I've thought of calling it *Sharp the Conquering* from the prologue of the *Parlement of Fowls*; but maybe *Poems* would be better. One of the longer poems has never been published and will take some overhauling—I haven't looked at it for almost a year; but I'll get the manuscript off to you at Faber, as

soon as I can. Also I'd like to name a list of poems from *Lord Weary* that I think you ought to include.

When we finally said goodbye, I had a wonderful feeling that happens scarcely ever—as if a whole life-time had welled up and we knew each other for ever, no matter what. I'll miss you very much.

Affectionately,

Cal

P.S. I do hope you get to see Bill—I'm sure you will be converted to each other at least.

136. To Léonie Adams

[n.d. late November 1948]

Dear Léonie:

Like the statement very much—especially the "acts of charity" and the *comfort* dig in the last paragraph.

One or two things though. The poetry *could be infected by his crime* and still be good. This is in fact partially so. We seem to be saying either a) the content doesn't matter i.e. we enjoy Pound's matterless style, or b) that Pound's right hand doesn't know what his left is doing i.e. when he writes verse he forgets in "an act of charity" all about his politics. Now, there's some truth in both these alternatives, but neither will really hold water. A smart "patriotic" journalist could go to town with us on this.

The "shortly before" in the last paragraph is a nice rhetorical point, but probably untrue. I doubt if the Pound who wrote the *Pisan Cantos* differed much from the one we know at St. Elizabeths, the Confucian translator.

I'd cut your second sentence (paragraph one) at "Ezra Pound," or do something to lighten it; but this doesn't matter.

Perhaps "shortly before" could just be dropped; but if you agree with my first point, why don't you get Allen to re-work his second paragraph?

Cal

137. *To William Carlos Williams*

[n.d. late November 1948]

Dear Bill:

Ezra doesn't know yet about the $1000. It has to be *approved* by the librarian; and then theoretically some Dante might appear in the month of December to take it away from him. The prize is called the Bollingen Poetry Award (the best book[,] fellows excluded[,] published during the year) of the fellows in American letters of the Library of Congress—the money comes from the Bollingen Foundation, but you see the library (and ergo the government) can't help but be connected. We're levelling all our guns on the librarian. He's away, but his subordinates are scared to death.

I think Ezra's *Agenda* (hard G) is deadly and frivolous—his map of the world is an enormous Italian boot with a little fringe of lace at the top, labelled "Europe." Damn little to offer us who face the terrible future—the Russian war! The conspiracy is all stuff; I saw so many people like that in and out of jail—their minds toppling with it. Yes, the *usury* is something; but he's so *simpliste*—out of a book; our lives and the world will *not* be right if we just read Ezra's hundred "masters." There's a real innocence, freshness, nobility, carelessness and magic to Ezra, but it's off the *Agenda*,—in his anecdotes about himself & others, in his best translations and poems—particularly in the *Pisan Cantos*, his most human and nuttiest work.

What a sermon!

The Eliot-lion figure was wonderful—all wrong in a way. He's maimed somehow, but not dull, not untrustworthy. When I finally said goodbye to him—I felt I could say anything to him, and be understood and sympathized with. That happens once in a blue moon, you know. There are many layers to be gotten under, when you do there's something wonderfully warm and human.

I go from despair to elation on my poem too—so I can't say anything.

Affectionately,

Cal

Ezra on Cummings: A razor blade without a handle.
Cummings on Ezra: You're humane without being human.

138. To Elizabeth Bishop

[December 18, 1948]

Dear Elizabeth:

This is a before breakfast letter—I'm sure this practice isn't habit-forming. I've been fingering & weighing and wondering about my present—what happens if you open presents before Christmas?

But I wish you'd come instead—not for a day, but for the winter. Or summer, I'll settle for that. There are times of dry loneliness at Yaddo. I'm a bit aghast when I think of how long I'll be on this damned poem. Is anything worth so much work and isolation? Anyhow I wish you weren't so far away.

The two people at Yaddo are pleasant, (particularly the little Catholic novelist; the painter has a rather withering old-maidish torpor) but they're not celebrating types. My suggestion that we have bottled egg-nog for Christmas breakfast fell rather flat.

Two excerpts from a Randall letter "I *sure* do like Elizabeth Bishop." Edith Sitwell: "A skull fattened for the slaughter."

Here's what happened at Washington—since I can no longer use it to lure you to Yaddo. If Miss Moore declines, you will be the next consultant, unless you decline. You'd better keep this to yourself. The details of the election are intriguing, but you've got to come here to hear them. You see what pressure I'm putting on you.

I had a long discussion with Auden one evening at the Cosmos Club and the conversation turned to the Southerners. A: "I wish they'd stay off criticism. That's not what they're good at. They're not really very bright." I'm not sure that Auden shouldn't too—his ingenuity seems often to exceed his intuitions when he writes; but the remark did my wicked New England heart good.

A final shot. *Look, please, when you are sick tell me, so I won't worry!*

Affectionately, love & merry Christmas,

Cal

I got a huge book from Cairns, with passages in Greek, Latin, Italian, Spanish, Portuguese, French, Provençal, German and Anglo-Saxon—all with translations and have been groping for my almost forgotten Greek. Did you know that Vergil spent seven years on the Georgics—2,000 lines?

Now to breakfast, just in the nick of time and unshaven.

(Did you ever see Miss Stafford again?)

Wouldn't you like to call on your neighbors, my mother & father: see postcard.

[December 24, 1948]
Christmas Eve,

Dear Elizabeth:

The Jew-fish sure is homely; but seeing that I mistook him for a Sea-robin in your poem, I can't say the picture was a shock, still the one with his (her) mouth part open . . . !

Now: No number of ingenious post-cards is the equivalent of a letter; so really I've written you more than you've me. But I will stock up on what Saratoga has & send them at brief frantic intervals—each one ending, "Let me hear from you."

Now something I can't tell anyone else. Yesterday Peter Taylor called up from Indiana mostly to warn me that I mustn't pay much attention to his brother-in-law (who is arriving here in ten days) because he is Peter's bro.-in-law. I: "Eliz. Hardwick is arriving on the same day." Peter: "She's dangerous for you too." I: "Maybe I can interest them in each other." Peter: "Cal, that would be the most blessed thing in the world for you." Somewhere a parenthesis, Peter: "Eleanor says her brother is nice, but absolutely mad." Ah me!

My poem's like the Grapes of Tantalus. Every time I feel I'm almost done with *Book IV* (doesn't that sound grand): New stanzas and new revisions! It's now about 600 lines with a hell of a lot of re-writing to do. I tremble to think of other "books." I had a big messy spurt in the last few days; but, damn it, each spurt means that the remaining books will have to be longer, and that the one I'm writing will have to be further & further revised. God!

Spent a holy evening listening to (A) the *Gloria* from Bach's B Minor Mass (B) the *Gloria* from a Gregorian mass (C) the *Gloria* from a Palestrina mass; so I too can look at a Jew-fish and cry "Rainbow, Rainbow."

Now my refrain & ending from now on:

Do come to Yaddo next summer,

I miss you,

Cal

P.S. Delighted about your apartment. Got a *dies irae* note from Flint which I'll enclose, if I can find it.

"A screen porch in a tree" (if I read the Jew-fish postcard right) wouldn't do for a Jazz-Blue-song?

Been reading scraps of the *Iliad* in my Cairns anthology. It has everything in the world—but T. Weiss says it's just as good in translation!

Tell me something funny about Randall at the Sitwell party in your next letter.

I suspect this is a silly letter, but I can't re-read it. The Carroll book is wonderful, especially the pictures—my only other palpable present was Allen's essays from Aunt Sarah, so it was an event.

I'm reading *Pride & Prejudice* aloud to the two Yaddonians—what a lovely book and lovely woman!

140. *To Elizabeth Bishop*

[January 5, 1949]

Dear Elizabeth:

This is on your letter and two "Manhattans on rocks" but I do want to write you—oh yes, a whole day of "stubborn" the last word to apply to imaginative work (taken from Eudora Welty's reply to Wilson on Faulkner in the Christmas *New Yorker*, which you will like), which produced: "Lycaon listened to Achilles speak" which must be about the bottom.

But the essential: Do come to Yaddo (I'm so lonely) this summer. Mrs. Ames would be delighted to have you, looks forward to you etc. But wouldn't it be a good idea to write now, and get it over with; then you wouldn't have to come, if . . . But you must, or I'll faint from the whole weariness of the thing. It's my dream to maneuver you & the Taylors here.

Tomorrow, the arrivals: James Ross; Eliz. Hardwick and a real Yaddo ringer who knows everything and everybody—is in on everybody—and is sort of a ~~pain~~ pain—the illegible letters have a sort of rhetorical effect.

———

(A day later)

James is here now; full of odd intro-extraverted experiences: training dogs, working in a cigarette factory, using a benzedrine inhaler till he ran 30 miles through North Carolina shooting at someone (actually sleety trees) he thought was out with his wife. He's very nice and good company. In a few hours: Miss Hardwick.

Of course, I won't tell Randall. I've only seen the "Night before Christmas"; last spring. It has lovely moments, but I don't know about the whole. Randall's defenses of his own poems are frequently overpowering. He always fills me with envy. God! Imagine writing: "Lycaon listens to Achilles speak." No black-tongued piratical vigor at all!

To my embarrassment Santayana sent me a Christmas-present. Now I'm

knocking off a day or two (with that mighty line "Lycaon listens to Achilles speak" ringing in my ears) to read *Dialogues in Limbo*. He sure is hot (a Randallism) and dazzling, when one is patient enough to slow down to his calm.

Affectionately,

Cal

The Yaddo summer list is being made out; so why not write now. No, I'm not trying to force your hand.

141. *To Peter Taylor*

Jan. 5 [1949]

Dear Peter:

James arrived yesterday afternoon and turned out to be very refreshing. When you're shut up writing all day; it's a relief to sit about & talk at night; so that's alright. You'll allow he's good company. You must know what you're talking about, though. Eliz. Hardwick arrives in a few hours. We'll see. [. . .]

I don't know about the rumors. It wasn't my picture of myself—here one drinks scarcely at all; but at the conference I drank steadily (I was never half as drunk as Allen; but that [is] the faintest self-praise[)]. But who didn't? The end was a party at the Tates for Eliot. When Eliot left, we had one of those fights (such as you can only have with Caroline) first whether Williams was any good as a poet. All very noisy and insulting. At one point Allen returning from the kitchen began, with rather surprising coherence, to answer a point that hadn't been made, then he began hiccupping; then continued answering the point that hadn't been made; then he hiccupped; then he went to bed. Through a lot of this sat Caroline's god-parents (a tiresome Catholic convert couple named Morgan) their emotions shifting from curiosity to bewilderment to disgust.

Then Caroline & I went on with it. Caroline: "Cal, everyone says you're getting worldly[."] But I think I had the better of it I said: Her god-parents were dull, her book-reviews were pedestrian and she knew unspeakably nothing about Catholic theology. But what was astonishing was that we couldn't get mad. It was (I wouldn't believe it) a good evening. The Church or something has really mellowed Caroline—her violence no longer burns.

Well, I'll tell you all about it. Eliot's a wonderful man—thinks all the right things are funny.[. . .]

I've just hit a tough spot in my poem and am stopping for a day or two to

read and write letters. Something big is terrifying: you get lost and helpless; belong to *it* etc.

 Love to you both,
 Cal

P.S. [. . .]Say a prayer for my poem. I've never gotten into anything of the sort before.

 I have an uneasy feeling that I've already written you about the Tate evening.

 What's become of Jean? I sent her a Christmas present; and not so much as an "I thank you."

142. To George Santayana

Jan. 5 [1949]

Dear Mr. Santayana:

 I was just nodding and I saw an image of a fat, yellowish dog receding down the center of a country road—the center was grass and the ruts clamshells; so much for flux.

 I had hoped to send you a book of my poems as a sort of Christmas present; but no. One thing written brings up another—somewhat as the *dog-image*. Should one shut these things out? It seems safer to let them come, take one's time to be helpless. The other day I thought of weaving in a passage from Homer—after [a] day, all I had was "Lycaon listened to Achilles speak." This seemed the right time to knock off.

 So I read your *Atlantic* chapters and *Dialogues in Limbo*. Vocation is love, I think: for beauty, or the muses or what you wish. At least, I seem to have the four kinds named by Stendhal. The first two in shallow moments, the others more deeply. Now at 31 it's just there—I can't send away for long or find alternatives. There's the power side, the making side, the craft one learns. But now I am struck by the other, the *powerless*—powerless, when it does not come; most of all powerless, when it does, like the dog taking you God knows where!

 I don't know how to describe my subject, but imagine my last 3 long poems, the "Death of the Sheriff" and "Between the Porch" all thrown (no, not thrown!) together. Right now I'm on a section of something over 700 lines spoken by my heroine. The characters and action are the poem—a lurid (gently treated, though, I hope) incest-suicide plot—descriptions of Maine (history and nature: setting) my characters' Catholic faith & practice—a lot of Greek & Christian myth (done dramatically), the *War* (the hero is a

lieutenant-commander in the last war) but this only comes in by illusion—mainly the heroine imagining where he is. I try to stay to what I know. Pretty romantic material—not its development, if all goes well. I don't know if politics will come in except as they did in *Lord Weary*—only I hope it will be worlds fuller, and this in itself may have its *broad* political bearing.

You can see I haven't tried very hard so far in this letter for order and clarity—after doing nothing else day after day in meter, it's pleasant not to—but I apologize.

I'm very eager to see *Power & Dominion*. I am trying to let your letters and books sink fairly uncritically, as one does with a friend and not as if I were to be examined.

The impression is now deep enough, but I intend to let it go on settling and sinking. I'd more or less stopped reading philosophy; and I am thankful it returned human.

Not much news. I had a fine time with Eliot. He thought all the right things funny and is going to publish a selection of my poems—mostly *Lord Weary*, the 3 I sent you and 4 other shorter ones. Also I saw Conrad Aiken full of stories—some devoted ones of knowing you as a student at Harvard. He'd just lost his third copy of *Three Philosophical Poets*.

I don't want to attempt your instructions in the "cryptic" poets by letter. I think if we talked and read some aloud I could show their merits; certainly what they have for me. I think you would understand and like Yeats, Eliot, Wallace Stevens, Auden maybe Tate and Ransom. Frost you'd understand easily enough, but not *like* perhaps. Marianne Moore you might think of as prose; Pound & Williams chaos, with lovely passages. It might be profitable to go into illogical associative structures.

Sorry I said "agree to differ" I meant those things ask for experience, really a lot of time. Growing up with the verses and knowing some of the authors makes a difference too. I don't think the poets I've named are harder than I am—some are less formal, but that's a difference of craft and superficial. I'm sure you'd see a good deal of what I see; but I would take so much of your time.

You might give me a philosophical book list that I can follow up as the years go by and at my leisure. We are alike in ways—in enough ways to make the differences in vocation, age, temper, background etc. shocking and wonderful. I wait for what you give. If the part of the Kavanaughs I'm working on comes out (God help me) I [will] make some sort of return.

Two new people here to liven things. A good, unintellectual novelist, the brother-in-law of my best friend—full of Southern stories; he's farmed, trained dogs, played baseball, worked in a cigarette factory, been in the army, had

delirium tremens. Etc. Good company. And a Southern girl (a New York character now) full of gossip—which, alas, I enjoy and think the only subject most people talk any sense at all on—it's first hand.

Affectionately,

Robert

P.S. Thank you so much for the Tillyard. I liked his Milton book. When I get to New York, I'll find you a present. Hope you liked Fitzgerald—he & I have had good talks on the Church and the classics.

143. *To George Santayana*

Jan. 15 [1949]

(I hope this letter doesn't sound too youthful and swell-headed—everyone says I've gone from introversion to extraversion in the last few years)

Dear Mr. Santayana:

A note of thanks! I doubt if I will call on you for funds; but now I can say "if economy is all that is preventing your trip; why forget it." So the possibility comes much nearer.

The poem won't be done this year or even, maybe, next. So I'll have to live quietly much of the time and go on writing in Europe. A short trip doing nothing but look & listen might be fun; but somehow I have always thought of going for two years—long enough to forget returning, to forget being a visitor, being classed with the "summer people."

Eliot has been urging me to go, and he said two good things. 1) (I asked him why *I* should) That Europe was something I should let *happen* to me (with limitless & mysterious possibilities rather than something that might [be] this or that). 2) That it would be best to go *alone*—to have the solitude for Europe to sink in.

I can't say that I "like people" but I have many intimate friends. It terrifies me to know I will be so far. Some are old, and will, no doubt, be dead before I return. I think of the journey as sacrificial—much will have to be missed and given up—and that is autumnal and joyous and not without pathos.

I want to be here through the summer—I have been gently urging the "directoress" to invite my friends, and am looking forward to what will gather—most of them have never met. But next fall, or winter I more and more think I would like to come—maybe England a few weeks then through France to Italy, or through the Pillars of Hercules.

I should have about $5000 on hand then—$2500 saved & $2500 from a Guggenheim. I have no income. I inherit a trust from my father that will give about $3000 a year. However, I try to imagine that as non-existent. Here, I pay for nothing except liquor, cigarettes and laundry, and am rather spoiling myself with independence and leisure.

I see you *caste* me as Alcibiades. I'm pretty tame, pedestrian and earnest in comparison. Two groups feed on us: the frivolous, lion-hunting fools, and the pedantic, pious, teaching fools. Good souls; but God! Alcibiades is a bulwark when we are among them. I have been pondering yours in limbo and the fearful, glorious, ruining man in Thucydides.

Ah well, back to work.

Affectionately, (I can't think of another adverb, that wouldn't be silly; so perforce . . .)

 Robert

Your remarks on incest & suicide clarify my meaning to me—the political analogues are obvious. I've just re-read Thucydides (in English). He makes even Machiavelli sound like a Shelleyian idealist. The realism, folly, ignorance and hubris of man! But it's all woven into us from Adam, is human, and has its glory.

I had a long argument the other evening with a fellow named Alfred Kazin. I said I couldn't imagine "Socialism" (he favors the liberal international kind[,] but they are not so sure now) has anything one could "believe in." It's a technique, necessary in various degrees, but depending on its context and qualifications for its value. The statesman, artist, philosopher and saint occasionally win through, for a moment; and then the glory of God is a little visible (or anyone may for a moment); but there's no "side of the angels" no Manichean black & white world. Afterwards, a girl told me that except for the personalities, she would not have sympathized with me; for I seemed almost shockingly detached. Well, to be boisterous and detached; I wouldn't mind that. Without looking at things as they are, and spirit as it is, the militant man is a nuisance.

I don't belong to Eliot's "school" whatever that is; and his problems are not mine; but in an odd way, I felt he was closer in sensibility (not personality) than anyone I'd ever met, young or old. There'll be no introduction or money in his selection.

I wonder if you ever got *Paterson Book One*. *Book Two* depends on it and is less brilliant.

144. To Peter Taylor

[January 1949]

Dear Peter;

[. . .]James is marvelous and just what we all needed to keep from getting piddling and literary. However. We've had a few *serious* single conversations and, you know, he isn't, to tell the truth, really comprehensible. He's wonderful though and I'm crazy about him. I hope he'll stay for a long time and "*sedate*" himself—a barbarism Eliz. Hardwick has added to my vocabulary. Miss Hardwick is slip-shod, good humored, malicious (harmless) and humorous—full of high-spirits ~~talking~~ rattling a lot of sense and sheer stuff—very good company and likes James (not dangerously).

So glad you had a good time with Randall and Mackie—there's no one like him. I thought his Salzburg ball game poem was magical and wrote him a fan letter. But you don't report any of his similes. Somehow one needs them living out here in the sticks.

Now Mrs. A's letting you come depends partly on the directors (they have to consent) however she can put over about what she wants to. They meet in March. I'll keep you up to date.

God, long poems are long. I think I'll be working on mine the rest of my life, like Ezra's cantos. No, but a couple of years more anyway.

Love to you both,

Cal[. . .]

145. To T. S. Eliot

Jan. 18 [1949]

Dear Uncle Tom:

I'm just back from an "audience" with Mrs. Ames—my first. One of the peculiarities of Yaddo is the uncertainty of the tenure—people are told they can stay a month or two months (I guess it makes sense, but it's tough on those who dangle) so I've spoken up for the flowers, and said nothing of the woods. (I see I have *flowers dangling*, but there's a parenthesis.) It went O.K. (an expression she detests) the visit.

According to Bob Giroux you have my new poems: six, but about 500 lines. The Werfel adaptation isn't much; but I like the others. I think I'll offer no suggestions on the selection from *Lord Weary* till you've made yours. I think I took all that was any good from *Land of Unlikeness* (about ten [or] 12 (?) po-

ems, more or less revised) and put it in *Lord Weary*. I don't have a copy, but I guess I could get you one from Jarrell or Bob or my mother or my former wife or some one. Four or five poems in *Lord Weary* have been slightly revised, and I'll mail you the changes when you've made your selection.

After Washington, I had a tough two weeks of writing rubbish and knew it; then by rather sweating blood I got back. The poem is going to be long and long in doing. I have one book between 600 & 800 lines coming into shape; I hope to have it all together in a couple of months. I'm not sure how long the whole will be; maybe some 3000 lines—I don't want to hurry—rather brood over it like a mother bear, till the form flashes. (Another fine mixed figure)

The Mallarmé-Valéry kind of revision seems miraculous to me, but excessive[—]a blind alley for most of us. It's comforting to think of Vergil, working all the time, casually and steadily—and turning out a line a day! Comforting till you realize what that line was! . . . Not line, though; after the *Eclogues* it's groups of lines, as you say of Milton. V. is an even more incredible craftsman and more anonymous. I've been thinking (doing too, I hope) a lot about an open, organized gentle style (harder than the loaded) to sort of counter-theme against the dramatic. John Ford is wonderful at that—with not quite enough to say; and of course *Antony & Cleopatra, Cymbeline & The Winter's Tale*.

This is boring chatter. I wish we had had the leisure to go into these subjects. When you return I'd like to visit you with a hunk of the *Kavanaughs* (my long poem) and let you stir it, if you have time. (Or you could stay with Mrs. Ames at "Pine Guard." I mustn't be catty. I guess everyone here feels like Timon's guests, and has to blow off steam, at times.)

I would like to get the judgment of Eliot the poet on my poems—off the record. Not so much judgment as the pointing out of things that are good or on their way to being good, that I might usefully explore further. The limiting negative kind of criticism I think I know something about (I always appreciated that too) but the other is limitless.

Ah yes, Europe! I'd like to go. This is perfect, though barbarous and isolated. If I could travel a little, then settle down and write day in and day out, till my poem is over—with a little good company & joy. We'll talk about it when you return.

Yours affectionately,
Cal

I hope the captains and the kings have departed from your life and you are "sedating" (horrible new verb, a girl up here produced) as dear old Ezra says we must (I got some baffling agenda: the English equivalent of "life" with

nothing in it but Huxley and a lot of pretty girls in pretty dresses). Omar was up here—(they sure are a marvelous family; exhausting as hell) and I introduced him to our Yaddo child, Miss Flannery O'Connor. Weird scenes of Omar trying to help her into her muskrat coat—a new experience for both.

No news of the Library prize.

FORGIVE ALL THIS CHATTER

This is sort of a monk's life, so you bend some one's ear off when you have a chance. Monk isn't right, of course. This letter is about as organized as one of Merrill's; God help me. By the way, *I do not drink here the way I did in Washington*. I begin to think burgundy's about perfect for the long run.

Wish Eliot the Poet & Eliot the Editor would take a look at Jarrell and Bishop (Elizabeth)

If you are keeping up with Spender's auto-biography, you will learn that you are dearer friends, than you had perhaps imagined. You know he bites the boot he licks.

146. To Elizabeth Bishop

[January 24, 1949]

Dearest Elizabeth:

I was just making my bed (if you could call it "making") when I became aware of a dull burning smell. "God, I must have left my cigarette burning." I rush into my other room—no cigarette. Absent-mindedly I feel in my pocket. There, lighted cigarette on holder consuming a damp piece of Kleenex. The pocket was also stuffed with kitchen matches. Oh my!

They can't "change their minds" poor souls! Dr. Evans has to OK our choice, but he always does. Nor can we re-consider.

I've had a reading jag—*The Tempest*, bits of *Othello* (a Ring Lardner character says: "Tho I'm no Othello, I'm not as ugly as Joe Bean") *Tartuffe*, *Le Misanthrope*, *Les Précieuses*, all of Thucydides. Isn't Molière swell!

Also your "In the Prison" a just wonderful thing. You must get together a book of short stories—you're one of the best people writing them—and I thought all along from the way you talked that they were about like Carley's water-colors—no I didn't, but . . .

We wondered if you'd read Kafka when you wrote it. Anyway the tone, humor, description etc. is all yours. The hero is a sort of Scrooge-Miss Elizabeth. I know him well.

You & Peter Taylor always make me feel something of a fake—so I love you both dearly.

The Randall German poem I liked was a short one in *The Nation*—also a lovely translation from Rilke. I wrote him that I couldn't make up my mind about the "Night before Christmas," but that it struck me as an "excursion" a fine piece of style but a little idle and long.

A secret: Santayana has offered me a trip to Italy. I don't see how I can accept, but it's terribly touching and I'm thinking more and more of the ~~trip~~ pilgrimage.

Did I tell you about Cousin Mary and Alexis Léger? Cousin Mary is a tall red-headed woman in her early sixties—awfully nice, mannish, worked in the Labor Department, likes to hike, drive in difficult traffic—a pure Washington Puritan. Francis Biddle was an old beau of hers. The Biddles love Léger, and Cousin Mary has always detested him. Well at the party you were at, she heard him saying something to her in French ("Je veux vous embrasser") "Of course I didn't listen; it's pure affectation for him not to speak American." Suddenly she found herself embrasser. She's much taller; and it came out all wrong—wooden, shuddering, towering, humorous, red-headed figure.

I told Eliot the story; but after seeing him kissed by Djuna Barnes, the devil in me made me write him the rest: Cousin Mary's way of describing Léger: "This greasy little Frenchman, who dyes his hair, that Bobby says is a good poet." Then E.'s reply: "I'm inclined to agree with both you and Cousin Mary on Alexis Léger." So I could hug *him*. This is sheer malice and don't repeat it.

I would like to visit you. Maybe in June and we could travel back together.

I guess I meant your tone and humor was moral; but Flannery O'Connor's tone and humor isn't much like yours, so I don't know what I meant.

Now back to the Kavanaughs (a man-hunt section) after my vacation. It's fun *not* writing one's poems, I find.

Affectionately,
 Cal

You won't have to give readings; but I think the Library one pays $500.

Read Peter's play, if you can get hold of a *Sewanee Review*.

1949–1954

Preparation of *Poems 1938–1949* • Marriage to Elizabeth Hardwick

Baldpate • *Red Hook* • *New York City* • *Iowa City* • *Boston* • *Europe* • *Iowa City*

Lowell and Elizabeth Hardwick in Europe, 1951 (courtesy Elizabeth Hardwick)

147. To Allen Tate

[New York City?, March 29, 1949]

—ARRIVING BY PLANE 435 THIS AFTERNOON WITHOUT OLD ROB-
BERT AND LIZZIE LOVE—

UNCLE LIG—

148. To Elizabeth Bishop

Baldpate, Inc.
Georgetown Mass.
[April 10, 1949]
Palm Sunday,

Dear Elizabeth:

I don't know whether you got my last letter or not. I'm in grand shape. I have your letter about beginning to write again with me. The world is full of wonders.

Love,
Cal

Thanks for being anxious about me, but I'm O.K.

149. To Gertrude Buckman

[April 10, 1949]
Palm Sunday,

Dearest Gertrude:

I'm in an odd place but Arms is with me with no one to talk to. I'm swell though. It was grand having breakfast with you. Hope you'll feel like getting in touch with Eliz. Hardwick. & me.

Love,
CAL + ARMS OF L/$_{\text{Law}}^{\text{Lowell}}$

150. To George Santayana

[April 10, 1949]
Palm Sunday,

Dear ~~Mr.~~ Santayana:

I can't at the moment tell you how much your last letter meant to me in detail. I've been having rather tremendous experiences.

Love,
Robert

P.S. I'm in sort of the same kind of place you are.

151. To Jean Stafford

[April 10, 1949]
Palm Sunday,

Dear Jean:

I'm going through another Yaddo, but with flying colors. I think we're still married in a sense, but not meant to be together. My normal celibate life!!! I'm beginning to feel how much you bore with when we were married.

Love,
Cal

152. To William Carlos Williams

[April 10, 1949]
Palm Sunday,

Dear Bill:

I hope some one told you why I couldn't spend the week-end with you. I'm taking sort of a rest. But I think the doctors are learning about as much as I am. Hope to see *Paterson III*.

Love to all of you,
Cal

P.S. Get in touch with me through Elizabeth Hardwick
28 E 10th St. N.Y.C.

153. To John Berryman

[April 16, 1949]

Dear John:

I ~~hope~~ hope Allen explained my complications to you in time. I've just had a horrid vision of the Kenyon administrative machinery turning loose on you because I failed to appear.

I'm flourishing in an odd way.

I hope very much to get out to Kenyon for a week or so with the Tates this summer.

Affectionately,
Cal

154. To John Thompson

[April? 1949]

Dear Jack:

This is health and a rest ~~and~~ but not too unlike a combination of boarding school, jail, and Yaddo. Rest is damn hard work.

What we said about Time Inc. strikes me as fairly true, but we (or I did) left out the good side.

Also my Father's vocation was to be a naval officer, not a child. Look up Elizabeth. Love to you 3

 ARMS

155. To Robert Frost

<div align="right">[April? 1949]</div>

Dear Robert:

I wish you could arrange through Merrill to come out and visit me. I have a Dante and Shakespeare, but it's tough sledding not *seeing* another poet.

 Love,

 Robert

156. To Peter Taylor

<div align="right">[April 27, 1949]
Low Sunday,</div>

Dear Peter:

Oh dear! The senile swindler who runs dear old Baldpate has been holding up my letters, or else you would have gotten a note I wrote you over two weeks ago.

This has been like purging the Augean stables, but I'm in mysteriously wonderful and rugged shape—better than ever in my life and each day better.

I *must* visit you (what a group of decadents you've gathered!) How do you feel about Eliz. Hardwick; we want to be together.

I've been calling & calling you and you've always answered.

 Love to Nellie & Kate,

 Cal

157. To Allen Tate and Caroline Gordon

<div align="right">May 5, [1949]</div>

Dear Allen:

This is Father's Day, though I believe it's the feast of Monica or something of the sort. I'm in wonderful shape in all ways; but the days are long, long, long!!!

I've seen my mother & father once, Frank Parker many times and Robert Frost once. Robert was worth all the others many times.

Can you and old Tate give me a hand, love to you both,

Cal

158. To Gertrude Buckman

<div align="right">May 21, [1949]</div>

Gertrude Darling:

Letters do not reach me, tho perhaps mine go out. I have thought of you with thanks.

I am a poor man and getting no richer. I have little to offer you. Giroux wants to publish my poems between *Lord Weary* and *The Kavanaughs of the Mills*.

<div align="center">

King David's Garden

for

Gertrude Buckman

"FILIAE REGUM IN HONORE TUO, ADSTITIT REGINA A
DEXTRIS TUIS IN VESTITU
DEAURATO CIRCUMDATA VARIETATE."

</div>

If you can still read Latin; and will be so kind as to permit me, your humble servant.

Sharp the Conquering[,] L. W. and the new poems are coming out in England, the whole business dedicated to Elizabeth. Hardwick.

I've had a funny feeling that you'd hit it off with Hyman Bloom. You're sort of the same and unsame. I haven't his address. You could get in touch with him thru Jack Sweeney or Elizabeth Bishop.

I wish you could harp Mozart to me again. I keep hearing you in my soul thank God.

Love,

Cal

I think I have your silver whistle here, but in my suit-case.

159. To Randall Jarrell

Baldpate
I'm pro-Truman, I doubt if any one is more so.

May 21,

Give my love to the Starrs
Ah Randall,

When shall I see you!!! It's almost a year now since you took Omar and me on that crazy drive, a year since Ezra said "Let me see the animal." When I left for Yaddo, he said "God go with you, Cal, if you like the company."

At Yaddo and at the Tates I played your "Lady Bates" with tears in my eyes—surely that's *even* nearer the *one story* than Graves' poem.

There are two people you were wrong as hell about Eliz. Hardwick and Gertrude Buckman. You must love more of the *wonderful* people. God! I can hear you re-quoting yourself to prove me wrong. But I'm not!

Well, it's 12 years now I think that we have been teachers of each other. 12 years. Re-read Allen's Christmas sonnets; the last four are really *much* better than the first two; but crabbed and cryptic. When we were together and writing—he didn't know even darkly how much he was saying.

You know you're not unlike the R. C. Church—"One more horrid thing" but the right thing.

If you will re-read Paul and the Gospels you'll see that the truth is both with the Jews and the R.C. Church; or so God said.

I've been thinking that you're perhaps the best poet in America[—]where are there better poets?—unless I am.—I'm poor, helpless, and conceited here—so bear (arms) with me.

I've read Vanzetti's letter to Sacco's son for the first time. Their cause is mine—I'm sure the pro-Russian traitors are secretly supported by *certain* rich men—those who have sold us (the poor—who's worse paid than the poet—even carpenters get more and work less) sold us for "a pair of shoes."

When I get out I'm going to do everything in my power to get the Sacco case re-opened, so that those responsible are imprisoned and *electricuted*.

Mother of God, old Randible, there's no *man* I love more than you.

My love to Mackie, and my humble affections to Kitten. I'm not mad at him because of what he did to my black suit.

160. To Elizabeth Hardwick

> [The Inn, Baldpate Hospital
> Georgetown, Mass.
> July 1, 1949]

Dearest Lizzie:

All goes well. New doctor an Italian literatus. Another dope in our room—all went to an unstrenuous play. No news. (Haven't talked to Schlomer yet.)

Here's Randall's letter. I was all wrong about *Nag's Head*. If it's impossible to get a house right away we might visit them, but let's keep to our plan.

This is scribbled off in the middle of all my room-mates and a nurse making beds—like a boy's letter from camp.

Gosh, your visit was wonderful and *saning*. Hope you can stand me still.

Love,
Cal

Miss you terribly.

161. To Elizabeth Hardwick

> [July 4–5, 1949]

Dearest Lizzie:

Arms has just been sent off to St. Elizabeth's after a visit here much like mine to the Tates. In a blast of manic elation he'd been calling my father "Daddy Bob." Refrain "Why, you're not such a baby as every one says." "Shit! What's the matter with being a baby! Josh Logan's a baby" Of my father's principle actions: Watering the sward grass, polishing the furnace, making charts for where the furniture should be placed etc.— "I'll tell you another; Daddy Bob, you're an artist; as Uncle Ransom desiderates, all you do is purely gratuitous." Then he'd hug Daddy, sometimes more roughly than he knew. When he left in the padded wagon, he was talking a combination of Merrill and Uriah Heep.

All goes well—grave and tame. Mother has finally accepted our arrangement—with cordial (?) diffidence—faux mieux. Long talk with Merrill who is all for us—so he says except for the Church.

~~Everyone~~ Merrill wants me to leave Baldpate and start house-hunting—I have a pocket-full of difficult Moore suggestions.

Tues.

I've just gotten back and read your second letter—one from Flannery, one from Omar.[. . .]

Arms (back from St. Lizzie's) and I are concerned to get us on/into a respectable, God-fearing status. Blair says Jean spoke of the annulment to help me—he's going to see her again. I'll see Father Dunagree in few days, if he's back. All this doesn't interest you. How would you like to be engaged? Like a debutante. WILL YOU?

My heart is with you—in all the New York heat and all the "nagging" indecision of renting your apartment and our house-hunting. Ah, it will be very soon! How happy we'll be together writing the world's masterpieces, swimming and washing dishes.

All my love,
 Cal

Reading *The Idiot* again.

162. To Peter Taylor

July 7, [1949]

Dear Sub:

This will have to go to Bloomington, and on; because I don't suppose "Scuppernong N.C." would reach you.

I'm well and about to leave—feeling rather gravelled and grim and dull, perhaps from rooming with 2 alcoholics and 2 dope addicts and a television set in a room like your barrack in Chattanooga.

Well, out of all my delirium I've come with the Catholic Church and Elizabeth Hardwick—and my unfinished poem. Add the crazy plan (approved by the doctors) of getting a house somewhere and settling down for some time with Elizabeth—unmarried, because according to the Church Jean's divorce doesn't count unless annulled.

It's an odd plan, but so are my circumstances. Finding a house is not easy.

I'd like to write a lot, but I don't know how to say it—my room-mates have returned and the "Red Sox" are on the screen.

I miss you and think of you and hope to see you and Eleanor before long.
 Love,
 Cal

I'm sorry for all the foolishness and trouble of my stay in Bloomington.

163. To T. S. Eliot

15 Grove Street
Beverly Farms, Massachusetts
July 25, [1949]

Dear Tom:

I agree about the title. I don't quite know what to do about dates[,] *Poems 1938–1948* (earlier versions of some of the *Land of Unlikeness* poems existed in 38—final versions in 1943). Take your choice. You're right about *Sabre*, of course; and I'll revise the detritus line in the galleys. I hope my answers to Bob made sense; when he called on me in the hospital, I was completely unilateral—ready to give you or anyone else an *agenda*.

The hospital is still too near a memory for me to find much amusement or pleasure in describing it. But all my friends and even my mother and father were wonderfully helpful. I am so moved by your interest—editorial and personal.

I'm spending a few days with my parents. On the 28th—my real news at last—I am marrying Elizabeth Hardwick. We have rented a house in Red Hook (a town about midway between New York and Albany) and will be there from the first of August till next June.

I feel that you have vicariously suffered my vicissitudes with me. Now I am taking to heart your comment on Huxley's comment on Lawrence—about the foolishness of a spectacular life—I mean mine, not Lawrence's, of course.

Yours very affectionately,
Cal

164. To Peter Taylor

[Red Hook, N.Y.]
Aug. 6 [1949]

Dear Peter:

Elizabeth Hardwick and I were married on the 28th of July—a small heterogeneous wedding with the Clarks, Parkers, Uncle Cot, Mary McCarthy and my parents—more like your wedding than any I can think of.

Red Hook is a little way from the Hudson, not far from Bard College—our house is picturesque and ancient—it belongs to Fred Dupee and once was the headquarters of General Israel Putnam—it even has a sign in front and to one side; however it's not very grand.

We are learning everything from the beginning: cooking, burning garbage, lawn-mowing etc. We are very isolated, see no one and have nothing to do but establish a routine and write.

I've had two letters from you since Baldpate, but no story—before receiving electric shocks, I had a comical mad period singing ballads (very badly and baldly with made up tunes) and destroying furniture—all letters sent to me then were destroyed, or are circling back to their senders.

Please forgive my not writing to you in the last month and announcing my marriage. It's been tough shaking all the unease, torpor, desire to do nothing—and now this plan, now that—and now, at last, how lucky!

We will be here till next June.

My love to you and Eleanor,
Cal

165. To Robert Fitzgerald

[n.d. August 1949]

Dear Robert:

We have rented Fred Dupee's house near Bard College and have settled down to country living. We are very clumsy, but we like it.

~~Coming out~~ I think of your account of the first part of my break-down in a great moil of confusion, embarrassment and gratitude. I am still far from having digested it all, but I realize that my experiences were like those that might have resulted from a narcotic—terrific lifts, insights, pourings in of new energy, but no work on my part, only more and more self-indulgence, lack of objectivity; and so, into literal madness i.e. I had to be locked up and went through all the usual clinical antics. Coming-to, after the shock treatments, was proportionately dismal.

I'm not in the Church now—nor do I know, except gropingly, what I believe. However, "the world is all before us" before us all and life and happiness.

We are so delighted that you have your new house, and hope to see you in the fall.

Love to you and Sally,
Cal

166. To Dorothy Pound

<div align="right">Aug 13, [1949]</div>

Dear Mrs. Pound:

Elizabeth Hardwick and I were married on the 28th of July and are living in an old quiet house that we have rented until next June. Red Hook is a bit north of Poughkeepsie and near a small college called Bard—far from everything if you don't have a car.

My "experiences" that led to the hospital now seem like a prolonged dream—and so they were, then almost unbearably dull and depressing. I have thought of you and Ezra often—the astonishing jolt of having things happen to you, being put somewhere, the surprises you never planned. Of course, the similarities are only external, and my treatment was all for the good.

I'm very excited about the "Odes." You might try Harcourt Brace (Robert Giroux is my editor) 383 Madison Ave. But all publishers are slow. Eliot is bringing out a collection of my poems, probably next spring.—In England there's a paper shortage, so all publishing dates are indefinite.

I haven't seen the "news" note in *Poetry* yet.

I'll be seeing you next winter—but now my love to you both,

Cal

167. To Gertrude Buckman

<div align="right">August 16, [1949]</div>

Dear Gertrude:

[. . .]I've written you and started to write you and thought about you and writing to you daily. Nothing I can say will really do to tell you everything that happened, or why. By the time I reached the hospital I was completely out of my head—strange physical sensations—I was a prophet and everything was a symbol; then in the hospital: shouting, singing, tearing things up—religion and antics. Then depression (extreme) aching, self-enclosed, fearful of everyone and everything anyone could do, feeling I was nothing and could do nothing.

I'm sorry about the mix-up on writing to Bald-Pate, that you heard about our marriage the way you did—sorry because of all my ill, inconsistent, selfish and so on actions toward you. You gave me so much color and grace and love—and now in this beginning of rest and happiness, beginning to be calm,

at last, about the whither of the future—where is this sentence going?—anyway I try to accept myself and hold on to the joyful.

This is all romantic, vague and probably foolish—but I want to be forgiven and to stay friends. No harm or coldness was ever meant.

Elizabeth sends her best wishes. We hope you will visit us sometime in the fall.

Cal

168. To T. S. Eliot

August 30, [1949]

Dear Tom:

I am sorry for the delay. I have been spending more time than I like to admit on "Thanksgiving's Over," the only poem in the book that I had never seen in print—revision on revision, then worst of all tinkering, sometimes just for change. This could go on; but I think I killed almost all that struck me as cumbersome, padded or obscure. I enclose an entire new version along with a few pages of minor corrections.

For the old introductory note substitute this:

The first sixty-nine pages of this book were published in America under the title *Lord Weary's Castle*. A few of these poems were taken from another book called *Land of Unlikeness*. When I use the word *after* below the title of a poem, what follows is not a translation but an imitation. Here and there elsewhere I have adapted ~~a line or a sentence~~ lines and phrases.

The title should now be *Poems 1938–1949*. The dedication: *For Elizabeth Hardwick*. Please cut out the old note and the Latin sequence, Suscipe Domine . . .

I guess with the Congressional suspension we've taken our final licking on Ezra's award.

Affectionately,

Cal

169. To Elizabeth Hardwick

Payne Whitney [Hospital]
New York, N.Y.
[n.d. September 1949]
First night,

Dearest Lizzie:

Not much news. This is like the inn with more organization and routine. Everyone talks about himself, so I seem more extroverted. There's one literary patient who has read much what I have and we've talked and played Russian Banker. (Borrowed the Sept. *P.R.* of all things.)

Talked to my doctor all about Yaddo, Chicago etc. I think all is going to be well; but it's sad without you.

Dearest, dearest, dearest Lizzie I think of you all the time; and worry so about all I have dumped on you. We are going to work it all out, dear, be as wonderful as you have been.

Love,
Cal

I am going to write Merrill soon; you mustn't take on everything by yourself.

170. To Peter Taylor

[n.d. 1949]

Dear Peter:

I am now in the Payne-Whitney Clinic, where Jean was and will probably be here two or three months for therapy. I seem to be in the other half, the down half of what you saw in Bloomington—self-inclosed, unable to function, depressed.

171. To Elizabeth Hardwick

[September 15, 1949]

Dearest Lizzie:

This is a thorough and solid place—what I have long needed. I had another long talk with my doctor yesterday afternoon—pouring out acts and facts.

Events: Game of badminton with ping pong racquets, arrival of a Catholic priest (a patient) full of facts about the Navy, Missions and St. Paul. (The city.) Tried to learn the rules of perspective—unavailingly. Bridge (against an expert) Russian Bank. Trying to read *Cakes and Ale*. Slept well.

I hope you are seeing people. You mustn't worry about me, please take every care of yourself, in a week or so the craziness and insecurity will begin to go.

All love,
Cal

172. To Elizabeth Hardwick

[September 20–21, 1949]
Tues–Wed.

Dearest Lizzie:

So glad to get your letter and know that Jack is going to drive you down. Things are going much better here and I think I am on the brink of some sort of results.

Now another morning—it's obviously cold outside, and I wonder what you are doing to keep warm. I hope you've gotten Mr. Moore to start the furnace.

O Lord, how empty I am. However, this letter is just to tell you ~~that the depression~~ that I am well. Please don't worry.

When you come on Saturday, you will see improvement.

Love,
Cal

173. To Elizabeth Hardwick

[September 28, 1949]

Dearest Lizzie:

~~Trying to purge my personality~~ You seem to have converted Dr. Blitzer. After I'd told all the sordid and awful things about myself I could think of, he said it was 95 percent due to my condition. Things are much the same[:] mornings, the unbearable; afternoons, the numb—both dumb and diminishing fast. I guess all's well.

Badminton, sanding a table[,] vague memories of many factual conversations—Helen Hayes, Mohammedan fairies, St. Louis compared with Kansas City, Russian Bank etc. Not much to report.

I hope Susan is with you. Tell all about the moving and what's going on with you. Oh God, I wish I were with you—real and in the real world!

Love,

Cal

174. To Charlotte Winslow Lowell

Nov. 5 [1949]

Dear Mother:

I was delighted to get your letter with its love and good-will. For many fairly obvious reasons I have not wanted to write about coming here—but ashamed and puzzled by it, to shut up like a clam.

All is going well, though slowly. We have a little apartment off Central Park and I go out Wednesdays and week-ends. I am looking for part time work and am beginning to really learn something from the psycho-therapy.

We have little money and much uncertainty; yet I'm sure that this is the way to sense and happiness. Elizabeth is marvelously brave, ingenious and sympathetic.

Not much news: We have been seeing the Clarks and Thompsons. This afternoon we [are] going to paint our apartment.

We would like to come on for Thanksgiving.

My love to you and Daddy,

Bobby

P.S. I've been trying to understand my first six or seven years, and have many questions to ask you.

175. To Elizabeth Bishop

November 18, [1949]

Dear Elizabeth:

I'm afraid I'll be in Boston from Wednesday to Sunday. Is there any chance of your staying longer? We so want to see you.

Things are much better with me. I stay in our apartment weekends and go to the Public Library almost every afternoon—to prepare a course in modern poetry for next summer at Kenyon! Also I'm hoping to get a job teaching in February. Psycho-therapy is rather amazing—something like stirring up the bottom of an aquarium—chunks of the past coming up at unfamiliar angles, distinct and then indistinct.

Any of the January dates for the meeting except the 6th will do for me. I'm supposed to give a reading at St. John's then.

Well, it has been long since we've seen each [other] and there's much to say. I'm dying to hear about Washington and Yaddo.

Love,
Cal[. . .]

176. To Robert Fitzgerald

[29 West 104th Street, New York, N.Y., n.d. December 1949]
Dear Robert:

After two readings of the Oedipus: Like it all, the verse varied and sustained enough to hold together stately passages like the opening speeches and the flatness of the stichomythia and Creon—I read it all in a tone of quiet declamation, the Chorus's rising to a chant. Like particularly the Prologue, Parodies and Ode IV.

I found myself wondering at times what could be done with stricter verse, straight blank or run on couplets at the same time making the phrasing and rhetoric a little less classic—probably it would make it clotted, unactable and cheap. As soon as one hears a voice, all the loosenings of the rhythm seem just right. Isn't the Greek, though, a little less rhythmed less lofty—somehow more prosy in tone and more formal in its metrics? Anyway, it's a gracious and beautiful translation.

A strange pathos to the Prince—sorry I didn't take down the magazine's name and save you the typing—the jeweled homely virgin and scenes, so perfect so ordered that their very perfection is their distance both from us as we are, and from God whose reality reduces them to dolls. Art able to approach, the artist able to approach but only by his craft, and so for the moment analogous to the Virgin—where neither we nor the artist can settle—pathos and something between acceptance and resignation—all done by the slow delicate rhythm, the images and the little, spoken phrases of reflection and theology.

We spent an hour and a half in the station with Flannery—more or less on

tip-toe because her train was "reported" an hour late, which meant it might leave any minute.

I'm hopeful about the Iowa teaching, but won't know for a week.

This is scratched out with a short pencil and maybe almost illegible. But now clearly: A Merry Christmas to you and Sally and Hugh and Benedict, from us both.

Cal

P.S. Let's get together soon after Christmas.

177. To George Santayana

Dec. 22, [1949]

Dear Mr. Santayana:

I'm rather afraid of writing you after so long and inexcusable a lapse. But I want you to know what I have been doing and what has happened since last April; though I am not sure even now if I have the courage and good sense to be altogether clear.

Late in July I married Elizabeth Hardwick, a girl I have known several years, but only well the last two months we were at Saratoga. She is a novelist, a good one, with marvelous tenderness and humor and a mind that flashes. We are now living in a little New York apartment and I expect to be teaching English from February to June, then again for six months this summer and again in the fall.

Well now for the confusion—the *mystical* experiences and explosions turned out to be pathological and left me much in the state of your Oliver in his last days—inert, gloomy, aimless, vacant, self-locked. (I have always been something of an Oliver who turned to images rather than duty.) In September it got so bad that I had to go to a hospital and take psycho-therapy. There I have been ever since, but am now about done and am living half in and half out of the hospital.

During all that blind mole's time—the fascinated spirit watching the holocaust of irrationality[,] apathy tormenting apathy—somehow I couldn't write you. But now please accept this brief note[,] a Christmas card, forgive me for my involuntary foolishness, and write me again from all your wisdom and culture as a wise uncle. I so want to know how you are.

Yours,
Robert

P.S. I see I've said little. Reading the *Last Puritan* in the last few weeks, I've had a curious feeling that we had been talking together for hours and hours—I mostly listening—and that all had been said and understood.

178. To Allen Tate

December 29, [1949]

Dear Allen:

Many thanks for all the trouble you've taken for me. Last night Paul telephoned to offer me the job, and I quickly accepted. We plan to leave for Iowa in about two weeks.

Elizabeth has told me about your letter to Paul and your efforts to find some money—now luckily unnecessary. You are a wonderfully generous friend, and I shall never forget.

Christmas has come and gone without much excitement—but I've decided to follow in Caroline's tracks and limit myself to wine and beer.

Couldn't you drop in on us one of your afternoons, say the Thursday the week after next—I'm going to read at St. John's next week, and am not sure whether I'll be able to make the poets' meeting. We'll have to find an apartment and get acclimated before the term starts.

My love to you and Caroline,

Cal

P.S.[. . .]Now the check has arrived. The Lord knows we can use it, but we'll have about $1000 when we reach Iowa; $2300 more for the four months, then Kenyon. Shouldn't it go to two still poorer people? I'll hold the check until I hear from you. Please be blunt about this.

179. To George Santayana

Jan. 8 [1950]

My Dear "Uncle":

The terms of your adoption were intended to *confine* you to a strictly spiritual relationship. Now I have endorsed your embarrassing check, and know that I am an imposter: a happy imposter, however, who leaves with his wife for Iowa feeling bank-worthy and grand. Many thanks, but be good, and send me only your valued letters.

After a week-end at St. John's College in Annapolis, reading poems I hadn't looked at for months, answering the students' bright metaphysical questions—often not knowing where my sentences would end: I return to re-read your letter, and marvel. I cannot say all I want to; but I see you writing letters in the half-light, reading "with pleasure" in a glare of light; and know that there can be sympathy but no sorrow for your green old age, your failing eyes your confinement. You are so clear and elaborate, and flat—harmonize so many seemingly opposed qualities: your scrupulously difficult and anxious writing and awareness with a calmness that is somehow skeptically resigned, yet enjoying and rejoicing. A clumsy stab at defining you; and now I meditate on your self-knowledge, and my imagination exists there for a moment and I feel as though I were knocking over a lighted lamp when I say that your life [is] still a triumph and all in character. Long, long may you continue!

In answer to your questions: I am back where I was in my faith—fallen or standing in disillusion. Only the bull who has been burned out of a barn looks at the sunset and trembles. Often I long to walk in the great house of the Church, but the candles would set my clothes on fire long before I reached the altar. I too can cry out "O Altitudo"—all Christ's violence and love, and all so instituted and work-a-day that a bee might be at home in that house. So I am back where I was with a difference, at first with a vengeance, taught more than I could take. You can't imagine how unpleasant I found making sense. I must think of some smug saw at this point, or an effusion on *pain* and *profit*.

The poem is fragmentary—much too allusive, tenuous and fantastic. I haven't been able to go back to it or look at it much, but there's stuff in it I'll eventually use. When we get to Iowa I'll try and comb out something for you.

Now I am looking forward to your "traditional" Tibullus in the right mood, quite diffident about all the "untraditional" squibs and fire-crackers in my own verse. I am delighted your old secretary is with you and waiting for the chapters of *Dominations and Powers* with excitement.

I'll mail you some of my wife's writings—almost over her dead body—so passionate is her modesty.

Yours affectionately,
Robert Lowell

P.S. The Pound is largely idiosyncratic trash, with lovely lyrical, reminiscent and auto-biographical stretches—his arcadia, how hard it came to him.

180. To Dorothy Pound

Dept. of English
Iowa City, Iowa
[March 7, 1950]

Dear Mrs. Pound:

I'm anxious to hear from you and Ezra—I was only in Washington for a few hours for the poets' meeting and couldn't make St. Elizabeths.

I've been through a long, burdensome dull period of the mind and now am myself again or better—and teaching student-poets English. Some are intelligent, a few talented and the rest, poor things, perhaps will learn to read.

I saw part of the great and wonderful torrent of E.P. letters at Harcourt Brace—their publication ought to stop many slanderous mouths.

Affectionately,
 Cal

181. To Robert Penn Warren

[728 Bowery St., Iowa City, Iowa]
March 10, 1950

Dear Red:

Your hospitality leaves one rather breathless and gasping, and I almost forgot to thank you, and tell you I enjoyed it all tremendously—particularly talking with you. I'm sorry the visit was so short and that Elizabeth was unable to come.

On the way home, the train had a hot-box, then the steam-line broke down and I finally walked leading an old lady into West Liberty. By that time I had listened to three engineers discuss every complicated and spectacular wreck in the last twenty years, and knew that train-accidents were part of life, something to look forward to and treasure in the memory; but the old lady kept saying: "I don't see how this happened; I've been on trains for sixty years."

Your section on the sources of poems covers more than I would have imagined possible in the space. One thing that might be added would be translations—prose originals of Shakespeare and Jonson; Pound's "Seafarer" with a literal translation—some of Wyatt; the hardest of all—plagiarizing, lifting, improving; then Valéry's idea of revision as both improvement and change, many versions and possibilities, none final. But I think you've covered enough,

and your section on "The Immortal Part" is about the best analysis of anyone's revisions that I have read.

Wish we could move the restaurant where I had the double martini and you, no longer on the wagon, here next week for Dylan Thomas's reading.

Best wishes for your health and everything else to you and Cinina,

Affectionately,

Cal

182. To Peter Taylor

March 30, [1950]

Dear Peter:

You must stop withholding all real details of the Randall Blackmur meetings. I've tried to imagine—but all I get are two monologues, never connecting, but licking their bruises. And then Randall left astonished, seeing it all as clear as day.

This is a bare stretching gray place. We see a lot of Robie and Anne, and little of anyone else. The people are really quite pleasant, intelligent, and friendly, but it's a world of the New Criticism, the young hatching into professors, the old hardening, and the virtues are very solid.

Perhaps, you've heard of the Bednasek trial. Last November a girl was strangled, or maybe not. And now the trial—gruesome, blurred, silly, pitiful—sororities, fraternities, "pinned" "chained," "they seemed happy" psychologist Irish policemen—money, justice, and no good answer. Elizabeth goes eight hours a day as an accredited reporter for the New York *Post*, and has talked a book.

Robie and I want you to spend your Guggenheim at home, and get us jobs at the Woman's College—Robie will teach the 18th century Russian novel and I the Scottish Chaucerians—no more creative writing. I have 25 poets, and some are not as bright as others.

Last week Dylan Thomas was here—Frank Parker, Harry Brown and Avery Handly all thrown in together and all at once and all the time. Somehow he was kept on beer most of the time, but he'd begin at 7 in the morning and end at 12—no meals except breakfast. About the best and dirtiest stories I've ever heard—dumpy, absurd body, hair combed by a salad spoon, brown-button Welsh eyes always moving suspiciously or fixing on the most modest person in the room—usually Anne Macauley, a great explosion of life, and hell to handle.

I was delighted with your *Two Spinsters and a Married Woman* (I hope you recognized my reference to the Scottish Chaucerian Dunbar) so don't tell me it's part of a play. It brings back another journey to Memphis—also Miss Anna Guiddon of Damariscotta, who should have met them and the man traveling with "Mother" who met me in the Men's Room.

I'm palming off Eleanor's poems on my class as mine and telling them to use their mother-wit and write about what they know—as I do.

Teaching is rather awful—boning up on what you can't use, then faking. My greatest success has been reading Burns aloud with a Scotch accent. I really enjoy it, I guess, and intend to dedicate my life etc. But it's all stuff about learning by having to explain—I've unlearned almost all I ever knew.

We want to visit you about the middle of August—after Kenyon and after a visit to Elizabeth's mother and thirteen brothers—God help us!

Love to you both,
 Cal

183. *To Peter Taylor*

Kenyon College
Gambier, Ohio
July 29 [1950]

Dear Peter:

I hope our invitation was more than some sort of Southern gesture. We plan to leave here on the sixth of August, spend two or three days with Elizabeth['s] mother and 13 brothers and sisters and then come on to you, arriving say the night of Wed. the 9th. I have to be in Cambridge on the 14th for a poets' conference that will pay my passage.

We're flourishing. I managed to write and deliver my assembly speech, finish my long poem and talk myself through hours and hours of two hour classes but also, in spite of every opportun[ity] I landed us in the worst house in Gambier—one with no porch, a two foot kitchen, and a surly theology-ridden black cat. Elizabeth is developing humorous hypocondriacal complaints and in general taking after you, for how else can I explain her beginning now on a 24 hour dieting program. She's not large, you know.

I'm just back from a faculty retreat, somewhat sobered for me by being put in a little house with Uncle Ransom, who toward 12 o'clock when the conversation was opening out into controversy and wildness, would suggest that we

retire, and as the voices gurgled and rolled in the distance would say "Well, I guess we're well out of it."

Thought the *Woman of Means* was tremendous, and was filled with envy for it is what I've tried to do with my Kavanaughs of Damariscotta.

Love to you both,

Cal

184. To Kenneth Burke

[Cambridge, Mass., n.d. but probably August 16, 1950]

Dear Burke:

Just a note to say that I am grieved at the treatment you received, and that I think it is abominable that you were shut up on political grounds, and that I can curse myself for not getting up last night and protesting against that son of a bitch Elliott for talking to you as he did.

Too much politics! But I think you spoke on a nobler and more realistic level than anyone else—more toward the political future that we are all beginning to breathe. My support is not worth much to anyone, but I hope you won't doubt the vehemence and loyalty of my feelings towards you.

Yours,

Robert Lowell

185. To George Santayana

Wadsworth House, [Harvard University]
Cambridge 38, [Mass.]
[n.d. August 1950]

Dear Santayana:

I've been meaning to write you an entertaining and sensible letter—and so have kept delaying, in fact there's one some 3 months old lying about somewhere unfinished. This is just a note to tell you that we will be arriving in Naples or Genoa about the first of October. We are taking a freighter and the sailing date is uncertain.

I'm out of my dumps (the religious mania seems to necessitate a kind of hangover of melancholia), and feel much as always.

The teaching went well and the long poem (long for me 600 lines) is finished.

Could you drop me a note at my parents' address *Beverly Farms*, Mass. and let me know how you are?

Yours sincerely,

Robert

I read an ode here last spring and after it was over (I thought I'd been rather resonant and impressive) an old gentleman named William James told me I read as though I were ashamed of myself. I'm sure he suffers from some inversion of New England diffidence.

The Harvard address is because I'm at a sort of poets' convention. I'm in a building with Canadians and Viereck.

186. To Elizabeth Bishop

15 Grove Street
Beverly Farms, Mass.
August 20 [1950]

Dear Elizabeth:

Our freighter, called the "Fernhill" suddenly emerged with Aug. 30 as the sailing date, so unless you could be in New York on the 29th, I guess there's not much chance of our meeting.

The conference was a crazy jumble with Viereck talking like an incoherent manic Merrill Moore, and Randall tense and inspired very profound, cogent, rude—full of disgusts and enthusiasms—Miss Moore was our one Belle. Some anonymous person gave her an orchid and she was very cute and full of crushing compliments for her critics such as the Harvard *Wake* that had never accepted one of her poems—after I read my "Dead Brother" she said the reading was bracing and did her good. Spender was all over the place and, I'm sorry to say, very pleasant and intelligent.

Peter Taylor and I have agreed that Randall is a terror for his friends in public—you are either corrected, ignored or expected to loudly agree. You end up feeling like a boor for supporting as much as you do and a hypocrite for not going further.

I wonder if you would do me a favor and buy some flowers for my Cousin Pearson Winslow who is dying (?) of cancer. They should be sent through my Cousin Harriet rather than directly. I hate to involve you with more florists. But this seems like the only way for me to do anything.

I guess the best way for you to reach us is through Harcourt Brace or the

American Express in Rome. We'll write you at Yaddo as soon as we are settled. You must try to join us—things are bad politically, but it looks like they will be indefinitely.

My Daddy is impatient to be off to the post-office, so I'd better conclude. God bless you for the coming year. Love from us both,

Cal

P.S. Give my love to the Pounds—I had many small brushes for his sake; though almost everyone seems to be on his side now.

187. To Elizabeth Bishop

September 18, [1950]

Dear Elizabeth:

My father died quite suddenly on the 30th of August and we have been rusticating and maundering with my mother. His death was painless—not really tragic, for he had little besides filling the days to look forward to. He was not a suffering or heroic man, but rather as some one said "happy-seeming" always smiling or about to smile—and deep under, half-known to him: apathetic and soured. There was at least one great might-have-been—a first-rate Naval career. The death seems almost meaningless, as is perhaps always the case when the life has long resigned itself to a terrible, dim, diffused pathos.

We sail now on the 28th a Thursday and plan to go to New York on the Monday or Tuesday before—now I think there's no escaping us for you. You must name some days you can see us in N.Y. or perhaps you'd prefer to come here for the week-end. *IN ANY CASE* don't slip away.

I'm boiling mad at Randall—I think his reading of the agèd Goethe was fatal. He gave a tremendous Philippic at Harvard against our culture that has no time or taste for poetry—something that would have made Jonathan Edwards sound like Montaigne. Then what with his tennis tournaments, swimming and new enthusiasms had no time to read my poem and never apologized. Ah me!

Love,

Cal

Thanks for your goodbye wire. How did you know the ship's address?

188. To George Santayana

Dear Mr. Santayana:

Many congratulations on your book. I don't suppose either you or your philosophy would favor such a brusque violent phrase as a "terrible pull" but so it seems—particularly since the sad dark sentences of your letter to me last January. It seems that you can relax and take your ease in the sun or shade and reflect that you've now done what you set out to. Oh it's never done of course for the writer or for anyone; and five or six times, or maybe fifty, you must have felt, for the moment, "satisfied" with yourself. Even I (after this year) with no reason in the world, out of pure foolishness, feel quite contented—but you have a *right* to.

A little over two weeks ago, my father painlessly and quite suddenly died from a heart attack. His first attack came in 1941 and since then death was always an instant possibility, but he was never exactly sick, though of late a little breathless and mentally unpersistent. We were familiar in an impersonal way without ever knowing each other well. His death is illusive to me and hard to take in—memories that emerge late in the afternoon.

We sail on the 28th on a freighter called the *Hopeville* and will arrive in Genoa on about the 10th of October and in two or three days will proceed to Rome. We plan to be in Italy until June with only a comfortable blur of plans. What a joy it will be to see you.

Yours ever,

Robert Lowell

189. To Ezra Pound

[n.d. September 1950]

Dear Ezra:

We are sailing for Italy next Thursday and expect to be gone for ten months. I wonder if you could take the trouble to write us some addresses and even advice. The last year until about four months ago was one of wading in the muck and weeds and backwash of a depression—all very remote and mysterious now, but at the time the world and my friends were fairly gone to me.

America seems clenched, and somehow nervous and muscle-bound—a grand time to be off. I wish you both were going with us. There's a lot to say, and I've been hoping to get down to Washington for an afternoon's talk, but

don't see how it can be done. Let me know if I can do anything for you, and save some time for me next summer or autumn, when we are back.

Affectionately,
Cal

P.S. How did you like the guy I sent on to you from Kenyon—heavy but a worker?[. . .]

190. To John Crowe Ransom

POSTCARD of San Miniato by Jacopo del Casentino, Palazzo Degli Uffizi

2 Lungarno Amerigo Vespucci
Florence
[November 9, 1950]

Dear John:

A rather Ohio face on the other side—"virtuous and honorable." Could you mail my proofs to—

2 Lungarno Vespucci
Amerigo Vespucci
Florence

We're enveloped by sun, draft, woolen underwear and the ages.

Cal

191. To Elizabeth Bishop

December 6, [1950]

Dear Elizabeth:

Out the window there is a statue of the 18th century playwright Goldoni; he looks like Alexander Hamilton and had a hand blown off five years ago when the bridge was mined. The city is gray and sand-colored, Bostonish, compact, very unvegetable. You live on a little more than you would in America and about 4 times as well—a maid, wine and lovely furniture for what a moderately good apartment would cost in New York.

The language, the architecture, the art, the people, the politics, the places one might go, the history—you cannot turn your head without starting up occupations, abundance in every direction, so that it seems one's energy and interest could never tire. It's another world, and we are floating.

But nothing is cheap, except time, labor and roots—a cultivated starkness. Politics are very up-to-date, fierce, irreconcilable, a funny mixture of Dante's factions and what I'd imagine you'd find in South America. All the old buildings, and history, yet the facts, necessities, and impossibilities of life rawer and more nervous than with us; and the whole culture trying to forget that it is a provincial France.

Florence has a communist mayor, every so often you see scribblings on the walls such as *Death to the criminal MacArthur*. But the people are boisterous friendly and fearfully orderly, and except at political meetings, you'd never know anything was wrong; yet in a day you could have utter civil war or more likely a communist government.

You absolutely must leave Yaddo and your horrible archeologist lover and join us, if the world survives into another temporary calm. Nothing will happen here by itself, and life is so much more sensible and joyful that you cannot imagine ~~having~~ losing again what you have lost all your life.

Do write me what you think of the *Kavanaughs*. My proofs have come and I am hammering at the fuzzy places and trying to add a stanza or two—filled with Miltonic mythology, hard for a rhetorician to resist.

Miss Hanson's book finally came. The language and stanza made it hard to take seriously, it's as though she had no experience except such as would make little refrains of Tennyson and Fitzgerald often very clumsy; but that's original and I've come on awfully good bits. She really seems to be interested in the metrical craft of her masters. I don't know anything quite like it.

We had a cold, uninformed, hurried visit to Rome, saw a good deal of the Assumption ceremony, but somehow arrived always an hour late. We missed the Vatican and Capitoline Museums and except for a tremendous feeling of having now been there, probably had no new impressions. The Roman ruins are at last contemporary. I went to see Santayana daily—the talk ranged from autobiography, philosophical theories on world politics, Aristotle's theory of sensation, Spanish quotations, ideas on Boston, lots of very catty and very good gossip and above all Boston and religion. The meetings were delightful for me and perfect; except that he is deaf and couldn't hear a word—shouted or whispered—that I said.

The strangest people have turned up—a room-mate of Bowden Broadwater's; a theosophist and composer I used to know at Harvard (a very able man who used to drink lemon juice, wear yellow ties and play Bach to balance his bodily fluids). He told incredible Frank Parkerish stories about Roman-American society and then said that St. Augustine was the incarnation of Judas, but that he couldn't prove it. Pearl Kazin, Dunstan Thompson, Gertrude

Buckman and at the far end of a huge cocktail party at the Roman Academy someone—courage failed to look twice and make sure—who looked like Carley.

O well, this is the moment to end this rambling letter. Write us and try to come soon. We hope to stay three years now.

Love,
Cal

192. *To George Santayana*

Dec. 6 [1950]

Dear Santayana:

A slow enjoyable life—reading, looking, going out two or three times a week. The Americans and Englishmen who settle in Italy for long fall into two types 1) (Usually women and "Voice of America" officials) very earnest, dissatisfied and bewildered by the political situation with an idea that the moral thing is (must be) the realistic thing—heroines from Henry James with jobs. 2) The leisured—a little effeminate, cultured, good gossips, a bit pathetic and flotsamish—the best once had great talents or ambitions. There's also a third class who bring the graduate schools of Chicago with them. The most unlikely people are always the most likely to appear—the Theosophist you knew 15 years ago at Harvard, who once tried to put you on a diet of lemon juice.

Saw Berenson (not yet Sibille). He started off by asking me personal questions about my first wife across the dining room table. However, the meeting was entertaining and went fairly well. He seems to approve of little in the arts or the world since 1900, which is natural enough, except that what must have most startled people about him once, was (along with his energy) his up-to-dateness. His book on the Florentine painters strikes me as still useful and fresh—an impressionist work by a professional collector, hence its thoroughness and flatness.

I've been doing some hard work revising and adding a stanza or two to my long poem—unlike you, I take a long time to get wound up and only strike fire when faced by the verbal, rhetorical and compositional densities of the verses in front of me; only at that point do I find significance among the narrows and obstacles—out of triviality, solid craftsmanship, clarity psychological sincerity etc. One likes to have the hammer in one's hands.

Our meeting was what it should have been, except that it was hard for me

to relax into speech, otherwise I felt silently at home with you. You have opened windows on ~~the old~~ this world, and left me wondering.

I'll see you in January or February when we expect to return to Rome for a week or so.

Affectionately yours,
 Robert Lowell

P.S. Must mail those copies of *Seven* to you which I forgot to give to Cory.

193. To Charlotte Winslow Lowell

December 26, [1950]

Dear Mother:

Today a white fog, so that the rooms are strangely gray, and you can scarcely see the river—all this to remind one, along with the day, of many things—mostly the New England coast, and many of our summers.

People loiter and roister about our square, one has a feeling that Korea is in the next county and that the city registers every political vicissitude in the world; and as a matter of fact the people are divided every which way, and seem to be marking time—waiting for the giants, Russia and America, to act.

Nothing is outwardly alarming, and no one is unfriendly or truculent. Walking in the streets, or lying in bed at night listening to the sounds—if you are at all absent-minded or drowsy, it seems like America—a slightly older America, such [as] that of my childhood in the early Twenties. At five in the morning the stones are alive with hundreds of scraping cart sounds—like blue crabs in a tub.

We see one American family constantly and a few other people, among them the art critic Bernard Berenson, every so often. Many transients—since we arrived I've seen acquaintances of friends of acquaintances from Boston, Harvard, Iowa City, New York, Louisiana, Chicago, etc. Soon there will have been a sample from every group or place either of us has ever known.

Ones that might interest you: A rather agile, ladylike friend of Aunt Sarah's friend Dorothy Courtney. Her sister has married a man from the first Florentine family, the Corsinis. Unfortunately, he sounds rather like your idea of me—his only practical accomplishment is amateur fishing—and now he is off for America with his wife to find a job and everyone is worried or amused because all that any could imagine him doing is managing an estate but someone else would have to do the dirty work and no such estate exists. (I don't know

why I have rambled on so about this rather mythical man we've never met; but his prospects in America are everywhere a matter of speculation, and the world is happier because of the absurdity.)

The other person—Lady Berkeley, met briefly at Berenson's. Strange extraverted replica of Ralph Lowell, talking a thousand words a minute and with a partially adopted child who has become a movie star—very celebrated and only eight and dominates Lady Berkeley—who is really a good simple soul.

You absolutely must join us next year or whenever the world looks safely at peace for a few months. I'm sure you'd enjoy Florence, find acquaintances everywhere, live much better on less—and above [all] we miss you and want to have you with us.

Thank you so much for the money—so much! We are going to spend a little of it on a 3 day's New Year trip to Monte Carlo—no gambling, just sightseeing—with our friends.

Love,
Bobby

I really do love you, in spite of my inertia about writing.

194. To Elizabeth Hardwick

Domaine de Fortis
Luynes
France
[January 5?, 1951]

Dear Elizabeth:

Quiet has come with a jolt—after a long red wine evening with Frank I spent a night of indigestion and vomiting, then a foodless and non-alcoholic day of aches and sweats. Now I feel better than I have for weeks—stilled, and free of twenty conniptions.

We are going to Arles this morning, later to Avignon and maybe to Paris. The P's house is half grand villa and half empty farm-house, the country is something like Kenyon and something like Ipswich and not [at] all like Italy.

I have hundreds of things to say about France and Italy, the Parkers etc.— all new and never before thought of. Frank now has a group of some ten engravings, much his best work, they really should seem original and impressive to anyone. I think he has broken through.

Please send the *Mills* if you haven't.

Miss my pretty girl—get a good rest, and I'll promise not to run you ragged again. Wish you were here to see France.

Love,

Cal

Write.

This is my first letter since P.W.[;] give my best to the poor little thing and the sweet little thing who have made it possible. The pace really was getting terrific by the time we left Monte Carlo. I've written Bob, I think we can get Frank's engraving in the mail by the 20th. I'll be coming back by this time next week.

195. To Peter Taylor

<div align="right">

[2 Lungarno Amerigo Vespucci, Florence]
13 Gennaio, [1951]

</div>

Dear Peter:

I have a theory that I can learn Italian simply by tossing about bizarre words and phrases—a new language is a joy as soon as you can be incomprehensible to your friends. Already, helped by Latin I can say things to our maid that no one can understand; Elizabeth says things I cannot understand, and the maid says things anyone in Italy can understand except us.

We have a wonderful, almost historic apartment. Looking out on one side you can see the statue of an eighteenth century playwright with a hand chipped off, and out the other, the remains of a blown up bridge, and a new one going up twenty-four hours of the day (they take away each night what they have built during the day) and the Arno river where not so long ago a woman and child were drowned and you could see long sort of dug-out boats poling up and down, as men threw out weighted lines like Balaeric slingers or something so difficult that you must be trained to it from childhood . . . and never found the bodies.[. . .]

Elizabeth is working on her Iowa City murder-trial novel, and for the last two months I have been fussing with my *Kavanaughs*, until the whole thing has been half re-written from galleys. Bob says that the printer's bill is likely to be "stiff"; but the book will be out in March or April much improved, I hope. All this plus grammars and art books, has kept us pretty retired; but everyone on earth that you almost want to see turns up in Florence, and you do see them and are glad of it. For New Year's we drove to Monte Carlo with some acquaintances who had more money to spend than we had, so that there

were constant, mild obstinate ripples of conflict. At the end we saw the Park-ers—gallons of raw red wine, tons of raw red steak, Lesley sometimes silently and sometimes acidly fuming, no harmony among the wives . . . and the meet-ing, like many others with the Parkers, was and wasn't a success. Frank has done some awfully good engravings.

We hope to stay another year—two if possible. All in all, it is a complete shake-up, and life is more various and enjoyable than one could believe possi-ble. But the future, whatever it is, is so close, you can touch it and breathe it: and it is rather lonely, and I think we would give our hearts to have you both living near us.

Love,
 Cal

P.S. Want very much to see the *New Yorkers* and Eleanor's poems in *Poetry*. We both seem to be getting fairly good reviews in England.

196. To George Santayana

Feb. 1 [1951]

Dear Santayana:

This is the day after the day after a night when I drank a good deal too much and behaved stupidly and wandered about the streets alone and came home at four in the morning and woke everyone up and had an argument with my wife into daylight. So I am full of gray realizations and feel like the styl-ized young fool in the old plays who is usually called "Mooncalf"—only I am not a schoolboy and the situation is odd and senseless.

This is opening into a subject which your letters touch on and which I think I am forever taking up with you. What a heavy way of saying that *the* peculiarity I seem to have been born with is a character made up of stiffness and disorder, or lethargy and passion. These words are not necessarily the best. The two horses, judgment and emotion perhaps, take many names; but they go together but ill at best, and at bad times, one is lying down immobile, the other galloping.

When I came on the Catholic Church, it was a museum to contemplate, of course; but what I was after was a way of life. Truth had to be considered, but a truth short of absolute, ideal, universal imaginative truth and literal histori-cal factual truth. At least I thought I could take such truth on trust if (1) the Catholic life could be lived by me and (2) I could respect and feel at peace and

at home with that lived life. I ~~can~~ never got very deep. There was discipline, gentleness and understanding, but not at the heart, or rather, not at my heart, or if at the heart it never circulated from there into the fingers.

Your whole description of my way of writing in your first letter was more accurate than anything I myself could have said. When it came I was just winding up about two months work revising my galleys of the longish poem I showed you. Some 200 or more lines are changed, some of the obscurity and quaintness is gone, and the ending is much clearer and stronger—still it is essentially the same and its weakness is, as you say, fuzzy, simplified, unthought-out motivation. There's plenty of wonder, fierceness, and polish,—too much. I am sure I lack most of Racine's kind of knowledge. Still I am casting about for a firm plot, maybe one along the lines of Phèdre and Hypolyte—though at the moment this is too close to my "Dead Brother" etc. Another subject is my father—no plot there but he is sure and close in my memory. Another is Hitler—a series of scenes—there the importance, typicality and catastrophe of the subject are given. The poet has only to use his head and saturate himself. However, keep all of this to yourself—the themes are still gestating and will probably come out in other forms.

We have been reading about Russia and are never able to forget politics. It's not only that the war is already on and merrily burning and seems about to flame into Europe—but the war is mysteriously internal and almost spiritual—almost an Armageddon or war of the gods and the giants. It's black and white only in essence. Thus, one might say that the giants or Russians are just, international, crude and cruel only by inheritance, intense, dogmatic, puritanical and simple-minded only because their cause is a faith. But I think that their good qualities are accidents or rather shams and that at heart they are nihilists—wolves really after blood, after power, power for Russia, power for the Party, and in the end power for the will of the leader. I suppose evil is a desire for the annihilation of the spirit, and that consequently it can never be completely externalized because visibly it is only negation, and in that sense everything that *is* cannot help but be good and the very desire to destroy must not only feed on the good, but also be continually and temporarily incorporating and digesting the good in itself.

In retrospect the rulers [of] Germany appear to have been possessed—that is, after you have allowed for all possible qualifications, mixed motives, historical and material determinations[,] exceptions, confusions obscurities etc. that is even after you have made all possible allowance it seems clear as day that they were animated by the desire to destroy. This seems to be even more clearly true of the men who rule Russia. It seems to me that this kind of pos-

session has always been part of experience, we all know it somewhat in our lives, in fact it can only come into [the] world through human beings—what is extraordinary today is the fury and clarity with which it shows itself. Not only is it a roaring blaze in Russia, but it is flickering everywhere.

I've been too long-winded about this, and even the use of such words as *evil, possession* etc. is likely to make one monotonous and boring. I'm sure you cover the ground more intelligibly in *Dominions and Powers*. From your conversation and little bits I've seen I gather that like your Christ book, it will be about ideas rather than historical events. I can't think of a time when the world and all of us more needed your thoughts.

I haven't seen Berryman's book yet. Crane's Civil War novel is sort of like a series of Tate and Brady photographs done in the style of Claude Monet— fresh, compact, impressionistic—the best of all imagist poems, perhaps, and the opposite of Stickney in that he throws out all show of a grand style, symbolic experience etc. His (Crane's) subject is a slice of life, while his technique like Monet's is a tour-de-force. Looked at one way there is only the subject; but looked at another, there is only the art, the execution and the subject is only an excuse. It's a wonderful book, though.

I may be in Rome for a few days, sometime next week. It's been a solace to write this letter this long morning, and I hope it won't be a toil to read it.

Affectionately,
 Robert Lowell

197. To George Santayana

Feb. 25 [1951]

Dear Santayana:

I send along this old letter of a month ago, though it now sounds harsh and vacuous, in fact like what it is, a hangover letter.

We will be here until the end of April and I'll be back in Rome at least once before we set off for Venice. My book will be out *early* in April and you'll have a copy as soon as they arrive. There [is] nothing new except my revisions and a fine title-page with a picture of a swan by my friend Parker.

I get so used to looking on you as my exact opposite—though I'm sure this is a half-truth—that I imagine any experiences I may have will radically differ from yours. Right now it's being full of notions yet having no strength to harness myself to write. I have a feeling—it's a lazy comforting one—that soon enough a dark time will come when there will be nothing left but to

write. The present seems a time to loosen up, wander about, see people, see Europe, enjoy being married. Italy, however, is full of sensitive, worn people, whose intelligences and personalities exceed their accomplishments—they face one like death's-heads.

I don't suppose maturity comes of itself. But I think I've gone as far as good sense allows the young with a certain sort of fierceness, violence, madness, enthusiasm. This morning I was reading some religious verses by the old French poet Desportes. They are a bit tame and full of pious platitudes for my taste. But their calm polish is enjoyable. Also I find something more.

> O Dieu! Tousjours vivant, j'ay ferme confiance
> Qu'en l'extreme des jours, par ta toute-puissance,
> Ce corps couvert de terre, à ta voix se dressant,
> Prendra nouvelle vie et, par ta pure grace,
> J'auray l'heure de te voir de mes yeux face à face,
> avec les bien-heureux ton sainct nom benissant.

In the first four lines, there is nothing to look at except that the words are justly placed, and perhaps the phrase *en l'extreme*. But in the last two lines the *auray l'heure* along with *face à face* and *bien-heureux* and the diffident emphasis of the trailing participle give silent touches to the whole scaffolding of the prayer—it now seems a personal experience, worldly-wise in its way—it's [no] longer naïve or a cliché. This is not what I want to write, but I would like my writing to have such virtues.

Well, many thanks for your picture—a combination of Voltaire and Thomas Hardy; and trust me to grow up to you. Had a good evening with Corey.

Robert Lowell

(We'll be in Rome late in March)

198. *To Elizabeth Bishop*

c/o American Express
Florence
April 24, [1951]

Dear Elizabeth:

We are on the brink of what looks like almost unceasing movement—till mid September! In a little more than a week we are sailing for Constantinople

stopping in Athens—early in June Venice (2 or 3 weeks), Vienna (a week or two) Paris by the 7th of July to meet old friends (the Macauleys) a trip through Germany for about a month beginning July 20, 20th of August Paris again to meet my mother [for] a tour of the chateaux country with her, then by early October Naples I think for the winter and oblivion.

I am writing this on a hangover—wobbling toward a resolution to stay off hard liquor; one must I guess. What a lot of people (mostly Americans) we have seen going down the drain or crashing—for all sorts of almost unbelievably spectacular reasons. I suppose people come here for odd reasons, and then their lives are so visible and discussed. Well, we have had an enjoyable winter—day in and day out, incredibly so—but idle. Elizabeth's novel has bogged down and I've done nothing but a draft of [a] short poem; oh no, for the last week (to forget about packing) I've spent hours and hours reading *Gerusalemme liberata*, a real technician's poem—everything reminds you of something else[,] Dido in Virgil, The Knight's Tale, Spencer's Bower of Bliss, Milton's Eden, *Phèdre* and Dryden's translation of the *Aeneid*. It's wonderful, though, curiously anonymous in style, full of melancholy and tormented undertones, heroines like mine, but less muddied.

We've been to Pisa, Siena, seen 5 or 6 of the wonders of the world, and visited the Princess (*Botteghe Oscure*) Caetani—a mad, sympathetic aristocratic Mrs. Ames, not deaf and really nice and kind, at least to us—but mad, so that though a grand and tireless manager, she thinks of nothing except her magazine—like an only child, a simile I understand so well.

I seem to have made up with Randall and really one misses and one feels rusty without him. Every time I drop some vague critical bromide, I hear the jump of his voice—a figure of speech, I'm not having hallucinations.

I'm cheered in a way by your difficulties finishing your book, planning your travel etc. Not really, of course, but it makes our similar difficulties seem more dignified.

I think I've almost given up expecting you—you'll only come suddenly after swearing you'll never move, or are on your way to Alaska—but do try to come and join us either this summer or next winter or both. As an old veteran of Europe, I think I can promise you—or anyway as an old friend.

Had a note from Pound "Think at last Monsieur Lowell is larnin' to write—going into it hindquarters first like E.P."

Write us care of the American Express Florence and your letter will be forwarded. Doesn't anything on our long route allure you? Paris, anyway.

With love,
Cal

April 26 [1951]

Dear Bill:

Many thanks for your review. I like particularly the parts about rime and my meaning—the two are the same but most people don't understand that. One difference—I certainly see rime as joy and colour, not just an obstacle, or perhaps, when the obstacle is accepted there is colour, joy and a certain sad glory. My women are not New England, I think; they are a little like Dido and some of Racine's heroines, they sop up and gentle some the torture and gritting. Don't you also have much of the "unwonted" tragedy too; and isn't it a kindness, with life as it is and the world as it is, to feel it?

Some of the contemporary Italian poets have a juicy, green, untired rush to them that makes one wonder, at times, if France's day as *the* European country isn't over. You're rather like that. Reading over your volume of later poems, I've been wondering if my characters and plots aren't a bit trifling and cumbersome—a bit in the way of the eye, and what one lives. But I'd feel as unhappy out of rime and meter as you would in them.[...]

We hope to be somewhere near Naples next winter, and may even stay another after that—we are still new enough to it for that. Not being able to know how long you can stay, makes you want to all the more.

My best to all of you—I hope somehow we will be spending another evening together before long.

Cal

200. *To Elizabeth Hardwick*

Cadogan Court Hotel
34/9 Queen's Gate Gardens
Kensington, SW 7, London
[late July or early August 1951]

Dear Elizabeth:

Please write me right away, and forgive me for all the fret and harrying of the last 3 days—I'm afraid our nerves were all in tassels. But it's all a trifle. If you want me back in a hurry wire and I'll be with you in a few hours. I've already cooled off and feel ridiculous and guilty and lonely and want my Uncle.

Particularly here, for London is like Marlboro St. or Philadelphia after

Paris—slow, dark, wide, respectable, Victorian etc.—and: They all (a miracle in Europe) speak American.

No impressions yet except England is much more like New England—factories in the country, waste vegetation, piles of ugly black industrial waste, ugly machine-made peaked houses, lovely Connecticut New York country, thousands [of] houses projects—even quonsets—and they all speak English.

When I get back I'll tell you about telephoning, the only really Kafkan experience I've ever had—an interminable utterly reasonable and competent process with only a verbal relation to its end. They never find your number, but after hours you learn the system, never feel that either you or they are going about it the wrong way, or that the number doesn't exist—you know that you started investigations that will last for months. Information is called Inquiries and so it is. Travelling is only a degree less hard; mostly because each turn does bring you physically nearer to your end.

I haven't done anything yet except read my clear as day French guide to Holland.

I have hopes this everlasting leaking pen is done—and it is!

Honey, I love you more than all the world and am worried to death and please write. All my love,

Cal

201. To Elizabeth Hardwick

[late July or early August 1951]

O Dear!

Your letters are so much more to the point than mine! We have had [a] hard, witless time of it! And we must settle and take care of ourselves. The unmarried life is too much for me—a whirl of impressions around one's bruised pulp!

Try not to get all nerve-wrung and hysterical. I do think you ought to go and have a check-up. What we both need is regularity which I guess we'll get with mother. Nothing matters so much as our own lives—we need each other so desperately—at least I need you, and I am really going to be more considerate from now on and take care of you and myself in doing so.

After not seeing anyone suddenly a flood—Kermit (really a good serious fellow with the jitters) Derek for what I thought would be a quiet drink and turned out to be a cocktail party for every minor gallery director and writer of

monographs in London—he's much too Beau Monde for us—a fascinating assemblage of English fossils. Then the opposite, the W. S. Graham Bohemian world—less interesting and more congenial, but not so very. I have a lot to tell you.

I can't wait to be back to my old Uncle.

Love,
Cal

P.S. I've learned to wash my socks and send out laundry—and made marvelous strides toward becoming a travel bore.

Come to Amsterdam if you're lonely, it might be calm after Paris.

202. *To Elizabeth Hardwick*

Hotel Bristol
Pau, Basses-Pyrenees
France
[September 18?, 1951]

Dear Elizabeth:

Here's the opening of a letter, I started before receiving yours about going to Florence. For about an hour now I have been lying under a pale blue double-spread. I am aware of the crumbs of my breakfast and can feel the vigorous gray sky of Pau blowing moistly through a large window. The world of this town, the world outside, is shrewd and careless: It is full of tree-sounds and traffic-sounds, and wears the weather like an "impermeable." I don't. I am knotted in my nerves and keep asking myself where the Hell we are going. Where is there any help for either of us to give, or to take? . . .

Dear Uncle, I am at the end of my road. I want to be located as soon as possible, and preferably in Holland. I have good reasons for this choice: The Anglo-Saxon's encounter with the Latin cultures has been worn to exhaustion. Holland draws me because of the novelty, the freedom to pick and choose and the privacy which is so necessary for reactions that are at all personal or profound. The paintings, Motley, and my own Protestant New England background give me a host of other suggestions. I *feel* I can make something out of living in Holland—one can never know, but the hunch seems crucially worth following.

I don't know whether what I have written sounds sensible or not; but when

it comes to giving you *instructions*, I am in complete confusion. I suggest you look at Amsterdam patiently (you might visit The Hague which everyone considers charming, and which Fromentin, alas, a hundred years ago, recommends as ideal for persons in our emotional state) then send for our things; after that we will join either here, there or in Paris.

To sum up: either our possessions should be on their way to Holland, or we should be looking for a place in France together.

I miss you, I need you, I need sympathetic, level-headed encouragement. I want to give it. We've got to stop this state of "sauve qui peut."

Love,
 Cal

P.S. I read *The Way of All Flesh* in jail—with venomous consent. Please don't go to Florence until we have found where our things are going. I'm ready to accept sight-unseen anything that *satisfies you* in Amsterdam. I didn't mean the underlined words to be mocking; I know they are, but please, old charmer, try your best.

203. *To Charlotte Winslow Lowell*

17 Nicolaas Witsenkade
Amsterdam
[October 1?, 1951]

Dear Mother:
 We've just spent a night in our new quarters, and find them tremendous after our various hotels—already we've had two home-cooked meals—home selected too with blue-berries, quarts of milk, grapes[,] canned soup and other difficult recipes such as scrambled eggs. I have a nook in a bay-window over a canal where I read Motley's history of the *Rise of the Dutch Republic*—Boston, Harper's Bros. 1855. But I am a power-house of help about the apartment.
 We are still waiting for our clothes from Florence and really aren't equipped to come to Paris. I suggest that you stay a few days at the France and then come on here. We'll find you a splendid hotel with a bath or a view. You might stay here until about your sailing time, then go either directly to Havre or back to Paris and then on to Havre. I could go with you to Paris or not, depending on how long you intend to stay there.
 Amsterdam is on the whole a much handsomer (less beautiful) city than

Florence. Life is more like it is in America and one feels more in control. We feel that we have been very lucky to get an apartment that has a good kitchen, is clean and not remote.

Cold days are cold, sunny days are magical. When you come there are quite a few little excursions we can make and things to see.

Love,
Bobby

P.S. We are well established with the American Express, American Information Service, and the British Consul. Tonight we are going to *Tosca* (in Dutch). Let me know what I can do to assist your plans. Our stay in Pau was delightful.

204. *To Randall Jarrell*

[October 6, 1951]

Dear Randall:

Breit wrote asking me to review your book for the *Times* saying that he had long ago felt that you deserved a push or something of the sort. Then he wrote through his secretary that I should keep to 500 words. I've gone to about double that length, and, though no critic, think I've done a fairly good job and hope you'll be pleased; but I don't know how much will be printed.

We've covered a lot of [ground] since I last wrote you—from Florence to Rome, to Turkey (mostly Constantinople but also Greek ruins in Asia) then Greece, then France, then London, now here. I feel and talk like a guide-book—full of gaps, irrelevance and amnesia. But it's overwhelmingly astonishing—so much that is harmonious, unbelievably wonderful, odd, unforeseen, varied—all one's European history to learn over, at least in [the] sense that all one's old facts and theories are hung onto new images.

It's like going to school again—I fill up on everything indiscriminately, and hope it will settle—a lot of French and Italian poetry, even some German and Latin, thousands of paintings, a lot of history, plays, opera, ballet—one feels so ignorant, so conscious that one won't have forever, that it's hard to stop.

So now we are stopped—after a trying and tumultuous visit from my mother. Amsterdam is outwardly a sort [of] eighteenth-century Boston—all canals and lovely, small, baroquish brick houses, worldly, Protestant, English-speaking. The people sound and look German—last night we watched a fan-

tastically homely and magnificently-singing Dutch chorale society do Haydn's *Seasons*.

I'm in the middle of Motley's *Rise of the Dutch Republic*, a magnificent, rather obtusely and fiercely Macaulayish anti-Catholic affair. The Spanish occupation, the wars of religion, taxation and trade seem much more real to me than they would have a little while ago, but I think I have been slow in catching on to what is happening now. Catholic apologetics are more a splendid lawyer's harangue than the story of what happens.

It's been tough getting down to writing—so many much more engaging distractions, and most of all I think a wavering between a desire not to repeat, and the void and formlessness of what I haven't tried and really imagine till I've done it. I have six or seven medium length more or less historical things in mind—one on King Abdullah of Trans-Jordan whom I saw in Santa Sophia last Spring. Beginnings are a hell of a mess.

I've meant to congratulate you on your award and Princeton. Robie says you've written a novel that you read aloud to yourself between tennis sets and that Peter admires and thinks (as a veteran novelist) you had no right to write. I think your Stevens is about the best of your critical essays. Why don't you write on Tate, Crane and a few others and then publish a book on modern American poetry. It would be much the best anyone has done; then you could suit yourself and go back into the past.

Europe is much more lovable than America, but I feel woefully remote and out of touch [with] my friends and everyone I want to talk to. So please write a letter, full of news about yourself and what you are thinking.

Love to you and Mackie,

Cal

P.S. Eland is the name of a street here with a tremendous modern police station on it, and a man who issues permits to stay, and won't believe that there is an English word *poet* that designates a legitimate form of writing. I say poet, not a journalist, dichter, words in meter, like Vondel—but he looks at me like a doctor.

I've seen all 3 Uccello panels—the one in Florence is almost black, the one in London perfect and the one in Paris worst of all—somewhere between blackness and garishness. Uccello seems to go with Masaccio, Botticelli, Piero, Mantegna, and Bellini (Michael Angelo & Leonardo) the freshest and most revolutionary period in all painting.

205. To Peter Taylor

Oct. 6 [1951]

Dear Peter:

I've been meaning to answer your long letter all summer but as Robie and Anne can tell you we have been perpetually moving, with plans to live in at least a dozen diverse European cities—each place, it turned out when we paused to discuss and argue, had unanswerable drawbacks. It's all been very clownish, messy and childish—to climax it all my mother arrived, a far more formidable character than your father. We all went to a Basque beach-resort and hit it off worse than can be imagined—long meals comparing food and hotels, or silent or arguing about whether we could afford a cup of filtered coffee—a frightful drink that burns your fingers and freezes for half an hour while it *filters* into your cup.

We finally broke away and took an apartment here. Mother arrives on Monday and I write this letter while waiting for the second wave. Amsterdam now that we are here and settled turns out to have unanswerable drawbacks— Elizabeth finds it dull and depressing, completely! So now I feel like the grasshopper writing to the cricket. (I've just finished a long letter to Randall telling about the good things and of course leaving all this out) The funny thing is that this has been the most exciting and instructive year I've ever spent, and yet a mess of cross-purposes personally.

Well, I'm telling you the blue side—because there are moments when I can't see the future at all and no one besides you that I would like to admit it to.[…]

Europe for the first time is literally too good to be true.[…]

I'm only determined to get some of it written down and lodged before we come back. Then I suppose I will teach, have five daughters, a complete set of china and join the Republican party.

Love to you both,
 Cal

206. To Elizabeth Bishop

November 6, 1951

Dear Elizabeth:

It's so long since I've written you that I don't even have your address, so I'll send this to Houghton and Mifflin, hoping that they will hand it to you at

the moment when you are giving them your finished manuscript. At this point you must be saying "why Holland?" Everyone has. I suppose it's the carless automobileless man, who has no command of foreign languages or scoutsmanship's substitute for burying himself in Ischia or Sardinia. It is quiet and still—as far as the outer world goes, I guess it has been still since the seventeenth century, when it was at the full tide, a baroque, worldly, presbyterian, canal-and-brick, glorious Boston. I've been reading Motley and Fromentin, and rather luxuriate in it; but it is prosy and empty, and Elizabeth doesn't like it at all. However, we have no money to unsettle again until May. By the way the returns from my book have been rather a shock: the royalties just about cancel off the cost for revisions.

The summer was a tremendous whirl—like going through college and graduate school in one year on pills that prevent your sleeping at night. We went everywhere I wrote you we would, except Venice and Vienna. I can't resist putting down the names: Naples, Bari, Lecce, Brindisi, Athens, Istanbul, Bursa, Smyrna, Athens, Delphi, Corinth, Sounion, Naples, Genoa, Paris, Versailles, Chartres, Mont Saint Michel, the Loire country, Fontainbleu, the Basque country, Lourdes, Pau, Brussels, Antwerp, The Hague, Haarlem, Amsterdam . . . and London, and Eton. Also I've read gobs of Italian, German, French and Latin poetry, Greek, French and Turkish history, and art books, till my head rocks, as though it held the lantern-slides of the world. I'm convinced none of us can possibly survive on into our forties, except as hermits, unless we become bores; and that takes some doing, you can't be a happy bore without talking, without having a line that will bore anyone of any age and in any circumstances, one that is stereotyped, demands no spontaneous thought, and yet is universal enough to find openings everywhere, and blanket conversation. Since this summer I'm well on the road.

We are just finished with Mother's visit. She is a very competent, stubborn, uncurious, unBohemian woman with a genius for squeezing luxury out of rocks. That is, she has a long memory for pre-war and pre-first-world war service; and thinks nothing of calling the American ambassador if there's no toilet-paper on the train etc. Well, under the best conditions, of course, I can't begin to make sense out of her or to her. Each year since I was eighteen, it's gotten worse. I don't suppose you can imagine three months with the three of us, all behaving very badly, then being very self-sacrificing, and fuming inside like the burning stuffings of an overstuffed Dutch chair. Now it's over; we have emerged triumphantly—so we thought, but there's a relapse and weakness, such as one gets from sulphur drugs.

At first I thought *Concordance* was too snug; but I see it's right and im-

pregnable, as my more flashy, high-sounding titles are not. I still wish you'd put your short stories in, first because I'd like to see them all together, but secondly because I think your poems and stories explain and light each other up, and that anyone will or should be dazzled by the combination.

Elizabeth has just finished a story that I think is much her best and sent it off to *PR*. I'm deep in the thin first drafts of a long monologue about a sort of 16th century Mrs. Dawson. Write me some American gossip, and heavens' sake hurry over here.

Love,
Cal

How's your poetry residence going? I've applied for Salzburg next summer.

207. To Randall Jarrell

February 24 [1952]

Dear Randall:

My old indulgence for putting off letters has grown so monstrously this winter that I now owe about thirty—I am only counting those that *must* be answered, those that *should* are as many again. For this purpose I borrowed the house-boat of a Dutch friend for three days. It is far from communication, is filled with oiled skiing boots, and wherever you turn there are books in Dutch, French, English and German. (Every Dutch intellectual is about equally fluent in all four languages.) This is the afternoon of the third day and this is the first letter.

From your letter and also from a note (unanswered) from Flint, "Dear Jarrell, he annihilates us all, and by our stripes is he healed!" I was expecting ugly treatment in your review, and had worked up an imaginary rebuttal. My defense was the same as your attack, i.e. that I had poured every variety of feeling and technique into it I knew of. The poem is meant to be grandiose, melodramatic, carried on by mixture of drama and shifting tones, rather like *Maud*. I agree with most of what you say, except the heroine is very real to *me*, and that in a freakish way the poem has more in it than any of my others. Anyhow I am delighted with your review and have read it many times out of vanity. Perhaps, I agree with it all, but since I've still finished nothing new, I go on overrating the Kavanaughs.

Peter or Robie had written us about your divorce, and I was surprised enough to hardly believe it. I can understand perhaps what brought it about,

but you and Mackie seemed to discount your differing enthusiasms and indifferences. You mustn't mind my saying that we all envied you and Mackie because your difficulties seemed to have nothing in common with the difficulties of other marriages, none of the open deliberate unkindnesses, scenes etc. Well, one mustn't say anything about the wisdom of divorces or proposals, except that your friends feel the same toward you and know they know less than you do about it. A cold-comfort compliment: Your [divorce] seems to have [been] the most calmly and humanely conducted I know of.

What I really want to say should have been said long ago. You must be feeling relieved in some ways and very much at loose ends in others—a turtle that has just walked out of its shell. Elizabeth and I have long been wanting to ask you to come and live with us, only we didn't know where we'd be. It's now pretty certain to be Florence or Rome. We've written the Taylors. They say they are coming. But with all Peter's indecisions I won't believe it till they appear. In any case we intend to go to Italy again. Couldn't you get a grant or borrow a little money (it would cost very little with us) and join us in September? There are almost innumerable attractions such as wonderful cheap opera, paintings, wine, sunlight, but the best is getting into an ancient green world utterly unlike America.

At the moment, I am feeling nervous. Small Dutch boys are making splashes outside my portholes, and seem to be tampering with moorings of the houseboat. I feel I lack both the language and presence to stop them. This has been a sedentary winter. We sit a few feet away from each other in a room that looks as though it were furnished with Mackie's stitched red stuffed beavers. We read continuously, except when interrupted; then we sigh querulously, "But I never have any time to read." In this way I have gone [through] twenty volumes of the Nuremberg trials, a book by a psychiatrist on the prisoners, Hannah Arendt, Macaulay's *History*, Motley's *Dutch Republic*, a lot of Clarendon, a lot of North's Plutarch, and a thousand other things—all of which you could no doubt have finished on a bus trip to North Carolina, and been at a loss for more before you were half there. However I feel waterlogged with miscellaneous knowledge. All this is too much to comment on. The Arendt is written with a fairness, exhaustiveness, and earnestness—even its boa-constrictor style helps—that makes other books on her themes seem light and heartless (I followed up her bibliography and tried Brogan, Dallin etc. and was disappointed.) As for Macaulay and Motley, I'm struck by their massive assurance; they are willing to see the past on their own terms, and are moral and easy-going in a way that seems a lost art. I've become very keen on the opera. In London we saw the *Rosenkavalier*, *Fidelio*, and *Wozzeck*. Well di-

rected and rather spottily sung. You ought to look up Büchner's libretto for *Wozzeck* and Spender's translation of his *Danton's Death*. It's as though Mann had suddenly emerged out of Beddoes, or rather Webster.

Holland is a flat country with a flat grey climate and features that too often remind one of Mount Vernon and Columbus. All the intellectuals read and speak English, French and German, and it is unheard of to review any of these languages in translation. The country is small, overcrowded and slowly getting poorer; the people, though more rooted than we are, are also more dependent. Their literature I think, is a sober review of other literatures. Nowhere is the gay commercial bourgeois seventeenth century so present; nowhere do you meet so many people who put you at your ease. But this winter has been enough.

This is almost enough writing: the boys are gone, and I must start thinking of the most simplified possibilities for supper. I hope you are not living on your own cooking, but if you are, I have one or two timeless recipes: bread-and-nothing sandwiches, uncooked oatmeal allowed to expand in a bowl of milk. Every bachelor is his own Timon. To think that before this three-days exile, I thought Elizabeth too scholarly and chic to attend to her meals!

I've been saving this till the end: I like parts one and three of the last *Paterson*. Maybe, it's being away from home, but he seems able to get everything material in as no one else. I wrote something of the sort to him in a letter, and saw it turn up in your review for derision. Well, we'll wrangle it out when I see you.

I go to Salzburg this summer, and am memorizing the idiomatic German in your poems in preparation.

Affectionately,
 Cal

Really try hard to come, hardly a day goes by when I do not wish you were here to talk to.

I see we are no longer on the top of that great inverted pyramid of Viereck's favorites.

208. *To William Carlos Williams*

[n.d. February or March 1952]
Dear Bill:
 After your Lawrence poem, and the many unkind things said in your autobiography about people who don't answer your letters; I feel I should offer

you some sort of defense for the entire species, i.e. all those who out of lassi-tude, the inertia of original sin or whatever, put off from day to day answer-ing *anyone*. One muses over what might be said while going to sleep one night, then wakes feeling the letter is for all practical purposes written, and so delay follows delay, and yet no harm or indifference is meant or even felt. What better way of keeping your friends in mind than always being on the point of writing. But enough of this.

I enjoyed the autobiography a lot. Pound twists through your whole book, your whole life, I guess. The picture is wonderfully eccentric and will seem newly painted forever. One gets the inhumanness, the generosity, the whirl of idées fixes, the live wire. In the end he is sympathetic, real, noble, absurd, as he is; he ought to feel disgruntled and flattered. H. D. is Flossie's version of her: "she was so dirty." You'd better hope there'll be no answers from *her*. Also liked the Paris parts, now that I've been there and am still travel-crazy. It's somewhat the same now, only it's becoming a city of Fulbright fellows, or rather of Fulbrights who have stretched their money for a second or third year, and are living in stoical penury, while their wives work at secretarial jobs. When they come home there'll be a new race in America.

I think I get what you mean about Eliot for the first time. You say, I think, that at the time *The Waste Land* appeared a whole flood of "American" poetry, that is poetry more in the present and more congenial to you, was about to prevail. Then it was driven underground, into small privately printed edi-tions, non-paying, ephemeral little magazines, etc. There's a chance you are right, and of course you are right in a way. But it was fairly heroic of Eliot, whose personality and opinions are after all very special, not in tune with the time, not at all what anyone in America or England really wanted—to have set out with all those disadvantages, and then by one's artistry and sincerity to dominate . . . No, that's something! For the counts that you would think are against him, and they are against him, are more amazing than what is superfi-cially fashionable about his work. I think the field was open, and that the other poets had the more direct road. You shouldn't complain. Then for your method. I don't think it's good or bad. Your way of writing doesn't help with-out your eye, experience, and sense of language. Your followers are mostly dull because none of them combine these qualities. Still I wish rather in vain that I could absorb something of your way of writing into mine.

I'm interested in what you say about Góngora. I've been looking at him lately—a real original, not like Donne or the Marino-Crashaw baroque con-ceited poet. I get from him something of the rhetoric of Milton along with the honest controlled obscurity of Mallarmé. This, together with what you say

about his hard tongue and his card-playing. Maybe he's the place where our ideas join.

We've been in Amsterdam since October . . . a dull, gray, mid-western city, very beautiful in the old seventeenth century center (where we're not) and fascinating historically for a New Englander. We've made some good Dutch friends and have been quite out of the rush of café and tourist America. I'm going to teach in Salzburg this summer, then a winter in Italy or Spain, then home.

I don't know what happened with the Princess Caetani and your check. She's a healthy, rushing, rather mad woman, very mad about getting contributions for her magazine. I can't say what caused her to forget you, bustle, [I] guess. I'm sure she meant no harm.

I thought Jarrell was hay-wire on *Paterson*, and to the point on you and Eliot and Europe. You see my prejudices are as incurable as yours, but it mustn't make any difference with us.

Affectionately,

Cal

209. *To George Santayana*

March 10, [1952]

Dear Santayana:

The trouble with writing a philosopher and master letter-writer is that one has to come up to the occasion—one likes to drop from the quotidian and gossipy to the banal instead of touching on the eternal; at least, that's how most letters get written. However, you're long in arrears to me, and only a certain awe makes me stand on formality.

We have been worried about you and have asked everyone coming from Rome for news, and no one knows anything for certain, but all have insubstantial intuitions; they say they think you are well and invisible. Please write.[. . .]

I've written drafts of two longish poems, but the results are mannered and too full of travel-impressions. I don't know how it is, or rather I don't know whether you've had the same experience; but I think I have written enough in one style for its virtues and limits to stand out baldly. I noticed this before I sent my manuscript away, and I see the reviewers notice it too: their praise and their blame runs into ruts. It's time to start again when your critics repeat

themselves; it's high time to let my form swim again in the inexhaustible. From all this you will see that I am going to teach American poetry at Salzburg this summer, and have been re-reading Emerson and Whitman. I think stretches of inertia and idleness are helpful, even necessary to a writer; but idleness is what it is, that is, nothing.

I've been reading Russell's *History of Western Philosophy* lately. It's delightful just as a series of opinions, character sketches etc. The empiricist, mathematician, logician and old-fashioned liberal moralist—a sympathetic person for me; but one who seems to reduce philosophy to a few scattered accurately-stated and verifiable scientific laws, not necessarily very coherent or momentous in themselves. As far as I can judge the old fixed wooden Aristotelian perennial philosophy that I painfully studied as a Catholic still stands. Russell and say Maritain use such different criteria, that I suppose they are irreconcilable. The writer, perhaps, shrinks from both: from the set mould of the Catholic and from the system-breaking of such a man as Russell, who breaks all the great philosophers like clay pots. The abilities and inspiration that make the imaginative writer timeless, work so poorly for the thinker! I think you largely agree with Russell, that is accept as true much [of] what he does, then build your system with skepticism, or even some one else's system, as in your Christ book. I have been pondering his comparison of you and William James, and it seems to me that Russell himself is a sort of irregular, modern, improper (in a good, engaging sense) Macaulay-Whig. If Macaulay were living now and had Russell's bent and knowledge of philosophy, he would no doubt think much the same. I mean this as a compliment. In your new book (many thanks for sending it, and for the inscription) and in all your books for that matter, it is a mixture of Whig empiricism and Catholicism that keeps you from being either. I mean this as a compliment too, to have been torn between the two noblest and most solid western intellectual and moral traditions is something.

We leave here in May. I may go to a big anti-totalitarian conference in Paris about the 15th. It will probably be pompous and exciting. Every European writer I have ever heard of, has been invited, and most of the American. Then to Vienna, then to Salzburg, then to Venice and Rome in September.

Take care of yourself, and drop us a word.

Yours affectionately,

Robert Lowell

210. To Elizabeth Bishop

<div align="right">April 24, [1952]</div>

Dear Elizabeth:

Our apartment is right now full of half-filled half open suit-cases, leaves are beginning to hide the canal, the sun is shining, the radio is playing a sort of Indian summer Mozart minuet, and each [of] us knows that if he can only stall long enough the other will do the packing. Our long green coffin-like trunk that we counted on to hold almost everything is brimful of books.

I've gone music-mad, have just heard Bach's two Passions each twice, and now we are going to Brussels to hear five Mozart operas in six nights. I know all about the sonata form (a misnomer according to Tovey) canons, and modulations, but have difficulty distinguishing them when heard, and have so far failed to convince the cynical and skeptical Eliz. H. Lowell that I am not tone-deaf. I always reply by asking her, "just what is a quaver?" or, "When is Hayden going to modulate back into C minor?" Her replies are more airy than clear.

We have quite a group of Dutch friends. They are all very loving, urbane and hard-headed about each other. The way one would like to picture, alas, the *PR* people. One in particular likes to talk intellectual shop even more than I do. We spend days that go from 11 in the morning till one the next morning reading Dutch poetry. He is able to quote Goethe's maxims, Stendhal, La Bruyère, Auden, Valéry, Valery-Larbaud and Randall by the hour. He can now do the same with you. He's rather like Mann's Leverkühn, dry, enthusiastic, exact, and with a terrifying knowledge of German philosophy. The other day Bill Burford was here. He was full of himself because he is writing a long autobiographical poem, and as you know his conversation is a pure centerless flux. The three of us spent a long night. Burford managed to drink an entire quart of Dutch gin, so one had the contrast of unimaginable coherence and unimaginable incoherence. The next day my Dutch friend said, "you always felt he was about to make a point."

Elizabeth is rather down on our abode and I think your Brazil is the one trip taken by some one else that she can bare to contemplate without envy. However, it sounds delightful. You always make me feel that I have a rather obvious breezy, impersonal liking for the great and obvious—in contrast with your adult personal feeling for the odd and genuine; but I'm not sure that Holland doesn't beat Brazil—it's not picturesque, healthy, spectacularly on the up or down, just like or just unlike home, had a post-war literary revival, not

very much anything except flat, canal-checkered and Dutch. It's probably odd and genuine; but then what isn't? Well, it *was* odd and genuine to have come here.

Elizabeth has just said the only advantage of marriage is that you can be as gross, slovenly, mean and brutally verbose as you want. This was re my asking her if she had ever told Mary McCarthy off. Can you imagine anyone telling off either Mary or Randall? At Harvard I once heard Mary say to Randall, "I think your poetry is much more obscure than Cal's." This was an obscure but hurting blow at both of us. Somehow I got caught between them. Randall laid down the law, but it wasn't a pleasure for anyone. How did you like your fresh girlish appearance in R.'s polemic on the critics? I think this was one subject in which he might well have called names.

Wonderful comic strip scene: man large and smiling stretched out on a sofa with a glass of milk; nervous, puzzle-faced wife standing by a chair piled with books. Husband: "I'd get a step-ladder if you are going to fix that roller-spring. It's dangerous to stand on books, you might fall and hurt yourself. Remember how George Fink warned his wife about dragging that trunk upstairs." We're very light-hearted about leaving.

Write us care of the American Express in Vienna. We'll be there and at Salzburg most of the summer. My usual refrain: When are you sailing so I can meet you at the dock with champagne.

Love,
Cal

211. *To Flannery O'Connor*

[late May or early June 1952]

Dear Flannery:

A copy of *New World Writing* arrived here yesterday (I see from this opening that I've been expatriated now for so long that I'm getting like Pound—imagining myself as an institution to which missives arrive). Anyway you're as good as ever, only really and enviably professional. Ford used to say that you could tell if a writer was any good from the first sentence—I found this advice useful when manuscript-reading for Sheed and Ward, though it led to fatal misunderstandings in my interviews with students at Iowa . . . Your first two sentences show you know your craft, and the end of the first and the word "downpour" in the second do even more. When I was through reading I

could have hugged the gorilla. The whole incident is rather epically dismal—
I'm reminded of Jean Stafford's little girl who puts on her bathing suit to take
a bath and makes a list of all the people she hates, the list was pretty universal.
I'm delighted to see that your novel is about to be published; I think it will be
something absolute of its kind and want to hail it and promise that we will
keep a copy under our pillows so that we can always say "Isn't it wonderful
that life is so awful, and that man's misery is without grandeur."

We've been drifting and getting stuck all over Europe from Bath to Smyrna.
It [is] all almost infinitely intoxicating and scatter-brained, the sort of thing one
ought to have done after two years of college. Elizabeth has become a great
reader of out of the way French novels, and I have been dabbling at studying
just about everything: paintings, music, history and poems in many languages.
I've even spent several strenuous days with a friend on the Dutch classics, and
whole evenings have been wasted on such blind-alley topics as modern archi-
tecture. After a while you realize that your ignorance is a treasure.

We are going to Vienna in a few days and I'm going to spend the summer
teaching at the American school at Salzburg, where we expect to join up with
Robie and Anne. We were all together last summer in France and experienced
complications because Robie and I are tireless sightseers, while Elizabeth and
Anne aren't—especially Elizabeth who doesn't even believe she should be
and expects the wonders of the world to file past her here on a news film, a
short one at that with lots of politics.*

Write us care of the American Express in Vienna if you have time. I've
been very anxious to hear about you for a long time.

Elizabeth sends her love.

Affectionately,

Cal

*Robie beats me though, and knows obscure parts of Paris history as one (par-
ticularly Robie) might know a murder. Your next book, by the way, ought to
be your version of Lizzie Burden or one of the Scotch trials. Forgive this let-
ter for being so light-headed, it was an apology and eulogy.

212. To Peter Taylor

[Vienna or Salzburg, Austria, n.d. June? 1952]

Dear Peter:

I feel about the way you do. When there's someone to talk to, I talk. When there isn't I plot or read a book. By now we've met a dozen or so people we're enthusiastic about (it's hard to believe) and it breaks my heart that you and Elizabeth Bishop and Powers and Robie aren't with us. I mean I'm wild about them the way I am about my American friends—each one is impossible to imagine coming from any country or even region except his or her own—as hard as imagining you coming from New England.

Allen (don't on your honor repeat this) came to Paris loaded down with rosaries, letters to Catholic notables from Maritain, Maritain's translation of the "Confederate Dead," orders for Christopher medals done by modern French medieval craftsmen, arguments against Descartes, leather-bound pictures of Caroline. After lunch he said, "I've never seen the inside of St. Germain des Pres (14th century church)[."] We go in. Allen looks at nothing; but kneels and crosses himself before an altar where the Host isn't. Next day he met Mrs. Spender and the whole Catholic facade vanished. I must say Caroline has it coming—she's utterly wonderful, of course; but it's against nature—I mean really, not just Allen's as a wolf, but everything that is honest and intelligent and gay and intuitive in him. He's really gloriously effervescent and unacademic. Now we're all to meet with the Spenders in Venice for another conference in September. I'm not anti-Church by the way, but it's intolerable that a man of Allen's vitality should go the Tartuffian dumbshow of a fraudulent conversion—the real Catholic is himself, his faith is part of him, just like anyone else's.

Reading your letter, I felt I [had] been living it all; we were having the same emotions at identical moments—each in his own character. Goodbye old friend; can't you all get away from it all for a month or two?

Love from us both to you both.

Cal

Please, for God's sake, don't repeat the above.

213. *To Robert Frost*

Salzburg Seminar
Schloss Leopoldskron
Salzburg, Austria
July 12 [1952]

Dear Robert:

I've been meaning to write you for a coon's age, and thank you for your Christmas cards and their notes. There's a joy in putting off letters you really want to write. But we're old enough friends to be near each other in silence.

When I was teaching a tossed together course called "the dramatic monologue" two years ago at Kenyon—Tennyson, Browning, Eliot, Robinson, you, etc.—I found that much to their surprise my best students were thinking much harder on you than on anyone else. There was no formula that the universities supplied for explaining how, say your poem about the Canuck and the ax-handle, held together—they had to think it out themselves. I have also been struck by how much your supposedly old-fashioned and provincial poetry is really in the great current—if one can call it that—of the best and most daring European work of the past fifty years—above all their plays. Well enough adulation.

We're having the time of our lives wandering and ~~looking~~ gaping—one tends to be ignorant and hard about such a hell of a lot. I think we'll be back in August or September, a year from now—so keep an empty chair in your rooms for me. Yes, many thanks for the many critical times, such as your trip with Merrill to Baldpate, the times when you were a solace. All's well now, only like you, I feel too young for the young.

Affectionately,
Robert

214. *To Ezra Pound*

July 12 [1952]

Dear Ezra:

Some sort of follow-up on my crazy joint post-card with Laughlin—if you ever got it. I've just been reading the *Cantos* over to freshen up for a little teaching I'm doing here this summer—also Hugh Kenner, who seems to have read no one except you and Eliot and Dr. Leavis (his style is [a] barbarous earnest parody of you and Leavis) and I don't think the young have the pha-

lanxes of particulars to go in for criticism, unless they're geniuses. Be that as it may, I learned something from him, which is perhaps why I'm annoyed.

Second thoughts: long stretches, particularly in the *Pisan Cantos*, have a loveliness and humor that's hard to find anywhere else. But damn it—I wish you'd read them over, they're too long, the drift must be *cut* some where. I think I get, or can suppose most of the connections; yet there's something that blankets me. This is fresh on my part, but I'm saying it with awe and humility. Anyhow I wish you'd read them again, and then, above all, finish them up. I'm wild about them after two years in Europe—particularly the sound the *hil* æ *eritas*; your Confucius is a stone to throw at the pedants who memorize instead of live their system.

My love to Dorothy, and I hope you'll be walking in the air soon.

Affectionately,

Cal

215. To Charlotte Winslow Lowell

Pensione California
Via Aurora [43], Rome
October 19, [1952]

Dearest Mother:

Unless a remarkable bargain-apartment turns up, we've settled on the above address for the winter. We're on the Pincian Hill, just off the Via Veneto, between the Villa Borghese and Piazza di Spagna—that's the most grandiose way of describing it. The reality is two smallish, almost Emma-immaculate rooms in a sort of Beacon St. going into the Fenway part of Rome. It's so proper that I fear we'll turn into two nineteenth century spinsters, deathly afraid of colds, and doing water colors of antiquity while waiting in vain for answers to letters of introduction.

I'd better be frank about the rumor you heard of from Frank, I mean from the Parkers, this isn't an occasion for a pun. What happened to me was a very mild repetition of the trouble that reached its climax before in Chicago and Bald Pate. I spent a few days in a hospital in Munich, then rested for ten days at a place that was something between an inn and a sanitarium on a Swiss lake. Due to Elizabeth's alertness the attack never went much beyond a state of nervous excitement—in a period of twenty days I went through the three stages of exuberance, confusion and depression, and can now safely say it's all definitely over, without any likelihood of relapse or return. In fact, I feel far more

relaxed and healthy-minded than I did two years ago on first arriving in Italy. I write all this to ease your mind, and perhaps, a little out of pride so that you will appreciate my dear and intelligent Elizabeth.

We have many friends and acquaintances here, and are settling down to routine and work.

Love,
Bobby

P.S. I'm not anxious to build up a reputation for poetic instability, so please reassure the Parkers.

We saw the Clarks and various other American friends in Venice. I'm beginning to want very much to be back in my familiar American world. We plan to return either in the summer or fall to teach.

216. To Allen Tate

Pensione California
Via Aurora 43, Roma
November 5, 1952

Please write us here. American Express only forwards for a month.

Dear Allen:

Our address has an allegorical touch to it as though we were living in the new American dawn. In fact we are in a rather American section of Rome—big new widestreeted houses just off the old city wall, pine trees and large view of the Pincian Hill. We'd been picturing to ourselves a cinquecento apartment, Dantesque, crenellated, yet sunny; but Rome turns out to be crowded like every other city.

I think you've struck the wells of personal experience in your "Buried Lake." I mean by personal my feeling the push and tone of the poem are somehow the full you (more than ever before) not that this or that or any of the details are autobiographical. What your terza rima means to me, I think, is the terrific formal wrestling to speak out: "imitate me if you have the presumption, Reader; what this has cost me is in the open." My only kick is that the struggle, perhaps, slides at times into muddiness. In Shelley's "West Wind" say, you feel how like breath the form is—with you, here and there, how like choking. You're more like Wyatt in the form than Dante. Also I find a few repetitions of the Seasons, and Allenisms, i.e. tough wrenched words in-

stead of the *mot juste*. There are signs that young poets are going back to free verse; as an old follower of yours, it cheers me up to see you use meter to smash into new ground. I take my hat off!!

We're feeling blue about the election. Ike is a sort of symbol to me of America's unintelligent side—all fitness, muscles, smiles and banality. And Stevenson was so terribly better than one had a right to expect. We too feel too hurt to laugh. However, it's made me break into song. How's this to the tune of Yankee Doodle?

Came to Boston, gave his spiel—
 Smart as a buck pheasant:
All those teeth inside his smile—
 My God, they're incandescent!

His face is on your T.V. screen,
 Got up with pancake powder;
When he's scraped the barrel clean,
 You'll see him swim in chowder.

"See me like an octopus,
 A-hugging up Bill Jenner;
I'd like to bust the bugger's puss,
 But Mamie loves a winner.

"My ghosts have told me something new:
 I'm marching to Korea;
I cannot tell you what I'll do
 Crusading's the idea["]

Yankee Doodle keep it up etc.

This is for Caroline to sing while belligerently making spoon bread. Marvelous letter from Caroline and I feel incommensurably repaid for lost Venetian glass. It was rather an inconsiderate bulk for you to carry. We're peeved though: it wasn't just glass, but awfully special—a real moving design and real silver, and cost ten dollars which go a long way in such things in Venice.

We're working like monks i.e. not like ravenous tourists—much harder than we've ever done since we've been married. Elizabeth has a good draft of a

long story that's stirring to become a novella and ought to be her master-work. I've got four poems more or less finished and an armful of inchoate scraps. Here's the best of the finished poems. Its avatars that I've met are legion.

EPITAPH OF A FALLEN POET

When England gives the laurel to some dope
Or screw who scrubs Catullus' tongue with soap,
Perhaps, he will consider why I took
This crooked turn, instead of Uncle Sam's
Good offices that only health can buy.
Because I knew my classics like a book,
Stranger from England, tell the British: I,
Catullus Redivivus, once the rage
Of Rome and Paris, used to play your role
Of homosexual wolfing the stray lambs
Who hunger by the Place de la Concorde.
My profit was a pocket with a hole.
Who asks for X, the Shelley of the age,
Must pay pound sterling for his bed and board.

I think I'm going into new country, and will not be repeating my old tricks; at least I'm full of stuff I had no notion of saying before.

Glum faces at the embassy listening to the election returns with the Foxes. Best comment from a girl in back of us, "It would have been thrilling to have had a bachelor in the White House." But one seems to feel a cold bright flash of war in the air. That's probably sour grapes.

It's heavenly being in Rome this winter. Things from layers on layers of history seem to sprout about one, even without one's looking. But there's a bleak, detached loneliness to this third year of ours, and I'm certain we must go home next summer. If you hear of anyone who wants an earnest teacher of poetry, please lend your good offices.

I think something happened forever when we saw you in Paris and Lake Garda. My love to Caroline,

Affectionately,

Cal

217. To W. F. van Leeuwen

Dear Huyck:

I feel like a dog not having written sooner—there's something abstract and distant about letters even at their best. As you overlook the black keyboard of your typewriter, it's as though you were facing yourself in the mirror and trying to hold the attention of what you see there by what you see there. This opening is meant as a counterthrust to your classified list of depressions, which I find very sympathetic—as long as it's not myself, I feel like cheering when one of my friends grows darkly thoughtful and philosophic, what the expression *self-possessed* should mean literally, but doesn't. I mean to . . . I'm trying to get around to some good optimistic New England American moralizing, such as saying it's only our long aimless periods that prove we are alive; I guess they do do something, but I mustn't put it that way. You know there's a wintry, wordy American character, half manic-depressive and half booster, who puts the tragic European to shame.

I'm just finishing a second persimmon that Elizabeth has brought me after a dart at shopping. Heavenly fruit, and surely the apples of Eden and idleness that told Adam of a better life, one in which he wrapped himself in a hair-shirt and spent all his days in bed cursing himself for not naming and numbering the animals. We're living in a Pensione on the Pincian hill over the Piazza di Spagna. A stone's throw away, there's a view of St. Peter's, an old medieval brick gate, and the Borghese Gardens full of umbrella pines and ~~people~~ men taking their one to four siesta. Elizabeth has just finished a dazzling story about a couple in Constantinople—Constantinople is Rome's faded twin, and one keeps thinking of them together like the two balancing weights of a scale. E's story, however, is about a healthy, unimaginative couple who are bewildered and distressed at finding a country that only wants to quite unblushingly ape America. Through their own mouths the couple condemn themselves to Elizabeth's feelings! I've piles and piles now of tangled revisions. So far each grandiose dramatic monologue has dwindled to a sonnet. Here's one to Santayana.

SANTAYANA'S FAREWELL TO HIS NURSES
The spirit giveth life; will letters kill
The calm agnostic, if by heaven's will
He found the Church too good to be believed?
"You'll die," the Sisters answer, "as you lived."

One wonders how they riddled what I wrote,
Or if the nuns were too pragmatical
To nurse illusion wrong. Believing Paul,
Most miserable of men, had missed the boat
By preaching truth was what his hand could reach,
I gave the bottomless Evangel soul;
Essence took heart and landscape from my speech.
Dying, I fancied the Blue Sisters pressed
Like geese-girls, hissing, "Rome must give her best,"
Till Curtius in full armor filled the hole.

You probably are familiar with the old Roman legend about Curtius and the abyss by the Capitoline. Santayana died about two weeks before we arrived. He sternly remained an *ideal* but unbelieving Catholic. His mind seems to have been in full power, and he was writing and translating until almost the end. His last three days were physically agonizing, in spite of doses of morphine. It was terrible to have missed him.

We shall be going home to America either next summer or in the fall. It depends on my getting a job teaching somewhere. We'll leave from Holland, so I think we can be certain of meeting in one or the other place. I wish we were settled in America, and you were paying us a long visit, also that we could drift through Rome together. Rome is glorious: it seeps into you when you are not looking or thinking, and you feel cozily anonymous and a piece of the ages. If the United States were around the corner, or even if I spoke fluent Italian, I think I'd stay forever. But as it is we are feeling ever more footloose and unworldly. It's no go[od] being always the stranger. I miss not being planted in human society, I miss my friends, I miss even not having a job. Also I foresee a possible reversal of all these feelings when I get back. The election is symbolically discouraging. We were frantic Stevenson fans, buying three papers a day, reading the complete speeches etc. I think Stevenson was the most human, intelligent and decent person who has run for president in my lifetime. Eisenhower isn't a bad man, I think, just formless, banal, efficient—smiles without personal wit or passions. He's so appallingly typical—I come back to my figure of a country looking at itself in the mirror for instruction.

I can see how you must be thinking about Judy. I already picture a honeymoon for you—tilting Manhattan skyscraper, mixed with skis in Vermont, as though both scenes and you both were jumping about in a glass cocktail shaker. It's really hell being all alone after a while. I don't think I could live a month without Elizabeth.

We're expecting and greatly looking forward to Bep's coming here in January. We hope *Botthege Oscure* will gobble up large sections of the autobiography, so that she'll go home wealthy. Like McCormick a lot. I hope to go to Berlin in the course of the winter and give a lecture or reading at the college where he is teaching. We may do an edition of Emerson's Journals together. The horses I tried to describe to you are by the Quirinale; they're just alike and have *opus Phidias* and *opus Praxideles* written under them—gallantly unconvincing and an affront to all archeological science. I'll try and send you a picture.

Many thanks for your letters, and yours very affectionately,
　　Cal

P.S. I'm writing a note to R. P. Warren about you. He's the best of men, though it's hard for any to get through a certain shell of impersonality with him. Rather like Shapiro without the bitterness—he had a rather fearful marriage and is now divorced and perhaps utterly changed.

218. To Allen Tate

Burlington Apts.
Burlington Ave.
Iowa City, Iowa
April 15th [1953]

Dear Allen/Father Tate:

I liked the idea of the Newburgh Conference, the Catholic Worker people are old friends, and it would be pleasant to get away from the usual professional, stereotyped college writers' conference show. But I see no way of doing it. I'll be at Indiana the full term, and teaching French poetry, an attempt which my ignorance and pronunciation make nervy. I don't think I'd better gad about. A week is quite out of the question (that's what I'd enjoy most) and even a single lecture is fairly complicated.

I'd like to come next summer, and maybe have a sort of discussion class in poetry. I'd like to make the proposal that art and religion per se have nothing to do with each other, but that in this imperfect world they are always colliding—they are always exploiting, avoiding and abusing each other, and that this is as it should be. By taking ten or twelve English poets, I would try to muddy up the waters—sympathetically and intelligently—then we would try to clear them as far as the facts allow. I don't see how I could avoid learning a lot. But I don't think it can be done until next summer, I mean the summer after this.

It's a pity your conference is not going to be in August. There's a friendly, and casual debate I'd like to have with you along the lines that one must at times condescend to Descartes and be inexhaustibly fair to him, otherwise there is always the danger that he will be fair to us and annihilate our critiques.

It was good to hear your voice. In the next few weeks I am going to Grinnell and Illinois to lecture and think I'll probably stay here until the term ends. We're sure to cross in the course of the summer.

Affectionately,

Cal

219. To Allen Tate

April 29th [1953]

Dear Allen:

[. . .]*Father Tate* was a joke. God is holding you, and you are standing up almost better than a man can. It seems to me that in the last two years or so, something human has grown in you without your really knowing it, all you could ask for has, though it's not what you would ask for, gives no pledges, or cushions. I liked what Arthur and Delmore said in their reviews. The poems show the same things only with far more blood and body. But I was talking personally.[. . .]

I have been thinking about Caroline a lot lately. I think we look at each other for the moment from behind fences, which is natural and right. One has to will and take positions, and once those positions have been assumed, there's no communion or even communication or talking without fences. But some day we will look at mushrooms or pictures together and talk ourselves blue, and all will be the same.

Thanks for your backing at Cincinnati. Elizabeth sends her love.

Cal

We'll miss you, but are delighted you're going to Italy.

220. *To Elizabeth Bishop*

June 14th, 1953

Dear Elizabeth:

Medias res:—We've just bought a seventeen year old Packard that an old professor looked after like a baby, or rather far better. I've just gotten my driver's license, and discover unexpectedly that I am slow and reliable. We go for pleasure drives along the unscenic Iowa River, and are almost senile with joy and fatuousness.

I'm tied up with teaching from now until next June: Indiana till the first of August, back here in September, Cincinnati from February till June. After that we hope to get a house and write as worldly people with a stake in the world, or President Eisenhower—wasn't the election a misfortune!

I gather from Nathalie Rahv and other people that Brazil is incredibly the perfect place for you, and that you have good friends there. But you must keep covering the entire Atlantic seaboard with long stops in New York and Massachusetts, so that I can see you. I don't like your removal at all.

Last night I had a dream. I was in France. Paris was again falling to the Germans, but it had become such a habit that one had to look closely to see that anyone really cared. I arrived in Paris (from the front, I think, but there wasn't much of one) went to a party, where I was surrounded by acquaintances. They became distant and shadowy when I approached them. Suddenly I saw you and gave you a tremendous hug. You moved to another table. I said: "I know where there are a couple of good French restaurants." You said: "They're all French here."

You see. You must come back.

What are you writing? Elizabeth has just finished two good essays and a story, and I've three or four poems that are coming out in *Kenyon* and *PR*. Also a pile of unfinished stuff.

Write and tell us how you are, and I'll answer with a good letter. Elizabeth sends her love.

Love,
Cal

I had your address from Nathalie, but [it] vanished in a cleaning of my billfold. I'm sending this through Houghton & Mifflin. If you stay in Brazil ten years we might drive. Are there bridges over the Panama Canal?

221. To Elizabeth Hardwick

33 Marlboro St.
Boston, Mass.
[September 10, 1953]

Dear Elizabeth:

O dear! Berium gulpings and bismoth enemas. I've been grayed utterly and there's nothing wrong except habitual constipation. At the same time I've been gulping Freud and am a confused and slavish convert. I keep saying: "How could Delmore have so understated one's buried intentions." Every fault is a gold mine of discoveries—I am a walking gold mine—with ten (sinisterly) forgotten names or impressions to one I remember. It's all too much (especially while staying with Mother). I long to be back.

Down to business. I'm going to visit the Starrs tomorrow and the Parkers Saturday and Duxbury Tuesday—3 regions to get some idea of houses—2 others are Brattleborough Vermont and the lower Maine coast. I think we ought to see quite a few alternatives before deciding. Merrill has offered us his boat-house for the winter months. It's furnished and heated and rentless and we could step out of our car into it. The money won't be hard to raise. It does look easy now. I've done all my shopping except the shirts—also two of Daddy's suits, a jacket and my old Ohio gabardine really decently altered. Two dresses, a suit and five jackets for you.

Oh honey I'm all clogged with berium and bismoth, have lost weight but would burst like the moon if I fell on my belly.

Give my best to the Wests.

I love you and am lonely. Are you sure Browning didn't just believe he wasn't writing. He couldn't have averaged less than 20 lines a day. (I can prove I haven't.)

Cal

222. To Elizabeth Bishop

232 Summit St.
Iowa City, Iowa
Nov. 29th, 1953

Dear Elizabeth:

I think about you continually—you and your studio and your Brazilian world. I'm sure you are as happy as you sound. But I don't approve at all. Like

a rheumatic old aunt, I would gladly spoil all your fun just to have you back. I think I'll try and have payments on your trust fund stopped.

We've just "bought" a house in Duxbury Mass.: 1740, red cedar shingled, 1950 oil furnace, eight rooms, kitchen, garage, three acres, stream, flag-pole, ten miles from Plymouth, forty from Boston, ten thousand dollars mortgage owing—it's ours! We'll be moving in early in May when I finally get through the last of my teaching. You must come then and we'll build a replica of your Brazilian house, and you can swing through the years back and forth from one to the other like a pendulum.

This letter may have a peculiar rhythm—that's because I've just read in *Time* that I'll have cancer of the throat in six years if I go on smoking fifty cigarettes a day (Elizabeth's figure for me). I don't think I'm scared enough to stop, but I'm starting my second day. It's surprisingly easy (anyone can do it) and unpleasant. Writing this letter is difficult; it's as though I were drunk or asleep. (You wish you were both as soon as you start to do anything that requires any thought or concentration at all.) Elizabeth started stopping a month ago, and was very Spartan and undemonstrative about it; I don't think she suffered. Now after listening to me for a few hours groaning and boasting she's ready to quit.

I guess you've heard about Dylan Thomas's death. He died four days after a brain stroke which seems to have immediately finished his mind. The details are rather gorgeously grim. He was two days incommunicado with some girl on Brinnin's staff in some New York hotel. Then his wife came, first cabling "eternal hate," and tried quite literally to kill *and* sleep with everyone in sight. Or so the rumors go in Chicago and Iowa City. It's a story that Thomas himself would have told better than anyone else; I suppose his life was short and shining as he wanted it—life, alas, is no joke.

What other news is there? Randall's writing a college novel with Mary McCarthy as the heroine. *PR* has refused to print sections; they all say it is bad and not fiction etc. and wait with watering mouths for Mary to read it. Fiction or not, it's rather terrific writing. Randall and I are doing an anthology of modern poetry—we want things like fifty Yeats, fifty Hardy etc. that cost like hell. I fear we will be paying Harcourt Brace a hundred dollars a month for the rest of our lives. Elizabeth is finishing her novel. I'm teaching Homer. My car won't start in the snow. We want to have a child as soon as we get to Duxbury. (Really!) I've been so busy finding ways to make teaching easy that I haven't done a stroke of work. Write us soon and come and stay with us next summer.

Love,
Cal

223. *To Allen Tate*

December 2nd, 1953

Dear Allen:

How are you doing? All we know about you comes from John Berryman and a note from Shapiro, and of course the newspaper accounts of your rioting. I was hoping to see you in the news reels. Randall says somewhere that a poet can only become famous through his personal disasters. I guess it's no joke to be mobbed though. I am sort of hoping you'll turn into an unreasoning Yugo-Slav partisan, rather a nut on the subject like Pound's usury.[. . .]

Rather dreadful summer at Indiana, heat, all of us cross at each other, and almost no students. I don't think anyone wants to go again. I've gotten to quite like teaching and the university world, but it's very undermining, and whatever happens we are going to take next year off, live in our house and write.

Elizabeth has almost finished her Iowa City murder novel, and is going to give an informal reading later this week—rather ticklish—the victims are really the Iowa City mind, and the little group of painters and musicians who listened last week astonished to Marguerite Young's work in progress, will, I am afraid feel that both Elizabeth and her subject are mere prose, a return to Grant Wood.

Write us soon and remember us to the Devlins, the Shapiros, Peggy Erskine and the Princess Caetani.

Love to you both,
Cal

Adventures of the mind! I've been reading all the drama recommended by Bentley. If someone would do the dialogue for me I could write a second *Oresteia*. Also all Freud and I have been teaching Homer. However, I would I were in Rome and sight-seeing with Caroline, I know I am the only man who could keep up with her—I feel cheated by only having lived through Caroline's mushroom days.

224. To Elizabeth Hardwick

POSTCARD: The White House
[Washington, D.C., December 16, 1953]

Dear Uncle:

Here I am—serene, rested and arrived. Such a lovely house. My cab driver said we wouldn't see another Republican president in our life-times (sanguine man!) in answer to my question *How has Washington changed in the last three years*. Miss you so much love ~~Cal~~ IKE.

225. To Flannery O'Connor

Christmas card of sleigh ride
[Iowa City, Iowa, n.d. December 1953]

Dear Flannery:

Our car is coëval with the vehicle in the picture, and almost as hale. Soon you'll be known as the "swan of old cars." I read your stories as Eliot would say with *continued respect*. Both the baptizing and the homicidal lunatic are fearfully good. What a relief it is to get back to the quiet waters of Elizabeth's Iowa City murder novel. She's almost done and last week we had a reading.

You've made a strange convert through me: Philip Rahv who now goes about enraging New York literati by telling them they should write a *Wise Blood*. What else have you written? Some one said you had something in *Harper's Bazaar*, but I can't believe it. I'm full to the gills with teaching, and wish I lived on an income in a world of illiterates.

We've just bought a house in Duxbury Mass. and will move in next June and stay there for over a year. You must visit us. I hear from Mrs. Winslow that you say you are "disgustingly healthy." Why do all women say that? I suppose you mean "fat," but what vanity. I wish I could. Elizabeth thinks all fat people should be burned in Calvin's institutes. O! Elizabeth has learned to cook this fall.

Love from us both,
Cal

226. To Elizabeth Bishop

January 1, [1954]

Dearest Elizabeth:

We have your photograph perched high on our little foot and a half Maine Christmas tree, sent us by my Cousin Harriet. I'm sure you remember her from Washington. I'd never dare take the wheel holding a kitten, and I doubt if my car would be up [to] reaching to that roof of the world you seem to have attained. Nevertheless, I want to take a colored photograph of my own car green glorious sedate and empty, and engraved underneath, "merry Christmas from the Lowells." Maybe Williams would write some verses for us. I think it's thrilling about your losing twenty pounds, though I'm sure I shouldn't remark on it, and I wouldn't want you any different—still it's a haunting idea. But alas, if I don't watch out I'll be gaining each ounce you drop. Except for football games, I've become a pure creature of books during the past three months. That's the trouble with living in a pioneer undecadent world.

We're both sick of Iowa City. Also I'm sick of explaining to Elizabeth why she shouldn't be. She has just finished her novel. It "centers" about a student murder that happened in 1950 when we were first here. It's the best thing she's done, very stern with a subdued satirical edge. And everything she tactfully didn't say about the local[e] is tearing through her. So here we are in the beginning of the New Year. It has just occurred to me that I haven't done a lick of preparation for my nine one hour lectures on American poetry to be given in Cincinnati in a little over a month. How I wish I'd been reading Americana instead of Homer and Pindar! By the way I had a long talk with a girl about one of your lectures. She said you were such a wise sympathetic person, but it was a pity that you stuttered. She said she really couldn't get a word, but loved your books so. Well, after five minutes it turned out to be Elizabeth Bowen. You ought to have heard how I sweated to merge the two characters.

Your *New Yorker* story is wonderful. A great ruminating Dutch landscape feel of goneness. I could weep for the cow. I've been dragging up old conversations with you and wondering just how autobiographical both this and that other two little girls story are. I feel they are perhaps parts of a Nova Scotia growing-up novel—though of course they are rounded short stories—the second is much more considerable, but somehow it raises the first. So I think of some Education of E. B. or E. B.'s Downward path to Wisdom. What K. A. Porter's childhood stories aim towards, or a super Miss Jewett. But it could be less than a novel—something in three, four or five sections that would go for

about a hundred pages. You see I'm back on my old *Mills of the Kavanaughs* rage for putting pieces together.

Glad you found Elizabeth's and my things had life in them. My best poem lately, I think, is a long thing on leaving Europe that came out in the summer *Kenyon*. I'd send you a copy, but haven't one. And the thought of copying it out makes me groggy.

I am rather groggy from a three days head-inflaming cold, from lying in bed (it's almost over now) and reading Carlyle's *French Revolution*. Overpowering, and almost as good as *Moby-Dick* when you give in to it. Our century really can't match the best Victorians for non-fictional prose. But I am not going to start a lecture.

Do you stop in the States on your way to Europe? I wish with all my heart that you could somehow stretch things and see us. We seem attached to each other by some stiff piece of wire, so that each time one moves, the other moves in another direction. We should call a halt to that.

Now, to end impersonally. I saw Pound some two weeks ago at St. Elizabeths, the first time in four years. It's a shock how unchanged he was, the same list of books (when he learned I was only to be there for the day, he brushed aside human amenities, plunged in medias res, and told me how to teach history from 1830–1860) the same rhetoric. But he's much fatter and healthier, jumps about, dances like a bear and no longer complains of memory gaps. O I think he has lived because he has wanted to, and Thomas didn't—No I don't mean that exactly, Thomas wanted to live burning, burning out.

So we. I want to live to be old, and want you to.

Love,
Cal

227. *To J. F. Powers*

[January 22, 1954]

Dear Jim:

Your visit washed me out and put the fear of God into me. The prose workshop is ruefully stumbling to its feet—I think most of them are planning to enlist in the navy.

Elizabeth and I wish we could make you sign a blank committing you to paying us a visit this summer—either you alone or you and your family. We will be in Duxbury all summer except for the first two weeks in August.

I think you ought to burn through your novel as fast as you can let yourself. Once it's done, you'll wake up in Ireland—probably as head of the Catholics for Union Party. I'm about to wake up on the platform in Cincinnati speechless. We'll be tarred out of town. My best to Betty—

Affectionately,
Cal

1954–1959

Writing of *Life Studies* and *Imitations* • Birth of Harriet Lowell

Rapallo • *Cincinnati* • *New York City* • *Boston*

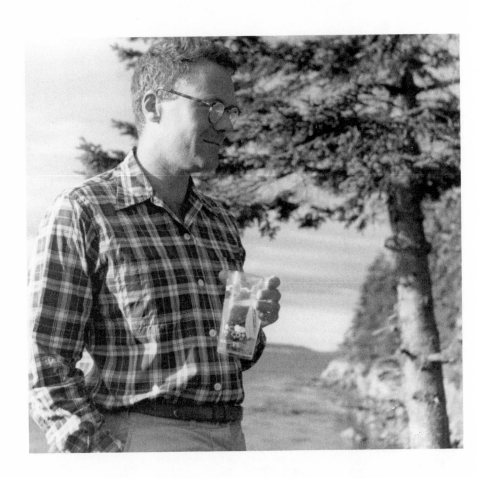

Lowell in Undercliff, Maine, 1955 (courtesy Elizabeth Hardwick)

228. To Elizabeth Hardwick

[Boston, Mass., February 11, 1954]
Thursday 11:30 p.m.

Dearest Lizzie:

I'm flying tomorrow at 9:30 a.m. so by the time you get this I'll have long been over the ocean. The reports are conflicting. Mother is up and talking, has no paralysis—but her blood pressure is 200 and something, which is alarming. I saw Merrill at the airport. He doesn't think Mother can be moved for over a month. I'll stay until she is out of danger (but there's no telling what is up) then either Merrill or the Cottings can go over. Mother's mind is all right (she's mostly sleeping). She doesn't know what happened to her, thinks it was indigestion. She's not in Genoa but Rapallo.[. . .]Well, I'm over my H.O. Wish you were in my arms.

Love,
Cal

Would you like to come on here and stay with the Moores?

229. To Elizabeth Hardwick

Albergo Europa
Rapallo, Italy
[February 15, 1954]

Dear Sweetheart:

I must give it all briefly. Mother died very suddenly fr[om] a second attack just an hour before I arrived. She was quite wandering i[n] her memory all the time and I don't think there was ever much chance. She didn't suffer and didn't altogether know where she was. They thought best not to announce my

coming to her, and I don't think she suspected the need. Pretty rough—I spent the morning with her nurse who only speaks Italian, both of us weeping & weeping. I mean I spent it in the room with her body!

I expect to sail with her on the Constitution from Genoa on Sunday, and will arrive in New York the 4th or 5th of March. Tomorrow I go to Florence to pick up her things. We'll have a small ceremony Friday or Saturday. Some of Mother's friends will come, also probably Blair, Rolando and maybe Allen.

I'll tell you about the trip later. It was a nightmare of planes missing connections. I think my only connection that connected was a Milan tram from the Air France terminal to the Stazione Centrale—a tram because it was raining and there were no taxis. The Cottings were almost miraculous in getting things arranged, but who can arrange weather or even airplane engines?

Don't worry about me—everything at this point is in a groove and almost arranges itself. I'll be back here[,] Rapallo[,] Wednesday night and here until sailing time.

I want you to do whatever is easiest for you. You might come on to Boston about the first and then meet me in New York. I think we'll have a funeral in Boston almost immediately after I arrive and then drive on to Dunbarton.

Well I feel dead on my feet, but otherwise am holding together. People are very helpful here.

My love, my sweetheart,
 Cal

P.S. Mother's doctor is Max Beerbohm's.

I don't know where you are, but am sending this to your mother's.

230. *To Elizabeth Hardwick*

Pensione Tornabuoni Beacci
Firenze, Italy
[February 17, 1954]

Dear Sweet-Heart:

The worst sledge-hammer blows are over now—I think the only technicality left is the vaccination which I've managed to have Thurs. Tomorrow I'm having a service for Mother at Rapallo. Sunday I sail on the Constitution from Genoa (the undertaker handles all arrangements for putting the body on the ship). March 1st I arrive in New York—ominous date.

This morning I see various old ladies mother knew here, and get the Am. Express to send her trunks on to Rapallo.

It's been rather hell, but the worst is over. I got Dr. Bacigalupo to give me a box of sedatives. Rolando spent the night with me here. Robert Fitzgerald met me.

I know you worry about me. But I am taking great care to sleep. The nine days voyage will be a great easing.

Love and love, Dear

Cal[. . .]

231. *To Giovanna Madonia Erba*

S.S. Constitution
Feb. 22nd [1954]

My Dearest Giovanna:

(after about twelve hours sleep) I live only in you too, your heart beats in mine, I feel you heavy in my arms—all this voyage I seem to have been carrying you—every bone in my body, every drop of blood, every nerve and sinew in my mind, are yours!

For some eighteen or nineteen months (it seems five years) since that late July or early August when you left Salzburg, I haven't dared look inside myself or hope. And yet we were together, and didn't know it, and were growing closer and closer each day. It has been as though there were deep inside me some great festering wound, as if I had rolled some great stone over it (to pretend it wasn't there) and thus I went on half alive. And now that I know that you still love me and are waiting, the wound is purifying and draining. I am alive again. I'm not saying this in exaggeration or self-pity. In a way I have made out quite well. I have grown older and abler, almost a professore like Rolando. But I was half-dead.

I think you must have had a terrible year. You must rest and keep yourself emotionally "stable" as they say. I'm an expert on this subject of stability now. Correspondence will be simple. For the present write me simply care of The Department of English, University of Cincinnati, Cincinnati, Ohio. I'll be there from the eighth of March till the 20th of May. After that we'll arrange something else. I'm very devoted to Elizabeth and don't want to hurt her. But O my Giovana, I am not alive without you.

Figaro was uneven. I missed Seefried, Kuntz, and Jurinac. Gatto (?) was quite charming as Susanna, whoever sang "la Madre" was fun; but what made

the performance sublime was Schwarzkopf. I've never heard anything like her *Dove sono* nor had Blair Clark. I wish you could send her my compliments or flowers, or whatever a poor poet offers the immortals. A lady and the finest singer I've ever heard, still! She seems a little stouter than when I heard her in Salzburg. Well, I know we disagree on this subject.

This is a quiet roomy voyage, just what I need. My room-mates are an Italian father and son going from Chiavari to Canada. They correct my spoken Italian, which God knows needs it.

O my Giovana, my Giovana! I cannot live without thee! I'll send you a good photograph and you do the same. I will look up the Angel Tosca in Boston, though.

I feel your great hands on me and rest like a child.

All my love,

Cal

P.S. I can send you some American money in a month or two, which you can keep for a trip to America. Only a day and a half by plane from Milan to Boston! I had a long talk with Blair, one of my oldest and most level-headed friends. You could write him if anything came up.

232. *To Giovanna Madonia Erba*

Department of English
University of Cincinnati
Cincinnati, Ohio
March 6th [1954]

My Dearest:

Well, I'm back a little earlier, writing a little earlier, and *waiting for a letter a little earlier*. I know I am a foolish man, but don't don't keep me waiting—it's like hanging on a meat-hook, going through a vegetable grinder, like being one of those pictures of flayed men—all purple and nerves—on an anatomical chart!

Mother's funeral was Thursday, and after the service in Boston, we drove some seventy-five miles into New Hampshire to an old family graveyard, where some of our people have been buried since the end of the 18th century. That's as old for us as the Coliseum, you know. It's an old journey for me. I used to go up there as a boy with my Grandfather, rake leaves, burn brush, catch newts etc. At that time there were still ancient New Hampshire farmers there, who had fought under Grant at Shiloh in 1861. The graveyard is on a

small hill. The stones are surrounded by a black iron and granite fence and overlooked by a statue of Christ that my Grandfather had copied from one (modern, alas! but simple) that he admired outside San Miniato in Firenze. There are pine trees on the hill, that they say have never been cut. The day was bright and sharp. The pond below was frozen. Everything glistened.

I guess funerals are for the living. Anyway, it was a catharsis. We all repeated the Bible-words, gave off our sorrow and felt closer to each other. Besides my Aunt and Uncle and Elizabeth, there was Mother's reading club, a little group of old ladies who had been meeting once a week in the winter, not to read but to talk—for over fifty years!

Now I'm back, feeling rather flat, and getting my lectures in order. And waiting, waiting, waiting! Please write. Please trust my mind to do the planning for us this time. That's what I'm good at. Did you get my letter from Gibraltar and the others? You can write me at the above address and no one will see.

All my love,
Cal

P.S. I have your De Sabata Scala picture. It cost me a dollar and three cents. It's gloriously dramatic, but not recognizable. I look at it and say "that's her."

233. *To Blair Clark*

2901 Clifton Ave.
Cincinnati, Ohio
Thursday, March 11, [1954]

Dear Blair:

Your letters are written with too much fullness and ease for me to be able to answer in the slap-dash, telegraphic manner that I find pleasant. I see the notice in the *New York Times* describes you as a "free lance writer living in Paris." I hadn't thought of that caption. But you are a writer. I was really amazed by your sitting down half-dead and typing off deliberately your words on Father Pierre. I like the article. You know Joseph II said to Mozart after hearing *Figaro*, "too many notes, my dear Mozart, for our poor Austrian ears." You have too many facts for me. But of course you have to. So I am dazed and amazed.

I can't go into Mother's funeral again. After all the strain and delay, it brought great relief and calm. There were red roses on the casquet that Mother

might have arranged. The casquet itself had a big brass crucifix on it, and Mother's name misspelled *Charlotte Winslon*. That's what she brought back from Italy with her. A beautiful sharp bright day for driving to Dunbarton. The minister got lost. There's more. In a funny way one felt close to Mother's friends and especially the Cottings, in [a] way that had never been possible before. I guess I am a black sheep forever, but it's calming not to be for a moment.

Very little news. We drove with Frank to Duxbury. You would have been reminded of Signor Drago's chauffeur. Elizabeth nearly fainted when she saw the bright yellow ugly new shingles, and must have talked on this subject for an hour and a half—Frank's driving all the while getting more violent. Well, some very capable woman under Elizabeth's direction is now doing $2000 worth of interior remodelling.

We are very much back and in harness. I've met my first seminar—a surprise, it had shrunken from seven to four. And I have given my first public lecture on Robert Frost—another surprise this audience—two to three hundred—was undiminished. Oh for the life of you free-lance writers!

Thank you many many times for your company in Italy, neither of us will ever forget that day in Milano, or Signor Drago, I suppose, either. Please thank Holly too for her sympathy. We hope to see you both this summer.

Love to you all,
Cal

P.S. If this letter sounds rapid, it's because I can type faster than I can think.

234. To Giovanna Madonia Erba

Saturday, March 13th [1954]

My Darling, Darling, Darling Giovanna:

I am writing in a moment of great peacefullness and verbosity. As you may imagine, until your last letter arrived, I was wound up like a bow-string, and there was a swelling tension between me and Elizabeth. The evening of your letter, I went to a party drank a lot of martinis, ate like a pig, and then came home and let my mind flow out to Elizabeth. I didn't tell [her] we were writing or anything descriptive about you; but I said I wanted to marry you. Well, a seething night. Then in the morning, like a carbuncle it broke. I realized that I loved E. and wanted her with me, and she realized that I was *in* love with you. Now though it seems eccentric, we are at peace. I think Elizabeth will

eventually marry some one else (in the next year or so). So she says, and [I] think so too. She was on the point of doing this at Salzburg. She has no one in mind, I think. And she won't marry anyone she can't love. Meanwhile it is peace for us to be together. Our marriage is hard to explain. We are like first cousins or brother and sister, though of course nothing is really like anything else.[...]

Our record library here amounts to nothing. However, to my surprise I actually found the mad scene from Lucia di Lammermoor. Not quite what you ordered. Instead of Callas, Erna Sack doing coloratura show pieces. Instead of our Italian, German. "*Nu Ich bin dein, du bist meine.*" In the next room a student was playing blues on a piano. He was very audible. Both victrola and record were in bad shape. But it was heavenly. I'll look up the true version in a record store down town.

Cincinnati is almost southern. Today the air is full of warmth and seed. I am getting my dear old seventeen year old Packard out. It still runs without a splutter. I wish you were in the seat with me.

Melodrama on Italian soil! You don't remind me of any literary heroines. Intense scenes though bring you closer. I think the crown of English literature i[s] *Antony and Cleopatra*. Worlds swelled in them. They weren't like us. Far more than Paolo and Francesca, they "sommettono la ragion al talento." It goes against life to kill one's mind. An American psychology professor once said that Cleopatra was just a maladjusted girl with a father-complex. I have no patience with such cant. But they were they, not us! (By the way, I spent a large part of last fall reading Freud. He [is] not like Freudians, but marvelous, like Proust, the most revealing mind of our age.) Who are you like? In your strength (mental and physical) like some of the heroines in the Latin Elegies: Lesbia, Cynthia. But they were hell on wheels and wore their men to death. Read that late elegy of Propertius where Cynthia, dead and a ghost, comes back (the sixth Book IV?) She has ~~something of~~ your voice. O we are we. I am yours undeviatingly forever. Insieme, insieme . . . per sempre!

There's a scene. White sheets. Salt air from the Mediterranean, far below. Sound of waves. Then you in your bridal dress. Nothing very fancy, for such wouldn't do for us. Maybe some stiff, close-fitting brocaded dress. And I am undressing you. WE are together, our mouths are together, our hair is together. Ah, there! I speak of mysteries, and I kneel now and throw salt, or whatever one throws, over my shoulder to prevent ill omens. All is humbleness and joy.

Here's a poem by Herbert ("Love III," the last lyric in "The Church"). He [is] talking of God, but we can secularize his words.

Love bad me welcome; yet my soul drew back,
 Guilty of dust and sin.
But quick-eyed Love, observing me grow slack
 From my first entrance in,
Drew nearer to me, sweetly questioning
 If I lacked anything.
"A guest," I answered, "worthy to be here:"
 Love said, "You shall be he."
"I, the unkind, the ungrateful? Ah, my Dear
 I cannot look on thee."
Love took my hand and smiling did reply,
 "Who made the eyes but I?"
"Truth, Lord, but I have marred them: let my shame
 Go where it doth deserve."
"And know you not," says Love, "who bore the blame."
 "My dear, then I will serve."
"You must sit down," says Love, "and taste my meat."
 So I did sit and eat.

There, there, there! You are at rest, my Darling Giovanna!
 Cal

235. To William Carlos Williams

<div align="right">

2901 Clifton Ave.
Cincinnati, Ohio
Saturday, March 13th [1954]

</div>

Dear Bill:

I want to write you right off, rattle-brained and enthusiastic as I am tonight—after my second slow reading and my third day with your book. Maybe the best way is to go through naming things I like—as though I were a reviewer, but this way saves time. *Desert Music* is very racy, and I'd like to hear you read it. When I read at the Harvard Phi Beta Kappa, I couldn't muster up an ode, not even within the very broad limits they allow. So I gave part of a long poem. I think they enjoyed my introductory remarks. The poem left them flat. After the reading, there was a meal, and I met for the first time my famous and very rich cousin, Ralph Lowell. We talked about our cousin the president of Harvard. When that gave out, I said, "I think you know Robert Frost." He

answered, "Yes, I've heard the name." Then to express himself accurately he added, "I am absolutely sure I've heard the name." When I got up to speak, he walked out. There was no discourtesy or awareness of what he was doing. He had to go somewhere. I wish I had had your poem about the Mexican whores.

In your poem to the Monahans, the part on pages 18 and 19 about the birds through "both of us go down," is wise and tender like one of the psalms—one written in southern Palestine, if the Jews had that same difference between north and south that all nations no matter what their latitude seem to have. The tone of the "Garden" is lovely. I like the "Host." Two weeks ago, coming back on a boat from Italy, I sat with a YMCA couple. They didn't smoke. They didn't drink. They looked reproach at people who did smoke and drink. They were anti-Jew, anti-Catholic (I asked them what their religion was. They answered Baptist. But we believe the Lord's supper should be open to all (in grape juice!) They asked me mine. I said, "I am a bad Catholic." The woman answered, "There are plenty of your sort of kind in the States." I didn't say anything. She repeated. I said, "I think you may have misunderstood. I don't have any religion, if I did, I'd be a Catholic." They shut up.) They did calisthenics (in their sixties) every day. I joined them one morning, but it lamed me for the rest of the voyage.

My favorite poems in your new book are "Work in Progress" and "To Daphne and Virginia." I think they are the wisest, the most relaxed, the most penetrating poems you have ever written. "Work in Progress" is bigger, but the other is of the same quality. I cannot express how they moved me, and my wife to whom I read them aloud—they are poetry and go beyond poetry—so it must always be if our art is worth the candle.

I mentioned a return from Italy. You will wonder why. My mother suddenly had a stroke. I flew over from here and arrived just one hour after she died. The cable sent to us from the consul went to the wrong address, so we didn't hear for five days. Four days later she was dead. Two cerebral hemorrhages. She died in full health not knowing a thing. The day before her stroke was like any other day. Even when she was sick, she thought it was indigestion, and wanted to put on her clothes and be out.[. . .]My Mother and I somehow competed. It took us a lifetime to be off guard with each other. Last fall I was with her for some ten days in Boston, and we talked over whatever we had in us. In the last moments of her life, she was free and like a little girl. A sort of triumph.

I hope I will see you and Flossie this May, either alone after the Institute induction, or about a week later with my wife when we drive to New England.

Love to you both,
 Cal

236. To Harriet Winslow

Saturday, March 13th, [1954]

Dear Cousin Harriet:

I have been meaning to write you of all people a really long and thought out letter. But I have been writing so many letters lately! So this can't at all be what I was planning. I know I never have to raise my voice for you to understand.

I am glad Mother spoke to you of my visit last fall. Not knowing anything of the future for Mother, we *did* get on so well and said so much. It takes the bitterness out of my late arrival in Rapallo. For she had slipped far after her first stroke, and I would have only seen and talked to a part. She gave out of her heart. It took us both a long time to learn.

Well, I am back here talking on poets. Two members of my class are ladies in their fifties who have given up housekeeping to write poetry. They think more people should write poetry. I don't. The public lectures are more fun. It's surprising what things you can say to some people in public that you would never dream of saying in private.

Yes, I got your cable just as I got on the steamer. Thanks so much. I was so moved by your telephoning Mrs. Hardwick. You were the only member of my family who did. (There was no occasion to, of course.) I'm sure she was pleased. She's a wonderful woman, who has had eleven children. Ten *and* Elizabeth! When Elizabeth was home they had twin beds in the same room and talked all night. Now, until I see you about the 24th of May,

Love,
Bobby

P.S. They also spent three nights listening to TV programs. It pleased their Presbyterian consciences to feel what a waste of time it was.

237. To Allen Tate

Monday, March 15th, [1954]

Dear Allen:

I can tell from our telephone conversation and your letter, that you've *had* it. Our winter in Florence was much the same—rain! No one to talk [to] who had ever had a thought of his own except Berenson. Our great companion was a fairy friend of Elizabeth's, Tony Bower (I can still hear him saying "Ducky, my Dear!") The Spenders know him and Natasha tried to make him exercise.

Italian literati *can* rub one wrong. They are brash where we are polite, formal where we are simple. The experts on Americana are the worst. There was a dreadful friend of the Frankenbergs from Lucca or Pistoia. Meetings with him were like being received by Prince Metterich's imbecile nephew, if he had one. This guy was always being offended, always trying to get a testimonial. O and when you are fatigued they are gay, singing verses on your name, and when you are drunk, they aren't.

But as an old tourist (I've been three times to your two) the country is *gloria mundi*. After a while you've hit Italy from many different angles, and make one or two of the best friends you have anywhere. And they are unlike any of your other friends. Then, then, the ice breaks. I think I would have hated the South, if it hadn't been for you and Caroline and John and Peter. This is gush, but after a while you do feel that terrible wine, olive oil and soil power—the Italy of Vergil and Juvenal and Propertius. But what a film you have to go through before you get there—before you begin to get there, for I suppose one never does. The Church *even* has this casualness and force. The "even" is just to get Caroline's goat. But I guess you can see why I went to the Nederlands—no one has ever been able to understand. But *I* at least wanted an utterly unItalian and unLatin Europe. We made more friends in Amsterdam than anywhere even in America that I have ever been. I wish you and Caroline could stop there on your way home. There are no hills to climb, no distances. And we could give you about ten letters of introduction.

What you say of Mother hits home. At the end, she really was trying to free herself from me. And in her last months she *had*, at least for the moment. I am surprised how many people loved her. You won't understand this. But when they met her without me or my Father, marvelous qualities came out. A boldness and humor—all her own. I saw this more and more last fall when I was with her. Together, except sometimes when we were alone, we sat like stones on each other's heads—inhibiting and inhibited. But with a drink or two and me in the distance people were charmed.

Can I say something about *The Fathers* which I've just re-read? The first hundred pages or so are absolutely charming and I think as perfect as anything you've ever written. Then for me at least something goes wrong. One feels that the melodrama is conventional, like some Elizabethan tragedies— Tourneur for instance. One has been there before, but your characters aren't there, never could be, the air withers them. This is fresh on my part. But your poetry is different. There you have a hand of iron. I think the lynching section of your new poem is the best thing you've ever done, the best terza rima in English. Better than Shelley even, for you have more weight. You know now

how to write from what you are instead of fancying. Would I did! I have about a third of a book now and may send the lot on to you one of these days. The first part of your novel, by the way, really has the atmosphere that I was trying (and occasionally *do*) get in my Kavanaughs, which you have never read.

You must have disliked my review of Red. So did he. When I read at Yale he never mentioned it. Writing it was like pulling one's teeth out. I was very depressed after a sweltering sheer *PR* summer at Bloomington—so I simply put down all the best things I could believe. I don't take anything back, but that's no way to write criticism.

Well, to wind up on the minor key. Isn't Cleanth a lovely and absurd man! How can one become an Episcopalian? It's easy to be a Catholic or an atheist, or both in different moods, but Church of England in America when you weren't born to it! In Northford the Catholic church is ugly and streamlined, the Congregational church is rich gothic, and the Episcopal church looks like a meeting house. Cleanth told me without the slightest note of humor or contention that his rector kept both Catholics and Congregationalists at a distance. He said he wasn't high Anglican, but that he didn't want to speak rashly, for some men whose minds he most admired in other fields were. He told me New England wasn't his tradition, but being a professor at Yale, he thought it right that he should make an effort to conform. His effort was to buy a 1710 salt box house which he has restored so that it is far more like itself and in period than when it was built.

Love to you both,
Cal

P.S. I think Montale is one of the best poets alive—infinitely better than René Char. But one can't talk to him at all. I don't think he ever understood a word of my slurred Yankee, Southern, mid-western English.

I'll repeat what you say of Ben. I would like to drive him through Cincinnati traffic. Elizabeth, by the way, thinks you have jaundice. One can without knowing it or turning yellow. We think Elizabeth had it now for over [a] year.

238. To Giovanna Madonia

[March 17, 1954]

NO EMERGENCY PREPARE FOR PASSAGE TO AMERICA LETTERS FOLLOW — CAL

239. *To Giovanna Madonia*

Wednesday, March 17th, [1954]

My Giovanna—

I hope my cable wasn't over-dramatic. I think of two things. 1) We ought to be together as soon as possible. 2) You should get out of the strain and tension of Milan. You might come by boat instead of plane; the sea-voyage is soothing; but I incline to think that neither of us can enjoy delays at the moment. We are the best medicine for each other.[. . .]

I don't think you need worry about the lawyer and divorce for the moment. You can stay with me in my house in Duxbury as my secretary and housekeeper (music-teacher, Italian teacher, pupil) with perfect propriety. God knows, a man needs some woman to keep things in shape when he settles in a country house. Duxbury is on the Atlantic, about forty miles south of Boston, and ten north of Plymouth where the Pilgrims, my ancestors landed. (They weren't much intellectual shakes, but for some reason the Mayflower descendants are thought of as the elite of the American immigrants.) Sorry for all this family business, I too find it tiresome and alien.

Well, Elizabeth has left! She insisted on arriving at the station an hour and a half early, and the train was twenty-five minutes late. If there's one thing that gets on my nerves it's waiting. Nevertheless, I feel today like a man who has been on a two months Riviera vacation.[. . .]Don't misunderstand me. She is a sweet, good and charming person. When I met her I was a much simpler, more muscle-bound man than I am now. She was an education, like going to a chiropractor. But I don't see how [I] could have stood another summer with her. I must say I am enjoying my bachelor life—in the past year I have made several trips by myself, so I already know the feeling. But this is so relaxing beyond belief. I feel like a bear rolled up in snow, holly leaves and honey waiting to drowse off into his winter hibernation.

O with you it will be rest, rest, rest forever—rest and hard writing. O I so want to marry you, and it won't be long; but now it's enough to be simply together.

Love and love and love,

Cal

E.'s version and mine is that *she* left me, that we both liked and still like each other, but that marriage wore us out. You say this too; if there's ever occasion.

240. To Ezra Pound

Dear Ezra:

["]Much conversation is as good as having a home." "To say many things is equal to having a home." ["]The primitive ages sang Venus: the last sings tumult." I have been meaning to write you for some time, and it is better that I gabble on, and write badly, than that I say nothing.

My mother died very suddenly in Rapallo on the 14th of February. I flew over and arrived an hour *after* her death. All my plane connections were late—the only move I made on time was catching a trolley in Milano—because it was raining and there were no taxis—to the Genova train. You didn't know my Mother, so there is no point in going elaborately into our relationship. We were very much alike—only for most of her life she had no idea where or who she was. Most of our lives were weighed on each other like stones, but at the end (during the last ten months or so[)] we were in a funny way, speaking different languages, very close—the same metabolism, the same humor, the same boldness, and slowness.

Well now to my reason for writing you—she died in the clinic of your friend Dr. Bacigalupo—the young man, not his father. So for a week or so—I was also in Siena picking up Mother's belongings—I was very close to you. And I think I know better now my old friend, the man under the masks, under the "agenda" much better than I did—say when I was in Washington last November or December.

Lately I have been reading over your Propertius—it and the *Pisan Cantos* seem to have more of the heart of you than anything else—or perhaps it is just my mood at the moment. I see the whole thing now for the first time as one poem. It's no more Propertius than Campion is Catullus; it's you—a much more graceful, airy character (Propertius was something of a Christian *poète maudit*, an iron, violent, paralyzed, and pierced and piercing beyond belief man.) But you are a man writing in the Occident of the First World War—humorous, skeptical, shocked that such a thing could happen, *quia pauper amavi*. But you do get the Roman feeling, like your friend Marlowe—less sinew, but much better organization.

Let me ramble on . . . The Italian poets I like best are Vergil and Dante—Dante knew what he was talking about, no one ever read Vergil better. Now Vergil, I am thinking for the moment of the Bucolics, really did see Empire etc. (along with knowing it was necessary) somewhat as you imagine Propertius did. I am sure he knew he was more than Augustus's equal as a man,

though less than his equal of course as head of the state. And God knows the land needed peace, so that the fields could breathe! Vergil everywhere by his indirections, his passions, for this one and that one, but above all for his friends, mostly people who either were, or were about to be, in the opposition—he shows he can stand up to Augustus as a man. He is saying "I feel things you could never imagine, but you are a man, and the country must have you etc." By the way you ought to see this. I can't think of anyone that would have disagreed with you more on Augustus than Mussolini. Well, Augustus didn't die hanged head downward like Saint Peter, with his mistress in Milano. That's a drawback; but Augustus was a vastly abler man of the same kind. So our old friend Ford—he was old and I was young, when I knew him—would have said.

Now I want to end this letter by quoting a poem I did a little while ago on Ford, and which I have been meaning to send you for some time now.

FORD MADOX FORD

The lobbed ball plops, then dribbles to the cup.
A birdie, Fordie! But it nearly killed
The ministers. Lloyd George is holding up
The flag. He gabbles, "Hop-toad, hop-toad, hop-toad!
Hueffer has used a mashie on the green!
It's filthy art, Sir, filthy art."
You answered, "What is art to me and thee?
Will a blacksmith teach a midwife how to bear?"
Always the English teacher! What is art?
New thresholds, new anatomies? Or was
It war, the sport of kings, the your *Good Soldier,*
The first French novel in the language, taught
Those Georgian Whig magnificoes at Oxford,
At Oxford decimated on the Somme?
Ford, mustard gassed and buried seven miles
Behind the lines at Nancy or Belleau Wood,
And five times blackballed for promotion: you
Emerged, a Jonah—O divorced, divorced
From the whale-fat of post-war London. Boomed,
Cut, plucked, and booted! You had learned your art.
Sandman! Your face[,] a childish *O.* The sun
Is pernod-yellow, and it gilds the heirs
Of all the ages there on Washington

and Stuyvesant, your Lilliputian squares—
Here writing turned your pockets inside out.
But Master, mammoth mumbler, tell me why
The bales of your left-over novels buy
Less than a bandage for your gouty foot.
Wheel-horse, O unforgetting elephant,
I hear you huffing at your old Brevoort,
Timon and Falstaff, while you heap the board
For publishers. Fiction! I'm selling short
Your lies that made the great your equals. Ford,
You were a kind man, and you died in want.

Not your kind of poem, or meter, but it's real and been on my mind to write
for some fifteen years.

Please excuse this disorderly letter—I've had a hell of a lot of business on
my hands lately, and little leisure to sit down and contemplate till things were
done exactly right. I think we both love Italia. Now vale, and love to you and
Dorothy, till I see you, as I hope to, toward the end of May,

Affectionately,
Cal

241. *To Blair Clark*

Sunday, March 21th [1954]

Dear Blair—

I'd better start off with the *coup de foudre*, as Merrill Moore would say.
(You ought to have heard him struggling with various incorrect forms of this
expression the last time I saw him, even spelling them out on an envelope, and
explaining to me that *coup* meant lightning. Poor man, he was so abashed and
for once wordless about Mother's death!) Elizabeth and I are separating.
You'll hear from her, and may have already; but my self-respect demands that
I write too. But we don't have two camps and two versions. I'm not going to
plumb the causes; briefly, we were ~~exhausted~~ worn thin by each other. We are
on perfectly good terms and E. is now in New York at the Algonquin looking
for a comfortable apartment.

Now for the moment *basta*! You can of course make your guesses (I'd love
to hear Jean's). If I have more to say, I'll tell you. I know I have no need to

urge you and Holly to go on being friendly with Elizabeth—nor even with me. I suppose we had both reached the limit of our metabolism—E. more than I, but both had.

I am back in my public lecture groove. We should confer on this subject. I have found a line of talking in anecdotes that both my Cincinnati audience and I can follow. I don't write my speeches out as Stephen did; but I say nothing that I am ashamed of. There are few human *coups de foudre* in Cincinnati; on the other hand, they make the pleasantest little community that I have struck outside of Amsterdam. People couldn't be kinder or more informal.

Now for politics . . . Wasn't Nixon's speech the most servile mush you ever heard. I was amazed by Stevenson, the first long speech of his I've heard on the radio. You really learn from him. This sounds patronizing, but how rare it is for a political man to do this—even Roosevelt seldom did this, at least to my mind. I thought your boss, Murrow, was good, but rather over-reaching himself—who cares if that fine voice is on committees with the late John Dewey and the great of the world. Still he is about our best radio man. Except for you, but you are so hard to hear at eight in the morning.

I've been reading a lot of Henry Adams lately. Our greatest man maybe, certainly the greatest New Englander. Not as a writer; James and Melville are more professional. Emerson is more massive as a thinker (though much less to the point for me). For Emerson not only spoke America's mind; he emerged like a whale adding something that wasn't there, and never would have been if Emerson had never lived. I sound like an English teacher—well, I am one. Nor can Adams be compared with Lincoln and Jefferson as a statesman—he never was in a position of responsibility. But as an all around man, no one touches Adams. He's wonderful, by the way on his and our manic-depressive New England character. I've been reading the letters, the life of George Cabot Lodge, the *Education*. What a game-cock. He's so much more Boston than I am—like Frank, like the Englishman on the boat.[. . .]But in this way Adams was more mature at twenty than I am at thirty-seven and wrote better prose—read his letters to his brother, Charles Francis[,] written from Germany and Washington and London. All this is to draw from you the facts about Elizabeth Cameron. Adams was fifty-two about when their correspondence began (just after Marian Adams' death—there's no connection there I am sure, Adams was hit beyond speech or belief by her suicide) and E. Cameron was about thirty-two. Nothing in the letters indicates anything, except that she was one [of] the about ten people in the world that Adams treated as his human and intellectual equal.

But I can't run on like this any longer. You are a fine man and my dear friend. Hope I'll see both of you this summer. As far as I know, I still plan to move into my Duxbury house. Mother's death (to mention the material, as she would herself) has about doubled my income and given some fifty thousand dollars in cash. All very handy at this point. Most of her estate is in another of those State Street Trust Co. trusts.

My love to you and Holly,
 Cal

242. *To Flannery O'Connor*

Wednesday, March 24th, [1954]

Dear Flannery:

I'd better give you my news. Elizabeth and I have separated. The event has been brewing for years, and we are both better off and still good friends. I am not sure you won't want me to dilate on this subject. I am not, however, rejoining the flock. I'm sure I do more good outside, at least for myself. Henry Adams called himself a conservative, Catholic anarchist; I would take this for myself, only adding agnostic. I don't think my prayers would cut much ice for you, so I omit them.

However, you have my good wishes. I have been hearing many fine things said about you. Jim Powers who was staying with me a month ago is wild about your novel and stories. I said, "*Wise Blood* is even better than Taylor's *Woman of Means*." A real compliment: you know how highly I think of Peter Taylor, a much wiser and bigger writer potentially than you or I, my Dear. And he's getting better all the time. Caroline, according to Robert says you have the best ear since James, or was it Homer she meant? One thistle, however, to throw among your bouquets—Bowden Broadwater says, "I still can't read Flannel Mouth." He went to work during Christmas vacation at Macy's packing cartons (after Mary had supported him for ten years). Each night coming home weary and worthy, he had a nervous breakdown.

What the hell do I care about your damned poultry? Even if they are all geese, even if one is named Claire Booth Luce Goose. I don't think she should breed even god-children. Allen, by the way, says she is a "remarkable woman." She's also pretty, which your goose isn't. She's also a goose, which your goose is. I sound like Charles Lamb.

Flannery, I love you very much (this isn't a proposal; I have other eggs to fry) and think you can write English, as Omar Pound would say. Sometime let

me tell you about Pound's ménage at Rapallo. His Doctor, a very good and conventional one (Ezra's, not Omar's) was my Mother's.

Love,
Cal

243. To Ezra Pound

Thursday, March 25th [1954]

Dear Ezra—

Thanks for your comments on my Ford[—]Hardy & Browning are good company; I did get the guy into it; I loved Ford, though he would hardly speak to me half the time, because (God Damn it!) he thought I would write undignified gossip about him in his old age, and (on the strength of that, I suppose[)]) become president of Harvard. You speak well of him; there was a great heart (the greatest perhaps I have known) in his fat. Not a good novelist? Yes; most of the time; but *The Good Soldier* couldn't be better—it's part of my knowledge, my life.

Why cry like a baby about reading the Bucolics? Your Latin is a hell of a lot better than mine, and even I could tumble through seven of them in one evening while waiting for sleep. By the way, I think Latin ought to be read like Italian i.e. with all the so-called illisions sounded, and with the accents running strongly counterpoint the quantities. But I still hold to the German pronunciation I was taught in school, except for V which I sound as V, not W.

What else? Get one of your visitors to copy out my Ford in triplicate. I'm a working man—till June. O try and wangle me a free copy of *The Classic Anthology* from Harvard; I am getting a divorce from my wife and can't afford to pay for anything I can get for free. Don't you admire the casual way I introduced this all-important item to me. I am going to marry an Italian girl—have been waiting half-dead, Ezra, now for two years. Don't go running about whispering to ANYone, or you'll get me into legal difficulties. Not with my wife, who has been grand, but in the other world i.e. Italy.

What do you make of R. Fitzgerald's *Odyssey*—slight and charming compared with Homer, of course, but the best we have for a complete translation—rather Irish early Yeats and Synge, I think.

Basta! Look forward and send my love to you and Dorothy—Au plaisir de vous revoir, aussi.

Cal

Caligula (how I hate what I know of the original, poor mad boy pushed to the head of the state.)

P.S. My Ford poem is going to Spender's *Encounter* (April). You'll curse me for that but Spender's a friend and the English may just possibly see it there. My devoted Principessa Caetani turned it down—after begging me for five years for anything, anything . . .

244. *To Giovanna Madonia*

Friday, March 26th [1954]

Animula Blandula (or however it goes) Giovanna—

I am reading Juvenal and Ovid's De Amatoria to take my mind off my students' poems—I think I told you they write about letting dinner burn while they dream of writing lousy poems. Now I must return to you. All that matters now is that we get together quickly—my barber says that in ten years I'll have a bald spot on the back of my head—carpite florem. Let's meet at least by June. We can honey-moon any where—England, France, Austria, Palestine, Greece—except behind the iron curtain. Child, I trust I'll turn your head once you can touch and see me. Vati parete perito!

"Tre mesi!" Surely, you are heavy-footed. I am having a lawyer friend of mine here look up the question of visas. Still, there's a lot to be said for our starting in Europe—only, if you were here tomorrow, it would be late for my desires. Are you sure your silly Sicilian head can handle such things as negotiating for a visa. Remember what Professor Babbitt said about your abstract musical knowledge—what's the use of having spent thousands of hours hearing the best singers in the world, if you can't turn it all into something that sounds like Russell's mathematical logic? It's funny how none of our American music, except for negro jazz, seems to make a splash in Europe! Poor Babbitt, if he had only had American poetry to teach you might have fallen in love with him instead of me—he already has *his* bald spot and is a full professor at Princeton!

"Lettere seguono." But they haven't yet. Damn the air planes! I know you are doing your best. A good day yesterday: listened to the Cincinnati symphony rehearse Prokofiev's second piano concerto—the rehearsals are vastly more fun than the full-dress performances—unlike you and me, Thor Johnson, Cincinnati's conductor, doesn't know how to wear a "black tie." Then an

evening spent reading Rilke with a German professor, and listening to a recording of Schubert's last Quintet. I live the life of Riley, and sleep and eat like a bear.

Dear heart, mia Venus, O Magna Mater, puella: I love, you, I love you, I love you. Also I want to get you to work housekeeping, so I can have the leisure to write love poems to you.

Il tuo Cal

IL tuo Cal

245. To Giovanna Madonia

[Greensboro, N.C., March 27?, 1954]

My Giovanna—

A strange day: I have just been with the Jarrells to Randall's very fancy sports-wear store and bought before I knew it $100 worth of colorful new clothes. A wonderful green vest that looks like a neck-tie. All to shine before you!

Dearest, your Italian letter is all about me and inside me; I can think of nothing else. It's as though everything I knew about you were now doubled, and refined and made wonderful beyond possibility. You are the best woman in the world. I want to be worthy. I want to kneel and hold you.

I have thought now for two nights on certain points. Famiglia. I will do anything I can to honor and love them—to be honored and loved by them. But I think the real point is this—I don't want you to become an Americanized Italian, nor I an Italianized American. We must each keep our roots, our languages, our personalities. We are (if I may use this theological figure) one substance, two persons—talking to each other in our separate languages, our separate voices, forever understanding and loving each other more and more, forever and forever. I don't think we differ on anything—it's only that we ~~are forever~~ keep understanding each other better.

I am sure the music can be arranged. I don't want you to stop—it is part of your life and won't interfere with your giving yourself entirely to me.

For some reason, after your letter, I feel so utterly with you, that I can hardly write at all tonight. I am not here in this bedroom typing on my friend's slow type-writer, but somewhere where there is no space, somewhere there is only you and I. I am a shadow lost in your light.

No, I plan to fly from Cincinnati on the night of the 9th of April; I'll be in

Nice by the night of the tenth or the morning of the eleventh. I think we might take rooms, or better one room in Cannes, (it's such a charming town with yachts etc.[)] We could then have six days together, and I would then fly back here in time to make my first after Easter vacation class. The cost will be no hardship to me at all. I can think of nothing but being with you—as you can see, this is a dull letter in comparison with your beautiful one—perhaps it's the strange house, perhaps it's talking all day to my friends and their children, perhaps it's buying those new clothes—Monday I'll write again like a writer, but now I am only il tuo, your friend who waits only for you. It seems so close now, and nothing else exists.

 Goodnight,
 Cal

YOU HAVE SAVED MY LIFE.

246. *To Flannery O'Connor*

[March 29? 1954]

Dear Flannery:

 We *do* speak the same language—in spite of your Georgia accent. Only— like Ezra—I'm not so quick on my feet as the young.

 Thanks,
 Cal

P.S. I've just been visiting Randall Jarrell in Greensboro—he only gets half your jokes.

247. *To Katherine Chapin Biddle*

2901 Clifton Ave.
Cincinnati, Ohio
Tuesday, March 30th [1954]

Dear Mrs. Biddle:

 Thank you for your very kind, slow-paced and human letter. Yes, it is very strange and autumnal realizing that I am my own elder generation—like retiring from politics, I suppose, but more fun.

I wish at the moment that I had Francis's training. Elizabeth and I are getting a divorce—we are quite chatty and cozy about it, and there is no bitterness. I am getting married again, to an Italian girl whom I have known for some two years. She too is getting a divorce from a husband who is *not* d'accordo, which makes a hell of a mare's-nest in Italian law—a reform of the Italian legal code should, by the way, have been part of the peace treaty. What's the per centage in an unconditional surrender, if you can't at least do that. I protest as an American citizen! (Apparently, I *am* one again, for I no longer am refused pass-ports.)

I don't think I am entirely [on] good terms with your Sister (from her side) for she refused one of my poems—a good one—and I told her gently that I am a professional poet and can really judge the quality of my produce better than she. Gosh, I haven't had a poem sent back to me for some ten years—I was beginning to take this as one of the gifts of age—like gray hairs and the Winslow bald spot.

I have told most people about my divorce, but not Harriet. I am not upset, but am afraid she will be. Poor Dear; she's had so much, so much.

Yours affectionately,

Robert Lowell

P.S. I say "Francis" so you'll know whom I mean; but really I am very conservative on these matters—too much so.

248. To Ezra Pound

Tuesday, March 30th [1954]

Uncle Ezra—

Pardon this spate of letters, but for the moment you speak my language, and there's no telling how long that may continue. Yes, in spite of your Idaho humor, which is hardly the Tuscan of Ovid. Not reading Vergil is your funeral, not his or mine. Imagine you thinking poor Mr. Dryden's translation had anything to *do* with the original! Sometimes I think you were born in Sioux City instead of Venezia.

Iambics—yes, you are partly right; but a man must sweat with his meters, if he is ever going to be a fabbro, and not just a prophet. Thirty-seven years has been none too long for me. You've got a point, but I knew that in my cradle—you must have told me.

I can push my own Jambics where I want to—you can scratch your own back with your own. i.e. jambics.

Here's a new poem—no iambics—see what your cigar-store wooden Italian solid Kansas humor can do with it. Every syllable is meant to be there.

Con amore,

Cal

ADOLF HITLER VON LINZ
(SIEGFRIED)

Hitler Adolphus? Shall I weigh him?
Expende Hannibalem: quot libras in Duce summo
Invenies? Crepat ingens Sejanus;
The lungs of Luther burn. You might say
He laid his cards on the table face-up, and called the hands.
Short suits, short suits: a ten year Marathon talked
For ten years talking the State on his talking tongue
To plum-pudding. For what?
For six million Jews?
The salt of the earth has burned like flax
To dirt in the craw of the lime-pits of Auschwitz.
Ach, das schrecklichste UnMensch in dieser unmenschlicher Welt!
Vielleicht. Vielleicht? Das schrecklichste!
He was. You were. *Du! Du!* Believing in Germany
Enough to break the Prussian spine,
Or the stiff neck of Europe?
Chiropractor, I went to jail
In my own country to save those German cities
You smashed like racks of clay pigeons,
Gyring through colored glass balls on Christmas trees
And Manchesters of Chicago Gothic—broken windows!
And my gorge stuck in my bowels,
When they sent me down the Hudson, through neat Connecticut,
Through an alchemist's autumn, and hand-cuffed to two two-bit
Puerto Ricans for Danbury, for my place of correction.
You nothing, whom we might have called Lucifer,
If only you'd lasted, *un poco—*
Una cosa piccola, animula blandula, believing in Italy,
Believing in Mussolini; like no other Italian,
Like no other German; no, not the Duce

Dragged for four hours by his bootstraps
down the Uffizi *a Firenze*
By a thick Linz dumkopf cracked on the paint of Florence,
By a Barbarus Induperator, a German tourist,
Federigo Secondo, Manfredi, Winkelman,
By Freud!
Six million . . . Ma Basta, un poco . . .
May the bastard rest in peace,
May the burnt-out dust rest.

249. *To Giovanna Madonia*

<div align="right">

Thursday, April Fool's Day,
[April 1, 1954]

</div>

La mia Siciliana, sopratutto in amore—

I am in my big library study in my shirt-sleeves and encircled by a man's disorder of books—livres de toutes sortes—mostly verse, in all languages. The coat of the suit I had on during our castello (reconstructed) walk, and Randall's soft scarlet sweater—it makes my sober Scotch suit quite Arabic—are on a chair angled off my right arm—in riposo.[. . .]

Yesterday, I was a Spaniard, or a modern German, or one of my Calvinist New England forebears. For two days, I had been infusing and fil[l]ing a poem of some seventy-five lines on Hitler—a poem I had been intending to accomplish now for some eleven years—ever since the day in September of 1943 about the time of Badoglio's surrender—when I was driven with two small scarcely English-speaking Puerto Ricans to a federal jail in Connecticut, for protesting against saturation-bombing and unconditional surrender—a democracy might at least be able to name conditions—then we might have the Italian divorce laws Americanized. C'est dommage!

I spent last night drinking sherry and reading Luis de Góngora aloud—a thunder bolt of a poet—like Pindar and De la Fontaine. However—I learned more about you in the process. Both you and Luciano—in different ways have a quite unItalian steeliness and swiftness to you. Reading some of the Romances of the young Góngora

"Dejadme llorar
orillas del mar"

I can quite imagine our nightly Milanese "conversazioni di ora in ora." I apologize for having been the cause. I leave your soul to Luciano, if I can only have your body "infinitamente."

"vaya a los Moros el cuerpo
y quede con vos el alma."

I think Luciano has behaved like a man—I wonder if I could have stood up against you this long? To do that took guts and cortesía. Now why can't he drop all claims on my life and let us get married!!!

"This is my dancing day" and soon our bridal day—all in scarlet like Sicilian Arabs. A week from the day after tomorrow I'll be flying over the Atlantic. If you can't come to Nice, I'll come to Milan. Have no fear, Machiavelli to the contrary—it's only the *armed* prophets who are killed—who can hurt me or you if we drink double-rich malted milks and have a gift for talking?

Quedéme y olvidéme,
el rostro recliné sobre el amada,
cesó todo, y de jéme,
dejando mi cuidado
entre las azucenas olvidado
Madonía-Cal
Madonía-Cal

Another Giovanna photograph! But you haven't time to mail it really.

250. *To Elizabeth Hardwick*

[April 3, 1954]
(How do I know where you hid the Chelsea ware-house check!)
Dear Baby:

I guess you are right about week-end flying. Truly, in the past, it has made my ears ring! When you come back from the Virgins, I'll pick a steady. For you. I think we have the same one in mind. Guess who mine is? The Toddle needs T. Roosevelt's big stick or Eddie Vincent's (not mine!) Now drink beer, and don't "communicate" so much. "Much talk is . . ." But I've forgotten my Bible.

251. To Giovanna Madonia

Saturday, April 3rd, [1954]

Cara, Freude! Freude! How can I leave thee? We have, alas, already so many children, anche io! Love, Cal

I was going to cable the above, but realized that there was little chance of both the Italian and American offices getting the message right. Honey, I am never going to leave you after we meet next Sunday—you're on my hands now for keeps. Why do *all* American girls caste themselves as their husbands and their fathers' little daughters, little mothers? See my Mary Winslow poem, if you can get hold of a text. Because the men love it. I don't, thank God. That's how I discovered me, or maybe you discovered me. Isn't it a pillow to windward (i.e. a comfort) that neither of us is superior to the other, except in the way a man must be, and a woman must be.

I am off down town to buy more clothes so that when I arrive in Nice (I enjoyed the American pun in your cable Nice/nice) I won't look like say a carpenter or a house-painter, but like a Arab or a gypsy. By the way, can you walk. Some times one sees more that way than by car or plane, though I like all modes of motion. By the way anche, I'd rather be weighed down by you than with a lot of children. They do so impede the insatiable tourist. Well, what suits you, suits me.

I ~~may~~ will not write again, for I dislike the idea of having my letters knocking around La Voce del Padrone after you depart for France, the country for a recontre.

AH, CARA!!!!!!!!!!!

252. To Peter Taylor

[The Jewish Hospital]
Cincinnati, Ohio
[May 13, 1954]
5/13 ONE p.m.

Dear Peter:

Here's the certificate of title for Jack. I can't even remember anything you said the other day at the hospital. Your visit was shortly after "shock" treatment, a time the patient cannot remember—time of almost total amnesia.

I hope very much you *can* drive my car to New York. By the time you

arrive I'll be ready to drive it again. Excuse the graceless laconic style of this note. Two weeks from now when I see you all again I expect to be myself again.

Love to you both from us both,
Cal

253. *To Giovanna Madonia*

New York Hospital
525 E 68th St.
New York, N.Y.
June 2nd, [1954]

Dearest Giovanna:

Elizabeth tells me that she wrote you from Cincinnati. What she said *è vero ma* . . . you must not consider yourself in any way connected with my relapse—a slight one. Elizabeth visits me here Wednesdays, Sat. and Sundays—at times I feel rather like a character in one of Allen Tate's poems that ends I believe, "The wall-paper, imperishably old / Uncurls and flutters, it will never fall." I have given everyone a lot of trouble; now I am sweating my confusion out of my system. Please pardon me.

I am here by my own choice, and will leave by my own choice. Amo et amabo te / Scrive me.
Cal

P.S. Letters sent here are delivered and not read by the doctors. I hope you will write in Italian, for then your own voice is audible.

254. *To Giovanna Madonia*

[June 25, 1954]

My Dearest:

I am undergoing at the moment injections of chlorochromozene or something similar, with the result that each pen-stroke is like lifting fifty pounds. Your mere wire brings me unspeakable relief. I have always known by faith that our re-union and final union was only a matter of time—but oh to know you are not overcome by all this, and I say London sounds like a wonderful advance—

far better than Paris—I've been looking at pictures of salmon fishing in *Life* magazine, and my mind jumps at the idea of a Canadian honeymoon for us.

Dearest Giovanna: I am well and doing well medically. I've talked about you to the doctors at great length. And Dr. Renny commented that this time my marriage should be one that would last fifty years.

I am mentally all there, but weary, weary, weary—Oh just for the moment. So will you go on taking charge of how we must act. You're my boss, for the time being.

Love,
 Cal

P.S. Don't you love England! But since your London cable gives no address I sent this to your old one in Milan (I just today got it from Randall.) God bless you!

255. To Giovanna Madonia

July 7th [1954]

My Dearest Giovanna:—

This is going to be a short letter; but a hard one to write and hard to mail. I want to ask you your advice. I feel about you just as I did on our two walks in Salzburg, and sitting under the Sforza castle in Milan. You are everything! But I see more and more clearly that I will never be over my disturbance and back to my health and work again without Elizabeth. That is I've got to be (and above all now) *with* some one and living a life that I understand already and feel master of. Except for you, Elizabeth has always been a good wife, and one who understood my disease far better than I myself. On the whole, even in this, she hasn't been interfering.

Now, dearest, tell me what we should do. I am much better and have been moved down a floor.

If all goes well, I should be out in a month or a month and a half.

Love,
 Cal

P.S. Please write back right away. Your letters won't be read by anyone except me. I wish to God I could see you! Hope Spain was fun.

256. To Giovanna Madonia

My Dearest, Darling Giovanna:

My last letter was too short, inadequate and far from clear. Let me expand on it. First on my relationship with Elizabeth, then on what is nearer *us*.

Elizabeth and I have an apartment here in New York. The way for me to convalesce is this. First I visit the apartment on week-end afternoons, then I spend week-ends there, then perhaps I'll spend days there working; then finally I'll live there and come back here or to a doctor the clinic recommends for therapy. None of this will take long except the last. I've really been quite sick and this time I want to get to the bottom of it all. Now Elizabeth has really been very faithful and good about everything. She wants very much to stay married to me. I need her knowledge of me and encouragement to get well. I think I must act in good faith and keep married to Elizabeth, for the time being, perhaps forever. She loves me, I love her.

Now you are the great moment, the great passion of my life. Away from you I dry up like grass. What I'd like you to do (I know I have no rights, but this is what I pray for) is to stick by me through this, and if you can for always. Is there any chance of your company's sending you here (New York) or to America? At worst you can still I hope make the trip in October with Callas. I think I have enough money to pay for everything; but it would be better from almost every point of view: morals, passport, occupation I should think for you to be employed. On this point I feel like your father, for the moment. But by the time I'm out of here I will have money.

I don't have to re-read my letter to realize th[at] my 2nd and 3rd paragraphs seem wildly contradictory. Perhaps they are. But can't help feeling that with patience and love all will work out. There must be some sort of *modus vivendi* for all *3* of us. A lot may and must clarify when we are together again. Please answer and advise.

All my love,
Cal

P.S. I want you in every way spiritually (among other things this means forever) and physically. I know I can't ask any thing and will be content (or fairly so) if you'll just let me hold your hand, sit at your feet, and stare. Write about this, and write about Paris and Barcelona, and Lorca. We have such worlds to talk over.

257. To Blair Clark

<div style="text-align: right">August 6th [1954]</div>

Dear Blair—

I've been out of my *excitement* for over a month, I think, now, and am in good spirits, though I don't feel any rush of eloquence to talk about the past. It's like recovering from some physical injury, such as a broken leg or jaundice, yet there's no disclaiming these outbursts—they are part of my character—me at moments; hence the protracted stay here, hence the continued therapy.

From your letter I can see that our plans already have your enthusiastic O.K. We'll go to Boston about the middle of September and take an apartment—for the next two years I will be go[ing] to a doctor, and even after that time I will probably go to some one every month or every two months. If I can get some equivalent of my part-time teaching at Iowa, I think we may stay in Boston and Duxbury more or less the rest of our lives. According to Paine-Whitney, I have made remarkable progress and the whole business is curable. It's also been imbecilic, inhuman, dangerous, embarrassing, and hell on Elizabeth. Now the world is beginning again for us.

Though at the clinic we live in a climate of radio and TV, it's quite difficult hearing you, because you collide with breakfast. But I've heard you several times, in fact just this morning. You are awesome, and still to my unattuned ear enormously unrecognizable. Your voice has that husky, clipped, lofty overseas urgency that reminds me of Murrow from London during the summer of 1940. I'm not being funny; the daily preparation must be terrific. I think of the agonies I've occasionally gone through with book reviews, but no one cares much if you are wayward and unobjective in a book review.

I wrote Giovanna early in July saying that I now saw that I was staying married to Elizabeth, however I wrapped my letters up in emotions (really felt at the time) and made them as soft as I could. I haven't had an answer, and don't quite see what I can write her at this point. The whole business was sincere enough, but a stupid pathological mirage, a magical orange grove in a nightmare. I feel like a son of a bitch. I wonder if you could find out without too much awkwardness without opening the old injuries what has become of her, and how she is. Don't take this as a demand. However I do know that I am responsible for whatever disturbances have happened in her life.

People have kept in touch with me much better than I have with them. I've had letters from my relatives, Iowa, Dick Howard, Holly. Tomorrow Elizabeth,

Jack Thompson and I are going trout-fishing on Long Island for the week-end—a fabulous place where you get half a mile of stocked stream for ten dollars, see stag, and I think wild boar.

Blair, a hundred thanks for the fatiguing help you gave us in March and April. We look forward to your return and to being with you all again.

Affectionately,

Cal

258. To John Berryman

33 Commonwealth Ave.
Boston, Mass.
October 6th, 1954

Dear John:

No, I'm a reformed character, more or less starting today, on writing letters. We've been hearing rumors for the last two weeks about your leaving Iowa, but nothing that gave much idea of the real inside. You got a lousy deal, and it looks as though the whole business was impossible from the start this fall. I was much luckier, not to have Paul, Marguerite or a landlord to mess with. You are too good a writer to fit their system, and too much of a scholar and professional teacher to find much in a stop-gap job. I can see that Minnesota is a hundred times better, and am awfully glad all has ended serenely. Somehow just having the Tates to gossip with puts one in a steadier and higher world.

We've been moving into two places at once, and discover that we are such nomads that everything has to be learned from scratch. You wire a lamp and the disassembled parts are worse than any Chinese puzzle; you paint a floor and find you've sealed off your clothes for the day. I've also had my one police trouble—because I lost my Mass. driver's license in 1938 for drunken driving, I have to be investigated by a Mr. Hayton from station 16. Mr. Hayton doesn't exist, but has always just left whenever you call. Each step in the process takes a month. We have a huge apartment, bigger than our house[,] on Commonwealth Ave. and Elizabeth has done miracles with it and everything else.

I've just started messing around with my autobiographical monster. Prose is hell. I want to change every two words, but while I toy with revisions, the subject stinks like a dead whale and lies in the mud of the mind's bottom. I marvel already at your story.

We live around the corner from the Boston Public Library and borrow records by the arm-load. We are doing the Schubert lieder with text-books, scores and conversation.

Elizabeth is finally through her settling tasks and has started a story. We are getting very Bostonian and pretend to live in an armor of regularity—there's an hour for this and half an hour for that. I hope to take a daily nine o'clock stroll that people can set their watches by.

Give our affectionate respects to the Tates. Elizabeth sends her love.

Affectionately,

Cal

259. To Harriet Winslow

Sunday, Oct. 24th [1954]

Dear Cousin Harriet:

The Purcell arrived safely in Duxbury, and we have been scanning the score with eagerness and wonder. The former tenants of our apartment finally on the day before we moved in insisted on taking their piano—so I'm afraid our practice will have to be postponed.

This has been a very traditional Sunday—this morning we strolled down to King's Chapel (very white, sparsely attended and Unitarian) this afternoon I've been painting my halls with black enamel and puzzling at an old book [of] Daddy's which explains such matters also the advantages of an "Igloo" incinerator. From painting to portraits—I want very much to see the doubtful Jane Stuart Charlotte Stark owned by the soi-distant John Stark. Her face has a trembling, inquiring firmness that stays with me. I'm probably the last person to be able to qualify as a judge of the price—anyone selling anything immediately wins me and I jump from under to over-evaluation in the twinkling of an eye. I hope to drive to Dunbarton later in the year and look forward to gazing.

Seeing you recently in Boston meant worlds to me, and I was glad you and Elizabeth could really talk together. You are a dear and constant friend. At last we are just about settled in both our abodes and can return to writing. Next Wednesday I'm going to Columbia to attend a symposium called rather grandly "the Unity of Knowledge." I am bracing myself to insist that poetry really is a form of rational thought—despite your doubts.

Last night we talked to some people who told us Quebec is the most beautiful city in North America; thereupon in our minds we moved it bodily to

Castine, where we hope it will rest contented till our August visit. But before I get any deeper whimsy let me say goodbye for the moment.

Very affectionately,

Bobby

260. To Elizabeth Bishop

Sunday, November 14, [1954]

My Dearest Elizabeth:

So glad your letter to Lizzie came yesterday, for I have been meaning to write you ever since your wonderful photograph arrived, and somehow, somehow . . . A lot of water has gone under the mill-wheel, since we were last writing almost a year ago now, I have been sick again, and somehow even with you I shrink both from mentioning and not mentioning. These things come on with a gruesome, vulgar, blasting surge of "enthusiasm," one becomes a kind of man-aping balloon in a parade—then you subside and eat bitter coffee-grounds of dullness, guilt etc. Well, your letter moved our hearts. Please don't worry anymore all the pieces have been picked up, and (but I see I have already used at least five discordant metaphors) life has licked up.

I wish you could see our sunny-side of Commonwealth Ave. apartment. We are three twenty foot flights up and look on two decaying churches and Boston's two hugest and most imperial life-insurance buildings. We have great rooms, look down on society, see at least one parade a month, and can't get the former tenant out of our heads—she had made her own world here, for twenty-six years she lived buried in ice-packs, syphons, trash, mammoth rose-wall-paper, signs of the zodiac and twenty-six birds, half of them uncaged. We are very, very tame in comparison. We've been moving into here *and* Duxbury for the past month and a half. Our nomadic heads are in a whirl, we don't know ourselves. Have you ever tried picking up your roots?

I think Elizabeth's *Simple Truth* is much the biggest and brightest thing she has ever written—it seems so simple, one forgets that it's a wonderful invention—I don't think any other murder trial has been its audience. There have been quite a lot of good letters and blurbs about it already. Yours is the best.

I don't have too much news. I've been reading Dickens, getting records[,] Berg, Schubert, Glück, not old New England lore from the Public Library, getting a Mass. driver's license (my old one was revoked after my accident with Jean in 1937 and that means I have to be investigated, gently but at a snail's pace) and trying to write prose—a hell of a job, it starts naked[,] ends as fake velvet.

Do write and tell us about your trip to Portugal much more about Brazil, very much about you. We send our love,

Cal

261. To Ezra and Dorothy Pound

POSTCARD: Etching of Trinity Church and Copley Square, Boston

[n.d. late 1954]

Dear Ezra & Dorothy:

Here is more or less our view in Boston—an Episcopalian church in the shadow of a life insurance palace. I don't suppose there's any symbolic meaning. We will be in Washington between the 4th and 5th of January and hope to see you both. Please forget the personal non-sense I wrote you last spring. I am very eager for you to meet Elizabeth.

Affectionately and wishing you a merry Christmas,

Cal

262. To Peter and Eleanor Ross Taylor

February 18, 1955

Dear Peter and Eleanor:

A thousand congratulations on the boy, the "new one" as I started to say to disguise my admiration in casualness.[. . .]

I hope the brushes arrive safely. They have a short history: they were my Father's, then mine, and now Peter Ross's. The bristles are black as a wild boor's in appearance, but sparse and giving when applied. On my own hair, their action has been perplexed, like clearing a swamp with a toy-lawn mower, yet they have always left behind them what I might call the *sincere ravages of effort*; if Peter Ross brushes before and after every meal and whenever he has a minute to spare, he [will] have no trouble. Enough of these flights.

The cautious Giroux says Peter's play is his masterpiece and can be produced—nothing like it since Ibsen and Chekhov. Wish we could see a copy. On the whole friendly and on the whole uninspired reviews of Elizabeth's *Simple Truth* are coming in—we are awfully tired of hear[ing] the phrase "novel of ideas," and the "irony of Miss Hardwick's title."

Life isn't simple either, I've just been trying to fit a forty-two and one eighth inch shade into a forty-one and seven eighths inch window frame, and

now I am off to see a Doctor Winslow (sic) about a part time teaching job at Boston University. We will go back to Iowa next February, but the heart of man is never quiet and now that I'm idle, I burn for duties. I'm also turning out yards of prose, and excel in two styles. A) the magical detail, that at first you mistake for a misprint, then cherish but can't explain, and B) the plain, bare as a piece of unpainted wood statement, that all writers must fall back on, "On the morning of August 24th 1927, a boy of seven was counting the four alcohol spirit lamps that heated the long copper warming-plate between two windows forty-two and one eighth inches apart.["]

Now congratulations and God bless you all, as I start off for Dr. Winslow. I do hope all is serene and idle for Eleanor.

love,

Cal[. . .]

263. To Babette Deutsch

Thursday February 24th, 1955

Dear Babette Deutsch:

My apologies for my "silence." Recently I did some readings for Professor Packard at Harvard, and found I had a definite block about talking to a disk—talking, not reading, for it's easy enough to declaim verses into nowhere.

I wish the poems could stand by themselves. "Colloquy," I think is the only poem that came to me Wordsworthian-wise—walking. I hadn't written a line for a year, and had just come home one evening from mopping floors as a conscientious objector. I was strolling about and staring at the low-tide litter, and wishing. That the War were over, and that the event in the last stanza would lift me out of my pails of dirty water. Then the lyrical outline came. In "Mr. Edwards" I was trying to get a little prose piece and two Edwards' sermons into Donne's St. Lucy stanza. I thought it was odd that Edwards liked real spiders as a boy and figure-of-speech spiders as a preacher. There were several years when he seriously thought through morbidity that he was the worst man who ever lived; but he was really a modest, rational, mystical sort of man—not all the terror and brimstone one I picture. "The Dead in Europe" has somewhat the same theme as *Colloquy* i.e. life coming out of St. Stephen's stoning or the bombing of Europe. The "Dead" and "Colloquy" were written about the same time; the *Dead*, I think, exaggerates and pushes further the other's rhythms—not too well, perhaps. The "Exile" is the same

story written a year later, but I drew on Mann's "Tonio Kröger" and tried to make the scene more objective—flowers coming out of stone; I put great store on the uncertainties of the last line. I don't think I have much to say now about the "Graveyard" except that it started as a translation of a Corbière poem on Paris night life that was a little like the litter in my "Colloquy." Then I grew drunker and drunker with the sea. I put all my chips on rhythm, more than I have ever done since.

No revisions; the "new look" I'm afraid is only a new reading voice, and new poems *in posse*.

Many thanks for your letter, prods and patience. Yours truly,
Robert Lowell

264. To Peter Taylor

April 11, 1955

Dear Peter:

At first I was, how shall I put it, *surprised and hurt*—that's how the history of St. Mark's School speaks of my Great Grandfather's novel, in which it was noted with surprise that Dr. Lowell's gentle humor had used members of the faculty as characters. If you'd used one of my poems instead of one of yours, I think I would have sued. So I felt after reading; but since then I've [had] so many compliments—nothing I've ever written myself has ever gotten me such attention . . . Well, I stand off, hat in hand, and thank you with grudging bewildered incomprehension. But were we really quite such monsters? Seriously, though[,] the whole thing fascinates me—I've been trying to do the same sort of thing with scenes from my childhood with my Grandfather, Old Aunt Sarah[,] Cousin Belle etc. I want to invent and forget a lot, but at the same time have the historian's wonderful advantage—the reader must always be forced to say, "This is tops, but even if it weren't it's true." I think you've done the trick.

Since starting this letter, we have had a long unannounced visit from your friend Pugatch—an able fellow and calming down, but even on his own account, he rather makes one's heart go out for Chalmers. He said your Pruit (?) was true to life. Later that day an old Harvard acquaintance accused me of writing under a pseudonym.

Spring is with us. I am trying [to] tell an oak from an ash. We are reading about planting hardy annuals. And our car, shark gray and robin's egg blue, looks like a tulip with chemicals injected in it.

Red has some very touching poems on his child in *PR*. I'm so sorry Eleanor had a hard time, and trust she "improves."

Love from us both,

Cal

265. To Ezra Pound

April 17th, 1955

Dear Ezra:

Yes, one of S's pictures would give us brightness. If she can send it to us C.O.D. on a loan, I will feel very much honored. I wish you would tell me more about the artist—as people are fond of saying in the Gospels, "How can a man live without selling?" Morons sell pencils, millionaires are paid a silver dollar for their directors' meetings. Let me know if we can do anything?

We have been playing with the idea of driving South, and then putting it off. This has been a funny, eye-opening winter i.e. living in the Boston I left when I was seventeen, full of passion and without words. I suppose all young men get up the nerve to start moving by wrapping themselves like mummies from nose to toe in colored cloths, veils, dreams etc. After a while shedding one's costume, one's fancy dress, is like being flayed. I've just been doing a little piece on *Why I live in Boston*. I made it impersonal and said nothing about what I was looking for here—the pain and jolt of seeing things as they are.

Pardon this rambling. I am looking out my window at a church and two life insurance buildings. It's an icy spring day. Magnolia blossoms are freezing as they decay. It was a joy seeing you and Dorothy last January. You've lost none of your thunder and generosity.

Affectionately,

Cal

266. To Elizabeth Bishop

[Surplus Street,] Duxbury, Mass.
July 16th, [1955]

Dear Elizabeth:

No, your two earlier letters never arrived, but I've just read your last again, and feel as though it were many letters, and almost as though you were here in the house talking to us. I'm enclosing some photos of us and also one of [a]

house here that we looked at and imagined buying—it's bigger than Longfellow's house and would have been quite beyond us to keep up, but for a week we dreamed of living in it, and persuading you to stay with us permanently.

E. is learning to drive too—only it turns out she already knows, because once a long time ago she was out with a suitor who passed out, and then E., never having driven drove home twenty miles and through traffic.

Random notes:—The doll is 18th century (?) Dutch and came from an antique store on Charles St. Her best angle is from the back, but she looked wonderfully alien and taking last January, so I bought her though she wasn't at all what I had intended. The customs in Boston were also quite confusing. Brazil seems to have a changing, and half-concealed rate.

Saw Randall who is living further down the Cape at Dennis—brown, knotted, and with a great black beard with a white splash in the center. He blows hot and cold on one, and both moods are disturbing. Now he is chilly, and I think of him as a fencer who has defeated and scarred all his opponents so that the sport has come to be almost abandoned, and Randall stands leaning on his foil, one shoulder a little lower than the other, unchallenged, invulnerable, deadly, salt marsh and deserted tennis court stretching below him. Really though, he is as "good as ever,["] and is writing a long review of you for the fall *Yale Review*.

I'm just back from a Harvard Summer School Symposium on drama. An Englishman wrote a three hundred page play in heroic blank verse on a king of Portugal who died fighting in Morocco. Some one told MacLeish that Eliot and Robert Speaight had said that this was the best play in English since *Murder in the Cathedral*. So sight unseen the author was brought from England, his play, cut to a fifth was staged without costumes or motion, and a panel made up of myself, Wilbur, MacLeish, Lillian Hellman, and Francis Fergusson set to talk about it. But Eliot had only said that he didn't suppose the play could be staged. The action was all but incomprehensible because the critics had no text, and cut and costumeless, it hardly made sense to the author. And the author! (in a few minutes he is about to arrive here for a day's visit). Bald, red-faced, spectacled, long amber hair curling down his neck, stuttering, humorous, flattering, modest, and knowing an immense play by heart down to the last and least word. At one point during the symposium, he was asked to give a brief pithy synopsis of his play, he talked for three quarters of an hour, scene by scene, with each promising to accelerate—then suddenly as he was within seconds of his climax in which the hero is hanged, MacLeish, who wasn't following, stopped everything with a flowery little speech praising the usefulness of the synopsis and asking for questions.

(Two weeks later and after your letter.) I guess my not writing has no particular meaning, just my old habit of putting off *all* letters and then brooding about it. This has been a house-choosing summer—our set-up: an apartment in Boston and a house here hasn't seemed workable, but rather too expensive, too cramped, too cumbersome, too impermanent, too much trouble. So we've been through every sort of alternative, a larger house in the country, England, and even Iowa. Each choice carries a whole way of life with it, and we have lived through them all. Our income is now sufficient for me to live quite comfortably without earning anything at all. But I don't feel much tempted that way. So I have been rocking this way then that—each ~~pull~~ push gentle at first, a cat tap, but later strong. Nettled, irresolute, now wanting to be with people now wanting to be alone, and so the summer has passed. We have just—a week ago—bought a house in Boston; it is on Marlborough St. 239, and only [a] block from where I grew up. It's gray stone, rather Parisian, four floors, two windows to a floor, white, neat, dainty Italian fire-places, a lovely foyer, a sort of stream-lined Victorian.

There's a strong piece on art and old age in the summer *PR* by Gottfried Benn. By the time you are old you have broken with convention, broken with your models and heroes, and finally broken with yourself. Our time of life is apparently one of the breaking times. The thought of going back to Boston sometimes makes me feel like a flayed man, who stands quivering and shivering in his flesh, while holding out a hand for his old sheet of skin. Excuse this image, it comes from bathing suits on the line, our washing-machine which became overloaded and stopped, looking at pictures of Pollaiuolo, and the heat—it is almost a hundred in the shade today.

In a few days we are moving to Castine for a month to stay in a little house near my Cousin Harriet, then in late September we will be moving into Boston. We'll have a huge airy guest-room, and offer it to you indefinitely as lure to bring you to America this fall.

We had another much better day with Randall and Mary. He is like a knotted, brown old gladiator, and will be still more so when his Mercedes racer arrives. Elizabeth says he is much stranger than Dylan Thomas, and that when Randall turned up, Nature has never seen anything like him, and instantly broke his mould.

I think most people who are Christians find profession and practice something commonsensical, cow-like, customary. I'd like to take it that way. Doing much more seems extravagant. It doesn't seem possible to act, except for a few ritual motions, as though we really began to really believe. That God should really be Christ—that does seem strained, and so unlike our usual and sober-

est ways of seeing things as to be improper. Then often our belief, our creed, seems like some simplified abstraction only intelligible to people who can no longer use their senses, a way of going to a country by not going, but by staying at home and buying a book of maps. Then you tell other people who also stay at home looking at maps that they are not getting anywhere because they have the wrong directions. This is getting off the deep end. I don't think anyone has much kick against what the Christian would like to want, we can't help seeing the same objects and the same colors.

 Cal

P.S. Don't take my heat-wave joke too seriously.

267. To Elizabeth Bishop

<div style="text-align:center">POSTCARD</div>

<div style="text-align:right">[Castine, Maine]
August 24, 1955</div>

Dear Elizabeth:

 The world moves in circles: Stonington, the Eberharts, sea-fishing etc. Mighty proud of my doll, and think I am learning to like it—my Cousin Harriet saw it out of the corner of her eye for a split second when it arrived—her rejection of it was utter. We've been having a dim, cool, lazy, delightful time here—reading Cousin H.'s *who done its* and listening to Monteverdi records. How I wish you were with us!

 Love,
 Cal

268. To William Carlos Williams

<div style="text-align:right">December 2nd, 1955</div>

Dear Bill:

 I have wanted to thank you for your kindness in writing me a year and a half ago when I was in the sanitarium. Such letters are hard to write, hard to reply to sometimes. At least it was so then—it seemed indecent to voice the mood I was in, but trifling to assume any other. Well, all that is long past now, and your letter was a help.

 We've just bought a house in Boston a block from where I grew up. It's an

unimpassioned, darkish, bricky, Londonlike street, still the mirror of propri-
ety, but lately filling up with rooming houses and cramming schools—they
are for boys who were too stupid to go directly from high school to college.
They look it, and stand about far under my window from nine a.m. to one a.m.
But this is wrong, most of their time is spent in trying to park their cars, only
the ones who room directly across the street, and can consequently walk over,
I think, make a class. This is the first year since 1940 when I have spent two
successive autumns in the same city. We're fearfully relieved to be settled and
doubt if we will ever move. We might even become Boston worthies, if it
weren't for the worm of life in us.

I've read *Journey to Love* many times. You are pouring out, and I know I
shall be hearing your voice speaking the words to some inner ear in me, for as
long . . . for as long as I journey myself. So, thanks again. I expect to be in
New York with my wife on the sixth or seventh of January, and would like to
travel out to pay my respects to you and Flossie. Would the afternoon of Sun-
day the 6th do?

Affectionately yours,
Cal

269. To Elizabeth Bishop

December 29th, 1955
Dear Elizabeth:

I shall have to write more of the champagne than of the poems for the mo-
ment, because Christmas with its maelstrom of cards, ornaments, sweets, extra
cleanings, scattered wits etc. has hidden them completely, and I with my old
woman's memory trust myself with nothing factual. Well, a little. I like the
long one with Lota speculating on the Brazilian Indian with his varnished hat
and praying for her enormously. You seem to have a loose seemingly careless
style, very humorous, very "I am saying what amuses me and saying it with-
out breaking my back"; but of course I know all [the] fierce labors you really
go through. What I mean to say is that this last poem and your long wonderful
Nova Scotia story both give themselves, as though you weren't writing at all,
but just talking in a full noisy room, talking until suddenly everyone is quiet.
I like your short poem too very much and the two in the *New Yorker*, particu-
larly the second—more later, when I have the texts near me.

The fine, Brazilian S.S. Pierce champagne came at a good time. We gave a
little Christmas party for eight unmarried people—it had to be on Christmas

night when everyone was bursting at the seams and blue in the face with over-eating and new dieting resolutions. If it hadn't been for your champagne, costly, exotic, glorious with your name, and amazing everyone with the fact that anyone in Brazil could bring Boston's Pierce into action, (now for an anaphora) if it hadn't been for your champagne, we would never have gotten off the ground. There were bad moments. Two guests whom we had rather wickedly intended to throw on one another, defied us, and invited friends of their own, whom we had never met. At any moment one might look up and see each guest and each stranger off in a corner, musing sullenly, silently. I sound like notes for a Mary McCarthy novel. Have you read her last in which Mary (divorced and remarried) is seduced by Wilson (divorced and remarried) after a Wellfleet reading of Racine's *Bérénice*. In the last chapter Mary driving to Boston for an abortion is run into and killed by a red-headed Millay-like Cape poet driving on the wrong side of the road. Who can doubt that Mary really *lives* in her books. If she ever loses her mind, she'll never know which parts of her life she lived and which she wrote. She is somehow rather immense with-out her books ever being exactly good form or good imagination.

Last night I was reading Lord Acton's introduction to a series of lectures on modern history. He offered as a truism that needed no underlining or am-plification: "Historians, learn by writing, rather than by reading." This had never occurred to me. Don't you think we could mak e a fortu n e (my type-writer splutters and skips spaces with anger) by starting a sanitarium to cure victims of ceaseless reading. Across the alley in back of our house, there is a reducing school. No one eats anything; but pyramids of garbage pile up—so high I sometimes can't force my car through them. This is the food they have left untouched, and the odor of its corruption is like incense, for each betokens a triumph of the will. So it would be with the book-cure; think of all the wonderful-really-necessary-for-one's-occupation-and-peace-of-mind-books one could *not* read each day! At a Christmas lunch we met a sweet old lady who was going out of her mind second by second as we watched. The reason was that on this one day out of the whole 365 she was missing her television. *Channel two* was on and there she was eating turkey and flaming pudding. She had come to Boston from Milton in a taxi; after thirty minutes the taxi re-turned to take [her] home. Her soup was unfinished and she had left presents apparently intended for the next year, so that she would never again be dis-turbed. That's how I've been about reading during my vacation, la chair n'est pas triste.

I hope my present has arrived and not caused you a world of trouble at the customs.

We stay on here. I am going [to] continue teaching at Boston University. We are very pretentious and sociable, sort of Poobahs; and are trying to memorize Lionel Trilling in defense of manners.

Love from us both,

Cal

270. *To Harriet Winslow*

January 16th, 1956

Dearest Harriet:

This is an old-fashioned candy-box day, and a lonely one as I look out my window at snowflakes as big as fingernails, and think on time, with your fierce totem-like abstraction glaring at me from a big old needlepoint chair where I have posed it. Despite your explanation I feel your real meaning has something to do with our world after the last atomic bomb has knocked sun, moon and earth into a new and uncordial relationship. However Santa cheers me up; but I wish you hadn't bowed, with this one spot of representationalism.

I'm sad this morning because I have just seen William Carlos Williams off. He had been giving a reading at Wellesley and spent the night with us. Since I last saw him, he has nearly died four times, been psycho-analyzed (at the age of sixty-nine and on Merrill Moore's advice) been partially paralyzed, and he might die suddenly any day. All this gnaws at him, and since he is a doctor, there is nothing that he can hide from himself. Still he is very gloriously alive, and says he had always had a mother-complex (his mother died three years ago) and no sense at all before his analysis.[. . .]

A last word on your picture. You are fearlessly conservative—the new style is all Edwardian. No arrows, no spheres, no bare spaces, no paste. Robert Graves calls for "punctilious and intuitive realism." Mary McCarthy whose book was lent you, has just assembled an apartment that is the envy of all literary New York. Nothing in it is older than 1880 or newer than 1910.

Heigh-ho the Boston snow! Better men than I are already shovelling it out of existence, and still it falls.

Love,

Bobby

271. To Flannery O'Connor

Dear Flannery:

I have been meaning to write and thank you for your note of last summer. And I am proud when I read my blurb in your advertisements. It's hard to say anything at all in a small space, without being overly epigrammatic. *Wise Blood*, I think, is impossible to improve on; but your stories are almost exhibition pieces of how a story should be written. Jarrell was talking last summer about the first paragraph of your "Artificial Nigger." He uses it on his students and wants to add it to Saintsbury's *History of English Prose Rhythm*. Well, models of form; and I admire so many other things about them. You never get off your subject into emptiness, and you never write mere Flannery stories, i.e. stories in the marvelous manner of the master. Instead each move, each image has to be sweated out and seen. Lately, I have been working at an autobiography. I find it hard to be neither sugary nor acid; and Oh the effort to keep one's eyes open and see what one describes! After doing a page, I wish I were born blind, or born you.

Sorry to have missed you last spring. I had to *fly* to Iowa and judge a fellowship contest. Flying sounds very important, but when I arrived, I found that Paul had exhausted the travelling expenses. We tried to get you on the Iowa TV, but I think you were banned in rural areas.

How are you? We [hear] one rumor, and then another. Giroux, Ransom, and Katie Carver. I worry and want to wish you health for the new year.

Love from us both,

Cal

272. To Harriet Winslow

Dear Harriet:

I feel an improper, but probably immemorially Bostonian squeamishness about acknowledging your kindness in your will. We are grateful for the lifehold on the brickyard house, and the generous yearly subsidy . . . and what touches me to the heart is that you have always seen Elizabeth as Elizabeth, and not just Elizabeth née Hardwick Lowell, a sort of Winslow in-law at one remove, though of course she is that too.

Katherine Biddle just telephoned about your "stroke," and was as unalarming as possible. I sit at your Uncle Arthur's long desk here in the sunlight, and see you too in the sunlight and lying in your bed, at ease and peaceful like a Sargent water-color and draw all the most peaceful conclusions. But it hurts to think about it.

I have just been reading Charles Francis Adams' *Autobiography*. It ends as follows:—"Were I to undertake in my own case to guess whether the number of my days of pure and genuine happiness had been more or less, I am confident that they exceed in number those of any one of my forebears." That's one way of living loyally in one's family groove!

More cheerful occupations have been hearing I Musici and seeing a collection of Rubens drawings at the Fogg, which are running simultaneously with a group of Sargents at the Fine Arts, and make a curious fat woman and thin woman contrast. I am writing away furiously at last; but Elizabeth is out shopping for a TV set, and a small one for Anna, and I feel that idleness and the common touch are about to engulf us, and wish you would say you wanted to see us, and we would hurry down to spend two or three days with you at Easter, and I can document the Washington Potomac school part of my autobiography.

Love, and please take care,
 Bobby

273. To Harriet Winslow

February 13th, 1956

Dear Harriet:

How goes it? This is a grand day; all the florist-windows are blooming gorgeously with their pre-Lenten displays, the sun is very much out, one can walk out without a coat, and I have a new FM radio that plays programs with Purcell's *Fairy Queen* and Vivaldi's *Seasons* almost daily. Please be flourishing.

I had a little ancestor worshipping spree the other day, and read up all we had in the house written by ancestors, and even worked out on four type-written pages my family-tree. How quickly it runs into the sands of the unknown. What sort of man was my Grandfather Lowell, who died in his twenties, leaving only a Phi Beta Kappa key, a photograph, his name on a wall at St. Mark's School? He had only been married a few months, and Daddy, his first child was not yet born. There are many of these wistful early deaths; Sarah Stark, poor Julian-James, not an ancestor but my patron, and benefactor, as Dickens would say.

One is glad my Grandfather collected what was known of his father Francis who died when he was two. Well how dim many of them are! I think I would know Joshua Winslow if I met him, the young man's vivid slightly burlesqued descriptions of France etc. the old man's letters of ashamed high-sounding morality—not trying to deceive, though—from the Barbados. I think I would know Francis Winslow, Grandmother Devereux, Mordecai Myers perhaps, and my Great Grandfather Lowell, who wrote with bland Trollopian humor in a novel about St. Mark's. But Lord, what would one make of one's 64 great-great-great-greats, if one met them all in a room, all of one age, all in 1956 cloth-ing? You can see what a silly state I have been in. I'm all mixed up on the little girl at Childs [Gallery]. Is she really Elizabeth Savage, whose portrait hangs at the Athenaeum, and whom Granpa describes briefly by saying that she cer-tainly contributed her share to Boston's population by having sixteen children? It's a lovely, determined gaze; she looks able to Mother a city, and no doubt rule it. I trust Elizabeth has written you about the "Pierpoint Limner," the vaguely emerging tree in the left corner, the patch on the right temple etc.

I've been writing hard thank heaven, and feel back in my swing. The other day a friend of ours brought his perhaps girl over to see us. She was a singer, very fat and full of herself, and with a good pious Catholic nature and a heav-enly big voice. We spent a big evening listening to her records of Beethoven['s] *Ah perfido*, Schubert's *Der Zwerg*, the last movement of Mahler's Fourth[,] Fifth and others. Oh dear, how simple-minded and full of toughness, stamina and glory one must be to be a singer! In a sense, I think, real singers give their lives away, body, breath and memory, therefore it's only right that they should talk about themselves, their teachers and music forever and forever. The girl's teacher is a Mrs. Adams, whom we meet yearly at the Cottings on Christmas Eve, a drunk at parties, full of just the sort of talk I have been describing rather to the astonishment of Sarah and Cot, and really a great teacher I think, and oddly enough at this very moment talking to Elizabeth a mile a minute, with mad emphasis on the telephone.

Dear Harriet, please pardon this disorderly nonsensical writing. You are much too bright to be one of my relatives or even a singer. Miss McCready and Mrs. Ames are coming to tea Thursday and we will report the outcome. Miss McCready says you are the best friend she has ever had, and other ex-cited, less solemn things said about you. I can't think of any more news, except that your friend Nat Winslow, Cameron's wife, is having an exhibition at the Art Institute in a few weeks.

Love,

Bobby[...]

May 16, 1956

Dear Jim:

Glad to get your Lenten reading. I started Lent full of resolves: Dante's *Paradiso*, no sweets, sweet replies to Elizabeth's running analysis of my driving. My driving is now beyond criticism, I never have accidents while really in motion, and daily splinter a fence or an opposing car while parking. Did you ever notice that if you back a normal-size American car against a small foreign car, you leave sad gouges?

What a saving sourness your stories have! The raw middle west, the raw Catholic Church, the raw Irish . . . or are Early, Fabre, and Udovic good Swedish names. (I've been tuned up for your world by visits from a Norwegian, over here for medical treatment, the brother-in-law of a good Dutch friend of mine. Thin, icy, Alger Hiss–looking, polite, knowing Boston better than I do in two days from his superior Norwegian maps, having read Lionel Trilling's novel and *both* his short stories, and really a nice guy and really up to his teeth in himself—he has collected every letter he has ever written, every photograph ever taken since his birth and . . . but I've digressed from *Grace*.) I like all the stories: "Grace" best maybe, then "Dawn," then the "Death of the Favorite." The "Devil," which I think I was rather numb on when you came to Iowa, now seems epical in its boisterous dreariness—I couldn't let that last phrase pass, but am not sure what it means. Anyway you are awfully cantless, and salty, and sour and at least as good as ever.

Did you read Caroline Tate's novel about Allen's conversion? An important character is Dorothy Day, sublimated, canonized, the book dedicated to her, but made to perform a black mass and on the last page kissed on the mouth by Allen, or rather kissing Allen on the mouth, meaning peace. Dorothy saw the book in page proofs, blew up, and forced the removal of both the black mass and the dedication. The novel is somehow lovely, silly, maddening, and ~~bold~~ took nerve to write. I guess I feel catty about Caroline because I wrote her what I took to be a shyly complimentary fan letter and got back a blast quoting praises from Jacques Maritain, who "knows more about the *form* of the novel than any one living," but whose praise fell short of Caroline's own in which she claims to be the perfecter of Henry James and the heir of Jung.

We are in a state of tremendous excitement. Anxious, eccentric, middle-aged, we have just learned that like almost all other mortals we are to have a child . . . months ahead, but for certain unless there is some accident. It's terrible discovering that your one moral plank, i.e. an undiluted horror of babies,

has crumbled! We're so excited we can hardly speak, and expect a prodigy whose first words will be *Partisan Review*.

Wish you and Betty could get to Boston: we live in a rather spick and span Victorian house in a district, once the summit of fashion but now the home of schools for backward highschool graduates who can afford college but cannot pass their college entrance exams. I have given up Iowa, teach one day a week at Boston University, haven't written any verse for ages, but am in the middle of what I hope will be a murderous and urbane autobiography. However, I am beginning to see my parents with a new and beaming eye.

Again I wish we were together. Elizabeth sends her best, mine to Betty.
Affectionately,
Cal

275. To Elizabeth Bishop

June 18, 1956

Dearest Elizabeth:

We are going to have a child. It will come sometime in January and already *we* are exhausted. We lie about on sofas all day eating cornflakes, no-calorie ginger-ale and yoghurt. Elizabeth never moves except to turn the page of an English newspaper or buy a dress. I never move except to turn on my high-fi radio or go on expeditions for second-hand books. E's doctor has decided that we had better not go to Maine, so we will probably spend the summer here . . . However E has been told not to spend *all* her time shopping, so we may go to Maine after all. This isn't quite how it really is, but the last four days here have been scorchers, ninety-four on our coldest floor and we are very disorganized and cynical. But how we boast! People whom I had utterly felt cut off from: my barber, my dentist, the head of the Boston University English department, wives of friends, children . . . to all of them I can't stop talking and bragging. Elizabeth had a rather painful first month and still feels languid but is much more comfortable. We hear of women (Eleanor Clark) who ski all through pregnancy, give birth in bomb shelters without doctors etc. But we don't approve, and are timid, delicate and ante-bellum.

I had no idea that the Christmas present would be so late, and had begun to fear that you were somehow offended, or had had to pay a fine at the customs. It really was mailed early in December . . . Five months arriving in Brazil! I must mail your next year's present early in July. The pitcher came from Treffery and Partridge, a little silver shop opposite the State House. The

pitcher looks suspiciously like one we once inherited from my Aunt Beatrice, who for the first sixteen months of her marriage lived in India and had a staff of sixty servants. For the sixty remaining years of her marriage she lived in Boston and could never adapt.

I think the man in E's story is really *us*, but already several people we never met are having persecution break-downs because they recognize themselves. I saw Andrews Wanning at Bard last week-end where I read a paper on art and bad characters. Apparently Andrews' wife is famous for dreading Tom, a sort of portent of what her husband might become if his art for enjoying life were to develop any further. Ah me, how grateful I still am to Tom for driving Carley Dawson homeward from Stonington!

I am so delighted about the Pulitzer. I was on the Bollingen and National Book Award committees and tried to get the prizes given to you and/or Randall. Your chances were killed by Phyllis McGinley who thought you were serious or a woman or something. The National Book Award went to Auden, a wonderful poet with not so good a book, while the Bollingen went to Conrad Aiken, not such a good poet but with one of his best books. Everyone said you and Randall were young and would have hundreds more chances. Phyllis McGinley dominated one meeting and Mrs. Biddle the other. Did you hear about Randall being made the consultant for the next two years? We were driving through Virginia at the time of the announcement. The early morning edition had a small front page picture of Randall very bearded and looking like a seedy French Second Empire baron. Slowly the editors began to realize that they had a sensational photograph. All day it grew larger and larger till by evening it almost covered the entire page, blotting out the whole world!

We are liking Boston and have quite a few friends—in some groups we seem unspeakably strange and bohemian, in others we seem very grand and social. It's fun to puzzle people. But oh it's wonderful to be in one spot two successive autumns. And now a third is coming! How I wish you would come and pay us a very long visit, several years. Couldn't you translate Howells into Portuguese and spend a long time boning up on local Boston color to be used in your introduction. We can't be much farther away from you than the sources of the Amazon.

You should see the Rahvs' new house. It's what Philip calls good material, and must have cost a hundred thousand dollars once to build. It has a hundred acres or so of land. Meadows that have [to] be mown, woodchucks that Philip traps and hires some one to take away, a stream that could be dammed for a swimming pool, a kitchen that was once exhibited in *Home Beautiful*. Inside it is full of vast empty spaces, staggered modern book shelves designed by Nathalie,

a clock that runs without winding for three years, but then has to be taken to the factory and re-charged for $25, dried pine trees in vases, a whole nursery wing for children, a quarter of a mile dirt driveway which the swimming pool stream overflowed and washed away for leagues and leagues this spring. The Rahvs' only neighbors are an old men's home, a girls finishing school and a society of retired fox hunters and active professional farmers. Philip boasts of knowing no one within forty miles, and one has a feeling of Tolstoy, versts, owned serf villages, and the grand old *PR* whisky drinking gossips in that old immense room with its small bed in the back occupied by a sick and murderous cat.

I've got a big chunk of autobiography coming out in *PR* this fall—fifty pages and hope you will approve, though it seems thin and arty after your glorious Nova Scotia mad mother and cow piece. Liked your Brazilian man better than ever in the *New Yorker*—the most feminine of character sketches with you and Lota both speaking through each other. I very much liked the short tourist poem and hope I wrote you about it.

You are on Mary McCarthy's good books, though few others are. She boasts on her book jackets of editing a college magazine with you, was very eager for you to get all the poetry prizes and gave your childhood background but not you to one of the characters in her last novel. But she is very high horse with success, has said that my poems are brassy, that Elizabeth's next to last *New Yorker* story sounds like Jean Stafford, and advised Arthur Schlesinger not to publish his ten year opus on F.D.R. I think I have a lot more news but feel I'm running down like the Rahvs' three year clock. So goodbye and all our love,

> Cal

276. *To T. S. Eliot*

June 19, 1956

Dear Tom:

This is just a note to wish you health and good spirits. We were very much upset to read about your illness in a newspaper. We called Bob Giroux and the precise details seemed far more cheering than the solemn uninformative language of the reporter implied. Some one, confusing you with President Eisenhower, said, "Eliot is able to run again." I hope you will soon be on your feet and enjoying cigars and martinis.

I was sorry to read this morning about the death of your sister and to see you described as still in a hospital. Ah me, this has been a year of deaths and

accidents for our friends and their friends. Auden somewhere speaks of the "fattening forties," and sure enough now that I am a few months away from my fortieth birthday I find that I am, as if by nature, taking saccharine in my coffee, weighing myself each morning, and . . . but the forties are a sad time perhaps made endurable by the ridiculous.

To change to a better subject: I meant long ago to write you a fan letter on the *Confidential Clerk*. I keep wondering about the young man setting out in hope and solitude—without friends, parents or wife—to be an organist. He gives a new twist to an old voice in your soliloquies, and seems an answer—a young man's more grieved and hopeful answer—to "Gerontion."

It meant much to us that we saw so much of you during your visit and we look forward to your return next spring or the following fall.

Affectionately,

Cal

277. *To Ezra Pound*

September 17, 1956

Dear Ezra:

I am a lousy correspondent, in arrears to all my dearest friends, as Hardy might entitle it. But now I am stirring and want to know all about "the Rémusat family and froggland in 1871." I've just been through, slowly and mostly in French, Flaubert's *Education* with a Guide Bleu map of Paris. I have been reading *Nana*, *Candide*, bits of Michelet, looking at old photographs we took while driving through Chinon, Chambord, Blois. I feel I know Paris like . . . I was going to say Boston, but Boston, rather impervious, is no Paris, just a lovely heap, Yankee, Italian, Negro, Irish, with its head, Harvard, cut off by the Charles River. The city though a culture isn't cultured; the college, though cultured, isn't a culture. So tell me about France in 1871.

Reading Lincoln Steffens the other day, I was astonished at the wonderful job you had done on his beginning of the Russian Revolution. Your section has been in my mind for twenty years, yet the original is only a piece of buoyant journalism. A few phrases cleaned up, a touch of setting, the right rhythm. You beat anyone at opening windows and letting air into your poem.

I admire *Rock Drill*, but don't quite know what to make of it. When I was midway through, a biggish paperbound book called, I think, *15 Poets*, arrived. Here were all our best American poets from the ages of 30 to 50, I among them. Really some of us, Bishop, Jarrell, Roethke, Wilbur, Shapiro, Scott,

looked pretty good. We scanned, we had a beginning, middle and end, and we were really very different. Then I went back to *Rock Drill*. You are much more different than any of us. I wish we could keep up with you; we don't have the life. But I wish sometimes you had a beginning, middle and end. I look forward to the next lot of cantos.

Meanwhile I think affectionately of you and Dorothy. I hope to be in Washington sometime toward the middle of October and look forward to seeing you.

Cal

P.S. Reading over your famous canto 90 again after writing the above, I feel that *amor* gives me more eyesight with each re-reading. I don't think I've told you that we are expecting a child in January; Elizabeth is now large and blooming.

278. To Elizabeth Bishop

October 24, 1956

Dearest Elizabeth:

U R 2 good 2 B 4 got 10. What a grand line! I'm just back from a week in New York and Washington. In New York I was on some poetry committee to give a poetry prize for Brandeis College in memory of Judge Brandeis. When I arrived at the 5th Avenue palace Marianne Moore was sprawled like some Boucher goddess in a print dress and black cartwheel hat on the huge marble disc of the huge marble banister. Next to her Louise Bogan looking a little stiff, proud and shocked. We went into the ballroom, a room a mile wide and long with a green carpet, nothing anywhere except a green carpet, little rickety iron chairs hugging the wall, and a green baize-covered lop-sided ping pong table. We ordered into the elevator, a matchbox that would only scarcely hold me and Miss Moore. Arriving, we entered on a man dictating, who waved us away and said without raising his eyes, "Oh heavens, first floor." But some one at the end of the corridor welcomed us. We entered a narrow room about as big as three matchboxes. There sat two secretaries and Mr. Warburg, "Piggy" as I later learned from Louis Kronenberger. Mr. Warburg immediately began spouting in a stately drone and couldn't be forced to wait for the other three judges. It never stopped for an hour and three quarters. I don't think he really had any effect on our voting, nor did we have much of any effect on him. At one time he talked for fifteen minutes on the climate and sloping banks of the islands off Vancouver, a "place where all poets should

go." His voice was terrible in the little space and made one feel as though it were an airplane descending forever from a great altitude. Moore sayings: Some one proposed Padaric Colum. "Well lately he has split apart." She meant his poetry had. Referring to you, "Poor Elizabeth, she does her best to bear up and rejoice." To W. C. Williams, "And his is sometimes ASTONISH-INGLY RIGHT, sometimes!" To Mr. Warburg, who seemed on the point of proposing a second meeting for a second ballot, "But these meetings are death to me." Some one said that he didn't suppose she often undertook the trip in from Brooklyn. Miss Moore: "I am just back from California." However, she was always small, gracious, mobile, and beautiful. I feel utterly in love with her. At the end of the meeting, Mr. Warburg, tanned, bald, brown-patched, Buddha-nosed, beaming, growing as big as Huntington Cairns, and having to be prodded by both his secretaries each time one of us spoke—at the end Mr. Warburg said to me, "Goodbye . . ." long pause. "Mr . . ." pause. "I have always wondered if your name were pronounced Lou-well or Lowe-well."

Well, Randall! Like the earth he carries his atmosphere with him and is no different in Washington than he is in Greensboro. In the office he has his big Degas, Munch, Klee, and Vuillard (?) reproductions and a spectacled photograph, like a picture of one's wife and baby, in a leather frame on his desk: Chekhov. At his home in Chevy Chase he has big reproductions of Klee, Degas, Munch, etc. Photographs in the shadowy hall of Wallace Stevens and Marianne Moore and on his desk another photograph—this time without spectacles—of Chekhov. Randall is just back from the west coast and tells an unconsciously blood-curdling story about how he spent the evening with two young poets. One he took a shine to. The other . . . "Well he could see that I didn't like him near as well." I'll bet the guy did! Peter Taylor speaks of the time when Randall "dropped" his little daughter age five. Randall is in grand shape, and is enjoying the library where he will work 20 hours a week and have three months vacation. He sounds like Bernard Shaw when he is quoted in the papers. He also has a little white patch in his beard and is ageless—almost. Lonely and wonderful.

I loved your description of the blue-and-brown-eyed beauty—how like my mother I seized on the vulnerable detail! I've shot my wad. Bear up, my dear, and come back to us. Elizabeth is grand, enormous, lovely and sends you her love, and I send mine.

~~Robert Lowell~~ Cal

P.S. My poor Cousin Harriet, frail and wonderful, she had a stroke last winter and her right arm and leg will remain paralysed forever. I had a good visit

with her and she talked just as someone my own age, only wittier and more natural. I think going out that way is even better than instant death, late in life and in full health. I saw Ezra, but I'll save that for another letter.

P.S. There's a review of Auden's *Faber Book of Verse* in the *New Statesman* by Walter Allen, who calls you the best woman poet since Emily Dickinson. I know you like neither E.D. nor being called a "woman" poet.

279. *To Ezra Pound*

October 24, 1956

Dear Ezra:

What a grand middleman you are to deal with! What can I afford? How do I know? I would like to offer $50 to *lease* the painting. Then I could perhaps send more from time to time and borrow others.

One would have to be hard-hearted and pig-headed not to be taken by Miss Martinelli; she has a rather unearthly grace and precariousness. I hope her Mr. Lee is a kind fellow and able to survive.

Now for your gospel. I love you, laugh with you, know you are a great poet, and always feel either talking with you or reading you that you open the windows. Still I have no mind for your gospel, and don't let us talk about the Jews. I have several on my family tree, and . . . but let's drop it.

Is H. D. coming up this way? I would very much like to meet her. I think that her later poems, those about Isis, Mary and the War really do what people claim for the new Edith Sitwell. I believe your friend Sheri would like them.

Well, it was good seeing you so hale and erupting and jolly. Give my love to Dorothy.

Cal

280. *To Ezra Pound*

239 Marlboro St.
Brunnenburg
October 29, 1956

Dear Ezra:

I am sending off the check made out to Miss S. Martinelli right away. What does S. stand for? Not Sheri, or does it? Painters, like owners of London

houses, should *only* lease their pictures . . . a ninety-nine year lease with rights for the painter to reclaim the picture for short periods from time to time. This would be a real producers' contract and not one that would spur buyers, I suppose, to boost prices. I would very much like to see the booklet and would welcome the loan of any other disposable paintings.

Tiberius hadn't occurred to me as a name for our dear forthcoming; it's no worse than Robert Traill Spence Lowell Jr. the 5th, which we are set on.

Love to you and Dorothy

281. To J. F. Powers

October 29, 1956

Dear Jim:

I rather hoped to hear from you and am enormously touched that you wrote. I started without the dimmest idea of how to write possible prose and had a hell of a time seesawing from limpid clichés to dense intolerable poetic darknesses.

The other day I came across a note that you must have written in January or February of 195[4] and in reply to what must have been outrageous comments of mine. You have a sentence saying "I have no intention of burning my novel!" Please pardon me. I think you are a wonderful writer and want to welcome your novel with open arms. An acquaintance of mine here is Ed O'Connor, author of the *Last Hurrah*, with astronomical sales and movie rights. He is really an entertaining and modest man, but success has fairly lifted him miles from the earth. We have rather onesided conversations in which Ed says that Elizabeth's novel (sales well under three thousand) deserved to sell more. ["]Nor are sales a sure index to merit, witness Joyce and Katherine Anne Porter only in Modern Library after ten years in the wilderness." But when I mention you my stock goes up. If Ed doesn't write the great Irish novel himself, you will he thinks.

How I wish I could see you! You seem so much nearer at Michigan. Austin Warren is convalescing from his heart attack about a block away from us. A sad picture there—Austin (much better, however) under a bust of Buddha and nearby a curious carved ebony Greek crucifix. His host is a man dying of arterial sclerosis, then a delinquent nephew of eighteen in a T-shirt, a wife ailing with pneumonia, and a long black book-lined corridor one foot wide, the apartment's only through-way, and unchanged since a visit I paid there in

1938. Do not mention all this in Ann Arbor. Austin looks quite well actually and is finishing, planning and publishing five books.

I [am] going on [a] short poetry-reading tour of the west coast sometime late in April and hope I can stop for a day at Minneapolis and see you and Allen. I expect to see Ted of course, growly as ever according to Jarrell, who was just out there and made the mistake of trying to admonish Ted into smiling.

Love to you and Betty,
 Cal

Our coming one, little Hattie or little Spence, draws nearer and nearer. I have such fears that he will be born ovoid and never forgive us.

282. To William Meredith

December 19, 1956

Dear Bill:

The other side of the page will puzzle you . . . in my poetry class I have a trick of having unidentified poems mimeographed. Then the class examines and guesses. Yesterday my prize student handed me this page and asked me to guess, and as I was beginning to see your mild face appearing like a polar bear in its shaving soap, he said, "Meredith." They are mighty fine poems, I wish they were mine. And the new one! "Some winter nights impel us to take in whatever lopes outside." You can't go wrong as a poet or human being with such sentiments.

Little question mark is almost on us. Elizabeth is barrel-shaped and delicate peach-colored, and we expect the baby in about twenty days. We have bought: six shirts, six kimonos, six blue blankets, a hundred diapers, one bassinet, one bathinet, one stroller, one bottle warmer, one electric burner, one small upstairs refrigerator, and one Miss Elsinore, expert baby nurse, for six weeks. So we are ready as we will ever be.

The Hungarians! I have a paranoid girl-cousin who fastens on the old and frail, T. S. Eliot, Edwin Muir, and twenty years ago, Lawrence Lowell. Now to give me a feel that my time is limited, she has fastened on me. The telephone rings. "This is Diana Reeve." "Yes." "What are you doing about the Hungarians!" They are a nightmare of guilt to me. The other night I was talking to Frost, and he spoke of the horror in living in one of those countries where you had to dare to die or dare not to die. Yet you would never know

whether you were right or what it could come to. I have a Hungarian American girl in my class who writes me bad love poems. I have ordered her to buy and memorize Marianne Moore and keep for a Christmas present.

Bill, we miss you and hope you will visit us and the Booths next summer in Castine.

Affectionately,
Cal

283. To William Alfred

December 21, 1956

Dear Bill:

Your letters are like ones I have gotten from Elizabeth Bishop and Santayana: they are too good to be answered. We once had such a letter from Mary McCarthy and it was so good that she never made the effort again, failed even to write us bread and butter letters, and now two years in arrears, is just able to drag out of herself a postcard saying she is thinking of our coming baby, (our third person singular, the most important person in the universe!)

We are told that it may come any day now for the next three weeks. [If] it comes before New Year's, we save six hundred dollars income tax. O blessed dependent! Elizabeth is the most delicate peach-bloom-color, bulged, cherubic, nervous and "tinse" as a wasp. In our hall is a white iron bassinet in which was reared fifty years ago Peter Chardon Brooks, great great great grandson of Peter Chardon Brooks, Henry Adams' grandfather. That is called being born on the right side of the tracks. But outside pimply, imbecilic lunk-students from the Newman Preparatory College (non-Catholic) leer in, baleful, duncifying, American. Think twice and at least once about your fighting husband and wife Cambridge neighbors before you are entirely homesick.

There's good news, though, from Cambridge. Last night your Mother called up and reported the white toothy dog, named Dusty, had vanished. Cross your fingers and make a wish—I really think that Dusty is irreplaceable. Your Mother seems to be bearing up, but says that you are a Mr. Milk Toast in the hands of the designing Black and Tan MacNeices, who she thinks are preventing you from ~~escaping~~ changing the *1984* dank of London for Italy.

Bill, we treasure your letters and miss you much.

Love from us both,
Cal

P.S. Really about the letters . . . we both think you are one of the wittiest and most interesting prose writers in America. Not that you are writing through us essays to the world at large! You should be.

P.S. (2) Our best to the MacNeices.

284. *To Natasha Spender*

December 21, 1956

Dear Natasha:

We have a very important baby doctor, who after much deliberation and soul-questioning was lured away from his native Iowa to take charge of the Boston Lying-In Hospital. Unfortunately he is utterly woman-shy and Elizabeth returns from her periodic inspections as suspicious and uninformed as she went. But last week Dr. Reede said that the baby was ready to come as soon as Elizabeth was. So it may be here tomorrow, next week or the week after. We don't know.[. . .]

We loved your visit. Delightful in itself, it also lifted a little the close veil of ignorance that darkens so many great things for me. I have been listening furiously to music from Gesualdo to Webern and have even, like Bouvard and Pécuchet, absorbed terminology. I drive Elizabeth almost livid and speechless now by suddenly saying, "isn't that an augmented canon in cancrizans reversed?"

Dear Allen was through here briefly and bearing seven Hindo veils for seven Boston girls. Some evening, I fear, they will all meet. During his absence, I used frequently to be talking to some one (feminine between the ages of eight and eighty) and she would say casually, "When is Mr. Tate coming back, I just had a post-card from him, you know?" He looked much ruddier and sturdier, wore a black bowler, and really seemed reborn from the restraints of India.

We think of you often and lovingly. We hope you thrive in the famous western air and return to the east. I make Boston sound like the Orient.

Love from us both,

Cal

285. To Peter and Eleanor Ross Taylor

[WESTERN UNION STORKGRAM]

[January 1957]

—HARRIET LOWELL BORN MOTHER AND CHILD FLOURISHING—

—CAL

286. To Harriet Winslow

January 10, [1957]

Dear Cousin Harriet:

I am trusting my better judgment and *not* sending you a first picture of Little Harriet, aged by five minutes. I mean I am trusting to Elizabeth's instinctive judgment. Five minutes old, Little H. looked strangely like both her parents and like you but also more like Dylan Thomas than say, Audrey Hepburn. Staring with glossy, bulging little eyes, she is withering with contempt some importunate bystander trying to make conversation by asking her if she accepts the universe.

Today the mother's milk has triumphantly begun to flow to our overwhelming relief. We are both fearfully up on all the organic details and rather surprise Aunt Sarah by our verbosity in bringing them up. We are nothing naturally compared with E's neighbors, mothers twenty years younger and still doing college themes.[...]

This is all in one key and could go on for pages. However, even I can/must have limits. Our cleaning woman, good as gold, a stone-age Celt in mind, makes up in flattery what her cleaning misses—quite a lot. We have been compared with Mary and Joseph, Arch-bishop Cushing, Ralph Lowell, and Owen, her husband, a morbidly tidy and monastic old man, who won't drink coffee unless Catherine boils it for him. In Elizabeth's absence I have a lot of talk with Catherine. This morning I have learned to crawl with Little Roxanne Murphy, whose father made *and* drank Murphy's beer; I have learned to ride in a baby carriage with Little Susan Selby, the daughter of another of Catherine's ex-employers. I strongly suspect that none of these people ever existed, or even Murphy's beer, but are like Sarah Gamp's Mrs. 'Arris.

Dear Harriet, we are so glad to have a daughter and to have her named af-

ter you. Under your name, we trust that she is pointed toward an intelligent and sweet-hearted life.

Love from us both,
 Bobby

287. To Robert Duncan

January 10, 1957

Dear Mr. Duncan:

Let us regard the dates, March 20–April 7, as set. I should have written sooner and thanked you for your kind letter, but I have been anxiously waiting for the birth of our first child, a little girl born last Friday. For ten days the world and the baby too, who wouldn't come, seemed to stand still.

I hope the western colleges will not be having their spring vacations at the same time as ours. With trembling modesty, I look forward to treading in the wake of Marianne Moore.

Yours sincerely,
 Robert Lowell

288. To Elizabeth Bishop

February 7, 1957

Dearest Elizabeth:

Tremendous news about your coming here in April! We have a room all ready for you with a patchwork quilt rescued from a blazing Tennessee (Hardwick) mansion, a confederate flag, a toy Robert E. Lee on horseback, an abstraction pasted together by Cousin Harriet . . . and I'll even loan you your rash little statuette so that you'll not miss Brazil. You must come and I hope for long. I may go to the West Coast late in March—eastern poets (Jarrell, Eberhart, Wilbur, Marianne Moore, all in six months) are now being shipped west by barrel-load to give readings. I wish you would come to us in the second week of April. The mud will be beginning to crack, and here and there a little green will be stirring.

I reread Amy Lowell on the strength of your fellowship and the half affectionate and half malicious proddings of Robert Frost, "some one ought to unbury Amy." There [is] a childish bluntness to her: all the Chinese scenes that

her brother Percival wrote about, the little girls (Oh a pretty little girl!) dancing behind her formidable form, all those counterparts—fragile, effete Watteau ladies. Poor lady, she broke her ankles, one twelve and the other, I think, fifteen times, really liked writers better than society, and died at fifty-two—a life briefer ~~in its way~~ than Keats'!

Upstairs, Harriet Winslow Lowell is crying as rhythmically as breathing. Lizzie and our beaverlike professional baby nurse, Miss Elsemore, are not in theoretic or emotional agreement. Miss Elsemore, red-haired, dumpy, in her late fifties, supported by forty years' practice and pre Dr. Spock's baby book, believes in letting a baby cry before eating. Miss Elsemore doesn't really believe that Lizzie can enter a room correctly. Poor Lizzie isn't allowed to play with Harriet except for thirty minutes between six and six-thirty when she would like to be relaxing over an old fashioned. Morning, noon and night, our house shakes, quakes and continues to stand while the opposites war—thesis and antitheses, lion and unicorn and nothing resolved except that Miss Elsemore remains in the saddle but not unchallenged. The worst is that Miss Elsemore is so devoted, accomplished and even in her expert style, gentle, that any substitute would be unthinkable and we have even committed ourselves to hiring as her eventual successor and *long*-term nurse, Ann (no Miss) an elderly very talkative and ladylike Anglo-Irish Quebec spinster, Miss Elsemore's girl-friend. Miss Elsemore is already foreseeing and planning Ann's regime, "with Ann toilet-sitting should begin in the eighth month." Frank Parker says we are very lucky not to have a nurse that contemns *both* Father and Mother and eats all meals with the family and never allows conversation to stray from baby-virtue and baby-care.

I'm really mad about my little daughter and feel as though I had been up to now lacking some prime faculty: eyesight, hearing[,] reason.

Hyman is a neighbor and we see each other every so often and he misses you. He has a young wife, a society girl, very much of a rebel. Hyman's friends whisper that she is only interested in riding at the Myopia Hunt. Her relatives accuse Hyman . . . But what don't they accuse Hyman of! Their hours are peculiar: Hyman gets up at noon and goes to bed at two maybe; Nina gets up at seven and goes to bed at ten. Yet she is a fine and devoted girl and I think the marriage is very happy. Hyman is awesomely consistent, brilliant, ascetic—more and more people say he is the best painter in America, and so he is, I guess, along with Graves and Ben Shahn.

I've been stalling on my autobiography—so many relatives don't like it. But that isn't the trouble; rather it's laziness and feeling that I must store up more drive and wisdom.

Boston is becoming a center. Edmund Wilson is here: to educate his daughter; Ransom may retire here, if he can find a duplicate bridge group (he and his wife are expert and passionate players); and surprise: Philip and Nathalie! I think Philip is going to teach at Brandeis and bring *PR* and even William Phillips, perhaps! with him. So spurn your rich expatriate's prize, return and be a resident poet amongst us.

Much love from us both,

Cal

289. To John Berryman

March 1, 1957

Dear John:

"A harmless and good woman, rather too young": your description is along the lines of Henry Adams' "She dresses badly . . . We shall improve her . . . I cower before her . . ." I detect a sleek, seal-like smile. But what are years? Will any of us equal the old master and marry a generation and a half younger than ourselves. Today I am forty years old, and my baby daughter weighs ten pounds. You can't match that. Also Elizabeth's forty and the newest (youngest?) mother I've met.

Give our love to Ann. We are awfully glad you are married again. Perhaps, you'll come and see us this summer in Maine. We go to Castine, an ailing little town with one admiral, two retired Episcopal bishops, and a population fifty percent over 75. It's about seventy miles north of Damariscotta and very near Blue Hill where the Blackmurs used to go.

We keep up with you through various sympathetic but imperfectly informed sources: Allen, the Camerons, Eileen, Ben Shawn.

I long to see you,

Cal

P.S. I'm taking the easterner's Pacific Coast poet's tour beginning March 20 and getting back here April 7. I might just be able to stop for a day in Minneapolis . . . probably returning. I'd like to see you and Ann and the unvanquished Allen. Do you know, by the way, my friend Jim Powers, the short story writer, 509 First Ave. South, St. Cloud. I think you'd hit off and wish you'd look him up. He makes rather poker-faced dry Irish sardonic [jokes] about his not being a scholar. However . . . I think you would be pleased with each other.

Wish Anne Bradstreet had gotten all the prizes, as she deserved.

290. To Elizabeth Hardwick

[San Francisco, Calif., March 29, 1957]
Friday, 3rd day in San Francisco

Dearest Darling:

Time rushes by with a mixture of fun and boredom and sleeping pills. I had a grand rather too active stay with Ted with visits to his wife at the tuberculars' barracks. She is getting well fortunately but the convalescence takes months. A lovely sensible girl, a sort of young Dido. The Vancouver was very hurried in hours but very calming and weak-teaish in tone. I stayed with a charming half British half Canadian couple and was reminded of Hamish.

San Francisco! Glorious city, too many readings! Too much Leonard Wolf, too many dull black magic poets. Mrs. Witt-Diamant reminds me somewhat in looks and character (would you believe it?) of Miss Elsemore. Utterly efficient, tirelesss, unpoetic, unprudish—being under her wing is a little like being in a pressure boiler with the metal top gabbling tirelessly and usefully away. Tomorrow I drive to Carmel, Sunday I see Winters. Tuesday I go to Santa Barbara and have lunch with of all people, Barbara Ward, also a visitor. Then Harry. I may fly directly back to Boston on Sunday the seventh and skip Las Vegas.

I'm in pretty sober shape and long to be back with my three girls and especially my big old Kentucky girl. Give the Numples a lovely kiss from Daddy and tell her I've mailed her a lot of two-bit Chinese garish and noisy toys. Best to good Miss E. Take care of yourself, Darling.

Love,
Cal

291. To Theodore Roethke

239 Marlborough Street
Boston 16, Massachusetts
April 10, 1957

Dear Ted:

My stay with you was [a] big moment of friendship and it is a joy to feel so close and delighted and at ease with you. Oh Lord, the parties, the noonday reading of verse over the (kitchen-litter) dining-room table, the consumption of food! I liked many things. Your best students knew enough to teach me new

knowledge. They all seemed very drilled and devoted and quite likely superior to any in the country. Then many people, the Heilmans, Miss Clower, the wonderful Mary McCarthy of Seattle (and here let me apologize: in a moment of what I took to be boozy cordiality I told her that her conversation was far superior to her poems. Please apologize for my boorishness somehow. I liked Wagoner very much and am curious about the future). I gather that I wasn't terribly original in my discovery of Rae Tufts. In San Francisco I met Ann London and was even for a few minutes in a room where there were *four* former Seattle students who had more or less been in love with her and been ditched. She has *something*. Please forgive my silly behavior, I reached Vancouver more or less a deaf-mute and stayed more or less on the beam for the rest of the trip.

I was awfully touched by our afternoons with Beatrice. What a flat way of saying something that went to my heart. I suppose one shouldn't dramatize, the barbed-wire, the colored neighbor, the gray wood, the hectic R. L. Stevenson flush of many of the patients etc. I think you have one of the most charming wives in the world and that you do well together.

Now I'm back here, once more a school-teacher and all bent up to start writing again. I wonder if you could send [a] photograph of you both to stand with other friends on my mantle-piece.

> Love to you all
> Cal

P.S. Please tell Graves that I treasure the honor of passing part of an afternoon and evening with him.

P.P.S. Yes, I do think you are tops as a poet in the new book!

292. *To Anthony Ostroff*

April 10, 1957

Dear Tony:

I'm mightily grateful for your conversation and ingenuity as a host. On my way home I stopped off for a couple of days at Kenyon—wisely in lieu of a day in Las Vegas. Ransom was very familiar with your about-to-come-out story and talked at some length on the plot, or rather he retold the plot and loosely connected it with what he knew of you from your letters. I'm sure that

with your wit and amazing history you have the steam and edge to become a very good writer.

Ah me, brick and cold and sunlight and God knows it's a relief to be back in Boston and Christendom! Now please tell me in your amused, intricate, and frank manner all about Nancy. Jesus what a presence. I suppose my sketch of her character would have bits of the truth . . . (oh the uncanny quickness and realism of woman! I was just typing these last sentences when my wife suddenly ascended three floors with clothes for the linen closet and was in a jiffy glancing over my shoulder where all she could read was the correct and ~~masculine~~ manly first paragraph of this letter which I had rolled back to.) Well, I really meant a good deal of the non-sense I spoke to Nancy that night. Only I know she is probably, or rather I'm probably, quite off her line. I'm delighted and dote on Lizzie and my little daughter, and am not looking for distraction. And yet, and yet I look forward with my gray old heart in my mouth to the possibility of Nancy's return in June. Imbecility!

I liked Miriam very much and hope you liked me as well as I did you.

Vale and write me [a] good letter addressed to the Department of English[,] Boston University[,] Boston, Mass. (I write in full knowing your knack for losing the road.)

 Cal

293. *To Peter and Eleanor Ross Taylor*

April 17, 1957

Dear Peter and Eleanor:

I must have been a noisy and elated guest and beg your forgiveness for many things and still feel grateful for that last ride without brakes or windshield-wiper or even much possibility it seemed at one time of making the plane. However, I had the time of my life and treasure it all now in recollection, tranquility and sobriety. I had a grand time talking Peter down and being talked down by him. I wish I had dared answer Eleanor back on the subject of Uncle Ransom's greatness. I'm not in the least convinced by her two crushing indictments. Still even on paper and a thousand miles away, I don't feel I have the steam to argue her down.

My beloved Henry Adams, who was so gracious and infallible on the Southern mind, has this to say about the American woman. "Sometimes at

dinner, one might wait till talk flagged, and then, as mildly as possible, ask one's liveliest neighbor whether she could explain why the American woman was a failure. Without an instant's hesitation, she was sure to answer: 'Because the American man is a failure.' She meant it."

I had such a swimmingly good time with Eleanor and Sally. I can't believe either one would make such a statement; let alone mean anything so tough on us. As I was saying there is no one in the world I can pour out to as I do to Peter. And now to prove it, I am off on a long, low intensity rambling and wise poem, which begins: "Dear Peter." By the time I'm through, I hope to have covered age, parenthood, baldness, re-won the Civil War for our side put in a plug for Saul Bellow, prosateur, and God knows what.

Sometimes I wish little Harriet were as gentle and even as old as dear Katie. Harriet has learned one new trick during my absence: She clenches her lips tightly and whitely shut whenever approached with a spoon of fluid meat extract and demands her nipple-bottle. Also she can no longer be made to laugh by her father merely singing discordantly and thinking his foolish abstruse thoughts. She *knows* when one just *pretends* to be solely thinking of her.

We are well and wish we could come back to Kenyon for Peter's opening. Love from us both, us three,

Cal

294. *To William Carlos Williams*

April 19, 1957

Dear Bill:

John Brinnen tells me that you will be coming to Brandeis on the 7th of June to receive our joyful homage. Our *hommage*! But I hope we will all talk with more pith and less ore rotundo than the usual Frenchmen. Still there's nothing wrong with the French: they have more of the animal's sense and more of Descartes' intelligence than we.

I wonder if I could persuade you and I hope Flossie to stay with us in Boston. It might be pleasant for you both to be here on Marlboro St. (William James once gave his classes this example of understatement: "Marlboro Street is hardly a passionate street.") You would miss the crush of the university, the deference of strangers, the teas with the president's wife, the calls from all

and sundry. But I am being quite unscrupulous. We so want to talk to you at leisure again.

Affectionately yours,
Cal

P.S. I've been on the poets of the Atlantic seaboard's tour of the west coast and enjoyed it mightily and everywhere I went I met Williams' (plural) fans. In San Francisco I met a guy who took my picture and promised to give me a fine one of you.

295. To Elizabeth Bishop

April 29, 1957

Dear Elizabeth:

Too much like myself! We had been having martinis and I was in a very foolish, exalted and exhausted state from my reading trip. Never again; I'm really very tame and will be all the time we see you in N.Y.

I live so far from seconds in Boston that I have never even made a stab at nominating Randall, but I have been hoping that we might combine and have even been keeping the *nominating* blank out on the top of our TV so that we could do something when you came to Boston. I'll fill my blank as soon as it arrives. I guess nominating people, once you've done it, is simple, like taking a plane or going to Europe. However, the Academy is so full of dopes that one is not hopeful. I met Jacques Barzun the other night; his candidate for fiction was Anne Goodwin Winslow, Marcella's mother-in-law. He also said, re Tate arriving boiled and unprepared for his lectures . . . well, I forget what he said, but he blamed our age of poet-teachers. The poets rob the university and the university kills poetry. But he didn't quite put it as outright as that. I pointed out ragged lives in the past, and he said, "Darn it, Melville fulfilled his con- tracts."

We'll be in New York on the 22nd for two or three days. Perhaps we could have an evening with just you and Lota. I would like to see you sometime with Miss Moore but also want to see you without her.

I read your "Roosters" and "Prodigal Son" to Jack Sweeney's class and at the end felt I'd learned a lot about roosters and pigs. I am afraid I sounded a little like some sort of centaur fusion of both the other night.

Honor bright, I'm not a rowdy. Perhaps you both will reconsider staying with us.

>Love,
>>Cal

P.S. Rizzardi showed me your Pound. I've read it aloud to people several times. Just as with "The Prodigal" and "Roosters," you are very womanly and wise. A lot better than Robert Fitzgerald in his rather pious and trap-doorish review that I've now seen in three magazines. Harriet weighs 14 pounds and Elizabeth is already getting her to reduce.

296. To William Carlos Williams

<div align="right">May 6, 1957</div>

Dear Bill:

You're in with a galaxy of the great: Copeland and Truman, good company for anyone; but I hope you won't feel that courtesy compels you to attend more than your own show. You are *Dr.* Williams, though, thank God! and need no advice.

I've been reading some of old Ford's poems lately and feeling that he is a hell of a lot more interesting and shady (I'm really not punning and mean a casual, dawdling, tree and memory-covered world). So unlike America in this our great hour!

You are awfully fierce and right about our U.S. speech and emotional rhythms being unlike the British. I sometimes wonder if that difference is not rather an ill business. Well, we are what we are and that's endurable to say the least.

I am returning the Brandeis letter. I take it you and Flossie will be getting in sometime in the afternoon of June 6th. Get off at the Back Bay Station and I'll be waiting for you. No snow this time and I hope some shade.

>Love to you both,
>>Cal

P.S. They are planning to have a panel of New England poets read in your honor. I don't like the category—a bunch of dry provincial sticks dressed up in the fine and speech of a college commencement.

297. To Anthony Ostroff

Dear Tony:

I should have written you long ago, for long ago the fine puff of madness died. My one intense foolish letter to our friend was never answered. Of course, it shouldn't have been. So all is over. *I* can see it all with humor (and a hangover), I hope everyone else can.

This rather exhausts my letter. But it does not exhaust my pleasant memories. I hope to see you sometime during the summer. I'm sure we'll remain friends through the years. My best to Miriam.

Yours affectionately,
Cal

298. To Elizabeth Bishop

June 10, 1957

Dearest Elizabeth B.:

Coming home from dropping the Williams for their visit with their cousin, an 82 year old Episcopalian nun, I stopped on Charles Street to buy Sunday papers, then drifted to the wine-basket florist, and, while debating buying you a little bouquet of miniature roses, forget-me-nots, pinks etc. all arranged to look like flowers in china, I saw the pianists' car swing round the corner, big as a battleship and you sitting, great car spaces about you, in the back seat. Being a Yankee, I raised an arm you couldn't have seen, and made sounds you couldn't have heard. I sent the flowers to Bill Merwin's wife—he had caught a cold from me and she had caught bronchitis from him. So . . . but I wish the flowers had journeyed on with you to dazzle your old cross aunt in Worcester!

The last morning with the Williams was touching. The delivery poem was read to Harriet and a coyly chuckling Miss Elsemore. She is gobbling up the Williams *Autobiography* and one sees it stuck between stair-rails on top of her *Reader's Digest* and her *Real Meaning of Jesus*. The book begins something like this: "I'm not going to tell you about the women I've been to bed with. They're not the story." When I left them at the nuns' house we all kissed goodbye, and Bill said, "You're my son. That's what I do to them." Age, Oh age!

I've read your poems many times. I think I read you with more interest than anyone now writing. I know I do, but I think I would even if it weren't for personal reasons. "The Armadillo" is surely one of your three or four

very best. I thought the title mistaken at first, a Moore name—though I suppose the armadillo is a much too popular and common garden animal for her—for an out-of-doors, personally seen and utterly un-Moore poem. However, "Armadillo" is right, for the little creature, given only five lines, runs off with the whole poem. Weak and armored, I suppose he is those people carrying balloons-illegal-to their local saint.

Your crucifix and torture (?) wheels in Flanders poem has a grave girlish jump to it. I've always wanted to write on this subject. Wilenski's *Dutch Painting* gives a fierce description of the reality of the Spanish soldiery in Breughel's "Crucifixion." Apparently he could get away with that. Maybe I'll do my poem, sad, resonant, ferocious, as a counterpiece to yours. Remember the Bad thief we saw at the Fogg?

Also reread the poems you recited. How true that treasure of white sunlight and energy one has in the morning, how often I've blown it off into reading a novel. "A Summer's Dream" seems to me a flattish (Jarrell adjective) variant of your exciting "Sunday, 4 a.m." I like best the mackerel-crying stanza. "Armadillo" was surely by far the best poem read by anyone that day.

How easy it is for me to lay it on, and mean it. I remember reading as a boy in Bartlett's *Quotations* this arresting and immortal sentence: "Peace reigns in Warsaw." I wonder who the author was? Today and yesterday, more peace has reigned in our house than we've seen for ages. See what you bring. It *kills* me that you are gone and I do want to make a stay in New York toward the end of July.

Love,
 Cal

P.S. I'm awfully relieved that Lota has my number and still likes me best of your poets. It's comforting too that you find most of the new poetry tame.

299. *To Elizabeth Bishop*

Castine, Maine
July 3, 1957

Dearest Elizabeth:

I've been rather carelessly waiting for your long letter before answering your wonderfully chosen postcards. We do want you and Lota to come for the visit you suggest, but why not come much sooner and for much longer. While you vanish away in the heat, we are so cool that we've used furnace, heaters,

flannel shirts and a fire-place stuffed with oak logs. We say to newcomers, such as the Dupees who've just arrived: "we can stand it, we're used to Maine." Why not spend the summer with us? We have lots of room in our house (now that Miss Elsemore is on her way out) and after that in August we can give you a little house to yourselves on the Castine shore that looks like Japan from one angle and like Castine from another.

I meant to write you about Cummings' reading on the public garden, but its colors have somewhat faded on me after a week in Maine. Most colorful was Allen Tate, who arrived at our house for the occasion dressed in a very pale, very delicately made khaki coat, a khaki hat with a plaid hat-band, loafers that shone like armor in a Rembrandt painting. He was smarting from the night before when Elizabeth, determined to raise his mode of existence from gossiping and violin-playing with girl graduate students, invited him to meet [a] terribly distinguished, awfully nice, awfully Bostonian former Miss Cabot, the wife of Ellery Sedgwick, nephew of the *Atlantic Monthly* man. She is the most brilliant talker about Bostonians in Boston, and so charming that ordinary mortals soon forget that one hand has been paralyzed from birth, one eye squints a little. Allen rose to the occasion enough to tell an anecdote about some one named Beezie Cabot, showed a surprising knowledge of Cabot genealogy. Then the air suddenly went [out] of him. He said, "At my age one never feels *absolutely* well you know," grew distracted when Mrs. Sedgwick suggested that he visit her at Stockbridge, and finally had to be prodded to escort her home around the block. This couldn't have been the night before the Cummings' reading because Allen seemed to go underground for days thereafter. Well, Cummings was introduced by MacLeish as someone who had been against Communism when it was still dangerous to take such a position. "Unlike Archie," Allen said loudly. And there we sat, a rather conspicuous and hateful row, the two Merwins, us, Allen, Moira Sweeney, Bill Alfred—all ages, all degrees of innocence and cynicism—while Cummings read outrageous and sentimental poems, good and bad of both kinds. About eight thousand people listened and those who couldn't hear crowded in huge masses under awnings across the Public Garden pond to look at non-objectivist paintings. The Revolution has come, I guess, yet we're still creatures of flesh and blood.

Maine is restful for our jaded Boston nerves. Except for driving up it's been pure rest cure—one much needed. Oh the drive up! We had to have a trailer. Due to some uncharacteristic oversight in my planning, I found myself faced with fearful alternatives. There are two kinds of U-Haul-it trailers, the

open, and the covered, little ambulance-like wagons that blot out all back-view and are entirely dangerous. The covered may be returned to the nearest large city (Belfast 25 miles from Castine), the cozy uncovered ones must be brought back to Boston, an additional drive of 458 miles. I hadn't understood, hadn't securely bound the agent to the terms I had imagined. I took the uncovered trailer. For two hundred of the two hundred and twenty-nine miles, we analyzed the flaws in this choice. And we had Miss Elsemore, furious at her dismissal, loaded with token forbearance from a last minute reading of her "What Jesus really thinks," blaming everything on Elizabeth, sweetening the journey by saying to the baby, "You're fickle, you'll soon forget men. . . . You'll have to take what comes . . . Your *Daddy's* one person you'll never forget." At Wiscasset, still gloomy with the boredom you felt there many summers ago, I got out—I was beginning to nod at the wheel—and went swimming off the town dock. While I was in the water, a freight-train slowly came to a stop and cut me off from my car and family. Getting out, I cut my big toe on the step, a barnacled tire. Oh when we got to Castine we found a young resident poet—off to the wedding of his favorite Wellesley student, and he drove the trailer back.

I want more than anything in the world to see ~~more of you than~~ as much as I can of you before your return. Lizzie has an old Kentucky friend, a Miss Turner, who teaches at Vassar, coming here for the month of August. I'd like to come and see you both in New York then, and perhaps I could guide you both here from there. Elizabeth is full of praise and affection for you both and is most eager for you to come.

Love,
Cal

P.S. At the end of Cummings' reading, while I stood in line waiting to shake hands with Cummings, I ran into Paul Brooks, who said breezily to me, "It seems absurd that I should have to ask you the address of our own author, Miss Bishop." All the age-old author and publisher rifts began to widen in me and I said, "But isn't she a Farrar and Straus author." Then I said something about how much I admired your stories and we parted rather coldly. I hope [I] haven't made things more of a mess.

300. To Elizabeth Bishop

Dear Elizabeth:

Thanks for speaking to Lizzie about your misgivings. I see clearly now that for the last few days I have been living in a state of increasing mania—almost off the rails at the end. ~~It's as if~~ It almost seems as if I couldn't be with you any length of time without acting with abysmal myopia and lack of consideration. My disease, alas, gives one (during its seizures) a headless heart.

I am not going to write very much now, but I do want you and Lota to know that I *am* at last in reverse. I am taking my anti-manic pills—75 mgs. of sparine, no more than what my doctor prescribed on the bottle but too much to drive a car or even see people much. The effect is something like the slowing and ache of a medium fever. One's thoughts are not directly changed and healed, but the terrible, over-riding restlessness of one's system is halted so that the mind can again see life as it is.

I want you to know . . . Oh dear, I wanted you to know so many things . . .

(Next morning) Yesterday was mostly bed, sparine and letting my beard grow. Today I feel certain that I am not going off the deep end. Gracelessly, like a standing child trying to sit down, like a cat or a coon coming down a tree, I'm getting down my ladder to the moon. I am part of my family again, I love my lovely family again.

When I said goodbye Lota said I was like an archangel! I see what an ass I have been. Lota has her head screwed on and is one of the loveliest and most amusing ladies I've ever met. Ask her to forgive me. And forgive me yourself, dear old friend, Boba. I'll make no solo descents on you either in New York or Brazil.

As I dully drove back over the Bango[r] toll bridge in my gray and blue Ford, the nut still rattling in the hub cap as though we were dragging a battered tin can at our heels, I looked up and a sign said, "When money talks it says, 'Chevrolet.'"

Love,

Cal

P.S. The George Herbert! I've really always wanted you to have it—ever since it turned up in storage four years ago. Perhaps you can add some stumbling block of humor to the dedication. I'll be mortally hurt if you don't keep it.

301. To Elizabeth Bishop

August 15, 1957

Dearest Elizabeth B.:

Your letter, besides bringing its cheerful tempering of the spirit, has brought me terrific relief. I feared that I was forever in exile, along with those other clinging, clutching, fevered souls, Muriel, your worst Nova Scotian relatives, all those bramble-armed bugbears that have so boringly tried to tangle up your life. God be thanked, and let this letter begin as a scherzo lest my last, though true and necessary, seem my one voice.

First I must solace you for having missed the voyage with Eberhart to Somes Sound. It was rich in undramatic mishaps. When the plans were being made, Dick managed to tell me ten times in the course of five sentences and five minutes that we must be off by ten. Ferried by Booth in Fred's outboard, I arrived at 9:35 at Goose Falls. We sat, blue-jeaned on the cable of the Falls' bridge. Time passed. We had a rather vexatious and repetitive talk about Phil's poem, a long narrative about a friend of his that was actually frozen to death while canoeing down an uncharted Canadian river. I had made the point that both in his letter applying for his Guggenheim and in the poem itself it would [be] disastrous to leave out the real adventure (which by the way he tells very powerfully in conversation) and substitute his reflections on the destructive element, ~~wish and~~ his aesthetic notions of how difficult such a poem is to write. Good points made for the second time began to pall, the cable ate into our behinds, Phil began to talk to me his maddening line about wanting to write like Muir and Merwin and Brewster Ghiselin. At eleven Eberhart appeared in his sky-blue beach wagon, and mumbled something about never being able to start on time when there are women. This became clearer when we reached the little red bungalow under Undercliff where Betty and the second ex-Mrs. Rexroth were waiting. The second ex-Mrs. Rexroth, tall fading red-haired, figury, black-sweatery said that she had heard me read in San Francisco but had had to leave before the end. I: "Which reading at San Francisco?" Second ex-Mrs. Rexroth: "The one at the museum. I heard all of Dick's readings but couldn't do that for anyone else." She had gone to six consecutive Eberhart readings (sometimes two a day)! In fact she was all too much astride the high, foamy wave of Eberhart's élan, and Betty was rather balky and unpoetic about obeying Dick, still a bungalow man and not yet the skipper of the *Reve*. First mishap, our skiff loaded with all our clothes, movie cameras, can of crepe suzettes etc. began to move gently out from under Undercliff into the great sea. At first it seemed to be coming back ashore, then

like Kitten diving through Randall's legs for its beloved coal pile, the skiff shot toward Stonington. Suddenly Dick was splashing in all his girth, and underwear and sneakers over razor sharp rocks and bouncing on floating sea-kelp and the skiff was caught. We were off, and I began to study steering with the chart. Dick's chart-reading, though miles ahead of mine, was encouragingly incomplete and there were many pleasing puzzles for the beginner to grow strong on. We passed gloriously under the Deer Island Bridge and into Eggommoggin Reach and the many islands. Each spar and island that came up could be checked off the chart (and in Dikkon's log book) but it was as though one were fitting some twenty screens in the twenty similar but each slightly different windows of country house and had somehow gotten the order wrong. Still everything with straining and pushing *would* go on the chart. We looked at the compass (the one that Dick described as working well North and South but not so well East and West) we were going somehow due west instead of due east! There were Blue Hill, the Camden Hills, the mountains of Mount Desert. A great brown mountain loomed ahead of us like Atlantis in Dante's Ulysses canto; we could already see white waves breaking. But there was no sign of what should have been the small-business-power blue smoke of the Bass Moccasin factory of Bass Harbor Mount Desert. We were entering the Isle au Haut! Things then went swimmingly, only Dick was disconcertingly officious, old school-teacherish and skipperish about my steering; he stood at a different angle and it was impossible for me to make a turn without little shifts and corrections. Then without warning he vanished utterly and was deaf to all my calls for even the most needful advice. Then came the sinister Casco Strait. Philip Booth, who has a way of making the serenest outboard trip across Castine Harbor seem a clash of thews, seamanship and foundering, had made this part of our voyage seem an almost maniacal act of hubris. Dick put down his movie camera, ordered Betty and the ex-Mrs. Rexroth on the alert, assumed command. The Casco Strait, however, was wider than the broadest part of the Boston Basin. Yet there was a difficulty, Dick is color-blind and at this supreme moment with the eyes of the ex-Mrs. Rexroth on him he reverted to his old heresy that colors have no functional difference and spars are painted now red, now black, merely to vary their monotony. Now the *Reve* is a perfect craft, about forty feet long, it looks as though some Alice in Wonderland accident had befallen some much smaller boat and that it had doubled its size without somehow readjusting its design. Broad and covered with dark mahogany, it looks some Gothic, episcopal church built for a small town about 1900, something from that last gasp of Victorian design when the old massive designs still held but when the quality

of the old massive materials was fast failing. It was, as Betty said, too big for those who might have liked it but couldn't have afforded it, yet too unsporting and bulky for those who could afford it. It developed one defect; not a ray of sun could pierce its massive after-cabin where everyone sat and watched the helmsman, a little stooped lest he bump his head, steer. We nearly froze, yet it was a broiling day.

Glorious entrance in to Northeast Harbor, all the most beautiful ~~ten~~ forty thousand dollar Atlantic class 31 foot sloops racing in the yellowing late afternoon sun. We entered Southwest Harbor and by this time I had so much mastered my chart reading that for the first time I understood the meaning of the names Southwest and Northeast, an experience denied the land automobile tourist. All our fish in Castine and even the fish in Bucksport comes from Southwest, and all summer we'd been hearing that one had never really tasted haddock unless one had had a Southwest Harbor haddock fresh off the fishing boats. I had determined to treat our group to a sea dinner and even had us all headed toward a famed place called Andy's when we became aware of a scarlet convertible that for several minutes refused to pass us and almost tread on our heels as we strolled down the dust dockside road. The car stopped, asked about Andy's the driver offered to drive us. Red-faced as his car, laughing, he really made Dick seem gaunt, speechless, Charles Adamsish. Asked about Andy's he put a hand over his mouth and said "Shh-h, Andy's my neighbor." He then proposed a place where he and his wife went when they wanted a real meal. He said he was Captain Claaussens, he said, "I'm a gambling man, that is in my calling I risk my life against sea-hazards. I'll make you a gambling proposition: if you are not a hundred and one percent satisfied with the meal you are going to get you can telephone me and I'll pay for it." So we abandoned Andy's and obeyed. On the way, we passed Caruso's, Captain Claaussens said, "I'll be honest with you, if you like Italian food you can get [a] real meal there." We reached our destination, it was a sort of very provincial country version of the Northeast Harbor *Lighthouse*. Hard hunched quarters, apricot paint, spotless Maine souvenirs, no liquor. We had real bread, there was a little butter in the clam chowder, the haddock was fried in fat as thick as the deck of the Reve, for dessert we had horrible "rainbow superbs."

Glorious evening, Maine food-filled cruise down Somes Sound. Everything I had hoped you and Lota would see on our trip now materialized. All the great lawns, birch and elm groves, frail expensive wharves, new Swedish racing craft at the moorings, here and there a private plane; you felt you were seeing the great Roman villas described by Horace and Juvenal as examples of the glorious *sic transit gloria mundi* of the imperial Roman's middle age (his

own middle age, not Rome's!). We landed at Somesville, went ashore, a rather ungracious little group, I in khaki socks, pants and shirt, Betty in blue shorts and sailor blouse looking like a boy of twelve, the ex-Mrs. Rexroth, figury, black sweatery, faded red haired, Dick, home-made Commander Whitehead, fringe-bearded, sunset red-faced, wearing a plum and beige lumber-jacket. Sweeping for a moment into control, I showed everyone the Somesville herring-run. Then foot-weary and languid, we all climbed a little hill to an old white hotel, *The Somes*. It wasn't for us. Elderly, wealthy, speechless lonely people sat about drinking carbonated water at candle-lit tables. In reply to Dick's "Do you serve the soft drink?" And Betty's, "We mean beer," the manager answered, ["]I could give you some ice tea but that would not do you any good." Ice-tealess then we sat conspicuously on the front veranda and tried to decide whether a man named Saigan, married once to someone he called Isa Gardner, and twenty years ago followed by the ex-Mrs. Rexroth from San Francisco to New York was really *Belle* Gardner's first husband. The clientele seemed to be entirely women, in evening dresses, they would rise from their little tables where they were playing probably Auction Bridge, stare at us then turn away in fatigue and horror. When we went back to our skiff it was moonlit dark, Dick with a bunchy, musclely leap pushed off, there was a blaze of phosphorous water like a Fourth of July sparkler, and poor Betty had fallen into the water, fortunately only three feet deep, but full of jelly-fish causing the phosphorescent blaze. On board the *Reve*, half the company began drinking a kind of boiler-maker, manhattans followed by beer. The ex-Mrs. Rexroth, really a rather gentle sympathetic soul, turned out to be a nurse, the ideal wife for Rexroth. The conversation turned to hospital stories. Betty showed an unexpected gift for really eccentric macabre recollections: the man with a bleeding amputated leg who asked her to kiss him on the lips her first day as a volunteer nurse; the man who had put a proposal of marriage in the back end of a hen so that the hen laid an egg containing the offer of marriage, which the girl opened at breakfast; a horrible man who had had "his tubes tied," so that he could enjoy sexual intercourse without the danger of procreation. Dick said, "Cal and I are haunted and harassed by a disaster which you girls are relieved of." We discussed the prostate operation in saturating detail. The *Reve* now offered from its hold, a set of canvas curtains that completely enclosed the back cabin, and which for no reason could fasten down completely on one side but not the other. Shut in, the hurricane lantern fuming, the cabin heavy with a thick canvas and coal oil dew, I took a last look through our canvas curtains at the Sound. Captain Claaussens questioned

about anchorage, had said, "Why a fish line will hold you." And yet an unfamiliar, tremendous ridged shadow, like the back of [a] crocodile seemed nearing. We had anchored correctly letting out five and a half times our depth of rope, only we had forgotten the tides, and our anchor was actually floating a fathom or so from bottom.

I can't go on in this detail, and the rest of the *Reve*'s cruise was uneventful. Dick demanded orange juice and blueberries, blueberry pancakes and bacon and eggs and sausage. At noon we reached an island off Blue Hill where we joined up with the Wanning ketch carrying Elizabeth and Susan, Philip and Margaret Booth and two small Booth children. First manhattans and beer on the *Reve*, then martinis on the Wanning ketch. Andy Wanning is of course beautiful on his boat, lazily, gently, absolutely, softly in control. Only we seemed to be drifting nearer the *Reve*, Andy slowly said, "This the strangest thing, we *are* drifting but the anchor rope is always slack." This was no Eberhart ignorant paradox, but a puzzle supported by thirty years of the most patient and skillful seamanship. Meanwhile the drinks, continued, Eberhart, red-faced, manhattan-breathing, began to focus his movie camera on the approaching boats. No one did a thing. Pat Wanning appeared from the hold, where orange-sweat shirted, khaki shorted, a pretty-grayed curl in the middle of her forehead, she had been working with unstopping efficiency. She said, "I am going to make a speech. I know my speeches are very unpopular in my family, nevertheless I am going to make a speech. I have prepared cold consommé, hot Canadian bean soup, hot dogs with relish and mustard, cucumber and tomato salad, coffee, tea and cocoa, but I haven't hands enough to serve you individually. When I pass the food out you must divide it yourselves." Behind her Andy, unlistening, filling another pitcher of martinis. She said to me re schools, ["]of course I like yachting and my free summers too, but I think colleges and schools will have to run twelve months a year; I can't bear it when my husband and children get up in the morning with nothing they *must* do." The great beautiful ketch, costing forty thousand dollars, according [to] the petrified Philip Booth, had drifted within a foot of the *Reve*. It really had. Then Andy started his motor and dragged our anchor away in safety. Meanwhile Elizabeth had drunk a whole water tumbler of the martinis to which she is allergic. She sprawled on the fore-cabin and just (?) out of hearing began [to] discuss sotto voce an amazingly frank and detailed reappraisal of our entire marriage. It went on for an hour and a half. She said that we were all leaving the next day with a trailer for Boston where we would both go [to] doctors. Susan already had her reservation back to Vassar. When we got home

and ever since, it seems as though we were at last in better agreement than we have been since Harriet's birth. I think we will both go to doctors, but we are staying here, *and* poor Susan has gone home two weeks early, the one unplanned outward event of the whole summer. Elizabeth had suddenly turned gray in the face at the thought of a whole month of Susan, who cannot cook, is too recessive to carry on conversation, will talk about nothing but her doctor's thesis with Trilling and Versailles Kentucky and finds ~~anything~~ nothing Elizabeth and I do half as interesting as her own health. Now we are in one another's arms, and feeling a thousand years younger. Of course, Susan's departure was perfectly friendly, not another dislodging of Miss Elsemore.

Oh one last sailing scene. We are in the ketch, sailing under Blue Hill, before the wind at capacity speed, nine and a half knots an hour, carrying full canvas, mainsail, *Geneva*, jigger, and an exotic thing, the mizzen stay-sail that stretches almost vertical in the air between the main mast and the little stern mast. Philip Booth is at the wheel utterly transformed with excitement, quoting Merwin sea poems, Shakespeare, calling Andy "Sir." He looks up and shouts, "By G-god Sir, Sir if this boat is going to j-jibe unexpectedly I'm not going to be resp-ponsible." Then Andy sleepy, floating lightly and indifferently as a cloud is back at the helm and Pat says, "Andy knows everything about boats but all his commands sound like questions."

Once I got started writing about the cruise, I found going on too pleasant to stop, but after so much buffoonery, like Pat Wanning I want to make a little speech. Your advice about going to a doctor and keeping up one's patience, sobriety, toughness and gaiety is dreadfully true, and I am sure that all is beginning to be well and that Elizabeth and I really profoundly love and are charmed by one another and we will be a safe happy place for little Harriet. All will come and one begins to see the ways.

Also I want you to know that you need never again fear my overstepping myself and stirring up confusion with you. My frenzied behavior during your visit has a history and there is one fact that I want to disengage from all its harsh frenzy. There's one bit of the past that I would like to get off my chest and then I think all will be easy with us.

Do you remember how at the end of that long swimming and sunning Stonington day after Carley's removal by Tommy, we went up to, I think, [to] the relatively removed upper Gross house and had one of those real fried New England dinners, probably awful. And we were talking about this and that about ourselves and I was feeling the infected hollowness of the Carley business draining out of my heart, and you said rather humorously yet it was truly meant, "When you write my epitaph, you must say I was the loneliest person

who ever lived." Probably you forgot, and anyway all that is mercifully changed and all has come right since you found Lota. But at the time everything, I guess (I don't want to overdramatize) our relations seemed to have reached a new place. I assumed that would be just a matter of time before I proposed and I half believed that you would accept. Yet I wanted it all to have the right build-up. Well, I didn't say anything then. And of course the Eberharts in-laws wasn't the right stage-setting, and then there was that poetry conference at Bard and I remember one evening presided over by Mary McCarthy and my Elizabeth was there, and going home to the Bard poets' dormitory, I was so drunk that my hands turned cold and I felt half-dying and held your hand. And nothing was said, and like a loon that needs sixty feet, I believe, to take off from the water, I wanted time and space, and went on assuming, and when I was to have joined you at Key West I was determined to ask you. Really for so callous (I fear) a man, I was fearfully shy and scared of spoiling things and distrustful of being steady enough to ~~do you~~ be the least good. Then of course the Yaddo explosion came and all was over. Yet there were a few months. I suppose we might almost claim something like apparently Strachey and Virginia Woolf. And of course there was always the other side, the fact that our friendship really wasn't a courting, was really disinterested (bad phrase) really led to no encroachments. So it is. Let me [say] this though and then leave the matter forever: ~~it has a~~ I do think free will is sewn into everything we do; you can't cross a street, light a cigarette, drop saccharine in your coffee without really doing it. Yet the possible alternatives that life allows us are very few, often there must be none. I've never thought there was any choice for me about writing poetry. No doubt if I used my head better, ordered my life better, worked harder etc. the poetry would be improved, and there must be many lost poems, innumerable accidents and ill-done actions. ~~Now will say that the~~ But asking you is *the* might have been for me, the one towering change, the other life that might have been had. It was that way for these nine years or so that intervened. It was deeply buried, and this spring and summer (really before your arrival) it boiled to the surface. Now it won't happen again, though of course I always feel a great blitheness and easiness with you. It won't happen, I'm really underneath utterly *in* love and sold on my Elizabeth and it's a great solace to me that you are with Lota, and I am sure it is the will of the heavens that all is as it is.

I wish we had three more weeks in low gear, drifting with the wind, sustained by three or four servants here, when you and I and Lota and Elizabeth could have passed the time without hurry or pressure. But that too will come and I am sure everyone loves, admires and approves of everyone else and are

far closer happier than a month ago now because a great block and question mark is gone.

We go to Boston on the fifth of September. Perhaps the fifteenth or there abouts would be the ideal time for you and Lota to make your visit and I promise to take Lota to Raymonds and Iver Johnson and Charles Street and my father's old tacky beloved army navy stores—wherever there's hardware, there we'll go.

Love,
 Cal

P.S. The last part is too heatedly written with too many *and*s and so forth. I guess it doesn't much matter though. The records are French Renaissance Vocal Music (Nadia Boulanger) Decca; there and old and new French song concert also directed by Boulanger put out by Decca Vox. The Prévert songs are Les Frères Jacques Polydor 1st series. Have you seen the huge monthly record catalogues. They list everything under five or things crossing classifications and would be handy to take home. I guess you're wise about the readings, though we wish we could hear you. Certainly there are trifles, not interesting challenges. Why doesn't Miss Baumgarten tackle Straus himself, surely he won't dare be so miserly as Giroux.

302. *To Anthony Ostroff*

August 23, 1957

Dear Tony:

Sorry not to have answered sooner; usually I am slow at answering *all* letters yet each time try to think of a new explanation[,] for we New Englanders can never get over the idea that simple experience is marked with pointers left here by providence, that all is allegorical and has its clue. Well, for the last two weeks I have been having a split life, from more or less noon on: tennis, outboarding, guests, clambakes, children's home-made circuses, records of old music, blue bay and green elm leaves; but in the morning from seven thirty on, a dark room, a glaring electric light bulb, stinking pajamas, a rising surf of cigarette butts, and reading and writing. The days are gone before they begin.

Do come on the tenth or eleventh and [spend] some time with us, all our time if we have a nurse. I look forward to introducing you to Elizabeth. I've tried to tell some of your fine narratives, the Chicago opera, the house built

not to house a baby, the young Heifetz, but my versions are indeed starved and pale and wait the voice of the master. We have lots of people we want you to meet around Boston if there's time and I'm sure you'll enjoy yourself.

Yours,

Cal

P.S. Yaddo! Ah me, it's nine years now since Elizabeth and I blew our lids there and tried to blow the roof off. The results were fortunate. Elizabeth Ames stands where she has always stood and we ended up married.

303. *To Elizabeth Bishop*

239 Marlborough Street
Boston 16, Massachusetts
September 11, 1957

Dearest Elizabeth—

I've put off writing you till I could proudly report that I had nailed down Dr. Taves; however, he's out of town, so that will have to wait.

Really things have turned the corner! We're getting on very cheerfully and sensibly. We have been back in Boston, almost a week and have spent the time mostly with ourselves, calling up no one. The only trouble with this is that one must take what comes, and what comes is the editor of the *Yale Review* with his white shoes, his fashionable conservatism and his young minister friend or our very icy Norwegian friend [(]have noticed how every young man of talent is now a minister or a playwright or a baby-doctor? The *50's*[)] who thinks he's Stendhal and who looks like Alger Hiss, and who is always explaining what a success his last visit to his about to be abandoned Dutch wife has been.

I've been furiously writing at poems and spent whole blue and golden Maine days in my bedroom with a ghastly utility bedside lamp on, my pajamas turning oily with sweat, and I have six poems started. They beat the big drum too much. There's one in a small voice that's fairly charmingly written I hope (called "Skunk Hour," not in your style yet indebted a little to your Armadillo). If I can get two short lines and a word, I'll mail it to you. The others, God willing, will come to something in the course of the winter. At least I feel I have armloads of lines and leads.

Back here I've gotten side tracked into reading. Emerson on Montaigne,

the two terrible senate scenes in Sejanus, they beat anything of their kind, and though not exactly contemporary, yet are—change a little decor and the blank verse—almost unbearably what has happened in Russia under Stalin, might happen anywhere. Jonson has a bold steadiness and here hardly ever flinches away into parody and the clichés of exaggeration. Went through John Ransom's complete selected poems (75 pages of big print) again. They are almost all queer Chaplinlike charades of himself: looking at children, young girls, the heaven and more often the knotted ravel of marriage. Then I went through Graves—more force than Ransom, more poems and kinds of poems. There is not a banality, I think anywhere, though a somewhat sparring, boxerlike and too steely man. But what a wonderfully nervous and ever exercised mind—each poem knocks me in a corner with a wet towel over my head. I liked the Morgenstern—He's not in the main and perhaps too glowing and grandiose German line. Have you read Heine's "Morphine," and "Der Sheidende" (the ending[,] very Jewish and German with its bluster, comicality, clicking sounds, confusion of pronouns[,] is about the wittiest poem I know of). Two long poems seem magnificent to me[:] Hebel's father and son dialogue in dialect, as good as Frost or Wordsworth, and much more serene, humorous and peopled; then Carossa's long lament for destroyed Germany . . . it reminds me of some of Randall's and some of mine (like me he even has the Cologne Cathedral, though I suppose that's not such a coincidence) it's [a] good deal deeper than we are, and if it's a little steady and too massive in expression, that too seems right and felt. Then there's the long Hölderlin that [I] guess goes the furthest of all, and almost all the Goethe—he has an even tempered agility that seems now too nimble and then too usual, there are no earthquakes, yet if one could take him, one might shed the poet's worst temptation, the temptation to get off the ground, roar and go blind. Goethe doesn't. My last reading has been Keats' letters, but I've just finished them, finished myself, and will keep quiet. Ah though! all of it just four years (in Trilling's selection) and young enough to make Booth and Merwin seem gray—all the foolery, and gaiety and shouldering into what life gave.

I have meant (talking about shouldering) to ~~reply to~~ wave a flag at your "so filthy rich and hideously uncomfortable." I agree mostly and we seem to strike everyone from away very harshly—vibrant, stiff, sickly. But I don't know, if it's the water one must swim in, where most of what one knows about life comes from, most of one has to love—it doesn't hurt so much. It is liveable.

So Harriet finds. She can now manage a few consonants *Da Da dadada*—though the immensity that these words designate doesn't seem to have sunk

in. She can't cook[,] she can now pull herself to her feet (first occasion on a cage of guinea ~~pick~~ pigs belonging to my cousin Alice's baby and removed from Harriet who had in two seconds half depilated them) and yesterday we caught her going through my Salem cigarettes and drooling a sweet trickle of brown juice. Come and ~~see~~ stay with us, Dear, with Lota.

Love,
Cal

P.S. Thanks for Lora the seal; Why can't *I* carry a tune!

304. To William Carlos Williams

September 30, 1957

Dear Bill:

I don't know why I've been so slow in thanking you for the volume of your letters. I am awfully proud to be in it. I was talking to Dick Eberhart about it this summer and he said "darn it I wish they had printed my letters to Williams." Well, I don't feel that way about mine, or his really either, but I do wish the Marianne Moore letters to you had been printed. You are mighty versatile—plays, criticism, history, autobiography, novels in different styles, every kind of poem—but here I'm struck by the variety of your personal voices—yours to Miss Moore is not the same as yours to Ezra, or again yours in the very beautiful, tender letters to Flossie. You know how to hit like thunder (Ezra) and yet you can be most practical and courteous. I think being a doctor made you as a writer, and that that freedom for full artistic concentration and perfection would have taken away far more than it would have brought you. Your best work couldn't be more perfect and it has that lifeblood of the arts, the real world. Well, we all get it in our different ways, according to our calling.

I've been writing poems like a house a fire, i.e. for me that means five in six weeks, fifty versions of each. I've been experimenting with mixing loose and free meters with strict in order to get the accuracy, naturalness, and multiplicity of prose, yet, I also want the state and surge of the old verse, the carpentry of definite meter that tells me when to stop rambling. There's no ideal form that does for any two of us, I think; I much enjoyed your rebuke to Viereck's rash claims for rime and conservative politics. However, these too have their place, if decently used.

I read at the *Y* on the 23rd and hope you will be free for a visit sometime around then. Elizabeth and baby Harriet are full of fun and vigor this fall.

Love to you both,

Cal

P.S. I see I forgot to say that I feel more and more technically indebted to you, growing young in my forties!

305. To William Empson

October 9, 1957

Dear Empson:

One really must write when one likes something. I thought your piece on Graves' Oxford lectures took him down without being in anyway less bold than he is. I liked your bit about being the underground against fairies. I think Graves is being Irish perhaps rather than splenetic when he hits below the belt. I like his boxer's way of doing it and don't believe a word. His own poems do make most other poets seem tame—how it must have burned him up to have been written off for thirty years as academic, except when he wrote light verse. Also, in a crazy way, I think he has something about man against woman that the new religious people have missed.

Your Joyce seemed madly screwy at first, but I end up feeling that you must be right even down to the affair with Molly. There is the blasting side too; I was reading Virginia Woolf's diary that "Tom came in. The first time I've seen him enthusiastic about anything. He said that the end of *Ulysses* was so good that it would make any writing (including anything more by Joyce) impossible for the next twenty years." (paraphrase)

And now your Donne. I know little science, and can't read the college critics and text-men; however, love, pluralism, man with woman etc. mean something, God knows. And here too, I think I agree with you. I rather enjoy Church, hymns, communion and all; but intellectually so many Christians are almost paranoid about everyone else. The number of beliefs and non-beliefs that will work well enough in practice must be infinite (if time and the world are).

We have a baby daughter, Harriet, nine months old, very strenuous and delightful, also thank God, a nurse. I guess we were rather late about it—last January I sat with another almost father—He was gray with anxiety because

his wife had been in labor for fourteen hours and he was about to miss his undergraduate midyears. He had been a paratrooper and told me the peace-time mortality was one in 50! All our younger generation writer friends (mostly women) have had two or three children at thirty and listen to us gray-faced with experience when we tell our mistakes. It makes us feel very impertinent, young and jaunty.

I've been writing poems again lately (five in the last seven weeks and my first in four or five years). And this has taken me back to rereading poets I used to like. "The Ants" (to start at the beginning) is a wonderful underground business—we underground men! Often I get all netted up reading you; but you make most poets seem very precious and wooden and arty.

Write us how you are. I find among the photographs that have stayed around on the mantle-piece of my study is one of you, bearded, fists clenched, trousers unpressed—everything atilt—as you rush around the baseball diamond at Kenyon.

Elizabeth sends her love,
 Cal

P.S. Thanks for looking me up years ago when I was sick in New York. That's all over.

306. To Randall Jarrell

October 11, 1957

Dear Randall:

I was just rummaging through a carton of old poems, envelopes, pictures etc. and came on some of my poems all marked up, stabbed, puffed, and dissected by you. You had such wit and patience and such generosity and justice, at least in your jokes: "these divisions roll on square wheels"; "you generally have one line in a poem when the rhythm gets not just harsh but gets tetanic like a muscle under too long tension." The times come back and I feel excited all over again.

There's a catch in this prologue. I've been writing poems lately again, my first in a good four years. And I want to try them out on you! Do you feel in the mood? I'll send one, and then if I get a peep out of you, will follow it with four or five more. I've been loosening up the meter, as you'll see and horsing out all the old theology and symbolism and *verbal* violence.

I suppose we shouldn't swap too many compliments, but I am heavily in your debt. I've been going through your selected poems quite a lot, and marvel again at how supple, scientific and personal they are. The War poems are perhaps still the best to me as a group. This reading I find I like particularly many of the short quatrain Heine-like ones. I think you and Elizabeth are worlds better than anyone else. The next is Shapiro—mostly in early poems, though there have been some good ones in the last year or so. He has a really Donne-like smash and something racy and Jewish added to Auden's wit. Something, however, clots for me in almost all the best and fierce pieces. There's a new English poet, Larkin, that I like better than anyone since Thomas. I've been reading him since last spring and really like him better than Thomas. He is by far the most interesting, I think of the Amis, Wain bunch, and unlike our smooth younger poets says something.

Elizabeth Bishop showed me a sheaf of your poems last spring and I liked particularly one about death and a statue(?) I only saw them a few minutes. And now your Jamestown again. The first part particularly is terrific, the newt! Everyone in the collection looks awfully good on the first reading; the historic quotes help. Then they all begin to level off into Paul Engle. His by the way strikes me as one of the best—simplified Hart Crane (in Crane's laureate manner). You, however, are yourself, unhurt by the occasion. I liked the beginning of Meredith's about Mozart, but the end made me feel very irreverent about our country.

We expect to be in Washington sometime around the sixth of December, when I give a Phi Beta Kappa reading at William and Mary. They only pay fifty dollars, but said: "We hope your wife will be our guest." So I caught them, and said, "Does that mean you'll pay her air-transportation?" So they did.

Best to Mary, affectionately,
Cal

307. *To Robert Giroux*

October 11, 1957

Dear Bob:

This is an author to publisher letter. My autobiography is on the shelf (or rather in my desk-drawer where I have a hundred tousled pages) for the moment. However, I've been writing poems for the last two months and now have half a book and hope to have a whole book by June. Would you like to

buy out my old stuff from Harcourt Brace? Or do whatever is necessary for you to publish my new poems? I don't know anyone really at H&B and would like to stick with you.

Also I have a publishing suggestion. There's a young English poet, Philip Larkin, who strikes me as more exciting than any English poet since Auden. His book is called *The Less Deceived*, Marvell Press, which you should be able to pick up at the Gotham or the Holiday. He has an earlier book which I haven't read put out by Faber, and there's an article about him in the current *Sewanee* by John Wain. He hasn't an American publisher and would be a real scoop for you. I'd be glad to write an all-out blurb.

We hear about you from Elizabeth Bishop, & wish we were getting to New York soon. I'll be reading at the *Y* on February 23. Do you suppose we could have our annual opera outing with you and Eileen some time around then, say the Friday or Saturday before?

Have you heard anything about Eilot's coming here this spring or possibly next fall? I thought his essays got very hasty and inadequate reviews.

Yours so ever,

Cal

308. To Randall Jarrell

October 24, 1957

Dear Randall:

Buy a copy of the Hall, Simpson *The New Poets of England and America* [(]Meridian[)], and read the Snodgrass selections. I'm sure you remember him with his silly name and his Mahler songs. I had him off and on in classes at Iowa for years and thought he had done the one or two of the best poems that my students had written there; and I let it go at that. I now think he is incomparably the best poet we've had since you started. The "Heart's Needle" series, written to his little daughter after his divorce are heart-breaking and dazzling technically. And he's just as good on other subjects, see his "April Inventory." Tell me what you think. I don't see how I can be wrong, and when I showed them to Elizabeth, who has ~~knot~~ patience with the slick new poets, she felt just as I did. I really think he can stand with Larkin.

It was good to talk to you again and terribly refreshing to know that you and Mary liked my *Skunks*. I've been working like a skunk, doggedly and happily since mid-August and have seven or eight poems finished(?) some quite long and all very direct and personal. They are mostly written in a sort of free

verse that takes off from the irregularities of my Ford poem. I'll get them typed up for you next week and mail them off. I'll be very sad if you don't like them. I don't see how I could ever have finished *Lord Weary* without your quips and praise.

My teaching is very easy—two seminars, both on Tuesday. One is of course the usual poetry writing class. In the other, I take short bits of prose, such as *Kiriloff's death* and read them carefully just as you would poetry. It's very interesting. In prose you have to be interested in *what* is being said. I teach, I'm afraid, like a painter, almost no preparation but very hard work in class. In that way it's very exciting for me, like going fishing.

What you were saying about Dostoyevsky raises questions. I'm sure I like bad men much better than you do. They are God's creatures too, and I don't know what writing would have done without them. I think the French poets from Baudelaire through Apollinaire have really renewed poetry, they are modern poetry (except for Hardy and Hopkins). And Rilke and Yeats and all our own best people (except Frost) have come from them. But what a lot! as Arnold would say. Laforgue and Apollinaire are lovable men, but not Baudelaire and Rimbaud, or Corbière or Valéry. This is getting a bit off the point I'm trying to make. I'm really talking about the semi-criminal poets, . . . in a queer way they do connect with Mallarmé and Valéry, who were utterly proper in their conduct, though deep and explosive in their souls. Well, Dostoyevsky seems to me to be simply by far the greatest of all the *poètes* and novelists *maudits*. And I do think Alyosha must have been part of him just as much as Stavrogin and the Underground man. An old letter of yours says that Allen actually seems to "look on violence as a *virtue*." No, it's not. Yet darkness honestly lived through is a place of wonder and life. So much has come from there.

I agree with you more and more about Graves. He is a mischievous soul, but few poets have more dash and charm, and he makes almost any poet seem repetitious and conventional. I gave my class his "Blue-Fly," and thought it was as fine as *The expense of spirit*. There's so much good Graves! This letter rambles on, unparagraphed . . . I've been reading quite a little lately: Catullus, Wordsworth, Keats' letters, Baudelaire, Rimbaud, a very useful for me German Penguin Anthology with literal translations at the foot of the page. The man isn't too good on Rilke, but I made many discoveries: the late Heine again: "Morphine," "Der Scheidende"; a marvelous long poem in Nord Deutsch by Hebel (as good as Wordsworth?); Goethe again; Hölderlin's "Brot und Wein" (which I stole my moon images in my David and Bathsheba from)[;] some good 17th century people, Gryphius and Fleming; a wonderful

war elegy (much in our line) by Carossa; a magical 13th century poem about children (like a whole group of Grimms) by someone really named Der Wilde Alexander; Morgenstern, etc. Really it's almost as good a poetry as English.

I saw quite a lot of Elizabeth Bishop when she was here saying goodbye to her Aunt Florence. It's [a] great joy to see her so thin and beautiful and healthy. Before she had gone we had told each other almost everything that had ever happened to us. She certainly has risen from the ocean's bottom! I like some [of] her latest poems, the "Armadillo," the Pound poem and one about a queer Brazilian old man who works for them. I really groaned to see her go back to Brazil.

I've been endlessly garrulous, and haven't even said anything about my little daughter, who is beginning to captivate me. Absolutely unbelievable robustness and delicacy and so many pretty dresses! However, I can't describe her.

We are awfully distressed about your illness, and hope the X-ray will show that all is well. You sounded very dim and hoarse at first on the telephone, but in a few minutes you were exactly yourself. Let it be so! I've been worrying quite a lot about you.

Love from us to you all,
 Cal

309. To Elizabeth Bishop

October 25, 1957

My Darling receding Elizabeth:

I guess I can match Miss Moore in explosive openings! However, you never recede and I seem to be always with you in the doorway of your aunt's brown apartment, ringing the bell for her to open the door again. You are with me always.

Otherwise, my poems still go on. I now have a jail one, a three and a half page one about my being five years old and seeing my Uncle Devereux for the last time (at my Grandfather's country place) before he died of Hodgkin's disease, another on my Father, one on flying to Rapallo for Mother's dying—all very personal! I'll type them out next week and mail them along with the others to you. I sent "Skunk Hour" with fear and trembling to Randall—he's never acknowledged the existence of my autobiography chapter. However, he's the most incredible reader—I have been looking over his comments on drafts of my old *Lord Weary* poems, so witty and enthusiastic: "This certainly is a just right poem; you were smart not to put in any of the unpleasant, stomach-upsetting details you love. (You and me both, for that matter.)" Re

my "Exile's Return." Well, he's delighted and wrote me back air mail saying, "I like the poem *very* much. The motion really has changed and is much clearer and easier." You know Randall has his own flippant natural language— I'll never forget John Ransom's writing an essay attacking Shakespeare's sonnets (with which Randall couldn't have been more in disagreement with!). Randall and Ransom sat talking one evening and every minute Randall got more enthusiastic about Shakespeare and more & more breezy about Ransom's critical points. At the end Ransom said, "That boy just doesn't have a critical vocabulary." Well, I couldn't be more pleased, so I'll mail (with fear and trepidation) my other poems to the consultant in Washington. Poor fellow, he's been quite sick for the last *two* months with flu and some kind of respiratory infection. We talked on the phone and he sounded very croaking at first, but then he was soon the old Randall, telling me "You know I've just read Dostoyevsky through. He was a very bad man, it seems."

I must tell you an indecent story about Frank Parker and the Bloom marriage. You know after six o'clock, Frank has only two interests: drinking red wine and talking about the sexual act. He was here the other night and had soon finished two quarts of red wine[,] stuttering and sunrise-color he moved over to the needle-point foot-stool in front of Elizabeth. First he said, "Wasn't Hyman Elizabeth Bishop's *Grande passion*.["] My Elizabeth answered rather sourly, "*One* of Elizabeth Bishop's grand passions!"—marvelous picture! you like George Sand scattering your heart up and down the Atlantic sea-board: Hyman, Hart Crane, Neruda, me . . . oh dear. Then Frank began on the Blooms saying that at first Nina threw herself on Hyman, almost forced the marriage, after the marriage used to dress up and ask him, "do I look pretty?" And Hyman would contract. Frank feels they are closer now, but he is watching like a falcon, ready to swoop—nothing attracts him more than his heroes' wives. In the middle of this rather nettle-like conversation, Lesley suddenly appeared and said, "How do you pronounce *zucchini*?" as though she and Elizabeth had never met! By the way, I have two mean verbs for an evening with the Rahvs: one *blows* and the other *sags*. They are warm-hearted in their immense immobile way and have quite changed Charles Street, which their apartment looks out on. You feel you are back in the twenties, lights, sounds, hole-in-the-wall Bohemian bars.

I haven't much news and have been staying at home writing. I had a good evening with I. A. Richards alone, both of us reading our poems—he's so much quicker and more innocent than I am. Saw Wilson at the Schlesingers; we all got quite drunk and I forgot all the things he said. He thinks Waugh is a Calvinist—to his credit, Wilson thinks that he too is a Calvinist. He said,

"You know some women are wonderful when you are sick["]—he has just built himself a gout-box (for sleeping) ["]and some loathe it." (Mary) We are going to visit them at Wellfleet about two weeks from now and I'll try to stay sober and report to you. (I do not drink much really, and for daily use I have found a mild all year round Bock Beer, made by the Haffenreffers, old Rivers' School-mates.[)]

Dearest Elizabeth, I always think of you. Send me your poems and a long letter. I loved your postals dropped like Persephone's pomegranate seeds.

Love from us both to you both,

Cal

I must tell you that I've discovered a new poet, W. D. Snodgrass really his name, as he well knows; one poem has the line: "Snodgrasss is drifting through the universe"—he was once one of my Iowa students, and I merely thought him about the best. Now he turns out to be better than anyone except Larkin (Randall, by the way, likes Larkin as much as I do: "I was just delighted with what you said about Larkin. I'm crazy about him. Say what one will, there['s] a surprising amount of objectivity in taste.") His [(]Snodgrass's[)] poems are much more personal than Larkin's, remind one a little of Vaughan and Traherne with a Laforgue-like wit and a perfect ear. I'll send you a bunch that are in an anthology gotten out by Hall and Simpson; I'm really stunned. Elizabeth was as moved as I was by a group called "The Heart's Needle" written to his little daughter after his divorce—very amusing and heart-breaking all, in modern idiom and as measured as Herrick. Maybe you'll agree with me.

I'm sending a picture of me to be followed by one of the family, as soon as we can get one that does Harriet justice.

310. *To Flannery O'Connor*

October 29, 1957

Dear Flannery:

We've just finished reading your "View of the Woods," and the margins are now fouled up with blue pen-marks for lines I like. But I like it all really; there [are] no flies on your craftsmanship. I have one hesitant kick, I guess, and am afraid of sounding like my Mother, "Bobby, why don't you write about nice things?" Or your Mother?

Well, you know Jarrell can qualify for having a *poete maudit* view of the

world. Last spring he almost had a stroke protesting to me about a *New Yorker* piece by Auden on fairy stories. Auden had said, "When the girl says she wants to kill Grandma, she really means *I wish Grandma would leave me* alone now." Randall said that "I really did want to boil my Grandmother!" However, reviewing one of my poems Randall wrote, "It would be hard to imagine a more nightmarish poem than "Thanksgiving is over" . . . It is almost with a sigh of relief that one concludes that all this is the possible [with] which art does not have to deal."

And so I do have one little kick to make at your "View." You are too much of a moralist; it's as though Mary Pitt were writing the story, inspired by playing the old Jehovah a little with her imagined world. I don't really mean all this carping and am mailing you my two favorite funny books, Laforgue's prose and the *Good Soldier Schweik* (my third favorite is Bouvard and Pécuchet, but I'm sure you already have it). They are both unbearable enough in God's truth, but they don't play Jehovah quite.

I heard about you last spring from a guy at Santa Barbara, and now again from Denver Lindley who told the story of the Negro hunt almost as you ~~would~~ might. Dear Flannery, write us a note and send us your picture so I can put you up on my mantelpiece with a few other old friends, E. Bishop, Taylor, Allen Tate.

This has been a wonderful and turning year with us. We adore our little baby and fortunately have a nurse, age 17, a child, to do the dreary work. Even then Elizabeth was almost a ghost after the early months. It's something becoming parents just at the age when our friends are beginning to sigh for their grandchildren. Also I've been writing poems again. They are much freeer and better I think than my old ones. You might enjoy both the humor and the anguish, and I would mail you a few, only there'll soon be a group in *PR*. I find you and Salinger much more up my alley than the young poets. But a wonder, an old Iowa student of mine (and of others) W. D. Snodgrass suddenly turns out to be inspired, the terrible group "The Heart's Needle," to his little daughter more or less lost to him by divorce. They are full of Iowa City scenery that you'd enjoy, even trips to the zoo, "bringing life-savers for the footpad coons to scour"; and there are a hundred other details as good.

We are sending you a couple of pictures of Harriet, knowing your weakness for children—along with our love,

 Cal

P.S. I have a Georgia girl in one of my classes, small, yellow-haired, glasses—a sort of ghost of you, if anyone could be. Her name is Miss Yeats, Irish but

a Baptist. Somehow today we got off the Balzac and Flaubert we were supposed to be reading onto you and Georgia scenery. I used the opening paragraph of the "View" to show how description can [be] bare yet all new and alive. Soon Miss Yeats was talking about your region. She thinks of you as the local goddess and would like to send you a note during her Christmas vacation and call on you. I hope you feel as boisterous and fresh as you sound in your work.

311. To Elizabeth Bishop

November 8, 1957

Dearest Elizabeth:

Here are my poems and a picture with them if I can get some sort of cardboard to protect it. I won't try to write a letter now because we are setting off on our Wellfleet Wilson week-end in a few minutes and I want to get my poems off now.

Did I tell you I've been deep in Laforgue (Smith's prose and the poems in French); it's [the] saddest story since time began; yet as he says contrasting himself with Corbière, "I have humor." It never leaves him. How few writers are readable after one has finished his *Hamlet*! Read two good poems of yours in Humphries' anthology—I like the outcast children very much. Wish I weren't such a rough writer, and could be inspired to do such a subject. I guess we all have our own fiddles—toute la Lyre! This non-sense came into my head—I guess it means, all our different sounds are part of the show.

 Love to you both,
 Cal

312. To Ezra Pound

November 8, 1957

Dear Ezra:

We expect to be in Washington the week-end of December 6, and I look forward to seeing you. Here are some poems, I've been writing like a house a-fire for the last three months. I hope you'll like some of them. I've been bolder about meter, and taken no count of the scansion in many of the new ones. I like regular meter too though, and don't feel I have to choose. Still after twenty years of writing in harness, it's not suicidal to cut loose a bit. My

stuff is small and self-centered compared with yours and perhaps needs a certain tightness to come off.

We've enjoyed seeing Omar, and will have an evening with him again before I see you. He is tireless about his teaching and has little time to loaf. I guess next year will be a lot lighter for him. Hope you are booming and flourishing as you were last year.

My love to Dorothy,

Cal

313. To J. F. Powers

November 13, 1957

Dear Jim:

It's a great sorrow to me that we live such continents apart and only get together once every four or five years. No one rouses me out of myself more than you. The Wilson was very timely: I found it waiting for us just after a week-end with the Wilsons at Wellfleet. It sort of Ok'd the visit. What a visit. Wilson drinks like an ox, like Ted Roethke, and yet it does no harm. Only at about 11:30, he becomes rather speechless. The rest of the time conversation pours back and forth. I know no one who has read so much and is so good company about what he has read.

Did I tell you about my reading in Seattle last spring and staying with Ted. He has a lovely young (early thirties) Bennington student wife. Much prettier and more mature and frailer than Ted. She was in a strange barbed wired hospital for TB, and Ted was on the town. He only serves whiskey to his students. After four days, I was all but dead: eating, reciting poetry, hearing Roethke poetry, losing at bowls, inspecting a fifty thousand dollar modern house with Irish Victorian furniture that Ted, feeling he was Von Hindenburg, wished to buy from the painter Morris Graves. It was really great fun. When June came Ted's wife returned to him and he bought a much simpler house, then late this September I had a wild letter: "Well, it's happened again! Same old routine: 4 or 5 city police (as the boogs say) dragging me off to the same old nut-bin." "I want *something* from Harvard quick either a promise or a final commitment about Archie's job . . ." Then ten days later, he was much better and home again and writing, "you may have got a garbled or semi-garbled letter from me." I think he's OK now.

I envy you Ireland. We hope to go to England a year from next June. Baby

Harriet is a huge handful. You wouldn't know Lizzie, cooing, blasting the skin off nurses, talking a whole new baby language. We're awfully delighted with her and glad she's not a boy that I would have to take mountain-climbing.

I've had a fine spell of writing that began about the middle of August and seems to be still going. All poetry, but much loosened up from the toil of writing the prose of my autobiography. I think it's the best writing I've done, and Oh how welcome after four silent years.

Last summer Elizabeth Bishop came to see us in Maine and we spent an evening with the E. B. Whites. Mrs. White said that you'd just sent her a new story that astounded her. Either it was a masterpiece or she couldn't get it at all. I trust it is a masterpiece in any case.

Do write us at length and tell me about your life and what to read my baby daughter.

Love from us both to you both,

 Cal

P.S. Is there really a Victoria Road in Ireland?

314. To Elizabeth Bishop

December 3, 1957

Darling Elizabeth:

"Come ye sons of art," arrived this morning and I played it in the sunlight of my study, and felt that I myself not Queen Mary was having the birthday celebration. I've liked Ritchie for a long time. And the two counter tenors! I know nothing male that sounds so much like what I imagine the castrati must have been—unearthly, glorious. This won't be a long letter. You must feel inundated to death with letters gifts, manuscript etc. from me. I was awfully proud of getting your cable from Brazil. Please write me your slow and cool critical opinion when you are in the mood.

I sent copies of my poems to Randall, Allen and Ezra Pound. Allen wrote back boastfully that he was expecting a visit from Smith and Barbara Howes and would write me after they left. (I wonder if Allen hasn't got a crush on Barbara Howes! Brandeis gives a yearly fifteen hundred dollar poetry prize for a poet under forty—or almost under forty—Katherine Hoskins got it last year.) Allen was a judge and it went unanimously to Barbara Howes. I've never heard of anyone who could read her. Randall hasn't answered at all. Pound wrote:

"Mr. Lowell of Boston
 No light Baby-Austin
but when the garbage froze or
the vast accumulation of residues
caused exacerbation,
 a bulldozer
was wanted for deep excavation . . .

whether I can corrugate
castigate or elevate this nonsense
into somthink worthy the occasion
 REEMains to be sawn
rough, hew them as we will."

This does seem unusually clear for Ezra. But, whose non-sense? His or mine? I'm not sure if enthusiastic flattery is meant or fierce abuse. My other fan is Philip Rahv. Who says, "Diss is da break-through for Cal and for poetry. The one real advance since Eliot." You guess how my head is turned. But really I've just broken through to where you've always been and gotten rid of my medieval armor's undermining. They are taking "Skunk Hour" and three others. I'm dedicating "Skunk Hour" to you. A skunk isn't much of a present for a Lady Poet, but I'm a skunk in the poem.

We've talked over a lot of things together I've never mentioned to Elizabeth. If you ever feel like writing me privately (I don't mean anything by this) you can address the letter c/o The Dept. [of] English, Boston University. I really glory in the memory of your visit and miss you terribly. Our love to you and Lota. Cal P.S. I'm flying to Williamsburg tomorrow to read a phi beta kappa poem ("Skunk Hour"!) and will spend four or five days in Washington seeing Randall and Cousin Harriet.

 Cal

P.S. I enclose 3 more poems; you've seen them all before in cruder version. Jesus! I've really exploded my powder writing and feel I have no force left. I hope for more next year.

315. To William Carlos Williams

<div align="right">December 3, 1957</div>

Dear Bill:

Here's a bunch of poems—all that I've done since the book you reviewed six (!) years ago. At forty I've written my first unmeasured verse. It seems to ask for tremendous fire, if it is to come off at all. I've only tried it in a few of these poems, those that are most personal. It's great to have no hurdle of rhyme and scansion between yourself and what you want to say most forcibly. I think even the best of us have much more trouble than we like [to] admit getting our rhymed and metrical verse to even make clear sense. Look at the trouble Allen Tate has, and he's surely one of the most passionate and practiced poets alive.

I've worried a little not hearing from you, but trust that you and Flossie are well. Lizzie and Harriet send their love. Harriet can't talk yet (eleven months) but I've had *two* dreams in which she spoke.

Affectionately,

Cal

P.S. I have been framing my photographs of old friends and hanging them up in my study. I wonder if I could have one of you and Flossie? I was promised one by the guy in Berkeley, but it never came through.

316. To William Carlos Williams

<div align="right">[n.d. December 1957]</div>

Dear Bill:

I'm off in a few minutes to teach 3 Ulysses—Dante, Shakespeare, Joyce . . . not yet Homer! I want to say right away that I consider your letter the greatest honor of my life. You are one of the most cultured men alive, an eternal poet, and one of the greatest ever. I reverence the kind of ipse dixit on my short poems. Who else can speak, if not the masters? Had a sweet poem to me on my poems from Ezra. You and Flossie grow younger each year—I'm young enough but too fat to fly over Grand Canyon.

Love from us three,

Cal

317. To William Carlos Williams

January 22, 1958

Dear Bill:

I will look up Bloodsoe—there aren't too many who are a "hell of a good guy," even in Boston. It'll be exciting to read your book on poetry. I feel it has taken me twenty writing years just to begin to understand your refinements of metrical and idiomatic technique. I have no master, only masters, you are about the first among them.

Ah money! I live on it, i.e.: unearned income. And intend to because it lets me loaf as freely as Walt Whitman. And I get paid about enough to buy neckties for my poetry, for my real work, and little enough for my leisure work, teaching at Boston University. But unearned trust fund income *is* a racket, a lot of boobs live in clover for doing nothing except paying for plates at fundraising dinners for the Republican party. (And Ezra too!)

Have you looked at all recently at Hawthorne's *House of Seven Gables?* It has enough economic history to set the Commonwealth of Massachusetts back on its toes again. Read the opening three or four paragraphs down to the dramatic "God will give him blood to drink." I read them to my prose class and told them that anyone who could digest this much wouldn't elect simpletons like Senator Saltonstall or the bone-headed Irish blow-hards that we seem content with. Why is New England, once the flower and really Attica of American culture now a museum useful for drawing talent to it from other sections of the country? Men who come here because Boston and Cambridge are good addresses?

I've just passed through another of my periodic mental crack-ups, but have been back teaching for three weeks now. I only teach one day a week, so with Christmas vacation coming at a timely time for me, I only missed one class during my entire break-down. I'm fine now.

I read at the Hebrew Y on the 23rd of February and would like to get a friend to drive me out to Rutherford to have lunch with you all on either the 21st or the 22nd—whichever suits you.

Love to you both,
 Cal

P.S. Got the big photograph—wish it had Flossie too. It's now hanging by my study fireplace.

P.P.S. What is the matter with Dave McDowell? I got Katherine Hoskins to send him the manuscript of her new book of poems. And now two or more months have passed and he has never answered her.

And now I see I've almost forgotten to say how much I liked your long murder story. Wonderful episodes like the minister and his bells—odious man. I just met his double, a young doctor, quite out of life, and horning in on others who had lives. The death is done with masterly command, and of course I enjoy my old friend the doctor. You clutch onto life like some fibrous root.

318. To Ezra Pound

January 22, 1958

Dear Ezra:

I'm enclosing a letter from Bill Williams just to show you what you no doubt well know—he speaks mighty reverently about you at least behind your back. Please return the letter.

What are the chances of your giving me a photograph of you and Dorothy? I'm hanging up all my friends and masters in my study, and won't feel the job is at all complete without your picture being there—your beard balancing off the now lonely beard of my old college friend Jarrell.

My visits to you seem to mellow through the years, and I want to say that they have always been a high point in my existence. When Dorothy said the other day that I was one of your oldest new friends, I felt like pinning a banner to my coat, a controlled money banner perhaps. Hope I didn't bend your ear off and appear impervious to your wise explosions. I have to temper your teachings with a good deal of waywardness to get along. One must have many masters not to be a slave to one—I'm talking about the arts, not government!

Yours with love to you both,
 Cal

319. To Allen Tate

January 24, 1958

Dear Allen:

Let's not have a fight about my poems. I like them, and people as different as my Washington Winslow relation, Elizabeth Bishop, Philip Rahv and T. S.

Eliot have liked them and thought they topped my work. But you don't have to, and I want us to stay as good friends as ever. I was going to say that you Southerners are always jamming Picketts charge into a Stonewall. But forget it—I'm Southern.

You *were* uncannily right about my getting sick again. I had a bout of about a month in the Boston Psychopathic and am now back—in fact I've [been] back teaching now for three weeks. Everything seems OK.

I am sorry you don't like my stuff because you are such a generous and good judge. I've been going to school to you for years and hope to life-long. Perhaps even Horace nods. At any rate I'm completely sold on *your* new poems and feel your terza rima lynching is probably your biggest (and most technically perfect) achievement. The rest of the poem too is full of dynamite.

Anyhow, even if I have betrayed the persona you have of me, I hope you won't cut us when you come here in March.

Affectionately yours,
Cal

320. To William Empson

January 29, 1958

Dear Empson:
Your bulling letter and even more your poems have been strangely invigorating to me during the last few days. I won't go into details;—but it can't be denied that almost no praise would be too high for your poems. You have the stamina of Donne, yet a far more useful and empirical knowledge of modern science and English metrics. I think you are the most intelligent poet writing in our language and perhaps the best. I put you with Hardy and Graves and Auden and Philip Larkin . . . All this—because recently the scales, so to speak, have dropped from my eyes and your work is now as clear to me as, say: Frost's.

I wish your theological letter could in some way circulate. It would do our world worlds of good. I, a Christian, have two or three minor bones to pick with your statement.

1. THE GARDEN OF EDEN:—The apple is just an apple (though fenced with airy boogies and taboos). The serpent is free will. Our first parents left the garden, not because of the old Father-God, but because of Adam's failure of nerve. If Adam had stood up, fig-leaved or without, we would still be living the lives of Riley in the garden. Father God was pre-Verbal, of course, and not very articulate.

2. The Christ was killed by the Jews under Caiphas and the Romans under Pontius Pilate. He was manic (just as I—four times—and hundreds of others have been) shortly before his capture. At the time of his capture h[e] was in the depth of a depression. Sweating blood, all but speechless. He didn't quite die but was smuggled by Nicodemus and Joseph of Arimathea from the tomb, and kept reappearing on the margins of activity, at least up [to] the time when he met and commissioned Paul as his Captain general. Did you ever notice what [a] superior job Paul did to the Christ's when he too had to appear in Jerusalem before Lysisas, Festus, Felix and King Agrippa?

3. The machine set up by the Christ and Paul of Tarsus wasn't really a machine biased towards hate and torture but rather one that was all but foolproof. But, of course, pinheaded Goy converts soon stupefied the Catholic church—all the sects, too—into petrifaction.

4. The Mass. The composers, Palestrina, Bach, Beethoven[,] Hayden, Schubert, Verdi, Berlioz, Stravinsky, made a garden even here, i.e.: in the ~~dreary lit~~ crumby liturgical desert of the R.C. Mass. It's not human sacrifice and sadistic torture that is being celebrated, rather it's Christ's climbing to his feet after the cruelest of all electric shock treatments.

Excuse the long rant. I'd rather jammer Bible with you than anyone alive. I do agree a thousand per cent with you about Xtianity (Pound's phrase) stinking up [the] world—Christianity as it is now mostly taught and lived.

Yours very affectionately,

Robert Lowell

P.S. Joseph, the husband of Mary and offshoot of King David, must have been Jesus' real father—any other conclusion would have been *contra naturam*, immoral, and chimerical.

321. To Ezra Pound

January 29, 1958

My dear Ezra:

I guess I can cut out the photo of you at the beginning of the collected *Cantos*. It's [a] shame though to remove an essential organ from that beautiful book, i.e. America's epic. Someday you will be on the stamps, if that's the immortality you want.

I'm sending you a letter [(]please return[)] from William Empson, the most brainy poet writing in English. I'll try and get you a copy of his poems,

but suppose he is out of print, like Hasek's *Soldier Sweik* and Heine's prose in translation.

Do you think a man who has been off his rocker as often as I have been could run for elective office and win? I have in mind the State senatorship from my district—the South End, Back Bay Boston, and your son's Roxbury etc. The incumbent is an inconspicuous Republican. His rival is a standard loosing party democrat. I'd run as a democrat, and if I could edge out in the very difficult primaries, then I'd cream the Republican. And then there'd be vistas before me as I sat in the Boston State Capitol on my little $5,000 a year job that would cost me about $10,000. What's your advice.

Love to you and Dorothy,
Cal

P.S. I may drive with a friend to see you sometime next week. Don't mention this in your reply.

322. *To Isabella Gardner*

[McLean Hospital] Waverly, Mass.
Wednesday, February 12, 1958

Dear Belle:

I'm delighted to be your valentine—what a lovely old-fashioned and large card it is! My illness has brought me deep into your family, George, Bob, and even on the side-lines, John. I even had a short financial chat with your father. I have a nice little lump sum of about $50,000, the only money I own that is not a trust fund, and I am giving it to George to manage. So I am now almost a Gardner.

This business at McLean's isn't exactly very serious. As you probably know, I have been having periodic manic upsets for some nine or ten years. I am here voluntarily to see if I can't get rid of them for good. I have a private room, my typewriter, my FM radio, a door that will shut and frequent visitors. I've been reading Kant and Joyce's *Ulysses*, and have actually finished a poem that has the admiration of I. A. Richards.

Some of my B.U. students have been coming out to me with poems; however, I'm not teaching this term. I rather hope [to] make my Chicago engagement though. And if nothing goes wrong I will read on the 23rd of this month at the Hebrew Y in New York.

I suppose that I should tell you that Lizzie and I are getting a divorce. It's difficult to toss off such a statement in a short letter from a mental hospital. We are both very much of one mind in this decision, and feel harmonious about it. It's a funny thing, our marriage in so many ways was gloriously successful, and yet for nine years there has been a back-breaking (to mix metaphors) jangling of nerves—eventually almost killing to us both. Now we are at peace.

Thanks again for your Valentine and for writing Elizabeth Bishop about me. I shall hope to see you and Bob in March.

Yours affectionately,

Cal

323. To M. L. Rosenthal

Saturday, February 15, 1958

Dear Mr. Rosenthal:

I have just been reading Cargill's interesting piece on Crane. I have always thought the *Bridge* was a triumph of sustained power, and have wondered why the best critics—Tate, Winters and Blackmur, and they were the best—so badly gummed up its achievement. I enclose a sonnet of mine that you might like to print in the *Nation*. It looks rough at first, but it was written with a world of pain and I hope enthusiasm and sympathy.

WORDS FOR HART CRANE

When the Pulitzers showered on some dope
or screw who flushed our dry mouths out with soap,
few people would consider why I took
to stalking sailors, and scattered Uncle Sam's
phony gold-plated laurels to the birds.
Because I knew my Whitman like a book,
stranger in America, tell my country: I,
Catullus Redivivus, once the rage
of the Village and Paris, used to play my role
of homosexual wolfing the stray lambs
~~that~~ who hungered by the Place de la Concorde.
My profit was a pocket with a hole.
Who asks for me, the Shelley of my age,
must lay his heart out for my bed and board.

I'll be interested in hearing from you.
Yours sincerely,
 Robert Lowell

324. To William Carlos Williams

Wednesday, February 19, 1958

Dear Bill:

Thanks for your card. I am afraid I won't be able to see you and Flossie just yet. I am still resting off my attack and am actually staying at McLean's hospital in Waverly. It's all rather free and comfortable—not unlike Yaddo without race courses, night life and literati. I have a sunny private room, read, listen to good music on my radio, and am writing poems, revising my autobiography, etc.

I hope you will send me *Paterson V*. In a month or so I'll mail you another little group of my own stuff, God willing. I now have four or five things you haven't seen. I wouldn't like ever to completely give up meter; it's wonderful opposition to wrench against and revise with. Yet now that I've joined you in unscanned verse, I am struck by how often the classics get boxed up in their machinery, the sonority of the iambic pentameter line, the apparatus of logic and conceit and even set subjects. Still, the muscle is there in the classics, we reread them with joy, and in a sense wherever a man has really worked his stuff outbraves time and novel methods. We would always rather read a good old sonneteer, such as Raleigh or Sidney, than some merely competent fellow who is on the right track. The excellent speak to the excellent.

You're very famous now, but I have been thinking a lot about how bone-headed most of the popular and even good critics have been about you most of your lifetime. It must be fearful to have done something with deadly originality and lucidity and beauty, and then be ignored, scolded, patronized!

Love to Flossie, it will be good to talk to you again.
 Cal

325. To Ezra Pound

Dear Ezra:

Awfully pleased with Martinelli's *two* drawings, an unexpected windfall—
I was just about to cut out my photograph from the collected *Cantos*. Soon you
will be hanging above my hearth like a Chinese ancestor. They are both beau-
tiful jobs and bring their original home to me.

I've been sick with one of my periodic mix-ups. Otherwise I would have
written immediately.

I've been rereading Joyce's *Ulysses* to fill my hands and mind, empty for
the moment of new poems. Your Joyce and Pécuchet essay seems wonderfully
fresh and piercing now after so many years and so many tons of academic
explanation.

Congratulations to you and Dorothy on Omar's coming son. He seems to
be in the highest spirits.

Affectionately yours,

Cal

P.S. I've done a metrical but unrhymed translation of Rimbaud's "Rages de
Caesar," and am embarrassed to see how good it is without my adding much
of anything, even with my subtracting the original's formal sound effects.

326. To Elizabeth Bishop

Saturday, March 15, 1958

Dear Elizabeth:

Oh dear, the record, the record! Almost immediately after writing you my
last letter, I wanted to write another taking it back. Elizabeth and I are happily
back together; I spend long week-ends at home and will soon leave the hospital
entirely. All the late froth and delirium have blown away. One is left strangely
dumb, and talking about the past is like a cat's trying to explain climbing down
a ladder. One would like to look at it all without moodiness or bravado.

I live in an interesting house now at McLean's, one in which no man had
entered since perhaps 1860; suddenly it was made co-ed. It was like entering
some ancient deceased sultan's seraglio. We were treated to a maze of tender

fussy attentions suitable for very old ladies: chocolate scented milk at 8:30; a lounging and snoozing bed-spread after meals, each announcement of an appointment gently repeated at ten minute intervals, an old crone waiting on table barking like television turned on full to pierce through deafness. On the other hand, it took three days to get a shaving glass. The man next to me is a Harvard Law professor. One day, he is all happiness, giving the plots of Trollope novels, distinguishing delicately between the philosophies of Holmes and Brandeis, reminiscing wittily about Frankfurter. But on another day, his depression blankets him. Early in the morning, I hear cooing pigeon sounds, and if I listen carefully, the words: "Oh terror, TERROR!" Our other male, assembles microscopically exact models of clippers and three masted schooners. Both men, and I too, shrink before a garrulous Mrs. Churchill, sometimes related to the statesman and sometimes to the novelist. Each of her sentences has a proper and usually Massachusetts' name. "But of course it was really Francis Xavier Beamis Todd's son?" "How are you related to Thomas Arnold Lowell?" I assumed she meant James Russell Lowell, and was abysmally wrong and have never been [able] to explain. Pointing to the classical moulding on a mantelpiece, she will say, "That's Cameron Forbes, the ambassador to Japan," or begin a dinner conversation with, "Speaking of Rhode Island reds . . ." Sometimes with a big paper napkin stuck like an escaping bra on her throat, she will dance a little jig and talk about being presented to Queen Victoria. She was.

I've done another family poem, a translation of Der Wilde Alexander's poem in the Penguin German anthology, and several Montale pieces from the Penguin Italian, and have improved my poem to you, but it's still too fragmentary to mail.

I've filled this letter with trivia. Things are really very well. I seem [to] have come out of this awfully quickly and easily, I am faithfully contracted to a very keen doctor, and Elizabeth and I are very much at ease and thankful to be together. Let's not let my ~~late~~ slip into the monstrous cloud our love. Love to Lota.

Cal

327. To Peter Taylor

Saturday, March 15, 1958

Dear Peter:
Well, it's almost worth having been sick to have your letter to Elizabeth; I lap up your Saturday staring at the gray gleam of the Ohio Sunday School

tone. It's not much fun writing about these breakdowns after they themselves have broken and one stands stickily splattered with patches of the momentary bubble. Health; but not of kind that encourages the backward look.

I'm back home now for long week-ends, have begun my systematic therapy, and will probably leave the hospital entirely in about two weeks. Life is serene: we go to movies, and concerts; Harriet takes us for long walks over the Public Garden grass on Sundays; I've been translating some Italian and German poems, and have a desk drawer full of fragmentary poems and bits of autobiography. Elizabeth has been terrific, and we're awfully glad to be together.

I've been meaning for several weeks to write you about your *New Yorker* story. After seeing the *Entertainer, Gervaise*, and even a feverish ten day turning to the hospital television—under obstacles: the house I was in was divided between ex-paranoid boys and senile old men—the old men would wander balmy and morose and dripping crumbs of cake in front of the screen, idly pushing the buttons, while the boys would ask them jeeringly when they were born, or exclaim, "I feel more and more like the custodian of a morgue."— This sentence will have to die syntactically dependent—it was leading up to saying that the surface of actors leaves me with wonder. What can you do after having been Henry VIII or even a cock of the walk weekly sheriff? You get beautifully your character's living for the moment he is seen or heard. All life for the flashes! Everyone has a lot of that, and we writers more than most, only the words, the structure, the tune come out of us, are us. The Father—a sort of no man's land between you and Father Taylor—came off wonderfully.

Dear Peter, you too fill me up to the brim and have for twenty years; no one is closer and better company. Hope we'll get together en famille very soon.

Love to you and Eleanor,
Cal

P.S.[. . .]Glad we are both such Randallites.

328. *To Theodore Roethke*

Saturday, March [15], 1958

Dear Ted:

I look forward very much to your stopping with us during your eastern sweep; we'll have a large room, a large heap of reading matter, a large bed,

and a large bottle all in readiness. I haven't heard you read publicly since that night at Breadloaf under the eyes and ears of Frost and in the idyllic pastoral setting of "Doc" Cooke. Sorry I can't introduce and tout (?) you and repay my Seattle debt.

Our troubles are a bond. I, too, am just getting over a manic attack. Everything seemed to be going swimmingly, then suddenly I was in the hospital— thorazine, windy utterances, domestic chaos . . . the old story. Now it's passed; I'm back typing in my study; my feet are on the floor. When you come we can spill out to each other.

Thanks for calling me *the 1 cat*. I had a wonderful run of inspiration and hard work from mid-summer till about Christmas, and discovered a new style for myself. It's rather unbelievable being any sort of poetic cat at all again. You remember how little new I had at Seattle; now there's almost a book. I haven't seen any of your English reviews except for one by Muir, mild as he always is even with Kafka, but very friendly and enthusiastic. He reviewed me once, and objected I think, to my explosions and redskins. We enjoyed him a lot when he was here giving the Norton Lectures—so unlike the Cambridge notables with their sparring and ambitions.

Let me know when you'll arrive, and I'll be at the airport in my two-tone, Tudor Ford.

Affectionately,
Cal

329. To Harriet Winslow

Saturday, March 15, 1958

Dearest Cousin Harriet:

I am back in my study. Elizabeth is napping[,] snow's falling, the streets are empty except for a bareheaded man waiting in a toy city-snow-colored puddle. This is my second long comfortable week-end at home. As you know from Elizabeth, my mania has broken, we are reunited, and soon I'll be home for good.

I've long been wishing I could obliterate that foolish, harsh letter I wrote you from McLean's. It's funny how the head fills with monstrous determination; all one's real loves and knowledges fly away; one stands reborn, scheming, lonely, silly. Please accept my brief and simple apology. I am deeply sorry the whole business happened and sorry you had to hear about it.

The future is much less alarming than might have been feared. I have a very good doctor whom I'll be seeing regularly. We both feel these attacks can

be permanently cured by therapy. Elizabeth and I have good times ahead, and little Harriet will never see the shadow that has darkened us and gone. I don't think this is whistling in the dark; we have a great store of sympathy and much has been learned.

Thank you for being so firmly and penetratingly with us.

Love,

Bobby

330. *To William Carlos Williams*

[March 17, 1958]
Saint Patrick's Day

Dear Bill:

"I sought for a subject, that would give equal room and freedom for incident, description, and impassioned reflections on men, nature and society, yet supply in itself a natural connection to the parts, and unity to the whole. Such a subject I conceived to myself to have found in a stream, traced to its source in the hills among the yellow red moss and conical grass-shaped tufts of bent, to the first break or fall, where its drops become audible, and it begins to form a channel; thence to the peat and turf barn, itself built of the same dark squares as it sheltered; to the sheepfold; to the first cultivated plot of ground; to the lonely cottage and its bleak garden won from the heath; to the hamlet, the villages, the market town, the manufactories, and the seaport."

Coleridge, *Biographia*, Chap. 10

Odd that you not he should have written this poem!

Many thanks for the beautiful little Italian flower book. There's some prospect of their doing something similar with a selection of my poems. Then with our two books and Ezra's we'll have a set.

Love to you both,

Cal

P.S. Don't write off Jarrell, I was just visiting him and he thinks your "Asphodel" is your finest poem.

331. To Randall Jarrell

Dear Randall:

I think this is the first April Fools' Day letter I've ever written, however it carries no portable hoax. I've been restored to "my friends and my relations" since a couple of weeks now and am flying to Chicago next Tuesday for their spring poet, playwright and novelist session.

I'd like very much to see your Rilke. While I was in the hospital and nothing original came, I tried a few translations, mostly from an Italian poet of Eliot's generation, named Montale. From there it seemed easy to do a few Italian scenes from the *Neue Gedichte*. Somehow they evaporated when they lost the gentle, groping weight of the German, the more direct German language, and its greater possibilities for word-displacement and placement. A literal translation is monstrous, an idiomatic English version, heartless and glib. The same with meters—a rhymed sonnet has little to do with the original, a free or blank verse sonnet seems unbelted. And so on. Your pieces in the *Seven League Crutches* are much the best Rilke in English. I imagine they took as much pain and intuition and humble uncertainty as your own work.

I hope we can count on you and Mary coming for your visit in May. Boston's spring will just be breaking then—Katherine Hoskins and Adrienne Rich and all your enthusiasts will be out in bloom for you.

Affectionately yours,
Cal

332. To Theodore Roethke

Saturday April 19, 1958

My dear Ted:

Agitated depression! I know only too well and frequently how you must feel. I hope the agitation at least animates and lessens that awful feeling of lowness and idleness that comes after our dizzy explosions. I keep thinking of Housman's phrase for Meredith, "a galvanized corpse." And Housman himself must have often felt he was half dead.

Glad to have your comments on my *PR* poems. I think my readings last spring did something to get me in the mood both to write and to write in a new style. Anyway these came in a rush—if my slow revisions can ever be called a rush. I worked from mid-August till mid-November and have almost a

book. I have some very free verse autobiographical poems, which you haven't seen and which I intend to combine with sections of the autobiographical prose. I have also a lot of unlicked fragments, and it's tantalizing and stunning to find that in my present leveled off state there is hardly a breath of inspiration. Remorse without conviction; life with a flat gray glare. However, things are picking up.

I've just been doing classes in Chicago, and heard how Berryman, substituting for you, gave a Roethke reading and keen eulogy. We both have books and lots of things to come back to.

I wonder if you will forgive me for interfering in something that's none of my business and which I only know about probably erroneously and by rumor. I heard somewhere that you and Beatrice had separated. I hope this won't be final. She seems such a beautiful person and wise wife. To my grief, I too tried to break away from Elizabeth. It was all part of my mania and nonsense. For two months, I was striding and posturing, writing letters, making wild plans. Then it all passed—again I was home. You mustn't feel you have done anything irreparable. All that was lost is returned. We even bring back certain treasure from our visits to the bottom.

I don't suppose I have any ideas on teaching poetry that you haven't tried. I like to take poems by new poets, particularly some of the younger ones, such as Philip Larkin and my old pupil W. D. Snodgrass, and mimeograph them without identification[—]any puzzle helps. Bad poems work well this way. Also bits of prose. Have you ever tried French poems?—there's a good Penguin anthology of the later 19th Century French with English prose translations at the foot of the page.

Dear Ted, take care, and let me, as Claudel used to write Gide, "grasp your hand."

Affectionately,
Cal

333. *To Elizabeth Bishop*

Sunday April 20, 1958

Dearest Elizabeth:

There's a saying that the true Bostonian has "a share in the Athenaeum, a lot in Mount Auburn and an uncle in McLean's." Well, "all roads lead to Rome," ["]God writes straight by crooked lines," etc. No matter what I do now, I shall end up as a true Bostonian.

You make sanatoria sound like ports for poets; however, I am now well out. On the last day I began *Helena Morley*. I was in a terrific room—cream mantelpiece, cream ten foot windows, in the next room a depressed Harvard law professor, reading, *Look Back in Anger*, and the *Unpublished Decisions of Brandeis*, making sounds like a pigeon (sometimes it was pigeons) and moaning, "Decades, Oh decades!" and "HorrOR, horrOR." The *Helena* is really overwhelming, everything's a story. I found I was underlining on almost every page. She has so much that a real author—I've been reading *The Princess de Clèves* and *Père Goriot*—never happens on in hundreds of pages. I like the "protector" the tattle-tale priest, her amused paraphrase of bad adult stories and flat charades. I couldn't have her worldly fresh ease in a million years. Your translation reads like an original.

Marianne Moore was here reading at Brandeis. There's no more "poor, brave Elizabeth." She is delighted with your life, knows Lota's whole history, down to the names of the "grandchildren," and has no end of praise for her competence and kindness and charm. Her reading, hard to hear and parse, was full of gentle and sharp things, as she complimented Rahv, Harry Levin, Cowley, put on her glasses, took them off, looked now like my grandmother, now like a clear-browed girl. She spoke of the "devious and interminable" introductions—this for John Ransom—to a Frost evening. The Fontaine read very dramatically; I must buy them. Also saw Zabel in Chicago, where I was meeting classes etc. for a week. He gave the most old Empire picture of Brazil. Each of his visits was preceded by "six months before I could even begin to make up my mind." On one he was kept up till three before flying by Allen Tate and Jean, and then shipped on to Caroline, who was driving Katherine Anne Porter out of her house. On another he had charge of Faulkner, drunk, photogenic, secretly supplied with some two hundred per cent Mexican drink, and lying in his shirt sleeves on the floor at some old Empire reception. Zabel lives twenty miles from the university and commutes by subway. When I saw him off and had to walk two blocks home unaccompanied, he was terrified lest I be mugged. Poor man, he is pouring out books, yet is still crushed by the *eight years* he tended his dying sister.

Chicago, magnificently waterfronted, filled with exiled Eastern seaboard professors, was like some one you've made a huge effort with all evening, and even quite converted yourself to, and in the end you find your enthusiasm is shared by no one, and you sigh with relief at your release. I used your "Armadillo" in class as a parallel to my Skunks and ended up feeling a petty plagiarist. I've tried other things in similar stanzas; nothing comes. The muse seems quite gone.

Sorry about Sammy. We are about to get one of those pigmy chinese bull dogs. Lizzie has delusions that they are too small to need exercise or even watering. Do you remember the Gardners'? Harriet has gone on a strike against solids, but is two pounds overweight. "N-no, n-no," she grunts and wraps us round her wrist. We need the dog for a pseudo diversion.

Pound is out. Going to a Chinese restaurant and using a telephone for the first time in 13 years, he told his daughter-in-law "the ancestral voice is once more on the air." A joke, I think, not the beginning of a Jeremiad.

I'll try *Marius*; I used to be amazed at how *there* it was, but somehow never finished.

Love,
Cal

P.S. You are the one whose letters are poetry, such a full sail, such witty stories!

334. To Elizabeth Bishop

June 21, 1958

Dearest Elizabeth:

I should have set your mind at rest about Pound weeks ago. Mrs. Pound was here just after the liberation seeing her son, Omar. I gather it's pretty certain that Pound is returning to Italy sometime towards the middle of July. He seems rather to hibernate through his winters—a relative hibernation[,] for us it would seem fierce activity. But of course when he was released, exhausting energies appeared—a trip to Charlottesville, lunches with colonels, professors, fans, suggestions that he was about to study old Egyptian, tour Germany, France, and England. Mrs. Pound had a long list of addresses and high-spots to see in Boston. We cut down to them a morning at the John Adams' House—very grave and cool after Ezra and the pealing traffic-wrung environs of Boston.

Last Sunday, Marianne Moore read before thousands on the Public Garden. I went rather fearing that neither her poems nor her delivery would carry. They didn't very much, yet that seemed irrelevant. She entered with a black cloak and black jacket and a diamondy green dress. The cloak came off, then after slight hesitation the jacket, then another pause and the cloak went on again. She *had* her audience. Each obstruction fell into her hands: a whistle from the amplifier ("I see I have a rival") trucks rumbling down Boylston

Street, a mute bean-shaven young man, who kept pushing her back to the speaker, an unexquisite mass of red flowers, received with a disgruntled, admiring "gorgeous"? Each epigram was cheered. Jack Sweeney's Irish wife said in amazement, "Why this is the only real American."

We're about off for Maine. Our house has a dock atmosphere as boxes of heavy clothing move downwards towards our new, shining, gun-metal-gray and meekly utilitarian ranch wagon. I return on the thirtieth of June to teach at the Harvard Summer School. It's disappointing to be away from my family, but doing something seemed altogether preferable to commuting weekly from Maine to my doctor.

We like Ives too. As soon as I put him on the phonograph a year and a half or so ago, Lizzie pricked her ears and felt he was firmly new and not just another advanced American copy of the big Europeans. I suppose he reminds one of Emily Dickinson, the queer mind, old-fashioned yet way ahead, and somehow superior to publication. I like hymns and feel assured getting them with so stern [a] discovering intelligence.

Awfully good to hear that you are writing poems again. I too have a lot of old lumber. Somehow it won't light. However, I have about enough for a book, and feel half-happy to let it rest in a drawer until the next awakening. I like the language of my new poems, but feel fatigued by their fierceness, my old serpent in the perfect garden. I wish I could be described as stubborn, hopeful, summery, utilitarian.

Just read the Agee. He has something of Ives' earlier America. There's a heart-breaking brevity to its ungainly, wooden, doomful little action. I add Agee's death to his hero's and can't forget the epitaph. Wish I enjoyed the telling as much as the overall momentum.

I am sending you one little new poem. The ending grows untimely and needs an upstroke. We are all very jolly and close, and marvel at Harriet bursting into words. "Shoe" is her favorite and she calls mounted policemen in a forsythia-yellow oilskin ambling down the Back Bay checking parking meter violations "doggie."

Love to you and Lota,
　　Cal

P.S. I must write you about Eliot and his new bride next letter. They danced so dashingly at a Charles River boatclub brawl that he was called "Elbows Eliot."

I am getting a pleasing and unexpected honor, an honorary doctor's degree from Kenyon.

335. To Robert Frost

July 3 [1958]

Dear Robert:

Thanks for your kind letter and for your kindness in holding off these many months so as not to mar or bruise me. The poems I ~~sent~~ gave you seem to me a gift of the muse . . . for me they breathe, seem engagingly put together. And yet, and yet! The direction rather appalls me—such a narrow fierceness, so many barbed quills hung with bits of skin. Another book will come, and perhaps there I will "see myself through others," as you do. Compared with your work mine is self-locked, more that of a man cut in two. I guess my last poems have the minor aliveness of a harrowing moment. Maybe not so harrowing; at times they seem gay with color quickness and humor. Indeed, I meant the poem on my Father to be all pathos and sympathy, a true recapture of the true man or part of him.

Pardon the jerky haste of this letter. I am writing it after a sweltering day of teaching at the Harvard Summer School, while collecting myself for a long Fourth of July escape to Maine with my family. Your friendship and refreshing bigness have been a treasure to me now for more than twenty years.

Affectionately,
Robert

336. To R. W. Flint

[August 7, 1958]

Dear Robert Flint:

One reads into the air and the faces and soon the occasion is over, like carving in snow; no more is heard of it. So, it's always a pleasure to get your calm interested letters. My old way of writing wore out for me, and it seemed Sisyphean to continue. And I felt nettled and too crisply labeled when a writer on metrics in the *Kenyon* found that all younger poets except me required new more flexible laws to be scanned. Also I found reading aloud that I wanted more humor, more immediate clarity, fewer symbols, more of the good prose writer's realistic direct glance. Then so much of my direct experience seemed ruled out. So, there were [a] few years of silence. Now I have an extra string to my fiddle and can go on. Hope *very* much we can meet early next fall.

Robert Lowell

337. To Anne Sexton

September 11, 1958

Dear Miss Sexton:

Of course your poems qualify. They move with ease and are filled with experience, like good prose. I am not very familiar with them yet, but have been reading them with a good deal of admiration and envy this morning after combing through pages of fragments of my own unfinished stuff. You stick to truth and the simple expression of very difficult feelings, and this is the line in poetry that I am most interested in.

I don't see how you can get a scholarship at this date and for only one course. However, I am keeping my fingers crossed and hoping that nothing will prevent your taking my course. I'll be at my office during registration next Thursday. If you have trouble finding me, tell the officials that I have OK'd you.

The course meets on Tuesdays from two to four. There will be somewhere under fifteen students, I think, the best two or three or four quite good. Perhaps it will all seem too simple and a waste of time. Still it's only poets who don't need such courses that can get much out of them.

Glad to hear about the Snodgrasses.

Yours sincerely,

Robert Lowell

338. To Harriet Winslow

September 16, 1958

Dearest Cousin Harriet:

Well, we are back in Boston with our old friends, the old warmth, the old flights of stairs, our new, unexpectedly house-trained and docile (except for chewing off curtain-pulls) cat, and our now old but very much changing from day to day daughter. Rather ajar from the change, we took off two days and drove through southern New Hampshire and the Massachusetts Berkshires, visiting a number of places that friends had just left—Dublin, Stockbridge. The first night I woke up with a sense of groping questioning and realized I was thinking of Castine, and feeling fearfully glad that I was now somewhere not just anywhere in the summer.

I guess the last year means something of the sort to me. Profound discoveries about one's life are cheap and suspect, and I find it congenial to lighten

and darken the colors almost in the same breath. We are still a bit nervous and beaten from last winter. Yet ~~more serene, cool and~~ now we look at each other, we are glad to be where we are, as we are. Last fall, I see now, I [was] walking on stilts. Now there seems to be much more time. [. . .]

We haven't too much news. I am getting ready for my courses and seem to be getting several quite good special students, going to Boston University just for my poetry-writing class. It's the excellence that can't be taught that makes such classes worth giving. I am at work on the last two or three poems for my new book. Lizzie's planning an article for *Harper's Bazaar* on a selection of William James' letters to women, and perhaps another on Boston. We were reading Oliver Wendell Holmes on Boston and rather sighing for the old days, yet Holmes almost thought as an after-dinner speaker—all praise and epigrams, a real old gorgeous wedding cake, with a model of the Statehouse dome on top of it. Yet life never could have been very much like that and just that.

We hate to think of your stationary life, and yet not to be dull or bitter is wonderful. How we marvel at your memory. Often at Castine, I felt like putting a hand over my eyes and challenging you to a guessing game as to what was in the room in front of me, or even what any of a score of Castiners we both know have been doing for the last few days. I know I'd have lost.

Give our love to Cameron and Elizabeth and John and Blanche.

Love from us both,
 Bobby

P.S. A quaint Boston domestic moment is ahead—I am driving to the Athenaeum to pick up Elizabeth and drive her to the supermarket. The last pages of Pasternak's *Zhivago* are still reeling through my mind. It covers most of our century with a tragic weary hero who loathes the stereotyped and has a Graham Greene-like willessness and worlds besides. For a moment the stone facades of the new Russia blow away like gauze, much of our own too.

339. To Elizabeth Bishop

October 16, 1958

Dearest Elizabeth:

My book's done I guess. At least I've mailed it off to Farrar and it's meant to come out in April, though there may be a delay because Harcourt is being edgy about releasing me from my old contract. I'm mailing you a copy and wish you'd point [out] any correctable flaws. *Correctable*—the big ones alas

I'm stuck with. There's quite a bit you haven't seen. I've been puttering away rather numbly since last spring and at last this fall quite a few came out. I hope you like the whole works as well as the bunch you have.

This has been a quiet fall. Lizzie's just gotten her Massachusetts driving license. We're both on the wagon. I work without killing myself at my two classes and have been reading and rereading a lot of old Russian fiction. Did I write you about Pasternak—really an earthquake—bigger perhaps than anything by Turgeniev and something that alters both the old Russia and the new for us—alters our own world too.

Gossip. The Rahvs are now finally separated, and Philip seems to have a girl, a young Viennese woman, pretty and teaching sociology at Brandeis, who talks, and thinks Philip isn't aesthetic enough in his literary criticism. Philip is as devious as Stalin about it all and we haven't met her. Nathalie has lost seventeen pounds and intends to lose seventeen more and is drinking rather less and is looking quite pretty. Still there's the awful sag when she stops talking on an evening. And last night we went with her to an exhibition of primitive art arranged by a friend of Bob Gardner's and Nathalie's shoes began to crucify her after ten minutes and one room.

Everyone is talking about Belle Gardner and Allen Tate and no one knows anything for certain, though there was great fear in Wellfleet that Belle's husband would hear something. Allen's at Oxford and Belle's planning a trip to Europe in April which includes England. Coincidence? but no one knows. Belle was here last night. I do wish she were brighter and more sophisticated. One sinks into the wet sand of her good works, good will and enthusiasm for young poets, fresh and already trailing heavy gray clouds of ennui and oblivion.

Stanley Kunitz is teaching at Brandeis, a small, sharp, orderly Bohemian little gray man, looking rather like Kenneth Burke. We have grand talks about Ted Roethke escaping from a sanitarium dressed like a woman—and (believe it?) unrecognized for three days! And we talk metrics. I really like him immensely. Bill Alfred has written a ferocious wonderful play in blank verse, full of Irish violence, Irish alcoholism, Irish politics, religion and Brooklyn Irish eloquence. Adrienne Rich is having a third baby—one that defied all preventative science—and is reading Simone de Beauvoir and bursting with benzedrine and emancipation. She and Lizzie had a forty-five minute argument, carried on in [the] dining-room, pantry and library about two people neither liked or really knew. We like her very much. Also Richards glistening with mountain-climbing—last week he slept in a sleeping bag with a frozen aluminum bottle of supposedly boiling water in zero weather—also glistening with his first book of poems and carbon copies that he hands out and reads—

just as well, because some are replies to Wittgenstein and Oppenheimer and Coleridge and the obscurer Plato and are written in Welsh rhyming schemes which are as intricate as Provençal poems that Pound quotes and where most of the words rhyme and are so complicated that Pound says nothing more intellectual than falling leaves can be versified in them.

I really think we'll go to Spain in January. Wish you'd join us and help us with directions. Give our love to Lota. As always your absence is an aching gap for me.

Cal

340. To Peter Taylor

October 31, [1958]

Dear Peter:

You see sights and no people; we see people and no sights. That's the American groove. I remember getting full of Frascati wine and wandering home alone one night from the Piazza Navona to the Piazza di Spagna and getting lost—baroque church after baroque church. I must have seen a hundred, several of them twice or thrice I guess without knowing it. Then an all-Irish New Years at Denis Devlin's. A lovely old man, the Irish ambassador to the Vatican took us all to Ostia Antica for a Roman dinner. He didn't feel we should recognize Tito—otherwise there could be a "cr-rr-sade against Russia of Christian powers." Later, he said, "do you suppose England will *invade* us if we are neutral in the next war."

I've got my book off at last—all poems, and it is coming out in April with grisly Frank Parker illustrations. I'm in the fine mood of an author with a new style and feel nothing else I've ever done counts. Ransom tells me that Randall is going to do a preface for Eleanor. I'm very excited and hope she'll allow me to throw in a blurb.

Ah me, the Ransoms' new house has a bar[,] the architect ran one once (very proper it only sold beer), and a magazine rack in the john. Rob said, "I could not quite compliment the architect on this, so I said you'll have to give me an extra bathroom key to get John out." John is awfully hale, rather lonely though I think. He said "of course I won't have much companionship here or intellectual conversation but other things are more important."

Getting my doctor's degree took me back æons to our old Douglass House interior decoration quarrels and our long fantasies of Randall as a mouse. The air was heavy with the widows, Kitty Rice and Mary Coffin. How frightful to

die in your mid-fifties! So many people I know have. We too, perhaps. Eliot says he feels as foolish at seventy as he did at seventeen. I'd like to live long enough to say that. As a matter of fact Eliot is much more foolish and happy now than he could have been then.

What are you writing? When are you coming back? Where are you going in the summer? We can find you a nice place in Castine. It's a sort of white church New England town, with Japanese scenery and two bishops. I think you'd both love it. We want to steal you from the Transues.

I'm shatteringly impressed by Pasternak, and have changed one of my courses just to read Russian—it was meant to be on something precise like the new critics as prose writers. Now I am at sea, trying to teach Tolstoy and Dostoyevsky to people who've read nothing and hardly even seen the Hollywood Russian movies through.

Aside from this the only thing in the world I care about is gossip about my friends. So write me in detail about the meeting of the Fitzgeralds and Jarrells. Surely, a foredoomed occasion. I have another installment of Allen's endlessly picaresque and phallic life. He's in much better health and now at Oxford. You'll probably be seeing him in Italy.

We do miss you every day, and feel life is truncated without you. I want my daughter to experience the civilizing influence of Katie.

Love to you both from us,
Cal

P.S. Do look up Iris Origo through the Princess Caetani. I have a dear friend Rolando Anzilotti who lives in Pescia near Pisa and Lucca that you would like if you are ever near there.

341. To John Crowe Ransom

November 6, 1958

Dear John:

I am in awful hot water on the Léger. I think I can appreciate the magnificence of ear and the cultural loftiness of *Amer*. And yet, and yet, the whole thing leaves me completely cold and seems to me to be about nothing except those great Gallic oratorical shadows, the sea, the poet, Greek religion. Sometimes Léger's matter seems close to Valéry's, but without the electrical anguish and joy and verbal and metrical excitement. Really, I am not the right reviewer. I know Léger slightly and don't want to throw stones at him. Also,

we know the Biddles very well, and still less want to upset them. Then, probably my feeling about *Amer* is my own blind spot. However, many readings haven't cured me of my prejudice.

We are so looking forward to your visit. Please tell me if there is anyone that you particularly want to see. The Richards are much hoping to see you.

Affectionately,

Cal

342. *To Elizabeth Bishop*

<div align="right">November 19, 1958</div>

Dearest Elizabeth:

Many thanks for your comments. I feel that I write only for you and Lizzie. I was just up at Dartmouth reading and talking. I read one of my old poems, "Salem," I think, and then your "Man-Moth," and said I felt like a mastodon competing with tanks, and determined to reform.

We've just had a visit from Snodgrass, touched with the fire of heaven I feel in a few of his daughter poems, but green and hysterical personally and rather unhinged by ten days in New York after three years of being buried and unknown at Rutgers. He wore plaid socks, wooly white underwearlike trousers[,] a coat made of white fibers and carbon and Ithaca New York tailoring, spoke in a profound persuasive, hypnotic Jarrell-like whisper then giggled. The Eberharts liked him unreservedly; Lizzie disliked him unreservedly.

"The bad gray poet." Frost. Monstrous vanity—talking about controlling elations, he said he thought of how little his success did for his relatives. This cooled him down. Yet a mountainous, marvelous man. He's about the only friend I have who wants to hear the details of my crack-up, what I think of girls, etc. Quite a contrast to the aerial Richards, the gentle Ransom—talking about women Ransom said, "Early in life, I pitied them," and even the giddy, philandering Tate. I'll never forget Peter Taylor's amazement in discovering that Allen was no traditionalist, but a whole-hearted masher and anarchist. I think Tate's plotting to divorce Caroline and marry Belle Gardner, but breathe a word of this to no one.

Please send me a full uncensored version of your Brazilian National Geographic picture. You've heard the story of a Brazilian cannibal boy watching a jet plane and asking his mother if it were good to eat. She said, "It's like a lobster, hard to get into, but sweet inside." Glad you are still outside.

We go to Spain, I think in mid-May. Then, I'll have five weeks instead of

two. I see my doctor three times a week and will continue to through next summer till August. He does me a lot of good, and I am learning not to throw my weight around the household every minute to prove I am not like my Father. Oh, and much else!

Just now the Academy ballot arrived. What a list! Still it's a pleasure annually *not* to vote for Harry Levin.

I'm sending you the American Pasternak for Christmas and they promise it will arrive on time. But who knows? Wilson had a terrific review of it in the *New Yorker*. By the way, have you seen Pritchett's review of your Diamond in the *New Statesman*, if not I'll mail it. I liked his crack at Nicolson.

Do try, try, you and Lota, to join us in Spain!

My dearest love,

Cal

P.S. Harriet now says, "I am a pick up," and calls me Cal.

343. *To William Carlos Williams*

November 21, 1958

Dear Bill:

I am mailing you the ms of my new book, about double what you've got. I hope it still holds up for [you]. I had a ragged and rugged winter for a while after last fall, but ~~seem~~ am still in my shoes and joyful.

I forget if I ever thanked you for your kind references to me in your Edith Heal book. The book's a beautiful lapidary job. I think you under-rate your autobiography rushed perhaps in places, but blazing fire in others. You and Fitzgerald catch the moment of the twenties better than anyone except Lawrence. By the way, I've been reading Lawrence's animal poems with rapture, and remember to my shame how I once thought you overpraised him in your fine elegy.

Our love to you and Flossie. I am sure you continue undaunted.

Cal

344. To William Carlos Williams

<div align="right">November 29, 1958</div>

Dear Bill:

I am terribly touched that you and Flossie read through my poems and aloud. And of course it's a joy to me that you found them alive and decently written—art and the life blood of experience can't live without each other. I suppose the book is terrible, however, there was great pleasure in the writing, in the quick flashes and the hundreds of re-writings. Dropping rhyme does seem to get rid of a thick soapy cloth of artificiality. The true spoken language beats any scholarly alchemists pseudo-language.

I won't believe what you say about your strength. You still have worlds in you. All of which I hope to see and hear again early in February, when I'll be in New York reading at the Y and will call you about getting out to Rutherford. You too take care of yourselves, dear old friends,

Cal

345. To Elizabeth Bishop

<div align="right">December 12, 1958</div>

Dearest Elizabeth:

Pleasant to have my book done, and this fall and winter has gone into joyful dissipation i.e. reading and seeing people. I've read "The Nose," "The Overcoat," quite a few of the *Sportsman's Sketches*, about ten long short stories of Chekhov, Rahv's anthology of Tolstoy's novellas, several of Dostoyevsky's, and now a jag of Americana, Chase's brisk over-sharp, *American Novel*, and once again *The Scarlet Letter*, *Gatsby*, James, Lawrence, and Melville on Hawthorne. Then a good two and a half days in New York staying with Kunitz, whose wife belongs to the Gustin, De Kooning, Klein group, saw three Balanchine Stravinsky Ballets in one night, the Audens, the McCarthies.

Boston's a pleasant place, but the home product is all dandification and jelly. The woodiness of the old caution, now these 50 years no longer sprouting, the jelly of *Vogue* and *Literary Digest* literary tastes. We want awfully to get away for a year or two. We have been thinking of Brazil again. Do you think some little poetry teaching and reading program could be gotten for me that would pay our way. We would like to come and see you and then rapidly a little more of South America.

People. Mary McCarthy beautifully plainly dressed, hair knot, long severe

stringy camel's hair overcoat, collecting donations for Spanish Civil War derelicts, her Florence book done, a novel on the thirties started, marking off her list of friends all who don't like *Zhivago*. Their god now, after Hannah Arendt, is an art scholar critic, Pope-Hennessy, who has written on Donatello, and is now on the verge of fatally alienating Kenneth Clark through the Broadwaters' over-eager partisanship. This I saw uptown at a rather splendid Italian restaurant, called the Baroque. Then downtown to the borders of Italian Manhattan to see Auden. Two messy rooms, expensive Oxford Press books heaped on plainness, Chester silently in another room. Then with Chester listening to records of the Brecht-Weill *Seven Deadly Sins* sung in German with the Auden-Kallman translation as a trot. Auden and Mary don't agree at all on Italy—A is about to be crossed off their list for his departure poem. However, he really knows worlds more about Italy in a personal non Madison Avenue way. Ah the British beefy, slow, eccentric normality, as against our own high-strung intensity.

I had lunch with Hyman a couple of days ago. He is shy of coming to our house. So I meet him at the Hotel Copley (on Exeter St.) Grille. Drear, bare, noisy. He seems in his new half bachelor life—he's moved off to an apartment on Beacon St. just behind Philip Rahv's new Bachelor apartment on Marlboro St.—rather gentle and haggard. Wanly himself and easier to talk to, and waiting for his next spring sale of paintings to start travelling.

What else? A good letter from Bill Williams. "Floss has just finished reading me your terrible wonderful poems . . ." and at the end, "The book took too much out of me which I don't have any more to give." A rather boozy night with Wilson loaded to the gills with Pasternak and Mosby's Civil War memoirs. On Mary and Pasternak, "Eh, eh, It seemed strange to hear Mary so sold on something. It's her severe religious back ground—" that *Zhivago* appeals to.

Being Harriet's father quite changes Pearl for me, a rather realistic portrait of the Hawthornes' Una, bursting like the Congo on their shy seclusion. James gives as examples of the old New England democracy Hawthorne's, "A shrewd gentlewoman who kept a tavern in the town was anxious to obtain two or three gravestones for the deceased members of her family, and to pay for those commodities by taking the sculptor to board." Pure John Ransom! James, "He speaks of all his friends as being Mr. even the unconventional Thoreau and the emancipated brethren of Brook Farm."

Old nineteenth century New England must have been fearful—in what other country would Thoreau, Melville, Whitman and Dickinson have been so overlooked! Yet it did sprout in a way there are no signs of now, and so

many of the best writers were hardly literary men—Parkman Motley, Adams, even Webster.

Well, I am trying to jolly you up for being in a new country. How wise and sad of you to be out of it!

The present from Brazil hasn't knocked on our door yet. I await it. Harriet awaits it. Maybe you shouldn't wait for my *Zhivago*; Edmund says the French translation is much the best, "though as usual the French squeeze all the juice out." i.e. let it escape. Love to Lota. I mourn your farness.

Love,
 Cal

P.S. My *page* proofs have just gone back to Faber.

Randall on MacLeish's *JB*—"as exaggerated and vulgar and awful as the mass media if they had unlimited freedom to express themselves."

Peter Taylor, "I am mad about painting. My favorite is Raphael. I love him as much as Chekhov." How deliciously un-*au courant*, after Randall and Mary M.! Remind me to write you a disastrous evening with the Cummingses, Ransom, Richards and William James's son.

346. To William Meredith

January 18, 1959

Dear Bill:

I am awfully slow on thanking you for poem and picture. We've been rather down under—all three of us—with some sort of nausea without fever that has been flying around. Rather a pleasure in a way for it gave us time to pause and contemplate, a void rather than an uproar to celebrate the new year. I've been letting things slide and wallowing in reading, and putting off honest work until my book is out—late March or April.

Now that I've been thinking for two years or so that content, passion and ugly experience are what poetry cries out for, I am beginning to feel a certain revulsion. I foresee and am beginning to actually see waves of sanitarium, low life and confession poems. If this happens and such things for a while become the style, it will be quite humorless, craftless, unbearable. Though much good may come. I am struck by how much more felt your Christmas poem is than poems that say all. *How not to say all*—this is as necessary as its opposite.

Not much local news. I'm still weak from a night with Allen and Stanley

Kunitz here that ended staggering and at four-thirty. The picture is very closely you, and what could be better. It will soon be on the wall.

We'll be in New York the week of February 5th and count on seeing you. Give my love to Mackie and thank her for her Bear card. Harriet will soon be mature enough for bears.

Affectionately,
Cal

347. *To William Carlos Williams*

<div align="right">February 15, 1959</div>

Dear Bill:

I [have] just been reading through Hart Crane's letters and came across, "What a clean manly fellow Williams is. I wish I could meet him!" A glorious, short, roaring life, like Dylan Thomas's but more an underdog and of course American, so with more meaning for us. Well, I'll go down to my grave in time thanking God that I have met Williams.

Poor Lizzie was in bed with a temperature the day of your play and the day after and sad to have missed it. I like the Pirandello opening, the wonderful, delicate, realistic long scene two, the doctor scene,—the main Protean girl was all there. The only thing I wasn't sure about was the poet playwright, hardly even the dimmest shadow of you—I suppose he wasn't meant to be, couldn't have been within the limits of the drama. I read my Breughel poem at the Y, and then quoted what I could remember from yours as much more inspired, "hand on stick, triumphant to disaster."

Many thanks to you and Flossie for my day with you. I hope I didn't stay too long. One feels so serene and at home in your house that it's easy to stay on and on. Ah, we are brothers—it is hard to follow the art and be neither dry, nor crackpot, nor a stuffed shirt.

Love from us both,
Cal

P.S. I'll write a better letter presently. Now I am buckling back to my classes, no great task compared with delivering babies, still it's something and has to be done professionally, though not professorially. Still laughing over the 2+2+1 visit.

348. To A. Alvarez

March 8, 1959

Dear Alvarez:

I am more or less between books and taking it easy and doing nothing except some rather free translations, not yet in shape. You could take what you want from the Faber book, but I imagine there won't be time. I think I come out in April.

I much admired your critical book. It really changed my feeling for Lawrence—he's really a very good poet. The good poems are almost all in *Birds, Beast* etc. I wonder if his poems aren't in a way his most felt, perfect and original work?

I have a few friendly bones to pick with you. 1) on me—the Bewley piece is serious writing of course and I guess rather generous for a *Scrutiny* article, but I think he misses my rough style—"Between the Porch and the Altar" strikes me as a much better poem than the "Quaker Graveyard," though there's no blue ocean in it. Jarrell's is the only criticism I've had that bit in very deep. Of course, it's too favorable probably, but I have other reasons for liking what he says. I take rather his line on American poetry. The poets I like are: Eliot, Frost, Pound, Stevens, Moore, Williams, Crane, Ransom and Tate, then of my generation E. Bishop, and somewhere behind her Shapiro and Jarrell, and somewhere behind these: Roethke, Kunitz and Eberhart. There's a trace of the old *Scrutiny* razor and ex cathedra in your tone and line. I don't particularly adore Cummings, but you sound a little foolish tossing off so clever a man (in verse and prose) so grandly. Jarrell says somewhere that no one tells the critic, "You have a delicate lyrical vein, but of course you're no Sainte-Beuve."

I liked very much your *PR* review and your *New Statesman* Dryden. When you are right you ring with sureness and are very fresh and clear. I think I can imagine how hard it is to write criticism that changes things and is reread. You are moving.

We hope to be in London toward the end of May or sometime in June. Very much want to see you. My family is ruddy and talkative. Hope yours is.

Cal

349. To John Berryman

March 15, 1959

Dear John:

Odd—the other day I was sifting old letters and came on the photograph of you and Ann and Paul, and since then it has been standing on my study mantle-piece among all my other pictures of my best friends.

I am just back from Greensboro, where Randall and [I] enjoyed (?) ourselves lamenting the times. It seems there's been something curious twisted and against the grain about the world poets of our generation have had to live in. What troubles you and I, Ted Roethke, Elizabeth Bishop, Delmore, Randall—even Karl Shapiro—have had. I hope your exhaustion is nothing very drastic; these knocks are almost a proof of intelligence and valor in us. However, all in all, each year grows better and gayer and more serious.

Your poems (shall I say it?) have a strange heart-cutting poet *maudit* and late Elizabethan tragedy quality. I like "Venice" (particularly the end), "Poet's Final Instruction," somehow middle western, *Spoon River* and Fitzgeraldish—(what had become of all that old middle western Chicago renascence, loathing and fascinated by capitalism?), the piece about Paul and his wild bad father, "They Have," and "Note to Wang Wei." I wonder if you need so much twisting, obscurity, archaisms, strange word orders, &-signs for *and*, etc.? I guess you do. Surely, here as in the *Bradstreet*, you have your voice. It vibrates and makes the heart ache.

Funny I should write you in this graveyard way; from all we hear you are top of the world, stunning audiences, milling out work. I don't suppose there's any chance of your getting to New York on the 29th or 30th of April for my publication party. I'll get Straus to mail you an invitation.

We miss you over these years and want to see your new family and want you to see ours. My daughter says, "I'm daddy's pick-up."

Love from us both,
Cal

350. To Randall and Mary Jarrell

[March 17, 1959]

Saint Patrick's Day—not a gush of religious fervor, but just Boston, where section II of our paper has a full-page green map of Ireland.

Dear Randall and Mary:

So much to chew on from my visit and little articulate to say. I liked seeing the South again and remember how it really saved my life once, and still does I guess. Sometimes it seems as though the crooked streets of Boston actually made the people think in knots. While I was away Lizzie sat next to an old St. Mark's class-mate of mine, one of the presidents of United Fruit, on the board of the Shawmut Bank, a very gifted fellow etc.—all he could talk about was balancing the budget, nor could he admit the image of a world, where our now drastically favored capitalism was much altered. Then at the other extreme, a talented fellow, Groton, once almost a flutist for the Boston Symphony, now forty-two, working two months on a five page drama review (which he probably won't write) for a little local highbrow magazine, called *Audience*.

I had a wonderful visit with the Taylors, joshing, fussing, squabbling, much as we used to at Kenyon. I agree on Eleanor's book. Literally it's as hard as Thomas or Crane and almost unintelligible. And yet it all comes through, and I don't see how else it could have without her strong invented style. A Protestant Flannery O'Connor. They quoted you as saying Peter's work was like a glass-bottomed boat, while Eleanor's was like actually going down to the bottom—the bottom, touching, clutching, murk, slimy green stems, staggered perspectives. Good too the quantity of it, the elegant workmanship, the new voice.

Randall, I wish you were here. Maybe Harvard can be coaxed into offering you MacLeish's job when ever it falls vacant. The trouble is that none of them know how you really differ from say Richard Chase, or worse.

Also, Randall, I don't know that I ever explicitly thanked you for your many spurs and reviews in the past. I couldn't have gone on, I think, without them. And now all seems good (personally) and I hope we and our families will find some way of living near each other. We can play the parts of Faust and Mephistopheles. But who is which? I guess everyone must have both inside him.

Love to you both,
Cal

351. To W. S. Merwin

March 19, 1959
Dido, "nec nos pigebat meminisse, tibi."

Dear Bill:

We got your letter about the jaundice, alas, but I am fuzzy about the details

of your summer plans. We are, God willing, flying to London on the 19th of May, and should be there for a couple of weeks at the Cavendish (!).

Rather a full winter somehow, though with little to report. Lizzie has just finished another story for the *New Yorker* and is working on an essay on Boston. My book comes out here on the last of April, and something like that in England. I've got two thirds or three fourths of a book of free translations: Rilke, Montale, Pasternak and others.[. . .]

Our poet this year has been Stanley Kunitz, at Brandeis three days a week. I've gotten to like the Ted Hughes's very much. They are *both* very good writers, and he especially seems as good or maybe better than any British young poet except Larkin. Adrienne has just had a baby, Jacob, and is reading Simone de Beauvoir. The Richards had an awful car accident, which has laid Dorothea up all winter[. . .]

The other day a young New Zealand poet called, Mr. Doyle, six months in America to sell us New Zealand poetry and see what he can gather from us to revive New Zealand, in chronic danger of Parnassianism. First he saw the Beats then Yvor Winters. "What do you think of the Beats, Mr. Winters?" "Run-of-the-mill garbage."

Excuse this hurried out letter. We long to see you both in May.

Cal

352. To Elizabeth Bishop

March 30, 1959

My dearest Elizabeth:

I have been meaning for a good many days to write you a rather calm, almost Confucian letter. I think the Brazil trip had better wait another year. My therapy (three days a week) is really doing great things and I ~~feel~~ begin to hope that by this time next year the knot inside me will be unsnarled. I do so want to live on into gray and white hairs, still growing. All the battering of the last ten years now seems to be paying off.

My trouble seems (just one angle for looking at it) to be to bring together in me the Puritanical iron hand of constraint and the gushes of pure wildness. One can't survive or write without both but they need to come to terms. Rather narrow walking—I can always go off the beam into hallucinations, or lie aching and depressed for months. This year I've held off depression by

working or drinking rather too much. That's had its run. Lizzie and I are both loosening up a lot and have much joy and variety together.

We've got our tickets to Europe and will fly on the 19th of May, then I'll be back teaching at the Harvard summer school from July to mid-August. We are going to London (2 weeks?), Amsterdam (4 days?), Rome and Florence (2 weeks?) Paris (4 days), home.

The trip to Randall and Peter Taylor was good fun. I feel much less fed up with Boston. Greensboro North Carolina and Columbus Ohio really are worse. No one to talk to but the flat local English departments. The stay with Randall was like a Jesuit retreat. I'd be lying on my bed reading R's "St. Jerome" poem and in he would come, wrinkled brow, hypnotic eye, to talk of our doom. The two great facts since the war are the decline of the west and our *probable* total nuclear extinction, he says. He's nuts on this. Still, it's all true, and the crass commercial vulgarity of our country goes beyond belief. Sometimes I think we will all die fighting some terrible Fascist reform movement. Randall gave me a grand introduction. "One of my two close friends"—I think he was telescoping you and Peter together—Peter said he should have said, one of his "*only* two friends"—"I would be glad to introduce him every other week." Then after I'd read and explained some of the autobiographical poems, he made a concluding harangue, "Here is something you haven't heard before, some one on the platform talking naturally. If you ask is this what it is to be a poet, you might ask what it is to be a human being, even a Greensboro student . . ." They are naïve people. Mary, "You and Elizabeth are the kind of people that make friends. Mary and Randall just aren't, if we couldn't in Washington, where could we?" Then she thanked me for writing warm letters to Randall the many times he had dropped me cold, and said ["]this time it's forever." "I never knew what you were like before. You were always either wild or so grave." It's fatal to be depressed with Randall. We were talking about Mackie, and I said tactfully that things end and that Jean and I also found staying married impossible. Randall, "Now I always thought you and Jean were more alike than any two people I'd ever met. I guess you would have been perhaps a little *too* spooky and haunted together. You know, I really think Jean is queerer than you are. She really is *very* queer."

I do treasure Randall, though. He has the pure, narrow steadiness of the prophet. He has a steadiness, and stands by his intuitions, while I flub and bull hither and thither. His life would kill me in a month, still he has refreshed me for twenty years.

I wish you and Lota could find some way of translating your usurious in-

comes into dollars and come here for a year. Boston is shining a little. Edmund Wilson is going to be at Harvard next year, Eliot and his bride will be here in the fall—maybe for the winter. There are flocks of engaging youth—Allen Tate—drifting through. Now if we could add you!

I want to mail you my free translations if I can find a big envelope. I've almost 40 pages and hope with a few more to have a book in next fall and out in the spring. I'll only teach one class at B.U. next fall and ought to have gallons of time.

The jacket has just come through with Frank's picture and no comment except your lovely blurb. I wish now it were printed inside as an introduction. I hope you won't have a hangover when you see how much you've said.

Love,
Cal

P.S. Yesterday Harriet made a tremendous family hit in her Brazilian waistless dress—Couldn't you mail me copies of all your new poems since *A Cold Spring*.—Let's think more about how we must get together, here, Brazil or Europe, and very soon.

353. *To Allen Ginsberg*

April 1, 1959

Dear Allen Ginsberg:

Glad to have your postal, because I have rather wanted to write you a few, scattered, inconclusive thoughts on the various writings you left with me.

What I like in the *Big Table* is Dahlberg's prose, really original, almost Plutarchan and Montaignelike. He's a tremendous and good writer. His poems are good, but much less so I think than the prose, too atomized into single not entirely memorable epigrams. The Kerouac seems to me uninspired Joyce, the Burroughs very real, but partially of psycho-pathic interest. I think Corso is good in some of the short poems you name in your preface, and say, "Dolls." The long seem rhetorical and void to me, for the most part. By the way, I think the paeans by you and Kerouac are a huge mistake. Besides being a lot of bull, they are tactically (?) unpersuasive. Corso is a small attractive poet, not in the same universe as Williams, or Moore or Pound or many others that I like, such as Auden. I can't see why *Big Table* should be suppressed, it strikes me as perfectly moral and serious. Forgive this bluntness, not, I hope, the usual famous New England kind.

I enjoyed talking to you all and look forward to the Creeley and your *Kaddish.*

Robert Lowell

P.S. By the way, the other evening led to getting hold of Barrett's Zen Buddhist book, fascinating, but monkish. What wonderful quotes!

354. To Elizabeth Bishop

April 7, 1959

Dearest Elizabeth:

What can be worse than crossed letters, and now I am continuing the asynchronation inextricably by answering your last which just missed my last.

Don't *altogether* abandon plans for our coming; I think we might do something, say, next May (1960), if a quick paid-for swoop could be arranged. History mustn't be deprived of the scene of your pleading with Mrs. Luce to OK me. She won't, will she? A lapsed Catholic! I feel very Montaigne-like about faith now—it's true as a possible vision such as *War and Peace* or *Antony*—no more though.

Oh we won't ever fall out, God help us! Aren't people difficult. I think, perhaps I have almost more warm intellectual friends than anyone, and have lost none except Delmore Schwartz. But it's like walking on eggs. All of them have to be humored, flattered, drawn out, allowed to say very petulant things to you. I'm sure they have to bear the same things from me—however, I don't feel the need to be diplomatic with you and Peter Taylor.

I'll read O'Hara. The other night Ginsberg, Corso and Orlovsky came to call on me. As you know our house, as Lizzie says, is nothing if not pretentious. Planned to stun such people. When they came in, they all took off their wet shoes and tiptoed upstairs. They are phony in [a] way because they have made a lot of publicity out of very little talent. But in another way, they are pathetic and doomed. How can you make a go for long by reciting so-so verse to half-jeering swarms of college students? However, they are trying, I guess to write poetry. They are fairly easy to listen to. There was an awful lot of subdued talk about their being friends and lovers, and once Ginsberg and Orlovsky disappeared in unison to the john and reappeared on each other's shoulders. I haven't had the heart to tell this to Lizzie or anyone else. They also talked a lot about entering the lion's cave, a reference, I think, to my "David and Bathsheba." I think they'll die of TB.

Sorry to hear about Marianne's stroke. Did I write you about visiting poor old Bill Williams, very mournful, enjoying one day out of seven, waiting for the end, the nervous system cracking, but not the mind and courage. But it would be heaven if somehow something could bring you back for a visit next September. I feel so forlorn without you, though this has been a happy year. There's no one else I can quite talk to with confidence and abandon and delicacy.

You can't understand Allen's appeal to your sex? Me neither. Except that he assays to assay your sex more than anyone I know. By the way, though, I think thru something misunderstood that I said to Blackmur, all Princeton for three days thought Allen was engaged to you! "Does she really love him? Isn't he too old?"

Keats—I read the letters fall a year ago. Better than anything except Laforgue's. I think his bold opinions on his friends impressed me more than anything. I wouldn't be that mature, if I lived to ninety, and memorized Montaigne and had hallucinations that I was Santayana.

I hope you have recovered and are not too inspired from having been thunderstruck. Neither thunder nor the muse has struck me for ages.

My love to you both,
 Cal

355. To Allen Ginsberg

April 10, 1959

Dear Allen:

I think letters ought to be written the way you think poetry ought be. So let this be breezy, brief, incomplete, but spontaneous and not dishonestly holding back.

Creeley and Levertov are careful, disciplined poets. If I were writing [to] them, I could truthfully say a good deal for their ~~honest~~ sensitive care. But in the rough and tumble of what is alive today? Creeley is [the] tamest imitation of Williams' tricks, tone, mannerisms, rhythms. I guess poetry as a technique means much less to me than to you. I can hear Creeley's polite, dim halting voice behind the barrage of Williams—I can just hear it, and not to much purpose, while Williams' manner drones at me in Creeley. Levertov with more observation and less skill also seems to come from Williams. Also I find everywhere a bit intangibly the humor and quirks of Pound—the hardest of masters, if you yourself are a quiet little person and so unlike him.

Well, I enjoy *Kaddish* much more. It's really melodious, nostalgic, moving, liturgical. Maybe it ought to be shorter—the manner sometimes almost writes itself—probably there's too much Whitman. And I do find it a bit too conventional, eloquent and liturgical. Well, it's well done, felt and a good poem.

Your letter says a good deal I sympathize with, and of course reams more that I don't. Yet I rather wonder if I didn't say most of my objections the other night. It's not a matter of argument, but of experience—what one's mind, heart, soul and stamina have gone through. I couldn't make you agree with me in a million years. We can, however, tolerate each other, at least I can tolerate *you*, and hope you'll put up with my rather splenetic joshing.

Yours,

Robert Lowell

P.S. A reason for the rough brusqueness of my letter is this. I see a great deal that fascinates me in your wave of writers. Yet as a whole? There's so much that is timid, conservative, intolerant of other kinds of writing. The times are bad? But not as bad as you think. 10,000 noodles to one competent writer; 10,000 competent writers to one interesting writer; 10,000 interesting, honest writers to one inspired writer; 100 inspired writers to one of great moment. But why drown out what there is? Just to name Americans in this century: James, Frost, Robinson, Wharton, Dreiser, Ring Lardner, Fitzgerald, Hemingway, Nathanael West, Salinger, Saul Bellow, Mary McCarthy, Flannery O'Connor[,] J. F. Powers, K. A. Porter, Pound, Williams, Ransom, Tate, Warren, Jarrell, Crane, Kunitz, Roethke, Eliz. Bishop, Faulkner, Winters, Blackmur, James Baldwin, Santayana, Eliot? I've given these people in no particular order. They differ enormously in interest. There [are] others just as good I've intentionally or absentmindedly passed over. But all these are first rate, nor should they be taken for granted in the welter of commercial writing, movies etc that we live in. Your wave of people may add a name or two to this list—or more than a name or two; who can foretell the future—you can't drown out what is already there.

356. To I. A. Richards

April 18, 1959

Dear Ivor:

In the hurly-burly of our argument on whether writers existed, I forgot to

bring up a problem for you and Omar Pound. He's going to be studying Chinese and Japanese at Harvard this summer and is looking for an apartment for himself, wife and eight month baby. Would you and Dorothea dream of renting or lending yours? He is tidy and quiet—more than is possible for pure Americans, so is his wife, Toronto, university professor family. Anyway I've asked him to call you while we are gone. Please don't feel any pressure. I told him that you didn't let your apartment and probably wouldn't want to. However, I'd like for him to talk to you—he has a curious crooked humble idealism—the opposite of Ezra—and is teaching in a secondary school, giving all his time, correcting a hundred blue books a week, never going out at night— also he has a doctor's degree in Persian.

I got rather a rave review from Alvarez in the *Observer*, so my book is off beyond my dizziest hopes in England. Awfully impressed with Fraser. He ruminates more than the post-Empson critics and writes better and more humanely. By the way, he has some interesting sentences—page 189, re Louis MacNeice—"It is probably an error, at least of tact, to bring into an appraisal of a living poet one's impression of his personality as a man. But there is a real sense, as Roy Campbell once remarked about Dylan Thomas and William Empson, in which good poets are, when you meet them, like their works . . ."

Our love to Dorothea. Hope she'll be with you when we return.

Cal

357. To Elizabeth Hardwick

[n.d. Spring 1959?]
Tuesday at breakfast

Dearest Lizzie:

I don't know what possessed me to come home to you so high, unseeing and careless and then over-drink. Now in the calm of a good sleep and the post dexadrine morning, it all seems very adolescent and rowdy and I can't blame you for finding my manner and manners impossible. I see-saw up and down and still haven't learned very well not to season my worry and depression with manic spoon-fuls, like Harriet's Kean-Kongs.

I do think calm is coming back. I admire and love and delight in you so much and really have no deep desires that aren't centered on my girls. Somehow often at home and *elsewhere* I get fearful, assertive, anxiety-ridden. I dream away and sulk. But changes have been happening. Last week did me a lot of good. You are where I am alive.

Hope you have slept and polled no more trees, dear heart.
All my love,
 Cal

I want to get this off before class and for you to know that you and Poggie are ever in my mind and that never have you seemed so utterly in my heart. This is a love letter and comes from my heart—excuse its lack of mind.

358. To Edmund Wilson

Bowditch House
McLean Sanitarium
Waverly, Mass.
May 19, 1959

Dear Edmund:
 I've always meant to improve my poem diamond-pointed on your window pane. Here's a new version, gnomic and round-headed enough, I hope, for any man's taste.

FOR EDMUND WILSON'S WELLFLEET WINDOW
Burning, burning, the unburied grain.
All trigger-happy by Jerusalem's light.
Alden's broad-bosomed stun-sails shrouded Plymouth?

Those Iron-Sides overcharged with righteousness,—
Let's say, they'd wrung out blood from stocks and stones,
fenced their mean garden with the Redman's bones,
established here their serpent-seed of night . . .
Say also, their nearly non-existent culture,
cheese paring, clipping Christos from cross and altar,
now pivots the Searchlight thrusting to shock
our riotous glass houses built on rock.
1942–1959

I've been conditioning here for about a month, and feel swimming, and looking forward to tanking up again on your conversation.
 Love to you and Elena,
 Cal

1959–1966

Writing of *Imitations, The Old Glory, Phaedra, For the Union Dead,*
and *Near the Ocean*

Boston • New York City • Cambridge

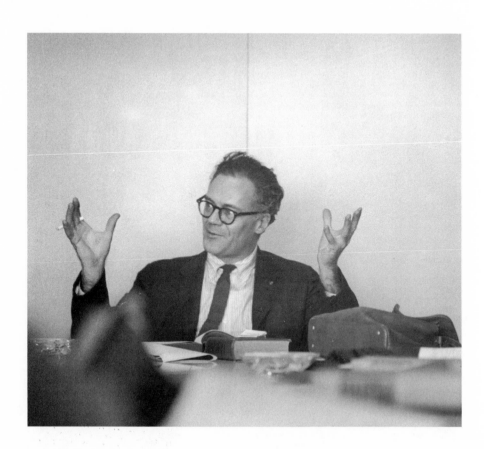

Lowell in Cambridge, Massachusetts, circa 1964 (courtesy *Life*)

359. To Elizabeth Bishop

<div align="right">

Castine, Maine
July 24, 1959

</div>

Dearest Elizabeth:

I feel rather creepy and paltry writing now to announce that I am all healed and stable again. So it is. Five attacks in ten years make you feel rather a basket-case, and it's excruciating having Brazil snatched out of my gloating jaws. Maybe when ten years have passed I'll be a sort of monument of the norm—Eberhart and Wilbur combined.

We're back in Maine, awfully tennis-playingish and beachy. Eberhart's boat still lands, heavy with strangers and heartiness; Phil Booth still writes sea-poems. Lesley Parker is just finishing a week with us, stonelike, sleeping in the sun, full of intense unreal gossip that tries to be heroically ungossipy. I sit typing, surrounded by chintz and Cousin Harriet's somber 19th century oils of Alpine valleys. The sun comes in the window. We are really very happy and companionable. I still click but can't believe it.

I can't believe somehow that you and Lota aren't just around the corner and about to arrive here. Or maybe that we are about to disembark in Rio. Never has there been a time when we would have all enjoyed one another as neighbors—together at length and at leisure.

In the hospital I spent a mad month or more rewriting *everything* in my three books. I arranged my poems chronologically, starting in Greek and Roman times and finally rose to air and the present with *Life Studies*. I felt I had hit the skies, that all cohered. I was mostly waste. However, I did four or five more translations, Heine and Baudelaire and have almost enough now for a book. I've just finished a little prose sketch for Tate's *Sewanee Review* 60th birthday number. Some one with strong off-Broadway connections has just called asking if I would translate Claudel's *Partage de midi*. We now plan a two or three weeks' trip this mid-winter to Spain or Italy.

<div align="right">

| *351*

</div>

Let me get this scrappy, whistling little letter into the afternoon mail. I want to write you something with a little thought soon, but this is just to relieve your mind, and cheer your mind towards thoughts of that long-promised return trip to North America.

All our love,
Cal

360. *To William Meredith*

239 Marlborough Street
Boston 16, Massachusetts
September 18, 1959

Dear Bill:

Thanks for your good letter and poem. We set big traps for red squirrels this summer; they were full of native guile, however, and happily escaped, and somehow or other I managed to stop up *all* the holes in the woodshed passage, so we escaped from them. For months now, I have only been able to do translations, though now and then I beat out a dry repetitious version of something already sufficiently and better said in *Life Studies*. I much admire your serious and cheerful accomplishment.[. . .]

There was no point in getting in touch with me during my "absence." I know all too much about the uninstructed heart, and it is wearisome and quite fruitless for human ears to try and catch its clamorous babble. HY wasn't babble, but my shorthand for the YMHA on 92nd St.

Very good to hear from you,
Cal

361. *To John Berryman*

September 19, 1959

Dear John:

I have been thinking much about you all summer, and how we have gone through the same troubles, visiting the bottom of the world. I have wanted to stretch out a hand, and tell you that I have been there too, and how it all lightens and life swims back. And it's a sorrow to think of you alone, seeing your son and not being with him. I've thought of your dazzling brilliance, so astonishing to

your friends, of reading in Chicago two years ago and hearing the uproar of admiration you had left behind you, the moment you introduced the "finest Haiku poem." Then our talks in Maine, meetings in New York. There's been so much fellow feeling between us, and for so long now. I am afraid nothing of this got said last night, yet it was as though we had been waiting for months for your call.

Well what is there to say? The night is now passed, and I feel certain that your fire and loyalty, and all-outedness carry you buoyantly on. The dark moment comes, it goes. Last night Natasha Spender was with us. She had just spent a day picnicking with Thomas Merton, very talkative and at ease—so much so she wished she had brought wine and pigeons instead [of] ham sandwiches, a seemingly more Trappist repast. We speculated briefly on you and Bob Lax and Bob Giroux. You seemed close enough.

So much for all that. We have been delighted with the English reviews of "Mistress *Anne*." The new poem about Harry in its sixty parts must be a deluge of power. It will be exciting to see the parts you are about to publish. I wish you'd send me more of it. You must believe that it will reach its finished form.

My child too is extraordinary, full of little courtesies and whimsies, often noticing more than we do. I muse it all in, and Lizzie's eagle eye misses little. The day after tomorrow, she starts at nursery school, the first step, a mild one but dramatic, toward her own separate life. Not so separate at first because Lizzie goes with her the first week with a crowd of new nursery school mothers, all circled about as a council for the teacher.

I still haven't at all said what I want to, but our hearts are with you and we love you very dearly.

Cal

362. *To Charles Monteith*

October 1, 1959

Dear Mr. Monteith:

Many thanks for your letter and for your trouble in acting as my proxy for the Guinness prize. I much admire [the] Guinness peoples' belief in the occasion; they seemed quite surprised that I wouldn't be there—jetted in perhaps. I feel in touch with some old tradition, such as Ben Jonson's barrel of claret.

We much look forward to Mr. Eliot's arrival and return here.

Yours sincerely,

Robert Lowell

October 3, 1959

Dear Mr. Smith:

John Holmes, the poet, was here last night and told me about going with you to see Robinson, shy, quiet, looking most of the time at you instead of Holmes, not out of arrogance, but because he knew you and felt at home. All this, coming on the heels of your moving letter, brought you very close, almost breathing flesh and blood in the room.

I don't know about greatness. I've just published, a new book of poems, my first in nine years. It's all quite a different style, uses a lot of free verse, is intelligible to anyone on the surface, and heavily and directly autobiographical. Everything went into a concentrated, rather imagistic directness, and for a while my old stuff seemed like something from the ancient extinct age of the reptiles, cumbersome creatures, bogged down and destroyed by their protective hide. Now the need to be more impersonal has come again, with it a need for some third style, still unfound. There are times when nothing you do seems really yours.

Lately I have tried to keep religious imagery out of my poems. However, the dramatic dark of Calvinism remains. It's a strange thing now as it lingers on, long after its iron web of theory and fiercely debated and lived theology have perished. Yeats says "Nature is blossoming, where the body is not bruised to pleasure soul." I like this better than the Calvinist ride through the dark till by grace and courage the darkness becomes light. Still one does what he can.

Now to be a little personal. It's in the last ten years, the years of my second marriage, and the birth of my daughter, that I have written to my mind what I really have had to say, in a book of poems which I don't think you've seen and which I'll mail you. During this time I have had five manic depressive breakdowns: short weeks of a Messianic rather bestial glow, when I have to be in a hospital, then dark months of indecision, emptiness etc. So the dark and light are not mere decoration and poetic imagery, but something altogether lived, inescapable. Even survival has had to be fought and fought for.

I put this down briefly and with some doubts about the geniality and good manners. However, I have been much moved by your letter, and really couldn't answer honestly without a bit of confession.

More than ten years ago, the philosopher, George Santayana wrote me out of the blue about my first book. A long correspondence followed and we finally met many times in Rome. He talked and wrote much about Boston, puri-

tanism, the Catholic Church and modern poetry. Your letter brings back those times most pleasantly, and I trust we will meet and talk before a year is passed.

Yours sincerely,

Robert Lowell

P.S. I am eager to get into your works.

364. To Harriet Winslow

October 12, 1959

Dear Cousin Harriet:

I'm just back from a short visit and reading in Buffalo. The feature in my line there is a collection of manuscripts, first drafts etc. by the more important modern authors. Many of them are dead, or at least much altered from their records. Recollections of their lives and even their visits to Buffalo hovered like cigarette smoke in the air. The room for my reading was called the "exhibit room," and all about me were the works, lined note-books and doodlings of Joyce, Yeats, Dylan Thomas, Elizabeth Bishop and many others. Glass cases, locked and weighted down by bronze frames, almost too heavy to lift. I felt I was myself an exhibit. At the end, I met a little old lady in black with a black crutch. She was descended from two nineteenth century poets named Stoddard, wrote poetry as a solace for arthritis, and looked like Ezra Pound's wife surrealistically aged by twenty years. I seemed to have drifted half a lifetime back in time, or to have become a small, hardened, purified vestige of literary history.

Back here, another world! Harriet had advanced in three days from four to ten piece puzzles. Letters were pouring in to Elizabeth congratulating her on a piece in *Harpers* she has just published, a polemic on contemporary American reviewers. In the drawing room Mary McCarthy, looking a little like a Quakeress, gray dress and black hair-knot and a head full of very un-Quaker projects and accomplishments.

We've had several week-end visits, and quite a flow of evenings with friends. What stands out this fall though is Harriet leaving three times a week at nine for nursery school. Like an artist, she brings back huge colored scrolls of paper covered with her first abstract expressionist paintings. She drives a tricycle, catches a big rubber ball, gulps observations like a vacuum cleaner. Or rather, her foot is on the ladder.

[. . .] You are always very near to us and achingly missed.
Love,
 Bobby

365. To David Posner

October 12, 1959

Dear David:

Day-dreaming back on Buffalo, I see a series of arrangements in rows, church, school and college following one another down the long levels of Main Street, rows of folders, rows of glass cases, the regular, irregular lines of your fine home museum in the apartment, the Abbots' two white dogs moving weightily, harmlessly but like a pair of land sharks for my heels.

Another curious and much deeper impression is one I felt about time, the motionless manuscripts, the dead or altered authors and in between the reminiscences, fading somewhat each day, yet already showing their carved and permanent form. One feels motion running through the seemingly still years since the War and can almost pick up one's own, purified and fossil remains.

This is a bit far-flung. My visit has left an impact and even wonder that somehow pushes beyond any of its events. I was delighted with the care, cooking and freedom of your hospitality. Remember me to your friends, Silverman, Friend and the lovely ex-air-plane stewardess who did so much toil for us.

With all best wishes,
 Cal

P.S. We are much pleased with your picture. We have just returned a Wyndham Lewis to Ezra Pound's son and now have filled the sore space on our wall.

366. To Stephen Spender

October 19, 1959

Dear Stephen:

I'll be glad to do the Richards piece. I like his simple sensuous and passionate poems often very much; the other more semantical and obscure ones are rather beyond my interests, quite likely because they are over my head. These are of course his own favorites. Most poets seem rather usual people

with at best a talent for words and form. With Richards the sly, subtle delicate spirit takes one in odd directions.

We wish you were coming to Boston. Natasha's visit was a great joy and full of glorious conversation. On the last day, we rather overdid things I fear by taking her on a drive to Plymouth—much confusion, ever thickening Sunday traffic, Harriet growing more animated with each mile.

I read your review excitedly when I was still sick and in a hospital and in no state to write you coherently. The kind of poem I'd like to try now would be much more impersonal, one bound together, not with iron hoops, but with hundred[s] of wavering and broken spider lines.

I could have guessed from Mrs. Pasternak's own translations and notes that my "nipples" for "breast" wouldn't pass. Still she grinds him down to a pretty and innocent neatness and in remaining perhaps true to his spirit, falsifies and extinguishes his powers.

I have the happiest memories of being with you in Washington, and hope I didn't behave like an arrogant bull. Lizzie sends her love,

Cal

367. To I. A. Richards

December 19, 1959

Dear Ivor:

We wanted to call Dorothea, but rather felt freedom from intrusion would be more welcome during the brief, stopping, plan-filled moments between London and Florida. Finally we called on Thursday and you had gone. The sun is perfect here today, and I imagine you are enjoying the full substance of it by your swimming pool, without our cold air, strips of sheer ice, and candied grass. We have been imagining the ease and vivacity of your at last reunion. What a time and twist, it's been!

Glad I was of some use on the poems. I felt I had left little behind me except the slow mumbled queries of my slow mumbling mind. Your mind flashes perpetually and it's quite a stint reaching its high altitudes, though aided by a thousand crossing wires of speculation. I was taken by passage after passage and would gladly give my whole book to have written your "To D. E. P." By the way, a copy of it fell out of my pocket at the Brooks's, and they read it in innocence and ignorance saying, "Cal is back in his best vein again." How heavily thinking we have an author's note and number weighs

on our reading. I remember reading a poem I didn't recognize by Ben Jonson and being lofty about its fluffy Victorian lightness.

We are impatient to see you both. Here in the cold clear January, we'll mix our Yucatan impressions with your Florida. Love from us both,

Cal

368. To Harriet Winslow

Friday, January 8, 1960

Dearest Cousin Harriet:

I went on a weird trip yesterday with Aunt Sarah and Emily to Concord New Hampshire. The object was to confer with the Historical Society and the army engineers about the graveyard. We made a contrasting group, three vague Winslows full of family reminiscence, three suave, friendly engineers full of facts and unrolling a map of the graveyard which included everything down to the widths of each tree, and three New Hampshire people, country New England accents, folk-lore, a sinewy hold on regional history—an office full of antiques, including a small bronze Napoleon from the Stark mansion. I think I was the vaguest, but the historical Society chairman kept calling Aunt Sarah's lawyer (Mr. Wade) Mr. Lowell, and Aunt Sarah would whisper, "Isn't it funny, he calls Mr. Weight (sic) Mr. Lowell.["]

Well, the flood-control floods must come, and our only choice is whether to leave the graveyard where it is or move it. Left where it is, it will be covered by a foot of water about once in five years for a day or two, and with twenty feet of water about once in thirty years for ten or fifteen days. The government would pledge itself to recover any damage, and many letters were produced to show that tree, stone, water and health experts thought there's no damage. Yet we all thought this was a gruesome and perhaps dangerous future. (We all, the Winslows.) So now the question is where? Somewhere on [the] heights of Dunbarton near the village? Somewhere near the Stark Mansion? Or near General Stark in Manchester, my brainstorm, but one that made the quiet Emily say that she would then move her family to Newport. I think we are all inclined toward the Stark Mansion. The government will move everything down to the outer stone wall and seem anxious to do all that may be done to change as little as possible. They can even seize suitable land, but that won't come up. What are your ideas? So much is fading humanly and physically, still something will last, unswallowed by flood, city building and the woods.

Harriet takes her white muff everywhere. It's just gone from her bed to the Public Garden. One night she called us up three flights of stairs. When I saw her, she was standing up in bed like a woodchuck and waving her arms. What did she want? She had to improvise a reason. "What this string on muff?" Another time, she said "potty isn't against the wall." She'll always know where things go, and her iron hand will keep them there.

We had a stuffed but easy Christmas. I am preparing my new courses, taking daily walks and getting ready for brief trips to Amherst, New York and Chicago for readings. Lizzie is full of plans after a bout of sinus infection. Harriet is trying to decide whether to be a cook (specializing in tea) or a zoo keeper, or a parent keeper. The other day she said I was her daughter. "The child is father to the man."

We are framing your two fine pictures, and will be happy to see them first hanging here and then in Castine.

Love,
 Bobby

369. To Randall Jarrell

January 30, 1960

Dear Randall:

How goes the Goethe? And what's happening to you? Flores' German anthology just arrived in the mail, and I have read your bunch of translations with increased wonder. It's amazing how close you are, and yet the solemnity and vibrance remain. I think I even prefer you at times to the original, which can seem a little too like itself. Why does he so resolutely always write in German? I say this humorously, of course, but feel there are moments for all of us when our imperfectly mastered foreign languages seem the crowning mannerism of some admired author. Just as at other moments, German or Italian seem languages that it is impossible to be trivial and conventional in our way.

I'm deep in translations and have only finished one poem of my own since last winter. I have to bend and bend to enjoy new English and American poems, but easily become pious and uncritical reading Pasternak and Montale. One wants a whole new deck of cards to play with, or at least new rules for the old ones. Maybe it's the times, or maybe it's being well in one's forties or maybe, it's all a private thing with me; but I feel wrung with altered views and standards—more than I can swallow. So many questions, one is almost speechless.

Well, I don't mean anything quite so hectic and dramatic. One keeps alive, and changes and wonders. You are one of the very few people I feel deeply enough in with to talk deeply with. I hope I'll see you before long. Lizzie sends her best to you and Mary.

Affectionately,
Cal

370. To William Meredith

March 3, 1960

Dear Bill:

I've just finished a long, long morning of giving a recorded interview for the *Paris Review*—one in which strain gave no edge, and hesitation no civilized tolerance. I feel flat and flattened. However, the opera came up, a strand to pick up with you now.

I am getting the grant, and have reread *Benito*. A few thoughts and questions: How would we do Delano's soliloquies? Half the drama—James's innocent abroad—is his growing saturation in this new Spanish and Negro world, his false guesses, his darkening suspicions. He could talk to some other American but that would be grotesquely cumbersome, or he could soliloquize to himself—Melville too is forced to leave him alone periodically. Could we do this without tedium, drones of half-verbal sound? Secondly, how can we handle the whole plot so as not to make it rather shockingly anti-Negro? What I'd hope for would be something neutral, rather what's happening now, wrong blazing into a holocaust, no one innocent. But the action—in Melville the Negroes with their bloodthirsty servility are symbolic demons—on the stage will be much more unbearable than read, or even worse, likely to seem a sadistic, unfelt farce. Otherwise the story is already almost more opera than novel, the big scenes, the shrouded master, the shaving, then the recurrent disappearing Spanish sailors. I wish we could have some sort of prologue with a back drop—perhaps changing—of the nearing Spanish ship. I'll look up Britten's *Billy Budd* and see what he does with dialogue. *Benito* has an awesome mixture of bravura, melodramatic bravado, etc. and a terrible subject.

I'll start off in New York about mid-September. It's a great comfort that we are starting our exploration together. Could you give me a reading and listening list? I hope my ignorance won't merely slow and confuse you.

Affectionately,
Cal

P.S. Have you ever thought of *Danton's Death*, the best modern political play I know of?

371. *To Richard J. Fein*

Dear Mr. Fein:

I don't believe much in answering questions. In a way the poem is no longer the poet's when it is done, and it takes almost as much care as the original writing to say anything useful. However, your questions have set me thinking.

1. I suppose war is a dark shadow of Christian experience, its tragedy, its reckless risk, its sacrifice, its tendency to tear up the world.

2. I don't believe the justice of a war is much help to a poet. The human part is more to the point—war's sordor, heroism, the death and adventures of friends, the blow brought home to one's whole being. Unlike us, a German or Japanese poet couldn't publish poems that criticized his country. He had that disadvantage.

3. I suppose patriotic poetry is usually marred by a brassy eloquence that some how makes it unbelievable like speeches at political conventions. We think the poet wouldn't talk that way when he descends from his platform. Stevens, Auden and Marianne Moore have all found ways of being patriots and yet themselves. I suppose irony and bitterness somehow seem more respectable to us now. I am not sure that I know why; I have this feeling too.

4. I've never tried to be a New England poet. When I was in the South, I discovered that I was a New Englander, and liked to muse on local facts and landmarks.

5. The *Life Studies* poems were meant to be entirely art, yet they are meant to give a sort of notebook effect, an impression of truth and a fragmentary naturalness, that would lose all its point if too worked up. A poem could stop, when its lifeline ended and didn't have to break its back to [be] a poem. I wanted a style and rhythm that could say anything that conversation or prose could say. I don't know about the pitfalls to this style, for me it only works on personal subjects and is always in danger of falling into a lazy flatness; in a more formal style the metrical obstacles expose and reveal the writer's honest labor.

I hope these notes will serve to some purpose.
Yours sincerely,
 Robert Lowell

372. *To Harriet Winslow*

<div align="right">April 26, 1960</div>

Dearest Cousin Harriet:

We had a smooth, sunny trip home above the clouds, and then descended to the leafless, overcast cold of Boston. Quite another world, one that touched as I looked out the window, and then watched Elizabeth bracing herself to pull her gloves on, and I wrapped Harriet in my spring coat. Now we are all back to our vertical city-house life.

We have just moved our high-fy with its refrigerator-size speaker down into the "library" and the first record would have been the Lili Boulanger, but Harriet flew into a paroxysm of distress at the first strange chorale sounds, and said "I don't want grown-up music." So we hurriedly shifted to a scratchy, boisterous, play-worn record of Dixi, the Blue-tailed-fly etc.

Well, time will deepen Lili Boulanger for us, but the first playing seems perfect. All the pieces are personal, and seem to come out of her marrow, her doom and expectation—personal and quivering beyond belief, once one knows her story. Yet it is formal and impersonal too—the public psalms, the difficult, unsentimental control. I think I expected the heart-break, but not the delicate magnificence, particularly in *du fond de l'abîme*. Dominguez's voice is splendid. I will write Nadia today. I have no technical knowledge or language, but I think I know by analogy what was attempted and done.

I seem to have no language to reply to your love for us. These yearly moments with you enter our hearts. I have to rub my eyes and shut my ears to realize how much ache and weight lies under your appearance of calm strength and fullness. I suppose your will struggles up-stream like a salmon, and somehow always finds itself in the same place, halfway up the falls, perhaps. We don't see this. You seem to carry all you touch, your friends, your house, your life, in your arms. We live in light and shadow, as much light as God and nature allow us to offer. You offer so much.[. . .]

Love from us all,
 Bobby[. . .]

373. *To Elizabeth Bishop*

April 28, 1960

Dearest Elizabeth:

Your marvelous second post-Amazon letter arrived yesterday, while Ted Roethke was just ending a visit. Poor thing, a mammoth yet elfinlike, hairless, red-faced, beginning the day with a shot of bourbon, speechless except for shrewd grunted asides—behind him nervous breakdowns, before him—what? He is off to Europe with his frail wife on [a] Belgian freighter in June. We had *all* the Boston poets in to meet him. I. A. Richards read, then Ted read, saying, "I feel like a punk or a hog-caller following Thomas Hardy." Then Philip Booth read, saying, "I feel like Ted," and Ted said, "Honey, that's work." When Ted read at Harvard, everything showed, the delicate glistening nerves, the wallow of flesh, the obscenity, the shyness. Well, it's awful to be driven on like a great baggy blue serge sail before the wind. Somehow, all this contrasted with you, the most all there of anyone I've ever known.

I wouldn't worry about the Amazon poem—it's the best fairy story in verse I know. It brings back an old dream of yours, you said you felt you were a mermaid scraping barnacles off a wharf-pile. That was Maine, not Brazil. Your new book with this and the Pound and the armadillo ought to be your very best and all in different styles.

Yes, the Tate-Gardner tape was crude and cruel and cheap. I made an awful blunder last spring when I was getting high. I called up Caroline and told her she mustn't let Allen get a divorce, that Allen really loved her and that Belle was extremely stupid. Actually, the marriage is a good thing—Allen much more settled down after all his gadding. They are both a little unreally cordial and dramatic—however, there's effervescence and happiness, and who knows? love, I think.

What tremendous descriptions in your letter! The sick man on the Amazon, the monks and nuns and Lota, the sacred heart on your bosom. I have nothing to reply with except a prosaic trip to Swarthmore. I was visiting a minute, intelligent dry poet Daniel Hoffman, midway in a book on vegetation and other myths in Melville, Hawthorne, James, Faulkner etc. and other American humorists, and all the way through a dry, intelligent, unreadable book of vegetation myth poems in strange ballad meters and the alliterative stanza of Sir Gawain. Exquisite Shaker and European baroque and Swarthmore stone house; nervous, charming near-sighted wife, poetry editor of the *Ladies Home Journal* (ten dollars a line) and a friend of Marianne Moore's—both industrious and armed with a Columbia graduate school culture, oppressed by the

lazy, social non-book-writing and non-New Criticism world of Swarthmore. (After their huge cocktail party, I asked them who was interesting and they said, "We are."[)] In the morning I read to the Swarthmore "Collection." A churchlike hall, an organ playing and the entire faculty behind me; the entire student body, many reading papers in front of me. A silence, an introduction. I made Quaker references and jokes—the little group of Catholics and atheists who met Quaker leaders once a month when I was in the Danbury jail— and gradually realized that only the building's frame was Quaker, not the students. Then my *"Three millionaires'* day.["] First the Barnes Museum,— the obligatory one year ahead application having been waived, Hoffman drove me to the back door of a sort of Frick museum in the country—one felt one was entering Germany for the first time since the war—sinister, silent men trained on Barnes aesthetics driving power rollers. A knobbed oaken door opened a crack, so as not to let Hoffman slip in. A little old lady with dyed red hair, Miss de Mazia, Barnes collaborator and supposed mistress brought out the guest book—whispered instructions: in an hour and twenty minutes a bell would ring to tell us to leave the floor where a lecture was about to begin, but we were to be allowed our full two hours. The pictures were hung in uniform gilded oak frames on a sort of de luxe burlap, about them bits of burnished iron, keys, hinges, scissors. The paintings were glorious—two hundred Renoirs, good Cézannes, Matisses, Demuths, Soutines, everything, even the trivia seeming to have really been *chosen*. A great feeling of the brevity and difficulty of the visit. Barnes had a great flair for nudes, done sometimes by unlikely people: a hideous Van Gogh, a Dounaier Rousseau, Cézanne's late nudes. But over all, oppressive and awesome, as if the earth panted to be released from its clothes, the innumerable Renoirs, sometimes seeming mere air and nothing, and sometimes the fullness of the world. After a while Miss de Mazia lectured. Heavy Italian (?) accent: "Tradition is how man dominates his sufferings." Then later, the dates of Fra Angelico. As I left a tall Negro student said I had been pointed out to him as Mr. Lowell from his town. He said it took time to get Miss de Mazia's style, but then she had it.

(Jack Sweeney just called, and I suggested that you would welcome a grant. He was full of the highest admiration and optimistic and will let me know in a week. I do hope you and Lota will touch on New York, and not just briefly while we are there.)

Second millionaire. The Frankenthalers', a modest bulging Commonwealth Avenue house on Rittenhouse square. Maid, both Hoffmans received with open arms, incredible Empire furniture, about ten paintings, a pittance after the Barnes, particularly as the pictures repeated on a small scale others I'd just

seen: Seurat's models for the *Grande Jatte*, a fifth the size of the Barnes's, Renoir's *Three Graces*, somehow small and alone and shivering, a wonderful graceful Degas of Mary Cassatt looking like a James heroine, furs, small waist, face invisible. Mr. Frankenthaler's sister appeared, expensive print dress, most interested in pointing out photographs and semi-famous paintings of Orlando, her poodle, and saying "I wouldn't sell this one to my brother. Oh, here's Willie, at last." A heavy young man with a doeskin waistcoat, a seducer's tough upper lip, a tilting posture. Then a table of drinks and sandwiches, and "I wonder where Willie has gone to." He was gone; later it turned out we were supposed to be a part of Willie's cocktail party. We left hearing Mr. Frankenthaler's sister murmuring, "I've never seen the Barnes collection, I can tell you no one will regret Miss de Mazia's passing." I thought I would.

Third Millionaire. (This will come to a stop) After a reading at Haverford—this time real Quakers, and I felt all my poems were as soiled and disreputable as Baudelaire on his mistress—a reception by Mr. Hires of Hires root beer. A crew hair-cutted, black and gray haired man with a heart condition, who had put up a hundred dollars for me to read. He told [me] that whenever some one had told [him] a book was supreme, he read it. He then named ancient poets I'd never heard of and Buckle's intellectual history of the world, which he had read nine times, and I think Ingersoll. The guests, Haverford faculty, fawned. One said, or maybe two separately, that Mr. Hires loved books so that he had at first built a library and no dining room in his house; though, of course, he could afford a dining room. And so, home to Boston, taking in on the way a dinner at Hartford, everyone standing around for two hours before dinner, the men in one group telling memorized smut, the women in another talking about Dale Carnegie speech courses, my hostess, whom I'd just met, apologizing for labelling my place card "Robert" instead of "Bob."

I don't know why I've stuffed all this in, except to plaintively suggest that even here one can see the world in a grain of sand. Dearest, how I miss you. Some day, we will be in the same spot and long, long, long. Love to Lota.

 All my love,
 Cal

P.S. I enclose a translation of Heine, almost an original poem from three of his. How marvelous to have had a life that could be so written about even in terrible pain. I hope to have my translation book done by September. Bentley has asked me [to] try *Phèdre* for his French-classics series, and I've tried a few pages in crisp unscanned verse, and am astonished that everything *isn't* lost.

Then I've half contracted to [do] a modern poetry anthology for Anchor. I hope to give large gobs of the people I like, but it's harder now to be very original; Oscar Williams and others have gradually spread and lapped up most of the good things. Let me know of anything you like a lot. And please, if you have copies, send me all you've done since *A Cold Spring*. I carry the armadillo in my bill-fold and occasionally amaze people with it. And more photographs. The Amazon ones were real but you were missing. Lizzie sends her love. Flannery's book is for next year; do you want to propose her for the Academy. I'll second. I wrote Randall to this purpose, but have had no answer.

374. To William Empson

May 16, 1960

Dear Empson:

I've just read your Satan and Delilah pieces—everything you do interests me, but the Milton stuff is particularly close. Lewis's book has always struck me as unusually alive and somehow perverse, and hard to answer. You have a wonderful way of talking sense yet of being unpredictable. I remember years ago feeling what you wrote about Lear was all self-evident, yet each new development took me by surprise. So with the Milton; the essays show marvelous energy and thought in refusing to simplify. Several thoughts of mine that touch on yours are: 1) Samson really is the last great verse play in English; 2) Samson is an appalling character, yet one that something subtly deep in Milton goes into—i.e. the usual descriptions of him bluff the ease with which he becomes a hero and the author, or they take him as a dry rock of hatred. You find another way and change things. Also with Satan, you make him eventually quite seamy, creased and terrible, in the end more like Macbeth, neither the shining angel nor the hollow, air-filled blusterer of the conservative. I suppose your idea of Milton's God is that Milton holds him but finds dwindling aridity, as though God were not of Milton's choosing but something he was stuck with and in the end hanging on to out of honor perhaps by his finger-nails. I say this too simply, but I like the way you hold on to character, and your personal moments speak out with a generous stubbornness and fury.

Here, and in the more genial Joyce and Fielding pieces even I think you take a fairly tragic line, but somehow the withering all black charred claws view has been destroyed. I feel I have been taught something about life as well as about the classics.

I wonder how you are doing. I *did* get my Ford opera grant. I'll be doing

a number of small jobs next winter, and we will be living in New York. Things alter for the better, and one rests and waits for something honest to say. Sorry I am not going to be with you.

Yours,
 Robert Lowell

375. To Elizabeth Bishop

<div align="right">August 9, 1960</div>

Dearest Elizabeth:

I've been coming to Boston at intervals during the summer to keep up my therapy. This is the last and I am gathering a clutter of things together to take to Maine in a few hours. Strange times, like a retreat, mostly alone here in the empty house translating, and usually a wonderful letter from you waiting for me.

In "The Drinker," I've half put the soap-dish back (a little cute) with "the keys and used silver razor blades / shine in a saucer." The junket was a joke, I know milk turns to clabber. Liked your Sexton and old silver remarks. I feel I'm her half-discoverer and now can't keep up with her new admirers. One lags. I don't think anyone could admire the best Snodgrass more than I do, but a fellow named George Elliott Jr. to whom I once made some qualifications on Snodgrass, now takes a swipe at me in the *Hudson*, and calls my book a fake *Heart's Needle*. I guess I'll soon be fake Sexton in the *Hudson*. (I have your letter in front of me and am avoiding the pains of organization by now running through it commenting.) You're not facile to be different in each poem, and except for the Trollope and perhaps the Pound in another way, your [poems] are always very much you. I just meant, you never let mere style and mannerism write your poems for you as everyone else does. "Randall never lifts a finger!" I feel solaced; I find it so hard to lift a finger and pine over it and feel it's a racket husbands ought to treasure, but a low, maddening furtive vice not to be confessed to so I'm glad to share this with Randall, all of whose vices, unlike mine, are like Cato's, and extraordinary ones he is proud of. (I'm joking.) How truly and easily you see through people like May Sarton! That's dangerous. I think most people—I seem obsessed with this expression, and don't exactly feel so lofty—see faults out of pique and are just like the people they criticize—you're not. We have swapped with Bentley and will be at 194 Riverside Drive after mid-September. Do think again about skipping New York and going straight to Europe. I'm not going to Copenhagen, alas, the trip would have come just in the midst of moving and I do occasionally "lift a finger."

More on solitude and meter—I've just been doing some Baudelaire in meter as strict as his, and have never had such a work-out. Three poems have about killed me. I think he is unlike any of the later Baudelairean French poets—in him the fire comes from the descent of his Racinian rhetoric into the material of Flaubert and Balzac, or something of the sort, so that if you remove the finish he's gone, though still rich in a flat prosy way. In Rimbaud and Laforgue, the finish goes; in Mallarmé and Valéry the material. This is a horrible simplification, but he is different. I never realized that such wonder could be done with a sentence, moving through its terrible balances and metric and so seldom turning into a mere fireworks of syntax. I've also done Rimbaud's "Poet at Seven" in rhyming irregular lines and think I've lost his terrible bull-like perversity, jamming and crush, the detestable (as Louise Bogan would say) alexandrine, yet keeping it. I think he rather hated meter and syntax, though a great master of both, while Baudelaire gloried in both.

I guess I don't really like solitude. The fun is hammering bits of it out of a crowded life. For one's self, I think one should keep [the] door open for strict, disorderly and free meters. God knows the chances are so slim of breaking through the crust writing something alive—one ought to have several possible techniques ready.

Gombrich, funny, just after your [letter] I had dinner with Spender and he brought up Gombrich. I must read him. Isn't poor Karl's a dull roar of bombast; it's the resonance I mind not the opinions, though[,] and think the opinions aren't real at all but were chosen to let him thunder. But what a curse to thunder and say nothing!

Harriet is terrific, like living with the new forces. I don't think she knows how frail we are, but being a child, she is heavy on her feet and we can almost keep up with her by cheating and using cunning and withdrawing into the shadows she can't understand.

Well goodbye, my Dear,

Love,

Cal

376. To Stephen Spender

Castine, Maine
August 9, 1960

Dear Stephen:

Many thanks for your letter. I was feeling rather hang-doggish the next

morning and felt I had been boringly self-preoccupied and full of writers' talk—almost enough to write you an apology. Suddenly I remembered next afternoon that I had even forgotten to ask the latest news of Mary. Tell me what is happening. We've had no news since she stayed with us last April, first giddy then rather dampened by Bowden's refusal to divorce. I don't know what to think about the new man sight unseen. One suddenly realizes that Bowden was flesh and blood!

I'm encouraged by what you say about my "Union Dead," just what I feared was that it lacked the kind of lived history that you and Auden discovered for English poetry in the thirties. Mine has a stern pathetic mystery about it, I think. Somehow, it took months to write and came in a time of drouth for me. In a couple of months, I'll send you some translations for *Encounter*. I have piles to pick from: Rimbaud, Leopardi, Baudelaire, more Pasternak and Montale.

Give my love to Natasha. Perhaps, next year we'll be in England. I want to write the Taylors to look you up, they are about my closest friends and good friends of Allen's.

Affectionately,
Cal

P.S. Your taxi driver is rather appalling. I remember how aghast Jarrell was once while listening to a book-store old gentlelady talk about the *Book of Changes*, and realizing that his great desire, the spreading of high culture was coming true!

377. *To T. S. Eliot*

194 Riverside Dr.
N.Y.C.
October 28, 1960

Dear Tom:

Here's the story on my *Phèdre*. Last spring Eric Bentley suggested that I do it for one of his Classic Theater anthologies. I think he was rather surprised when I actually finished it this fall and had no written contract with him. Then Giroux and Straus wanted to bring my play out as a separate volume—hell! Would Bentley delay his anthology long enough for Farrar and Straus to sell enough copies to break even? Each morning a letter or a postcard in green ink would arrive from Bentley. His great anxiety was that Jacques Barzun had done Beaumarchais's *Figaro* for the same volume, was

threatened by a rival translation, wanted to have his play produced this spring in Detroit, couldn't get a separate volume publication. Now the arrangement is that Barzun and I will be published by Farrar and Straus, Bentley will hold off till August. All rather a mess, but my play will come out here in March or April. Now about Faber, Bentley wants rights to let his anthology circulate (no separate publication) in England, about a thousand copies. Would Faber care to publish me later in England after Bentley's Classic Theater anthology— six plays, paper cover, sells here for $1.45[—] has been distributed in England. I don't think I can exactly morally prevent Bentley from distributing his anthology in England—the other volumes in the series have been. Otherwise there's nothing I would like better than to have Faber publish me and the two year delay doesn't matter.

I don't know whether I have the technical training to do a libretto, but of course I think of Stravinsky as the best composer alive and would rather write for him than anyone else. It would have to be something much more passionate and simple than Auden's *Rake*. I was thinking of trying an operatic version of *The Changeling*, keeping Middleton's words and meter wherever possible. I would try anything Stravinsky suggested. The composer—even a minor one— should call the tune. For Stravinsky, I would want to bend completely. I don't know about my competence but I have a colleague, William Meredith, who knows much more about music and guess that together we could produce. How should I get in touch with Stravinsky?

I also have another book that Faber might be interested in. It's to be called *Imitations* and will be about 50 free translations I've been working on for the last three years. 11 or 12 Montale, 4 Rilke, 15 Baudelaire (the hardest and done in rhyme and meter) 3 Leopardi, 3 Heine, 5 or six Pasternak and so forth. The poems are all done, but I need three or four months for polishing and intend to have a manuscript for Farrar and Straus by April, and they will publish in the fall. Some of the translations are almost original poems and I think some of my best work.

What a rush of business! Miss Kray has asked me to introduce you again this winter. I hope you won't wince at this. I intend to be more brief and impersonal this time. I feel very close to you, but I don't know how to say this from the platform.

Sorry the trip is not a pleasure to you. Lizzie and I think a lot about travelling with rather mixed minds. Excuse this messy letter. We both send our love to you and Valerie.

Cal

P.S. Allen and Belle have just hit town. Allen's doing nothing whatever but looks better than he has for twenty years. Can you hear his voice saying (re a trip to Lexington Kentucky) "And the pay-off is that my portrait is being hung in the courthouse." I hope it isn't a ghastly one done by Mary Aiken.

378. To Adrienne Rich

November 18, 1960

Dearest Adrienne:

My unanswered letters have dwindled to a little group of real letters, all to poets: Elizabeth Bishop, you, Allen Tate, Roethke in an asylum in Dublin, and Donald Davie with a pile of interesting poems mislaid. How lovely to hear from you! I made some 200 corrections in *Phèdre* since you saw it, several speeches have been rewritten and about half your suggestions had been taken care of. I'll catch the rest in galleys. They were all very much to the point, only I am momentarily weary of patching. Great, perhaps unbelievable things have been happening. I now have a producer, a Mrs. Bel Geddes, widow of Norman Bel Geddes. Blond, sixtyish, looks rather like Mrs. Adlai Stevenson, Belgian accents, 4th wife of 4 husbands, international field hockey champion, what my editor the sober Bob Giroux calls, "rather an adventuress"; but rich and full of energy and sympathetic and bristling suggestions. People like Callas (we got a favorable reply, I think i.e., that she was about to open at the Scala and couldn't make any immediate decisions[)]—also Edwige Feuillere, and Melina Mercouri and perhaps a director, Zeffirelli, who has done Callas and had rave Tynan reviews from Tynan for *Romeo and Juliet* at Stratford (England). So, there seems to be a real perhaps outside chance for a big Broadway success, money etc. It's all more like winning the Irish sweepstakes than writing.

Your poems are awfully good. The two country house pieces seem perfect and the long history poem has something new for you (?), an overriding voice and tone. I have been trying to think where I've heard it—nowhere really but there are touches of Williams and I think Tate. At least, you for the first time seem Southern—interruption: Harriet has just come with her toy telephone— "my Cousin's on the phone. Do you want to talk maybe?" I guess history is a Southern Agrarian discovery and Alf's studies have brought that out in you. What I mean is that you set a tone of so much interest and authority that the reader swallows everything uncritically. I haven't gotten to the point of being

critical, but doubt if I would find anything. The "kitchen" opening in the third poem is a great stroke.

The opera is good fun, really fascinating and an obsession. Yet if I miss a few days it all seems to fade. It seems to have about as much connection with writing as a grant to watch the Yankees practice for a season. Yet anything that you like and that absorbs you must be worth the time. Interruption: Harriet has come clattering in in Lizzie's high heels. Unintelligible dialogue, mostly contralto laughs at my typing. Fielder says children are moral imbeciles. Lizzie's favorite quote after a day with Harriet and Eileen.

Back to opera. I've seen about 5 Puccinis, 3 Mozarts, 3 Verdi's, 3 Strauss's, *Carmen*, *Boris*, Della Piccola, Monteverdi, Eck, and more things than I can remember, and at every stage of imperfection and probably could write a perfect Puccini libretto if he would rise from the shades. At the Met they only speak German and Italian, and everyone except Bing needs to be on Metro-Cal. Grotesque scenes. Straus's *Arabella* being done in an English translation by a German by singers who only know German. Diva—"Ist es *leeps* or *lips*." Translator's phrase, "we come perhaps from very dubious people." Torrent of German dialogue between German diva, German conductor, German stage-director: Ist es ~~dubious~~ dübee-us oder doobyus. No one really knew. The Italian tenors are another group. They look like comic strip goons and chatter away in little groups about their income taxes and singing teachers and mothers and have to be told by the choir master not to put their feet up on the Met's plush seats, and yell bravo when every thing is going haywire. The stage directors are always trying to make the operas into plays while the conductors try to make them into oratorios, both very keyed up and oblivious of the other's world and threatening to quit, while Bing rushes on the stage to complain because a plastic glass has refused to shatter or there's no sound of breaking glass when Cherubino jumps out a window. Raging German voice to an out-of-control chorus, "Dü I speakk Schinese?"

And so it goes. The great people now take pride in being able to tell me and Meredith apart and are right about half the time.

Queer jumbled world. Dag Hammarskjöld reads my poems. Kenneth Koch and Ginsberg disputing which is the dullest of the other's poems. Hollander full of writing lyrics for a Broadway musical. Philip Rahv with a Long Island Society divorcee, crushing trip to the Bronx with Harriet, the Epsteins and their son, Jacob. Bill Williams paralyzed and unable to hear me and Mary McCarthy's brother Kevin read[ing] *Paterson* at the Y. We are the only gentiles at every party we go to, and really love New York and feel a little seedy. Lizzie

has flatly given up asking people to dinner, because the West side is so far away and we only have the Bentleys' dishes. Bentley is very nice by the way and full of German literature information and absolutely hell-on-wheels as an editor. I have had two hundred letters and postcards signed in green ink and coming on different stationery: Boston, Columbia, Doubleday etc. so I won't recognize them and not read them, all with minute fussy outraged queries about publication and screams against Roger Straus.

Enough. Excuse this outpour. I've almost forgotten how to write. We both miss you and Alf sorely.

Love,
Cal

379. To Allen Tate

November 18, 1960

Dear Allen:

I have been meaning to write you [a] note expressing my regrets at getting so plastered the other night—god knows what I said or did. Next day on the way to Washington I felt I was living in an aquarium. Life's been quieter since you and Belle left, though we stayed up till six waiting for the Minnesota returns that never came. How good the election came out as it did! What fun it was seeing you both! I really meant half the sentimental things I said the other night and none of the foolish ones. Stanley said it was hard to tell which of us made the least sense. Then he confessed that he literally has *two* stomachs which somehow means he cannot get tight. So, it's all his fault and he is a dangerous companion, some one who can walk on water while mortals drown.

Really awfully glad I've at last written something that pleases you. The "Union Dead" poem took all winter and I suppose is the most composed poem I've ever written. My *Phèdre* which took about the same time to write now looks as though it might be done on Broadway. All very odd and strange!

We've both had three week colds. Lizzie has just finished reviewing thirty books to pay for an hour at Bergdorf Goodman's. We like it here, and find now that Lizzie has given up entertaining (How can I invite anyone to the West Side?) that we are less rushed than in Boston and often have an evening together or go to a movie.

The opera is rather far from my calling but great fun. I wish I had your presence. The opera officials still can't tell me and Bill Meredith apart, and

have heavy German-American guessing games trying to. I've been translating a lot of Baudelaire and sometime when I can get it a bit more polished and re-typed would like to send it to you.

You and Belle seem so happy together. It's a great joy to us. So unlike Philip. By the way his lady was the one person very apologetic about drinking too much at Stanley's.

Lizzie sends her love to you both,

Cal[. . .]

380. To Edmund Wilson

December 16, 1960

Dear Edmund:

I've lately met about ten Englishmen who have been in Boston. They all feel you are *the* living person in your new northern world. Or perhaps in any world—their reverence is incredible, though of course deserved. Meanwhile we sorely miss you [and] Elena. Wouldn't you like to come down here and perform for Harriet's birthday party on January 7th?

We really love New York after five years of Boston, and Lizzie's even roaming about town looking at houses—she has even figured out a way to live rent-free by renting two floors. I've been enjoying the opera very much and have finished two books of translations, and soon the day will be on me for more work of my own. How is your Civil War book? I like the Callaghan piece. I used to read his stories in my old Catholic convert days.

We both send our love to you both, and Merry Christmas from Harriet to Helen,

Cal

381. To T. S. Eliot

[December 18, 1960]

COULD WE GIVE YOU AND VALERIE A SMALL TEA FOUROCLOCK WEDNESDAY JANUARY FOURTH MADE OF LIVELY PEOPLE YOU LIKE

CAL

382. To Elizabeth Bishop

December 23, 1960

Dearest Elizabeth:

I hope these will reach you sometime near Christmas, and that you will like them and that you will let me dedicate them to you. The book will come out next fall—I still hope to make changes and perhaps add two or three more poems. My Racine is on its way to you, not air mail, and should reach you soon. It will come out this spring.

We like it here so much, we have finally decided to sell our Boston house and are about to buy an apartment—15 West 67th, duplex, one huge room two stories high, artist's window, bedroom kitchen and dining room on first floor, three bedrooms, all fairly large, fireplace, exposed beams, elevator man, near new Lincoln Center, improving neighborhood, Central Park a few feet away for Harriet. I make this as dull as I can in haste, but we are thrilled with the move and figure we can live here for about what we can in Boston.

I've talked to Marianne Moore a couple of times on the phone—"Robert, I am in eclipse." Meaning she, poor thing, had been suffering from dysentery. About the Mid-Century [which] gives her book and mine away together and our photographs have been combined into one—"like Pompeii and Herculaeum." We had a little contest saying how much we loved and admired you—Brooklyn accent, "Of course she venerates you."

Dear Elizabeth, let me know your plans. We will probably go to Boston for a month in May. I may go to England sometime in the late summer or fall if my *Phèdre* opens there. Where can we meet?? Love to you and Lota and Merry Christmas.

Cal

More news and gossip later.

383. To Elizabeth Hardwick

December 26, 1960
The Day after Christmas

Dearest Lizzie:

The apartment still looks out on a sunlit Hudson, but inside it's awfully hollow and lonely without mother and child. I had a pleasant evening at the

Epsteins'. We argued about the Prophet Amos and Harriet's fur shoes for Jacob were a hit after a while. Three Podhoretz children! After seven, children grow quiet.

I've just cooked myself my usual breakfast, only remembering to put the coffee pot back on the stove. Now for my two thankyou letters and back to my Baudelaire revisions. Mr. Badman misses the both of yous. Love and happy New Year to everyone,

Uncle Dad

Cal

384. To Hannah Arendt

January 9, 1961

Dear Hannah:

Here's the Rilke, almost unrecognizable, and really more my reply or extension than a translation. Stanza 3 which I added is something I have wanted to write since I first read military history as a small boy—and especially somehow all this winter. I want to put it out of chronological order and away from my other Rilke pieces and let it end my book, for it's really my own credo, and hope you'll let me dedicate it to you in gratitude—I wonder if it isn't quietly my finest poem? This is said in the first blush of accomplishment!

Lizzie and I will miss [you] here in these months of your exile and ours.

Yours affectionately,

Cal

385. To Hannah Arendt

January 27, [1961]

Dear Hannah:

Thanks for your letter. I couldn't be more pleased! The poem, with three or four slight verbal changes, will come [out] in the *Nation* in a week or so. I've sent a copy of the translation book to you. Please make objections if the spirit moves you, and I can make improvements before it goes to galleys. I see to my embarrassment, that I didn't get in the changes you suggested in my two Rilke portraits. However, I've made them in my own copy. I'm still of two minds about including the "Self-Portrait."

We got invited to Washington along with 165 other intellectuals—all very

white and dramatic, and full, as Washington hasn't been for years, with bright people who aren't poets and teachers. I feel the country is green again and wrote in the Kennedy's guest book: "Robert Lowell, happy that at long last the Goths have left the White House."

We and I are having a more quiet life than so far this winter. Just as well, our new apartment is ours now, and we are New Yorkers. We miss you very much.

Affectionately,

P.S. A rather silly but not necessarily misleading woman Mrs. Geist, has seen Mary in Paris, and says she is in high spirits, very much in love and that her fiancé is very attractive. I had lunch with Bowden.

386. To Elizabeth Bishop

February 15, 1961

Dearest Elizabeth:

Isn't this Valentine's Day or near it? Such an age since I've heard from you. Your telegram was a joy, but I was grieved to think of the lost letter. Please write it again. The translation book keeps growing—I've added "Mémoire," "Bateau Ivre" and "Les Chercheuses" of Rimbaud; Baudelaire's "Le Voyage," a Victor Hugo, and 12 pages of Villon's *Testament*, probably my best translations along with the Baudelaire. Let me know things you question. I am supposed to have my manuscript in by April, but the book won't come out till September. The *Phaedra* will be out in April—a Greek movie and Greek tragedy girl, Melina Mercouri may do the part of Phaedra. I see her next week. We have just submitted the manuscript to the Edinburgh Festival. If they should take, I'll be in England in August and September and hope we can meet at length, and at last.

Mary McCarthy was here last night *fresh* from her Alabama divorce. Her new man in photographs looks like a combination of Lionel Trilling and Jim Farley—though a year or two younger than Mary, he looks of an older generation. He works in the foreign service in Warsaw. Mary's more at ease and generous than we have ever seen her—no more nervous Broadwater rundowns of everyone under the sun. Bowden's improved too and really very touching—he's still Bowden.

We were invited along with 170 others—writers etc.—to the Kennedy inaugural. Strange scenes with Allen Tate, tails, white gloves, "my duty to the Republic etc" and Belle, very at ease with Allen at least, huge, described by Francis

Biddle as a "sponge wrapped in a quilt." The Kennedy business is very inspiring—with a lot of reservations, I feel like a patriot for the first time in my life. I wrote in the Kennedy guest-book, Robert Lowell, happy that at long last the Goths have left the White House. Bobby Kennedy read it, and said, "I guess we are the Visigoths[."] Incredible dinner at the Eberharts with the Tates, Madam Perkins, K. A. Porter, Auden, Ted Spencer's sister and Betty Eberhart's German cousin. Allen very tight gave two identical very formal toasts to the memory of Ted Spencer, and Auden helpfully took out all our plates, still unfinished, to the pantry, and Katherine Anne announced that she was seventy.

I am now on my second month of contact lenses and feel a new man—I can see and be seen about twice as well. They're really miraculous—you can swim, sleep, dive, play football or anything under the sun in them.

[. . .]Living in New York after Boston is like discovering that there is oxygen in the air—people to talk to, plays, opera, and something in the air that somehow makes the same people very different here from what they are in Boston. Lizzie has stopped giving dinner parties and now has lunches out with friends. Somehow everything is much merrier, easier and more serious. Other American cities may honor writers, but they can't digest, or worse, they can, and expect you to live as they do. Harriet's a woman now, the most beautiful in New York, I tell her, if she would stop talking 24 hours a day about what she's wearing.

I run into your old cronies: Pearl Kazin and Loren and am green with envy because they have letters from you. Dearest, please write me! Our love to you and Lota.

Cal

387. To Marianne Moore

Neurological Institute of Presbyterian-Columbia Medical Center
New York, New York
March 26, 1961

Dear Miss Moore:

I've been reading the new Oxford and Cambridge Protestant *New Testament*. The translators offer a new version of the Lord's Prayer. This has given me the arrogance to try my own hand.

"Our Father, help us to revere your name,
To hold your truth on earth & to enter the kingdom.

Give us today sufficient bread;
Forgive us our injuries,
As we forgive those we have injured;
Guide us in the day of tribulation,
And save us from Hell. Amen."

Could one say of our Lord what a Harvard House Master said of Protestant Pusey: "He is a real pigmy in a world of fake giants"?
Affectionately,
Robert Lowell

388. To Stephen Spender

194 Riverside Drive
New York City
May 7, 1961

Dear Stephen:

I have put off writing you partly because I wanted to have the Rimbaud I am sending you ready, and partly because things have been confused and changing with me and I hardly know what to say. I have been well for about a month and I think Elizabeth and I are coming back together. I was never very sick, but have been through rather a dark time which I still don't want to go into much. I was very much touched by your letter and the message from Natasha. Life is good, but how turbulent and tangled it gets sometimes.

I hope you can use the Rimbaud. The selections are supposed to form a unit—Rimbaud's story up to the *Saison* more or less. I rather hope you can use the whole sequence, but I know it is a good many pages. Take what you can. The book that this is part of will probably come out in November. Look forward to seeing you next winter in any case.

Affectionately,
Cal

The Beverly Hills Hotel
Beverly Hills, California
Friday, June 16, 1961

Dearest Elizabeth:

Days of things not people. Yesterday morning a long block away on 86th St. I saw a figure I knew I couldn't escape—dirty untucked shirt, red, bulging, drink-gone face, a sort of pirate, all shapeless red and waiting—and when I got nearer it held a dollar bill and asked me to buy him a bottle of wine. Morals and squeamishness joined and I hurried on—to have my lens fitted. Then 8 hours later, 1st Class jet, a second vodka martini brought without asking, two sparkling burgundies, part of a chicken stuffed with yellow butter—I read about Pasternak's train-themes and looked on 1000 miles (ten miles a minute) of uninhabited Rockies and deserts—real dust oceans—and felt like a last parasite of the Tsars.

My room cost $25 dollars a day exclusive of services, it gives on a patio, the bath-tub is enclosed in a plastic cabinet. The two CBS men have moved to a cheaper hotel because of the "low budget." They talk to me too much about money, feel they are unadorned weak men, & despise California. After two days of the Beverly Hills Hotel and screening actors, they seem to have gotten an all-New York caste for Pasternak. We have an hour or so's meeting today and tomorrow the real work begins. I'm not allowed to meet Olga's plane on Saturday, so I can rest for the ordeal. (This isn't personal, but a general policy.) I haven't dared mention Dr. Bernard, my one Hollywood connection.

There are two beds here, and I wish to God you were in the other and enjoying our usual Marlborough St. breakfast on a twin acre-wide table. Tony and I both felt dull and grieved when she told me the house was sold. All that life! It haunted me during the long, whizzing, ten miles a minute jet flight. How I miss you and how.

390. *To Elizabeth Hardwick*

[June 18, 1961]

Dearest Lizzie:

The morning after—somewhere else in the hotel Olga is sleeping till eleven, but I can't. I haven't seen the performances yet except in bits and pieces and have no idea whether it was good or bad (to show it to us would have cost $400 or maybe $4,000). It might be very much either.

My part may not have made sense, or have made very queer sense. I don't think anyone would have noticed. I was given tremendous praise for knowing my cues, but nothing else was mentioned, or perhaps even listened to.

We are flying back Tuesday morning. We wanted an extra day here, but flying back on Monday would get us in at 2 a.m. All's at CBS's low-budget expense. Meals for two at the hotel will cost something like $30. I feel like Sherman Adams. Blair will end like Gold[fine] in Stockbridge and I'll be in jail. Today we'll rent a Hertz car and drive off through the fog and flatness to something called the O-HI Valley, I think. I am carnation color from the swimming pool.

Olga is nice, but as Silvers says, her one subject is Russia. I am not sure that she even hears or understands the English language on any other subject.

Dr. Bernard, by the way, met at a similar lady psychiatrist's modern bungalow, has decided my dreams are more rewarding than my actuality. This adds great plot, color and imagery to our sessions and seems to remove them to the for me safe and detached world of fiction—my disease in life is something like this.

In the back of my mind is Boston and you and Harriet always, and I feel if I listen carefully I'll hear something slip or fall. I can imagine many scenes for you and hope you are not furiously under a toppling debris of problems. I hope you are not, and wish you were here all the time.

All my love,
Cal

P.S. I think my first letter went air-mail Europe—whatever that does to delivery. The hotel seems to expect at least that.

Saturday night (after TV)
Dreams—

a) Aunt Sarah's old maid complaining that I had been rude to her, also to Aunt S. (who might have been m[y] grandparents) and she didn't want to see me for the present—this connected with my sickness—Lizzie's To hell with your relatives then? We would live without them. I wonder how I was rude.

b) Someone's assistant inspecting room next to the one I was in[,] uninvited—followed by his boss, inspect room where I am— though I've been withdrawn from people to avoid even less disturbing things than this. They wear old fashioned formal clothes—part of a dinner jacket combined with something else.

c) Surrounded by a ring of line[s] of people, problem as in a game to meet or manipulate their moves.

1. Images—a girl's legs said to have nothing on under her dress, but this merely meant no slip. Not particularly sexy image.
2. A girl in flamingo red dress beautiful, California tan & figure.
3. Small cannon, hand-sized, a toy but acquiring the strong hard materials and precise mechanism of a real cannon. (Modern)
4. Left with a bicycle somehow defective and forced to ride (uncertain result).

Sunday night
Discussion with R. P. Blackmur about an imaginary recent longish poem by Harry Brown. The poem had rather derivative, unauthentic emotions and technique, but was wonderfully inventive (opposite of a Blackmur poem). We were both trying to prove that the Brown poem was really *very* good despite its defects. This was a critical discovery.

391. To Elizabeth Bishop

85 East End Ave.
Apt. 14G
N.Y.C.
June 27, 1961

Dearest Elizabeth:

I'm O.K. and have been since April and have been meaning to write you since April but I shy away from giving a lot of personal history—this has happened so many times one feels a little cut off from one's kind. I was in a hospital for five weeks or so, less high and in an allegorical world than usual and not so broken down afterwards. Once more there was a girl, a rather foolish girl but full of a kind of life and earth force, and once more a great grayness and debris left behind me at home. Now we are back together, wobbly but reknit almost.[. . .]

My book is a lot bigger: a long selection from Villon, more Rimbaud—"Les Chercheuses," "The Drunken Boat," "Mémoire," now a total of eight sonnets (I took all your suggestions) Baudelaire's "Le Voyage," more Pasternak, and some scraps of Homer and Sappho. The whole is much more worth dedicating to you now and I hope you'll be pleased.

I have a rather large plan, risky to mention at this point when not a line has been written, but I would like to try a long long poem about Hitler and the Second World War, done more or less chronologically, short scenes, prose, strict and free verse, and many styles. It would take many years to do, if it could be done at all, and almost anything could go in it. I could get away from the too personal, use history and perhaps catch a great chunk of the times we have endured.

I must say your Brazil book sounds much more achievable and good sense. I think you do catch that revolutionary under pressure quality of the earlier poets—most poets tho seem like crusts of hardening lava. By the way Jason Epstein at Random House would very much like to see the manuscript of your stories, if it is clear of ties to Houghton and Mifflin. I have been reading over the long *New Yorker* childhood story. Really no one is better either in an open Russian way or symbolically as in your "Prison"!

Harriet will be almost five when you arrive, strong long legs, a powerful climber, an actress whenever men are around, she has two boy friends her age and many mine, including me and is learning about life in large scoops.

I loved your last letter as always and am thrilled at your visit, really come this time. Write again soon. Write again soon and I will be less hang-dog and more fun.

Best to Lota and love to you,

Cal

P.S. Lizzie tells me there's another letter from Boston, so I'll write again then. Somehow it's hard to write very fully, or interestingly or honestly about personal matters. I always feel my Mother's moralizing wrestling with my father's optimism. Almost from birth I decided they were both wrong and the truth lay elsewhere. Then from time to time I talk like both of them at once.

There's a long bit about Quadros in the last issue. When you wrote you were accepting a job, I thought at first that you were entering the government like Lota and were perhaps rebuilding a city. I miss you greatly.

392. *To T. S. Eliot*

Castine, Maine
June 30, 1961

Dear Tom:

Many thanks for your two letters and the criticism. I have taken most of it. "Cythera" now ends, "to see my heart and body without disgust." I am a lit-

tle uneasy about the sound of the two nouns after "courage and strength" in the preceding line. But the sense is better. I am also taking the subtitle translation away, and have written a short preface which clarifies what I am trying to do. I accept all your changes for the English text of *Phaedra*. Monteith has written me asking if the contracts for the two new books should be the same as for *Life Studies*. I think they should.

We drive to Maine tomorrow. Our troubles are over and Lizzie and I are together again. The whole business has been very bruising, and it is fierce facing the pain I have caused, and humiliating to think that it has all happened before and that control and self-knowledge come so slowly, if at all. I have a very good doctor though and have unravelled many things. Life still has blood in it, and love has come back to our small family.

I gather from Bob that you will be back here next fall or winter. We look forward to seeing you and Valerie then.

Affectionately,

P.S. This is a rather inadequate letter. It might have all been in one sentence because for the last two days I have been reading Milton's polemical prose for a course I am giving next fall.

393. To Elizabeth Hardwick

85 East End Ave.
Apt. 14G
New York, New York
July 10, 1961

Dearest Lizzie:

We circled the Bedford airport for hours, then the pilot announced that we should look for a Northeast agent, *if there was one*, if we wanted to continue to New York. I got in here at twelve-thirty. Read *Time* from cover to cover, also my two chair companions, first a young lady from Bar Harbor working in personnel for R. H. Stearns, worried like us about the drift to the suburbs, "the Chestnut Hill branch claims they are carrying us." Then a young German from Hamburg, recently divorced and returning from visiting his two children, about Harriet's age, in North East Harbor. A sort of thawed Per and beginning a novel [about] his divorce, a testament for his children, in the style of Jacques Prévert. I gave him a huge reading list of things like *Washington Square*, and stared out the window at an image of my hand, big enough to fit the

Sphinx and dizzily distorted in the window. And thought, heart-drenched, of how much I wanted to be gentle, humorous, modest, both feet on the ground and in the bosom of my family.

I love you and miss you and wish I were back. Love to you both,
Cal[. . .]

394. *To Harriet Winslow*

<div align="right">

Castine, Maine
July 31, 1961

</div>

Dear Cousin Harriet:

Here I am back at my desk in the barn and once more working on a play. This time it is a dramatization of Melville's little novel, *Benito Cereno*, the story of an honest but rather thick-skulled American sea-captain from Duxbury, Mass. who spends a day on board a Spanish slave ship in 1799, unaware that the slaves have seized the ship and killed most of the Spaniards. The hero is a sort of Henry Jamesian Innocent abroad. All this is to satisfy my Ford opera grant, though I think of a play rather than anything that could be sung. Soon Lizzie will be down blowing her horn, and we will be off to our staff of life, tennis.

Yesterday, a ceremony: taking my Grandfather out of his two ton gold frame, and hanging him weightless, dark and frameless between the two windows facing the dining-room fire-place. Perhaps he belongs emotionally rather than artistically. He is my first experience of both country life and family background, and Harriet who watched every motion of the hanging had her first felt experience of a great grandfather, and said, "Now I want to see my grandmother, not your grandmother but mine." She meant Mother.

I woke up the other morning with a curious feeling of continuity, due I think to my surroundings. Great falling festoons of loose green vines, trees and white woodwork. One thing dropping, slightly tangling and touching another indefinitely. And a feeling that as we pass through our fairly brief lives, we stay long enough to pass something on that some one else catches by his fingertips. A little bit of my grandfather and that old world seems to touch Harriet. As a father I could use his out of doors abundance and invention.

By the way, I think the Commons house needs new paint, shutters, kitchen and possibly some of the outside. I want to ask the expert eye of Mr. Farley and he can write you. The barn is marvelously strong, snug and permanent. Thanks for the hot-plate, toaster curtains and running water. It's now an in-

dependent house. And thankyou a thousand times for the continuity you have given my wayward but always rebounding life—continuity, sympathy and warmth. We both love you very dearly!

Love,

Bobby

395. To Elizabeth Bishop

August 7, 1961

Dearest Elizabeth:

The other night I had a dream about you, one of those dreams where there were many scattered people moving about like bits of wood in a current, much maneuvering and confusion. Somewhere on the edges you were, but we couldn't come together, and all was a headache of difficulties and distances. Finally you appeared in our apartment and said I am ready to take a walk, unless you intend to keep me waiting longer—it's already been hours. Well, I am expecting you this fall in New York and I won't keep you waiting.

There's something else. For the last two weeks, I haven't had a drop to drink. At first one feels removed from the living, that sociable drop gone that makes us all one species, in warmth, weakness and talkativeness. Then the air clears and steadies. I have so many holes in my soul, I imagine this is the only way for me to go through the rich jungle of New York on my own feet. So come soon, and we will gaze on the riches of the world in our odd sobriety. I can't say that you ever seemed to lose the slightest gaiety, rather the opposite!

We never seem to write what we plan. For a year or so, I've had a vague idea of making an opera libretto out of Melville's *Benito Cereno*. It was mostly my fellow Ford Foundation Fellow, Bill Meredith's notion, and I kept delaying, sure in my heart that I would always put it off. Then after I got back here I started. Now a draft is done, 47 pages of iambicky free verse, full of horror, charade and scenes. The grand "Gerontion"-like Elizabethan monologues I proposed for myself never materialized: all is terse, rapid and direct. Lizzie is all for it, but it has gone so fast, I am very dim on what I've done.

I'll give you two of my days. First day: New York, in bed tight after too gay a time with an old Kenyon class-mate and Léonie Adams. (By the way Bill Troy died this spring after a long speechless drag with cancer of the throat. The funeral was a high mass with a little group of Columbia atheists, mostly women and Russian translators, with a man or two in a beret. No one knew when to stand or kneel except for Caroline Tate. Later Léonie kept getting letters from

intellectual priests, who all assumed that Bill was in Purgatory and would need a lot of prayers.) Back to my day. With a terrible head-ache, I look at my watch: 7:15. I rush with a heavy head to the Lexington Avenue Subway, take a local by mistake. Stones along the side seem to crawl by, one by one in slow motion. On the Staten Island Ferry, the refreshments girl announces, "we have no coffee." I drink something that is neither tea nor coffee. Worrying furiously with this question, I read that Kennedy is calling up the reserves, and some sort of estimate that seventy million people may be killed on both sides at the first blow. Pictures of the New York common man, all saying that they don't intend to be pushed around and that for the first time they feel we have a president. Leaving the ferry, I meet the conference leech, natty beret, pressed suit, a two pound portable Olivetti typewriter. In his wake, the two conference morons, tieless shirts and trousers held up by neckties. My two hour class; I am very distant, ascetic and philosophical. Lunch: ham mostly fat and terrible things, egglike, that look like they've been through a steam laundry. A joint conference on drama, poetry and fiction in which the conference director, a Mr. Rust Hills, makes more and more surly references to my colleague, Saul Bellow's heroes. Mounting explosive heat. I side-step the conference nymphomaniac. Swimming. Something has gone wrong with the tide, at every six inches there are deflated contraceptives. Boys of five blowing them up like balloons. Hideous blue and bloated things floating. The water striped with reddish algae that stains. Red sand on the beach, that also stains. On the horizon, the houses of Brooklyn and the *Queen Mary* making for Manhattan. Saul Bellow goes off for a long killing fiction-discussion meeting with the conference nymphomaniac, leaving me with the conference leech, who invites me to dinner. Supper: at six, after two minutes for drinks—more laundered food. Discussion on Wagner College dormitory steps. First two shy literary agents, then Molly Kazan, deep practical New York voice, an answer for everything, obviously a woman who touches nothing that doesn't turn to gold. She is challenged by Will Maas, the Wagner poet and poetry professor, quietly alcoholic, less quietly homosexual, a man who hasn't published for twenty years and never, at best, sold anything for a nickel. He questions the lastingness of Broadway at best. Stifling sleepless heat, sounds of intimacy, outrage and drinking. A young bearded poet announcing that he is the best poet of 24 in America, then rapping each dormitory door with a toilet brush. From the next room belonging to my other colleague, Edward Albee, a playwright—the low endless Tennessee voice of the conference nymphomaniac reading aloud a play. At about four-thirty, all is quiet.

Second day (if I have the strength to tell it!) Our annual trip from Castine to Mount Desert. Lizzie, Harriet, I and Betty Dawson, our colored nurse.

Betty is a first-rate housekeeper, a novelty in our family, but she is a slow, retiring soul. On the drive up, one of her few remarks was, "I don't make friends easily." Lizzie says, if most people have 12 spark-plugs, eleven and a half of Betty's are clogged with chewing-gum. She fears nature, "why don't the folks living up these back roads get out of here?" She knows the woods are full of snakes, won't go to the ladies' room alone, and has a hundred and seventy-five dollar polaroid camera. Showing Betty the world turned out to be impossible. After two miles: "We almost there? They have dinky roads like this in Virginia." Harriet, mistakenly bought a two-note wooden flute, begins deafening, then prodding, then (this is the worst) questioning Betty. "Why is it wood? Why does it have two notes? That's funny, isn't it. Tell me something else you know!" On the great Ocean Drive, pointing out things was a failure. Betty glumly gaped inland, afraid that snakes might run out of the woods. At Thunder Hole, the polaroid pictures first came out gray outlines on blinding white, then formless gray on white and finally pure white. At the beach, we trampled about in the much too-cold-to-swim water, while Betty sat in the shade, head unraised, as she shifted the film in her camera. At last a real picture, of Elizabeth, but a brawny unknown man in trunks occupies two-thirds of the film-space. That night we slept ten hours. In the morning, Harriet woke me up and I had to tell her about the domestic life of Aunt Jemima. "She only reads her children cook-books."

I work from about ten to three-thirty, then we play tennis, then we eat and listen to music. It's really very quiet and beautiful. We go to New York about the 7th. I feel like some one washed up on land and given a new suit, after six months of floating. A cancerous impatience is wearing away, and I guess life is really much too lovely not to live out.

A few facts that I may have given you before. Our address will be 15 West 67th St. Harriet weighs forty pounds and comes to my belt. We all miss you and long to see you. My best to Lota, love,

Cal

396. *To Isabella Gardner*

15 West 67 St.
New York, New York
October 10, 1961

Dear Belle:

I should have written you a note on your book earlier, but it disappeared

in the debris of settling and just now turned up again. We have been doing this that and the other, of course, getting settled—all the workmen arriving in the wrong order and having to be brought in again. I have re-written my plays, and busied myself trying to work up enough Milton scholarship to talk about him two hours once a week. And so on. Now we are in, nothing very heavy remains to be done, and I can answer letters.

What I like best about your book is your freedom to dart into all sorts of subjects and passions that would scare me. Some of the poems I like are the "Snail," "Mea Culpa," the long one about acting, the "Looking Glass," "Little Rock." Few give so much of themselves in so small a space. The language is rich, and nervous and has a lyrical jump to it. What next? You have many useful styles started, and I suppose can only wait and see what the various chances and pressures draw from you.

Writing's hell, isn't it? I tire of my turmoil, and feel everyone else has, and long for a Horatian calm. I find that you plan one thing and something unforeseen breaks through it and carries you God knows where. So there's always surprise, adventure and imperfection, much better, I guess than a tame certainty. Then after a while, you do see a tantalizing sameness—limitation and consistency. Well, excuse all this—I've just finished reading a review that says I lack the gentle humble touch of Roy Campbell.

Love to you both. We look forward to seeing you at the month's end. I have to go to Johns Hopkins and then Harvard about then, but hope not to miss you entirely. Bob was here for a night, rather weary, but bringing the excitement of New Guinea.

Love,
Cal

397. To William Carlos Williams

October 25, 1961

Dear Bill:

Many thanks for your note. I guess there are two languages to bother about. There's one's general style, one's own American idiom, something part received and part developed by each poet for himself. This goes into all poems and is ever ready once it has been acquired, though it takes some watching. The other is the style that will work for each separate poem, and this is always impossible until one finds it. At least this is how I explain my own slowness and many mis-steps once I get started—what makes one poem

work for me and another go rotten. The fun of my translations was that the first sort of language seemed to come pretty readily and steadily during the three years I was working.

You hit the mark much more often than I do. I hope you'll like a little thing I've done for *Hudson*, to go with your poems there, though about you in general. I'd like to come out for a visit, if you and Flossie feel like seeing me.

Affectionately to you both,
 Cal

398. To A. Alvarez

November 7, 1961

Dear Al:

Your remarks on my Villon are very opportune—*Time Magazine* in a longish panning review says half my poems bear the smudge of translation and the other half seem to have been written by some talented foreigner. Dudley Fitts in the *New York Times* says they should be read in a salt mine, with a grain of salt, and three hysterical Frenchmen writing to *Encounter* say my Rimbaud is an insane slaughter and hopeless trash. On the other hand, every decent judge from Edmund Wilson down likes them or some of them. I feel misunderstood, not a bad feeling.

Sorry you've had a black time and sorry divorce is coming. I suppose it's a mercy at this point. I had an attack last spring which put me in a hospital for a month. It was mixed up with a girl and caused a lot of havoc, but the last four or five months have been good. Our family is calm, I've written a play taken out of Hawthorne and Melville, another sort of imitation and quite strong I think though in need of dramatic tinkering. I am enclosing my only poems, I haven't sent them off here. The elegy is perhaps a little too "Movement" in tone; the other is my farewell to contact lenses. You want to write about the nuclear world and end up with your shoestring. I like your Tynan and Empson reviews and also a number of short things. I too am blind to Aiken beyond an enjoyment of his graces. Tate's really talking for the blurb, I fear. I found Empson somehow quite heroic and moving—the only critic who really seems to like Milton and thinks his matter is important. The Christian stuff, particularly at the end is a bit cracked, but I must say I was reading my class the end of Faustus. It really is hellish of God. That may have been what Marlowe meant. I find Tynan better reading on the theater than anyone else, though my dramatic line is something he detests, Elizabethan, though very disguised.

I hope to see you in May. We have bought an apartment just off Central Park, grand for Harriet and with a big room with an 18 foot ceiling, and feel much more happily placed. Lizzie is finishing up a book of her essays, Harriet is a little lady.

Affectionately,

Cal

P.S. It must be hell to be cut off from your child, I hope you're not entirely.

399. *To Randall Jarrell*

November 7, 1961

Dear Randall:

Lying awake the other night after my reading, I thought of the joy of seeing you. I meant to write you a note but time slipped by. I wish I had heard your reading and paper. Viereck was rather appalling wasn't he, both in delivery and content. You stand out very much from other people in brilliance and freshness. I have been quoting your professor of Lithuanian translating *War and Peace* crack. I seem to be getting a rain of mangling reviews, *Time* magazine and now Dudley Fitts who says my poems should be read in a salt mine with a grain of salt. I must know something about what I am doing. I'm sure I do.

I remember once, the last time at Greensboro, I think, when you came into my room and began talking out of a blue sky about the ills of our culture, and Mary said that I worried about personal matters while you were upset about the world. The world is very much under my skin and really seems like a murderous nightmare when one looks outward. I am sick of nations armed to the teeth. It can't be true we must raise a finger or a whisper! Otherwise my life is pleasant enough.

Elizabeth Bishop has just blown in from Brazil for a month. I find the talk and companionship here, particularly in little groups more up my alley than Boston. We are right off the park, and I get a lot of nature taking Harriet to the amusements. The other day, Anton Webern's music was on the radio. She heard it and said, "It's like wild animals thru the woods walking," and then, "It's like a lot of spiders crying together, but without tears."

I'm in an awful wrestle trying to get my play reworked so it will act.

Love to you both,

Cal

400. *To Stephen Spender*

Dear Stephen:

I have tried to answer a certain kind of critic by writing a preface to my book, and thought of sending you a few paragraphs. But I think a direct reply might be more to the point. My rather peculiar attempt seems to goad people into talking through their hats.

"I want to offer Aury, Leyris and Thomas two answers. The first has to do with Rimbaud's literal meaning, the second with my attempt to turn his French poems into English poems.

I know perfectly well what Rimbaud means. Exact prose translations are very useful. There should be accurate scholarly editions of the great modern European poets with literal translations and footnotes. Such editions would replace the innumerable slap-dash free renderings which are neither informative nor good poetry on their own.

This isn't what I was trying to do. Robert Frost says that poetry is what can't be translated. To make something that is poetry in another language into something that is poetry in one's own language is impossible unless one is a poet ~~and inspired~~. My method is nothing new; the example I had in mind when I was working [on] Rimbaud was Sir Thomas Wyatt's versions of Petrarch. Whether I have succeeded or not cannot be demonstrated by line by line comparisons. In my "buffalo" passage I was trying to build up a mélange of exotic places, not just one place. In my "cabbage-green mould" I was trying to give a sordid, rather Dickensian setting. I object to Aury, Lyris and Thomas' hysterical foaming. Their ability to judge English poetry is probably on par with my French scholarship. Their letter has about as little to do with my intentions as the notes of a Brazilian geographer would have had to Rimbaud's."

Thanks, Stephen, for your own courteous and eloquent reply. We get news of you from Elizabeth Bowen and others, & send our love to you both.

Affectionately,

Cal

401. *To Anne Sexton*

December 1, 1961

Dear Anne:

Let me pour out my scattered general impressions first. If they are inconsistent, that won't matter. The best thing about your book is its unstopped fullness. I get an impression of increasing supply and weight; indeed your first book, especially the best poems, spills into the second and somehow adds to it. Perhaps, you shouldn't be too critical, and should have no fears, except the fear of losing your material and screaming off into vagueness. This you haven't done. My favorite still is the *Hudson* one on your Father, print perhaps helps, but I feel a passion and concentration here. You have any number of poems that roll along in something I'd call your version of my *Life Studies* style; the method, and often the emotions, (this comes from similar experience not imitation—I often think, I've felt this too, but never written about it) are familiar to me, and now that I've lost the supply I envy you. I'm glad you've tried new things, the religious poems and character sketches. They are variously successful, I guess, but give the book a professional air of not just confessing, but of liking to write poems. Your final "Letter" is a good idea, and reads like one of your own letters. I doubt if it's your best poem. Maybe I'll find myself imitating it too.

Faults? I don't think they matter. Or perhaps they are unavoidable human limitations—yours! There are loose edges, a certain monotony of tone, a way of writing that sometimes seems to let everything in too easily, bald spots, uninspired moments that roll off disguised by the same certainty of voice, poems that all one can say about them is they are Sexton and therefore precious. I sometimes feel that you are one of the few people who could write a whole book, like the *Spoon River Anthology*, where the little moments would prop the big moments and there'd be little waste. To an extent, you have done this, and have made your life your treasury. This sounds very gnomic! After all these years *Spoon River* doesn't really do this, and survives in a large handful of its best moments. Still it was a grand stab at writing a whole book of short poems!

I have been struck lately by the fact that we can do this and that, but we are always the same. Most people, however, don't begin to get out what's in them. When some one does that as you have and gotten out more than even you probably imagined was there, it seems absurd to carp at little faults. You have many, but they really don't matter, and the book gives the impression generally of laborious revision, I mean of having already made the essential re-workings. I tend to think that further effort should now go into your third book.

I'll be in Boston from the 7th through the 9th staying at Bill Alfred's. I'm afraid I'll be in a terrible rush of engagements, but we might work in something, say Saturday or Sunday, otherwise it would be better to talk on the phone or for you to come here for a day. I doubt though if a poem by poem discussion would be worth your time. You are riding the tide and really *are* on your own. I'd love to see you though.[. . .]

Thanks for your letter and book.

Affectionately,

Cal

402. *To Peter Taylor*

January 13, 1962

Dear Peter:

Well, at last we are able to boast of having been somewhere—only to Columbus Ohio, we say, then, *but* we were visiting the Peter Taylors. Each time there is an astonished shock of recognition, no one thinks you are Elizabeth Taylor Fisher. We all had a lovely time.[. . .]

Allen was brisk and sober at Yale, though he was pushing the candidacy of a sweet old dud of a poet, John Hall Wheelock and we finally split the prize between Wheelock and Eberhart. Queer conversation between Allen and me and Cleanth about such things as the Incarnation. Cleanth was taking an iron-clad 100 per cent orthodox Episcopalian line, sparring at Catholics and non-believers. Allen was very slippery and Tartuffian. Then came a staggering day here from one to ten thirty with the Tates, Woods and Aikens, Allen fixed and transfixed by Bourbon.[. . .]Once he asked Lizzie to kiss him. Then he embraced me and said I was his best man friend, my only faults were too much generosity and no sense of reality. He denounced Ed O'Connor for not marrying and living periodically in ~~original~~ sin, and not receiving Belle and Allen when they were living in sin. Harriet was summoned to him with great pomp—he was then wearing one of her cardboard green birthday derbies. "You are a Kentucky Belle because your mother is a Kentucky Belle. You are very dear to me because your parents are very dear to me. You will be dear to me when you are older." (One had a feeling she would be much more dear to him then.) At that point Harriet stared at him in wonder, and slowly said, "If you are still alive." I had to quickly explain that we would all be alive forever. At one point he said he was a Southern puritan, and Lizzie said he was about as Puritanical as an ape. All fun to tell, but rather deadly to live through. He's so smart and

alive sober, which I suppose he is most of the time, but I get his vacation evening side. This was the third in four months.[. . .]

All our love,
Cal

P.S. All this should have been a bread and butter letter to Eleanor[. . .]We know she was both the underpinnings and the ornament of our stay. What a figure! I mean what a figure of speech!

403. *To the Editors,* Partisan Review

[n.d. Winter 1962]

1.–6. I want to write a few sentences on the first six questions as a whole, and then go on to the seventh. What we have to offer the world is some sort of what I would like to call parliamentary socialism. That is an administration that provides for its subjects, guarantees a good many human rights, and can be voted out of office. This very great good is unfortunately, however, poisoned and confused by a crusading nationalism and the amoral power struggle.

7. I am trying to think of some way of answering the seventh question simply and strongly. No nation should possess, use, or retaliate with its bombs. I believe we should rather die than drop our own bombs. Every man belongs to his nation and to the world. He can only, as things are, belong to the world by belonging to his own nation. Yet the sovereign nations, despite their feverish last minute existence, are really obsolete. They imperil the lives that they were created to protect.

404. *To Frederick Seidel*

February 4, 1962

Dear Fred:

You will be glad to receive the enclosed. I have held off writing to you until the judges' decision was made. We all with our different tastes, or at least practices, came up to the same decision on you, and even on the runner up.

Your book is a landslide of power. What the beats, perhaps, have been trying to do without wings. It's hard for me to think of any book of poems as

powerful, and I think you can now consider yourself an important poet, one who will be much abused and who will have fanatical defenders. My critical judgment is that the poems are ragged, have needless obscurities, needless rhetoric, needless violence, echoes of me, and maybe Crane, & unevenness. But what does that matter? Neither I, nor anyone else has gone where you have gone. A great variety of characters come to life, your spirit is behind them turning them into important poetry, and yet they are not you but real dramatic discoveries. I think no book in English gives such a feeling of, say, Propertius and Suetonius combined. So—

After this it's an anti-climax to say that Mr. Kolodny, who is in charge of this part of the YMHA is a conventional man, who literally nearly had heart-failure when Mailer read some of his free verse at the Y. There may be more adventures to this award. Atheneaum, I believe, has no choice but to accept our choice. The money, by the way, goes to the publisher, not to the author to cover their possible losses. I guess you get it back in the end, if *Final Solutions* has any sort of sale, which is in the cards.

I want to get this off, so I won't go on with personal gossip. We're all in all fine. I've written a verse play and quite a few poems. Lizzie's essays are coming out this spring. We miss you and Phyllis, and hope you'll return soon.

Can I give you a little advice?—Strange from me! You are coming into the glare of fame and being known. For God's sake, take care and keep alive. It would be shameful not to trust yourself and to know that you have done more than can be added to you.

Affectionately,
Cal

405. *To Elizabeth Bishop*

March 10, 1962

Dearest Elizabeth:

I meant to answer your lovely full letter instantly. Then I put it off meaning to send you some new poems, then more poems kept coming in a little trickle, and I kept waiting, and somehow shying away from copying them out. We have had a succession of little pricking winter illnesses: chicken pox, tonsillitis, piles, tonsillitis, coughs—all these for me, Harriet much the same plus scarlet fever, over in three days with drugs but involving hundreds, I think, of inoculations because Mary came here before the diagnosis was made then went to several parties and households with children.

We are very keen on our Brazil and feel heaven would be a new atmosphere. I think the Congress for Cultural Freedom will arrange for me to do readings in other countries and help pay the bills. Lizzie is planning a lecture on "plot" that might be given and would have more critical substance than my offerings.

Glad you liked Sandra. The whole business is a slightly malarial memory for me. She has surprising energy and freshness a slice of the new age, full of references, interests and rhythms that are strange to me, a bit of what one once was or might have been at that age.

Did you see what *Time* did to us? Very impertinent, vulgar and often meaningless. You are warm, interested in people and unslick—all just the opposite of what they said. Still in their ugly way, they did their best by us, putting us at the top of our little decadent, post-war empyrean. It's funny being a poet, working in the medium that can't and shouldn't have much public. You find you want a little publicity as a by-product. Something to tell you you are no worse than the rest of the human race on their own terms, terms we never sought. I wrote a little squib for Bill Meredith's guest-book.

> "Are we couth or uncouth?
> Oh it's best to be both,
> both sides of the coin,
> half man and half horse,
> poor creatures of rhyme,
> who want to rejoin
> the human race
> and life and time."

A word about the poems I'm putting in. You'll find one to you, unidentified, about that time in Stonington after the Carley Dawson departure. More romantic and gray than the whole truth, for all has been sunny between us. Indeed it all started from thinking about your letter, how indispensable you are to me, and how ideally we've really kept things, better than life allows really. Also I tried versing your "In the Village." The lines about the heart are Harriet's on her kindergarten society, the rest is merely your prose put in to three-beat lines and probably a travesty, making something small and literary out [of] something much larger, gayer and more healthy. I let the scream throw out the joyful *clang*. Anyway I send it with misgivings. Maybe you could use it for raw material for a really great poem. My other things don't need comment. My inspiration seems to have become minute—little lines, little sub-

jects. By the way, I thought your *New Yorker* child was awfully good, Mary and I both read it aloud one weird evening with Ted Roethke.

Roethke is in a strange monstrous state of acting himself, never happy unless he is thinking about himself, and asserting he is better than anyone else. Under the fat man, less fat now but looking like a blown up Churchill even with the cigar, is a thin, sensitive, very intelligent soul, all wound up and quivering. Most of the evening he was pawing Mary in front of her husband and his wife. Meanwhile Jim was taking him behind the scenes in our kitchen hallway and offering him Scotch, "the house is yours," while Mary sat on the sofa hearing his wife say only people who really hate Ted give him anything to drink. At the end Jim said "I've never seen you in better form (their first meeting). I think it's fifty-fifty you'll get home without a quarrel with your wife." A riddling picture of us all, but rather awful!

We've rented a little two room apartment above us, and now I sit there in great sunlit silent space and it seems as if we had a house again.

Dr. Baumann has become part of our lives. Brisk sunny visits, pills, shots, conferences behind closed doors, conversations with her all-German nursing staff, bargain suppositories for piles. She's wonderful, and makes illness a treat.

Kunitz's address is 157 West 12th St. His wife's name is Elise. He's my great stand-by, and every Monday after class, I stop at his house and we talk till two, both coughing. I saw Mackie Jarrell the other night when I was reading at the Conn. Women's College. She sent her love and apologies for never having answered a letter. Like Randall, she somehow can't[,] to anyone. What an imprint to have been married to Randall. She is now a Ph.D., a full professor, and an expert on Pope, Swift and the modern Irish, but the old stamp remains. The strong prejudices without Randall's buoyant self-certain euphoria. She can't bear his fairy stories, thinks something tragically limiting happened to his life and still seems to love him.

I feel we all do less than we might in every way, yet somehow discover we are real and human, as those before us have been—all shuffled forward so rapidly through this life, aching, puzzled, too good to be true. I look back on my parents as people perpetually about our age.

I think we are all at last going to Puerto Rico in ten days. We all thirst for the heat and change. It's been a rather low-tide and pinching winter getting settled in our minds here. I feel on the verge of some howling platitude, such as how stunning it is to find you are almost living exactly what you would like to. That's about it. All our love to you and Lota.

Cal

P.S. Lizzie is very anxious to know more about the climate, can she wear summer dresses, what fall or winter things will we need? Thankyou a thousand times for what you've already done. By the way have you run into Keith Botsford, an old Iowa acquaintance of mine, and now in charge of the Freedom Congress things in Rio? He's quite attractive in slightly too sharp and shiny way. Also friend Fred Dupee has written from Rome wanting your address for some lady coming to Brazil, attractive and a reader of yours—"Loves English poetry, especially E. Bishop."

406. To Cleanth and Edith Brooks

March 10, 1962

Dear Cleanth and Tinkum:

Many thanks for your kindness and conversation at Yale. I think with a blush of embarrassment and pleasure of Cleanth coming into my room with coffee at eight. I've just been to two other Conn. country houses, all charming, but none so perfect and visionary as yours.

The fellow I talked to you about as a possible Elizabethan for your department is John Thompson. He was a class-mate of Peter Taylor and me at Kenyon, and John Ransom thinks very highly of him, as we do. His book, *The Founding of English Meter* was published by Columbia here and I forget who in England. Hollander is reviewing it and can tell you all about Thompson.

I've been thinking about Cleanth's remarks on making poetry religion. I don't think something you make is at all the same as what you live by, though there's an overlapping. Perhaps written revelation is in a sense poetry, each man's lunge into the depths, the truth of life, even the whole truth, in so far as our partial beings allow and the words turn up. I see poetry as a mixture of deep-seeing and a game or craft. Perhaps we are all false prophets with a bit of truth splashed in. The battle between religion and poetry is that the truths of one quite often don't fit in with the truths of the other, no system can really include the pluralism of the arts, nor can one man's art very well include another man's. These are hasty thoughts.[. . .]

Affectionately,

Cal

March 18, [1962]

Dear John:

I meant to write immediately and thank you for your sympathetic and in-spired piece on me and "Skunk Hour." During the first reading, I started out saying, "Why it doesn't mean that at all. Nothing's let out about the author." But you've made an amazing guess, more or less a bull's-eye thrust into what was going on when the poem was written—all very dazzling and disturbing.

I'll limit myself here mostly to a few impersonal notes. The "sob in each blood-cell" is meant to have a haggard, romantic profilish exaggerated qual-ity—true, but in the rhetoric of destitution, here the more matter of fact de-scriptive style gives out, won't do, and there's only the stagey for the despair. Then one leaves it for the skunk vision. Most people take the skunks as cheer-ful, one of my cousins said in disgust they were the only happy note—however, they are horrible blind energy, at the same time as in Herbert's "I wish I were a tree" there's both a wish and a fear of annihilation, i.e. dropping to a simpler form of life, and a hopeful wish for that simpler energy. My feel-ings about Christianity are confused, and I'll have to say something in my printed comment. My Ovid stanza looks better I'm afraid in your essay than in the original poem, though I think I'll put it back. It somehow won't stand by itself, or quite fit the poem.

I hear, mostly I guess from the Tates, that you have a charming wife, and are flourishing. Congratulations! It's almost ten years since I've seen you. Re-member that night at the opera in Giroux's tails? When you said Lizzie wouldn't know me? I've felt very near you through that time, and fed on the various contradictory rumors that came—mostly that you had just given a dazzling lecture somewhere.

I've been through a wearying mid-winter, tonsillitis, flu, bronchitis, one lit-tle fever giving ailment after another, so that for a month I've gone to bed every other night with a temperature. In two days we are all going to Puerto Rico. In about a month we are coming to Minnesota to read and lecture, and stay with the Tates. I hope we can get off together at length. This summer, we are going to Brazil. This started as a visit to E. Bishop but now it's a sort of Cultural Con-gress tour with readings and lectures in several countries for us both.

I've written a long play out of Hawthorne and Melville: "Endecott and the Red Cross," "Major Molineux," and "Benito Cereno"—three plays that make one and are called *The Old Glory*. They are rather Brechtian and different in tone and meaning from their sources, and are pretty strong, but need techni-

cal changes to act—which I've done with one, but keep putting off for the others. As I put them off, I write poems, and now have a third of a book, small clear half anguished things that I want to show you.

All winter I've had an uncomfortable feeling of dying into rebirth. Not at all the sick, dizzy allegorized thing such words suggest and which I've felt going off my rocker. But the flat prose of coming to the end of one way of life— whittled down and whittled down, and picking up nothing new though always about to. I had a dream the other night about Philip Rahv, who has just married a society lady and bought a house on Beacon Street. He was picking up everything I had carefully thrown away all my life—golden keys of social ease, till at the end, I think his two sons had just entered Groton. I said to myself, "What['s] the point of throwing away so much?" Well, that isn't what I want to pick up, but I feel the time has come for some kind of Yeatsian somersault.

What you said about the other poets of our generation is something I've brooded much on. What queer lives we've had even for poets! There seems something generic about it, and determined beyond anything we could do. You and I have had so many of the same tumbles and leaps. We must have a green old age. We both have drunk the downward drag as deeply as is perhaps bearable. I feel we have better work and better lives ahead.

What a Longfellow-note after your searching essay! Forgive me, I am trying to break the ice and start talking where we left off ten years ago. In our insides we never stopped. Still one has to grunt and sweat a bit to get the talk going. I feel we are very close and see things with the same mixture of cheerfulness and sourness that make life livable.

I have an incredible little daughter. Also Lizzie, who sends her love and whom you'll soon see.

Affectionately,
 Cal

408. To Elizabeth Bishop

March 18, 1962

Dearest Elizabeth:

Our letters crossed, and I again feel abashed at having let so much time slip by. The Cultural Congress is going to back our trip. We'll get traveling expenses and a per diem $40. I think we'll ~~sail~~ fly about the sixth of June. We are now taking a Radcliffe girl (one we know and who is marvelous with Harriet) and have to wait for her exams. We want to stop at one or two places,

Trinidad, maybe Haiti, Surinam and Brasília on the way, and should arrive in Río about the 15th, and plan to stay there about a month. Then on to other countries reading and lecturing. Then either back to Brazil with no lectures or home to Maine. The Cultural Congress man is Keith Botsford care of Stefam Baciu, Associaco Brasileira do Congresso Pela liberdade da Cultura Caixa Postal 89, Agencia Copacabana, Río. I copy it all out to advance my Portuguese and for its strange likeness and unlikeness to your address.

Oh dear! Colds aches, tonsillitis, bronchitis, sweaty days, low fevers at night for a month now, though Dr. Annie's last drug seems to have killed the troubles. I weigh 173, less than at any time since school and look all too much like a poet. We are going to Puerto Rico on Tuesday for ten days and hope to return reborn.

I can't seem to find your last letter anywhere, and while I seem to remember it all I've probably forgotten just the things that need an answer or comment. I carried it to my study intending an instant full answer. Now where is it? Please forgive me if I am blank on something important.

I had a strange dream two nights ago about Philip Rahv, ascending the social ladder rung by rung as I climbed down. I think at the end his two sons were safely in Groton "de only place to send them," while Harriet was graduating from the local public school. We whittle away our inheritance. I think my last words were, "Is this what *PR* was all about?" And Philip said "of course." Have you ever noticed how snobbish the old rebel bohemians are. No one believes in society now except Mary and Philip. I'm rather sick of being so literary, but still turn green at the thought of Fred Morgan's coming out parties for his daughter, Natasha Spender's list of dukes they see, and the Epstein's sending their son to St. Bernard's with conferences with Bowden— they were caught by the headmaster, while Bowden was showing them the backgrounds catalogue. The child doesn't want to go, because "there is no goldfish bowl." Questioned, he says he's made "a thorough investigation."

I love the idea of the coming summer. Write soon dear, so I'll have a letter waiting when we get back. Your little Arthur looks beautiful in the *New Yorker*. I don't seem able to use that much remembrance any more. Hope you liked my things. I feel I'm about to discover the common man or cooking or something homely and earth-shaking.

Love to you all,
Cal

P.S. Big change! I find the blighting tone of Henry Adams, my old Bible, a terrible bore, coals to Newcastle, though I wouldn't want anyone else to say it. I

guess what is so good about him is that he did too, and knew it was a real illness in him—one he loved to exploit. I think his tone is a state anyone from our background should go through to be honest and alive, and then drop. I suspect anyone who hasn't been that bitter. Still, staying there is like calling malaria life. I guess what I mean is that there was real malaria under the jokes, exaggerations and epigrams, a sort of Baudelairian gallantry. But who could *want* what Empson says somewhere *to learn a style from a despair?* I'm thinking of the white sand and full of deep non-sense today.

409. To Alfred Kazin

March 18, 1962

Dear Alfred:

I have just started *Contemporaries*. I've just had a month of tonsillitis, bronchitis and little feverish things, nothing serious, but all told very low tidish and maddening, and Tuesday, we are off for ten days to Puerto Rico. So if anything I say seems confused blame it on the moment.

You seem to be the only critic besides Edmund, who reads new books. I mean in some deep way they are relived inside you and come out again heavy with their old actuality, but reformed by your character and digestive system. Dare I say that this is an odd gift, like all gifts, almost as bad as being a poet—life for its possessor, but something too real and occupying to be exactly desired. I like what you say about Mailer. I find an elephantiasis in him that is contemptible, then a real mind and real energy that leaves me envious and empty. Then you are good on Powers, an old friend, who has the opposite disease, a whittling away of bigness toward some ironic integrity. I don't [know] which gains the most. I suppose I think most big things should go through the wringer, and that then Mailer or Styron would look more like Powers than like Tolstoy. But for many inflation is almost a formal necessity, like plot or meter.

I feel about Pound that his content is very important, and that it is a content we are scared to define. The disciple, of course, only makes it worse. The mixture of malignancy and nobility may not be different than in other writers, but the voice of anti-semitism is like the voice of a drunkard telling people in cars to drive through the pedestrians—nothing can condone for that. Yet as a poet he is a hero, full of courage, and humor and compassion. Somehow more than most writers, his ideas aren't exactly part of him, though they are. It's hard really to find him hateful. I think everyone who has known him has found him maddening but not hateful—maddening with a kind of gorgeous

generosity, that puts us to shame. Ray West's list of how writers ought to be is asinine. Reading Karl Shapiro's book lately for the first time, I found long stretches orotund and terrible, but the push behind it, something I rather agreed with. I could go on for pages. As yet I've read only a fraction, but what strikes me is that you keep your own strong feeling, and prejudices and yet lose yourself in the difficulties of each writer. You neither let them swallow you, nor lecture them. What you say about my old too literary side is surely true. Let's all get together in the spring.

Affectionately,

Cal

P.S. I can't read one of your pieces without feeling changed.

I wonder why I bring in Pound? The other day I talked to Norman Pearson who [had] just been to see him, very courteous sick, weighing 130. He was thinking of old ailing friends and asking to be forgiven his harshness to each, among the people he loved he named me, and I've had twinges of ingratitude.

Lizzie wants me to say she feels as I do about your book and sends her love to you and Anne.

410. To Ezra and Dorothy Pound

March 18, 1962

Dear Ezra and Dorothy:

It seems and is a long age since I have seen or written either of you. An embarrassing image comes to me of the day we visited the Adams' House and of the many times we got lost, I think ending up on a ten mile peninsula, a stone's throw from Boston, if there'd only been a bridge, which there wasn't.

I had a pleasant day with Omar last fall, and a few days ago saw Norman Pearson at a big Yale party, where we sat in a corner, ignored everyone and talked about you and his visit. I am glad you remember me warmly, for I think of you both all the time and relive our afternoons in Washington, the cookies, the arguments, the dangerous rides home with other visitors.

Ezra, I think you should feel happy about your life, and the thousands of kindnesses you have done your friends, and how you've been a fountain to them. So you've been to me, and I miss the old voice.

I'm asking my publisher to mail you my two last books, translations, but real translations in their way I hope like yours. You may like some of them,

perhaps the Leopardi, Villon and Rimbaud, first read by me after reading your criticism. Don't bother to comment.

We have a beautiful daughter, now five, and always in motion and asking questions, and rather quicker and surer than we are. Tomorrow we all go to Puerto Rico to bake away our colds and the midwinter grayness and grind of the city. Next winter I have a sort of commuter's professorship at Harvard to teach there for three months[,] then we'll be free and hope will get to Italy, and see you. This summer we are going to Brazil and other parts of South America. One cries out at times to get away from one's own America, though we are all very well.

Au revoir, I remember you both with love.

Cal

411. To Edmund Wilson

March 31, 1962

Dear Edmund:

I'm just back from Puerto Rico, sunned and shaken—partly by the country, all the sun and water, all the creeping Puerto Rican life, which is all around us here on the West Side, but which is revealed there in greater purity perhaps, that creeping life that will survive all the crust of our culture—or will it? Shaken too by nights in a single bedroom, where I could wake up at all hours and read and smoke and speculate, and seem flooded by what is, without being able to define it, and somehow rejuvenated by it. Oh what could be less youthful than youth, mine anyhow, walking in its stiff necessary armor!

I've spent much of the day drinking in your *Patriotic Gore*. The preface stings. I guess I pretty much agree, but it all seems even sadder. The States have become a menace, sea-squids, as you say, and I guess they never were too good. Their wars and deification were never right. Still we have to swim in them and when they die, if they don't kill us all first, the world will be still worse, though less murderous maybe and horrible.

I am braced by your portraits. I see now, I think, that all your life you have been writing a sort of Plutarch's Lives. These last seem the most passionate of all. But they all go together. One might use the phrase: *moral aristocrats* for them. By this, I mean some queer tense twist of principle, changed to virtue by having been lived through the undefineable multiplicity of experience. No two persons are alike, all are glaringly imperfect, still there are heroes. You

can see I've just come from your Holmes, whose principles mean nothing to me literally, but whose life seems so shining and cantless.

Pardon this sprawl, and let me salute you, dear old fellow questioning Calvinist, on your triumphant book.

Our love to you both,
Robert

412. *To Elizabeth Bishop*

April 14, 1962

Dearest Elizabeth:

"The piles are gone, no 19th Century decline"—how's that for an opening—my alternate is "we've just been invited to the White House again." Somehow I can't combine the strong points of the two, but what intolerable euphoria they give together!

[. . .]I was rather on tiptoe that my poems had been intrusive, and read your letter with great relief. Your suggestions on "Water" might be great improvements. By the way, the Mermaid wasn't your Millay parody, but something in one of your letters, inspired by Wiscassett probably. Glad this and my tampering with "In the Village" didn't annoy you. When "The Scream" is published I'll explain, it's just a footnote to your marvelous story.

We're just back from visiting Belle and Allen. They are best at home and you really feel Belle saved Allen's life from the long inspired nightmare of Caroline. She's slow, imperious, though not to Allen, and sane—no crazy agrarian axe to grind! Fortunately Allen had a slight ulcer and could only drink three drinks a night. Also saw John Berryman, utterly spooky, teaching brilliant classes, spending week-ends in the sanitarium, drinking, seedy a little bald, often drunk, married to a girl of twenty-one from a Catholic parochial college, white, innocent beyond belief, just pregnant. They live in two rooms—in one Kate is asleep, getting through the first child pains, in the other, a thousand books, and John going into the 7th year on a long poem that fills a suitcase and is all spoken by John, first son (seven) from his second marriage. The poem is spooky, a maddening work of genius, or half genius, in John's later obscure, tortured, wandering style, full of parentheses, slang no one ever spoke, jagged haunting lyrical moments etc. One shudders to think of the child's birth.

Also saw Jim Powers, and had a marvelous time, talking ironic banter with him, just as though no time had passed. Wonderful moment, John in his exag-

gerated way and unbelievable accent, saying, "Why this man is the best *prose* writer in *America*. He is as good as *Chekhov*. His 'Lions and Harts' is like 'The Bishop!'" Then Jim smoking, saying slowly, face unchanged, "I don't know, I always thought Chekhov wrote too much." Jim, buried in St. Cloud all these years is as confident as Randall, though all is irony. Now his novel is coming out [after] 11 years and should be a masterpiece.

I'm either getting soft, or good books are suddenly pouring out. K A Porter's huge novel, very grim and the only *long* novel since *The American Tragedy* that needs to be long, I mean long by an American. Randall's essays are very dashing and satirical and sad. I guess he's better writing about poetry than about American culture—this book is almost entirely culture, a sort of *Culture and Anarchy*, but he's terribly good reading. Then Wilson's civil war book, his best I think, with Plutarchan portraits of Lincoln, Grant, Justice Holmes etc. Then Alfred Kazin's great heap of essays, surprisingly tougher and less long-winded than he is. And a little Jewish book that Jason Epstein discovered, "I the Money" almost as good as Nathanael West. I'll bring all these things to you when we come, if you don't have them. (Oh, and wonderful, Isherwood's new novel, particularly the end.)

I'm very shabbily prepared to talk to Brazilian audiences. Botsford seems to assume that I can pick up a fluent reading knowledge of Portuguese in a few days, but of course I never will. I quite like a few poems of Bandeira, also [Jorge] de Lima, and am half thru Assis' *Epitaph of a Small Winner*—awfully good I can see the Brazilians will make me feel like a barbarian, with their French and Latin cultures we never had. It's much more bruising to find the Brazilians have it, than to see it in France where you would expect it. I am beginning to believe Eliot's rather high-handed quips at us about the maturity of the Latin mind. I'll bring a lot of anthologies etc. and guess I can spout and read aloud endlessly the poetry in English of this century. I suppose they already know the big people—or are they as ignorant as we are? No one here except for young enthusiasts knows even Neruda. We do want to talk to little groups and not put on a rhetorical show. Lizzie has a grand lecture on plot, which can be given when we want to put our best foot forward. I guess I can make nice readings of selected poets with a few quick explanations, facts etc.

Where am I? I'm rushing through this letter skimming things and assuming that we'll pour out gossip to each other for hours. We seem almost in Brazil now. Oh the White House—we are going there to dinner sometime next month to meet Malraux; Edmund and Allen are going and I suppose legions of others. Only black tie, not white.[. . .]

Damn the young! My students, after I gave them a laborious six weeks on

Pope, Dryden, Dr. Johnson, Goldsmith etc. turned out to have read only one poet before Hopkins—Donne of course. I feel taken in the flank. I am all pointed to explain the new poetry as a continuation, change and revolution of the old. But no one reads the old, except English professors. I'm on a Wordsworth and Blake jag. I'd like to do poems that would hit all in one flash, though loaded with subtleties of art and passion underneath. Or great clumsy structures like Wordsworth's Leech Gatherer, that somehow lift the great sail and catch the wind. Most of our poets are so weak on brute, energy, flash, power, driving a sentence or a stanza to its mark, though it's good to be clotted, obscure, ingenious etc. But the typical modern poem is taken over by pedants people who bore you to death. How wearisome the swarm of accomplished[,] youngish poets are after some one like Powers or Mary! The poet ought to be at least as interesting a person as the prose writer!

Dearest, we can't wait. Our love to Lota.

Cal

413. To Frederick Seidel

April 14, 1962

Dear Fred:

The prize is all in confusion. The Y, over even Kolodney's head, has refused to award it and sent an insulting letter to Athenaeum; Betty Kray has resigned on this from the Y (though this is partially a threat, which she thinks will make them cough up the $1,500[)]. Ford at Athenaeum says they don't give a damn about the money and are going to publish you anyway. Somehow on the blurb, it will be said that you *did* win the prize, there will be ways of publicizing the fact. It's all a head-ache, but more or less to the advantage of your book, which will go out with a certain storm of attention.

So, there it is in a nutshell. There's nothing for you to do, or worry about. This seems to be censorship year. English faculties and unlikely persons such as Harry Levin and Dick Wilbur are everywhere testifying for Henry Miller. We are all signing testimonials for Miller, between signing other ones against using the bomb.

We go to Brazil early in June and will be in South America all summer, mostly in Rio. I'm glad to be away. A lot of good books have come out lately: K. A. Porter's, Wilson's, Isherwood's, Jarrell and Kazin's essays, and [a] strange brilliant New York Jewish book, *How Much?* which has a violence that

reminds me of your poems though nothing is really alike. Also Alan Dugan whose poems got the National Book Award this year and is full of wit and outrage.

Your book is really astonishing. I eagerly wait to see it explode.

Our love to you both,

Cal

414. To Edmund Wilson

May 31, 1962

Dear Edmund:

We are off to Brazil on Monday and are both topsy-turvy with planning, seeing South Americans, making an anthology of English and American poetry to be literally translated into Spanish and Portuguese. And so on.

I am very set up by your *New Yorker* interview. The part on me is a wonderful piece of picture—writing and judgment, and along with two early essays by Jarrell moves me more than anything that has been written on me. *Imitations* got such a mauling from the popular reviewers.

I meant to write you a little fan note after Washington. Except for you, everyone there seemed addled with adulation at having been invited. It was all good fun but next morning you read that the President has sent the 7th fleet to Laos, or he might have invaded Cuba again—not that he will, but I feel we intellectuals play a very pompous and frivolous role—we should be windows, not window-dressing. Then, now in our times, of all times, the sword hangs over us and our children, and not a voice is lifted. I thought of all the big names there, only you acted like yourself.

Our love to you and Elena. We'll see you in September.

Affectionately,

Cal

415. To Elizabeth Bishop

[Buenos Aires, September 10, 1962]

DEAREST ELIZABETH COME HERE AND JOIN ME ITS PARADISE! ALL MY LOVE

CAL

416. To William Alfred

[n.d. 1962]

HAVE BEEN AT DEATHS DOOR FROM FLU & MALARIA IN BUENOS
AIRES FOR THE LOVE OF GOD PLEASE GET SOMEONE TO TAKE MY
CLASSES UNTIL ABOUT THE END OF OCTOBER

C.A.L

Robert Lowell ROBERT LOWELL

417. To Elizabeth Bishop

15 West 67th Street
New York, NY
November 3, 1962

Dearest Elizabeth:

I come home days now from the hospital, and will be entirely finished
with the hospital in four days. So all has passed over, not too gruellingly, at
last now, it seems. I meant to write to you much sooner, but somehow till
today I put off answering everything even details on reading engagements
for next month that I have through Lizzie already accepted. I just sit in my
study and read and snooze, or listen to records. It sounds like old age, but it
isn't, I was really quite run down from "over-exuberance" (I guess that's
the word) and a lung infection, gone now without a trace, I got in
Argentina.

I hope our summer wasn't too taxing on you and Lota, because we had a
wonderful time—almost a mirage, the beaches seem at this distance and on
this heavy fall rainy day in New York.

I don't have any real gossip, except Stanley's reports on the poets' confer-
ence in Washington, at which Delmore was put in jail for shouting while
drinking by himself I think, and was rescued by John Berryman! Stanley was
insulted by Oscar Williams, called Williams a worm, and nearly knocked him
down. Randall apparently read a tribute to both of us, along with Frost and
others, which the library will print, and I'll mail to you, if they don't. Each
poet I've met has a different account of what was good, odd or great at the
conference. Allen and Belle were here. During their visit, it chanced that
Cousin Harriet called from Washington, saying "I know what you are in for,
they were here." She meant Washington, not her house, but I think she re-

gards all visitors to Washington, such as poets and ambassadors, as planned insults to the old Washingtonian.

Loved your letter with the account of the open air meeting and Lota's medal. She must wear the big one when she comes here next.

Love,
Cal

418. To Elizabeth Bishop

December 24, 1962

Dearest Elizabeth:

The day of Christmas Eve, pure summer with you I imagine, but with us rather grimy, the sound of the snow-chisel banging through sidewalk ice to pavement. Today is sunny, but Harriet surprised us by slipping down the stairs unnoticed during our breakfast and curling up in a blanket in the big living room. No temperature, but several aches, urine to be taken by the hospital. Dismay that she may not be up to the various Christmas preparations. She has really had a swimmingly good fall, ice-skating with her new nurse, bringing artifacts home from the Dalton School. I wish you and Lota could see her.

Last night, my friend Jack Thompson brought over a Mexican poet and a young Brazilian play director whom we met at Belem. After the usual comparative literature comparisons, the Brazilian started on America, a tale of woe. He was almost tearful, and even admired Brizola. We gave our defense of Carlos, but somehow one had the impression of a man determined to get away from the agony of self-criticism and scorch whoever was nearest at hand—not us but the United States. Nietzsche says that thoughts of suicide got him through many hard nights, and I guess this turning on someone else has saved thousands of souls.

Here, the atmosphere is very different from South America, and very different, I think, even from last fall. We were all either exalted or scared out of our wits by Cuba, and then relieved. Now suddenly there is no criticism, and I think no government in my life time has been less hated. Yet there seems to be great malaise with our culture and a kind of numbed contentment with our place and fate in the world. Last night I felt we had given up having strong feelings about ourselves and left this to the South Americans.

After I got well, I buried myself in writing. I have finished the old poem to you that I begun after you left Maine, and another about dropping in a dream on the Copacabana beach. I'll send them both to you. Then other things

which I won't send, including a translation of Juvenal's Tenth Satire, "The vanity of human wishes," and a long unfinished dramatic monologue on my namesake Caligula. To my surprise, I have mostly written in very strict meter, even sonnets, not at all my intention, and a fact that I find disturbing to my theories of how poetry should be written. I have always thought one should be able to shift from free to counted verse and mix the two, but I am surprised to find myself shifted despite my desires, seized by the muse or perhaps only the spirit of rhetoric.

I have thought of you, Dear, frequently every day. I hope our visit wasn't crushingly fatiguing to you both. I don't think any visitors were ever so sensitively and tirelessly entertained. I guess I was beginning to go off during the last two weeks in Brazil, and this must have been painful for you to watch or at least sense. When I got to Buenos Aires, my state zoomed sky-high and I am glad you didn't see it. It's hard for the controlled man to look back on the moment of chaos and claim. I shan't try, but it was all me, and I am sorry you were touched by it. Please let us be as dear to each other as always.

I am sending you some records. We had a more original present, an antique wooden shield with cranes, alligators and jungle trees but the post office said it was hopeless to try to get it through and that if it got to you at all, you would be months negotiating with the customs.

Giroux says that Houghton and Mifflin have released your manuscript. Let me know if I can do anything. The unfinished poems should be tremendous from your descriptions. I guess it's grating to have fragments lying about waiting and waiting for a breath to blow. I've had the worse experience, 1 of grinding out like a machine things I'll never use. Ten sonnets of Nerval, that vanish to nothing in English, words for a symphony for the dead, that Leonard Bernstein wanted me to try and have so far produced a bilge of declamation.

Are you still trying to translate Lispector stories? Jack Thompson says that the Farfield Foundation which he works for could probably subsidize a translation though at a very low rate, five dollars a 1000 words. I wonder if anyone in Brazil could and would undertake her novel at that amount, though of course there'd no doubt be more from the publisher on acceptance, and later from sales. They also might be able to finance a trip by Nelida to New York. She might too get a Ford if you and I and Keith sponsored her. I think she would have to apply first.

Our love to you and Lota, and mine to you.

Cal

419. To Harriet Winslow

<div style="text-align: right">December 26, 1962</div>

Dear Cousin Harriet:

I hope the pandemonium of voices and successive speakers wasn't unnerving yesterday. We hardly knew we were caught in a swirl of children practicing with their new toys, while the adolescent and the old gestured above them. Lunch soon followed, and we sat in a grand chartered hotel room overlooked by a small rotating Santa Claus. As the toasts went round, we wondered whether it or we were in motion. All very pleasant and full of family feeling. When we left, we were ready to take a plane and follow the Meades to Puerto Rico, and more extreme, Elizabeth was considering adopting a beagle puppy!

Today, stillness, the old New York, no pets except the squeaking straw-stuffed toys, though we are considering a kitten. The new year seems to have begun, I am thinking ahead now to my weekly trips to Harvard, and Maine seems closer. We will be glad to get Harriet back to her country base, and glad to get back ourselves.

The golden Lincoln Memorial, strange comment on the Emancipator! shines on Harriet's wrist. She will grow up thinking she owns the United States. Yesterday, she lost her belief in Santa Claus, when after a rather thin, suspected performance, I unveiled and took off my Santa suit in front of her. But she still believes in God. A little Jewish boy laughed at her credulity, and said that there was only nature, if that. Harriet said, "Imagine not believing in *such a great personality* as God!" From time to time, I look at her and foresee a long-limbed restless girl in her teens, the last day when I will lift her up. How long childhood is for a child, and how short for the parents!

Too much talk of time. We hope your days will pass pleasantly. Whenever Easter vacation comes, I hope we will make our descent on Washington. Till then, our love! Our love too to Cam and Libby, also John and Blanche and Briney, all of whom I was sorry to miss on my quick visit.

Love,

Bobby

420. To Elizabeth Bishop

Dearest Elizabeth:

We've been in a great flurry lately. Lizzie is on the board of a new book review about to be set floating during the lull of the newspaper strike here that has temporarily put the *New York Times* book section out of existence. Meetings, arguments, telephone calls, and now at the end of two weeks, a fairly dazzling first number has been promised and will come out in the middle of February. One of my side-line duties was to phone Randall, who said he promised himself never again to write anything he could use in a book of essays. There was nothing he wanted to review. Then he paused and said there was one book, yours. He has been following all your new poems in *The New Yorker*, and is choosing a good many for a new anthology.

I pass this on to cheer you and perhaps prod you. The wolf with its head on its paws lies looking at the desolate yellow wastes of our present civilization, ready when your book comes to howl its welcome. This makes a difference. I remember my second book seemed lost in the dust of carping and the mildest praise, when Randall wrote a long piece violently liking and disliking. In a preface to Emily Dickinson, John Brinnin asks if she isn't the greatest woman poet, brushes away the past, and then says only Marianne Moore and Elizabeth Bishop (of the English poets of this century) reach her level.

I don't suppose you need praise, but I find there are sinking times when everything I do looks about like what dozens of others are doing, or worse. It's pleasant to have an art that can never make money or much sensation; then in dry times it hardly seems to exist. You have more to offer, I think, than anyone writing poetry in English. On, Dear, with those painful, very large unfinished poems!

I am at the end of something. Up till now I've felt I was all blue spots and blotches inside, more than I could bear really, if I looked at myself, and of course I wanted to do nothing else. So day after day, I wrote, sometimes too absorbed to even stop for lunch and often sitting with my family in a stupor, mulling over a phrase or a set of lines for almost hours, hypnotized, under a spell, often a bad spell. Now out of this, I have seven poems and seven translations, just about a book when added to what I had before. Now I say to myself, "Out of jail!" I look back on the last months with disgust and gratitude. Disgust because they seem so monstrous, gratitude, because I have lived through the unintelligible, have written against collapse and come out more or less healed. Oh dear, have you ever felt like a man in an unreal book?

I begin my Harvard teaching next week, and have been boning up on the standard old Americans, Emerson, Longfellow, Bryant etc. They are much farther away than they were when I was in school and college. Then they were almost something one shouldn't read much of lest they led astray. Now the times have brought them back maybe,—hardly imitated still, they are like our own kind of revolt and competence. The beats have blown away, the professionals have returned. Sometimes they flash—Emerson is a funny case of the poet who was all flash in theory and desire and even gifts, and somehow his equipment and instincts wouldn't let him. Then a lovely moment would come.

Harriet has had a rather hard winter getting over being shy at school. There was group dancing and singing, and she somehow got off on the wrong foot and wouldn't join, and even told us trying to change "made her heart bleed." But now there's bursts of luncheon invitations, exchange house-visits, dancing class, swimming lessons with a friend and the sorrow is gone. She is beginning to be the girl she will be for the next ten years, living in our dense world of conscious attractions, liking this person, disliking that one. It's that time of sheer survival of energy boxing with ignorance, when I suppose only exuberance and a thousand things to do get us by the impossible obstacle of growing into something definite—Oh bold, cheerful changing little creature!

Write and tell me about yourself, and how the hot months are going and give lots of gossip. Our minds are still in last summer. Love to Lota,

Love,

Cal

421. To Keith Botsford

January 25, 1963

Dear Keith:

I have long owed you a letter of thanks and apology. I suppose it's a bit like the cat painfully backing down the telephone-pole it scooted up. Anyway I am deeply grateful for the time, pains and ingenuity of your help through the summer, and most of all, I guess, for seeing me through the rough-house and phantasmagoria at the end of Argentina. I hope our tour did some good and left limited damage. I am ashamed of what I did.

It's sunny today, but seven above zero. Brazil is far away, and yet it has somehow accompanied us: yellow, blue, and red boat streamers hang from our balcony, our big silver slave's bangle is handed to visitors as we guess at its fruits, and whenever we give a dinner, we have Lizzie's special Brazilian

black beans and Doreen's special green peppers. We try to describe Goulart, Aleijadinho[,] Burle Marx, *Rebellion in the Backlands*. I've written a poem about walking in my sleep, leaning on a large standing globe, and then falling through the air southward till I land on the Copacabana, and another quite long about walking through Buenos Aires and trying to guess its history, present and past, from its statuary.

One day the play directing young man from Belem and São Paulo turned up with a pearl gray muscovite hat, and a long wail about United States exploitation. I've never realized till lately how wonderful it is to shift the streams of self-criticism from one's self to anyone else. I mean to do this deliberately and almost wickedly. But at some point one should own up to what one's doing. Most of the evening really went pleasantly.

From time to time, people from our common worlds turn up and we think of you—Spender, the Bellows, Jack Thompson who rushed off from his wedding in our house to a honeymoon in Quebec. How has your writing been going? I've been doing little else, and have now come to a stop to get ready for my Harvard seminars which start next week. How are your family? Mine are (a) Lizzie, starting a new book review to replace the *Times*, and (b) Harriet, going from ice-skating, to swimming to dancing lessons.

I met a young negro writer 24 and former student yesterday. He said he's stopped writing until he could understand America, and was up to his neck in *New Statesman* reviewers' reflections. I said, "just absorb it." Actually America has never been harder to understand. After the great gambler's stroke of luck in Cuba, we are all stunned, grateful for the lull, and feeling strangely that we had little to do with it. Or perhaps the summer in South America has wonderfully disoriented us. The problems are never the same—here one feels the huge gap between efficiency and the true bloom. Shades of Brasília!

Well, our love to you, Ann, A[lb]erta and the children.

Affectionately,

Cal

422. To Elizabeth Bishop

February 10, 1963

Dearest Elizabeth:

So much to catch up on! a big burly letter written at different dates, the two lovely Sydney Smith volumes, and now a note asking if they had arrived. They have and I have been dipping in. Their sociable, minute, witty life far

from all cant and extravagance is very attractive. I was going to say a life free from enthusiasm, but of course a continual air of enthusiasm blows through them—they are free from anything so extravagant as pessimism. That August afternoon of last summer comes back when you were picking your companions for heaven up on that tea-house on the mountain. Strange now to think how I imagined I was sipping in moderation and tolerance from you all summer! I think I was, Dear, though I hardly gave a convincing demonstration.

I suppose you have read about Frost's death, though we, through the absence of New York papers, had to be told by telephone. He has been much with me: I've written a short piece on him for a new review (guided by us which will be a sort of intelligent *New York Times* section), talked on television, re-read quantities and talked on him to my classes at Harvard. Walking by his house in Cambridge last Thanksgiving, I thought with some shame about how wrong I was to be bothered by his notoriety and showing off. Under the great display the life was really very bounded and simple. Pound's daughter was here, looking like him and strangely like Jack Sweeney's Irish wife, Moira. Somewhere there was an awakening from father—not a disillusionment but surprise: "Until six years ago I never questioned one of his thoughts . . . Of course I wasn't prepared to be impressed by T. S. Eliot . . . When he came back, we didn't know that even he couldn't do anything . . . two years of sitting hardly raising an arm and thinking all his contemporaries' careers had gone better than his . . . stopped me from translating the *Cantos*, saying they were no good. Do people in such a state really feel the terrible things they say? . . . at first it was *Cantos* at every meal.["] She saw Frost the day before he died. "I wanted him to know that some one who loved Father didn't have bad manners." Frost said he loved Ezra and hoped to see him in Venice, where he now is in a rather better state. She and her husband live in a Tyrolean castle, cold, too large, isolated; Dorothy Pound stays with them. (["]It seems she and father exhausted all they had to say to each other at St. Elizabeths") and they talk about cats and flowers, and each winter some one in the small family launches off on the New York edition Henry James—"his subtle qualifications hardly seem to fit the circumstances of my life." A strange shy, pathetic, in no way ugly life. She hardly knows what country she belongs to and has just taken a short course in filing at Yale to take care of her father's papers. I have been thinking of the great callousness and bravado of Ezra's existence, so free one might of half-thought of most men's waverings, feelings of being a copy, of not pursuing the goal etc. Then the shell breaks and the cold air tortures the exposed flesh. Then partial recovery, though the other was a recovery of humanity.

I've started commuting to Harvard, enter my classes with apprehension, then enjoy them. One student, however, said the room seemed made up of 18 frozen introverts. I guess we'll all thaw as we get used to talking to each other. I live in Quincy House, very modern, all glass, with walls of unfinished cement brick. Their designer and installer came into my room the other day to display them. Papers with titles like *India News* come for the former occupant, Mr. Sinha, who has left behind him something I've always dreamed of, a library made up of books I've never read. And never will, alas, for they are all problems in logic and recent English philosophy.

My *Phaedra* contract has at last been signed! Now it may go on next fall, either here or in London. My next book is done, I think. I have 22 original poems and about twelve translations. It has the gentle title, *An Eye for an Eye*. I'll get copies typed and send you one next month. Often it seems all acid and mannerisms to me. I may have gotten into a rather mechanical appetite for publishing. Habits come hard to me, and then seem excessive and possessive. I get a curious pleasure from getting a book off my hands and out.

I enjoyed your limerick on Keith. I finally wrote him a sort of apology and bread and butter letter. Poor thing, all ticks and angles. I gave him a hard run.

In the mail the other day came two drawings: one a very accurate Dureresque head in a surrealist design with entrails (?) and a huge thumb, the other a precise flame pattern in diamonds like good wood-carving. With them a pitiful letter about break-downs and wanting a friend. "I went to your Milton class, but didn't dare speak." And, "Oh God, why can't God be good to us!" I felt I had to ask him over. A tall young man of twenty arrived, sandy mustached, talking in images only, the son of a captain for the Grace Lines, and carrying his poems wadded in a paper bag. He had spilled milk on a bird drawing he was doing for me, and then, more out of fancy than rage, had poured milk on his poems so they stuck together. They read like [a] young man of twenty's version of the most obscure Thomas; each was finished in a day and ended where his page ended. He wanted a friend.

Let's not argue politics, I feel a fraud on the subject. One has, or I at least, such a feeling of things are in the saddle here. The great machine rolls on, all in all efficiently enough, but it doesn't at the moment seem as if anyone in our lifetimes will have the force to deflect it. We trust, I suppose.

Goodbye, Dear, and our love to you and Lota. Send another letter.

Love,

Cal

Hope to see your Lispector in the *New Yorker*. Do you want me to get in touch with Jack Thompson about getting your other friend[*] I know perfectly well who she is—the young Brazilian who was here said she and Clarice were the best prose writers in Brazil—but your letter isn't at hand and I don't trust myself with the spelling. I'll show him your sentences and ask him to write you.

[*]Rachel de Queiroz

423. To Ezra Pound

February 10, 1963

Dear Ezra:

Last fall I wrote you a fan letter on your *Paris Review* interview and the *Cantos* there and in *Poetry*. Then I somehow lost the letter and neglected to write again. Last week I met your daughter, Mary, and went out to see Bill Williams with her and remissness came back to me.

The *Cantos* are some of my favorites, very beautiful and heart-felt. The words stay with me and sing, and are not just the words of a poem but a message and a record. Nothing new I've read so breaks through the crust of its making. The interview too is very gentle and urbane—the best statement of our and your case that anyone has made.

Thinking all this, it was sad to hear that you have been suffering greatly in the last two years. There's no reason. But I know it does no good to say this. I think there are times that cannot be softened or explained off, but which can only be lived through—that blank sense of failing. Now I gather it has lifted and you are reviving. Don't let me intrude. I sympathize and suppose I've lived in the same cellar for moments.

We liked your daughter very much. She has a touching, embarrassed grace that should make you very proud. Be proud too that for so much of your long life you have been a fountain for your friends and readers.

Affectionately,

Cal

424. To Hannah Arendt

February 25, 1963

Dear Hannah:

I am just sending you a little note to say that I think your first two Eichmann pieces are an almost miraculous job of accumulation, narration and sifting of truth. To have collected so much and to have told it plainly would have been enough, but you have morally lived through it all and separated all the varied shadings of truth and lies. I liked your sentences about the "gusts of elation," and also what you say about the Dutch Jews being tortured when they resisted. This seems to answer Bettelheim's argument which I could never take. At every point you both tell the story and push beyond into us all.

It was good seeing you the other afternoon. I like to imagine you now out of all this confusion and free from your labors, relaxing and resting.

Affectionately,
Cal

425. To Elizabeth Bishop

March 10, 1963

Dearest Elizabeth:

I think of you daily and feel anxious lest we lose our old backward and forward flow that always seems to open me up and bring color and peace.

Things are gayer now, but we indeed live in the current. Each Monday I fly to Boston, each Wednesday or Thursday morning I fly back. This gives me two short weeks, each with its own air and pace, instead of my old all of one cloth New York weeks. The teaching is enjoyable, not too much work really, unlocking in a mild way, except that of course one sees too many people and talks too much about poetry to too many embryonic poets. Here we are in the hectic whirl of putting out the new book review. I'm very much a bystander and admirer. But Lizzie is furiously engaged and in a way making inspired use of her abilities—for God knows we need a review that at least believes in standards and can intuit excellence. The bad side is a rush around us of the excoriated and excoriating—nerves and people. We live in the fire and burnt-outness of some political or religious movement.

I want to send you a few books or two at least. Hannah's book on revolutions is somewhat diffuse and theoretical but is full of things that give me pause and I think we would both feel. She approves of the American Revolu-

tion but finds it somehow somewhat abstract and inspired no serious thought after Jefferson and the founders. The French Revolution however which she thinks doomed to violence and tyranny began with pity for the miserable, set up standards of violence and unlimited desire and has inspired generations of thinkers. She is wonderful on how sentiments of compassion get changed into blood power-lust and dictatorship. This is a very garbled way of expressing her dense thought, but she brings home to me frighteningly how certain red-capped liberal feelings can go with a sinister acceptance of the terrible.

The other book is quite different, a magical little essay on Herbert by Eliot.

This is a rushed letter, much more so than my state of mind. This last week-end has been full, a trip to Washington for the magazine, then when I got back Dorine, our nurse from Rio, who had immediately gotten engaged and pregnant when she arrived here, had a miscarriage. She is now in the hospital but well and seems on the whole relieved for she and her husband are not in any position to support a child.

We are terribly interested in having you write a Brazilian letter for the book review—in your wonderful letter style and about anything that you want.

Love to you and Lota,
Cal

426. To Elizabeth Bishop

May 8, 1963

Dearest Elizabeth:

[. . .]I spent a week-end with the Ransoms at Kenyon. Before my reading John and I went to an exhibition of African masks, etc. put on by a six-foot, thirty year old patroness, rather charmingly dizzy with such things—some of her notices would say, "I really don't know what this was for." John stared at something, all grass and grimace, and said, "They may not have been good neighbors to each other, but they never harmed the rest of the world." John has been re-writing old poems; Randall thinks the results absolutely wooden. I can't judge really, because I find it so touching that he should now after twenty-five years be painfully living through his old work again, questioning not only the style but the experience. He has a lecture on music (in poetry) decaying into prose, fable into whimsy and drama into horror. He has made a map of his little garden—no Burle Marx work of art, but all genuine, and all

day he and his wife solve *Nation* crosswords. He is having a delightfully innocent and firm old age.

Randall was here reading at the Y. Eric Bentley introduced him, said little about him except that he liked their common generation and loathed that before them, good art produced by hideous personalities such as Pound, Eliot and Wyndham Lewis, and also loathed the sewer of the "beasts." He said a lot about fake Oxford accents from St. Louis. When Randall got up he said he had listened to Mr. Bentley and even tried to understand him, that Eliot had said James had a mind too fine to be violated by ideas, and that he hoped his audience had such minds because the ideas they had heard would only confuse what they got from his (Randall's) poems. Then he said Eliot had started out superior to everyone else but had become such a *good* man that he no longer needed to write poetry. I'm not probably giving the true impression, but Randall got rather gracefully out of a coarse simplification. Randall has written an awfully good nineteen page terza rima poem on his childhood in Hollywood "The Lost World," and really in his way seems to have reached a gentle honest and inspired state of life. I have been thinking of what you said about Pound and Chekhov, and of course it's true. Alas, we are most of us splinters, but I see more and more that it is death to cultivate one's creases and seams.

I'll mail you Randall's "50 Years of American Poetry" lecture. The paragraph on you is only a sketch of an essay he wants to do on you. He is keener on you than on any one else, and has read and liked most of the poems since your book. Why couldn't Giroux do *all* your poetry to date? I was talking to him a week or so ago, and he seemed to like the idea.

I suppose you have been reading about the fierce and awful race riots in Birmingham. We've sent a telegram and signed a petition. I can imagine the Southerners, but what they are doing is barbarous, and all for a nightmare of the nerves, something that exists there, but not in fact. One felt this so strongly in Trinidad and on the whole in Brazil.

I've seen several of your friends, the Summers, Gold and Fizdale, Marianne Moore, who is coming here next week on the annual Academy Meeting day. We all get very bubbly about you, and of course Gold and Fizdale are wild about Lota. I don't like to think of Brazilian conditions for you, so much seems stirring under the mist and reports that one gets. Our country here seems the opposite since the fall Cuba business—a strained calm, with a little hopeful half smile, as we sit on our cushion of strength and corruption. I think there is even a slight fear that the future will be a windless monotonous ocean of order and no wars. It's easy now to hope, and under the hope lies God knows what.

I see Jack Thompson tomorrow and will speak again about Rachel de Queiroz. Your letter arrived too late for me to hear Tourel sing you. My *Phaedra* may be done next fall, Siobhán McKenna would like to do it at the Dublin Festival, Peter Hall and Peter Brook are considering it for their London company, Olivier is reading it, the Phoenix Theater here is interested. Bubbles perhaps, still something will probably happen. A wonderful young Englishman, Jonathan Miller wants to direct my American play, and now we are trying to find a producer. So—but I feel by now my plays were written by some one else. In [the] next few weeks, I should have my poems typed and will send them to you. The stone phallus was meant to be awfully raw and obvious, but maybe the poem ought to end earlier. I really want to write in a new way, one I can't describe, but one that is free from a kind of shadow I still often walk under but no longer believe. The best I have done seems wizened, and yet I feverishly hope that each new trifle will catch fire.

Another *New York Book Review* will be out next Monday—long pieces by Wilson and Kenneth Burke, then the review will lapse till next September and then we hope come out every other week. We would [be] very eager to print anything you wanted to say about any book, or a series of Brazilian letters.

The weather is lovely now, and the time of last year's departure is with me, and hundreds of rich moments with you return.

My love to Lota—all my love to you.

Cal

I have a feeling from the gap of time since your last letter that you must have found the clothes to go to Peru. I hope all has been well. I wish we were flying back to you.

427. To A. Alvarez

May 12, 1963

Dear Al:

It would be a privilege to write a keen letter about you to the Bollingen. As I am not sure about who I should write there, I'll wait till you answer. As you know I am very indebted to you and in a way that I can hardly repay for your many reviews and remarks on me. I don't think you are right in regarding your stream of brilliant short pieces as hack work, besides the *Observer* pieces which cover the younger better than anyone else, there's the Dryden essay, your review of Hannah, the liquidation camps and many others.

Sorry to hear of your alimony tangle. Don't think me light-hearted, if I say that bad as it might be, you are lucky, it's something objective and outside you. The other . . . however, I know well these things have a way of combining and mounting on one till all one is or does is acid. Anyway don't believe it. I'm sure the Bollingen will come through and you will caste off your pressures by writing *Under Pressure*.

I enclose a poem. It will be good to see you next fall.

Yours as ever,

Cal

P.S. I was haunted by Sylvia's poems and your remarks in the *Observer*. I read another good one by her in a more conventional style about bees. She used to come to a few of my classes. I knew a little about her depressions but never saw anything, and thought the gods were smiling on her and Ted. I gather the death was suicide and that they had split up. How is he making out? I wish I could help.

428. To Elizabeth Bishop

June 19, 196[3]

Dearest Elizabeth:

Tell me where you would like Flavio to apply? Some of the best colleges for English would be Columbia, Harvard, Berkeley, and Minnesota. Rutgers would be good too. I can write to people in most of these, probably all, and recommend him highly. The best thing would be for him to apply and put me down as a reference, and I could fill out the blank they would send me. Your word on him is law with me, but of course I remember him well and think very highly of him.

I'll mail you more records tomorrow. I didn't send any more, but want to. Can books too be sent through Mrs. Theodorides? If so, what would you like? I still owe you an Oxford 17th cent. verse, and would like to mail more, if they would go through.

I wasn't hurt by the correction of my macumba, and now think I have it right. It's coming out again in next winter's anniversary number of the *Kenyon Review* for Ransom. I tried to make something of all your wonderful Yemanjá observations (much better than my poem) but could not verse them into any style that was poetry for me. I have a few other poems I'll mail you.

Now a puzzling project. I've more or less been asked to adapt a German play *Der Stellvertreter*, *The Representative*, by a man named Hochhuth. It's

mainly about gas chamber Germans, but its real edge comes from a group of scenes of Catholic high officials, finally ending up with one with Pius XII in which the Pope refuses to say anything concrete about the German extermination of the Jews, even though they are being removed almost before his eyes in Rome. It's a seven hour play, in loose verse, no artistic masterpiece but with a crude O'Neill-like power with a little Brecht and Schiller thrown in. I'd be adapting it with Lillian Hellman, whom I couldn't like better personally, but I suppose there'd be artistic and ideological differences, though no doubt I'd learn a lot about playwriting. In Germany it has been defended by Catholics and of course attacked by many more. The hero is a Catholic priest who ends up in Auschwitz. Well, I'm not interested in an anti-Catholic diatribe, but I think the play makes a case [that] must be heard, and I see it as an analogue for any institution or religion—something I personally perhaps ~~could~~ ought to do, only partially artistic, a bit like my C.O. business. Well, I'd like to try the writing, if I could do it strongly and honestly.

A couple of weeks ago I went at Nabokov's invitation to a little conference at Mrs. Agnes Meyer's estate—great luxury with almost monastic regularity, a sweet old lady, nearing 80 with displaced retina trouble, bluntly bright, full of good works, personal memories of Claudel, Mann, and even Rodin. Oppenheimer presided, quivering like a humming bird with difficult elliptical quotations on every field, beautiful-looking, rather like the monk in the Giorgione or Titian piano player scene; Nicolas subdued Rabelaisian and Russian reminiscences, kind to me, but not very interested; the architect who built Radio City, conservative in his craft but full of a gentle worried humane wisdom— what he would build would be the opposite of Brasília; Stuart Hampshire hesitant, humorous, gossipy, pure British, and a Miss Hersch, a Jaspers student and the epitome of that kind of intellectual, Hannah A without the genius and humor; George Kennan with views almost like Khrushchev's on the arts—in a really noble old-fashioned uninformed way, wishing the world would go back to 1800, wishing the bombs were buried. Nabokov said Oppenheimer was Callas, and Kennan was Robeson and the rest of us were just honest singers. Well, I felt very young, small, ignorant and fascinated, trying to play the role of the hesitant, muddled, intuitive poet.

What marvelous letters you've written me. You must tire of my dark inwardness and shop talk. All winter I've been full of my insides, and now for a week I've stopped drinking, dead! and really mean to make it stick. Meanwhile all my twists squirm on the surface.

A little English magazine has an interesting interview of Empson—rather sad. He says most nineteenth-century English poets began well, had a dismal

middle-age, then wrote well again. That he himself stopped when he couldn't bear what [he] was writing. That he was interested in a kind of poetry prompted by Graves that was the working out of problems that in life one had no answer for, so that one tried to be clear as one could for the art and the working out, but really wrote for no audience, "not even Laura Riding." In middle age one is too busy living, working to send a son to college etc. to live with this kind of problem, even though underneath one seethes with scorpions. He hopes to write grand poetry when he is forced to retire at 65.

I've just been to Bob Gardner's documentary on his New Guinea expedition—horrifying ritualistic wars, full of clear rules, such as stopping at night, never pushing things to much killing, skirmishing like cops and robbers, with celebrations after the death of an opponent rather like our Groton St. Mark's football games, rather like Homer, but allowing awful things like the spearing of stray children, the men doing little else but fight, all feathers, courtesies, psycho-somatic magic, and death, death, death—maybe a score or so on each side a year, but constant, utterly without an ideology or even purpose, except to externalize and drown the pains of the soul, wars every day, though gentle compared with ours and fun like a game, even the clamor of mourning, and it all happened, I had the guilty feeling of having gone to a gladiatorial fight.

The family's fine, awfully athletically alive, Harriet with her little girl visitors, climbing etc. Lizzie with her magazine. Dorine is about to leave to marry. She was a good sport with Harriet, but toward the end she has become almost a call girl with gruff Argentine voices calling, "Iss mith Dorine ~~there~~ dere?" We have a new maid and nurse, very gentle, Argentine, meals served, clothes washed and ironed, Jehovah's witness tracks, no English, the only old-fashioned servant we've had. On the 27th we leave for Maine.

All my love, and to Lota,

 Cal

Two days later—I've just sent a little group of records through Betty Theodorides APO, a couple of Richters, the only Messaien I could get (no Henze) Sutherland selections from Lucia, and extra the last two Elliot Carter quartets. I'll keep her APO number and try to send some books through the summer while her APO is still possible.

The German play looks dimmer and dimmer as something I might do. It has a note of nobility coming from a West German that would all too easily seem sensational, revelling in horror etc. in English and on Broadway. I seem to teem with unused energies, one should watch this I know. I have a notion now of trying a play on Eatherly. You probably know his story, he was one of

the Hiroshima pilots. He became conscious-stricken through what he had done, or maybe it was in his character anyway, sent checks to Hiroshima, forged checks, twice tried to kill himself, held up banks, then didn't take the money, and wound up in a Texas sanitarium, divorced given up by his family, somewhere between sane and insane, living to tell his story and protest against nuclear war. Noble and pitiful, hard to dramatize. I would want to write a tragedy, not a piece of peace propaganda—not at all that for I don't think it could be done in a way that would do any good. Part of the poor man's tragedy is that although he exploded as one should and as practically no one else did, yet he has little to say, and is condemned to an almost monomaniac whittling down of his life to this one subject. Well, we'll see.

Excuse these messy copies of my poems. "Caligula" is perhaps too ugly! I wrote it last December and cut it down from four hundred lines. Hope you like something. The harshness grates on me, but I suppose it's all on the road to something less clenched. Anyway the drive to write this sort of thing seems to be dying in me—down to its roots.

Do write me in Castine.

429. To Theodore Roethke

<div align="right">July 10, 1963</div>

Dear Ted:

I'm glad you brought up New York two years ago, because I too had a feeling that we never really got together properly. Somehow with all the rush, the big parties, so many people to see, it's harder than Seattle for the meeting of friends. New York in a way is everyone's city, and no one's. Almost everyone I know, except Elizabeth Bishop, gets through it by drinking.

About the rest, with all your comparisons of our careers, backgrounds etc. I think you must know that the other man's pond, or house or country always seems to have perfections that we have never possessed. But it's all more or less the same when you get inside. I mean really, it's the insides that make the difference. I remember Edwin Muir arguing with me that there is no rivalry in poetry. Well, there is. No matter what one has done or hasn't done (this sounds like a prayer) one feels each blow, each turning of the wind, each up and down grading of the critics. We've both written enough and lived long enough perhaps to find this inescapable. Each week brings some pat on the back or some brisk, righteous slur, till one rather longs for the old oblivion. Well, it would be terrible if there weren't many frogs in the pond, and even many toads. It

does make me happier that you exist, and can do so many big things that I have no gift for. We couldn't be more different, and yet how weirdly our lives have often gone the same way. Let's say we are brothers, have gone the same journey and know far more about each other than we have ever said or will say. There's a strange fact about the poets of roughly our age, and one that doesn't exactly seem to have always been true. It's this, that to write we seem to have to go at it with such single-minded intensity that we are always on the point of drowning. I've seen this so many times, and year after year with students, that I feel it's something almost unavoidable, some flaw in the motor. There must be a kind of glory to it all that people coming later will wonder at. I can see us all being written up in some huge book on the age. But under what title? Anyway, Ted, I do love and honor you. Our love to Beatrice and her painting.

 Cal

P.S. About the enclosed poem. I'm not a good judge or audience for ballads usually. I like the coarseness, and the great push to get it in the right form, stanzas, anapests etc. One of the things I marvel at in your poems is the impression they give of having been worked an extra half day, when another writer would have curled up with exhaustion.

430. To Elizabeth Hardwick

POSTCARD: Jan van Eyck, *The Marriage of Giovanni Arnolfini and Giovanna Cenami*,
National Gallery, London

[London, July 18, 1963]

Dearest Lizzie:

I miss you so much, and you are missed and admired by so many people I meet. A good part of this trip is like a prolonged college reading, but the city is delightful, a New York run like Boston with hundreds of humane and irrational obstacles to slow the pace—a Brazilian intricacy that is somehow efficient and enormously male. I had a fine afternoon with Randall, the only other person in the world not drinking. I love London and wish I had another unengaged week, but it will be a relief to go to Nice this Sunday, and more still to return home. Today the Faber party, tomorrow the Embassy, in a few minutes I'll be off to Harrods for the sweaters.

 All my love to you & H.

 Cal

431. *To Beatrice Roethke*

Castine, Maine
August 3, 1963

Dearest Beatrice:

Terrible news! I just heard last night when I returned from a two days' boat race, and I seem to be still tossing about sleeplessly, and trying to recover my old memories of Ted. He was nine years or so older than I, but we always seemed much of an age, and now I feel as though a great chunk of myself has dropped into the pit. Outside, there's a close cold Maine sky, smoke, smoke-colored clouds, a sense of summer's having drifted between our fingers into winter. There are a couple of birds, reptilian, unsocial, loonlike but all one gray shade, we call shag, flapping about outside—Ted could have made something charming out of them, but I can't.

This morning I read over the spring examination that Ted had enclosed in a letter mailed three weeks ago, and felt under examination myself, and in some doubts as to the result. I think I wrote him last that he had the strength to go on for an extra day's work when anyone else would have given up. One felt this in the exam and of course much more in his poems. I hope it's some consolation to you, and was to him, to know that what was published in his last year showed he was at the top of his powers. I have been in London and Paris for the last two weeks. I had enthusiastic talks with John Davenport, Mary McCarthy and her husband, and indeed everywhere I went about Ted. About his work, about him. It's sad, and still unbelievable to think of all that delicacy of touch and ear, that Rabelaisian energy—gone.

I suppose the scenes I remember best are from the summer we met at Yaddo in 1947—fierce glistening croquet games, champagne at breakfast, the quick one sentence jabs, Ted and I sitting on the porch at Breadloaf with Frost, the curious lift one had of joshing with a large man, and through it all the feeling of living close to some one very intensely and very innocently dedicated. He was just at the edge then, I think, of his later fame, and I see him very tensed, in earnest and willing to stumble and learn, and I can still hear the last two sections of one of his long poems ("The Shape of Fire?") about "that minnowy world," singing. So much freshness, loveliness and innocence of the right earned kind.

Another scene, is visiting you at the hospital in Seattle, those narrow gray, barracks buildings, barbed wire even, I think, at the gate, you terribly frail, we, clumsy and substantial. My last letter from Ted ended with an addition that your painting was "really rolling," emphatic gray penciled lines rounding off five pages of looping green ink.

1963 | *429*

Well, I loved him very much and I love you very much. I trust and hope our last letters cleared up the fog of our never quite speaking through to one another last year in the tumult of New York. Lizzie sends her love and grief. Please let me know if I can do anything.

Love,
Cal

432. *To Mary McCarthy*

August 7, 1963

Dear Mary:

I have been back a week, but almost immediately I went off on a two days' yawl race with Andy Wanning, and now the autumn seems to be advancing with lightning speed with London and Paris swirling off, now almost invisible, in the receding wake. I don't know how to thank you and Jim for all your tenderness, labor and invention that filled every minute with novelty and joy. Each item asks for a letter. I think of being twice met at Orley with waits, the Church at Senlis, St. Genevieve, the somehow huge Turkish bath bareness of the Pantheon, then your apartment with every inch shining with the dash and care of your selection, and finally the shadows deepening on the grass of Saint Cloud, the dachshund trotting off to safety, and the fruit still holding out and lasting with Flemish splendor. The best of it was the feeling of happiness and refreshment that you and Jim give. Betjeman said that Australia made him feel twenty years younger. Well, I can't imagine Australia doing that, but you two do.

Two days ago we heard that Ted Roethke had died apparently of a heart attack in a swimming pool. I guess one had been expecting this for months, he looked so bruised and overcast when we last saw him in New York. And yet he seemed to live with a kind of knowingness, as if he saw all the holes in the road better than we did. Last June, I was reading the stage-directions to a German play that used historical characters. The directions said one should forget all about the photographs, and remember the actions and essence of these people. But I think it must have been hard for Ted to forget what he looked like, all the awe and comedy he necessarily carried about with him, all that delicacy of ear and touch under the great wallow, all the suffering and phosphorescence of his last years. It's hard to get used to knowing that it's not just the very remote and old that die, but someone who used to beat you at croquet a few months ago.

I am about midway in *The Group*, and have just reached the fine section

seen through the stately eye of Hatton. Somehow he makes them all seem smaller and younger, and I am reminded more than ever of our curious clubby monosexual, but seething with tentacles world of St. Mark's. How close the eye was for changes and vicissitudes of character! I think the whole form's popularity chart could have been made from one to thirty-seven, and each week two or three digits would have to be changed. Of course we were four or five years younger, straight Republicans, and hardly aware of any counter-currents, and expecting to move ahead on our advantages along the shining grooves of business. Twenty-five years later, many of the most brilliant and promising are selling real estate. This brings me to the point I meant to make at the beginning. I think you have done something I've always wanted to do, and never had the knowledge or slant to try—you show these cloistered, pastoral souls breaking on the real rocks of the times. What is troubling, shocking and hard to swallow about your story is realizing that we were so compact and ignorant,—dependable little machines made to mow the lawn, then suddenly turned out to clear the wilderness.

Well, we are enjoying the quiet. Taking the children for a drive to see the red moon rise, and a raccoon cross the road is an event. I trust you are getting the same ease and rest at Bocca di Magra (?). We look at the signs pointing to Old Town with an insiders feeling of special knowledge. We can't wait for your next visit, and have five designs for drawing you here next summer.

Love,
Cal

433. *To Nicholas Nabokov*

August 9, 1963

Dear Nicholas:

I am here in Maine sitting in the old barn I use for a study, gray wood, raw wood[,] water I can almost touch by stretching out a hand, silence except when one listens carefully, the waves lapping, chirps, whirs, a distant rooster the slow climb of a car. The houses are very different here, but nature is much the same as at Verduronne. I can almost hear the grasshoppers falling into the moat [by] the old house next to yours, and nothing here seems as new and practical as its efficient stone tower. Life at the moment seems a great swirl of the new and old. I am so saturated with memories that I cannot write a line, and almost wonder why I or anyone ever tried.

Lizzie and I have talked about Berlin for next summer. I take it that the in-

vitation was tentative, and I suppose our acceptance should be too at this point. However, the idea of being there and being there with you is very tempting, and we have gone as far as thinking it would be a good idea to spend the spring studying German. We might take along a child for Harriet to play with, and spend the August vacation by the sea somewhere, perhaps Spain. To earn my keep, I thought it might be a good idea to get together a little group of four or five and talk over English and German poetry. Then we could give readings or lectures, if such were desire[d.] Anyway let me know what you think.

The only address I have here for the Trinidad poet is, Derek Walcott, Port of Spain, Trinidad. His book was published by Jonathan Cape in English with a blurb by Robert Graves. He is an attractive, live young man, and writes with great power, and is the best Negro poet writing in English that I have read. He is also about the only Trinidad writer who hasn't migrated to London.

All morning I have been reading Herman Melville's Civil War poems. His great mind is half smothered in the somewhat mouldy poetic style of the time, but that only makes him the more real and truly part of the past. He speaks of Maine soldiers, and one can almost hear them marching out of this village, where a Union Soldier's statue stands unaging. Melville was a good Northerner, what he really felt most was the pain of so many young men dying, with "golden mottoes in their mouths." Perhaps Berlin and the meeting of Negro and white poets is the place to understand how war can stop.

Lizzie sends her love. I miss you very much, your great fullness of warmth and speech.

Affectionately,
 Cal

434. To Elizabeth Bishop

August 12, 1963

Dearest Elizabeth:

Your letter has been around the world. It arrived here yesterday forwarded by Faber. I feel we have had a most vicarious joint visit to London together. I feel a terrible fraud. I was sent first class by the State Department. When I got on the plane at 8 in the evening, I found six match-boxes with my name inscribed in gold, then scarlet knitted shoe-socks, then the menu. Well, I was not drinking at all, but they offered cocktails (as many as you wanted) chilled vodka to go with the chilled caviar, red and white wine, champagne and liqueurs, then an awful elongated Elvis Presley movie of jumping 14 year

old girls. When I landed at two-thirty our time, I had breakfast with some American friends and was shown by car every sight I had ever seen in London. It took me a day in my stunned one night's sleep lost state to understand people talking British. They all do. I guess the London weather is terrible, they all say so, but it seemed glorious to me, a sort of big Boston that functioned, or a New York with at every step some little detour or hurdle to make things more human and less sheer. *Sheer* seems to be the American's most refreshing and vexing quality.

I must tell you about seeing Randall and later Mary McCarthy, the sheerest of all American pilgrims, both rather marvelous almost saintly in their buoyant go ahead intensity. Randall loves England, and had spent two months with guide books planning his summer, cathedrals, plays, a long string of German castles, visits to *all* the Donatellos in Italy. He avoids all English literary people, but listens avidly to the *real* English ("England is everything the visiting Englishman isn't"). He rents chairs in Regent's Park, they wave to the children, carry bread crumbs for the pigeons, and absolutely hate France. The French customs men wouldn't look at them. I suggested language difficulties, but Randall said wistfully, "They might smile!" Randall is having suits made, quotes his tailor, is incensed that such artisans are not considered artists, has bought a Jaguar, which he won't risk in London. And so on. I laugh a little, but they gave a lovely sparkling salt water feeling of Jamesian purity. And I too felt crazy about London, even the literary people.

My whole trip was minute little readings, stage, radio, TV, little lunches, rehearsals (six hours[)] for a minute and 15 seconds BBC TV recital of "Man and Wife," though of course I was with a mob of other people and didn't even rehearse more than four minutes. I saw quite a lot of Empson. They live in a hideous 18 room house on the edge of Hampstead Heath. Each room is as dirty and messy as Auden's New York apartment. Strange household: Hedda Empson, six feet tall still quite beautiful, five or six young men, all sort of failures at least financially, Hedda's lover, a horrible young man, dark, cloddish, thirty-ish, soon drunk, incoherent and offensive, William Frank Parker redfaced, drinking gallons, but somehow quite uncorrupted, always soaring off from the conversation with a chortle. And what else? A very sweet son of 18, another, Hedda's, not William's, Harriet's age. Chinese dinners, Mongol dinners. The household had a weird, sordid nobility that made other Englishmen seem like a veneer.

I don't know that I have the wind to go on with Mary. Nothing could have been less like the Empsons'. A lovely apartment, William Morris wall-paper, every item clean as a ship, and mostly brought over from England, meals

planned and worked on for days, elevating, industrious trips to churches and museums, everything performed and executed to the last inch, though Mary had just gotten over a bad attack of jaundice. Jim doesn't gossip, and Mary really seems to have become a remarkably kind, generous person, and as happily married as anyone I know. All real, I think, but there is a bubble or two. One is Mary's new novel, which will bring her maybe a quarter of a million (she is already planning to set up a foundation for peace or something with it, though they really don't have much money). She has refused the cover of *Time*, but accepted the cover of *Newsweek*, and a story in *Life*. We had an incredible picnic on the grass of Saint Cloud with the Spenders, Sonia Orwell, the *Life* photographer, minor expatriates, minor embassy officials, a sixteen foot Polish table cloth, magna of champagne, Flemish dining room groups of fruit. But no one in the know likes the book, and I dread what will happen to it in the *New York Book Review*. I've now read it through, and in my usual seesawing, indecisive way, have formed two opinions: 1) bad, that it is a very labored, somehow silly Vassar affair, awfully girlish girls, a chapter on the pessary fitting, a chapter on breast feeding, a chapter on a commitment in Payne Whitney, rather commonplace known material, documented as though she were writing about Florence; 2) good, a kind of clearness and innocence, trying to be kind to the characters—one feels she often made them dull so as not [to] resemble any of her real class-mates. The plowing and smiling through a long hard, impossible task. After all there was a kind of breathless courage and perhaps folly in giving her Vassar girls' view of the thirties. I doubt if she feels it's much of a masterpiece, still the excitement of a first commercial success is intoxicating. I'll feel wretched, if the reviewers are cruel, and take the chance to go to town on her.

Forgive me for saying that I felt comforted by your saying your Muse is dead. Mine is dead as lead, and when I try to write I feel full of a hollow aimlessness, though otherwise quite happy. What I mean of course is that if you, so much better than I, can coast along, I am somehow released for a while. I have no doubts about you, you seem much richer and more interesting than anyone else, and you *never* write junk, seldom write anything that isn't a kind of landmark, so your slow pace must be the one that wins the race. Still I brood about all those rich and unfinished fragments, such a fortune in the bank, but you have done so much better than I could advise you, that I won't prod. You mustn't waver in knowing how much you have.

Thanks for your comments on my poems. I meant to bring them and your letter down to my barn today, and retouch, but I forgot. The raw gobs of hash was meant to be the turtles' food and not the turtles, and probably should have

the word *fed* or something of the sort put back. Maybe I had a perverse desire to blur the picture for a second. I really was too slow-witted to realize the turtles were dying. I detest the "Caligula" for feeling but find it alive as a poem. I'll get the Y of the goddess right, the *the* before *macumba* was an afterthought to make the rhythm more conversational. You are no doubt right about the jumpiness. By the "as many holes as a fishnet" I meant the screen to be some kind of metaphorical veil that shelters the past, now open and defenseless as one looks back with a feeling of distant detachment. *Leaf*-green is what I remember, perhaps in imagination, I hoped for a pathos in the rusty tin and the growing green, the freezing of that growing time. Glad you liked *Night Sweat*. My only product this summer is finishing another sort of like it with Maine scenery. I'd copy it out now but no copy here is close enough for me to remember the right version. I thought [of] you in Nice, a small Rio with a rich country behind it.

All my love,
 Cal

P.S. Oh I had a letter about Flavio from the Harvard Dean. No hope this year, but I am sure it can be done next. He seemed very well disposed. Let me know what I can do. Our love to you both.

435. To Elizabeth Bishop

15 West 67th Street
New York, N.Y.
September 11, 1963

Dearest Elizabeth:

Well, we are back in town. How strange the sticky weather, and all the big architecture and lives seem. As we were driving into town along the Hudson, I half expected to [see] the buildings and even the horses of 1900, perhaps a recoil from expecting London last summer to look like New York. After going to a movie you feel in one.

I've never seen anything like Lizzie and the magazine. Instead of her somewhat murky Kentucky Scottish reserve, all is smiles, flutter and superlatives. The first regular issue comes out on the 26 of this month, and from then on it will be every two weeks. The editors have been interviewed for *Newsweek*, and Lizzie comes home from the office talking as Eve must have about work. I am collecting poetry for the magazine. There'll be one or two in each issue,

about 35 or so for the year. Please send me anything you can spare from the *New Yorker*. The Drummond would be wonderful. The poem seemed marvelous to me, probably the best modern Brazilian poem (?). Could you write a few sentences explaining it and describing Drummond? I think that would help a lot. A short paragraph would do.

You are so sweet about my poems. I think I must write entirely for you. I finally cut the "Buenos Aires" down to 8 stanzas from 14. The phallus is out, and the whole tone is now rather wistful and gentle—much better, I think, and I hope you'll approve. I enclose one more little thing, written a hundred times I guess since last fall, and still very slight. I also have a nightmarish terza rima thing, that I don't know how to finish.

I've put in a clipping from the *N.Y. Times* on Carlos, a harshly simplified account, though meant I think to be friendly. It's nice to think he's gaining ground.

Well, saintly isn't quite the word for Mary, or what anyone would think reading the *Newsweek* spread on her. However, she was so kind to me and easy to talk to that I was rather stunned, and the new marriage does make for almost a transformation. "Unsordid" "no gossip," silly, but after Bowden, high praise.

Hannah has been getting a flood of attacks, Lionel Abel in *PR.* and Podhoretz in *Commentary*, wrong-headed but on rather a higher level than Musmanno. Lizzie suggested Abel to *PR* under the impression that he liked the book (which he did at first) and all this has had to be explained to Hannah. She seems unshaken, and says this book is [the] only one people can understand, so they strike at her.

What a mortality year for poets! Did you read about MacNeice's death? I saw him in London looking very firm and in good spirits, though Bill Alfred said he would be dead soon from drinking. I liked some of his poems, more the early ones, very much. Always a smart mind and eye, and a spring to the rhythm.

I begin again at Harvard at the end of the month. My American play will definitely go on in March, and there will soon be readings etc. at the strange roomy old church where it is being done. So, a full year is coming. I am beginning to enjoy not drinking and am almost vain about it—what a change from last fall with its mania followed by gloom.

Let me know if I can buy anything for you and Lota. All my love, and please excuse the ~~rather~~ chipper banality of this letter.

Love,

Cal

436. To Mary McCarthy

<div align="right">October 2, 1963</div>

Dear Mary:

This is an autumn of crackling controversy. The entire *PR* world seems to be throwing bricks at one another. I find it all vexing and sometimes distressing, though one doesn't fall asleep somehow.

I don't know whether you've seen the book review's Norman Mailer piece on you. It's rather as though he had taken up the boxing fight, he had proposed in person with you at Edinborough (?) and taken a swipe at you when your head was turned. Well, it's not too bad maybe. At least it didn't irritate me the way *Newsweek*'s spread did, that mixture of flattery and venom. More Mailer! He rather lays himself open, and I wonder if I would be impertinent if I suggested that you should, at your leisure, write a reply—not a reply but a serious consideration of Mailer's own work?

I feel that if *The Group* had appeared anonymously, it would have been considered very brilliant, though imperfect and uneven. Instead, it is being buried in the irrelevancies of controversy. You come out very well, but I hate to think of your being ~~distressed~~ knocked. Please believe me I am your loyal friend and I hope a formidable one.

Our love to you both,
Cal

P.S. That last sentence seems to conclude with quite unnecessary swagger. However, I'll leave it. We are looking forward enormously to your visit. Do take care of your health. I wish some one would send Philip Rahv and Jason Epstein on a goodwill trip around the world.

437. To Elizabeth Bishop

<div align="right">October 27, 1963</div>

Dearest Elizabeth:

What a time you all have been through with sickness and political turmoil. I waited breathless while Goulart's martial law was hanging in the air. Sometimes I've wondered, almost enviously, what it must have been like to have lived in the Paris of revolutions, faction barricades. But I can see it is only deadly, waiting with fever in your joints for your temperature to rise.

We had our little New York outburst[,] a Hannah Arendt evening presided over by Irving Howe. Hannah wasn't there and most of the talk went against her. One was suddenly in a pure Jewish or Arabic world, people hardly speaking English, declaiming, confessing, orating in New Yorkese, in Yiddish, booing and clapping. The fire of the evening fell, not on Hannah, but on Raul Hilberg who had written a documentary book on the Jewish exterminations, a book hitherto uncontroversial, but which he now quoted original documents from and ended rather unadvisably by suggesting that the Jews were passive by religion and even now couldn't face the facts. Then Lionel Abel, frothing gesturing, thumping on the table, called him banal boring etc. And from then on the Jews were anything but passive. Well, it was alive, but very rash, cheap, declamatory etc. a sort of mixture of say Irish nationalists and an Alcoholics Anonymous meeting with contending sides. A lot of mud was thrown at Hannah, and one left disheartened and even a bit scared. However, the next night there was a party, where all the contending factions were represented, though only the more articulate intellectuals. And somehow, there seemed to have been a catharsis, and everyone was friendly and relieved that what had been brewing for months had somehow boiled off. There's nothing like the New York Jews. Odd that this is so, and that other American groups are so speechless and dead.

I'm not speechless, what with teaching, occasional readings, a TV show with Kunitz on Roethke. I feel always in motion and quite frivolous and rattle-brained, though pretty calm and even dull by not drinking. Life's fairly enjoyable, but every so often I look back and see only the confused flotsam of a hundred quickly done, half-done, ill-done efforts. I'll be glad when the term's over, and wish I could spend a week on [a] hospital bed, like you, resting. So, I suppose, one fills up, but can anything be well-done that isn't accompanied by dreaming, sloth, contemplation, leisure? I feel I am tied by a wire to a plane swooping back and forth between Boston and New York.

Have you read the posthumous poems by Sylvia Plath? A terrifying and stunning group has come out in the last *Encounter*. You probably know the story of her suicide. The poems are all about it. They seem as good to me as Emily Dickinson at the moment. Of course they are as extreme as one can bear, rather more so, but whatever wrecked her life somehow gave an edge, freedom and even control, to her poetry. There's a lot of surrealism which relieves the heat of direct memory, touches of me, and I'm pretty sure touches [of] your quiet and humor. She is far better certainly than Sexton or Seidel, and almost makes one feel at first reading that almost all other poetry is about

nothing. Still, it's searingly extreme, a triumph by a hair, that one almost wishes had never come about.

Harriet is having her tonsils out this week. She is quite a little lady now, learning to read, answering the phone, assembling collages of corks, package handles, drawings of boats etc. Oh, oh, oh, how time whirls us on! Do you realize that we have already outlived more than half the classic English poets. I suppose they knew no more than we what it all meant. What scatterings of experience. I do feel though that I've lost a few unbelievably narrow and stubborn poses. Do you ever feel that you have almost learned enough at last to be ready to be reborn with profit?

Pardon this flurry. It's just in the nerves. I wish I could spend a few weeks with you. Let us know if we can do anything to help in this troubled moment.

Love,
Cal

438. To James Laughlin

Nov. 20, 1963

Dear J—

Here's a blurb for Stevie Smith.

"On gray days when most modern poetry seems one dull colorless voice speaking through a hundred rival styles, one turns to Miss Stevie Smith and enjoys her unique and cheerfully gruesome voice. She is a charming and original poet."

Could you send me Ezra's present address. I've just read the *Pisan Cantos* again, and feel that no poetry since Thomas Hardy so moves the heart. Our best long poem, and as remarkable an advance over the earlier *Cantos* as "Mauberly" was over the earlier *Personae*.

As ever,
Cal

January 24, 1964

Dearest Elizabeth:

You have a right to be rather flurried by my silence. As you probably now know from Lizzie's letter I have been in a hospital for the last six weeks. It was never really bad, and now seems like a brief fevered moment in a year that now takes up where it paused. Well, six weeks of retirement, looking at TV, talking to casual acquaintances in the sanitarium, and I am sorry to say not answering letters. These attacks still come, but on the whole they throw me less and less off balance.

Today I have been home a week, and am spiritless and loggy from commenting on my Harvard term papers and poems. Pardon my languor, Dear, if I don't answer everything or write a very entertaining letter. The 12th Night poem is marvelous. It has the form, tightness and charm of some of your early poems such as the one about the little horse and rider, but translated into nature and direct observation. I carry it around in my bill-fold, and it seems comparable to the "Armadillo" that I have long cherished. I think you and Auden are writing the best poems now in English, only you two have the form and personality and fullness of great poetry. Could I have mislaid "The Table"? I don't seem to have ever gotten it. I am sure the review will want it. In my letter I only meant to say that Drummond was the best Brazilian poet. I too wouldn't think he had the power of Neruda.

[. . .]The whole series of the reviews will start flooding toward you. There's tons to disagree with of course but the whole is awfully readable and dazzling. Lizzie unfortunately is up to her neck in controversy, first Mary (for her parody and Mailer's review) and now Arthur Schlesinger for a Washington sketch. She has decided to my relief to lay off people we know. Hornets buzz outside but we are at peace at home.

I think I now have a book done, to be called *For the Union Dead*, and adding up to 35 poems. It will be out in September and I'll send you galleys when I have them. I think there are half a dozen poems you haven't seen. I suppose the book tries to be an advance, whatever that means, or a sort of combination of *Life Studies* and the more metrical style of my earlier stuff. I hope you'll like it. It's a little like your work, each single poem an entity, unhelped by previous poems, though I am afraid I have far more monotony and haste.

I worry about each notice from Brazil, and have no way of telling how really threatening each new disturbance is. One prays that Carlos is inde-

structible. I had a talk with Arthur Schlesinger the other day (while in Washington reading a little piece I had written on the Gettysburg Address) about Carlos, and found he felt much the same as we do.

Kennedy's murder was a terrible trauma for all of us. At first it seemed the work of a Southern fanatic, then of a leftist plot. I found myself weeping through the first afternoon, then three days of television uninterrupted by advertising till the grand, almost unbearable funeral. I guess it had something to do with my crack-up. The country went through a moment of terror and passionate chaos with everyone talking wildly, and deeply fearful and suspicious. Then there was the unbelievable relief of everything seeming to go well under Johnson. Now there's the let-down, a general prosiness perhaps, and the return to thousands of every day personal and national problems. Maybe it's just my nature, but one seems to see-saw from a sort of rosy blandness to a blank, bare cracking feeling. It's like swimming across a pond littered with pieces of wood; one wonders if one has the energy to push through it all, then one floats gaily and the curry draws one forward.

I wish every now and then and quite often, we two could have more days on the beach, talking unhurriedly and watching the surf break.

The place where I was staying was called the Hartford Institute of Living, a grand Utopian title. It's much better being out and alive. My Harvard appointment has been renewed for two years. This week will be my last until next September. Rehearsing for a reading of my play begins in two weeks. The play will go on in September. We plan to go to Castine this summer. Harriet can read and write.

My love to Lota, and all my love to you.

Cal

Thanks worlds for everything: letters, present and poem.

440. To Mary McCarthy

February 20, 1964

Dearest Mary:

I too have been delaying writing with the idea of waiting till I was sufficiently collected to do the moment justice. But I am afraid I would wait till doomsday before I could match your letter.

I *was* getting sick, and about two weeks after the assassination, I went to a hospital at Hartford, ~~gloriously~~ grandly called The Institute of Living. All

was really rather soft and subdued. I was never very sick and the recovery was gentle and gradual: a dull fairly agreeable month of small crafts, chaff with the other patients and popular television. It softens the critical mind for a while, but does no harm. It's a little painful prodding the formless, embarrassed mind to pick up the pieces. You weren't in any way a cause. These things come from the air. The stir of a feather can start them, though no doubt I would be immune, if I had a different soul.

Enough of that! I thought your *PR* piece showed great courage and power of argument. It was the right way to stand up for a friend, and the clanging polemical tone was probably the right way to shout down the fury on the other side. Outrageous—but called for, and who else dared? I admire, because I feel so unable to hold a mass of facts together, then argue, clearly, forcibly, and at length. You showed the same skill when you described the language of *The Group* at the Y.

A lull here, but we have just been to a Town Hall Meeting to hear Lee Oswald's Mother speak. There was the sad, fierce, unattractive, provincial and somehow pathetic ex-Stalinish crowd, vague declamatory speeches that wouldn't have worked with any other crowd, a hugely for the moment effective and fact drenched speech by a man named Mark Lane, delivered with professional defense lawyer's fluency and sarcasm—then at last Mrs. Oswald rather frightened and stage-struck talking non-sense about the American way—however, she was much better in private. Well, I suppose Oswald did the murder, otherwise not only the Dallas police, but the FBI would have had to plot, frame and lie. Still, one feels the case has been handled in a cruel, sloppy, hit-or-miss hustle of confusion—two or three damning bits of evidence that no defense counsel has been allowed to test, and then a litter of difficulties and inconsistencies.

Each Sunday, I see that you are still condemned to be a best-seller, but you must feel that your old true character has returned by now; you've passed through the raised clubs. What a roar, what a forest fire, of praise and abuse! I don't suppose it's possible for human nature to become a public figure and creature of publicity, and that those who have to live that way have ways to grow deaf and survive. Thank heavens, you are just you, the same person with another strong book added to your list.

Next week we begin rehearsing for a reading of my play. The performance won't be till next October. Hannah came over the other night, in calm spirits though somehow frail. I've spent a week or two imagining a play about Trotsky in exile, but it would take Dostoyevsky to carry it. Now, I've just finished a more modest effort, the translation of a long sequence by Anna Akhmatova

on her son's exile to Siberia under Stalin. Love to you both, and excuse this floundering letter.

Love,

Cal

P.S. I haven't said anything about you and Lizzie, but I pray for everyone's happiness that we drop and forget the past and go on as we used to. We all want to with all our hearts.

441. *To the Editors,* Partisan Review

[n.d. 1964]

Both Hannah Arendt and Lionel Abel have written with such intelligence and force that any comment by me is likely to seem weak and impertinent. I particularly wish to avoid saying anything about the Jewish committees, or Abel's unanswerable, "What would you have done?" and "What could you have done?" I do think he distorts the painfully patient examination Miss Arendt gives this question. Her portrait of Eichmann, far from being lenient, is a masterpiece in rendering the almost unreadably repellent. I never felt she was condescending, or hard, or driven by a perverse theory, or by any motive except a heroic desire for the truth.

442. *To Adrienne Rich*

February 25, 1964

Dearest Adrienne:

I am very mortified about "In the Woods." It was about to be printed when I got sick, then somehow it got delayed and put aside. I've just talked to Bob Silvers, and he is going to see that it is printed as soon as possible. Your card to Lizzie doesn't seem to have arrived. Please forgive me.

I have often thought of that morning when I last saw you. I practically stepped from the church into a taxi. The radio was going in a confused way, and the driver was grinning and giggling in a compulsive way, and saying, "The President has been shot." The death hadn't been announced, but seemed probable. I asked the driver why he was smiling, and he said, "Because it hurts so, it just hurts." Then the chaos of the afternoon when it looked as though the murder had been done by a rightist fanatic. I must have been very wrought up

anyway, because I lay for a long time on my bed listening to the reports and weeping. One felt as if a civil war were beginning. No rational daylight law seemed to hold, and it's easy to see how Johnson rushing to his plane feared lest an atomic war might be beginning. What destructive almost abstract dynamite we are all sitting on, though all seems comfortable, safe and controlled.

How glad I am to have your favorable impressions of the plays, particularly today when we are beginning rehearsals for a reading on Sunday. I know so little about what will act and what won't, that this might as well be my first manuscript. The church-theater won't be ready till late summer, so our opening will be in October.

Glad to hear you have written more and done so much absorbing reading. I went off to the hospital armed with a suitcase of classics: Freud, the complete Aristotle, Dante, etc. and then spent most of my time looking at popular television, even waiting breathlessly for the next Thursday's Dr. Kildare. However, I've finished off a number of fragmentary poems, and will have a book out in September.

I hope Alf enjoys Pakistan.[. . .] I won't be back in Cambridge till next fall, I think. But I hope we will see you. Maybe you would like to come down in April and see Randall's version of the *Three Sisters* staged with tremendous stars by the Actors' Studio.

Love from us both,
 Cal

Have you heard anything about the Richards in Ghana? It seems a terrible time to be there.

443. *To T. S. Eliot*

March 4, 1964

Dear Tom:

I want to apologize for plaguing you with so many telephone calls last November and December. When the "enthusiasm" is coming on me it is accompanied by a feverish reaching to my friends. After it's over I wince and wither. Fragments of the true man, such as he is, are in both phases. You are very dear to me always.

I have just been through a baffling week of hearing my play read, and find myself talking like some of my more pompous and farcical characters, so

much so that I wonder if their foolishness wasn't some held down slice of my character that I've tried to banish from my poems.

I gather from Bob that the Caribbean has been health-restoring and very pleasant. We have [been] going on a series of Sunday-morning pipe-dream trips, even studying the course of an oriental family cruise, but instead we will be going to Maine. And instead of going to the Caribbean, I am starting on a broken series of teaching and reading trips to such diverse places as Delaware, Toronto and New London.

Someone at Faber sent me a copy of Philip Larkin's new poems, which by their mildness move me more than anything I've read lately in prose or verse. He has such a chipper, modest and personal language for describing the almost undetermined, the sad, proud accident of his unattached middle-age. Very different are the last poems of Sylvia Plath with their dare-devil desperation. She came to my class one spring in Boston, and I only thought of her as sensitive, accomplished and anonymous—now she seems as brilliant to me as Emily Dickinson, and with something of the same nervous compression.

I've just finished proof-reading the manuscript of my new smallish book of poems for Farrar and Straus. I'll send that and my play to you at Faber in the next month or so.

Our love to you and Valerie,
　　Cal

444. To Elizabeth Bishop

<div align="right">March 10, 1964</div>

Dearest Elizabeth:

It's an iron-black warm New York morning that reminds me of Europe. With the heat turned off in my study, I hear the great huffle of nature outside and almost feel I were voyaging off into the Atlantic, till I look up and see the stationary sky-line of little sky-scrapers and wooden water towers.

There was a piece in the *Times* this morning about Goulart taking over the oil refineries and a lot of land—gloomy U.S. ponderings on continued unrest. I hope there's no new trouble.

I have been listening to readings of my play for a week, and feel it is something a ghost wrote and signed my name to. I have a brilliant bubbling young Englishman, Jonathan Miller, directing, and some rather optimistic but heavy drama people managing the production. I feel in a very alien element, and

back Miller whenever there's division of opinion. The play has power, I think, and great length, almost four hours.

Well, the daze of returning to myself seems to be clearing and cheering. I've just finished my first new poem in months, the inner stirrings of a character, half me and part Gerard Nerval. I once translated a lot of his sonnets, but the French was so simple that they almost seemed to exist already in English, and somehow their Keats-like richness was rickety and stilted in my words. I've also done a long dirge by Anna Akhmatova on her son who was taken off to Siberia in the 30's. Her style is a graceful, feminine pre–Marianne Moore one, but her grief has great grandeur. Strange to write from behind such a mask!

Next week a series of readings begins, Greensboro, Toronto, Delaware, Kenyon, Baltimore. The map! Last week I did my first, and answered all the old questions that I know no answers to, the roles of [the] poet, obscurity, what do I think of John Brinnin. By the way, there's an awful, pale dull play now running on Thomas, called *Dylan*, Alec Guinness badly miscast in the lead and a tall full-haired youth, playing John Malcolm Brinnin.

I haven't read much that held me lately except [a] short autobiography by Dahlberg, *Because I Was Flesh*, a marvelous, realistic, loaded with Montaigne-like classical references dirge on his Mother, a lady barber, and now Larkin's new book. Rather sad now about his unmarried middle-age, but always witty, quiet and his own in style. Reading him, I had a feeling that you were the crown of his whole group, humor, the authentic tone, nothing put in to make poetry. But none of them have your splendor!

Your poem will be out in the issue after the next, I think. Everyone is very excited and proud of it. We must thank you for your present, we finally got a delightful *Goldberg Variations*.

I think about you both daily. Send some news and another poem or poems. The family sends its love, and I all mine,

Cal

445. To Elizabeth Bishop

April 3, 1964

Dearest Elizabeth:

All sounds calm and at peace in Brazil for the last day and a half, but I am still reeling as I try to imagine the stir of the last few days and surely the last weeks or months. I dimly followed the marine mutiny, but our last direct Brazilian report was several months ago from Keith, who said Goulart was of-

fering Carlos's police higher wages in the army, and that C. was in an increasingly perilous position. So, the overturn came without a whisper of warning.

Our cable must sound unduly worried, but the news changed rapidly. I was in Toronto on a two days' visit and reading. The last news I read there was that the marines were attacking the barricaded governor's palace and at the same instant Carlos's police were trying to storm the little Copacabana fort. As I flew home, there was a clear sky over the Atlantic when we reached it, and I pictured the same moon, thousands of miles south, shining on the same ocean, everything strangely nearer because the sandy shore led like a road to you, and in the mind one might walk it, and be lost as I then thought in conflicting knots of thin helmeted soldiers. Thank God it's all over. I realize that since I left Brazil all was simmering and that one week told little of what would be the reality the next. I trust the change has lessoned the darkness for you and Lota and the country. Do write and tell what has been going on with you, and all that your eye lit on.

What is your personal news? I gathered from Howard Moss the other night that you have written a new long poem and that you are planning very soon a trip to London. Will you come by here—not much on the way I fear. Do you want to be in Brazil for the new order or are you eager to get away from it temporarily? I hate to think of all the strain you must have had. Here one had at times a wild wish to be on the scene. Goulart seems to have disintegrated like one of those sand houses or churches on the Copacabana beach, but it must have seemed much more fearful and hazardous from moment to moment. Carlos is everywhere here: news accounts, pictures, editorials, interviews, talking English on TV. The picture is very favorable to him, but simplified and less brilliant, bold, colorful than memory remembers. Give him our warmest wishes etc. I felt very stricken when I thought he was in danger.

Not much news with us. We both went to the Greensboro writing festival and saw Randall, older, smaller, grayer, and still rather shaken by the jaundice he had over a year ago and aggravated by Italian cooking this fall. He is still full of intuitions, knowledge and certainties, a grizzled belief in joy and excellence, noble and a little sad. I gave him my new book with misgivings, hardly knowing what I thought of it myself, and sure that his dislike would be unbearable. But he liked it, and thought it was my best book, and said I had the same absolutely right details that you have. On Monday I go to the University of Delaware for ten days, where I'll be received by an accomplished but unintelligible poet named Huff, but my old friend Peter Taylor will also be there, so it should be fun. Then Kenyon for two days, then nothing else till Maine, except for a reading in Baltimore.

The old get older. I've seen Marianne Moore a couple of times, once introducing Auden very wittily calling him a "fantast who was also a sage," and ending with a humorous quote from Auden that all ills of the body were ills of the soul, and "I give you Mr. Auden." Then later at a small poets party for Vernon Watkins, where for all her fragility she stayed with us 7 hours talking. Her baseball is way over my head. So is John Ransom's aesthetics and philosophy. He came here for the National Book Award with his post box key instead of his suitcase key, no money except his ticket, and hardly knew his hotel, yet talked with fascinating merry complexity on Kant, Valéry and Stevens. Eliot too is apparently very weak and old and fearful to be far from his wife, yet sang me a humorous song called Mr. Caruso on the phone.

Oh dear, let me say goodbye. Things in Brazil still sound a bit confused, but I feel such relief for you both. Dear Lota must have had her hands and mind full. How we trembled for you when the first ~~news~~ vague news began to break! Dare I say that I hope there was humor and pleasure, as well as trouble for you in the simmering days before the overturn?

All my love,
 Cal

We are both so unspeakably relieved for you and Lota! Rio scenes and memories have been spinning through my head for the last three days like movie shots.

446. To Randall Jarrell

<div align="right">May 11, 1964</div>

Dear Randall:

I have been meaning to write you and Mary a note of thanks or remembrance for weeks now—weeks of reliving the past first at Delaware with Peter, then two days at Kenyon at the strange ecclesiastical ceremony of dedicating the old library to Ransom. I've just gotten my twenty-fifth reunion class-book from Harvard. Face after unremembered face tells how it married so-and-so luckily after a "protracted siege," has three children who will soon be ahead of it at golf and fishing, joys in an 18th century farm, is fighting a losing battle against the lawn and the waist, is conservative in religion, politics and the community—well, we're all flesh and blood and middle-aged.

You stay young, and it's good to think of you, still so honest and hopeful and full of brilliant talk and knowledge, able to judge and to make. Your great

parade of women have a delicate splendor, more like bits of Tolstoy than other poets. It's awkward thanking you for liking my new book, but this came at a good time. One can judge so ill one's self, and sometimes I find a mean tameness and sour monotony which I detest. *Life Studies* gave me an opening, and the problem for the last four or five years has been a hunt for the knack and power to fly.

I've just done a review of Berryman which you won't agree with, I think. I've always felt he threw all he had into writing, and more and more as time went on, though his top, I think, is Bradstreet. As I wrote, I tossed in all my larger more enthusiastic impressions, though he'll probably feel I've hemmed him in with barbs.

Just like our Harvard '39 colleagues we were out in the park with our little girl yesterday, watching her plunge thru the press on her extra-wheel supported bicycle. Last night we skipped for a few steps, and she said neither of us was much good, I because I didn't do it much and she because she had just started. For a while she wouldn't at school, now just as I was writing about Berryman, Lizzie called—the spring interview—Harriet is blooming and blossoming in all directions.

I gather your opening will be sometime in June. We'll celebrate when you and Mary come. Our love to you both,

Cal

447. To Adrienne Rich

June 3, 1964

Dear Adrienne:

I'm afraid in the nervous self-preoccupation of travelling, the little drive to New York is itself rather [an] expedition after so many months of non-driving life here, I'm afraid all that prevented my showing how much I was struck by your new poems. You go on exploring and accumulating more resources. It seems you more and more have worked out a style of your own, one that combines the casual and the splendid, the organized, and the wild leap. And now there's perhaps no one in the country one can expect more from. Almost everyone is caught in the dilemma of either starting again, a little threadbare having junked too much in desperation, and the desire to be fresh, or there is a hardening, a sticking to the old good, but predictable, means. Loss and gain—no one is managing this more powerfully and solidly than you.

All this is too abstract, but I feel the method has a lot to do with what you

are saying, that the renewal of life, the taking in of its generous detail, the keeping open, the keeping daring etc. has everything to do with having some frame or form to hold with. It does with you. "In the Dark" and the poem about the bowling alley are incredible jobs of inclusion, and then, with [the] first in particular, of invention.

I was thinking of something more personal though yesterday as we sat at coffee, chatting about various people, Berryman, Susan Sontag, the Dutch paper on the table, and near you, all around you, your house, your children at school, Alf in Pakistan, and somewhere throwing shadows, your recurrent images of the doomed elms. I think you are saying that this last image is not what we are, it's rather some vein of decay, fatigue, tearing imperfection, and impatience that we carry about in us. As we grow older, moments of pause come, and we say, "This too is part of it, life is inescapably this too"; and then somehow we feel it's all rich and merciful. I was thinking of Berryman, his troubles and his power, and with what smash and vehemence he carries himself. It's too near me, I would crumble in a minute. I suppose that is why he troubles me more than he does you. Parts of his character are so close to me that I cannot look on him even in the imagination without a drowning feeling. I feel oxygen coming into my lungs and then failing. Well, we are always failing and succeeding in different ways, and we are all constantly finding and not finding courses that will do for us. We walk our own roads more or less, but we all walk, make our different lines on the same surface. Yesterday I felt something of this was shared by us, and something was lived together without invasion.

Affectionately,
Cal

448. To Elizabeth Bishop

June 15[–16], 1964

Dearest Elizabeth:

I am returning Flavio's letter because you will probably want to keep it. It certainly is charming and shows a kind of innocent yet wise devotion to you that seems to ring from another age—youth's, but something more. I would also like to have read your guide to U.S. manners, also of another age I gather with its buoyant Nova Scotia gallantry. I thought he was charming too in parrying some of your suggestions—to say "I was always pretty yellow," shows he has great courage. He has a lot of lively-witted compassion—what more

could one ask for? I hope and trust all will go well with him and Harvard and later life.

Everyone here very much needs your guide to U.S. manners. Civil Rights seems the clearest of black and white issues. But the road is a rough one. There's a great flow of aimless violent incidents. Very ugly attacks, mostly by little Negro gangs, and with no purpose whatever. But the effort must go on to give the Negro equal rights and what is harder, and almost impossible, chances. Meanwhile, one walks the streets with a perhaps silly feeling of dread. Rich and poor, black and white, liberal and conservative might be at each other's throats. Nowhere, I suppose, is such a peril less likely, and yet we are beginning to be afraid of each other.

This kind of feeling has been growing on everyone for the last few months. Television flashes it home, but of course isn't a cause. I rather exaggerate. For the last few days I've been reading Hugh Thomas on the Spanish Civil War. It simmered and simmered, then overnight it became merciless on both sides. Looking back, I would choose the Republic, but without conviction. Everyone then seems on a bloodthirst[y] drunken binge, or worse, soberly, apathetically or furiously directing forces on a drunken binge. And there is no tolerance or place for the unconvinced bystander.

There's a connection between how the world is and what the imagination lights on. What it usually lights on now is some gruelling murk or release at all costs. Well, why not? It has always been so. Nothing could be more terrible than *Lear* and the *Oresteia*, both of which I have been reading. And there is no more harmless way for the elemental and black to come out than in words, paint and notes, where nothing can ever be hurt. Still life is a struggle for some equally inspired calm and balance. That sounds a little smug, and cheap and inconsistent coming from me—it's a hope not a law, or rather it's law and support that is often unavailable.

Your Piero remarks have sent me back to the little Christmas volume of his pictures that Lizzie gave me. If he was lazy his laziness makes others' industry reckless waste. And here's the classic calm! But no, only the technique is calm in the *Scourging*, all the classic order squeezes like a vise on Christ. According to my text, the young man in red in the foreground is the Duke of Urbino betrayed by the other two, his evil counselors. There's a suggestion of Poussin's harsher style. I have been thinking of the curious versatility of the man who could do both the *Nativity* and the *Scourging*, opposed worlds in meaning, yet the same world in style, a breathless peace beyond the horror, and beyond the singers.

I went to sleep last night leaving the shade up over the open window at my

ear because of the heat. What I looked at was the gorgeously rectilinear facade of an old-fashioned yellowish brick abandoned building. In the day, it is drab enough, and pigeons fly in and out of its broken windows, six to each of its five low stories. It seemed like South America, staid and vibrant sweep through the city. I woke with a half dream vision of the utter metaphysical impossibility of our existence. Yet we had got by, we were, I was. And behind me stretched limitless spaces of glowing, pale, empty sky. It was a kind of peace. The sky of the *Scourging*. I felt how silly the dark speculation in the first part of my letter written yesterday was.

I guess Spender, now back and reachable through *Encounter* and Karl Miller at the *New Statesman* might be the best people for you to look up for a start. Larkin is the librarian at Hull, a legendary figure, seldom seen in London. I know you will find great warmth and many admirers. We just had lunch with the Biddles who sent their tenderest love to you. We saw the Tates, sailing for Naples, Allen very brisky and witty, Belle rather morosely intense, moments of a sort of boiling vagueness under what is of course a very happy and devoted marriage.

We are staying on here about a week longer to see the opening of Randall's *Three Sisters*, done by the Actors' Studio. I hope they surpass themselves as indeed they must.

Love,
Cal

P.S. How strange the new address, though Pastoria sounds as though you had brought a little of Brazil in your suit case.

449. To Elizabeth Bishop

August 10, 1964

Dearest Elizabeth:

Marvelous letters about England, Portugal and the boat. I think of you rather buoyantly taking in all you could contain at your own pace and seeing more than all the rushing and rushed swarms straight from the U.S.[. . .]

Did you read about Flannery O'Connor's death? I know nothing except the longish notice in the *Times* that described her career mostly. I gather she must have died of the bone disease, lupus, that plagued her all these years. A book of short stories will come out in January. It seems such a short time ago that I met her at Yaddo, 23 or 24, always in a blue jean suit, working on the last chapters of

Wise Blood, suffering from undiagnosed pains, a face formless at times, then very strong and young and right. She had already really mastered and found her themes and style, knew she wouldn't marry, would be Southern, shocking and disciplined. In a blunt, disdainful yet somehow very unpretentious and modest way, I think she knew how good she was. I suppose she knew dimly about the future, the pain, the brevity, the peacocks, the life with her mother. She was 38 when she died, and I think always had the character of a commanding, grim, witty child, who knew she was destined to live painfully and in earnest, a hero, rather like a nun or Catholic saint with a tough innocence, well able to take on her brief, hardworking, hard, steady, splendid and inconspicuous life. I think the cards seemed heavily stacked against her, and her fates must have felt that they had so thoroughly hemmed her in that they could forget, and all would [have] happened as planned, but really she did what she had decided on and was less passive and dependent than anyone I can think of.

Tell me how Brazil is, Lota and the political world. It must be good now to be home, no longer moving from place to place, but with new memories inside you. Our love to you both,

Cal

450. *To the Editors,* The Village Voice

[New York, N.Y., November 19, 1964]

Dear Sir:

I am shocked by Ruth Herschberger's malicious account of my play *Benito Cereno* (*Voice* Letters, November 12). It is only my regard for *The Village Voice* and its readers that makes me answer this deliberate falsification. It is perfectly clear that I am horrified by the American tendency to violence when in panic, and that is what the ending of my play—the killing of the slaves and their leader on the mutinied ship—means.

The play is set about 1803, in Jefferson's time, and the remarks so outrageously attributed to my own feelings are meant to show the ambivalence toward slavery, even in the mind of a Northerner like Captain Delano. He literally cannot see what is before his eyes because he thinks of the Negroes only as servants and primitives. But most important to me in this historical play is my lament for the decision made both consciously and unconsciously in the United States to have the most repressive slavery in history. A reading of Stanley Elkins' brilliant book, *Slavery*, gives a most instructive comparison between our condition and that of South America. Ruth Herschberger's notion

that I am Captain Delano and wish to put down the present Negro revolt either by guns or by anything else is slanderous. In my poem "[For] the Union Dead" I lament the loss of the old Abolitionist spirit; the terrible injustice, in the past and in the present, of the American treatment of the Negro is of the greatest urgency to me as a man and as a writer.

Ruth Herschberger says that I made news in the 1940s by "going after Commies." It is not ridiculous enough that I am made to be Captain Delano in the 1800s, I am also in her mind apparently confused with the detestable Senator McCarthy.

Robert Lowell

451. To Elizabeth Hardwick

Institute of Living
Hartford, Connecticut
January 30, 1965

Dearest Lizzie:

I should have written sooner but conditions are really not very propitious. I am writing on one elbow on my bed. The corridor to this "unit" and the only place we meet in common is about five feet wide. The patients are senility cases, no cuckoo like Judge Rohrabach (now dead alas) but dim slow and talkative. During most of the day I transfer to a unit called Butler II, where the patients are adolescents, some wear long hair and almost none have finished high school. I won't go into the boredom of "leather appreciation" and ceramics appreciation, of watching basketball games for an hour without smoking, or of trying to converse with the oldster reading Francis Bacon sentence by sentence and complaining but never specifying about the difficulties of the Elizabethan vocabulary, then turning to the boy, three months a freshman at some unknown university, [who] carry[s] around the *Modern Library* giant collected Keats and Shelley, but who had never heard of the "Ode to a Nightingale."[...]

My only solace is a Mrs. Shirley Clark, who made the Frost film (later wrecked), *The Connection* and many others[...]a sort of youngish Lillian with a dash of Susan Sontag. Very sardonic and good company, and under exactly the same privileges and restrictions as I.

Well, the papers—I really need less medication to handle them properly. They are not here yet, but I assume are on their way from Fred. I'll absolutely need my November grades which [are] in one of the desk drawers in my

study. Sorry about Harriet's mumps. These children's diseases do hit her hard. I hope to hell I don't get. I have memories of Red's troubles. Thrilled about the new writing, "Our years," write anything you want. I want to see out of curiosity, but won't censor. It's funny, for years I have suspected that you might write a masterpiece on this subject, though God knows what you can do with your sedentary manic poet. Thanks for all your trouble.

Love,

Cal

452. To Elizabeth Hardwick

Istitute of Living
Hartford, Connecticut
February 5, 1965

Dearest Lizzie:

I can't even spell my absurd address correctly. Thanks for the stream of letters on yellow paper and pastoral postcards. It's monotonous and lonely here, of course. And now more so because Shirley Clarke[. . .]has been moved to another "unit."[. . .]Now there's no one who can talk here.

Mournful thoughts on death! It seems so irrational for Frost, Eliot, Blackmur and Roethke all to have died in about the same twelve months, all different in age and the consummation of their careers. No, everything that is *isn't* right.

Nothing doing here except that I suppose I am rather steadily getting better. Last night I was on a grotesque little "group IV" entertainment. People read things like *The Congo*, *Archy and Mehitabel* etc. and I read two little Ransom poems. Health to those still alive! I really feel very sad about Blackmur. He was in lousy health for a long time, but he always seemed to me like a young man, just a little my senior, an awesome critic, but . . . Oh well!

Love,

Cal

Lots and lots and lots of love to Harriet for her dear postcard.

453. To Elizabeth Bishop

15 West 67th Street
New York, N.Y.
February 25, 1965

Dearest Elizabeth:

The wonderful lithograph is hanging to the left of our fireplace in the big room. One can stand with one eye fixed on it and the other on the silver slave's fertility decoration we bought in Brazil and have set in the middle of the dining room table—amulets against the evils of New York. Further on in the kitchen hangs the modern primitive banana painting of Keith's friend from Recife. Keith, by the way, has an article in *Commentary* entitled "My Friend Fuentes," in which he makes sure that his personal adoration doesn't blind him to flaws in the thinker and novelist. Back a few sentences . . . many thanks for your lovely present. I hope the bundle in customs is our Christmas present, an unworthy return, the complete Guesaldo, two records, one of which I'm sure you already have, and a joke record. I sent them air-mail, hoping that timeliness would make up for their meagerness.

I am back from a month in the sanitarium. It was a quiet stay this time. I went in almost well and so had little of the jolting re-evaluation that usually comes. These attacks seem now almost like something woven in my nervous system and one of the ingredients of my blood-stream, and I blame them less on some fatal personal psychotic flaw. Who knows? They are nothing to be blithe about, but I feel rather composed about it all. Here I am back in the bosom of my family, and back in my study, and getting ready to finish the *Oresteia*. Life and work go on.

One can talk more easily of Randall, now that he has shaved and walks the same earth we do. Gone the ~~moment of the~~ noble air of pained, aloof nobility. Something touching and imposing to look at is gone, but what a relief for his friends! I'm afraid I like the perverse savage new poems best: "In Montecito" and "Three Bills," and of the straight serious poems, "Next Day." Most of the opening poems except I think for the long "Lost World" are good and I found I was underlying a lot of lines in poems I didn't entirely like. His worst fault is the repetition of a style and subject, as though Housman had written rather voluminously and slopped up his meter, and strung individual poems out. Endless women, done with a slightly mannered directness, ~~repated~~ repeated verbal and syntactical tricks, an often perverse and sadistic tenderness—but I am getting into clichés in describing. I like him better than any of us except you when he is good.

I think and hope and know that I have reached the end of my publicity splash. There's a rather crude, hair-blown series of pictures and remarks by me in *Life*. They threw out most of the quotes I wanted, and chose clumsily and meaninglessly from the pictures they had. Rather better is an interview with me in *Encounter*. I'm awfully glad and excited that Giroux will soon be bringing out your poems. We have all been waiting, it seems for years and years to get them all together, so many favorites in this last lot, probably your best book.

While I was in the sanitarium, I went into Hartford, our town, and saw a not very good but touching performance [of] *Uncle Vanya*. On leaving, I heard one of the audience say, "Of course, it's hardly dramatic in our sense." Her friend answered, "Yes, it's like all Russian plays." First voice, "Yes, *The Cherry Orchard* and *The Wild Duck* are like this." Tomorrow we are going to see the Russian Arts Theater do *The Cherry Orchard*.

Sorry Lota is tired. Maybe you should scoop up a bribe and both come here in the spring.

All my love,
Cal

454. To Valerie Eliot

April 12, 1965

Dear Valerie:

Too long a time has passed since Tom's death. I wept when I heard about it, and for weeks caught myself rather inanely saying, "This is sheer loss, without recompense." Sheer loss for us. I have reached an age when all my elders are disappearing, and can't reconcile myself to the fact. Their wit and guidance are irreplaceable, and each year one seems to withdraw further from the friendly shade and walk in the noonday glare.

I don't want to go into a critical tribute now, but I must say that there was no one else who could both write and tell us how to write, no one who spoke with such authority and so little played the roll of a great man. There was no doubt of the greatness, even in the modest silences and the patient courtesy with the boring and humdrum, and least of all in the loud laughter and little phrases and whole narrations of wild irony.

He was a good and patient friend. I think we laughed at the same things and hated the same things, and no older man so touched something personal in my depths.

I'm sure everyone tells you that you gave Tom his greatest happiness. We all think this. Somehow I think, the long spiritual pilgrimage, that gruelling, heroic and yet inwardly at peace exploration and purgation—all that shines through "Ash Wednesday" and the *Quartets* was inevitably going to end in the surprise reward of a joyful marriage.

Elizabeth and I both send our dearest love,

Cal

455. To Randall Jarrell

April 29, 1965

Dear Randall:

I have thought twice about intruding on you, but I must say that I am heart-broken to hear that you have been sick. Your courage, brilliance and generosity should have saved you from this, but of course all good qualities are unavailing. I have been through this sort of thing so often myself that I suppose there's little in your experience that I haven't had over and over. What's worst, I think, is the grovelling, low as dirt purgatorial feelings with which one emerges. If you have such feelings, let me promise you that they are temporary. What looks as though it were simply you, and therefore would never pass does turn out to be not you and will pass.

Please let me tell you how much I admire you and your work and thank you for the many times when you have given me the strength to continue. Let me know if there's anything I can do. And *courage*, old Friend!

Affectionately,

Cal

456. To William Doreski

May 4, 1965

Dear William—

You need to pay more attention to the way your images interact. The poem beginning with "Altars rest among the weeds" begins strongly, but declines into a rather hazy abstraction through the middle, then finishes strong with a fine image which has nothing to do with the rest of the poem. All of the poems suffer to some degree from this disorganization.

I think you will become more catholic in your reading. Merwin isn't just

gimmicky, although he's heavily mannered. Not quite the same. Bly is less promising, to me. He is sensitive, politically, but treats language like a pair of someone else's shoes.

I would be happy to see you in New York. We could easily supply you with shelter for a few days. If you could come the first week in September perhaps we could pick you up on the way from Maine and drive you down. You could take the train, or fly, home. Don't feel shy about staying with us, please. I would enjoy talking to you at length.

Yours,
Robert Lowell

457. To Lyndon B. Johnson

May 30, 1965

Dear President Johnson:

When I was telephoned last week and asked to read at the White House Festival of the Arts on June fourteenth, I am afraid I accepted somewhat rapidly and greedily. I thought of such an occasion as a purely artistic flourish, even though every serious artist knows that he cannot enjoy public celebrations without making subtle public commitments. After a week's wondering, I have decided that I am conscience-bound to refuse your courteous invitation. I do so now in a public letter because my acceptance has been announced in the newspapers, and because of the strangeness of the Administration's recent actions.

Although I am very enthusiastic about most of your domestic legislation and intentions, I nevertheless can only follow our present foreign policy with the greatest dismay and distrust. What we will do and what we ought to do as a sovereign nation facing other sovereign nations seems now to hang in the balance between the better and the worse possibilities. We are in danger of imperceptibly becoming an explosive and suddenly chauvinistic nation, and may even be drifting on our way to the last nuclear ruin. I know it is hard for the responsible man to act; it is also painful for the private and irresolute man to dare criticism. At this anguished, delicate and perhaps determining moment, I feel I am serving you and our country best by not taking part in the White House Festival of the Arts.

Respectfully yours,
Robert Lowell

458. To W. F. van Leeuwen

June 17, 1965

Dear Huyck:

Here I am rereading your letter that stirs up so many thoughts just as we are about to drive off for Maine. I see, alas, we've done nothing about getting in touch with the de Groots. I hope they'll still be here next fall. "Driving to Maine," I wonder if I wrote you that your stop with us in Iowa made a small revolution in my life. Almost immediately, I brushed up on my driving and bought a nineteen year old Packard. I hadn't driven for more than ten years after having a messy accident with my first wife.

A Dutch review, probably Judith's, arrived from Faber and Faber the other day, but the last part was on someone else and clipped away so I couldn't find the signature. The one on *Imitations* was read to me and I admired and was grateful.

How have the years gone? I really can't say whether well or ill. A bit of both. Every year or two, I have a breakdown and am in a sanitarium for about a month, never much more. Often there are girls or a girl, and it's all messy and hard as hell on Lizzie. Then there is a lot of wear and tear and rocks to life at best. Still we are rather deeply happy together and have a lovely, boisterous eight year old child. I teach and have written more in the last few years than all the earlier ones. After awhile, one feels familiar with life's joys and pains. They are old friends. I think I know that that's what we are here for, and not to discover some allegorical key that doesn't exist.

We were in Egypt shortly before you were in Palestine, a ghastly unforgettable country. The delta looks superficially much like Holland, green, flat, canals, but all about it is the desert dust and in it poverty, mud brick villages, waterwheels, colorful water buffalo. The habitable area is much the same, but there are thirty million people. Maybe modern western life spoils us, for Egypt once the pride of civilization, must have always been this way, and though the talk is all about the advances of Nasser and socialism, one thinks nothing will move much. Maybe the old fixed art will return and repeat itself for another four or six thousand years. The people had a pleasing, passive sophisticated gentleness, particularly the ones who had been moved from houses to apartments and yearned for the Oxford and Paris they could no longer visit. Meanwhile plans, parades, police, worthy motives, inefficiency, rasping anti-Israelism, hot arguments about classical and spoken Arabic, gloomy, probably provincial circles of the Writers' Union. America after that seemed fearfully solvent and tough and rough, but thank God with a varied landscape.

I feel blue about this country's future.[. . .]

We have been bad correspondents, but you and Judith are ever in our minds and we keep promising ourselves a return to Amsterdam. Someday, not far off I hope, we will turn up with Harriet and renew the years. The Richs and Jarrells speak of the great happiness they had with you, so we don't feel far away.

Our love to you both,

Cal

459. To Stanley Kunitz

Castine, Maine
August 16, 1965

Dear Stanley:

You've been in my mind a lot—sorely missed, but somehow the flood of letters about the White House has left me not even answering personal letters. Wasn't the "Dover Beach" grotesque? Some one from the *Times* called me at eleven thirty after a party and asked me if the lines were mine. All I could think of were the words "world" and "before" and I said, "Oh no, they are by John Milton." Teddy Kennedy stopped here with a group of young friends mostly congressmen and Phil Booth who had found them a mooring, had me over to meet them. I felt like a white raccoon. Ah youth that runs the world!

Glad you liked my poem. I really felt through, and was dawdling and diddling away without fire at my Eumenides when it seized me. I'd have felt a terrible fraud, if I hadn't tried. Since then I've done another long poem, but lower-keyed in the same meter, and a short piece I think good. An ill summer for the native here, but lovely for the vacationer. We've played tennis every day, and Harriet, rather a tough, has begun sailing lessons, and knows many knots, the five parts of a sail and many things I never learned and Liz can't even follow. Congratulations, dear friend, on your birthday. At our age, it would be consoling to believe in repentance, reformation and eternal life, like the Catholics. Well, we've all remained pretty hail and should rejoice.

Love to you both, we'll be back around the tenth. This has been a good summer, but oh God how it has whizzed by!

Cal

460. To Robert Graves

<div align="right">

15 West 67 St.
N.Y.C.
Oct. 6, 1965

</div>

Dear Robert:

I meant to write you long ago to say that I was bowled over (not surprised) by your fine poems in the *New Statesman*—great power with a kind of charm and easy impertinence, that are yours to command perhaps, but always a miracle when you really catch fire. This is heavily put. Your marvelous cough poem comes back to me now, my chest congested and recovering from flu.

Yours with warmth and admiration as ever,
Robert Lowell

461. To J. F. Powers

<div align="right">

Oct. 6, 1965

</div>

Dear Jim:

Coming back here from Maine and finding a mountain of old magazines waiting, ready to divert from the toils of getting settled, about the first thing I read was your wonderful review in *Commentary*. I don't see how it could be stronger or clearer, yet without purple patches or hysteria. It should be a classic, and I think could only be written by a Catholic. Now it brings back my own experiences, searching for authorities on just and unjust wars. I can't kick at the difficulty of the definition—life is that difficult, and absolute pacifism seems possible to few, and usually under conditions that make it either easy or inconsequential—only I think that it ought to [be] assumed that many or most wars are unjust, and that just wars have a habit too of deteriorating and changing. Anyway there ought to be an unrelenting chaos of people kicking against wars, people frequently risking and giving their lives to prevent or soften wars. Well, we risked little, and we had little help from either our society, American priests, or the vague sublimities of Pius XII.

It's your first statement I can think of on this business, and that's right. One must speak and not make a career of it. You may have heard about my White House business. Nothing I've ever done had such approval, and I've been plagued ever since to sound off on Viet Nam programs till I wish I could

go to sleep for a 100 years like Rip van Winkle. Well, I'm just writing to say I admire and sympathize with you. Such things keep the air breathable. Perhaps they give us a little iron and kindness. I gather you are at another novel— wonderful! We miss seeing you and Betty.

Affectionately,
Cal

462. To Eleanor Ross Taylor

October 6, 1965

Dear Eleanor:

Good talking to you. When I called the Jarrells, Randall had gone to the hospital. Mary was cheerful about things in general, but I think maybe she takes a different line with me than with you and Lizzie. Poor Dear Randall, I feel he is our own special thorn and pearl, vexing and noble beyond any of our acquaintance! He's had a hell year. May it be over.

Liked "Victory" in the *Kenyon* tremendously. I wouldn't have thought so much could have gotten through except in a short story, and of course it would have had the same easy fibre of concentration. You really are one of the best poets writing, and have your old special voice, subject, cadence etc. but I think with a new directness.

Our love to you and Peter,
Cal

463. To Elizabeth Bishop

[n.d. October 18 or 19?, 1965]

My Dearest Elizabeth,

I imagine you may have heard by now of Randall's death. He was under-going treatment of an injured wrist at Chapel Hill, and "lunged" in front of a car on a main highway near a bypass. He had a bottle of pain-killer in his pocket. I've just come from the funeral and must soon leave for Harvard. I'll write you soon in detail. It cannot be told for certain whether the death was suicide or an accident. I think suicide, but I'm not sure, and Mary's version, the official version, is accident. All heart-breaking and ghastly. Poor Dear, he wanted to take care of himself! I'm Desolate. He was starting on a review of

your book, very enthusiastic, but I think got nothing written. I know he thought "Manuelzinho" a masterpiece.

My dearest one, please take care of yourself. All my love,
Cal

P.S. I should know in a couple of weeks whether the Rockefeller grants are going to be continued. If they are I feel almost certain you will get one.

464. To Elizabeth Bishop

October 28, 1965

Dearest Elizabeth:

It was fun looking up echolalia (again) chromograph, gesso, and road-stead—they all meant pretty much what I thought. Oh and taboret, an object I've known all my life, but not the name. All the poems are good and the book reads with the steady excellence of some perfect short story, say my beloved "Coeur Simple." "Santos" gains a lot by being the opening door to the Brazilian section. My favorites are "Brazil"—how I envy the historical stretch at the end, so beautifully coming out of the vegetation—"Manuelzinho" a dazzling masterpiece—"Armadillo"—how proud and swell-headed I am about the dedication, one of your absolutely top poems, your greatest quatrain poem, I mean it has a wonderful formal-informal grandeur—I see the bomb in it in a delicate way—"The Riverman," a sort of forsaken Merman, and a very powerful initiation poem that somehow echoes your own entrance in Santos—"Twelfth Morning" has lovely, strange touches—"The Burglar" ballad is a special poem, and gives a huge sweep of Rio, and again though a true narrative and ballad tells a lot about your own judgments on your society, obliquely—"Death in Nova Scotia" haunts me (It was weird this summer when I drove through New Brunswick and Nova Scotia on a short salmon fishing trip, to see everywhere the pale Maple Leaf Flag, more like (and pleasantly at last) a boy scout flag than a nation's—embittered anglophiles still fly the old Union Jack[)]—the poem is doubly provincial and remote, in time, the Prince of Wales and all, and in place, very sad and lovely—"Filling Station," just as good I think, one of your best "awful but cheerful" poems—"Trollope," the more I read it the more I think he was right about Washington—at first I took the poem as a spoof at the superficial condescending Englishman—by the way your rhythm and riming are extraordinary, and of course unobtrusive— then Ezra is marvelous, you get bits of your old monument in it, nicely, and the

whole is a success against every impossibility. By the way I am talking on the educational TV with Marianne Moore about Pound for his 80th birthday. He seems to be completely sane now. You were very right to put your story in, it's one of your finest poems, and bridges the two sections. I rather wish you'd thrown all, or almost all, your stories in, even though it would have made jags in the book's pattern.

The Randall business is very awful. Did I tell you his wrist injury was from putting his hand through a window last spring, though no one knows this. There was also a girl (late thirties) that Hannah met at Goucher College in Baltimore. (No one else knows this.) He finally wrote to her that he couldn't cope with life unless he went home to Mary. He should have had a doctor who made clear to him that getting over his manic depressive attack had nothing to do with returning to his wife—my doctor has always made that point, even to the extreme of once several years ago letting me go from the hospital to an apartment where I went on with my affair, and then went back to Lizzie, knowing that I really wanted to in my soul's center. Of course the new girl would probably have been like Randall's other wives, but she might have tided him back to health. Nothing on earth can be as bad as ending your own life—I mean medically not morally—except murder. Well, and there was a bang up quarrel with Mary just before he went to the hospital for the last time, not mental but to have ice treatments on his wrist, made much worse by an unsuccessful operation in September. There's a small chance of accident—he was planning to have dinner with his step-daughter the next day, had begun teaching, had written one or two people that he was well and writing again, and had notes on a review of your poems which he was very keen on. In his pocket a bottle of demerol, pain-killer, that might have fuzzed his senses. I think it was suicide, and so does every one else, who knew him well. Hannah said to me, "What is so awful was that it was so fitting." Mary was in California when he died, and didn't drive him to the hospital, the Taylors didn't think she was coming back. They are very bitter. Mary's story, of is that he was well, and had only temporarily turned on her in his manic state—no one knows about the suicide attempt, and she insists that the death was an accident—naturally I guess. He seems to have been begging her for a divorce, *before* he was sick last fall. I want to stay out of it all. I've just written a ten page memorial and eloge for the *Review* which I'll have them mail you, and which I hope you'll like. His worst flaw was forcing his wives into becoming false assents to himself, agreeing on everything, having the same critical opinions etc. making them dishonest, as one of his poems even says. When Peter called up Mackie, she was astonished that Randall had ever been

sick, then she said, "This may sound strange, but I think this means more to you than it does to me." She meant Randall's death, not his illness. Oh but he was an absolutely gifted, and noble man, poisoned and killed, though I can't prove it, by our tasteless, superficial, brutal culture.

Dear Heart, I see you've had another *golpe*—unhappy Americas, unhappy world! Hope, there's nothing ominous for you and Lota.

All my love,

Cal

What a full and glorious book, even grander than I foresaw, thinking of the poems in ones and twos. There are marvelous things in poems I haven't mentioned—I think particularly of the title poem.

465. *To Stephen Spender,* Encounter

[n.d. late February 1966]

Dear Stephen:

Please substitute this for my earlier rhetorical diatribe on this subject. Thanks for your very kind remarks on the Blunden business. The whole thing is a marvelous English comedy. I guess I would feel quite remorseful, if I'd won out. Hope to see you here soon.

Affectionately,

Cal

NABOKOV'S ONEGIN

I suppose every translator dreams of writing a version that will stand on its own feet, new, important, and yet relentlessly loyal to its original. In poetry this is almost impossible, and perhaps even in prose. Something very odd and catching has happened in Nabokov's *Onegin*, or so it seems to the reader with no Russian. Maybe a merely literal and literate prose reproduction rightly struck Nabokov as an appallingly commonplace assignment, and a stifling test for his zany genius. What he has written is a weirdly eccentric minor English poem, one that suggests that Pushkin's *Onegin* is not, as everyone claims, a national classic, but some wildly queer miscarriage, like Marvell's "Appleton House," a poem whose idiosyncratic freshness is so peculiar that it reduces the translator often to a stutter of whimsicality and gristle. It's as though Nabokov swore to be faithful, and then felt that faithfulness would only bring him one of those coarse plaster busts of Homer, that doom of the usual conscientious

translator. And aren't there dark moments when almost anyone suspects that most of the official classics are plaster busts? Yet both commonsense and intuition tell us that Edmund Wilson must be nine-tenths unanswerable and right in his criticism of Nabokov. The long arguments about Russian gerunds, the devious dictionary meanings of English and Russian words etc. cannot conceal what is obvious, that Nabokov's *Onegin* is really, and perhaps only half intentionally, a spoof at its readers, rival translators, Pushkin, and Nabokov himself.

Robert Lowell

466. To Elizabeth Bishop

February 25, 1966

Dearest Elizabeth:

Wonderful your letters are pouring out again. I had terrible pictures of you despondent and lost in the new toil of teaching—lonely, cold at sea. Lizzie taught last term at Barnard for the first time in her life. Her first comment was "the students aren't very good, but I am." She gave them various non-fiction books such as Levi-Strauss and *In the American Grain* and found them agape. Then they almost all wrote *A* papers, and she got quite enthused, had another offer from Bryn Mawr and got her Barnard salary raised. Then you can now teach probably almost anywhere, more or less on your own terms, and a year here might be a pleasant change for you and Lota. New cars are cheaper.

You are too good as always about my writing. I've just been through agonies hammering out a three page introduction to Sylvia Plath. I think it does now, but the first few drafts were beneath any of my graduate student papers. No, I am laborious, too much like everyone else, and a bit harsh and perverse. While you . . . Your book is another species from most everything else. I think even the reviewers now see that there's no one, except Marianne Moore at all comparable to you. I guess I struck Roethke under a bit more favorable circumstance. I mean last year when I came to Seattle, I was to give the Roethke Memorial reading and had worked myself into the proper state of awe. I gave a Yeats reading at Columbia at about the same, and my head rang with resonance, all of which may show in the long metered Marvell couplet thing I wrote all last summer. Ted's ~~worth~~ worst fault was a sort of tender hard-heartedness, too great a wish to be big, so that much of the poetry is a little dead under the ringing cadences. But then he really was big and it took great courage to burn out with such a big flare—nothing much left then to his body, and very like a drunken baby to meet here on visits.

Bobby Kennedy never showed up for the dinner, but Jackie did, full of wild vignettes spoken in her breathless, almost parody voice. I thought Lizzie was horrified and discovered she was charmed. Once in a blue moon—I thought this about Alice Longworth—someone from the grand world is really delightful. Sometimes, I think I would die, if it weren't for a few platonic relations with women. Adrienne Rich used to come out twice a week to see me in the Boston hospital, and a couple of hours would whirl by in what seemed like a few minutes of talk.

I have a formidable new doctor, Kurt Eissler, sounding (I mean just his name) like a Nazi in a film, and of course out of Germany with forty volume sets of Goethe, Wieland etc. and books of his own on Goethe, Genius and Environment, Depression etc. Maybe I'll get well, this doctor is the first I've had who is really much like an artist, though it took several days for us to speak a language intelligible to the other.

I pray you get the National Book Award. Did you say the day was the fifth? I don't leave for Florida till the 10th. You must stay with us. You wouldn't know us, we are so soften[ed] by our doctors and guinea pigs. When we drink together, we talk about how well we get on, squeaks in the background, even splintering hopping sounds from our little laconic bird, long angora (pig) hairs on the sofa, now sinking into fluff from Harriet's turns on it.

Do tell Reed to come and see us. He must have saved your heart in exile. What a difference an intelligent voice makes. Our Guadeloupe beach was restoring, but one felt stupider than the stupidest tourist—and was!

All my love,
Cal

467. To Robert F. Kennedy

Feb. 25, 1966

Dear Senator Kennedy:

I see Pushkin goes far beyond Shelley, who only called poets "the *unacknowledged* legislators of mankind." Alas, I am fairly blessed with the things of this world, am hungry for fame, and nobody has ever bowed down to me. Still, unlike the dervish, I do have a country. It was very gentle of you to write me in long hand, and to struggle with the elements to make Blair's dinner. Your presence was in the wings, and we sorely missed you. I trust our meeting will come about.

I have always been fascinated by poets like Wyatt and Ralegh, who also are statesmen and show a double inspiration—the biggest of these must be

Dante, who ruled Florence for a moment, and would never have written about Farinata and Manfredi without this experience. Larger parts of the Commedia are almost a Ghibelline epic. Then there are those wonderful statesmen, like Lincoln and Edmund Burke, who were also great writers.

Well, I do think you are putting into practice that kind of courage and ability that your Brother so subtly praised in his *Profiles*, and know how to be brave without becoming simple-minded. What more could one ask for in my slothful, wondering profession?

Yours sincerely,
Robert Lowell

468. To Ezra Pound

March 8, 1966

Dear Ezra:

Olga was kind enough to send me a tape of your reading of my "Brunetto." I must say your voice stays in my head constantly and that the lines really sound like Dante, like you and Dante, so much that I now think of them as yours. I've been doing a little piece on Ford's last poems, and you have been much in mind—I think of you both as comrades and travellers on the long shining road from Provence to pre-War London.

I follow the news of you and read your rare public statements. I think you rather stand alone in facing those purgatorial moments we all face and don't, the good and ill of our lives—you do it with glorious humor and sorrow. Hope to get to Italy sometime and renew the years with you.

Affectionately,
Cal

P.S. The Dante took me about a month of hard work. Sometime in some pause in my life and time, I'd like to do ten or so more. May the gods go with you and all your family!

469. To John Berryman

March 10, 1966

Dear John:

This is really just to say that I love you, and wonder at you, and want you

to take care. Your reminiscences of Randall were the height of the evening, and seemed for a moment to lift away all the glaze and constraints, that dog us, and yet it was all in order. All so like what you have done in your poetry, freedom for us too, if we had the nerve.

I felt a whole generation was taking a bow to Randall, some to the work, others to the discerning disturbing courage, so often trampling on the mediocre, in order to truthfully stand up for the good—the boldest and most brilliant spokesman for our common profession. The evening at Princeton comes back—I had blacked out the imitation Lowell poems, but that too comes back—two race-horses, I guess three, and all of us secretly uneasy. In the sand-colored hard interior of the train home, I remember putting my coat over Randall, who was shivering, and feeling some crisis had passed.

Let me beg you to take care of yourself. You must be physically fragile. If anything happened to you, I'd feel the heart of the scene had gone. Our love to you and Kate.

Cal

470. To Olga Rudge

May 6, 1966

Dear Olga:

Here I am back, almost as high as at Rapallo, but looking out on the rooftops and water towers of New York, worlds and worlds away. I would be much honored if you will accept the enclosed check. Ezra seemed so convinced that he was eating into your savings, and this might cancel some of the winter's expenses.

I had a good talk with Ezra, though everything I said seemed fuzzy and platitudinous after the crisp carving of his scattered sentences. I tried to tell him that he was about the only man alive who had lived through Purgatory, and come through white with a kind of honesty and humility. So, so—he was the most awesome encounter I had in Italy, and somehow wonderfully the same and wiser than when I used to go to St. Elizabeths. So much owing to you.

I won't bore you with more, but want to thank you for your courtesy and hospitality. I'm afraid I rudely stayed through the siesta hour.

Yours,
Cal

471. To Edmund Blunden

Castine, Maine
June 25, 1966

Dear Edmund Blunden:

Many thanks for your letter. I've admired your poetry for years, and rather felt as though an old friend were being set against me, when the controversy began to boil. I really should have withdrawn, when you were entered, but somehow didn't through inertia. The lectures too would have been a problem. Criticism comes slowly and imperfectly to me. Something might have come, but who knows? I hope you will find pleasure in the work you are bound to do with distinction. May cheerfulness set in immediately!

I trust someday we will meet, and maybe read poems together.

Yours sincerely,
 Robert Lowell

472. To Elizabeth Bishop

July 16, 1966

Dearest Elizabeth,

It seems months and months since I've written you, and it is, though we've talked on the phone, and you seemed during your Washington months close in a way . . . a visit, but one I almost missed. I have a guilty feeling of almost having let something die—in me, I guess. Do you have moments of relaxing, or relaxing to let in life, that may be a letting go.

All this comes to me on a clear day, bush and grass in the sun, bush and grass in the shadow, the sea high, like a lake shore, a few feet off now from my window. For about a month, ever since coming here, I have been working steadily on an expanded prose version of the *Prometheus*. Now a first full draft is done, almost seventy pages, and I wonder why I buried myself in it so, five days a week, and sometimes six. Can any truth come through the old Greek plot, the few, ever-recurring grand words? Somehow though, I find myself in a rut, where it's easier to write than not to. Oh to break away for months! (and sometimes I feel very tired, in a not quite physical way,) find ways to dream—I am always dreaming inside myself—do nothing! And I do, but am made glazed, stiff and nervous by the near at hand. I have been thinking of Whitman's huge sweep, mostly in his thirties and forties, lines pouring out, a hundred poems a

year, yet with long, idle afternoons of sauntering, chatting, at ease nearly with what the eye fell on.

A couple of days ago Delmore Schwartz died from a heart-attack, just outside his room in a cheap New York hotel—alone, out of touch, for a year, a shadow, a rumor seen here and there, gone underground, after he vanished and hid from Syracuse University, angry he hadn't been given tenure. Maybe the heat killed him; the death rate has risen lately in New York, but really his end was in the cards for long, too much drinking, a paranoia that cut him off from jobs, even friends—for a day, there was no one to claim the body. I think back on the time, when Caroline Gordon said, "This is the one mature young man I've ever met." This hurt me, but I felt dismissed with a great swarm of other young men. And it seemed true in a way. *In Dreams Begin Responsibilities* had just come out, and reasonable, intuitive essays, the old new criticism, but with a new touch, in all the Quarterlies. He was much more bruised and swollen, when I knew him well, an intimate gruelling year, a year or so before you and I met—Jean and he and I, sedentary, indoors souls, talking about books and literary gossip over glasses of milk, strengthened with Maine vodka, the milk intended to restore what the vodka tore down—Delmore in an unpressed mustard gabardine, a little winded, husky voiced, unhealthy, but with a carton of varied vitamin bottles, the color of oil, quickening with Jewish humor, and in-the-knowness, and his own genius, every person, every book— motives for everything, Freud in his blood, great webs of causation, then suspicion, then rushes of rage. He was more reasonable than us, but obsessed, a much better mind, but one already chasing the dust—it was like living with a sluggish, sometimes angry spider—no hurry, no motion, Delmore's voice, almost inaudible, dead, intuitive, pointing somewhere, then the strings tightening, the roar of rage—too much, too much for us! Nothing haunts me more than breaking with friends, I used to think he was the only one I broke with.

Are you glad to be back in Rio, or are you up in the hills? I feel I had a hand in your going to Seattle, though I didn't really, and didn't suggest it. It must have been trying and empty a lot of the time, but aren't you glad—I sound like my Mother—that now you know how simple teaching is, that you can always fall back on it? Write soon and tell me about yourself, what you did then, what you are doing now. Are you and Lota going to Italy this fall? We may go to Spain next summer. Lizzie is at work on two books, one we are supposed to do together, a high school English and world literature text-book for Harcourt Brace, the other hers, a book on poverty from five or six parts of the country, helped out with a tape-recorder. She has been going shyly and

sharply around with it, no, mostly shy, to our local figures, the laundress, the caretaker's widow, Phil Booth—hard to unearth the Maine poor, or rather open them up, for they are everywhere. When the debris is finally sorted, I think she will have something brilliant, but starting is hard. I am dying to hear more of and see your Brazilian book. I suppose life is at our fingertips, millions talking prose all their lives, if one could only, not gather, but arrange it!

I miss you so much, Dear, and feel a third of me is dead, when we stop writing.

Our love to you and dear Lota, all mine to you!

Cal

P.S. I don't know when this will arrive, all the air lines, except, oddly enough, Maine's eccentric North East, are on strike.

473. To James Laughlin

August 31, 1966

Dear J:

Let's get together in New York. The visit to Ezra was awesome and rather shattering, like meeting Oedipus—he said, "I began with a swelled head and am ending with swelled feet." And many other things, then long stretches of silence. He is very worried that he is using up Olga's money. He has a nobility I've never seen before, the nobility of some one, not a sinner, but who has gone far astray and learned at last too much. I told him he was one of the few men alive who had the courage to go through Purgatory. He answered, "Didn't Frost say you'd say anything once?" I felt I was talking cant, when I tried to cheer him. No self-pity, but more knowledge of his fate than any man should have. I wonder if he could make a trip here, but I gather he changes from week to week. I'll feel out Harvard, though I have no real position there. I named him for the national gold medal, but no other nominator backed me. He deserves some fine act of homage, but who will make it?

Ah Delmore! He has been in my mind all summer, though we hadn't been close for years. Still the old is always there, those shining humorous early days—all good sense and all promess! I think much of this lasted in flashes, mostly with young acquaintances in bars.

Yours as always,

Cal

474. To Elizabeth Bishop

<div align="right">
15 West 67th Street

New York, NY

September 15, 1966
</div>

Dearest Elizabeth:

What's up? It seems almost a year since I've had anything in writing from you. I spent a summer almost without event or narrative: work through the day, two hours of doubles, evenings at home or with our undrama-torn Castine friends, though no one is untorn. I can think of almost nothing. In midsummer, following my desire and ignoring my better judgment, I went to a birthday party for Jackie Kennedy—white turrety inn building at Cotuit, rooms rented for the guests by our hostess Mrs. Paul Mellon, through the afternoon glimpses of what must be fellow guests, women with hair a foot high, smiles but no introductions, information that the launch would arrive for us at eight, that we could have a free drink, or drinks, a solitary swim—water after the ice of Maine—a solitary dull drive through Cotuit, return to assembling and drinking guests, the nearest I came to knowing any were Mike Nichols, Charles Addams, and Jerome Robbins—most of them were people like Forestall's son, Paley, the CBS President, people with names like big figures in news, business or politics, but often not related, or poor cousins. Launch with champagne in paper cups, harbor boat pacing our boat, wonderful sunset over Cotuit accredited to Mrs. Mellon's plans—then landing, swarms of new known-unknowns with lanterns, big tent, air of very expensive rustic simplicity. Hours of waiting, feeling that no one was known from our world to any of the other guests except Mike Nichols. Air of drama and waiting for Jackie, the chartered plane (chartered by my old friend Blair Clark[)], for Lillian Hellman and the Styrons. After a while, Jackie suddenly present and talking to Mike Nichols, Hellman group there, both senator Kennedys, McNamara. Later, a luxuriously simple dinner, all I can remember are blood-red lamb chops, Mike Nichols next to Jackie, later, middle-aged people dancing the new dances, not very wildly, but too young for me, a slightly tawdry untimely Marie Antoinette feeling of a festival when the age for being whole-hearted about such things has passed, the flash of the jet-set, a little lurid and in bad taste in a world of poverty and blood, a certain real ease—meeting with McNamara, Jackie putting her hand over my mouth and telling me to be polite and I saying something awkward about liking him, but not his policy, then Jackie saying "how impossibly banal, you should say you adore his pol-

icy, but find him dull." Few minutes talk with Styron and me arguing with McNamara, no great impact on either side, except that McNamara seemed a simple brilliant administrative soul, who [had] given little thought to moral complications, and who might have even taken the usual liberal line against Viet Nam more easily than I would. The party didn't get into the news, but somehow a month later, a gossip column in Norfolk Virginia reported that I stayed up till five with McNamara and we had gotten on famously, and the columnist hoped I'd learned something—all non-sense. A vague feeling of a heterogeneous opposition to Johnson group. The most interesting person to talk to was Bobby Kennedy, but like Carlos, there is a scary feeling of ambition and power about him, along with frankness. Well, next day, driving rather dull and stunned to Provincetown and the Stanley Kunitzes, I was parked in traffic, looking at a road-map to find some less travelled road, something more like the backwater of Castine, when suddenly I moved forward with a jolt, found the car had stopped, a hole through the windshield a little of my hair in the spider web of smashed glass, the car no longer able to move. The car ahead of me wasn't damaged, no blood drawn from me, though $500 injury to my car, paid by Hertz insurance. After hours of waiting, papers, police, a wrecker, I am off to Provincetown in an *Avis* car—the Hertz and Avis booths touched each other and I was at both, making out accident papers at one, and car-rental papers at the other. Two days later I had to appear at the Barnstable Court for inattentive driving, a roomful of indicted, adolescent carelessness, I by now in fear of losing my license, taking from my pocket a birthday poem written by William Jay Smith to Francis Biddle, beginning "In life's great court all men are judged." Relief. I plead "Nolo [contendere]," and get a twenty-five dollar fine. That night I lectured at Harvard on the dead, Randall, Roethke and Delmore Schwartz, and reflected that I myself might have been dead without even knowing it. Then home and back to work. In the course of the summer, I have finished *Prometheus* at last—how like him I felt as I labored on interminably—and my new book of poems heavily revised.

Now Harriet's school, my teaching and everything is starting. It's exhilarating to be still alive. Hope you will do something on Randall, the deadline has been pushed forward to May. And do write.

All our love to you and Lota,
Cal

P.S. Forgive me for sending off this little gulp of incident. If I waited for a second wind to go on, it might be days.

475. To John Berryman

YOUR POSTHUMOUS POEMS ARE A TREMENDOUS AND LIVING TRI-
UMPH LOVE
 CAL

476. To Ted Hughes

October 8, 1966

Dear Ted:

I think I would like to come to the festival. We may be here in Spain, so the expense wouldn't be great, though I'd like the fifty additional pounds. You have a fine roster. When I came before, the readings were fun, but a little rushed and ragged, but London was glorious. You will give the thing great distinction.

Oh, I don't think Sylvia's book, and even things like her legend and the *Time* Magazine story have hurt anyone. I wondered whether I shouldn't have been more impersonal in my introduction, and then decided every reader would already know at least as much as I let out. It must be maddening to run into pseudo-Sylvia's, like the pseudo Dylan Thomases, but that's no one's fault. I do hope the rest of her poems will be published. Certainly the Napoleon and Lesbos ones are tops. I don't know how to say this and may be on the wrong track, but I feel the whole thing is terrible for you, almost a dying twice, or a prolonging of the dying, though it's really consoling that the poems are there. I'd know at times that I would wish they were at the sea's bottom. Let me say that I love and admire you, but you don't need testimonials.

Affectionately,
 Cal

I've just finished a version of *Prometheus*, all my own, that somehow seems like both a triumph and a fake.

477. To Daniel Berrigan

Dear Father Daniel Berrigan:

I have been going through your manuscript with great interest and enthusiasm. I don't think, though, that I should write a preface. Mostly, I am afraid of spreading myself thin, of finding myself sounding off on all sorts of things I am not an authority on. I'd be coals to Newcastle too, a lapsed Catholic and C.O. giving you a puff. I was telling Arthur Schlesinger the other night that I liked his anti–Viet Nam article, and he said "your approval is all I need to really make me with Johnson."

Your whole line stirs many thoughts. I don't think we can look on war and poverty as people have for ages. I am teaching the Bible (just as writing, but I constantly stray into forbidden waters) at Harvard now. Well, it's troubling how much of it's inspired by a war society, and a slave society. Particularly war. It's easy to call the figures mere metaphors, but they are real enough— Jaweh is a war-god whatever else he is. Well, I'm not naïve, all societies were like that then, and I like all the ragbag of anthropology and oddity and brutality—one of the great moments is Deborah's song. And how dull an ethical, cleaned-up Bible would be! Still, as a model, though it's an advantage to be able to look at it a-squint and interpret for one's self! As a model, in this century of God's absence and the Church or churches' absence! As you may guess, I've just been reading Bonhoeffer, who seems often so much like you in feeling and situation, though not in thought. It was fun too coming on your thoughts under such heading as Belem, São Paulo, places we went to one summer three years ago. I thought at times more concrete detail would help, but this might spoil the rhythm of your speculation. Bonhoeffer, in one of his letters, says that Christ seemed like a man, while John the Baptist to his disadvantage, somehow seemed like a cleric. Well, I think you are a very brave and lively man. I am really surprised you haven't gotten into even more trouble than you have. Let's try and have an evening together sometime this fall. Forgive this tumbling note. I am gathering myself for my weekly trip to Harvard.

Yours as always,

Robert

478. *To the Editors,* Partisan Review

[n.d. Fall 1966]

1. Yes, nothing could matter more than who is in the White House. It's not like the arts. Two very foolish novelists with opposed beliefs or temperaments would write equally foolish novels, but two equally foolish presidents would have widely differing effects on our lives, the difference between life and death. Yet a great president somehow honors his country, even if what he effects is debatable. I suppose Lincoln was our most noble and likeable president. The country is somehow finer for having had him, yet much that he accomplished was terrifying and might have been avoided by the run-of-the-mill Douglas. I wish Stevenson had been elected. Maybe he would have done nothing (I don't believe this) but at least he would have registered what he was doing. I can't imagine him not losing a night's sleep over Hiroshima, even if he did drop the bomb. I think he might not have.

2. Inflation is over my head, but I think we can never again forget poverty. Man throughout time has been very lighthearted about poverty in a way that we can never, with decency, be again.

3. I don't know what the split between the President and the intellectuals *means.* Something very horrifying about our country has been brought home to us. I don't know how profound this is, or how much it is a passing twinge of remorse, how much is due to Johnson and how much was almost inevitable with almost any president. We've swallowed worse things than Vietnam, yet it's hopeful that we are now appalled. We may be going through a deep change of heart as to what can be allowed to nation-states, or maybe our present mood is only a sort of temporary, superficial and hangover "profundity."

4. As far as honor goes, I think white America is committed to granting equality to the Negro. How much equality actually will be granted is another darker and unanswerable question.

5. I think our foreign policies are quite likely leading us to the third and worst world war, not right away probably, but over a stretch of time, within twenty or thirty years. When we have said the worst we can about our American foreign policy, and I think as citizens we must say this, still it must be admitted that the future

depends on other countries besides ourselves. Who can be happy, when he looks at the great contenders?

6. I have mostly answered this question. I have a gloomy premonition though that we will soon look back on this troubled moment as a golden time of freedom and license to act and speculate. One feels the steely sinews of the tiger, an ascetic, "moral" and authoritarian reign of piety and iron.

7. Doom or promise must be found in youth. I think perhaps the young hope for things that neither we nor any previous generation dared hope for. But how much like us, and what a slender reed, they often seem!

479. *To Mary McCarthy*

November 19, 1966

My dear Mary:

I'm afraid I never write you, because of realizing I ought to write you something worth saying, then the muse brings nothing very amusing to mind. I haven't even thanked you and Jim for the lovely pendules (?), which now hang over our fireplace. What are they? What were they?

I liked your Burnett very much, much what I think if I had a gift for words. I've just finished a play (I now have the formula for my stuff) a play "based on" Aeschylus's *Prometheus*, about twice as long as the Greek, and in prose. And my *Dies irae* to a *PR* questionnaire on the state of the nation. It's getting pretty scary, but we with talents and souls seem to like one another better than usual.

Liz and I will be in Germany for a couple of weeks from mid-January till the end, then later about mid-March, I'll be in London for a performance of my Benito at the Mermaid. Maybe that would be the best time to see you. You might like seeing the play. My friend, Jonathan Miller, will be directing. He did a miraculous job here.

Oh me, I'm teaching the Bible as writing at Harvard, a virgin field, and what things I read! Meyer Schapiro said a group of Jewish children read the Book of Joshua in Israel, and then similar goy atrocities through the ages. And were asked if they approved of Joshua, then if they approved of all the others, or none. Most approved of Joshua, more than half approved of all, and a small minority of none. This seemed to prove that reading the Bible was a dubious

moral adventure. Then what can one make of Revelations, a non-naturalistic masterpiece, that Susan Sontag would approve of, and what hideous morality. The Bible world is almost as bloody as ours—more instructive than all the theologians. Don't suppose your Catholic Childhood ever exposed you to it.

Miss you and Jim terribly, and trust will have a reunion before many months roll by. By the way have you seen Hannah's Brecht, marvelous and marvelous to quote German poetry without translation in the *New Yorker*. But don't you think he might have written nothing of importance in East Berlin, because he was old and interested in his theater? Did the old Wordsworth sin against the poetic holy ghost, or was he just old and exhausted? Hannah is really a Hebrew prophetess, a sort of Prussian Deborah. Still, I guess she's close to being the moral heart of the country.

Poor Philip is having high blood pressure, very somber about it. Meyer Schapiro said Philip was like a heavy-weight boxer, who thought no one was a boxer at all that didn't weigh over 157 pounds. That leaves only the big Russians and that strange saint of the *PR* left, T. S. Eliot.

Our love to you all,

Cal

480. *To William Empson*

December 5, 1966

Dear William:

Just a fan letter for your recent Hough Frye piece—as always in your work I read each phrase and sentence with heart-felt joy and understanding—perhaps all the more in some of your late short pieces. Let me say again that ever since I first met you in 1939 I have loved and reverenced you as my friend and teacher, as the most important teacher in England, the greatest Englishman.

Yours as always,

Cal

[Seven]

1967–1970

Writing of *Notebook 1967–68*

New York City • Cambridge • Oxford

Robert and Harriet Lowell in New Haven, Connecticut, 1967 (courtesy Elizabeth Hardwick)

481. To Elizabeth Bishop

<div align="right">Friday, February 26, 1967</div>

Dearest Elizabeth—

I gather from Dr. Baumann you've been going through a sea of troubles—asthma, a hospital, trouble with Lota, God knows what. I've been keeping informed as best I can, but really don't know too much. I dread thinking of you in trouble, exposed, and a-wash in Rio. Somehow another country, language, Spanish nuns etc. make it all seem more gruelling and uncertain. My yearly attacks, tho bruising and troubling to everyone, and even to a degree unpredictable, *do* seem to fall into a groove of repetition, making everything easier to handle. I've just gotten over another. Nothing new worth writing about, except that I have another doctor now, and there seems to be the real hope that my manic seizures can be handled by a new drug, Lithium, and that all my giddy reelings come from a kind of periodic salt deficiency in some lower part of the brain. At least, this drug is now working with many.

I'll have Giroux send you my new book. There are quite a few changes from the version you saw, translations added, and pictures, which you may not like, tho I do. Nolan has done over a hundred, mostly in color illustrations for my *Imitations*, much more ambitious and inspired than these.

The day after tomorrow, I'll be fifty, and Lizzie is arranging a party of almost thirty, our big room lined with long tables. Doubt if I can rise to the occasion—tho I guess still being around and hale, is a triumph for our stricken generation of poets. Last fall, Berryman wrote a marvelous sequence of new dream poems, entitled, "Opus Posthumous"—they really seem ex humo, from beyond the tomb. I thought he was gone, but the experience seems to have resurrected him. In four days, I fly to London for the opening of my *Benito*. I wish you could see it done, it moves very slowly, and at least on the stage, surely. One reviewer said it was unconventional in that it had nothing shocking, no sex, no perversion, just the explosion of a country, 170 years in the past.

I've been writing like a beaver for the last week revising and re-typing my Prometheus, pages and pages of words, it will either stun [or] stupefy an audience, if it doesn't work. It's a sort of Shelley, or generic European declamatory romantic poem—alive maybe, if anything can breathe under the formidable armor of its rhetoric and stance.

I hear rumors that you may come here. I'll welcome you with open arms, joy, and whatever stability and wisdom my hereditary granite New England morality still retains.

All my love. Do let me hear, do let me know how I can be of help.

Love again,

Cal

P.S. I carry your "Under the Window" in my bill-fold, and even read it aloud to Dr. Baumann late in December before I went off to the hospital. Much to say. Your style never seems mannered, just marvelous, unguessable description, now as natural as your letters, but full of design and compression. Yes, you have man's journey, his seven ages, many wonderful flashes, like the second car's syphilitic nose, all the way through, then the great rise, just where it is needed, with the "morpho." It's like going on the pilgrimage of your Fish, or the poem ending awful and wonderful, yet the journey is as utterly new and surprising as a first discovery of what life is all about. And so it is. If I can't stop what I've already done, I must stop. Maybe, if I carry your "Window" around long enough, I'll learn. It's a kind of patience and freshness.

482. *To the Editors,* Partisan Review

[n.d. Spring or Summer 1967]

Refusal to report to the army is certainly the most effective way a young man can protest an unjust war.

483. *To William Doreski*

May 16, 1967

Dear Bill—

Congratulations to you and Jean! Where in Boston will you be living? I will of course be at Harvard in the Fall—surely we can meet then. I think you'll like the changes I've made in "Waking Early Sunday Morning." The

middle stanzas are tighter and more visual, as you suggested. The book will be out in a month or so; I'll send you a copy.

I'm sorry you fought with your father. I went through much the same thing. It is difficult for men sometimes to admit to their sensitivity and appreciation of things which as children they were discouraged from approaching. I think I knocked my own father down out of a sense of injury to art as much as for his meddling in my love life. Of course it was melodramatic and adolescent, but I was a very melodramatic adolescent indeed.

If you get to Maine this summer we would be happy to have you stay a week or two. I know Elizabeth would enjoy meeting Jean.

Yours,
Cal

484. To Elizabeth Bishop

June 14, 1967

Dearest Elizabeth:

I guess you've seen the *Time* thing. I was almost out of my mind with dread and indignation. They had collected about 1000 pages, questioning people I hardly knew, and asking impertinent personal questions. I feared the notoriety and the heavy wounding hand. Well, it was harmless and even rather delicate and tactful for them. I liked your responses, but not the description of your genius (theirs not yours) at the end. It seems to me you are full of passionate feeling, as well as a serenity, a fullness, not a coolness. By the way, the optimistic James Dickey is one of the most desperate souls I know of, dreaded by the faculties where he has read. Rather good poet though, particularly on horrible things like fire-bombing. I really have a much less agonized German existentialist life than they indicate. More frivolous, I'm afraid, too.

Loved your sour letter. I've been seeing quite a lot of Irene, who surely made my play at Yale. She's a bit resonant and over interested in culture. Quite gallant, one of the best actresses, living from hand to mouth, or at least job to job. The whole production was lovely, a wonderful Prometheus, Kenneth Haigh, and Miller's marvelous direction. After two weeks, we were in consternation. Two hours of undramatic heroic Greek speeches—a very long two hours. Somehow it worked out for those of us who liked it. What a spring of plays, travelling, readings, and *Time*!

Did the late war scare you to death? It did me while it was simmering. We had a great wave of New York Jewish nationalism, all the doves turning into

hawks. Well, my heart is in Israel, but it was a little like a blitz krieg against the Comanches—armed by Russia. Nasser is like a Mussolini ruling some poverty stricken part of India. I never saw a country I would less like to stay in, yet the Egyptians were mostly subtle and sad and attractive.

Every so often, I have a vague acute feeling of missing something or someone, and it's you—long talks on some rock, or sandy knoll, or Copacabana Beach. Letters are no substitute. You [must] come back for a long visit.

No news. I'm drained of anything to write. Not a poem for a year and a half. I wish I had a suitcase of unfinished possibilities. (I've just [looked] at Eliot's juvenilia. Some of the best lines in the *Waste Land* come from an early quite hopeless lyric on Saint some one.[)]

I've been seeing Dr. Baumann, slightly high blood-pressure, which turns out to be nothing, but I was depressed because my mother and father had this kind of trouble. But it's nothing. By the way, don't doctors love to explain how [you] have asked the wrong question. If you say, "Aren't fingernails part of the hand?" they explain that there's no such thing as the hand that anything could be part. Both Annie and my "shrink" do this. I have a probably irritating seminar teacher's habit of doing just the opposite i.e. making sense out of non-sense.

Goodbye, my dear old love, and love to Lota. Tomorrow we set out for Castine with four angora guinea pigs.

Cal

485. To Shozo Tokunaga

Castine, Maine
[June 26, 1967]

My Dear Shozo:

First the questions. *Stocks and stones* is a little joke on Milton's Piedmontese sonnet—it was the Catholics according to Milton who were idolators and worshipped stones. The rest of your interpretation is right. *Glass houses*, people who live in glass houses shouldn't throw stones etc. of the proverb— expensive houses later built by [a] plutocratic civilization with sea-views. You are right on *Mole-tide*, surrealist, but ridged and muddy as the tunnels of moles, who of course couldn't be in the harbor. Glad you like "Between the Porch," I think it's my favorite in the book. You are completely right on the *mover. Them* is the eyes. *Green* statues, because bronze turns green, also some kind of pun or joke on the statues being the same color as the almost tropical

summer vegetation of Washington. *Liberators* statues—the Spanish South Americans seem to go in most for this sort of art and sentiment. *Breeding*—the poor South American countries are of course out-~~producing~~ breeding us. What can I say about "Central Park"? It took me a long hopeless month's work. I connect it both with Juvenal's 10th and Marvell's "Garden," and perhaps "Coy Mistress." It was quite a job fitting in both Egypt (I'd just been there) and the abandoned kitten. "Waking Early" I've read Kirkup's ingenious essay. He'[s] all astray about the fecal business throughout. No hangover is intended. The speaker has no bowel trouble, or erection trouble. He never leaves his bedroom. The poem is about energy (Too much and too little, both dangerous, a sort of non-clinical manic-depressive state, resembling the world and the American national character[,] mine too[)]—then about the pathos and impotence of the old religion, belief in the state etc. Then, of course about American imperialism, Viet Nam etc. *Ten* is only vaguely symbolic, suggesting spiritual progress, but also the many steps the salmon must climb to surmount the salmon run. No Moses, no Ten Commandments—only literal wooden steps the poor salmon must climb up on his literal ladder. I think I meant to pay Stevens some sort of little compliment with my title. I'd be happy to have someone sometime read our two poems together for their contrasts.

I think I may go to Australia next March for their Adelaide Festival, and then would stop in Japan, and then at last, we will meet, my dear old unseen friend.

> Affectionately,
> Robert

486. To James Kirkup

June 29, 1967

Dear James Kirkup:

Oh dear—where you go off the rails is the entire fecal business. This was not only not intended, but could not have been subconscious because this is an ailment I've never been afflicted with, I mean constipation is a very rare occasion in my existence. The waking is meant to be simply insomnia, and was in fact, though the poem is of course a mosaic of partly true and partly fictional autobiography. The opening salmon is a sort of waking dream or meditation. He's a memory of an Oregon stream, and stands for energy, poetic, sexual, maybe mostly heroic moral energy. He's not phallic, except in the way

popular Freudian symbols encumber the air, and take some ingenuity to avoid. I enjoy Freud as a sort of marvelous Borges, E.A. Poe novelist—much greater, but his clues are more and more becoming opaque clichés. Like Hopkins saying "nothing is cheaper in devotional poems than angels"—so are Freud's Oedipal and phallic symbols. I suppose one should think of the speaker in "Waking Early," as someone in a sort of rambling dramatic monologue. He begins in the dark with the rambling gloomy thoughts of insomnia, and never leaves his bed (a sleeping bed, not a writing bed), in trying to escape the graceless tedium of Sunday (my title has the words and rhythm of a conventional dead hymn), he tries to build up some kind of imaginative, and spiritual energy—sex is of course in the poem, but only in hints that will be developed in the last two poems of the sequence. No bathroom, no toilet, no fecal images except the refuse, and the metaphorical dreck (a real woodshed, cluttered up as is so common in the country).

What else? No hangover, just the gloom of the world, and life and lying in bed—I wrote the poem directly after my White House business, and felt impotent to write anything worthy the rather false notoriety I had received for what I'd done, also after many months of block on short poems. The Jews collected foreskins of their defeated enemies. Humor and temperament, and also the Sunday morning made me load the poem with half pious half blasphemous Biblical allusions. The Baudelaire is wrong. I'm fairly saturated with him, but hardly know the prose poems. I believe I was thinking of *Voyage*.

So, I fear I have left my poem in tatters for you. You've constructed a sort of Eric Erikson-Osborne prose poem on my structure. If you will think it over, you may see that it is not hermetic, but has as deep a meaning as that which you wrongly attribute to it, one parallel to your meaning, but no shit.

I am at Harvard at Quincy House from Monday to Wednesday from October till Christmas. Let's meet and have dinner and beware of drinking ourselves into constipation.

Yours,

Robert Lowell

P.S.—I appreciate the pains and intelligence of your piece, but please don't have Shozo print it without my letter (the copy I'm sending you is my only one). But better not at all. If the subject still interests you, I think you might take a deep second thought and re-write.

487. To Adrienne Rich

Dearest Adrienne:

I've been in a coma of sloth or industry, writing to *no*-one, answering no-one. This is the first letter for weeks. Thanks for your kind remarks on *Prometheus*. The Weil essays really stunned me, and I read them often with moist eyes, partly because of how I was feeling, but mostly the tone and content. I've been poeticizing (hideous word, shades of Richard Eberhart) furiously, and now have three poems, all *momento mori*s about summer and being fifty. One, long, about a hundred lines, takes phrases and more from Simone Weil, and somehow I connect it with you mostly (I have the laurel wreath, but as a symbol for the earth, and nature that kills us[)]—

this circlet of friable laurel,
a funeral wreath from the despotic gangster

I'll enclose the whole thing, if I can find a readable copy.

Went back to New York for a few days and check-up, at the end of July. Check-up, OK, and saw Elizabeth Bishop, temporarily separated from Lota by Lota's doctor's orders, but to be reunited in September. We had a lovely afternoon walking through the Park, for once cool, and discussing, reminiscing—unable to believe our ages. I expect to go to Russia early in September, and so won't be in New York. I wish you would look her up—c/o Lloyd Frankenberg, 61 Perry Street. She likes your work very much, particularly the last books—she who likes almost nothing. I'm sure you would get on beautifully. So few people—I almost said especially poets—are kind, humorous, charming and interesting.

Funny summer! We've just had our first two successive clear days since June. Mary and all her family are very much here. Once a week, we have our old French readings with our friend, who teaches French at Exeter. But we've been rather frighteningly improved by Mary, who always does her homework—in everything, it might be said, cooking, dressing, responses in the local Episcopal service—and knows the language. Lizzie gets drunk, asks something out of order like "Did Pascal live before Plato?" then vanishes to read the *New York Review of Books* or have a heart to heart talk with Harriet. Two Margaret Fullers in one little village! The first night, one of our great local talkers said, I know I am not in a class with your wife and Mrs. West. A picnic, everyone

dressed in blue jeans except Mary, Balenciaga dress, and umbrella brought by her stepson—however, she stayed in the horrible Maine water for half an hour. We have arguments as to whether *grand maistres* in Villon means masters of the monastic orders, or just the great. When the Gowries were here we almost got the giggles as she was telling of her affair with Jim in Poland. Gowrie: ["]Did you ever have a liaison in Edinbro?" I: "None of your business." He thought her a fascinating, rather terrifying woman. She is painting her baronial white Main Street house yellow—unlike the others. Very sweet though, a lift to our sagging decadent little community.

Dear Adrienne, I hope you are not too lonely, off by yourself, with no Mary McCarthy, with no Alf. I couldn't have had a better time with you, and have been thinking back on it all summer.

My love,
Cal

P.S. I enclose the poem to show you that I can still be serious and sad. Be sure to read the third side.

488. To Elizabeth Bishop

October 9, 1967

Dearest Elizabeth:

I write so few letters that I see with surprise again that the number of my street is the same as the number of the year. A gray coolish day here; my Bible reading's done; and I am getting ready to set out for the University. This troubled fall!

I hope I have been of some slight help to you. I worry until the trip to Brazil is over and you can arrange your life with fixed routine—not very fixed, just a place where you know you will be, and can go on at your leisure with your poems and Brazil book. You seem so marvelously healthy that I grieve at the thought of trips, business details, disturbing meetings etc. The woes of your heart are enough.

It's been a joy to sit chatting with you, even in this sad time—all the more perhaps because the sorrow can be shared a little. You make most people, even the most charming, seem as if seen through a glaze, as if they lived in a glaze. And your poems and prose animals have the same freshness, the wood is exposed, clean and genuine.

I won't go on. I feel for Lota, though I've no right to, rather as I did after

Cousin Harriet's death; a part of my life has fallen away, a part of my life in you.

No news here. Liz and I went to a good negro movie, *Jason*. Otherwise we haven't seen or *heard* from a soul.

All my love,
Cal

489. To Edmund Wilson

Dear Edmund:

I have a memory of being rather loud and drunk and rude to you the other night. I was feeling tired and trying to relax. This can be a pain in the neck to one's friends. Please trust in my love and admiration forever. I am enjoying your memories, particularly World War I, such a relief in this world where we live up to our ~~necks~~ eyes in boloney.

Our love to you both,
Cal

490. To Mary McCarthy

December 16, 1967

Dearest Mary:

I'm glad to say that I named you too, in the *Herald Tribune* 3 books of the year, along with Styron and a philosopher soldier friend of Hannah's, Glenn Gray, *The Warrior*. We weren't asked to comment; many thanks for the affectionate humor of yours; however after standing irresolutely on the shore during our picnics, and watching you swim forever, I must give you the ocean, your element, not mine.

Interesting idea, that Elizabeth is a poet of terror. I have never been able to quite connect what I know of her life with the seemingly dispassionate coolness of the poems. Your few lines are one of the best things said about her; on me too, though my honest simplicity has fewer mysteries. Why aren't such notes collected in symposia, instead of the academic tripe usually assembled?

Gossip. About a month or more ago, Elizabeth B. came over here, while I was still at Harvard, had a few vodkas, and had to be taken up stairs without clothes by Lizzie and Nicole. Next morning, when I came home, she was in

the kitchen with a can of beer—all else had been hidden—during the night, she had made a foraging trip downstairs over the barricade of Harriet's bicycle—(back to my sentence) chattering in Portuguese to Nicole. I put her to bed with a sleeping pill (mild). Later, going to the bathroom, she slipped and broke her shoulder, quite badly. A worse injury maybe than anyone's in the marches and demonstrations. Then what a time of ambulances, waits in the hospital[,] calls to Dr. Baumann. Well, I think it cooled her down, so that finally she was in very good shape to go back to Brazil, and handled all the very vexing duties and encounters. By the way, there is a girl, about thirty, in Seattle, divorced, perhaps because of Elizabeth, with a child of two. She seems to be a very decent and good sort according to Dr. Baumann and Lizzie who was asked to phone. I think Elizabeth will set up with her in San Francisco. Reassuring, I think, and the best that could be hoped for. Pardon all this; I wouldn't write it to anyone else and know you won't spread it.

Sorry to hear you've been ill, and hope you'll take care if the Hanoi comes off. Not much news with us. Lizzie's written a "definitive" review of Lillian Hellman that practically has us ostracized—none of my doing. I've been agitating a little, but mostly writing. My summer's poem is now 800 lines, practically an *Iliad* for my short-winded symbolist talent. It has what you name, all my usual stuff, plus Napoleon, Cato, the Duc de Guise etc. Things seem to swim out of the happenings of the day, including distant things, the ponderings and vagaries of thought.

Oh dear, we miss your esprit and wit; we miss you both, and trust we'll be together another summer. We're fighting a plan to run the new sewage system through my barn. Not quite that bad, but near it.

Love,
Cal

P.S. Lizzie sends her love to you both too. I enclose a land poem, part of my sequence.

491. *To Ted Hughes*

Christmas 1967

Dear Ted:

I should have written you earlier about *Wodwo*, but this has been a pressed and pushed fall for me, teaching, writing, agitating. A wonderful book, a continuation not a repeat, shifting for the most part from animals, as much as you

should. I haven't read the prose which everyone likes yet, but among the poems my favorite now are "Crabs," "Jaguar," "Root," "Rescue," "Scapegoats," "Kreutzer," "Rat I," "Mountains," "Bibroch" and "Wodwo." That's a lot; and who else has your shaggy, electric energy?

I am buried in a long poem, a sort of notebook or journal in 14 line unrhymed sections. It's now reached about 850 lines; a *Ring and the Book* among my short-winded works. Hope all is well with you; you should look on *Wodwo* as a triumphant emergence and return.

Affectionately,
 Cal

492. *To Elizabeth Bishop*

January 12, 1968

Ah my Dear—

I guess one could be vexed with you or anyone, but I don't see how anyone could be *cruel* to you—never, and alone there and a woman! I wish I could have been at hand to shield you. I want you never to suffer. Well, the troubles of the last couple of years and above all this last, won't be again. I'm glad though that you are keeping Ouro Prêto; something of Brazil will be kept, and I'm sure many dear friends.

Glad you are on what seems to me the very solid ground of San Francisco, glad Roxanne is with you. Dr. Baumann described her to me at great length and with the completest praise—rather like Hannah on Rosa Luxembourg. I'm laying it on a little, but not much.

Marvelous stay in Cuernavaca with a radical priest friend of mine, Monsignor Ivan Illich (!). Doing I don't know what, only I hoped to combine this trip with one to Cuba. However, the State Department would not authorize my passport as a journalist. Just as well; only Mexico where I could forget everything. Queer gathering; at one moment I'd be talking to heavy Chicago nuns, and the next to Brazilian refugees with forty year sentences waiting for them. Lots of climbing Toltec ruins, New Year's midnight in the market.

Now back to the cold, draft-evader protests, jury duty, my last trip to Harvard. The Spock etc. indictment may have been a bad tactical error by the government—all sorts of tepid withdrawn people, like Auden and Jason Epstein are signing protests. I've signed something which pledges my support to the men indicted—saying we will take their places if they go to jail. Honor demands that one does this, but how I loathe the claptrap, the polemical stirrers,

one, alas, must agree with! I feel like a month of bass and pickerel fishing; still, there's a thrill—sort of like being a soldier one day a month, then sunning and gossiping the rest.

Lizzie has written a review of Lillian very blasting (and ill-judged, I think) which has got us into a hornet's nest of abusive letters to the book review. I've never cared too much when I've been attacked, but this riles, I feel almost physically forced to cut the writers of the letters. Strange, because as I've said I don't think the piece should have been written—on personal grounds, not critical. I've learned that it is sometimes right and necessary to be angry, even when wrong.

Yes, I'm well. The pills I am taking really seem to prevent mania. Two or three years will be necessary, but already critical months have passed. Ordinarily I would certainly have been in a hospital by now. The great thing is that even my well life is much changed, as tho I'd once been in danger of falling with every step I took. All the psychiatry and therapy I've had, almost 19 years, was as irrelevant as it would have been for a broken leg. Well, some of it was interesting, tho most was jargon.

My long poem is now over a thousand lines, and will probably go on another 500, will go on till June when it began. Then I'll polish through the summer. I am writing it as if it were my last work. Someone asked me if [I] expected to die when I finished it—no, but trying to write with such openness and not holding back.

Goodbye and all my love, and Darling, forget your troubles in Brazil,
Cal

493. To Jacqueline Kennedy

Jan. 18, 1968

Dear Jackie:

A sort of bread and butter. I write so seldom now, but nothing written on the impulse is to be regretted. Walking home mostly through snow, whitish, or brain-gray, or ink, the more or less familiar little tangle of Central Park between the 80's and 70's twisting by me, foreseen and changed (what can I do to end this sentence?) it seemed that you'd held the afternoon with a certain kindness and poignance for us all, but also for me. I mean really that I felt I wanted to thank you in some firm unextravagant way, that would ring true for you.

Yours as always, Dear,
Cal

494. *To the Editors,* New York Review of Books

February 4, 1968

We should have a national day of mourning, or better our own day of mourning, for the people we have sent into misery, desperation—that we have sent out of life; for our own soldiers, for the pro-American Vietnamese, and for the anti-American Vietnamese, those who have fought with un-equaled ferocity, and probably hopeless courage, because they preferred an-nihilation to the despair of an American conquest.

Robert Lowell
New York City

495. *To Mary McCarthy*

February 5, 1968

Dear Mary—

Let me answer for once while your letter is fresh in mind, also because I've been saying the last two or three weeks that you ought to be here. Not a sug-gestion, rather I have been feeling the absence of your kind of talent. We have been to several draft-resistance meetings, somewhat arranged by Mitch Good-man, Denise Levertov's husband and one of those indicted with Spock. These things are on a level at which honesty is impossible. Little groups of non-G.I.s or draft-evaders are placed on the stage (samplings of the common man) few can speak at all, except in erroneous clichés. The one who got the most ap-plause, was an oldish boy, obviously on dope, with a rented Viet-Cong uniform a Viet Cong flag he waved and an unintelligible story of facing a 23 year sen-tence for being caught with the needle, instead of attending a resistance rally.

Elizabeth is now at 1554 Pacific Ave. San Francisco, Roxanne and her child ~~restored~~ installed. I think all's in harbor and more or less at rest. She had a hell of a time in Brazil where most of Lota's friends were very cool and rude to her, but she went through it sober. I've only seen her drunk two or three times in my life. What helps is an ox-like power of character and imagination which nothing can break.

Hasn't the last week been hideous? I think somehow of the Indians throw-ing their lives away with scornful courage, and often my eyes water. I wrote this sentence to say at the meeting, after a short impromptu urging the stu-dents to consider how they might honorably *avoid* going to jail: "We should have a national day of mourning, for the people we have sent into misery,

desperation—that we have sent out of life; for our own soldiers, for the pro-American Vietnamese, and for the anti-American Vietnamese, those who are fighting with unequalled ferocity and probably hopeless courage, because they prefer annihilation to the disgrace of an American conquest." But nothing can be heard at such rallies, so I left.

Away from this; we are so happy you all will be back in Castine. Envy you Sicily. My poem is almost done, almost 1400 lines, with the start progress and end—only spring to throw in and round out my year. Liz sends her love and is looking forward to your Gilliatt.

Love to you both,

Cal

496. To Elizabeth Bishop

February 21, 1968

Dearest Elizabeth:

Just a line or two to fling you my love before I set off for a short trip to Charlottesville and the Peter Taylors—reading etc. much chaff with friends. I have your painting on the wall, gold frame, blue mat suggested by the framer, and oddly right. Lovely and cozy; it replaces my now exiled Baskin Nuclear Man, shut in a closet. I love you so much, and have an intuitive feeling that all's much better now, a place of light and human warmth for you! I've been happily buried; my Endecott play rewritten for performance in April; the long poem now 100 sections, and in the formal shape it will end with[,] after 20 or more sections. Just been reading Trilling on Joyce, the heroic annihilation of most human things to doing *Finnegans Wake*, not approved or disapproved by Trilling. Thank God for my small (God knows what) talent! But even I seem to get absorbed, stop writing. Do you know what hell is? Forever meeting a new English faculty, coed, all older than one is, cup of coffee in a paper cup in one hand, in the other hand a cookie and cigarette, and always standing, and signing copies of one's least liked book (I'm thinking of poetry readings). The other half is the pre-reading cocktail party meant to last half an hour and lasting two, so that you can hardly walk or see.

I must stop. So looking forward to introducing you when you come here.

Much love,

Cal

March 16, 1968

Dear Peter and Eleanor:

I saw your name on the envelope with a gasp of shame. Each day or every other day I've been writing down a long list of things to be done, writing you at the head, then writing Elizabeth Bishop. Then I read a good book. I had the best time with you all—never such talk, and the house Blue Ruin, is etched, engraved seared on my memory. It was all joy including the two meetings with the English department and breaking my watch; apparently I over-wound it to brace myself for Monticello—he was a New Englander at heart, more like a literate Kennedy than like William Yandell Elliott.

I've been all over the place, and followed McCarthy three days in New Hampshire, going through two sweater factories, one shoe factory, one wood factory, one Lyons and Kiwanis Club, two ladies clubs. In one factory there were only 25 registered Republicans, and 120 unregistered machines. My line was that if I spoke he'd lose the few votes he had. It's a miracle how such a quiet and in many ways soporific campaign worked. No reservations on McCarthy. His freshest side is mostly off the record—dead-pan Jim Powers Irish jokes. It's hard to imagine anyone less like a literary man, and more like a good writer. Well, it all looked hopeless ten days ago, still does I guess, but much less so—in a way he has already succeeded by smashing light into New Hampshire. Tho God knows, it seemed anything but smashing at the time.

I don't agree on Kennedy, tho remembering your clairvoyance on Johnson and Goldwater, I hesitate to breathe. In the heat of the evening before Bobby's announcement I was talking to someone at the New York McCarthy head-quarters and rashly asked if I could do anything (intending to get out of a suggestion that I address 3 New Jersey country clubs to raise money[)] (Wouldn't I be expelled from the Institute if I did such a thing—my rosette ground to powder[)]—and was asked to call the senator Kennedy. So I did and left my number and he called (leaving no stone unturned) He said about what he did the next morning only the tone was somehow much gentler and more reassuring. My heart, such as it is, will have to be with McCarthy to the end, personally, & because he is much the better candidate as far as I can judge, and then (this means almost most) because he hoped and dared when no other politician in the whole country hoped or dared, when there was no hope. I'm going to Milwaukee on Thursday, I think, for a few days, as a camp-follower, to see the cows. McCarthy said if all cows had to be milked the way Romney milked them, milk would cost $25 a quart.

Excuse all this chatter. I have few people to talk this way to. My poem is all but finished, anyway inspiration has stopped and I feel I may have said what I had in me. Four or five more pieces maybe. I haven't said anything to Eleanor who *made* my visit. We all send our love. Harriet has written a contrapuntal composition, so intricate she is unable to play it. What can be played sounds post Schoenberg, but that may be due to her faulty command of what Allen would call traditional skills.

Love,
Cal

P.S. I almost forgot the whole point of this letter. I do want to become permanent visitor to U. of V. Nothing more. That's what I am at Harvard. How can I name my price? You must, then I'll know what you really think of me. About to meet John Berryman; we're having a memorial reading for Randall, Roethke and Schwartz tonight.

498. *To Elizabeth Hardwick*

March 22, 1968

Dearest Lizzie:

I'm off with somehow a heavy heart, and no doubt heavily breathing for Milwaukee. My address is the Sheraton-Schroeder. Ah dear, the odds seem set against our getting any but the two worst candidates. What a nightmare to be in all this. However the trip with Sidney will be fun—it's clouds waiting where the land under us ends in sky. Lonesome for you two, red and healthy this Friday night.

All my love,
Cal

499. *To Mary McCarthy*

April 19, [1968]

Dearest Mary:

Your McCarthy letter arrived, and I've sent it off to his house, special, and garlanded with stamps. I took it I was meant to read it, anyway I did, but showed it to no one except Lizzie. It can now live in rumor from day to day[,] new things being attributed to your letter—alas, if any had the brilliance to

add them! Of course I loved it all—the horrible vision of the old frontier re-
turning, the sheer wood a little grayer—tarnished by power, discredited and
famished by exile! McCarthy particularly loathes being compared with
Stevenson, though he shows this by silence, and will surely like your compar-
ison—I think it's a distaste for the kind of person who liked Stevenson, dis-
taste for the rich, polite East. I saw it last night at Marietta Tree's in a half
transparent black mourning dress for King, loving *all* three candidates of the
Dem. Party, the one person who can't be disappointed almost, working for
Kennedy, favoring Humphrey, charmed by McCarthy, though embarrassed
by his voting record, "I'm always with the Lefties." Well, what is left; I said
changing Adams somewhat that I was an aristocratic, Christian atheist. I
think Bob is about to call you about possibly covering the Indiana campaign,
if you will after [you've] finished Hanoi. You might. You would see strange
things, the Lions Club of Spring Point Oregon, sweater factories. All very
merry and trivial in this sad world. Yet it does matter, and sometimes my eyes
water in anticipation of the inevitable defeat. The Senator is best—this sounds
silly, but isn't—in deep humorous images taken mostly from sport and farm-
ing—they are all political. After Bobby announced, he said: "They are treat-
ing me like a horse about to [be] turned into glue."

God, where will we be next fall, next year? We are dying to hear and read
about Hanoi. I've become more and more aware this year that ideologies and
government systems can easily fade into skeletons of clay. I don't like the other
line either, that the good things in our political tradition are in *essence* meaning-
less. Enough; it's good that one handful, you and I and Dwight and Hannah,
who have agreed on as many things as we should over twenty years, still agree.

Love to you both as ever,
Cal

We were so touched by your making Lizzie your executor. Now you're back,
alive still.

500. To William Empson

April 24, 1968

Dear William:

Strange, I was about to write having just heard that you had been ill last
year—I'd heard some rumor before, but somehow it slipped my mind. Any-
way, I grieve and hope all that is over now.

You must take our apartment. It's quite pleasant, a room twenty feet high, three little rooms next to it and three more on the next floor. Very near both Central Park and Lincoln Center. We go to Maine in mid-June and won't be there, but hope you will visit us. You can take a plane from either Buffalo or New York to Boston, and from there to Bangor and I will drive to meet you, the whole trip about two hours. The only out to our apartment is no air-conditioning—even our big room does little to cool the tropical American summer. I'll try to put something in.

I saw your little shot at Arthur Schlesinger and another I think in *Encounter*. Even these small things you do as no one else. I was on a panel with Conor O'Brien in which he gave a shortened version of his Yeats fascist essay, plus a reading of Yeats' poems. When I followed mostly reading a little of myself, I said, "It's hard to follow William Butler Yeats, harder still to follow Conor Cruise O'Brien." He was more or less proving all writers were irresponsible. Best to Hetta.

 Yours as ever,
 Robert

501. *To Grey Gowrie*

April 26, 1968

Dear Grey:

How much I miss you. I've just mailed an ardent and graceful letter in your favor to Secretary Giltrap of Trinity. I might have been there, for I just had an invitation to read at some Trinity poetry society on May 2, an impossible date that would have given me about nine hours rest between trips to Ohio (Ransom's 80th) and Texas. When you are firmly a part of the Trinity get them to invite me again, with advance notice.

I feel in your five years tenure of Castle Martin, the whole caste will turn up: Larry Scott, Wooffer, Lewis Mumford, James West's children, McCarthy and Kennedy, exiles to Ireland facing extradition, Kissinger, Bob Silvers, Caroline, Aunt Sarah, Harriet with her first date etc. Someday, we will.

My *Endecott* play has opened, rather terrific, if I dare say so and despite the fact that plays cannot by definition (at least American ones) be art. The writing is enormously improved and the production is about as good (nothing could be better) as Miller's.

The campaign is like the horse-races or roulette, constant motion, bets, guesses, momentous possibilities, frivolity of action. And the country is in a

curious state of carnival and cháos. All is much less somber than last February. It seems so, it seems so to me; and yet it all has the unreal aspect of a lanternslide landscape flung on the real one. *Momento mori*!

We are fine. Harriet has *composed* a saraband, a nocturn and a tremendous nameless chordal construction. I have finished 108 sonnets and am about done.

Oh Lizzie regards McCarthy as a great American and candidate but an unreliable and unserious companion for me, another Frank Parker.

We are really looking forward to the fog and emptiness of Maine. Wish you and Bingo and Brer were going to be with us.

Love,
 Cal

502. To A. Alvarez

<div align="right">May, 1968</div>

Dear Al:

I have been meaning to thank you for your large book of essays and your critical kindness to me. Two months ago, I would have had more precise observations, but now, such is the whirl of time, I would have to restudy you like a student being examined. It seems to me, there's nothing written without an edge of mind and wit and a clear simplicity. Also your pieces, unlike most things of their kind do not fade with the passing of their first publication. They grow grander with their bulk.

What *is* in my mind is your interview with Hochhuth. I wonder if you intended him to come out rather pompous and tame bull-like? Strange that the author of this reputedly scandalous play should be embarrassingly pro-Churchill. He seems another example of a kind of character that troubles me much lately—one that can be capitalist, socialist, democratic, communist, (what have you?) yet thick-hided and coarse brained, too toughened for nuance or profundity. I haven't seen this play, but know the other one which I was invited to adapt.

A lot has happened to me this year. These pills for my manic seizures seem to have made a cure, tho I will take them to my dying. This has changed my life, not only no attacks, no hospitals, but even, and perhaps most, health itself is different, freer and out of the shadow. The other is a long poem, *Notebook of a Year*, in 14 line sections, now about 1500 lines and close to done. I follow the seasons loosely, but the real structure is personal happenings, moods, brushes

with the great events etc. Accident gave it such form as it has, yet a true one I hope, and I hope too it's the best thing I've done, one to end on if nature should wish. Congratulations on your new child, your wife, your book. Miss you.

Cal

503. To Richard Wilbur

[May 23, 1968]

EUGENE MCCARTHY CAN AND MUST WIN IN CALIFORNIA. WE URGENTLY APPEAL TO YOU TO SPEAK THERE IN HIS BEHALF. THE VOICE OF THE EASTERN INTELLECTUAL COMMUNITY CAN INFLUENCE MORE VOTES AND IMPEL MORE POLITICAL ACTION IN CALIFORNIA THAN THE APPEARANCE OF A MOVIE STAR. AT NO OTHER TIME AND IN NO OTHER PLACE IN THE CAMPAIGN HAVE YOU BEEN SO NEEDED. BILL STYRON, ARTHUR MILLER, JULES FEIFFER AND I ARE GOING TO OREGON THIS WEEKEND AND THEN ON TO CALIFORNIA. WILL YOU JOIN US? PHONE FRANCES LEAR, ARTS COMMITTEE 212-757-8715

ROBERT LOWELL

504. To Kingman Brewster

May 30, 1968

Dear President Brewster:

I have been trying to reach you by telephone, but it has been difficult because you have been away or at a meeting, and I have been away following Senator McCarthy's campaign. I wish in some part of the ceremony, preferably just after receiving my degree, to speak the following sentence: "I know that I am being honored mostly, and probably entirely, for my poetry; still I wish to express my gratitude, to this University for now honoring me, when I stand in much the same position, and perhaps in some of the same danger as William Coffin of Yale and Benjamin Spock of Yale, and the other defendants at Boston."

Now the point is to get this uttered or at least printed very openly and very quietly. I think I owe this to my honor and to the occasion, and have tried to

make my words as uninflammatory, unrhetorical and unembarrasing as possible. Of course we are all grateful to you for your gentle and skillful handling of the Coffin business.

Yours sincerely,

Robert Lowell

505. *To Jacqueline Kennedy*

June 10, 1968

Dear Jackie:

I have been thinking of writing you a long letter, a letter of mourning, but also of apology, because I think I might have done something for Bobby that might have helped, a word of caution. Many times I tried, not by conscious intention but by instinct. Still he knew well enough how the cards were stacked for him, and chose—a life glorious though brief. And perhaps this was best. I hope you won't hold my business in McCarthy's campaign against me. I could do nothing else, and wouldn't have. I think I was perhaps one of the few people in either party who ardently wanted either your Brother-in-law or McCarthy.

Because I cannot in this tired moment write a long letter, please take this short poem (it's part of a long series, 120, in this form, called *Notebook of a Year*) as a tribute.

R. F. K.

Here in my study, in its listlessness
of Vacancy, some old Victorian house,
air-tight and sheeted for old summers,
far from the hornet yatter of the bond—
is loneliness, a thin smoke threat of vital
air. What can I catch from you now?
Doom was woven in your nerves, your shirt,
woven in the great clan; they too were loyal,
you too were more than loyal to them . . . to death.
For them, like a prince, you daily left your tower
to walk through dirt in your best cloth. Here now,
alone, in my Plutarchan bubble, I miss
you sorely, you out of Plutarch, made by hand—
forever approaching our maturity.

I can't say more. I share your sorrow.

As ever affectionately,

Cal

506. To Adrienne Rich

Thursday, [July] 18 [1968]

Dear Adrienne:

Thanks for the parody—almost too close; one has so few stylistic tricks in the end. Like best the second sponge line. When you publish it, even if very soon, you'll need a footnote explaining who Grayson Kirk was, not a branch of the Scotch Church, but a poor, odious, pitiful creature, once president of Columbia.

God, what ease to be here. Ache and fatigue have been running out of my body like discharged swill. Two tree swallows nest outside my barn door in a forbidding little wooden house bought at last year's yacht club fair. A family of skunk paid us a visit last night—smelled but not seen.

What do you think was in McCarthy's suitcase a week ago? Mitch's novel. In America, even our statesmen are literate. Do rest, and, contradictory advice, if the spirit moves you come and see us.

Love to you all as always,

Cal

507. To Anne Fremantle

August 9, 1968

Dear Anne Fremantle:

I was about to apologize for not answering sooner, but I see I am not late, for how to teach the Bible fascinates me although I haven't had too much success, have less advice. I simply used the King James text. I began with the poetry: Deborah's Song, then David's lament, then the psalms; asking which were the worst psalms, which the best; do they begin and end etc. does the language fall into stereotype; are ones the enlightened moralist, who ever he is, might consider inspired less imaginatively inspired than the bad ones. How do the poems of the Bible compare with English religious poems? Are they religious? What does this mean. Then Job, a kind of play, and again is it too

long, uneven etc. Do the speakers differ. What kind of play, compared with Prometheus, Samson etc. I found the histories and stories the easiest to get at. They can be read much like other stories, character, narrative etc. Something like David is the best introduction to the style and meaning of the Gospels. Then Christ and Paul as stylists, people. What was hardest is the prophets; they are so formless. I tried to compare them, find what caught fire in them, what didn't. Ecclesiastes and Canticles are easy to teach. So it went; I made no attempt to do much more than a third; I used neither scholarship, nor religion, but assumed that the value of the texts should be as self-evident as Proust or Shakespeare. I must have thumbed through a number of things, but all I remember as of much use (aside from one's general reading) was Jung's little Job book, and the Kierkegaard chapter on Abraham.

Oh about the old God, I agree with you. If you try to make him good, you can't. He's a war-god, often a criminal tyrant. Still, He's still close to the nature of things, ergo profound, also more real than God usually is in writing; the odious God of Job, unlike Milton's, is alive, an Arab god, almost an African god; somehow he's a necessary tho mostly vile and barbarous ancestor of Christ, who really does stand up.

Good luck. I hope you can use this. I learned a lot, I think, from my teaching. If you see Ivan, give him my love.

Yours as ever,

508. To Adrienne Rich

August 23, [1968]

Dearest Adrienne:

I can't write much. In a little while I am taking Harriet and Best Friend, Johanna, Cynthia Pyle's daughter, to the fish hatchery. Last night, we went to the Cemetery, and Jan Hughes appeared sheeted (but with a visible dog and car) as a ghost, then the kids collected phosphorous water in a jar; it didn't flash. You can guess I don't do much of this sort of thing, so it's fun.

Oh but poetry readings for peace, McCarthy or any other cause on earth, except free alcohol, are never fun, or morally permissible. The last ditch argument is that they make money for the cause, but never do in proportion to the energy killed and the affliction inflicted. I don't like poets generically. Yet today, I am only writing to poets (and I seldom write to anyone else) you, E. Bishop, and Holub.

Just a day before the Russian invasion, I had a letter from him, happily remembering that evening when he read, and we ended up at your house; then he spoke of the revolution, much as you talked about Columbia (including rather limited expectations)[,] still an experience such as he'd never had, and as far as it went had no reservations on; then he said it was [at] last easy to get me an invitation to go to Prague when I wanted to . . . So, the bottom's gone. Fortunately, he was and is, I hope, lecturing in England.

I did two Ghazals: 14 lines made out of about a 100; meaning almost the opposite. Give my warm greetings to Bill. Sad about Dear Dido.

Tomorrow I go to Washington to go on to Chicago with McCarthy. No hope; I think we'll be licked, worse than Rockefeller. We'll be home on the 11th, and will soon see you, but even that won't quite restore the passage of this beautiful summer, the best, the most productive I've ever had. Good about your book; mine is now 153 sections. I want no more, but there [will] probably be one or two. I am turning the book in when I get to New York.

If I had the verve, I'd try to match your poetry evening night with my day at the Eberharts, equally deadly (except for Buckminster Fuller) but just the opposite in its "camp" (old sense) inelegance.

My love, as always,
 Cal

509. *To Elizabeth Bishop*

September 5, 1968

Darling Elizabeth:
 Let me answer the thing I can in a word or two: I'll certainly be at Harvard for your reading, and look forward to introducing you in New York, whenever it is. The guy at the Gotham seems pleasant and capable met in passing, but I really know nothing. Eberhart had a good poem, I think, in the last book: "Cape Rosier Wedding."

Oh I've had a lovely summer, but when I look inside it's sad and acid: age, death of friends, aging of everything in sight, the bad immediate future of this country, most countries, talents and decency misused etc. The stuff of life always. And now for a second, as I sat on my dry grass lifted above the harbor, and reread your letter, I was almost you—at least I could remember back last fall and Rio. The things that cannot be done twice! I think of my parents, the *I* who lived then! Ah courage!

Chicago was as it seemed. I wasn't at the Amphitheater, or in the marches.

I spent much of my time in McCarthy's apartment, chatting, watching him throw an orange to his brother, hearing his rather beatnik daughter say we would have to have our gas and pistols now, and maybe, tanks. The rest of the time, I spent with Lizzie, Styron, Mailer etc. In bars. Every so often I went out into the park and sidewalks by the Hilton. One night boys with bloodied heads were brought into staff headquarters, the next our staff headquarters were raided by about twenty policemen, because some probably imaginary beer cans were thrown out the window. A club was broken. One boy had twenty stitches, another six. It was horrible and looked like the old Gestapo movies. We were terrorized. The demonstrators, on the whole, behaved beautifully, about as dangerous as a church congregation. Still, I can't sympathize much with the people who sent them in to be bashed. Gene did nobly, I think, the only man of importance in either party to defy the parties, nor did he overdo it. His defeat in the voting was no surprise, but the violence was.

Five more days here. I feel my book is done, and I must read Shakespeare for Harvard, so it's not untimely. But it's hard as giving up whiskey, to give up seeing and hearing live things at every turn of the head. Oh, and to see my friends again—lovely, but so turbulent. Death to politics! The jargon is migraine; and they all seem to be activist. I seem to stumble into actions—not grand enough to suit the imagination of Keith Botsford, but I have no faith. I don't suppose Harvard will erupt on Bill Alfred, Harry Levin, and me.

Imagine two very cheerful paragraphs I was intending to write. I must get this into the mail. I feel sore since Chicago, as if a man had hit Harriet.

Look forward so to your visit.

Love,

Cal

510. *To Donald Junkins*

15 West 67 St.
N.Y.C.
September 21, 1968

Dear Don:

Nothing bores me more than McCarthy campaign rhetoric—or anyone else's. But you make points that interest me. I knew both McCarthy and Kennedy well, particularly McCarthy, but at first when the year began I think I knew Kennedy slightly better. They were both very ugly on each other long before they were running against. Gene at least had the advantage of putting

his Bobby-criticism in the form of sardonic jokes, which had the advantage of being imaginative and polemically true. Bobby's were frontal slurs, sometimes true, sometimes untrue and platitudes.

When you speak of power as something the Liberals don't understand—well I've never been a Liberal tho I have a liberal vein—but by power I understand charisma, charisma used to obtain power. Who can judge it? I had a good telephone conversation with Bobby the night of his entrance, but in San Francisco, a week before his murder, when I talked with him, exchange was impossible. What he said had no relation to what he said later in the day at the debate. He was a noble man, and much was frightening.

Now the poem. It's the first of three, themselves part of a sequence of 170. I had several abusive notes from anti-Kennedy *New Republic* readers; but an almost embarrassedly aroused letter from Jackie, thru whom I'd come to know Bobby, saying the truth of what I'd written was almost unbearable. Well, she's no poetry critic, but she must have understood her brother-in-law as well as anyone. The last line, you don't understand. *Our* is not an editorial we; the secondary meaning, the only one, would give *our* the meaning of *man*'s or *mankind*'s, or the possible future maturity of the country. He may have been our hero; he was never mature; nor would anyone who knew him well and loved him, have thought so. To say he was our maturity robs him of most of [his] true seriousness and pathos.

I don't have ties with many publishers; my own is filled. Why don't you mail your book to Harry Ford at Athenaeum, saying I suggested this. He's done several people I proposed: Snodgrass, Katherine Hoskins . . . I'll be at Quincy House and look forward to seeing you this fall.

Yours affectionately,
Cal

511. *To John Berryman*

[September 22, 1968]

Dear John—

I've now read most of the poems, my admiration still rolling up. I'm dumbfounded at how many of the same things we have: rough iambic lines, often pentameter (for me mostly), short sections that are not stanzas; wife, wives, child, old flames, new ones, sex, love, loves, portraits of writers (I have Frost, Jarrell and Williams too), landscape (I have more of this) portraits of the dead, full middle age, humor, death etc. Well, you have a hundred things

I don't: rhymes, Henry, more jokes, Delmore, Ireland; and you must be the best Irish poet since Yeats. What I like is your ease in getting out everything—I mean everything in your experience, learning, thought, personality etc. is possible mills thru the poetry. I think age helps; but most poets are dwindled by age. Like you I want to go out walking.

Affectionately,
Cal

P.S. Thinking of the differences on my side. Of course, my tone is mine. We both have a good deal of gaiety and desperation; but I would say your world is rather more comic. My universe, my 16 months of time are tragic. I don't think of the *I*'s in either of our poems as tragic, except mostly as all men are, and rather less. Tragic and comic aren't quite the right words, but you will understand.

512. *To the Editor,* Commentary

[n.d. November or December 1968]

A fog of rumor came to us last April of a black descent on Columbia, then the mice stood up at attention with rifles in their hands, nerved for blood, but with fingers stretched to their typewriters. Still, there's no gravy in hitting a respected, not too much on target, though a great lady, controversialist. No one can be in much disagreement with Diana Trilling's desire for more reason, sense, and seniority in our "confrontations and protest." What's crossed then? The fussing at thought, the patter of smear. No one thought Mrs. Trilling heaves into my thoughts lands straight. All's twisted in the current of ignorant, unseeing didacticism, in the rattled sentences of her "On the Steps of Low Library."

Robert Lowell
New York City

513. *To Elizabeth Hardwick*

January 9, 1969

Darling—

I hoped you might call, but all that came was a voice asking for (I think) Mr. Dioscorides. I have been hard going the last couple of years, though when

haven't I been? I am going to do everything to cut down on the drinking, even stop if I must. Not today of course at Bill's birthday, but I'll try to go light. Also, even harder, a pledge to try to do my duties and answer things. Can I become the pillar never absent from the family hearth? I love: your varied interests, your refreshing teaching, your neat clothes, your capacity for keen conversation and argument and most for our lovely child. You know it's hard, I seemed to connect almost unstopping composition with drinking. Nothing was written drunk, at least nothing was perfected and finished, but I have looked forward to whatever one gets from drinking—a stirring and blurring? I'll really try as a child might say, but even the Trinity can't make the crooked stick straight—or young again.

Love, Dearest.

Cal

514. To Shozo Tokunaga

Jan. 10, 1969

Dear Shozo:

I've almost answered nothing for months so busy have I been writing. Let me tackle some of your questions.

QUAKER GRAVEYARD.

1. "Bark" means take the bark or skin off. "Void" is Ahab's death or absence.
2. "Blocked," yes block letters; I guess—on the coffin. I meant the sailor [to be] somewhat symbol[ic] and generic (not necessarily the one the poem's about[.)]
3. "Pitch this portent" troubles me now; portent was the corpse; why portent? Maybe a sign of death and the end of the world. See Hart Crane's Melville poem.
4. Yes, "hell-bent" is right. "Deity," the devil, the god of war; "dreadnaught" pun on a kind of heavy warship and the literal meaning of the words, implying hubris.
5. "Chaste," in the sense of inhuman, sterile, "steel" like a warship.
6. "Roped-in," yes happens, the wharf would have to be very small and run-down; most of the phrases you touch on have something

hyperbolic and exaggerated about them. Too much? (Trying to load lines does make them rather surrealistic, then I didn't quite know this. Now I do a little more with the unreal[.)]

7. Someone in Nantucket once told me if I kept going east I'd come to Spain (enemy of England)[;] maybe "westward" should be "eastward," but I meant looking west toward New England! You know "Castles in Spain" are illusory hopes or possessions.

8. "Eel grass" is grasslike seaweed growing mostly in the shoals, not weeds on ship; "waterclock" is really the globe, a kind [of] round clock, touched by the hours, changes of season. Clear??

9. "Wooden" etc. a cliché maybe: a simpler less complicated older time. You are right about wooden, but it's also pre-steel ships. Also, stiff.

10. Right on "slick." Yes, *even* "if," or an emphatic *if*.

11. Can't quite answer "packing"; sent off quickly and rudely etc. I think the expression is oldish, slang of New England, the South, England still current more in the 19th century. I have a few more slang expressions "swallowed up quick," "barked." "Three quarters," I meant one quarter of *each* was not a fool, but not this precisely.

12. Right on "shoals." "Crabs" may be Eliot, but I got it from Corbière in a poem about Paris. "Quaker Graveyard" began as a translation of that poem, then black turned into blue and nothing but this maybe is left of the original.

(a few lines here)

13. "Unstoned," yes, both sea and Quakers' Graveyards which once had no or few tombs, so a little spot might have hid bodies you could guess.

14. Swept bare of trees. No, the "swingle" is torn, but your inversion is nice and maybe possible.

15. "Stoven"; yes. No comma after "hide"; Jonah a type of Christ, but Christ by my bitter jugglery becomes the whale not the Whaleman.

16. Good on munching, but this word is never used the way I use it. The grass or leaves by the lane could be munched, I guess by some twist I made the lane become its cows.

Dear Shozo, my answers are not as good as your questions, but now I must stop exhausted. Another installment on another day, not tomorrow. Thank

you for your beautiful Kyoto dragon boats, your Christmas card. I go now to a friend's fiftieth birthday, and rush this off.

As ever,
 Robert

Taking up on my way to the station the wife of the outgoing secretary of the interior. How's that for name-dropping, but [she] is someone I've never met.

515. To Peter Taylor

Dear Peter—

How do you like my new stationary? No, it's just a new fold. On the same day as yours I got a letter from Harvard to be there on the 14th and 15th (not for the overseers' meeting as you, but for the Quincy House festival, our equivalent of the Southern spring festivals so charmingly characteristic of your region[)]. So, stop here and we will travel to Cambridge together. I can *show* you some of the ropes, and it's good to know a man on his own ground. I am looking forward to Virginia. I am sad about your mother. I knew you'd want to leave.

I am back today from Newfoundland, the setting of my Grandfather's longest and best loved novel, *Priest of Conception Bay* (really; you can look on a large northern map). End of February, I go to Israel, in a bullet-proof car; middle of March in the same to Spain with Lizzie and Harriet who has always wanted to see the great Velasquez's first-hand and improve her Spanish accent. Then in a float of roses to Charlottesville. As you can see I've finished my long poem? Has anyone told you, you *are* in it?

Love to Eleanor,
 Cal

P.S. Ah Peter, this world of strife! I am in a long tiresome controversy with Diana Trilling. We each seem to think the other is a Maoist. We have a Burmese kitten (small chocolate-covered Siamese) named Sumner for our great somewhat chocolate-covered Senator. Sumnie drops at your feet incessantly a small tan-colored part of a Straus and Giroux envelope and waits. Making sounds in heat. Remember Feather Taylor. When I told Adrienne I was going to Israel she told me she was anti-semitic this winter. Yes, I said eagerly, ["]and anti-Negro." We paused.

P.P.S. Did you read Edmund Wilson's extirpation of everyone I met at your party last spring?

516. *To the Editor,* Commentary

[n.d. Winter 1969]

Controversy is bad for the mind and worse for the heart. I know it's rude and ludicrous for me to have entered this one, and now follow my first "grim communication" with a second. I apologize to Mrs. Trilling the person for my attack on Mrs. Trilling the polemicist. In this game, may the opponents use its wooden swords fairly.

Mrs. Trilling's original article was so haunted with apprehension, and bristling with the professional logic of prosecution, that I did not think it of sufficient interest to "answer." My quarrel is with the part that heavily banters Dwight Macdonald and me. We were not in the picture, but perhaps the article was once planned as a sequel to Mailer's "Steps of the Pentagon," and her plot forced her to borrow two of his supporting characters.

Her rather majestic irony about my "radical piety," and my signing petitions, appearing at rallies, seems to suggest that I act to draw applause from the young, get in fashion, whatever. This may be consoling to her own picture of herself as some housekeeping goddess of reason, preferring the confines of her mind to experience, and pronouncing on the confusion of the crowd, unconfused herself and unpronounced on. Surely, she will not be indicted for activism. On the great day, when she meets her Maker, John Stuart Mill on his right hand and Diderot on his left, they will say, "Liberalism gave you a standard; what have you done for liberalism?" Then she will answer that her record is clear of agitation about the Vietnam war, clear of a feverish concern for the drafting of reluctant young men to fight it, free of a nervous fear about the militarization of our country. Terror of the nuclear bombs never forced her to lose hope. She seems more preoccupied with the little violence of the unarmed student uprisings than with the great violence of the nation at war. She implies that we who are horrified by napalm on human flesh are somehow indifferent to the piss on President Kirk's carpet. She wants to be sure where I stand on this. She asks me many questions.

I answer that I might wish to be a hundred per cent pro-student, but the other morning, or some morning, I saw a newspaper photograph of students marching through Rome with banners showing a young Clark-Gable-style

Stalin and a very fat old Mao—that was a salute to the glacier. No cause is pure enough to support these facts. We are fond of saying that our students have more generosity, idealism, and freshness than any other group. Even granting this, they are only us, younger, and the violence that has betrayed our desires will also betray theirs if they trust to it.

I would like to tell Mrs. Trilling one thing very clearly. I had nothing to do with the student strike at Columbia. I was at Columbia just once two or three weeks before the troubles. I spoke for four or five minutes against President Johnson's Vietnam war. I received tame applause. Also, I want to explain to her, finally I hope, that I have never been New Left, Old Left, or liberal. I wish to turn the clock back with every breath I draw, but I hope I have the courage to occasionally cry out against those who rule us, and wrongly lecture us.

> Robert Lowell
> New York City

517. To Elizabeth Hardwick

> Holyland Hotel
> Jerusalem, Israel
> [March 6, 1969]

Dearest a million miles away Liz:

I never knew I'd miss you so. You go around this queer indescribable country, [. . . from] armies I & 7 II pointed toward the Syrian & Jordanian borders, to a club of friends of Isaiah Berlin's, to fooling utterly at home, Yiddish joking [with] a college president, to the failed Jewish English professor at Iowa in whose gentle hands I am—

But I have the shakes. When I lift the coffee cup to my lips at breakfast table, I don't know whether I can get it there. God, have mercy on me may I not die far from you!

Love (this is lovely if I were a 100 years younger[)]. Love again I miss you so.

> Cal

518. To Elizabeth Hardwick

[March 6, 1969]

My dearest, adored Lizzie:

My hand almost shakes too much to write. I'll see a doctor in a few minutes. I only pray to God that I see you and Harriet again, dearest!

Love

Cal

519. To Elizabeth Hardwick

King David Hotel
Jerusalem, Israel
[March 9, 1969]

Dear Heart:

I guess this has time to arrive before you depart. So loved to hear your voice—4 days ago I went thru a trauma and daze of thinking it couldn't be possible I'd never meet you again. Not so much trouble—just high blood pressure, trembling of foot and hand—remedy don't climb high places, over-drink, stay up too late (all the old things) and take pressure pills. I'm really some ~~enormous~~ high places' percent better than when I wrote & 1000 than 4 days ago.

Thrilling perplexing country—Hakeldama, the Field of Blood for always. I have simple and bulky presents for you both.

All my love,

Cal

520. To Jacqueline Kennedy Onassis

15 West 67 St.
New York City
April 12, 1969

Dear Jackie:

I meant to write you long ago but from the papers you were so mobile I had no idea where to send my letter. Then I expected you might turn up in New York. And then I've been like a mole till lately working on my long poem. I have been a mole to everyone.

I want to wish you joy of your fresh marriage, and liberty from all the vexations and trials of the last few years when you must have felt like someone stationed in a window, and almost tied.

We were in Spain a week or so ago and even in Seville where I thought of you riding. We had a homicidal Spanish driver (they all are, but seem to have few deaths) whose only aim was to keep us on "main" highways, and ours to get off them on terrible winding ribbons blocked by craters and donkeys. Yet we had a lovely journey.

If you get back here do let me see you and meet your husband.

Affectionately as ever,

Cal

521. To Jerome Mazzaro

May 26, 1969

Dear Mazzaro:

How can I say something nice about the care, interest and distinction of your thoughts in reviewing me, and at the same time say that something troubles about the unreality and abstraction. Your baroque music for Berryman, tree for Miss Bishop and citizen, politics etc. for me seem best as good poetic intuitions. As critical insights they are either untrue or murky.

But these are errors, I think: *variously rhymed*; but except for two [or] three old sonnets reprinted, I have only about ten rhymes in my book; *Chekhov*; but I only meant a sensitive prose language, using like his many images—if I had caught something of his spirit, I would be surprised and delighted; I can't imagine Jarrell as taking the State as an index of God's purpose—we began publishing in a time when *the* State was Hitler's Reich—most of Jarrell's references to the state regard it as a sort of malign giant, Calvin's God, but Jarrell didn't believe in God; in the same way somewhat,—I think of politics as real, a possible subject, but not remotely as truth, whatever that can be in actions?

I don't think any of the other poets you name ever thought of themselves as belonging or not belong[ing] to a Lowell Circle. I don't think I ever heard the words till yesterday in your piece. A graver matter is the competition, the boxing match. Without it, I think we miss some of the pleasure of writing: part of it is rather like a tennis match. Who would play without scoring? But how can you score in poetry? In what contest that means anything can we enter our poems and books? The scales do not exist to weigh art. Yet some

things are better or greater. I must call the contest emulation. Probably the periods when many artists, not just one, are excellent, are ~~caused~~ helped by this emulation. But fame or reputation is another thing sometimes having little or nothing [to do] with works of art. I suppose it's the flaw in us that makes us dance with such jealousy and keenness for this prize. In this too, some good.

Pardon these stray sentences. Now that I am happily ~~(?)~~ through writing for a while, I have leisure to do a little of this sort of thing. Thanks again for your piece.

Yours truly,
Robert Lowell

522. To Jacqueline Kennedy Onassis

June 25, 1969

Dear Jackie:

Tomorrow we drive off to Maine, wife, child and cat (Charles Sumner[)] (named after the great Massachusetts abolitionist, and a sable-brown Siamese)

Ah so much time! I kept thinking of it. I can't even grope back clearly to the short time ago we met (64?) I mean here in New York. It was at the Liebersons (with my book displayed on the table) with Stravinsky still quite hale; or was it with Morris Graves talking about a nose he had designed for the moon-ship? Anyway a continent seems gone since Joe's in Washington. Each week I get a request to say what I would say on getting out on the moon. All I can think of is, "We're here." But that's not for publication.

You have always written me thrilling letters about my work. I don't think anyone cares more, tho I've never been ill-dealt with. I'm glad you feel my lines on Bobby ring right. The first was a windfall, but I had to blow long on the coals of the second two for my flame. He stays young in many minds.

It amused me rather to entitle the poem after yours "Another Friend," the second friend was a purely fictional wraith. I too am always your friend. Surely we will meet next fall and winter.

Love as always,
Cal

523. To Stephen Spender

15 West 67 St.
NYC
June 25, 1969

Dearest Stephen:

I think your criticism is about the most acute I've had. All the reviewers nearly point out the unevenness of my sonnets. Something fairly even is often written in prose, or blankverse, or continuous rhymed stanzas—never in discontinuous sonnets. I would have liked each line to have been better than the last, and knew this was impossible. If I had expected somesort of non-stop inspiration, I wouldn't have finished a ~~section~~ poem. Instead of a collection of anthology pieces, I have a note-book. You very truly point out how there must be ups and downs. All were worked as much as I had the strength. If Karl Shapiro hadn't written something called *Essay on Rime*, I might have called my book *Rhymes* (in contrast to Pound's *Cantos*) to underline my book's highly-wrought, bumpy short scope. But to me it's a world.

I imagine I must have been reading your student book at the same time as you were reading me. I like it all, particularly the humorous narrative parts, Paris, meeting Ginsberg. And I have puzzled with your speculation as much as my imagistic mind would let me. I think it's one of your best books, one people will keep coming back to on the subject. Strange, even as I was reading it it was somehow in the air, or more likely in the news that the great student bubble was dropping in flakes. And what was poignant, fascinating, threatening and boring had left its vacancy. Who can accept what will fill that vacancy?

Now an apology. With you I always feel that in my exuberant callousness I am liable to sound off before you on some subject you are expert on. Well, not Oxford, but German poetry, or even Wystan. No, you can never be an old, old man of terrifying tantrums like Ivor. Thank heaven!

Lizzie heard from Natasha that you had been troubled with skin cancer on your back. May it go clean away. The surprising sorrow when our own bodies bite us!

Dear Stephen, thanks for your two letters and your many years of love and affection. Lizzie and I send our love to you and Natasha.

Cal

524. To Richard Tillinghast

Dear Dick—

I am writing you from casual notes "the morning after" going thru your two fascinating and heady for me chapters. I've made notes at random and not on everything, or everything that struck me.

First *Union Dead*—this hasn't ever been written on in much detail, so your criticism seems fresher than on *Life Studies*, tho this probably isn't true.

Introductory remarks—generally very intuitive—but here is more or less my order and principles of the writing. A hard book: 2 poems[,] "Drinker" and "Union Dead[,]" written painfully in the winter of 58–59 before going to New York. One personal, tho a fiction, one a public "ode" tho autobiographically truth. In both I was trying to give the "free verse" of *Life Studies* greater resonance and rhetoric (sound effects, history). Nothing more for a year while I did *Phèdre*, *Imitations* (partly written earlier) and *Old Glory*. Winter of 60–61 most of the "Williams" poems: 1st six (only "Hudson" took a year and a half to write (cut from two long pages) and was finished after the metrical poems)[,] "Eye and Tooth" (no, I don't think your symbols of masturbation, pubic hair etc. are much to the point[)]. I very consciously meant the Tiresias Voyeur symbolism, the eye seeing sex, the women's bodies for which it is punished. This is all true and/or intended. Did you see my first draft of this in my Williams essay? Rest of your examination is very good and true—the highly personal nature of the poem . . . I did more or less drop this line—weariness or had I done it? Then, I think, I wrote "Edwards," biography in free verse stanzas, a correction of a kind to my ~~harsher~~ more dramatic earlier "Edwards." He was an ancestor, but this doesn't make our relation exactly personal—another grandfather. Next wave, winter of 61–62, the metrical poems. "Caligula" was an exercise in writing a poem of my own in couplets, after doing Racine, a more open style maybe than "Falling Asleep"; "Severed Head" also a metrical exercise, started in spring chipped at interminably during the summer; it's influenced by Tate, even a bow to him—he rather naturally thought it the best thing I'd written, but I have always found it a gloom of toil, much better tho if the last short section went. I think "Brazil," "Buenos Aires," "Night Sweat," New York fragment came about this time. You see I was deliberately using meter, "Public Garden." Others partly regular come earlier I think, but after the "Williams" poems: "Florence" (you're very good

on this)[,] "Urn," "Tenth Muse," "Hawthorne." This order is only half true, so much revision, faulty memory. Yet they are generally true; as you acutely say there's another obscure, more Montale group: "Going," "Myopia," "Law" (its image half remembered, half composed in my mind that haunted me—this time I may really have meaning I am largely unaware of). "Returning," it started from a late Ungaretti called "Stanze" or something, or "Ulysses"? "The Lesson," where I had Stevens in mind (a tribute?) just as I had Ransom in mind in "Those Before Us" (very good on this). So, you riddled the book more or less correctly, perhaps too faintly noting its painful start and stop composition. I think [I] never had less to go on from poem to poem—I clutched at different methods till they wore out.

Additional notes on *Union Dead*. The oriole's nest is a real nest, not part of the clock; I meant to link moon on clock and oriole, from metal to nature, a joyful ending that isn't. "Brazil"—ending isn't a breakdown, tho there was one, and the poem was written after recovery—maybe it's better as a breakdown, but who could ~~know~~ tell this? Aunt Harriet is *Cousin* Harriet; everyone makes this mistake. "Lesson"—*you*, I've never known; your *one* and quite likely your other interpretations might do, but I felt a tremor of addressing someone loved, a close friend, myself, a girl. I never wrote syllabics knowingly. I took a lot of pains with my free verse rhyme, tho they work more or less as you say. The heroine of "Water" is Elizabeth Bishop; this doesn't change the poem perhaps, but if it were to Jean Stafford, the whole scene would be more symbolic. I of course didn't plan four elements in the first four poems, no Seasons of the Soul.

Your page 58 is a brilliant example of what interesting things can happen when you are both personal and generalizing. The only trouble with the book is too much paraphrase. Now your paraphrases almost always tell something very perceptive, but they are necessarily more lucid and in a different tone. Do you know Winters' description of Tate's "Subway" sonnet in *Primitivism*, where he shows that the insanity of experience in the poem ending in numbness is almost the opposite of what the poem does? What the poem says is not what it does.

More notes. Trilling is interesting in his anthology on my "Union Dead" poem. I feel "Flaw" is one of your favorites; mine too! I spent a whole summer rewriting less than ten lines (along with "Soft Wood" done in two days, two drafts, maybe)[,] labor lost mostly on "Severed Head"—like "Caligula," he is my *debased* alter ego—he really existed tho, before I Hawthornized him into allegory. In *Notebook*, if you've seen it, I cut "Night Sweat" to [the] first sonnet—I have so many other poems to Lizzie there that this doesn't maybe matter, and I think the first much the stronger, despite the turtle.

Life Studies—Rosenthal is far from a natural critic, but I find him best and very good on *Life Studies* part IV. He covers the ground. What you do which is refreshing and different is to be interested not just in the poems, but in their subjects, subjects which often live only in the poems and could be learned about from no [o]ther source—my parents. My Father: of course, I can't judge whether my picture is sympathetic. My interpretation and yours wouldn't be entirely contradictory. It's possible to see him in my poems as a helpless suffering thing that Hardy would [have] been hurt for. I put on the satire, but if it's all satire, easy game and no anguish, the poem narrows. I weep for him when I read the poem, maybe that's private. Maybe I throw in too much Freud, I try to use him two thirds (?) skeptically and playfully. Even then I found his Faith harder to take straight than the Pope's. And for Faith,— I hadn't been a Catholic for about four years when I met Santayana in '50. Like what you write on him. The joke about "oldman on the Yangtse" is his youth, but I guess you get that. Very good on people and me in hospital. If your interpretation is penetrating, it doesn't matter if it isn't mine, or even one I might have thought of. Some of your interpretation is very unclear without the text (which you ask the reader to have at hand) while most [of] the interpretations don't need the text; maybe just to me. Isn't the Richard, *Richard II*, not *III*? That would fit my meaning much better. We talked didn't we last summer about the Ovid stanza. I wish the poem could be clear without it. Berryman aggrandized my work on this stanza to 100 hours, tho God knows how much I spent—much less. The prose in *Life Studies* was never therapy, except as my own therapy for a long period of not being able to write new poems. (I had forgotten the man in "L'Azur" was in a hospital, if I'd ever known it—a break![)]The man who said "hardly passionate" about Marlborough St. was either Henry or William James, but I don't know the source. Jarrell's caution on proposing and disposing comes from his *Kavanaugh* review, particularly the long poem, where I am most bossy. You speak of *millions* of Germans killed by our bombing, but this seems high and worse glib, even if the numbers were over a million, as they must have been. Not too happy about your occasional vacations into political polemic; they are a little quick and light.

Let me finally give the order of the autobiographical parts of *Life Studies*. First in 1954 (?) while in a long depression in the Payne Whitney Clinic, came "Uncle Dev." and possible the little poems after "Commander Lowell." These were very rude prose sketches, to be worked up into what I don't know, but they ~~impressed~~ surprised Lizzie and I put them away for years. Then came the long published prose piece in 1956, no fragment but hard work (I had Henry Adams and Flaubert's *Education*, which I was painfully reading in

French—as models[)]. I found the problems and possibilities of a sentence, a paragraph as charming as anything I'd done; yet revision and retyping so much was detestable—so impossible not to find holes, so tedious to ~~retype~~ plug them. I think that's why the autobiography stopped. I had other difficulties—a dread of more of the same, impossibility of honestly showing the living, at loss for a plot to pass beyond childhood. I did write more tho, a sketch of Dunbarton. Now 1957 the poems began (I'd written none for four years) with the first part of "Man and Wife" (after a too strenuous reading tour of the West Coast) which seemed to open things pressing inside of me. I couldn't finish. Then at summer's end and a visit from Elizabeth Bishop, I began "Skunk Hour" as a loose rendering of Hölderlin's "Brot," and heaping on Maine scenery. I think no Hölderlin is left. Then (roughly, I was working on five or six things at once) "Commander Lowell," drawn from Rimbaud's "Poètes de Sept Ans" (half my pieces come from something) "Crane" revised, "Terminal Days," "Sailing Home," "Lepke," "Man and Wife" finished, "To Speak" (from a late bitter poem of Catullus, but maybe nothing's left of that). Then I had a breakdown, quite a jolt, the first in four years (from then on they were to come yearly, until lithium pills, now none). After the *three months* I wrote the poem with that title. The fury of composition had gone. I had a feeling from certain criticism, tho most [of] the old poets were kind (Eliot, Pound, Williams) about my handful of new work—I felt I should perhaps be more formal. Also I wanted to write a complete book and was unsure how to on ~~mere~~ push. It took almost the rest of the year to write the remaining poems: "Waking"—done most while sick, but not the ending which makes it a poem; "During Fever," "Dunbarton" and the two short poems were fairly easy; "Grandparents" was a try at joy in a loose formality. People have different opinions on the unity and success of *Life Studies*; for me, a decent unity came after staring into impossibility. Earlier a new style had come, freedom and an accomplishment after more or less staring into the wall. I meant the skunks at the end to move with their thud of triumph. My whole sad, hesitating journey to their walk is perhaps no less so—tactics of ~~survival~~ stopping so as not to stop.

Here are my marginal thoughts. I think your piece is brilliant. Am grateful more than I can write. Wish you'd consider a book, if you cared to waste the time.

Affectionately,

Cal

525. To Hannah Arendt

August 16, 1969

Dearest Hannah:

Paradise? I guess your wonderful letter is a plant or flower tossed me from there. To answer your questions. I knew I had something else from Gray, but couldn't find it, had even forgotten its source in Nietzsche. I'm afraid I would add twenty pages to my book if I put in acknowledgements for such things—and the reader would be enraged at my pretension. The Mao is entirely a parable and unverified. It came from I. A. Richards, who refused to say he ever told it. Maybe he didn't[,] there's a chance for confusion in evening discussion. Many good reviews, but none better than Meredith's, none memorable, tho many with good things. None of the authors were known to me, and I mix them now hopeless[ly] in my mind.

I fear I have been adding new poems all summer. Influence of environment—they all fit into my last year's sections on summer. I hardly see in the city. I have 15 more, and may have two or three still, before mid-September, my deadline for the English printing. I don't know what I've added, but a crack inside me was filled. I think they stand up with the old, and, scattered here and there, fill out hollows. This must end. We've had a wonderful summer with Mary, the very best; and she actually spent three days, (three half-days,) helping me find flaw in the old poems. Excuse all this talk. I forgot for a minute and thought I was finishing a new book . . . one done last March.

Could you come up here? I think we'll all stay till the 10th or so. Also there's a good house for sale, about $25,000 (?) near the water.

Harriet has had an against-the-current summer. No friends, the full shyness of twelve. She has spent day after day with the little twenty year old Spanish girl who works for us. They do three things: TV, jigsaw, and talk about the cat. Maybe not too bad; I spent most of a summer listening to professional baseball on the radio, in a store room and many more trolling alone for pickerel. Still, it's broken, she has started swimming cooking, picking wild flowers, and now her friend has come, and they are like people about to announce an engagement—this figure is out of hand, this experience is more than innocent.

Today, the whole village has been on tiptoe for the "Old Skippers' Race," Maine natives sailing the summer people yachts—we have 16 in the harbor, 3 Castine owned. And as usual, this has been one of the three days all summer too foggy to race. Tonight Senator McCarthy is coming to us—with Mary

and Jim supplying the roast, Mary cooking, Jim carving and we providing the house and liquor.

Ah the going of the summer! The only news I've attended [to] is the miserable Kennedy business. A real summer tragedy, I've known it in the past, have almost lived it, long in the past, still might etc. Otherwise I feel better, better physically but also irrationally better about things. Maybe it's an empty mood, or maybe I mean everyone seems to have gotten over practicing for ~~calamity~~ crisis. Mary and we had dinner with a local leftist clergyman, one who had invited Foreman to his church in New York, but the most innocent of men. He said, "~~Don't feel guilty~~ (no, doesn't one) feel guilty up here away from all suffering and problems?" And Mary said haltingly, excitedly, "No, I feel just the opposite."

Lizzie and I send our love to you and Heinrich. Do try and come up. Vacation must last till Christmas, had one the nerve to stay.

Love,
Cal

526. To John Berryman

15 West 67 St.
N.Y.C.
September 9, 1969

Dearest John:

I'm really just back an hour or two from Castine. I've come to New York for some reason with feet of stone. I suppose I couldn't take a winter in the country—a whole winter with its lack of cronies, the people I love, or rather a winter in the country with the society it must give you. Loneliness would do better. But this place hammered together with stone, dirt and bad sounds! Anyway I feel autumnal, my feet drag.

How good, tho sad to get your letter. I take it awful as your optical nerve is, you will get over it. I've had nothing like that, but troubles with blood pressure. One day in Israel I couldn't get my coffee cup to my lips, my hand shook so. I thought I'd had a stroke, but it turned out to be largely a wrong prescription. These wretched little black splinters mortality hits us with. Well, we both know it. I'd like to scorn it, not quite as Yeats. It seems silly to triumph that much. He too knew he couldn't. At the beginning of the summer I felt embar-

rassed and hesitant about getting on the tennis court; at the end tho I think I was better (quicker) than for two years or so—I wouldn't go back farther.

About my book. It does seem to have to be read through. At least several people have said so. It's kind of [an] oddly plotted novel, a very short, dense, rather difficult novel. My fear was of being over crusty and wrought. During the summer, I could do nothing else. So, against intention, I added 20 or so new poems. Scattering them through the book, so its hard for me to judge their effect or effectiveness. I guess they're up to the others and enough different. Also I revised retouched some 20 or thirty old poems in *Notebook*. Now I'm done; this last will be the first English edition and third American printing. I don't know whether I have anything more in me worth ~~printing~~ adding.

But you? There were new and top Dream Songs in the *Advocate*. If you can go on that way, why stop ever? (Blackmur)

Sometimes, it's only love that lets air in our lungs.

Now our love to you and Kate, thanks for your large letter. I'd rather have your praise than anyone else.

> Cal

What chance of seeing each other? I might manage the journey out to you.

527. To Elizabeth Bishop

November 10, 1969

Dearest Elizabeth:

I've owed you a letter forever; and you me! Dr. Baumann has just read me over the phone a sort of joint letter from you and Roxanne to her. You've had a buffeting time. But I see you are mending, indomitable. I saw Pound here last spring, very silent and gone, he and Marianne Moore weighing less than 140 pounds. He was in a stately chair at the Public Library; whenever a woman came up, he stood up and bowed. Once he said to me, "These chairs of state were a mistake." (That's about all he said, except once when Louise Bogan came to see him, and said, "I was on the Committee," and Pound seemed at sea, then he said "I always thought that was one of Cal's jokes.") What I'm getting to is, I finally said, "For God's sake sit down, Ezra," and he, "I've done nothing but sit down all afternoon." You've been doing nothing

but getting to your feet. I mean this as a great tribute, but of course you've seldom been off your feet. I keep thinking of Coleridge—you know he was medically right in his treatment of ~~yourself~~ himself. No, you must take care, my Dear.

Here, it's Washington March week, a fever of activity. Slightly unlikely people in the van. Mary McCarthy, here from Paris for dentistry, marshalling signatures for a proclamation; my old friend Blair Clark, speaking at Purdue[,] Chicago and Washington. I get less leftist, if that were possible, every day, but am going to the march again with Dwight. It's a mammoth ball, fed and checked by hopes of danger. I trust it will be mostly tame. You can't tell, quite.

I go on writing: 56 more sonnets to go into the book, scattered, for the first British edition next fall—bigger, more expensive, the title now simply *NOTEBOOK*. I don't seem to do much else, though my Harvard teaching is good fun. I'm doing Shakespeare's English histories. And as far as I prepare at all, read mostly history, not criticism. My dearest regards to Roxanne, and all my love as always to you. I seem to spend my life missing you!

Love,
Cal

528. To Marcia Nardi

[n.d. 1969]

Dear Marcia Nardi—

I woke this morning with a start of shame to realize I'd completely forgotten to get in touch with you. Then at breakfast a second letter was in my mailbox. Here's the story. I've read your poems rather hurriedly and feel their great strength, but haven't yet anything very close to say about them. The reason why this is so is that all fall I've suffered from some sort of thyroid excess or deficiency, both at once in different "areas," I think. It leaves me with waves of languor; I can't sit through a movie, my meager preparation for classes is a toil etc. Probably the thing isn't serious or dangerous but absolutely nothing can be done till more tests are made. I think I am even forwarding science. Anyway about everything has gone unattended to, except my writing. Here, strangely, the weariness doesn't touch and I can sometimes work 15 hours a day, I think, when I get back to New York from Harvard.

I very much want to see you; I guess I've known you with admiration for 20 years, since *Paterson* II and of course the other names you give such as

Randall. I can't open gates really; I'm always failing. Still, if one publisher won't leap, somewhere another will. My best luck has been with Harry Ford at Athenaeum. Let's have lunch sometime soon after the 18th when I'm through here and have decently studied your text.

Yours with apologies,
Robert

529. To Richard Tillinghast

December 12, 1969

Dear Richard—

I have owed you a letter for some time. I've been tied up, writing furiously, finishing up the term. I like the preface. I lacked the chance of course of reading it as it should be before knowing anything else in the book. It gives it a powerful shove. I felt, I think, a little as Bill did (tho maybe for slightly different reasons) about the politics. A couple of weeks ago, at Boston College someone asked me from the audience for the first time what I thought of the Revolution. I said, "This is a question, I'm prepared to handle. Tell me what you mean by revolution, and I'll tell you what I think." He repeated his question without increment; so I gave a rambling, confused and to me satisfactory description of my adolescent fascination with the French Revolution. I think the word is a dead word for the critic (of literature?) until he makes it live and think. I've just read a five page review by a man named Feldman in *Dissent*; he takes me (tho he notices contradictions) as a public figure of the extreme radical new left, then in alternating paragraphs of fierce polemic and almost fiercer admiration, treats me as a radical propagandist. He finds "Leader of the New Left" sentimental praise, and my light verse on President Kirk bitterer than my Stalin. Still, his politics are almost frantically real. I think someone might question whether yours are. They give you liveliness and freedom to describe and judge. You are usually uncannily right, and seldom wrong—whatever that means. I thank you for so much time, brilliance and warmth. You mustn't be gone too long, because I and many others will deeply miss you.

Affectionately,
Cal

P.S. Even you might have been a little overamused if you had met in 1943 during your first moments in jail a kooky doped up black.

530. To William Meredith

February 17, 1970

Dear Bill—

Your letter I had mislaid turned up in a coat pocket, and tho you say not to answer and I shan't, I must, I want to say something. Probably you've never had a *real* depression. I think I have. Tensing at the thought of each new meeting, never speaking more than one sentence, and that dull, and other things that, however, would [not] at all bear on your life: Two happy moments a day, that of falling asleep, of waking with a dream I thought would continue (if I were in luck). None seemed to mind, tho occasionally I was chided by people for being restrained.

What I am aiming at is that you shouldn't avoid your friends for fear of being below yourself. They won't notice, alas, or won't care. I won't care. You are always the same to me.

Since I really saw you, I guess my life has [had] many shadows and slips, but I've been too generally happy to really remember. We go to Italy for 3 weeks on March 18, then I guess I go on to Oxford for two months.

Let's try to see each other before we leave.

Affectionately,

Cal

531. To Elizabeth Bishop

March 11, 1970

Dearest Elizabeth—

Your letter cheered me up in a somewhat shadowed moment. But also you *sounded* so calmly high-spirited, amused, at ease and easily sure. Well, it's not that way, but this exuberance must be in you despite your affliction. You cheered me too by liking the poems to you which I feared you might not. I had always wanted you in the first *Notebook,* yet nothing came and I even wrote an inferior sonnet form of "Water" which got as far as galleys and then I withdrew it.

Ah, the award! I like to make a cut at boldness occasionally, ~~but~~ this I think I had to do. The rather curious jury, due to Rexroth, left Pound off the listings of poets to be considered (Meredith put him on). No one even noticed the omission, but there was great clamor about *Ada* and *Portnoy* not being listed.

I came from the wings to the bright stage (first twenty red plush rows absolutely empty) as "recipients" do and said more or less this: That I felt very shy receiving the award for you, that you had always been my favorite poet and favorite friend, I said it was hard on the stage to say anything of much critical worth. I spoke of your enormous powers of realistic observation and of something seldom found with observation, luminism (meaning radiance and compression etc.) and so on for a few ~~more~~ sentences. Then I said I was going to say something perhaps ungracious, but that I cared not, because I would [have] considered myself dishonored if I didn't say it. Then I spoke of the complaints (named no names) and said that on the whole I agreed with the complainings but that a much more important author, Ezra Pound who had published a little book in June, one of his good books and quite possibly his last, had been mentioned by no one. (Just before me a long communication from the author of the prize-winning Huey Long biography had been read—not a word of criticism, it was like Humphrey speaking of Johnson five years ago—And before that Lillian Hellman had made a "courageous" attack on Agnew.) I said you've just heard about two great statesmen; Pound was a very small statesman and a very great poet. Then I read your St. Elizabeths poem (in the beginning I'd said I would read one of your poems, because your cable hadn't arrived). I said it was a clear poem whose meaning was hard to determine, the tone was reverential mockery or mocking reverence. I went back to my seat on stage—decent applause. Behind me a voice saying, "I announce that I sever myself from this antisemitic fascist performance." Rexroth in sideburns, tho I didn't know at the time. Well, the master of ceremonies, he was a silly little man who made nonstop afterdinner jokes. Just one was quite good: Some author was writing a novel about eight bicycle thugs. He was asked how he found his plot, and answered, By taking the plot of *The Group* and changing the sex. But he saved my life by instantly saying, I want to announce that I disassociate myself from anyone who could say what you've just heard was antisemitic or Fascist. There was faint applause for Rexroth and more for the master of ceremonies. And so things passed off.

On the way out, I got congratulations. Eric Erikson, an acquaintance from Harvard, said, "Why did the guy do that to you?" And I, "He's one of the poetry judges." (Rexroth had made the short citation of your award break into two about equal parts describing you and some protégé of his named Whalen.) Then I said (Rexroth wasn't there) "The bastard." And Erickson looked at me in red-faced amazement then repeated, "The bastard."

Now. Then two days later—I was away in Cambridge and later Province-

town—the telephone rang at 5:30 a.m. (unlisted number) and a voice, quite calm and clear, said ["]this is the voice of the shofar["] (the Jewish ramshorn for war). Quite good music; Lizzie listened a minute or so, then expecting it to change to the usual anonymous obscenities, hung up. Next morning, same hour, another call. Confusion of connections. Apparently long distance. Voice of operator, saying to Lizzie, "Do you want to speak to Mr. Levin?" Disconnection, or she hung up. In about an hour, another call; voice asking for me, something about ["]tell him to make peace with his God." Lizzie "I never heard anything so impertinent and absurd. He is at peace with God." Voice, something about "last rites" then "tell him on this day he is going to die." Vain threat! It sounds buffoonish as I tell it, but that was not the effect, it seemed dignified and terrifying. No more now for five days. I assume it's over. But how lousy!

 All my love to you,
 Cal

P.S. Awful week for Lizzie and Harriet. Harriet was the cooler. "Tell him if they call again, Dad is off on his trip to Israel." Also, "What do they mean by *his* God, there's only one God."

 Lovely translation of Vinícius & story about him. I met a man, drunk, yesterday who said his only ~~true~~ fault was a reprobative wife.

532. To Allen Tate

March 19, 1970

Dear Allen:
 I tried to get you on the telephone but was told you had gone to Nashville. I know I can't apologize adequately. Somehow all the Tate material has been lost. I brought it back from Maine in a special carton, then placed it on a shelf in my study bookcase, then back in a carton. When I was away recently, my study was cleaned all too thoroughly by the maid and she threw out the carton. When your letter arrived, I remember telling Lizzie that I'd have the stuff off to you in a minute because it was all collected in one place. Hell!
 I feel like Mill with Carlyle's *French Revolution*. Only I trust nothing I had was the single existing copy. I feel this is my final impertinence to you after my very bad performance with the book. Sometimes, it's impossible to admit one won't or somehow can't do something. Your poetry and probably everything

else you have written needs a fresh angle, a new word. I think of Gothic for lack of a better, but this has misleading suggestions of Poe, and old horror novels. A grand style, often very clean and blunt, a mixture of symbol, courtesy and terror, caught up in history. There's nothing like it, tho I and many others have imitated here and there. When the future reader picks you up, he will pick up your world, its earth and memories.

We leave today for Italy, all three of us[,] Harriet interested in Venice but certain she'll see as few churches as possible—those stately similar monuments of outworn superstition. Then I go on to Oxford and won't return till late June. Love to Helen and the children. Please forgive me.

Love,
Cal

533. To Allen Tate

All Souls College
Oxford
April 25, 1970

Dear Allen:

You have plenty to be sore about. I of course can't excuse my undertaking to do the book, then delaying interminably, then not doing it, then losing the material you sent me.

My stumbling block was writing the essay. You claim a mysterious intuition into my motives which I do not possess. But you know why one doesn't write something—the reasons why you didn't write your novel in 1942, or I my Jonathan Edwards book. That good winter. It would be hard to say, but our motives were nothing sinister; neither were mine in again writing poetry and putting off the essay. I could answer all your other accusations (tho none of us can ever be as white as this piece of paper) but I only wish to take up one. I certainly wouldn't have embarrassed or patronized you in New York. You know what you say isn't true.

Ah Allen, which of us has insulted the other more. You have, as is right. I was your student and younger friend. Your letter isn't a good way to keep friends. Please forgive me for the book business, which I trust will come out happily. And forget your diatribe, it's too inspired by half. And please believe that I love you,
Cal

534. To Elizabeth Hardwick

April 25, 1970

Dearest, here I am not quite a day yet, a half lost soul in All Souls about to have lunch with the Berlins. The first two people I met here were Charles Monteith and A. L. Rowse. It's a bachelor world, but very beautiful. Oxford is rather like Bath—Bath and Yale, quite Italian. I have eaten in gown, handled a 14th century psalm book, not much else.

Thanks for your lovely letters (I had good ones from Elizabeth, Farb and Donald Davie, who is at Stanford and suggested that I might like getting out of my country, just as he wished to leave England[)]. I'll go to Essex next week and phone or write you immediately, when I know a little more. I think we could live in London and I could do the sort of thing I did at Havrd. London is fifty minutes by train. I think the change of air might be refreshing and clear the mind. In fact, if I like Essex and hear good things about it, I am inclined (if you and Harriet are willing). We could begin this October or next.

Holland. I stayed 16 days with Huyck and Judith and loved it all. I think I saw literally everyone we saw before, except that strange couple with the lovely father who read *Finnegans Wake*. All sent their love, and Hank van Galen Last, three times. I suppose they are all what we would call Old Left, but without the unpleasant features of many of ours. They are all still friends but with many rifts.

Waiting [for] me of course was a blistering letter from Allen, a rather paranoid reading of my motives. I wrote him a gentle, I hope, rather appeasing letter back. I don't want to excuse my failure with his festschrift. Give H. my love. I miss you both so. This must go now.

Cal

[typed on the envelope:]

P.S. We are now enjoying a hail storm, crystal peas bouncing off mouldy parapets. Winter is long. Huyck's Mother, old and sick, said "It's nice to have a nice guest since summer is late."

535. To Donald Davie

<div align="right">April 27, 1970</div>

Dear Donald Davie:

Yes, I think the expatriate business is much more important than whether one likes England and Holland (where I have just been) or America better. I suppose I am Leftist in a rather removed way, or is it that I am Conservative in a rather middleclass and dissolute way. The labels don't work. I have no faith in idealist violence or in revolution. I don't like the drear safe/unsafe iron frame of what is established.

No doubt what troubled you, troubles me: we suck the strife in with the air we breathe, we suck in too much controversial argument from our friends. Just after the War, I was in New York, seeing almost no one but my dear gone friend, Jarrell. He was editing the book section of the *Nation*, and he kept quoting Nijinsky: "Politics is death." Well, it gives us alms, but a writer really has very different cravings and necessities.

I think I'll take, or may take, the Essex job. My wife and child can live in London, and I'll commute. From Edwards' letter, I think they'll give me four thousand pounds for teaching from October till Easter. Two years. Not quite as good as I have here. Then I'll go back. In the summer too, we'll probably go back, like you.

Your poem is lived. Could I say that your style and inspiration embody the sincerity and ~~awkwardness~~ embarrassment you find wanting in the Argentine poet? You'll have no trouble finding another American publisher. I would be glad to write anyone if you should feel in need of a backer, which you won't.

Drop me a note when you get here. I expect to leave sometime in the late 20s of June.

Robert Lowell

P.S. Thank you for your sensitive, kind letter. I very much want to see you.

536. To Elizabeth Hardwick

POSTCARD: Caravaggio, *David with Goliath's Head*, Borghese Gallery, Rome

[April 30, 1970]

Dearest—

I am sorry I was so mute on the phone. At the start two others seemed competing with you. The stones here are beginning to soften. Everyone is very kind and casual. All love to you both, I'm off to London.

Cal

1970–1977

Writing of *The Dolphin* and *Day by Day* • Separation from Hardwick •
Birth of Sheridan Lowell • Marriage to Caroline Blackwood

Oxford • London • Bearsted • Cambridge • New York City • Ireland

Lowell with Caroline Blackwood, Ivana and Evgenia Citkowitz, Bearsted, England, circa 1971 (courtesy Xandra Bingley)

537. To Elizabeth Hardwick

Dearest—

What delightful letters you write! Your little jokes and Mr. Menzies (whatever the papers man is). I've seen the Caroline McCulloch movie, and found it surprisingly good, tho I can follow myself always in print or picture with a certain suspension of disbelief and even of boredom. Everyone feels a strange feminine person, at first unseen and merely a Southern voice, crowns the show, or is the darling of the show. Mary is very good and I think about half the movie is that long wine dinner at Castine. It's like life, only I'm allowed to talk enormously more.

I have accepted Essex and will receive confirmation in a day or so from the Vice-provost, or what ever the queer anomalous title of the head of the university is. I get 4000 pounds about 8000 dollars, but much more in buying power. A minimum this, but it will be more and go up. Appointment for two years, but I can make it one, or permanent—but then the taxes would be much higher. Apparently for two years it does not have to be taxed (?).

Not [much] news since calling. I gave my first student reading last week, of me and others. In a little while I have dinner with Sir Maurice Bowra, very affectionate, loud and deaf. The Berlins have him for a guest each summer, and have two plans: to persuade him that the [illegible] Junta is becoming liberal so he can go back to Greece or marry him to Sonia (my idea). But he is very nice and distinguished. People shower me with offprints, nevertheless I've found time to walk under Arnold's Cumner Hills. Everyone is keeping an ear open for a house or flat for us, if possible on one of the parks.

All love,
Cal

Dear Harriet, this is me at the end of a dinner. Hope your eyes are removed. O.K. Dal (Dad)

538. To Elizabeth Hardwick

May 26, 1970

Dearest Lizzie—

What's up? Such boiling messages, all as public as possible on cables and uninclosed postcards. It's chafing to have the wicked, doddering, genial old All Souls' porter take down your stinging cable. It matters not; everything must be pressing you this moment in New York.

Grey and Bingo, but mostly Bingo, are flat or house hunting. She is in touch with three or four agencies. I think something near Regent's Park or Hampstead would be best for Harriet. Not too far from the center of the city, yet parkish. I crave not to look out on traffic, even here in Oxford, it goes on like the ocean.

I've just given a reading at Bristol for Christopher Ricks; Grey drove me over and Mary McCarthy took a train from London to arrive with a guide book of Gloucestershire. Lovely day of Bristol strolling and supper in the country.

I've written Harriet a letter without funny pictures and animal jokes.

What else? Bingo thinks it will be perfectly possible for us to find a place without forcing you to come over. They have three. Things can be found, nice places, tho probably their main heat will have to be supplemented with plug-in heaters.

About letters—I can't pour them out, Dear. Every mail alas brings in a new tide, and some must be answered. Today, a nice one from Desmond Harmsworth with a translation of Valéry's *Cimetière*. Also letters from All Souls seem to arrive four or five days after mailing.

Miss you both—Luv,
Cal

539. To Elizabeth Hardwick

May 31, 1970

Dearest Lizzie:

Very Oxford day: in the crowds watching the bumping (8) boat races on the Isis, lunch with Iris Murdoch and her husband, Aline, Lord David Cecil, Father Peter Levi; funeral of Enid Starkie at St. Mary the Virgin; afternoon of reading Warden Sparrow's Shakespeare books—and yesterday an immense walk from Godstow to Oxford over a three mile meadow covered with buttercups, peacocks, cattle and skylarks. Blythe spirit—but no, the skylark's nagging wearied twitter like stars in the sky above us. This I did with Sidney. Brisk telephone conversation with Al Alvarez.

Bingo and I (if that's the right way to phrase it) are putting an ad in the *Times* for a house or less. We should hear next week. I'm steeling myself to do something about my teeth. There are now five holes I can stick my tongue in; none yet painful.

Not much happens. I read to the Oxford poetry society and answered questions. Much like home, only I was asked to read Marianne Moore. Oxford incredibly beautiful with all the flowers, I think, I've read about in English poetry—a bit too like a college. What's happening? I read as much as I could of the last exhaustive review—Saturday I must do something with Ronnie Dworkin on the unreal world. I must stop, my ribbon is screwy, high table dinner. I feel when I'm through here I'll receive my sixth form degree.

Love to both,
Cal

540. To Christopher Ricks

June 1, 1970

Dear Christopher:

I shan't forget that week-end either. I had images of at first everyone you knew arriving, but eventual[ly] being outnumbered by droves of Americans, all asking dinner and ice. All of us with our peculiar feuds. It was lovely having Mary.

I've been browsing through your interesting Housman and Milton, partly to avoid writing letters. Much joy in joyful stalling. I think I have All Souls fever, a dry slothfulness. I must stop now anyway. Someone is coming to instruct me for a taped symposium tonight. [O]n Cambodia. Oh ignorant heart.

I find Housman suits this place and time in my life. What would he not say to A. L. Rowse at breakfast, over port? My love and thanks to Kirsten, and I pray we may be dear friends now that we are friends.

Yours,

Robert

541. To Elizabeth Hardwick

June 14, 1970

Dearest Lizzie:

Lovely to hear your voice, clear as tho we're across the yard[—]quad. I'll reserve passage on the 24th or possibly the 23rd. This is a day or two later than I said on the phone. The reason is I hope to go to Poland with Blair next Tuesday, or Wednesday. He is going to see his friend, now separated from her husband. This is a stand-in trip for our age-old "ancestral" tour of Scotland.

I am going this morning to see Huyck and Judith at the Wains's. Everyone I know knows someone else I know fortunately. Then on to Cambridge driven by Omar to see D. P. Not too much fun really, but something decided more than a month ago, and a debt to old times.

Wonderful drive through Cumberland, Lancashire and Northumberland and a visit to Basil Bunting. A Wordsworth fan and a Pound disciple. (This trip to Europe seems to circle around Pound.) I told you about Empson, "I now find the glare at the end of the tunnel to the afterlife (his retirement) oppressive." And "the afterlife is now assuming almost Egyptian proportions." About art critics writing catalogues, "a steady iron-bar jet of absolutely total nonsense."

I think my study better be rented. We can't pay over a thousand dollars for storage. I trust Harvard will make out a catalogue so I can get hold of (know) what I have or want. I wonder if there are old lost poems, salvageable? Perhaps not.

You've had a terribly chafing stint of schools, Lowell "material." ~~Inadvertently~~ Tastelessly, I used this word in my first letter to Allen, and each letter of his sends it back to me in quotes. I wonder if colleges will have to buy this kind of stuff by weight rather than interest. It seems horrible to think of warehouses stuffed with papers and papers. When machines do all, pedants can spend lifetimes listing and living variants. Or will computers do this too?

I guess I've taken it easy. This is almost the first time since lithium that I

am mostly unemployed—take leisure to be wise. I'm not ~~quite~~ what I was when one groping and reaching summer I began *Notebook*.

Give all my love to Harriet, tell her I am bringing you both nice but modest presents.

Love from your soul among the "Souls,"
Cal

542. To Elizabeth Hardwick

[Maidstone, Kent, June 20, 1970]

PERSONAL DIFFICULTIES MAKE TRIP TO NEWYORK IMPOSSIBLE RIGHT AWAY
LOVE CAL

543. To Elizabeth Hardwick

[London, July 1, 1970]

THANKS FOR YOUR SWEET LETTER AFTER CHRISTMAS OUR BEST TIME LOVE
CAL

544. To Caroline Blackwood

[Greenways Nursing Home, London, n.d. July 1970]

I love you with all my heart and mind, what can I do, if you give me nothing to go on? I can't crowd in on you. Let's for God's sake try again, cool and try. So much love should go on to something.

P.S. If I were with you I'd do all within my defects. Can you pretend to be the same? O try!

545. To Elizabeth Hardwick

[August 6, 1970]

~~August 6~~

~~Dearest Lizzie— You have always been a gentle courageous, courteous,~~
~~witty, generous. how I can~~

August 6, the day of your departure

Dearest Lizzie—

You[r] last not[e] and much else that you said and have said through the years go to my heart. You couldn't have [been] more loyal and witty. I can't give you anything of equal value. Still much happened that we both loved in the long marriage. I feel we had much joy and many other things we had to learn. There is nothing that wasn't a joy and told us something. Great joy.

Love,

Cal

546. To Elizabeth Hardwick

11 Fellows Road
London
August 11, 1970

Dearest Lizzie:

There's cold in the the air, enough to make me rub my feet for warmth. And then a colder, perhaps truer air in Maine. Illusions, surely! The true Maine is always at a distance. You are there. And this morning I can reach to you. O I hope I have reached Harriet Lowell, To whom I have sent many postcards, terrible things like the horseguards which you were so gracious as to buy, stamp and leave me.

Goodbye, My Love,

Cal

547. To Caroline Blackwood

[n.d. 1970]

I assume ceteris paribus that when I am in a certain state you are too. I could come out in a week or two, if I could have a place to stay. Do come and see me,

it's the best slow step we could make. Then I'd like to have the bottom rooms. We could be together without meeting till evening.

548. To Elizabeth Hardwick

80 Redcliffe Square
London
August 27, 1970

Dearest Lizzie:

Nothing worthy to answer your beautiful letters. I've been rambling about getting a studio, toying with revisions, feeling the deadest poet as so often, and getting my textbooks ordered for Essex. Very cordial department head who found an actually much better anthology for the one I'd ordered, also one much worse. No pressure. Also my students are already picked for me in very small numbers, so I avoid that agony. Not much else a lunch with Karl Miller, stay in Kent. I don't feel very boastful, but I don't think I'm a bastard. I rather look forward to Essex; teaching is so much easier and more dependable than writing, tho so much less.

I've thought much and wonderingly about Harriet's picture. Since Venice she's turned into a woman, or is that only the photographer's angle? Then the profound in the second line and rather sad camp note. I wish I could be with her and let her let fly her random thoughts. We were good at deep jokes. When Can I see you both? I thought of a trip leaving here around the 10th of December, or a little later. Would that confuse? Well, God bless you, all the sorrow in joy. Thanks for liking my revolutionary sonnet group. They'll have a different arrangement in *Notebook* but this pleased me.

All my love,
Cal

549. To Frank Bidart

33 Pont Street
London S.W. 1
September 11, 1970

Dear Frank:

I've lost my address book and must write you care of Harvard, though wondering if they still list you.

I thought your Frost a remarkable bit of criticism, concentrating cleanly and calmly on what seems a small point and making a very telling one. . . . The poem seemed very good in itself and up [to] the others in the sequence. Wonder what your new work can be!

I was touched by your offer to come here and go through the last proofs. I got all [of] them done, though missing you, last late spring. First galleys, then page proofs, tons of corrections, additions. Better than any version you've read I hope. I got help from Oxford students and various friends, but not your mind which remembers all versions.

I'll be teaching at Essex and living at the above address till spring, but I hope to be in New York for a couple of weeks through Christmas. To go into my affairs is somehow too long and confusing in a letter. On the more public side, I've written thirty or so new poems in the old meter. I feel you will enjoy the occupation of your new teaching. On the whole, I always have. Did you know that Elizabeth Bishop will be at Harvard roughly teaching my courses this fall? Do make yourself known to her as my friend. I'll write her. No one is as interesting to know.

Affectionately,

Cal

550. To Elizabeth Bishop

September 11, 1970

Dearest Elizabeth:

I am living in a silly Back Bay part of London, there are many, near the Cadogan Hotel where Wilde was arrested, leading a silly but not unhappy life. I expect to get back for a couple of weeks at Christmas, and trust I'll have much time to see you.

I meant to answer your last radiant letter, the gladdest I think you've ever written me, but I lost my address book, with every address in the world. Have you been getting letters in Ouro Prêto from some brassy and intrusive unknown? It isn't me. I hope your good spell has held. I was almost in the same mood. Now I am not, but in a very good one. Lizzie and I have more or less separated, though as good-naturedly as such things can be. I have someone else. And future looks cheerful, but who at our age can ever tell? I still feel I can reach up and touch the ceiling of one's end. Yet I have nothing more serious than a tooth to be capped. I sometimes think our age is as full of unknowns as seventeen. We really couldn't see at all clearly then.

You'll find drawbacks and deadwood at Harvard, but I think you'll find the work light and exciting, and from time to time make permanent student friends. I'm glad they are new and not all the age of Jason Epstein. I have many friends; one I'll recommend, Frank Bidart, American Basque, and who knows my poems much better than I do—a great help in corrections and proof-reading.

Love, I wish you were with me, or I with you, and assume we soon will be. All my love,

Cal

551. To Elizabeth Hardwick

[September 1970]

Dearest Lizzie—

[. . .]Glad to have the checks and have added a thousand dollars to my small account. Saw Gertrude two days ago, who was temporarily in the house of the man I rent from. Somehow fated. We had a pleasant evening. She has a little job with a little publisher, which she complains of, though bravely. Yet, miracle, she is as she was twenty years ago to my dim eye.

School begins in two or three weeks. I've been assembling my texts, and Essex has been helpful, a good American anthology, which costs ten pounds, more than any student can buy, and something made up of Ginsberg and the Black Mountain for the moderns. Am I a wolf in black fleece offering myself to the very advanced classes of Essex?

Not much more money will be needed; soon my salary will be rolling in. I would like what I get from royalties. Is that too much? When I come in Christmas time I'll clean up the papers business, which should set us up better. All love to you and Harriet,

Love,

552. To Elizabeth Hardwick

September 12, 1970

Dearest Lizzie:

Suddenly after mailing my letter I realized I hadn't thanked you properly for the checkbook and making the whole business of cashing so easy. Even if we think of ourselves (not practical) as still on the old basis of a joint account, still nothing could be done without your help.

No news here. This is one of those rainy dark European city days, pleasing at times, but at others they almost make one ~~see~~ touch eternity as Baudelaire wrote. I am reading the Shakespeare I will teach, mostly the Roman plays. I rather need a library, but I've always more or less gotten on without using one, except for the random, accidental offering of Quincy House. But now instead of Hazlitt's characters, I have Professor Dorsch's defense of the character of Julius Caesar. Professor Dorsch is the editor of my edition, and is too off even to effectively disagree with. Love to Dear Harriet.

Love,
 Cal

553. To Elizabeth Hardwick

September 18, 1970

Dearest Lizzie:

In a postcard you said you realized that there was nothing I could do about your problems. I was sad of course when I read this, and knew in a way you were partly true. The distance is farther than a hand can reach or mind can perhaps attend. Nothing for me to do, and as for my feeling it's an acute, useless undifferentiated ache. I can't imagine the inside of your lives, yet I am not free at all of what I've done to you.

Very soon I'll begin my teaching and am pointing toward it—getting classbooks even reading them. It's all very shadowy but I guess my feet are on earth. I do miss you both and would ask to be forgiven, if that had active meaning. All's well. Do let us keep in touch, closely in touch till I come at Christmas.

Love to you both,
 Cal

The last few days, after finishing Shakespeare's Roman plays, I've had the London sights with a guidebook. The Tower is more Roman than Fellini's *Satyricon* which I also saw.

554. To Elizabeth Hardwick

September 25, 1970

Dearest Lizzie:

I see we are using the same ornate letter-paper. And if you were to use my old typewriter, it would be the same type or at least the same machine. So much for continuity. I would have written sooner, but I've been spending a few days in Amsterdam with Huyck and Judith.

Adrienne came up naturally often in our talk but no one knew of the separation. I am sorry, knowing nothing about it. Mostly because Adrienne seems such a matchstick, tho gloriously, to live by herself. Again, knowing nothing about the facts, I don't think the separation will last long and because Adrienne will need Alf if she goes to the hospital again, and because after all they shared and agreed on many things. I don't quite know how to write into her confusion and don't know the address, but give her all my love. What are Street Schools?

When I first came to England, people gave me quite a few old long pieces, so that naturally there seemed to be the world's abundance and enthusiasm. I suppose I'm liked in one country about as much as another. These buildings can fall in a minute.

I do want to hear all your communication and gossip. It could never be too much. I too can't state my feelings even to myself. The past is almost more with me than today. I look on it with all pride and joy, but it is piercing to look back, especially when I have no reproaches. Shall I say that I, or rather we, are alright? There's much to be said at length at Christmas. Love to yourself and to my Harriet. She has gone into a void, but I can't imagine she would find writing to me pleasant. In your next letter, quote something she has said.

Love,
Cal

555. To Elizabeth Bishop

[October 5, 1970]

Dearest Elizabeth:

Didn't I write about your beautiful poem? It's the nearest thing you've written to a short story in verse—an *I*, you or not you, telling a naturalistic narrative, more heightened than prose fiction would accept, very personal, the way a short story can sometimes be, without too much stress, because you

always, till well on in waiting, seem to be just quietly talking. One of your poems that most stays with me. My dentist, I feel!

I've written thirty more poems in the meter of *Notebook*, but somehow unlike *Notebook* in tone—more strained, the Romantic romance of a married man in a hospital. Mostly I'm not very very forthright. A few may be good, but I am disheartened by the whole, and keep trying to comb out the unnecessarily grand obscurities I somehow began with.

Like you I depended on Bill for everything all my years at Harvard. Once I was a year behind on my health certificate. Perhaps much more, I depended on him for companionship. I could always drop in and have drinks or a dinner or meet students. Often they, not I, came to his house at four in the afternoon and left at four in the morning. Give him my love; today I am going to Essex to teach for the first time and dreading the undefined errors I am bound to make without Bill. Give him my love.

By now you will probably have fifty poet-appliers, manuscripts double at first meeting. I tried to cut them down to 12 but usually couldn't. Then I made the mistake of letting in auditors, usually wives of physics professors, who wrote better often than most of the students in worn styles that couldn't be digested by the students. Other classes were comfortably small but insultingly so. I had three for the Bible. Some were too large to talk, others too small. Yet the students mostly in the end were ideal, or at least in class they were. I don't think you'll have troubles. I almost always left a class ~~happier~~ happy.

Natasha Spender speaking of her husband teaching English students for the first time, says he is like a boy going off from home to school for the first time.

My "someone" is Caroline Citkowitz. She is 39, has published stories in the *London Magazine*, has three very pretty daughters, eldest ten, and was once years ago married to Freud's grandson, Lucian. You might have ~~meant~~ met; Caroline lived some time in San Francisco and later in New York, but you haven't or she would remember. However she reads you with great admiration and thinks you much brighter than Mary whom she knows. What a bare list, but how can I make the introduction? She is very beautiful and saw me through the chafes and embarrassments of my sickness with wonderful kindness. I suppose I shouldn't forget Harriet and Lizzie, anyway I can't. Guilt clouds the morning, and though things are not embattled, nothing is settled. I'll be back in New York for Christmas, then there will perhaps be more decision. I could be happy either way, if things could be settled. But nothing is. I am happy to be in presentable spirits.

This is somewhat in the mood of waiting [to] take a train to my new work later this afternoon. If only life could be as manageable as teaching. Didn't Faust say this? England, I speak from the wisdom of a six months stay, is wonderfully unstirred after New York.

All my love,
Cal

556. To Blair Clark

October 9, 1970

Dear Blair:

When I first read your postcard, through some macabre mistake I read that Peter White had *raised* the list of class suicides to four—I only know of two excluding Al Clark. What a grim way of holding the suspense then suddenly springing it. Glad he's alive.

I expect to come over to New York during the Christmas holidays. There's a problem whether to come with Caroline. The only time she can come is before Christmas, while Lizzie wants me to come later when Harriet like Caroline's children will be out of school. However, it seems callous humanly for me to *arrive* in New York, in Lizzie's home city, with Caroline. Or am I being meaninglessly scrupulous? Until the divorce is made, and it looks as though it will, and that I will marry Caroline—it still remains uncertain in my mind. When friends of mine have been in this dilemma, I've always thought they should stop torturing themselves and everyone else, and make a quick clean severance. But it's not easy, unless one becomes some sort of doll only capable of fast straightforward action.

I am beginning to teach and enjoy it, also getting away to London. Sometimes the change is small, tonight Caroline and I are having dinner with an angry young Hindu novelist whom I met in a pub near my sanitarium. Sunday, a higher life, the Spenders. Just talked to Mary finishing her novel and depressed; we'll see her here in a few weeks. Hope you'll see Joanna and all moves toward, not heaven, but paradise. I miss you. Could I or we stay with you in mid December? Love,
Cal

557. To Elizabeth Hardwick

October 11, 1970

Dearest Lizzie:

This has been a gray warm Sunday until now at twilight it is cool and clear. For the last three or four hours, I have been home and on bed reading forty or fifty pages of Emerson's poems for teaching. The unease of distance and severance are on me. He says of his child that his lips could pronounce "words that were persuasions."

Why don't you write and tell me what is happening? I know it's hard in this uncertain, changing time. You wrote something—like so many phrases and feelings in your letters, it stays with me—like it was hard to state your thoughts accurately, even in your thoughts. I feel that too, and so find it hard to write, though not-writing I'm afraid was always one of my gifts. Let me hear of you and Harriet, and at length, if you can.

Essex, my part of it, is enough like Harvard to sometimes seem a mirage. The same students, tho half audible from their good manners and foreign idiom, the same old classes, the same with fresh textbooks, a taxi drive along the Thames that is like the East River and even the Charles. I suppose my low-toned, conversational teaching is safe from the falls of ambition, but I feel wobbling in talking. You can seldom tell what the students think, or what is perhaps more important, what good you've said. It's all fairly pleasant. "The gentle lifesaver of routine," as Emerson might have said, if he had had less searing comforts.

Did you get the three thousand dollars? It deserves a note, even if it has already melted into the flow of costs. I really haven't very much. I have enough, but wish I could hear.

Love,
Cal

558. To Elizabeth Hardwick

October 18 [1970]
(Shortly after our phone-talk)

Dearest Lizzie:

I don't know whether I've said or written ~~that~~ I feel like a man walking on two ever more widely splitting roads at once, as if I were pulled apart and thinning into mist, or rather being torn apart and still preferring that state to

making a decision. Is there any decision still for me to make? After all I have done, and all that seven months have done, can I go back to you and Harriet? Too many cuts.

Time has changed things somewhat since we met at Greenways, I am soberer, cooler. More displeasing to myself in many little ways, but mostly about you. A copy of my new book came the other day, and I read through all the new and more heavily revised poems. A sense of the meaning of the whole came to me, and it seemed to be about us and our family, its endurance being the spine which despite many bendings and blows finally held. Just held. Many reviewers saw this; though it was something I thought pretentious and offensive if claimed to push in my preface, I saw it too. I have felt as if a governing part of my organism were gone, and as if the familiar grass and air were gone.

I don't think I can go back to you. Thought does no good. I cannot weigh the dear, troubled past, so many illnesses, which weren't due to you, in which you saved everything, our wondering, changing, growing years with Harriet, so many places, such rivers of talk and staring—I can't compare this memory with the future, unseen and beyond recollection with Caroline. I love her very much, but I can't see that. I am sure many people have looked back on a less marvelous marriage than ours on the point of breaking, and felt this pain and indecision—at first insoluble, then when the decision has been made, incurable.

I don't think I can come back to you, but allow me this short space before I arrive in New York to wobble in my mind. I will be turning from the longest realest and most loved fragment of my life.

I'll arrive mid-day or so on Thursday. I'll probably stay with Blair. We won't feel tied together at all hours, but all my time will be yours. I don't expect to see anyone except Blair and probably Stanley.

I don't want to scrap over details.

My love to you both,
 Cal

559. To Elizabeth Hardwick

[October 21, 1970]

Dearest Lizzie—

I phoned you just before leaving for Essex, and now am writing just after returning and reading your letters. Alf's face was with me most of the time, large in the foreground, and what was nearer, you and Harriet and of course

thoughts of Adrienne, peeping out behind, as if behind a poster. He always seemed in such full health and discipline, that nothing pointed this way. It's as abrupt as Randall's death, and these last days hits me with the same force, though we weren't close and my real friend was always Adrienne.

You have written so much and so many things, the same repeating contra-dictory things since last summer. Poor thing, what else could you do under the circumstances? The last letter is relaxed, more relaxed, and ends with more of an up-note. And the last terrible sentence is "hell and damnation . . . Life is so terrible." Even if I returned for good, if that has meaning, almost all would be unsolved. I realize all three of us (crushing realization) have lived a depres-sion, lived through our darks, at more or less the same time. Mine, waking up pricked through with my guilt and hollowness; the same ache you have felt has hurt me, but with time the feeling lifts. It's the usual, once annual depres-sion, lighter than most, but enough to make me peculiarly indecisive and use-less to you now. I suppose I've made my choice, I and my seven months absence have ~~have chosen~~, and you are right to say you wouldn't have me back. I feel whatever choice I might make, I am walking off the third story of an unfinished building to the ground. I don't offer this as good description, it's too vague and grand, but to show you why my useless, depressed will, does nothing well. Just the usual somberness after mania, jaundice of the spirit, and yet it has so many absolutely actual objects to pick up—a marriage that was both rib and spine for us these many years.

Caroline isn't (if you really want me to be free to talk to you about her) one of my many manic crushes, rather this and everything more, just as you were at Yaddo and after. She is airy and very steady and sturdy in an odd way. She has been very kind to me. I think we can make out. I love her, we have been together rather a long time—often and intensely. I have ~~fears~~ doubts that I by myself, or anyway, can make out[,] that dear you and Harriet can make out. I think somehow that Christmas will help us all, great troubles but no longer everyone unreal to everyone, and Christmas is the season to lighten the heart. All my love to both—

 Cal

Hold on my Dears. Making out is so much stiffer than making it.

560. To Adrienne Rich

Wednesday, October 21, 1970

Dearest Adrienne:

I heard about Alf's death last Monday from Lizzie on the telephone and then went off to my teaching at Essex carrying the wound and a sort of composite picture of him, now short-haired now long and a gay green or blue turtle-necked sweater—accurate thoughts and figures and an ardent moonlight glow. His death seems to me the most tragic I have known since Randall's. In both, the end seems so unproportioned to the previous lives, full of health and promising its renewal. We knew him less well than you, but Lizzie and I have felt we lost part of ourselves, a part of our old lives of the last fifteen years.

You've heard of course from Lizzie about our situation. I am with another girl, Caroline Citkowitz. I love her and we've been together a long stretch by now. Still, it's all somber and unreal. Both Lizzie and Harriet are disturbed, and so am I. Hard to tell what is right or even possible. There's an old picture somewhere, mostly as frontispieces, where Dante stands against an elaborate tapering tower with galleries—it is Purgatory, and it seems to lean. That's how the last twenty-one years seem to me now. This week especially with its many letters. I'll be home for two or three weeks at Christmas. Perhaps things will [be] better and flatter then. Meanwhile the useless inescapable time of the two mutually exclusive choices. I imagine I'll get divorced, and all may be well, but the loss will never go.

I am talking for you in a way in your much greater trouble. I have thought of you much when I heard of your separation, and felt my ignorance was too great to express itself in a letter. Terrible things happen, that have causes of course, but which can't be answered. Maybe you'll try not to, as is best, and your marvelous courage will carry through these new obstacles as it has through so many of the old. At Christmas, I pray that we may have more of our vodka or saki luncheons. My love to the children and all to you.

Love,
Cal

561. To William Alfred

October 21, 1970

Dear Bill:

I've just gotten back from Leicester and read your caring letter. Telling

Elizabeth plainly and without ambiguity in a letter what I am going to do is hard. It's hard for me to be that certain even in my quietest thoughts. I am coming to New York over Christmas and [will] stay two weeks or so. Then we can talk at leisure, then we can talk it out, which can't be done by letter or long distance phone. This helps no one I have said, and you more or less say. Still such an old and passionate love cannot be ended like slicing pie. The time hasn't been very long after all considering how much is still hanging. I have written Lizzie several times that I felt we would get a divorce, but that we should decide when we met.

Oh yes, you are right about Harriet, I lie awake about her. Jewelry is a good idea. We talked the other day on the phone and things seem less frantic.

Love,

Cal

562. To Elizabeth Hardwick

[n.d. late October? 1970]

Dear Lizzie:

I have had letters from Blair and Bill, rather different letters. Bill's was about Harriet and making my intentions absolutely clear. Blair was about Caroline's coming to New York. From both I see I must be more open and certain. This was hard for me to do and seemed rough. I merely wrote out of my feelings, which was probably unkind and without purpose. I must say now that I definitely want a divorce whenever arrangements can be made. I don't see why you should veto Caroline's coming to New York. There wouldn't be much sense in my coming if you and Harriet were in the Caribbean. Harriet should meet Caroline sometime[. T]hen, though this would have to be awkward, she would feel less bewildered by the possibility of visiting us.

Oh dear, these sentences seem stiff and unreal to type out.

I've sent you a charming little present along with one to H.

Love,

Cal

563. To Peter Taylor

November 1, 1970

Dear Peter. I weep for your eyes. Years ago I had a little foretaste of some-

thing similar. I kept seeing a little black nit or gnat worrying oddly over any white surface I looked at. At times it became a hair with little legs. Nothing more happened. Your business is really terrible, so many flashes, then thought of the operation. I wish I could comfort.

When I got your letter I was going out to breakfast, and hardly dared open it. I thought the first words would be: we are appalled, *we* meaning you, not Eleanor, then you and Eleanor. It's all about as silly, in a way, as Allen on the mountain, and that is very silly. (I thought of him this morning, when I read a review that spelled his name Allan.) I needn't sketch in the full narrative. I fell in love part manic, was sick in a hospital a good part of summer, got well, stayed in love. There was great joy in it all, great harm to everyone. I have been vacillating. I think Lizzie and [I] will come back together. If that can be done. Anyway, I'll be home in New York during Christmas.

I'm glad you are writing one act plays, a length sympathetic to the craftsmanship and short windedness of writers like me. Doesn't writing something keep you afloat and breathing? I've been turning out poems at a great rate. They almost keep out ~~depression~~ the shadows. I love England and London, tho I lead a mole's life, but for teaching and two or three friends.

You have a new friend, Dick Howard, friend of Jean's and once of Blair. Maybe he is a little below both Randall and Proust. I once got letters from him contrived beyond reading. It's good news that he's writing a preface to Eleanor, and better that she is publishing.

One London note. I rent an apartment from a man named the Knight of Glyn, the only title of its kind in England; his mail comes addressed that way, and his towels are marked *K of G*. I don't know him, except to speak to, but he is a young man who has written a monograph on good Irish houses and takes pot or worse watches people taking pot. Have I escaped the snares?

Love to you and Eleanor,
 Cal

564. To Mary McCarthy

November 2, 1970

Dearest Mary—

I've put off writing because I draw back from seeing what I am going to say ~~in~~ typed. It's a kind of decision which I haven't yet talked about to anyone. ~~It looks as~~ I think I'll end up by returning to Lizzie and Harriet. I've done great harm to everyone and bemused myself. To go on seriously toward marriage

with Caroline against the grain, the circumstances, our characters etc. is more than can be got away with. We don't think we can, and are in accord. Still—

I won't go on much. I do find though that even for such a careless person as me one is cemented in habits beyond belief. I had to come to England and live with practically a new wife to learn my whole being is repetition of things once done. I don't mean quite that. With time we build up an organism, an artifact, that is mysteriously complex, quite beyond our intelligence. You most have found that. Still, it seems nothing merely to know what one can do. As if that were ever enough, as if one ever did.

I'll see you on the sixth. Maybe *we*'ll see you. I love the idea of your naturalistic check-up in Rome. I've been writing furiously too. It's too far from publication for me to be pierced with acute discontent, and good enough to ~~engage~~ grip the day. Dying to see you, and love to Jim and you. I've talked on the phone to Lizzie and I ~~suppose~~ know we can make up. I feel a little ~~someone~~ like a Russian who has lost his own fortune and his uncle's at Baden Baden. ~~Other OK, pardon all this.~~

Love,
 Cal

P.S. Excuse the pencilling.

565. *To Elizabeth Hardwick*

November 7, 1970

Dearest Lizzie:

I wonder if we couldn't make it up? It's hard to put this in a letter, and no doubt will be far harder in fact. I have thought this might be for about ten days now, and people have noticed, and thought I was more like my once self, what I must have been.

A cold way of putting it is that long burned-in and accepted habits never leave us. One can make out with the family he has long endured, which has a long time suffered him and his ways. Maybe you could take me back, though I have done great harm. Maybe now that the possibility is really possible, you will quite rightly draw back, happily rid of your weary burden.

I don't know. I'll be back around the fourteenth of December, so soon we can almost reach out [a] hand and touch it. If we should come together, there's one hard problem, among many I would like you to consider. I don't think I

can very honorably drop my Essex appointment which lasts into March—more self-inflicted messiness and alteration than I can face in myself. That would mean I would have to return etc. Things have reached a kind of tolerable balance for me here, that will continue, I think, but not conceivably forever.

My book is out and has had gratifying, and more than that, reviews from Alvarez and Connolly in the Sunday papers, not like Benito.

Dying to see you and Harriet.

Love,

 Cal

566. To Mary McCarthy

<div align="right">November 15, 1970</div>

Dearest Mary:

Heinrich's death seemed on the horizon so long that one forgot. At least I did being out of touch. Poor Hannah! I suppose crossing bridges beforehand may make the final thing a little less jolting, less jolting anyway than the suicide of our friend [(]though mostly [we were the friends of] his wife Adrienne[)], Conrad. Friends dying comes now like increasing raindrops.

Thanks for your remarkably clear letter. You rather sharpen the horns of my dilemma. Everyone has vacillated, though I the worst. I hope you will write Lizzie. There's nothing you can tell her that she doesn't already know from me, but your sympathies and views would help. I think the jag that hit Caroline and me was whether to get married, she not wanting to and I not wanting to go on in perpetuum unmarried. Or maybe this was just the surface manifestation of some deeper unsurmountable gap. Pray God it all washed out.

My number here is 235-2270. Please let me know your plans. I hope we can do more or less as we intended to on your ghost visit last month. My love to you, hope your book is off. I almost have a new one, a small scale sequel to *Notebook*. It will probably be ages before it goes off to the publisher.

Love again to you both,

 Cal

P.S. I have [been] puzzling on your mysterious sentence about Lizzie and Woman's Lib. What's that? Do you mean it's in the air or something closer?

567. To Elizabeth Hardwick

November 16, 1970

Dearest Lizzie:

I didn't write sooner because I didn't want to fly off into crossed letters. I will do all I can to make things work; I think we can,—we have after all for more years than I have the wits to count, tho all remains remembered. Perhaps everyone involved will get in the end what was most deeply and secretly desired. I'm no better than I was, unless it's better to discover the hardness of old habits. I won't put you through more.

I have been pouring out poems, and almost have a little book, in the same form as *Notebook*, but much smaller. I've even anticipated my landing in New York. You see I am back home.[. . .]

I have a vague idea I know about "groupies," it's like some Greek or archaic English word, I once knew and forgot. I guess the new idiom is here to stay; it keeps seeping in in tiny trickles when I try to write. You and Harriet seem to have been having a week of pre-Thanksgivings. Give my derelict love to Sarah and Cot.

My classes are small and quiet, the Poetry Writing rather retarded after Harvard, a good one in Shakespeare, where I have twice spent two hours reading one act of *Antony and Cleopatra* aloud. The college looks like Brandeis, if Brandeis had been built on a fiftieth the money, and with no Jews. The people are young and lively, most of my colleagues being just beyond graduate student age.

I think about you and Harriet. I am jealous. Let me into your circle again, but not see the groupies.

Love,

Cal

568. To Blair Clark

November 21 [1970]

Dear Blair—

It must be like migraine getting stuck with all my affairs, from all sides. Here's what's going on in me. I am haunted by my family, and the letters I get. There seems to be such delicate misery. Lizzie's letters veer from frantic affection to frantic abuse. Then somehow she and Harriet are fused as one in her mind. It's not possible, but I get the impression they really are in Lizzie's

mind. It's crazy, yet I can't from a distance do anything about it, perhaps less on the spot.

The thing is I am ~~really much~~ perfectly happ~~ier~~y with Caroline. At first I was frightened of not being married—old feelings of being outlawed. But I see it doesn't matter much. We can go on permanently as we are. We are permanent no matter what our status. Caroline has always been afraid of legal marriage. Not being married, somehow loosens the bond, man and woman's mutual, self-killing desire to master the other. Then we might get married anyway when we knew we didn't have to. I don't yet know what will happen, but I increasingly fear the blood I'll have to pay for what I have done, for being me. Anyway, I'll be coming to you around the 14th alone.

I want to hear all about you, and your heart if you wish. Long deep talks.

Love,

Cal

569. To Elizabeth Hardwick

November 28, 1970

Dearest Lizzie:

I'm back from reading at Cambridge, and tomorrow it's a reading at the Mermaid, scene of *Benito*'s triumph. All went well enough at Cambridge and I was told I had a record small audience. Somehow it leaves one with a feeling of tarnish and fraudulence. Two lunches a breakfast and a dinner at various faculty tables and high tables—too much like St. Mark's, too much like college. Still good conversation, warmth of a kind. Essex on the other hand is in great disgrace, a protest with bonfires, then the next day by accident, a long-prepared *Daily Telegram* attack on our leniency. The protest was what is talked of as pitifully non-political: pot. Not much to arouse the demons, or amuse them.

I may have been short about Jack's well-meant cable—I was worried, unknown troubles for you in New York, and then I hate having friends tilt my hand. I have enough tangles now to occupy me for years, on top of my pills, a delicate matter to keep one from scumming up another. Nothing new though. Only new thing is I notice spreads in my teeth, rather like Mary's before her patching.

Not much that might interest you. Most [of] the people I see wouldn't even be names to you, my colleagues. Once a week I have lunch with Sidney, and come away with lines for poems. Poems at a great rate, even scribbling lines down during a dinner. I suppose I may have a book, a little *Notebook*, ready by

next fall. Then a new tune, a new meter, a new me . . . The last never, I guess. The surroundings here are not disappointing, I mean for the eye, but perhaps mostly humanly, the famous more mumbled and muffled pace. Well, it will be very soon. All my love to you and Harriet.

Love,
Cal

570. *To Elizabeth Hardwick*

November 30, [1970]

Dearest Lizzie:

A line before I set off for Essex. The Mermaid reading was as good as I could make it and went over. Somehow, it's a show I can stage too easily. But why shouldn't it give the satisfaction of a well-played tennis game? I don't [know] what that would be, just a very occasional ace serve. I guess, reading gives more satisfaction than tennis. But who could face it daily, or weekly. I'm through for this year.

I still do nothing much but bury my indecisions in many many poems. I think I have ninety now and a tall house of draft and discard. I am very bad company because I am so removed. You won't enjoy me. However I am coming to see you and dear Harriet, not Blair. So you'll hear from me at once. If I'm not hung up in red tape. The Home Office still has my passport, and my bank account is an impenetrable mist. No, I'll be there.

I thought you were better informed than I on my reviews, but later in the day, clippings came from Faber, the one new to me Elizabeth Jennings. She is a sad, touching person, rather like Claude Edmonde in appearance and habits—but shy, poor and poetic.

I dread the *Review* circuit and the buzz of American politics. An American isn't expected to ~~the great~~ follow issues. He can miss the papers for days without being pulled up and informed. But even for Englishmen, all's mumbled and distant. Can't see us as Mary and Bowden, even with my lack of engagement.

Love to both dear ones,
Cal

571. To Elizabeth Hardwick

December 3, 1970

Dearest Lizzie—

My pay seems to be mostly old-age deductions, something that demands more optimism in me than in the government.[. . .]

I went to a great Vanderbilt game with Ben; Caroline's dachshund was lost; I think permanently, a tragedy Ben didn't rise to, nor did Caroline rise to the dangers she had put Ben in by letting me drive him back to Clarksville. I remember Allen and Ben yelling when the girl band came on, "Get those women off the field." O blessed old days before Woman's Lib. I liked some of John's poems in some British or Irish magazine; he had gotten rid of Henry, and good and tender things made up for show-off obscenities. Can't believe it's all bad; it isn't. Folly to answer, even in a single sentence. I got a rather sour review from Denis Donoghue, who seems to think the book is about the breaking and final break up of our marriage. That's not in the text. I wouldn't trust Carruth too much, tho he has a gnarled integrity.

I'll be seeing people this weekend, Mary, Gaia, Francis Bacon and Sidney. I'll be with you both soon, if I can leave England.

Love to you both,

Cal

P.S. I was a little testy about politics last letter. I feel like someone naked under his raincoat—though I guess that's always a girl—coming back to be inspected.[. . .]

572. To Elizabeth Hardwick

[n.d. December? 1970]

Dearest Lizzie—

I'm just off to lunch with Sidney, but yes it's a date for the Messiah on the 17th. Hope you feel much better by the time this reaches you. Here in London, we've reached weather like one of the worst Maine summers. Less disturbing maybe because it's the usual thing. You see a streak of indirect sunlight some day at three and everyone hymns the weather.

Love to my two messianics,

Cal

573. To Elizabeth Bishop

[n.d. December 1970]

Dearest Elizabeth—

I fear I may owe you an apology for versing one of your letters into my poems on you in *Notebook*. When Lamb blew up at Coleridge for calling him "Frolicsome Lamb," Coleridge said it was necessary for the balance of his composition. I won't say that, but what could be as real as your own words, and then there's only a picture that does you honor. Still, too intimate maybe, and if so I humbly ask pardon.

The other night, part of a weekend alone, I was in a Knightsbridge Portuguese restaurant *Offado*, more people worked on the tables, half in the kitchen etc. than there were guests; even the guitarist and singer helped, then sang things like *Girls from Majorca*, while I ate and consumed a carafe of rosé, their table wine. After a while I expected you to come in the door any moment, even began nervously looking at my watch. So much I wanted to see you.

So much I do. I'll be in New York staying with Blair Clark about the time you get this. I think Lizzie and I are going to break. I should have done it much more cleanly some time ago. But I can't. I wonder if anyone in his right mind could. I am back to see Lizzie and Harriet, things are not even now quite settled, but they must be.

I must see you. I can easily come to Cambridge, or it could be New York if you'd like—you must be ripe to leave Cambridge by now, but I'd rather like to see Harvard. Give my love to Bill. All my love to you,

Cal

574. To Caroline Blackwood

[New York, N.Y., December 21, 1970]

THANKS FOR LETTER IM NOT A CRIPPLE ALL MY LOVE

575. To Caroline Blackwood

[229 East 48th Street, New York, N.Y. 10017, December 1970]

ALL WELL MERRY CHRISTMAS LONG FOR YOU

CAL

576. To John Berryman

33 Pont St.
London SW 1
December 27, 1970

Dear John:

I've read your marvelous prayer at the end of your book, and can hardly find words to praise it. Though cunning in its skepticism, it feels like a Catholic prayer to a personal God. I like the humorous, anguished admission of faults, somewhat like Corbière to whom your book is appealingly dedicated. I think too of Verlaine's religious poems, you too noble, down under, improper. Anyway, it's one of the great poems of the age, a puzzle and triumph to anyone who wants to write a personal devotional poem. Along with your posthumous poems, to my mind, the crown of your work. The rest of the book though full of flashes seems a little casual and shaggy, but I haven't read it enough.

You write close to death—I mean in your imagination. Don't take it from your heart into life. Don't say we won't meet again. I am writing at home with Lizzie and Harriet, but I give my London address. A new life. One to be envied, but today it fills me with uncertainties that mount up terror.

Well, may your God and mine bless you and our families.

Love,
Cal

577. To Elizabeth Hardwick

[33 Pont St., London SW 1]
January 7, 1971

Dearest Lizzie:

In my thoughts I planned a much more ample personal and bread and butter letter, but still feel the jar, loss of sleep etc. of the flight. If I'd taken a later or earlier plane I would probably have been diverted to Birmingham.

I thought of a lot of kind charming things you did. Above all you stand out at the airport with your curled hair and beautiful smile that survived the long dull wait. Then the blue wash cloths, the buttermilk, the calm Christmas day, and the wonderful wit and good spirits of Harriet, surely rather owing to you—I mean your old undeviating loyalty.

I haven't done much, rested, read *Hamlet* for class, Henry Adams on the

English, a mountain of mail asking me to read various places without fee. I worry about your blood-pressure. Mine went back to 180, due to the journey no doubt. I'm sure both our pressures will go down. Would that all pressures might. And thankyou for breasting the problems and trials of my visit, so often turning trial into joy.

Love to you both,
Cal

578. To Elizabeth Hardwick

[March 8, 1971]

Dearest Lizzie—

I think our letters on the agency tax-money must have crossed. I wrote as soon as the States Street letter arrived.

Through long hours of revising, a leisurely bath and a quick dressing, I have been thinking about our long past. What shall I say? That I miss your old guiding and even chiding hand. Not having you is like learning to walk. I suppose though one thing is worse than stumbling and vacillating, is to depend on someone who does these things. I do think achingly and bewilderingly about you and Harriet.

Tell Harriet that last Tuesday my taxi was twenty minutes late. I missed my train, got another taxi at Essex that took someone in the opposite direction, reached my class half an hour late, just as it had been dismissed. However, I made it up in the afternoon. Even muddlers survive, though shaggily.

Do miss you both. All my love,
Cal

579. To William Alfred

80 Redcliffe Square
London SW 10
March 20, 1971

Dearest Bill:

[. . .]Caroline and I are having a child. It will be born early in October, and most people we've met know by now. Many problems, but somehow a calm has come for the last month and a half that is quite surprising. Like walking through some gauze screen that allowed one to see real things without

touching them; but what we see is different. Anyway, for me and Caroline a peace we haven't known, perhaps ever. Ah well who knows ... what's around the corner? It's easier to face.

I expect to be in America for an appearance at Purdue on the fourth of May, and then will be in New York a week. I hope to see you, either there or in Cambridge.

Love,
Cal

580. To Elizabeth Hardwick

March 29, [1971]

Dearest Lizzie:

Letters are very slow, but this and an earlier one (if you haven't got it) will be waiting when you return. I almost wept over yours. Ah we must keep it so. Our time on this earth is so poignantly short. Two additional lives would be too little to cleanse my character, to go the rounds of amends.

In Norway, someone came up to me and said that your Hedda piece had solved the problem they had been debating for a hundred years. It was at a party, and I never could discover what problem. Hedda's ~~soul~~ nature, good and evil? I guess there was more.

Reed Whittemore's letter seemed strained, pushed by something unexpressed. A *nasty instance*, or whatever he said my review was. I answered cordially, I think. Miss van Duyn writes witty and intelligent reviews, I guess her verse is witty and intelligent. She *must* be better than Corso, but I haven't read him for years.

A haunting letter from Adrienne. Woman seems to have ousted the blacks. I thought of a made-up folk saying, A man whose profession is finding needles in haystacks will soon see them everywhere except in pincushions. I don't know who this applies to.

Can I say that Caroline's children are already planning things for Harriet? Ones a little below her age perhaps like the Hyde Park maze. She is warmly awaited.

Oh dear, Scandinavia. Per is improved by his homeground, warmth under the ice. Norway is a country country, a bit of Oregon, Colorado and Vermont. Bergen partly made of wood and cliff-hung is one of the most beautiful cities I've seen. Oslo is one of ours, Boston in the setting of Portland. Then Copenhagen, and Amsterdam, but I was tired and knew no one, and had rec-

ommendations to people withdrawn by flu. My hotel was like a Volkswagen, efficient, uncomfortable, cheap and small. My shower was a hole in the ceiling separated by a movable board from the basin but not from the toilet. At breakfast, a cheerful middleclass man in spectacles chanted Danish hymns.

I think you are heroic to make the trip to London. It's you who is the dearest soul that ever breathed. Or is it Harriet. Again my eyes water. All must be for the best.

Love,
Cal

581. To Adrienne Rich

March 29, 1971

Dearest Adrienne:

How lovely to hear from you at the beginning of my 54th year of grace and pardon. I haven't read my Stanley piece in print and forget exactly what I wrote about obscurity. I think I was putting in [a] plug for the difficult poetry I grew wise and confused on in the thirties. I don't think obscurity can be put on like an overcoat, any more than the style of the *Rape of the Lock* can be. Still there's always an effort of will, whose other name is choice. I'm uncertain what you mean by dream, but I am sure you don't mean sleep walking. The poetry of the future? I'm not sure I have read any, then again I think I've read a lot—Rimbaud, *Othello*, wherever poetry is straining to its uttermost. Most art, even the best hardens to a convention, yet the very best can't be imitated by the future, no second *Moby Dick*, and hundreds more.

Women? Randall and Peter and I found them even in our Kenyon exile, we were all more or less engaged. I know too much about women to be entangled into an argument. We are having a child because we stumbled into it and then found we dearly wanted one, and had a moral horror of abortion—I mean for ourselves, not for others. We feel a calm and awe. I don't think you know what you are talking about. Why shouldn't our having a child be profound? The times are difficult, almost impossible today, yesterday, always. If one lived in East Pakistan, Biafra e[ven] Vietnam. Character and private conditions may make having children fearful, but I don't believe the *times* make it harder for anyone we know.

Oh well, dearest Adrienne, it's lovely you are writing. I hope to be briefly in New York around the first of May. I'll spare you a lecture on repetition and change based on a trip to Norway and reading the *Burnt Njál Saga*. What

could be less like our lives than theirs of honor and hack, yet at every point a responsive cord is struck. In sad moments it seems that man and woman advance from one black bog to another. To look at the worst, as Hardy says. And the joy is incredible too. Please forgive my chaffing, my heart is with you.

Love,

Cal

582. To Allen Tate

March 29 [1971]

Dear Allen:

Your letter arrived just the other day due to the postal strike. I would be very happy to add my second to Howard Nemerov. I thought he was in long ago, he certainly deserves to have been.

What a lot has happened since I saw you last June. Caroline and I are going to have a child in October. The months whirl round and the day grows nearer. We are happier than we could have imagined. An eager anticipatory calm.

Lizzie and I are going through the steps of a legal separation, which will be much the same I think as the later divorce. It's all very sad, I have no wish to talk about it now. It could have been much worse. I was in New York over Christmas, will go again in May, then Lizzie and Harriet will come to London for a week or so in June. We've done our best, and [at] least Harriet won't experience a divorce in which her parents hate each other.

A last thing. Please Allen don't quarrel with me again. You and I have held on to each other for almost thirty-five years. I have always, or almost always, been charmed by you and thought of you with reverence and gratitude.

Love to you and Helen and your family. I feel rather like you at this moment.

Cal

583. To Elizabeth Hardwick

April 13, 1971

Dearest Lizzie—

Our letters seem doomed to cross. I woke up this morning silently saying *Flavio*, and for the first time in the twenty-four hours since I'd read your letter—realized how deeply terrifying his death must be for Elizabeth. Where is

she? I've sent a cable to [the] Brazil address, saying "Dearest Elizabeth, can I help?" I do hope she is in this country. How almost like something in Hardy would it have been if the little group in Rio could have looked eight years ahead. Even Keith has had vicissitudes.

Think carefully about not bringing Harriet to London. Are you coming yourself? Of course it is all delicate and uncertain, and the success of her trip would have to depend on the moods of so many persons, so many swayed persons. Maybe you have been getting the wrong advice, from yourself among others. Anyway, it's [a] great blow to me. I suppose I'll make the early May flight, though the flying is like six hours of giving blood. [(]For you and Harriet too![)] And [it] isn't really a serious and honorable assignment.

You seem to have found a curious new stylistic trick, the phrase, uncertain between two meanings, *id est*, ["]Harriet's not interested in what has happened to you." Happened has two meanings, but I don't suppose you knew that you couldn't have both. Poor Carolina South!, it is nature wearing the mask of city slum. Sorry you didn't have a better trip. Love to you both. I'll be seeing you.

Love,
Cal

584. To Allen Tate

April 13, 1971

Dear Allen:

What a sweet letter! I don't read the *TLS* very regularly and haven't read the attack on you, but I did see Conrad's sharp rebuke. Good, but I don't think man of letters, or "service to letters" fit you these days. You should put on your other mask, the mask of Dionysus. It's your fire that counts. Last term I gave my students a day on sonnets, reading them you, Longfellow and Tuckerman. (I teach something they insist on calling "North American Literature.") Longfellow has charming open lines, and Tuckerman something more, a Tennyson turned hard, but their energies are scattered and left me with only haphazard praise to give after reading you carefully. Fury, music and wit, not a word to be dropped or moved in whole poems. I am talking about the Christmas, Subway sonnets. You can afford to ~~worry~~ nag at criticism, when you have left so much that will stand.

Poetry and poetry criticism now are like twenty moving currents ceaselessly sloshing and twisting against each [other] in a bucket—for there must

be a container even to confusion. So many parties each with its heroes. Let them go freely, but it's [a] pity there [is] so little talent, and that so buried, and so stepped on often by the rude hacks. Everything liked till nothing's liked. I don't find the literary moment bad compared to most things.

It's unlucky to pray for a boy or a girl. Even God can't alter ours now. I prefer little girls; still, another added to Harriet and Caroline's three would make five. Woman's Lib! You shall certainly be a godfather, if you can find radiance for someone not outside Providence, but the church. Should the child follow your example or your words? Or mine?

I won't see you in New York because I will be gone by the end of May. Caroline sends her best wishes to Helen and your two. My love to all of you.

 Cal

Again apologies for the festschrift. I was writing all the time, as if I might die before I gave out. Idle time was kept to be idle, and mostly to revise. The difficulties in phrasing strategy etc. for my opening essay. A hundred times I was tempted by strong phrases; when they stopped, I stopped, and fled to the protection of my own work. It would be tactless to thank you for this, it's a little like felony, but I must.

585. To Stanley Kunitz

April 25, 1971

Dearest Stanley—

I wrote the review knowing that many of the poems were written when death was near enough to you to put out your hand and touch it, and that you might be in that position when you read it. How lovely to know you feel tough again, back to your lifelong state. Once or twice, I felt I was likely to die. Can't say I enjoyed the realization much, yet what a relief to have been there. Have we though? Someone said death isn't an event in life, it isn't lived. Thank God. You must be sick of people bothering you about my review. I wanted to put you dramatically, and think (without exactly admitting it to myself) I was angling for a good place in the review.

Several of my books, especially *Notebook*, I assumed might be my last. Now with this one (no doubt it will be) I don't. It's about done, many taken out, many put in, total a little under 120, title *Dolphin* (a very different title than *Crow*—which by the way I don't like at all, tho I like him personally better than any other poet here). I'm playing with the idea of bringing out the

book in a limited edition, in a sort of Cummington Press run by Ted Hughes' sister, about 500 copies, printed any way I want, expensive. That might be the most tactful thing I could do for Elizabeth short of burning the ms. Then in a year or so I'[ll] bring out commercial editions. I'd hate to leave [the] book in type if I were run over or something. Lawsuits between Lizzie and Caroline etc. Lizzie is the heroine, the eel I try to ensnare and release from the eelnet, but she will feel bruised by the intimacy. She should win all hear[t]s but what is that when you are left, and left again in print?

Everyone in America seems to think this is too dire a time to breed. I had an impertinent lecture from Adrienne, but for us it's a calming joy. We already have three rather lovely little girls, so the coming of another child is not alarming—tho always there is a frightening mystery and uncertainty. Caroline is comparatively physical[ly] healthy, we breathe now as the cattle breathe. Caroline sleeping and eating double, looking as though she'd deliver tomorrow, tho it's not till October 9. We mustn't talk as if we were living in East Pakistan.

We live in the same house now, next week Caroline will take my name—this isn't marriage yet, I don't want to jostle Lizzie at all. Will the hailstones of the gods fall on me, if I say I've never been so happy, nor knew I could be?

Don't know when I'll reach America. Maybe in September. It seemed too jolting to come this spring. The plane trips in themselves are murder,—and so much else added! Oh my Dear, who to talk to? I love it here, but the English are generically horrible, just like New York Jews and New Englanders. Alas, I've been all three. But the countryside, and the ~~eccentric~~ changeful slowed pace of life here are lovely, not that feeling one sometimes gets in New York of screaming, metallic, poisoned ice.

All my love to you and Elise.

Cal[. . .]

586. To the Editors, New York Review of Books

[May 6, 1971]

JUDGMENT DEFERRED ON LIEUTENENT CALLEY

A principle may kill more than an incident. I am sick with fresh impressions. Has no one the compassion to pass judgment on William Calley? His atrocity is cleared by the President, public, polls, rank and file of the right and left. He looks almost alive; like an old song, he stirs us with the gruff poignance of the

professional young soldier. He too fought under television for our place in the sun. Why should the bait be eaten when the sharks swim free? I sense a coldness under the hysteria. Our nation looks up to heaven, and puts her armies above the law. No stumbling on the downward plunge from Hiroshima. Retribution is someone somewhere else and we are young. In a century perhaps no one will widen an eye at massacre, and only scattered corpses express a last histrionic concern for death. We are not hypocrites, we can learn to embrace people outside society—President Nixon, our own Huckleberry Finn who has to shoot everyone else on the raft.

—Robert Lowell

587. To Peter Taylor

May 13, 1971

Dear Peter:

Every so often it occurs to me that you are only a few days away from me by mail. Then I think, "He's an awfully clever fellow and won't appreciate my heavy jokes." It's a beautiful spring here. I've spent an afternoon in Kew Gardens, met two charming dolphins, Baby and Brandy, gone trout fishing in a reservoir where the neighboring anglers made record casts, but also caught nothing. Every week some new and wrong American literary friend turns up. About the end of the month we go to Italy for about ten days.

We. But we're more than that. Caroline is almost five months pregnant, and looks nine. Fearful dread of twins, and indeed Allen, who behaved very badly about us to Lizzie, has already offered himself as a godfather. Even so. If there is only one child, we might call him, until after the divorce, Lowell Guinness. It's a great comfort, soothes us and somehow takes away from the willfulness of my action. I feel I've more than half lost Harriet, not through anyone's fault but through distance. It's more than I can bear sometimes, but this will make up. We have three other children, lovely little girls so "Lowell" will have a nest waiting. One child is already knitting him mittens. I doubt if it will be *HIM*! Everything in our house is girl except me.[. . .]

I worry about your eye, and expect my own to advance to your stage. I've had a low aching virus which was cured by a low antibiotic that still gives me nausea.

O, now I know why I am writing. Do you think you might ever come over here? We could give you a wonderful brick ruin, and a stocked trout stream about the width of a typewriter ribbon. England has everything you love, safe

schools, no Negroes, quaint old people, absolutely nutty ones our age, whiskey without ice. You could renew your old academic and ecclesiastical connections. We would love to have you and Eleanor visit us. Or we could find you a house.

I miss America, and thought of coming over this spring, but it seemed too complex and jolting. It would be better probably after the baby is born. I've just more or less finished another book of poems, after working frantically, sometimes six days a week. Now I am utterly empty. What are you doing? I have my old *Prometheus* play being done here this June. Isn't Eleanor bringing out a book?

My love and loneliness to you both.
 Cal

Since writing you last fall, I was home for Christmas and tried to call you, but I think you were visiting one of your houses. My visit of course was good and bad. More good. I think I am happier than I've ever been, even tho Henry Adams' brother says happiness depends on digestion. Caroline and I haven't quarreled for four months, an absolute record for me with anyone. We are both slovenly, but essentially sane. I do miss you!

588. To Elizabeth Hardwick

[n.d. May 1971]

Dearest Lizzie—

Such good reports of you and Harriet. Both Jonathan and Stephen used the word radiant of Harriet, and reported you were in fine confident spirits, electric. I'm sorry to have sent you that fussy letter about money. I really can't make out on my Essex salary. At our age its hard to live on nothing, taxis etc. I think the only article of clothing I've bought in a year is an overcoat. If you need money at any time from the Farrar royalties I'll give it you. I am keeping the fourteen thousand as a reserve. I admit this sounds like an anti climax to my money groans, but I think you can understand the mental relief just having it gives me.

Rather homesick for America now in the heavy summer weather, Americans arriving like summer birds, returning Englishmen. I had some sort of virus without fever that made my head and bones ache. The antibiotic cure of course brought a slight nausea and depression. Otherwise all is well. I'll go to Rome at the end of May. Then my play comes out on the 24th of June. I've

been through it three times, brisking it up, making Zeus a little more like God or nature and less like a Gestapo boss. Elizabeth Bishop is coming here I think in the second week of June. I don't know how she has taken the boy's suicide and dread knowing. I think I'll spend the summer revising my imitations. I made two or three much better I thought by being more quiet and accurate. I am tired by so much original writing, almost four years without stop.

I think of you constantly and long in a way for America, but not just a hurried glimpse. Maybe next Christmas would be best. Or I could dash over in September. I am beginning to get habituated to being here, really quite a job but it brings peace. I think a writer never for long feels he has done well. One of the most exciting things here has been Borges' visit. I've had two nights more or less alone with him, talking about Tennyson, James and Kipling, and almost wept when he talked "without pity" to an audience about his blindness.

I started this letter meaning to talk only about missing you, but that though true would be boring. I guess all is well as far as mortality and one's large failings allow. Jealous of you and everyone else seeing Harriet.

Love,
Cal

589. To Elizabeth Hardwick

[Milgate Park, Bearsted, Maidstone, Kent]
June 23, [1971]

Dearest Lizzie:

I've just cabled Harriet a small sum of money, an unadventurous, impersonal gift, but I couldn't face the disaster of import duties, delays, choosing the wrong thing. At least this can't wholly miss fire.

Tomorrow *Prometheus* opens at the Mermaid, once more beautifully directed by Jonathan. The Wernicks (!) went last night to the preview and liked it. I've only seen the dress rehearsal, very finished, except Ocean improvised his lines—maybe he should, but we hope he won't. Io very good, but less than Irene, and young. Hermes better. Gulls better. Kenneth the same. Reading the text and speeding it with little changes, I kept coming on suggestions of yours like *a hailstorm of gifts*. This happened many times because I was following with the lines to see that the actors got my emendations. Feelings of tender and lonely gratitude to you. I can't judge the play. How did I get into so much Greek? And I may finish up the *Oresteia*. Jonathan says Sir Bernard Miles who runs the Mermaid Theatre is like old Cronus. Quite a change from Bob Brustein.

I may go to Russia to see Madam Mandelstam who wrote me a touching letter in reply to mine on her book. But O the filthy Russian regime and the maddening precautions one must take, such as not writing her before I arrive. I've conferred with such Russian authorities as Gaia, Weidenfeld and Mary. They all agree, but of course no one knows what the government intends to do with Madam M.

I keep looking for your *Scarlet Letter*. I like almost all of it, tho perhaps the non-fictional historical shadowing most. I see I learned all I know about the Puritans from Hawthorne. I'm reading Hogg's *Justified Sinner*, a similar very Scotch book, only the women are in the background, Chillingworth is the hero-fiend. No use to say how much I think of you. My blood-pressure is down.

Love,

Cal[. . .]

590. *To Adrienne Rich*

80 Redcliffe Sq.
London SW 10
June 23, [1971]

Dearest Adrienne:

I wonder if this will reach you before you leave for California? I trust it will trail you there. O I think you might want to live somewhere else this summer, and then return to Vermont in the cool of another year.

I mustn't advise or judge you, but I feel an air of relief in your letter, as if you had emerged from a very long fever. As indeed you have. The loneliness and freedom of a new life. We are never born again I think, nor would want to be. Yet there are new starts. A marriage ends, and nothing stays unchanged. We face the freshness and fears and release of looking at what we really are. (What is THAT?) And the awful pains of improvisation and invention.

It wouldn't be correct for me to defend myself to you, but you may be able to see that we are in somewhat the same position, by different paths. You know a lot about me but nothing about my situation. You hold half the broken eggshell and see things thru Lizzie, not exactly through Lizzie's eyes. The only important thing wrong with marriage with Lizzie was our unending nervous strife, as tho a bear had married a greyhound. We were always deeply together and constantly fascinated and happy together, and constantly sadly vexed. When you talk about romantic sexual love, Dear, you are surely talk-

ing through your hat. I doubt if you are through with it. And anyway, it is only very partially true of me. No one sees a woman steadily for over a year and remains only romantically in love. I think you are thinking of people like Sandra. This has nothing in common with that. It's not for nothing that in the old days I always came back to Lizzie. Sometimes I think your sense of justice wants Lizzie to be happier and me to be unhappier. But you can't wish that— and I do think she will be happier, tho to say so sounds like cant. I think you will be happier, and now are. These are hard sayings and life is hard, but only fatal in the end.

I see the people you can imagine and a few you can't. Our weekends are much like yours—sun, grass children. Sometimes I go trout fishing and fail to land them. God go with you on your summer. I wish you weren't so far.

Love,
Cal

591. To Elizabeth Hardwick

[Milgate Park, Bearsted, Maidstone, Kent]
August 3, 1971

Dearest Lizzie:

It's hard to believe letters cross the Atlantic in less than the months of the old ships at sea in the nineteenth century. It does something to smother expression maybe. Or is it that I feel you would not much welcome details of my daily life? Not that we have drama. I've been mostly settling in, and am now fairly at ease and glad to be out of the press and smother of London. It's easy to go there, but the call isn't strong this summer. And summer so queer and cool and short. The children's school ends the sixth of July and begins the sixth of September. Another reason to be here instead of interrupted almost ten months in London.

Events—this morning two swallows flew in my window and out . . . those old friends who used to scare me into my old barn. I have a rabbit who dogs me around the house, and can't be housebroken. I've just corrected a thirty-five page interview for a little magazine called *the Review*. It's mostly shop, though we took care not to repeat Seidel's old one. It seems double its ten years or so ago, I'm very valetudinarian, free with my wisdom of age. Last weekend, separately Bob Silvers and McCarthy were here, Gene rather pricking up his ears toward campaigning, or backing someone. Bob told me about your letters from Harriet. I rub my eyes—suddenly from cats and pigs to full adolescence. Liked particularly the garbage and newspaper bits. I had one

lovely card from her before she left—tender and gracefully humorous. We hardly bring out the most severe and ideological in one another, tho I write her like another grown-up—almost. Funny, just yesterday, I took *Villette* out of the bookcase—and put her back. I'm deep in *Dombey*—almost to where I left off in Maine four summers ago. I am terribly proud of Harriet—the flower has come to her, about five years earlier than anything came to me. Whatever else, she won't be a wooden lady.

Bob brought your Sylvia—dazzling, as usual. In a way I want to see it in contrast with your book's other heroines—you feel strong attraction, strong ~~repulsion~~ disgust. "Daddy" is too much for me, and I think it [is] weakened by being too much Sylvia—Oh stridently! Some of her new poems (not the intermediate book) but more *Ariel* are terrific—one on unfaith. Remember how Dr. Eissler said Freud ~~shifted~~ transferred from the benign Joseph to the far more dangerous Moses? Don't.

Love,
Cal

592. *To Elizabeth Hardwick*

August 18, 1971

Dearest Lizzie:

May I say it? The last is the sweetest of your letters—only one crack. How could you compare my gentle Flaubertian elegy on my father to "Daddy"? Oh how I too wish that in some turning of time and doubling of matter you might be meeting my plane in New York this late summer. I don't see how I will get to America sooner than Christmas or Easter. The date of the child's (Lowell-Guinness, I've been holding this back from you) [birth] is little more than six weeks off. Yes, the country is already much better for the children, and will be for the next one's entrance. They have so much more at their age to distract them—much of it will last through winter: indoor swimming (at an awful country hotel, The Great Dane) various horse things, and even ballet, and mostly running about the house, indoors and out. Pets go on snowballing, Bosun, a miniature, long-haired dachshund, liable to be eaten by the cats, Tigger and Kitty—and Goldie and Carpie liable to be eaten by everyone. Oh this is like one of Harriet's old letters.

Guests pile in—the Empsons, Sonia, and now perhaps Alice. I don't think McCarthy is doing much—that makes him refreshing after the other

polls.[...]Your book seems a big thing: a more passionate, personal style, Woman, a subject untouched in our time by anyone of critical and literary vocation. Are [you] going to use any of your old women pieces, particularly Emily Brontë, and maybe *La Deuxieme*? You've given this out of the way subject quite a little time. The one advantage I find in Woman's Lib is that I can start off humorous or angry arguments with *any* woman. Last winter, a Lady Norwich stopped speaking to me with the furious remark, "I have as much right as a man to crank a car." I said I had always prayed for such a woman.[...]

593. *To Elizabeth Hardwick*

[September 24, 1971]

Dearest Lizzie—

I only partly understand your second paragraph about "recent shocks." One of course is my book, but it doesn't have a publication date, need not come out ever. It's not defamatory, it's like your "Notebook," probably less astringent. My story is both a composition and alas, a rather grinding autobiography, what I lived, though of course one neither does or should tell the literal or ultimate truth. Poetry lies. I'll send it to you if you wish (when it's in neater shape), you won't feel betrayed or exploited but I can't imagine you'll want to scrape through the sadness and breakage now.

I can't write much. Everything has fallen on us this week—false labor pains, rushed midnight trip to hospital, discovery that the child is upsidedown, feet-first, and must be turned. For over a week I had continual nosebleeds (high blood pressure?) now stopped and cured by an expert wicking my nose. No more worry? Our whole household seems to be catching scabies from Bosun the toy dachshund. What a moment![*] I guess all will be well.

Mail is queer. Some reaches me. I guess more doesn't. Harriet's didn't. I'll write her soon. Mary and Jim were here, sad over your illness and gloating over the reactionary Dr. Russell's misdiagnosis. Poor Mary! She got some of the worst reviews I've ever read—worse than my *Prometheus*, more inconsequential entertainment journalists. She seemed shaken; but a brave soul never shows it except involuntarily.

I can't write more; all my love to you and Harriet.

*All must be washed/boiled, all us, clothes, rabbits and *hedge*.

Cal

594. To Blair Clark

BOY ROBERT SHERIDAN BORN LAST NIGHT LOVE
 CAL

595. To Elizabeth Hardwick

October 1, 1971

Dearest Lizzie:

We had to dash from Maidstone to London on the next to last day in order to get proper medical attendance; then after *inducement*, twelve hours of labor. Even fathers get tired, but all is well. Not enough to write letters.

Whatever you do, don't burn *your* "Notebook"! I hope to live in it long after I'm dirt. What you showed me was some of your tenderest, and easiest writing. I wrote you that mine need not be published ever. It won't be published, but kept. I won't burn all but a few blue parts so you mustn't. Maybe in calmer times we can publish the two books in one volume. I think in time to come, if we are still here, my poems will seem less disturbing to you. It's my best/last work maybe—isn't an author always his own best critic? Particularly of a lately finished book.

My blood survives the tense last two weeks, two midnight ambulances etc. Not for me! It's my old high wavery bloodpressure. Now I'm back on aldumet, have had and will, all sorts of tests. All's well, heart, liver etc. Only the blood goes high then drops—not with inner anguish, but mysteriously. I guess it's not too serious. Like me.

Oh the will—I mean the settlement—can't your friendly lawyer draw up what seems right, and then I without a lawyer will object to what I wish to. I'd like to avoid lawyer costs. Though I pay less than my share, my expenses for the baby are heavy, will be.[. . .]Oh I'm well enough off. Of the common possessions, I'd like [a] few family ~~possessions~~ tokens for *Robert*; I'd naturally like to leave him something—maybe royalties. For myself, a few of the books. I have much of what I want in paperbacks. Thankyou for your *dear* concern.

Love,
 Cal

596. To Frank Bidart

[December 6 or 8?, 1971]

Dear Frank:

[. . .]I am writing to take you up on a favor. Could you come here after Christmas or early January? Here's the agenda, as Pound would say. My new book, *The Dolphin*, about eighty poems, shorter than when you saw it, but with many new poems (it now ends in a long pregnancy and birth (one poem) sequence)[,] everything endlessly rewritten, and about 40 poems about English statuary, demos etc. taken out, not because they are bad, but because they clog the romance. 2) To find something to do with the rejected poems; they can't be a narrative, but could have a mounting drive of similarity. 3) Here's where I need you most: I've tried to reduce *Notebook* to personal narrative. Mostly the Historic, the metaphysical and the political go, tho it keeps bits of each, then go the personal poems that fit well enough but are inflated, uninspired or redundant. I've done a sort of jerry-built first draft, and am not sure whether it works (half my new revision will go? etc.). You can see how your advice and care would be unique and invaluable. This all began by trying to get around the mounting pressure on me not to publish *The Dolphin*. (For moral reasons.) And indeed, it must wait.

Now my confession, I haven't yet gotten around to your book and will in a few days and will write you. I've done nothing but schoolwork and my own work for a month—uneasy to have so much unfinished on my hands unfinishing.

Anyway Caroline and I would love to have you here. I of course want to pay your passage. Do see if you can come. Miserable about Elizabeth B. With asthma you think you cannot breathe at all. I'm writing her but give her my love.

Affectionately as ever,
Cal

597. To Peter Taylor

December 9, 1971

Dear Peter:

Doesn't Conrad's *Victory* end with a scene in which the hero Heist or Geist or something is so etiolated and uninvolved that he lets three thugs de-

stroy and kill his girl, his best friend and his favorite raspberry patch—but no, what I remember is that everyone's safety depends on his answering seven letters—three are bills, one is a book of poems sent for criticism in longhand, and the other three . . . one was to you, the other two, answers to two answers Harriet never wrote to two of his.

We've been through—I feel it's undemocratic to have such problems—help problems. Our under thirty, former machinists division of the Royal Navy, "boy" who did everything, drove, fixed[,] cooked, had a violent seizure (something between paranoid and criminal—anyway frightening) and had to be fired. Suddenly from large numbers of people roaming in the house we were none, baby, two little girls, and Caroline and I—nothing very near and no one able to drive the car. Visions of our former employee wandering the downs of Kent—our minds much like Allen's when he imagined that girl's imbecile twin brothers making for Sewanee. How we could have used his higher style. Now we have two Canadians, Pam and Perry; they look like students, but not in English. They do everything; apparently everything that takes hard work and a clear mind in England, has to be done by Canadians or Pakistanis. Caroline and I have expired American licenses—it's been suggested I not renew mine, but Caroline has just failed two tests. People go a little insane if they can drive your car, and you can't.

I called up Harriet, and talked to Lizzie, and will try again next week for Harriet. Since the baby we've been pretty much out of touch. I suppose I don't want to stir the embers. I think if Harriet were to come, all would work, but she gazes at so many uncertainties, new country, so many new people—a new father . . . in her mind. She'll come here, or maybe I'll come to New York at Easter. Maybe I should try to renew my ten days at U of V. ———O voluminous One, with your five volume set of shorter plays, I have only a brilliant unpublishable forty page poem, and also brilliant revisions, cuts etc. of *Notebook*, which I have learned is impossible to read through. It would be more joy than I can write to have you and Eleanor stop with us this winter.

 Love
 Cal

598. To Charles Tomlinson

Dec. 13 [1971]

Dear Charles:

Sorry not to have written you sooner about your little book that gave me

such delight. Teaching and a baby have made my remarkable inefficiency more remarkably inefficient. I can't say anything worth putting down now without carefully rereading your text. My impression is that the ten poems are harder than the smaller selection I had read. He is still *the* poet to discover, at least for me.

Are your poems concrete? I've always thought they could be charming as "graphics" as you call them, but have no particular relation to read poetry. They are to be looked at, like pictures. This is too simple—I mean what I am saying.

We are here most of the time with brief forays to London. Could you come down sometime? Maidstone is only an hour by train from London. I would love to see you and yearn for someone to talk shop to—even on graphics.

Yours as always,
Cal

599. To Frank Bidart

December 23, 1971

Dear Frank:

You take a taxi from Heathrow (London airport) to Victoria Station (continental side) in London, then a train to East Maidstone (they leave twice an hour and the trip is about an hour—*you need to be careful to get in the right end of the train* or you will end up in Rochester, Folksstone or Dover) then get a cab to Milgate Park, Bearsted. I'd meet you at any of these points, but knowing the unevenness of plane schedules and my inefficiency, I think the chances of a bad slip are great.

You will come here in a moment [of] comparative calm for us. In the way one does, we've piled up an incredible number of people at Christmas time: our four children, two of their friends—one called the naughty Armstrong—two Spenders who make each other age, the Mary McCarthys with a depressed son, the Grey Gowries, separated but momentarily reunited with son—and then The Staff, more than I dare name, all eccentric or nervous, with friends, imbecile mothers. When you come all that will be gone, except for us, almost enough for a village.

I just had a letter from Morton Bloomfield accepting my resignation, which I hadn't offered. It's through misinterpreting a letter I wrote Bill. Yet I now think we might come spring a year from this one, or fall 73. I would very much like to get back to America temporarily; it's beginning to have the

glamour of a foreign country for me, even one unknown. We are settled here and unwieldy to move.

I've been through the whole of *Notebook* now making changes, some very good, I think, though many botches—I can't read an old changed poem without putting back some of the original text—making more changes. The strategy for us is [to] read the short new book, then tackle the old tangles. I can't tell you how I look forward to your coming and how grateful I am. We must find things to do, here, around here, and in London, that you will like.

Affectionately,

600. To Elizabeth Hardwick

February 5, 1972

Dearest Lizzie:

Just a note of delight about Harriet's trip. I enclose the check (in another envelope). Of course I would be glad to come and escort her here, but plane trips kill me—two in about two days! Also this isn't a moment when I feel like a swift, a rapid motion glimpse of all my dear New York friends. So I sigh with relief. I'll be at Heathcliff airport with a car at the exact hour.

I can't write much. This week was hell, just ending. Ivana's case was and is very grave; doctors reports conflicted; no point was reached when we could feel she was out of danger. Then difficult drives through one of England's worst snow storms (nothing to ours, but looking like Napoleon's retreat from Moscow to the English eye). Then the skin-stripping operation; then next the plastic surgery. I think she [is] out of danger (but for the unforeseen) but will be two more months in the hospital—one of the best in England and with manners like Miss Elsemore.

I will write Harriet either today or tomorrow. Tell her the thought of her coming has been to me the happiest of all happy thoughts. (Do I sound like Wordsworth? I am Thrilled and half-marveling that you and Harriet are reading *poetry*. To me *poetry* means poetry written before 1906.[)]

I appreciate your accommodation.

All my love,

Cal

601. To Elizabeth Bishop

February 6(?), 1972

Dearest Elizabeth:

You seem to have been here during Frank's visit, both by voice and reference (if Caroline had met you, you would have been as here as we). (Change in type caused by my disastrous stopgap of putting an Olympia ribbon on a Hermes, meaning rolls stop rolling every five minutes and have to be exhaustingly switched.[)]

You are so here that I started to phone you about Marianne. The end of her life already ended by infirmity—she was a star in my sky 35 years ago when I first read Dick Blackmur's essay. Last week I was teaching her to my poor dim students, along with Cummings whom they of course liked and got much better. For you though, it's losing *the* person. What can I say? Maybe you'll write a little book of memory and thoughts. I have never heard anyone describe her so well—or anyone else. Her death has made little stir, unlike Berryman's—on whom each English week or arts page has a bad elegy. This is right, though I thought him doomed too ever since I ate with him last year[,] then it was drink, later he must have died from not drinking. She was much more inspired—his heroism was in leaping into himself in the last years, ~~amazingly~~ bravely.

I think Frank and I revised 405 poems in a month. That's no way to write, but it was made more sensible by Frank's amazing filing code and total memory for my lines. Even for rejected versions. The three books are my magnum opus, are the best or rather they['ll] do. Are they much? Read *Dolphin* when you have leisure. I'll send the other two fairly soon. I am going to publish, and don't want advice except for yours. Lizzie won't like the last. What else can I offer her? There's something creepy about deliberately writing something posthumous. (Love, Cal)

I have no heart to write about Ivana's accident. We have been ~~like~~ a lost ship.

602. To Frank Bidart

February 9, 1972

Dear Frank:

One of my rare letters. My reflexes still say you are here. Your bedroom now much colder and no longer glowing with its coal-red heater, seems to hold you; at breakfast, we wait for your appearance at 9:37 moving simulta-

neously for your black coffee, and *The Times*. This afternoon I fell asleep reading and woke up saying, "Frank, where, where have we gotten?" You are much missed. I don't know what either my books [or I] would have done without you. I dare not think of the books, lest all need as much more revision as the last we added, and they again need as much, on without advancing to infinity, where parallel lines meet. I did however "resolve" as Caroline says, the 16 you left behind.

I cannot imagine you weren't dead when you landed in Boston . . . and buried after the poets' dinner. I've just shaken loose my leaden shroud, and feel light again. Not light enough to write more. While waiting for the taxi, I bought Caroline and me, identical *electronic* lighters. Perry is going to mark them, so no theft will be concealed.

Affectionately,
Cal

603. *To Frank Bidart*

March 1, 1972

Dear Frank:

Your Pound book so absorbed me that [I] haven't read the *Lear* I teach tomorrow. This letter must be a note. Many thanks for both books. The Eliot has lost many marvelous lines, that would have been among the most famous, if he'd found a way to chunk them in. Now never.

I think if you could come for a while in the summer, I'd be ready to start on the Russian. Olwyn Hughes is satisfied, though not out of her mind with my offer.

For my birthday I bought myself (like John) some magnificent, very cheap and ill-cut chocolate corduroy trousers. And Caroline, a silver chain bracelet, Victorian, with Faith, Hope and Charity tokens. Such were our gifts when we [were] poor and young and admired Mexican folk art in Greenwich Village.

I told you, didn't I, that Ivana will be home in about two weeks. Scarred but sound. I finished my Berryman. It's nothing extra, publishable.

I wish now we had all our revision to do over. At the time, I thought we'd [be] dead before it was done.

I look forward so much to seeing you this summer. Caroline sends her love.

Affectionately,
Cal

604. To Stanley Kunitz

Dear Stanley,

I am sending you a huge, perhaps exhausting package: my new book, *The Dolphin*,—all the history poems from *Notebook*, and quite [a] few more, heavily changed and arranged chronologically (300); a small book (60), all from *Notebook*, of personal poems, more than half about Lizzie and Harriet. I have decided to publish in about a year, and don't want a lot of stir and rumors. The only copies I'm sending out are to you and Elizabeth Bishop. I hope they catch your fascination, so your toil will be lighter than it would otherwise be.

Spring is coming fast here, crocus and snowdrop, and many green shooting things and ground leaves whose names I do not know. Out walking, I found a big blueblack rook, dead yet reminding me of your famous bird with a whole in its skull. I feel the old yearning of adolescence and earlier. If one could walk far enough and in the right ways, one would meet love and immortality, and make a marriage. I am fifty-five today, no time to be a boy. We've had a hard winter. In January my six year [old] stepdaughter tipped an electric kettle on herself (not knowing it was there) it fell in her lap and the top came off. It's hard to remember when she was not in the hospital, but now she'll be back with us in two weeks. The first two weeks, it was all pain and a risk of death.[. . .]

How are you and Elise? I wish you were here to take our garden in hand. In return you would b[uy] unlimited wine and the conversations that go with [it.] Was the Yevtushenko gala as awful as it sounded in the papers? I don't think you and I could pl[ease a] big audience, unless Yevtushenko read us aloud.

Harriet comes here on the 25th for 8 days very gracefully blessed by Lizzie except that [it] is underlined that she is to see as much of me as possible and as little of Caroline. Maybe she and I could visit the Isaiah Berlins alone. But things are much better with Lizzie and me, much of the fever is gone, so I am doubly anxious not to smash all with my b[ook] a very tender though embarrassing for [her] necessary[. . .]

605. To Elizabeth Hardwick

Dearest Lizzie:

Sweet of you to remember old times, even my now rather rusty sight-

seeing: the "horrors of the Vatican," the mosque at the Cordoba that didn't look like a church, the Carpaccio with the dragon Harriet pitied, the poets' feast, Grace Stone, and the many walks when we didn't arrive quite where we intended, or when. Don't worry, I have many things to go, *romero*, with Harriet. More than the pitifully short time will allow. I'll make out a loose schedule when she comes. I had no intention of marching her in a caravan of small children.

Huyck van Leeuwen read of a theory in an Italian historian, Guglielmo Ferrero, that Napoleon's mobile Italian Campaign was controlled by fast dispatches from *The Directoire* in Paris. But they must have left something to Napoleon who was there. I'm here. The plans will be alright. But is anything alright? We make so many mistakes and age rubs them in, almost indelibly. God rest us all, and Tiny Tim.

You must change the departure date. I teach till very late on Thursday afternoon, and then again on Friday morning. Friday night will be alright, tho the earlier plan would have been better. I know how hard and dark Harriet's trip is for you. I mustn't go into this. When she comes back you will wonder at some of your fears. When things loosen up, I'll try and get to America— *North* America as my Essex Literature classes call it.

Love to you both,
 Cal

606. To Elizabeth Hardwick

Sunday, March 19, [1972]

Dearest Lizzie—

This probably won't arrive before Harriet, but I have put in for a call to you this afternoon. Thanks for your lovely letter.[. . .]

Sorry about your kidney. I live on mutually antagonistic pills. Nothing much wrong though but teeth. I feel my mouth is falling to chalk but the dentist will find only one urgent hole.

Ivana to the doctors' surprise is already climbing the stairs. Because most of the water boiled on her middle it's hard for to stand straight like a ramrod, or rather walk upright. She's to go back to school next month. In six years, she'll have to have another plastic operation (less bad than this one) because she will outgrow her surgery. All done in half a second!

· I wait for Harriet like a bridegroom, or a sinner waiting the priest. The weather has been heavenly for nearly a week, so warm it's a relief to go in the

windowless hall and cool from the heat. I know we'll have a happy time. She comes in the awe of full spring.

I can't judge my Berryman. It looks denser in proofs. It's fiction in a way, but may not be far from the truth. Anecdotes about John could be made up for miles by his cronies and students, monotonous, wearying, like Dylan Thomas's, because the escapades even when they happened, lived on the imagination. I was on a program for him in London. It centered on a movie interview with Alvarez—John, close-up, just off drunkenness, mannered, booming, like an old fashioned star professor. His worst. I think of the young, beardless man, simple, brilliant, the enthusiast . . . buried somewhere with the older.

Goodbye, my love. One seems to have no age in this season—I don't mean I feel twenty.

Love,
 Cal

607. To William Alfred

[March 20, 1972]

Dear Bill:

Many thanks for your letter bringing home the loneliness of being here without you. I wonder if you got the poems on page 47 right. They are meant to be about Caroline and me, in a sort of pastoral analogue. If you took them [to] be about Elizabeth, they might be better . . . sadder and about more. Food for thought, when I get a little more time.

On the Auden, I have been indiscreet. How could he stop speaking to me about a book he hadn't seen. I think he's not a snubber and has never stopped talking to anyone, except Rudolf Bing[,] even then I think it was the Met he stopped talking to. Pretty rough to me, unpleasant too to wait for his appearance in England . . . to be cut. So, about ten-thirty at night, a too ardent hour, I sent him this cable: "Dear Wystan—astounded by your insult to me with William Alfred." I didn't mean to get you involved, but without naming you it seemed impossible to rescue my charge from complete vagueness. Well, now it seems Auden has been behaving this way lately when drunk and then doesn't remember. I probably should have done nothing, but sending the cable made my life sweeter. I apologize to you. Poor Wystan, still marvelous and calm in things he writes. I think it's desertion not marriage that cuts him. For some reason, though once warm, not intimate, friends, we have cooled more

and more for the last four or five years. He has cooled, I haven't and would be glad to stop it.

I am going to do everything not to make my book offensive to Lizzie; the poems you name could go without too much loss, but others couldn't.

Love as ever,
Cal

Sonia Orwell is a few feet away waiting for a picnic; Harriet arrives Saturday.

608. *To Peter Taylor*

March 20, 1972

Dear Peter—

Lovely news. I answer immediately since who knows how long a letter will take to go from my backwater to yours.[. . .]We're an hour by train from London. The house is early 18th century Palladian, and very Old South messy, a just housebroken miniature dachshund, about a thousand children, numerous, very unreliable, even dangerous, Old South help, strangely dressed. My New England creed that morality is tidiness and incessant action has failed. So has Caroline's Anglo-Irish breeziness. (How does Eleanor stand on Belfast? When Caroline talks on the subject, New Left London intellectuals change the subject to something non-controversial like Hitler.) We call our house cozy. One mastering element is my son, who has already learned to talk without using words—interminably, a blessing to the insomniac.[. . .]

I am to show another "charming Southerner" London next week: Harriet is coming for the first time. What were you interested in at 15? Harriet has read Donne, but "likes the 19th century better." Do you think you and Eleanor would like to see the same things Harriet would? The Tower? The City? Sonia Orwell?

Somehow this winter commuting to my college which looks like the University of Southern Florida, and talking to students who wouldn't answer questions—"Is Lear tragic or senile?" They mutely thumb through their texts. I got so weary, I hardly read the brief assignments I gave. I am hoping to live off my royalties and "papers." Each letter from you is a day's vacation. I'll teach again here next October, then next year, Fall 1973, 3 months at Harvard. By then I'll be tragic and senile. I've done a lot of work, a small new book and bales of rewriting, *Notebook*, version 3, called *History*. I expect it to

be a school text—an entirely old-fashioned history only considering Wars, Heroes, women, and myself.

I so long for you to meet us and for us to meet you!

Love to Eleanor,

Cal

609. To Christopher Ricks

Dear Christopher:

My book problems are complicated and I would like to ask your advice. My new book is a small one, some eighty poems in the meter of *Notebook*—the story of changing marriages, not a malice or sensation, far from it, but necessarily, according to my peculiar talent, very personal. Lizzie is naturally very much against it. I am considering publication in about a year; it needn't be published, but I feel fully clogged by the possibility of not. This awkward exposition shows my painful embarrassment.

I have two other books that are re-arrangement and rewriting 1) *Notebook*, now about 300 poems, is called *History*, through the ages from the reptiles to 1970. It takes me a hundred poems or so to get to Verdun, so the bulk of *History* is in my lifetime, sometimes heavily autobiographical—The Twenties are mostly seen as my adolescence. 2) A short book, 60 poems, called *For Lizzie and Harriet*, which also comes from *Notebook* and is about my marriage. My three books are related, though not in sequence exactly. The new one, *The Dolphin*, would come out by itself; the other two would come out as separate books under one cover. All to be published at the same time.

I know so much published revision is silly, but the confusions of my composition, looking for my form etc. made it necessary. I am still making small changes on a fairly clear manuscript, and almost feel that I have made the improvements within my powers and gifts. Afterwards, something new, but not before I get my great load published.

I wonder if we could confer sometime toward the end of April? We'd love to have you stay here. You see how all this involves your article.

Affectionately,

Cal

610. *To Elizabeth Bishop*

March 28, 1972

Dearest Elizabeth—

Let me write you right away . . . thoughtlessly, casually, first scattered impressions—my thanks. The smaller things. Most of your ~~questions~~ reservations seem likely to [be] right and useful. I can't tell from a quick reading and haven't checked your remarks with my lines. I think they will help; please give me more. I am talking about your brief line to line objections. 2) The transition back to London is a hard problem maybe. I'd like to do [it] in two or preferably one sonnet. The pregnancy isn't meant to come crash on New York, though it was only a month later, i.e. when we knew or suspected. It's [a] problem of finding inspiration for a link, I think.

Now Lizzie's letters? I did not see them as slander, but as sympathetic, tho necessarily awful for her to read. She is the poignance of the book, tho that hardly makes it kinder to her. I could say the letters are cut, doctored part fiction; I thought of it (I attribute things to Lizzie I made up, or that were said by someone else. I combed out abuse, hysteria, repetition.[)] The trouble is the letters make the book, I think, at least they make Lizzie real beyond my invention. I took out the worst things written against me, so as not to give myself a case and seem self-pitying. Or maybe I didn't want to author them. I promise I'll do what I can to answer your piercing ~~objections~~ thoughts. I've been thinking of course these things for years almost. It's oddly enough a technical problem as well as a gentleman's problem. How can the story be told at all without the letters. I'll put my heart to it. I can't bear not to publish *Dolphin* in good form. I am in no hurry for time, and would love to spend the summer working if the muse lets me.

Salary is complicated. I got $9500, I think eventually at my highest. After three years, I was given rooms at Quincy House free for two or three days a week for three months. I didn't teach after Christmas. I had the expense of commuting. I think all salaries must be higher now. Every two or three years I got a little $500 raise. I may have started at $8500. Also I wasn't around when I wasn't teaching. I'm sure you will get more. Maybe the best thing is to have someone practical and forceful to handle it for you, but even lambs like us can kick the bucket over.

Harriet is with us now, and though the weather is now suddenly wintery, [I] think it is May with us.

I feel like Bridges getting one of Hopkins letters, as disturbed as I am grateful.

Oh, I forgot. If you can get the revised *Notebook* from Frank, particularly the section *For Harriet and Lizzie*, but also the latter part of *History*, you might get a slightly different slant on the meaning of *Dolphin*. The three books are one heap, one binding, so to speak, though not one book.

All my love,
Cal

611. To Elizabeth Bishop

[April 4, 1972]
Easter Tuesday, 1972

Dearest Elizabeth:

Harriet has come and gone, and I'm left in a mood of wonder, so well she carried off what had to be difficult, impossible I almost thought. We talked more freely than we ever have (this is age but only partly) yet not too much, and no sides had to be taken except humorously. And things went well with Caroline, Harriet's brother and the other children. A moment not to come again, for there never can be such a moment again, but it is a promise of future happiness.

Let me rephrase for myself your moral objections. It's the revelation (with documents?) of a wife wanting her husband not to leave her, and who does leave her. That's the trouble, not the mixture of truth and fiction. Fiction—no one would object if I said Lizzie was wearing a purple and red dress, when it was yellow. Actually my versions of her letters are true enough, only softer and drastically cut. The original is heartbreaking, but interminable.

I thought of doing this: It's just a sketch, because I've really only had yesterday to read through *The Dolphin*, and scribble and sketch. *First*, the entire "Burden" section should come after "Sickday," after "Burden" come "Leaving America," and "Lost Fish," then all the "New York" (new title). This leaves rough edges, and falsifies the actual time sequence, but gets rid of the rather callous happy ending, and softens E.'s role in the New York group— she seems rather serenely gracious (I overstate) about my visit after the birth. I can go this far, but won't bring any post facto business about the baby into the "New York" section. *Two*, I take [it] your moral objections are confined to the letters, and not to all of them. Several can be handled and perhaps improved by using some of the lines in italics, and giving the rest, somewhat changed, to me. "From My Wife" would be called "Voice." Other poems do not need change maybe. "Fox Fur" and "The Messiah" become gentler when the reader assumes the child is born.

This is a sketch and not exactly what I'll do. The problem of making the poem unwounding is impossible, still I think it can be made noticeably milder without losing its life. It might be much better, for who can want to savage a thing. How can I want to hurt? Hurt Lizzie and Harriet, their loving memory? Working my poem out is a must somehow, not avoidable even though I fail—as I must partially.

What are your plans? I hope to come to New York for a week at the end of May. I wish I could talk to you face to face about this and everything. The cloud of winter seems to have lifted.

Love,
Cal

612. *To Frank Bidart*

April 10, [1972]

Dear Frank:

In the confusion of Harriet['s] visit and the arrival of the Taylors, I have mislaid your letter—left it in London. So I start again from scratch. It's important, since I am your friend, to state the thing soberly. Blurbs tend to stiffen into honorary degree citations, a form, unlistenable, unbelievable, even when true. I think they exist to make reviewers intelligent, natural and brilliant. Here goes:

> "For three or four years, I haven't forgotten the story and atmosphere of Frank Bidart's California sequence; it is very painful, and moves in a dry, gruesome glare, heightened—perhaps this is my anti-Californian bias—by flashes of a modern 'western,' when the gunslingers are fossils. Bidart's poetry, unlike most, doesn't distort or glaze or stand between the reader and the subject."

I've read and long thought on Elizabeth's letter. It's a kind of masterpiece of criticism, though her extreme paranoia (For God's sake don't repeat this) about revelations gives it a wildness. Most people will feel something of her doubts. The terrible thing isn't the mixing of fact and fiction, but the wife pleading to her husband to return—this backed by "documents." So far I've done this much: 1) Most important—Shift "Burden" before "Leaving America" and "Flight to New York." This strangely makes Lizzie more restful and gracious about the "departure." I haven't changed a word to this effect, but

one assumes she knows about the baby's birth. "Burden" now begins with "Sickday," and I think gains much by the baby's birth not being the climax. 2) Several of the early letters, "From my Wife," are now cut up into "Voices" (often using such title) changing mostly pronouns, as if I were speaking and paraphrasing or repeating Lizzie. Most of the later letters I haven't been able to change much or [at] all. 3) Changes for style, not to do with this business.

Now the book must still be painful to Lizzie and won't satisfy Elizabeth. As Caroline says, it can't be otherwise with the book's *donnée*. However, even fairly small changes make Lizzie much less a documented presence. A distinct, even idiosyncratic voice isn't the same as some one, almost fixed as non-fictional evidence, that you could call on the phone. She dims slightly and Caroline and I somewhat lengthen. I know this doesn't make much sense, but that's the impression I get reading through the whole. Then Sheridan is somewhat a less forced and climactic triumph; as E.'s problem of the getting back to England and into pregnancy is gone; and the very end of "Flight," with the shark is less Websterian and Poeish.

Harriet's visit scared me to death naturally beforehand. But never have we been able to talk so easily. One age. Surprisingly, she both knew about and liked Blue Nun, Irish coffee and champagne. Then she and Caroline would argue with me about socialism and women, both pitifully incoherent to a man, especially Caroline, but to my delight agreeing. I want to get this off in the car, so will stop. Trust you'll come sometime in June.

Affectionately,
Cal

Give my love to Elizabeth and Bill

623. To Frank Bidart

May 15, 1972

Dear Frank:

I've neglected answering because I was waiting for your *History* notes, and also because I imagined I would soon be in America. But Ivana will have to have another operation in the next few weeks, and the time doesn't seem very fortunate with Lizzie before the divorce gets planned.

Your remarks on *Dolphin* are too profound and detailed for me to handle in a letter. Besides you would have to see the new text before we would have our feet on the earth. The thing is I *must* shift the structure and somehow

blunt and angle the letters. The new structure, with the alteration of a few lines here and there, seems a big improvement to me. I had meant to end with the "Flight to New York" sequence, even after R. S.'s conception, but feared I would be lying. The "departure" is the real, though not chronological ending; it will of course seem to be *both* the real and chronological ending because I place it at the end—not from anything I say. Sophistry? No, not entirely. This is the real truth of the story and is in a way happening again now. The letters are not really changed to improve—the most I can hope is to lose nothing . . . to both lose and gain. I do think Elizabeth is mostly right, though she is peculiarly (almost unintelligibly) sensitive to private exposure. Her letter to me was as powerful criticism as I've ever gotten—usually she only writes me about this phrase or that.

Affectionately,
 Cal

P.S. What can we say of the War! Sorry you've been ill. We've had rather a hard winter; it's better now.

614. To Christopher Ricks

[July 22, 1972]

Dear Christopher:

Thanks for your letter. If you think Hallam Tennyson is an intelligent person to talk to about his forebear, and if he can do it sometime in mid-September or later—I will. The name is like a great shadow—Hallam Tennyson interviews C. Day Lewis.

Read your Tennyson with fascination, and of course thought of your father while reading the early chapters, all more or less new stuff to me. Curious that I made the point before reading you—What would T's reputation be if he had died at thirty-two? Less accomplishment, greater glory?

Quarrel a bit about your Milton essays. *P.R.* has always been a favorite of mine. It's as though two voices both Milton spoke the dialogue—all the inspired things nearly are Satan's, but Christ is another side of Milton (a losing side?) that acts as a breakwater. It doesn't seem to me a minor poem compared with great things of its length, the *Dunciad*, *Hyperion*, Johnson's two Juvenal's, "Michael." Oh well.

We had such a happy warm time with you. I'm furiously doing last revisions on my three little books, two thousand changes I think. I was interested

in your chapter on Tennyson shifting lines to new and unforeseen settings. It [is] so easy to bog down trying to complete a group of lines directly. Then you find you've unwittingly done it already somewhere else.

Affectionately,
 Cal

P.S. O I left out my only real point about *P.R.*; you say nothing about all the really glorious lines and speeches. I wonder if I'm the only person under 65 who really likes the poem?

615. *To Elizabeth Bishop*

September 10, 1972

Dearest Elizabeth:

Love to have "Poem" again; why don't you call it "Small Good Picture"? I don't mean this.

I think we will fly on about the 16 of October, not sooner. Rather a grim trip. Sad go-over what can't be again—and lousy position of being the person who wants the divorce. And then can there be two Mrs. Lowells in one city? Our best local county council doctor turned out to be a bigamist and had to flee back to Australia—with his new wife to support his old. As far as I know Lizzie will not dispute the divorce, but the details are complicated—trusts with different terms etc.

Many thanks for the lovely seal slippers; they fit Sheridan and he wears them. He has just learned to walk—like that, in two days. So they were timely. Would you (seriously) like to be a godmother? We would both be honored. I would like to have Peter Taylor and Bill Alfred for Godfathers. Then we can have an English set, mostly relatives.

Don't know whether you can make Frank rough it. He must have the most fixed habits I've ever met. Once we got his eggs and toast a minute different from ours, he was actually an easy guest with predictable wants. An English friend read his "Herbert White," and wondered what the parents of his Wellesley students would say if they read it. Years gone before it became part of him in my imagination, I took an agonizing double-take when I looked at him. He was an angel of light to me this summer, liked as one of the family by all of us.

The other night, I was reading Sylvia Plath, then you to one or two friends here—I'm afraid she seemed rather gothic and arid in comparison. All spearhead.

Today all my books go to the publisher. They are like a guest who wouldn't leave, so I'm relieved. What to do though? Soon I'll be teaching—an exercise I seem to like less and less. Also I teach at a pleasant (hideous new architecture though) but 2nd or third choice college, and the commuting is very tedious.

I had troubles twice with visas, so am not unhappy you didn't like Russia. Loved the Viking ships; I still have them, only I took out Oslo and its museum,

all my love,
Cal

616. To William Alfred

[September 22, 1972]

Dear Bill:

I never write you except to ask favors. This is an exception, almost. We'll arrive, Caroline Sheridan and nanny—in New York on the 8th of October. I think we'll come to Cambridge on the 16th or so for a couple of days. I don't know the date yet. I think Caroline must see the splendor of an American university, and see my friends. Is it easy to get hotel rooms. We'd need two. Sheridan is very destructive—even to books and even after Milton appeared to him in a vision saying, "If you kill a man you only kill a body, but if you destroy a book you destroy an immortal soul"[—]and walks.

Ah, it is long since I've seen you. I've utterly lost myself in writing almost steadily since January, and think I have all my poems as good as I'll ever make them. I think you'll like the way the ~~close~~ sharp parts of *Dolphin* are now written much better—both for art and kindness.

I love England; often I wish it were entirely inhabited by Americans. Couldn't we give England New England in exchange. Swamps would be drained, slums and wasteland redeemed—as T. S. Eliot would have desired.

Love as always,
Cal[. . .]

[October 31, 1972]

Dearest Elizabeth—

I'm so glad you wrote because I didn't think we parted on the right note—so much so I didn't quite know how to write. The trip has left us bone-tired, not in spirit so much as physically—I could use one of Mailer's irritating metaphors, a boxer who has been punished for ten rounds.

I am sore about my alimony, though it's quite bearable and more or less what I outlined in my mind two and a half years ago. I keep what I make: salary, manuscript sale, royalties. I lose everything inherited, all trust interest, NY apartment, Maine house and barn—I thought they were Lizzie's in Cousin Harriet's will, but as I had forgotten, they were half mine by Maine law—all this is OK, but it's the small things, the difficulty of getting personal or family things, my books, silver spoons etc. I have no need of furniture, but all of ours I paid for, and some pieces were in my parents' house when I was five, or seven or eight. Well, I want little, not even many books; there's a clause in the alimony agreement saying we should agree on what should be mine—and doubtless when emotions are less keen we will agree, since not more than a couple of thousand dollars at most is in question. What really bothers me though is that Harriet will receive nothing of consequence from me—the alimony provides for her tuition through graduate school and further, but to be handled by Lizzie. I feel Harriet has been stolen from me like the dozen silver spoons. Of course, there are provisions for mutual consultation on her life and education—uninforcible if we are in a temper, as we are now, and mustn't be later when our blood cools—for everyone's good. So it will be, God willing,—today I am enjoying the luxury of steaming. Frank's dedication—here's what happened (but no one concerned can tell the same story about something even as simple as this). I think I said to Frank last winter that I ought to dedicate *History* to him, but that this seemed odd because he was really a collaborator. Anyway I totally forgot and dedicated it to Kunitz, who had written me a powerful letter about it, had recently nearly died, to whom for ages I had wanted to dedicate a book, etc. Frank was so upset, I made a double dedication, a solution like splitting a Bollingen, that no one quite relishes, but the only possible way out for me. I haven't dared tell Kunitz and meant to if I had had a chance to see him, not just talk to. Now I will. It's hard to express how much Frank's work with me was worth, and is—without giving an immodest evaluation to my poem. There's no other book to dedicate—the *For Lizzie and Harriet* is itself a dedication, and the *Dolphin* must

be to Caroline. I'm so glad you really like her—I assumed so somehow—perhaps Frank has copies of some of her things. He must have. We're so bad about parcelling and mailing, and only have one copy of most things.

Oh God, Dear one, I do feel you must have security. I don't think I've undermined you, cannot remember not being open about my return—somehow Bloomfield assumed I had resigned when I hadn't.

If I weren't still tired I'd tell the humors of our San Domingo days—I'd say with my whole heart, we (you & I) are together till life's end.

All my love,
 Cal

618. To Elizabeth Bishop

[November 1, 1972]
(a day later)

Dearest Elizabeth— I must write more softly to you, or promise I will. My late trip hardly softens one's surface, or one's depths. I feel a large something infected has been removed from me—it was not really my fault or Lizzie's. Gone it is, but I cannot take it in yet, and remain at a loss, a little tired and cross trying to reassemble myself. I pretended to be angry at first about the alimony, then found I really was. Somewhere deeper than I can reach the anger has gone.

If I have ~~written~~ spoken to you in less than my old admiring and loving voice, forgive me.

All my love,
 Cal

619. To Elizabeth Hardwick

[January 10, 1973]

Dear Lizzie:

Back at last to teaching, my sixth term of teaching Modern North American Poetry. How different it seems than the poets of Philip Larkin's *Oxford Book of 20th Century*—even when Eliot and Auden are in both lists. I'm doing a review of the Larkin because it might give me an opening to write unpretentiously about the poetry of the century—some of it, all British, Americans only used to point up differences. I suppose we all thought of ourselves as more modernist than we really were, our tastes were more experimental than

our own ~~chosen~~ styles. But in Larkin (a felt anthology, in no way defiant, but a sign of the times) modernism might never have been.

Why have I gone on this way? It was good to see so much of you and Harriet. Sad, too because at best nothing is repeatable for us. ~~in time.~~ I felt when Harriet came here a year ago, that this would never be again—I mean that no matter how many times she came, and how happy the visit was, we would be different persons, at a different moment in our lives. I felt that with you. What did Peter Ross Taylor say after we left Columbus so long ago?

I am out of work now. No more of my old—6 or 7 years—can be written. Nothing much new comes even as a desire. Maybe my prose bits. They'll need more—small stuff and too hard to do, but probably better than play or verse at the moment. Could I call my few essays *Men*. I see to my embarrassment, they all are.

Give all my love to Harriet, and tell her I'll write soon—very. Liked Mary's using Stalin, almost no one who is against Vietnam violently makes this qualification.

Love,

Cal[. . .]

620. *To Frank Bidart*

[January 16?, 1973]

Dear Frank:

Just as I put this sheet in the typewriter, Faber called saying the page proofs are ready and will go off tonight to you and me. They go to press on the 19th of February. Don't feel obliged to do anything, but if you have to choose, take *History*. I can do the short books fairly thoroughly.

I've revised the poem you saw and already stuck it in; and now there's another (the very last!?) in "Marriage" section of *Dolphin*, "Careless Night" between "Overhanging Cloud" and "Morning Away" (morning, night morning). Miss Skelton of Faber's voice went dangerously numb when she heard.

I have a bad case of after-book blues. All day we have been under the belief that peace in Vietnam has at last been made. Somehow, I'm not sure why, the burial of a bad chapter never to be salvaged, is like a funeral. Well, nothing to do after so much occupation and purpose. While you are naked and running, you don't feel your nakedness. Etc. The room is full of puppy-dolphin blimber, because Ivana didn't have an orange in her lunch-bag.

Servant things are better. We have Devie, Jan's very efficient Kent friend,

and her efficient mute boy-friend working. Lights we didn't know existed now shine. Another honey-moon with another couple.

Bad reading for a lonely country house, I just skimmed through Capote's *Cold Blood*, mostly thriller hack work, diffusely competent, but somehow killers take on life, surprisingly.

We are bracing ourselves to having our house famed and visited as a Fludd shrine. Suddenly in the last weeks hermeticism, (his and others), has become an almost universal admiration. Perhaps Fludd's ghost will be a tutelary spirit for us?

Miss our long days and eloquent evenings together. We must find a pretext to extend our next collaboration. All seems well between me and Elizabeth and the other Elizabeth—thank God, but don't trust him. Caroline sends her love; she now wears everywhere a coat that makes her look like a large sheep.

Affectionately,
Cal

621. *To Christopher Ricks*

January 16, 1973

Dear Christopher—

Doing something on William has long defeated me, I'm afraid. No poem comes; a considered critical essay is beyond my uncritical talents; I can't somehow catch hold of him briefly in a paragraph or two. My kind of judgment edged out of reminiscence would be impertinent in a festschrift. I've been through this with my old friend Allen Tate, and finally did nothing. William is one of the few (only?) people I read every scrap of and am never disappointed. I don't want to disappoint by promising a piece I won't write.

As ever,
Cal

P.S. We hope you both will visit us some weekend before the winter rolls on much further.

622. *To Elizabeth Bishop*

January 24, 1973

Dearest Elizabeth:

I felt almost with the address-words of your letter, that we were so airily

and happily beyond the days of our clouds. And of course I felt this the times I saw you last in Cambridge. What a lovely long night of drinks, gossip, memories, everything.

The Wilbur poem annoyed me too. Which way is the irony meant? Against Dick? Against some conventional person much like Dick, yet slashed as his opposite? Or against Sylvia? All probably. I seem to have run into people lately who are his old friends, and welcome being bitter on him. He has really always been a model acquaintance, almost friend to me, though I felt a fragile shell kept his rivalry from muddying me. Still, a good man. I've always thought, I'm afraid that Ransom did his kind of poem (Wilbur's) with genius and a character.

When Eliot made his statement about teaching contemporaries, the New York Radio or some paper called me up for comment. All I could think of was that I would be out of a job. Here, by brute force I managed to teach Shakespeare for 2 months or so, and then was hurled back by the head of our department into semester . . . term on term of modern North American poets, my specialty. I think a *writing* course in poetry might be half *reading* modern poetry. But now must think up something for Heimert. How about Milton. Is Satan the hero usually starts the students talking for several meetings. But maybe that's past. I think maybe English 19th century poetry.

I have read somehow about six defenses of hermeticism in the last ten days. An impassioned text (new for the Mariner) of Coleridge by Empson. The passionate anti-Christian and the passionate Christian (Empson and Flannery) have much the same tone. Empson believes the Mariner really experienced the spirits and Coleridge really really hid them—almost in a burning sulphur air of Tory-Trinitarian persecution. Then Kathleen Raine on Yeats['s] Journals, his hermeticism that has outworn Eliot's A. Catholicism. Then Graves speaking the fourth and even fifth dimension at seventy-five in his love poems. And finally (this is my whole point) a great outcry about John Dee and his successor Robert Fludd, scientists and the Magi of the hermetic movement under Elizabeth and James. We live in the house Fludd lived in (visitors come and we can tell them nothing—but I'm ordering books). His Jacobean bust is in the village church, and Caroline has an authenticator friend who told her the Lowells and Fludds were related. A few years ago the Lowells would have spurned this connection; now it's at a premium. But do you believe you have experienced eternity, or immortality? Another article says that Hardy did with his first wife, then denied what he had actually known by experience. I think I am unreconstructible. But it would be merry to believe such things. Particularly now, when I am having strong after-book blues, feel I've written nothing and am incapable of the minimum necessary practical effort.

The Pelican must be Marianne, but aren't all her animals her? Their carefully noted anatomies given Moorish virtue? Oh thanks thanks for your lovely magnifying paperweight. Will I someday stare thru the white flower or coral, half-blind, to read letters. Caroline sends her love—I as ever all mine.

Love,
 Cal

623. To Robert Boyers

February 17, '73

Dear Robert Boyers:

Here are 3 poems from my poem *History* (I want however to use [the] title I've given them for your magazine). I have three books coming out this spring, about two thirds taken rewritten from the last *Notebook*. I have a lot of unpublished stuff on hand, but it is either personal or doesn't gracefully detach from its context.

I've never gotten the point about Harold Bloom. Isn't he the Yale professor with a theory about the Romantics? I was impressed by the Ashbery review. Wheelwright, of course, has been long lying about—the sort of true eccentric I somehow dreaded coming also from Boston and almost the same family. He seemed like a knotted Cummings, so knotted it stopped reading, though not admiration. I've read a book or so of Ammons and like his uncharged, natural style—a nature poet. I haven't read enough to know what he is—at least it's true writing at best and mostly fresh. I don't know what Ashbery means by eccentric; of all the poets he names only Wheelwright is classifiably eccentric. I must [not] go on in this pompous, casual way. This is an idle scattered time for me. I look forward to reading *Shagbark*. Is it a vegetable?

My best as always,
 Robert

624. To Elizabeth Hardwick

[n.d. 1973]

Dearest Lizzie:

I am in a stupefying muddle of mind from several weeks of work and now a touch of flu..This letter will show it. Then I'm in a snarl on how to get money out of England. Living in two countries almost doubles the forms and

stops. The money thing will work out, but it'll take two weeks or so to clear. . . . Harvard papers at a standstill. Debts, immigration—I expect to be deported from England, refused entry to America, jailed or fined in both countries. This sounds wild.

I see I have no Blake in my library, but isn't *Daughters of Albion* one of those vague bombastic long-lined Ossianic things? His only long poem I find wonderful is *Marriage of Heaven and Hell*, as good as Nietzsche or Rimbaud's *Saison*. My library doesn't have my preface to Sylvia Plath. As I remember, it was quick and tender. There was a similar ghastly Plath meeting here last spring, with Greer who could read poetry to illustrate her points. I've hardly met the real Lesbian storm troops, but I think they talk like hysterical Negroes and other fanatics—the meaning of words, the object they denote[,] mean nothing. Glad you saved me, if you could ~~bare~~. Your Woolf has something people will quote on her—rather Bloomsbury writing (university people with a style) on Bloomsbury. Can't understand you on Carrington and Stratchey. (Have you read her letters?) Then Stratchey's best books are more inspired and readable than anything by the group except *Passage to India*. And then Leslie Stephens, admired by Leavis and J. R. Lowell? But more startling, what are your 100 pages? More of *woman*? It's your most passionate writing and therefore best.

What about Harriet coming here in her vacation? I'd love so to have her. Our local antique dealer is looking for a beautiful old picture frame. If she comes I'll have to know the dates as soon as possible. I wonder if she wouldn't enjoy an early April trip to Italy, Brookses, Anzilotti, poets etc.

I so sympathize with your positive will-lessness. I've had none for anything practical for weeks.

Love,
 Cal

Let me know if I can sign anything to help with the Trust transfer. Do they think I am not in my right mind? Ever? But maybe that isn't anything to do with it. It's like a very cold end of April American day here—green with no leaves, a great shushing gale blowing outside that could move a sailboat if one were in my room.

625. To Blair Clark

February 18, 1973

Dear Blair:

I was sorting old letters and astonished and humbled by how many I had from you. This must be our longest recent period of not writing. As I remember Joanna will have her child in March—you are in the anxious last month. I know it from Harriet and Sheridan (though Sheridan was made more hazardous by my having a series of continual nosebleeds).

I had a good time with Frank, tho I also had my usual three hours at the Athens lunch and at the end bought a Parker painting for $1500. The check came back, I had written it for seven thousand pounds in letters, and for seven pounds in numerals, and dated the check 1972. Drunkenness my guardian angel. I do want to buy the painting, if I have the money. It's wonderful seascape (was to my Athens Olympia eye)[,] green water rolling in on the roughest North Shore. Hester Pickman said it was a nineteenth century, only they would not have painted that way. This wasn't a slur.

You must be very tired after McGovern, so much time and hopelessness. Time? Lost? Or anyway crushing to last through. So much travelling; when I get back from America, I sleep off and on for three days. Day-sleep is not only a life-restorer, but evidence that we need life ~~restored~~.

Didn't you have some plan of coming here? On Joanna's return from Poland? We could give you part of Redcliffe Square, I think, though you might prefer a Hotel to getting your own breakfast etc. I think we have a house near Harvard. The Taylors, Elizabeth Bishop and Frank and Bill Alfred will all be there. More very close friends than I have anywhere in one place.

Give Joanna our love in this anxious time.

Affectionately,

Cal

626. To Frank Parker

[March 20, 1973]

Dear Frank:

The *Ocean* is at Hounslow Airport, cargo section and will soon be on its way here, perhaps in time for Harriet to see it on her vacation. The lady in cargo section made filling the forms easier than I can imagine, but I hope I've

been correct. My forms have a way of returning to me, sometimes with angry reproaches.

We are crazy about your pictures for my books; they really fit better than Sidney's for the British edition—except for a wonderful colored Dolphin, he took old pictures from my *Imitations* done ten years ago, fine but far-fetched. Don't repeat this. He and I are very close friends and have frequent lunches, but his wife, described by Kenneth Clark as a German abstract expressionist painting of the angel of death done without passion, refuses to see us. An embarrassment. I like above all the dolphin[,] a hard subject; you get so much motion into her—Sidney's is a fish, very exact, but not like the books. The pine tree is gay and fits the scenery. History is a little like old Jacobean frontispieces, which is right in a way because I am partly writing an old careful ~~but~~ inaccurate history—Ralegh's *History of the World*—I'll be accused of being a systematic hermetic—sun and moon. What's the box? Coffin? Ship of Death? Train to London? New York?

Can we wait on my $1500? I have screwed up my bank account by thinking that having an account called *internal* would free me from such harassments as work permits etc. but it means that I can only mail out a hundred pounds at a time from here. My American account is small, Giroux having mistakenly sent my royalties to England, and I have to pay the lawyers' fees this month. I'm not hard up, just in confusion.

I was very touched by your letter: I've been searching for the last ten minutes to find it and comment, but it's carefully treasured away somewhere beyond loss and finding.

Love to Judy. Tell her our son has given up talking altogether, to improve his walking and acting. Rather comforting.

Love,
Cal

627. To Elizabeth Hardwick

[March 24, 1973]

HARRIET ARRIVED SAFELY MATURELY AND GLORIOUSLY LOVE
CAL

628. To I. A. Richards

April 6, 1973

Dear Ivor:

Congratulations on your 80th, a solid, provable achievement, even if we didn't know how much younger you are.

I have your delicate New Hampshire water color landscape on my mantel-piece. We had only one snow this winter, but made the most of it with photos and children in scarlet. The snow lasted five days and the snowman ten. Apparently, the New England climate is coming here—snow, cold and brightness. This morning almost frost, sunlight and a shivery wind. Not too bad!

I have mixed feelings about my friend Caligula, so beyond my living up to. How much he once looked like one of my St. Mark's form-mates! Moving in his turtleneck sweater to his roadster—handsome and terrible. In another head, he looks like one's 25th reunion. Charming to have him arrive from your hands for breakfast.

I was 56 last March, forty years older than Harriet, fifty-five than Sheridan. I made so much of the first figure, that the second staggers me—it's almost beyond witticism.

Is everything growing more or less? The sheep fields about our house are up for sale at 7 times what they sold for 7 years ago. No houses will supposedly be built on them for 15 or even 20 years. It gives us a feeling of being crowded.

My books are finished, galleys, page-proofs corrected, everything—six years work, but somehow much more, though most authors must feel this. I feel almost the hollowness of having finished a life's work—or just moved to nothing new.

We'll be in Cambridge for mid-September. No house as yet, but I guess that will work out. I think Harvard won't be the Harvard of the sixties, but a strange country—less so because of you and dear Pocohontas.

My love,
Caligula
(this is a unique signature)

629. *To the Editor,* Encounter

[n.d. April 1973]
Lewis A. Coser writes, "Robert Lowell urged the poet to go into 'the bull-ring.'" But I don't want my significance to extend beyond context; the bull-ring I wrote about was the poetry reviewers.

 Robert Lowell
 Maidstone, Kent

630. *To Elizabeth Bishop*

April 30, 1973

Dearest Elizabeth:

I wonder if my last ever reached you? In my woolly-witted way I mailed it to Harvard. I can't find any American to talk to about Watergate, though the English are glad to, but without one's own anguish and fervor. Sickening, fascinating gobbets come out in each paper. But it's too much, unless the country can somehow be cleaned up. I think the corruption has been going on long before Nixon, yet he is a criminal silhouette on things—government almost by the Mafia—the day of Goulart. It's strange though, so many worse things have been happening to our country for the last—but what *is* the precise date?—years. One feels dirtied, or rather as if one's insides were force and money.

I am reading for ten minutes for something on behalf of paralytics and repairing the old Banqueting Hall. I suppose there's an analogy. I was asked to choose some poem not by myself and one by myself to go into a booklet. I took your "Nova Scotia," and my old "Water" (I see I've again [made] a mistake that I made in my *Benito Cereno* play, of making someone talk of someone's water.) A good pare, I think, and clear to read.

Philip Larkin spent last weekend with us. He looked older than T. S. Eliot—six foot one, low-spoken, bald, deaf, deathbrooding, a sculptured statue of his poems. He made me feel almost an undergraduate in health, and somehow old as the hills—he is four years younger. I asked him about a poem, "Wild Oats," where he speaks of a girl he met a few times in his twenties—"a bosomy English rose," and had kept two photos of her in his billfold—and there the two photos were, her breasts invisible under a heavy coat, small, the same and no more than passport pictures. He is the best poet still writing here I think, perhaps by far.

A cut up month is on me, short reading trips to Rotterdam, Pisa—Berlin, not reading. We are trying to get up courage to go blind to Paris.

How do you like Washington? Has it dimmed since we knew it? Is Ted Roethke gone yet? I'm having a wonderfully worthless life—Caroline has just finished her book too—fishing, magazines, bits of fiction by people I've just met, movies.

Frank rather disapprovingly says you are in a motel. I wish I could fly to see you. Is Frank's book causing a heartening shock. All my love,

Cal

631. To Elizabeth Hardwick

June 1, 1973

Dearest Lizzie:

It was miraculous to have your letters and pictures. It always seems to have been an unfulfilled craving in my life to have a scrapbook—as the drawers overflowed with unsorted photos. I had just bought one, and now its filled, artfully arranged pages, sequences, like my long poems, full of profundity for me if no one else. Way back, I have Allen and Mrs. Ford Madox Ford, Peter and me and Jean in New Orleans, looking hung over, except unbelievably for Jean. I have no old ones of you because two and a half years ago I left my bill-fold in a restaurant or taxi—early in the evening going home—and lost about eight small snapshots and a hundred dollars (?) in Per's Norwegian money. What I miss is that wonderful wild one of you smoking, taken on the Loire (?) by Robie. Please send me more. We can call it *Notebook's Scrapbook* and sell it [to] the *Sunday Observer* like Waugh's Diaries. . . . No, I really want more. Do send lots of you!

My books? I've written Bob to send you all three and just *History* to Harriet, so as not to force them on her. They'll be out June 20, almost three weeks late due to some unaccounted delay by Farrar—tho they may have had to because of Frank's drawings. They please me very much. I mustn't write of your feelings about the book. I wish the publication and reviews were over; I seem to be a mark for all sorts of dissimilar people in both America and England. The books are so many and they cost so much, less here than in America. It would have been slovenly to have brought them out in one volume, though cheaper.

The sale of the commons house is a kind of death, but I think it was unavoidable. If you are willing, since you write the house is mine to use, we

might make some sort of *access* agreement, something less binding than with children and really meaningless except psychologically. I would be too shy to live there until after my death. Maybe Sheridan could come as a visitor. I don't think he and Harriet are likely to become intimate—if he were five years younger he could easily be her son. When you write me, I'll sign the dower. It came too quickly and undescribed.

I am having a hell of a time with Henshaw. First he didn't call back, then came the long weekend bank holiday. Now he is incommunicado somewhere in Europe till the week end. You must feel everyone in America is a Nixon bugger; we feel everyone here must have a title and sordid photographed sexual orgies, a long suffering wife and a thousand acres—Somehow aided or hindered by Henshaw. I'll try again to get some one else. Don't tell me about house decay. In the last month we've had two flooded cellars, the remove of a partition, leadshallows stolen from an outbuilding, a dog lost, an unfindable fuse, a skylight leak, the disappearance of all our napkins and handkerchief, a plastering job done by Dixie's husband's brother, a three days' cook with a son who went insane—the mother, Dean Crook's of Harvard's marvelous daughter[,] married to a hippy[,] buying a donkey without asking us—the donkey had a bad cold and had the vet for six pounds, the dryer stopped, and so on. Houses really ail more than we do, they never cure themselves. I watch time go too, and love thinking about you and writing.

All love, and H. All day I've lived thru her life in your pictures.

Cal

632. *To Peter Taylor*

June 1, 1973

Dear Peter:

Let me warn of some of the troubles of a *large, old* house: Leak in the main line, inability to find the cesspool mouth or the main water tank, groups of pipes that warm nothing and cannot be removed, lead valleys stolen or corrupted, fuses undiscoverable and defunct, death-trap murals, water that heats from 3 to 6 am only, keys that unlock nothing, hippy plasterers, a nanny that without warning buys Joshua a donkey that immediately eats 3 of our five rose bushes, three times the vanishing of a vital part of the automatic orange squeezer. And so on—this is just a drop in the bucket to what we've had. On the other hand our stables are being saved at very little cost.

Surprised you found Harriet ages older than Peter Ross Taylor, I would

have thought just the opposite. The high point of her visit, for me too, was a restaurant found by Caroline's brother which played silent Laurel and Hardys on the wall during lunch. Do you realize what geniuses they are? They refreshed us from the banality of *The Doll's House*. Lizzie has suddenly gone to an extreme of carefreeness with Harriet. Idea: to go to Lake Como alone sending Harriet and her friend Cathy more or less alone to Redcliffe for all July, with a dim notion of doing, that savior of vacationless youth, ceramics. I may be permissive about myself, but only exhaustion could let me give it to children. We've made, are making, another plan. I write Lizzie veiled hints about responsibility. Talking about permissiveness: for a month I've stuck to a bottle of wine a day, and most often half a bottle. My hands no longer shake over coffee, I can leave a taxi deftly like a man of forty, I wake with a feeling of vaguely and gently infinite time ahead of me—I hang up my clothes.

We still don't have a house at Harvard but Blair, perhaps worth all the rest, has just joined our searchers. We could have the gigantic Mason Hammond house, bigger than we are used to, but would have to rent it impossibly for a year.

I was so thrilled by *Time*'s article on Senator Irvin that I almost wired you. I suppose a huge cleaning out of course including Nixon might purify us. There are so many dreary people to follow; like the mafia without submachine guns. And I'd think some of the bugging is necessary and at least legal. European view: *all* Europeans love New York and change the subject when I'm cynical about it; *all* Europeans dislike Americans—I was going to say from Mailer to Senator Fullbright, but this doesn't make sense. I'm violently pro-Iceland and find little knots of fierce intimidated fellow-partisans—every large London party has at least one. It's dangerous trying to find him. Caroline directly or indirectly knows dirt and picturesque description on *all* the people involved in the Lambton scandal and is frantically trying to get in touch with Margaret-Ann at the [Cannes] Movie-festival who (in a deeper sense) knows most of the principles. His interview speech was the best I suppose since Malcolm X, but in life he is an ineffectual sordid Tiberius-like person.

What else? My books come out in 3 weeks. I dread them. I have to spell my name to the Faber's secretary, then she says *Loywall?* Tomorrow we all go to Calais in a boat that doesn't touch water—to escape our mouldy house.

Love to you both,

Cal

P.S. In solitary moments I remember that Allen more or less saved me, once in 1937 and then again in 1941–42. I resolve to write him and don't. Always the same old Allen, yet he was once wonderful.

To my bewilderment, my mute stoned students (in class) write perfectly good term papers?

633. To Elizabeth Hardwick

July 4, 1973

Dearest Lizzie—

Fourth of July—the only sign of it here was an article in the *London Times* by Ralph de Toledano explaining that the Declaration of Independence was not revolutionary, but that George III was the revolutionary. Maybe there'll be banners for Red George and Red Mao. The two lost American Holidays, This and Thanksgiving, leave a funny sort of present-absence here.

I'll take the deed to the consulate and mail it off probably Friday, not later. We have guests coming and the trip to London and back in one day is somehow too much. Harriet is on the verge and by the time you get this she'll be in Amsterdam. You had better send me her address and phone number. Everyone is turning up, Jean Valentine, the Eberharts, Mac Rosenthal. Are you going to Lake Como?

Love,
Cal

Good summer!

634. To Elizabeth Hardwick

July 10, 1973

DEED MAILED TO MAINE THE REVIEWS FRIENDLY OR UNFRIENDLY ARE MORE OR LESS ONLY CRUEL PUBLICITY POSTERS GOD HELP US AND SPARE US LOVE

CAL

635. To Elizabeth Hardwick

July 12, [1973]

Dearest Lizzie:

I think of you all through these five sultry days, and haven't called again lest I further trouble things. I swear I never in all this business have wanted to hurt you—the very opposite. The gloomy picture of us in *Newsweek* is due to Richard Howard and his friend Victor who took pictures here for some poetry anthology, and must have sent this one to *Newsweek* without our knowledge. Ivana's not at her best; nobody is, . . . a family from Utah.

Most of the hurting reviews are flashed up for news and will look very dim by September. Miss Perloff I would guess to be an instructor or young professor, earnestly, waspishly, pursuing her career, too stiff to be much of a critic. The Hopkins comparison is so eccentric, one thinks someone wrote it into her paper when she wasn't looking. I suppose one shouldn't blame her for stupid cruelty that mistook itself for truth. I'm sorry I brought this on you, the ghastly transient voices, the lights.

Love,
Cal

636. To Elizabeth Bishop

July 12, 1973

Dearest Elizabeth—

I suppose you've seen some of my American reviews, a lampooning! I think they all have a jarring effect on Lizzie, but one by a Miss Perloff in the *New Republic* has been a calamity for Lizzie—what it says about her and Harriet. The distortion of the "fictional" characters becomes a slander on the people themselves. I have been talking to people who are seeing her and to Lizzie herself. Last weekend she seemed to be suicidal, and friends had to drop in and telephone to see that she didn't take too many pills. All was confused and increased by her having total insomnia. Now her mood has quieted, but I have no certainty. We dread the telephone.

In *Newsweek*, in an otherwise discreet review, an unflattering photo of Lizzie was published, and above it a family portrait photograph (taken by Victor when he was here and given without our knowledge to *Newsweek*) Caroline, I, a wild Ivana (labeled *Harriet*) and Sheridan[,] looking like a secret

polygamous poor white family. This was so grotesque that Lizzie seems to have thought it funny. Unfortunately, she reads all the reviews, though no possible one could be pleasant.

The weather for the last three days has been close and sultry. My study is a very long room with a view of cows, fields, trees—all becalmed. If I stroll up and down, I can feel Lizzie with me, and no escape but arguing, though the past all in all gives a more joyful picture . . . and the future is only dread of what will happen. My intuitions hope, but what is that?

Your old letter of warning—I never solved the problem of the letters, and there and elsewhere of fact and fiction. I worked hard to change the letters you named and much else. The new order somehow makes the whole poem less desperate. And the letters, as reviewers have written, make Lizzie brilliant and lovable more than anyone in the book. Not enough, I know. And then I didn't want to imagine reviews in magazines with big circulations that would reduce my plot to news or scandal, politicians or actors.

My immorality, as far as intent and skill could go, is not[h]ing in my book. No one, not even I, is perversely torn and twisted, nothing's made dishonestly worse or better than it was. My sin (mistake?) was publishing. I couldn't bear to have my book (my life) wait ~~hidden~~ inside me like a dead child.

All the while I've been writing, I've thought of you in the heat, and been happy to think of Alice's room among the air-conditioned trees. We could use air-conditioning here in the middle of the day, but at night it's cool.

all my love,
Cal

We still have no house.

637. *To Robert Giroux*

July 18, 1973

Dear Bob:

I don't know where the business with Lizzie will go to. After the divorce our relations were as good as one deserved. For the last month or so we were having a complicated unimportant little dispute about Caroline signing a quit-claim to the Maine property. On the same day as your letter, I had one in her old delirious style (I had said something about being sorry to have nothing left from the past except my grandfather's gold watch and a few books)

rhetorically offering to give me "everything." I think what she says about her feelings is more or less true. What most set her off was the Perloff review, published two days later than her letter to you.[. . .]

Of course I can't clear myself from one angle: publishing "versions" of her letters (I hope no reviewer will call them Imitations). They are made up of a mixture of quotes, improvisation, paraphrase. The revelation particularly in the glare of reviews, ~~must be~~ is shocking, but the portrait is very careful and affectionate, the essence of her charm and bravery, her own words humor and sharpness . . . out of the outpouring of her actual letters and conversation. The number of sentences quoted is a fraction of the whole *Dolphin*, though to me very clear and wanted.

I think this will blow off without a lawsuit—who knows? We did become very friendly again after the divorce. I have nothing left really to pay for a lawsuit; any further wrangle would be a tragedy for Harriet, Lizzie and me. The letters are the legal, arguing problem—the real trouble for Lizzie is the picture of Caroline . . . the two things combine. I did everything I could to make my book ~~inoffensive~~ kind without killing it.

The best reviews here are on a higher level than the American ones so far—their technical suggestions are almost more galling than the ~~hints~~ grin of scandal. I wonder if you could send the following to *The New Republic* (under your signature or the Firm's, because I mustn't pour my ~~own~~ fuel on the fire).

The lines, "from the dismay of my old world to the blank now" are misquoted by Professor Perloff who also flaunts them for her title "The Blank Now." The lines actually are "From the dismay of my old world to the blank new." The tone and meaning have been lost by changing ~~one letter~~ the letter *e*.

I am asking Karl Miller to airmail you the Ricks review, it's [a] kind of lawyers summation of the defense in a difficult but just case. It's not meant for court of course.

Well, I pray none of us get further entangled. Harriet is arriving in two days, greedy for London.

As ever gratefully,
Cal

638. To William Alfred

August 31, 1973

Dear Bill—

The summer's end and the month's end, and now the English heat wave has so far retired that my hands are still and cold as I write. In a week we will be in Brookline. Harvard seems ~~another~~ a recovered universe; if I looked in the mirror, I imagine I would have the white beard of father time.

I don't know why I am writing you this way. From not having written verse for months perhaps. It does seem strange returning. The summer tho quiet has been worrying. I am afraid relations with Lizzie are broken off; at least I haven't heard from or about her for two months. The reviews fanned the fire, but I now think the exposure of publication was bound to do it. She roughly had seen the contents, but this was less than seeing them printed, hearing other people see them. (Pause, while I look for my lighter and find it inexplicably under my ashtray.) Harriet came here ten days or so on her way to biking in Ireland. Lizzie has kept her out of the quarrel; so much so that H. thought the trouble was over an imaginary real estate dispute—long since settled in Lizzie's favor. I do think the business is blowing away. Was it Calvin or Harry Levin that said acting is a choice of evils. It so often is in little things (that makes them so irritating) then every so often something *big* is. I must have been right to publish, how could I know?

[. . .]It will be lovely to be with you again and have our long religious and gossipy talks; it will be stunning after 3 years to have students who talk. Thank you for your very troublesome work in house hunting. We gave you much too fuzzy instructions. I have the opening Harvard date, and have written to Frank to try and meet us on the early afternoon of the 7th—weary, plane-squashed, all ages, hardly able to speak our language.

Caroline adds her love to mine,

Cal

639. To the Editor, Agenda

18 Maple Street
Brookline, Mass. USA
[Sept. 20, 1973]

I tried to answer your questions from 1 to 20, and found the results assertive and dryly unreadable. I'll slosh my various prejudices together.

REGULAR METER: I was slow to learn meter and slower to learn how to leave it if I wished, or what was perhaps harder, slack the regularity. Its difficulties entranced—anyone can play tennis to rule, the possibilities of further skill and accuracy are almost infinite. I cannot write ~~a line~~ meter without feeling the chances, though my tennis has never advanced. It's a happy way to write meter to counterpoint it with conversation, letting voice and meter coincide then run to cross purposes, often in the same line. Weak or split words at the end of a line should be rare, I think, and used for some effect of slash or casualness. I don't know why I enjoy making meter unslur a word and artificially draw out the syllables, but I do. I scan by accent alone. I first published and, with a few exceptions, only wrote accentual syllabics. Several times I attempted Hardy's line *based* on twisted extra syllables, and always felt ramshackle. After twenty or more years, I didn't.

FREE VERSE: The ~~point~~ rule of free verse is that it is unscanned, and seems as free as prose or talking to one's-self—where the true lines begin? I often tense and vary my free verse with rhymes, part-rhymes, uniform stanzas and lines in meter. Or I am more catholic and do none of these things, though I find myself falling into some loosely normal line-length. Is each line a rhythmic whole? I feel it must be, even when unprovable by punctuation or even sense. No one wrote better free verse than Marianne Moore's measured, unscannable run-on syllabic stanza, or equalled her triumphs of meticulousness and largeness. Just as fine are Williams' short lines, often in quatrains, sure in their line divisions, though these divisions might be hard to guess if we first saw his poems in prose.

LEFTOVER QUESTIONS: Lines visually stop at the end, like our spines—even against punctuation and sense. Whether there should be a line-end pause when sense doesn't require one is a problem for recital not composition. A good ear depends less on sound than on meaning and tone of voice. Sound poetry isn't poetry but music or unaccompanied recitative, just as concrete poetry is a form of graphics. They might be taken more seriously if classified with singing and drawing. In short-line poems, metrical or free, the line-ends can serve as caesuras. Only the exceptional poet is a metrist in the sense that he uses meter as some special form of machinery—Milton, Campion, Tennyson, Bridges, perhaps Auden and Graves, and Pope[,] though his laws could be counted on one hand. Lively exceptions, but such scaffolding is seldom the main concern, though all poets at their best write by sound and most often by rhythm in measure. Saintsbury's prosodic rules overflow from his saturation and pleasure; they are confidently sloppy and caught in movement. Alas, I haven't reread him since college.

THE PENTAMETER: If the pentameter is dead, scanned verse is. Blank verse and even meter might mysteriously die like the old novel and Jacobean tragedy. I don't see that they have. Blank verse would have imposed a heavy burden of continuity and monotony on *The Waste Land* and *Cantos* and most late epics. But the most ambitious poems of Frost, Stevens, Hart Crane, Thomas and Allen Tate are in pentameter. The number of modern poets who haven't written well in this meter is small. Long poems like boa constrictors tend to crush meter.

 Robert Lowell

640. *To Seamus Heaney*

<div align="right">Oct. 4, 1973</div>

Dear Seamus Heaney:

As you will see, we are too far away from Belfast to come. I expect to be back in England by February or March, and might be able to read in Belfast then. I don't suppose a poetry reading would be an incendiary incident. Let's not make even a hypothetical date till I return.

I am very glad to have your letter so that I can write you directly and thank you for your review, the only one from someone mainly a poet, and a good poet, and except for Ian Hamilton the only one from any poet. My English reviews were on the whole as good as I had a right to expect, probably more than that. But in America a month or two passed before I had a good or bad review, and they were more often bad, that was even literate,—jargon and heavy journalistic joshing. This isn't because American criticism is worse than English, but because here what is intelligent goes into the quarterlies not the weeklies. Well, one shouldn't chafe too much at this, but your generous piece was terribly welcome at a blue time.

I have liked your work for some time. I remember knowing nothing about Belfast once, and being told by a friend Grey Gowrie that there were more good poets in Belfast than in all the rest of Ireland, or any city in England. This seemed strange, but I imagine it's true. Of course I am roused by the ring of meter in you. And in others, I think,—someone well-known but whose name slips me that wrote a verse letter to you in the *Listener*, I think. It would be a great joy to read in Belfast under your auspices. One can make a lot of money reading here, but to go places without a friend to meet you is like going into a furnace or ice-chest. A melancholy thing—I've just this morning

turned down an offer to substitute for Auden on his circuit, eighteen readings in a month, everywhere from Rhode Island to California.

Again thanks for reviewing me. I hope to see you in the spring. Perhaps you'll visit Caroline and me in Kent.

Yours,
Robert Lowell

641. *To Elizabeth Bishop*

January 18, 1974

Dearest Elizabeth:

Sorry to be slow in answering your sweet letter. I'm getting, I guess, into the pace of being back—a happy change and place full of space, quiet and coalfires.

You bring up the bad review in *Agenda*, I didn't want to show it to you when I was fresh from reading. All in all, the reviews haven't been bad, about three to two unfavorable, many journalism, too little tested in poetry to know very much. The moral criticism, I pass by,—that is for me to take up with myself—something can be learned—the mind can change, though not the acts. I think I allow a good deal of the technical criticism.

Mistakes. Only one reviewer has shown this. I took 14 poems from *Notebook* called "Long Summer" written out of, tho not about, our 1966 summer in Maine. They are dense, symbolic, almost hallucinated (this a mixture of the style and the mood behind it). In *History* I ~~clear~~ calm them up, make them poems about boyhood in Maine. But the first version is much better—I've spent days and days, like other revisers, spoiling by polishing. I think my great fault is rhetorical melodrama, a laborious maneuvering of this.

I see in a blurb you've written you object to confession and irony. I suppose confession is the use or exploitation of painful experience that gets one's conscience, that must out—but must it? Irony is being amusing (or worse acid about) about what we can't understand. I guess one can't write much without possibly falling in with both—well they don't get one to heaven.

I feel our friendship has passed out of some shadow. Cambridge is a crowded place. Too much brushing from one friend to another, too many required shifts of attitude ~~are required~~, and we are hardly allowed to move. It's too academic. I'm sure I am ignorant of most of what I dislike, but what I've tenderly liked stays—you. Send me your sad poem. I now have nine or ten, about being 56. I mean they set off from that time of life, more interesting, less

promise. Is this impertinence . . . after your sad poem? I think we are much happier now, but how [to] say it unless we get together in place? Love,
Cal

PS. Won't it all be freer visiting, journeying to you in your new home, alone, and on the ocean?

642. To Elizabeth Hardwick

[January 18, 1974]

Dearest Lizzie—

Sorry about the unexpected call. I had forgotten that cable in England means "telephone." I was caught by surprise having just telegraphed what I thought was a "cable."

Delighted with your Philip. It seems to say everything for and against imaginable in your short space—and more than what is possible in a funeral speech. Yet I don't imagine anyone is hurt. I started a piece on him for *Commentary* and had actually written a little less than two pages . . . when I read you. I felt a great relief of not having to go on, you made it unnecessary; mine was a rambly reminiscence beginning during the War with going with the first Rahvs to hear Randall lecture at Princeton with Allen very himself presiding.

I suppose the drop into the void is always a few weeks ahead, but for the moment we are so much more at ease than we were in Brookline that no hardship can be felt. I wonder if Harriet would like to come for a week or so at Easter. We have two, not first rate, but safe horses. And surely something more wide ranging, like London, can be arranged. When is Easter. I may come home to go to Skidmore and Vanderbilt sometime in April!

Nothing much with us. I write without much steam on me—quite a few free verse poems now, redrafts of some of my perversely wild translations (it's a mistake to invent something of one's translating *only* if faithfulness does better; the trouble is a *faithful* may do nothing, be undistinguishable from another of the kind.) And then I have a prose book (*Occasional Criticism and Reviews*, like poor Philip's last magazine.) All the youthful stuff would have to be not just revised but re-imagined. It never ends.

Have I thanked you for the relief of my visit? I had that settled-in fever-cold that's run through all my family, and psychologically and through physical weakness could hardly make my trip. Through physical complication and pinchedness Brookline was like one of these vexing d reams where innumer-

able little objects will never stay in place. All to disappear. I hope so I didn't leave my cold behind. How much briefer letters are than words.

Love,
Cal

I like best almost Philip not being particularly autobiographical, and his refusal to accept his friends' versions of their actions being complete. I am bugged about "provincial." Almost no English or American intellectuals (except sometimes Jews and the foreign-born) have ever *tasted* another country or culture. It's not a matter of dipping in other languages, though this could help—it's their spirit which can't be ours, and isn't.

643. *To Robie Macauley*

January 29, 1974

Dear Robie—

I've known for some time about Anne, and somehow out of flu, inertia and pain haven't written you. Out of many times together with you both, the two quite long and intense ones stay with me—summer and winter. Remember when Lizzie and I came to Iowa, almost apartmentless, waist-high snow and Paul Engle? Then the dessert contest, or rather emulation, Lizzie's weekly labor to equal Anne's marvelous foam and canned strawberry things—didn't one or two at the last moment collapse amid tears though to everyone's ease, for I think no one really liked desserts, and Lizzie was in a Spartan discipline to keep emaciated? Well, other things—Anne saying in the snow to the wife (in shy ecstasy) of some workshop student that she was just pregnant—Anne without consideration or embarrassment, but with a voice of contralto compassion, "O, that's too bad." And your great knack criticizing a novel as if it were a story in life that we wanted to hear. And so much Iowa gossip—Ray-Lu, Mrs. Engle.

After that, meeting in Paris under the Eiffel was a honeymoon. More Poulard, the Folies Bergères, getting caught in the equipage museum, the historical scandals of the chateaux—how young and green one must be to do such things, though a trip with Mary McCarthy to any cathedral even now is an even more serious and guidebook task. Wasn't it at Chinon where there wasn't really a chateaux, but where Jeanne D'Arc had recognized the king, that we had what we thought was a 16th century dinner very cheap, and marched in the Bastille Day parade? All so many times—I see myself under

the heap of guests at your wedding—all some twenty-five years, gone almost without visible alteration, like a quarter-of-a-century ice-cube. I owe much happiness to Anne's fullness and graciousness to us, and to you for so much friendship. Aren't the great years in [a] way those of the most embarrassment and accomplishment, those just after, and a little after, college? Memory now looks like the closing of a very good book. Why didn't I write about it that way?

I know you ~~must~~ feel blanked and the dark. I am glad my last memory of Anne is in New York when her plane was hours late, and we all sat about with the Taylors (?) and Thompsons rumor-riddled—no, trying to guess about Anne and explain—then she came floating, easy, amused. Fortunately nothing in my immediate memory helps me to imagine the end.

I wonder when I'll see you. I want you to meet Caroline. Much of the last years has been so happy, it is not real. And of course, it's not, for all things are short, especially at 56, that golden age you haven't reached. Poor old Peter tries to pretend to this age, though in every step belies it—at Harvard parties I would try to unostentatiously get up and give him my chair. I have a son of two and four months. But I won't wag on about time—a show too sad to stop with for all its humor. Did you see Caroline's brother's movie on Hefner? The reviewers wonder if it is subtle satire or formless reportage.

Oh all my love to you, Dear Robie,
 Cal

644. To Peter Taylor

[n.d. Winter 1974]

Dear Peter,

As if lying all night on the bed-springs
I wake to a hundred arthritic aches
to answer the telephone unexpectantly ringing at 7,
announcing the old car can't take the children to school—
this time the windshield wipers.

I have lost a dream longer than a novel—
I'd been called to the little dome library
of New Englandia in the Boston State House.
The thing was to avoid being shown the books by Old Mackie (a man,

who would keep me there for seven hours not Mackie J.)
and talk us deaf under the little dome.
I was to speak at the Bicentennial in Charleston S.C.
Charlestown to Charleston uniting North and South—
hurrah for integration, but no more busing—
It [was] insulting they expected a peaceful paper from *me*.

In a skyscraper hotel on the South Carolina beach,
I saw my friends the Gardners sunning
in the cold and dusky air—I thought I saw—
but who can see without glasses . . . not I.
The trouble with the skyscraper hotel is
we could only buy Jack Daniels
or any other whiskey in the basement.
I have been to three Seven Up parties.

But the interesting thing was that a boy
we thought had already come to nothing at 15,
was talking to me about psychiatry—
not over my head, but far better than I could.
He talked with a dense friendly little frown.
I said do you think Freud is as inaccurate
as the Book of Genesis? (I remembered guiltily
arguing with an Israeli poet that the King James'
Bible was better than the Hebrew because a new tongue
added a another layer of subtleties . . .
so much needed because there was
no question of truth in the Bible.[)]
I really wanted an answer.

I had the answer myself, but I woke up,
and lost it to the telephone.

Dear, dear friend, reality beats fable or dream
by being twice as dull.
Caroline wakes, I wake. We huddle over heaters,
reading the unbearable and brutal news.
I am putting the prose dialogue of my *Prometheus*
into free verse—the writer of free verse

is never free! 20 pages—
I feel as though I were embarking on *War and Peace*.

How can I end this letter without structure?
I miss you so.

Our love to you and Eleanor,
 Cal

PS. Despite this crude recoil from your beautiful poem, I admire it very much. I really am trying to put the Io and Prometheus part of my play into free verse, and am having a hell of a job. I want it to complete my essays and reviews called *Makings* because Giroux said I had the promising makings of a book. It was already much my longest work, 180 pages. And we do miss you both, and sometimes feel we are losing our minds without you.

645. To Steven Axelrod

<div align="right">February 10, 1974</div>

Dear Mr. Axelrod:

Let me without planning run through answering your questions. The Williams-Larkin thing in my interview was for the English audience which would consider Larkin a major poet (if anyone here is) and all the more so for being provincial. I feel much the same way, and was trying to pay a humorous compliment. Maybe the most noticeable thing to imitate is meter. Williams seems nearest to my heart and hand when I am writing free verse, regardless of my content. In my last books, my guiding angels were writers of blank verse or rough blank verse. There are so many! One curiously was Wallace Stevens—his obscurity, his love of generalization, his occasional simplicity, his improvisation, and his Tennysonian sweetness so far from my bent. I'll say something on Tate later. Perhaps most revolutionaries are only so in their moment of action. I think I was a professional who was forced, who forced myself, into a revolutionary style in writing *Life Studies*, the biggest change in myself perhaps I ever made or will—to continue it, tho I'm at times tempted, would be pastiche. I haven't the bravery to hail my revolution as glorious, or the cowardice not to ~~admire~~ sympathize. One gets such wonderful and miserable cell-mates. The changes in "Waking Early" are as you say; the earlier lines seemed weak and not to fit. *Global* is a heavy burden; the call to write that

way must be once or twice in a lifetime, and a surprise. I think if I had Schopenhauer's bubbles in mind, as I probably did, it would only be true as a matter of associational thought. The "choose life and die" comes from a short speech by Justice Holmes; he has something like "live" and I made the change at [the] last minute while musing with my wife Elizabeth. How we mean the opposite of what [we] first say or habitually say—what we understand but do not know. I think Cooper's book is [a] friendly doctor's thesis affair; pleasing for me to read, gentle—no judge or definer, tho sensitive.

I read your *Dolphin* review with a large xeroxed review pile sent me by my publisher, two to one unfavorable, a tally hard to make because few are significant either way. Yours seemed flatly written till I got to the end and realized that the simple word *wonderful* had your entire review behind it, that everything had meaning. I feel rather happy about my book, tho it's mostly lost ~~at the moment~~. It's unlike *Life Studies*, which wasn't lost, in having a plot and action like a novel, in not being written in immediately clear and imagistic language—someone who liked *Life Studies* mightn't like it, which I think of as a stylistic achievement for me. You are accurate about your summary of the fact and fiction—my problem, more than in any of my other books, was that I had something I had to find a way to write. That something is its raison d'etre, and what, if achieved, is the bone of its merit. Tate is a long story. In the beginning he was not only an influence but often *the* (my) style of writing; not writing like Tate meant not echoing specific phrases, that for me was freedom from Tate. Ages later even the external of meter, his terza rima, made me write a pure Tate pastiche, "Severed Head." Yet I think he was a kind guide. I just reread "Swimmers," inspired ~~thing~~, even its rhetorical Southern flourishes live. The meter with its run-ons, lumpy inverted accident etc is akin to my sonnets. I'm writing single poems, short free verse lines about being 56. What *are* they about? Thanks for your letter and review. I do think your fine style goes too far toward bare statement in the Tate piece—there's no telling what he is. Can't we meet sometime?

Your

Robert Lowell

646. To Elizabeth Bishop

February 22, 1974

Dearest Elizabeth—

Time flies on so, slides so, a whole month has passed since your last let-ter—a month of sitting by red coals, enjoying desultory reading (reviews of other people) and flu, chronic. Frank did tell me of your shoulder before I wrote last but I meant to wait for you to write. I think about it, and sorrow be-cause I suppose it must be painful and now slow.

In another envelope I am sending a long piece by Ehrenpreis in the *TLS*, the whole piece because tho you only come in at the end, it all accumulates to a powerful tribute to you. A thing it says which I have always known with envy and been unable to say exactly is how inventive you are. Many of your poems start obliquely, the fire balloons, the Nova Scotia Picture, the hen in New York—something beside the point and unimportant (seemingly) but is not; or a story, the Amazon, the thief, a servant. I've always thought using oneself was fine because I could test the feeling by memory in revision, or bet-ter still draw on and correct the details of description. But of course anything so close allows too little for the imagination, the pleasure of pure invention, the control of plot and form. Browning was never too good, almost[,] when he came close to being directly himself—he had almost limitless invention, yet there seems too much Browning-voice in his people, and then, I don't know how to say it, too little of Browning. How rich he was, and long! Your personae quite avoid this in the "Man-Moth" and "Crusoe," both you in some transformation or dream they seem so well lived. I won't send you my new poems till they come out with the power of print in April. I have 9 or 10. They really reveal nothing, except the most intimate of things, being 56, and are quiet. I would like to claim that I have turned the rhetoric, the flow etc. of my sonnets. This had to be, though one's style, one's self really must not change. By the way is a confessional poem one that one would usually hesitate to read before an audience? I have many (they are a perfectly good kind) but have none in my last lot, and you have none ever.

I'll be coming back to America on the 5th or 6th of April with Harriet, and then giving a few readings in the South. I might read something at the Signet on the 27, tho it stretches my stay a bit. I'd like to see you. No word from Frank. Somehow I think he'll live it out more steadily than we might have dreamed. There was a terrible harassment as well as dependence on his mother. Do I dare come back to Cambridge? Either I or Harvard, or the

British mails seems to have mislaid most of my term papers? They would all, I suppose, have been As and Bs but I can't improvise. Caroline sends her love, and Sheridan who talks now, monologues.

> Love,
> Cal

647. To Elizabeth Hardwick

May 1, 1974

Dearest Lizzie—

Here I am in the country half-frozen and out of touch with Mayday. Tomorrow I start a final performance of reading, & discussion of translation at Essex, amid the dying embers of a month-old strike. I'm still tired from travelling about America.

Sorry things blew up with us just at the very end last Thursday—I can't believe almost a week has passed. I'm sending the Clive James to Michael Rubenstein my lawyer—still unread. I suppose only a lawyer knows what is libel and what isn't.

Letter from Wynn Handman wanting to do the whole *Old Glory* on some kind of grant. Also someone here wanting to do *Phèdre* at Edinburgh. Ah, the old flowers of last year!

Except for the end, nothing could have been more tender and considerate of old "patriarchal" than your treatment of me—your treatment and Harriet's.

What do you think turned up here from Paris? A letter from Giovanna Madonia, taking her ten years child to Glyndeborne. Oh where is Sidney Nolan who used to go there this time of year?

> Love to you both,
> Dad-Cal

My first day I slept 18 (?) hours.

648. To Giovanna Madonia

May 1, 1974

Dear Giovanna:

I do want to see you; I live in Kent an hour by train from London, but can

easily come up on Whitsunday. It's a very long time ago—all time for everything, for everyone, seems to have doubled in the past five or six years. I have been in America teaching last fall at Harvard, and have just gotten back from a 3 weeks' reading trip mostly in the South, the American South. It frightens me to resee people, to see myself in them. I know we think of seeing each other again with excitement of course and surely fear.

I haven't put this particularly well. I am married again (Caroline Blackwood) and have a two and a half year old son. You don't even know Harriet (17) very gracious, or is that the word?, my daughter by Lizzie. I don't know your son. How much we suddenly don't know about each other! May we be gay and gentle when we meet.

Affectionately,
Cal

649. *To Frank Parker*

May 1, 1974

Dear Frank:

Courage; I feel I have seen you in a low moment. But 56 or 57 or 58 is an ill moment for us all. There's little we can do for our friends or for ourselves. My images of you are from almost all our years except your captivity. I start with Godfrey Brinley's French class, where for a few weeks I got the name of "the man from the middle west," for sitting in the wrong seat or wearing smelly gym socks; and you sat stuttering unintelligible French with greasy handkerchiefs wrapped around your raw scabby ankles—your glasses forever coming out of your case to be ineffectually polished. How did we even come near to passing? Was it that that first made us friends in our weakness? Weren't drawing and buying books on Napoleon considered exotic and rather unmanly? There's hope. I just saw Allen reading an essay on Robert Frost at the Library of Congress—in no way deaf or senile, though dying at 75 of emphysema (?). And Ransom, my father's age, still hale though seldom recognizing friends. And Godfrey Brinley himself till two or three years ago still alive. See, we have more than 25 years ahead, as much as we've known each other.

Dear old friend—if you last another five years, as you will, *you* will see yourself much more famous as a painter—you are already. And then there are our minute inexhaustible little children. Don't they enter *halcyon* days at about five?

Forgive this chatter, Dear one; somehow I too will be better, if you are.

Our love to you and Judy—none for your ferocious real estate man. Did I tell you that I found something that is convenient, if I can sublet it, on Hilliard St.?

 Cal

650. To Marjorie Perloff

May 13, 1974

Dear Marjorie Perloff:

I can't really argue with any propriety on your critical opinion of *Dolphin*—the author must make his book as good as he ~~kind~~ can while still writing and revising. He may even try to make each new book better than any of the others. If he succeeds—he can hardly tell. Perhaps you have a blind spot for English ~~material and~~ place names.

Thanks for your apology for the tone, which did hurt and bother us. I'll be interested to read your Rimbaud. I always thought Crane *was* Rimbaud in a weird, perhaps almost too, American way.

Thanks for liking my criticism. I keep meaning to have the boldness to gather what there is of it, and publish in a smallish volume. I'll be at Harvard from February to May next year and hope to see you (off stage.)

 Yours sincerely,

 Robert Lowell

651. To Allen Tate

May 13, 1974

Dear Allen:

Time, or at least the season, seems to be moving backward since I saw you. It's so much colder here. We only have fireplace heat, and it's as bad as the windy days during our Monteagle winter of 42 and 43. Nothing could be—I remember going to bed then, and read the three volume St. Simon. Our famous fire must have been a protest against the cold.

I liked your Frost essay enormously—I might say I was amazed . . . so long it has been since you wrote an extended piece on one poet. I think somehow it's the rhetoric, the work-up that carries the feelings of the mind—how

you work up to your analysis of "Stopping in a Woods," how you work up to your final conversation with Frost at Yale. It is like a real meeting . . . in words.

What is it that Eliot says, *Fare forward?* So we must. My love to Helen.

Love as it has been,

Cal

652. To Peter Taylor

June 3, 1974

Dear Peter:

Sorry to hear this morning that you are in the hospital. I know this is slight, the strain of selling one more house. I can't bear such news, above all about you. Everyone I know—and more—so many hearts—Frank Parker phlebitis and something that prevents his drinking and makes him look different, Lillian Hellman here, Hannah Arendt in Scotland, now both recovered. For a month we have been living under the shade of Israel Citkowitz'[s] death. It would take a book to tell about him, a book by a Russian—we were all as good friends as the chance allowed us to be, a friendly part of my life really, but of course most real to the children all in different ways according to their ages and temperaments. Yesterday, a second death: his apartment filled with rubbish, plunder, a piano, books in French and German, piano things, was finally cleared. Unlike most flats, it was as much him as the shell of a turtle, so that its end was like the last sigh of a soul.

Disturbing also for us, tho one doesn't feel quite fraternal complaining, is the new budget, 93 per cent of incomes like Caroline's. All such confiscation comes to little, we say, (I'm not sure on what authority), to three bombers. I think your new old house must be a good thing, not to be trapped without a car in, tho the old new house must have been your prettiest. Aren't you happy with your untaxed Virginia income and untaxed Virginia real estate—the names sound like two girls in a Southern allegory one act, too abstract for a story-poem.

An old letter of yours opens with two dreams, one about meeting an elderly gentleman angel, saint of kites. Last night Caroline and I (this is a rather unusual duo in my dreams) met Auden, and I explained to him, citing 11 poems, that he was really a religious poet. We seemed to be having a cordial sensible conversation, when he suddenly mouth-squirted water in Caroline's face (a female ape once did this in life when C. was pregnant). One could not

tell whether he was odd, sick or insulting. We thought the last, left, lost in a maze of Cambridge Mass, streets—behind me Auden on his bed propped on his elbows reading his own poem—to see if he were religious?

I am so garrulous. You have been touched maybe as we are all liable to, by the wing of the angel. My love to Eleanor and to Jack Thompson for writing me. God bless you and keep you, Dear.

Love,

Cal

653. To Philip Larkin

June 12, 1974

Dear Philip:

Thanks for your inscription; I've been reading your book every day or so since it came. It's a good length to read through, none of the poems are the kind of empty thing one writes to write poetry.

I like the title poem best maybe; all the poetry is in the last lines, these would count for little without the others. Then the big terrible poems that everyone likes "The Old Fools," "Building"; "Livings," "To the Sea," "Sad Steps," "Cut Grass," "Explosion," then perhaps more privately "The Royal Station," "Homage,"—I could go on—"Vers de Societe."

I suppose if one reads enough of your late reviews they say everything. The poems are really very sad, and are meant to be, despite the joy of their humor and the triumphant trudging—or whatever it [is] that makes each line personally walked, hand-made. I think you resemble Graves and maybe Auden at times, but the poet I most think of is still Herbert—elegance and homeliness. You could only so write at all. "High Windows" is like "Love" or "Church Monuments." You surely (more than anyone else living maybe) have added to the literature . . . but I am not talking as Verlaine would want me.

We loved having you here and hope you will return sometime soon. I am writing short poems about being 57—when I started, it was 56. I didn't know how lucky I was. Age, the best of subjects—it's amazing this statement can give any pleasure.

Affectionately from Caroline too,

Cal

654. *To the Editor,* New Review

[n.d. June or July 1974]

Sir,

Clive James's sentence of derision on my Plath sonnet has been quoted at least five times in passing by reviewers to expose my bombast and kitsch. Meaning is lost when lines are detached, then punched shapeless and enveloped in formidable critical prose. I wasn't trying to refute John Bayley's witty and imaginative, "Plath, *a miniature mad talent.*" My heroics were meant as brass; I was parodying and gibing when I wrote with inflation, "rising in the saddle to slash at Auschwitz," and "*I am a woman.*" John Carey judges Plath (and me) with his disquieting lucidity: "shouting, extremism, and unreason," as if we were the UDA. Sylvia was a rash writer, but not as Carey implies "brandishing." It's hard to write now of her posthumous royal shadow, her honest cruelty, her insolent rightness.

My critics' confusion comes perhaps from my trying to mix high poetic style with a lower, quicker style that talked to the character of the person with love mockery and awe.

Robert Lowell

655. *To Alan Williamson*

Sept. 23, 1974

Dear Alan:

I should have written you the day I finished your monsters, when I was delightedly oozing with it. I have been working on a new poem, and am dimmer on the details of your book now. My favorite chapter is (I might say, of course is[)] *Notebook*, the best I've read either in book or review—and more than that, it's a sort of book of fiction in itself, so that I read it with the absorption and sense of discovery and surprise that I'd read a new narrative. I forget disagreements. There are many; tho not many matter, and maybe most give a feeling of veracity to your prejudices and judgments.

At random: the country not quite ready for self-determination was ironically ~~charmingly~~ said by Lizzie and is not male chauvinism. The king at the end of "Guevara" is Charles and many—what kings liked best usually throughout history was hunting (like Guevara perhaps including, but not necessarily, man-hunting, war[)]. When a King, a powerful man, is himself hunted, he must in a degree be sympathetic—so Che. I was aware of the ab-

surdity of the similarity. But unlike you, as you say, I am not against the right or the left per se, just bloodthirstiness, meanness and stupidity. For that reason, the pictures of Tom Hayden and Irving Howe strike me as not much more controversial than Richard III. I once taught the Bible, and read it fairly firmly by bracing myself against the God of cruelty—nature really. Nature is more richly like what one reads in the Bible, than like most of the great historians, the English ones. I could hold this position in *Notebook* and *History*; and now that it has partially slipped (the splendor, the indignity) I still hold it, but slide (wisely?) toward another more stopped and gaping style.

When I was at Iowa—'50 or later in '52[—]I read 2/3 of Freud, like reading Tolstoy. In that sense (memory randomly renewed) *Life Studies* is full of him; a replacement to the Christian Church, more intimate but without boundaries or credo, or philosophy. I have never taken him as gospel, been psychoanalysed, suffered an emotional or intellectual transference in therapy—my own decisive trouble was, as with all manics, a *salt* deficiency. I picked up Freud from reading, talk (I knew about his way of thinking vividly from Delmore Schwartz before I read a word). I think you use Freud too piously, or rather too much in quick unexplored references. One could use Thomism to "explain" Proust, Nietzsche and Yvor Winters, usefully up to a point (if you were deeply and perhaps skeptically, versed in Thomism[)], but the method might become skimming and hard. You don't always really give yourself to Freud, sometimes he is inappropriate, sometimes just a curious parallel; however mostly he is your hard working shovel.

Of the other chapters, of course I'm delighted with your case for the defense of *Lord Weary*—for long I felt I was fleeing from its style with my life, and couldn't be fair. *Notebook* was deliberately an attempt to get back to its present instant, moment of struggle and occasional grand style. Somehow *Life Studies* is your second best chapter; I think you are most profound and surprising when you stare and burrow into my actual experience—as written.

I worry about your getting your poems published and finding the right job. I hope all your powerful work on such an esoteric subject: me, will help. I trust something will.

I have been worrying months now about Peter, but have faith he is safe. I am a tremendous fan of his story-poems—is it just a matter of writing lines that is so wonderful.

Caroline and I send our best as always to you and Anne. My deepest gratitude.

Affectionately,

Cal[. . .]

656. To Elizabeth Bishop

October 6, 1974

Dearest Elizabeth:

My most guilty apologies! Your letter was slow in coming, and arrived almost two weeks after Frank left. Things with us haven't been quite as untroubled as he thought. The *Depression* is just dawning on us, and brings enormous problems and irreconcilables. The question is whether I should return to America where I can earn, have friends, etc. I have been thinking of trying to get an arrangement like yours at Harvard and teach full time. I don't feel particularly persona grata there—still, it seems weak and demoralized not to do something for my family more than royalty payments at this time, but I can't do much here—even someone like Spender has a hard time getting a decent university job, and his pay is small. ON THE OTHER HAND—we have our house (houses) here and four children, and transplanting them might be murderous, and the cost of moving huge. Nothing will or can be done till some time after I return to Cambridge, but these are thoughts to trouble my noon's repose.

Caroline (don't repeat this) isn't too well and is having what I think of as an oldfashioned nervous breakdown That is there is nothing wrong with her reason—she is not manic or depressed—but is full of jerks, ups and downs, panics, moments of excitement, fear[,] grandiosity, inertia—tho most of the time she is calm and full. Like you, she takes in everything, and this adds to the strain. I think I am describing a change of life, or its prelude. There are so many children, their troubles little and big—I make things sound more intense than they are. I know everything is working out. I wish I weren't gravely impractical by nature and habit.

I assume you will assume that I love all your poems. I have been brooding on this last one since it arrived, and I have ached to live in such a house too—I have all my life—cut my losses and live the life of severe deprivation, idleness and imagination. I think I have felt this at least from Kenyon on, and in a queer luxurious way have achieved it. What is interesting is that your rhythm slows and forces one to read it as prose—prose perhaps like M. Moore's poems, tho your rhythm has a much slower wandering quality—I don't think she'd choose such a shack. All this from memory; but now rereading, I remember all sorts of talks with you: that room I got near (?) you in Brazil, filled with proletarian callgirls—the meter I see is steadily iambic . . . any number of terrific seemingly tho quiet details—you arrive at your castle safely. I am troubled by one thing, a sort of whimsical iambic Frost tone to the last five

lines or so, though I think they are needed. New lines might make a fine poem into one of your finest. Nothing else needed.

I'm arranging my pieces and reviews—good enough to publish maybe. Not too bad. What strings them together is my scattered firsthand descriptions of many of the poets. I have a marvelous dull title—*A Moment in American Poetry.* Tell Frank what I have just written, and ask him if he can locate my Harvard collection New England piece, and my first *New York Review of Books* Berryman. I have 18 poems now, all in the same free verse—18 if I count generously calling a poem in two parts two poems. Ask Frank, if you wish[,] to show you his zerox edition of my new poems. Tell him too that it now looks as though it will be impractical and too expensive to bring my whole family to Harvard, that I wonder if Harvard can give me some sort of two room setup in one of the colleges (houses). Today Caroline is recovered and about to see a doctor.

We both send our love,

Love,

Cal

Oh dear, Lewis Wharf rings a bell, but perhaps it is only Rolls or Rose Wharf, I never knew which, where Daddy used to go to mysterious (naval?) banquets.

657. To Peter Taylor

October 9, 1974

Dear Peter:

The other night at a large party I suddenly felt an acute nausea (as if I had been drinking heavily,) then a rather comforting feeling of changing inside to ice, then I was being rolled about by about six merry people on a low table, like a gentle practical joke. I had fainted. It may have been from accidentally drinking something like vodka in orange juice, or it may not. The doctors can't tell. Anyway it's not serious, ~~except that~~ but it made me feel close to you. I've written you a second poem about this, and about the years that brought us to now. It's all too abstract and saturnine, but that the fault of the genius of poetry.

I've been through your collected stories again. My old opinions hold, as they must; but I see the stories somewhat as one long novel, or a *Spoon River* of the living. You were very bold I think (for it brought you freedom) to keep your mother['s] father's high middleclass background always in sight—a go-

ing, not quite destroyed world that no one has tried much to sentimentalize like the Old South or the Twenties. I like the way you always waver away from the too simple and partisan. One I like (did I always) is Venus etc. the double incest. Auden once told me incest was a subject without meaning—why try to give it one, it has so many? The shadow on what's youthful and close. Isn't allegory a way of getting out the tabooed?[. . .]

We are having troubled times with the stockmarket for Caroline. She is having what we call an "acute nervous depression," tho none of the three words really fits, because she is quite lively, oxlike and functioning. I don't think we are up to the great expense and weight of moving our whole family to Cambridge this spring. I'll come alone. There's the now insoluble question of whether we should live in England or come to America where I can earn, and make connections. Well, this will solve itself?

Give our love to Eleanor. The story-poem is fine, wonderful—not the best tho of the three I read it could [be] in your book. I was surprised by the *short* lines, then about how to read them—then I realized that I myself had written two whole plays in this meter—I *see* lines, and forget to measure or scan the rhythm in any way.

Our love to you both,
 Cal

658. To Elizabeth Hardwick

October 13, 1974

Dearest Lizzie:

I just had an examination by some very great heart-expert (they all look like sons-in-law to me now), and was cleared of any heart-trouble, as earlier of lung trouble. So now I am pushing crates and carrying buckets of coal upstairs.

[. . .]I don't know if Harvard would be better. We are upset by the riots, which tho they'll of course die down will remain smoldering in the air. I wonder if the Negroes are pro Ulster Protestant. It's horrible; I think the busing in such an atmosphere is criminal. We decided not to take our family to Cambridge—3 or 4 big difficulties—new schools for the children, the hell of finding a house for four or even six months, the rough feeling everywhere, cost.

I'll come over alone, toward the end of January. Can I stop a couple of days with you and H?, and disturb the studio?

Doesn't something like a foot take forever at our age? I'm sorry for you. I

had a bump then a bruise on my shin for a year or more. I think if I stared intently I'd [see] a vague yellow now.

I wonder how States Street is doing for you? Are cautious investors the worst? I suppose it's just the opposite, but still they lose.

It's an indescribable consolation for me to be near to you so happily.

Love,

Cal

659. To James Laughlin

<div align="right">October 23, 1974</div>

Dear J—

Thanks for your letter. You seem to be the only editor in England or America who actually reads his authors with critical enthusiasm. Of course you can have the Ransom; I am anxious to have it come out in America in a good context.

Please give my love to Flossie; I am in America so much on the run that I haven't had a chance to get someone to take me to Rutherford. I didn't know too if she wanted visitors—it was so surprising to like her and Bill equally. I don't feel the same about poor Olga, tho Mary is nice. Ezra's money has always fascinated me since I read the *ABC* as an undergraduate. I think tho there are so many other things, hence our dispute and joking on the stage in New York. I think you *took* the evening with your humorous poignant memories of Rapallo—a little after your visit I wrote Ezra from Harvard asking if I could study with him—he wrote back on a postcard—that I should consider the implications and that Amy wasn't a skeleton in anyone's closet. I had written apologizing for her vain attacks on him.

Thanks for liking my last books—some people didn't—I can't think of a phrase I like better than "think meat and lovely technique."

Affectionately,

Cal

I'll be at Harvard from February to May. Hope to see you.

660. To Jean Stafford

<p style="text-align: right">October 30, 1974</p>

Dear Jean—

I must clear up one thing—I didn't drink on top of antabuse knowingly. I *may* have taken an orange juice with vodka or something. It's impossible to tell. It's hard at a big party to be sure what one is handed. Or the fainting may have been something else entirely. I am Ok, lungs and heart, as far as tests can tell. I am alarmed about *your* drinking, but it might be more dangerous to stop. For all your varied physical troubles, your life must be a triumph of defying doctors and going your own way. Sometimes they seem to forget our poor lives, the lives we must actually get through and try to enjoy. All this is lost in their solutions of craft.

The last two days here have been cold and bright for England, almost like New England. We keep from freezing by coal, electric heaters, and an inaudible oil furnace. I am reminded of Damariscotta Mills: two cook-stove-oil-burners, two airtights, one plug-in radiator, electric heaters, something with coal. How did I keep it all going—I was even more inert and unhandy then.

Well I pray for your novel, and even more for you, the book a part of you. Do you realize all of us are the older, not yet senile, generation, the long-on-view whose shadow falls on all who are younger? What can we do about it? I write about being 57. This morning I. A. Richards told me he had written three poems on Allen Tate—"curious poems, not on him particularly, but age." I said, "The grand subject." But started to add, I'm writing on it too, when I realized I could not say this to a man of 82.

~~May we have that far to go.~~

Caroline sends her love—is that peculiar from [someone] you've never met? Love,

 Cal

Did you notice I live in Bearsted?

661. To Elizabeth Bishop

<p style="text-align: right">December 18, 1974</p>

Dearest Elizabeth:

Now that Caroline is back fresh from seeing you and Cambridge and everyone, I feel almost as if I had made the trip myself, and talked to you at

some length. This letter is difficult because if I don't pay attention my most pressing news will be Caroline's trip. It's a terrific thing to have house and schools settled and know we'll be together. No three or four months that could [have] been borne perhaps because they had to be.

My suggestions for the end of your poem must have been troublesome. I think I've spent more futile hours trying to perfect something satisfactory— always pressing and invisible, the unimagined perfect lines or ending, for there it usually falls. Often I've given up, and wondered why I ever found fault. There are the experiences we haven't had, working in a spool factory etc. and can't imagine, and there are others like the end of "Lycidas" where all the experience is easily ours, but we can't turn to it or find the right sound. I've just [spent] a week or more on three lines which finally ended in changing the position of two words (I did other things). I hope you won't bother any more, you were probably right all along.

I think a lot about getting things right, when I haven't enough to make it matter—and often there is scrawl that cannot be arranged. We seem to be near our finish, so near that the final, the perfect etc. is forbidden us, not even in the game.

I see us still when we first met, both at Randall's and then for a couple of years later. I see you as rather tall, long brown-haired, shy but full of des. and anecdote as now. I was brown haired and thirty I guess and I don't know what. I was largely invisible to myself, and nothing I knew how to look at. But the fact is we were swimming in our young age, with the water coming down on us, and we were gulping. I can't go on. It is better now only there's a steel cord stretch[ed] tense at about arms-length above us, and what we look forward to must be accompanied by our less grace and strength. Well, no more dies irae; I wonder if Christians believing in immortality saw their lives as less circular.

Just had a letter from Peter Taylor. He writes that all his letters begin by philosophizing and end with trivia. I think he meant he felt at home with trivia. We are getting ready for Christmas, 2 families in our house, each with four children. It's like Aunt Sarah's family Thanksgivings; unlike her, none of us can make audible feast speeches.

Give my best to Alice; Caroline sends love.

Love,

Cal

662. To Seamus Heaney

[34 Cypress St., Brookline, Mass.]
April 29, 1975

Dear Seamus:

Put us down for the Kilkenny last week in August festival. I'm afraid I'm worse than you and literally haven't written any letters since coming to America. Bills from there seem like something stopped in time. Peacocks—but I once spent an endless day or weekend in a sort of Mexican hacienda. The owner unhappily terminating his marriage on that day, but we didn't know. Yet how hideous and in harmony seemed the cries of the beautiful peacocks.

I too remember with refreshment our trip to the Belfast Airport. Where is Kilkenny? Isn't there a Mother Goose about the cats of Kilkenny?

Caroline sends her best.

Robert Lowell

663. *To the Editors,* New York Review of Books

[Milgate Park, Bearsted, Maidstone, Kent, June 12, 1975]
I am glad the war is finished, despite the poison it leaves behind: it leaves more than we can face, the catastrophic moral and military disaster, 55,000 dead, a half million unpardonably unpardoned deserters, half Vietnam killed, robbed, and scrapped with our complaisance—the Waterloo of anti-Stalinism. How can we get out of the indignities of the display window? The black prophet is now drowned by his truth. In our defeat communism is inevitable and cleansing, though tyrannical forever.

664. To Elizabeth Bishop

September 11 [1975]

Dearest Elizabeth:

I haven't done well on letters to anyone; and how can I write you who jam more into a postcard than I can on this long blue scroll? It must [be] a freedom [to] have your books out and on the wall. When I moved from Boston to New York, there were no bookcases for two months, and the books stood in their boxes ten feet high, like some backward child's pyramid. I couldn't even despair.

I've read Helen Vendler's Herbert too—quite a lot of it really, and found new poems. But mostly I didn't agree too much with her taste, and worse, didn't [see] how her various schemata bear. He's a strange poet, and if we don't go on reading him without thinking or questioning too much and loving our old favorites (the best way to read him)[,] then it seems a miracle that he ~~could harmonize~~ didn't sink under so much sophistication, metrical craft, clergyman discipline and religious genius. Helen, I guess, sees that; but her language is worried.

Worried too, I feel is Frank Bidart. I hope he is not getting his contributors to realign, repunctuate and revise. I now have a young Mr. Stewart at Farrar Straus, with Frank's care but not his depth, who takes out my comma-dashes, and gives basketball *center* a small *c*. I am in fear I'll leave a line out and neither I nor anyone else will ever know. Occasionally, I realize I have done this in typescript. The realization a gradual blundering feeling of discovery.

We've had a good and level summer. No excursions, but a brief one to Ireland. The two countries for an American look so much alike, that it turns one topsy-turvy to realize they are not alike. Two sisters, faces and dresses the same; characters opposed.

We've almost decided to try New York for the winter; then I could commute for a night or two each week as I used to. Brookline turned out to [be] almost as far away as New York for me—rare visits, rapid returns. This way I would be in Cambridge longer, and then away. I think I give you every so often compliments on how well known you are. Even in Ireland, it is impossible to find anyone who knows poetry who doesn't know you. They all seem to admire, often violently. I've finished selecting my poems (a lot, I fear) and have a new book done—to come out in 1977.

Caroline sends her love.

Cal

665. To Elizabeth Hardwick

September 11, [1975]

Dearest Lizzie:

What lovely reverie and remembering letters from you! So much I partly remember and imperfectly conjecture: Fitzgerald's marriage (we found him heavy, but surely fate stepped too heavily on him)[,] Gillian, lovely and right, but I think back with a September sadness on poor Bill, though I'm sure this marriage will make him happy. He looks mostly like an old man now, slightly

humped and bald-grizzled. His adoption of Don is an underworld task, like drawing water eternally in a sieve.

I wonder if you have my marked copy of the collected Stevens—*my* selections built on Randall's. There are too many I like: much of *Harmonium*, "Sailing after Lunch," "Esthétique du Mal," half *The Rock*, (his own elegies and the most felt of his poems). He endlessly speculated on whether the actual or the imagined was the real thing—at his dying this question was more poignant. I can see how much you enjoy returning to New York; especially with that second Castine, the pastoral Smith, looming on you.

I am about to phone Harriet, and can hardly think she could be at the end of that new address and number. I envy her her classes—I could learn so much I think, as if I'd never been to college. You speak of changes, and I think you mean changing from one place to another—but another is reaching, the age when the whiplash of college is no longer held over you . . . and you descend to revising your own writing, and learning history from short book reviews. I gather from your use of the term "partying" you at least know what it means. But what can one do, children are so soon on their own as we are—independent in all ways except financially. I think one should worry over dangers, not morals, but what can one do?

I feel the worst of old maids ending on that last phrase—so far from Wallace Stevens . . . or just from his poems.

Love,

666. *To Seamus Heaney*

September 11 [1975]

Dear Seamus:

We might try a trip to Dublin when the fall gets on, late October, early November, if that is convenient for you. I haven't much new to say in an interview. Elgy had new things but I blushed to read her through, I seemed like an infirm and twice lifesize balloon. And there were many factual errors. One I remember is that an unfriendly critic said Caroline really didn't like people. But it was a friendly critic trying to be friendly, who said it; meaning, it's stylistically brilliant and honest not to like people, or maybe only that the world is full of hypocrisy and fraudulence and ought to be disliked. I'm sure Elgy intended the best—but compliments that no one will believe are a little like a stone in a snowball.

I've read the sonnets a good many times. Two that I like best are "The

Train" and "A Drink of Water." In general, I like all your description. Your Nature pours out images with a full hand; the cup (to work this figure to death) is so often dry for me, a town man in the end. Sonnets seem in two ways perhaps the wrong form for your sequence. First the somewhat too full-dress, particularly the final couplet; then the whole sequence makes me think of Wordsworth, and that something that goes so well should have gone even farther. At worst, you should [be] able to mine many poems out of your many strong lines—perhaps in quatrains, or more drastic changes. I've been so long netted in my own unrhymed sonnets that I'm no judge. The "Pigeons" must be one of your best—a fine fur or richness of description, the feeling of going through mystery, a sorrow. The material seems close to the sonnets, and perhaps you could use them to make a sequence of four or five in the looser form. You couldn't ask for more than what you are writing of your migratory life.

I don't know how to word how much I felt at our meeting, as though something unchanging had come into my life. Best to Marie (spelling wrong) and the children.

Affectionately,
Robert

667. To John Haffenden

September 15, 1975

Dear John Haffenden:

To answer your critical questions first—I have since college admired Heredia, though in my slow way of reading, I only know him from anthologies—about twenty poems read many times. What do I owe him? I can't say exactly. *History* started with short personal poems in free verse, then as 14 line free verse, then blank verse. I must have written fifty of these before I tried historical vignettes. I'm in another style—fray, shamble and conversational idiom. I think in my historical poems I had Heredia constantly in the back of my mind, and felt honored by the contrast.

I've just gotten [a] list of letters written to me up to 1970 from the Houghton Library at Harvard. There are 15 from John, mostly short, I think. If you will write to Rodney Dennis, the Librarian[,] you can read them, but you have to have Kate's permissions to publish them. I too should see them, if you are intending to publish. If there's an afterlife, I think I'd spend it living and reading everything written to me. It becomes so rapidly vague, one forgets almost everything in old letters, particularly the brilliant details.

Thanks for the Sheffield invitation. I go to Harvard after Christmas (almost now!) so I think I'll do no readings. Hope very much to see you again.

Yours,

Robert Lowell

668. To Peter Taylor

October 6, 1975

Dear Peter:

Congratulations on your story—are you really buying a house with it? How many *New Yorker* pages are 35 of yours?

Our free verse letters have an uncomfortable resemblance to the letters in couplets Keats' friends and Keats himself wrote. Yours however somehow obliquely stirred a buried piece of conscience in my mind. I know I must have been very hard on you during my manic period. I really remember almost nothing. It is in the tone—a tone that covered up what I said—or a tone that worsened what I said? Caroline and I and Mary McCarthy the other night debated which of us was the most tactless. But what I said went further; in the euphoria of sickness, I coast without hearing.

In the mail today with yours a request to read at a Walt Whitman celebration, end[ing] "Walt wants you" and another for contributing free to a Pound Symposium, with more or less the same phrasing. I think Kenneth Clark is boasting when he claims he can stay awake reading for an hour. One night last August in a time of insomnia, I stayed up three. Usually both of us can only read book reviews—enough to fill two volumes come weekly. It's strange the most ambitious books lack the taste and polish of the average reviewers, even when they are written by people who are themselves grade A reviewers.

Ten days ago Ivana went off [to] the boarding school. We miss her and always notice she is gone, and feel in our big house like dwarfs living in giant's clothes.[. . .]

I only read Clark's I Tatti in a magazine, and it seemed quite feline and intuitive about Berenson. Isn't it usually considered the high-water point of his reminiscences? Sidney Nolan has a Clark story—going to his house and preparing what he would say, he arrived to see a dignified man standing behind Clark—more or less pushing Clark aside Sidney said, "You are to be congratulated on your splendid son." Or something even fuller. Then Clark turned to the old man saying, "You must see that the hors d'oeuvres are warmed." He speaks too of Clark looking at one with impartial sympathy.

I dislike tentative moving of furniture worse than anything on earth. And wreck the most sensitive of plans by asserting, "Are you absolutely sure you want it there?" You are having sport with human beings, even if the human being is you yourself.

Both our arthritis troubles must come from this. Even to hang light pictures causes pain.

Caroline sends her love to you both; she has just reviewed a book so dirty for the *TLS* that it can't be given to a local typist.

Love to you both,
 Cal

669. To Frank Bidart

February 15, 1976

Dear Frank:

So good to hear your voice. I had just been talking to Lizzie, and felt a rush of health. My recovery has been easy in most ways, but I am weighed down by the new frequency of attacks. How can one function, if one is regularly sick. Shades of the future prison. But all's well for the present. The doctors differ somewhat but are optimistic. So am I. We sit by the fire paying bills. Caroline has written three chapters of a novel. I've written a short heart-felt poem.

It will be good to have you with us on the 19. Like old times and not like your last visit.[. . .]

Sorry you are depressed about teaching. It comes to almost all this time of year. Think of the glorious things you are teaching, and still learning from, or renewing yourself from, no matter how old they are. Caroline sends her fire-lit love.

Love,
 Cal

670. To Elizabeth Bishop

March 4, 1976

Dearest Elizabeth:

Thanks for your card, finally perfectly deciphered, and for your reassuring letter to Caroline—for months she meant to answer, saying "This is a real letter."

I had a longish though not violently troubled stay in the hospital, and have been out a month—mildly depressed as the cheerful doctor insists. Mildly is bad enough. Though I can't make too much of it. I fear the frequency of these things, fear becoming something that must be categorized as a burden. Yet I put my trust in my doctor's unruffled trust in lithium. The past was quite livable.

Your poem came to the right buyer. An aching subject, as the *art* even of losing must be. Your stoical humor persuades me that loss is ~~almost~~ an advantage. Or is it the form—each rhythm, rhyme and pause right? The last 4 lines are the triumph, here the poet's voice rings out. I am reminded of Wyatt or Herbert. You command your words.

I have been writing furiously in my doldrums, and always feel on the edge of being too raw . . . and more than on the edge. This book is almost entirely free verse; but the next, God willing, may be metrical. One needs to hold a shield before one's feelings and the reader. Meter might, but really it's a matter of character and imagination. Right now I'd like to borrow your villanelle armor.

I hear you are going to Holland. I trust you'll see our friend Judith Herzberg. She is a good poet and thinks you the best alive. She looks like a pretty Virginia Woolf.

Spring came on my birthday and Harriet flies in tomorrow.

Love,
 Cal

671. *To Blair Clark*

March 4, 1976

Dear Blair:

I finally deciphered the crucial word "tricky" in your lithium warning. I think you mean the blood has to be taken every month or so to check the amount of lithium in the system. I've been doing that, though hating the blood-needle. However, the air is full [of] rumors against lithium, hard to check on because it is almost a universal faith with English doctors. It's the preventative effectiveness that shakes me, I can't really function against two manic attacks in one year.

This one was drawn out, but not too bad. I've been home a month, rather downlooking at first, then thawing, all the while writing with furious persistence. Now I have little to grumble at.

We have a haunting transAtlantic problem. We, both Caroline and I, would be decisively better off, if we lived in America, yet the move would be a shattering one for us as a family, getting the children resettled etc. or paying them flying visits, the groaning effort of abandoning houses, finding something anew. A dilemma, almost two impossibles. I see myself changed into an expensive, parasitical burden. This is in blue moments; meanwhile I have Harvard and considerable royalties, yet I feel less employable than 1 White Russian in England.

I should really tear this letter up. Outside, the sun is shining. Harriet is arriving tonight. A coal and wood fire warms the large bright-window room, and we swim along happily writing and rewriting.

I didn't realize you were already *writing* the *Nation*. Please send us copies. I always admired your Boston *Globe* editorials, so free of clichés, so muscled to say something. I have written a farewell to Hannah Arendt for the National Academy, about seven typewritten pages. I might mail it to you, if it could possibly fit in.

I can see the problem of living in New York with children. We plan on getting an apartment in New York next fall, but with only one child, Sheridan, aged five, and too young for school. Is New York getting any safer or gentler? If it were as it was, such ages ago, I think we could almost live there.

I sent Martha Ritter a note care of you, which she doesn't seem to have gotten. I just said I had worried about her since we last saw her, and that I thought her poem remarkably perfectly natural, yet self-telling, and that it should be published. O the ghosts of the past.

Forgive me this worry; it is like an insomniac reverie—one that wakes up happily squeezing oranges and making coffee, and the lovely companionship of Caroline.

Love to you both,
Affectionately,
Cal

P.S. Tell if you come across anything more detailed on lithium. I am trying to find a substitute.

672. To Stephen Berg

Dear Stephen:

I started a letter a year or so ago saying I couldn't honestly blame you for Adrienne's slash. I was barraged with crude bashing reviews at the time, and took them as one does. I don't see how you could have turned it down, particularly for your magazine whose lifelines are opposing prejudices and judgments. However, Adrienne in her pre-prophetic days and for more than ten years was one of my closest friends. I could say she has become a famous person by becoming cheap and enflamed; but that isn't it. Her whole career has been a rage for disorder, a heroic desire to destroy her early precocity for form and modesty. And wasn't she right? And wasn't she unrecognized mostly when she first became a better poet and before the time of her fevers? And who knows how the thing will turn out—such a mixture of courage and the auctioneer now?

I suppose the hodge-podge and tabloid side of your magazine puts me off. However, that's your power and freshness—the magazine is a fair where you can buy almost anything you want or don't want.

I don't think you have been a bad friend or mistreated me. Mazzaro's ~~unreadable~~ hard to read defense irked me almost more than Adrienne's clear attack.

I like your poems—the easy quiet language, the quiet grief, the rises into eloquence usually at the end of a poem. It's a style so many of us have with nostalgic images and the slow tolerance of prose. I am troubled a bit by a glibness maybe in the sex, and sometimes with a feeling you might have exerted more—yet I can hardly count the lines I might underline to remember. We neither of us write as we did when we met a third of a lifetime ago.

Yours as before,
 Cal

PS: Thanks for picking McClatchy for my *Selected*. I want to avoid the honor of a front-page picture. This would have gone off months ago, but I wanted to say something about your poems which I had unfortunately lost.

Sorry[,] have no[thing] unpublished and really finished on hand now.

673. To Elizabeth Bishop

Dearest Elizabeth:

My typewriter ribbon dimmed, as you can see from the date above, and I thought for a minute I would [be] sending you something unique since I was writing my mother from school—my illegible printed capitals longhand. However the unused *red* ribbon comes out beautifully.

I called you as often as I could both before and after your message but got no answer. Our trip to New York was driven, exciting, crowded as all such trips are—the small smoked-drenched bedroom, the noisy stopping and starting trucks worst at dawn, the cross-biased friends who could only be warily mentioned to one another, the warmth of many dear meetings, the nervous publisher with many page-proof errors. Frank caught about 40. The printer's favorite slip was putting a period for a comma but without capitalizing. My play was rather splendid I like to imagine and magnificently endless—six to eleven-thirty. The actor playing Captain Delano looked into the audience, perhaps with his telescope, and saw five people in a row asleep. I was in mortal fear I might be one of them, and kept crossing and recrossing my legs, moving to the edge of my seat then almost through the back . . . and never nodded, but must have seemed afflicted. Or did I wink and was seen? Anyway, a bicentennial production, fifty players and more than fifty costumes and always the problem of racing the plays beyond their rhythm or killing the audience.

I liked your interview but must disappoint you by saying I'm still in free verse, written in the blue period after sickness, when I felt I could nothing else well. On the balance side and on the side of formality, I am told all my lines are lines. I do scores of revisions to make them so. I use iambics often loosened into anapests. I suppose definitions of words in the dictionary can be made to do this—anything can be scanned but not be made into decisive lines. I meant to say that I agreed with everything you said, but not in practice. How different prose is; sometimes the two mediums ~~just~~ refuse to say the same things. I found this lately doing an obituary on Hannah Arendt. Without verse, without philosophy, I found it hard, I was naked without my line-ends.

New York is weird now, or so it seemed coming from the calm of Kent or even London. America and England are mirages and happy islands to each

other, both an escape from prices. Caroline and I both felt that New York was too anxious and running on tiptoe for us—despite of (or because of) too may friends. Typical and almost first symbol, the Straus and Giroux elevators jam and have for months, and the only stairway is permanently locked, even to Bob Giroux because of dangerous school children. One is almost congratulated for arriving in the office without much delay.

I am alone in London for a few meditative self-help days, in exile from my family because Sheridan has mumps (fast recovering) and Caroline has to join the girls in The Hebrides, where there is a mumps epidemic.

Getting to Boston and above all seeing you was a delightful gift I was promising myself, but all was too hurried. Caroline sends her love.

All my love,
 Cal

674. To Frank Bidart

April 15, 1976

Dear Frank:

Writing you is about the first thing I am doing—after writing Elizabeth, after failing with the Hoover, after sleeping off the plane trip and all New York. Letters are a way not to be alone, like Captain Delano without his ship.

Caroline is much more rested than when you last saw her. When we reached Redcliffe a little before noon, she slept unstirring almost till seven, then again from nine-thirty till about nine in the morning. (I did almost as well.) Now she is beginning another voyage, no Atlantic, but a chain of small laps—a quick look-in at Milgate, then London, then Glasgow, then the Hebrides. Once there, the sea air, the children, and a Cousin her best friend—but she is still exhausted and I am keeping my fingers crossed. Sheridan is rapidly recovering[. . .].

Nothing really went wrong flying home, but it was slow and chafing enough for me to partly live through the kindness of your many trips to us. So little occurred, I'm at a loss to fill out this paragraph. The worst was the hour's wait and watching uncountable benches fill to capacity with passengers who didn't look as if they could afford passage. Once on board, one of the staff told us we were probably on the biggest plane in the world. He said this sadly. To get out of our seats, we had to arouse a dark soundly sleeping figure slumped over a book in French. Caroline thought he must be Fanon's brother.

Then in spasm of economy, Caroline bought four custom-free bottles of vodka. They went into a mammoth, flimsy bag of children's toys. When we were lining up and leaving the plane, first one bottle of the vodka made, then slipped through, a hole, then another bottle, then the toys. Well, all was gathered up.

Many thanks for calling in the "Long Summer" titles. Three minutes later, you would have caught Caroline returning from Cornelia's. Thanks too for finding some forty errors. I noticed some of the periods for commas, but gave up in adding to my already record-length cable to Giroux. Did you notice how symbolic the "Myopia" substitution would have been?

Back here, I put on my old for-all-uses reading glasses. The type-page grew clear and all else filmed. So it has been for four years—without damage.

I've had another go at the Hoover. Usually with a simple contraption there's a chance that by pushing something will happen. This time, it whirred and hissed, but wouldn't suck. My type is dimming, I must stop.

Our love,
Cal

P. S. I just turned something (the ribbon) on the typewriter, and look . . . it's a beautiful black. After our exciting whirl through New York, we both feel it is too fast and fallen for us. Everyone is trying to sell not rent apartments. This is just one sign.

675. To Marcia Nardi

[Milgate Park, Bearsted, Maidstone, Kent]
May 25, 1976

Dear Marcia:

I am upset and full of self-accusation about your letter. I don't mean to turn away from you. When Frank Bidart brought me the letter you speak of, I am afraid I put it aside rather flinching from a sad appeal I could do nothing about. Then the letter disappeared.

I doubt if I will outlive you many a year, but surely I don't want to leave you in the dark and shattered by my neglecting your appeal. It's a little like the drowned helping the drowned. I have had two breakdowns, and stays in hospitals in the last twelve months. My wife is very ill at the moment. One prays for strength to meet the day. Well, it will all work out, won't it? One [good] season follows bad.

I really can't be of help to you at the moment. Please forgive my evading

to answer you. I want to do something. Tell me about the two small favors that would, or might, make such a difference.

Yours as always,
 Robert Lowell

676. To Elizabeth Hardwick

June 8, 1976

Dearest Lizzie:

I remember Ivor once startling me by saying he sometimes didn't know whether he existed. That was in my *Life Studies* day, and I couldn't believe it. Now your nice letters bringing me back [to] Maine almost from the blue . . . assure me I do exist.

Caroline has been ailing for almost three months, not back this time, but some obscure stomach trouble, difficulty in swallowing, difficulty in keeping food down. As hospitals and tests approached and receded, first London, then Zurich, she rapidly got better—is almost well now but not quite.

Elizabeth Bishop is about to visit here for two days—an informal visit, but not one to take lightly. The dog must be sent away because of her asthma but will that be enough? Half our chairs are tainted with dog hairs. Then so many things she can criticize, the disheveled garden, the carefree garden man, our care of Sheridan. Should he be sent away too? So many things down to my not writing meter, making errors in description. Of course no one is more wonderful, but so fussy and hazardous now. Her set subject in person and letters is scolding with affectionate fury over Frank Bidart (whom she half-depends on) a safe thing though grating.

Next week I am to hear sections of my *Phèdre* set by Benjamin Britten. Do you remember our dinner with him and Pears (?) ages ago when I mortally wounded Bob Giroux by ordering another bottle of his expensive wine? The meeting otherwise went cordially, but I never heard again from Britten. This winter I learned he had had a very severe and incapacitating heart attack and had just now finished *Phèdre* (only her tirades) his first work since partial recovery.

My students go in heavily for incompletes, it's the catch to assigning papers instead of exams. So Harriet is in vogue. We hope she'll come here, if New York gets too hot. Don't envy you City College in July. I suppose you feel awfully looked-at yet limited in motion at Castine. It all—the landscape—came back to me with Phil Booth's poems—meditations like photos, but solidly something.

Look forward to August 21 and your London arrival. You'll mail me your address. Our country number, if you will call, is 0622-38028 Maidstone. Why amn't I asked to the Penn Club? Dues? Tact? The Democratic Convention sounds like the heat of New York doubled. Won't you see it on television, as I did Chicago?

Love,
Cal

677. To Elizabeth Hardwick

July 2, 1976

Dearest Lizzie:

You caught our James appearance. We went with Rolando, who was disappointed that no one at all except literary people went—so different from the crowds of senators and members of parliament to receive [the] gold replica of the Magna Charta, also at Westminster, which we also went to. We seem to be on their list, this morning an invitation came to hear the embassadoress speak in the 900 year old Cathedral close, accompanied by soldiers and officials in dramatic many colored costumes—an advertisement for the disembarking tourist?

Just heard Stephen and Isherwood in a public conversation on the poets of the Thirties. Stephen giggling, "Unfortunately, it seems that poets do have to be educated["] (on the limitation of their group not being proletarian.) Isherwood matter of fact, no cant, his only cause homosexuality[,] this too his motive for going to Berlin. Auden dominated the whole thing, the only name the audience could ask questions about—poor Day Lewis, his wife, there, only cited as a plagiarist. Others have distinction, but only Auden has a brilliant changing intellectual outline—even his oddities: "Frogs won't do . . . Why go to plays, it's so unEnglish."

Thanks for Percival Lowell. I hadn't realized his errors were so fruitful, I suppose that's the rule in science. In the family, we always doubted his Mars, but swore by the accuracy and orthodoxy of his Pluto . . . once to have been called Percival.

I regret the letters in *Dolphin*. The only way to make a narrative was to leave a few. I hesitated to send you a copy of the *Selected Poems*, but Giroux acted on his own, which was right because the bulk of them were written under your eyes. I'm glad some of it stood up for you. I read all in one day, trying to proofread—so much I hadn't taken in for ages—one doesn't really

absorb what one is reading at readings. Autobiography predominates, almost forty years of it. And now more journey of the soul in my new book. I feel I, or someone, wrote everything beforehand. If I had read it at twenty would I have been surprised, would I have dared go on?

For a month, I think, the heatwave has been here, like an American city, like inland America—to the English the melting of the icecap.

Love,
 Cal

P.S. Greatly looking forward to your August.

678. To Peter Taylor

July 2, 1976

Dear Peter:

We are enjoying a month of heatwave—I suppose you must have it double—but avoiding anything that takes intelligent effort. My will, corrected for pages to accord with New York State law, has lain on my bed imploring me since May. I'm sorry not to have answered your letter. Of course, we are not mad, only disappointed . . . it's like the loss of an unexpected gift. You have missed the heatwave, supposed to be so much more insufferable in London because unfamiliar.

Looking for your last letter, I only can find a very old one, and am left wondering if Mary Jarrell turned up for your honorary degree. Two months ago, I got Goethe's *Walpurgis Nacht* (?) in two not very inspired translations, along with the German to complete for Randall's *Faust*—after a horrible two days of trying to write facetious rhymed verse in short lines . . . my admiration mounting for rival translators, I dubiously accepted Randall's saying it wasn't really good in German. Or did he say it was too good to translate? I gave up. By the way, one must admit that Mary and Michael have done a fine job of carefully and slowly bringing out everything. Randall is still a currently alive writer—so many genres in reserve.

Have you ever tried to stop writing? It's harder than alcohol, which I also foreswear as the very early sun crashes at about four through faults in the blinds. The trouble is I've become a sort of orange-squeezer expected to produce new and better juices. My method is formidable enough to turn out new poems, but not new subjects. Have you ever hit on something marvelous, impossible to anyone much under sixty, only to find you had already printed it?

I have just been days changing Caroline's appalling stepfather into a woman, into my mother, into an imaginary English friend's mother . . . ending it by hollowly asserting we are all in his shoes—hollow, though of course we are. I think you've finished verse mothers for the century . . . as Auden drained his colleagues. This season the English poets of the Thirties have replaced Bloomsbury. It brings back our own Thirties when we were still peeping over our college, trying to make sense of the embattled sides. England doesn't seem to have any Agrarians to be recaptured.

Caroline inscribed a copy of her novel to you both, but Duckworth sent it to a reviewer in Florence. Don't be insulted if you get an uninscribed copy. Her American book is a problem because her unpublished things should come out in an English book first, while American publishers don't want a hundred page novel. Doubleday is interested and the answer may be to reprint the fiction of [the] first book with the new novel. She got bushels of rave reviews.

A pleasant, delightful surprise was a visit from Elizabeth Bishop—more relaxed than ever in Cambridge. We talked on and on, we seemed as young and accepting as we were thirty years ago. We weren't too accepting then, but accepted each other. She left almost ready to write autobiography in free verse. Only when Caroline came into the room, would she say something like, "I don't like strawberries,["] Then [Caroline], "They *are* dry." She [Elizabeth], "I don't see why you say that."

I guess we'll [meet] back in Brookline or Cambridge. Frank Bidart has been alerted, the slow summer creeps away.

Our love as always to you and Eleanor,

Cal

679. To Elizabeth Bishop

July 12, 1976

Dearest Elizabeth:

Frank has just told me you arrived back in Boston in a wheelchair, a sad surprise because you seemed in such good health here and safe with your new English drug. I am mailing this to Lewis since I gather you will be out of the hospital by now.

I still thrill to your visit. After a little, it seemed as if almost thirty years had rolled back, and we were talking brownhaired callow and new in New York, Washington or Maine. Voice and image seemed much more what we were than what we are—or is the essence as it was? Glad too you liked my

new poems, for I feared you mightn't. Today they are off to Bob Giroux, and though I already miss their presence pressing on me to change, polish, do more, I have an almost physical sense of lightness, as though my shoulders weighed less, and my baggage was stored in the station for a day.

I'm sure Frank told you he found us an apartment, "better than any you've had," so say nothing to deter us. The uncertainty is so much more formidable from here. I think Cambridge will really be much more convenient academically and socially than Brookline. We only have a non-driving (like us) nurse.

Everything now seems to carry me backward. One thing I was certain of was that England didn't have real summers like my Grandfather's farm or the Tate's house in Tennessee—or at most did for no more than three successive days. But it goes on—nature's still now hidden and real heat. Sometimes I almost move to set off for the lake with my trolling rod for pickerel. How Grandfather would have pulled the place and us into order. But the soil and everything on it is crumbling and wilting, sand-browns with a blush of green.

We should be moving in about the 20th of September. Hope you are now recovered and moving to North Haven. I think on clear days you can see Castine from the northern shore. I miss it all, and am now looking forward to getting back.

Caroline sends her love,

Love,

Cal

680. To Frank Bidart

September 4, 1976

Dear Frank:

We arrive Flight BA 561, 2:05 p.m. on Wednesday the 15th. There, I've spelled it out. I gather you are not teaching then, but feel courtesy and consideration demand that I release you from your offer. But it would be such a treat for us, arriving so Atlantic-worn and foreign. We can go to Bailey's afterward and have something intoxicatingly sweet. All the more for me; I've been on the wagon for two months and have developed a morbid taste for what we call here, coffee with ice. That's only in company, when I feel a need to be verbose. Coffee is like benzedrine, at first I woke up tingling unpleasantly. Now I drink mostly hag.

Caroline is up to her neck enlarging that long story you liked about Great-

Granny Woodhouse. More and more less (or mostly more) doomed descendents are creeping out like moving shadows from the immovable, desolating G.G. Woodhouse. When it's finished, her third book will be finished. At the moment, I can count them by turning my head from the typewriter, there are ten piles, typescript, notebooks, pages wrenched from notebooks. The race is to get a publisher's clean copy before flying.

Now a huge favor. I handed in my book about two months ago; and then haven't stopped adding, deleting, etc. Yet I had wonderful illusions the long, blind task was over. And now there can be no more. I can rub my hands over the bottom of the pot and find no ~~more~~ material . . . I think I've even thrown some of the metal of the pot in. And yet, nothing is ever perfect, even within its crippling inevitable human limitations. I want you to read me through for the last time, using your fine-toothed comb and good sense. Then my words can sleep with the publishers till they hatch as a book. I apologize for these nervous, jaunty figures of speech, Dear Old Collaborator.

I gather from your phone calls the summer has had some very hard moments for you. It's miraculous, as you told me about yourself, how often writing takes the ache away, takes time away. You start in the morning, and look up to see the windows darkening. I'm sure anything done steadily, obsessively, eyes closed to everything besides the page, the spot of garden . . . makes returning a jolt. The world you've been saved from grasps you roughly. Even sleep and dreams do this. I have no answer. I think the ambition of art, the feeding on one's soul, memory, mind etc. gives a mixture of glory and exhaustion. I think in the end, there is no end, the thread frays rather than is cut, or if it is cut suddenly, it usually hurtingly frays before being cut. No perfected end, but a lot of meat and drink along the way.

I'm surprised how glad I am to be getting back to Harvard this fall, and to you the center of it.

Caroline sends all her love, I mine,

Cal

P.S. I guess I told you we put Milgate on the market. It won't go soon, I suppose. The unfixed future is bewildering. We think of a less costly to run house near Oxford.

681. To Jean Stafford

September 4, 1976

Dearest Jean:

I have been thinking of you daily since our phone talk in New York. I'm no good on telephones unless the other person floods me with leads and ~~quste~~ questions, and I am ~~faria~~ (my electric typewriter has the jumps) afraid I wasn't much balm in your suffering. We were five days in New York and then had to rush home because Sheridan had the mumps and his nurse a psychotic paroxysm. Our whole time was taken up with seeing my play, three and a half hours, plus a stupefying hour and a quarter dinner break, Blair and his wife; Harriet and Cathy, Cornelia Foss, all of us returning impoverished and nodding to the final climactic play. The chief actor looked out into the audience with his captain's telescope and saw five people snoring. I had to squirm and shift horrifyingly like an arterial-sclerotic to stay awake. It was all pretty good and got good reviews except for an annihilating review by Clive Barnes, which Blair in some unaccountable seizure-amnesia of generosity mailed to me. Brief impressions must be even more illusory than calm long considered ones, but New York seemed so fragile, disintegrating before one's eyes. A rather lovely paper palace—Israel and New York, like Moscow and Leningrad under siege in 1942.

1940. Remember Chimes St. and Baton Rouge and Jamie Caffery and . . . Cinina? I got a letter last month from Vanderbilt to write for Red's 70th festschrift. After struggling with a laborious prose compliment, I dropped it for a poem, more of the tone, the humidity, less critique. A hundred unusable things came back to me—the arrival of Gaga's chairs, Peter's earplug falling out at bridge with Edith Kelso, Peter and I in pajamas sick over taking out Cinina's cat-shit, waiting still in pajamas outrageously for you to return from the office to get our lunch, Christmas with Red staring long at a sheep that looked like Cinina and saying it reminded [him] of someone he couldn't place. You could toss up fifty times as much in the same number of words. How can I thank you?

Time, but we must call it age, they are so inextricably married, is really full of novelty, and even wisdom, never quite enough to say we have repaired our losses or smoothed our distortions. Do you see I am trying to thank you for the past? Last weekend I was reading a famous old book on Napoleon's stay at St. Helena. No one would accuse Napoleon of over-severity to past faults and crimes, rather too easily, like a president-emeritus, with nothing to do, he teems with answers and solutions. On Waterloo, "But it's strange, there must be a reason why the English have always beat us." In his will he died as a

Frenchman and a Catholic; in life he preferred Mohammedans, the sun, said about deathbed confession, "Who knows, there's so much we can't imagine." What does it matter? Once we thought we could potentially imagine everything, or anything. But I couldn't have imagined these "mellow" days, and gentle as they are what a mercy.

I gather from Peter that he is probably seeing you now. We are flying to Cambridge in ten days. I look forward to teaching, but except for reading reviews of familiar books I am an old number. Let me know if I can do anything. Will call soon after we deplane.

Love,
 Cal

682. *To Elizabeth Hardwick*

September 4, 1976

Dearest Lizzie:

I can't find the words or maybe the style to say how comforting and enjoyable your visit was. It was so strange seeing you and Caroline easily (?) together, that I almost feel I shouldn't refer to it. People with us seemed to take it as naturally as we did, one wondered if they were making an effort. I want to thank you for the strain you may have felt, but never revealed. I can never have too many compliments from you, and loved your liking what I said.

Also Susan. In my thickness, I think I wouldn't have known how sick she had been or have had doubts about her future wellbeing. She has always been a warm polite person to me and I felt she went further than that in London. (Sometimes I think I am the enemy of womankind, and sometimes coming in from the country, I feel I can't keep up a conversation, even with old friends like the Spenders. Two nights before our Murdoch-Spender dinner, I ate alone with them. For half an hour I prayed that I wouldn't have to go. When I went, at first I couldn't talk, and never to Natasha, then it loosened, so much so Natasha suggested we go on shop-talking and she'd go home.) End of long parenthesis. You must have felt lonely arriving in a largely strange city, stuck in that Penta Hotel with such mobs of unknown, unmysterious clubmates. And to get back to Susan, how nice to hear her say, as she has more or less said in print that you are the best prose-writer in America, and isn't it wonderful that she is someone younger not Mary's nannying age. Lord. Lord, I have been writing to Allen Tate and Jean Stafford (very sick) and wondering if I wasn't writing last letters.

I can't contain this paragraph. It fascinated me that your Billie Holiday was written as part of your novel. I wouldn't have guessed, but now I think I see the cause of the more delicate, more poetic(?) prose. Don't tell me anything, but let me surmise that you are writing something close to autobiography, closer than plot will usually allow, ~~yet~~ that the style and selections will be artfully angled and chosen, so that the form might seem startlingly experimental even. Don't tell me either if, where and how I turn up. Shall I say you are welcome to anything about me in *Smiling through* you can use . . . even what you haven't shown me. What a ludicrous offer (what you have already). I do think you should use anything you can control. Caroline at this moment is piecing a book review of a leaking Irish house into a piece of childhood autobiographical fiction.

We fly on the 15th, 46 Sacramento St. Cambridge. I can see how poor Randall a little before his death, wondered how he could talk through a class—the great teacher. I don't doubt now, though I am a very old number, replenished, I think in dour moments, by new reviews of old familiar books. How odd to talk about James's *American* I last read first year [at] Kenyon.

I think all the time about Harriet, with stiff, bearish affection. Could I meet David (?) sometime in your apartment—not to approve but to acquaint myself. This is a moment, I suppose, before another unforeseeable moment. In my darkness, I am reassured.

No more really. I can't write these air-mail letters without running my last words into the fold. . . . I chose the sonnet you particularly detested because of the woodchuck lines at the bottom and didn't notice, I guess, the top.

Caroline sends her love. Let me phone soon after I arrive.

Love,

Cal

P.S. Will you ever see Sheridan? He came to breakfast helmeted in a huge pot, which has now burned the soup, so the whole long house asphyxiates. He's at a movie about a car without a driver, a masterpiece like the *Red Balloon*.

683. To Elizabeth Bishop

September 4, 1976

Dearest Elizabeth:

We'll arrive on the 15th, almost as soon as this does.

I've been writing sad letters this morning, one to Jean Stafford and one to

Allen Tate—each may be my last. Then more cheerfully to Peter Taylor who is planning three trips for the winter, dreaming of renting or even buying as many houses, but who writes jokingly, "never in my life could I imagine being alive six months in the future . . . now less than ever."

I fear I've confused you again about teaching. I've written Perkins that I will again teach poetry-writing and 19th century English poetry. I am grateful to your tact in teaching prose instead of poetry, but it's [a] gesture I should have made. Could I? Years ago, I had [an] anthology made by Malcolm Cowley that printed key chapters of novels. I usually knew the whole novels and often the students didn't. I found fiction much easier to talk about, and it drew so much more talk from the students. Teaching Shakespeare was much the same. The Bible, however, turned my small seminar into mutes. But I've never tried to teach people to actually write prose.

We've just put Milgate on the market, not expecting any acceptable offers for some time. Unless the imaginary golf course grabs us for a casino. The living expenses have doubled in a year, and it's more than we can safely carry. Our sketchy plan is to buy something smaller, as expensive to buy but less to run, somewhere near Oxford. It's all very sad and only fragmentarily imaginable.

Caroline is fixedly finishing a third book, two longish stories, and a third much longer—and this is the catch—on a seemingly trivial visit to a desolating great-grandmother when she was ten. Though once finished, it is now growing and growing, in piles of longhand notebooks—absorbing more and more daughters, grand-daughters grandsons, mostly with tragic lives . . . withered but often more interesting branches of the great-grandmother. Typing it out in order is like rebuilding a house. Even the size is uncertain.

My book is done. It's the opposite of yours, bulky, rearranged, added-to, deleted two months after submission—as though the unsatiated appetite were demanding a solid extra course when dinner was meant to be over. I have no more to say . . . of course. Yet after reading Wilbur I found myself musing in iambics, not meaning to. I spent days even trying rhyme—it was no marriage, rather more like parody, but fascinating. So fascinating, that after a while one would gladly ruin a poem just to complete the exercise.

We had a dreadfully pedestrian international PEN club meeting here—"The truth of the imagination." All middle-aged people who have published two books but can't write, can't talk, but want to talk or at least hear people who can't talk talk. The intoxicating thing about rhyme and meter is that they having nothing at all to do with truth, just as ballet steps are of no use on a hike. They are puzzles, hurdles, obstacles, expertise—they cry out for invention, and of course in the end for truth, whatever that is. It's queer though,

Lawrence's "Figs" is de gustibus as true and surprising as Herbert's "Affliction." But the task of composition is different. No more. I think Frank has had a hard, surprisingly lonely summer. Best to Alice. Caroline sitting on her heels on the floor. Staring, sorting, scribbling on more than ten [piles] of script and typescript to finish before flighttime. Ivana and Sheridan and the nanny have gone off to a movie about a car without a driver, more or less engaging to three different ages. The drama of the PEN club was frequently seeing and hearing Lizzie. It couldn't have gone off more happily, . . . but the immanent sorrow.

684. To Fanny Howe

October 30, 1976

Dearest Fanny—

It was weird, almost murky, coming home from the hospital and reading through a month's mail and find your letter—it's almost prehistory since our last communication, a disturbing telephone call from Carl . . . he spoke of the decadent Gowrie set to which I belonged. Later I wrote a sonnet on assassination, but it was about *Les enfants de paradis*. Then to hear Skimper's voice from your house.

I'll be in Cambridge this weekend, staying with my friend, Frank Bidart. Does the name ring a bell from my old writing classes? You must know a good deal about Caroline and her panic at my coming. Fortunately she is delighted to have me stay near but not with her. She has been partly sick from overdrinking for many months. She can make marvelous changes. Like you, she is fond of straightforward shocking prose. I liked what you wrote in *Agenda*. We must get in touch and you must meet Caroline.

affectionately,
Cal

This letter is more breezy than I feel—it's all very terrible but very hopeful.

685. To Frank Bidart

[63 Sparks Street, Cambridge, Mass., n.d. Fall 1976]

Dear Frank—

I'm spending the night with Caroline. Be back in the morning. Have keys.
Cal

686. To Elizabeth Hardwick

[Milgate Park, Bearsted, Maidstone, Kent]
January 11, 1977

Dear Lizzie:

To thank you for so much kindness during my time in America—everything has been much quieter here. The great headache is how and where to move from England before the new tax laws which cut unearned incomes to nothing, or so it seems. A rather undemocratic necessity. I wonder if we haven't all been unconscious secret capitalists for years. The real trouble of course is where to take or put the children. Nothing can be done until it is.

We spend our time writing. I am more than half way through the Eumenides working from translations. Terrible the Aeschylean translator's hackneyed grand rhetoric—it keeps smearing to my version. With luck I'll have the whole *Oresteia* ready to be acted late spring in New York. The best translations I've seen are Yeats' Oedipus and Pound's Sophocles, an odd mixture of early Pound and Browning. Most [of] the important poetry in the world, plays in particular, has never been done into English and perhaps never will now.

I must tell you later about our Christmas with the Mostyn-Owens—the Wests, seven children, seven hour train trips and seven hour dinners.

My socialist-anarchist earned income half-person will be at Harvard by the first of February with a room or rooms in Dunster House.

Aunt Sarah has told Jackie she wants to see me, and I realize how much I've wanted this too. Jackie says she is so absent-minded she may forget.

How is Harriet's job-hunting? Natalya is doing more or less the same, but is now seriously trying to get into college and pass O-levels. Genia lives in a world of rapidly changing holiday romance. Ivana is still a little girl doing charades, collecting dolls and wanting to become a professional actress. Sheridan is a force ~~embodied~~ in person.

See you soon,

love,

Cal

PS. Tell Bob that reviewing Elizabeth is too much for many reasons—and on top rushing Aeschylus to a deadline in March.

687. To Caroline Blackwood

[63 Sparks Street, Cambridge, Mass.]
Jan 31, 1977

Dearest Dolph:

This morning I move to Dunster House, an old student among the stu-
dents. I am a little apprehensive. It's about 10 above zero now.

—shortwindedness, not only when climbing steep stairs, but sometimes
when merely sitting, a feeling one can never draw enough breath. I sleep sit-
ting up,—good for breathing, bad for sleep. I've been to the college infirmary,
and will have more exhaustive examinations this morning. No diagnosis ex-
cept it's not anemia or asthma. However there's no question but that there's
something 'objective' and physical the matter. One of those temporary, soon
healed things that affect adolescence—so I trust.

Do you think we had better settle in America, and maybe here rather
[than] in Ireland?

688. To Caroline Blackwood

Feb 10, 1977

[Estate agent—Redding—$250,000]

There don't seem to be enormous cheap houses.

The hospital business, despite the usual rough useless and dramatic ambu-
lance at McLean's, was painless eventless; perhaps what death might be at
best. A feeling that one was doomed like Ivan Illich, but without suffering.
Then there seemed to be no danger at all,—except that there may still be—
but all so quiet it hardly seemed to matter. Death where is thy sting? But it
couldn't be heard? . . . If that's all life is, it's a coldly smiling anticlimax—
gone the great apocalypse of departure.

689. To Caroline Blackwood

[Dunster House, Harvard University, Cambridge, Mass.]
Feb 12 [1977]

My first day in residence

I don't think I've ever been so on my own, so firmly pinned down to
emptiness.

The mind goes numb grading through about thirty student papers. The body goes numb in its little room, too enervated to read through Anna Karenina as one resolved.

In heart-hospitalization . . .

690. *To Bishop Maurice Schexnayder*

February 13, 1977

Dear Father (bishop) Schexnayder:

I always think of you as father, a humbler more authoritative title. I knew nothing about your elevation, or dreamed of it, though now it seems right and inevitable. Only your retirement seems wrong, but that comes to all.

Last week I was in the hospital with water in my lungs and some damage to the heart's muscle. I think I was in the very room my grandfather had shortly before his death forty years ago—three before I met you. Now all's well, but for a day or two I seemed to lie under a ~~very~~ low gray ceiling.

I remember well your long patient explanations to me of catechism. The books we discussed, I still have. You were a road over a dark stream.

A year or so after leaving Louisiana, I turned out to be a poet, and so it continued. All my thanks and best wishes to you.

Sincerely yours,
Robert Lowell

691. *To J. D. McClatchy*

February 13, 1977

Dear Mr. McClatchy:

Many thanks for your grand review, itself it would seem longer than all I've written. My book to be a selection had to give an impression of much having been left out—much that a kindly critical judge might want to retain—not just trash and verbiage. Still I feel I have written too much. I can't help it, and can't stop. If I had ground down as perhaps I should have, I would only perhaps have three books, themselves defective and not altogether my best. A selection however doesn't abolish. At the last minute I suggested putting "91 Revere St." in. I think I still accept Jarrell's adverse criticism of the *Mills*. It

was meant to do more or less what you say—but with such wordiness and contortion.

I suppose anyone except an academic would say that Browning's *Ring and the Book* is unreadably long, yet it might be claimed that any cut would mar . . . It's ecstatic for once not to have too much, even if some silver is lost.

I mustn't run on. Thanks again for your defense of the *Dolphin*. I very much hope we can meet, while I am still in America. It looks now as if we were partly moving back. Look forward to your confessional book and Anne Sexton.

Yours sincerely,
 Robert Lowell

692. To Caroline Blackwood

Feb 27 [1977]

I am back from New York, having read with Allen Ginsberg, been heckled by Corso (not calamitous)

693. To Caroline Blackwood

Feb 28 1977

Ireland—I only make abt. ten thousand now teaching. Do readings & prizes deduct? How long will your income not be taxable? When will you be able to be with me in this country?

I should tell you about the hospital, though it is a tame story—that's the point. After my cardiograph came out irregular, I wavered a long moment, then was practically handcuffed in a sort of sitting up stretcher, bounced down a stairless gangway (all this was in McLean's) then banged in an ambulance to Mass. General. More waits, while I absorbed the imaginable seriousness of my condition. Death? Ivan Illich? But there was no pain at all, and it seemed to me that death would be nothing. What gentler thing could one ask for, except, though painless, it had absolutely no meaning, no long ~~expected~~ private message. Of course, I was soon reassured, when new drugs I had already been given at McLean's removed the drama.

[lungs filled with water because heart can't squeeze enough]

694. To Caroline Blackwood

What strikes me in this order is the teenager flat, the likeness to the Louvre, (a vague feeling that one will live there as old royal Louvre pensioners[)], and the nearness of the Liffy.

. . .

But it has taken away a huge, undefined vagueness, my only way since I left of imagining our future—an infinite stairway of Dunster House cafeteria dining halls.

[Birthday in New York—given a laurel wreath by Harriet & Lizzie]

I've written or rather finished five poems since arriving—mostly chaste subjects like the hospital. I never want to be in Dunster House without you. Ever.

All my love
 Cal.

695. To Caroline Blackwood

March 17, 1977]

I've [been] thinking all the time, reimpassioned old poems to you, and also waiting for a letter.

I love you so much and I wish I could do everything for you. What did you mean on the phone when you said I had nearly lost you? I am excited about the house. But do you really want me back? Sometimes you sound indifferent. I'm not, though my voice may sound low and subdued coming from so far.

696. To Caroline Blackwood

[n.d. Spring 1977]

I have written a minor *Union Dead* fifteen years idler—fatigued, bright and elegiac.

Even though I see many people, I'm mostly to myself a prey to [] scattered reflections—that try to get into poems

697. To Caroline Blackwood

April 14, 1977

I don't know what to say, our problems have become so many-headed and in-superable. Nothing like the sunshine of the years we had together—when it shone, as so often—so blindingly.

. . .

The plane trip wasn't too bad; I immediately took two dramamines and slept four hours, then another long sleep after dinner.

698. To Caroline Blackwood

April 19, 1977

Us? Aren't we too heady and dangerous for each other? I love you, am more dazzled by you, than anyone I've known, but can't I be your constant visitor? Then there will be no wrinkles to steam-iron out. Ireland seems so far from home and help . . . who and what I know, though a kind of paradise to come to with you and Sheridan and all the girls there, and the big winey dinner in big rotting house.

699. To Caroline Blackwood

April 22, 1977

[C. need psych. in Ireland]
Maybe now I am away and the stress is less, you won't need a doctor at all.
. . .
I got a medal from Brandeis.
I have an invitation to go to Russia with all the great American novelists Bellow, Updike, Vonnegut, Cheever.
[June 28 for 10 days]
And us? I really feel too weak and battered by it all. I fear I do you more harm than good. I think your blackness would pass if you didn't live in fear of manic attacks. And they don't seem curable—almost thirty years. How's that for persistence? I miss you sorely.

700. To Caroline Blackwood

April 30, 1977

(Off to Southern reading tour—Knoxville, Charlottesville till 19th May)

How is Sheridan? People are rather taken aback when I tell them about the burnt-cork Hitler moustache . . . However television is the source of all dreams.

[In Ireland] . . . in a way you are nearer to neighbors and a part of your past. But how lonely and dark it might become. But of course I know nothing about what is going on in your heart.

701. To Caroline Blackwood

[May 3, 1977]

Dearest—

I'm writing about three or four hours after your call—in great confusion, not knowing how or what to say. I am afraid of your visit, because I am afraid nothing will be done except causing pain. How many lovely moments, weeks, months, we had. Sunday I sat by the Charles River watching the strollers, the joggers, the sunners—and the river. And I seemed to follow it back through our seven years, the great multitude of restaurants, the moment when everyone was in the bathroom when I bathed, the long summer of your swelling pregnancy, the rush to London, the little red man's appearance—or earlier trapped in All Souls, and a thousand things more. But the last two years have been terrifying for us both—and neither of us have made it any better for the other. It hasn't been a quarrel, but two eruptions, two earthquakes crashing.

Well, we should talk . . . always. I really can't do anything till June in New York or the end of May here, or I could visit Ireland mid- or later summer. I feel you ended things during my Irish visit, ended them wisely and we can't go back. I have had so much dread—the worst in my life—that I would do something, by my mere presence I would do something to hurt you, to drive you to despair. Who knows cause . . .

702. To Caroline Blackwood

[15 West 67th Street, New York, N.Y. n.d. late May? 1977]

Strange unfamiliar small type. It's so hard to explain things. I've been completely rattled by the last year and a half or so—dreading what might happen

and almost dreading more my inability to do anything. Here in my own country I really have much more to lean on, more friends, chances to make money etc.

Life can never be as good as it was with us. It's wonderful news that you haven't been drinking much. I haven't been drinking very much but more than I should. I am trying to follow your example.

. . .

Coming directly from Russia to Ireland would crack my summer in two— the best part is going to Maine and escaping the urban whirl of Cambridge and New York. I do love you—two eggs colliding.

P.S. I'm told I mustn't let anyone call me Cal in Russia because it means something like dogshithead.

703. *To the Editors,* New York Review of Books

[n.d. late May? 1977]
In response to "The Hard Case of Yeats" (May 26, 1977)

"Hence, as Robert Lowell has asserted, Yeats couldn't see anything" (*NYR*, May 26).

Why should one blind man say this about another? I suppose such a patronizing phrase might slip from one's tongue in conversation or in an interview. However Denis Donoghue has a gift for isolating, slanting, and distorting when he paraphrases—often to make an unfair point, strangled in a web of qualification. In a short poem of mine called "Truth," I have a half fictitious British poet, hostile to Yeats, say, "He had bad eyes, saw nothing." Dare I say in this place that Yeats saw beyond the reviewer?

Robert Lowell
New York City

704. *To Caroline Blackwood*

May 29, 1977
[—chatty, impersonal—seeing Brodsky next night]

I am trying to find a genuine *Mein Kampf* with a young photograph of Hitler to checkmate Sheridan.

. . .

I miss my rash gallant fish and feel doubly a bad father.

705. To Alfred Corn

June 8, 1977

Dear Alfred Corn:

Rather overwhelmed by your ~~letter~~ cher maître, and the evening ran on gaily . . . very. Now of your poems, I'd roughly say the Darwin one is the best. It has the most variety of voice, humanity keeps breaking in etc. It's usually fascinating to attend. The others are made up almost entirely of strong lines—too strong because they tend to cancel each other out; the powerful rhythms steamroller (though this is much too strong a word) the meaning, the feeling. I've lifelong been bothered by this problem, and am oversensitive to it. Yet as you go on, I think you will more try to vary your eloquence—as you do in Darwin and elsewhere. It's a good fortune to have such a fine sword to bend and rumple. (What a figure!)

The reviews—I belong to an older more myopic to the new generation. Ashbery is always rather astounding for the carpentry of his lines. You wonder at a loss how he will finish each sentence. And he does. Yet the pressure makes him wearisome reading except in a few clear poems. As I think you suggest in saying form and content can't [be] boiled to form or a particularly ingenious rhetoric. Even the very great Valéry has too little content, as compared to Baudelaire, except in his very great poems. Eliot suggest[s] that much of his prose is more readable because written with more passion.[. . .]

I look forward to many more evenings with you and Sandy and Frank.

Yours, gratefully,

706. To Caroline Blackwood

June 24, 1977

[leaving for Russia] in almost a matter of minutes.

Awful about Sheridan. Did you jump in fully clothed? It's so hard to maneuver, and someone drowning is so hard for the unexpert to help. You can drown yourself. I trust he is safe now & recovered from the shock.

I feel almost suicidal when I think how I have failed you—little person. We'll meet in September. You and God willing.

707. To Caroline Blackwood

[Castine, Maine]
July 17, 1977

I feel broken by all conversation, and a voice inside me says all might be well if I could be with you. And another voice says all would be ruin, and that I would be drowned in the confusion I made worse. If I were to get sick in Ireland? But here it all can be handled. But it's the effect my troubles have on you. It's like a nightmare we all have in which each motion of foot or hand troubles the torment it tries to calm.

. . .

I'm sending Sheridan a card, & have another. Castine sights when Russia is exhausted. Hitler cards are unattainable.

708. To Steven Axelrod

July 27, 1977

Dear Stephen Axelrod:

Thank you for your careful, sympathetic piece, the longest *Dolphin* has had, and I think the closest to my intentions. The counterpoint about introspection and art speculation was chance[,] probably from having to speculate so much in *History*. Or is it merely that in age one speculates as naturally as growing gray hair? I'd like to be entirely concrete, but the stream of impulse runs differently.

My new book *Day by Day* comes out in August. It [is] longer, written in free verse, yet carries on the old story. I fear it comes close to tragic, though that's not clear either in the book or life. When I get back to New York in late September I'll have my publishers send you a copy. I'll be interested in what impression it makes on you, and whether it disrupts or confirms your interpretation of *Dolphin*. I've reached a dry or vacation moment in writing poetry and am collecting my old prose.

By the way the opening poems in *Dolphin* were written on a very bad typewriter and under heavy thorozine. Of course, they were doggedly rewritten later, but retain the confusion of their circumstance.

Again let me thank you, as so often, for your kind criticism. Look forward very much to your book.

Yours as always,
Robert Lowell

709. To Caroline Blackwood

[n.d. Summer 1977]

I talked to Bingo who said you were fine; but Natalya didn't say you were fine but were on the verge of tears all day. And needed a rest. You are always with me—deep and in rapid images.

710. To Caroline Blackwood

[n.d. August 1977]

[12 Noon Aer Lingus 1 Sept.]

I haven't quite lost my muse. Isn't she a presence, like God, and not like Robert Graves' young girls? I had an old piece of prose—about Maine for a page or so, and then giving a series of vignettes: Cotton Mather, Ben Franklin, Emerson, Hawthorne, Thoreau, Lincoln, Wallace Stevens, Santayana—almost all New England, and worthies. I've got 19 pages and at worst as many again to write. Because I'm working on it, I think it my best critical prose.

711. To Caroline Blackwood

[Castletown House, Celbridge, Ireland, September 9? 1977]

I spent until about two with Sheridan. We had a merry amiable time except that he (wisely) preferred people to swans and a rubber-tyre swing to people.

Notes

Lowell's Addresses

Locations of Letters and Manuscripts

Selected Bibliography

Acknowledgments

Index

Notes

This edition is edited with a view to the general reader and the student. I have tried where possible to identify people, historical events, and literary allusions. Lowell had a highly social imagination and a mind that delighted in making connections between texts and people. He read voraciously. The notes are not exhaustive (Lowell often provides an adequate identification or explanation himself), but they attempt to give texture to some of his remarks and to help the reader gain a general understanding of his world.

Lowell learned that he was manic depressive in 1949 after his first acute manic episode. I have indicated which letters were written during this episode and ones that followed. Acute mania is characterized by "euphoria, grandiose thought, rapid speech expressing loosely connected thoughts (flight of ideas), decreased need for sleep, increased physical activity, and sometimes delusions or hallucinations" (*Oxford English Dictionary*). However, Lowell went through mildly manic (hypomanic) cycles before 1949 (in 1957, he retrospectively called his 1943 letter to President Roosevelt a "manic statement"). Also, not every manic episode Lowell experienced after 1949 resulted in psychosis and the need for hospitalization. Some letters appear to have been written in mildly manic states, in which he experienced many symptoms of mania (gradiosity, loss of judgment, irritability, dissociation, volubility) but did not become profoundly delusional or psychotic. However, I have only found it appropriate to indicate mildly manic letters rarely, when evidence from the biographies and the letters justify doing so.

From the first letter, Lowell's correspondence is saturated with events, images, and phrases that occur in his poetry; to mark each instance would require an extra volume of notes. I have therefore identified only direct references to Lowell's poems and prose. The discovery of correspondences with his work I leave to the reader's pleasure.

The titles of Lowell's books referred to are abbreviated as follows:

LOU	*Land of Unlikeness* (1944)	N70	*Notebook* (1970)
LWC	*Lord Weary's Castle* (1946)	HIS	*History* (1973)
P50	*Poems 1938–1949* (1950)	FLH	*For Lizzie and Harriet* (1973)
MK	*The Mills of the Kavanaughs* (1951)	DOL	*The Dolphin* (1973)
LS	*Life Studies* (1959)	SP76	*Selected Poems* (1976)
IM	*Imitations* (1961)	SP77	*Selected Poems* (revised) (1977)
FTUD	*For the Union Dead* (1964)	DBD	*Day by Day* (1977)
NTO	*Near the Ocean* (1967)	CPR	*Collected Prose* (1987)
N67–68	*Notebook 1967–68* (1969)	CPM	*Collected Poems* (2003)

1. To Ezra Pound

Letters 1 and 2 were published in the *Yale Review*, January 1999, 54–62. Lowell enclosed "Madonna," "The Earth," and "part of a chaotic long poem called *Jerusalem*, on the 1ˢᵗ Crusade."

Amy Lowell: American poet (1874–1925).

turtles: See letter 434.

translation: See "The *Iliad*," *Vindex*, St. Mark's School, June 1935, reprinted in *CPR*, 145–51.

Eberhart: Richard Ghormley Eberhart (b. 1904) taught at St. Mark's School in Southborough, Massachusetts. Lowell never took a class with him, but they discussed poetry and he gave Lowell and his friends lists of books to read (he had studied with F. R. Leavis, Gilbert Murray, and I. A. Richards at Cambridge at the same time as William Empson). They sometimes called him Cousin Ghormley.

2. To Ezra Pound

mediating on: meditating on?

Ear, ear for the sea-surge . . . : Pound, *A Draft of XXX Cantos* (1935); canto 7, lines 5–6.

With hollow shriek . . . : Milton, "On the Morning of Christ's Nativity," line 178.

"Near Perigord": Pound, "Near Perigord," *Lustra of Ezra Pound* (1916; 1917 American edition).

nor can Her heart . . . : Shakespeare, *Antony and Cleopatra*, 3.2. 47–50.

Eliot's "Ariel" poems: Eliot, *Collected Poems 1919–1935* (1936).

Relatives . . . : Pound's reply has been lost. His attitude to a young relative of Amy Lowell and James Russell Lowell might be guessed from a letter Merrill Moore wrote to Pound in 1938: "I think your letter is swell, but you've got me wrong. I don't mean to give you the impression that Robert T. S. Lowell (known to his friends as Cal) is anything like (in personality and so forth) the ones who have gone before. . . . Cal Lowell is no hooey" (quoted in Mariani, *Lost Puritan*, 68). Pound may have written to Lowell a second time at Moore's suggestion when he was at Kenyon; see "For Peter Taylor I," *HIS*, and letter 659. Pound later changed his mind. In the late 1950s, he said to Harry Meacham: "I had thought I had done with Lowells after Amy, but Robert came to see me several times. He is probably the best poet and the best human value in the U.S." (Meacham, 66).

3. To Frank Parker

Francis S. Parker (b. 1916), American painter; he is referred to throughout Lowell's letters as Frank.

Madaket: For two summers in a row, Lowell stayed in a small house near the Madaket Coast Guard station on Nantucket Island with his best friends, reading, writing, and studying in a disciplined manner. Having survived one such summer already, Parker delayed his arrival in 1936, preferring Ipswich and, perhaps, less of Lowell's rigor, while Lowell and Blair Clark set up house together.

Blair: Blair Clark (1917–2000), journalist and editor. Clark recalled that Lowell "made me read all the minor Elizabethan playwrights. . . . He assigned himself Shakespeare, Milton, Homer . . . and the English lyric poets" ("On Robert Lowell," *Harvard Advocate*, November 1979, reprinted in Meyers, 255–56). Clark also remembered the cuisine: "We had dreadful health food all the time. The diet was eels—cooked by me, badly—and a dreadful cereal called Beckie's Puddy and raw honey. All decided by Cal" (Ian Hamilton, 24).

Anne: Lowell and Anne Dick started to date in the spring of 1936. See Ian Hamilton, 30–34.

Sunswick: Summer house in Ipswich, Massachusetts, that belonged to Anne Dick's grandmother.

My indirect work with her: Anne Dick recalled that after the engagement "came the letters. The instructions for me to work, first on *Troilus and Cressida*. So I would go into my grandfather's study and I would write about *Troilus and Cressida*. . . . And my grandmother, who still didn't

know anything, would come banging on the door and say, 'All the biggest men'—that's what she called psychiatrists, she didn't know the word—'All the biggest men say that studying is the worst thing for the mind.' . . . But I had to study because my fiancé wanted me to study" (Ian Hamilton Notebooks, British Library). See also Ian Hamilton, 32.

Bobo: A nickname for Blair Clark.

think on those things: Cf. Matthew 1:20 and Philippians 4:8.

Grolier: A poetry bookshop in Cambridge, Massachusetts.

Cal: Lowell's nickname. See letter 77.

4. To Anne Dick

Printed in the *Harvard Advocate*, November 1977. Few of Lowell's letters to Anne Dick survive. William Alfred copied this fragment from the original, the location of which is unknown.

6. To Charlotte Winslow Lowell and Robert T. S. Lowell

your stand: Lowell's parents disapproved of his engagement to Anne Dick and his impatience with Harvard (Ian Hamilton, 39). As a crisis brewed, Charlotte Lowell forwarded most of his letters to her psychiatrist, Merrill Moore. Many of Lowell's letters to his parents survive only in typed transcriptions from Dr. Moore's files at the University of Texas, including this one.

Elmer Bright's: Lowell's father worked at the Elmer H. Bright & Co. brokerage firm on State Street in Boston.

John Parker: Frank Parker's father.

7. To Richard Eberhart

Several letters to Richard Eberhart that Ian Hamilton read at the Dartmouth College Library have not been located. This transcription is copied from Ian Hamilton's Notebooks in the British Library.

Your "Alphabet": Eberhart, "Alphabet Book," *Transition* (June 1936).

your book: *Reading the Spirit.*

your novel: Eberhart never published his novel.

McCreary: Possibly Frederick R. McCreary, friend of Amy Lowell (see Robert Lowell Papers, Harvard, bMS Am 1905/802).

8. To Charlotte Winslow Lowell

Charlotte Lowell wrote "*This is not true*" across the top of this letter before sending it to Merrill Moore.

Rock: Arthur Winslow's summer house near Mattapoisett, Massachusetts.

Gaga and Aunt Sarah: Mary Devereux Winslow, Lowell's maternal grandmother; Sarah Winslow (later Cotting), Lowell's aunt.

Cinder: In Lowell's autobiographical prose, Cinder is the Airedale (Harvard); in "My Last Afternoon with Uncle Devereux Winslow" (*LS*), he is "our Scottie puppy/paralyzed from gobbling toads."

9. To Robert T. S. Lowell

churning about: In December 1936, Lowell's parents tried to end his engagement to Anne Dick. His father accused Anne of "visiting Lowell in his rooms at Harvard, unchaperoned. That same evening Mr. Lowell followed up his lecture with a note: '. . . Such behavior is contrary to

all college rules, and most improper for a girl of good repute'" (Ian Hamilton, 39). Anne passed the note to Lowell, who drove home and hit his father, knocking him to the floor. See letter 483.

10. To Sarah Winslow

I don't know how to sign myself: Lowell was called "Bobby" by his family. In his youth, he sometimes signed his letters "Cal" rebelliously; in this instance, however, "Cal" was presumably a friendly and intimate gesture. When he grew older, he reverted to "Bobby" when writing to Aunt Sarah, his mother, and other female members of his family.

11. To Anne Dick

The trip: To ease family tensions, Merrill Moore suggested that Lowell accompany him to Tennessee to meet John Crowe Ransom, Allen Tate, and other writers of the Southern Fugitives group. Lowell could finish the semester taking Ransom's classes at Vanderbilt University, and instead of spending another summer on Nantucket—he admitted to his parents that "the only flaw [was] a slight inadequacy in the cooking"—he could attend two writers' conferences (RL, "A draft on *what I am trying to do,*" Merrill Moore files, Harry Ransom Humanities Center, University of Texas, "received Wed., March 17, 1937"). He wrote to Anne Dick en route to Tennessee.

Miss Rogers: Possibly a secretary in Moore's office. Moore sometimes allowed his assistants to treat patients (see Ian Hamilton, 47).

Tate: Allen Tate (1899–1979), American poet. See "Visiting the Tates," *CPR*, 59.

Norman: Norman Johnson, a Harvard classmate.

Granny: Anne Dick's grandmother.

12. To Norman Johnson

His wife: Caroline Gordon (1895–1981), American novelist.

Mr. Ransom: John Crowe Ransom (1888–1974), American poet and critic, taught at Vanderbilt University until 1937, when he joined the faculty at Kenyon College. See "John Crowe Ransom," *CPR*, 22.

Brown: Harry Brown (1917–86), American novelist and screenplaywright; Lowell met him as an undergraduate at Harvard. Of Lowell's student friends, Brown had the earliest success. He published two books of poetry with New Directions during the war.

13. To Richard Eberhart

Original not located; this edition reproduces Ian Hamilton's transcription in the British Library, including his bracketed summaries, remarks, and omissions.

Ford: Ford Madox Ford (1873–1939), English novelist and critic.

Mrs. Ford: When Lowell met Ford Madox Ford, his companion was Janice Biala (1903–2002), Polish American painter.

her sister in law: Wally Tworkov.

Rossetti: Christina Rossetti (1830–94), English poet.

the ideograph: See Ernest Fenollosa, *The Chinese Written Character as a Medium for Poetry* (1919).

Jarrell: Randall Jarrell (1914–65), American poet and critic.

no doubt: "This interim between Harvard and the writers schools has convinced me more than ever that my vocation is writing, and that if I should fail that I should certainly fail in anything

else: fail to make good and fail to gain happiness" (RL to Charlotte Winslow Lowell, June 5, 1937, Harvard).

14. To Charlotte Winslow Lowell
secretary to Mr. Ford: Ford was writing *The March of Literature* (1938).
Bill: Blair Clark's brother.

15. To Anne Dick
sorry: Lowell and Dick drifted apart during his long absence and they ended their engagement. Only a fragment of this letter survives.
"horrentia Martis": Mars' bristling [arms]; from an editor's prelude to a first-century edition of *The Aeneid*, line 4 (courtesy Warren Myers).

16. To Frank Parker
Cousin Lawrence: A. Lawrence Lowell (1856–1943), president of Harvard, brother of Amy Lowell and Percival Lowell; Robert Lowell's distant cousin.
"la plus belle de la monde": *King Henry V* 5.2.210, slightly misquoted.
Chirico: Giorgio de Chirico (1888–1978), Italian painter, lived in New York from 1935 to 1938.
printed envelope: Lowell's Kenyon address is engraved on the envelope.

17. To Richard Eberhart
Ian Hamilton transcription.

18. To Merrill Moore
Mr. Jeffers: Probably Robinson Jeffers (1887–1962), American poet. "I've been reading . . . an Oxford American Literature compiled in the late thirties, and full of names, now rather fading: Sandburg, Jeffers, Lola Rudge, MacLeish. . . . Jeffers, a sort of country cousin to Eliot in his pessimism, is almost a great poet. I wouldn't like to be that dark, though no doubt I am" (RL to Elizabeth Bishop, August 16, 1965, Vassar).
H. D.: Pen name of Hilda Doolittle (1886–1961), American modernist poet.

19. To Arthur Winslow
Phillips House: Private wing of Massachusetts General Hospital.
get better: Arthur Winslow was dying of cancer.

20. To Robert T. S. Lowell
Santee: Frederick Santee, Lowell's classics professor, "lived across the street from Douglass House. He was a brilliant man. I think he graduated from Harvard at 14. He'd been a prodigy and was very eccentric. He was a very sweet man and gave his time entirely to his students" (Peter Taylor interview, Ian Hamilton Notebooks, British Library). See also *CPR*, 22.
poems: "The Cities' Summer Death" and "The Dandelion Girls," *Kenyon Review*, Winter 1939.
essay in this issue: His review of John Crowe Ransom's *The World's Body* was published by *Hika:*

An Undergraduate Journal of Arts & Letters in October 1938; see Ian Hamilton, 59. David Mc-Dowell was a *Hika* staff member and a fellow Douglass House resident.

remembered me: Lowell met Frost in his freshman year at Harvard in 1935. "I'd gone to call on Frost with a huge epic on the First Crusade, all written out in clumsy longhand on lined paper. He read a page of that and said, 'You have no compression.' Then he read me a very short poem of Collins, 'How Sleep the Brave,' and said, 'That's not a great poem, but it's not too long'" (Meyers, 64; see also "Robert Frost," *CPR*, 8–11).

Cousin Alfred: Alfred Lowell, a cousin who helped manage the Lowell trusts.

21. To Merrill Moore

trial: Lowell met Jean Stafford at a writers' conference in Boulder in the summer of 1937. During the 1938 Christmas vacation, he took her to a nightclub in Boston. Driving home, he turned on a dead-end lane and drove into a wall. Stafford's face hit the windshield. She spent a month recuperating at Mount Auburn Hospital, then endured five operations over the spring and summer to reconstruct her nose and cheek. Lowell was fined $50 for "driving an automobile while under the influence of liquor" and $25 for driving to endanger; his license was also revoked (*Seattle Times*, December 29, 1938; Ian Hamilton, 62–63). Stafford and Lowell agreed that she should sue the Lowells' insurance company to cover her medical bills. Although they were forbidden to see each other on the advice of their lawyers, they continued to meet ("and had a glorious affair," Ian Hamilton, 80). Against Lowell's wishes, his parents decided to fight Stafford's suit. They went to Europe in the summer of 1939 to avoid the trial, leaving it to their lawyers, and gave Merrill Moore power of attorney over Lowell's finances while they were abroad. See Ian Hamilton, 60–67.

Starr: Lowell met Milton Starr through Merrill Moore in Nashville in 1937 (see Ian Hamilton, 47). Milton Starr was associated with the Fugitives through his brother Alfred; he was also a friend of Randall Jarrell's. See Pritchard, 27.

the rights of the Jews: "The rights [of Jews] have got to be maintained. Milton Starr is doing a great deal towards this by contributions to the refugees and by his help to individuals" (Moore to RL, July 11, 1939, copy at the British Library).

22. To Charlotte Winslow Lowell

Copy transcribed by Charlotte Lowell; she wrote "This made Bob see red" across the top.

about Jean's accident: After two trials, Stafford was awarded $4,000. She and Lowell were engaged at the end of 1939.

23. To A. Lawrence Lowell

sensuous, passionate . . . Milton, *Of Education* (1644); cf. RL to Stephen Spender, October 19, 1959, letter. President Lowell replied: "For you, not yet! not yet! . . . Dr. Moore thinks you had better not come back to Harvard at present, and I suspect that in this he is wise" (Ian Hamilton, 70).

24. To Charlotte Winslow Lowell

Chilton Club: Exclusive women's club in Boston.

forced marriage: Stafford and Lowell were married on April 2, 1940, at St. Mark's in the Bowery in New York City. Neither Stafford's nor Lowell's parents attended. Allen Tate gave Stafford away and Blair Clark was best man.

my ways are not your ways: Isaiah 55:8.

25. To Charlotte Winslow Lowell and Robert T.S. Lowell

valedictorian: Lowell's graduation speech was published in *Hika*, October 1940, reprinted in *Hika: Fiftieth Anniversary*, Winter 1985. A copy is at Harvard (bMS Am 1905/2792).

27. To Robie Macauley

Robie Macauley (1919–95), American novelist, editor, and CIA agent, befriended Lowell and Peter Taylor at Kenyon.

Kitty Rice: The wife of Philip Blair Rice, a philosophy professor at Kenyon.

Nerber: John Nerber, author of *The Specter Image* (1944), was "tall, blond, and very handsome[;] he wore 'strange, poetic clothing,' and, as Jack Thompson quipped, 'You couldn't get a straight story out of him about anything.' Nerber never graduated, drifted to New York . . . and died an early death" (McAlexander, 50–51). See also *CPR*, 21–22.

Brooks and Warren: Cleanth Brooks (1906–94), American critic, was coeditor of the *Southern Review* from 1935 to 1942 with Robert Penn Warren and Charles W. Pipkin; Robert Penn Warren (1905–89), American poet and novelist. "I must take this opportunity to tell you what I have told many other people: you were the best teacher I ever had, and that I hardly knew what poems and stories meant before I met you" (RL to Warren, 4/8 [1946], Yale).

hell and damnation poem: A poem that became "Dead Briton's Vision," never published; see RL to John Crowe Ransom, July 10, 1944, letter.

Peter: Peter Taylor (1917–94), American prose writer; he was Lowell's roommate at Kenyon.

Virginia Jett: A former girlfriend of Peter Taylor's (McAlexander, 62).

Peter's story: Taylor, "A Spinster's Tale," *Southern Review*, Autumn 1940.

29. To Peter Taylor

Middleton Murry: John Middleton Murry (1889–1957), English journalist and critic.

Communion: Lowell was baptized by Father Maurice Schexnayder and received into the Catholic Church on March 29, 1941.

Philip and Bartholomew: The feast of St. Philip the apostle and James the Less is May 3; the feast of St. Bartholomew is August 24.

Philippe, qui videt me, videt et Patrem meum: "Philip, he that hath seen Me hath seen the Father" (John 14:9).

consumption: A doctor found a spot on Stafford's lung.

31. To Charlotte Winslow Lowell

Typewriters: First typed letter.

32. To Peter Taylor

The correspondence nearly ended . . . : See Hopkins to Robert Bridges, January 19, 1879, *The Letters of Gerard Manley Hopkins to Robert Bridges*, ed. Claude Colleer Abbott (1935), 60–61.

33. To Violet Otis Parker

Monteagle: Lowell and Stafford shared a house with Tate and Gordon in Monteagle for the winter.

Frank's disappearance: Parker, serving with the Canadian Black Watch, disappeared in August 1942 during the Dieppe raid; it later emerged that he had been taken prisoner.

John's letter: Parker's brother John (Jr.); their father was killed serving with the British Navel Reserve in 1941.

35. To Charlotte Winslow Lowell and Robert T. S. Lowell

Probably written while mildly manic.

my poem on Granpa: "Death from Cancer on Easter" (part 1 of "In Memory of Arthur Winslow"), *Sewanee Review*, Summer 1943; the series is reprinted with revisions in *LOU* and *LWC*. Lowell was revising the manuscript of *LOU* while working for Sheed & Ward.

recover our ancient freedom . . . : "This neglect then of rhyme . . . is to be esteemed an example set, the first in English, of ancient liberty recovered to heroic poem from the troublesome and modern bondage of rhyming" (Milton, "The Verse," *Paradise Lost* [2nd ed., 1668]; William Blake, Preface to *Milton* (1808), lines 13–16.

my title: *Land of Unlikeness*: The title of Lowell's first book comes from St. Augustine's *regio dissimilitudinis* in the *Confessions* (413), which scholars suggest Lowell found in Étienne Gilson's *The Mystical Theology of Saint Bernard* (1940); see Staples and Hobsbaum.

Manchester: Lowell's parents spent the summer in West Manchester, Massachusetts.

36. To Franklin Delano Roosevelt

Probably written while mildly manic.

This letter appears in *CPR*, 367–70. Although Lowell dated it September 7, 1943 (listing his parent's return address in West Manchester, Massachusetts, as his own), and although an envelope containing the letter to his parents is also postmarked September 7, Lowell appears to have written both in his apartment in New York City on September 5, 1943, as the "Sunday" on the letter to his parents indicates.

39. To Frank Sheed

Probably written while mildly manic.

Mr. Sheed: Frank Sheed (1897–1981), Lowell's boss at Sheed & Ward, founded the Catholic publishing house with his wife, Maisie Ward, in 1926.

40. To Peter and Eleanor Taylor

Probably written while mildly manic.

Peter Taylor married Eleanor Ross (b. 1920), American poet, on June 4, 1943.

Yaddo: See Roberts, 209–10, and Hulbert, 166–68.

Stephens College: Stafford taught at Stephens College in Columbia, Missouri, in 1937–38. See Roberts, 124–28, and Hulbert, 57, 64–65.

41. To Peter Taylor

Probably written while mildly manic.

Sub: Lowell's nickname for Taylor. Lowell had a running joke with his friends about a group of animals, primarily bears, who resembled his acquaintances. Peter Taylor recalls, "he had various bears—they were spelt bert" (Ian Hamilton Notebooks, British Library). David Roberts writes, "In Baton Rouge the Bears were modified into the Wuberts, pronounced 'Wu-bear,' in the French manner" (193). "Sub" may have been a bear's name. Chief (or sergeant) among these was "Arms of the Law," a Boston Irish policeman bear who arrested the unruly others. Arms appears to have been invented in Lowell's childhood (Ian Hamilton, 15).

I will certainly go to jail: On October 13, 1943, Lowell was sentenced to a year and a day. The extra day on his sentence made him a felon. After spending ten days in the West Street Jail in New York City, Lowell served five months in a federal prison in Danbury, Connecticut. "I corrected proofs. . . . I queued for hours for cigarettes and chocolate bars, and did slow makework like wheeling wheelbarrows of cinders. I found life lulling. I slept among eighty men, a foot apart, and grew congenial with other idealist felons. . . . I was thankful to find jail gentler than boarding school or college—an adult fraternity. I read—*Erewhon* and *The Way of All Flesh* . . . two thousand pages of Proust" (Meyers, 163).

43. To Richard Eberhart

mop-work: Lowell was released on parole on March 15, 1944. Stafford and Lowell moved to Black Rock, Connecticut, in early April, and Lowell served out the remainder of his sentence working at St. Vincent's Hospital in Bridgeport, cleaning the army cadet nurses' dormitory. He was paid $15 a week (Ian Hamilton, 96).

About the play: Eberhart sent Lowell a copy of *The Crystal Sepulcher*, which he never published. His *The Mad Musician*, however, is about the staging of a play very like it; its characters are crudely based on Lowell, his parents, and Anne Dick, among others. See Eberhart, 133–60. See also Ian Hamilton, 27–28.

don't print: Eberhart obliged, though he published an excerpt of the poet's speech in "Verse More and Less Topical" in the *Kenyon Review*, Spring 1944; section 3, "Speech from a Play," is reprinted in *Burr Oaks* (1947).

your gunnery: Eberthart served as a gunnery instructor in the naval reserve in several places, including Dam Neck, Virginia; see Eberhart, "Dam Neck, Virginia," *Burr Oaks* (1947).

not a pacifist: The poet in Eberhart's play creates a scandal by becoming a pacifist.

44. To John Crowe Ransom

my long satirical poem on England: The only complete version of "Dead Briton's Vision" known to have survived is in the collection of Richard Henry Levey. Drafts are in the Lowell Papers at Harvard.

impressions: Herbert Marshall McLuhan, "The Analogical Mirrors," Josephine Miles, "The Sweet and Lovely Language," Austin Warren, "Instress of Inscape," and Harold Whitehall, "Sprung Rhythm," *Kenyon Review*, Summer 1944. Lowell's "Note" appeared with Arthur Mizener, "Victorian Hopkins," and Austin Warren, "Monument Not Quite Needed," *Kenyon Review*, Autumn 1944. Lowell's essay was reprinted (as "Hopkins' Sanctity") in *Gerard Manley Hopkins*, by the Kenyon Critics (1945). It is also reprinted in *CPR*.

the point about *buckle*: McLuhan discusses the function of "Buckle!" in Hopkins's "The Windhover" (lines 9–10: "Brute beauty and valour and act, oh, air, pride, plume, here/Buckle! AND the fire that breaks from thee, then"). Cf. "Colloquy in Black Rock," lines 25–26.

45. To Allen Tate

The Ruggles . . . Bennett's: Eleanor Ruggles, *Gerard Manley Hopkins: A Life* (1944); Joseph Bennett, *Baudelaire: A Criticism* (1944).

Baudelaire: To learn more, Lowell was "reading 19th and 20th century French Anthologies with terrific excitement" (RL to Allen Tate, n.d. Summer 1944, Princeton). The anthologies have not been identified; but they may have been the first place Lowell encountered Tristan Corbière. "I don't think I have much to say now about ["The Quaker Graveyard in Nantucket"] except that it started as a translation of a Corbière poem on Paris night life that was a little like

the litter in my Colloquy. Then I grew drunker and drunker with the sea" (RL to Babette Deutsch, February 24th, 1955).

I am a *little* anemic: "I don't think Cal is any too well, but it may be only the heat and the tedium of mopping floors. He had a terrifying seizure of some sort in church last Sunday and I thought he was going to faint at the communion rail. He doctored himself with brandy (Cal's drinking at 9 in the morning indicates something unusual)" (Stafford to Peter Taylor, July 12, 1944, Vanderbilt, quoted in Mariani, *Lost Puritan*, 117).

the seven poems: The seven poems were not preserved with the letter; they might have included "The Dead in Europe," "France," and the "On the Right Hand of God" sequence, as well as an early draft of "Colloquy in Black Rock." He also wrote "The Quaker Graveyard in Nantucket" in Black Rock, published in *Partisan Review* (1945).

the story of Peter's: Probably "The Scout Master," *Partisan Review*, Summer 1945.

on the Fugitives: Oliver W. Evans, "The Fugitives," *Commonweal* (1944).

46. To Peter Taylor

Frederick Kuh: Named for Frederick Kuh (1895–1978), war correspondent for the *Chicago Sun* who reported the surrender of Italy four days before it happened. See "Frederick Kuh, Manx Cat (for Jean Stafford)," *HIS*.

Fanno schifo tutti: They're all disgusting.

Orthodoxy: Taylor and Lowell had been discussing G. K. Chesterton's *Orthodoxy* (1909), "a magnificent book and psychologically the *right* one to read now-a-days" (RL to Peter Taylor, [n.d. January? 1945], Vanderbilt).

book of poems: *LWC*.

47. To Selden Rodman

not a s[ubject] on which I can feel loquacious . . . : Selden Rodman (b. 1909), poet and art critic, solicited poems for the Modern Library's *New Anthology of Modern Poetry* (1946) and the journal *Portfolio*. Rodman's papers were later burned in a house fire; only portions of this letter are legible. The rest is my conjecture.

War: "At worst life is pretty wonderful; although anyone who has escaped this war has no right to talk. I don't care about anything except writing and trying to be a half-way decent Christian. Politics is a spider's web of unreality" (RL to Peter Taylor, 7/18 [1945], Vanderbilt).

the other six: A ten-sonnet sequence, "On the Right Hand of God," first appeared in *Portfolio*, December 1945; reprinted as "Caron, Non Ti Crucciare" in *New Anthology of Modern Poetry*, ed. Selden Rodman (1946), and *CPM*.

48. To Peter Taylor

Partisan Review story: Taylor, "The Scout Master," *Partisan Review*, Summer 1945.

Schwartz: Delmore Schwartz (1913–66), American poet, was an editor of the *Partisan Review* when Stafford and Lowell befriended him.

Ronald Knox: Monseignor Knox (1888–1957), English Catholic theologian; the limerick appears in W. H. Auden's *Oxford Book of Light Verse* (1937).

even the personified Time: "Where the Rainbow Ends," *LWC*, lines 18–20.

49. To Caroline Gordon

Your divorce: Caroline Gordon left Allen Tate in the fall of 1945. After brief stays in New York

City and Princeton, she traveled to Damariscotta (where she quarreled violently with Stafford). Gordon and Tate were divorced in January 1946; they remarried three months later.

50. To Selden Rodman

Dec. 3 issue of *Time*: "Ezra Pound, in Washington awaiting trial for treason (pro-Axis broadcasts from Rome), was freshly re-indicted for 19 overt acts, and became the center of a literary flurry in Manhattan. Pulitzer prizewinner Conrad Aiken considered him 'less traitor than fool'; E. E. Cummings whipped up a paraphrasing of 'To thine own self be true . . .'; Louis Untermeyer favored life imprisonment among the works of Eddie Guest. Random House hastily dropped Pound from a forthcoming poetry anthology" ("Pigs and Poets," *Time*, December 3, 1945, 31). The article refers to Conrad Aiken and William Rose Benét's *Anthology of Famous English and American Poetry* (1946), which was to include twelve Pound poems. After Pound's reindictment, Random House tried to remove his work but the ensuing controversy made Bennett Cerf, president of the company, back down (see Wilhelm, 263, and Carpenter, 791).

52. To James Laughlin

your symposium: Poet and publisher James Laughlin (1914–97) was an upperclassman when Lowell was at Harvard; he had attended Pound's Ezuversity in Rapallo during a leave of absence in his sophomore year. His New Directions publishing house reprinted the *Kenyon Review* symposium on Hopkins as *Gerard Manley Hopkins*, by the Kenyon Critics (1945).

53. To Blair Clark

Lesley's match-box analysis: Frank Parker and his English wife, Lesley, visited the Lowells in Damariscotta in the fall of 1945. According to a Stafford letter, Parker told Lowell that "Jean's attitude toward Cal in public is 'satirical'" and that "Lesley seems to have told Holly [Clark] that Jean is enamored of Peter [Taylor]" (Ian Hamilton's summary of an unidentified Stafford letter dated January 21, 1946, Ian Hamilton Notebooks, British Library). This is corroborated by an innuendo in Stafford's letter to Taylor the following year: "The year [1946] had started off very badly with the Tate business and with a perfectly hideous misdeed of Frank Parker's about which you may or may not know. I don't think you do, but I shall one day tell you" (Stafford to Peter Taylor, December 19, 1946, quoted in Ian Hamilton Notebooks, British Library).

54. To Peter Taylor

Claudel: Paul Claudel, *Ways and Crossways*, trans. John O'Connor (1933).

"at bottom": A common figure in Matthew Arnold's essays; see in particular *Literature and Dogma* (1873), 47.

Father Flye: Father James Harold Flye (1884–1985), mentor of James Agee.

staying with Delmore: See letter 472. The visit ended badly. "Delmore, the intriguer, had hinted . . . that [Jean Stafford] was interested in another man (himself perhaps?). He had even insinuated this to Cal, whereupon Cal had socked him. The fist fight that ensued brought the Ellery Street winter to a dramatic close" (Simpson, 123–24).

O'Donnell: George Marion O'Donnell (1914–62), a poet who studied under John Crowe Ransom and other Fugitives at Vanderbilt, was teaching briefly at Harvard.

Eleanor's story: Eleanor Ross [Taylor], "Mr. Milkman," *Sewanee Review*, Spring 1947.

55. To Peter and Eleanor Taylor

Birds of New England by a Mr. Forbush: Cf. "The Mills of the Kavanaughs," stanza 28, lines 8–15. Edward Howe Forbush, *Birds of Massachusetts & Other New England States* (1925); *The Domestic Cat: Bird Killer, Mouser and Destroyer of Wild Life: Means of Utilizing and Controlling It* (1916).

56. To John Berryman

John Berryman (1914–72), American poet. See "For John Berryman, 1914–1972," *New York Review of Books*, March 30, 1972, reprinted in *CPR*, 112. "If it was Cal and John's turn to clean up, Jean and I would hear them reciting to each other—Hopkins, Donne, Marvell, Crashaw. . . . At a poem a plate, the work went slowly" (Simpson, 135). In a letter written to his mother from the Lowells' house, Berryman remarked: "Cal (Lowell) & I are working our way, comparing opinions, through the whole of Western poetry" (*We Dream of Honour*, 223–24). See also Jean Stafford, "An Influx of Poets," *New Yorker*, November 6, 1978.

the Rahvs: Philip Rahv (1908–73), American critic who founded the *Partisan Review* with William Phillips; Nathalie Swann Rahv, architect, was married to Rahv from 1941 to 1958. See "Man and Wife," *LS*, line 17.

Eileen: Eileen Simpson (1918–2002), John Berryman's first wife.

your stanza: Not preserved with the letter.

58. To Gertrude Buckman

Gertrude Buckman, editor, was married to Delmore Schwartz from 1938 to 1943. She befriended Jean Stafford in New York when Lowell was in prison, the year her marriage to Schwartz ended.
Maurice Mulligan: One of the bears; see note to letter 41.

60 and 61. To Mr. and Mrs. Robert T. S. Lowell

Cornell: Coincidentally, Julien Cornell was Ezra Pound's lawyer. Charlotte Lowell urged Jean Stafford to retain him for Lowell's defense in 1943. His books include *The Conscientious Objector and the Law* (1943) and *The Trial of Ezra Pound* (1966).

64. To Peter Taylor

transplanted southerners: Taylor wanted to write a story about a family of "Southerners living out of the South." He also wanted to write "a story about Douglass House. . . . There will be three principal characters. The first of these has read the *Confessions* of St. Augustine. The second has read the *Confessions* of Rousseau. The third has read *The Education of Henry Adams*. Each is (or tries to be) a reflection of his reading. And each is busily writing his own confessions. I'll obviously have to use the word *confessions* in whatever title I choose" (Taylor to RL, January 15, [1947], Harvard). "One of the things we had fun about always was this Southern/Yankee thing. Most of it was just joking and corn. . . . We read Henry Adams that first year at Kenyon and Cal always loved the part when Henry Adams speaks so scornfully of Roony Lee [Robert E. Lee's son], who was at Harvard with him and says he had no intellectual power" (Peter Taylor interview, Ian Hamilton Notebooks, British Library). See Taylor, "1939," *Happy Families Are All Alike* (1959).

David and Bathsheba: "David to Bathsheba in the Public Garden," *Nation*, December 7, 1946, and "Bathsheba's Lament in the Garden," *Nation*, May 17, 1947; reprinted as "David and Bathsheba in the Public Garden," *MK*.

65. To Louis Untermeyer

your anthologies: Louis Untermeyer (1885–1977), American poet and anthologist.

Why was each blade "a singular knife": Lowell conflates "The Wayfarer . . ." and "In Heaven . . . ," *War Is Kind* (1899), reprinted as "The Wayfarer" and "The Blades of Grass" in *Modern American Poetry: A Critical Anthology*, 5th ed., ed. Untermeyer (1936).

an open-air school: From 1927 to 1930, Lowell attended Rivers School, "an open-air, i.e. unheated school where scholarship was low, health was high, manners were hearty" (Ian Hamilton, 16).

Shapiro: Karl Shapiro (1913–2000), American poet.

66. To Gertrude Buckman

Giroux: Robert Giroux (b. 1914), American editor. Lowell met Giroux through Jean Stafford; he was the editor of *Boston Adventure*. Giroux became Lowell's editor with the publication of *Lord Weary's Castle*.

Dilly: Nickname of Heather Keeler Thompson, first wife of John Thompson.

official conference: Writers' Forum at the Woman's College, Greensboro, organized by Taylor.

***Life*:** "'Prize Poet' Robert Lowell Wins the Pulitzer Prize," *Life*, May 19, 1947.

Academy reward: Grant from the American Academy of Arts and Letters.

General Greene: Greensboro, North Carolina, is named after Nathanael Greene, Revolutionary War general who commanded the southern army from 1780 to 1783.

the villain in Pickwick: Alfred Jingle, the rascal in Dickens's *Pickwick Papers*: "'My friend Mr. Snodgrass has a strong poetic turn,' said Mr. Pickwick. 'So have I,' said the stranger. 'Epic poem—ten thousand lines—revolution of July—composed it on the spot—Mars by day, Apollo by night—bang the field-piece, twang the lyre.'"

Red: Robert Penn Warren's nickname.

67. To Gertrude Buckman

I feel lonely and dreary: Lowell's mood was low throughout the spring. "Things have been going very badly with Jean, and I feel so depressed that I almost dread seeing anyone" (RL to Peter Taylor, [n.d. early March? 1947], Vanderbilt).

68. To Peter Taylor

Engle's . . . Greenslet: Paul Engle (1908–91), American poet who directed the Iowa Writers Workshop from 1937 to 1965; Ferris Greenslet (1875–1959), editor in chief of Houghton Mifflin, author of *The Lowells and Their Seven Worlds* (1946).

Kitten: Jarrell's cat.

Awards: Lowell won the Pulitzer Prize for *Lord Weary's Castle* and grants from the Guggenheim Foundation and the American Academy of Arts and Letters.

your raven: At the end of the war in London, Taylor had a "glimpse of a literary giant as one of a group of thirty at a lecture given by T. S. Eliot. Speaking on the writings of Poe, Eliot reminded Peter 'of nothing so much as a great lanky raven'" (McAlexander, 90–91).

Luce: Henry Robinson Luce (1898–1967), publisher of *Time*, *Life*, and *Fortune* magazines.

Mrs. Ames: Elizabeth Ames, director of Yaddo.

69. To Elizabeth Bishop

Elizabeth Bishop (1911–79), American poet, who became Lowell's lifelong friend and correspondent.

you have had a miserable winter: Lowell and Elizabeth Bishop were introduced by Randall Jarrell in January 1947. They had various plans to meet again that winter and spring but Bishop's asthma forced her to cancel.

70. To Paul Engle

Library of Congress job: Consultant in poetry to the Library of Congress. Working in an office at the top of the library's Jefferson building overlooking the Capitol and the city, the consultant administered projects to improve the library's poetry collections.

Blackmur: R. P. Blackmur (1904–65), American literary scholar and poet.

71. To Gertrude Buckman

Pumble: Buckman had signed her previous letter "Pumblingly, [Gertrude]" (Buckman to RL, [n.d. late spring 1947], Harvard).

Young: Marguerite Young (1909–95), American novelist.

Lexei: Alexei Haieff (1914–94), Russian American neoclassical composer; his work includes *Caligula* (1971), based on Lowell's poem. The other guests included Marianne Hauser (b. 1909), novelist; Austin Warren (1899–1986), literary scholar; Ruth Domino (later Domino-Tassi), fiction writer; Ulysses Kay (1917–95), composer; Seymour Krim (1922–89), essayist; T. E. Doremus (1922–62), novelist; Jean Pedrick (b. 1922), novelist and poet; Michael Seide (1911–2001), fiction writer; and Charles Neider (1915–2001), literary scholar.

Mr. Bontemps: Arna Bontemps (1902–73), American poet and novelist, worked as a librarian at Fisk University in Nashville. His books include *God Sends Sunday* (1931) and *The Poetry of the Negro 1746–1949*, ed. with Langston Hughes (1949). His "juveniles" include *The Story of the Negro* (1946), *The Story of George Washington Carver* (1954), and *Frederick Douglass: Slave, Fighter, Freeman* (1959).

MacLeish: Archibald MacLeish (1892–1982), American poet and playwright, was librarian of Congress from 1939 to 1944.

Thomas: Dylan Thomas (1914–1953), Welsh poet.

Empson: William Empson (1906–84), English poet and literary scholar.

Spencer: Theodore Spencer (1902–49), American poet, professor of English at Harvard.

Richards' delivery: I. A. Richards (1893–1979), English literary scholar and poet. His books include *The Meaning of Meaning*, with C. K. Ogden (1923); see "Waking in the Blue," *LS*, line 3.

Levin: Harry Levin (1912–93), writer and scholar, professor of English at Harvard; Elena Zarudnaya Levin translated Leon Trotsky's *Diary in Exile* (1958), among other books.

72. To Gertrude Buckman

Roethke: Theodore Roethke (1908–63), American poet.

Powers: J. F. Powers (1917–99), American novelist and short-story writer. He spent thirteen months in prison as a conscientious objector during the Second World War.

Roskolenko: Harry Roskolenko (1907–80), American travel writer and poet; Buckman reported that Roskolenko contacted her on his return from Australia and Japan (Buckman to RL, July 6, 1947, Harvard).

Stead?: Christina Stead (1902–83), Australian novelist.

Tolstoy's great story . . . : Tolstoy, *Hadji Murád* (1912); Maksim Gorky, "Reminiscences of Leo Tolstoy," *Reminiscences . . .* (1946); Earnest Joseph Simmons, *Leo Tolstoy* (1946).

the lovers in Central Park!: Buckman wrote that lovers in Central Park were amorous in an embarassing but nice way (Buckman to RL, [July] 6, [1947], Harvard).

73. To Robert Frost

"The Witches": Frost, "Two Witches," *New Hampshire* (1923).

a language that *speaks*: When Lowell was a student, Frost "read me the opening of Keats's 'Hyperion,' the first version, and I thought all of that was sublime. It's Miltonic verse and every line was equally good and terrific and unapproachable. And Frost just passed through the opening and then came to that line about the naiad, 'No stir of air was there.' He said, 'There it comes alive.' Now that's not superficially a dramatic line, and he didn't mean the other lines were poor, but he meant that it was building up for that, and the voice tone is something I think he's just extraordinarily sensitive to" (interview with Cleanth Brooks and Robert Penn Warren, reprinted in Meyers, 38). See also Frost to John T. Bartlett, Fourth-of-July[,] 1913 and 22 Feb '14, *Collected Poems, Prose, and Plays*.

74. To Robert Frost

Merrill is wonderful to watch: Frost wrote that they had Merrill Moore to thank for their friendship, "if for nothing else. I have found Merrill wonderful in performance to watch" (Frost to RL, July 16, 1947, copy at Dartmouth).

worlds have "changed and decayed" since 1936: "Isn't it fine that [the] young promise I began to entertain hopes of when it visited me on Fayerweather St. Cambridge in 1936 should have come to so much and to so much more promise for the future. . . . I read your genuineness in every line of verse in [the] book you sent me. So come along and bring your other poet with you. We can have a good talk about change & decay and Him that changes not" (Frost to RL, July 16, 1947, quoted in Ian Hamilton, 129). Cf. "Change and decay in all around I see;/O Thou who changest not, abide with me" (Henry F. Lyte, "Abide with Me," lines 7–8).

Your farm sounds like Ezra Pound's child: Frost bought the Homer Noble farm in Ripton, Vermont, in 1939. Ezra Pound's father's name was Homer Loomis Pound; his son's name is Omar.

75. To J. F. Powers and Bucklin Moon

Bucklin Moon (1911–84), American writer and editor.

Beast's slugged brandy: "Beast" was Lowell's nickname for Roethke; Roethke's for Lowell was "Rattleass from Boston, Mass" (Mariani, *Lost Puritan*, 153).

Wilder: Thornton Wilder (1897–1975), American playwright.

76. To Gertrude Buckman

on my review: "Paterson I," *Sewanee Review*, Summer 1947. Williams's letter thanking Lowell for the review is printed in *Selected Letters*, 259–60.

Brustleins: After Ford Madox Ford's death, his companion, Janice Biala, married the painter Daniel Brustlein.

77. To Elizabeth Bishop

Fish poem: Bishop, "At the Fishhouses," *New Yorker*, August 9, 1947.

the *Sun* . . . : "A Report on Verse," *Chicago Sun Book Week*, July 20, 1947; photographs of Bishop and Lowell appeared on the cover, Lowell's "Fat Man in the Mirror" on page 2. Winfield Townley Scott's article, "Looking at Poetry East and West," included Lowell in a group of "one-book youngsters worth keeping an eye on"; Bishop is not mentioned in the Scott article. For Bishop's view, see *One Art*, 146–47. John Ciardi (1916–86), poet and translator; John Mal-

colm Brinnin (1916–98), poet, author of *Dylan Thomas in America* (1955); Howard Moss (1922–87), poet and editor.

reviewing you: Jarrell, "The Poet and His Public," *Partisan Review*, September–October 1946; Lowell, "Thomas, Bishop, and Williams," *Sewanee Review*, Summer 1947, reprinted as "Elizabeth Bishop's *North and South*," *CPR*.

78. To Gertrude Buckman

the librarian: Luther H. Evans (1902–81), librarian of Congress.

Mrs. Biddle: Katherine Garrison Chapin (1890–1977), American poet. She was married to Francis Biddle (1886–1968), attorney general of the United States (1941–45), member of the international tribunal at Nuremberg. Biddle indicted Ezra Pound for treason on July 26, 1943.

fellows: The Fellows of American Literature at the Library of Congress included Allen Tate, T. S. Eliot, Louise Bogan, Robert Penn Warren, Katherine Anne Porter, W. H. Auden, Karl Shapiro, and Theodore Spencer.

Cosmos Club: Lowell lived at the Cosmos Club in Washington, D.C., on the advice of Allen Tate, who was a member. "I stay at a place called the Cosmos Club, to belong you must have published a book (but the only author-members I've ever heard of are Allen & President Chalmers). The resident members are uncles of Marshall Pétain. There I took Williams and Bishop, and Williams with his wife in the next room and two whiskeys began telling stories about women, the 20's, Pound's illegitimate daughter and French culture. Gradually we were cordoned off by gaping and horror-struck ~~French~~ colored maids—every so often one would come and touch our table to remind us that we were still there. Then in my embarrassment and excitement I mistook the oldest member for the head-waiter" (RL to Peter Taylor, Nov. 3 [1947], Vanderbilt).

79. To Ezra Pound

Dr. Overholser: Winfred Overholser (1892–1964), superintendent of St. Elizabeths Hospital.

80. To Ezra Pound?

The letter, which survives only as a fragment, may have been addressed to both Ezra and Dorothy Pound; it may otherwise have been a letter of application to Pound's doctor for visiting privileges.

81. To Elizabeth Bishop

nun poem: "Mother Marie Therese," *Kenyon Review*, Summer 1948, reprinted in *MK*.

82. To William Carlos Williams

Draft of a letter written on the verso of a letter from Williams to Lowell, dated September 26, 1947. Williams's letter is printed in *Selected Letters*, 261–62.

Saturday the 18th: Lowell invited Williams to record his poems at the Library.

Van Buren's autobiography: Martin Van Buren, *Autobiography* (1920), a recommendation from Pound, whom Lowell had just seen for the first time.

about American names: "Mrs. Williams and I have been reading *Lord Weary's Castle*, it's interesting to me that you have found a way to mention local place names without jumping out of context which so often occurs to make a work false sounding. It's very hard to treat American things and name them specifically without a sense of bathos, of bad sentimental overlap resulting" (Williams, *Selected Letters*, 262).

83. To Gertrude Buckman

Evelyn: Evelyn Katz Shapiro, Karl Shapiro's wife.

Stark house: General John Stark's house in Manchester, N.H.; the Starks are Lowell's maternal ancestors.

Woodward: W. E. Woodward, *A New American History* (1936); Ezra Pound corresponded with Woodward and cites his books and letters in the *Cantos*.

Adams: Brooks Adams, *New Empire* (1903).

the Colliers: Buckman was working for *Collier's*.

84. To Theodore Roethke

"Ordnung! Ordnung!": "Scurry of warm over small plants. / Ordnung! Ordnung! / Papa is coming!" (Roethke, "The Lost Son," lines 141–43).

85. To William Carlos Williams

Lyle—the paragraph with *Forever Amber* . . . : David Lyle, Paterson resident whose correspondence with Williams is incorporated into *Paterson*. See Williams, *Paterson*, 259. Attempts in Massachusetts to ban Kathleen Windsor's *Forever Amber* (1944) for obscenity were unsuccessful because the judge deemed it "conducive to sleep, but not to sleeping with a member of the opposite sex."

(*Chimera—I think summer 47*): Kenneth Burke, "Ideology and Myth," *Accent*, Summer 1947. His ideas about epic, presented in twelve clauses, appear in an appendix to the article.

Jarrell writes me: See *Randall Jarrell's Letters*, 185.

Sewanee Review article: Frederick Morgan, "William Carlos Williams: Imagery, Rhythm, Form," *Sewanee Review*, October–December 1947.

86. To Gertrude Buckman

"Sweeney Agonistes": Eliot, "Sweeney Agonistes," *Collected Poems 1919–1935* (1936).

Swiggett: *The Divine Comedy of Dante Alighieri: A Translation in Terza Rima. Intro. and Arguments Glen L. Swiggett (1956).*

Polish cultural attaché: Czeslaw Milosz (1911–2004), Polish poet, worked from 1947 to 1950 as a cultural attaché for the Polish embassy in Washington. An interviewer asked Milosz if any of his books survived the end of the war: "I remember seeing a copy of [Milosz's second book of poems] *Three Winters* with a bullet hole in the cover in your library in California." Milosz recalled that "the floor we lived on collapsed when the shell hit the building. Later on, after the war, we searched through the rubble for our things. That was when we found that book, and there really was a bullet hole through it" (Ewa Czarnecka and Aleksander Fiut, *Conversations with Czeslaw Milosz*, trans. by Richard Lourie [1987], 89).

Spanish cultural attaché: Unidentified. The community of Spanish writers in Washington at the time congregated around Juan Ramón Jiménez (1881–1958), living in exile from the Franco regime and working as a consultant to the Library of Congress.

trace Carlos: Unidentified; possibly the family of William Carlos Williams.

Léger: Aléxis Léger (1887–1975), French poet who wrote under the pseudonym Saint-John Perse; he lived in Washington from 1940 to 1957.

Corbière selections: Tristan Corbière (1845–75), French poet. Lowell was reading Corbière in French. He sent Elizabeth Bishop a copy of Walter McElroy's translations (1947) and inscribed on the flyleaf, "Dear Elizabeth, You'll probably feel insulted by any translation, especially this bad one; but I got two for Christmas.—Cal" (from the library of Elizabeth Bishop, Houghton Library, Harvard).

a new poem: "Thanksgiving's Over," *Partisan Review*, Winter 1950, reprinted in *MK*.

87. To J. F. Powers

By the Waters of Babylon: Psalm 137, trans. Miles Coverdale (1535), line 1; incorporated into *The Book of Common Prayer* (1662).

his story: Delmore Schwartz, "The Child Is the Meaning of This Life," *Partisan Review* (1947), reprinted in *The World Is a Wedding* (1948).

K.A.P.: The Powers named their first child Katherine Anne Powers after Katherine Anne Porter.

what you did in *Great Expectations*: A joke hinging, perhaps, on the "Aged Parent": "Do see the movie [of *Great Expectations*] i[f] you get a chance, if only to see Jaggers, the Lawyer, and the parent of his clerk, referred to by the clerk as 'Aged P'" (Powers to RL, November 26, 1947, Harvard).

88. To Elizabeth Bishop

your questions: "Falling Asleep over the Aeneid," *Kenyon Review*, Winter 1948, reprinted in *MK*. See Bishop, *One Art*, 151–52.

two spigots: "I have been working some on another poem called 'Faustina.' . . . I am also doing a couple of Cape Breton ones started this summer and am beginning to worry lest I have only two poetic spigots, marked *H & C*" (*One Art*, 152).

a wonderful poem: Jarrell, "Lady Bates," *Nation*, February 28, 1948.

Admiral Nimitz: Chester Nimitz (1885–1966), commander of the Pacific Fleet during the Second World War.

Mackie: Mackie Langham Jarrell, Randall Jarrell's first wife.

89. To Katherine Anne Porter

your Stein piece: Porter, "Gertrude Stein: A Self-Portrait," *Harper's*, December 1947.

the shot at Laughlin: "Americans in general [Stein] found to be rather childish about money: they spent it or gave it away and enjoyed wastefully with no sense of its fierce latent power. 'It is hard to be a miser, a real miser, they are as rare as geniuses it takes the same kind of thing to make one, that is time must not exist for them. . . . There must be a reality that has nothing to do with the passing of time. I have it and so had Henry Green . . .' and she found only one of the younger generation in America, a young man named Jay Laughlin, who had, she wrote, praising him, avarice to that point of genius which makes the true miser."

the Mathers: Richard Mather (1596–1669), Increase Mather (1639–1723), and Cotton Mather (1663–1728), three generations of Puritan clergymen. In 1927, Porter started to write a biography of Cotton Mather but never completed it. Cf. "New England and Further," *CPR*, 182.

Essex Junto: Some of Lowell's ancestors from Essex County, Massachusetts, were part of the "Essex Junto"(so named by their opponent John Hancock). They wanted to create a confederation of New England states to fight against the influence of Thomas Jefferson (whom John Lowell called an "anarchist"). Vigorous supporters of Alexander Hamilton and John Jay, they felt the government should oppose revolutionary France and be friendlier to Great Britain.

90. To J. F. Powers

the car: In early September 1947, Lowell drove with J. F. Powers to Chicago in Powers's 1931 Chevy coupe. The car became animated in Lowell's storytelling along the way, a character "tired, out of sorts, critical of today's world" (Powers to Paul Mariani, n.d. 1992, quoted in Mariani, *Lost Puritan*, 153).

Quisling . . . Gesell: Vidkun Quisling, leader of the Norwegian national socialist party; he was executed in 1945. Silvio Gesell (1852–1930) and Clifford Hugh Douglas (1879–1952), economists whose radical ideas interested Pound.

91. To George Santayana

George Santayana (1863–1952), Spanish American philosopher. Lowell sent Santayana a copy of *Lord Weary's Castle* when it was published in a gesture of admiration. Santayana wrote to say how much he liked the book. He was particularly struck by "the flashes of Catholic piety that appear repeatedly, contrasting with the Bostonian and Cape Cod atmosphere of the background." He also admitted that there were some poems "that I can't make out clearly. I seem to need to know your personal history and the circumstances and the books that you had in mind." He asked Lowell to send him some new work. See McCormick, 454.

anarchical conservative: "Bay Lodge and Joe Stickney had given birth to the wholly new and original party of Conservative Christian Anarchists, to restore true poetry under the inspiration of the 'Götterdämmerung.' . . . The conservative Christian anarchist, as a party, drew life from Hegel and Schopenhauer rightly understood" (Henry Adams *The Education of Henry Adams* [1931], 405–06). Cf. also "New England and Further," *CPR*.

***Opinion in America* . . . or the Gospels:** Santayana, *Character and Opinion in the United States: With Reminiscences of William James and Josiah Royce and Academic Life in America* (1920); *Persons and Places: Fragments of an Autobiography* (1944–53); "The Poetry of Barbarism," *Interpretations of Poetry and Religion* (1900); *The Idea of Christ in the Gospels: Or, God in Man* (1946); *Dialogues in Limbo* (1925).

two new poems: "Falling Asleep over the Aeneid" and "Mother Marie Therese," *MK*.

a long poem: "The Mills of the Kavanaughs," *MK*.

Edwards' book: Jonathan Edwards, "Narrative of Surprising Conversions" (1736).

lines from his sermons . . . : Edwards, "Sinners in the Hands of an Angry God" (based on Ezekiel 22:14) and "The Future Punishment of the Wicked"; *Of Insects*.

92. To Carley Dawson

Carley: Lowell met Carley Dawson at a party in honor of St.-John Perse (Aléxis Léger), hosted by poet and publisher Caresse Crosby (Ian Hamilton, 131). A divorced socialite who had "been the mistress of St.-John Perse" (Kalstone, 140), Dawson lived on O Street in Georgetown with her ten-year-old son. Lowell soon started to attend concerts with her. Dawson worked for her mother's cosmetic company; she later wrote a series of juveniles, beginning with *Mr. Wicker's Window* (1952).

Age of Anxiety: W. H. Auden, "Age of Anxiety: A Baroque Eclogue" (1947).

Rubinstein: Arthur Rubinstein (1887–1982), Polish American pianist.

93. To George Santayana

the Trojans and Italians . . . : Santayana remarked on their similarities: "For instance in being attracted to the Church, feeling its historic and moral authority, and yet seeing that its doctrine is not true you have placed yourself exactly in my position, though reaching it by a different path. And so too about this late war. The bombing for the sake of 'frightfulness' (in imitation of the Germans) and the insolent demand for unconditional surrender." About "Falling Asleep over the Aeneid," he wrote that Aeneas, "not as a theme in himself but as a witness and observer, has evidently left you full of strong images and tragic perceptions. Virgil is no doubt too mild for your taste and you transmute his Trojans and Italian barbarians into something more like Red Indians" (Santayana to RL, January 28, 1948, quoted in McCormick, 455–56).

new dialogues: Santayana's *Dialogues in Limbo* (1925) was reissued in 1948 with three new chapters.

my new poem: "Thanksgiving Is Finished" (later "Thanksgiving's Over," *MK*).

94. To J. F. Powers

that Ted business: Powers had suggested that Lowell review Roethke's second book, *The Lost Son*, for the *New York Times*. "Let's put this kid over this time. He's got it coming and won't rest until he's appreciated" (Powers to RL, Jan. 12, 1948, Harvard).

Bill Williams attack on Eliot's Milton essay: Williams, "With Forced Fingers Rude," *Four Pages* (February 1948), which he wrote in response to Eliot's "Milton" (1947).

as Eliot reads it: Lowell may have heard Eliot read the poem at Harvard in 1947. Eliot recorded it for the Library of Congress later in 1948 (released on three 78-r.p.m. records on February 18, 1949).

95. To Gertrude Buckman

her science courses: Stafford "started a kind of tutorial in biology with a professor at Columbia University" who "ran what he called 'the mouse room,' where he was 'breeding mice with tails like bolts of lightning and mice that danced in circles counterclockwise.' Stafford had her own desk and microscope, and she attended Tuesday colloquia on tobacco viruses and kindred subjects" (Roberts, 278; the quotations are from a letter to Lowell, n.d., Harvard).

Flint . . . Haggin: R. W. Flint, American poet, critic, and translator, was engaged by Lowell's work and his views on faith; he wrote Lowell a series of letters on these subjects. Lowell was silent at first but finally wrote back in response to Flint's "Robert Lowell: The Tradition and Technique of Revolt," *New Leader*, December 27, 1947. B. H. Haggin (1900–87), music critic for the *Nation*, a close friend of Jarrell's.

97. To Elizabeth Bishop

Here's my poem: "Thanksgiving Is Finished" (later "Thanksgiving's Over," *MK*).

"Poète contumace": Tristan Corbière, "Poète contumace," *Les Amours jaunes* (1873).

the Nun: "Mother Marie Therese," *MK*.

Stickney's: Trumbull Stickney (1874–1904), American poet. Stickney met Santayana when he was an undergraduate at Harvard; they later drifted apart. "Stickney was one of the few [poets] whom Santayana admired without reservation and one of the very few whom he acknowledged among the living as having influenced his own thought, principally by arousing his interest in Indian philosophy" (McCormick, 116).

Aeneas: "Falling Asleep over the Aeneid," *MK*.

What's on the inside: On verso: to "Jarrel/Tate/Spender? discuss: Brooks Adams. Frobenius, Gesell, essential Loeb/Ford, W. L. to Tate. Barry Domvile 'Admiral to Cabin Boy' Has Tate anything of Devlin's/or has L? what any one else know of him. Tate's question re/Marianne/O.K. but see what others think/IN ANY CASE NEVER more than ONE wumman at a time. Tate's re/some prof/??usual time lag or not?" (Pound note, Bishop Papers, Vassar). Leo Frobenius (1873–1938), anthropologist; "W. L." is Wyndham Lewis (1882–1957), English painter and writer; Sir Barry Domvile (1878–1971), founder of The Link, a British fascist organization, author of *From Admiral to Cabin Boy* (1947); Denis Devlin (1908–59), Irish poet.

98. To John Berryman

Possibly written while mildly manic.

Three sorries: Berryman visited Lowell in Washington and stayed at the Cosmos Club at Lowell's invitation. Afterward, he wrote that he had seen both Stafford and Buckman in New York. As much as he did not like being a "link," he told them that Lowell was doing well and avoided

mention of Dawson. He also wrote that he understood why Lowell did not make time to read his manuscript, but his disappointment is palpable (Berryman to RL, March 8, 1948, Harvard). Lowell later recalled, "When we came back to my room, I made the mistake of thinking that John was less interested in his new poems than in mine" (*CPR*, 113).

let me pay: Berryman stayed at the Cosmos Club at Lowell's invitation but was billed for the room.

Salzburg idea?: Jarrell was invited to the Salzburg Seminar in American Civilization. He wrote to Lowell, "I have just learned—I called you last night but couldn't get you—that I can take somebody else to Salzburg, technically as an 'assistant.' He'd get room and board—in a Castle—and travelling expenses just as I will. . . . Some other faculty people are Margaret Mead and Reinhold Neibuhr. The students are European teachers or graduate students" (printed in *Randall Jarrell's Letters*, 189).

perhaps we'll make up: Berryman regretted the rift between Lowell and Delmore Schwartz.

100. *To Carley Dawson*

Possibly written while mildly manic.

Murder for Profit: William Bolitho, *Murder for Profit* (1926); the book recounts the crimes of G. J. Smith, who murdered his wife in a bathtub, and of Fritz Haarmann, who "was found guilty of exactly twenty-four murders."

101. *To Carley Dawson*

Possibly written while mildly manic.

more Bolitho: *Twelve against the Gods: A Story of Adventure* (1929).

Val[s]' lecture . . . Carmen Conde: "Vals" is probably the unidentified "poet from the Spanish embassy." Carmen Conde (1907–96), Spanish poet.

How slowly . . . my love: Spenser, "Epithalamion," lines 278–81; Lowell reverses the order of the lines. Cf. Dennis Barlow in Evelyn Waugh's "The Loved One," who quotes poems from the *Oxford Book of English Verse* as his own (*Horizon*, February 1948).

Auden says: "The girl whose boy-friend starts writing her love poems should be on her guard. Perhaps he really does love her, but one thing is certain: while he was writing his poems he was not thinking of her but of his own feelings about her" (W. H. Auden, "Squares and Oblongs," *Poets at Work: Essays Based on the Modern Poetry Collection at the Lockwood Memorial Library, University of Buffalo* [1948], 175).

102. *To Peter Taylor*

Possibly written while mildly manic.

Mr. Steele: Library of Congress recording engineer.

Scuppernong: "Scuppernong" was the name of Taylor's first country house, located near Norwood, North Carolina (McAlexander, 103).

104. *To Theodore Roethke*

Possibly written while mildly manic.

the flowers and the long ones: The flower poems make up section 1 of Roethke's *The Lost Son* (1948); the long poems are "The Lost Son," "The Long Alley," "A Field of Light," and "The Shape of the Fire."

Léonie Adams . . . Troy: Léonie Adams (1899–1988), American poet, married William Troy (1903–61), American literary critic, in 1933. They never divorced.

Washington: Roethke was living in Seattle.

105. To Elizabeth Bishop

Possibly written while mildly manic.

Budapest recital: The Budapest Quartet was in residence at the National Gallery from 1938 to 1962.

German pictures: *Paintings from the Berlin Museums*, an exhibition of 202 paintings from the Kaiser Friedrich Museum and other Berlin galleries hidden in salt mines during the war; they were discovered by the Third Army and brought to the U.S. "for safe keeping" in December 1945. A total of 964,970 people attended the exhibition at the National Gallery of Art during its forty days on view.

2,000 *Illustrations*: Bishop, "Over 2,000 Illustrations and a Complete Concordance," *Partisan Review*, June 1948.

106. To George Santayana

Possibly written while mildly manic.

the ghost of Cynthia: Propertius, *Elegy* 4.7 ("Cynthia from beyond the Grave").

you mentioned your interest: Santayana told a reporter for *Time* that he had been reading Lowell's poems ("Philosopher without Quest," *Time*, September 27, 1948).

107. To Jean Stafford

Possibly written while mildly manic.

Good luck: Stafford agreed to go to the Virgin Islands to finalize their divorce.

108. To Carley Dawson

Possibly written while mildly manic.

Harriet: Lowell's cousin Harriet Winslow lived in Washington and moved in the same social circles as Carley Dawson.

Mary Chess White Lilac: The Mary Chess cosmetics business was founded by Carley Dawson's mother, Grace Chess Robinson.

109. To R. W. Flint

Possibly written while mildly manic.

"Gallant": "the back country, waking their dreams—where the deer run/and the wood-duck nests protecting his gallant plumage" (Williams, *Paterson*, section 1, lines 86–87).

one in the winter Kenyon . . . : "Falling Asleep over the Aeneid," *Kenyon Review*, Winter 1948; "Mother Marie Therese," *Kenyon Review*, Summer 1948.

Tillich: Paul Tillich (1886–1965), German American philosopher and theologian.

111. To Elizabeth Bishop

Possibly written while mildly manic.

"The Grave," "The Sweet Dead Whale" "Silence": Marianne Moore, "A Grave" and "Silence," *Observations* (1924); what Lowell calls "The Sweet Dead Whale" is "The Steeple Jack," *Selected Poems* (1935).

Blackmur: R. P. Blackmur, "The Method of Marianne Moore," *The Double Agent: Essays in Craft and Elucidation* (1935).

the Canadian mountain: Moore, "The Octopus," *Selected Poems* (1935).

112. To George Santayana

First part of letter possibly written while mildly manic.

"He tried. That's Bostonian": Santayana, puzzling over "Thanksgiving Is Finished," wrote, "[The] self reproach of Propertius for not treating his old girl better and turning her down after she had inspired so many of his verses, is almost decadent Christian, rather than decadent pagan: might be Baudelaire. Your Michael, I understand, had nothing to reproach himself for. He was 'wild' and didn't know that shady side of the world or of the heart well enough. But he had 'tried.' That is Bostonian" (Santayana to RL, April 29, 1948, quoted in McCormick, 458).

Bridges: Robert Bridges (1844–1930), English poet who published the first edition of Gerard Manley Hopkins's verse in 1916. Lowell had copied "Low Barometer" into his notebook in the early 1940s (Axelrod, 246).

Testament: Bridges, *The Testament of Beauty* (1929).

his ideas . . . : Cf. Stevens, "To an Old Philosopher in Rome," *Collected Poems of Wallace Stevens* (1954).

The anthology: *A Little Treasury of American Poetry*, ed. Oscar Williams (1948).

[In] the quotes the *he* is recollecting: The "he" in "Thanksgiving's Over" recollects the speech of his wife, who killed herself.

philosophical visitor: "A young Russian, become a Canadian, came to see me the other day in an open brown flannel shirt, round goggles, and dirty yellow hair brushed back from a forehead already very high and like Josiah Royce's: and he began by demanding what I recognized for my principle in ethics" (Santayana to RL, April 29, 1948, quoted in McCormick, 458).

Royce: Josiah Royce (1855–1916), American philosopher.

Auslander: Joseph Auslander (1897–1965) was the poetry editor of the *North American Review* in 1937, when he was named the first consultant in poetry to the Library of Congress. His appointment was renewed yearly until 1942, when he became gift officer for the Library.

the Williams: Williams, *Paterson*, Book One (1946) and Book Two (1948).

"Acquainted": Frost, "Acquainted with the Night," *West-Running Brook* (1928).

114. To William Carlos Williams

Possibly written while mildly manic.

you're in the last *Cantos*: Lowell reviewed *Paterson*, Book Two, for the *Nation* (June 19, 1948). Williams wrote to thank him. He added: "It makes me think of my old friend Ez who knowing me since childhood, you might say, has never really digested anything I have put down. Never. All his favors have been 'friendship.' And you know what that means. Where in his Cantos which mention hundreds of intimates have you ever seen even my shadow?" (Williams to RL, June 16[, 1948], Harvard).

very lovingly: "and as for the solidity of the white oxen in all this/perhaps only Dr Williams (Bill Carlos)/will understand its importance,/its benediction. He wd/have put in the cart./The shadow of the tent's peak treads on its corner peg/marking the hour. The moon split, no cloud nearer than Lucca" (Pound, canto 78, lines 215–20).

116. To Elizabeth Bishop

the prose parts of *Paterson* . . . : See Bishop, *One Art*, 159.

on Burns: John Speirs, "Burns," *Determinations: Critical Essays*, ed. F. R. Levis (1931).

Fontaine: Marianne Moore was having trouble finding a publisher for her translation of the *Fables* of Jean de La Fontaine; Viking eventually published it in 1954.

It doesn't *drug* me . . . : "I like a moderate amount of solitude and dullness to work in but this is almost drugging" (*One Art*, 159).

praise his anthology . . . : *100 American Poems*, ed. Selden Rodman (1948); Selden Rodman, *The Amazing Year, May 1, 1945–April 30, 1946: A Diary in Verse* (1947).

117. To J. F. Powers

send Eliz. Hardwick . . . in *P.R.*: Powers, "Peter Taylor: *A Long Fourth and Other Stories*," *Commonweal*, June 25, 1948; Elizabeth Hardwick, "Fiction Chronicle," *Partisan Review*, June 1948.

Four Pages: *Four Pages*, a pamphlet series that had a brief life in 1948, was published by Dallam Simpson, an admirer of Pound's.

Mrs. Longworth: Alice Longworth (1884–1980), Theodore Roosevelt's daughter.

Fitzgerald: Robert Fitzgerald (1910–85), Catholic American poet and translator.

my nun's Rabelais . . . : "Mother Marie Therese," *MK*, lines 50–54.

118. To Carley Dawson

trailling: Trailing.

Cairns: Huntington Cairns (1904–85), American jurist and writer who was acquainted with poets in Lowell's circle; he was counselor for the National Gallery during Lowell's year in Washington.

Stonington: Stonington, Maine. "Once I had a wild notion of fishing for a living and wound up there and sold myself on a house and sold Jean on it—till she saw it! An odd little yellow thing that she called Fatso. It was tiny and beset with neighbors" (RL to Elizabeth Bishop, [July 29, 1948], Vassar).

119. To Ezra Pound

memorial for Eliot: Cf. "They that go down to the sea in ships, that do business in great waters" (Psalms 107:23); "And then went down to the ship" (Pound, canto 1, line 1); and "business as usual in eclipse / goes down to the sea in ships" ("Waking Early Sunday Morning," *NTO*, lines 27–28).

120. To Elizabeth Bishop

Bloom: Hyman Bloom (b. 1913), American expressionist painter, friend of Bishop's.

121. To Charlotte Winslow Lowell

Apple Sauce: Apple Sauce Cottage, the house in Essex, Massachusetts, that Lowell's parents rented in the summer of 1948.

122. To Richard Eberhart

the poem: Possibly a reference to Eberhart's "Speech from a Play," reprinted in the *Saturday Review of Literature*, July 1, 1950; see letter 43.

the females: Eberhart, "A Legend of Viable Women," *Poetry-Ireland*, October 1949, and *Kenyon Review*, Winter 1949.

Dikkon: Eberhart's son.

123. To Elizabeth Bishop

everybody died . . . When my mother died it made me nervous: "It was not dying: everybody died" (Jarrell, "Losses," line 1); "When they killed my mother it made me nervous" (Jarrell, "The State," line 1).

Carruth: Hayden Carruth (b. 1921), American poet, editor at *Poetry* (editor in chief from 1949 to 1950).

run-down sensibilities: "I had a wonderful letter here from *Poetry* magazine. . . . It requests a contribution & congratulates me on my poetry's having 'perceptivity' & 'sureness,' etc., that 'seem often to be lacking in the output of the *run-down sensibility of the forties.*' I think we should make a modest fortune by working out a prescription for run-down sensibilties" (Bishop to RL, [August 22, 1948], Harvard).

***Les Liasons Dangereuses* . . . Clarissa Harlowe:** Choderlos de Laclos, *Les Liasons Dangereuses* (1784); Chaucer, *Troilus and Cryseyde* (1483?); Samuel Richardson, *Clarissa* (1748).

the poem on me: Richard Eberhart, "Speech from a Play"; see note to RL to Eberhart, August 27, 1948 letter.

Parkman: Francis Parkman (1823–93), American historian.

the poem he sent Randall: Unidentified.

124. To Richard Eberhart

Wisconsin Lawrence poem: Eberhart, "At Lake Geneva," *A Little Treasury of American Poetry*, ed. Oscar Williams (1948).

125. To John Berryman

***The Possessed*:** Berryman, "The Possessed," *The Dispossessed* (1948); Berryman had sent Lowell a copy of the book in April.

beware of Richard: R. P. Blackmur, "The State of American Writing," *Partisan Review*, August 1948; see also *The Good European* (1947).

agree with Randall: Jarrell, "Verse Chronicle," *Nation*, July 17, 1948.

Tate and Pound reviews: Robert Fitzgerald, "The Poetic Responsibility," *New Republic*, April 26, 1948, and "Poetry and Perfection," *Sewanee Review*, Autumn 1948, reviews of Allen Tate's *Poems, 1922–1947*; "Addendum to Pound," *New Republic*, August 23, 1948.

126. To John and Heather Keeler Thompson

John Thompson (1918–2002), American poet and literary critic, friend from Kenyon College.

pictures: Of Robie and Ann Macauley's wedding reception; the photograph is reproduced in Ian Hamilton, opposite p. 149.

127. To George Santayana

***Dialogues in Limbo*:** Santayana, *Dialogues in Limbo*, rev. ed. (1948).

"Poets at Work": *Poets at Work: Essays Based on the Modern Poetry Collection at the Lockwood Memorial Library, University of Buffalo* (1948).

128. To Elizabeth Bishop

Cowley: Malcolm Cowley (1898–1989), American literary critic.

a student of a former Kenyon class-mate . . . : Flannery O'Connor (1925–64), American writer who studied with Robie Macauley at the University of Iowa in 1947. "Flannery reminds me a little of Eleanor[,] acute and silent. She's run through the local library, put out crumbs for birds, bought a sternostove—I think she's planning a sort of half-hibernation to never leave a small dark cheerless room where she'll subsist on vitamin B soup capsules, and Dr. E. Flan-

ders Dunbar's psycho-somatic summa. But we've learned her ping-pong" (RL to Robie Macauley, n.d. Fall 1948, Texas).

129. To Peter Taylor

Wallace: Henry Wallace (1888–1965), vice-president of the United States under Roosevelt, ran for president in 1948 on the Progressive party ticket.

the *Nation*: "Whatever idiocies he may have babbled into the Fascist radios (and I cannot help thinking that, even so, he was on riskier ground than Jeffers's Roosevelt-hating after the event), Old Ez, in my opinion, has never been a traitor to the republic of letters, for wh. (as he would abbreviate) not forgiveness is due him, but honor. I would rather see him saved from death by drowning, or the firing squad, than Bennett Cerf. Or even Clifton Fadiman; and if that be treason, etc., etc.," (Rolfe Humphries, "Jeffers and Pound," *Nation*, September 25, 1948).

Sired a baby: Katherine Baird Taylor was born on September 30, 1948.

130. To Elizabeth Bishop

The train connections: Lowell and Bishop attended the Bard Poetry Conference in the first week of November with William Carlos Williams, Louise Bogan, Richard Wilbur, James Merrill, Mary McCarthy, Elizabeth Hardwick, and others. See Bishop, *One Art*, 173–76, and Fountain and Brazeau, 103–08. See also RL to Elizabeth Bishop, August 15, 1957, letter 301.

Glugg: See letter 301; see also "The Mills of the Kavanaughs," *MK*, stanza 20, line 14.

Rexroth: Kenneth Rexroth (1905–82), American poet.

Frankenbergs and Summers: Close friends of Bishop's: Lloyd Frankenberg (1907–75), American poet and critic; Loren MacIver (1909–98), American painter; Joseph Summers (1920–2003), Renaissance scholar who was a conscientious objector during the Second World War; U. T. Miller Summers, writer. Joseph Summers was one of the organizers of the Bard conference.

131. To Ezra Pound

the Uberti: Probably Ubaldo degli Uberti, a friend of Pound's and a descendent of the Farinata degli Uberti who appears in canto 10 of Dante's *Inferno*. See Pound, canto 89, line 269; canto 95, line 37; and canto 97, line 239.

132. To George Santayana

your *system* is lost . . . : "If Santayana has a 'system,' it is hopelessly lost among the flourishes of such adroit naturalistic fencing. . . . A Catholic living in a Catholic retreat, he calls his religion 'a matter of sympathy and traditional allegiance, not of philosophy.' Says he mischievously: 'I believe I am the despair of the nuns here, who hope I'll become pious on my deathbed.' When he settles down in his armchair to read, he turns to the old masterpieces (two recent exceptions: the poetry of Pulitzer Prize–winning U. S. Poet Robert Lowell, which he admires, and a German biography of Albert Einstein, for whom he has great regard)" ("Philosopher without Quest," *Time*, September 27, 1948, 100).

Wilson's interview: Edmund Wilson (American critical essayist, 1895–1972), "Santayana at the Convent of the Blue Nuns," *New Yorker*, April 6, 1946, reprinted in *Europe Without Baedeker* (1947).

your essay and Mann's . . . : Santayana, "Goethe and Faust," *Goethe: A Symposium*, ed. Dagobert D. Runes (1932); Thomas Mann, "Goethe's Faust," *Essays of Three Decades*, trans. H. T. Lowe-

Porter (1947); Johann Peter Eckermann, *Conversations with Goethe in the Last Years of His Life*, trans. Margaret Fuller (1839).

133. To Caroline Gordon

the Cosmos Club: Lowell went to Washington for two days of meetings with the Library of Congress fellows. They decided that if Marianne Moore turned it down, Elizabeth Bishop would be offered the job of consultant for 1949–50. They also awarded the first Bollingen Poetry Award to Ezra Pound for the *Pisan Cantos.*

135. To T. S. Eliot

the Barnes kiss . . . : See letter 146.

Sharp the Conquering: "The lyf so short, the craft so long to lerne,/Thassay so hard, so sharp the conquering" (Chaucer, *Parlement of Fowles* [1477?], lines 1–7).

136. To Léonie Adams

Like the statement: Because the Bollingen Award would not be official until the end of the calendar year, the fellows were under pressure from Library of Congress staff to change their minds about giving it to Pound for the *Pisan Cantos.* Adams, at the library daily, faced the worst of what she called the "siege." She drafted the fellows' official recommendation, coordinating suggestions from Lowell, Allen Tate, Robert Penn Warren, and others. The final draft is published in *The Case Against the Saturday Review of Literature . . .* (Chicago: Poetry, 1949).

137. To William Carlos Williams

the usury . . . : See Pound, "Usura," canto 45. Williams visited Pound at St. Elizabeths when he was in Washington. "Now is that insanity or is it not? . . . A horrible misgiving comes over us that history may (more or less) prove that Ez was SANE! For usury is a public crime of such overwhelming proportions that no one in our day can even guess it. . . . Oh well, oh well. Oh well—I'm trying to reconstruct Ezra's 'mind' or mindlessness, his sense or nonsense" (Williams to RL, November 27, 1948, Harvard).

The Eliot-lion figure: "As for Eliot, I dunno, I dunno, I dunno. He is hiding too much for anyone to trust him far. 'The marsupial' as Ez now calls him is cute as a pussy-cat, I'd be happy to talk with him and to have him lie around the house any time he shows up but it would take a long, long time before I'd trust him . . . My private opinion is that the man is dull at some central point in his perceptions. To me it is like the tiger in the Assyrian wall decorations, the blue and yellow ceramics of sculptured tiles, you remember? There's one lion that has had a spear through his spine and is paralyzed from the haunches down. . . . O.k., Eliot is maimed, so what? (You'll reply to me) . . . On the other hand he is charming, I can see that. So am I, charming. So that cancels that. I don't intend to make him a buddy—nor would he want it" (Williams to RL, November 27, 1948, Harvard).

138. To Elizabeth Bishop

"I *sure* do like Elizabeth Bishop" . . . : *Randall Jarrell's Letters,* 213, slightly misquoted. Edith Sitwell (1887–1964), English poet.

Cairns: Huntington Cairns, *The Limits of Art: Poetry and Prose Chosen by Ancient and Modern Critics* (1948).

your neighbors . . . : Bishop was in Key West. Lowell enclosed a postcard from his mother vacationing in not-quite-nearby Winter Park, Florida: "Dear Bobby We arrived safely and Daddy is W. & H. It is warm and restful. I can pick oranges and grapefruit in the gardens just outside my window. We miss you. Love Mother" (Charlotte Lowell to RL, December 6, 1948, Vassar).

139. To Elizabeth Bishop

Jew-fish: Pictured on a postcard from Bishop.

your poem: Bishop, "The Fish," *North & South* (1946).

his brother-in-law: James Ross (b. 1911), Eleanor Ross Taylor's brother, who wrote one novel, *They Don't Dance Much* (1940), and later became a journalist in Greensboro, North Carolina.

Rainbow, Rainbow: Bishop, "The Fish," line 75.

Jazz-Blue-Song?: See Bishop, "Songs for a Colored Singer," *North & South* (1946).

T. Weiss: Theodore Weiss (b. 1916), American poet.

the Carroll Book: Lewis Carroll, *Phantasmagoria and Other Poems* (1869).

Allen's essays: Tate, *On the Limits of Poetry: Selected Essays, 1928–1948* (1948).

140. To Elizabeth Bishop

Probably written while mildly manic. Postmarked January 5, 1949, but was written over a two-day period, probably the 3rd and 4th.

Eudora Welty's reply to Wilson on Faulkner: "In practicing so far from such cities as produced the Flauberts, Joyces, and Jameses, Faulkner's provinciality, stubbornly cherished and turned into an asset, inevitably tempts him to be slipshod and has apparently made it impossible for him to acquire complete expertness in an art that demands of the artist the closest attention and care" (Edmund Wilson, "William Faulkner's Reply to the Civil Rights Program," *New Yorker*, October 23, 1948, 106–13). Eudora Welty's letter to the editors took exception to Wilson's review: "It's as though we were told to modify our opinion of Cézanne's painting because Cézanne lived not in Paris but by preference in Aix and painted Aix apples—'stubbornly' (what word could ever apply less to the quality of the imagination's working?)" (*New Yorker*, January 1, 1949, 50–51).

"Lycaon listened to Achilles speak": Cf. Homer, *The Iliad*, book 21. Lowell returned to this subject in *"The Killing of Lykaon," IM*.

a real Yaddo ringer: Edward Maisel (b. 1917), American writer.

I won't tell Randall: "Just before I left New York Randall sent me copies of 'The Olive Garden' and 'The Night Before the Night Before Christmas.' . . . When someone sends you something are you supposed to 'criticize' or merely appreciate? And I hesitate to tell you exactly what I do think somehow. I guess I'm afraid you'll tell him. But it does seem limp & more suited for a short story. But then one always feels he's 'been there'" (Bishop to RL, December 31, 1948, Harvard).

141. To Peter Taylor

Probably written while mildly manic.

the rumors: "Is it true that you are drinking too much and going to pieces and that that ungainly bird Eliot is worried to death about you? So the story goes, and I want to know if your spree at the poets' conference is the basis for it" (Peter Taylor to RL, January 1, 1949, quoted in Ian Hamilton, 138).

142. To George Santayana

Probably written while mildly manic.

Atlantic **chapters:** Santayana wrote three new "Dialogues" for the revised edition of *Dialogues in Limbo* (1948).

four kinds named by Stendhal: Stendhal, *De L'Amour* (1822).

"Death of the Sheriff" and "Between the Porch": In *LWC*.

Power & Dominion: George Santayana, *Dominations and Powers* (1951).

Aiken: Conrad Aiken (1899–1973), American poet. George Santayana, *Three Philosophical Poets: Lucretius, Dante, and Goethe* (1910).

the Tillyard. I liked his Milton: E.M.W. Tillyard, *Milton* (1930). The Tillyard book that Santayana sent to Lowell is undocumented.

143. To George Santayana

Probably written while mildly manic.

the fearful, glorious, ruining man in Thucydides: Santayana used Alcibiades (a subject of Thucydides' *History of the Peloponnesian War*) as a figure in *Dialogues in Limbo*. "Lowell . . . doubtless had been reading one of the three new *Dialogues in Limbo*, 'The Libertine'" (McCormick, 460).

Your remarks on incest & suicide: Lowell may have written his postscript some days later, after receiving Santayana's January 14 letter: "What you tell me of your new long poem also pleases me immensely. Incest and suicide may be romantic; they certainly express the Spirit rebelling against fate and taking the low into its own hands. But they also involve coming up against the ultimate; and that is classic rather than romantic. But Spirit, according to my view, should never attribute *power* to itself; and if it recognizes its dependence, as Christ in the Gospels does continually on the Father, the spirit becomes the spirit of observation and worship, rather than of adventure."

Kazin: Alfred Kazin (1915–98), American literary critic.

144. To Peter Taylor

Probably written while mildly manic.

his Salzburg ball game poem: Jarrell, "A Game at Salzburg," *Nation*, January 1, 1949, reprinted in *The Seven-League Crutches* (1951).

145. To T. S. Eliot

Probably written while mildly manic.

The Werfel: "The Fat Man in the Mirror," *Poetry*, August 1947, reprinted in *MK*.

Mallarmé-Valéry kind of revision: "One ends by working for work's sake. In the eyes of these lovers of anxiety and perfection, a work is never *complete*—a word which to them is meaningless—but *abandonded*. . . . I had contracted this sickness, this perverse taste for endless revision, and this indulgence in the reversible state of works at the critical age when the intellectual man is formed and fixed" (Paul Valéry, "Au sujet du *Cimetière marin*," published in 1933; trans. F. Codman and H. Baugh, *Southern Review*, Summer 1938).

John Ford: John Ford (1586–1640), English dramatist.

Timon's guests: See Shakespeare, *Timon of Athens*, 3.4; see also RL to Randall Jarrell, February 24, [1952].

the captains and the kings: Rudyard Kipling, "Recessional," line 8.

Spender's auto-biography: Stephen Spender, "The Life of Literature," *Partisan Review*, 1948 and 1949; "London Gray, New York Gold," *Nation*, May 14, 1949, reprinted in *World within World: The Autobiography of Stephen Spender* (1951).

146. To Elizabeth Bishop

Probably written while mildly manic.

"In the Prison": Bishop, "In Prison," *Partisan Review*, March 1938.

The Randall German poem . . . : Jarrell, "The Olive Garden" (a translation of Rilke's "Der Ölbaum-Garten"), *Nation*, December 18, 1948; "The Night before the Night before Christmas," *Kenyon Review*, Winter 1949.

Barnes: Djuna Barnes (1892–1982), American modernist writer.

moral: In an earlier letter, Lowell had written to Bishop, "There's a little Catholic girl named Flannery O'Connor here now, who will remain if she can—a real writer, I think one of the best to be when she is a little older. Very moral (in your sense) and witty—whom I'm sure you'd like" (RL to Elizabeth Bishop, January 14, 1949, Vassar). In reply, Bishop had asked what Lowell meant by "moral."

Peter's play: Taylor, "The Death of a Kinsman," *Sewanee Review*, Winter 1949.

147. To Allen Tate

Written during an acute manic episode.

Yaddo was under FBI surveillance because a former guest, Agnes Smedley, was suspected of espionage. In February 1949, *The New York Times* reported the Smedley story. Because Smedley was a friend of Yaddo director Elizabeth Ames, Lowell and the other guests became suspicious of Ames's role in the scandal. They organized a campaign against her, enlisting former Yaddo guests like Tate to their cause and pressing the Yaddo board to investigate her. An equally large number of former residents came to Ames's defense and she was vindicated. Then in March, at the Cultural and Scientific Conference for World Peace held in New York City, Lowell joined Mary McCarthy, Dwight MacDonald, and others in questioning Dmitry Shostakovich and A. A. Fadayev about the treatment of artists and dissidents in the Soviet Union. Lowell's reaction to these events was increasingly excited and he underwent a new religious conversion. On March 29, the eighth anniversary of his reception into the Catholic Church, he traveled to Chicago to visit the Tates.

OLD ROBBERT: A letter from Caroline Gordon to RL (n.d. Spring 1949, Harvard) suggests that "Old Robbert"—another "bert"?—may have been Robert Fitzgerald.

148. To Elizabeth Bishop

Written during an acute manic episode.

anxious about me: After seeing the Tates, Lowell visited Peter Taylor in Bloomington, Indiana, where he was arrested. He was committed to Billings Hospital in Chicago on April 3. On April 6, Charlotte Lowell, with the help of Merrill Moore, Blair Clark, and John Thompson, took Lowell to Baldpate Hospital in Massachusetts. For accounts of Lowell's first major manic episode, see Ian Hamilton, 143–63.

152. To William Carlos Williams

Written during an acute manic episode.

Hardwick: Hardwick stayed with Frank Parker off and on during this period and visited Lowell regularly (see Ian Hamilton interview with Hardwick and letter from Jean Stafford to Peter Taylor, April 26, 1949, copies in Ian Hamilton Notebooks, British Library).

155. To Robert Frost

Written during an acute manic episode.

visit me: Frost obliged.

157. To Allen Tate and Caroline Gordon

Written during an acute manic episode.

the feast of Monica: St. Monica (331–87), the mother of St. Augustine of Hippo, was Caroline Gordon's patron saint (see Gordon to Peter Taylor, n.d. May 1949, copy in Ian Hamilton's Notebooks, British Library). Her feast day is August 27.

158. To Gertrude Buckman

Written during an acute manic episode.

"FILIAE REGUM . . .": Psalm 44:10 in St. Jerome's Latin Vulgate Bible. In the King James Bible, the line occurs in Psalm 45: "Kings' daughters were among thy honorable women: upon thy right hand did stand the queen in gold of Ophir."

keep hearing you: Cf. RL to Carley Dawson [April 25, 1948].

silver whistle: A "silver bosun's pipe that I'd once given him" (Gertrude Buckman notes, Berg Collection).

159. To Randall Jarrell

Written during an acute manic episode.

the Starrs: Milton and Zaro Starr (see letter 21 and note; see also Pritchard, *Randall Jarrell: A Literary Life*, 29–30).

played your Lady Bates: One of the poems Jarrell recorded for the Library of Congress, released on 78 r.p.m. phonodisc as *Randall Jarrell Reading His Own Poems* (1949).

the *one story*: "There is one story and one story only" (Robert Graves, "To Juan at the Winter Solstice," *Poems 1938–45* [1946], line 1). Jarrell refers to Graves's "one story" in several essays, including a review of *Lord Weary's Castle* ("From the Kingdom of Necessity," *Nation*, January 11, 1947, 75–77). He singles it out for particular praise in his review of *Poems 1938–45* (*Partisan Review*, September–October 1948), calling it "one of the most beautiful poems of our century."

Allen's Christmas sonnets . . . : "Sonnets at Christmas," *New Republic*, December 26, 1934; "More Sonnets at Christmas," *Kenyon Review*, Spring 1943.

those responsible . . . : Perhaps a reference to A. Lawrence Lowell, chairman of the commission to review the Sacco and Vanzetti trial. Apart from rebuking Judge Thayer for a "grave breach of official decorum" for his widely reported remarks about getting "those anarchist bastards," the commission refused to overrule the conviction, consider new evidence, or recommend a new trial. Sacco and Vanzetti were executed on August 23, 1927. President Lowell received hate mail for the rest of his life on the anniversary of their execution but was unrepentant about the commission's decision.

electricuted: Electrocuted.

what he did to my black suit: See letter 68.

160. To Elizabeth Hardwick

Written while recovering from an acute manic episode.

The Inn: Lowell was moved from a locked hospital unit to "The Inn," a more relaxed facility at Baldpate.

Schlomer: Baldpate was "quite a good small hospital run by an adorable old German doctor, Dr. [George] Schlomer. . . . I went up to see him and I think both Merrill Moore and the family thought that was a very bad idea and got quite mad at the doctor, but the doctor—if I remember—got rather turned off them. He was a very reserved and distinguished old man, and

he seemed to look on my visits favorably" (Elizabeth Hardwick interview, Ian Hamilton Notebooks, British Library).

Nag's Head: A beach on the Outer Banks of North Carolina.

161. To Elizabeth Hardwick

Uriah Heep: Mr. Wickfield's clerk in Dickens's *David Copperfield* (1850).

Reading *The Idiot* again: Dostoyevsky, *The Idiot*, trans. Constance Garnett (1935).

163. To T. S. Eliot

I agree about the title: Eliot thought that a "fancy title" like the originally proposed *Sharp the Conquering* would not be appropriate for the English edition of Lowell's poems. Eliot also had several textual changes to suggest. He objected to the scansion of "detritus" in "Colloquy in Black Rock," and wanted to change the American spelling of "saber" to the English "sabre," among other things (Eliot to RL, March 8 and July 18, 1949, Harvard); see *CPM*, 1007.

Huxley's comment: See Aldous Huxley, "Introduction," *The Letters of D. H. Lawrence* (1932).

164. To Peter Taylor

Fred Dupee . . . General Israel Putnam: F. W. Dupee (1904–79), American literary scholar, *Partisan Review* editor; Israel Putnam (1718–90), American Revolutionary War general.

electric shocks: Electroconvulsive therapy (ECT) was "introduced as a therapeutic modality in the early 1940s; there were several clinical reports of its efficacy in treating acute mania" (Goodwin, Jamison, 625). Its use in American mental hospitals was common by 1949.

165. To Robert Fitzgerald

your account: Because many people witnessed and gossiped about the Yaddo affair and Lowell's breakdown, Robert Fitzgerald wrote an account to explain Lowell's behavior. He circulated it widely in the literary community. Excerpts are quoted in Ian Hamilton, 144–45, copies in the Robert Fitzgerald Papers, Yale University.

"the world is all before us": "The World was all before them, where to choose / Thir place of rest, and Providence thir guide: / They hand in hand with wandring steps and slow, / Through Eden took thir solitarie way" (John Milton, *Paradise Lost*, book 12, lines 645–48).

166. To Dorothy Pound

"Odes": Pound, *The Classic Anthology Defined by Confucius* (1954), reprinted as *The Confucian Odes* (1959).

the "news" note in *Poetry*: "The award of the Bollingen Prize to Ezra Pound for the *Pisan Cantos* was announced in February by the Library of Congress. It is, we believe, the first honor of the sort that has come to Mr. Pound since he received one of the annual prizes from *Poetry* about thirty-six years ago. In the interim he has seen some of his literary disciples enjoy, or endure, a great deal of public recognition . . . All this, while Pound's own reputation hardly existed beyond the more assiduous readers of little magazines. It must have been disheartening at times, and nothing is more understandable than that he should have adopted a rather cross attitude towards America" ("Notes," *Poetry*, April 1949, 56–59).

168. To T. S. Eliot

the Latin sequence: "Suspice, Domine, munera pro tuorum commemoratione Sanctorum: ut, sicut illos passio gloriosos effecit; ita nos devotio reddat innocuous" ("Receive, O Lord, these gifts for the commemoration of Thy Saints, that just as their passion made them glorious, so may our devotion free us of sin"; see *CPM*, 8 and 1006).

the Congressional suspension: After the Pound-Bollingen controversy, Congress abolished literary awards and prizes at the library. Several magazines, including *Poetry*, the *Hudson Review*, and the *Sewanee Review*, offered to take over the administration of the Bollingen, but it was eventually moved to Yale University.

169. To Elizabeth Hardwick

This is like the inn: See note to letter 160.

P.R.: *Partisan Review*.

170. To Peter Taylor

This letter was never posted.

where Jean was: Stafford entered the Payne Whitney Clinic at New York Hospital for nervous exhaustion and alcoholism in November 1946, after she and Lowell split; she spent the greater part of a year there.

171. To Elizabeth Hardwick

Cakes and Ale: W. Somerset Maugham, *Cakes and Ale* (1930).

173. To Elizabeth Hardwick

Hayes: Helen Hayes (1900–93), American actress.

I hope Susan is with you: Possibly Susan Turner, a friend of Hardwick's.

175. To Elizabeth Bishop

St. John's: St. John's College in Annapolis, Maryland; Lowell and Bishop hoped to rendezvous in Washington, D.C., in January 1950.

176. To Robert Fitzgerald

the Oedipus: Sophocles, *Oedipus Rex*, trans. Dudley Fitts and Robert Fitzgerald (1949).

the Prince: Possibly a poem that F. T. Prince (1912–2003), South African poet, later revised for *Soldiers Bathing* (1954).

177. To George Santayana

Oliver: The protagonist of Santayana's *The Last Puritan: A Memoir in the Form of a Novel* (1935).

178. To Allen Tate

Paul: At Allen Tate's urging, Paul Engle offered Lowell a teaching job at the Iowa Writers Workshop for the spring semester.

179. To George Santayana

your embarrassing check: When he learned of Lowell's recovery and marriage, Santayana sent
him $500 through John Hall Wheelock (McCormick, 461).

Tibullus: Santayana's translations of Albus Tibullus (55–19 B.C.), Roman poet, appeared in
Posthumous Poems (1953).

The Pound: Ezra Pound, *Pisan Cantos* (1948).

180. To Dorothy Pound

a long, burdensome dull period of the mind: The Pounds were aware of Lowell's depression. In a
letter to the Taylors, Hardwick quoted Dorothy Pound: "'We've just heard that Cal has had
to go back to the home and Ezra sounds you this message: Cal is not cracked but worried be-
cause the country is sick. He is too young to know what to do about it. I wish you could talk
about the case with Ezra, who feels he has an understanding of it. This relapse is most dis-
tressing and the causes most infuriating.'" Hardwick adds: "Horrors! I am happy to say that
Cal has changed so much that he no longer minds old Ez. Adorably sane" (Hardwick to Peter
and Eleanor Taylor, October 20, 1949, Ian Hamilton Notebooks, British Library).

myself again: Lowell reported to his parents that "I have been seeing a psychiatrist here about
once a week, and we agree that I am well out of my extreme troubles. There is a stiffness,
many old scars, the toil of building up new habits. However, I definitely feel out of the old,
perverse dark maze" (RL to Mr. and Mrs. R.T.S. Lowell, March 10, 1950, Harvard).

E.P. letters: *The Letters of Ezra Pound 1907–1941*, ed. D. D. Paige (1950).

181. To Robert Penn Warren

Your hospitality: Lowell read his poetry at the University of Minnesota, where Warren was
teaching.

the sources of poems: Robert Penn Warren and Cleanth Brooks, "How Poems Come About: In-
tention and Meaning," *Understanding Poetry*, rev. ed. (1950).

"The Immortal Part": A. E. Housman, "The Immortal Part," *A Shropshire Lad* (1896).

Cinina: Robert Penn Warren's first wife, Emma Brescia Warren, was known as Cinina.

182. To Peter Taylor

Randall Blackmur meetings: "Blackmur . . . served as visiting critic at the Greensboro Arts Forum
in the spring of 1950" (Pritchard, 199).

talked a book: See Hardwick, *The Simple Truth* (1955).

Handly: Avery Handly (1913–58), Nashville painter whom Taylor befriended during his years at
Vanderbilt.

the Scottish Chaucerian Dunbar: William Dunbar, "Trestis of the Tua Mariit Wemen and the
Wedo" (1507?). The Taylor story is possibly "Their Losses," *New Yorker*, March 11, 1950.

journey to Memphis: After graduating from Kenyon in 1940, Lowell, Stafford, and Taylor traveled
to Memphis to visit Taylor's family. "As the train pulled into the station, past the town's slums,
[Taylor recalled,] 'Cal was very disapproving and very critical: "All this will have to go." He
was speaking like an Old Testament Prophet'" (Roberts, 188); see also Ian Hamilton, 74.

183. To Peter Taylor

a faculty retreat: Among the faculty at the Kenyon School of Letters in 1950 were Kenneth Burke,
William Empson, John Crowe Ransom, and Delmore Schwartz.

Woman of Means: Peter Taylor, *A Woman of Means* (1950).

184. To Kenneth Burke

Kenneth Burke (1897–1993), American literary critic. This letter is copied from Burke's transcription in a letter to James Sibley Watson, Jr., Berg Collection.

the treatment you received: At the Harvard Summer School symposium on the Defense of Poetry, Kenneth Burke spoke against American intervention in the Korean conflict: "There should be but one plank in our platform, so far as human relations in general are concerned: To do all within our intellectual and imaginative power to turn the world away from the cult of the ultimate destruction." William Yandell Elliott (1896–1979), a member of the Fugitives, viciously attacked him without giving him an opportunity to reply. Burke left abruptly after the session. A number of the conference participants wrote supportive letters to him, including Harry Levin, Theodore Roethke, Randall Jarrell, Stephen Spender, and Lowell; see the Burke-Watson correspondence, Berg Collection.

185. To George Santayana

William James: William James, Jr., an artist who worked for the Boston Museum of Fine Arts, son of William James (1842–1910), American philosopher.

Viereck: Peter Viereck (b. 1916), American poet; see also note to letter 207.

186. To Elizabeth Bishop

"Dead Brother": "Her Dead Brother," *Nation*, February 22, 1947, reprinted in *P50* and *MK*.

for his sake: "There were some awkward moments that summer . . . when Delmore [Schwartz] attacked Tate at a cocktail party for backing Pound for the Bollingen. When Cal tried to placate him, Delmore stiffened and turned instead on Empson, who had also backed Pound, and was just back from China, still sporting a Mao suit. That was too much for Delmore, who shouted that Empson was a Communist and a traitor to England" (Mariani, *Lost Puritan*, 193).

187. To Elizabeth Bishop

IN ANY CASE: See note to letter 97.

Philippic: At the Harvard symposium, Randall Jarrell gave a paper entitled "The Obscurity of the Poet," which later appeared in the *Partisan Review* (January–February 1951).

188. To George Santayana

your book: Santayana had recently finished writing *Dominations and Powers*.

191. To Elizabeth Bishop

Communist mayor: Mario Fabiani (1912–74), communist mayor of Florence from 1946 to 1951.

Death to the criminal MacArthur: MacArthur was widely denounced in Europe for ruining the U.N.'s chance to negotiate a Chinese withdrawal from North Korea.

archeologist lover: "Bishop went to Yaddo for four months after she finished at the Library of Congress in October 1950. . . . [She] was pleased that Victor Wolfgang von Hagen [b. 1908], an archeologist and explorer, several of whose books on South America she had read, was there" (Fountain and Brazeau, 119).

Miss Hanson's book: Pauline Hanson, *Forever Young* (1948).

Assumption ceremony: On November 1, 1950, Pope Pius XII declared that Mary had been assumed wholly into heaven at her death; see "Beyond the Alps," *LS*, and *CPR*, 1032.

Pearl Kazin, Dunstan Thompson: Pearl Kazin, literary editor of *Harper's Bazaar*, friend and correspondent of Bishop's. Dunstan Thompson (1918–75), Anglo-American poet.

192. To George Santayana

Berenson: Bernard Berenson (1865–1959), Lithuanian American art historian.

Sibille: "Santayana sent a letter of introduction to Dr. Luciano Sibille at Florence to ease Lowell's way in Italy, noting Lowell as a 'particular friend of mine and sensitive in religious matters'" (McCormick, 461).

seven: unknown; possibly *Seven Types of Ambiguity* by William Empson (1930).

Cory: Daniel Cory (1904–72), Santayana's secretary who later edited his *Letters* (1955).

193. To Charlotte Winslow Lowell

like blue crabs in a tub: A sound lodged in Lowell's ear, particularly while he was revising "The Mills of the Kavanaughs" (see stanza 26, lines 2–4, *MK*).

Lady Berkeley: Sister of Ralph Lowell; see below.

Ralph Lowell: Ralph Lowell (1890–1978), banker and philanthropist from the richer branch of the Lowell family; Lowell's distant cousin.

194. To Elizabeth Hardwick

P.W.: Payne Whitney.

Frank's engraving: Parker engraving for the frontispiece of *MK*.

195. To Peter Taylor

the *New Yorker*s and Eleanor's poems in *Poetry*: Peter Taylor, "What You Hear from 'Em?" *New Yorker*, February 10, 1951; and "Two Ladies in Retirement," *New Yorker*, March 31, 1951; Eleanor Ross, "The Bine," "Adkins Rose," and "Sister," *Poetry*, October 1950.

196. To George Santayana

along the lines of *Phèdre*: Lowell first attempted to translate Jean Racine's *Phèdre* (1677) at Yaddo in 1947: "Did a little on *Phèdre*—the results rather dull" (RL to Gertrude Buckman, n.d. June 14, 1947, Berg Collection). He returned to the project in 1960 and published *Phaedra* in 1961.

Berryman's book: John Berryman, *Stephen Crane* (1950).

Crane's Civil War novel: Stephen Crane, *The Red Badge of Courage* (1895).

197. To George Santayana

a picture of a swan: "Frank has done a gorgeous frontispiece to my book—a great swan troubling the waters and getting ready to rise. It was not done especially for the book. I was looking through a pile of his etchings and liked it enormously" (RL to Charlotte Winslow Lowell, February [1951], Harvard).

O Dieu! Tousjours vivant . . . : Phillippe Desportes, "Plainte" ("Des abysmes d'ennuis en l'horreur plus extresme . . ."). "O Lord! In the midst of this life, I firmly believe that, come the last day, through your omnipotence, this body of mine, covered with earth, listening to your voice, will take on a new life and, by your absolute grace, the hour will come for me to see you with my own eyes, face-to-face, and with the blessèd bless your holy name."

198. To Elizabeth Bishop

Gerusalemme liberata: Torquato Tasso, *Gerusalemme liberata* (1574; "Jerusalem delivered").

Caetani: Marguerite Chapin Caetani (1880–1963), Principessa di Bassiano, was the editor of the international literary journal *Botteghe Oscure*. Her sister, Katherine Garrison Chapin, was married to Francis Biddle.

a note from Pound: Lowell misquotes Pound's letter slightly: "1st impression iz that Mons. Lowell is learnin' to write backin' into it hind-side before = /nasty comparison of Jarrell's on the *cover* don't yr. pubis—*like* yu yr EZ" (Pound to RL, n.d. 1951, Harvard).

199. To William Carlos Williams

your review: Williams, "In a Mood of Tragedy," *New York Times Book Review*, April 22, 1951, reprinted in *Selected Essays*, 324–25. "[T]he rhymes are necessary to Lowell. He must, to his mind, appear to surmount them."

200. To Elizabeth Hardwick

my Uncle: A term of endearment for Hardwick.

201. To Elizabeth Hardwick

suddenly a flood . . . : Kermit Lansner, a reporter for *Newsweek;* Derek Hill (1916–2000), English painter whom the Lowells had met at I Tatti; W. S. Graham (1918–86), Scottish poet. "I had a note from Uncle Tom [Eliot] and we are to have dinner at the Garrick Club 'unless your wife is with you' [He] reminds [me] of Cousin Alfred[,] more London than London" (RL to Hardwick, [n.d. July/August 1951], Texas).

202. To Elizabeth Hardwick

Holland: "He wanted me to go up to Holland, which I didn't want to do . . . We had spend a part of a month in France, and then he and [Mrs. Lowell] went to Pau and I went to Holland alone to look for a place. I found it absolutely terrifying—I didn't know anyone there, I didn't know what to look for and so on" (Hardwick interview with Ian Hamilton, Ian Hamilton Notebooks, British Library). Hardwick also recalled that, at this point, they had "no money" and were "carrying a paper suitcase, practically."

Motley: John Lothrop Motley (1814–77), American historian, author of *The Rise of the Dutch Republic* (1855), which Lowell first read in his youth.

Fromentin: Eugène Fromentin, *Les Maîtres d'autrefois* (1876; *The Masters of Past Time*).

The Way of All Flesh: Samuel Butler, *The Way of All Flesh* (1903).

204. To Randall Jarrell

Breit: Harvey Breit (1909–68), assistant editor of the *New York Times Book Review;* Lowell's review, "On *The Seven League Crutches*," appeared in the October 7, 1951, issue.

King Abdullah: King Abdullah of Jordan (b. 1882) was assassinated on July 20, 1951, by a Palestinian nationalist.

your award and Princeton: Jarrell received a grant for $1,000 from the National Institute of Arts and Letters and was invited to teach at Princeton for the 1951–52 academic year.

your Stevens: Jarrell, "Reflections on Wallace Stevens," *Partisan Review*, May–June 1951.

Eland is the name of a street here: "Today, in a German dictionary, I saw *elend*/ And the heart in

my breast turned over, it was—/It was a word one translates *wretched*" (Jarrell, "Seele im Raum," lines 46–49).

Vondel: Joost van den Vondel (1587–1679), Dutch poet, author of *Lucifer* (1654), a verse play about the angels' revolt against God. At St. Mark's, "I had come on a tantalizing passage from a freshman syllabus which had described the 'spirited' Corneille and Racine as dwarfed by their contemporary Vondel, the Milton of Holland" ("The Day of Atonement," Robert Lowell Papers, Harvard).

206. To Elizabeth Bishop
Concordance: An early title for *A Cold Spring*.
a long monologue: "The Banker's Daughter," *LS*.

207. To Randall Jarrell
your review: Jarrell admired many poems in *The Mills of the Kavanaughs* but had reservations about the title poem: "The people too often seem to be acting *in the manner* of Robert Lowell, rather than plausibly as real people act (or implausibly as real people act). I doubt that many readers will think them real; the husband of the heroine never seems so, and the heroine is first of all a sort of symbiotic state of the poet. (You feel, 'Yes, Robert Lowell would act like this if he were a girl'; but whoever saw a girl like Robert Lowell?)" (Jarrell, "A View of Three Poets," *Partisan Review*, November–December 1951, 696).

Maud: Tennyson, *Maud* (1855).

[divorce] seems to have [been] . . . : Lowell made corrections to his typed letter in blue pen. "Divorce" and "been" appear to be penciled by a different hand (Jarrell's?).

Nuremberg trials: International Military Tribunal, *The Trial of Major German War Criminals: Proceedings* (1946); Douglas M. Kelley, *22 Cells in Nuremberg: A Psychiatrist Examines the Nazi Criminals* (1947).

Hannah Arendt: Hannah Arendt, *The Origins of Totalitarianism* (1951).

Arendt: "Randall Jarrell had written me in Holland that if I wanted to discover something big and new, I would read Hannah Arendt's *Origins of Totalitarianism*. Randall seldom praised in vain, but my Dutch intellectual friends, as usual embarrassingly more into whatever was being written in America, were ahead of me, and were discussing *Origins* with minds sharpened by the Dutch Resistance, a hatred of Germany, and a fluency with German philosophers. I felt landless and alone, and read Hannah as though I were going home, or reading *Moby-Dick*, perhaps for the second time, no longer seeking adventure, but the voyage of wisdom, the tragedy of America" ("On Hannah Arendt," *New York Review of Books*, May 13, 1976).

tried Brogan, Dallin etc.: D. W. Brogan, *The Development of Modern France 1870–1939* (1941); David J. Dallin, "Report on Russia," *New Leader*, January 8, 1949, and *Forced Labor in Russia*, coauthored with Boris I. Nicolaevsky (1947).

Büchner's libretto . . . : Georg Büchner, *Danton's Tod (A Play in Four Acts: Death)*, trans. Stephen Spender and Goronwy Rees (1939); Thomas Lovell Beddoes (1803–49), English poet; John Webster (1580–1632), English dramatist.

Mount Vernon and Columbus: Mount Vernon, Ohio, borders the village of Gambier (where Kenyon College is located).

his own Timon: See Shakespeare, *Timon of Athens* 3.4.

Viereck's favorites: Lowell and Jarrell liked to joke about Peter Viereck's articles for the *Atlantic Monthly*; see *Randall Jarrell's Letters*, 185 and 226.

208. To William Carlos Williams

Lawrence poem . . . : "Once he received a letter—/he never answered it—/praising him: so English/he had thereby raised himself/to an unenglish greatness" (William Carlos Williams, "An Elegy for D. H. Lawrence," lines 9–13). "I always answer letters, but others seldom have answered those I sent out in my desperation. D. H. Lawrence never answered me, either, when once I wrote to him" (Williams, *Autobiography*, 51). See Williams's reply to Lowell, *Selected Letters*, 311–13.

Góngora: Luis de Góngora y Argote (1561–1627), Spanish Baroque poet; sections 3 and 4 of Lowell's "Ruins of Time," published in *NTO*, are translations of Góngora's "Esta que admiras fábrica, esta prima" and "Menos solicitó veloz saeta."

Marino-Crashaw: Giambattista Marino (1569–1625), Italian *secentismo* poet; Richard Crashaw (1613–49), English poet.

your check: Williams's "The Desert Music" was published in *Botteghe Oscure*, Winter 1951; presumably the check was his payment.

hay-wire on *Paterson,* and to the point on . . . Eliot and Europe: "*Paterson* has been getting rather steadily worse," Jarrell writes. Williams has "limited himself by volunteering for and organizing a long dreary imaginary war in which America and the Present are fighting against Europe and the Past. But go a few hundred years back inside the most American American and it is Europe: Dr. Williams is just as much Darkest Europe as any of us, way down there in the middle of his past . . . When we read the *Four Quartets* we are reading the long poem of a poet so temperamentally isolated that he does not even put another character, another human being treated at length, into the whole poem; and yet the poem . . . impresses us not with its limitations but with its range and elevation, with how much it knows not simply about men but about Man—not simply about one city or one country but about the West, that West of which America is no more than the last part" (Jarrell, "A View of Three Poets," *Partisan Review*, November–December 1951, 698–700).

209. To George Santayana

inexhaustible: cf. Ralph Waldo Emerson, "Intellect," *Essays* (1847).

Russell's: Bertrand Russell, *History of Western Philosophy* (1945).

210. To Elizabeth Bishop

Tovey: Sir Donald Francis Tovey (1875–1940), English composer and musical scholar, author of *Essays in Musical Analysis*, 6 vols. (1935–39), which Lowell read at Yaddo in 1948.

One in particular: Willem Ferdinand van Leeuwen, Dutch psychotherapist; with Hans Gomperts, he edited *Libertinage*, a literary magazine. He was given the nickname Huyck after the title character of J. van Lennep's *Ferdinand Huyck* (1840).

La Bruyère: Jean de la Bruyère (1645–96), French writer.

Valery-Larbeaud: Valery-Nicolas Larbaud (1881–1957), French novelist and critic.

Leverkühn: Adrian Leverkühn, protagonist of Thomas Mann's *Doctor Faustus* (1947).

Burford: William Burford (b. 1927), American poet, Fulbright scholar at the Sorbonne in 1951–52.

your Brazil: On a trip around South America in late 1951, Bishop stopped in Brazil. Her severe allergic reaction to a *caju* forced her to stay in Rio into the new year. After her recovery, Lota de Macedes Soares, who had been caring for her, invited her to move in.

fresh girlish appearance: "I have heard intelligent and cultivated people complain more times than I can remember, 'I can hardly *read* the quarterlies any more'; and I once heard Elizabeth Bishop say, 'After I go through one of the literary quarterlies I don't feel like reading a poem for a week, much less like writing one'" (Jarrell, "The Age of Criticism," *Partisan Review*, March–April 1952, 185–201).

211. To Flannery O'Connor

For O'Connor's reply, see *The Habit of Being* (1979), 35.

New World Writing: O'Connor, "Enoch and the Gorilla," *New World Writing*, April 1952.

Lizzie Burden: Lizzie Borden (1860–1927), accused of the murder of her father and stepmother in 1892.

212. To Peter Taylor

Probably written while mildly manic.

"Confederate Dead": Allen Tate, "Ode to the Confederate Dead," *Mr. Pope and Other Poems* (1928), translated by Jacques Maritain as "Ode aux Morts des Confédérés," *Sewanee Review*, Summer 1952.

Mrs. Spender: Natasha Spender (b. 1919), English pianist, wife of Stephen Spender.

213. To Robert Frost

Probably written while mildly manic.

your poem: Frost, "The Ax-Helve," *New Hampshire* (1923).

214. To Ezra Pound

Probably written while mildly manic.

Kenner: Hugh Kenner (1923–2003), American literary scholar; *The Poetry of Ezra Pound* (1951).

hil & eritas . . . their system: See Pound, canto 88, lines 5–14. Cf. also canto 76, lines 4–5.

215. To Charlotte Winslow Lowell

the rumor: Lowell became very ill in Salzburg. He was taken to the American military hospital at Salzburg for one night, then transferred to the military hospital in Munich. When Lowell was released from the violent wards, Hardwick moved him to the Binswanger Sanatorium at Kreuzlingen, Switzerland. For a full account of Lowell's breakdown, see Ian Hamilton, 188–96.

216. To Allen Tate

"Buried Lake": Allen Tate, "The Buried Lake," *Sewanee Review*, Spring 1953.

Stevenson: Adlai Stevenson (1900–65), American statesman who campaigned for the presidency against Dwight D. Eisenhower in 1952 and 1956.

A-hugging up Bill Jenner: During the 1952 presidential campaign, Senators William Jenner (R-Indiana) and Joseph McCarthy (R-Wisconsin) viciously attacked Secretary of State General George C. Marshall for being, in Jenner's words, "a front man for traitors." Instead of defending Marshall, his old mentor and supporter, Republican candidate Eisenhower remained silent. During a campaign stop in Indiana, Jenner embraced Eisenhower on the platform, which, Eisenhower later told his aides, made him feel "dirty." His failure of loyalty may have been due to his fear of Senator McCarthy's influence.

Mamie: Mamie Eisenhower (1896–1979), wife of Dwight D. Eisenhower.

EPITAPH OF A FALLEN POET: "Epitaph of a Fallen Poet," *Partisan Review*, January–February 1953; Lowell sent a copy of this version to Pound (see RL to Pound, 3/26/54, Yale). The poem was revised and reprinted as "Words for Hart Crane" in the *Nation*, March 22, 1957, and *LS*. See letter 323.

217. To W. F. van Leeuwen

First published in the *Harvard Review*, Fall 2003.

E's story: Hardwick, "Two Recent Travelers," *Kenyon Review*, Summer 1953.

one to Santayana: Published in *Perspectives USA* in 1953; rewritten as the sixth stanza of "Beyond the Alps," *Kenyon Review*, Summer 1953. Lowell later removed it from "Beyond the Alps" and never included it in a book. Later, he wrote a new elegy, "For George Santayana: 1863–1952," *LS*.

Judy: Van Leeuwen was engaged to Judith Herzberg (b. 1934), Dutch poet.

the autobiography: Bep, nickname of Elisabeth du Perron-de Roos, wife of the influential critic and poet Edgar du Perron (1899–1940). She was seeking an English publisher for her husband's memoir *Land van Herkomst*. Mrs. du Perron is also "the author of many subtle essays on French and English literature" (van Leeuwen to SH, April 29, 2003).

McCormick: John McCormick (b. 1918), American literary critic, lecturer at the Free University of Berlin from 1952 to 1953, whom Lowell met in Salzburg; see "Falling Asleep over Grillparzer: An Interview with Robert Lowell," *Poetry* 81, January 1953, reprinted in Meyers, 23–32. He later wrote *George Santayana: A Biography* (1987).

now divorced: Robert Penn Warren was divorced from his first wife, Cinina, in 1951.

and perhaps utterly changed: Cf. W. B. Yeats, "Easter, 1916" (1921).

218. To Allen Tate

Newburgh Conference: Tate tried to organize "Conversations at Newburgh," a Catholic writers' conference (see Allen Tate to RL, April 1953, Harvard).

219. To Allen Tate

Father Tate: In a letter calling off the "Conversations at Newburgh," Tate wrote, "You've got to stop saluting me as Father Tate. I am not qualified to be anything like that. My situation seems to get rougher all the time, and the lines drawn; but where it will end nobody knows but God, who has His reasons for not taking me into His confidence. I patiently await the moment of revelation" (Allen Tate to RL, April 28, 1953, quoted in Doreski, 107).

in their reviews: Arthur Mizener, "Among the Shabby Lucifers," *New Republic*, April 13, 1953; Delmore Schwartz, "The Forlorn Demon," *New York Times Book Review*, April 5, 1953.

look at mushrooms: Gordon was a passionate mushroom hunter (see Laskin, *Partisans*, 123).

220. To Elizabeth Bishop

essays and a story: Hardwick, "The Subjugation of Women," *Partisan Review*, May–June 1953; "Memoirs, Conversations and Diaries," *Partisan Review*, September–October 1953; "Two Recent Travelers," *Kenyon Review*, Summer 1953.

three or four poems: "Beyond the Alps," *Kenyon Review*, Summer 1953; "Inauguration Day: January 1953" and "A Mad Negro Soldier Confined at Munich," *Partisan Review*, November–December 1953.

221. To Elizabeth Hardwick

habitual constipation: Hardwick replied: "Darling, I tell myself that there is nothing wrong and I'm relieved the tests are over and what I gather to be the verdict justifies Mama's old axiom that diarrhea is nothing but constipation. (It takes a gift for paradox to arrive at that)" (Hardwick to RL, September 12, 1953, Harvard).

222. To Elizabeth Bishop

The details: For a vivid account see Berryman to RL, November 14, 1953, Harvard.

college novel: Jarrell, *Pictures from an Institution* (1954).

anthology: Jarrell and Lowell's notes for the anthology (never completed) are at Harvard (bMS Am 1905/2798).

223. To Allen Tate

your rioting: Police in Trieste killed several protesters during riots that erupted after the United States, Britain, and France stalled while negotiating the fate of Trieste. Italians in many cities rioted in sympathy for the slain protesters; in Rome, the American and British embassies were targeted by the crowds. Flannery O'Connor reported that Tate was trapped in his Austin by hundreds of demonstrating students, one of whom fetched an ax to force him to open the car. An old gentleman stood in front of the car to protect him; when some middle-aged people joined the man the mob was diverted. (Flannery O'Connor to RL, 1 January [1954], Harvard).

his personal disasters: "Tomorrow morning some poet may, like Byron, wake up to find himself famous—for having written a novel, for having killed his wife; it will not be for having written a poem" (Jarrell, "The Obscurity of the Poet," *No Other Book*, 11).

Wood: Grant Wood (1892–1942), American regionalist painter.

the Devlins: Denis Devlin (1908–59), Irish poet, worked as a career diplomat in the Irish Foreign Service; he became ambassador to Italy in 1958.

Bentley: Eric Bentley (b. 1916), Anglo-American playwright and critic; *In Search of Theater* (1953).

Oresteia: Lowell returned to this idea in 1964. His translation, *The Oresteia of Aeschylus*, was published posthumously in 1978.

Homer: "Cal and a member of the Classic[s] department are teaching Homer in Greek, which I am taking" (Hardwick to Blair Clark, October 16, 1953, Texas).

225. To Flannery O'Connor

For O'Connor's reply, see *The Habit of Being*, 65.

Wise Blood: O'Connor, *Wise Blood* (1952).

226. To Elizabeth Bishop

my Cousin Harriet: Harriet Patterson Winslow, Lowell's maternal cousin, "was more to me than my mother" ("Soft Wood," *FTUD*, line 38).

her novel: Hardwick, *The Simple Truth* (1955).

Bowen: Elizabeth Bowen (1899–1973), Irish fiction writer.

Your *New Yorker* . . . story . . . : Bishop, "In the Village," *New Yorker*, December 19, 1953; "Gwendolyn," *New Yorker*, June 27, 1953.

Miss Jewett: Sarah Orne Jewett (1849–1909), American fiction writer.

on leaving Europe: "Beyond the Alps."

Victorians for non-fictional prose: Thomas Carlyle, *The French Revolution* (1837), and Lord Acton, *Lectures on the French Revolution* (1910) (RL to John Berryman, December 31, 1953, Minnesota).

227. To J. F. Powers

burn through your novel: Cf. letter 281.

229. To Elizabeth Hardwick

Written while mildly manic.

Rolando: Rolando Anzilotti (1919–82), Lowell's friend and Italian translator.

Mother's doctor is Max Beerbohm's: Dr. Giuseppe Bacigalupo (1912–99); Max Beerbohm (1872–1956), English caricaturist and writer who lived in Rapallo.

230. To Elizabeth Hardwick

Written while mildly manic.

vaccination: For smallpox.

ominous date: March 1 being Lowell's birthday.

231. To Giovanna Madonia Erba

Written during an acute manic episode.

Lowell met Giovanna Madonia very briefly in Salzburg in 1952, when he "took up" with her during a manic episode (Ian Hamilton, 189). In 1954, she and her husband the poet Luciano Erba were living in Milan and she was working for the music publisher Ricordi. Lowell met her again in the manic episode following his mother's death. The complete correspondence between Madonia and Lowell can be found in the Houghton Library, Harvard University—Madonia's letters in the Lowell collection (bMS Am 1905), Lowell's under the catalog number *95M-0008. Although it spans only six months, the correspondence is quite extensive because Lowell, his mania igniting, was voluble. Madonia was one of many of Lowell's manic crushes but one of the few to preserve his manic letters.

My dearest Giovana: Not for another few days did Lowell catch his spelling error. On February 27, 1954, he wrote, "Thumbing through my Dante, I came across this: 'Giova*nna* o altri non ha di me cura.' I remember this line once hit through my heart at Salzburg; but now it only fills me with embarrassment—I have misspelled your name! And dropping an *n* spoils the euphony. Sweetest, really I am sorry, I wouldn't like it a bit if you were to write me as Robbert or Call" (RL to Giovanna Madonia, February 27, 1954, Harvard).

Seefried, Kuntz, and Jurinac . . . Schwarzkopf: Irmgard Seefried (1919–88), Austrian soprano; Kuntz, a baritone; Sena Jurinac (b. 1921), Austrian soprano. Gatto is probably Renata Scotto (b. 1934), Italian soprano. Elisabeth Schwarzkopf (b. 1915), German soprano.

Dove sono: Mozart, *Marriage of Figaro* (1785–86).

233. To Blair Clark

Written during an acute manic episode.

Father Pierre: Clark, "One-Half of France Is Ill-Housed," *New York Times*, March 1, 1954; the article mentions the work of Abbé Pierre, an advocate for the homeless.

Charlotte Winslon: See "Sailing Home from Rapallo," *LS*, line 36, and "Near the Unbalanced Aquarium," *CPR*, 350.

234. To Giovanna Madonia Erba

Written during an acute manic episode.

Sack: Erna Sack (1898–1972), German soprano.

mad scene from Lucia di Lammermoor: Maria Callas's 1955 Berlin recording was played at Lowell's memorial service in New York, September 25, 1977.

"sommettono la ragion al talento": Dante, *Inferno*, canto 5, line 39, slightly misquoted. It should read, "la ragion sommettono al talento" (submit their reason to their lust).

the sixth Book IV?: Propertius's elegy 4.6 is "The Temple of Palatine Apollo"; Lowell is thinking of 4.7, "From beyond the Grave."

Insieme, insieme . . . per sempre!: "Together, together . . . forever!" "We stood with tears running down our faces, and the nurse talked to me for an hour and a half in a patois that even Italians would have had difficulty in understanding. She was telling me everything she could remember about Mother. . . . And the nurse went out, and she said '*Qua insieme per sempre.*' She closed the door, and left me in the room" ("Near the Unbalanced Aquarium," *CPR*, 349).

Love bad me . . . drew back: "Love bade me welcome: yet my soul drew back"; Herbert, "Love (III)," line 1; line 9 is slightly misquoted.

235. To William Carlos Williams

Written during an acute manic episode.

Desert Music: Williams, *The Desert Music* (1954).

the Mexican whores: "The Desert Music," *The Desert Music*.

through "both of us go down": "For Eleanora and Bill Monahan," *The Desert Music*, lines 30–52.

the *Garden*: "The Mental Hospital Garden," *The Desert Music*.

the "Host": "The Host," *The Desert Music*.

237. To Allen Tate

Written during an acute manic episode.

What you say of Mother: "What one feels about one's parents after they are dead is subtly different as time passes. I am sure that my relation to my mother was quite as unhappy as your own; but after twenty-five years it is now something else; and I feel now that she is trying to get free of me, rather than the other way around" (Tate to RL, March 11, 1954, quoted in Doreski, 109).

Tourneur: Cyril Tourneur (c. 1575–1626), English dramatist.

my review of Red: "Prose Genius in Verse," *Kenyon Review*, Autumn 1953.

Montale . . . René Char: Eugenio Montale (1896–1981), Italian poet; René Char (1907–88), French poet. Tate wrote that he didn't see very many Italian writers because he couldn't bring himself to adapt to their manners of introduction (they expected him to come to them). He had heard that Montale expected him to call; though he liked Montale, he refused to do so (Tate to RL, March 11, 1954, Harvard). Elizabeth Hardwick recalled Lowell's encounter with Montale in a letter to Ian Hamilton: "In Italy, we met Montale, and had several sweaty, mute evenings of language difficulty and great displays of blundering affection. We walked up the Arno, I remember, and Montale, since we couldn't talk, sang into the night, 'In Questa Tomba Oscura' and other songs" (Hardwick to Ian Hamilton, copy at Texas).

what you say of Ben: An unidentified rumor about Tate's brother and coal mines (Tate to RL, March 11, 1954, Harvard).

240. To Ezra Pound

Written during an acute manic episode.

["]*Much conversation . . . a home.*": Pound, "Homage to Sextus Propertius" (1917), 4, lines 11 and 30.

***The primitive ages sang Venus: the last sings tumult.*"**: Pound, "Homage to Sextus Propertius," 5:1, lines 8–9, slightly misquoted.

a Christian *poète maudit*: See note to letter 112.

Marlowe: Christopher Marlowe's translation of Ovid's *Amores* "compensated, by his own skill, any loss in translation: a new beauty has . . . been created" (Pound, *Literary Essays* [1954], 249).

Ford: "Yu wil be glad to hear Cal Lowell has writ 2 poeMZ without fallin over his feet / a bit ob-sKEWer at 1st readin, but really got ole Fordie on the page" (Pound to Williams, Apr 8, 1954, *Pound/Williams*, 288).

241. To Blair Clark

Written during an acute manic episode.

Nixon's speech: In a speech broadcast on March 6, 1954, Adlai Stevenson said that the Republican Party was clearly "divided against itself, half McCarthy and half Eisenhower." The networks refused to allow Senator McCarthy free airtime to rebut Stevenson; it was given to Nixon instead, who delivered a speech on March 13. In a statement attacking Stevenson and the networks, McCarthy singled out CBS's Edward Morrow for particular censure. News analysts speculated whether the controversy might signal the demise of McCarthy's influence ("Turn of Tide?" *New York Times*, March 14, 1954).

Dewey: John Dewey (1859–1952), American philosopher.

reading the letters . . . Elizabeth Cameron: Henry Adams, *Letters of Henry Adams* (1938); *The Life of George Cabot Lodge* (1911). Blair Clark was distantly related to Elizabeth Cameron, Adams's close friend after the suicide of his wife.

242. To Flannery O'Connor

Written during an acute manic episode.

poultry: O'Connor kept peacocks, Muscovy ducks, chickens, geese, guinea hens, and other poultry.

243. To Ezra Pound

Written during an acute manic episode.

illisions: Elisions.

The Classic Anthology from Harvard: Pound, *The Classic Anthology Defined by Confucius*, published by Harvard University Press in 1954.

R. Fitzgerald's *Odyssey*: Although selections appeared as early as 1954, Fitzgerald's complete translation of *The Odyssey* was not published until 1961.

***Encounter*:** "Ford Madox Ford: 1873–1939," *Encounter*, April 1954; revised for *Shenendoah* (1955), further revised for *LS*.

244. To Giovanna Madonia

Written during an acute manic episode.

Animula Blandula: Little soul, wandering. Hadrian: "Animula, vagula, blandula,/Hospes, comesque, corporis;/Quæ nunc abibis in loca,/Pallidula, rigida, nudula/Nec ut soles dabis iocos?" (In Byron's translation: "Ah! gentle, fleeting, wav'ring sprite,/Friend and associate of this day!/To what unknown region bourne,/Wilt thou, now, wing thy distant flight?/No more, with wonted humour gay,/But pallid, cheerless, and forlorn.") Cf. also Pound, "Blandula, Tenulla, Vagula," *Canzoni* (1911); and Eliot, "Animula," *Collected Poems, 1919–1935* (1936).

carpite florem: "Pick the flower"; Ovid, *Liber Tertius Artis Amatoriae*, line 79.

Vati parete perito!: Obey the practiced poet/prophet; Ovid, *Liber Primus Artis Amatoriae*, line 29.

"Tre mesi!": Three months!

Babbitt: Milton Babbitt (b. 1916), American composer who was on the faculty at Salzburg in 1952.

Mathematical logic: Bertrand Russell, *The Principles of Mathematics* (1903) and *Principia Mathematica* (1910–13).

"Lettere seguono.": Letters will follow.

246. To Flannery O'Connor

Written during an acute manic episode.

language: "I wrote [Cal] that his not being in the Church was a grief to me and I knew no more to say about it. I said I severely doubted he would do any good to anybody else outside but that it was probably true he would do good to himself inasmuch as he would be the only one in a position to. I said the Sacraments gave grace—and let it go at that" (O'Connor to Sally and Robert Fitzgerald, 26 April 54, *The Habit of Being*, 71).

248. To Ezra Pound

Written during an acute manic episode.

your Idaho humor: Pound was born in Hailey, Idaho.

Mr. Dryden's translation: John Dryden, *The Works of Virgil* (1697).

fabbro: *The Waste Land* is dedicated to Pound, "il miglior fabbro."

Expende Hannibalem . . . Sejanus: Lines from *Juvenal 10*, which Lowell later translated: "Throw Hannibal on the scales, how many pounds/does the great captain come to?" and "Sejanus crackles" ("The Vanity of Human Wishes," *NTO*, stanza 11, lines 1–2, and stanza 5, line 8).

Ach, das schrecklichste . . . : "Oh, the most horrible monster in this monstrous world! / Perhaps. Perhaps? The most horrible!"

un poco—/ Una cosa piccola, animula blandula: A bit—/a small thing, little soul, wandering. Cf. RL to Madonia, March 6, 1954, letter 244, and note.

By Freud!: Cf. Freud, "The Material of Dreams," *The Interpretation of Dreams*, trans. A. A. Brill (1913), 164–66; and Paul Keegan, "Introduction," in Freud, *Psychopathology of Everyday Life*, xxxiii.

249. To Giovanna Madonia

Written during an acute manic episode.

La mia Siciliana, sopratutto in amore—: "My Sicilian, above all in love."

scarlet sweater: Lowell borrowed a sweater when he visited the Jarrells in late March and seems to have carried it back to Cincinnati; see also *Randall Jarrell's Letters*, 394–96.

Badoglio's surrender: Pietro Badoglio (1871–1956), Italian general who was prime minister after the fall of Mussolini. He announced Italy's unconditional surrender to the Allies on September 8, 1943, the day after Lowell mailed his letter to Roosevelt. He also announced Italy's declaration of war against Nazi Germany on October 13, 1943, the day Lowell was taken to the West Street Jail.

"Dejadme llorar/orillas del mar": Let me weep/at the seashores. The lines, which recur as a refrain in Góngora's "La más bella niña" (1580).

"conversazioni di ora in ora": Conversations from time to time, hour after hour.

"infinitamente": Endlessly.

"vaya a los Moros el cuerpo/y quede con vos el alma": "The body goes to the Moors/and the soul remains with thee" (courtesy Forrest Gander); "Servía en Orán al Ray" (1587), lines 47–48.

Quedéme y olvidéme . . . : "I stayed myself and I forgot myself,/against the beloved I laid my face,/everything stopped, and I let myself go,/letting my caution/fall to forgotten lilies" (courtesy Forrest Gander); Juan de la Cruz, "Noche Escura del Alma," lines 36–40. Although

Lowell never translated the poem, the line "One dark night, my Tudor Ford" in "Skunk Hour" points to it (RL to Richard Wilbur, January 8, 1962, Amherst). See also Frank Bidart, "Dark Night," *In the Western Night: Collected Poems, 1965–90* (1990), 6.

250. *To Elizabeth Hardwick*

Written during an acute manic episode.
The Toddle: "Toddle House" was another of Lowell's bears.
"Much talk is . . .": Cf. Ecclesiastes 10.13, 12.12, and Pound, "Homage to Sextus Propertius," 4:11.

251. *To Giovanna Madonia*

Written during an acute manic episode.
Cara, Freude!: Beloved, joy!
La Voce del Padrone: Madonia's street address.

253. *To Giovanna Madonia*

Written during an acute manic episode.
è vero ma: "Is true, but . . ."
"The wall-paper . . . never fall": Allen Tate, "Mother and Son," lines 41–42, slightly misquoted.

254. *To Giovanna Madonia*

Written during an acute manic episode.
chlorochromozene: Chlorpromazine, marketed as Thorazine; Lowell was treated with it just as studies about its effects on manic patients were being published (see Lehmann and Hanrahan, "Chlorpromazine: New Inhibiting Agent for Psychomotor Excitement and Manic States," 1954). "Since lithium was still essentially unknown at that time, particularly to American psychiatrists, chlorpromazine quickly became the treatment of choice for acute mania" (Goodwin, Jamison, 604).

257. *To Blair Clark*

hearing you: Clark was a CBS foreign correspondent.
Dick Howard: Richard Howard (b. 1929), American poet. Blair Clark introduced him to Lowell in 1952.

258. *To John Berryman*

your leaving Iowa: At Paul Engle's suggestion, Marguerite Young and Berryman taught a course together on the novel. Young and Berryman did not get along, however, and during class one evening Young accused Berryman of making sexist remarks. They fought. After class, Berryman went to a bar, drank heavily, lost his keys on the way home, and tried to break into his apartment. The landlord called the police and Berryman was arrested. The scandal, reported in the local newspaper, prompted the University of Iowa to fire him (see Haffenden, 242–44; and Mariani, *Dream Song*, 284–86).
set their watches by: "The neighbors knew it must be exactly half past four when they saw Professor Kant . . . step out of his house-door, and went towards the little lime-tree avenue, which is named after him, the Philosopher's Walk . . . and [they would] set their watches" (Josiah Royce, *The Spirit of Modern Philosophy* [1892], 109).

262. To Peter and Eleanor Ross Taylor

the boy: Peter Ross Taylor was born on February 7, 1955.
Peter's play: Taylor, "Tennessee Day in St. Louis," *Kenyon Review* 18 (Winter 1956).
man is never quiet: Cf. A. E. Housman, *A Shropshire Lad*, 31, line 15.

263. To Babette Deutsch

Babette Deutsch (1895–1982), American writer, editor, and translator.
Edwards' sermons . . . : Jonathan Edwards, *Of Insects*, "Sinners in the Hands of an Angry God,"
and "The Future Punishment of the Wicked." "The source of the stanzaic structure [of 'Mr.
Edwards and the Spider'] is Donne's 'A Nocturnal on St. Lucy's Day'" (*CPM*, 1022).
the last line: "*Voi ch'entrate*, and your life is in your hands" ("Exile's Return," line 24); "voi ch'en-
trate" is a quotation from Dante's *Inferno* 3.9 ("Lasciate ogni speranza, voi ch'entrate,"
"Abandon all hope, you who enter here"). See note to "Exile's Return," *CPM*, 1006.
Corbière: Corbière, "Paris Nocturne"; see letter 514, and *CPM*, 1009.

264. To Peter Taylor

surprised and hurt: Taylor, "A Sentimental Journey," *New Yorker*, March 12, 1955, reprinted as
"1939" in *Happy Families Are All Alike* (1959), a story about two Kenyon undergraduates who
resemble Taylor and Lowell.
my Great Grandfather's novel: Robert Traill Spence Lowell, *Antony Brade* (1874).
Pugatch: Eugene M. J. Pugatch (Kenyon '54), former student of Peter Taylor's.
Chalmers: Gordon Keith Chalmers (1904–57), president of Kenyon College from 1937 to 1956.
your Pruit (?): Prewitt is the Lowell character in Taylor's story.
on his child: Robert Penn Warren, "To a Little Girl, One Year Old, in Ruined Fortress," *Partisan
Review*, Spring 1955.

265. To Ezra Pound

S's pictures: Unidentified but possibly by Sheri Martinelli; see letter 279.
like being flayed: Cf. letters 232 and 266. See also Lowell's Autobiographical Prose: "For
two years I have been cooling off from three months of pathological enthusiasm. I go to sleep
now easily, but sometimes I wake up with a jar. In my dreams I am like one of Michael An-
gelo's bulky, rugged, ideal statues that can be tumbled down a hill without injury. When I
wake, it is as though I had been flayed, and had each nerve beaten with a rubber hose" (Har-
vard).
a church and two life insurance buildings: Cf. Autobiographical Prose, Harvard, and "Near the
Unbalanced Aquarium," *CPR*, 349; cf. also Henry Adams, *Education*, 3.

266. To Elizabeth Bishop

taking: As in "fetching."
Yale Review: Jarrell's group review of "Recent Poetry" in the *Yale Review*, Autumn 1955, did not
include Bishop's book, although a brief notice appeared in his article "The Year in Poetry,"
Harper's Magazine, October 1955.
An Englishman: Jonathan Griffin, *The Hidden King* (1955).
Speaight: Robert Speaight (1904–76), English actor and scholar.
Wilbur: Richard Wilbur (b. 1921), American poet.
Hellman: Lillian Hellman (1905–84), American playwright.

Fergusson: Francis Fergusson (1904–86), American literary scholar.

Benn: Gottfried Benn, "Artists and Old Age," *Partisan Review*, Summer 1955.

Excuse this image: Cf. Autobiographical Prose; "I'm in the country now splitting my time between small household chores and a piece of autobiographical prose that moves an inch a day" (RL to Ezra Pound, June 14, 1955, Yale).

Pollaiuolo: Antonio Pollaiuolo (1432–98), Italian painter.

267. To Elizabeth Bishop

my doll: Bishop sent Lowell a native Brazilian doll to thank him for his gift of a Dutch doll.

268. To William Carlos Williams

***Journey to Love*:** Williams, *Journey to Love* (1955).

269. To Elizabeth Bishop

the long one: Draft of "Manuelzinho (Brazil. A Friend of the Writer Is Speaking)," *New Yorker*, May 26, 1956.

short poem: Probably "The Shampoo," *New Republic*, July 11, 1955.

the two in the *New Yorker*: "Manners (for a Child of 1918)," *New Yorker*, November 26, 1955, and "Filling Station," *New Yorker*, December 10, 1955.

her last: Mary McCarthy, *A Charmed Life* (1955). Mary McCarthy and Edmund Wilson were married in 1938 and separated in 1944.

a red-headed Millay-like Cape poet: Edna St. Vincent Millay (1892–1950) and Wilson were lovers in 1920.

Lord Acton's . . . by reading: "Learn as much by writing as by reading"; Lord Acton, "Inaugural Lecture on the Study of History," *Lectures on Modern History* (1906).

la chair n'est pas triste: The flesh is not weary; "La chair est triste, hélas! et j'ai lu tous les livres," (Mallarmé, "Brise Marin," line 1).

Trilling: Lionel Trilling, "Manners, Morals, and the Novel," *The Liberal Imagination: Essays on Literature and Society* (1950).

270. To Harriet Winslow

abstraction: Cousin Harriet sent the Lowells one of her abstract paintings for Christmas.

271. To Flannery O'Connor

"Artificial Nigger": O'Connor, "The Artificial Nigger," *A Good Man Is Hard to Find* (1955).

on the Iowa TV: "[In 1955, O'Connor] goes to New York for appearance on television program *Galley Proof*, May 31, where she is interviewed by Harvey Breit of *The New York Times* and watches dramatization of 'The Life You Save May Be Your Own'" (O'Connor, *Collected Works*, 1248).

Katie Carver: Catherine Carver, editor at Harcourt, Brace.

I worry: O'Connor suffered from lupus erythematosus.

272. To Harriet Winslow

your kindness in your will: Cousin Harriet wrote that she was going to leave the lifetime use of one of her Castine houses to the Lowells, together with a small income to cover property taxes and upkeep. "I left the life income to Elizabeth instead of to you," she wrote, "so that if she outlives you she can have it" (Harriet Winslow to RL, January 25, 1956, Harvard).

Autobiography: See Charles Francis Adams, *Autobiography*, 211.

I Musici: Italian chamber ensemble.

273. To Harriet Winslow

Mordecai Myers: Cf. "91 Revere Street," *LS*.

"Pierpoint Limner": Hardwick had seen a portrait of "Elizabeth Savage at Mr. Child's gallery. He says the portrait is by 'the Pierpoint limner'—a fascinating appellation—" (Hardwick to Harriet Winslow, February 1956, Harvard).

a singer: Unidentified.

274. To J. F. Powers

a Norwegian: Per Seyersted; see note to letter 393.

Trilling's novel . . . : Lionel Trilling, *The Middle of the Journey* (1947); the stories are probably "Of This Time, of That Place," *Partisan Review*, January–February 1943, and "The Other Margaret," *Partisan Review*, Fall 1945.

all the stories: Powers, "The Presence of Grace," "Dawn," "Death of a Favorite," and "The Devil Was the Joker," *The Presence of Grace* (1956).

Caroline Tate's novel: Caroline Gordon, *The Malefactors* (1956). One character is based on Dorothy Day (1897–1980), founder of the Catholic Worker movement.

275. To Elizabeth Bishop

the man in E's story: "I just read yesterday Elizabeth's story about the man who lived in a hotel room for fifteen years, did nothing, etc. It reminded me uncomfortably of my friend Tom [Wanning]—remember him?—except that he is much richer and lives in a much worse hotel. The whole thing is so like him that I even wondered if E knew him. I think it's very well done, and the magazine editor scenes are awfully good" (Bishop to RL, June 7, 1956, Harvard).

Andrews Wanning . . . a paper on art and bad characters: Andrews Wanning (1912?–97), American scholar who taught seventeenth-century English literature at Bard College and liked to sail wooden yawl boats (see letter 301). Lowell's paper, "On the Diabolic in Literature" (Harvard bMS Am 1905/2799), is printed as "Art and Evil" in *CPR*.

the Pulitzer: Bishop won the 1956 Pulitzer Prize for *Poems: North & South—A Cold Spring* (1955).

McGinley: Phyllis McGinley (1905–78), writer of light verse.

Auden . . . Aiken: Auden, *The Shield of Achilles* (1956); Conrad Aiken, *A Letter from Li Po* (1955).

Howells: William Dean Howells (1837–1920), American novelist and critic.

autobiography: "91 Revere Street," *Partisan Review*, Fall 1956.

Brazilian man: Bishop, "Manuelzinho," *New Yorker*, May 26, 1956, reprinted in *Questions of Travel* (1965).

opus on F.D.R: Schlesinger's *Age of Roosevelt* was published in three volumes: *The Crisis of the Old Order, 1919–1933* (1957); *The Coming of the New Deal* (1958); and *The Politics of Upheaval* (1960).

276. To T. S. Eliot

your illness: Eliot had a heart attack while sailing from New York to England.

"fattening forties": Auden, "Under Which Lyre: A Reactionary Tract for the Times," line 54.

Confidential Clerk: Eliot, *The Confidential Clerk: A Play* (1954).

"Gerontion": "Here I am, an old man in a dry mouth,/Being read to by a boy, waiting for rain" (Eliot, "Gerontion," lines 1–2).

277. To Ezra Pound

"the Rémusat family and froggland in 1871.": "Cal ever glance at the Remusat fambly ? / OR frogg-land as in 1871 ?" (Pound to RL, n.d., Harvard). "Froggland" is France (cf. Ezra Pound, canto 86.17); Pound was writing the *Thrones* cantos and reading the *Memoirs of Mme. de Rémusat*, trans. Mrs. Cashel Hoey and John Lillie (1880).

Flaubert's *Education* . . . Michelet: Flaubert, *L'Éducation sentimentale* (1870); Émile Zola, *Nana* (1880); Voltaire, *Candide* (1758); Jules Michelet (1798–1874), French historian.

Lincoln Steffens: See Pound, cantos 16 and 19, and Lincoln Steffens, *The Autobiography of Lincoln Steffens* (1931).

Rock Drill: Pound, *Rock Drill: Cantos 85–95* (1955).

amor: "Amor" appears four times in canto 90, twice in the phrase "ubi amor, ibi oculus" ("where love, there the eye [is]").

278. To Elizabeth Bishop

U R 2 good 2 B 4 got 10: "I had a strange [fan letter] from a boy who loves 'all the arts'; his paintings and drawings are in Canada or he'd send them to me, so instead he appends a long list of all their titles . . . & on the back of the envelope (the letter's in Portuguese) he wrote: U R 2 GOOD 2 B 4 GOT 10" (Bishop to RL, September 24, 1956, Vassar).

Mr. Warburg: The meeting notes confirm the presence of Anita Warburg but the Mr. Warburg Lowell describes is not identified (Brandeis Archives).

Kronenberger: Louis Kronenberger (1904–80), American drama critic and writer.

Colum: Padraic Colum (1881–1972), Irish American poet and playwright; his most recent book was *The Vegetable Kingdom* (1954).

your description: "We've had a house guest for over a month now, one of a pair of famous sisters, Rio 'beauties,' old school friends of Lota's. She really is beautiful, too—tall, grizzled blond, magnificent teeth and one blue eye and one brown eye. But she is an extreme hypochondriac, and it's a little like having Proust to visit . . ." (Bishop to RL, September 24, 1956, Harvard).

Allen: Walter Allen, "Aristocracy of One," *New Statesman and Nation*, September 15, 1956, 316.

279. To Ezra Pound

Miss Martinelli: Sheri Martinelli, an artist whose work Pound had arranged to have published in a booklet entitled *La Martinelli*.

Mr. Lee: Gilbert Lee, Martinelli's common-law husband.

several on my family tree: See "91 Revere Street," *LS*, and RL to Peter Taylor, June 21, 1957.

H. D. . . . her later poems: H. D., *The Walls Do Not Fall* (1944), *The Flowering of the Rod* (1945), *Tribute to the Angels* (1946); see also "R.A.F" and "Christmas 1944" (*What Do I Love?* 1950).

281. To J. F. Powers
I rather hoped I would hear from you: Powers had just read "91 Revere Street."
Ed O'Connor: Edwin O'Connor (1918–68), American novelist.

282. To William Meredith
William Meredith (b. 1919), American poet.
the other side: The letter is typed on the verso of a mimeograph of Meredith's "Pastorale."
with such sentiments: William Meredith, "On Falling Asleep by Firelight," lines 8–9.
Miss Elsinore: Miss Elsemore.
Muir: Edwin Muir (1887–1959), Scottish poet, critic, and translator.
Booths: Margaret and Philip Booth, Castine neighbors; Philip Booth (b. 1925), American poet.

283. To William Alfred
William Alfred (1922–99), American playwright and scholar.
Dusty: The dog's actual name was Smokey (Alfred Papers, Brooklyn College).
Black and Tan MacNeices: Alfred spent the winter of 1956 in a flat in the London house of Hedli
 and Louis MacNeice; Louis MacNeice (1907–63), Irish poet. MacNeice was a poet who inter-
 ested Lowell early (see Axelrod, 246). By calling the Irish Protestant MacNieces "Black and
 Tan," Alfred's Irish Catholic mother is making a charged, inaccurate joke.

284. To Natasha Spender
Gesualdo to Webern . . . Bouvard and Pécuchet: Gesualdo (1566–1613), Italian composer; Anton
 von Webern (1883–1945), Austrian composer; Gustav Flaubert, *Bouvard et Pécuchet* (1881).

285. To Peter and Eleanor Ross Taylor
STORKGRAM: Lowell sent an identical telegram to other friends and family.

286. To Harriet Winslow
the universe: "I accept the universe" is attributed to Margaret Fuller; see *CPM*, 1032.
Arch-bishop Cushing: Cardinal Cushing (1895–1970), archbishop of Boston from 1944 to 1970.
Sarah Gamp's Mrs. 'Arris: See Dickens, *Martin Chuzzlewit* (1944).

287. To Robert Duncan
Duncan spent the winter of 1956–57 as assistant director of the Poetry Center at San Francisco
 State University.

288. To Elizabeth Bishop
your fellowship: "Lota and I are really planning to get to New York around the first part of
 April. . . . We also have to stay for six months, and I am in a quandary because I recently re-
 ceived an announcement that I can have an Amy Lowell scholarship if I stay *out* of the U.S. for
 a year, starting in September. I never heard of these scholarships before. Perhaps you had
 something to do with my receiving it? If so I certainly thank you. I'm hoping they'll give me
 an extension of a month before I have to leave, as they put it, 'the continent of North Amer-

ica.' It should be a lesson to us not to leave wills with strings attached. I imagine they have a hard time finding a rich-expatriate-already poet like me to give it to! But not so rich it won't be extremely welcome" (Bishop to RL, January 25, 1957, Harvard).

Percival: Amy Lowell's brother Percival traveled to Japan and Korea as a young man and wrote four books about Asia, including *The Soul of the Far East* (1888).

(Oh a pretty little girl!): Cf. Amy Lowell, "A Roxbury Garden," *Men, Women, and Ghosts* (1916).

a life briefer than Keats'!: Amy Lowell's two-volume biography of Keats was published in 1925; she died in May of the same year.

the Myopia Hunt: An exclusive club in Hamilton, Massachusetts.

Graves and Ben Shahn: Morris Graves (1910–2001), American painter; Ben Shahn (1898–1969), American social realist painter, photographer, and lithographer.

289. *To John Berryman*

rather too young: Berryman had recently divorced Eileen Simpson and married a graduate student named Elizabeth Ann Levine, "a harmless and good woman, rather too young" (John Berryman to RL, n.d. 1957, Harvard; see Haffenden, 255–56).

"She dresses badly . . .": "*We* shall improve her. She dresses badly. She decidedly has humor and will appreciate *our* wit. She has enough money to be quite independent. She rules me as only American women rule men, and I cower before her" (Henry Adams to Charles Milnes Gaskell about his future wife, Marian Hooper, 26 March 1872, *Letters of Henry Adams*, 223).

But what are years?: Cf. Marianne Moore, *What Are Years* (1941).

marry . . . younger: T. S. Eliot, sixty-eight, married his thirty-year-old secretary, Valerie Fletcher, on January 10, 1957.

290. *To Elizabeth Hardwick*

Ted: Theodore Roethke.

Dido: Dido Milroy Merwin; see letter 298 and note.

Leonard Wolf . . . black magic poets: Leonard Wolf, author of *Hamadryad Hunted* (1946) and *A Dream of Dracula: In Search of the Living Dead* (1972), among other books. Jack Spicer (1925–65), American poet and leading figure of the Berkeley Renaissance, taught a workshop entitled "Poetry as Magic" at the San Francisco Public Library.

Mrs. Witt-Diamant: Ruth Witt-Diamant, founding director of the Poetry Center at San Francisco State University.

Ward: Barbara Ward (1914–81), British economist.

Harry: Harry Brown.

291. *To Theodore Roethke*

Probably written while mildly manic.

the Heilmans . . . : Robert Heilman (b. 1906), Shakespeare scholar, professor at the University of Washington from 1948 to 1976; his wife was Ruth Champlin; Jean Clower, a poetry student of Roethke's; David Wagoner (b. 1926), American poet, student and friend of Roethke's; Rae and Paul Tufts, hosts of Seattle literary parties; Ann London, poetry student of Roethke's, part of the San Francisco Beat scene in the late 1950s, later a medieval scholar.

Graves: Morris Graves.

the new book: Roethke, *Words for the Wind* (1957, English edition).

292. To Anthony Ostroff

Probably written while mildly manic.

Anthony Ostroff (1923–78), professor of rhetoric at Berkeley in 1957.

about-to-come-out story: Ostroff, "La Bataille des Fleurs," *Kenyon Review*, Summer 1957.

293. To Peter and Eleanor Ross Taylor

Probably written while mildly manic.

My beloved Henry Adams . . . She meant it.": *The Education of Henry Adams* (1931), 442.

begins: "Dear Peter": Lowell attempted to write a letter-poem to Taylor several times. A draft of a poem about a walk in Central Park is in the Lowell collection at Harvard (bMS Am 1905/2237). See also RL to Peter Taylor [n.d. Summer 1976?].

Bellow: Saul Bellow (b. 1915), American novelist.

295. To Elizabeth Bishop

Probably written while mildly manic.

exhalted: Perhaps due to his jet lag; for the link between sleep cycles and mania, see "Sleep and Biological Rhythms in Bipolar Illness," Thomas A. Wehr, David A. Sack, Norman E. Rosenthal, and Frederick K. Goodwin, *Psychiatry Update: American Psychiatric Association Annual Review* 6 (1987), 61–80.

nominating Randall: For the American Academy of Arts and Letters.

Barzun: Jacques Barzun (b. 1907), American historian and critic.

Anne Goodwin Winslow: Anne Goodwin Winslow's books include *Cloudy Trophies* (1946); she was the mother-in-law of Marcella Comes Winslow, Washington artist and portrait painter.

Rizzardi showed me your Pound: Bishop, "Visits to St. Elizabeths," *Nuova corrente: rivista di letteratura* (1956). Alfred Rizzardi (b. 1927), Italian editor, poet, and first translator of Pound's *Pisan Cantos*, asked Bishop to contribute an essay or memoir to a special issue of *Nuova corrente* dedicated to Pound. Instead of writing prose, Bishop sent him her poem (Rognoni to SH, May 3, 2003). See also Millier, 280.

in three magazines: Robert Fitzgerald's review first appeared in *Nuova corrente*, January–July 1956; it was reprinted as "A Note on Ezra Pound," *Kenyon Review*, Autumn 1956, and "Gloom and Gold on Ezra Pound," *Encounter*, July 1956.

298. To Elizabeth Bishop

Bill Merwin's wife: Dido Merwin, first wife of W. S. Merwin (b. 1927), American poet.

delivery poem: Williams, "The Birth," *Massachusetts Review*, Winter 1962.

Flanders poem: Possibly "Sunday, 4 A.M.," *New Yorker*, September 20, 1958.

"A Summer's Dream" . . . : "But the sea, lying/blue as a mackerel,/our boarding house was streaked/as though it had been crying" (Bishop, "A Summer's Dream," *New Yorker*, July 24, 1948, lines 13–16).

"Armadillo": Bishop, "The Armadillo—Brazil," *New Yorker*, June 22, 1957, reprinted as "The Armadillo" with a dedication to Robert Lowell in *Questions of Travel* (1965).

299. To Elizabeth Bishop

Cummings': E. E. Cummings (1894–1962), American poet, read for 7,000 people at the Boston Arts Festival in the Public Garden on June 23, 1957.

Paul Brooks: An editor at Houghton Mifflin.

300. To Elizabeth Bishop

Probably written while mildly manic.

sparine: A low-potency anti-psychotic drug, related to chlorpromazine, used as a sedative.

George Herbert!: When Bishop and Lota de Macedes Soares departed for New York, Lowell presented Bishop with *The Works of George Herbert, in Prose and Verse* (1852), bound in brown morocco. The two volumes had first been a gift to the Reverend Robert T. S. Lowell of the parishioners of Christ Church in Newark, New Jersey, in 1859. They were passed on to "R.T.S.L. (3rd)" in 1892. Lowell reinscribed it to Bishop: "These two volumes given one August morning with ALL his heart by Robert T. S. Lowell (4th) to Elizabeth Bishop. 8/8/57 'Thy mouth was open, but thou couldst not sing'" (Harvard). "Thy mouth . . ." is line 4 of Herbert's "Death."

301. To Elizabeth Bishop

Published in Bishop, *One Art*, 344–46.

the second ex-Mrs. Rexroth: Maria Kass Rexroth married Kenneth Rexroth in 1940. Although they separated in the late 1940s, they remained legally married for many years.

***Belle* Gardner's first husband:** Isabella Gardner (1915–81), American poet, niece of Isabella Stuart Gardner, and a cousin of Lowell's. She married her first husband, Harold van Kirk, in 1938. Her later marriages were to Maurice Seymour (1943 to 1947), Robert H. McCormick, Jr. (1947 to 1957), and Allen Tate (1959 to 1966).

Strachey and Virginia Woolf: Lytton Strachey and Virginia Woolf were engaged for the length of a conversation on February 17, 1909 (Michael Holroyd, *Lytton Strachey: The New Biography* [1994], 256–57; Hermione Lee, *Virginia Woolf* [1996], 255).

French Renaissance Vocal Music: Cf. "Fourth of July in Maine," lines 77–80, *NTO*.

Straus: Roger W. Straus III (1917–2004) founded Farrar, Straus and Company with John Farrar in 1945.

302. To Anthony Ostroff

Heifetz: Jascha Heifetz (1901–87), Russian violinist.

303. To Elizabeth Bishop

Dr. Taves: "Here is the letter Lota just received from her ex-analyst—'ex' may not be right. The man's name seems to be *Taves* . . . [Y]ou might make an appointment to see him when he returns to Cambridge, and see how you like him. Lota's Dr. apparently has others up her sleeve, too. I do hope I'm not being awfully bossy about this—but everyone finds analysts through their friends, I think" (Bishop to RL, August 28, 1957, Harvard).

editor of the *Yale Review*: J. E. Palmer, editor of the *Yale Review* from 1954 to 1979.

Emerson on Montaigne: Emerson, "Montaigne; or, The Skeptic," *Representative Men* (1849).

Sejanus: Ben Jonson, *Sejanus His Fall* (1605).

Graves: Robert Graves, *Collected Poems* (1955).

I liked the Morgenstern . . . : "I got the German anthology right away and have found some wonderful things. Did you notice Morgenstern?—Klee-like and Stevens-like?" (Bishop to RL, August 15, 1957, Vassar); *The Penguin Book of German Verse*, ed. Leonard Forster (1957).

Hebel's: Johann Peter Hebel (1760–1826), "Die Vergänglichkeit. Gerspräch auf der Straße von Basel zwischen Steinen und Brombach, in der Nacht."

Carossa's long lament: Hans Carossa (1878–1956), "Abendländische Elegie."

the Cologne Cathedral: See "The Exile's Return," *LWC*.

the long Hölderlin: Friedrich Hölderlin (1770–1843), "Brot und Wein."

"... hideously uncomfortable": "But I really can't *bear* much of American life these days—surely no country has ever been so filthy rich and so hideously uncomfortable at the same time" (Bishop to RL, August 28, 1957, Harvard).

She can't cook: "I hope the baby is doing well—and able to do the cooking by now" (Bishop to RL, August 28, 1957, Harvard).

Lora the seal; Why can't *I* [car]ry a tune!: Bishop sent Lowell a copy of Rowena Farre's *Seal Morning* (1957). Chapter 3, "Lora and Music," recounts the seal's singing and her adventures with musical instruments.

304. To William Carlos Williams

your letters: Williams, *Selected Letters* (1957).

the Marianne Moore letters: For Moore's letters to Williams, see *The Selected Letters of Marianne Moore* (1997).

like a house a fire: Cf. "Near the Unbalanced Aquarium," *CPR*, 363.

your rebuke to Vierick's rash claims: See Williams, *Selected Letters*, 280.

305. To William Empson

underground against fairies: In the twenties, Graves and some other poets "wanted to combat a fashion for male homosexuality among intellectuals, a thing which was becoming tiresome for the boys as well as the girls, and they did this by saying it was sentimental to love other young men (because so reliably agreeable and comforting) whereas any man worth the name would take on a woman (because she would be certain to crucify him after stripping him of all his goods).... [I]n the mind of Graves, passionately supporting women against injustice, it became part of a universal truth about human life, that men are no good unless they practice Human Sacrifice to a goddess, who is also the Muse" (Empson, review of Robert Graves, *The Crowning Privilege: The Clark Lectures, 1954–1955* [1955], *New Statesman*, [October 1, 1955], 400).

Your Joyce seemed: Empson, "The Theme of *Ulysses*," *Kenyon Review*, Winter 1956; Empson suggests that "Stephen *did* go to bed with Molly, very soon after the one day of the book."

Woolf's diary: "Tom on Saturday. My talk with Tom deserves writing down, but won't get it for the light is fading; ... There was a good deal of talk about *Ulysses* ... the book would be a landmark, because it destroyed the whole of the nineteenth century. It left Joyce himself with nothing to write another book on. It showed up the futility of all the English styles" (*A Writer's Diary: Being Extracts from the Diary of Virginia Woolf*, ed. Leonard Woolf [1954], 49).

your Donne: Empson, "Donne the Space Man," *Kenyon Review*, Summer 1957; Empson addresses doubts about the sincerity of Donne's conversion to Anglicanism. "Surely it is much more probable, as well as more agreeable, to expect that he didn't feel committed to either sect, and saw no reason to give either of them an excuse to burn him."

we underground men!: "We tunnel through your noonday out to you." (Empson, "The Ants," line 1; originally "Sonnet," *Cambridge Review*, April 27, 1928).

306. To Randall Jarrell

the short quatrain Heine-like ones: See Jarrell, "Soldiers," *Selected Poems* (1955).

Amis, Wain: Kingsley Amis (1922–95) and John Wain (1925–1994), English writers; with Philip

Larkin (1922–85), Donald Davie, Thom Gunn, and John Holloway, they were associated with "The Movement."

death and a statue: Jarrell, "The Bronze David of Donatello," *Art News*, October 1957, reprinted in *The Woman at the Washington Zoo* (1960).

newt!: See Jarrell, "Jamestown," lines 6–8, *Virginia Quarterly Review*, Autumn 1957, reprinted in *The Woman at the Washington Zoo* (1960). Cf. also Pound, canto 14, line 11, and "Dunbarton," *LS*, line 50.

307. To Robert Giroux

an earlier book: Larkin's first book of poems, *The North Ship*, was published by Fortune (London) in 1945. The Faber book Lowell refers to is his novel *A Girl in Winter* (1956).

Eileen: Eileen Simpson.

Eliot's . . . essays: Eliot, *On Poetry and Poets* (1957).

308. To Randall Jarrell

Snodgrass: W. D. Snodgrass (b. 1926), American poet; *The New Poets of England and America*, ed. Donald Hall, Robert Pack, Louis Simpson (1957), included "Heart's Needle" (sections 2, 4, 6, 7, 8, and 10), "April Inventory," and "The Marsh." See *Randall Jarrell's Letters*, 286.

Kiriloff's death: A scene in Dostoyevsky's *The Possessed*.

bad men: See "Art and Evil," *CPR*, 129–44.

But what a lot!: "What a set! what a world! is the exclamation that breaks from us as we come to an end of this history of 'the occurrences of Shelley's private life'" (Matthew Arnold, "Shelley," *Essays in Criticism* [1888], 237).

Alyosha . . . Stavrogin . . . the Underground man: Characters in Dostoyevsky's *The Brothers Karamazov* (1879–80), *The Possessed* (1872), and *Notes from Underground* (1913).

"look on violence as a *virtue*": "Allen never feels the need for any *motivation* of violence—violence is to him, perhaps unconsciously, an intrinsic good" (Jarrell to RL, [September 1945], *Randall Jarrell's Letters*, 133).

. . . about Graves: Jarrell, "The Poet and His Public," *Partisan Review*, September–October 1948, "Graves and the White Goddess" (in two parts), *Yale Review*, Winter 1956–Spring 1956.

"Blue-Fly," . . . as fine as *The expense of spirit*: Graves, "The Blue-Fly," *New Yorker*, July 11, 1953, reprinted in *Poems 1953* (1953); Shakespeare, sonnet 129, line 1.

made many discoveries . . . : Heinrich Heine (1797–1856); Johann Peter Hebel (1760–1826), "Die Vergänglichkeit: Gespräch auf der Staße von Basel zwischen Steinen und Brombach, in der Nacht"; Johann Wolfgang von Goethe (1749–1832); Johann Christian Friedrich Hölderlin (1770–1843); Andreas Gryphius (1616–64); Paul Fleming (1609–40); Hans Carossa (1878–1956), "Abendländische Elegie"; Der Wilde Alexander (late thirteenth century), "Hie vor dû wir kinder wâren"; Christian Morgenstern (1871–1914). Cf. Lowell, *IM*.

my moon images: "David and Bathsheba in the Public Garden," *LWC*, part 2, lines 26–36.

the Pound poem and one about a queer Brazilian old man: Bishop, "Visits to St. Elizabeths," "Manuelzinho," *Questions of Travel* (1965).

309. To Elizabeth Bishop

My Darling receding Elizabeth: On her way back to Brazil, Bishop sent Lowell a postcard from Savannah, Georgia, that she signed: "Recessively yours—E.B." (Bishop to RL, Oct 19?, [1957], Houghton Library).

a jail one . . . : "Memories of West Street and Lepke," "My Last Afternoon with Uncle Devereux Winslow," "Terminal Days at Beverly Farms," "Sailing Home from Rapallo," *LS*.

"This certainly is a just right poem . . .": See Robert Lowell Papers, Harvard, *73M-90, bMS Am 1905/2063.

"Exile's Return": Lowell, "The Exile's Return," first printed in the *Nation*, March 16, 1946, when Jarrell was the magazine's poetry editor; reprinted in *LWC*.

"I like the poem *very* much . . .": Randall Jarrell to RL, [November 3, 1975], Harvard, printed in *Randall Jarrell's Letters*, 427.

attacking Shakespeare's sonnets: John Crowe Ransom, "Shakespeare at Sonnets," *Southern Review*, Winter 1938, reprinted in *The World's Body* (1938).

really his name: Snodgrass is also the name of the poet in Dickens's *Pickwick Papers* (1837).

"Snodgrass is drifting . . .": "Snodgrass is walking through the universe" (Snodgrass, "These Trees Stand," lines 6, 12, and 22).

310. *To Flannery O'Connor*

For O'Connor's reply, see *The Habit of Being*, 251–52.

"View of the Woods": O'Connor, "A View of the Woods," *Partisan Review*, Fall 1957, reprinted in *Everything That Rises Must Converge* (1965).

Laforgue's prose: *Selected Writings of Jules Laforgue*, trans. William Jay Smith (1956).

Good Soldier Schweik: Jaroslav Hašek, *The Good Soldier Schweik*, trans. Paul Selver (1931).

Lindley: Denver Lindley (1904–82), editor at Harcourt Brace.

negro hunt: See O'Connor, "Wildcat," "The Geranium: A Collection of Short Stories" (MFA thesis, University of Iowa), reprinted in *Everything That Rises Must Converge* (1965).

311. *To Elizabeth Bishop*

my poems: Probably "Memories of West Street and Lepke," "My Last Afternoon with Uncle Devereux Winslow," "Terminal Days at Beverly Farms," "Sailing Home from Rapallo," and "Skunk Hour."

"I have humor.": Jules Laforgue (1860–87), French poet. "I must say that I admit to a grain of temperamental kinship with that charming incurable madman, Corbière . . . Corbière has dash and I have humor; Corbière dazzles while I purr; I live by an absolute philosophy and not by eccentricity, I sit still while he frisks about; I know nothing of *amour jaune*—my love is not yellow; it is white and the deep mauve of morning" (Laforgue to Léo Trézenik, August 1855, in *Selected Writings of Jules Laforgue*, trans. William Jay Smith [1956], 251).

his *Hamlet*!: Laforgue, "Hamlet, or the Consequences of Filial Piety," *Selected Writings of Jules Laforgue*.

. . . outcast children: Bishop, "The Wit," "Squatter's Children," *New Poems by American Poets*, ed. Rolf Humphries (1957).

313. *To J. F. Powers*

conversation pours: "I was so pleased to find someone who talked like an old friend of the twenties—I kept telling him that he was a man of the twenties, that he seemed to me perfect: accelerating conversations, going off in all directions, interrupting one another, range of interest and reading, flares of imagination, general freedom of the world" (Wilson, *The Fifties*, 452). "What he says is probing and witty, sometimes perverse, with a desire to startle" (Wilson, *The Sixties*, 428).

". . . the same old nut-bin": "Well, it's happened again. Same old routine: 4 or 5 city police (as the

boogs say) dragging me off to the same old shit-bin, the same old commitment routine—what a bore" (Theodore Roethke to RL, October 8, 1957, Harvard).

Archie's job: Archibald MacLeish held the Boylston Chair of Rhetoric and Oratory at Harvard University from 1949 to 1962.

a new story: Probably Powers, "A Couple of Nights before Christmas," *New Yorker*, December 21, 1957.

314. To Elizabeth Bishop

"Come ye sons of art": Henry Purcell, "Come, Ye Sons of Art: Ode on the Birthday of Queen Mary II" (1694), performed by Margaret Ritchie, soprano (L'Oiseau-Lyre DL 53 004, 1954).

your cable: "POEMS LOVELY HAVEN'T FORGOTTEN YOU" (Bishop to RL, November 21, 1957, Harvard).

Smith and Barbara Howes: Poet William Jay Smith (b. 1918) was married to poet Barbara Howes (1914–96).

Pound wrote: "Mr Lowell of Boston/No light Baby-Austin/but as when the garbage froze or/the vast accumulation of residues/caused exacerbation,/a bulldozer/was wanted for deep exca-vation-/no Cabbot a suitable game,/goose or rabbit,/rhyming with . . . /But that divinity registered unsegragted in that vicinity/ seeking latinty./whether I can corrugate/castigate or elevate this nonsense into/somethink worthy of the occasion/REEMains to be sawn/rough, hew them as we will" (Pound to RL, 13 Nov [1957], Harvard). Lowell later sent Pound the "Life Studies" manuscript, " "8 years of work . . . It's a cry of the heart, to be written once in a lifetime and unrepeatable" (RL to Pound, February 10, 1959, Yale).

garbage: See "Memories of West Street and Lepke," line 6, and "Skunk Hour," line 45, *LS*.

worthy the occasion: "Even the Latin of his Lowell motto:/ *Occasionem cognosce,*/seemed too businesslike and pushing here" ("Sailing Home from Rapallo," *LS*, lines 28–30).

316. To William Carlos Williams

Probably written while mildly manic.

fly over Grand Canyon: Williams flew over the Grand Canyon on the way back from California. He wrote to Lowell, "Your occupation with unrhymed measures vastly broadens your poten-tialities. You have opened a new field. You needed that break, rhyme could not contain you any longer, you have too much to say for that. Suffice it to say that I am impressed and ap-prove. Many of the poems, their mastery of the language moves me deeply. . . . Glad you are writing again as you remain one of the two or three major poets of my generation which I count on to keep me abreast of my times. This book in unrhymed verse brings one of my dreams for you into full fruit" (Williams to RL, Dec. 4, 1957, Harvard).

317. To William Carlos Williams

Probably written while mildly manic.

Bloodsoe: Robert Bloodsoe, editor at Beacon Press.

your book on poetry: Williams, *I Wanted to Write a Poem* (1958).

lets me loaf: "I loafe and invite my soul" (Walt Whitman, *Song of Myself* [1856], line 4).

Saltonstall or the bone-headed Irish blow-hards: Leverett Saltonstall (1892–1979), governor of Massachusetts (1939–44), Republican senator from Massachusetts (1944–67). The "Irish blow-hards" would include James Michael Curley (1863–1958), the infamous and intermittent mayor of Boston during Lowell's childhood and youth who dominated Boston politics. In his

novel *The Last Hurrah* (1956), Edwin O'Connor based the character Frank Skeffington on Curley.

murder story: Williams, "The Farmers' Daughters," *Hudson Review*, Autumn 1957.

319. *To Allen Tate*

Probably written while mildly manic.

fight about my poems: "Of the unpublished pieces, only one seems to be at all up to your old standard: 'Skunk Hour.' . . . But *all* the poems about your family, including the one about you and Elizabeth, are definitely *bad*. I do not think that you ought to publish them. You didn't ask me whether they ought to be published, but I put the matter from this point of view in order to underline my anxiety about them. . . . [B]y and large, and in the total effect, the poems are composed of unassimilated details, terribly intimate and coldly noted. . . . The free verse, arbitrary and without rhythm, reflects this lack of imaginative focus. Your fine poems in the past present a formal ordering of highly intractable materials: but there is an imaginative thrust towards a symbolic order which these new poems seem to lack." Tate closes by saying, "Quite bluntly, these [personal family] details, presented in *causerie* and at random, are of interest only to you. They are, of course, of great interest to me because I am one of your oldest friends. But they have no public or literary interest" (Allen Tate to RL, December 3, 1957, Harvard, quoted in Ian Hamilton, 237, and Doreski, 120–21).

Picketts charge into a Stonewall: George Edward Pickett (1825–75), Confederate officer whose troops led a disastrous charge against Union soldiers at Gettysburg; Stonewall Jackson (1824–63), Confederate general, was accidentally shot by his soldiers at the Battle of Chancellorsville as he returned to camp at dusk on May 2, 1863.

You *were* uncannily right: "Tate suspected that these poems signaled another bout of mental illness and conveyed this belief in a letter to Perry Miller" (Doreski, 124). "Elizabeth Hardwick was indignant when she heard that Tate was originating rumors of this sort" (Ian Hamilton, 237).

your new poems . . . : Tate, "The Buried Lake," *Sewanee Review*, Spring 1953; "The Swimmers" (the "terza rima lynching"), *Hudson Review*, Winter 1953; reprinted in *Poems* (1960).

the persona you have of me: "The consequences of publication would be very, very serious. . . . It is not a question of a little poetic disagreement, as you put it; it concerns his eventual reputation as a poet and his immediate public persona" (Allen Tate to Elizabeth Hardwick, December 18, 1957, quoted in Doreski, 125).

320. *To William Empson*

Written during an acute manic episode.

in some way circulate: Lowell circulated it himself by enclosing it to Ezra Pound (see RL to Ezra Pound, January 29, 1958, letter).

jammer Bible: Cf. "Memories of West Street and Lepke," *LS*, line 26.

321. *To Ezra Pound*

Written during an acute manic episode.

loosing: Losing.

a friend: Possibly Ann Adden; see Ian Hamilton, 240–49.

323. *To M. L. Rosenthal*

Written during an acute manic episode.

M. L. Rosenthal (1917–96), American poet, poetry editor of *The Nation*.

piece on Crane: In "Hart Crane and His Friends" (*Nation*, February 15, 1958), Oscar Cargill is critical of Allen Tate's and Yvor Winters's misreading and mistreatment of Crane. For an analysis of the metamorphosis of "Epitaph for a Fallen Poet" to "Words for Hart Crane," see Hammer, 228–32.

the *Bridge*: Hart Crane, *The Bridge* (1930).

a sonnet of mine: "Words for Hart Crane," *Nation*, March 22, 1958, reprinted in *LS*.

325. To Ezra Pound

Joyce and Pécuchet: Pound, 'James Joyce et Pécuchet," *Mercure de France*, June 1, 1922; reprinted as "James Joyce and Pécuchet," trans. Fred Bornhauser, *Shenandoah*, Autumn 1952.

Rimbaud's "Rages de Caesar": See "Eighteen-Seventy," *IM*.

326. To Elizabeth Bishop

my last letter: The letter has not survived.

the statesman . . . the novelist: Sir Winston Churchill (1874–1965), English statesman; Winston Churchill (1871–1947), American writer of historical novels.

I've done another family poem . . . : "Home after Three Months Away," *LS*; translations of Der Wilde Alexander ("Children") and Montale are in *IM*.

the Penguin Italian: *The Penguin Book of Italian Verse*, ed. George R. Kay (1957).

327. To Peter Taylor

your *New Yorker* story: Taylor, "The Unforgivable," *New Yorker*, January 25, 1958, reprinted as "Promise of Rain" in *Happy Families Are All Alike* (1959).

the *Entertainer, Gervaise*: John Osborne, *The Entertainer*, starring Laurence Olivier and Joan Plowright, opened on February 12, 1958, at the Original Royale Theatre on Broadway; *Gervaise*, dir. René Clement (1956).

328. To Theodore Roethke

the I cat: Lowell always typed I for 1; a possible variant is "the I cat" (unverifiable, since Roethke's letter has not survived).

one by Muir: Edwin Muir, "New Verse," *New Statesman*, January 18, 1954.

He reviewed me: Muir, "American Poetry," *Observer*, January 14, 1951.

Norton Lectures: Muir, *The Estate of Poetry: The Charles Eliot Norton Lectures, 1955–1956* (1962).

329. To Harriet Winslow

harsh letter: The letter has not survived.

330. To William Carlos Williams

Coleridge, Biographia, Chap. 10: Coleridge, *Biographia Literaria* (1817), volume 1, chapter 10, 188–89, slightly misquoted.

Italian flower book: Williams, *Il fiore è il nostro segno. Poesie di William Carlos Williams*, trans. Cristina Campo (1958).

our two books and Ezra's: *A lume spento, 1908–1958/Ezra Pound*, ed. Vanni Scheiwiller (1958). For

bibliographies of Italian translations of Lowell's works, see *Robert Lowell: A Tribute*, ed. Rolando Anzilotti (1979), and Robert Lowell, *Giorno per giorno*, trans. Francesco Rogoni (2001).

331. To Randall Jarrell

my friends and my relations: many sources; cf. "I lamented my own folly and willfulness in attempting a second voyage against the advice of all my friends and relations. In this terrible agitation of mind I could not forbear thinking of Lilliput . . ." (Jonathan Swift, *Gulliver's Travels* [1726], page 10).

your Rilke . . . I tried a few translations: Jarrell published a series of Rilke translations in *An Anthology of German Poetry*, ed. Angel Flores (1960). Lowell's translations of Rilke poems from the *Neue Gedichte* (1907) are published in *IM*.

the best Rilke in English: Rilke, "The Olive Garden," *The Seven League Crutches*, trans. Jarrell (1951). Jarrell's other Rilke translations include "Evening," "Lament," "Childhood," "The Grown-Up," "Washing the Corpse," "The Child," "The Great Night," "Death," and "Requiem—For the Death of a Boy."

Hoskins: Katherine Hoskins (b. 1907), American poet.

Rich: Adrienne Rich (b. 1929), American poet.

332. To Theodore Roethke

Housman's phrase: "I hope you won't succeed in getting anything from Meredith, as I am a respectable character, and do not care to be seen in the company of galvanised corpses. By this time he stinketh: for he has been dead twenty years" (A. E. Housman to Laurence Housman, 9 August 1903, quoted in Laurence Housman, *My Brother, A. E. Housman* [1938], 168).

my *PR* poems: "Man and Wife," "Skunk Hour," "To Delmore Schwartz (Cambridge 1946)," "To Speak of the Woe That Is in Marriage," *Partisan Review*, Winter 1958.

unlicked fragments: Cf. "To shape my legs of an unequal size;/To disproportion me in every part,/Like to a chaos, or an unlick'd bear-whelp/That carries no impression like the dam" (*3 Henry VI* 3.2. 159–62).

Penguin anthology: *The Penguin Book of French Verse, Vol. 3: The Nineteenth Century*, ed. Anthony Hartley (1957).

as Claudel used to write Gide: Claudel closed many of his letters to Gide with "Je vous serre bien cordialement la main"; see Paul Claudel and Andre Gide, *Correspondence: 1899–1926* (1984), 46.

333. To Elizabeth Bishop

Helena Morley: *The Diary of "Helena Morely,"* trans. Elizabeth Bishop (1957).

Look Back in Anger: John Osborne, *Look Back in Anger* (first performed in 1956).

The Princess de Clèves . . . : Marie-Madeleine de La Fayette, *La Princesse de Clèves* (1678); Honoré de Balzac, *Le Père Goriot* (1835).

Fontaine: Jean de La Fontaine, *Fables*, trans. Marianne Moore (1954).

Zabel: Morton Dauwen Zabel (1901–64), American critic.

Sorry about Sammy: Sammy was Bishop's toucan. "My darling toucan died; I still can't bear to think about it. It was all my fault. I used an insecticide the man in the store said was 'inoffensive' to animals, and it killed him. There he lay, just like life only with his feet up in the air. I want to get another one, but Lota says we're having a little vacation from toucans now. I am trying to write Sammy an ode—incorporating a lot of poems I wrote about him from time to time—'Most comical of all in death'" (Elizabeth Bishop to RL, April Fool's Day [1958], Harvard).

I'll try *Marius*: Walter Pater, *Marius the Epicurean: His Sensations and Ideas* (1885).

334. To Elizabeth Bishop

about Pound: Bishop heard a rumor that Pound might visit Brazil, which worried her (Bishop to RL, May 8, 1958, Harvard).

We like Ives too: Charles Ives (1874–1954), American composer.

Just read the Agee: James Agee, *A Death in the Family* (1957).

I add Agee's death to his hero's: James Agee (1909–55), American writer, died of a heart attack in a taxicab in New York City, leaving *A Death in the Family* unfinished. It was published posthumously in 1957 and won the Pulitzer Prize. The book's protagonist, Jay Follet, is killed in a car accident.

new poem . . . needs an upstroke: "Home after Three Months Away," *LS*; see lines 39–40.

336. To R. W. Flint

metrics: George Hemphill, "The Meters of the Intermediate Poets," *Kenyon Review*, Winter 1957.

337. To Anne Sexton

Anne Sexton (1928–74), American poet.

your poems qualify: In an interview, Sexton explained that Snodgrass had "suggested that I study with Robert Lowell. So I sent Mr. Lowell some of my poems and asked if he would take me into the class" (*Anne Sexton: The Artist and Her Critics*, ed. J. D. McClatchy, [1978], 9). Sexton and Donald Junkins were Lowell's students in the autumn of 1958; Sylvia Plath and George Starbuck joined the class in the 1959 spring semester.

338. To Harriet Winslow

Zhivago: Boris Pasternak (1890–1960), Russian poet; *Doctor Zhivago*, trans. Max Hayward and Manya Harari, with the poems of "Yurii Zhivago," trans. Bernard Guilbert Guerney (1958).

339. To Elizabeth Bishop

Kunitz: Stanley Kunitz (b. 1905), American poet.

wonderful play: William Alfred, *Hogan's Goat* (first performed in 1965); he started writing it in 1956.

first book of poems: I. A. Richards, *Goodbye Earth and Other Poems* (1958).

Provençal poems that Pound quotes . . .: See Pound's translation of Arnaut Daniel's "Can Chai la Fueilla" ("When the leaf falls . . ."), *Literary Essays* (1954), 115–16.

340. To Peter Taylor

preface: Jarrell wrote the introduction to Eleanor Ross Taylor's *Wilderness of Ladies* (1960).

Douglass House: "I am moving from the Johnsons to the more casual and uncloistered Douglass House, as the elegant, enclosed letter will indicate. Here all the Kenyon poets and a few inconspicuous other students have been gathered" (RL to Charlotte Lowell, [n.d. November 1938], Harvard). Students living at Douglass House included Randall Jarrell, Peter Taylor, John Thompson, Robie Macauley, John Nether, and David McDowell.

the Transues: Friends of the Taylors from Kenyon.

Iris Origo: Iris Origo (1902–88), Anglo-Italian writer.

341. To John Crowe Ransom
the Léger: Ransom had asked Lowell to review St.-John Perse's *Amers* (1957).

342. To Elizabeth Bishop
"The bad gray poet": "Frost—the Bad Gray Poet" (Bishop to RL, *One Art*, 365; Lowell misquotes her slightly in *CPR*, 206). Cf. William Douglas O'Connor on Walt Whitman, *The Good Gray Poet: A Vindication* (1866).

your Brazilian National Geographic picture: "Here is a picture of me among the Vialapiti. I want to get copies of some of the better ones" (*One Art*, 365).

Wilson: Wilson, "Doctor Life and His Guardian Angel," *New Yorker*, November 15, 1958.

his crack at Nicolson: "I was not surprised to see that Sir Harold Nicolson, who has lately been telling us how ungentlemanly or unladylike our men and women of genius are, was shocked by this young girl. His attention to manners is making him censorious of the springs of nature. 'Helena Morley' seems to me like any little girl one has ever seen or heard of: remorseless" (V. S. Pritchett, "A Brazilian Diamond," *New Statesman*, October 25, 1958). Bishop at one point considered entitling the *Diary of "Helena Morley"* "Black Beans and Diamonds" because it takes place in the Brazilian provincial town of Diamantina.

343. To William Carlos Williams
Edith Heal book: Williams, *I Wanted to Write a Poem: The Autobiography of the Works of a Poet*, ed. Edith Heal (1958), 97.

344. To William Carlos Williams
read through my poems: "Floss has just finished reading me your terrible wonderful poems. You have lost nothing of your art, in fact you have piled accomplishment upon accomplishment until there is nothing to be said to you in rebuttal of your devastating statements or the way you have uttered them. I'm trying to be not rhetorical but to approach the man you are with all defenses down. . . . To be a successful artist means victory in the first place and then over the world you inhabit. Poverty in the case of the painters Cézanne and Van Gogh. . . . Your problem was the English language. Your use of the words is aristocratic, sometimes you use rhyme—but thank goodness less and less frequently and that is an improvement, you speak more to us, more directly when you do not have to descend to it, your language gains in seriousness and ability in your choice of words when you abandon rhyme completely. . . . The book must have caused you some difficulty to write. There is no lying permitted to a man who writes that way. (Next day) I couldn't go on. The book took too much out of me which I don't have any more to give. It's very impressive but I couldn't read it again. The one short lyric is really beautiful, finished and beautiful" (Williams to RL November 24, 1958, Harvard, quoted in Axelrod, 92).

345. To Elizabeth Bishop
The Nose . . . Sportsman Sketches: Nikolay Gogol, "The Nose" (1836) and "The Overcoat" (1842); Ivan Sergeyevich Turgenev, *A Sportsman's Sketches* (1852).

Rahv's anthology: *The Short Novels of Tolstoy*, ed. Philip Rahv, trans. Aylmer Maude (1946).

American Novel: Richard Chase, *The American Novel and Its Tradition* (1957).

whose wife belongs . . . : Elise Asher (b. 1914), American poet and painter; Philip Guston

(1913–80), American painter; Willem De Kooning (1904–97), Dutch American painter; Franz Kline (1910–62), American painter.

Balanchine: George Balanchine (1904–83), Russian American choreographer.

Florence book . . . : McCarthy, *The Stones of Florence* (1959); the "novel on the thirties" became *The Group* (1963).

Pope-Hennessy: Sir John Pope-Hennessy (1913–94), English art historian, wrote extensively about Donatello.

Clark: Sir Kenneth Clark (1903–83), English art historian.

Chester: Chester Kallman (1921–75), American poet. His libretti include several collaborations with his companion, W. H. Auden, including *The Rake's Progress*.

his departure poem: W. H. Auden, "Good-Bye to the Mezzogiorno" (1958).

Mosby's Civil War memoirs: John Singleton Mosby (1833–1916), Confederate ranger, author of *Mosby's War Reminiscences, and Stuart's Cavalry Campaigns* (1887).

Pearl . . . : Una Hawthorne (1844–77), Hawthorne's eldest child. Pearl is Hester Prynne's daughter in *The Scarlet Letter*.

James gives as examples . . . : Henry James, *Hawthorne* (1997), 37–39, slightly misquoted.

Randall on MacLeish's *JB*: Archibald MacLeish's *J.B.: A Play in Verse* (1958), a retelling of the story of Job, was produced on Broadway and awarded the Pulitzer Prize.

346. To William Meredith

beginning to actually see: Possibly a reference to poems by Sexton and other Boston University students.

Mackie: Randall Jarrell's former wife was a colleague of Meredith's.

347. To William Carlos Williams

a clean manly fellow: "Williams wrote Bill [Sommer] a memorable letter accompanying his check (for $25.00) in which he said that Bill got under his underdrawers!—and went on to say that he was potentially greater than Marin. It has heartened Bill wonderfully. Such a letter was worth more than the plaudits of a hundred Rosenfelds. I'd like to meet Williams! (Repeating this statement so many times won't do any good I suppose, but there's that directness about the man that I know I'd find cleansing)" (Hart Crane to Gorham Munson, Oct. 12, '22, *The Letters of Hart Crane: 1916–1932*, ed. Brom Weber [1952], 102).

your play: Williams, *Many Loves*, dir. Julian Beck, opened at the Living Theater on January 13, 1959.

"hand on stick, triumphant to disaster": Williams, "Pictures from Breughel," section 9, lines 19–24. Lowell's Breughel poems are "The Blind Leading the Blind," based on *The Parable of the Blind* (1568), and "The North Sea Undertaker's Complaint," based on *Gloomy Day* (1565), *LWC*.

348. To A. Alvarez

Alfred Alvarez (b. 1929), English poet, novelist, and critic.

Lawrence: Alvarez, "D. H. Lawrence: The Single State of Man," *The Shaping Spirit: Studies in Modern English and American Poets* (1958).

***Birds, Beast* etc:** D. H. Lawrence, *Birds, Beasts and Flowers* (1923).

the Bewley piece: Marius Bewley, "Aspects of Modern American Poetry," *Scrutiny* (1950). "Marius Bewley has written brilliantly and in detail on Lowell in *The Complex Fate*. He defines the tortured, harsh quality of his poetry as the result of 'a head-on collision between the Catholic

tradition and an Apocalyptic Protestant sensibility.' I can't argue with that, but would add that clearly neither force wins" (Alvarez, "Art and Isolation," *The Shaping Spirit* [1958], 185).

for a *Scrutiny* article: *Scrutiny*, edited by F. R. Leavis from 1932 to 1953.

"you're no Sainte-Beuve": "I never remembering hearing *anybody* say of a critic, 'He's all right, but he's no Sainte-Beuve'; but substitute *Dante* or some such O.K. name for *Sainte-Beuve*, and there are very few writers about whom the statement hasn't been made. When the first book of one of the best of living poets was published, one of the best of living critics said about it only that it was 'grating,' and lacked the sweetness of the Divine Comedy. So it did; the poet might have replied with the same truth that his critic lacked Matthew Arnold's yellow kid gloves" (Jarrell, "The Age of Criticism," *No Other Book* [1999], 284). Charles-Augustin Sainte-Beuve (1804–69), French literary critic.

your *PR* review and your *New Statesman* Dryden: Alvarez, "Poetry Chronicle," *Partisan Review*, Fall 1958; "John Dryden" (a review of *The Poems of John Dryden*, ed. James Kinsley), *New Statesman* (1959), reprinted in *Beyond All This Fiddle: Essays 1955–1967* (1968).

349. To John Berryman

Odd: In March 1959, John Berryman had just been released from the hospital and was living apart from his second wife, Ann, and their son, Paul; the couple divorced shortly thereafter.

"Venice" . . . "Poet's Final Instruction": Berryman, "Venice," *American Letters*, December 1948, retitled "Venice, 182—"; "The Poet's Final Instructions," *His Thoughts Made Pockets & The Plane Buckt* (1958).

Spoon River: Edgar Lee Masters, *Spoon River Anthology* (1915).

about Paul: Berryman, "A Sympathy, A Welcome," *New Yorker*, August 16, 1958.

"They Have," and "Note to Wang Wei.": Berryman, "They Have," *His Thought Made Pockets & The Plane Buckt* (1958); "Note to Wang Wei," *New Yorker*, August 2, 1958.

350. To Mary and Randall Jarrell

Chase: Richard Chase (1914–62), American literary critic.

351. To W. S. Merwin

"nec nos pigebat meminisse, tibi": We were not displeased to remember you (hence, we were missing you bitterly) (courtesy Warren Myers). Lowell may have wanted to allude to "nec me meminisse pigebit Elissæ dum memor ipse mei," Virgil, *Aeneid*, book 4, line 335 (in Dryden's translation: "Nor can my mind forget Eliza's name,/while vital breath inspires this mortal frame"; in Robert Fitzgerald's: "Never will the memory of Elissa/Stale for me, while I can still remember/My own life, and the spirit rules my body"). The full name of Virgil's Dido is Elissæ Dido.

the Ted Hughes's: Sylvia Plath (1932–63), American poet, and Ted Hughes (1930–98), English poet.

Mr. Doyle: Charles Doyle (b. 1928), poet and critic, was visiting the United States from New Zealand on a Unesco International Creative Artist's Fellowship.

352. To Elizabeth Bishop

"St. Jerome" poem: Jarrell, "Jerome," *Analects*, October 1960, reprinted in *The Woman at the Washington Zoo* (1960).

Frank's picture: "Frank has done a good picture in black and white of a relaxed, grieving or dreaming lion before a corridor of light bulbs—me, I suppose" (RL to Bishop, March 5, 1959, Vas-

sar); "Of course, I am thrilled that you want to do the picture [for the frontispiece of *Notebook*]. Do what you wish, I would almost rather see it after you've sent it in. A loose connection with the poems is often best, though I think of *Life Studies* and your McLean Lion—that was close" (RL to Frank Parker, January 18, 1970, collection of Francis S. Parker).

353. To Allen Ginsberg

Allen Ginsberg (1926–97), American poet.

the *Big Table* . . . Dahlberg's prose: The University of Chicago suppressed the publication of an issue of the *Chicago Review* featuring the work of William Burroughs. The editors resigned and founded *Big Table*, the first issue of which consisted largely of material from the suppressed *Chicago Review*. The second and third issues included excerpts of *Because I Was Flesh* by Edward Dahlberg.

The Kerouac . . . the Burroughs: Jack Kerouac, "Old Angel Midnight," and William S. Burroughs, "Ten Episodes from *Naked Lunch*," *Big Table*, no. 1 (Spring 1959).

the paeans by you and Kerouac: "Notes on Contributors," *Big Table*, vol. 1, nos. 1 and 3 (1959–60); Allen Ginsberg, "Notes on Young Poets," *Big Table*, vol. 1, no. 4 (1960).

Corso: Gregory Corso, "Rembrandt Self-Portrait," "EMILY DICKINSON THE TROUBLE WITH YOU IS," "Walk," *Big Table*, vol. 1, no. 4 (1960).

I can't see why *Big Table* should be suppressed: The U.S. Post Office banned the mailing of *Big Table*'s first issue in March 1959, impounding 499 copies of the journal. The ban was not set aside until a court ruling in July 1960.

Creeley and your *Kaddish*: Robert Creeley (b. 1926), American poet; Ginsberg, *Kaddish* (1961).

Barrett's Zen Buddhist book: Daisetz Teitato Suzuki, *Zen Buddhism: Selected Writings*, ed. William Barrett (1956).

354. To Elizabeth Bishop

O'Hara: See Bishop to RL, March 30, 1959, *One Art*, 371. Frank O'Hara (1926–66), American poet.

Orlovsky: Peter Orlovsky (b. 1933), American poet, Allen Ginsberg's lover and companion.

the lion's cave . . . : Cf. "David to Bathsheba," section I of "David and Bathsheba in the Public Garden," *MK*, line 19. (Lowell's *Life Studies*, with its frontispiece of the "MacLean lion" by Frank Parker, had yet to be released.)

thunderstruck: "I was hit by a thunderbolt, I believe, our last big storm. It felt like a large rock falling on my feet, so that I looked up at the sky, like Henny Penny, to see where it had come from. Bang!—it almost knocked me over. I was standing beside an outside base plug. (Lota's fancy is to light up the scenery at night. I tell her it makes the house look like a concentration camp.)" (Bishop to RL, March 30, 1959, *One Art*, 372).

355. To Allen Ginsberg

you think poetry ought be: "I think . . . (to carry my hutspuh to logical conclusion) that your broken line poetry is slightly unnatural—too worked on—to be really precise. Can you have a Crafty natural speech? a deliberate Flow? a forced artlessness? I mean the point of 'freeverse' is to make use of natural 'unpoetic'—really unpoetic—qualities—natural speech artless flow" (Ginsberg to RL, April 5, 1959, Harvard).

Creeley and Levertov: Robert Creeley, "The Awakening," "The Wife," "The Memory," and "The Snow"; Denise Levertov, "The Rainwalkers"; *Big Table*, vol. 1, no. 4 (1960). Denise Levertov (1923–97), Anglo-American poet.

poetry as a technique: "You know, really, I see W.C. Williams as a big Goof, piddling around with his idears, not at all the neat Technician that you see him. I love him, and his poetry,—but I was amazed (enlightened) and shocked to see you apply New Criticism to his 'indented' houses. Well, I'm speaking vulgarly, not new criticism—that wasn't it—it was the shadow of some Officialdom of Intellect applied to the appreciation of his Precision of language, & rhythm. HE DIDN'T WRITE IT THAT WAY. He didn't know—in those terms—what he was doing. He's just W.C.W. in Rutherford at a piece of paper writing—conscious of visual imagery, Imagism—and conscious of the rhythm of his speech, and how he could arrange it into symmetrical units—that much yes—and working by Ear and not Official Ear—his own individual ear—" (Ginsberg to RL, April 5, 1959, Harvard).

intolerant of other kinds of writing: Ginsberg replied: "There's no real intolerance on our part, or mine, for the older writers, tho I admire Wolfe and Sherwood Anderson & the Primitives more than some you mention (O'Connor, Roethke, Kunitz)—the Intolerance has in fact been reversed, I've been the object of much—that's made me a little hypersensitive, sure—you have no idea the barrage of garbage I've had to swallow from Kenyon, Hudson etc. without losing my temper the last few years" (Ginsberg to RL, April 16, 1959, Harvard).

356. To I. A. Richards

Fraser . . . page 179, re Louis MacNeice: G. S. Fraser (1915–80), Scottish poet and critic; "Evasive Honesty: The Poetry of Louis MacNeice," *Vision and Rhetoric Studies in Modern Poetry* (1959), 179, slightly misquoted.

357. To Elizabeth Hardwick

Kean-Kongs: Almost illegible; possibly a child's variation on King Kong?

Poggie: Possibly "poggy" or "poguey." The word has several meanings; with "bait," it is sailor's slang for candy, also related to prostitute. "Many thanks for Harriet's lovely dress. She is very keen on men now and knows how effective her new splendor is. Two weeks ago when Lizzie and I were having a somewhat impassioned discussion, she said, 'Daddy's Poggie. I am a pick-up. Nathan's a pain in the neck.' And we were instantly reconciled" (RL to Bishop, February 9, 1959, Vassar). "A messy letter, I am playing Burl Ives for my daughter, yelling 'I am Daddy's Poggie'" (RL to Jarrell, February 15, 1959).

358. To Edmund Wilson

Written during an acute manic episode.

my poem diamond-pointed on your window pane: "Lowell etched an early poem, 'Children of Light,' on a window in [Wilson's] Wellfleet house, and later sent Wilson a manuscript of the revised version" (Jeffrey Meyers, *Edmund Wilson: A Biography* [1995], p. 374). "Children of Light," *LOU* and *LWC*.

conditioning here: Robert Giroux planned a publication party for *Life Studies* in late April but Lowell, alarmed by his own behavior, checked himself in to McLean Hospital.

359. To Elizabeth Bishop

I was mostly waste: Probably "It was mostly waste."

prose sketch: "Visiting the Tates," *Sewanee Review*, 1959, reprinted in *CPR*.

360. To William Meredith

HY wasn't babble: In a previous letter, Lowell had written to Meredith, "I suppose you've heard that I've been through one of my manic swings with its jolting confusion and silliness. A dull story. All's fairly okay now . . . I am introducing Eliot at the HY on the fifteenth of October" (RL to William Meredith, September 14, 1959, collection of Richard Henry Levey, copy at Connecticut College). Meredith wrote back on September 16, 1959, apologizing for not having contacted him during his illness (Harvard).

361. To John Berryman

stretch out a hand: Cf. note to letter 332.

Bob Lax and Bob Giroux: Berryman befriended Lax and Giroux when they were students at Columbia University; with Thomas Merton, they worked for the *Columbia Review*. Robert Lax (1915–2000), American poet.

poem about Harry: The Dream Songs are "about an imaginary character (not the poet, not me) named Henry, a white American in early middle age sometimes in black face, who has suffered an irreversible loss" (Berryman, "Note," *The Dream Songs*, vi).

362. To Charles Monteith

Charles Monteith (1921–95), editor at Faber & Faber.

the Guinness prize: "In October 1959 . . . Lowell had been awarded an odd prize in London: a prize awarded annually by the brewing family's own poet, Bryan Guinness, otherwise Lord Moyne" (Ian Hamilton, 397). John Wain read "Skunk Hour" at the prize ceremony on Lowell's behalf (Wain to RL, 6 October 1959, Harvard).

Ben Jonson's barrel of claret: As poet laureate, Jonson received an annual "terse," or "butt of Canary wine" from Charles I.

363. To Chard Powers Smith

Chard Powers Smith (1894–1977), American writer and poet.

John Holmes . . . Robinson: John Holmes (1904–62), American poet who taught at Tufts. Chard Powers Smith befriended the poet Edwin Arlington Robinson in 1924 while at the Macdowell Colony in Peterborough, New Hampshire. See Smith, *Where the Light Falls* (1965).

"Nature is blossoming . . .": "Labour is blossoming or dancing where/The body is not bruised to pleasure soul" (W. B. Yeats, "Among School Children," lines 57–58).

364. To Harriet Winslow

Stoddard: Possibly Richard Henry Stoddard (1825–1903) and Elizabeth Drew Stoddard (1823–1902).

a polemic: Hardwick, "The Decline of Book Reviewing," *Harper's*, 1959.

365. To David Posner

David Posner (1938–85), American poet, taught at Buffalo and was the curator of Lockwood Library's poetry collection.

366. To Stephen Spender

the Richards piece: Review of I. A. Richards's *Goodbye Earth and Other Poems* (1960), *Encounter*, February 1960, reprinted as "I. A. Richards" in *CPR*.

simple sensuous and passionate: "Logic therefore so much as is usefull, is to be referr'd to this due place with all her well coucht heads and Topics, until it be time to open her contracted palm into a gracefull and ornate Rhetorick taught out of the rule of Plato, Aristotle, Phalereus, Cicero, Hermogenes, Longinus. To which Poetry would be made subsequent, or indeed rather precedent, as being lesse suttle and fine, but more simple, sensuous and passionate" (Milton, "Of Education" [1644], 6).

your review: Stephen Spender, "Robert Lowell's Family Album,"*New Republic*, June 8, 1959.

Mrs. Pasternak's ...: Lydia Pasternak-Slater, Pasternak's sister and English translator, "lives in Oxford—wrote very annoyed because you had brought the word 'nipples' into a poem related, however remotely, to her brother" (Spender to RL, Oct. 15 1959, Harvard). "Like water pouring from a pitcher, my mouth on your nipples!" (Lowell, "Sparrow Hills," *IM*, line 1).

367. To I. A. Richards

"To D. E. P.": Richards, "Hope: To D.E.P. in hospital for a broken hip," *The Screens and Other Poems* (1961).

368. To Harriet Winslow

"The child ...": Wordsworth, "My Heart Leaps Up" (1807), line 7; "Ode: Intimations of Immortality from Recollections of Early Childhood" (1807), epigraph.

369. To Randall Jarrell

the Goethe?: Jarrell was translating Goethe's *Faust*; see also note to letter 678.

German anthology: *An Anthology of German Poetry: Poetry from Hölderlin to Rilke in English*, ed. Angel Flores (1960).

370. To William Meredith

interview: "Robert Lowell: An Interview with Frederick Seidel," *Paris Review*, Winter–Spring 1961, reprinted in *CPR*.

the grant ...: Lowell's first idea was to turn Melville's "Benito Cereno" into a libretto; see *OG*.

what's happening: Sit-in protests, which started in Greensboro, North Carolina, on February 1, 1960, spread through the South and became a powerful protest strategy during the civil rights movement. News reports about nonviolent demonstrations that were met with excessively punitive, often violent force by local police and white communities appeared daily in the papers. On March 3, the *New York Times* reported "Alabama Expels 9 Negro Students; Governor Calls Action Needed to Prevent Bloodshed—Nashville Arrests 50."

Britten's *Billy Budd:* Benjamin Britten, *Billy Budd* (op. 50, 1950–51), based on Melville's story.

371. To Richard J. Fein

Richard J. Fein (b. 1929), American poet. His critical books include *Robert Lowell* (1970).

372. To Harriet Winslow

the first playing: Elizabeth Hardwick crossed out "early" and penciled in "first."

knows her story: Lili Boulanger (1893–1918), French composer, younger sister of Nadia Boulanger.

Dominguez's voice: Lowell was listening to a recording by Oralia Dominguez of one of Lili Boulanger's symphonic poems.

373. To Elizabeth Bishop

Amazon poem: Bishop, "The Riverman," *New Yorker*, April 2, 1960, reprinted in *Questions of Travel* (1965).

mermaid . . . : Cf. "Water," *FTUD*, lines 25–28; Bishop, *One Art* (1994), 170.

the Tate-Gardner tape: Jackson Mathews, "Conversation with Sylvia Beach & Co.," *Kenyon Review*, Winter 1960. During the interview with Sylvia Beach, Isabella Gardner and Allen Tate make an appearance at her bookstore. A toast is raised to their marriage, which struck Bishop as "gratuitously cruel to poor old Caroline" (Bishop to Lowell, April 22, 1960, Harvard).

descriptions in your letter: See Bishop, *One Art*, 381–85.

Daniel Hoffman: Daniel Hoffman (b. 1923), American poet.

Miss de Mazia: Violette de Mazia (1899–1988), close friend of Albert Barnes (1872–1951); she was vice president of the Barnes Museum board of trustees.

Buckle's Intellectual History of the world . . . Ingersoll: Probably Henry Thomas Buckle, *History of Civilization in England* (1957); Robert Ingersoll (1833–99), American orator and politician, author of *Some Mistakes of Moses* (1879) and *Why I Am Agnostic* (1896).

the world in a grain of sand: Blake, "Auguries of Innocence," line 1.

from three of his: "Heine Dying in Paris," an imitation of Heinrich Heine's "Morphine" "Der Scheidende," and "Mein Tag war heiter," *IM*.

374. To William Empson

your Satan and Delilah pieces: Empson, "The Satan of Milton," *Hudson Review*, Spring 1960; "A Defense of Delilah," *Sewanee Review*, Spring 1960; reprinted in *Milton's God* (1961).

Lewis's book: C. S. Lewis, *A Preface to* Paradise Lost (1942).

what you wrote about Lear: Empson, "Fool in *Lear*," *Sewanee Review*, June 1949; "The Horrors of *King Lear*," Spring 1949.

Joyce and Fielding pieces: Empson, "The Theme of Ulysses," *Kenyon Review*, Winter 1956; "Tom Jones," *Kenyon Review*, Spring 1958.

375. To Elizabeth Bishop

the soap-dish . . . : Bishop compared a draft of "The Drinker" with the version printed in the *Partisan Review*, Spring 1960. Lowell removed an image of a soap dish in the *P.R.* version, which she missed. She added: "As a cook I feel I should tell you that soured milk is NOT junket" (Bishop, *One Art*, 386). See "The Drinker," *FTUD*, lines 31–32.

old silver remarks: "That Anne Sexton I think still has a bit too much romanticism and what I think of as the 'our beautiful old silver' school of female writing which is really boasting about how 'nice' *we* were. V. Woolf, K.A.P., Bowen, R. West, etc.—they are all full of it. They have to make quite sure that the reader is not going to mis-place them socially, first—and that nervousness interferes constantly with what they think they'd like to say" (Bishop to RL, July 27th [1960], Harvard).

swipe at me: George P. Elliott, "Three Imaginary Autobiographies," *Hudson Review*, Summer 1960.

You're not facile . . . : "I don't know whether it is a virtue or not, never to sound the same way more than once or twice! It sounds too much like facility, and yet I don't feel a bit facile, God knows" (*One Art*, 387).

"Randall never lifts a finger!": At a party, "I remarked that I was afraid I'd had some sort of falling- out with Randall and [Anne Macauley] said 'Good!' All wives seem to feel strongly about Randall! 'Never lifts a finger,' etc." (*One Art*, 387).

May Sarton: "May Sarton much addicted to the higher cliché—but as Lota says, it's still better than the lower cliché" (Bishop to RL, July 27th, [1960], Harvard); May Sarton (1912–95), American poet.

More on solitude and meter: "By the way meter is a puzzle to me now. Metrical verse and un- metrical verse seem almost two different species. Something quite pleasant both to write and to read is added by meter, but it's something free verse doesn't want at all, and which seems to have little to do with experience or intuition, though I know all the standard answers to this. I think it's some architectural, building up effect that makes meter impressive. You have some- thing explicit and hard to do, and your reader can spot this, criticize the difficulties, and enjoy the obvious work. I'm fascinated by something in between like the great passages in [Middle- ton's] *The Changeling*, where meter is kept but its big applied, laid-on-thick billow disappear. What a figure!" (RL to Bishop, July 12, 1960, Vassar).

Gombrich: E. H. Gombrich, *Art and Illusion: A Study in the Psychology of Pictorial Representation* (1960).

Karl's: Karl Shapiro, *In Defense of Ignorance* (1960).

the new forces: "The new American must be either the child of the new forces or a chance sport of nature" (Henry Adams, *The Education of Henry Adams*, 501).

376. To Stephen Spender

my "Union Dead": "For the Union Dead," first read at the Boston Arts Festival in the Public Gar- den in June 1960.

377. To T. S. Eliot

Figaro: Beaumarchais's *Figaro's Marriage*, trans. Jacques Barzun, published with Lowell's *Phaedra* in *Phaedra and Figaro* (1961).

Auden's *Rake*: Auden and Chester Kallmann's libretto for Igor Stravinsky's *The Rake's Progress* (1951).

The Changeling: Thomas Middleton, *The Changeling* (1653); see also Eliot, "Thomas Middleton," *Selected Essays: 1917–1932* (1932).

introduce you: Eliot read at the 92nd Street Y in New York in January 1961.

378. To Adrienne Rich

Davie: Donald Davie (1922–95), English poet.

Mrs. Bel Geddes . . . : Barbara Bel Geddes (b. 1921), American actress; Norman Bel Geddes (1883–1958), theatrical and industrial designer.

Edwige Feuillere . . . : Edwige Feuillere (1907–98), French actress; Melina Mercouri (1923–94), Greek actress; Franco Zeffirelli (b. 1923), Italian film, theater, and opera director and designer. His production of *Romeo and Juliet* opened at the Old Vic Theatre in London in April 1960.

country house pieces: Rich, "September 21," "Passing On," *Snapshots of a Daughter-in-Law* (1963).

history poem: Rich, "Readings of History," *Snapshots of a Daughter-in-Law* (1963).

Alf's studies: Alfred H. Conrad (1924–70), Rich's husband, economist, co-author of *The Econom- ics of Slavery and Other Studies in Econometric History* (1964).

"kitchen" opening: Rich, "A Woman Mourned by Daughters," *Snapshots of a Daughter-in-Law* (1963), lines 1–3.

Fiedler: Leslie Fiedler (1917–2003), American literary critic.

Hammarskjöld: Dag Hammarskjöld (1905–61), Swedish economist and statesman, secretary-general of the United Nations from 1953 to 1961.

Hollander: John Hollander (b. 1929), American poet.

Koch: Kenneth Koch (1925–2002), American poet.

lyrics for a Broadway musical: In 1960 John Hollander was working on the lyrics of *Underworld*, written by Ben Hecht, with music by Jeremy Moross. "I must have told Cal of this in October '60 or thereabouts. The only traces of the musical exists in a few recordings of songs from it, most recently, six of them on a CD of Jeremy Moross' theater songs called *Windflowers*" (Hollander to SH, September 14, 2002).

the Epsteins: Barbara Epstein (b. 1928) worked in publishing and at the *Partisan Review*; she later became cofounder and coeditor of the *New York Review of Books*. Jason Epstein (b. 1928), Random House editor, cofounder of the *New York Review of Books* and the Library of America.

382. To Elizabeth Bishop

I hope these will reach you: A typescript of *Imitations*, which Lowell dedicated to Bishop.

the mid-century: A book club started by W. H. Auden, Lionel Trilling, and Jacques Barzun.

383. To Elizabeth Hardwick

Podhoretz: Norman Podhoretz (b. 1930), editor of *Commentary* magazine from 1955 to 1995; Midge Decter (b. 1927), essayist; their children are Ruth and John. Decter also has two children from a previous marriage.

Mr. Badman: Cf. John Bunyan, *The Life and Death of Mr. Badman* (1680).

384. To Hannah Arendt

the Rilke: "Pigeons," an imitation of Rilke's "Die Tauben," dedicated to Arendt in *IM*.

your exile: Arendt spent the 1961 winter quarter (January–March) at Northwestern University. Lowell and Arendt befriended each other in the winter of 1960; see "On Hannah Arendt," *New York Review of Books*, May 13, 1976.

385. To Hannah Arendt

I couldn't be more pleased!: "Your poem greeting me here right on arrival was such a consolated. And has been sitting in front of me on my desk ever since. To greet me when I come home from (not quite the rat-race in the arena) but something similar, perhaps the rat-race of education . . . The poem is very beautiful and a real reply (not response) to Taube die draussen blieb. I am so proud that you will dedicate it to me that I blush and get all embarrassed" (Hannah Arendt to RL, January 18, 1961, Harvard).

the *Nation*: "Pigeons," *Nation*, February 18, 1961.

"Self-Portrait": "Self-Portrait," *IM*.

We got invited to Washington: For John Kennedy's inauguration.

Affectionately: Lowell forgot to sign the letter, despite the fact that Arendt had asked how she should address him: "Dear Robert—(or is it Cal? And which is your preference?)" (Hannah Arendt to RL, January 18, 1961, Harvard).

386. To Elizabeth Bishop

lost letter: "BELIEVE MY LETTER LOST TRANSLATIONS ABSOLUTELY STUNNING

PROUD AND PLEASED RECORDS RECEIVED LOVE ELIZABETH" (Bishop to RL, January 26, [1961], Harvard).

I've added "Mémoire" . . . : "Nostalgia," "The Drunken Boat," "The Lice-Hunters" (by Rimbaud); "The Great Testament (for William Carlos Williams)," "Ballad for the Dead Ladies," "The Old Lady's Lament for Her Youth," "Villon's Prayer for His Mother to Say to the Virgin," "Villon's Epitaph" (by Villon); and "The Voyage (for T. S. Eliot)" (by Baudelaire); *IM.*

Her new man: James West, public affairs officer at the American embassy in Warsaw when he met McCarthy; they were married on April 15, 1961.

387. To Marianne Moore

Written during an acute manic episode.

try my own hand: Marianne Moore wrote a note to Lowell to praise his Baudelaire translations: "The metre and rhymes . . . illustrate my conviction that rhymes should be so inevitable as not to show, therefore stabilizing content the more" (Marianne Moore to RL, March 19, 1961, Harvard). Lowell replied to Moore from the hospital. Like almost everything Lowell wrote while he was ill, he later discarded the poem he sent her; however, he retained two lines ("Forgive us our injuries,/As we forgive those we have injured") for "Middle Age," *FTUD.* Moore replied: "Thank you for the improvement, Robert. All that detains me—the only word—is 'Hell' after the circumspect 'tribulation' and 'save' us. One thing certain:—people always automatically say deliver us from *evil* whereas the emphasis is on deliver or save (from the inevitable)—Well I tend to think more than is to the point I think!" (Marianne Moore to RL, March 28, 1961, Harvard).

Protestant Pusey: Nathan Marsh Pusey, president of Harvard from 1953 to 1971.

"He is a real pigmy in a world of fake giants"?: "When dragged into prominence by half poets, the result is not poetry,/nor till the poets among us can be/'literalists of/the imagination'—above/insolence and triviality and can present/for inspection, 'imaginary gardens with real toads in them,' shall we have/it" (Marianne Moore, "Poetry," lines 28–34).

388. To Stephen Spender

the Rimbaud: "Nostalgia," "The Poet at Seven," "The Drunken Boat," "Eighteen Seventy," "The Lice Hunters," *Encounter,* November 1961.

Saison: Rimbaud, *Une Saison en enfer* (1873).

389. To Elizabeth Hardwick

for Pasternak: Lowell was in Los Angeles to film *Pasternak: A Television Essay,* a half-hour documentary for CBS, broadcast on Sunday, June 18, 1961. Lowell described Pasternak's work as "'orderly, syntactical,' and noted that he was 'in every way a disciplined writer but he had a gift for a surging flow of images'" (John P. Shanley, "Pasternak Recalled," *New York Times,* June 19, 1961).

Olga's plane: Olga Andreyev Carlisle (b. 1930), Russian American writer who edited *Poets on Street Corners: Portraits of Fifteen Russian Poets* (1968).

390. To Elizabeth Hardwick

Sherman Adams . . . in jail: Sherman Adams, Dwight D. Eisenhower's chief of staff, used his influence to help the industrialist Bernard Goldfine avoid federal investigations into his business

practices. In 1958, a congressional oversight subcommittee discovered that Adams had received free hotel rooms, meals, a vicuna coat, and a valuable Oriental rug from Goldfine. The subsequent scandal resulted in Adams's resignation and Goldfine's prosecution.

O-HI Valley: Ojai, California.

Silvers: Robert Silvers (b. 1929), cofounder and coeditor of the *New York Review of Books*.

391. To Elizabeth Bishop

more Pasternak . . . : Pasternak: "September," "For Anna Akhmatova," "Mephistopheles," "The Seasons," "Sparrow Hills," "Wild Vines," "In the Woods," "The Landlord (the Wedding)," "Hamlet in Russia, A Soliloquy"; Homer: "The Killing of Lykaon"; Sappho: "Three Letters to Anaktoria"; *IM*. For Bishop's reaction to *IM*, see *One Art*, 394–96.

your Brazil book: Elizabeth Bishop and the Editors of *Life*, *Brazil* (1962).

the long *New Yorker* childhood story . . . your "Prison"!: Bishop, "In the Village" and "In Prison."

Quadros: Jânio da Silva Quadros (1917–92), president of Brazil from January 31 to August 25, 1961.

accepting a job: Bishop accepted a job to write about Brazil for *Life* books.

like Lota: Lota was the "adviser" and unofficial director of the Arterro of Flamengo park project in Rio.

392. To T. S. Eliot

criticism: Allen Tate thought the title of *Imitations* should be changed to *Versions*. Eliot disagreed: "I also think that the right title for this is *Imitations*. . . . I also think that the sub-title is a mistake: your translations are indeed imitations, and if you use the word translation in the subtitle it will attract all those meticulous little critics who delight in finding what seem to them mis-translations. You will remember all the fuss about Pound's *Propertius*. . . . All I can say about the book as a whole is that I have enjoyed it and the only criticisms I have made, which you will find on the pages themselves, are of poems of which I had a fairly accurate memory of the original. I would like to call your attention to *Voyage to Cythera* (not Cytherea, as you have it, but Cythera). You cannot use the term 'old boys' in England as the equivalent of 'vieux garçons'. 'Old boy' in England means an alumnus of a public school and is not at all the equivalent, so I have suggested 'gay old dogs' instead. It seems to me almost a pity that in the last line of the poem you have left out the important word 'heart' and in the following poem, *The Servant*, I suggest that the phrase 'large heart' suggests merely an anatomical misfortune and that the real meaning of the French is 'generous'.* [in margin:] *Somehow 'large-hearted' has a clear meaning but 'whose large heart' is ambiguous!" (Eliot to RL, 1st June 1961, Harvard).

393. To Elizabeth Hardwick

a sort of thawed Per: Per Seyersted (b. 1921), Norwegian literary critic. Seyersted was the "first husband of my youngest sister Ingrid, who visited [the Lowells in 1956] in America when they were separating" (van Leeuwen to SH, April 29, 2003).

395. To Elizabeth Bishop

calling up the reserves: Jack Raymond, "Speedy Build-Up of Army Studied in Berlin Crisis," *New York Times*, July 17, 1961.

Hills: Rust Hills (b. 1924), *Esquire* fiction editor from 1956 to 1963.

Kazan: Molly Kazan (1907–68), American playwright, wife of Elia Kazan.
Maas: Willard Maas (1911–71), American poet.
Albee: Edward Albee (b. 1928), American playwright.

396. To Isabella Gardner
your book: Isabella Gardner, *The Looking Glass* (1961).
I tire of my turmoil . . . : Cf. "Eye and Tooth," *FTUD*, lines 36–40.
Campbell: Roy Campbell (1901–57), South African poet; his version of *Fuente Ovejuna* by Lope de
Vega was published in *Six Spanish Plays*, ed. Eric Bentley (1959).

397. To William Carlos Williams
for the *Hudson*: "Dr. Williams," *Hudson Review*, Winter 1961–62; reprinted in *CPR*, 44.

398. To A. Alvarez
Your remarks: Alvarez wrote that Lowell's Villon imitation in the *Observer* was the best thing the
newspaper had ever published and one of the best modern poems he knew (Alvarez to RL,
October 31, 1961, Harvard).
***Time Magazine* . . . hopeless trash:** "The Limits of Imitation," *Time*, November 3, 1961; Dudley
Fitts, "It's Fidelity to the Spirit That Counts," *New York Times Book Review*, November 12,
1961; Dominique Aury, Pierre Leyris, and Henri Thomas, "Rimbaud," *Encounter*, March
1962.
The elegy: "Alfred Coming Clark," *FTUD*.
my farewell to contact lenses: "Eye and Tooth," *FTUD*.
your Tynan and Empson reviews: Alvarez, a review of Kenneth Tynan's *Curtains*, *New Statesman*
(1961); "Empson's God," *New Statesman*, September 29, 1961.

399. To Randall Jarrell
under my skin: Cf. "Fall 1961," *FTUD*, lines 6–15, and note, *CPM*, 1058. "This is a weird year—
less than last though. I haven't had a drink since July. The nuclear air gets on my nerves. It
seems a hideous comedy that we should charge the globe with so much ruin. I guess I felt that
way about the bombing in the last war, but somehow it's now come to a head, and seems to be
in everyone's head. I suppose I ought to join the unilateral group, but I hate that arid, logic-
chopping (sp?) debater's world of the righteous cause" (RL to William Meredith, October 20,
1961, Levey Collection, copy at Connecticut College). "We never got down to the world the
other night. Perhaps one never does. I must say I think things are terrible, a situation that is al-
most an historical grimace of terror. I don't mean the whole house is about to blow up in our
faces, but rather that unless things change and nations step down from their stockpiles, this
will happen. Anyway now the cards are all dealt wrong" (RL to Mary McCarthy, October 21,
1961, Vassar).

400. To Stephen Spender
two answers: Dominique Aury, Pierre Leyris, and Henri Thomas wrote a letter "in amazement
and indignation" at Lowell's Rimbaud imitations in *Encounter* (see note to RL's letter to
Stephen Spender, May 7, 1961). Their letter and Lowell's reply (changed slightly from this
version) were published in the March 1962 issue.
"buffalo" passage . . . "cabbage-green mould": "Here are only a very few of the mistakes, picked

at random in *The poet at seven* . . . we find: "*life in The Sahara/where ravished Liberty had fled*" for: "*la vie/Du grand désert, où luit la Liberté ravie*," *luit* having been flatly read as *fuit, le grand désert*, on the other hand, being identified as *the Sahara*, which makes rather surprising the apparition of *buffaloes* in the next line (a gift from the Boston zoo!). . . . Further on, we come on: *a Bible pocked with cabbage-green mould* for: *une Bible à la tranche vert-chou*. Madame Rimbaud's *green-edged* Bible pocked with mould!" (Aury, Leyris, and Thomas, *Encounter*, March 1962, 90).

your . . . reply: "[T]o attack them for not being exact translations seems to me rather like criticizing Van Gogh for having done inaccurate copies of Millett or Delacroix" (Stephen Spender to Henri Thomas, November 1st 1961, copy at Harvard).

401. To Anne Sexton

general impressions: "Did I ever say anything about your comments on Sexton? I'm rather abashed about my blurb—not too much, because, in an odd way she is much more inspired than she knows how to be, and has done what scores of young poets, some of them more knowing than she is, will never do: written a book that can be remembered. I don't really like the tone underneath, or care much about the experience, or rather the experience's impact on Anne Sexton" (RL to Bishop, October 3?, 1961, Vassar).

your book: Sexton, *All My Pretty Ones* (1962).

on your Father: Sexton, "All My Pretty Ones," *Hudson Review*, Spring 1961.

"Letter": Sexton, "Letter Written during a January Northeaster," *Hudson Review*, Summer 1962.

402. To Peter Taylor

the prize: The 1962 Bollingen Prize.

Woods: Tate and Gordon's daughter Nancy Tate Wood and her husband, Percy Hoxic Wood.

403. To the Editors, Partisan Review

Published in the *Partisan Review*, Winter 1962.

1–6: Written in response to a seven-point questionnaire: "1. What is your opinion of the position of the West in the cold war? . . . 2. To what degree is it desirable and possible for the U.S. to re-orient its policies as to identify with the movements and leaders of change throughout the world, instead of supporting the opponents of radical social reform, as the U.S. has tended to do in the past. . . . 3. Does the position of democratic socialism have any relevance . . . to the cold war . . . ? 4. What are we defending in the West? . . . 5. What has been the effect of the cold war on political thought and speculation in the Western world? 6. What are the objectives of the East and West? . . . 7. Do you think the issues at stake in the cold war so decisive as to be worth a nuclear war?"

404. To Frederick Seidel

Frederick Seidel (b. 1936), American poet.

Mailer: Norman Mailer (b. 1923), American novelist.

Phyllis: Seidel's wife.

405. To Elizabeth Bishop

Mary: Mary McCarthy.

Sandra: Sandra Hochman (b. 1936), American poet, with whom Lowell had an affair during his

manic episode in 1961. See Bishop to RL, January 22nd, 1962, Harvard, and Ian Hamilton, 284–86.

... unslick: In "Poetry in English, 1945–1962," *Time* described the "cool, eely slickness" of Bishop's work, finding it "sometimes repellent" (March 9, 1962, 93).

You'll find one to you: "Water," *FTUD*.

The lines about the heart: "The Scream," *FTUD*, lines 33–35.

New Yorker child: Bishop, "First Death in Nova Scotia," *New Yorker*, March 10, 1962.

Jim: James West.

Under the fat man: "Imprisoned in every fat man a thin man is wildly signaling to be let out" (Cyril Connolly, *The Unquiet Grave* [1945], 58).

Dr. Baumann: Anny Baumann (1905–82), Bishop's New York doctor and friend.

his fairy stories: Randall Jarrell translated stories by the Brothers Grimm in *The Golden Bird* (1962) and Ludwig Bechstein in *The Rabbit Catcher* (1962).

407. To John Berryman

piece on me: Berryman, "Despondency and Madness," *The Contemporary Poet as Artist and Critic*, ed. Anthony Ostroff (1964), 99–106.

you've made an amazing guess: "Our occasion is the approach of a crisis of mental disorder for the 'I' of the poem—presumably one leading to the hospitalizations, spoken of elsewhere in the volume, *Life Studies*, where it stands last. . . . One thing critics not themselves writers of poetry occasionally forget is that poetry is composed by actual human beings, and tracts of it are very closely about them. When Shakespeare wrote, 'Two loves I have,' reader, he was *not kidding*" (Berryman, "Despondency and Madness," 99).

a haggard, romantic profilish exaggerated quality: "I will now admit that I cannot like 'my ill-spirit sob in each blood cell'; the expression is just what it should not be, rhetorical, exterior, especially with 'hear'" (Berryman, "Despondency and Madness," 104).

"I wish I were a tree": George Herbert, "Affliction," line 57.

My Ovid stanza: Lowell's first version of "Beyond the Alps," *Kenyon Review*, Spring 1953, included a stanza about Ovid. He removed it when he printed the poem in *LS*. Berryman objected to this change in his essay. "Who cares to hand grades to a writer who could first *make* the Ovid stanza in 'Beyond the Alps' . . . and then delete it? . . . Mr. Lowell once told the present writer that the stanza took him a hundred hours; it is worth every second of the time, and may be read, despite its author, for as long as things not formular are read" (Berryman, "Despondency and Madness," 101). Lowell reprinted the poem with the stanza restored "at the suggestion of John Berryman" ("Note," *FTUD*).

grunt and sweat: "Who would fardels bear,/ To grunt and sweat under a weary life" (*Hamlet* 3.1.76–77); see also Matthew Arnold, *On Translating Homer* (1861), lecture 3.

408. To Elizabeth Bishop

St. Bernard's: Bowden Broadwater was the registrar at St. Bernard's School for boys, 98th Street and Fifth Avenue, New York City.

Your little Arthur: Bishop, "First Death in Nova Scotia," *New Yorker*, March 10, 1962.

to learn a style from a despair?: William Empson, "This Last Pain," line 37.

409. To Alfred Kazin

Contemporaries: Alfred Kazin, *Contemporaries, from the Nineteenth Century to the Present* (1962).

Mailer or Styron would look more like Powers: Kazin, "Gravity and Grace: The Stories of J. F. Powers" and "How Good Is Norman Mailer?" *Contemporaries* (1962). William Styron (b. 1925), American novelist.

West's: Ray West (1908–90), editor, English professor at the University of Iowa in the 1950s.

Shapiro's book: Karl Shapiro, *In Defense of Ignorance* (1960).

Pearson: Norman Pearson (1909–75), Yale professor, appears in canto 96 (Ezra Pound, *Cantos*, 682). He is also the editor, with W. H. Auden, of the Viking Portable Library's *Poets of the English Language* (1950), an anthology that Lowell favored for teaching.

411. To Edmund Wilson

sea-squids: See "Harriet," *N70*, sonnet 1, line 3, and Wilson, *Patriotic Gore* (1962), xi–xxxii.

412. To Elizabeth Bishop

how's that for an opening: "Speaking of piles . . . (wouldn't that be a good 'opening phrase' to use for a Creative Writing course?), I must tell you a nice Brazil-American misunderstanding over that word when you get here. . . . I am so glad Dr. Baumann is in attendance and I do hope you are better and gaining weight. Please don't go into a 19th-century decline!" (Bishop to RL, *One Art*, 405).

Your suggestions . . . : See *One Art*, 408; see also Kalstone, 199–202.

the Mermaid: "The boats bringing the men back from the quarries look like convict ships & I've just been indulging myself in a nightmare of finding a gasping mermaid under one of these exposed docks—you know, trying to teat the mussels off the piles for something to eat—horrors" (Bishop, *One Art*, 170).

'Lions and Harts': J. F. Powers, "Lions, Hearts, Leaping Does," *Accent*, Autumn 1943, reprinted in *Prince of Darkness* (1948).

K A Porter's huge novel . . . : Katherine Anne Porter, *Ship of Fools* (1962); Theodore Dreiser, *An American Tragedy* (1925).

Randall's essays . . . *Culture and Anarchy*: Jarrell, *A Sad Heart at the Supermarket: Essays and Fables* (1962); Matthew Arnold, *Culture and Anarchy* (1869).

Then Wilson's . . . Alfred Kazin's: Wilson, *Patriotic Gore* (1962); Kazin, *Contemporaries from the Nineteenth Century to the Present* (1962).

"I the Money": Lowell confuses "I the Money" (perhaps thinking of Williams's *In the Money?*) with Burt Blechman, *"How Much?" A Novel by B. Halpern as Told to Burt Blechman* (1961); see letter 413. Nathanael West (1903–40), American writer, author of *A Cool Million* (1934) among other books.

Isherwood's new novel: Elizabeth Bishop's copy of Christopher Isherwood's *Down There on a Visit* (1962), given to her by Lowell, is at Harvard.

Bandeira . . . : Manuel Bandeira (1886–1968); Jorge de Lima (1895–1953); Joaquim Maria Machado de Assis (1839–1908), *Memórias Póstumas de Brás Cubas* (1881; *Epitaph of a Small Winner*, 1952).

young enthusiasts: "When first the College Rolls receive his Name/The young Enthusiast quits his Ease for Fame" (Samuel Johnson, "The Vanity of Human Wishes," lines 136–37); see the reference to Johnson later in this letter.

Malraux: André Malraux (1901–76), French novelist, minister of cultural affairs during the de Gaulle administration.

Wordsworth's Leech Gatherer: Wordsworth, "Resolution and Independence" (1807).

. . . at least as interesting a person as the prose writer!: Cf. "Poetry must be as *well written as prose*" (Ezra Pound, *The Letters of Ezra Pound 1907–1941* [1950], 48); "[T]he language of a large portion of every good poem, even of the most elevated character, must necessarily, except with reference to the metre, in no respect differ from that of good prose, but likewise that some of the most interesting parts of the best poems will be found to be strictly the language of prose when prose is well written" (Wordsworth, *Preface to the Lyrical Ballads* [1802]).

413. To Frederick Seidel

The prize is all in confusion: The Y was alarmed by two poems in Seidel's collection that it deemed "offensive" to Jewish and Catholic communities; it later said that the poems contained "libel." The Y attempted to cancel the award. See Sanka Knox, "3 Poets in Break with 'Y' on Award," *New York Times*, July 16, 1962, and "Poems in 'Y' Dispute Will Be Published," *New York Times*, July 17, 1962.

testifying for Henry Miller: Miller's *Tropic of Cancer* was published in the United States in 1961. The book was banned for obscenity by several state courts. A 1964 Supreme Court decision overturned the lower court rulings.

Dugan: Alan Dugan (b. 1923), American poet; he won the National Book Award for *Poems* (1961).

414. To Edmund Wilson

your *New Yorker* interview: Wilson, "Books—An Interview," *New Yorker*, June 2, 1962.

next morning you read: Max Frankel, "U.S. Ships and 1,800 Marines on Way to Indochina Area; Laos Decrees Emergency," *New York Times*, May 13, 1962.

415. To Elizabeth Bishop

Written during an acute manic episode.

IT'S PARADISE: By the middle of August in Rio, Lowell began to show signs of mania. Hardwick returned to the United States with Harriet on September 1. Lowell flew to Buenos Aires on September 4 with Keith Botsford, who couldn't keep up with him and returned to Brazil. Lowell's wild behavior put him in political danger. See Ian Hamilton, 300–03; Bishop, *One Art*, 410–13; and Fountain and Brazeau, 175.

416. To William Alfred

Written during an acute manic episode.

HAVE BEEN AT DEATHS DOOR: When Bishop discovered that Botsford had left Lowell behind in Argentina ("He'd been talking politics, etc.," she wrote in a letter to Hardwick. "Strangers, or the police, would naturally just think he was a drunk; he doesn't speak Spanish—and he might get beaten up or thrown in jail, etc.—and you know the confused state of affairs in B.A. at present"), she was furious. At her insistence, Botsford returned to Buenos Aires to search for Lowell and, with the help of American embassy people, found him at a party for Rafael Alberti (whose friends tried to hide Lowell from what they thought was a C.I.A. attempt to kidnap him). Lowell had been drinking heavily for days without sleeping and had contracted a lung infection. He was committed to the Clínica Bethlehem. He sent this telegram to William Alfred from the hospital. Blair Clark, recently installed as vice president and general manager of CBS News, flew to Argentina to bring Lowell home. Hardwick and Lowell's psychiatrist, Dr. Viola Bernard, met the plane and drove Lowell to the Institute for Living in Hartford.

417. To Elizabeth Bishop

poets' conference: The National Poetry Festival, Library of Congress, October 22–24, 1962.

tribute: Jarrell, "Fifty Years of American Poetry," *Prairie Schooner*, Spring 1963, reprinted in the conference proceedings (Library of Congress, 1964) and *The Third Book of Criticism* (1969).

Lota's medal: "Just after you left Lota was given a *medal*—two, rather—a medal with grosgrain ribbon, etc. to wear for dress, and a miniature—a stick-pin for every day. I don't know quite how she can wear that; she said she had to acquire a lapel. It is for Public Service—speeches and her picture in the papers, etc." (Bishop to RL, September 11, 1962, Harvard).

418. To Elizabeth Bishop

Brizola: Leonel de Moura Brizola, governor of Rio Grande do Sul.

old poem to you . . . namesake Caligula: "Water," "Dropping South: Brazil," "Caligula," *FTUD;* "The Vanity of Human Wishes," *NTO.*

Ten sonnets of Nerval . . . : "El Desdichado (After Gérard de Nerval)," "Christ in the Olive Grove (After Gérard de Nerval)," *CPM,* 970–73; "Three Poems for Kaddish," *Ploughshares* (1979), reprinted in *CPM,* 981–83.

Bernstein: Leonard Bernstein (1918–90), American composer.

Lispector: Clarice Lispector (1925–77), Brazilian novelist.

Nelida: A friend of Bishop's. "Nelida has been here once to talk the higher Portuguese with me" (Bishop to RL, [September 1962], Harvard).

420. To Elizabeth Bishop

Published in *New York Review of Books,* November 6, 2003.

first number: Contributors to the first issue of the *New York Review of Books* (February 1, 1963) included John Berryman, Mary McCarthy, Gore Vidal, Richard Poirier, Philip Rahv, W. H. Auden, Adrienne Rich, Elizabeth Hardwick, and Norman Mailer. Lowell's "Buenos Aires" and his essay "Robert Frost" also appeared in the debut issue.

Brinnin: *Emily Dickinson: Selected,* ed. John Malcolm Brinnin (1960).

what dozens of others are doing: Cf. the magazine version of "Waking Early Sunday Morning," *CPM,* 933, lines 17–24.

421. To Keith Botsford

Goulart: João Belchoir Marques Goulart (1918–76), president of Brazil from 1961 to 1964. During his tenure Brazil suffered rapid inflation. His attempts to introduce land reform programs to benefit the working class caused enmity with the military, which eventually deposed him.

Aleijadinho[,] Burle Marx, *Rebellion in the Backlands*: Aleijadinho (1738?–1840), Brazilian sculptor; Roberto Burle Marx (b. 1913), Brazilian landscape architect; Euclides da Cunha, *Rebellion in the Backlands,* trans. Samuel Putnam (1944).

writer 24 and a former student: Unidentified.

Ann, A[lb]erta and the children: The ink after "Ann" is rubbed away; "A[lb]erta" is a guess.

422. To Elizabeth Bishop

Sydney Smith volumes: *The Letters of Sydney Smith,* ed. Nowell Smith (1953).

Frost's death: Robert Frost died on January 29, 1963.

one might of half-thought: one might have half-thought?

your limerick on Keith: "This was wrung from me somewhere along the line last autumn: A cultured acquaintance named K——/Faces life with a pipe in his teeth./He behaves,—well, in brief,/It would be a relief/To lay a small wreath upon K——" (Bishop to RL, n.d. but probably included in her January 8, 1963, letter, Harvard).

things are in the saddle: "Things are in the saddle/And ride mankind" (Emerson, "Ode Inscribed to W. H. Channing," lines 50–51). Lowell was teaching Emerson that term (see letter 420).

Queiroz: Rachel de Queiroz (b. 1910), Brazilian novelist.

423. To Ezra Pound

your *Paris Review* interview . . . : Donald Hall, "Ezra Pound: An Interview," and Pound, cantos 115 and 116, *Paris Review*, Summer–Fall 1962; Pound, passages from canto 113, *Poetry*, October–November 1962.

424. To Hannah Arendt

Eichmann: Arendt, "A Reporter at Large: Eichmann in Jerusalem," parts 1 and 2, *New Yorker*, February 16, and February 23, 1963.

"gusts of elation": Arendt wrote about Nazi euphemisms that "made self-deception easier": "Eichmann's mind was filled to the brim with [such] sentences. His memory proved to be very unreliable about what actually happened. . . . The point of the matter is that he had not forgotten a single one of the sentences that at one time or another had served to give him what he repeatedly called a 'sense of elation.' Hence, whenever, during the cross-examination, the judges tried appeal to his conscience, they were met with 'elation,' and they were outraged as well as disconcerted when they learned that the accused had at his disposal a different elating cliché for each period of his life and activities. In his mind, there was no contradiction between 'I will jump into my grave laughing,' appropriate for the end of the war, and 'I am ready to hang myself in pubic as a warning example for all anti-Semites on this earth,' which now, under vastly different circumstances, fulfilled exactly the same function—that of giving him a lift" (*New Yorker*, February 16, 1963, reprinted with revisions in *Eichmann in Jerusalem*, 53–54).

the Dutch Jews: "In 1941, in the old Jewish quarter of Amsterdam, [Dutch Jews] dared to attack a German security police detachment. Four hundred and thirty Jews were arrested in reprisal and they were literally tortured to death, first in Buchenwald and then in the Austrian camp of Mauthausen" (*New Yorker*, February 16, 1963, reprinted with revisions in *Eichmann in Jerusalem*, 12).

Bettelheim's argument: See Bruno Bettelheim, *The Informed Heart: Autonomy in a Mass Age* (1960).

425. To Elizabeth Bishop

Published in *New York Review of Books*, November 6, 2003.

Hannah's book on revolutions: Arendt, *On Revolution* (1963).

Herbert by Eliot: Eliot, *George Herbert* (1962).

426. To Elizabeth Bishop

about Pound and Chekhov: "I spent two days in Samambaia reading a long, bad, but fascinating new life of Chekhov—I bet Randall has read it, too. What a wonderful man, really—almost a saint. The son of serfs yet a greater gentleman than the estate-owning novelists. . . . I admire Pound's extraordinary courage, many things about him—but read this, Cal, and see how petty Pound appears, how horribly 'flawed,' as you say—and almost completely lacking in natural human feelings" (Bishop to RL, March 5, 1963, Vassar).

signed a petition: Dorothy Norman, Maria Willard, Alfred Barr, Stanley Kunitz, Robert Lowell, Andrew E. Norman, Mark Rothko, "Letters to the *Times:* Conduct of Officials towards Negroes Protested," *New York Times*, May 12, 1963.

Gold and Fizdale: Arthur Gold and Robert Fizdale, "the 2-piano team" (*One Art*, 394).

Tourel sing you: Jennie Tourel (1900–73), American mezzo-soprano, sang at Carnegie Hall on March 13; she set "Visits to St. Elizabeths" to music in a song entitled "Bedlam" (see Bishop to RL, March 5, 1963, Harvard).

Siobhán McKenna: Siobhán McKenna (1923–86), Irish actress.

Miller: Jonathan Miller (b. 1934), English physician, writer, and director; his productions of Lowell's plays include *The Old Glory* (1964), *Benito Cereno* (1967), and *Prometheus Bound* (1967 and 1971).

The stone phallus: "Buenos Aires," *FTUD*.

Wilson and Kenneth Burke: Edmund Wilson, "Every Man His Own Eckerman," and Kenneth Burke, "William Carlos Williams, 1883–1963," *New York Review of Books*, June 1, 1963.

427. To A. Alvarez

Under Pressure: A. Alvarez, *Under Pressure: The Writer in Society, Eastern Europe and the U.S.A.* (1965).

I enclose a poem: Unidentified.

Sylvia's poems . . . : Plath, "Edge," "The Fearful," "Kindness," "Contusion," *Observer*, Febuary 17, 1963; Plath committed suicide on February 11, 1963.

about bees: Possibly "Wintering" and "The Arrival of the Bee Box," published under the collective title "Bees," *Atlantic Monthly*, April 1963.

428. To Elizabeth Bishop

Flavio: Flavio Soares, Lota's nephew.

my macumba: See "Dropping South: Brazil," *Kenyon Review*, Winter 1964, lines 17–24. "I liked your poem about Copacabana. . . . But *macumba* is just the name in this part of Brazil for voodoo—(It's name in most of Brazil is *candomblé*). So I don't think you can address it. It's like saying 'Congregationalism!'—it's the whole practice. The goddess to whom the candles by the ocean, white flowers, etc. are offered is *Yemnajá*—goddess of the sea, also somewhat confused with the Virgin Mary" (Bishop to RL, May 28, 1963, Harvard).

Der Stellvertreter: Rolf Hochhuth, *Der Stellvertreter* (*The Representative: A Christian Tragedy*, 1964).

Nabokov's: Nicolas Nabokov (1903–78), Russian American composer and organizer of international festivals for the Congress for Cultural Freedom.

Meyers: Agnes Meyer (1887–1970), wife of Eugene Meyer, owner of the *Washington Post*.

Oppenheimer presided: J. Robert Oppenheimer (1904–67), American theoretical physicist, director of Los Alamos Laboratory's Manhattan Project.

architect who built Radio City: Edward Durrell Stone (1902–78), American architect.

Hampshire: Stuart Hampshire (b. 1914), English philosopher.

a Miss Hersch: Jeanne Hersch (1910–2000), Swiss philosopher.

Kennan: George Kennan (b. 1904), American diplomat and historian.

interview of Empson: See "William Empson in Conversation with Christopher Ricks," *Review*, June 1963, reprinted in *The Modern Poet: Essays from "the Review*," ed. Ian Hamilton [1968], 177, and *Argufying*, ed. John Haffenden (1987).

prompted by Graves: "When I started writing there was a lot being written—by Robert Graves as much as anybody—about how poetry ought to be about a conflict: it needn't resolve a conflict . . . but he thought the poem ought to be about a conflict which is raging in the mind of the writer but hasn't been solved. He should write about the things that really worry him, in fact worry him to the point of madness. The poem is a kind of clinical object, done to prevent him from going mad. It is therefore not addressed to any public, but it is useless to him unless it is in fact clear and readable, because he has to—as it were—address it to the audience within himself. It isn't expressed unless it's a thing which somebody else can read, so if it's obscure it actually fails in this therapeutic function, it isn't saving his sanity. But nevertheless he doesn't

write it for any group or—he doesn't even write it for Laura Riding" ("William Empson in Conversation with Christopher Ricks," *The Modern Poet: Essays from "the Review,"* 185–86).

Bob Gardner's documentary: In 1961 Gardner led an expedition to study the Dugum Dani in the former Netherlands New Guinea. His film about the Dani is *Dead Birds* (1964).

a play on Eatherly: Claude Robert Eatherly (1918–78), pilot of *Straight Flush*, the weather plane that signaled the *Enola Gay* to drop the atomic bomb on Hiroshima. See Edmund Wilson, "The Case of Major Eatherly," *The Cold War and the Income Tax: A Protest* (1963), and John Wain, "A Hymn to Major Eatherly," *Weep before God* (1961).

"Caligula": "Caligula," *FTUD*.

429. To Theodore Roethke

the enclosed poem: Possibly Roethke's "Otto," *The Far Field* (1964).

431. To Beatrice Roethke

Terrible news!: Theodore Roethke died on August 1, 1963.

"that minnowy world": "Morning-fair, follow me further back/Into that minnowy world of weeds and ditches/When the herons floated high over the white houses,/And the little crabs slipped into silvery craters" (Roethke, "The Shape of Fire," lines 64–67).

432. To Mary McCarthy

Betjeman: John Betjeman (1906–84), English poet.

The Group: McCarthy, *The Group* (1963).

Old Town: James West was from Old Town, Maine.

433. To Nicholas Nabokov

Walcott: Derek Walcott (b. 1930), St. Lucian poet; *In a Green Night: Poems* (1962).

Civil War poems: Melville, *Battle-Pieces and Aspects of the War* (1866).

434. To Elizabeth Bishop

Newsweek...: "Contrary Mary: Vassar '33," *Newsweek*, September 2, 1963; Jordan Bonfante, "Lady with a Switchblade," *Life*, September 20, 1963.

what will happen to it: Elizabeth Hardwick (writing under the pseudonym Xavier Prynne), "The Gang," *New York Review of Books*, September 26, 1963; Norman Mailer, "The Mary Mc-Carthy Case," *New York Review of Books*, October 17, 1963.

The raw gobs of hash . . . : See "The Neo-Classical Urn," *FTUD*. "Of course I can't take 'raw gobs of hash'—but perhaps I'm right and not just squeamish—'raw gobs' might be out of their legs, etc. but they are pretty well covered with shell and the flesh has to be very small bits, I'd think.—'hash' is the word that really bothers since it suggests a quantity heaped together—not random floating bits of raw flesh. 'Hash,' the noun, means a *dish of hash*, a stuck-together mass . . . ? Poor old turtles . . . what a dreadful boy you were! The poem suggests the horror of an exposed brain—(I've been reading about the Incas & their passion for trepanning)—the various *containers*, all vulnerable, for life—& maybe that's what it's supposed to suggest?" (Bishop to RL, July 12, 1963, Harvard). Cf. Also the turtles in RL to Ezra Pound, May 2, [1936].

the "Caligula": "I have no books about Romans here in Rio so I just take your word for all these grim details . . . and a lot of it's what I remember, vaguely. I like the bad rhymes—plans/dance, etc." (Bishop to RL, July 13th [1963], Harvard).

the Y of the goddess . . . : "Oh dear—my typewriter must have the tail of the Y missing—the goddess's name is *Y*emanjá—or usually Iemanjá. Y seems to be the English spelling, because that's the way it's pronounced. The poem now seems perfectly right to me . . . In the line 'macumba candles courted Yemanjá'—I see you've put in a 'the.' Well, I don't think the 'the' works, unless you want a very bumpy rhythm, because it's macumba—accent on the 2nd syllable" (Bishop to RL, July 2nd, 1963, Harvard). See "Dropping South: Brazil," *FTUD*, line 17.

"as many holes as a fishnet": See "Those before Us," *FTUD*, lines 14–16; "'As many holes as a fish-net' bothers me a bit—seems so unlikely! Aside from that the imagery is clear and just right—that muskrat, the spoor (one of those 1,000 time better last-minute changes, I gather) of cornflakes—" (Bishop to RL, July 12th [1963], Harvard).

Night Sweat: "Lota read NIGHT SWEAT and said simply, 'It's a beauty . . .'" (Bishop to RL, July 12th, [1963], Harvard).

435. To Elizabeth Bishop

The Drummond: Carlos Drummond de Andrade, "The Table," trans. Bishop, *New York Review of Books*, January 16, 1969.

one more little thing: "The Mouth of the Hudson," *FTUD*.

a nightmarish terza rima thing: "The Severed Head," *FTUD*.

on Carlos: Marshal Tito was on a state visit to Brazil. Because Carlos Lacerda was governor of Rio, he was able to make trouble for President Goulart by refusing to provide security for him; see "Brazil Revising Program," *New York Times*, September 8, 1963.

Lionel Abel in *PR* . . . : Lionel Abel, "The Aesthetics of Evil: Hannah Arendt on Eichmann and the Jews," *Partisan Review*, Summer 1963; Norman Podhoretz, "Hannah Arendt on Eichmann: A Study in the Perversity of Brilliance," *Commentary*, September 1963; Michael A. Musmanno, "Man with an Unspoiled Conscience," *New York Times Book Review*, May 19, 1963.

MacNeice's death: Louis MacNeice died on September 3, 1963.

436. To Mary McCarthy

the boxing fight: "When the BBC, spotting a good story, offered Norman Mailer one thousand dollars if he would appear on TV in Edinburgh and 'fight it out with Mary McCarthy'—who would also get one thousand dollars, Mailer assured her, leaving the subject of the debate up to her—she refused" (Brightman, 478).

Mailer: Mailer, "The Mary McCarthy Case," *New York Review of Books*, October 17, 1963.

437. To Elizabeth Bishop

Goulart's martial law: "President Goulart asked Congress for state-of-siege powers to 'suffocate a conspiracy' to overthrow him. He said Governor Lacerda was behind the alleged plot. . . . The clash was averted when Congress opposed the state of siege and President Goulart withdrew his request" (Juan de Onis, "Brazil Imperiled by Political Rift," *New York Times*, October 13, 1963). Goulart was overthrown by the military in April 1964.

a Hannah Arendt evening: *Dissent* magazine held a forum on Arendt's *Eichmann in Jerusalem*. "When Hannah's *Eichmann* was published, a meeting was summoned by Irving Howe and Lionel Abel, normally urbane and liberal minds. The meeting was like a trial, the stoning of an outcast member of the family. Any sneering overemphasis on Hannah, who had been invited but was away teaching in Chicago, was greeted with derisive clapping or savage sighs of amazement. Her appointed defenders drifted off into unintelligibly ingenious theses and avoided her name. When her tolerance was eloquently and unfavorably compared with Trotsky's, Alfred Kazin walked self-consciously to the stage and stammered, 'After all Hannah

didn't kill any Jews.' He walked off the stage laughed at as irrelevant and absurd. His was the one voice for the defense. I admire his bravery, and wish I had dared speak. Half my New York literary and magazine acquaintance was sitting near, yet their intensity was terrifying, as if they were about to pick up chairs" (Lowell, "On Hannah Arendt," *New York Review of Books*, May 13, 1976).

Hilberg: Raul Hilberg, *The Destruction of the European Jews* (1961).

the last *Encounter*: Plath, "Death & Co.," "The Swarm," "The Other," "Getting There," "Lady Lazarus," "Little Fugue," "Childless Woman," "The Jailor," "Thalidomide," "Daddy," *Encounter*, October 1964.

438. To James Laughlin

a blurb: Stevie Smith, *Selected Poems* (1964).

438. To Elizabeth Bishop

12th Night poem: Bishop, "Twelfth Morning; or What You Will," *New York Review of Books*, April 2, 1964.

horse and rider: Bishop, "Cirque D'Hiver," *North & South* (1946).

sketch: Hardwick, "Grub Street: Washington," *New York Review of Books*, January 23, 1964.

Gettysburg Address: "On the Gettysburg Address," Library of Congress, January 3, 1964, printed in *CPR*, 165–66.

Kennedy's murder: President Kennedy was assassinated on November 22, 1963.

curry: current?

440. To Mary McCarthy

your *PR* **piece:** McCarthy, "The Hue and Cry," *Partisan Review*, Winter 1964.

Trotsky in exile . . . : Lowell never wrote the Trotsky play; see John Gale, "Keeping the Lid on the World," *Observer*, March 12, 1967, reprinted in Meyers, 116–17. In an interview with Ian Hamilton, Jonathan Miller recalled that Lowell "continued to discuss theatrical projects with me and he'd ask me for things he might work on. There was some scheme to write a play about Trotsky on Principo" (Ian Hamilton Notebooks, British Library).

Akhmatova: Akhmatova, "Requiem," trans. Lowell, *Poets on Street Corners*, ed. Olga Carlisle (1968); reprinted in *CPM*.

441. To the Editors, Partisan Review

Published in *Partisan Review*, Spring 1964.

committees: One of the issues that excited controversy was Arendt's criticism of the leaders of the *Judenräte*.

442. To Adrienne Rich

In the Woods: Rich, "In the Woods," *New York Review of Books*, April 30, 1964.

the Richards in Ghana: I. A. Richards went to Ghana to see if he could interest the government in adopting his Basic English program (an attempt to build an internationally comprehensible language using 850 English words) for Ghanaian schools; see *Selected Letters of I. A. Richards*, *CH*, 165. Ghanaians held massive anti-American protests in February 1964.

443. To T. S. Eliot

Philip Larkin's new poems: Larkin, *The Whitsun Weddings* (1964).

444. To Elizabeth Bishop

the oil refineries: Tad Szulc, "Brazil Prepares to Seize Farms and Refineries," *New York Times*, March 10, 1963.

half me and part Gerard Nerval: "Going to and fro," *FTUD*; in a manuscript draft of the poem, Lowell dedicated the poem to "Nerval or someone" (*CPM*, 1060–61).

445. To Elizabeth Bishop

marine mutiny: On March 27, 1964, the *New York Times* reported that "leftist" sailors and marines had mutinied against their officers in support of President Goulart. A navy minister appointed by Goulart pardoned the mutineers, to the outrage of the Brazilian military, which used the controversy to execute its plot to overthrow Goulart. Carlos Lacerda supported the military coup.

lessoned: Lessened?

Howard Moss: Moss was Bishop's *New Yorker* poetry editor.

Huff: Robert Huff (b. 1924), American poet.

Her baseball: Moore, "Baseball and Writing," *New Yorker*, December 9, 1961, reprinted in *The Arctic Ox* (1964).

446. To Randall Jarrell

parade of women: Jarrell, *Selected Poems: Including the Woman at the Washington Zoo* (1964).

review of Berryman: "The Poetry of John Berryman," *New York Review of Books*, May 28, 1964, reprinted in *CPR*, 104–11.

447. To Adrienne Rich

"In the Dark". . . the Bowling Alley: What Lowell calls "In the Dark" is either "In the Woods" or "After Dark"; both poems and "Breakfast in a Bowling Alley in Utica, New York" were printed in *Necessities of Life* (1966). See Lowell, "Modesty without Mumbling," *New York Times Book Review*, July 17, 1966.

Sontag: Susan Sontag (1933–2004), American novelist and critic.

the doomed elms: Adrienne Rich, "After Dark," *Necessities of Life* (1966).

448. To Elizabeth Bishop

your guide: Bishop compiled for Flavio "a sort of Young Gentleman's guide to U.S. manners" (Bishop to RL, June 13, 1964, Harvard); cf. "Manners," *Questions of Travel* (1965).

little negro gangs: Possibly a reference to alarmist coverage of Malcolm X and the Harlem "Blood Brothers" in the *New York Times* in May 1964.

Hugh Thomas: Hugh Thomas, *The Spanish Civil War* (1961).

Your Piero remarks: Bishop sent Lowell a postcard detail of *Burial of the Holy Wood* by Piero della Francesca. "[T]he Piero card is identical with one Mary sent me last fall. She quoted from some Italian critic that the almond like ring in the grain of the wood of the Cross was a halo. Perfect picture, nothing could be truly more classical" (RL to Elizabeth Bishop, June 1, 1964, Vassar).

If he was lazy . . . : "[T]he Scourging is the most beautiful *now*—but the Resurrection is surely one
 of the most powerful and affecting—startling—pictures ever painted. P della F was supposed
 to have been very lazy—did you know?—it was almost impossible to get him to do anything
 or finish anything" (Bishop to RL, June 13, 1964, Harvard).
. . . abandoned building: See "The Opposite House," *FTUD*.
Pastoria: Bishop was staying at the Hotel Pastoria in London.

449. To Elizabeth Bishop
short stories: *Everything That Rises Must Converge* (1965).

450. To the Editors, Village Voice
Published in the *Village Voice*, November 19, 1964.
Elkins's: Stanley Elkins, *Slavery: A Problem in American Institutional and Intellectual Life* (1959).

451. To Elizabeth Hardwick
Written while recovering from an acute manic episode.
Mrs. Shirley Clarke . . . : Shirley Clarke (1925–97), American New Wave filmmaker; her work in-
 cludes *Robert Frost: A Lover's Quarrel with the World* (1964), which won an Academy Award,
 and *The Connection* (1962). See Lauren Rabinovitz, *Points of Resistance: Women, Power & Pol-
 itics in the New York Avant-garde Cinema, 1943–71* (2003), 131.
"Our years": Hardwick's project, "Our Years" (sometimes referred to as "Smiling Through"),
 was later abandoned (Hardwick in conversation with SH, July 2, 2003).

452. To Elizabeth Hardwick
Written while recovering from an acute manic episode.
everything that is *isn't* right: "And, spite of pride, in erring reason's spite/One truth is clear,
 Whatever is, is right" (Alexander Pope, "An Essay on Man," lines 293–94).
The Congo, Archy and Mehitabel etc: Vachel Lindsay, "The Congo (A Study of the Negro Race)"
 (1914); Don Marquis, *Archy and Mehitabel* (1927).
Blackmur: R. P. Blackmur died on February 2, 1965.

453. To Elizabeth Bishop
new poems . . . : Jarrell, "In Montecito," "Three Bills," "Next Day," "The Lost World," *The Lost
 World* (1965).
I was underlying: Probably "underlining."
Life: "Applause for a Prize Poet," *Life*, February 13, 1965.
an interview: A. Alvarez, "A Talk with Robert Lowell," *Encounter*, February 1965.
The Cherry Orchard and *The Wild Duck*: Chekhov, *The Cherry Orchard* (1904); Ibsen, *The Wild
 Duck* (1984).

456. To William Doreski
William Doreski (b. 1946), American poet and literary scholar.
Bly: Robert Bly (b. 1926), American poet, editor of the *Fifties* and then the *Sixties*, a journal.

457. To Lyndon B. Johnson

Published in the *New York Times*, June 3, 1965; a copy is at Harvard.

458. To W. F. van Leeuwen

de Groots: S. R. de Groot, physicist, and Silvia de Groot, anthropologist; friends of van Leeuwen's.

459. To Stanley Kunitz

Wasn't the "Dover Beach" grotesque?: In a speech to college students, Johnson said: "Robert Lowell, the poet, doesn't like everything around here. But I like one of his lines where he wrote: 'For the world which seems to lie out before us like a land of dreams.' Well, in this great age—and it is a great age—the world does seem to lie before us like a land of dreams." The lines (which appear as an epigraph to *The Mills of the Kavanaughs*) are from Matthew Arnold's "Dover Beach," which Johnson's speechwriter both misquoted ("For the world which seems to lie before us like a land of dreams") and misattributed.

the words "world" and "before": "Johnson Hails College Students as His 'Fellow Revolutionaries,'" *New York Times*, August 5, 1965. Lowell was thinking of the last lines of *Paradise Lost*: "The World was all before them, where to choose/Thir place of rest, and Providence thir guide:/They hand in hand with wandring steps and slow,/Through Eden took thir solitaire way."

460. To Robert Graves

poems: Graves, "A Shift of Scene," "Good Night to the Old Gods," *New Statesman*, July 23, 1965.

cough poem: "To life far off, in bed with a foul cough,/And a view of elms and roofs and six panes' worth/Of clear sky" (Graves, "A Shift of Scene," lines 1–3).

461. To J. F. Powers

your wonderful review: Powers, "Conscience and Religion" (review of Gordon Zahn's *In Solitary Witness*), *Commentary*, July 1965.

462. To Eleanor Ross Taylor

"Victory": Eleanor Ross Taylor, "Victory," *Kenyon Review*, Autumn 1965.

463. To Elizabeth Bishop

Randall's death: Jarrell died on October 14, 1965.

464. To Elizabeth Bishop

echolalia . . .: See Bishop, "First Death in Nova Scotia," lines 1–3; "Sunday, 4 a.m." lines 20–22; "Visits to St. Elizabeths," lines 16–21; and "Filling Station," lines 21–27; *Questions of Travel* (1965).

"Coeur Simple": Flaubert, "Un Coeur Simple," *Trois Contes* (1877).

"Santos": Bishop, "Arrival at Santos," *Questions of Travel* (1965).

"Brazil" . . .: Bishop, "Brazil, January 1, 1502," "Twelfth Morning; or What You Will," "The Burglar of Babylon," "First Death in Nova Scotia," "From Trollope's Journal," *Questions of Travel* (1965).

Ezra: Bishop, "Visits to St. Elizabeths," *Questions of Travel* (1965).

your story: Bishop, "In the Village," reprinted in *Questions of Travel* (1965).

as one of his poem[s] even says: Possibly "A Well-to-Do Invalid," *The Lost World* (1965).

golpe: "President Castelo Branco, in Sweeping Decree, Dissolves Political Parties, Increases Executive Powers, and Opens Judiciary to Appointment of New Judges," *New York Times,* October 28, 1965.

465. To Stephen Spender, Encounter

my earlier rhetorical diatribe: Copy in Nabokov papers, Berg Collection.

this subject: Nabokov's article "Nabokov's Reply," published in *Encounter,* responded to reviews of his annotated translation of *Eugene Onegin.* Nabokov took particular exception to Edmund Wilson, who reviewed the translation unfavorably in the *New York Review of Books* (July 15, 1965). Lowell first wrote to the editors of *Encounter:* "Such an arch, feline tone, such a feminine, ruffled tone, as he boasts of 'refuting practically every item in Edmund Wilson's enormous piece,' in Wilson's crushing nine-tenths, unanswerable review of Nabokov's ridiculous practical joke of a translation of *Eugene Onegin*—this too surely written by Pnin or the author of that ingenious spoof in couplets at the end of *Pale Fire.* And those babyish, unilluminating grimaces at the great, at Nabokov's betters: Stendhal, Balzac and Dostoyevsky!" He adds: "The following lines seem to be a dig at my translations—'an infernal vision to me who can distinguish in the most elaborate imitation the simple schoolboy howler from the extraneous imagery in which it is so pitifully embedded.' Poor Ezra Pound, poor Nabokov—it isn't his scholarship that Wilson is impunging, but the lousy English poetry Nabokov throws at us in the name of Pushkin" (RL to Editors of *Encounter,* n.d. early February 1966, copy at Berg Collection). For Nabokov, see *Selected Letters,* 385–87. See also his "On Adaptation," *New York Review of Books,* December 4, 1969, and *Ada* (1969). A letter from Nadezhda Mandelstam criticizing Nabokov and defending Lowell's versions of her husband's poems is in the Lowell papers, Harry Ransom Humanities Center, University of Texas, Austin. See also her letters to Lowell at Harvard (bMS Am 1905/823–25).

the Blunden business: Lowell's name was put forward for the 1966 Oxford Professor of Poetry. Enid Starkie organized a counter campaign to elect the English poet Edmund Blunden (1896–1974), who won.

NABOKOV'S ONEGIN: Published in *Encounter,* May 1966.

466. To Elizabeth Bishop

Levi-Strauss . . . : Claude Lévi-Strauss (b. 1908), French social anthropologist; William Carlos Williams, *In the American Grain* (1925).

three page introduction: "Sylvia Plath's *Ariel*," *New York Review of Books,* May 12, 1966, reprinted as a foreword to *Ariel* (1966).

a Yeats reading: See "Talk on the Poetry of William Butler Yeats at Columbia University, New York, NY," Special Collections, Butler Library, Columbia University (NXCP89–A271).

Marvell couplet thing: "Waking Early Sunday Morning" or "Fourth of July in Maine," *NTO.*

Eissler: K. R. Eissler (1908–99), Viennese psychoanalyst.

Reed: Henry Reed (1914–86), English poet.

467. To Robert F. Kennedy

legislators of mankind: Percy Bysshe Shelley, *Defense of Poetry* (1840), slightly misquoted.

Alas: "You have probably read it as I understand you have read everything but when I found the following in Edmund Wilson's book 'The Bit Between My Teeth' I thought of you. 'That

hour is blessed when we meet a poet. The poet is brother to the dervish. He has no country nor is he blessed with the things of this world; and while we poor creatures that we are, are worrying about fame, about power, about riches, he stands on a basis of equality with the powerful of the earth and the people bow down before him,' [(]Pushkin[)] When are they going to write those kinds of things about those of us in politics. See if you can start a trend in that direction" (Robert F. Kennedy to RL, February 18, 1966, Harvard, quoted in Ian Hamilton, 377).

Profiles: Robert F. Kennedy, preface, John F. Kennedy, *Profiles in Courage* (1964 edition).

468. To Ezra Pound

my Brunetto: "During the summer [of 1965], Pound appeared for the first time at the Spoleto Festival, invited by Gian Carlo Menotti. There he read from the work of Robert Lowell and Marianne Moore, but was otherwise silent" (Wilhelm, 340).

a little piece: "Ford Madox Ford," *New York Review of Books*, May 12, 1966, reprinted as a preface to *Buckshee* by Ford Madox Ford (1966) and in *CPR*.

469. To John Berryman

Your reminiscences: Berryman, "Randall Jarrell," *Randall Jarrell: 1914–1965*, ed. Robert Lowell, Peter Taylor, and Robert Penn Warren (1967).

the evening: A memorial service for Jarrell at Yale University on February 28, 1966, featuring Berryman, Eberhart, Hollander, Mary Jarrell, Kunitz, Meredith, Rich, Taylor, Warren, Wilbur, and Lowell.

The evening at Princeton: "My favorite recollection of this amazing man was one time when he came to visit me in Princeton, New Jersey, and he came down from New York for dinner with Robert Lowell. And he had a hangover, and that was very amazing because Jarrell did not drink. . . . So here's Jarrell walking up and down in my living room, miserable and witty. And very malicious, as he could certainly be, making up a brand-new Lowell poem full of characteristic Lowell properties, Lowell's grandfather and Charon, and the man who did not find this funny at all was Lowell. There was a complete want of humor at that point. At last we calmed Randall down" (Berryman, "Randall Jarrell," *Randall Jarrell: 1914–1965*, 15).

471. To Edmund Blunden

your letter: George Fraser copied for Blunden a "most generous passage" Lowell had written about the Oxford Professor of Poetry elections; Blunden wrote to thank Lowell and to say he hoped to see him before long (Blunden to RL, 27 May 1966, Harvard).

472. To Elizabeth Bishop

prose version: "In translation, the poetry seems lofty and dead, and the characters statues. . . . Using prose instead of verse, I was free to tone down the poetic eloquence, and shove in any thought that occurred to me and seemed to fit" ("Author's Note," *Promethus Bound* [1969], v–vi).

"In Dreams Begin Responsibilities": Schwartz, *In Dreams Begin Responsibilities* (1938).

talking prose all their lives: "Par ma foi il y a plus de quarante ans que je dis de la prose sans que j'en susse rien" (Molière, *Le Bourgeois Gentilhomme* [1670], 2.4).

474. To Elizabeth Bishop

Mike Nichols . . . : Mike Nichols (b. 1931), American stage and screen director; Charles Addams (1912–88), American cartoonist; Jerome Robbins (1918–98), American choreographer; William S. Paley (1901–90), American broadcaster.

the Styrons: William and Rose Styron (b. 1928), American poet.

McNamara: Robert McNamara (b. 1916), secretary of defense from 1961 to 1968; principal architect of American Vietnam policy.

I lectured at Harvard: "In the poetry room, I listened again to the voices of the dead poets: Ted's carved and musical, clear of the wallow of life, Delmore's husky and stumbling, too close to conversation, Blackmur's, not dead at all, but brisk and firm, as if newly shored up and painted—Randall's unbearable to me, because I could anticipate every cadence, pathos trying to make its lovely supreme cast beyond itself. The reading went well, particularly the amusing poems" (RL to Stanley Kunitz and Elise Asher, August 15, 1966, Princeton).

475. To John Berryman

POSTHUMOUS POEMS: Berryman, "Op. Posth.," nos. 1–2, 7–13, *Times Literary Supplement*, December 1, 1966; nos. 3–6, *New York Review of Books*, December 8, 1966. "Op. Posth., no. 13 was also printed in *Randall Jarrell*, ed. Taylor, and Warren (1967).

476. To Ted Hughes

the festival: Ted Hughes wrote to thank Lowell for the introduction to *Ariel* and to invite him to the International Festival of Spoken Poetry in London, July 12–16, 1967.

. . . have hurt anyone: "The Blood Jet Is Poetry," *Time*, June 10, 1966. See also Ted Hughes to RL, 14th September 1966. Hughes wondered if it would be wise to publish *Ariel* in the United States, since it might inspire others to imitate her (not the work but the suicide). "And the backlash onto her family has been considerable" (Hughes to RL, 14th September 1966, Harvard).

the Napoleon and Lesbos ones: Sylvia Plath, "The Swarm," *Encounter*, October 1963; "Lesbos," *The Review* (October 1963). Both were included in the American edition of *Ariel* (1966).

477. To Daniel Berrigan

Daniel Berrigan (b. 1921), Jesuit priest and social activist.

your manuscript: Berrigan, *Consequences: Truth and . . .* (1967).

Deborah's song: Judges 5:1–31.

Bonhoeffer: Dietrich Bonhoeffer (1906–45), German theologian who opposed Hitler.

in one of his letters: See Bonhoeffer to Eberhard Bethge, 21 July [1944], *Letters and Papers from Prison*, ed. Eberhard Bethge, trans. Reginald H. Fuller (1953), 369.

478. To the Editors, Partisan Review

Published in the *Partisan Review*, Winter 1967.

1. . . . : Response to a questionnaire from the editors of the *Partisan Review*: "1. Does it matter who is in the White House? Or is there something in our system which would force any President to act as Johnson is acting? 2. How serious is the problem of inflation? The problem of poverty? 3. What is the meaning of the split between the Administration and the American intellectuals? 4. Is white America committed to granting equality to the American Negro? 5. Where do you think our foreign policies are likely to lead us? 6. What, in general, do you think is likely to happen in America? 7. Do you think any promise is to be found in the activities of young people today?"

479. To Mary McCarthy

Burnett: McCarthy, "The Inventions of I. Compton-Burnett," *Encounter*, November 1966.

I now have the formula: "I [write] poems that [are] like writing a play in which I put the hero in a pit, and set him the problem of finding a way out, or living there. . . . Our nation and civilization seems to have gotten itself into just such a pit, man-made but perhaps unavoidable" (RL to Philip Booth, October 10, 1966, collection of Philip Booth).

Schapiro: Meyer Schapiro (1904–96), American art historian who taught at Columbia.

Hannah's Brecht: Arendt, "Bertolt Brecht: 1898–1940," *New Yorker*, November 5, 1966.

480. To William Empson

Hough Frye piece: Empson, "Graham Hough, *An Essay on Criticism*," *New Statesman*, December 2, 1966; "Northrop Frye, *The Return of Eden: Five Essays on Milton's Epics*," *Listener*, July 28, 1966.

in 1939: Lowell met Empson through Jean Stafford, who worked at I. A. Richards's Basic English Institute in Cambridge in 1939. A friend of Stafford's recalled a dinner party at Lowell's parents' house: "Mrs. Lowell was horrified with Empson because he was uncouth. He had a pair of overshoes which he never took off, and a suit that he obviously slept in, and he was talking about Wittgenstein and telling stories that had us practically on the floor. Mrs. Lowell didn't think it was a bit funny" (Roberts, 178).

481. To Elizabeth Bishop

Lithium: A mineral salt used to treat bi-polar illness. "Its therapeutic value was discovered by the Australian physician John Cade (1949) . . . Although a handful of American psychiatrists were among the pioneers, lithium was not widely used in the United States until the late 1960s" (Goodwin, Jamison, *Manic-Depressive Illness*, 603).

Nolan: Sidney Nolan (1917–92), Australian artist. See *The Voyage: and Other Versions of Poems by Baudelaire*, illus. Nolan (1968).

I fly to London: *Benito Cereno*, dir. Jonathan Miller, opened at the Mermaid Theatre on March 12, 1968.

Shelley: Shelley, *Prometheus Unbound* (1819). Lowell wrote earlier to Bishop: "Now I must go and read through Shelley's *Prometheus*, a task for me I'm afraid though scattered through it are many of his lovely verses. I like his politics well enough, but that universal European romantic rhetoric, grand without observation humor, or the heart-breaking loving-kindness of Hardy, wearies" (RL to Elizabeth Bishop, November [22], 1964, Vassar).

"Under the Window": Bishop, "Under the Window: Ouro Prêto (for Lilli Cotreia de Araújo)," *New Yorker*, December 24, 1966.

awful and wonderful: "All the untidy activity continues, / awful but cheerful" (Bishop, "The Bight," lines 35–36).

482. To the Editors, Partisan Review

Published as "In Clay's Corner," *Partisan Review*, Summer 1967. Cassius Clay (Muhammad Ali) refused induction into the army on April 28, 1967. "I ain't got no quarrel with them Vietcong," he said. He was stripped of his boxing title, criminally indicted, convicted, and sentenced to five years in prison. The *Partisan Review* solicited comments from writers about Clay's case.

484. To Elizabeth Bishop

Time thing . . . : Lowell was featured on the cover of *Time* magazine (June 2, 1967). Blair Clark's tape-recorded interview with the journalist is at the Ransom Humanities Center, University of Texas.

your responses: "Lowell's friend, Poet Elizabeth Bishop, says that confessional poetry 'is really something new in the world. There have been diaries that were frank—and generally intended to be read after the poet's death. Now the idea is that we live in a horrible and terrifying world, and the worst moments of horrible and terrifying lives are an allegory of the world.' Speaking of some of Lowell's confessional imitators, she adds: 'The tendency is to overdo the morbidity. You just wish they'd kept some of these things to themselves'" ("The Second Chance," *Time*, June 2, 1967, 68).

description: "Elizabeth Bishop, 56, one of America's leading women poets, is the epitome of the cool, detached, low-key observer" (*Time*, June 2, 1967, 74).

the optimistic James Dickey: "James Dickey, 44, is Lowell's polar opposite—facile, exuberant, bearing joy and affirmation" (*Time*, June 2, 1967, 74).

fire-bombing: Dickey, "The Fire Bombing," *Buckdancer's Choice* (1965).

Irene . . . my play: Irene Worth (1916–2002), American actress, starred in Jonathan Miller's production of *Prometheus Bound* at Yale.

the late war: The Six-Day War started on June 5, 1967. Lowell was asked to sign a public appeal to Lyndon Johnson to support Israel's war, which he declined to do: "I thought . . . we should have guaranteed the boundaries of Israel and, if necessary, helped to defend them. I did not think the United States should have forcibly opened the Gulf of Aquaba. President Johnson's handling turned out to be both correct and humane. However, this war should never have happened; for this, Russia and America, the suppliers of weapons, are heavily to blame" ("Robert Lowell Gives Reason for Not Signing War Plea," *New York Times*, June 14, 1967).

on Saint some one: Cf. "Come under the shadow of this gray rock—/Come in under the shadow of this gray rock,/And I will show you something different from either/Your shadow sprawling over the sand at daybreak, or/Your shadow leaping behind the fire against the red rock" (Eliot, "The Death of Saint Narcissus," *Poems Written in Early Youth* [1967], lines 1–5) with *The Waste Land*, section 1, lines 25–29.

485. To Shozo Tokunaga

Shozo Tokunaga (b. 1930), Japanese literary scholar, was writing a book about Lowell's poetry.

Stocks and stones . . . : Cf "Children of Light," *LWC*, lines 1–2, with "Avenge, O Lord, thy slaughtered saints, whose bones/Lie scattered on the Alpine mountains cold;/Even them who kept thy truth so pure of old,/When all our fathers worshiped stocks and stones,/Forget not" (John Milton, "On the Late Massacre at Piedmont," lines 1–5).

your interpretation: Unknown; Tokunaga's letter has not survived.

Glass houses: See "Children of Light," *LWC*, lines 6–7.

Mole-tide: See "Colloquy in Black Rock," *LWC*, lines 11–13.

on the *mover. Them* is the eyes: See "Between the Porch and the Altar," *LWC*, lines 16–20.

Green statues . . . : See "July in Washington," *FTUD*, 7–10.

Juvenal's 10th and Marvel's "Garden," and perhaps "Coy Mistress": "Central Park," section 4 of "Near the Ocean," "The Vanity of Human Wishes: A Version of Juvenal's Tenth Satire," *NTO*; Andrew Marvell, "The Garden" and "To His Coy Mistress."

Kirkup's ingenious essay: James Kirkup, "Between Wind and Water: Some Considerations of Robert Lowell's 'Waking Early Sunday Morning,'" *Iconomatrix* 1.1 (1975).

Ten: See "Waking Early Sunday Morning," *NTO*, lines 1–8.

little compliment: Wallace Stevens, "Sunday Morning," *Harmonium* (1923).

our two poems: Lowell's original and Tokunaga's Japanese translation.

486. To James Kirkup

Published in *Iconomatrix* 1.1 (1975).

Borges: Jorge Luis Borges (1899–1986), Argentinian poet and short story writer.

Erikson-Osborne: Eric Erikson (1902–94), German American psychoanalyst, Lowell's colleague at Harvard; John Osborne (1929–94), English playwright.

487. To Adrienne Rich

kind remarks: "I finally got hold of a copy of the *Review*, with Prometheus. It seems every bit as remarkable as it did in the other version you showed me, last fall, and hasn't lost, what I was afraid it might have lost, the presence of some gentle, touching helplessness to set against all that bloc-like force, on the one hand, and the Promethean intellect, on the other. Somehow that other spirit makes itself felt, and one is left with a vision of the world in which just these three powers exist—mental clarity, force, and innocence. It is an opera, yet more visual than any opera ever was—the landscapes in it are like Hardy's landscapes—realistic yet legendary" (Rich to RL, 19 July '67, Harvard).

Weil essays: Simone Weil, *Selected Essays, 1934–1943* (1962).

this circlet of friable laurel . . . : Rich and Alfred Conrad presented Lowell with a laurel wreath on his fiftieth birthday, March 1, 1967 (Rich to SH, May 7, 2003). The poem he quotes, "Half a Century Gone," is 105 lines long in stanzas of varying lengths. It was heavily revised into five sonnets for *Notebook 1967–68*. "This circlet of friable laurel,/a funeral wreath from the despotic gangster" (lines 4–5) became "our springtide's circlet of the fickle laurel,/a funeral wreath from the Despotic Gangster," "Half a Century Gone," *N67–68* (see Adrienne Cecile Rich Papers, Radcliffe).

Mary: Mary McCarthy and James West had recently bought a house in Castine.

teaches French at Exeter: Harris Thomas.

grand maistres in Villon: "Aux grands maistres Dieu doint bien fere/Vivans en paix et en re-quoy/En eulx il n'y a que reffaire/Si s'en fait bon taire tout quoy" (Villon, *Grand Testament*, lines 241–44).

The Gowries: Xandra Bingley and Grey Gowrie; Alexander Hore-Ruthven, earl of Gowrie (b. 1939), Irish poet and politician who worked as Lowell's teaching assistant from 1966 to 1968. He is the author of *A Postcard from Don Giovanni* (1972).

488. To Elizabeth Bishop

even in this sad time: "This fall has been saddened by the death of Elizabeth Bishop's friend, Lota, who flew here from Brazil, and on the same day took an overdose of barbiturates, was in a coma for a week, then her heart failed. She had troubles with the blood system which touched her mind. The mournful end of a marriage. Elizabeth, though lost, seems to be recovering" (RL to Eleanor Ross Taylor, October 7, 1967, Vanderbilt).

prose annals: Bishop, "Rainy Season, Sub-Tropics," and "The Hanging of the Mouse."

Jason: Potrait of Jason (1967), dir. Shirley Clarke, starring Jason Holliday.

489. To Edmund Wilson

rude: "Dinner at the Epstein's—Cal Lowell and Lillian [Hellman]. Cal and Jason had been down to the big Washington demonstration against the Pentagon and were very funny about it, but Cal said that it had been one of the fine moments of his life—had marched arm and arm with Norman Mailer and Dwight Macdonald, and had apparently been rather scared when soldiers pointed guns at him, Elizabeth [Lowell] hadn't come because she was writing a review slating Lillian's play. Cal, after dinner, began to go on to me about the Bible, which for some reason

he is teaching at Harvard. His line, when he had talked about it on a previous occasion, had been Wasn't it just a lot of old Jewish folk tales?; now, he would keep reiterating: 'Edmund, what do you think are the best things in the Bible?' Afterwards, he wrote me a letter in which he apologized for having been 'loud and rude.' I guess the subject of the sacred book arouses the New Englander in him: he doesn't know what attitude to take to it—downgrading or enthusiastic" (Wilson, *The Sixties*, 669–70).

World War I: Wilson, "The Army, 1917–1919," *A Prelude: Landscapes, Characters and Conversations from the Earlier Years of My Life* (1967).

490. To Mary McCarthy

McCarthy recommended Lowell's *Near the Ocean*, Elizabeth Bishop's *Questions of Travel*, and Gaia Servadio's *Tanto gentile e tanto onesta* in "Books of the Year: Some Personal Choices," *Observer*, December 10, 1967.

I named you . . . The Warrior: Mary McCarthy, *Vietnam* (1967); William Styron, *The Confessions of Nat Turner* (1967); and J. Glenn Gray, *The Warriors: Reflections on Men in Battle* (1967).

your element, not mine: "With Robert Lowell's *Near the Ocean* the scale is titanic; the verse reverberates and rumbles like Jupiter's thunder or ancient Ocean, his preferred element in this collection of new poems and classical imitations. Some of the poems I find difficult, because of the insistent pressure of references, a roaring and clashing of echoes. He makes his own imperious theogony, of ancestors, wives, child, brother poets, and, like a god, feels pity for modern men, inadaptive monsters out of their depth. Himself he sees as a trapped salmon charging a waterfall" (*Observer*, December 10, 1967).

a poet of terror: "[Bishop] is admired for her lucidity and control, but surely she is a poet of Terror. Under her lens, objects are magnified, creating an effect of strangeness and hermetic separation. For her the common world is made up of microcosms that imitate macrocosms; sandpipers' prints, children, the poor, the mad. She is fascinated by trade-marks, snatches of overheard conversations, and other hieroglyphs" (*Observer*, December 10, 1967).

Hellman: Hardwick, "The *Little Foxes* Revived," *New York Review of Books*, December 21, 1967.

a land poem: "Snake," *N67–68*.

491. To Ted Hughes

Ring and the Book: Robert Browning, *The Ring and the Book* (1869).
Wodwo: Hughes, *Wodwo* (1967).

492. To Elizabeth Bishop

Illich: Ivan Illich (1926–2002), Viennese-born philosopher. Lowell visited his center for cross-cultural studies in Cuernavaca, Mexico in 1968.

The Spock etc. indictment: Benjamin Spock (1903–98), American pediatrician opposed to the Vietnam War. He was indicted, tried, and convicted for counseling draft evaders; the conviction was later overturned on appeal.

494. To the Editors, New York Review of Books

Published in the *New York Review of Books*, February 29, 1968.

495. To Mary McCarthy

the last week: The North Vietnamese launched the Tet Offensive on January 30, 1968.

your Gilliatt: Possibly a reference to McCarthy's response to an exchange between Penelope Gilliatt and Elizabeth Hardwick about Hellman's *Little Foxes*; see "Lark Pie," *New York Review of Books*, February 1, 1968.

496. To Elizabeth Bishop

Baskin Nuclear Man: Leonard Baskin, *Hydrogen Man* (1954).

Trilling on Joyce: Trilling, "James Joyce in His Letters," *Commentary*, February 1968, reprinted in *The Last Decade*, ed. Diana Trilling (1979).

497. To Peter and Eleanor Taylor

William Yandell Elliott: William Yandell Elliott (1896–1979), member of the Fugitives, professor of government at Harvard University (where his students included Henry Kissinger). See RL letter 184.

McCarthy: Eugene McCarthy.

My heart . . . will have to be with McCarthy: "I feel no competence or longing to take on the burden of a political logician or polemicist. Of the announced or seriously offered Democratic or Republican candidates, only senators Kennedy and McCarthy seem morally or intellectually allowable. Of these, McCarthy is preferable, first for his negative qualities: lack of excessive charisma, driving ambition, machinelike drive, and the too great wish to be president. But I am for him most for what he possesses, his variable, tolerant and courageous mind, lungs that breathe the air. When the race against President Johnson was hopeless and intractable, he alone hoped, entered and won" (RL to Mr. [?] Harrison, March 28, 1968, copy at Harvard).

Romney: George Romney (1907–95), governor of Michigan, made a bid for the 1968 Republican nomination but showed poorly in the February New Hampshire primary.

498. To Elizabeth Hardwick

Milwaukee: Lowell's trip to Milwaukee with the McCarthy campaign was covered by the *New York Times*: "When candidates speed from town to town, they usually spend their time in close conversation with aides about the peculiar characteristics and problems of the next stop, rehearsing the names and sensitivities of the important local politicians. But not Gene McCarthy. He rides with Robert Lowell, whose knowledge of politics extends no further than the Guelphs and the Ghibellines in 14th century Florence and whose total interest in this campaign is embraced by his statement, 'I am for peace.' Arcadians both, Mr. McCarthy and Mr. Lowell discuss poetry and divert themselves with a kind of 'in' conversation, of which the following is a sample: LOWELL: Can they draft monks? McCARTHY: No. LOWELL: Well, that's a loophole. McCARTHY: Do you suppose we could get some bishop to give all our student supporters minor orders?" (E. W. Kenworthy, "Poet and Politician Orchestrate McCarthy Overtures to Voters," *New York Times*, March 29, 1968).

Sidney: Sidney Nolan.

499. To Mary McCarthy

the old frontier: See John F. Kennedy's "New Frontier" address accepting the Democratic Party nomination, July 15, 1960.

Marietta Trees . . . King: Marietta Tree (1917–91) worked on the staff of the United Nations Secretariat until 1967. Martin Luther King, Jr., was assassinated on April 4, 1968.

an aristocratic, Christian atheist: Cf. RL to George Santayana, Jan. 12 [1948], letter; "New England and Further," *CPR*; and Henry Adams, *The Education of Henry Adams*, 405–06.

the Indiana campaign: Mary McCarthy's four-part series "Hanoi" was published in the *New York Review of Books* between May 23 and July 11, 1968; her "Notes on the Election" appeared in the October 24, 1968 issue.

500. *To William Empson*

shot at Arthur Schlesinger: See Empson's contribution to *Authors Take Sides on Vietnam*, ed. Cecil Woolf and John Bagguley (1967), 27. Arthur Schlesinger's review of the book took exception to writers who "demand a new Nuremberg. William Empson wants to punish American airmen who drop napalm" (Schlesinger, "Two Questions about Vietnam," *Encounter*, December 1964, 73–78). Empson replied: "I said nothing of the kind. I said, 'A U.S. airman who has wrecked a village with napalm there is just as much a war criminal as the accused at Nuremberg.' The hypocrisy of approving both the bombing and the legal executions was plainly the target of this brief remark. I think that legal trials of the defeated enemy by the victors set a very bad precedent, and the part of it conducted in Tokyo undoubtedly had a disastrously opposite effect to that intended—the whole nation admired the behaviour of the heroes who were being made martyrs, otherwise they probably would have admitted that some of their behaviour was bad. Ever since *Encounter* was founded, I have noticed that its political contributors have great difficulty in opening their mouths without a lie hopping out" (Empson, "Authors and Ambiguity," *Encounter*, February 1968, 93).

O'Brien: Conor Cruise O'Brien, "Yeats and Fascism: What Rough Beast," *New Statesman*, February 26, 1965.

501. *To Grey Gowrie*

Trinity: Gowrie was applying for a teaching job at Trinity College, Dublin.

Castle Martin . . . : "In 1967 I inherited an estate in Ireland from a great aunt out of the blue" (Gowrie to SH, March 18, 2003). Laurence Scott, American artist who befriended the Gowries when they lived in Cambridge, Massachusetts; Woofer, Fanny Howe's dog ("Cal was attached to a stray dog Bingo and I adopted, a collie. We called him Doggo, which for some reason delighted Cal. When after a few years, Doggo died, Woofer became, as it were, a family dog"); Lewis Mumford (1895–1990), American architectural critic ("Cal and I dined with Lewis Mumford once or twice. I remember Mumford attacking something Cal said. . . . Cal got his own back by turning Mumford into an allegorically grumpy schoolmaster"); Henry Kissinger (b. 1923), American political scientist, a friend of the Gowries; Caroline Blackwood (1931–96), Irish writer who was dating Robert Silvers.

a nocturn: Cf. "These Winds," *N67–68, N70, FLH*.

Bingo and Brer: Bingo is the nickname of Xandra Bingley, Gowrie's first wife; their son is Brer Ruthven.

502. *To A. Alvarez*

book of essays: A. Alvarez, *Beyond All This Fiddle: Essays, 1955–1967* (1968).

your interview with Hochhuth: "If H. came over pompously that was my fault—mine & the interpreter's. I found him an attractive man & relieved, I felt, not to have to be on the defensive about Churchill to an Englishman. Maybe that's why he bent over backwards to praise him. And then, manners are hard to come by via an interpreter, however sympathetic he might be" (Alvarez to RL, May 9, 1968, Harvard).

503. To Richard Wilbur
Lowell sent an identical telegram to a large circle of writers.

504. To Kingman Brewster
the ceremony: Lowell received an honorary degree from Yale in 1968. This letter was published in the *New York Review of Books*, July 11, 1968.

Coffin: Yale's chaplain, William Sloane Coffin, an outspoken antiwar activist, was indicted by a federal grand jury in early 1968 for aiding young men who wanted to resist the draft. President Brewster faced intense pressure to fire Coffin but he refused to do so. Charges against Coffin were eventually dropped.

505. To Jacqueline Kennedy
mourning: Robert Kennedy was shot in Los Angeles on June 5; he died on June 6.

this short poem: "R. F. K.," *New Republic*, June 22, 1968, revised for *N67–68, N70, HIS, SP77*.

506. To Adrienne Rich
the parody: "AT THE BARRICADES Mornings, in Dacron pyjamas, I hog the john/where the Vergilian sun soaks through our reed blinds/and limelights our Victorian bidet./Our natural Puerto Rican sponge lies on the tiles/like an earlier incarnation of itself,/some marine Pyrrhus soaking up the bilge/of our master bathroom. /It is nineteen-sixty-eight,/the Old Left lies in its teeth about us,/Grayson Kirk, blanched to an almost revolutionary fineness/is addressing the troops on our Panasonic transistor;/I seem to hear him whisper: Paley, Sulzberger, Hogan you were my masters and I die in chains.—from the Yiddish of Mordecai Lowell" (Rich to RL, n.d. 1968, copy at Schlesinger Library, Radcliffe).

Grayson Kirk...: Grayson Kirk was president of Columbia University from 1953 to 1968. William Paley, owner of CBS; Arthur Ochs Sulzberger, publisher of the *New York Times*; and Frank S. Hogan, Manhattan district attorney, were Columbia trustees during the student protests of spring 1968.

Mitch's novel: Mitchell Goodman, *The End of It* (1962); he was married to Denise Levertov.

507. To Anne Fremantle
Anne Fremantle (1909–2002), Anglo-American Catholic writer, friend of Ivan Illich.

Jung's little Job book...: C. G. Jung, *Answer to Job* (1952); Søren Kierkegaard, *Fear and Trembling* (1843).

Ivan: Ivan Illich.

508. To Adrienne Rich
Holub: Miroslav Holub (1923–98), Czech poet; the location of Lowell's letter(s) to him is unknown.

Russian invasion: Soviet tanks rolled into Czechoslovakia on the evening of August 20, 1968.

two Ghazals: "Another Friend" and "Fame," *N67–68*.

Dido: Dido Merwin was recovering from surgery (Rich to RL, 16 August '68, Harvard).

Rockefeller: Nelson A. Rockefeller dropped out of the race after receiving 11 percent of the vote in the Republican New Hampshire primary in March.

Fuller: Buckminster Fuller (1895–1983), American philosopher, poet, and architect. Lowell found him "very Cambridge Yankee, with a quaint old-fashioned brilliance and knowledge of sci-

ence" (RL to Elizabeth Bishop, August 23, [1968], Vassar). His great aunt was Margaret Fuller; see "Margaret Fuller Drowned," *N67–68*, *N70*, *HIS*.

509. To Elizabeth Bishop

Cape Rosier Wedding: Richard Eberhart, "A Wedding on Cape Rosier," *Shifts of Being* (1968).
Chicago: Site of the 1968 Democratic convention.

510. To Donald Junkins

Donald Junkins (b. 1931), American poet, former student of Lowell's.
Now the poem: "R. F. K.," *N67–68*.

511. To John Berryman

the poems: Berryman, *His Toy, His Dream, His Rest* (1968).

512. To the Editor, Commentary

Published in *Commentary*, March 1969.
a black descent on Columbia . . . : Written in response to Diana Trilling's account of the Columbia uprising, "On the Steps of the Low Library: Liberalism and the Revolution of the Young," *Commentary*, November 1968. "Once the first buildings at Columbia were seized, one of them by black students . . . it was reasonable for the revolutionaries to hope that black dissatisfaction with Columbia, not only on the score of a [controversial] gymnasium but also because Columbia had engendered a considerable enmity as landlord of buildings largely tenanted by Negroes and Puerto Ricans, or only because it was a powerful white institution bordering the black ghetto [Harlem], might be triggered into a significant black uprising" (Trilling, *Commentary*, November 1968, 33–34).

513. To Elizabeth Hardwick

Mr. Dioscorides: Perhaps a joke about Dioscorides (c. 40–90 C.E.), Greek physician and pharmacologist who traveled as a surgeon with Nero's armies. In his study of drugs, he describes using opiate sleeping potions as surgical anesthetics.
Bill's birthday: January 9 being William Meredith's birthday.

514. To Shozo Tokunaga

"Bark" . . . : See "The Quaker Graveyard in Nantucket," *LWC*, lines 12–16.
hell-bent: Tokunaga queried Lowell about a misprint ("heel-bent") in the edition he was reading (Tokunaga to SH, October 4, 2004).
the one the poem's about: "The Quaker Graveyard in Nantucket" is dedicated to Warren Winslow, killed on January 3, 1944, when the USS *Turner*, recently returned from North Africa and anchored in the Ambrose Channel of New York Harbor, sank after an accidental explosion. See "At the Service Cemetery" and "Cousin Charlie," Robert Lowell Papers, Harvard.
"Pitch this portent" . . . : See "The Quaker Graveyard in Nantucket," *LWC*, section 1, lines 17, 19, 22; section 2, line 2; section 3, lines 4–5, 7, 15, 19, 21–22, 24; section 4, lines 4, 5, 9.
"Crabs" may be Eliot: "Quaker Graveyard in Nantucket," *LWC*, section 4, line 14; cf. Eliot, "Rhapsody on a Windy Night," lines 41–45, and "The Love Song of J. Alfred Prufrock," lines 73–74.

Corbière: "Entendez-vous gratter les crabes de la nuit?" (Corbière, "Paris Nocturne," line 4).

"unstoned" . . . : See "The Quaker Graveyard in Nantucket," *LWC*, section 4, line 20; section 5, lines 3, 10, 14, 17, 18; section 6, line 4.

wife of . . . : Ermalee Udall, wife of Stewart Udall (secretary of the interior from 1961 to 1969).

515. To Peter Taylor

Priest of Conception Bay: Robert Traill Spence Lowell, *The New Priest in Conception Bay* (1858).

controversy: See Diana Trilling, "On the Steps of the Low Library: Liberalism and the Revolution of the Young," *Commentary*, November 1968, and her letter to the editor, *Commentary*, March 1969.

Sumner: Cat Charles Sumner Lowell was named for Massachusetts Senator Charles Sumner (1811–74). Sumner and Henry Adams's father were founders of the antislavery Free Soil Party, believing that compromise with the South over slavery was impossible. Cf. "New England and Further," *CPR*.

extirpation: Wilson, "The Fruits of the MLA: 'Their Wedding Journey,'" *New York Review of Books*, September 26, 1968; "The Fruits of the MLA: II. Mark Twain," *New York Review of Books*, October 10, 1968.

516. To the Editor, Commentary

Published in *Commentary*, April 1969.

heavily banters . . . : Trilling takes Lowell, Macdonald, and Mailer to task throughout her article. See Trilling, "On the Steps of the Low Library," *Commentary*, November 1968, 34.

"radical piety": "I have no wish to deprive Mr. Lowell of his armor of radical piety, if he so badly needs it" (Diana Trilling, letter to the editor, *Commentary*, March 1969, 12–14).

She asks me many questions: "I address him not as a poet, not as a licensed sensibility, but as a powerful working member of the intellectual community, himself one of its most active controversialists, a signer of protests, a joiner of demonstrations, a writer of letters to the press, a much-valued speaker at meetings and rallies. What, for instance, does Mr. Lowell now feel about the use of violence as an instrument of social change? Does he still hold with the pacifism he professed in the past . . . ? Does he believe that no choice remains to us except either the anarchic disruptiveness of the New Left or compliance in the establishment, or does he think that the liberal tradition is still to be drawn upon? . . . What, in greatest simplicity, does Mr. Lowell think of the Columbia uprising as a moral spectacle: how does he feel about students kidnapping an officer of the University, rifling the personal files of the President and broadcasting their contents, urinating on floors, spitting at their teachers, destroying the research of one of their professors, shouting obscenities?" (Diana Trilling, letter to the editor, *Commentary*, March 1969, 12–14).

517. To Elizabeth Hardwick

[. . . from]: Lowell's handwriting is so shaky that several words are illegible. "I & 7 II" is an approximate guess.

Berlin's: Isaiah Berlin (1909–97), English philosopher.

519. To Elizabeth Hardwick

Hakeldama: See Acts 1:18–19.

520. To Jacqueline Kennedy Onassis
marriage: Jacqueline Kennedy married Aristotle Onassis on October 20, 1968.

521. To Jerome Mazzaro
Jerome Mazzaro (b. 1934), American poet, author of *The Achievement of Robert Lowell: 1939–1959* (1960), *The Poetic Themes of Robert Lowell* (1965), and *Profile of Robert Lowell* (1971).
reviewing me: Mazzaro, "Robert Lowell and the Circle," *New Republic*, May 31, 1969.

522. To Jacqueline Kennedy Onassis
Liebersons: Goddard Lieberson (1911–77), composer and president of Columbia Records.
the moon: Apollo missions 9 and 10, launched in the spring, made preparations for Apollo 11, which landed on the moon on July 21, 1969.

523. To Stephen Spender
Essay on Rime: Karl Shapiro, *Essay on Rime* (1945).
your student book: Stephen Spender, *The Year of the Young Rebels* (1969).
terrifying tantrums: See I. A. Richards to RL, [between 6 and 21 May 1969] and [after 21 May 1969], *Selected Letters of I. A. Richards*, 179–81.

524. To Richard Tillinghast
chapters: Tillinghast, "An Introduction to Robert Lowell's Recent Poetry" (Ph.D. thesis, Harvard University, 1970).
"Williams" poems: "Everything about ["The Mouth of the Hudson"]—the setting, the attitude, the technique—is so reminiscent of William Carlos Williams, that one is tempted to identify the main figure specifically as Williams" (Tillinghast, 120).
symbols of masturbation . . . : "In dreams, to have a tooth pulled is generally interpreted in psychoanalytic literature as symbolizing masturbation. That the tooth (the symbolic penis) should be 'noosed in a knot' obviously suggests guilt and the 'castration fear' that psychoanalysts associate with anxiety. Even the random visual associations are ominous in an unspecified way; perhaps the triangular blot of rot may be taken to suggest pubic hair" (Tillinghast, 135).
my first draft of this: Cf. "Eye and Tooth" (*FTUD*) with the second and third paragraphs of "Dr. Williams" (*CPR*, 37–38).
drop this line: "His loss of interest in the possibilities of self-revelatory poems informed by psychoanalysis was followed by an interest in less personal, culture-informed poems like 'Florence'" (Tillinghast, 137).
"Edwards": "Jonathan Edwards in Western Massachusetts," *FTUD*; "Mr. Edwards and the Spider," *LWC*.
you, **I've never known . . . :** See "The Lesson," *FTUD*, lines 13–15; "if 'you' equals 'one,' it may be paraphrased: One's childhood continues to exist because one lets it live in imagination. Another possibility is that 'you' is the childhood self being addressed by the adult self" (Tillinghast, 130).
four elements . . . : "Following the suggestion that *For the Union Dead* is a return from myth to reality, one could say that the first four poems are based on the traditional four elements: water, fire, earth, and air" (Tillinghast, 113).
Primitivism: Yvor Winters, *Primitivism and Decadence: A Study of American Experimental Poetry* (1937).

Trilling: Trilling, "'For the Union Dead': Robert Lowell, 1917–," *The Experience of Literature: A Reader with Commentaries* (1967).

I cut "Night Sweat" to [the] first sonnet: Lowell used the first stanza of "Night Sweat" as the second section of "April's End" (*N67–68*).

The joke about "oldman on the Yangtse": "Commander Lowell," *LS*, lines 71–73.

Isn't the Richard, *Richard II*, not *III*?: "Ironically comparing his rustication with Richard II's, he quotes Shakespeare: 'Is Richard now himself again?'" (Tillinghast, 86). See "Home after Three Months Away," *LS*, line 11, which slightly misquotes Colley Cibber's adaptation of *Richard III* 5.3.119.

the Ovid stanza: See note to RL's letter to John Berryman, March 18, 1962, letter.

"L'Azur": "'Waking in the Blue' has connections with *Les Fenêtres* and *L'Azur* by Mallarmé. *Les Fenêtres* is about a man in a hospital looking out the window, searching for the sort of clarity represented by the azure of the sky in *L'Azur*" (Tillinghast, 84–85).

525. To Hannah Arendt

Paradise?: "We leave here—leaving paradise, or sort of—on the 15th, go to Zurich for a week and fly home. (Home?)" (Hannah Arendt to RL, August 13, 1969, Harvard).

Gray: Glenn Gray, *The Warriors: Reflections on Men in Battle* (1967). "Glenn Gray wrote a very happy letter about your encounter at Aspen. By the way, did you tell him that you got another thing from the 'Warriors'—on p. 51, the last lines, the quote from Nietzsche, or did you get that from another source?" (Arendt to RL, August 13, 1969, Harvard).

The Mao . . . : "River God," *N67–68*; Richards and Lowell discussed the Mao story at the American Academy of Arts and Letters meeting on May 21, 1969. Richards refers to their conversation in his letter of [after May 21, 1969]; see *Selected Letters of I. A. Richards*.

Meredith's: William Meredith, "*Notebook 1967–68*," *New York Times Book Review*, June 15, 1969.

Kennedy business: On July 18, 1969, Edward Kennedy drove his car off an unmarked bridge on Chappaquiddick Island near Martha's Vineyard, Massachusetts. His passenger, Mary Jo Kopechne, drowned. Kennedy was found guilty of leaving the scene of an accident.

Heinrich: Heinrich Blücher (1899–1970), Arendt's husband.

526. To John Berryman

read through: "Thanks for your formidable and gorgeous book. . . . I read the whole book in page galleys but was too busy and ill to write to you. . . . [A] few days ago in 24 hours I read the book again from beginning to end and my objections dropt to the ground. Everybody will have to read the book twice. About the rhyme I have myself repeatedly given up rhyme altogether in the Dream Songs while preserving an effect of rhyme. I think you are right in this. Moreover the disjointedness disappears and it comes out as one poem" (Berryman to RL, Fri 5 Sept 69, Harvard).

***Advocate*:** Berryman, "Henry's Understanding" "Henry by Night," "Apollo 8," *Harvard Advocate*, Spring 1969.

527. To Elizabeth Bishop

Bogan: Louise Bogan was on the original Bollingen Committee in 1948.

Washington March week: The "March against Death," November 14–15, attracted hundreds of thousands of protesters to Washington.

again with Dwight: Lowell attended many peace marches with Dwight MacDonald, including the 1967 March on the Pentagon and a Nixon protest at the United Nations on September 18, 1969.

more expensive: more expansive?

528. To Marcia Nardi

Marcia Nardi (1901–90), American poet; see letter 116. "W. C. Williams incorporated *wholesale* into *Paterson II* a very long intimate letter which I wrote him, behind my back, and *without my permission*" (Nardi's marginal note, n.d.). See "Publication Day," *HIS*.

531. To Elizabeth Bishop

the poems to you: "Four Poems for Elizabeth Bishop," *N70*.

award!: Bishop's *Complete Poems* (1969) won the 1970 National Book Award.

and said more or less this: A copy of Lowell's remarks given at Philharmonic Hall in New York City on March 4, 1970, is at Yale.

Ada and *Portnoy*: Vladimir Nabokov, *Ada, or Ardor: A Family Chronicle* (1969); Philip Roth, *Portnoy's Complaint* (1969).

Pound: *Drafts and Fragments of Cantos CX–CXII* (1969).

St. Elizabeths poem: Bishop, "Visits to St. Elizabeths," *Questions of Travel* (1965).

a voice saying . . . : For more about this occasion, see Linda Hamalian, *A Life of Kenneth Rexroth* (1991), 321.

Whalen: Philip Whalen (1923–2002), American poet associated with the Beat movement.

Vinícius: Bishop had just sent Lowell her translation of Vinícius de Moraes's "Sonnet of Intimacy." See *One Art*, 517, and the omitted postscript: "Vinícius came here, or to the hotel, with a young girl, *not* his 5th, or is it 7th—yes 7th—wife. The 7th wife arrived the next day . . . almost nine months pregnant. Vinícius brought his wife to call . . . not mentioning the girl, although I'd heard about her, of course. He seemed very decadent and sick. In Rio he invited all his friends for an evening, didn't drink anything at all, and at midnight made a speech, with everyone present, ordering the pregnant wife from the house. The wife went on a rampage, smashed the apartment and almost finished off several friends—one man I know slightly had to have nine stitches in his forehead—police, ambulances, etc. Then poor Vinícius took himself off to his favorite clinic, for a 'rest'" (Bishop to RL, February 27, 1970, Harvard).

532. To Allen Tate

Tate material: When Lowell agreed to edit "a collection of essays about Tate and his work, which was to be published by the University of Minnesota Press" (Doreski, 179), Tate sent him all the essays he had collected over the years (see RL to Allen Tate, December 30th, 1968, Princeton). Lowell later admitted that he was not able to finish the project and Tate asked him to return the material.

Carlyle's *French Revolution*: John Stuart Mill's maid accidentally burned the only manuscript copy of Thomas Carlyle's *The French Revolution* in 1835.

533. To Allen Tate

what you say: "I fear I shall come near to insulting you when I say that I can't believe the 'Tate' material was lost that way. . . . At this point I don't think I ought to spare you my annoyance. . . . I asked Frank McShane to cancel the evening for Tate's 70th, in which you and Red Warren were to participate, because I could not face the possibility of your megalomania getting out of control, either through the condescension of 'ranking' me or in allusions to my private life. Your Napoleonic stance permits you to confess other people's lives. I hope that you will not again confess mine. I have thought all this for many years. A small crisis has brought it to the surface. Not quite yours as always" (Tate to RL, March 30, 1970, quoted in Doreski, 193–94).

534. To Elizabeth Hardwick
Rowse: A. L. Rowse (1903–97), English poet and literary scholar, fellow of All Souls from 1925 to 1974.

535. To Donald Davie
the Essex job: "I am accepting an offer to teach two years at Essex . . . The department is one Donald Davie set up and without having any great luminaries like Harry [Levin] and John Bullitt, is about as good as any I've seen—young, scholarly, Bohemian and interested in literature—a quality almost unheard of in an English department. But my real reason is I want us out of America—not a gesture of rejection—but a couple of years to breathe and forget the grit and steel and wind of our ~~present~~ now atmosphere" (RL to William Alfred, May 4, 1970, Brooklyn College).
Your poem: Davie, "Epistle: To Enrique Caracciolo Trejo."
publisher: Davie's *Essex Poems* (1969) had recently been rejected by Wesleyan University Press.

536. To Elizabeth Hardwick
I'm off to London: Faber and Faber hosted a party in Lowell's honor on April 30. Among the guests was Caroline Blackwood.

537. To Elizabeth Hardwick
Published in *McSweeney's*, Late Winter 2001.
Caroline McCulloch movie: A twenty-five-minute film about Lowell screened at the National Film Theatre in London.
Bowra: Sir Maurice Bowra (1898–1971), warden of Wadham College, Oxford, helped organize the campaign to elect Lowell Professor of Poetry at Oxford in 1966.
Sonia: Sonia Orwell, widow of George Orwell.
Cumner Hills: See Matthew Arnold, "The Scholar Gipsy," lines 66–70.

538. To Elizabeth Hardwick
house hunting: "There'd been a time when Lizzie had written to me saying could I find a flat for Cal in London and somehow Caroline had been in on this and she and I had tramped around estate agents looking for a flat for Cal. That was before the Faber party [when Lowell and Blackwood started their affair]" (Xandra Bingley interview, Ian Hamilton Notebooks, British Library).
Harmsworth: Desmond Harmsworth (1903–90), poet, artist, and publisher; his verse translation of Paul Valéry's *Le Cimetière Marin* was published in 1969.

539. To Elizabeth Hardwick
Iris Murdoch . . . : Iris Murdoch (1919–99), Irish novelist, married to John Bayley (b. 1925), English literary scholar and writer; Lord David Cecil (1902–86), English biographer and literary scholar; Peter Levi (1931–2000), English poet who was a Jesuit priest until 1977; Enid Starkie (1903–70), Irish literary scholar; John Sparrow (1906–92), English literary scholar, warden of All Souls from 1952 to 1977.
Godstow: "And, above Godstow Bridge, when hay-time's here/in June, and many a scythe in sunshine flames" (Matthew Arnold, "The Scholar Gipsy," lines 91–92). "As to the future—

God knows—or does he? Please get better Cal. I love you so much. Love[,] Godstow Marsh" (Blackwood to RL, n.d., Summer 1970, transcribed in Ian Hamilton Notebooks, British Library).

Blythe spirit: See Percy Bysshe Shelley, "To a Skylark," lines 1–5, and Matthew Arnold, "The Scholar Gipsy," lines 69–92.

Sidney: Sidney Nolan.

Bingo: Xandra Bingley; see note to letter 501.

Dworkin: Ronald Dworkin (b. 1931), American political philosopher; he and Lowell discussed Vietnam, civil disobedience, Nixon, and "a host of other matters" at the request of Oxford students. "It was just the two of us together with a large room full of students. I don't remember many details of our conversations, alas, but I do remember being impressed both with Lowell's outrage and his knowledge of politics and events" (Dworkin to SH, January 25, 2004).

540. To Christopher Ricks

Christopher Ricks (b. 1933), English literary scholar.

that week-end: See letter 538.

feuds: "No particular feuds, just some banter at what the English think of Americans, I suppose" (Ricks to SH, 20 April 2003).

Housman and Milton: Christopher Ricks, *A. E. Housman* (1968); *Milton's Grand Style* (1963).

541. To Elizabeth Hardwick

the Wains's: John and Eirian Wain's.

D.P.: Dorothy Pound.

Basil Bunting: "I go for a few days with Grey to the Lake Country, mostly to see the Wordsworth scenes but also to call on one of Grey's idols, Basil Bunting. Ford used to suggest that Pound must have made up such a name, but he is actually quite good" (RL to Hardwick, June 2, 1970, Texas); Basil Bunting (1900–85), English poet who served a jail sentence at the age of eighteen as a conscientious objector; he met Ezra Pound in Paris in 1923.

total nonsense: "A steady iron-hard jet of absolutely total nonsense, as if under great pressure from a hose, and recalling among human utterances only the speech of Lucky in *Waiting For Godot*" (Empson, "Rhythm and Imagery in English Poetry," *British Journal of Aesthetics*, January 1962, reprinted in *Argufying* [1987], 148).

Lowell "material": The library of the State University of New York at Stony Brook was interested in buying Lowell's papers. Harvard's Houghton Library eventually bought them for $141,000.

leisure to be wise: Cf. "But we, brought forth and rear'd in hours/Of change, alarm, surprise—/What shelter to grow ripe is ours?/What leisure to grow wise?" (Matthew Arnold, "Stanzas in Memory of the Author of 'Obermann,'" lines 69–72) and "Deign on the passing World to turn thine Eyes,/And pause awhile from Letters to be wise" (Samuel Johnson, "The Vanity of Human Wishes," lines 158–59).

542. To Elizabeth Hardwick

Written during an acute manic episode.

543. To Elizabeth Hardwick

Written during an acute manic episode.

544. To Caroline Blackwood

Written during an acute manic episode.
Ian Hamilton transcription.

545. To Elizabeth Hardwick

Written during an acute manic episode.
The envelopes for letters 587 and 588 are addressed to "Mrs. Robert Lowell, Castine, Maine U!S!A!"

547. To Caroline Blackwood

Ian Hamilton transcription.
bottom rooms: "Blackwood returned to London in August. Lowell was calm, she found, but 'he wasn't normal,' and she refused to allow him back to Redcliffe Square. . . . 'I told him he must get a flat of his own. Which he minded terribly—he was very wounded. . . . But Israel [Citkowitz, Blackwood's second husband] said rightly, was saying, "I really don't want a madman with the children." I had to tell Cal that. Because Israel could have taken the children away from me'" (Ian Hamilton, 402–03).

548. To Elizabeth Hardwick

sonnet group: "The Revolution," *Modern Occasions*, Fall 1970.

549. To Frank Bidart

Frank Bidart (b. 1939), American poet; he met Lowell in the fall of 1966. In January 1970, Lowell asked him to help ready the revised *Notebook* for publication. Bidart stayed in Lowell's studio for a week and together they put the manuscript together, noting hundreds of changes to individual lines and rearranging the order of the book.
your Frost: Bidart, "Robert's Rules," *Partisan Review* (1971), a review of *The Poetry of Robert Frost*, ed. Edward Connery Lathem (1969).
The poem: Possibly "Another Life," *Golden State* (1973).

551. To Elizabeth Hardwick

job: Gertrude Buckman was working for Thames and Hudson.

552. To Elizabeth Hardwick

Hazlitt's characters . . . : William Hazlitt, *Characters of Shakespear's Plays* (1817); Shakespeare, *Julius Caesar*, ed. T. S. Dorsch (1964).

553. To Elizabeth Hardwick

Fellini's *Satyricon*: Federico Fellini, *Satyricon* (1969).

554. To Elizabeth Hardwick

hospital again: Rich was hospitalized in 1967 for orthopedic surgery to treat her rheumatoid arthritis, a recurring condition.

Street Schools: See Rich, "The Case for a Drop-out School," *New York Review of Books*, June 15, 1972.

555. To Elizabeth Bishop

your beautiful poem: Bishop, "In the Waiting Room," *New Yorker*, July 17, 1971; see line 60.

thirty more poems: Early drafts of the *Dolphin* poems.

Freud's grandson, Lucian: Lucian Freud (b. 1922), English painter, was married to Blackwood from 1953 to 1957.

556. To Blair Clark

Al Clark: Cf. "Alfred Corning Clark," *FTUD*.

her novel: Mary McCarthy, *Birds of America* (1971).

Joanna: Joanna Rostropowicz, Polish scholar, Blair Clark's second wife.

557. To Elizabeth Hardwick

"words that were persuasions.": "For his lips could well pronounce/Words that were persuasions" (Ralph Waldo Emerson, "Threnody," lines 52–53).

routine: "smug routine and things allowed / Minorities, things under cloud! / Hither! take me . . ." (Emerson, "Mithridates," lines 29–31).

558. To Elizabeth Hardwick

Alf's face: Rich's husband, Alfred Conrad, had committed suicide the previous week.

565. To Elizabeth Hardwick

reviews from Alvarez and Connolly: A. Alvarez, "A Change in the Weather," *Observer* (London), November 8, 1970; Cyril Connolly, "The Private and the Public," *Sunday Times* (London), November 8, 1970.

569. To Elizabeth Hardwick

scene of Benito's triumph: Jonathan Miller's Mermaid Theatre production of *Benito Cereno* in 1967 was poorly reviewed.

***Daily Telegram*:** *Daily Telegraph*.

Jack's . . . : John Thompson's.

570. To Elizabeth Hardwick

Jennings: Elizabeth Jennings (1926–2001), English poet and critic.

Claude-Edmonde: Claude-Edmonde Magny (1913–66), French literary critic whom the Lowells befriended in Europe in the early 1950s.

571. To Elizabeth Hardwick

Ben: Benjamin Tate, Allen Tate's brother.

review from Denis Donoghue . . . : "The events which he does not list as public are domestic mis-

fortunes, notably a marriage breaking, then broken" (Denis Donoghue, "Lowell's Seasons," *Guardian Weekly*, December 26, 1970).

Carruth: Hayden Carruth's essays about Lowell include "A Meaning of Robert Lowell," *Hudson Review*, Autumn 1967, reprinted in *Robert Lowell: A Portrait of the Artist in His Time*, ed. Michael London and Robert Boyers (1970); Adrienne Rich and he were close friends.

Gaia . . . : Gaia Servadio (b. 1938), Italian novelist married to William Mostyn Owen, British art historian; Francis Bacon (1909–92), Irish painter.

573. To Elizabeth Bishop

versing one of your letters: Cf. Bishop to RL, February 27, 1970 (*One Art*, 515–17), with "For Elizabeth Bishop 3.," *N70*.

When Lamb blew up at Coleridge . . . : Possibly a reference to Coleridge's "This Lime-tree Bower My Prison" (1797), in which he addresses "gentle-hearted Charles." See Charles Lamb to Coleridge, Aug. 6th, 1800, and Aug. 14, 1800, *Letters of Charles Lamb*, ed. W. C. Hazlitt (1886), 245 and 249.

574. To Caroline Blackwood

229 East 48th Street: Blair Clark's apartment.

576. To John Berryman

prayer . . . : Berryman, "Eleven Addresses to the Lord," *Love and Fame* (1971). The book is dedicated "to the loving memory of the suffering lover & young Breton master who called himself 'Tristan Corbière' (I wish I versed with his bite)."

Verlaine's religious poems: Paul Verlaine, *Sagesse* (1880).

580. To Elizabeth Hardwick

Hedda's: Hardwick, "Ibsen and Women II: Hedda Gabler," *New York Review of Books*, March 25, 1971.

Whittemore: Reed Whittemore (b. 1919), American poet.

Miss van Duyn: Mona Van Duyn (b. 1921), American poet.

Per: Per Seyersted; see note to letter 393.

581. To Adrienne Rich

my Stanley piece: "I will stop and digress on the virtues of intelligible and unintelligible poetry. Take painting: if I were painting my father, I might do a mirror-likeness in one of a hundred styles, or I might distort him, give him staghorns, or do him as a river, a recognizable river, an unrecognizable, or as a pattern of gray and red brushsweeps. Most artistic transformations are symbols. The typist's 'seduction' in the *The Waste Land* is nature, Tiresias is symbol. When Crane writes of his soul's journey as the flow of the Mississippi from brook to the Gulf of Mexico, he is using symbol. When he begins another such journey with 'Where the cedar leaf divides the sky,' he is writing a symbolic line, which, despite its clear shock, must remain in mystery. Now that obscure poetry is perhaps out of fashion, one must pay homage to its supreme invention and exploration. I remember Empson years ago with a group discussing one of his poems, 'To an Old Lady.' Was it about the moon described as an old lady, or an old lady as the moon? Was it physics or metaphysics? Empson said, 'It's my grandmother. The

old girl would have been furious if she had known I was writing about her.' Wasn't he right? Think of the simple, heartfelt, offensive poems that have been written about friends, wives, children. What hope for the half-poet? The frank, open and vulnerable, the voice of a generation, fades as soon as the elitist incantations of the hermeticist" (Robert Lowell, "Words That Cats and Dogs Can Understand: *The Testing Tree* by Stanley Kunitz," *New York Times Book Review*, March 21, 1971).

To look at the worst . . . : "Let him in whose ears the low-voiced Best is killed by the clash of the First, / Who holds that if way to the Better there be, it exacts a full look at the Worst, / Who feels that delight is a delicate growth cramped by crookedness, custom, and fear, / Get him up and be gone as one shaped awry; he disturbs the order here" (Thomas Hardy, "In Tenebris II," lines 13–16).

582. To Allen Tate

Nemerov: Howard Nemerov (1920–91), American poet.

583. To Elizabeth Hardwick

Flavio: Lota's nephew committed suicide in the fall of 1970; Bishop heard the news in early 1971.

584. To Allen Tate

Conrad's sharp rebuke . . . : See Geoffrey Grigson, "Southern Gentlemen of Letters" (reviews of Allen Tate, *The Swimmers and Other Selected Poems* and *Essays of Four Decades*), *TLS*, March 19, 1971, and an exchange between Conrad Aiken and Grigson (*TLS*, April 9, 1971). Aiken wrote: "Tate's reputation, as one of America's most useful citizens of letters for the past forty years, can and will survive this disgraceful attack." The reviewer replied: "Mr. Aiken's various charges of bad manners, bias, malevolence and envenomed assault are fanciful: and I think that nothing in my review—which it was no pleasure to write—sinks to Mr. Aiken's own description of Allen Tate as 'one of America's most useful citizens of letters for the past forty years'—as if Mr. Tate had been a good pencil sharpener."

Tuckerman: Frederick Tuckerman (1821–73), American poet.

the Christmas, Subway sonnets: Tate, "Sonnets at Christmas," "More Sonnets at Christmas," and "The Subway."

585. To Stanley Kunitz

Crow: Ted Hughes, *Crow: From the Life and Songs of the Crow* (1971).

a sort of Cummington Press: Olwyn Hughes's Rainbow Press, a letterpress like Cummington, publisher of *Land of Unlikeness* (1944).

586. To the Editors, New York Review of Books

Published in the *New York Review of Books*, May 6, 1971, reprinted in *CPM*, 1125.

Lieutenant Calley: Officer commanding the troops who killed more than 300 people in the village of My Lai on March 16, 1968 (the public did not learn details of the massacre until November 1969). Cf. "Women, Children, Babies, Cows, Cats," *HIS*; see also the note in the *CPM*, 1127.

Why should the bait . . . : See "Leaving Home, Marshall Ney," *HIS*, lines 13–14. See also note to "Dolphin," *DOL*, *CPM*, 1139.

587. To Peter Taylor

Possibly written while mildly manic.

and indeed Allen: Allen Tate and his third wife, Helen Heinz, had twin sons, John Allen and Michael Paul; Michael died as a baby in a 1968 accident.

Prometheus: *Prometheus Bound*, dir. Jonathan Miller, opened at the Mermaid Theatre on June 24.

588. To Elizabeth Hardwick

Borges' visit: Jorge Luis Borges gave four lectures at London's Institute for Contemporary Art in May 1971; he discussed his latest book of poetry, *In Praise of Darkness*, during the third lecture, on May 10.

589. To Elizabeth Hardwick

The Wernicks: Robert and Marion Wernick, New York friends of the Lowells.

Brustein: Robert Brustein (b. 1927), director of the Yale Repertory Theatre Company from 1966 to 1979.

Madam Mandelstam: Nadezhda Mandelstam (1899–1980), Russian writer, widow of poet Osip Mandelstam (1891–1943). "Amusing pitiful letter from her, begging me to [travel to Russia]. 'Life is not imagination and harder to live than to publish'" (RL to Blair Clark, June 23, 1971, Texas).

her book: Nadezhda Mandelstam, *Hope against Hope: A Memoir* (1970); the location of Lowell's letters to Nadezhda Mandelstam is unknown, though her letters to him indicate they had a correspondence for several years.

your *Scarlet Letter:* Hardwick, "Seduction and Betrayal: I," *New York Review of Books*, May 31, 1973, reprinted in *Seduction and Betrayal* (1975).

Hogg's *Justified Sinner:* James Hogg, *Confessions of a Justified Sinner* (1824).

590. To Adrienne Rich

to defend myself: "I feel we are losing touch with each other, which I don't want. . . . I feel a kind of romanticism in your recent decisions, a kind of sexual romanticism with which it is very hard for me to feel sympathy. . . . [M]y affection and admiration for Elizabeth make it difficult to be debonair about something which—however good for her it may ultimately be—has made her suffer" (Rich to RL, June 19, 1971, quoted in Ian Hamilton, 433).

Sandra: Sandra Hochman; see letter 405.

591. To Elizabeth Hardwick

Villette: Charlotte Brontë, *Villette* (1853).

Dombey: Charles Dickens, *Dombey and Son* (1848).

your Sylvia: Hardwick, "On Sylvia Plath," *New York Review of Books*, August 12, 1971.

"Daddy": Plath, "Daddy," *Encounter*, October 1964, and *Tri-Quarterly*, Fall 1966; reprinted in *Ariel* (1966).

592. To Elizabeth Hardwick

my Flaubertian elegy: "Commander Lowell (1887–1950)," *LS*.

Alice: Alice Meade, Lowell's cousin.

Your book: Hardwick, *Seduction and Betrayal* (1975).

La Deuxieme?: Hardwick, "The Subjection of Women," *A View of My Own* (1962).
prayed for such a woman: The rest of the letter is torn.

593. To Elizabeth Hardwick
your "Notebook": See note to letter 451; the writing was not finished and is not a source for *Sleepless Nights* (1979) (Hardwick in conversation with SH, July 2003).
Poor Mary!: Reviews of Mary McCarthy, *Birds of America* (1971).

595. To Elizabeth Hardwick
aldumet: Medicine for high blood pressure.

596. To Frank Bidart
your book: Bidart sent Lowell the manuscript of *Golden State* (1973).

597. To Peter Taylor
Heist or Geist: Axel Heyst.

598. To Charles Tomlinson
Charles Tomlinson (b. 1927), English poet.
your little book: César Vallejo, *Ten Versions from Trilce*, trans. Tomlinson (1970).

599. To Frank Bidart
Bloomfield: Morton Bloomfield (1913–87), Harvard English Department chairman in 1971.

600. To Elizabeth Hardwick
Heathcliff airport: Heathrow Airport.
Ivana's case: "[I]n January 1972 Lowell's stepdaughter Ivana (now aged six) overturned a kettle of boiling water and was badly burned" (Ian Hamilton, 428). See "Ivana," *DOL*.

601. To Elizabeth Bishop
Marianne . . . Dick Blackmur's essay: Marianne Moore died on February 5, 1972; R. P. Blackmur, "The Method of Marianne Moore," *The Double Agent: Essays in Craft and Elucidation* (1935).
book of memory: Bishop began an essay about Moore in 1969 and continued to work on it until the year she died. "Efforts of Affection: A Memoir of Marianne Moore" was published posthumously in *Vanity Fair* (May 1983), reprinted in *The Collected Prose* (1984).
unlike Berryman's: Berryman "leaned" from the Washington Avenue Bridge in Minneapolis on January 7, 1972 (Haffenden, 419).

603. To Frank Bidart

Your Pound book . . . The Eliot: For Lowell's birthday, Frank Bidart sent him Hugh Kenner, *The Pound Era* (1971), and T. S. Eliot, *The Waste Land: A Facsimile and Transcript of the Original Drafts including the Annotations of Ezra Pound*, ed. Valerie Eliot (1971).

the Russian: Lowell originally considered publishing *The Dolphin* with Olwyn Hughes's Rainbow Press (see letter 586). He changed his mind and instead considered reprinting his Russian translations from *Poets on Street Corners*, ed. Olga Carlisle (1968), with Rainbow as a chapbook. The poems appear in an appendix to *CPM*.

I finished my Berryman: "For John Berryman: 1914–1972," *New York Review of Books*, March 30, 1972, reprinted in the *CPR*.

604. To Stanley Kunitz

. . . a whole in its skull: "The hole in his head, / cut whistle clean" (Kunitz, "Robin Redbreast," *The Testing-Tree* [1971], lines 26–27).

the Yevtushenko gala: Yevgeny Yevtushenko (b. 1933), Russian poet, read with Kunitz, James Dickey, Eugene McCarthy, Richard Wilbur, and others at Madison Square Garden in New York City on January 28, 1972. The event "celebrat[ed] Yevgeny Yevtushenko's belief that the era of static 'poetry readings' is over—that the presentation of poetry today is 'the common work of poet and audience'" (advertisement, *New York Times*, January 9, 1972).

for [her] necessary: The page ends here; the rest of the letter is missing.

605. To Elizabeth Hardwick

Grace Stone: Grace Zaring Stone (1891–1991), American novelist.

Ferrero: Guglielmo Ferrero, *The Gamble: Bonaparte in Italy, 1796–1797* (1939).

607. To William Alfred

the poems on page 47 . . . : "1 and 2 on p. 47 will tear Elizabeth apart, important though I agree they are to the wholeness of the book. I have to say that" (Alfred to RL, March 12, 197[2], Texas). Poems 1 and 2 on page 47 of the original *Dolphin* manuscript are "Fox-Fur" and "The Messiah" (the first two sections of "Flight to New York"). They are clearly about the Elizabeth character in the poem. Lowell may have mistaken the poems on page 47 for ones on page 46, "Before the Dawn of Woman" and "Dawn." In an interview, Alfred recalled: "Elizabeth [Bishop], Esther Brooks, and I were the only people who would dare tell Cal that he ought not to print the material from his wife's letters. He knew it. Cal first sent us mimeographed copies, and I wrote in my letter, 'You cannot print what is on page so-and-so.' He said, 'All right, I won't print that one,' but he'd pretended I'd gotten the pagination wrong and it was another poem" (Fountain and Brazeau, 309). See Bishop to RL, March 21, 1972, *One Art*, 561–64, and *CPM*, 1133–34. See also original *Dolphin* manuscript, Lowell Papers, Harry Ransom Research Center, University of Texas, box 5, folder 9; Bishop Papers, Vassar College, box 82, folder 82.5.

On the Auden: "Alfred also reported . . . that he had just met W. H. Auden for the first time: 'He spoke of not speaking to you because of the book. When I said he sounded like God the Father, he gave me a tight smile. I write to warn you'" (Ian Hamilton, 425).

Bing: Rudolf Bing (1902–97), general manager of the Metropolitan Opera from 1950 to 1972.

608. To Peter Taylor

Belfast: Beginning with Bloody Sunday, 1972 was the deadliest year of the Troubles; killings in Belfast were reported several times a week. On March 24, Prime Minister Edward Heath suspended Home Rule in Northern Ireland.

609. To Christopher Ricks

your article: Ricks, "Profile: The Poet Robert Lowell," *Listener*, June 21, 1973.

610. To Elizabeth Bishop

impressions: See Bishop, *One Art*, 562.

611. To Elizabeth Bishop

"Burden" section should come after "Sickday": The "Burden" section was retitled "Marriage"; "Sickday" was retitled "Sick"; *DOL*.

"Leaving America" . . . then all the New York (new title): "Leaving America for England," *DOL*; the New York poem is retitled "Flight to New York," *DOL*.

"From My Wife" would be called "Voice": In "Voices," *DOL*, the tone of the speaker is more resigned than in "From My Wife."

"Fox Fur" and "The Messiah": Lowell collapsed these two poems into "Foxfur," *DOL*. Some lines from "The Messiah" were also moved to a poem entitled "In the Mail," *DOL*.

614. To Christopher Ricks

Hallam Tennyson: See "A Colloquium on Tennyson," *Listener*, March 8, 1973, a selected transcript of the program that was produced by the poet's great-grandson, Hallam Tennyson, for BBC Radio 3. "HT produced programmes in which various hands (mouths) discussed someone's work. . . . The third voice to be heard [in the article] is that of Lowell" (Ricks to SH, 20 April 2003).

C. Day Lewis: Cecil Day Lewis (1904–72), English poet.

your Tennyson: Ricks, *Tennyson* (1972).

your Milton essays. *P.R.*: Ricks, *Milton's Grand Style* (1963) and "Over-Emphasis in *Paradise Regained*," *English Language Notes*, December 1961; John Milton, *Paradise Regained* (1671).

the *Dunciad* . . . : Pope, *The Dunciad* (1728); Keats, *Hyperion* (1819); Johnson, *London: A Poem* (1738) and *The Vanity of Human Wishes* (1749); Wordsworth, "Michael" (1800).

615. To Elizabeth Bishop

"Poem" . . . Small Good Picture: Bishop, "Poem," *Geography III* (1976); "Small Bad Picture," *Poems: North & South—A Cold Spring* (1955).

if they read it: See Bidart, "Herbert White," *Golden State* (1973).

Viking ships: "In Oslo we saw the Viking ships . . . Frank said you had some lines about them in a sonnet but later took them out?" (Bishop to RL, September 8, 1972, Harvard). See "Northmen," *HIS*.

616. To William Alfred

Milton: "Who kills a man kills a reasonable creature, God's image; but he who destroys a good book, kills reason itself, kills the image of God, as it were in the eye" (Milton, *Areopagitica* [1644]).

617. To Elizabeth Bishop

Frank's dedication: *History* is dedicated to Frank Bidart and Stanley Kunitz.

I don't think I've undermined you: "Back in Cambridge was the news that Robert Lowell . . . was 'all signed up' to return to teaching at Harvard the next year. Elizabeth's appointment had been as Lowell's replacement, and his unexpected return seriously jeopardized her job. . . . [She] was relieved when Harvard granted her a contract . . . independent of any contract of Lowell's" (Millier, 473).

powerful letter: "As for *Dolphin*, I should be less than honest if I didn't tell you that it both fascinates and repels me. There are details that seem to be monstrously heartless. I will grant that parts of it are marvelous—wild, erotic, shattering. (Who else had the nerve for such a document of enchantment and folly?) But some passages I can scarcely bear to read: they are too ugly, for being too cruel, too intimately cruel. You must know that after its hour has passed, even tenderness can cut the heart. What else need I say to you, dear Cal, not as your judge— God Save me!—but as your friend. In any event, these are matters that I have not discussed with another soul" (Stanley Kunitz to RL, April 19, 1972, quoted in Ian Hamilton, 422).

619. To Elizabeth Hardwick

the Larkin: "Digressions from Larkin's 20th Century Verse," *Encounter*, May 1973.

Mary's using Stalin: See Mary McCarthy, "Sons of the Morning," *New York Review of Books*, January 25, 1973.

620. To Frank Bidart

peace in Vietnam: "President Nixon Suspends All Military Action against North Vietnam," *Times* (London), January 16, 1973.

Fludd's: Robert Fludd (born in 1574 in Bearsted, died in 1637 in London), English physician, Rosicrucian, and mystical philosopher.

621. To Christopher Ricks

William: Ricks invited Lowell to contribute to *William Empson: The Man and His Work*, ed. Roma Gill (1974).

622. To Elizabeth Bishop

Wilbur poem: Wilbur, "Cottage Street, 1953," *The Mind-Reader* (1976). "A very *neat* poem by Wilbur about Sylvia Plath makes me angry—several people including Frank have admired it and I think it is very bad—really unfeeling. I tried to decide why and think it's because it is supposed to be ironic and isn't—'It is my office to exemplify/The published poet in his happiness'—it's full of words like that. Now Ransom could have written a poem like that, neat rhymes, cliché words, and all—and the irony would have been really there and somehow chilling and deep & sad—this just seems smug, I'm afraid" (Elizabeth Bishop to RL, January 14, 1973, Harvard).

teaching contemporaries: See Eliot, "On Teaching the Appreciation of Poetry," *Critic*, April–May 1960, 13–14, 78–80, and "T. S. Eliot Deplores Modern Verse Study," *New York Times*, December 30, 1960, 1. "I don't believe in teaching anything 'contemporary'—or even recent. I agree with Eliot's ideas on this subject—only the classics, some history, the sciences, *can* be taught—and certainly no 'literature' unless the author has been dead 100 years, or possibly was a 'foreigner'" (Bishop to RL, January 14, 1973, Harvard).

Heimert: Alan Heimert (1928–99), Harvard English Department chairman in 1973.

Coleridge: Empson, "Introduction," *Coleridge's Verse: A Selection*, ed. Empson and David Pirie (1972). See review in *TLS*, December 15, 1972, and Empson's reply, *TLS*, January 12, 1973.

Raine on Yeats['s] Journals: Kathleen Raine, "Life in Death and Death in Life: Yeats's 'Cuchulain Comforted' and 'News for the Delphic Oracle,'" *Southern Review*, 1973, and *Yeats, the Tarot, and the Golden Dawn* (1973).

Graves: Possibly Robert Graves, *Poems about Love* (1969) or *Poems, 1970–1972* (1972).

The Dee: John Dee (1527–1608), English mathematician, astronomer, and alchemist.

Pelican: Moore, "The Frigate Pelican," *Selected Poems* (1934). "You know the lines from 'The Frigate Pelican' . . . I've always thought they are autobiographical and could somehow be used to defend Marianne against the vicious gossip that is already in the air about her" (Bishop to RL, January 14, 1973, Harvard). See letter 111.

623. To Robert Boyers

3 poems: "Poems from Something Longer" ("History," "Man and Woman," "Last Things, Black Pines 4 a.m."), *Salmagundi*, Spring–Summer 1973, reprinted in *HIS*.

the Ashbery review: John Ashbery, "In the American Grain," *New York Review of Books*, February 22, 1973.

Ammons: A. R. Ammons (1926–2001), American poet; *Collected Poems, 1951–1971* (1972) won the National Book Award.

eccentric: Both Wheelwright and Ammons "are American originals (in the French sense of *un original* as someone who is also quite eccentric), and they are products as much of the American landscape as of the poetic tradition, in devious ways" (Ashbery, "In the American Grain").

Wheelwright: John Wheelwright (1897–1940), American poet from a patrician Boston family; he was killed by a drunk driver on September 15, 1940. Lowell knew him when he was young: "Yesterday afternoon brings back an evening with Howard Blake and Jack Wheelwright in 1938. The same dark defile of books was there and we argued about Virgil! Occasionally the name of the absent magister came up—Dr. Warren. We had come from the Athens Olympia and were in high spirits" (RL to Austin Warren, October 6, 1956, Brown University Library).

Shagbark: John Peck, *Shagbark* (1972).

624. To Elizabeth Hardwick

Daughters of Albion: Blake, *Visions of the Daughters of Albion* (1793).

Rimbaud's *Saison*: Rimbaud, *Une Saison en enfer* (1873).

Greer: Germaine Greer (b. 1939), Australian literary critic. See Richard Holmes, "Poetry International," *Times* (London), June 22, 1972.

Woolf: Hardwick, "Bloomsbury and Virginia Woolf," *New York Review of Books*, February 8, 1973.

625. To Blair Clark

the Athens: The Athens Olympia restaurant in Boston.

McGovern: Senator George McGovern (b. 1922), antiwar Democratic candidate for president in 1972. Clark was the communications director of the Democratic National Committee. The Nixon administration's attempts to sabotage McGovern's campaign resulted in the Watergate scandal.

626. To Frank Parker
The *Ocean*: The actual title of the painting is *The Wave*.

629. To the Editor, Encounter
Published in *Encounter*, June 1973.

Lewis A. Coser: "Robert Lowell urged the poet to go into the 'bull-ring,' and Jean-Paul Sartre has staked his literary reputation on the notion that 'the writer is speaking to his contemporaries and brothers of his class and race.' Their insistence on the writer's social responsibility has by now become conventional wisdom of most of the Western intellectual community" (Lewis A. Coser, "Julien Benda: On 'Intellectual Treason,'" *Encounter*, April 1973).

630. To Elizabeth Bishop
"Wild Oats": "In my wallet are still two snaps,/Of bosomy rose with fur gloves on" (Philip Larkin, "Wild Oats," lines 22–23).

Washington: Bishop spent the term teaching at the University of Washington in Seattle.

her book: Blackwood, *For All That I Found There* (1973).

631. To Elizabeth Hardwick
Diaries: On March 25, 1973, the *Observer* began printing excerpts from Evelyn Waugh's diaries.

632. To Peter Taylor
Senator Irvin: "Watergate Prober Sam Ervin," cover story, *Time*, April 16, 1970; Sam Ervin (1896–1985), Democratic senator from North Carolina, chaired the Senate's Select Committee on Presidential Campaign Activities.

the Lambton scandal: Lord Lambton, undersecretary of defense for the RAF, resigned after his visits to call girls were secretly recorded by pimps. "I have behaved with credulous stupidity," he said in his statement. Lord Jellicoe, leader of the House of Lords, resigned shortly afterward for the same reason.

His interview speech: "Asked by a BBC interviewer why a man of 'social position, charm and personality' felt impelled to visit a whore, Lambton replied: 'I think that people sometimes like variety. It is as simple as that. If a man tells another man he went to bed with two pretty girls, the man would say 'lucky dog.' Asked if he felt there was something like an international vice ring involved, he shrugged. 'It's a sort of international organization—like the Boy Scouts. You know, hands across the sea'" ("Talking to Teddy," *Time*, June 11, 1973).

633. To Elizabeth Hardwick
Times: Ralph de Toledano, "A Text for Reaction, Not a Licence for Revolution," *Times* (London), July 4, 1973.

634. To Elizabeth Hardwick
THE REVIEWS: A note in Hardwick's hand at the foot of the page reads, "Cal's answer to Miss Perloff's review in *The New Republic*." Marjorie Perloff (b. 1931), American scholar whose review, "The Blank Now," was published in the *New Republic*, July 7 and 14, 1973. Perloff's second book, *The Poetic Art of Robert Lowell*, was also published in 1973.

635. *To Elizabeth Hardwick*

The Hopkins comparison: "Poor Harriet emerges . . . as one of the most unpleasant child figures in poetry; only Hopkins's Margaret, grieving over Goldengrove unleaving, can rival her cloying moral virtue" (Marjorie Perloff, "The Blank Now," *New Republic*, July 7 and 14, 1973).

Victor: Thomas Victor, American photographer.

636. *To Elizabeth Bishop*

what it says about her: "[I]t is Lizzie who becomes the dominant figure in the sonnets, and she is depicted, perhaps unwittingly on Lowell's part, as Dark Lady or Super-Bitch par excellence. In her letters and phone calls, she is forever patting herself on the back for running to Dalton to pick up Harriet's grades or driving her to camp, and she dwells irritatingly on Harriet's goodness. . . . It is therefore difficult to participate in the poet's vacillation, for Lizzie and Harriet seem to get no more than they deserve. And since these are, after all, real people, recently having lived through the crisis described, one begins to question Lowell's taste" (Perloff, "The Blank Now," *New Republic*, July 7 and 14, 1973).

Alice's room: Alice Methfessel, Bishop's companion.

637. *To Robert Giroux*

misquoted: "Trapped by memories and bombarded by reproaches from his second wife Elizabeth, the poet can only move uneasily: 'From the dismay of my old world to the blank/now'" (Perloff, "The Blank Now," *New Republic*, July 7 and 14, 1973).

the Ricks review: Ricks, "The Poet Robert Lowell," *Listener*, June 21, 1973.

639. *To the Editor,* Agenda

Published in *Agenda* 11 (1973). The copy transcribed here is based on corrected proofs that Lowell mailed to William Cookson from Brookline.

640. *To Seamus Heaney*

thank you for your review: "I had done a radio review of *History*, etc. on RTE [Radio Éireann], in a books programme I presented at the time: 'Imprint.' The transcript was forwarded to publishers and to him" (Heaney to Jonathan Galassi, February 9, 2002).

except for Ian Hamilton: Ian Hamilton, "Ringing the Changes," *Observer*, June 24, 1973.

a verse letter: Michael Longley, "Letters: To Seamus Heaney," reprinted in *An Exploded View: Poems, 1968–1972* (1973).

substitute for Auden: W. H. Auden died on September 29, 1973.

his circuit: Cf. Auden, "On the Circuit," (1963).

641. *To Elizabeth Bishop*

the bad review in *Agenda*: Peter Dale, "Fortuitous Form," *Agenda* 11 (1973). "You know when you were here that afternoon I hadn't read that fearful review in AGENDA so I had no idea how bad it was" (Bishop to RL, December 27, 1973, Vassar).

in a blurb: "It's like turning the light switch off, and there in the dark—reality: all kinds of likely and unlikely things, incandescent on their own, beginning to stir and breathe. All that really needs to be said about Sandra McPherson's new poems is that they are very, very good—original, surprising, and *clean*—a delight and refreshment in the tedium of irony, confession

and cuteness of contemporary verse. The title of the collection, *Radiation*, is beautifully suitable" (Elizabeth Bishop, blurb on jacket copy, Sandra McPherson, *Radiation* [1973]).

642. To Elizabeth Hardwick

your Philip: Philip Rahv died on December 22, 1973. Hardwick, "Philip Rahv (1908–1973)," *New York Review of Books*, January 24, 1974.

my perversely wild translations: "I have nine poems, almost a third of a book, and am beginning redoing five or six Montales[,] also Mémoire. I really did shockingly turn, twist, some of the translations to my own morbid purposes!" (RL to Frank Bidart, January 9, 1974, Harvard).

Philip's last magazine: After Philip Rahv broke with William Phillips, he founded *Modern Occasions* in 1971. The journal published six issues.

d reams: Lowell's typewriter skipped.

autobiographical . . . : "Thinking over the life and the nature of this extraordinary person, I remember that he had a large number of friends and maintained an intimacy with many of them. And yet we must respect the fact that Philip was not especially autobiographical. Of course this was something of a puzzle because his curiosity about the biography of his acquaintances was relentless, just as his refusal to accept their version of their actions and their motives was complete. Still, for himself, Philip was reserved in a genuine way and much interested in his dignity, and beyond that fanatical about standards and opinions. His life and his views were complicated; his living out of both was turbulent and serious" (Hardwick, "Philip Rahv [1908–1973]").

provincial: "The outstanding theme of Rahv's efforts was, I think, a contempt for provincialism, for the tendency to inflate local and fleeting cultural accomplishments. This slashing away at low levels of taste and at small achievements passing as masterly, permanent monuments was a crusade some more bending souls might have grown weary of. But he was not ashamed of his extensive 'negativism' and instead went on right up to the end scolding vanity and unworthy accommodation" (Hardwick, "Philip Rahv [1908–1973]").

643. To Robie Macauley

Hefner: Sheridan Dufferin coproduced *The World of Hugh Hefner*, dir. Tony Palmer (1973); Macauley was the fiction editor of *Playboy* from 1966 to 1977.

644. To Peter Taylor

your beautiful poem: Possibly "Her Need," *Shenandoah*, Summer 1976.

645. To Steven Axelrod

Steven Axelrod (b. 1944), American literary scholar, author of *Robert Lowell: Life and Art* (1978) and editor of *The Critical Response to Robert Lowell* (1999).

Williams-Larkin thing: "What's good about [Williams] that Pound doesn't have is that he worked in his locale. . . . He knew things not on the Sunday walk, how his patients talked, what happened in their marriages. His hand was on the car-wheel, as Pound's could never have been in Rapallo. . . . Williams' provincial counterpart is Philip Larkin" (Ian Hamilton, "A Conversation with Robert Lowell," *Review*, Summer 1971, reprinted in Meyers 159.

"Waking Early": Cf. "Waking Early Sunday Morning," *CPM*, 383–86, and "Waking Early Sunday Morning [magazine version]," *CPM*, 933–36.

Schopenhauer's bubbles: "It is the future generation that presses into being by means of these ex-

uberant feelings and super sensible soap bubbles of ours" (epigraph to "To Speak of Woe That Is in Marriage," *LS*).

Justice Holmes: "Holmes once said of the casualties of the Civil War that 'our dead brothers still live for us, and bid us think of life, not death,' and on another occasion proclaimed that 'life is action, the use of one's powers. . . . To use them to their height is our joy and duty'" (Axelrod, 169).

the Tate piece: Axelrod had sent Lowell an early draft of "Starting Out: Learning from Tate," Axelrod, 14–42.

646. To Elizabeth Bishop

Ehrenpreis: Irvin Ehrenpreis, "Viewpoint," *TLS*, February 8, 1974.

fire ballons . . . hen in New York: Bishop, "The Armadillo," "Large Bad Picture," "Trouvée," *Complete Poems* (1969).

Amazon, the thief, a servant: Bishop, "The Riverman," "The Burglar of Babylon," "Manuelzinho," *Complete Poems* (1969).

"Crusoe": Bishop, "Crusoe in England," *Geography III* (1976).

with the power of print: "To Mother," "The Airport" (later revised as "Logan Airport, Boston"), "Fourth Year" (later revised as "We Took Our Paradise"), "Wellesley Free," "The Afterlife," "1. What We Were" (later revised as "Robert T. S. Lowell"), "2. Before We Are" (later revised as "For Sheridan"), "Ulysses Circling" (revised as section 6 of "Ulysses and Circe"), "The Exile's Return" (revised from the old version), "Homecoming," *Review*, April 1974.

he'll live it out: Bidart's mother died in 1974.

647. To Elizabeth Hardwick

month-old strike: After thirty-six Essex students were arrested for protesting university grant policy, hundreds of students occupied buildings and marched to support them; many more were arrested throughout the spring. "Back in England in early May [Lowell] returned to Essex to read and talk about translation in support of . . . students jailed for striking" (Mariani, *Lost Puritan*, 426).

the Clive James: Clive James, *The Metropolitan Critic* (1974).

I suppose only . . . : See letter 654.

Wynn Handman: Handman revived *The Old Glory* for a Bicentennial production at the American Place Theater.

650. To Marjorie Perloff

English ~~material and~~ place names: "Lowell is . . . our great contemporary American Puritan poet, the lyric historicism of '91 Revere Street' with its glacial Sunday dinners and Commander Lowell's lettered garbage cans. The intricacies of modern divorce, erotic love and the pastoral settings of Britain—these have never been congenial themes for Lowell" (Perloff, "The Blank Now," *New Republic*, July 7 and 14, 1973). Cf. letter 82 and note.

Crane *was* Rimbaud: Perloff was writing *The Poetics of Indeterminacy: Rimbaud to Cage* (1981). "I thought at the time there would be a whole chapter on Crane . . . since Crane was very much influenced by Rimbaud" (Perloff to SH, November 15, 2002).

651. To Allen Tate

Our famous fire: The fire was a creative one; Tate, Gordon, Stafford, and Lowell all finished books in the winter of 1942–43.

I liked your Frost essay . . . your analysis of *Stopping in a Woods*: Allen Tate, "Robert Frost as Metaphysical Poet," *Memoirs and Opinions* (1975). The Frost poem is "Stopping by Woods on a Snowy Evening."

Fare forward?: The phrase recurs in Eliot's work; see particularly "The Dry Salvages," lines 14, 26, 39, and 47.

652. To Peter Taylor

in the hospital: Taylor had a heart attack; see Ian Hamilton, 441.

Israel Citkowitz['s] death: Composer Israel Citkowitz, Caroline Blackwood's second husband, died on May 4, 1974.

653. To Philip Larkin

This appears to be the only surviving letter from Lowell to Philip Larkin. Three letters from Larkin to Lowell (dated October 8, 1957, March 31, 1959, and August 24, 1963) are in the Robert Lowell Papers at Harvard.

your inscription: Larkin sent Lowell a copy of *High Windows* (1974), inscribed: "From a Drought to a Deluge."

big terrible poems . . . : Larkin, "The Old Fools," "The Building," "Livings," "To the Sea," "Sad Steps," "Cut Grass," "The Explosion," "Friday Night in the Royal Station," "Homage to a Government," "Vers de Société," *High Windows* (1974).

"Love" or "Church Monuments": George Herbert, "Love," "Church Monuments" (1633).

654. To the Editor, New Review

Published in the *New Review*, July 1974.

Clive James's sentence: Lowell's letter responds to John Carey's review of Clive James's *The Metropolitan Critic*. Carey writes that James's "really penetrating criticism always starts from a distrust of rhetoric, of shouting, of extremism and unreason. There's no shortage of these in the modern work he takes the brunt of. Sylvia Plath and Robert Lowell particularly rile him by their tendency to commandeer the disasters of history and brandish them as if they were upsets in their own little psyches. He finds this epitomized in Lowell's sonnet about Sylvia Plath, apparently occasioned by John Bayley's article in *the Review* 24 which used the words about Plath that Lowell finds objectionable[:] 'A miniature mad talent? Sylvia Plath/who'll wipe off the spit of your integrity,/rising in the saddle to slash at Auschwitz,/life tearing this and that, *I am a woman?*' 'A lot of rhetoric had to go over the dam,' counters James[,] 'before all the concentration camps in the Reich and occupied territories got whittled down to that one word "Auschwitz"—hundreds of journalists and television anchor-men had to do their stuff. And at last, after the whole infinitely ramified nightmare had been trimmed to that one stub and the stub itself had been crushed to powder, it was time for Lowell to come along and toss off a line suggesting that in Sylvia Plath the *Endlösung* finally met its implacable opponent. Carrying a sword. Riding a horse'" (Carey, "The Metropolitan Critic," *New Review*, May 1974, 77–78).

UDA: Ulster Defence Association, paramilitary loyalist group.

655. To Alan Williamson

Alan Williamson (b. 1944), American poet and critic. He studied with Lowell at Harvard and befriended Taylor while teaching at the University of Virginia. He was married to Anne Winters (b. 1939), American poet.

your monsters: Williamson, *Pity the Monsters: The Political Vision of Robert Lowell* (1974).
self-determination: "Outlivers," *N67–68, N70, FLH*, lines 13–14.
Guevara: "Che Guevara (Central Park)," *HIS*, lines 13–14.
Tom Hayden and Irving Howe: "Leader of the Left," *HIS*; "The New York Intellectual," *HIS*.

656. To Elizabeth Bishop

this last one: Bishop, "The End of March," lines 24–26, 32–33.
New England piece . . . : "New England and Further," *CPR*, 179–212; "The Poetry of John Berryman," *New York Review of Books*, May 28, 1964 (correction, June 11, 1964), reprinted in *CPR*, 104–11.
zerox: Xerox.
Wharf: Bishop "had been eyeing across Atlantic Avenue a warehouse conversion project known as Lewis Wharf. Suddenly one day, she signed an 'intent to buy' agreement. . . . Despite her financial worries, Elizabeth refused when Lowell suggested that when he sold his papers to Harvard, the university should take the irregular step of paying her five thousand dollars for her wonderful letters to him. . . . A year later, when Harvard sent the money anyway, Elizabeth was extremely grateful and wrote warmly to Lowell that it came at a time of such financial anxiety that it alone allowed her to keep the Lewis Wharf apartment" (Millier, 482–84).

657. To Peter Taylor

I had fainted: An Antabuse reaction; see Ian Hamilton, 441.
a second poem: "Our Afterlife II," *DBD*, lines 11–18. Cf. also line 1 with: "For several years I haven't felt my 'true self.' Most embarrassing, when I get out of one of the large taxis, the driver sometimes asks if I need help; I take stairs too with a considered seriousness. I forget names and faces as always only more; if I give someone a comical name, like Nemo or Lynhurst, I am liable to think it is his name. I forget things, have no memory of where I put my cigarette-lighter after a few minutes, no recollection even after I find it irrationally lying on a distant bureau. I act, as all flesh must, my age" (RL to Peter Taylor, December 12, 1974, Vanderbilt).
Venus etc.: Taylor, "Venus, Cupid, Folly and Time," *Kenyon Review*, Spring 1958, reprinted in *The Collected Stories of Peter Taylor* (1969).
Story-poem: Taylor's three story-poems are "The Instruction of a Mistress," "The Hand of Emmagene," and "Three Heroines," *In the Miro District* (1977); Lowell refers to either the second or the third.

658. To Elizabeth Hardwick

would be better: That is, a better college for Harriet than Barnard.
the busing: On September 12, 1974, the start of court-ordered busing to achieve racial integration in Boston's public schools was marred by violence in South Boston, where black students were attacked and school buses were stoned. Riots continued into October.

659. To James Laughlin

the Ransom: James Laughlin asked Lowell if he could reprint Lowell's tribute to John Crowe Ransom in the 1974 *New Directions Annual* anthology. Laughlin also wrote to say how much he enjoyed Lowell's last books—"nobody else puts solid think meat and lovely technique together the way you do" (October 14, 1974, New Directions Publishers Papers, Harvard).

poor Olga: In a journal entry dated 21 September [1979], Stephen Spender noted: "I happened to be in Venice on the day, two years ago, when I heard the news of Robert Lowell's death. The same afternoon I went to a drinks party at the Cini Foundation. Olga Rudge was there and I told her the news of Robert's death. 'The best thing that could have happened to him,' she said, 'after what he wrote about Ezra.' Lowell had always written praisingly of Pound but had remarked somewhere that one could not ignore his anti-Semitism, but must balance it against his genius and generosity" (Spender, *Journals*, 373). What Lowell "wrote about Ezra" may refer to remarks Lowell wrote in the mid- or late 1960s: "First I must step over the pit of Pound's politics in support of Mussolini, and his anti-Semitism in support of Fascism . . . the writing on Jews is evil and dull, often not much above the level of Father Coughlin's newspaper, a now lost name in his forgotten yellow sheet . . . It's not my duty as fellow poet, critic and his friend to defend or clear Pound's record. I can't see him as a bad man, except in the ways we all are" ("On Ezra Pound," Robert Lowell Papers, Harvard, bMS Am 1905/2828–2829).

the *ABC*: Ezra Pound, *The ABC of Economics* (1933).

our dispute and joking: "At one point Mr. Lowell and Mr. Laughlin got into a warm exchange over Pound's economic theories. Mr. Lowell said he did not understand them. Mr. Laughlin thought that maybe Mr. Lowell did, but would not let on. Mr. Lowell countered by saying Pound's theories were like Christianity: One had to take them on faith" (Thomas Lask, "'Requiem for E.P.' Recalls Turbulent Life of Embattled Poet," *New York Times*, January 6, 1973).

660. To Jean Stafford

Did you notice I live in Bearsted?: See note to letter 41.

661. To Elizabeth Bishop

suggestions: Bishop, "The End of March," lines 24–26, 32–33; see letter 656.

662. To Seamus Heaney

the cries of the beautiful peacocks: "I had mentioned that the house where we'd be put up during the Kilkenny Arts Festival (with Barrie Cooke, painter, and Sonja Landweer, ceramicist, in Jerpoint) had peacocks in the walled garden" (Heaney to Jonathan Galassi, February 9, 2002). Cf. Wallace Stevens, "Domination of Black," *Harmonium* (1923), lines 10, 27, 36.

our trip to the Belfast Airport: "Cannot remember the date or the reason for the Belfast meeting. I do remember coming off the Dublin train, being met at the station by Michael Longley and Cal and one or two others—and for some reason talking over the driving of Longley's car. On that occasion Cal made the marvelous remark about the motor: 'Longley's car is just a bundle of wounds'" (Heaney to Jonathan Galassi, February 9, 2002).

663. To the Editors, New York Review of Books

First printed in "A Special Supplement: The Meaning of Vietnam," *New York Review of Books*, June 12, 1975.

664. To Elizabeth Bishop

Vendler's Herbert: Helen Vendler, *The Poetry of George Herbert* (1975). "You'll probably see Helen Vendler at that Irish Festival. . . . I am trying to read her G. Herbert Book but that kind of 'close reading' is pretty much beyond me, I'm afraid" (Bishop to RL, August 1, 1975, Harvard).

his contributors: Bidart was the guest editor of *Ploughshares*, vol. 2, no. 4, 1975.

Mr. Stewart: Tom Stewart, editor at Farrar, Straus and Giroux.

basketball *center*: "The Graduate," *FLH*, line 6.

665. To Elizabeth Hardwick

Fitzgerald's marriage: To Penelope Laurens, Fitzgerald's second wife.

Gillian: Gillian Walker, a close friend of William Alfred's, was briefly engaged to him; she later married Alfred Maysles.

poor Bill . . . His adoption of Don: William Alfred; Don was his ward.

Harmonium . . . : Stevens, *Harmonium* (1923); "Sailing after Lunch," *Ideas of Order* (1935); *Esthétique du Mal* (1945); "The Rock," *Collected Poems* (1954).

666. To Seamus Heaney

Elgy: Elgy Gillespie, "Robert Lowell," *Irish Times*, August 1975.

"The Train" and "A Drink of Water": Seamus Heaney, "Glanmore Sonnet IV" and "A Drink of Water," *Field Work* (1979).

Wordsworth: Cf. Heaney, "Glanmore Sonnet III," *Field Work* (1975), lines 9–14.

The Pigeons: Heaney, "The King of the Ditchbacks," section 3, *Station Island* (1984).

Marie: Marie Devlin Heaney (b. 1940), author of *Over Nine Waves: Myths and Legends* (1994).

667. To John Haffenden

John Haffenden (b. 1945), English literary scholar.

Heredia: José Maria de Heredia (1842–1905), French poet. "The man who told the history of the world in a thousand sonnet scenes is Heredia, not a guide to us now, I suppose, but done with a Tennysonian density and finish" (RL to Adrienne Rich, November 5, 1967, Radcliffe).

you can read them: Haffenden was researching his biography of John Berryman.

668. To Peter Taylor

How many *New Yorker* pages are 35 of yours?: Taylor, "The Captain's Son," *New Yorker*, January 12, 1976.

Pound symposium: Pound died on November 1, 1972, in Venice.

my manic period: In January 1975, "[Taylor] decided upon taking a two-week jaunt to England. . . . The only difficulty in the whole trip was provided by Cal, who was in the midst of another breakdown. 'I have never seen him quite the way he is this time,' Peter reported to Allen Tate. 'He'll be perfectly fine one day and quite mad the next.' Cal was in and out of the hospital several times during the two weeks, and a badly distraught Caroline was constantly changing her mind about how she wanted Peter to deal with Lowell" (McAlexander, 227).

Clark's *I Tatti*: Kenneth Clark, *Another Part of the Wood* (1974).

reviewed a book: Blackwood, "Lovesome Things" (a review of *My Secret Garden*, ed. Nancy Friday), *TLS*, October 24, 1975.

669. To Frank Bidart

heart-felt poem: Possibly "Thanks-Offering for Recovery" or "The Downlook," *DBD*.

your last visit: When Bidart arrived for his previous visit, Lowell was in Greenways Hospital.

670. To Elizabeth Bishop

the *art* . . . of losing: See Bishop, "One Art," line 1.

671. To Blair Clark

"tricky": Lowell took so much lithium in the spring of 1975 to forestall a manic episode that his blood levels became toxic and he had to be treated at Mount Sinai hospital in New York. It is possible that, to reduce toxicity, his lithium levels were brought too low to prevent his manic episode of November 1975.

downlooking: Cf. "The Downlook," *DBD*.

***writing* the *Nation*:** Blair Clark became the editor of the *Nation* in 1976.

Martha Ritter: Lowell's lover in the fall of 1969; see Ian Hamilton, 393–94.

672. To Stephen Berg

Stephen Berg (b. 1934), American poet, editor of the *American Poetry Review*; he studied with Lowell at Boston University.

Adrienne's slash: Rich, "Carydid: A Column," *American Poetry Review*, September–October 1973.

rage for disorder: Cf. Wallace Stevens, "The Idea of Order at Key West," lines 52–53.

Mazzaro's: Jerome Mazzaro, "Imitations," *American Poetry Review*, September–October 1973.

McClatchy: J. D. McClatchy, "Robert Lowell: Learning to Live in History," *American Poetry Review*, January–February 1977.

673. To Elizabeth Bishop

My play . . . : The American Place Theater revived *The Old Glory* for an American Bicentennial production, dir. Brian Murray and Austin Pendleton. Nicolas Coster played Captain Delano.

your interview: "The really youngest generation now tends to write in free verse, but it seems to me that the best poets set themselves some strict limitations. Wallace Stevens almost never got away from iambic pentameter. And Robert Lowell said in the last letter I had from him that he's going back to form, that he was tired of the loose free verse he was writing" (Anna Quindlen, "Book and Author: Elizabeth Bishop," *New York Post*, April 3, 1976, reprinted in *Conversations with Elizabeth Bishop*, ed. George Monteiro [1996], 57–58).

obituary: "On Hannah Arendt," *New York Review of Books*, May 13, 1975. See notes to letters 207 and 437.

674. To Frank Bidart

Fanons: Frantz Fanon (1925–61), West Indian psychoanalyst and social philosopher, author of *The Wretched of the Earth* (1963).

"Long Summer" titles: The "Long Summer" sequence in *Notebook* that became "1930s" in *SP76*. See headnote to *HIS*, *CPM*, 1075; the note to "1930's," *CPM*, 1102; and "Long Summer," *CPM*, 943–50.

Cornelia's: Cornelia Foss, American painter, one of Blackwood's closest friends; she is married to composer Lukas Foss.

the **"Myopia" substitution:** In the first galleys for the *Selected Poems*, the title of "Myopia" was mistakenly given to another poem.

676. To Elizabeth Hardwick

Britten: Benjamin Britten, *Phaedra*, dramatic canata, opus 93 (1975). It was first performed by Janet Baker, mezzo-soprano, with the English Chamber Orchestra, on June 16, 1976.

Pears: Sir Peter Pears (1910–86), English tenor, Britten's companion.

677. To Elizabeth Hardwick

our James appearance: A memorial stone to Henry James was placed in Westminster Abbey on June 17, 1976; Hardwick read about Lowell's attendance at the event in "Henry James, at Last, Admitted to the Abbey," *New York Times*, June 18, 1976.

Rolando: Rolando Anzilotti.

poets of the Thirties: Organized for an exhibition about the poets of the thirties at the National Portrait Gallery that opened on June 25, 1976.

his errors: Percival Lowell (1855–1916), American astronomer, brother of A. Lawrence Lowell and Amy Lowell. His hypothesis that a planet beyond Neptune existed in the solar system was confirmed after his death by the discovery in 1930 of Pluto (its planetary symbol, PL, stands in part for Percival Lowell). He also advanced the theory that grooves on the Martian surface were artificial waterways built by inhabitants of the planet. His books include *Mars and Its Canals* (1906) and *The Genesis of Planets* (1916). He founded the Lowell Observatory in Arizona.

678. To Peter Taylor

Goethe's *Walpurgis Nacht* . . . : Lowell completed the few untranslated lines of "Gretchen's Spinning Songs" for Jarrell's *Faust*. See Goethe, *Faust, Part I*, trans. Randall Jarrell (1976), 195–96. Lowell abandoned his own attempts to translate the Walpurgisnacht section of *Faust*.

Michael: Michael Di Capua, Farrar, Straus and Giroux editor, and a friend of Jarrell's.

the new novel: Caroline Blackwood, *The Stepdaughter* (1976).

680. To Frank Bidart

Great-Granny Woodhouse: Published as *Great Granny Webster* (1977).

681. To Jean Stafford

Barnes: Clive Barnes, "The Stage: Lowell's 'The Old Glory,'" *New York Times*, April 19, 1976.

I dropped it for a poem: "Louisiana State University in 1940 (for Robert Penn Warren)," *DBD*.

682. To Elizabeth Hardwick

Susan: Susan Sontag.

your Billie Holiday: Cf. Elizabeth Hardwick, *Sleepless Nights* (1979), 34–44.

how I turn up: If any character in Hardwick's novel resembles Lowell, he rarely appears; see *Sleepless Nights*, 7–8. In a letter to Hardwick, Mary McCarthy remarked that the genius of the book lay in the fact that its emotional center—"the huge fact of Cal"—was an absence (McCarthy to Hardwick, n.d., Texas, quoted in Laskin, *Partisans*, 263).

James's *American*: Henry James, *The American* (1877).

sonnet you particularly detested: Lowell included the sonnet "In the Mail" in the first edition of his

Selected Poems (1976). He revised the first seven lines of the poem for the second edition (1977). The first lines in the poem quote a letter to Lowell from Frank Bidart (Ransom Humanities Center, Texas).

a car without a driver . . . : *The Love Bug* (1968); *Le Ballon rouge* (1956).

683. To Elizabeth Bishop

Perkins: David Perkins (b. 1928), Harvard English Department chairman in 1976.
a third book: Caroline Blackwood, *Great Granny Webster* (1977).
Lawrence's "Figs": D. H. Lawrence, "Figs," *Birds, Beasts and Flowers* (1923).

684. To Fanny Howe

Fanny Howe (b. 1940), American poet and novelist.
Carl: Carl Senna (b. 1944), political journalist, Fanny Howe's former husband.
a sonnet on assassination: "Assassin! (Les Enfants du Paradis)," *HIS*.
Skimper's: Nickname of Malise Ruthven (b. 1942), Irish writer, Grey Gowrie's brother.

685. To Frank Bidart

spending the night with Caroline: Blackwood was living in the house they had rented on Sacramento Street in Cambridge. Lowell believed that he was making Caroline ill and asked Bidart if he could stay with him in his apartment on Sparks Street. "He was seeing her sometimes at my house, sometimes at Sacramento Street. . . . She arrived around the end of September and he arrived around . . . late October, and they were together till maybe mid-November? and then he moved to my place" (Bidart interview, Ian Hamilton Notebooks, British Library).

686. To Elizabeth Hardwick

Oresteia: *Oresteia* (1978).
Yeats' Oedipus and Pound's Sophocles: W. B. Yeats, *Sophocles' King Oedipus: A Version for the Modern Stage* (1928); Sophocles, *Women of Trachis: A Version by Ezra Pound* (1956).

687. To Caroline Blackwood

Part of a series of letters to Caroline Blackwood that Lowell wrote in 1977. They survive only in fragmentary passages transcribed by Ian Hamilton, which this edition repeats exactly.

shortwindedness: "I went to pick him up at the airport. . . . It was arranged he was to stay at Dunster House but he'd stay with me first for like a week or so. It was terrifically cold, and the second night about 2 in the morning—we'd both been asleep—he knocked on my door and he said that he couldn't breathe and he felt he had to go to the infirmary. . . . McLean has a general hospital as well as the psychiatric part. . . . They had found at McLean that he had liquid in his lungs and he had what's called congestive heart failure. . . . So McLean had sent him to the Mass General in an ambulance. He stayed there about a week, to get this liquid out of his lungs. . . . He missed [the] first week [of classes] and I believe that's the time Helen [Vendler] took over his teaching. At the end of the week, I believe I picked him up at the hospital and he stayed with me over the weekend so he wouldn't have to go straight from the hospital to being absolutely alone in Dunster House" (Frank Bidart interview, Ian Hamilton Notebooks, British library).

688. To Caroline Blackwood

Ian Hamilton transcription.

[Estate Agent—Redding—$250,000]: Ian Hamilton's summary.

Ivan Illich: Tolstoy, *The Death of Ivan Illyich* (1886).

691. To J. D. McClatchy

grand review: McClatchy, "Robert Lowell: Learning to Live in History," *American Poetry Review*, January–February 1977.

your confessional book and Anne Sexton: "I had just written my Yale Ph.D. dissertation on the confessional poets (Lowell among them), and was thinking of making it into a book. But never did" (McClatchy to SH, May 13, 2003); *Anne Sexton: The Artist and Her Critics*, ed. J. D. McClatchy (1978).

692. To Caroline Blackwood

Ian Hamilton transcription.

heckled by Corso: Lowell and Ginsberg read at the Poetry Project at St. Mark's Church on February 23, 1977. See Ian Hamilton, 459–60.

694. To Caroline Blackwood

Ian Hamilton transcription.

the likeness to the Louvre: "Lowell's sixtieth birthday [on March 1] coincided with news from Blackwood that Milgate had been sold, and that she had taken an apartment in a huge Georgian stately home at Castletown, near Dublin" (Ian Hamilton, 460).

[Birthday in New York . . .]: Ian Hamilton's summary; March 1, 1977, was Lowell's sixtieth birthday.

696. To Caroline Blackwood

Ian Hamilton transcription.

a minor *Union Dead*: DBD.

699. To Caroline Blackwood

Ian Hamilton transcription.

[C. need psych. in Ireland]: Ian Hamilton's summary.

700. To Caroline Blackwood

Ian Hamilton transcription.

the burnt-cork Hitler moustache: "Blackwood's fear of Lowell's mania was such that she could barely distinguish 'health' from 'sickness'; any sign of excitement, high-spiritedness, was now a possible symptom. For example, in several letters to Blackwood, Lowell referred to an incident in which Sheridan had corked a moustache onto his upper lip in imitation of a Hitler he had seen on television. Jestingly—in cheery one-line throwaways—Lowell would [refer to it] . . . For Blackwood, the mere mention of Hitler was a danger sign; thus, an otherwise quite sensible letter would take on a threatening glow. The constraint that this imposed on Lowell was intolerable; on the other hand, Blackwood could not simply unlearn the trauma of the last two years" (Ian Hamilton, 465).

[In Ireland]: Ian Hamilton's summary.

701. To Caroline Blackwood

Ian Hamilton transcription.

your visit: Lowell won the Gold Medal for Literature from the American Academy of Arts and Letters and Blackwood flew to New York to attend the ceremony. She stayed "about a week" (Ian Hamilton, 464–65).

702. To Caroline Blackwood

Ian Hamilton transcription.

unfamiliar small type: Lowell had moved into his old apartment on West 67th Street and was borrowing Hardwick's typewriter.

703. To the Editors, New York Review of Books

Published in the *New York Review of Books*, July 14, 1977, with Donoghue's reply.

a half fictitious British poet . . . : "Truth," *DOL*, lines 8–14; the half of the British poet who is not fictitious is Auden (see *CPM*, 1138).

704. To Caroline Blackwood

Ian Hamilton transcription.

[. . . seeing Brodsky next night]: Ian Hamilton's summary; Lowell befriended Joseph Brodsky (Russian poet, 1940–96) in the 1970s.

705. Alfred Corn

the "Darwin": Corn, "Pages from a Voyage," *All Roads at Once* (1976).

Sandy: J. D. McClatchy.

708. To Steven Axelrod

sympathetic piece: Axelrod, "Lowell's *The Dolphin* as a 'Book of Life,'" *Contemporary Literature*, Autumn 1977.

710. To Caroline Blackwood

Ian Hamilton transcription.

[12 Noon Aer Lingus 1 Sept]: Ian Hamilton's summary. Details of Lowell's impending flight to Ireland.

old piece of prose: "New England and Further," *CPR;* see RL to Elizabeth Bishop, June 15, 1965, Vassar.

711. To Caroline Blackwood

Ian Hamilton transcription.

I spent until about two with Sheridan: Blackwood left Castletown before Lowell returned to America. "After ten days of turbulence, Lowell telephoned Elizabeth Hardwick in New York. He was coming home early, he said, because things had become 'sheer torture' at Castletown. Lady Caroline, he said, had left for London, and he would get a flight to New York on the following day—Monday, September 12. (His original intention had been to fly to Boston on the

fifteenth.) On the Sunday night, Lowell was alone in Castletown, and as he wrote to Black-wood, he freakishly became 'immured' in the vast mansion: first the telephone failed, then the electricity" (Ian Hamilton, 472). He flew to New York on September 12 and died in a taxi from the airport. He was returning to Hardwick but carried in his arms a portrait of Blackwood by Lucian Freud.

Lowell's Addresses

91 Revere Street, Boston, Massachusetts: "In 1924 people still lived in cities. Late that summer we bought the 91 Revere Street house, looking out on an unbuttoned part of Beacon Hill bounded by the North End slums, though reassuringly only four blocks away from my Grandfather Winslow's brown pillared house at 18 Chestnut Street" ("91 Revere Street"). (1924–27)

170 Marlborough Street, Boston, Massachusetts: (1927–37)

Cottage near the Coast guard Station, Madaket, Massachusetts: "The climate is cool and we are secluded; yet it is not too cold to be comfortable, and we are not so secluded as to be shut off from life" (RL to Richard Eberhart, July 10, 1935, Dartmouth). (Summers 1935 and 1936)

Tent, Allen Tate's lawn, Clarksville, Tennessee: (Summer 1937)

John Crowe Ransom's house, Gambier, Ohio: (Fall 1937)

Douglass House, Kenyon College, Gambier, Ohio: (Fall 1938–Spring 1940)

1106 Chimes Street, Baton Rouge, Louisiana: (1940–41)

63 West 11th Street, New York, New York: (1941–42)

"Wormwood," Monteagle, Tennessee: (1942–43)

12 Gansevoort Street, New York, New York: (1943)

68 Ocean Avenue, Black Rock, Connecticut: (1944–45)

The Barn, Sturges Highway, Westport, Connecticut: (1945)

Damariscotta Mills, Maine: (1945–46)

202 East 15th Street, New York, New York (1946–47)

Yaddo, Saratoga Springs, New York: (Summer 1947, Fall–Winter 1948–49)

The Cosmos Club, Washington, D.C.: (1947–48)

Red Hook, New York: (Summer 1949)

29 West 104th Street, New York, New York: (Fall 1949)

728 Bowery Street, Iowa City, Iowa: (Winter–Spring 1950)

2 Lungarno Amerigo Vespucci, Florence, Italy: (1950–51)

17 Nicolaas Witsenkade, Amsterdam, The Netherlands: (1951–52)

Pensione California, Via Aurora 43, Rome, Italy: (Fall 1952)

Burlington Apartments, Burlington Avenue, Iowa City, Iowa: (Spring 1953)

232 Summit Street, Iowa City, Iowa: (Fall 1953)

2901 Clifton Avenue, Cincinnati, Ohio: (Spring 1954)

Surplus Street, Duxbury, Massachusetts: (Summers 1954 and 1955)

33 Commonwealth Avenue, Boston, Massachusetts: "We are now by some miracle just about in both our Duxbury house and a Boston apartment—the latter is half palazzo and half loft, and was occupied for twenty-six years by an aristocratic old woman dressed in Hellenistic pajamas, an ice-pack and (really!) twenty six live birds, some in a special sky-light room, but most of them

flying about her head and the book-cases. . . . [B]y Elizabeth's ingenuity and energy, the place is by now (despite my spur of the moment floor-painting) not even eccentric" (RL to Peter Taylor, October 24, 1954, Vanderbilt). (1954–55)

Castine, Maine: (Summers 1955, 1957–69, 1977)

239 Marlborough Street, Boston, Massachusetts: "We live in [a] house very much like my parents' house, which is a block down Marlboro and almost visible when there are no leaves and if one stands far out on the sidewalk. Outwardly our neighborhood, Back Bay Boston, has changed little in thirty years. . . . I begin the day in a dining-room that is a quietly down-grade and fraying reconstruction of my parents' dining room at 170 Marlborogh St" (Autobiographical Prose, Harvard, Harvard University). "The house, on Marlborough Street is of early Bostonian grandeur with black and white marble entrance (and a flat stone dish of the most exquisite flowers on the table), spacious stairs up to the drawing-room—the walls, entirely books" (Marianne Moore to Hildegarde Watson, August 5, 1956, *The Selected Letters of Marianne Moore*, 533). (1955–61)

15 West 67th Street, New York, New York: (1961–70, 1977)

All Souls College, Oxford: (Spring–Summer 1970)

33 Pont Street, London: (1970–71)

80 Redcliffe Square, London: (1971–76)

Milgate, Bearsted, Maidstone, Kent: "If you drive, you go through Maidstone and take the road to Ashford. After some three miles you come to an ugly sprawling thirties Tudor house called Tudor House—on your right, then we are the next right, a small, rough, semi-private drive. We are the last house, about a third of a mile up the drive and at it's end. It is large brick 18th century—Old South" (RL to Christopher Ricks, May 10, 1972). (1971–76)

18 Maple Street, Brookline, Massachusetts: (Fall 1973)

34 Cypress Street, Brookline, Massachusetts: (Spring 1975)

63 Sparks Street, Cambridge, Massachusetts: (Fall 1976)

Dunster House, Harvard University, Cambridge, Massachusetts: (Spring 1977)

Castletown House, Celbridge, Ireland: (1977)

Location of Letters and Manuscripts

William Alfred: Formerly in his private collection; now on deposit at Brooklyn College Library

A. Alvarez: British Library

Hannah Arendt: Library of Congress

Steven Gould Axelrod: Collection of Steven Gould Axelrod

Daniel Berrigan: Carl A. Kroch Library, Cornell University

John Berryman: John Berryman Papers, Elmer L. Andersen Library, University of Minnesota

Elizabeth Bishop: Elizabeth Bishop Papers, Vassar College Library

Edmund Blunden: Copy at Houghton Library, Harvard University

Keith Botsford: Yale Collection of American Literature, Beinecke Memorial Library, Yale University

Robert Boyers: Collection of Robert and Peggy Boyers

Kingman Brewster: Copy at Houghton Library, Harvard University

Cleanth Brooks: Cleanth Brooks Papers, Yale Collection of American Literature, Beinecke Rare Book and Manuscript Library, Yale University

Gertrude Buckman: Henry W. and Albert A. Berg Collection of English and American Literature, New York Public Library

Blair Clark: Formerly in his private collection; now on deposit at the Harry Ransom Humanities Center, University of Texas

Alfred Corn: Carter Burden Collection

Sarah Winslow Cotting: Robert Lowell Papers, Houghton Library, Harvard University

Donald Davie: Donald Davie Papers, Beinecke Rare Book and Manuscript Library, Yale University

Carley Dawson: Special Collections, University of Oregon Library

Anne Dick: Robert Lowell Papers, Houghton Library, Harvard University

William Doreski: Henry W. and Albert A. Berg Collection of English and American Literature, New York Public Library

Robert Duncan: Bancroft Library, University of California

Richard Eberhart: Rauner Special Collections, Dartmouth College

T. S. Eliot: Collection of Valerie Eliot

William Empson: Houghton Library, Harvard University

Paul Engle: University of Iowa Library Special Collections

Richard J. Fein: Collection of Richard J. Fein

Robert Fitzgerald: Robert Fitzgerald Papers, Yale Collection of American Literature, Beinecke Rare Book and Manuscript Library, Yale University

R. W. Flint: Collection of R. W. Flint

Anne Fremantle: Henry W. and Albert A. Berg Collection of English and American Literature, New York Public Library

Robert Frost: Rauner Special Collections, Dartmouth College Library

Isabella Gardner: Washington University Libraries

Allen Ginsberg: Special Collections, Butler Library, Columbia University

Robert Giroux: Henry W. and Albert A. Berg Collection of English and American Literature, New York Public Library

Caroline Gordon: Firestone Library, Princeton University

Grey Gowrie: Collection of Grey Gowrie

Robert Graves: Estate of Robert Graves

John Haffenden: Collection of John Haffenden

Ian Hamilton: Ian Hamilton Notebooks, British Library

Elizabeth Hardwick: Robert Lowell Papers, Harry Ransom Humanities Center, University of Texas

Seamus Heaney: Collection of Seamus Heaney

Fanny Howe: Special Collections, Stanford University

Ted Hughes: Robert W. Woodruff Library, Emory University

Randall Jarrell: Henry W. and Albert A. Berg Collection of English and American Literature, New York Public Library

Norman William Johnson: Robert Lowell Papers, Houghton Library, Harvard University

Donald Junkins: Collection of Donald Junkins

Alfred Kazin: Henry W. and Albert A. Berg Collection of English and American Literature, New York Public Library

Robert Kennedy: Kennedy Library

Stanley Kunitz: Firestone Library, Princeton University

Philip Larkin: Brynmor Jones Library, University of Hull

James Laughlin: New Directions Publishers Papers, Houghton Library, Harvard University

W. F. van Leeuwen: Collection of W. F. van Leeuwen

Charlotte Winslow Lowell: Robert Lowell Papers, Houghton Library, Harvard University (nos. 14, 23, 25, 32, 130, 205, 215, 227); Robert Lowell Papers, Harry Ransom Humanities Center, University of Texas (nos. 6, 8)

Robert T. S. Lowell: Robert Lowell Papers, Houghton Library, Harvard University

Robie Macauley: Robert Lowell Papers, Harry Ransom Humanities Center, University of Texas (nos. 28, 693); Collection of Richard Henry Levey (nos. 33, 118)

Giovanna Madonia: Houghton Library, Harvard University

Jerome Mazzaro: Collection of Richard Henry Levey

Mary McCarthy: Vassar College Libraries

J. D. McClatchy: Collection of J. D. McClatchy; Carter Burden Collection

William Meredith: Collection of Richard Henry Levey

W. S. Merwin: Collection of Richard Henry Levey

Charles Monteith: Faber and Faber Archive

Marianne Moore: Rosenbach Museum and Library, Philadelphia; copy at Henry W. and Albert A. Berg Collection of English and American Literature, New York Public Library

Merrill Moore: Harry Ransom Humanities Center, University of Texas, Austin

Nicolas Nabokov: Yale Collection of American Literature, Beinecke Memorial Library, Yale University

Marcia Nardi: Collection of E. M. O'Neill

Flannery O'Connor: O'Connor Archive

Jacqueline Kennedy Onassis: Kennedy Library

Anthony Ostroff: Special Collections, State University of New York–Buffalo Library

Francis S. Parker: Robert Lowell Papers, Houghton Library, Harvard University (no. 3), Collection of Judith and Francis S. Parker (nos. 16, 675, 698)

Violet Otis Parker: Collection of Judith and Francis S. Parker

Marjorie Perloff: Collection of Marjorie Perloff

Katherine A. Porter: Katherine A. Porter Papers, Special Collections, University of Maryland Libraries

David Posner: Cambridge University

Ezra Pound: Ezra Pound Papers Addition, Yale Collection of American Literature, Beinecke Rare Book and Manuscript Library, Yale University (nos. 1, 2, 200, 267, 286, 301, 304, 352, 357, 460) Pound Manuscripts II Collection, Lilly Library, Indiana University (nos. 84, 85, 128, 141, 226, 507)

J. F. Powers: Collection of Katherine A. Powers

John Crowe Ransom: Special Collections, Olin and Chalmers Libraries, Kenyon College

Adrienne Rich: Adrienne Cecil Rich Papers, Schlesinger Library, Radcliffe Institute for Advanced Study, Harvard University

I. A. Richards: Houghton Library, Harvard University

Christopher Ricks: Collection of Christopher Ricks

Selden Rodman: American Heritage Center, University of Wyoming

Theodore Roethke: Theodore Roethke Papers, Special Collections, University of Washington Libraries

M. L. Rosenthal: Bobst Memorial Library, New York University

Olga Rudge: Yale Collection of American Literature, Beinecke Memorial Library, Yale University

George Santayana: George Santayana Collection, Harry Ransom Humanities Center, University of Texas

Arthur Schlesinger: Kennedy Library

Frederick Seidel: Collection of Frederick Seidel

Anne Sexton: Harry Ransom Humanities Center, University of Texas, Austin

Frank Sheed: Department of Rare Books and Special Collections, Hesburgh Library, University of Notre Dame

Chard Powers Smith: Yale Collection of American Literature, Beinecke Memorial Library, Yale University

Natasha and Stephen Spender: Collection of Natasha Spender

Wallace Stevens: Huntington Library

Allen Tate: Firestone Library, Princeton University

Peter Taylor: Jean and Alexander Heard Library, Vanderbilt University

John Thompson: Estate of John Thompson

Richard Tillinghast: Collection of Richard Tillinghast

Shozo Tokunaga: Houghton Library, Harvard University

Charles Tomlinson: Harry Ransom Humanities Center, University of Texas, Austin

Louis Untermeyer: Lilly Library, Indiana University

Robert Penn Warren: Robert Penn Warren Papers, Yale Collection of American Literature, Beinecke Rare Book and Manuscript Library, Yale University

Richard Wilbur: Collection of Richard Wilbur; on deposit at Amherst College Library

William Carlos Williams: Yale Collection of American Literature, Beinecke Memorial Library, Yale University

Alan Williamson: Collection of Alan Williamson

Edmund Wilson: Yale Collection of American Literature, Beinecke Memorial Library, Yale University

Arthur Winslow: Robert Lowell Papers, Houghton Library, Harvard University

Harriet Winslow: Robert Lowell Papers, Houghton Library, Harvard University

Sarah Devereux Winslow: Robert Lowell Papers, Houghton Library, Harvard University

Selected Bibliography

Adams, Charles Francis. *Autobiography*. Boston: Houghton Mifflin, 1916.

Adams, Henry. *The Education of Henry Adams*. New York: Modern Library, 1931.

———. *Letters of Henry Adams: 1858–1891*. Ed. Worthington Chauncey Ford. Boston: Houghton Mifflin, 1930.

Anzilotti, Rolando, ed. *Robert Lowell: A Tribute*. Pisa: Nistri-Lischi, 1979.

Arendt, Hannah, and Mary McCarthy. *Between Friends: The Correspondence of Hannah Arendt and Mary McCarthy, 1949–1975*. New York: Harcourt Brace, 1995.

———. *Eichmann in Jerusalem: A Report on the Banality of Evil*. New York: Viking Press, 1963.

———. *The Origins of Totalitarianism*. New York: Harcourt, Brace, 1951.

Auden, W. H. *Collected Poems*. Ed. Edward Mendelson. London: Faber and Faber, 1991.

Axelrod, Steven Gould. *Robert Lowell: Life and Art*. Princeton: Princeton University Press, 1978.

Axelrod, Steven Gould, and Helen Deese, eds. *Robert Lowell: A Reference Guide*. Boston: G.K. Hall, 1982.

Berrigan, Daniel. *Consequences: Truth and . . .* New York: Macmillan, 1967.

Berryman, John. *Collected Poems, 1937–1971*. Ed. Charles Thornbury. New York: Farrar, Straus and Giroux, 1989.

———. *The Dream Songs*. New York: Farrar, Straus and Giroux, 1969.

———. *The Freedom of the Poet*. New York: Farrar, Straus and Giroux, 1976.

———. *We Dream of Honour: John Berryman's Letters to His Mother*. Ed. Richard J. Kelly. New York: Norton, 1988.

Bishop, Elizabeth. *The Collected Prose*. New York: Farrar, Straus and Giroux, 1984.

———. *The Complete Poems, 1927–1979*. New York: Farrar, Straus and Giroux, 1983.

———. *One Art: Letters*. Ed. Robert Giroux. New York: Farrar, Straus and Giroux, 1994.

Blackwood, Caroline. *For All That I Found There*. London: Duckworth, 1973.

———. *Great Granny Webster*. London: Duckworth, 1977.

———. *The Stepdaughter*. London: Duckworth, 1976.

Blotner, Joseph Leo. *Robert Penn Warren: A Biography*. New York: Random House, 1997.

Brightman, Carol. *Writing Dangerously: Mary McCarthy and Her World*. New York: Clarkson Potter, 1992.

Burt, Stephen. *Randall Jarrell and His Age*. New York: Columbia University Press, 2002.

Caramagno, Joseph C. *The Flight of the Mind: Virginia Woolf's Art and Manic-Depressive Illness*. Berkeley: University of California Press, 1992.

Carpenter, Humphrey. *Serious Character: The Life of Ezra Pound*. Boston: Houghton Mifflin, 1988.

Coleridge, Samuel Taylor. *Biographia Literaria*. London: R. Fenner, 1817.

————. *Coleridge's Verse: A Selection*. Ed. William Empson and David Pirie. London: Faber and Faber, 1972.

Davie, Donald. *Collected Poems*. Ed. Neil Powell. Manchester: Carcanet, 2002.

Doolittle, Hilda (H. D.). *Collected Poems, 1912–1944*. New York: New Directions, 1983.

Doreski, William. *The Years of Our Friendship: Robert Lowell and Allen Tate*. Jackson: University of Mississippi Press, 1990.

Eberhart, Richard. *Collected Verse Plays*. Chapel Hill: University of North Carolina Press, 1962.

Eissler, K. R. *Goethe: A Psychoanalytic Study, 1775–1786*. Detroit: Wayne State University Press, 1963.

————. *Leonardo da Vinci: Psychoanalytic Notes on the Enigma*. New York: International Universities Press, 1961.

Eliot, T. S. *The Complete Poems and Plays of T. S. Eliot*. London: Faber and Faber, 1969.

————. *Inventions of the March Hare: Poems 1909–1917*. Ed. Christopher Ricks. London: Faber and Faber, 1996.

————. *On Poets and Poetry*. London: Faber and Faber, 1957.

————. *Selected Essays, 1917–1932*. London: Faber and Faber, 1932.

Empson, William. *Seven Types of Ambiguity*. London: Chatto and Windus, 1930.

————. *Milton's God*. New York: New Directions, 1962.

————. *Argufying: Essays on Literature and Culture*. Ed. John Haffenden. London: Chatto and Windus, 1987.

Fountain, Gary, and Peter Brazeau, eds. *Remembering Elizabeth Bishop: An Oral Biography*. Amherst: University of Massachusetts Press, 1994.

Freud, Sigmund. *The Interpretation of Dreams*, translated by A. A. Brill. New York: Macmillan, 1913.

————. *The Psychopathology of Everyday Life*. Ed. Adam Phillips. Trans. Andrea Bell. London: Penguin, 2002.

————. *The Standard Edition of the Complete Psychological Works*. Ed. and trans. James Strachey. London: Hogarth Press, 1953.

Frost, Robert. *Collected Poems, Prose, and Plays*. Ed. Richard Poirier and Mark Richardson. New York: Library of America, 1995.

Gerard Manley Hopkins, by the Kenyon Critics. New York: New Directions, 1945.

Goodwin, Frederick K., and Kay Redfield Jamison. *Manic-Depressive Illness*. Oxford: Oxford University Press, 1990.

Gordon, Lyndall. *Eliot's New Life*. Oxford: Oxford University Press, 1988.

Graves, Robert. *The Complete Poems in One Volume*. Ed. Beryl Graves and Dunstan Ward. Manchester: Carcanet, 2000.

————. *The Crowning Privilege*. London: Cassell, 1955.

————. *The White Goddess: A Historical Grammar of Poetic Myth*. London: Faber and Faber, 1948.

Haffenden, John. *The Life of John Berryman*. Boston: Routledge and Kegan Paul, 1982.

Hale, Nathan G. *The Rise and Crisis of Psychoanalysis in the United States: Freud and the Americans, 1917–1985*. Oxford: Oxford University Press, 1995.

Hamilton, Ian. *Robert Lowell: A Biography*. New York: Random House, 1982.

Hammer, Langdon. *Hart Crane and Allen Tate: Janus-Faced Modernism*. Princeton: Princeton University Press, 1993.

Hardick, Elizabeth. *The Ghostly Lover*. New York: Harcourt, Brace, 1945.

————. *Seduction and Betrayal: Women and Literature*. New York: Random House, 1974.

————. *Sleepless Nights*. New York: Random House, 1979.

————. *The Simple Truth*. New York: Harcourt, Brace, 1955.

————. *A View of My Own: Essays in Literature and Society*. New York: Farrar, Straus and Cudahy, 1962.

Hass, Robert. *Twentieth Century Pleasures.* New York: Ecco Press, 1984.

Heaney, Seamus. *Field Work.* London: Faber and Faber, 1979.

———. *Finders Keepers: Selected Prose, 1971–2001.* London: Faber and Faber, 2002.

———. *The Government of the Tongue.* London: Faber and Faber, 1988.

———. *Station Island.* London: Faber and Faber, 1984.

Heymann, C. David. *American Aristocracy: The Lives and Times of James Russell, Amy, and Robert Lowell.* New York: Dodd, Mead, 1980.

Hobsbaum, Philip. *A Reader's Guide to Robert Lowell.* New York: Thames and Hudson, 1988.

Homberger, Eric, ed. *Ezra Pound: The Critical Heritage.* London: Routledge, 1972.

Hopkins, Gerard Manley. *The Letters of Gerard Manley Hopkins to Robert Bridges.* Ed. Claude Colleer Abbott. London: Oxford University Press, 1935.

Housman, Laurence. *My Brother, A. E. Housman.* New York: C. Scribner's Sons, 1938.

Hughes, Ted. *Collected Poems.* Ed. Paul Keegan. London: Faber and Faber, 2003.

Hulbert, Ann. *The Interior Castle: The Art and Life of Jean Stafford.* New York: Knopf, 1992.

James, Henry. *Hawthorne.* Ithaca: Cornell University Press, 1997.

James, William. *Selected Letters.* Ed. Elizabeth Hardwick. New York: Farrar, Straus and Cudahy, 1961.

Jarrell, Randall. *The Complete Poems.* New York: Farrar, Straus and Giroux, 1969.

———. *Kipling, Auden and Co.: Essays and Reviews, 1935–1964.* New York: Farrar, Straus and Giroux, 1980.

———. *No Other Book.* Ed. Brad Leithauser. New York: HarperCollins, 1999.

———. *Pictures from an Institution: A Comedy.* New York: Knopf, 1954.

———. *Poetry and the Age.* New York: Vintage Books, 1953.

———. *Randall Jarrell's Letters.* Ed. Mary Jarrell. Boston: Houghton Mifflin, 1985.

———. *A Sad Heart at the Supermarket: Essays and Fables.* New York: Atheneum, 1962.

Kalstone, David. *Becoming a Poet: Elizabeth Bishop with Marianne Moore and Robert Lowell.* New York: Farrar, Straus and Giroux, 1989.

Kenner, Hugh. *The Pound Era.* Berkeley: University of California Press, 1971.

Kunitz, Stanley. *Collected Poems.* New York: Norton, 2000.

Laskin, David. *Partisans: Marriage, Politics and Betrayal among the New York Intellectuals.* New York: Simon and Schuster, 2000.

Lawrence, D. H. *The Letters of D. H. Lawrence.* Ed. Aldous Huxley. London: William Heinemann, 1932.

Lowell, Robert. *Collected Poems.* Ed. Frank Bidart and David Gewanter. New York: Farrar, Straus and Giroux, 2003.

———. *Collected Prose.* Ed. Robert Giroux. New York: Farrar, Straus and Giroux, 1987.

———. *Giorno per giorno*, translated by Francesco Rognoni. Milano: Mondadori, 2001.

Lowell, Robert, Peter Taylor, and Robert Penn Warren, eds. *Randall Jarrell: 1914–1965.* New York: Farrar, Straus and Giroux, 1967.

Mariani, Paul. *Dream Song: The Life of John Berryman.* New York: Morrow, 1990.

———. *Lost Puritan: A Life of Robert Lowell.* New York: Norton, 1994.

———. *William Carlos Williams: A New World Naked.* New York: McGraw-Hill, 1981.

Mazarro, Jerome. *The Achievement of Robert Lowell: 1939–1959.* Detroit: University of Detroit Press, 1960.

McAlexander, Hubert M. *Peter Taylor: A Writer's Life.* Baton Rouge: Louisiana State University Press, 2001.

McCarthy, Mary. *The Group.* New York: Harcourt, Brace and World, 1963.

———. *The Writing on the Wall, and Other Literary Essays.* New York: Harcourt, Brace and World, 1970.

McClatchy, J. D., ed. *Anne Sexton: The Artist and Her Critics.* Bloomington: Indiana University Press, 1978.

McCormick, John. *George Santayana: A Biography.* New York: Knopf, 1987.

Meacham, Harry M. *The Caged Panther: Ezra Pound at Saint Elizabeth's.* New York: Twayne, 1967.

Mendelson, Edward. *Early Auden.* New York: Viking Press, 1981.

———. *Later Auden.* New York: Farrar, Straus and Giroux, 1999.

Meyers, Jeffrey, ed. *Robert Lowell: Interviews and Memoirs.* Ann Arbor: University of Michigan Press, 1988.

Miehe, Patrick K. *The Robert Lowell Papers at the Houghton Library.* New York: Greenwood Press, 1990.

Millier, Brett C. *Elizabeth Bishop: Life and the Memory of It.* Berkeley: University of California Press, 1993.

Moore, Marianne. *The Selected Letters of Marianne Moore.* Ed. Bonnie Costello with Celeste Goodridge and Cristanne Miller. New York: Knopf, 1997.

———. *Selected Poems.* New York: Macmillan, 1935.

Nabokov, Vladimir. *Selected Letters: 1940–1977.* Ed. Dmitri Nabokov and Matthew J. Bruccoli. San Diego: Harcourt Brace Jovanovich, 1989.

O'Connor, Flannery. *Collected Works.* Ed. Sally Fitzgerald. New York: Library of America, 1988.

———. *The Habit of Being: Letters.* Ed. Sally Fitzgerald. New York: Farrar, Straus and Giroux, 1979.

Ogden, Charles, and I. A. Richards. *The Meaning of Meaning.* New York: Harcourt, Brace, 1923.

Ostroff, Anthony, ed. *The Contemporary Poet as Artist and Critic.* Boston: Little, Brown, 1964.

Paulin, Tom. *Writing to the Moment.* London: Faber and Faber, 1996.

Perloff, Marjorie. *The Poetic Art of Robert Lowell.* Ithaca: Cornell University Press, 1973.

———. *The Poetics of Indeterminacy: Rimbaud to Cage.* Princeton: Princeton University Press, 1981.

Phillips, Adam. *On Kissing, Tickling and Being Bored.* Cambridge: Harvard University Press, 1993.

Plath, Sylvia. *The Collected Poems.* Ed. Ted Hughes. New York: Harper and Row, 1981.

———. *The Journals, 1950–1962.* Ed. Karen V. Kukil. London: Faber and Faber, 2000.

Porter, Roy. *A Social History of Madness: The World through the Eyes of the Insane.* New York: Weidenfeld and Nicholson, 1987.

Pound, Ezra. *The Cantos of Ezra Pound.* New York: New Directions, 1998.

———. *Literary Essays.* Ed. T. S. Eliot. London: Faber and Faber, 1954.

Pound/Williams: Selected Letters of Ezra Pound and William Carlos Williams. Ed. Hugh Witemeyer. New York: New Directions, 1996.

Pritchard, William H. *Randall Jarrell: A Literary Life.* New York: Farrar, Straus and Giroux, 1990.

Rabinovitz, Lauren. *Points of Resistance: Women, Power and Politics in the New York Avant-Garde Cinema, 1943–71,* 2nd ed. Urbana: University of Illinois Press, 2003.

Ransom, John Crowe. *The New Criticism.* Norfolk: New Directions, 1941.

———. *Selected Poems.* New York: Knopf, 1945.

———. *Selected Poems.* New York: Knopf, 1969.

Rich, Adrienne. *Collected Early Poems, 1950–1970.* New York: Norton, 1993.

Richards, I. A. *Goodbye Earth.* London: Routledge and Kegan Paul, 1958.

———. *Internal Colloquies.* New York: Harcourt Brace Jovanovich, 1971.

———. *Practical Criticism.* New York: Harcourt, Brace, 1929.

———. *The Principles of Literary Criticism.* New York: Harcourt, Brace, 1925.

———. *The Screens.* New York: Harcourt, Brace, 1960.

———. *Selected Letters of I. A. Richards.* Ed. John Constable. Oxford: Clarendon Press, 1990.

Ricks, Christopher. *Essays in Appreciation.* Oxford: Clarendon Press, 1996.

———. *The Force of Poetry.* Oxford: Clarendon Press, 1984.

———. *Milton's Grand Style.* Oxford: Clarendon Press, 1963.

Roberts, David. *Jean Stafford: The Life of a Writer*. New York: St. Martin's Press, 1988.

Rudman, Mark. *Robert Lowell: An Introduction to the Poetry*. New York: Columbia University Press, 1983.

Sacks, Peter. *The English Elegy*. Baltimore: Johns Hopkins University Press, 1985.

Santayana, George. *Letters*. Ed. Daniel Cory. New York: Scribner, 1955.

———. *The Works of George Santayana*. Ed. Herman J. Saatkamp and William G. Holzberger. Cambridge: MIT Press, 1986.

Saunders, Frances Stoner. *Who Paid the Piper? The CIA and the World of Arts and Letters*. New York: New Press, 2000.

Schoenberger, Nancy. *Dangerous Muse: A Life of Caroline Blackwood*. New York: Nan A. Talese/Doubleday, 2001.

Schwartz, Lloyd, and Sybil P. Estess, eds. *Elizabeth Bishop and Her Art*. Ann Arbor: University of Michigan Press, 1983.

Sexton, Anne. *The Complete Poems*. Boston: Houghton Mifflin, 1999.

———. *A Self-Portrait in Letters*. Ed. Linda Gray Sexton and Lois Ames. Boston: Houghton Mifflin, 1977.

Shorter, Edward. *A History of Psychiatry*. London: Wiley, 1997.

Simpson, Eileen. *Poets in Their Youth: A Memoir*. New York: Random House, 1982.

Spender, Stephen. *Journals, 1939–1983*. Ed. John Goldsmith. New York: Random House, 1986.

Stafford, Jean. *Boston Adventure*. New York: Harcourt, Brace and World, 1944.

———. *The Interior Castle*. New York: Harcourt, Brace, 1953.

———. *The Mountain Lion*. New York: Harcourt, Brace, 1947.

Staples, Hugh B. *Robert Lowell: The First Twenty Years*. New York: Farrar, Straus and Cudahy, 1962.

Stevens, Wallace. *Collected Poems of Wallace Stevens*. New York: Knopf, 1955.

Stuart, Sarah Payne. *My First Cousin Once Removed: Money, Madness, and the Family of Robert Lowell*. New York: HarperCollins, 1998.

Tate, Allen. *Collected Poems, 1919–1976*. New York: Farrar, Straus and Giroux, 1977.

———. *Essays of Four Decades*. Chicago: Swallow Press, 1968.

———. *The Fathers*. New York: G. P. Putnam's Sons, 1938.

———. *Memoirs and Opinions 1926–1974*. Chicago: Swallow Press, 1975.

Taylor, Peter. *Collected Stories*. New York: Farrar, Straus and Giroux, 1969.

———. *Early Guest: A Sort of Story, a Sort of Play, a Sort of Dream*. Winston-Salem: Palaemon Press, 1982.

———. *Happy Families Are All Alike*. New York: McDowell, Obolensky, 1959.

———. *In the Miro District and Other Stories*. New York: Knopf, 1977.

———. *The Long Fourth*. New York: Harcourt, Brace, 1948.

———. *Widows of Thornton*. New York: Harcourt, Brace, 1954.

Tillinghast, Richard. *Robert Lowell's Life and Work: Damaged Grandeur*. Ann Arbor: University of Michigan Press, 1995.

Travisano, Thomas. *Midcentury Quartet*. Charlottesville: University Press of Virginia, 1999.

Valéry, Paul. *The Art of Poetry*. Trans. Denise Folliott. New York: Pantheon, 1958.

Vendler, Helen. *The Given and the Made*. Cambridge: Harvard University Press, 1995.

———. *The Music of What Happens*. Cambridge: Harvard University Press, 1988.

———. *Part of Nature, Part of Us*. Cambridge: Harvard University Press, 1980.

———. *The Poetry of George Herbert*. Cambridge: Harvard University Press, 1975.

Warren, Robert Penn. *The Collected Poems*. Ed. John Burt. Baton Rouge: Louisiana State University Press, 1998.

Wilhelm, J. J. *Ezra Pound: The Tragic Years, 1925–1972*. University Park: Pennsylvania State University Press, 1994.

Williams, William Carlos. *Autobiography*. New York: Random House, 1951.

―――. *The Collected Poems*. Vols. 1 and 2. Ed. A. Walton Litz and Christopher MacGowan. New York: New Directions, 1986–88.

―――. *Paterson*. Ed. Christopher MacGowan. New York: New Directions, 1992.

―――. *Selected Essays of William Carlos Williams*. New York: Random House, 1954.

―――. *Selected Letters*. Ed. John C. Thirlwall. New York: McDowell, Obolensky, 1957.

Wilson, Edmund. *The Fifties: From Notebooks and Diaries of the Period*. Ed. Leon Edel. New York: Farrar, Straus and Giroux, 1986.

―――. *Patriotic Gore: Studies in the Literature of the American Civil War*. New York: Oxford University Press, 1962.

―――. *The Sixties: The Last Journal, 1960–1972*. New York: Farrar, Straus and Giroux, 1993.

Yeats, W. B. *The Poems*. Ed. Richard J. Finneran. New York: Macmillan, 1997.

Acknowledgments

This book was made possible by Lowell's children, Harriet and Sheridan Lowell, and it is for them. Thanks especially to Harriet Lowell for her care, and to Lowell's stepdaughter, Evgenia Citkowitz.

I am deeply grateful to many people who searched their attics for letters or answered queries. Lowell's oldest friends, Blair Clark and Frank Parker, as well as Judith Parker, were candid, warm, generous with their memories, and unfailingly helpful. For assistance in matters large or small-but-important, I would also like to thank Judith Aronson, Steven Axelrod, Massimo Baciagalupo, Xandra Bingley, Philip Booth, Bobbie Bristol, Esther Brooks, Stephen Burt, Kathleen Merrill Campognolo, Theo Cuffe, Janice Delaney, H. A. Drion, Barbara Estrin, James Fenton, Forrest Gander, Grey Gowrie, Jorie Graham, John Haffenden, Andrew Hamilton, Ian Hamilton, Langdon Hammer, Seamus Heaney, Daniel Hoffman, Michael Hofmann (for German), John Hollander, Fanny Howe, C. R. Hugenholtz-Wiarda, Janna Israel, Donald Junkins, Yun Kim, S. and N. Lambrechtsen-ter Horst, Ann Kjellberg, Patrick Lannan, Frank Lawler, W. F. van Leeuwen, J. Michael Lennon, Richard Levey and Sigrid Christiansen, Sharon Lipovsky, David Lynn, Paul Mariani, David Martino, Eugene McCarthy, J. D. McClatchy, Patricia Smith and William Melton, Stanley Moss, Warren Myers (for his ear for Latin allusion), E. M. O'Neil, Francis Q. O'Neill, Darren Overty, Tom Paulin, Marjorie Perloff, Joanna Picciotto, D. A. Powell, Katherine A. Powers, Adrienne Rich, Mark Rudman, Ianthe and Malise Ruthven, Peter Sacks, Lloyd Schwartz, Frederick Seidel, William Sessions, Natasha Spender, Rose and William Styron, Lauren Taylor, Charles Thornbury, Richard Tillinghast, Shozo Tokunaga, Mary Tonkinson, Meg Tyler, Helen Vendler, Margo Viscusi, David Wagoner, Rosanna Warren, L. van Wassenaer-Wiarda, Elise Wiarda, J. J. Wiarda, A. Wiarda-Moltzer, Richard Wilbur, Alan Williamson, and Anne Winters. I am also grateful for conversations about this book with my former colleagues at the Folger Shakespeare Library, the Lannan Foundation, Kenyon College, Stonehill College, and my present colleagues at Barnard College.

I transcribed most of the letters (and am responsible for any errors), but Julia Hamilton gave me invaluable help by transcribing one important group with perfect accuracy (my thanks to her extend to Ana, Sophie, and John Hamilton). Thomas Travisano, preparing the complete Lowell-Bishop correspondence for publication, shared his work with me and we were able to compare our versions and notes. I am very grateful to him for his openness and comradeship. Peter Ericksson in Santa Fe; Gregory Wrenn and Alice Yang in Cambridge; Rachel Abramowitz, Lauren Feinberg, Nicola Fucigna, Rachel Julkowski, Audra Noble, Vrylena Olney, Anne Russell, and Abby Walthausen in New York, painstakingly compared transcriptions to the originals for accuracy.

For enlightening conversations about the history of medicine and treatments for bipolar disorder, I would like to thank Michael Neve, Andrew Scull, Kay Redfield Jamison, and Thomas A. Wehr.

Many librarians helped me with research. I am particularly indebted to Christopher Fletcher

at the British Library; the staff of the Houghton Library at Harvard University, including Leslie Morris, Philip Capernaros, Rachel Howarth, Denison Beach, Elizabeth A. Falsey, Tom Ford, Susan Halpert, Sylvia Parsons, Jennie Rathbun, Emily Walhout, and Jozef Zajac; Isaac Gewirtz, Stephen Crook, Philip Milito, and Rodney Phillips at the Berg Collection, New York Public Library; Dean Rogers at Vassar College Libraries; Christopher Barth and Carole Marshall at Kenyon College Library; Sarah Hartwell at Rauner Special Collections, Dartmouth University; Corrina Flanagan at the Beinecke Rare Book Library, Yale University; Dorothy G. Knauss at the University of Oregon; Anne Engelheart at the Schlesinger Library, Radcliffe Institute for Advanced Study; Sean Noel at Boston University; Beth Alvarez at the University of Maryland Library; Anthony Bliss and David Kessler at Bancroft Library, the University of California; Michael Basinksi of the Poetry Rare Books Collection at the State University of New York at Buffalo; Brian Dyson, the Hull University Archivist; Chatham Ewing at Washington University Library; Christian Dupont at Notre Dame; David Horn at Burns Library, Boston College; Polly Armstrong and William McPheron at Stanford University Libraries; Stephen Enniss and Elizabeth Shoemaker at the Woodruff Library, Emory University; and Tara Wegner, Avi Santo, and the staff of the Harry Ransom Humanities Center at the University of Texas.

The Lannan Foundation, the Melton Arts Foundation, and the Whiting Foundation lent support for travel and research. The Bunting Institute provided me with invaluable access to the Harvard Libraries.

Three people read the entire first draft (a heavy duty, since it was much longer than the present volume): Francesco Rognoni, Robert Hass, and Christopher Ricks. Francesco Rognoni, the Italian translator of *Day by Day*, helped me track down elusive letters and documents and made many valuable, spirited observations. Robert Hass was an intuitive and engaged reader. When he might easily have despaired of his former student, he patiently improved my prose. Christopher Ricks responded to a letter from a stranger asking if he might take a look at the typescript. He read every page attentively. He then spent several hours with me and, with striking precision and an allusive wit to match Lowell's, pointed out many things that I'd missed, gently improving the book.

At Faber and Faber, Paul Keegan's suggestions were ingenious and efficient. I am also grateful to him, Jane Feaver, and John Bodley for locating letters to T. S. Eliot and Charles Monteith.

At Farrar, Straus and Giroux, Lowell's lifelong friend and editor, Robert Giroux, led the way with his edition of Bishop's letters and was very supportive. Annie Wedekind gathered all the loose ends and brought the book through production with graceful ease. Blessings upon Roslyn Schloss, the copyeditor.

At Russell and Volkening, Timothy Seldes was a warm and helpful agent and guide from start to finish.

Perhaps because I can't begin to articulate my debt to them, I have left for last the three people most important to the existence of this book: Jonathan Galassi, Frank Bidart, and Elizabeth Hardwick. Jonathan Galassi's learning, his beautiful ear, trust, energy, and patience made him an inspiring editor. No sentence I write can be worthy of Frank Bidart's special nature, or of his friendship to Lowell. He gave me hundreds of hours of help and companionship while I worked on this project. It's no coincidence that Lowell's prose became more sophisticated and subtle after he married Elizabeth Hardwick. Once she makes an appearance in these pages, her loyalty and love for him—never pious, always wondering and exact—is palpable to the end. If he stirs to life here, it is due in great part to her openness to the project. I am not insensible to her bravery (nor to her wit about "bravery") and am very grateful that she allowed me to work on it. "A whale ship was my Yale College and my Harvard"; the education that this book has been I owe to her.

I regret any errors to which I may presently be blind.

Index

Note: Robert Lowell's name is abbreviated as RL throughout the index.

Arnold, Matthew, 48, 51, 298, 537
 Culture and Anarchy, 407
 "Dover Beach," 461
 The Scholar Gypsy, 537, 539
 "Stanzas in Memory of the Author of
 'Obermann,'" 540
Art Institute, 255
Ashbery, John, 602, 670
Assis, Machado de, 407
 Epitaph of a Small Winner, 407
Associated Press, 107
Atheneaum, 396, 408, 508, 527
Auden, W. H., xxvii, 86, 90, 110, 115, 120, 125,
 186, 258, 260, 263, 302, 333, 334, 361,
 369, 378, 440, 448, 598, 616, 618, 630,
 635, 652, 654
 "Age of Anxiety: A Baroque Ecologue," 81
 cooling of friendship with RL, 587–88
 The Faber Book of Modern American Verse
 (ed.), 263
 "Good-Bye to the Mezzogiorno," 334
 "On the Circuit," 618
 The Rake's Progress, 370
 recording for Library of Congress, 92
 Seven Deadly Sins, 334
 The Shield of Achilles, 258
 "Squares and Oblongs," 90
 "Under Which Lyre: A Reactionary Tract
 for the Times," 260
 Vietnam War protests and, 493
Audience, 339
Augustine, St., 48
Augustus, 222, 223
Auslander, Joseph, 100
Austen, Jane, 122
 Pride and Prejudice, 122
Axelrod, Steven, letters to, 623–24, 671

Babbitt, Milton, 228
Bach, Johann Sebastian, 186
Bacigalupo, Dr., 210, 211, 222
Bacon, Francis, 454, 561
Badoglio, Pietro, 233
Baldpate Hospital, xxvii, 135–42, 143, 190
Baldwin, James, 345
Ballanchine, George, 333
Balzac, Honoré de, 112, 115, 303, 368
 Père Goriot, Le, 322
Bandeira, Manuel, 407
Bard College, 143, 144, 145, 258

Barnard College, 467
Barnes, Clive, 657
Barnes, Djuna, 131
Barnes Museum, 364, 365
Barrett, William, 343
Barzun, Jacques, 276, 369–70
Baskin, Leonard, 496
 Hydrogen Man, 496
"Bateau Ivre" (RL's imitation of), 377
"Bathsheba's Lament in the Garden," 60
Baton Rouge, Louisiana, 29, 30
Baudelaire, Charles, 44–45, 298, 351, 368,
 370, 374, 376, 377, 382, 488, 670
 "Le Voyage," 377, 382
Baumann, Dr. Anny, 398, 483, 484, 486,
 493, 525
Bayley, John, 631
BBC TV, 433
Beat writers, xxviii, 340, 345, 395, 415
Beaumarchais, Pierre Augustin Caron de, 369
Bednasek trial, 155
Beerbohm, Max, 210
Beethoven, Ludwig van
 Fidelio, 181
 "Ah! Perfido," 255
Bel Geddes, Barbara, 371
Bel Geddes, Norman, 371
Bellini, Giovanni, 177
Bellow, Saul, 275, 345, 387, 416, 667
Benito Cereno (Lowell), 400, 479, 483, 557,
 559, 607
Benn, Gottfried, 248
Bentley, Eric, 202, 365, 369, 370,
 373, 422
Berenson, Bernard, 163, 164
Berg, Alban
 Wozzeck, 181, 182
Berg, Stephen, letter to, 647
Berkeley, Lady (sister of Ralph Lowell), 165
Berlin, Isaiah, 515, 532, 537, 585
Bernard, Dr., 380, 381
Bernstein, Leonard, 412
Berrigan, Daniel, letter to, 477
Berryman, Eileen Simpson, 52, 109, 271,
 297, 372
Berryman, Elizabeth Ann Levine, 271, 338
Berryman, John, xxvii, 49, 92, 169, 202,
 406–407, 410, 450, 498, 516, 522
 critique of "Skunk Hour," vii, 400
 death of, 583
 RL's essay in memory of, 584, 587

"Church Monuments," 630
"Love," 215–16, 630
"Her Dead Brother," 158, 168
Heredia, José Maria de, 642–43
Hersch, Jeanne, 425
Herschberger, Ruth, 453–54
Herzberg, Judith, 196, 645
HIKA (Kenyon literary magazine), 22–23
Hilberg, Raul, 438
Hills, Rust, 387
Hires, Mr. (of Hires root beer), 365
Hiroshima, 427, 478
History (Lowell), xxx, 583, 585, 588–89, 594, 596, 605, 632
 after-book blues, 601, 606
 Bidart's help in preparing, 579, 582, 583, 584, 591, 593, 599
 the dedication and, 597
 described, 589
 publication of, 602, 608, 610
 reviews of, 617, 618
Hitler, Adolf, xviii, 168, 383, 668, 669
 Mein Kampf, 669
 RL's poem on, 232–33
Hochhuth, Ralph, 424–25, 502
 Der Stellvertreter, 424–25, 426
Hochman, Sandra, 397, 575
Hoffman, Daniel, 363, 364
Hogg, James, 574
 Confessions of a Justified Sinner, 574
Hölderlin, Friedrich, 292, 298, 522
 "Brot und Wein," 298, 522
Holiday, Billie, 659
Hollander, John, 372
Holmes, John, 354
Holmes, Oliver Wendell, 326, 406, 407, 624
Holub, Miroslav, 505
Homer, 4, 82, 98, 124, 202, 204, 382
 The Iliad, 121, 122, 124
 The Odyssey (Fitzgerald translation), 227
Hopkins, Gerard Manley, xviii, 35, 44, 48, 50, 100, 108, 110
Horace, 82
Hoskins, Katherine, 305, 309, 320, 508
Houghton Mifflin, 32, 178–79, 199, 383, 412
Housman, A. E., 110, 320, 539, 540
 "The Immortal Part," 155
Howard, Richard, 239, 555, 612
Howe, Fanny, letter to, 661
Howe, Irving, 438, 632

Howells, William Dean, 258
Howes, Barbara, 305
Hudson Review, 368, 390, 393
Huff, Robert, 447
Hughes, Jan, 505
Hughes, Olwyn, 570, 584
Hughes, Ted, 340, 570
 Crow, 569
 letters to, 476, 492–93
 Wodwo, 492–93
Hugo, Victor, 377
Humphrey, Hubert, 499
Hungary, 265
Huxley, Aldous, 11, 143
 Eyeless in Gaza, 11

Illich, Monsignor Ivan, 493, 505
Imitations (Lowell), xxix, xxviii, 365, 370, 375, 376, 377, 382, 404–405, 483, 519
 preface to, 392
 publication of, 377
 reviews, 390, 391, 392, 409, 460
Institute for Living, xxix, 440, 441–42, 454–56
Iowa Writers Workshop, xxvii, xxviii, 197, 198, 199, 202, 203
Isherwood, Christopher, 407, 408, 652
Israel, 515, 516
 Six-Day War, 485–86
Italy, 330, 334
"I the Money," *see* Burt Blechman, "How Much?"
Ives, Charles, 324

James, Clive, 626, 631
James, Henry, 76, 97–98, 128, 225, 333, 334, 345, 363, 422, 521, 573, 652
 The American, 659
 The Awkward Age, 76
 Washington Square, 384
James, Julian, 254
James, William, 185, 521
James, William, Jr., 158, 335
Japan, 39
Jarrell, Mackie Langham, 78, 128, 336, 341, 398, 465–66
Jarrell, Mary, 248, 463, 653
 letter to, 338–39

Lowell, Robert (*cont.*)
 New York Review of Books and, *see New York Review of Books*
 nickname "Cal," xxv, 69
 on nuclear weapons, 395
 on parliamentary socialism, 395
 pictures of, 28, 56, 134, 536
 pictures of his friends, collection of, 302, 308, 309, 315, 335, 336, 338, 356, 359
 plays, 389
 Benito Cereno, see Benito Cereno (Lowell)
 Endecott and the Red Cross, see Endecott and the Red Cross (Lowell)
 The Old Glory, see Old Glory, The (Lowell)
 Phaedra, see Phaedra (Lowell)
 Prometheus Bound, see Prometheus Bound (Lowell)
 poetry, ix, xxix, xxviii, 60, 80, 99, 139, 184, 194, 195–96, 205, 331, 337, 343, 364, 368, 369, 397–98, 406, 414, 416, 418, 424, 434–35, 444, 445, 446, 461, 475, 486–87, 625, 644
 begins writing, 4, 7
 on career as poet, 24–25
 Complete Poems, 529
 Day by Day, see Day by Day (Lowell)
 The Dolphin, see Dolphin, The (Lowell)
 For Lizzie and Harriet, see For Lizzie and Harriet (Lowell)
 For the Union Dead, see For the Union Dead (Lowell)
 History, see History (Lowell)
 Kenyon Review, early poems published in, xxvi, 22–23
 Land of Unlikeness, see Land of Unlikeness (Lowell)
 Life Studies, see Life Studies (Lowell)
 Lord Weary's Castle, see Lord Weary's Castle (Lowell)
 The Mills of the Kavanaughs, see Mills of the Kavanaughs, The (Lowell)
 Near the Ocean, see Near the Ocean (Lowell)
 Notebook 1967–1968, see Notebook 1967–68 (Lowell)
 Poems 1938–1949, See Poems 1938–1949 (Lowell)
 Selected Poems, 630, 634, *see also Selected Poems* (Lowell)

 "Skunk Hour," 291, 297, 299, 306
 writing, in 1957-60, 291, 293, 295, 296–97, 297–98, 299–300, 302, 303–304, 305, 306, 312, 318, 320–21
 see also titles of individual poems
 prose and, viii–ix, xxii, xxx, 11, 244, 264, 351, 619
 autobiographical, published as "91 Revere Street," *see* "91 Revere Street"
 Pulitzer Prize, xxvii, xxx, 62, 63
 Red Hook house, 142, 143, 144, 145, 151
 reviews by, 449
 satire and, 11
 at Sheed & Ward, publishers, xxvi, 187
 sixtieth birthday, 666
 smoking, 201
 sobriety, 386, 425, 428, 436, 438, 655
 Jean Stafford and, *see* Stafford, Jean
 summers in Maine, 271, 279–81, 324, 325, 351, 368, 384, 385–88, 431, 461, 500, 537
 teaching, 307, 321, 359, 387, 390, 407–408, 454–55, 475
 at All Souls College, Oxford, xxix, 532–34
 at Boston University, xxviii, 244, 252, 257, 265, 273, 275, 298, 302–303, 308, 312, 326, 327, 342
 in Chicago, 321
 at Essex University, xxix, xxx, 533, 537, 543, 544, 545, 546, 548, 549, 550, 557, 563, 572, 588, 596, 598, 611, 626
 at Harvard, *see* Harvard University, RL teaches at
 at Iowa Writers Workshop, xxvii, xxviii, 197, 198, 199, 202, 203
 at Kenyon College, xxvii, 150, 152, 154, 155, 156, 157, 190
 at New School for Social Research, xxix
 in Salzburg, xviii, 185, 188, 190
 series of trips for readings and, 445, 446, 447
 at University of Cincinnati, xxviii, 211, 213, 214, 218, 228
 translations, 315, 316, 317, 320, 340, 342, 351, 352, 359, 365, 368, 374, 376, 390, 412, 414, 653, 662
 Imitations, see Imitations (Lowell)
 typewriters, on writing on, vii, 33, 583, 648, 650

Thompson, John (Jack), xxvi, 149, 240, 399,
 411, 419, 423, 559, 630
 The Founding of English Meter, 399
 letters to, 110, 137–38
 marriage, 416
Thoreau, Henry David, 80, 334, 672
"Those Before Us," 520
Thucydides, 127, 130
Tibullus, Albus, 153
Tillich, Paul, 96
Tillinghast, Richard, letters to, viii, 519–23,
 527
Tillyard, E.M.W., 126
Time, 49, 115, 116, 201, 384, 390, 391, 397, 434,
 476, 485, 610
Times Literary Supplement, 568, 625, 644
Tokunaga, Shozo, letters to, 486–87, 510–12
Toledano, Ralph de, 611
Tolstoy, Leo, 48, 66, 330, 333
 Death of Ivan Illyich, The, 663, 665
Tomlinson, Charles, letter to, 580–81
"To Speak of Woe That Is in Marriage," 522
Tourel, Jennie, 423
Tourneur, Cyril, 219
Tovey, Sir Donald Francis, 186
Tree, Marietta, 499
Trilling, Diana, 509, 513–14
 "On the Steps of Low Library," 509,
 513–14
Trilling, Lionel, xx, 252, 256, 288, 496, 521
Trinity College, 500
Trollope, Anthony, 48
Troy, Bill, 386–87
Truman, Harry S., 77, 140, 277
Truman, Margaret, 75
Tuckerman, Frederick, 568
Tufts, Rae and Paul, 273
Turgenev, Ivan, 327
 A Sportman's Sketches, 333
Turner, Susan, 149, 281, 287, 288
Tworkov, Wally, 17
Tynan, Kenneth, 371, 390

Uberti, Ubaldo degli, 114
Uccello, Paulo, 177
University of Cincinnati, RL teaches at,
 xxviii, 211, 213, 214, 218, 228
University of Delaware, 447, 448
University of Vermont, 498, 580

Untermeyer, Louis, 62, 63
 letter to, 61
Updike, John, 667

Valentine, Jean, 611
Valéry, Paul, 154, 186, 298, 330, 368, 448,
 538, 670
 Cimetière marin, 538
Vals, Carmen, 90
Van Buren, Martin, 72, 73, 76
 Autobiography, 72, 73
Vanderbilt University, 16, 619, 657
 Ransom's lectures at, xxvi
van Duyn, Mona, 565
van Dyke, Henry, 114, 115
"The Vanity of Human Wishes," 487
Vendler, Helen, 640
Vergil, *see* Virgil
Verlaine, Paul, 563
Victor, Thomas, 612
Viereck, George, 158, 182, 293, 391
Vietnam War, 475, 477, 493, 495–96, 499,
 594, 599, 639
 RL's opposition to, xx, xxix, 459, 461, 463,
 488, 493, 495–96, 502–503, 513–14, 526
Village Voice, letter to the editors of, 453–54
Villon, Francois, 377, 382, 390, 405, 490
 Grand Testament, 377
Virgil, 20, 82, 120, 129, 222–23
"Visitors," xviin
Voltaire, 170, 260
 Candide, 260
Vondel, Joost van den, 177
Vonnegut, Kurt, 667
"Voyage, Le" (RL's imitation of), 377, 382

Wagoner, David, 273
Wain, Eirian, 540
Wain, John, 296, 297, 540
"Waking Early Sunday Morning," xix–xx,
 484–85, 487–88, 522, 623
Walcott, Derek, 432
Walker, Gillian, 640
Wallace, Henry, 113
Wanning, Andrews, 258, 287, 430
Wanning, Pat, 287, 288
Warburg, Mr., 261–62
Ward, Barbara, 272

PERMISSIONS ACKNOWLEDGMENTS

Grateful acknowledgment is made for permission to reprint the following previously published and unpublished material:

Excerpt from the unpublished letter of Hannah Arendt reproduced by permission of Georges Borchardt, Inc., on behalf of the Hannah Arendt Bleucher Literary Trust.

Excerpt from the unpublished Ian Hamilton interview with Frank Bidart is used by permission of Frank Bidart and the British Library.

Excerpts from the unpublished letters written by Elizabeth Bishop to Robert Lowell copyright © 2005 by Alice Helen Methfessel. Reprinted by permission of Farrar, Straus and Giroux, LLC, on behalf of the Elizabeth Bishop Estate.

Excerpt from the unpublished letter of T. S. Eliot is used with the permission of Faber & Faber Ltd.

Excerpts from the unpublished letters by Allen Ginsberg copyright © Allen Ginsberg Trust. Reprinted with the permission of The Wylie Agency, Inc.

Excerpts from the unpublished letters of Elizabeth Hardwick are used with the permission of Elizabeth Hardwick. The excerpt from the unpublished Ian Hamilton interview with Elizabeth Hardwick is used by permission of Elizabeth Hardwick and the British Library.

Excerpt from the unpublished letter of Randall Jarrell is used with the permission of Mary von S. Jarrell.

Permission for quotation from Marianne Moore's letter to Robert Lowell, March 28, 1961, granted for the Estate of Marianne Moore by Marianne Craig Moore, literary executor. All rights reserved.

Excerpt from "Canto LXXXVIII," by Ezra Pound, from *The Cantos of Ezra Pound*, copyright © 1934, 1937, 1940, 1948, 1956, 1959, 1962, 1963, 1966, and 1968 by Ezra Pound. Reprinted by permission of New Directions Publishing Corp.